2001-2002 CHURCH ALMANAC

GENERAL AUTHORITIES

VIEWS OF NAUVOO

WORLDWIDE CHURCH

MISSIONS

TEMPLES

CHRONOLOGY

NEWS IN REVIEW

FACTS, STATISTICS

Top left, President Gordon B. Hinckley, with counselors President Thomas S. Monson and President James E. Faust, visit Conference Center; shown at right shortly after its dedication Oct. 8, 2000. Below left is Boston Massachusetts Temple, the Church's 100th. Below right are participants of temple dedications during 2000, Martha and Genny Zapata of Juchitan, Mexico.

G AUT O
VIEWS OF NAUVOO
WORLDWIDE CHURCH
MISSIONS
TEMPLES
CHRONOLOGY, NEWS IN REVIEW
FACTS, STATISTICS

FOREWORD

In October 1997, President Gordon B. Hinckley established a goal, one he called a "tremendous undertaking" and it was indeed: to build and dedicate more than 30 temples in less than three years, giving the Church 100 temples before the end of 2000.

In making the announcement, he observed: "As I have previously indicated, in recent months we have traveled far out among the membership of the Church. I have been with many who have very little of this world's goods. But they have in their hearts a great burning faith concerning this latter-day work. They love the Church. They love the gospel. They love the Lord and want to do His will. They are paying their tithing, modest as it is. They make tremendous sacrifices to visit the temples. They travel for days at a time in cheap buses and on old boats. They save their money and do without to make it all possible.

"They need nearby temples — small, beautiful, serviceable temples."

Later President Hinckley commented: "I can only add that when these 30, or 32, are built there will be more yet to come," and he further observed: "We shall not stop at these. We shall go on building."

The growth of temples under President Hinckley's influence has been dramatic. The Church had four operating temples in 1900, eight in 1950, 16 in 1975, 37 in 1985, and 47 in 1995. During 1999, 15 temples were dedicated in six nations, which is more temples in more nations than were operating in 1973 after 143 years of Church history. As of Oct. 1, 2000, 32 of 35 planned temples have been dedicated in some 13 nations, which is more than were dedicated in 155 years of Church history. Another 21 are in various stages of planning or construction.

Yet the statistics, important as they are, do not tell the real significance of the expansion. Temples bring a strong local presence of the Church to a community. They open the doors for members to be more visible. Temples give members an opportunity to be more friendly. A temple in a community allows us to demonstrate friendship where the Spirit of the Lord is in greater abundance. Worthy members who have the missionary spirit will give greater service. The legacy of our temple-minded prophet promises to be lasting as the Church enters its most exciting chapters in the 21st century and third millennium.

We are pleased to provide in this Almanac a listing and photos of all 100 temples, as well as information about the original Nauvoo Temple, and the new one that is being built. We believe that this, the largest Almanac ever, will prove to be a worthwhile reference of a remarkable period of temple building.

We extend our sincere appreciation to the staff of the Church's Family and Church History Department and the many other people who have made significant contributions to this work.

Jim M. Wall
Publisher, *Deseret News*
Gerry Avant
Editor, *Church News*

Post Office Box 1257
Salt Lake City, Utah 84110

The *Deseret News Church Almanac* is prepared and edited by the staff of the *Church News*, a section of the *Deseret News*, in cooperation with the staff of the Family and Church History Department of The Church of Jesus Christ of Latter-day Saints.

Deseret News

Deseret News Publisher	Jim M. Wall
Deseret News Editor	John Hughes
Deseret News Managing Editor	Richard Hall
Church News Editor	Gerry Avant
Church News Associate Editor and Almanac Coordinating Editor	John L. Hart
Almanac Assistant	Dell Van Orden
Church News Staff	R. Scott Lloyd
	Julie A. Dockstader
	Greg Hill
	Sarah Jane Weaver
	Shaun D. Stahle
	Jason Swensen
	Linda Hamilton
Church News Artist	John Clark
Deseret News Photo Staff	Tom Smart
	Ravell Call
	Jeffrey D. Allred
	Paul G. Barker
	Michael Brandy
	Stuart Johnson
	Laura Seitz
	Chuck Wing
	Scott G. Winterton
	Carie Hicken
Deseret News Marketing Director	Stephen G. Handy
Deseret News Marketing Staff	Connie Smith
	Sharon Johnson

Family and Church History Department

Executive Director	Elder D. Todd Christofferson
Assistant Executive Director	Elder Charles Didier
Assistant Executive Director	Elder Spencer J. Condie
Assistant Executive Director	Elder Bruce C. Hafen
Managing Director	Richard E. Turley Jr.
Almanac Chairman	Grant A. Anderson
Staff contributions	Melvin L. Bashore
	Karen S. Bolzendahl
	Marie McBride
	Pauline Musig
	William W. Slaughter

CONTENTS

A statistical profile of

THE CHURCH OF JESUS CHRIST OF LATTER-DAY SAINTS

(Dec. 31, 1999)

CHURCH MEMBERSHIP

Total membership 10,752,986

CHURCH UNITS

Stakes 2,542

Districts 636

Missions 333

Wards, branches 25,793

CHURCH GROWTH

Eight-year- old children baptized in 1999............... 84,118

Converts baptized in 1999 306,171

MISSIONARIES

Total missionaries serving 58,593

EDUCATION

(1998-99 school year)

Cumulative total of continuing education enrollment ... 490,625

Students in seminary.................................. 373,887

Students in institute.................................. 285,250

Students in primary and secondary Church schools 8,707

Students in Church colleges and universities (Fall, 1999) . 41,627

Members speaking English 5,435,000

Members speaking Spanish............................... 3,226,000

Members speaking Portuguese............................ 780,000

Members speaking all other languages................... 1,311,000

(October, 2000)

TEMPLES

Temples in use 100

Temples approved or under construction 21

LANGUAGES

Full program 27

Partial program.. 75

Total languages.. 102

Complete translations of Book of Mormon in print...... 56

Translated selections of Book of Mormon in print....... 37

Triple combination translations........................ 16

Total membership (estimated) 11,000,000

Stakes 2,573

Missions 333

Visitors at President Gordon B. Hinckley's 90th birthday celebration enjoy dramatic interior of Conference Center as well as world-class performing artists on June 23, 2000.

MAJOR EVENTS

OCTOBER 1998 - OCTOBER 2000

Also see **News in Review** section

Administrative and Policy Announcements

• Changes affecting the Church's musical organizations on Temple Square were announced Jan. 2, 1999. The Mormon Youth Chorus and Symphony would be reorganized with the chorus becoming a training choir for the Tabernacle Choir and the symphony reorganized under a new name, the Orchestra at Temple Square.

• In a letter to members of the Church throughout the world, the First Presidency on Feb. 11, 1999, called upon parents "to devote their best efforts to the teaching and rearing of their children in gospel principles which will keep them close to the Church."

• The Church issued a formal statement July 16, 1999, after the passage of the Religious Liberty Protection Act in the U.S. House of Representatives, stating the act was "an important step in restoring freedom of religion to the protected First Amendment status it enjoyed for over 200 years."

• In a letter to local Church units, dated Sept. 15, 1999, the First Presidency launched a Churchwide effort "to revitalize and improve teaching in the Church."

• A Relief Society declaration reaffirming the roles and values of women was announced Sept. 25, 1999, during the General Relief Society Meeting, and what had been known as the Relief Society homemaking meeting was renamed "Home, Family, and Personal Enrichment Meeting" with a different focus.

• The First Presidency, in a letter addressed to members of the Church throughout the world," reaffirmed on Oct. 4, 1999, that Monday nights are reserved throughout the Church for family home evenings.

• The First Presidency announced Oct. 16, 1999, a uniform naming guideline for temples worldwide. The guideline, which applies to all of the 121 existing or planned temples, provides for the temple name to primarily include the city and state or province, or the city and country in which the temple is located. Some of the temple names were also altered to give clarity because of local usage.

• The Church's policy of strict political neutrality was reaffirmed Oct. 19, 1999, in a letter from the First Presidency to Church leaders.

• The General Welfare Committee of

the Church approved a name change for LDS Social Services, it was announced Nov. 27, 1999. The new name is LDS Family Services.

• The First Presidency on Dec. 1, 1999, sent a letter to priesthood leaders, reiterating the long-standing counsel to members of the Church to remain in their homelands and help build up the Church in their native countries, rather than immigrate to the United States.

• The Church's Family History and Historical Departments were consolidated into one department — the Family and Church History Department — on June 1, 2000.

Changes in General Church Leadership

Presidency of the Seventy

• **Elder Ben B. Banks** was called to the Presidency of the Seventy, effective Aug. 15, 1999, and sustained Oct. 2, 1999. Released from the Presidency of the Seventy was **Elder Joe J. Christensen**, who served in the presidency from Aug. 15, 1993, to Aug. 15, 1999.

• **Elder Dennis B. Neuenschwander** was called to the Presidency of the Seventy, effective Aug. 15, 2000, and sustained Oct. 7, 2000. Released from the Presidency of the Seventy was **Elder Harold G. Hillam**, who served in the presidency from Aug. 15, 1995, to Aug. 15, 2000, and was called, effective Aug. 15, 2000, as second counselor in the Europe West Area presidency.

First Quorum of the Seventy

• Two members of the Second Quorum of the Seventy sustained April 1, 2000, to the First Quorum of the Seventy were **Elders Lynn G. Robbins and Lance B. Wickman.** Also called to the First Quorum of the Seventy April 1, 2000, were **Elders Donald L. Hallstrom** and **Ronald A. Rasband.**

Emeritus General Authorities

• **Elders Joe J. Christensen** and **Andrew W. Peterson** of the First Quorum of the Seventy were granted emeritus status Oct. 2, 1999.

• Granted emeritus status Oct. 7, 2000, were **Elders F. Enzio Busche, Loren C. Dunn, and Alexander B. Morrison** of the First Quorum of the Seventy.

Second Quorum of the Seventy

• **Elders Adhemar Damiani, Stephen B. Oveson, David R. Stone, H. Bruce Stucki, Richard H. Winkel, and Robert S. Wood** were called to the Second Quorum of the Seventy April 3, 1999.

• **Elders Douglas L. Callister, Darwin B. Christenson, Keith Crockett, H. Aldridge Gillespie, and Robert C. Oaks** were called to the Second Quorum of the Seventy April 1, 2000.

• Released from the Second Quorum of the Seventy Oct. 7, 2000, were **Elders Eran A. Call, W. Don Ladd, James O. Mason, and Richard E. Turley Sr.**

Deaths of General Authorities

• **Elder Dallas N. Archibald,** 60, a member of the First Quorum of the Seventy, drowned Dec. 14, 1998, while fishing in the Biobio River near Santa Barbara, Chile, about 300 miles south of Santiago. It was the first accidental death of a General Authority since **Elder J. Golden Kimball** of the First Council of the Seventy died in an automobile accident in Nevada in 1938.

• **Elder Carlos E. Asay**, 72, president of the Salt Lake Temple, who served as a member of the First Quorum of the Seventy from 1976-1996, including 13 years as a member of the Presidency of the Seventy, died April 10, 1999.

• **Bernard Park Brockbank,** 91, an emeritus member of the Seventy, died Oct. 11, 2000. He was sustained as Assistant to the Quorum of the Twelve in 1962, and a member of the Seventy in 1976. He was granted emeritus status in 1980.

Auxiliaries

• **Coleen K. Menlove** was sustained Oct. 2, 1999, as Primary general president, succeeding **Patricia P. Pinegar**. Sustained as first and second counselors, respectively, were **Sydney S. Reynolds** and **Gayle M. Clegg**. Released as first and second counselors, respectively, were **Anne G. Wirthlin** and **Susan L. Warner**.

• **Elder Marlin K. Jensen** of the presidency of the Seventy was sustained Oct. 7, 2000, as Sunday School general president, succeeding **Elder Harold G. Hillam. Elders Neil L. Andersen and John H. Groberg** were retained as counselors.

Appointments

• **Senator Harry Reid**, D-Nevada, was named minority whip of the U.S. Senate Dec. 1, 1998, believed to be the highest-ranking position a member of the Church has held in Congress.

• Two new associate directors of the Tabernacle Choir — **Mack Wilberg,** professor of music at BYU, and **Barlow Bradford**, director of orchestras at the University of Utah — were announced Dec. 4, 1998, by President Gordon B. Hinckley.

• **Blaine Jay Smith** was appointed manager of administrative services for the Tabernacle Choir, it was announced Jan. 23, 1999.

• **Michael K. Young**, dean of George Washington School of Law, was appointed by the U.S. Senate to the United States Commission on International Religious Freedom, it was announced June 15, 1999.

• **Craig D. Jessop** was appointed by the First Presidency as music director of the Mormon Tabernacle Choir, suceeding **Jerold D. Ottley,** who retired Dec. 3, 1999.

• **Richard King** of the Central Park Ward, Fremont California, Stake, was named president-elect of Rotary International and will begin his service in July 2001 as world president of the service organization. This will be the second time in the history of the 95-year-old Rotary International that a member of the Church has led the 30,000 community-based service club organization. **Elder Richard L. Evans** of the Quorum of the Twelve was president in 1966-67.

• **David T. Warner**, a faculty member in the School of Education and the School of Music at BYU, was appointed chairman of the General Music Committee of the Church, it was announced July 15, 2000. He also directs the Music Division, as well as overseeing productions in the new Theater at Temple Square, located in the Conference Center.

• **Jim M. Wall**, executive vice president and general manager of the *Denver Post*, assumed his new duties Aug. 1, 2000, as publisher of the Church-owned *Deseret News*, which publishes the *Church News*. The Church Almanac is a publication of the *Church News/Deseret News*.

• **Roger L. Hunt**, a former regional representative and stake president in Nevada, and Kent J. Dawson, president of the Henderson Nevada Black Mountain Stake, were sworn in as federal judges in the United States Federal District Court in Nevada, it was announced Aug. 5, 2000.

Awards and Honors

• **Marjorie P. Hinckley**, wife of President Hinckley, was given the Heritage Award Oct. 31, 1998, by the Utah-California Women in Salt Lake City.

• **President Hinckley** received BYU's Marriott School of Business International Executive of the Year award Nov. 6, 1998.

• **Dr. Roger L. Hiatt** of the Memphis, Tenn., 2nd Ward and fomer president of the Philippines Baguio Mission, was honored Nov. 9, 1998, by the American Academy of Ophthalmology for his vast contributions in the field of ophthalmology.

• **Elder W. Eugene Hansen**, emeritus General Authority, was presented the Utah State Bar's Distinguished Service Award Nov. 20, 1998, for his exemplary professional career as an attorney.

• Former world champion and Olympic medal winner in the discus, **L. Jay Sylvester**, was inducted into the National Track and Field Hall of Fame in Orlando, Fla., on Dec. 3, 1998.

• **President Thomas S. Monson**, first counselor in the First Presidency, received the 1999 Distinguished Public Service Award from the Bay Area BYU Management Society and the BYU Alumni Association Feb. 12, 1999, in Oakland, Calif.

• The Department of English at the University of Utah honored **President Hinckley** in March 1999 with the establishment of an endowment in his name — "the Gordon B. Hinckley Endowment for British Studies."

• For outstanding contributions to genealogical work, the **Church Family History Department** was honored April 16, 1999, with the prestigious Silver Tray Award from the **Utah Genealogical Association** at a luncheon of the association's convention in Salt Lake City.

• **Jon and Karen Huntsman** were honored April 29, 1999, by the BYU Management Society for their generosity and accomplishments and given the "1999 Distinguished Utahns of the Year Award."

• **JaLynn Rasmussen Price** of the Potomac North Ward, Washington D.C. Stake, was named April 30, 1999, as the 1999 National Mother of Young Children by American Mothers Inc., at its annual convention in Honolulu, Hawaii.

• The **National Alliance of the Mentally Ill** on July 1, 1999, presented the Church with its Campaign To End Discrimination "Religious Advocacy Award" at its 20th anniversary convention in Chicago, Ill.

• The **American Society of Landscape Architects** honored the Church July 15, 1999, with a "once-in-a-century medallion award for its world-renowned landscaping and gardens at Church headquarters in Salt Lake City."

• **Christian and Karen Hardy** of the Oakland (Calif.) 1st Ward were among 17 Americans to receive the Friendship Award Sept. 29, 1999, at a state dinner in Beijing, China, for their work in improving conditions at a children's hospital in China.

• **President Hinckley** on Nov. 17, 1999, was honored as "Communicator of the Year" at the annual Golden Spike Awards luncheon of the Intermountain Association of Business Communicators and the Public Relations Society of America.

• **Lorna Fejo**, an Aboriginal member of the Church in Australia, was one of six Australians honored with the 2000 Australian Achiever Award for her work during the last three decades in Aboriginal communities in the Northern Territory.

• **Marjorie P. Hinckley** received an honorary doctorate of Christian Service April 20, 2000, from BYU for her love of learning, loving support of her husband, example of righteous motherhood, and positive influence on millions of people worldwide.

• **Jerold and JoAnn Ottley**, retired conductor and voice coach of the Mormon Tabernacle Choir, received Presidential Citations from BYU April 20, 2000. On May 5, 2000, they were honored by the BYU Management Society as "Distinguished Utahns of the Year."

• **Danny Ainge**, former BYU basketball star and retired professional player and coach, was inducted May 1, 2000, into the GTE Academic All-America Hall of Fame in Boston, Mass.

• **Calvin E. Smoot**, director of purchasing and travel services for the Church, was given the Presidents Award from the National Business Travel Association during the organization's global convention Aug. 2, 2000.

Deaths of Prominent Church Members

(As Of Sept. 30, 2000)

• **Robert K. Thomas**, 80, founding director of the Honors Program and former academic vice president at BYU, died Oct. 3, 1998, in Provo, Utah.

• **Albert Kenyon Wagner**, 78, the first director of Benemerito de las Americas — the Church school in Mexico City — died Oct. 6, 1998, in Mesa, Ariz.

• **Glenn E. Nielson**, 95, president of the Washington, D.C. Mission from 1973-77 and founder of Husky Oil Co., died Oct. 19, 1998, in Cody, Wyo.

• **John E. Carr**, 86, director of the Church Translation and Distribution Department from 1969-77 and president of the New England Mission from 1959-62, died Oct. 22, 1998, in Murray, Utah.

• **Boyd Frederick Schenk**, 76, a pioneer of the Church in the St. Louis, Mo., area and former chairman of the board and chief executive officer of Pet Milk Co., died Nov. 28, 1998, in Town and Country, Mo.

• **Johan Paul Jongkees**, 78, first president of the Holland Stake (now The Hague Netherlands Stake) from 1961-1971 and London Temple president from 1978-1982, died Dec. 31, 1998, in Holland.

• **Berkeley Bunker**, 92, president of the Southern States Mission from 1955-1959, who served in the U.S. Congress as a Nevada senator from 1940-1942 and as the U.S. representative from Nevada from 1944-1946, died Jan. 21, 1999, in Las Vegas, Nev.

• **Arnold J. Irvine**, 78, secretary to the First Council of the Seventy from 1951-1955, former education editor for the *Deseret News*, and former staff writer for the *Church News*, died Feb. 7, 1999, in Sun City, Calif.

• **Paul E. Felt Sr.**, 83, former president of the Southwest Indian Mission and director of the American Indian Institute and Studies, died Feb. 9, 1999, in Provo, Utah. He was the first institute director outside the United States.

• **Leonard J. Arrington**, 81, Church historian from 1972-1982, and director of the Joseph Fielding Smith Institute of Church History and the Lemuel H. Redd Jr. Professor of Church History at BYU, died Feb. 11, 1999, in Salt Lake City, Utah.

• **Daken K. Broadhead**, 93, former executive assistant to U.S. Secretary of Agriculture Ezra Taft Benson from 1953-1955, and former member of the general Church Welfare Committee, regional representative and mission representative of the Quorum of the Twelve, died Feb. 21, 1999, in Newport Beach, Calif.

• **Susan Ashby Brinton**, 81, BYU's first homecoming queen, Relief Society general board member from 1972-1984, and personal secretary to Presiding Bishop LeGrand Richards, died Feb. 25, 1999, in Salt Lake City, Utah.

• **Margaret Romney Jackson Judd**, 89, first counselor in the Young Women general presidency from 1961-1972, died April 1, 1999, in Salt Lake City, Utah.

• **Caroline Eyring Miner**, 91, 1973 Utah Mother of the Year, 1976 Utah Poet of the Year, and a member of the Young Women General Board from 1948-1961, died April 19, 1999, in Cedar Hills, Utah.

• **Glenn Russell Handy**, 87, former area construction supervisor for Asia in the Church Building Department, who oversaw the development of many Church building projects in 13 Asian countries, died May 3, 1999, in Provo, Utah.

• **Stewart B. Eccles**, 92, organizer and first manager of Deseret Industries and former member of the General Church Welfare Committee, died May 5, 1999, in Salt Lake City, Utah.

• **Wallace G. McPhie**, 77, former director of Church construction worldwide and director of and construction manager in Temple and Special Projects Construction, died May 9, 1999, in Salt Lake City, Utah.

• **L. Ronald Folkersen**, 71, president of the Sweden Stockholm Mission from 1972-75,and former regional representative and director of Church Service missionaries at the Church

Office Building, died May 12, 1999.

• **Virginia Pickett Backman**, 75, wife of **Elder Robert L. Backman**, Emeritus General Authority, died June 4, 1999, in Salt Lake City, Utah.

• **Kenneth Young Knight**, 72, former president of the Canada Vancouver Mission and retired vice chairman of Sinclair Oil Corp., died June 5, 1999, in Salt Lake City, Utah.

• **Carlfred B. Broderick**, 67, noted LDS author in the field of marriage and family relations, died July 27, 1999, in Cerritos, Calif.

• **Agricol Lozano Herrera**, 72, the first Latin stake president in Mexico and former president of the Mexico City Temple and of the Argentina Bahia Blanca Mission, died July 29, 1999, in Mexico City.

• **Daniel Albert Keeler**, 75, whose voice was widely used for many Church films, recordings, and pageants, including the Mormon Miracle Pageant in Manti, Utah, and the Hill Cumorah Pageant in Palmyra, N.Y., died Aug. 4, 1999, in Bountiful, Utah.

• **Ivan J. Barrett**, 89, a BYU professor for 42 years, lifelong scholar of Joseph Smith, and president of the Northwestern States Mission from 1964-1967, died Aug. 16, 1999, in Orem, Utah.

• **Thane J. Packer**, 85, a member of the YMMIA General Board who helped develop the Church's Varsity Scout program and who helped foster Scouting in the Church in the Pacific, died Aug. 22, 1999, in Provo, Utah.

• **Ruth Elaine Muir Gardner**, 72, author of LDS hymns "Families Can Be Together Forever" and "Go Forth in Faith," died Sept. 1, 1999, in Salt Lake City, Utah.

• **Edna Michelsen Faux**, 99, who during her service on the Primary General Board from 1947 to 1972 chaired the committee for integrating Boy Scouting into Primary, died Sept. 7, 1999, in Salt Lake City, Utah.

• **Belva Barlow Ashton**, 71, who as part of her Relief Society General Board responsibilies directed the 1978 dedication activities of the Relief Society Monument to Women in Nauvoo, Ill., died Oct. 8, 1999, in Salt Lake City, Utah.

• **James William Kuli Harris**, 63, the People's Representative for Parliament from Vava'u, Tonga and former Secretary of Labour, Commerce, and Industries in Tonga, died Oct. 23, 1999, in Hawaii.

• **Elizabeth Fetzer Bates**, 90, who wrote the Primary children's songs "Book of Mormon Stories" and "Pioneer Children Sang As They Walked," died Nov. 20, 1999, in Salt Lake City, Utah.

• **Maurine McClellan Haycock**, 82, widow of D. Arthur Haycock, who was secretary to five Church presidents, died April 1, 2000, in Bountiful, Utah.

• **Stan Watts**, 88, BYU men's basketball coach from 1949 to 1972, who guided the Cougars to two National Invitation Tournament championships in 1951 and 1966 (equivalent to national championships at that time), died April 6, 2000, in Provo, Utah. He was inducted into the Basketball Hall of Fame in 1986.

• **Albert Jay Blair**, 56, manager of historical sites and exhibits for the Church, died April 10, 2000, in Orem, Utah.

• **Alice Sheets Marriott**, 92, co-founder of Marriott Corporation with her husband, J. Willard Marriott, and a former trustee of the John F. Kennedy Center for the Performing Arts, died April 18, 2000, in Washington, D.C.

• **Helen Lee Goates**, 74, second daughter of President Harold B. Lee and Relief Society General Board member from 1974-1975 and from 1979-1984, died Arpil 19, 2000, in Salt Lake City, Utah.

• **Arnold R. Knapp,** 89, president of the England Bristol Mission from 1973-1976 and director of Church International Public Communications from 1977-1978, died May 4, 2000, in St. George, Utah.

• **Judith Wirthlin Parker**, 80, who was chairwoman of the Music Committee that compiled the Primary Song Book "Sing With Me" while a member of the Primary General Board from 1959 to 1974, died May 29, 2000, in Salt Lake City, Utah.

• **Wilford W. Kirton Jr**. 78, former legal counsel for the Church who worked with seven presidents of the Church on legal matters, died July 23, 2000, in Salt Lake City, Utah.

• **Sherman Bitner Hinckley**, brother to President Hinckley, died Aug. 13, 2000, in Salt Lake City. He had been instrumental, along with a cousin, in the acquisition and donation of historic Cove Fort in central Utah to the Church. The fort had been built in 1867, under the direction of Ira Nathaniel Hinckley, grandfather of President Hinckley and Brother Hinckley.

News Events

• **Madame Jehan Sadat**, former first lady of Egypt, visited the Relief Society general presidency in Salt Lake City on Oct. 1, 1998, and toured the Humanitarian Center and Welfare Square.

• **President Hinckley** dedicated the **Encampment Mall Monument** in St. George, Utah, Oct. 9, 1998, honoring the pioneers who first settled in the area.

• **President Hinckley** traveled through New England Oct. 14-18, 1998, and spoke to 1,600 members in **Burlington, Vt.**; visited the birthplace of Joseph Smith and spoke to missionaries in **Sharon, Vt.**; spoke to 5,500 members in Lowell, Mass; addressed missionaries and then to 3,500 members in **Worcester, Mass.**; and to members of the **Utica and Albany stakes in New York**. On the way back to Salt Lake City he spoke to 20,000 members from 16 stakes in five states in the United Center in **Chicago, Ill.**

• **Two missionaries, Elder Jose Manuel Mackintosh** of Hiko, Nev., and **Elder Bradley Alan Borden** of Mesa, Ariz., serving in the **Russia Yetakerinburg Mission**, were attacked and stabbed Oct. 17, 1998, resulting in the death of Elder Mackintosh and injury to Elder Borden.

• **President Thomas S. Monson** dedicated the **BYU Salt Lake Center** on Oct. 28, 1998.

• It was announced at a news conference Oct. 28, 1998, that the Church is playing a key role in the establishment of a new, state-of-the-art family history research facility in the **Ellis Island Immigration Museum in New York City**.

• In Australia, **Elder Vaughn J. Featherstone** of the Seventy and president of the Australia/New Zealand Area presented a check to **New South Wales Premier Bob Carr and Wollongong Mayor David Campbell** on Oct. 29, 1998, for $100,000 to help alleviate damage caused by a storm that pelted Wollongong with 33 inches of rain in a 12-hour period.

• The first shipment of more than 240,000 pounds of relief supplies was shipped by the Church Nov. 2, 1998, to victims of the devastating Hurricane Mitch in **Honduras, Nicaragua, and Guatemala**. Within two weeks, some 600,000 pounds of supplies had been shipped by the Church.

• **Ricks College** won an unprecedented fourth consecutive **National Junior College Athletic Association** women's cross country championship and established a new national team record Nov. 14, 1998, in Overland Park, Kan.

• **President Hinckley** visited three mid-Atlantic states Nov. 13-15, 1998, and spoke to 8,600 members in **Greenville, N.C.**; 7,000 in **Richmond, Va.**; and more than 7,000 in **Baltimore, Md.**

• **President Hinckley** visited hurricane-stricken areas in **Nicaragua and Honduras** on Nov. 19-21, 1998, offering comfort and assistance and promising them they would not be forgotten. He spoke to 19,000 members in three hastily arranged meetings in **Managua, Nicaragua, and in Tegucigalpa and San Pedro Sula,**

Honduras.

• When the 106th Congress convened in January 1999, 17 Church members were serving in the **U.S. Senate or the House of Representatives,** the largest number of Church members to ever serve in Congress.

• In Spain to dedicate the Madrid Spain Temple, **President Hinckley**, along with his first counselor, President **Thomas S. Monson**, and **Elder Jeffrey R. Holland** of the Quorum of the Twelve, paid a visit to **King Juan Carlos and Queen Sofia** at the royal palace March 18, 1999.

• The pioneer cemetery at historic **Winter Quarters,** Neb., containing the remains of more than 600 Latter-day Saints from the exodus of 1846-47, was deeded to the Church April 1, 1999, by the city of Omaha.

• On April 1, 1999, the centennial box of the **Sunday School**, created from 39 different woods sent from missions around the world and sealed in 1949, was opened in ceremonies attended by **President Hinckley**.

• A shipment of 78,500 pounds of food was sent by the Church April 10-11, 1999, to assist **refugees from Kosovo**, just one week after the assistance was announced by President Hinckley in general conference. A shipment of 200,000 pounds of clothing was also sent by the Church.

• Three people died and four others were wounded when a gunman opened fire inside the **Church Family History Library** in downtown Salt Lake City April 15, 1999.

• **President Hinckley** spoke to 57,500 members at a regional conference on April 25, 1999, in **Santiago, Chile**.

• Sixteen homes of Latter-day Saints were destroyed by tornadoes that struck parts of **Oklahoma and Kansas**. One member was killed in Kansas.

• BYU men's volleyball team won the 1999 **NCAA national volleyball championship** in Los Angeles, Calif., May 8, 1999, capping off a 30-1 season.

• **BYU-Hawaii** women's tennis team won the NCAA Division II national championship May 17, 1999, in Pensacola, Fla., in its first year of Division II competition.

• The **Mormon Youth Chorus and Symphony** performed its last tour May 11-13, 1999, to St. George, Utah, and southern California, and the last concert of its 30-year history in the Salt Lake Tabernacle May 21-22, 1999, before being disbanded.

• At a news conference linked by satellite between Salt Lake City and Washington, D.C., **President Hinckley** officially launched on May 24, 1999, the **FamilySearch Internet Genealogy Service**, a free Web site offered by the Church that promises to be the greatest boon to family research since the invention of microfilm.

• The first branch on **Christmas Island**, a 140-square-mile atoll in the South Pacific and part of the Republic of Kiribati, was organized May 23, 1999.

• The first LDS meetinghouses in two countries were dedicated in **Athens, Greece**, on May 30, 1999, and in **Ulaanbaatar, Mongolia**, on June 6, 1999.

• The **Tabernacle Choir** reached a major milestone July 18, 1999, as it performed its weekly network program "Music and the Spoken Word." The program has now been on the radio for 70 years, and is the longest continuous, uninterrupted network radio broadcast in the world.

• Nearly 22,000 members gathered in **Guayaquil, Ecuador,** to hear President Hinckley speak at a member meeting.

• **President Hinckley** spoke to 5,000 members at a member meeting in **Maracaibo, Venezuela** on Aug. 3, 1999.

• A rare **tornado** touched down in **Salt Lake City** Aug. 11, 1999, killing one person and injuring about 150 others and causing some damage on Temple Square and at the Church's new Conference Center across the street.

• **President Spencer W. Kimball** was honored Sept. 7, 1999, as **President Hinckley** dedicated a new building at Ricks College in Rexburg, Idaho, that bears the name of The Spencer W. Kimball Student and Administrative

Services Building.

• **President Hinckley** spoke to 1,000 people gathered in a remote corner of southwestern Utah Sept. 11, 1999, and **dedicated a reconstructed monument**, honoring the memory of 120 people who lost their lives in the "Mountain Meadows Massacre" of 1857.

• At least 20 homes of members of the Church were destroyed and hundreds of Church members were evacuated Sept. 15-17, 1999, when flooding caused by **Hurricane Floyd** swamped several areas in **Florida, Georgia, South Carolina, and North Carolina.**

• For the first time, general conference on Oct. 2-3, 1999, was broadcast on a wide scale over the Internet, reaching as many as 100,000 people worldwide in 12 languages. This was the **last general conference held in the Tabernacle** on Temple Square. In his closing address, President Hinckley bid "goodbye to an old and wonderful friend." General conferences in the Tabernacle date back to 1867.

• **President Hinckley** dedicated BYU's renovated **Ernest L. Wilkinson Student Center** Oct. 5, 1999. The center was originally completed in 1965, but, because of intense activity, was "reworked from basement to roof."

• After heavy rains and flooding in southeastern **Mexico,** more than 3,500 members of the Church in eight stakes were temporarily evacuated from their homes Oct. 5-7, 1999.

• Retiring director of the Tabernacle Choir, **Jerold D. Ottley,** conducted his last weekly network broadcast of "Music and the Spoken Word" on Oct. 17, 1999. He served 24 years as director of the choir.

• The premiere concert of the **Mormon Tabernacle Choir, the Temple Square Chorale, and the Orchestra at Temple Square** was held Oct. 29, 1999, in the Tabernacle in Salt Lake City.

• Several Church members were among nearly a thousand delegates and dignitaries participating in the **Second World Congress of Families** Nov. 14-17, 1999, in **Geneva, Switzerland.**

• On Nov. 22, 1999, the Church's **FamilySearch.org**, the world's largest Internet genealogy site, was augmented with 240 million names, enabling users to access more than 640 million entries.

• **"American Prophet: The Story of Joseph Smith,"** narrated by famed actor **Gregory Peck**, made its debut over the Public Broadcast System Nov. 26, 1999.

• On the eve of the sesquicentennial of the founding of the **Sunday School**, a time capsule containing nearly 200 pounds of mementos and artifacts gathered from all 29 areas of the Church was sealed in ceremonies Dec. 8, 1999. The capsule, an earth-shaped titanium sphere, is to be opened in the year 2049.

• **President Hinckley** was interviewed Dec. 24, 1999, by **Larry King,** host of CNN's national broadcast talk show "Larry King Live," which orginated from the Tabernacle on **Temple Square.** President Hinckley was one of three religious leaders interviewed on the program. The other two were linked by satellite from **Bethlehem** in the Holy Land and from **Washington, D.C.**

• **The First Presidency and Quorum of the Twelve** issued their testimony of the Savior Jan. 1, 2000, in a document titled **"The Living Christ."** The "Testimony of the Apostles," which later was translated into 41 languages, was the first of two pronouncements issued by the First Presidency and Quorum of the Twelve concerning the Savior during the year 2000.

• The first of two large shipments of food and other supplies from the Church arrived in northern **Venezuela** Jan. 1, 2000, where floods killed thousands and left legions homeless. The first shipment was 225,000 pounds of food, hygiene kits and medical supplies. The second shipment, which arrived in mid-January, was 200,000 pounds of food and clothing.

• In the midst of his Pacific Rim travels, **President Hinckley** met on Jan. 27, 2000, with the president of

Indonesia, **Abdurrahman Wahid**, at a dinner in the presidential palace in Jakarta.

• On Feb. 1, 2000, **President Hinckley** returned to Salt Lake City after an eight-stop excursion of the **Pacific and Australia that took him to Hawaii, Kiribati, Australia, Indonesia, Singapore, and Guam.** During the tour, he traveled 22,670 miles and gave nine major addresses to more than 26,600 people.

• In late February or early March 2000, the 100 millionth copy of the **Book of Mormon** was printed since it was first published in 1830, it was announced April 22, 2000. At year-end 1999, about **99.2 million copies** of the book had been distributed, and with about 15,000 books sent out each day, the date for reaching 100 million was estimated in late February or early March. Another milestone was reached in 2000 when the Book of Mormon was printed in its **100th language,** although some of the languages are no longer in print.

• **President Hinckley** spoke March 8, 2000, to a sold-out **National Press Club Newsmakers** Luncheon in Washington, D.C, the first president of the Church to speak to the club.

• As of March 20, 2000, the Church had sent 11 shipping containers of clothing, food, and medical supplies to **Mozambique** and 10 to **Zimbabwe** in Africa to help alleviate suffering caused by flooding as a result of weeks of heavy rains and cyclones.

• A new 60-minute movie, **"The Testaments of One Fold and One Shepherd,"** opened to the public March 24, 2000, in the Legacy Theater in the Joseph Smith Memorial Building in Salt Lake City. The message of the film is the reality of the Atonement of Jesus Christ for all mankind and affirms that both the Bible and Book of Mormon are testaments of the Savior.

• The first general conference to be held in the new **Conference Center** in Salt Lake City, across the street north of Temple Square, convened April 1-2, 2000. More than **400,000** requested free tickets to attend the conference, far exceeding the 21,000-seat capacity of the hall. During the conference, **President Hinckley** announced six new temples to be built in Aba, Nigeria; Asuncion, Paraguay; Helsinki, Finland; Lubbock, Texas; Snowflake, Ariz., and in the tri-cities area of Richland, Kennewick, and Pasco, Wash.

• A video production, **"Special Witnesses of Christ,"** was broadcast between general conference sessions April 1-2, 2000, and will be translated into 26 languages. The second of two pronouncements this year of the **First Presidency and Quorum of the Twelve** about the Savior, the video features each apostle bearing his testimony of Christ.

• At a press conference in Kirtland, Ohio, on April 17, 2000, **Elder Loren C. Dunn** of the Seventy and president of the North America East Area and executive director of the Church Historical Department, announced the Church's plans to restore or reconstruct six facilities in **Kirtland** that were prominent in Church history in the 1830s: construction of a new visitors center resembling a 19th century grist mill used by **Samuel Whitney**, restoration of the **Newel K. Whitney** home, the building of a replica of the **John Johnson** Inn on its original foundation, and the restoration of a tannery, ashery, and schoolhouse.

• Following a six-year effort, the rebuilt **Gadfield Elm Chapel**, the oldest LDS chapel in England that was constructed in 1836 by members of the **United Brethren** and given to the Church four years later after 600 members of that faith joined the Church en masse, was rededicated April 23, 2000, by **Elder Jeffrey R. Holland** of the Quorum of the Twelve.

• More than 20,000 women participated in the **BYU Women's Conference 2000** on April 27-28, 2000, that was preceded by a day of service on April 26.

• The **FamilySearch Internet Genealogy Service** received its 3 billionth hit May 13, 2000, less than a year after the site was launched.

• All three members of the **First**

Presidency spoke at a luncheon in Salt Lake City May 24 commemorating the **150th anniversary of the *Deseret News*, which publishes the *Church News*.**

• BYU concluded its **"Lighting the Way for the 21st Century"** capital campaign — the most ambitious campaign in the university's 125-year history, generating more than **$411.7 million** in donations — on May 31, 2000. The campaign was launched in 1995.

• The first stake in **Liberia** on the southwest coast of Africa was created June 11, 2000, in the captial city of Monrovia by **Elder H. Bruce Stucki** of the Seventy.

• The first LDS meetinghouse in **Bulgaria** was dedicated in Sofia June 18, 2000, by **Elder Charles Didier** of the Seventy and president of the Europe East Area.

• **President Hinckley** announced on June 21, 2000, that Church-owned **Ricks College** in Rexburg, Idaho, would become a four-year college and would be renamed **Brigham Young University-Idaho**. For most of its existence, Ricks, which was started in 1888 as a stake academy, has been a junior college, but was a four-year college for seven years, from 1949-1956.

• All three members of the **First Presidency** and other General Authorities addressed 103 newly called mission presidents and their wives at the annual **Mission Presidents Seminar** June 20-23, 2000. **President Thomas S. Monson** spoke to the group on June 20, **President James E. Faust** on June 21, and **President Hinckley** on his birthday, June 23.

• **President Hinckley** commemorated his 90th birthday June 23, 2000, at **"An Evening of Celebration,"** held in the Conference Center in Salt Lake City and telecast over the Church's satellite system. It featured distinguished LDS musicians of international reputation, the **Mormon Tabernacle Choir, and the Orchestra at Temple Square.**

• The legacy of the **Mormon Battalion** was celebrated June 24, 2000, at the 75-year-old Mormon Battalion Monument on the grounds of the Utah State Capitol. **Elder Marlin K. Jensen** of the Presidency of the Seventy was the featured speaker.

• A monument, honoring 410 Icleanders who immigrated to America from 1854-1914, was dedicated June 30, 2000, near "**Mormon Pond**," a tide pool on the rocky coast of the **Westmann Islands,** where many of the early Icelandic converts were baptized.

• A museum devoted to LDS Church history was opened as part of the new **Icelandic Emigration Center in Hofsos, Iceland,** on July 3, 2000. The next day, July 4, the first LDS meetinghouse in Iceland was dedicated in **Gardebaer,** a suburb of the capital city of Rejkjavik. Iceland's president, **Olafur Ragnar Grimsson,** participated in both events.

• The 150th anniversary of the **Church in Scandinavia** was celebrated in **Denmark** during the first week of July, 2000 with a series of firesides, dances, reunions, and the unveiling of two statues. The first statue, unveiled July 4 in **Rebild National Park**, is titled "The Family" and symbolizes a **Mormon family** as they prepare to make the voyage to Utah in the late 1800s. The second **statue** was unveiled July 6 in the harbor area of **Copenhagen**, where many of the saints boarded sailing ships for the journey to America.

• A database that included a worldwide catalog of Jewish records on film, microfiche, and books available at the **Family History Library** was presented July 9, 2000, to the **International Association of Jewish Genealogical Societies** meeting in Salt Lake City.

• More than 25,000 people gathered in **Snowflake, Ariz.**, July 21, 2000, for a Pioneer Day celebration during which **President James E. Faust** dedicated a monument honoring the founders of the northeastern Arizona town.

• The **Joseph F. Smith Memorial Grove** at This Is the Place Heritage Park in Salt Lake City was dedicated July 24, 2000, by **Elder M. Russell Ballard** of the

Quorum of the Twelve, a great-grandson of the sixth president of the Church.

• Four 19th century-style sailing ships will cross the Atlantic in August 2001, reenacting the **Mormon migration** from **Scandinavia to England to New York,** in anticipation of the 150th anniversary of European immigration that began in **Denmark** in 1852, it was announced Aug. 12, 2000.

• Legendary BYU football coach **LaVell Edwards** announced at a press conference Aug. 17, 2000, that he would retire at the end of the 2000 season. During his 29 years as head football coach, he has amassed the third most wins among active coaches in the United States with 251 victories.

TEMPLE NEWS

• The Church's northernmost temple in **Anchorage, Alaska,** the second of the smaller temples, was dedicated Jan. 9, 1999, by **President Hinckley.**

• The **Colonia Juarez Chihuahua Mexico** Temple, Mexico's newest temple in its oldest stake, was dedicated March 6, 1999, by President Hinckley. This was the last of the first three smaller temples announced in general conference in October 1997.

• Just 30 years after the first missionaries arrived in Spain to preach the restored gospel, the **Madrid Spain Temple** was dedicated March 19, 1999, by **President Hinckley.**

• In the closing session of general conference April 4, 1999, **President Hinckley** announced that the **Nauvoo Temple**, which was destroyed by fire in 1848 and virtually leveled by a tornado in 1850, would be rebuilt.

• Fifteen years after it was announced in 1984, the **Bogota Colombia Temple** was dedicated April 24, 1999, by **President Hinckley.**

• On April 24, 1999, **Elder Spencer J. Condie** of the Seventy presided over site dedicatory services for the **Copenhagen Denmark Temple**, which, like the Vernal Utah Temple, will be created by the remodeling of an existing edifice, the Church's Priorvej Chapel in Copenhagen.

• The **First Presidency** announced June 14, 1999, that a temple would be built adjacent to the pioneer cemetery in **Winter Quarters** in Omaha, Neb.

• Described as "the most beautiful building in Ecuador," the **Guayaquil Ecuador Temple** was dedicated Aug. 1, 1999, by **President Hinckley**, 17 years after it was announced.

• The **Spokane Washington Temple**, the second temple in Washington, was dedicated Aug. 21, 1999, by **President Hinckley** in the Spokane suburb of Opportunity.

• **President Hinckley** dedicated the first temple in Ohio, since the Kirtland Temple in early Church history, in **Columbus** on Sept. 4, 1999.

• The **Bismarck North Dakota Temple** was dedicated Sept. 19, 1999, by **President Hinckley** in a land with relatively few members separated by vast distances.

• The **Columbia South Carolina Temple**, located in one of the original 13 American colonies, was dedicated Oct. 16, 1999, by **President Hinckley**.

• The **Detroit Michigan Temple** was dedicated Oct. 23, 1999, by **President Hinckley** in the suburb of Bloomfield Hills.

• More than 5,000 people crowded onto the site of the original **Nauvoo Temple** Oct. 24, 1999, to witness President Hinckley break ground for the rebuilding of the Church's second temple in Nauvoo, Ill.

• The **Raleigh North Carolina Temple,** located in the suburban community of Apex, was dedicated Dec. 18, 1999, by **President Hinckley**.

• For the first time in the history of the Church, two temples, both in Canada, were dedicated on the same day. The **Halifax Nova Scotia Temple** was dedicated Nov. 14, 1999, by **President Hinckley** and the Regina Saskatchewan Temple was dedicated by **President Boyd K. Packer**, acting president of the Quorum of the Twelve.

• Nestled at the base of the 300-foot-high Rimrock cliffs on the outskirts west of the city, the **Billings Montana Temple** was dedicated Nov. 20, 1999, by **President Hinckley**.

• Serving some 14,800 members stretching hundreds of miles across the northern end of Alberta, the **Edmonton Alberta Temple** was dedicated Dec. 11, 1999, by President Hinckley.

• The first temple dedicated in the year 2000 was the **St. Paul Minnesota Temple**, dedicated by **President Hinckley** on Jan. 9, 2000.

• On the first leg of his tour to the Pacific and Australia, **President Hinckley** dedicated the **Kona Hawaii Temple** on Jan. 23, 2000, the second temple in the island state.

• The first two of nine temples that are expected to be dedicated in Mexico in 2000, were dedicated by **President Hinckley** in **Ciudad Juarez, Mexico,** on Feb. 26, 2000, and in Hermosillo, **Sonora, Mexico**, on Feb. 27, 2000.

• The **Albuquerque New Mexico Temple** was dedicated March 5, 2000, by **President Hinckley**.

• Two more temples in Mexico were dedicated by **President James E. Faust:** the **Oaxaca Mexico Temple** on March 11, 2000, and the **Tuxtla Gutierrez Mexico Temple** March 12, 2000. The Tuxtla temple is the 75th operating temple in the Church.

• **President Thomas S. Monson** dedicated the **Louisville Kentucky Temple** on March 19, 2000, the first temple in Kentucky.

• In an area that has been termed as "the breadbasket of the nation," the **Fresno California Temple**, the fourth temple in California, was dedicated April 9, 2000, by **President Hinckley**.

• The **Medford Oregon Temple**, the second temple in Oregon, was dedicated April 16, 2000, by **President James E. Faust.**

• The **Palmyra New York Temple**, built on what was once the 100-acre Joseph Smith farm and overlooking the Sacred Grove, was dedicated April 6, 2000, by **President Hinckley.** The first session was transmitted over the Church satellite system in 12 languages to meetinghouses in six time zones. An estimated **1.3 million members** participated in the session.

• For the first time in the history of the Church, three temples were dedicated in two days, bringing the Churchwide total of operating temples to 85. On May 20, 2000, **President Thomas S. Monson** dedicated the **Tampico Mexico Temple**. On the next day, May 21, 2000, President Monson dedicated the **Villahermosa Mexico Temple**. Also on May 21, 2000, **President James E. Faust** dedicated the **Nashville Tennessee Temple**, the second temple in Tennessee.

• For the second time in Church history, two temples were dedicated on the same day. **President Thomas S. Monson** dedicated the **Reno Nevada Temple** on Easter Sunday, April 23, 2000. The **Memphis Tennessee Temple** was also dedicated on April 23, 2000, by **President James E. Faust**.

• The **Montreal Quebec Temple** — Canada's sixth temple and Quebec's first — was dedicated June 4, 2000, by **President Hinckley**. On the same day, the **San Jose Costa Rica Temple** was dedicated by **President James E. Faust**. It marked the third time in Church history that two temples were dedicated on the same day.

• For the first time in Church history, a Church president dedicated four temples during one overseas tour. **President Hinckley**, on an extended tour of Asia and the South Pacific, dedicated the **Fukuoka Japan Temple** June 11, 2000; the **Adelaide Australia Temple** June 15, 2000; the **Melbourne Australia Temple** June 16, 2000; and the **Suva Fiji Temple**, June 18, 2000, making a total of six temples dedicated in June 2000. The dedication of six temples in one month also occurred in April 2000. On the trip, **President Hinckley** also visited **Thailand** June 12-13; New Caledonia June 16; and **America Samoa** June 17.

• The **Cochabamba Bolivia Temple** was dedicated by **President Hinckley** April 30, 2000, following five days of open house in which 65,570 people visited, resulting in 2,231 referrals.

• **President Thomas S. Monson** dedicated two temples in Mexico, the 9th and 10th temples in that country. On July 8, 2000, he dedicated the **Merida Mexico Temple**, and on July 9, the **Veracruz Mexico Temple**.

• The **Baton Rouge Louisiana Temple**, serving members in Louisiana and Mississippi, was dedicated July 16, 2000, by **President Hinckley.**

• The **Oklahoma City Oklahoma Temple**, serving Oklahoma and parts of Kansas, Texas, Arkansas, and Missouri, was dedicated July 30, 2000, by **President James E. Faust**.

• The first temple in Venezuela, announced in 1995, was dedicated in **Caracas** on Aug. 20, 2000, by **President Hinckley**.

• **President Hinckley** dedicated the **Houston Texas Temple**, the second temple in Texas, on Aug. 26, 2000.

• The **Birmingham Alabama Temple,** Alabama's first temple, was dedicated Sept. 3, 2000, by **President Hinckley.**

• Nearly seven years after it was announced in 1993, the **Santo Domingo Dominican Republic Temple** was dedicated Sept. 17, 2000, by **President Hinckley**.

• The **Boston Massachusetts Temple** — the Church's 100th operating temple — was dedicated Oct. 1, 2000, by **President Hinckley.**

TEMPLES IN OPERATION at year end

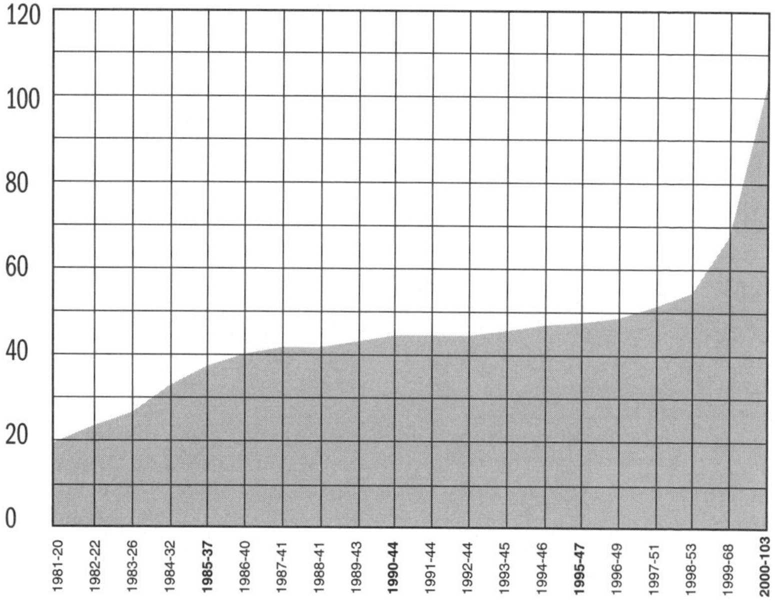

GENERAL AUTHORITIES, OFFICERS

GENERAL AUTHORITIES

(Current as of October, 2000)

THE FIRST PRESIDENCY

President Gordon B. Hinckley

President Gordon B. Hinckley was ordained and set apart as the 15th president of the Church on March 12, 1995, after serving 14 years as a counselor in the First Presidency and 20 years in the Quorum of the Twelve. Except for a short period during World War II, he has worked as an employee or General Authority of the Church on a full-time basis since completing his mission in 1935.

His ministry as president of the Church is characterized by a strong desire to be out among the people and to provide temples close to members wherever they may be in the world. In the first five years of his presidency, he has truly exemplified the injunction he gave in his first conference address after becoming president: "It is time to move forward without hesitation."

Since being called to the First Presidency in 1981, he has dedicated or rededicated 65 of the 100 temples now in operation, 39 of them since becoming Church president. Since 1995, he has traveled an estimated half million miles, speaking to members in more than 50 nations in Africa, Asia, the Pacific, Europe, and North, Central, and South America.

He has been awarded six honorary doctoral degrees.

President Hinckley was born June 23, 1910, in Salt Lake City, Utah, to Bryant S. and Ada Bitner Hinckley. As a young man, his ability with words won him a reputation as an outstanding speaker.

After graduating from the University of Utah in 1932 in English, he served a mission to the British Isles from 1933-35. Upon his return, he reported to the First Presidency in an interview that led to employment as secretary of the then recently formed Radio, Publicity, and Mission Literature Committee of the Church. During the next two decades he pioneered in the adapting of Church materials, particularly historical, for radio and later television programming, and prepared various materials for missionaries.

He married Marjorie Pay on April 29, 1937, in the Salt Lake Temple. They have five children and 25 grandchildren.

In 1937, he was called to the Deseret Sunday School Union General Board, a position he held until being called as counselor in the East Millcreek Stake in 1946. Ten years later, he was called as president of that stake, a third-generation stake president. In 1951, he was appointed general secretary of the General Missionary Committee, and assisted in introducing uniform missionary lessons.

President Hinckley was sustained an Assistant to the Twelve April 6, 1958, and as a member of the Quorum of the Twelve Sept. 30, 1961. He was ordained an apostle Oct. 5, 1961, at age 51.

He was called as a counselor to President Spencer W. Kimball on July 23, 1981, and as second counselor Dec. 2, 1982, serving until Nov. 5, 1985. He served as first counselor to President Ezra Taft Benson from Nov. 10, 1985, to May 30, 1994, and as first counselor to President Howard W. Hunter from June 5, 1994, to March 3, 1995.

Thomas S. Monson

President Thomas S. Monson was set apart as first counselor to President Gordon B. Hinckley on March 12, 1995. He was also set apart as president of the Twelve on that date. He previously was set apart as second counselor to President Howard W. Hunter on June 5, 1994, and as second counselor to President Ezra Taft Benson Nov. 10, 1985. He was sustained to the Quorum of the Twelve Oct. 4, 1963, and ordained an apostle Oct. 10, 1963, at age 36.

Before being called as a General Authority, he was general manager of Deseret Press. He began employment with the *Deseret News* in 1948 as an advertising executive, and was chairman of the *Deseret News* board for 19 years. Born Aug. 21, 1927, in Salt Lake City, to G. Spencer and Gladys Condie Monson, he graduated cum laude from the University of Utah in business management, and received an MBA degree from BYU. He has received an honorary Doctor of Laws degree from BYU and an honorary Doctor of Humane Letters degree from Salt Lake Community College.

He served in the Navy during World War II. He was ordained a bishop at age 22 and served in the presidency of the Temple View Stake in Salt Lake City. He was called as president of the Canadian Mission in 1959. He and his wife, Frances Beverly Johnson Monson, are parents of three children and have eight grandchildren.

James E. Faust

President James E. Faust was set apart as second counselor to President Gordon B. Hinckley on March 12, 1995, after serving as an apostle for 16 years. He was sustained an Assistant to the Twelve Oct. 6, 1972, and to the Presidency of the First Quorum of the Seventy Oct. 1, 1976. He was sustained to the Quorum of the Twelve Sept. 30, 1978, and ordained an apostle Oct. 1, 1978, at age 58.

President Faust has served as a regional representative, stake president, and bishop, and filled a mission in Brazil from 1939-42. He served in the Air Force during World War II, and in 1948 graduated from the University of Utah with a B.A. and juris doctorate.

An attorney, he practiced law until being called as a General Authority. He is a former Utah state legislator and was appointed by President John F. Kennedy to the Lawyer's Committee for Civil Rights and Racial Unrest. He was adviser to the American Bar Journal and the president of Utah Bar Association. In 1996, he was given the Distinguished Lawyer Emeritus Award by the Utah Bar Association and in 1997 BYU awarded him an honorary Doctor of Christian Service degree.

He was born July 31, 1920, in Delta, Utah, a son of George A. and Amy Finlinson Faust. He and his wife, Ruth Wright Faust, are parents of five children and have 23 grandchildren.

First Presidency and Quorum of the Twelve stand as witnesses of Christ.

THE QUORUM OF THE TWELVE APOSTLES

Boyd K. Packer

Set apart as acting president of the Quorum of the Twelve on June 5, 1994, and again March 12, 1995. Sustained as an Assistant to the Twelve Sept. 30, 1961; sustained to the Quorum of the Twelve April 6, 1970, and ordained an apostle April 9, 1970, at age 45. Former supervisor of Seminaries and Institutes of Religion; former president of the New England States Mission. Received bachelor's and master's degrees from Utah State University, and Ph.D. in educational administration from BYU. Pilot in the Pacific Theater during World War II. Born Sept. 10, 1924, in Brigham City, Utah, a son of Ira Wight and Emma Jensen Packer. Wife, Donna Smith Packer; parents of 10 children.

Sustained as an Assistant to the Twelve Oct. 6, 1972; sustained to the Quorum of the Twelve on April 6, 1974, and ordained an apostle April 11, 1974, at age 51. Served in the Marines in the Pacific during World War II. Graduated from Utah State University with a B.S. degree in finance; was vice president and treasurer of department store chain in Boston, Mass. Former stake president and counselor in stake presidency. Born Aug. 5, 1922, in Logan, Utah, to L. Tom and Nora Sonne Perry. Married Virginia Lee; parents of three children. She died in 1974. Married Barbara Dayton in 1976.

L. Tom Perry

David B. Haight

Sustained as an Assistant to the Twelve April 6, 1970; ordained an apostle Jan. 8, 1976, at age 69, and sustained to the Quorum of the Twelve April 3, 1976. Former regional representative, president of Scottish Mission, and stake president. Attended Utah State University. Former mayor of Palo Alto, Calif., district and regional manager of large retail store chain, assistant to president of BYU. Served as a commander in the Navy during World War II. Born Sept. 2, 1906, in Oakley, Idaho, to Hector C. and Clara Tuttle Haight. Wife, Ruby Olson Haight; parents of three children.

Sustained as an Assistant to the Twelve April 6, 1974, and to the Presidency of the First Quorum of the Seventy Oct. 1, 1976; ordained an apostle July 23, 1981, at age 55, and sustained to the Quorum of the Twelve Oct. 3, 1981. Received bachelor's degree in political science and master's degree from the University of Utah; has received four honorary doctorates. Former Church commissioner of education, former YMMIA general board member, regional representative, and bishop. Former executive vice president of the University of Utah. Born July 6, 1926, in Salt Lake City, Utah, to Clarence H. and Emma Ash Maxwell. Wife, Colleen Hinckley Maxwell; parents of four children.

Neal A. Maxwell

Russell M. Nelson

Sustained to the Quorum of the Twelve April 7, 1984, and ordained an apostle April 12, 1984, at age 59. Former Sunday School general president, regional representative, and stake president. Renowned surgeon and medical researcher. Received B.A. and M.D. degrees from University of Utah, and Ph.D. from University of Minnesota. Former president of the Society for Vascular Surgery and former chairman of the Council on Cardiovascular Surgery for the American Heart Association. Born Sept. 9, 1924, in Salt Lake City, Utah, to Marion C. and Edna Anderson Nelson. Wife, Dantzel White Nelson; parents of 10 children.

Sustained to the Quorum of the Twelve April 7, 1984, and ordained an apostle May 3, 1984, at age 51. Graduate of BYU in accounting, received juris doctorate cum laude from University of Chicago; was law clerk to U.S. Supreme Court Chief Justice Earl Warren, practiced law in Chicago, was professor of law at University of Chicago, and executive director of the American Bar Foundation; served nine years as BYU president, three years as Utah Supreme Court justice. Former regional representative and counselor in stake presidency. Born Aug. 12, 1932, in Provo, Utah, a son of Dr. Lloyd E. and Stella Harris Oaks. Wife June Dixon Oaks died July 21, 1998; parents of six children. Married Kristen Meredith McMain on Aug. 25, 2000.

Dallin H. Oaks

M. Russell Ballard

Sustained to the First Quorum of the Seventy April 3, 1976, and to the presidency of the quorum Feb. 21, 1980. Sustained to the Quorum of the Twelve Oct. 6, 1985, and ordained an apostle Oct. 10, 1985, at age 57. Attended the University of Utah; previously engaged in various business enterprises, including automotive, real estate, and investments. Was president of the Canada Toronto Mission, counselor in a mission presidency, and bishop. The grandson of Apostles Melvin J. Ballard and Hyrum Mack Smith, he was born Oct. 8, 1928, in Salt Lake City, Utah, to Melvin Russell Sr. and Geraldine Smith Ballard. Wife, Barbara Bowen Ballard; parents of seven children.

Sustained as an Assistant to the Twelve April 4, 1975, to the First Quorum of the Seventy Oct. 1, 1976, and to the presidency of the quorum Aug. 28, 1986; sustained to the Quorum of the Twelve Oct. 4, 1986, and ordained an apostle Oct. 9, 1986, at age 69. Served in the Sunday School general presidency, as stake president's counselor, and bishop. Graduate of University of Utah in business management; former president of trade association. Born June 11, 1917, in Salt Lake City, Utah, to Joseph L. and Madeline Bitner Wirthlin. Wife, Elisa Young Rogers Wirthlin; parents of eight children.

Joseph B. Wirthlin

Richard G. Scott

Sustained to the First Quorum of the Seventy April 2, 1977, and to the quroum presidency Oct. 1, 1983; sustained to the Quorum of the Twelve Oct. 1, 1988, ordained apostle Oct. 6, 1988, at age 59. Received B.S. degree in mechanical engineering from George Washington University, completed postgraduate work in nuclear engineering at Oak Ridge, Tenn. Worked on the staff of Adm. Hyman Rickover, developing military and private nuclear power reactors; was consultant to nuclear power industry. Former president of Argentina North Mission, regional representative, and counselor in stake presidency. Born Nov. 7, 1928, in Pocatello, Idaho, to Kenneth Leroy and Mary Eliza Whittle Scott. Married Jeanene Watkins; parents of seven children. She died May 15, 1995.

Sustained as an Assistant to the Twelve April 4, 1975, and to the First Quorum of the Seventy Oct. 1, 1976; sustained as Presiding Bishop April 6, 1985; sustained to the Quorum of the Twelve April 2, 1994, and ordained an apostle April 7, 1994, at age 61. Former first counselor in the Sunday School general presidency, president of the England London Mission; regional representative and stake president's counselor in the United States, England, Germany, and Spain. Earned bachelor's degree from the University of Utah, and master's degree in business administration from Harvard; served in the U.S. Air Force as jet fighter pilot; was an executive with four major national companies. Born Aug. 24, 1932, in New York City, N.Y., to John Rulon and Vera Marie Holbrook Hales. Wife, Mary Elene Crandall Hales; parents of two children.

Robert D. Hales

Jeffrey R. Holland

Sustained to the First Quorum of the Seventy on April 1, 1989, while serving as president of Brigham Young University; ordained an apostle June 23, 1994, at age 53, and sustained to the Quorum of the Twelve Oct. 1, 1994. Former Church Commissioner of Education and director or instructor at many institutes of religion. Received bachelor's degree in English and master's degree in religious education from BYU, and master's degree and doctorate in American studies from Yale University. Former regional representative, counselor in stake presidency, and bishop. Born Dec. 3, 1940, in St. George, Utah, to Frank D. and Alice Bentley Holland. Wife, Patricia Terry Holland; parents of three children.

Sustained as first counselor in the Presiding Bishopric April 6, 1985; sustained to the First Quorum of the Seventy Oct. 3, 1992; sustained to the Quorum of the Twelve April 1, 1995, and ordained an apostle April 6, 1995, at age 61. Commissioner and deputy commissioner of education for the Church Educational System. Former regional representative, member of the Sunday School general board, and bishop. Received bachelor's degree from University of Utah, and master's degree and doctorate from Harvard University. Former president of Ricks College, 1971-77. Born May 31, 1933, in Princeton, N.J., to Henry and Mildred Bennion Eyring. Wife, Kathleen Johnson Eyring; parents of six children.

Henry B. Eyring

PRESIDENCY OF THE SEVENTY

L. Aldin Porter

Sustained to the First Quorum of the Seventy April 4, 1987, at age 55; sustained to the Second Quorum of the Seventy April 1, 1989; sustained to the First Quorum of the Seventy April 6, 1991; called to the Presidency of the Seventy Aug. 15, 1992, and sustained Oct. 3, 1992. Former counselor in the Boise Idaho Temple presidency, president of the Louisiana Baton Rouge Mission, regional representative, stake president, and bishop. A graduate of BYU, he was an executive of a financial planning company. Born June 30, 1931, in Salt Lake City, Utah, to J. Lloyd and Revon Hayward Porter. Wife, Shirley Palmer Porter; parents of six children.

Called to the First Quorum of the Seventy Dec. 5, 1990, at age 56, and sustained April 6, 1991; called to the Presidency of the Seventy Aug. 15, 1996, and sustained Oct. 5, 1996. Former regional representative, president of the Australia Sydney Mission, counselor in the presidencies of the Eastern States, Utah North, and Utah Ogden missions, and bishop. Formerly corporate attorney for Kennecott Copper Corp.; graduated from the University of Utah Law School and earned a master's degree from New York University. Born June 11, 1934, in Bountiful, Utah, to William W. and Sylvia Carr Tingey. Wife, Joanne Wells Tingey; parents of four children.

Earl C. Tingey

D. Todd Christofferson

Sustained to the First Quorum of the Seventy April 3, 1993, at age 48; called to the Presidency of the Seventy Aug. 15, 1998, and sustained Oct. 3, 1998. Former regional representative, stake president, stake president's counselor, and bishop. Received bachelor's degree from BYU, juris doctorate from Duke University. Former associate general counsel of Nations Bank Corp. in Charlotte, N.C.; practiced law in Washington D.C., and was volunteer chairman of Middle Tennessee Literacy Coalition and Affordable Housing of Nashville, Tenn. Born Jan. 24, 1945, in American Fork, Utah, to Paul V. and Jeanne Swenson Christofferson. Wife, Katherine Thelma Jacob Christofferson; parents of five children.

Sunday School general president. Sustained to the First Quorum of the Seventy April 1, 1989, at age 46; called to the Presidency of the Seventy Aug. 15, 1998, and sustained Oct. 3, 1998. Former president of the New York Rochester Mission, regional representative, stake president, and bishop. Received bachelor's degree in German from Brigham Young University and juris doctorate from the University of Utah; was attorney specializing in business and estate planning. Born May 18, 1942, in Ogden, Utah, to Keith G. and Lula Hill Jensen. Wife, Kathleen Bushnell Jensen; parents of eight children.

Marlin K. Jensen

David E. Sorensen

Called to the Second Quorum of the Seventy June 6, 1992, at age 58, and sustained Oct. 3, 1992; sustained to the First Quorum of the Seventy April 1, 1995; called to the Presidency of the Seventy Aug. 15, 1998, and sustained Oct. 3, 1998. Former president of the Canada Halifax Mission, stake president and counselor, and bishop. Was chairman and chief executive officer of North American Health Care, a hospital chain, and board vice chairman of Nevada Community Bank in Las Vegas, Nev. Attended BYU, Utah State University, and University of Utah. Born June 29, 1933, in Aurora, Utah, to Alma and Metta Amelia Helquist Sorensen. Wife, Verla Anderson Sorensen; parents of seven children.

Sustained to the Second Quorum of the Seventy on April 1, 1989, at age 56; called to the First Quorum of the Seventy June 6, 1992, and sustained Oct. 3, 1992; called to Presidency of the Seventy Aug. 15, 1999, and sustained Oct. 2, 1999. Former president of the Scotland Edinburgh Mission, stake president, and bishop of three different wards. Attended the University of Utah and was owner and president of lumber company; formerly employed by two road machinery equipment companies. Born April 4, 1932, in Murray, Utah, to Ben F. and Samantha Berry Banks. Wife, Susan Kearnes Banks; parents of eight children.

Ben B. Banks

Dennis B. Neuenschwander

Sustained to the Second Quorum of the Seventy April 6, 1991, at age 51; sustained to First Quorum of the Seventy Oct. 1, 1994; called to Presidency of the First Quorum Aug. 15, 2000, and sustained Oct. 7, 2000. Former president of the Austria Vienna East Mission and counselor in mission presidency. Was manager of International Area of Acquisitions Division of the Church Genealogical Department. Received bachelor's degree from BYU, master's degree and doctorate in Russian literature from Syracuse University in New York. Born Oct. 6, 1939, in Salt Lake City, Utah, to George Henry and Genevieve Bramwell Neuenschwander. Wife, LeAnn Clement Neuenschwander; parents of four children.

FIRST QUORUM OF THE SEVENTY

Angel Abrea

Sustained to the First Quorum of the Seventy April 4, 1981, at age 47; first Argentine General Authority. Former president of Argentina Rosario Mission and the Buenos Aires Argentina Temple, regional representative, and stake president. Graduate of University of Buenos Aires; certified public accountant; served as secretary of the treasury in San Miguel, Argentina. Born Sept. 13, 1933, in Buenos Aires, Argentina, to Edealo and Zulema Estrada Abrea. Wife, Maria Victoria Chiapparino de Abrea; parents of three daughters.

Carlos H. Amado

Sustained to the Second Quorum of the Seventy April 1, 1989, at age 44; called to the First Quorum of the Seventy June 6, 1992, and sustained Oct. 3, 1992. Former president of the Guatemala Guatemala City Mission, where he was assigned to reopen the El Salvador San Salvador Mission, chairman of the Guatemala City Temple Committee, regional representative, stake president and counselor, bishop, and branch president. Received degree from the Technical Vocational Institute of Guatemala City; former technical draftsman, and later area director for the Church Educational System. Born Sept. 25, 1944, in Guatemala City, Guatemala, to Carlos and Rosario Funes de Amado. Wife, Mayavel Pineda Amado; parents of five children.

Neil L. Andersen

First counselor in Sunday School general presidency. Sustained to the First Quorum of the Seventy April 3, 1993, at age 41. Former president of the France Bordeaux Mission, stake president, and stake president's counselor. Graduated cum laude with a bachelor's degree from BYU, received master's degree in business from Harvard University. His business interests included advertising, real estate development, and health care, all based in Florida. Born Aug. 9, 1951, in Logan, Utah, to Lyle P. and Kathryn Andersen. Wife, Kathy Sue Williams Andersen; parents of four children.

Merrill J. Bateman

President of BYU. Called to the Second Quorum of the Seventy June 6, 1992, at age 55, and sustained Oct. 3, 1992; sustained as Presiding Bishop April 2, 1994; called to the First Quorum of the Seventy Nov. 2, 1995, and sustained April 6, 1996. Former regional representative and stake president twice. Owner of two management companies; former dean of BYU College of Business and served as business consultant to nations in West Africa. Received bachelor's degree from University of Utah and doctorate in economics from Massachusetts Institute of Technology. Born June 19, 1936, in Lehi, Utah, to Joseph Frederic and Belva Smith Bateman. Wife, Marilyn Scholes Bateman; parents of seven children.

Sustained to the First Quorum of the Seventy Oct. 3, 1975, at age 41, while president of Chile Mission; lived in Latin America and Asia for several years while in Church leadership positions. Was in fruit growing and shipping business in Texas, and owner of a company that grew citrus and tropical fruits in Texas, Mexico, and Central America for distribution in the United States and other countries; attended BYU. Born Oct. 25, 1933, in Springville, Utah, to Rawsel W. and Mary Waddoups Bradford. Wife, Mary Ann Bird Bradford; parents of six children.

William R. Bradford

Monte J. Brough

Sustained to the First Quorum of the Seventy Oct. 1, 1988, at age 49; sustained to the Second Quorum of the Seventy April 1, 1989; sustained to the First Quorum of the Seventy April 6, 1991; called to the Presidency of the Seventy Aug. 15, 1993, and sustained Oct. 2, 1993; served until Aug. 15, 1998. Former regional representative, president of the Minnesota Minneapolis Mission, member of Young Men general board, and bishop. Received bachelor's degree and doctorate in business administration from University of Utah; former president and founder of financial management company. Born June 11, 1939, in Randolph, Utah, to Richard Muir and Gwendolyn Kearl Brough. Wife, Lanette Barker Brough; parents of seven children.

Sustained to the First Quorum of the Seventy April 7, 1984, at age 52, while president of Idaho Boise Mission. Former regional representative and stake president. Received B.A. degree from BYU, law degree from University of California at Los Angeles. An attorney, he was president of a law firm in Los Angeles and past president of Westwood Bar Association; former legislative assistant in California Legislature. Born May 10, 1931, in Winslow, Ariz., to Cecil E. and Gladys Bushman Carmack. Wife, Shirley Fay Allen Carmack; parents of five children.

John K. Carmack

Sheldon F. Child

Sustained to the Second Quorum of the Seventy April 6, 1996, at age 57; sustained to the First Quorum of the Seventy April 5, 1998. Former area authority in the Utah North Area, president of New York New York Mission, stake president and counselor, and bishop. Was president of R.C. Willey Home Furnishings in Utah. Studied at University of Utah and Utah State University. Born May 8, 1938, in Ogden, Utah, to Mark Fay and Viola Criddle Child. Wife, Joan Haacke Child; parents of six children.

Gary J. Coleman

Called to the Second Quorum of the Seventy June 6, 1992, at age 50, and sustained Oct. 3, 1992; sustained to First Quorum of the Seventy April 5, 1997. Former president of the California Arcadia Mission, counselor in the Utah Ogden Mission, stake president's counselor, and bishop. Was associate director and instructor at Weber State University Institute of Religion. Received bachelor's degree in physical education from Washington State University, master's degree and doctorate from BYU in counseling and guidance. Born Sept. 18, 1941, in Wenatchee, Wash., to Benton Joseph and Evalin Barrett Coleman. Wife, Judith Renee England Coleman; parents of six children.

Sustained to the Second Quorum of the Seventy April 1, 1989, at age 48; called to the First Quorum of the Seventy June 6, 1992, and sustained Oct. 3, 1992. Former president of the Austria Vienna Mission, regional representative, stake president, and bishop of two wards. Former professor of sociology and ancient scripture at Brigham Young University. Born Aug. 27, 1940, in Preston, Idaho, to Spencer C. and Josie Peterson Condie. Wife, Dorthea Speth Condie; parents of five children.

Spencer J. Condie

Gene R. Cook

Sustained to the First Council of the Seventy Oct. 3, 1975, at age 34, and to the First Quorum of the Seventy Oct. 1, 1976. Former executive secretary to the First Council of the Seventy, president of Uruguay-Paraguay Mission, and lived in Latin American countries for many years while on Church assignments. Previously was consultant, agency manager, and trainer for life insurance firm and former management trainer for Church employment. Received bachelor's and master's degrees in business administration from Arizona State University. Born Sept. 1, 1941, at Lehi, Utah, to Clarence H. and Cora Myrl Thornton Cook. Wife, Janelle Schlink Cook; parents of eight children.

Sustained to the Second Quorum of the Seventy April 6, 1996, at age 55. Sustained to the First Quorum of the Seventy April 5, 1998. Former area authority in the North America West Area, regional representative, stake president and counselor, and bishop. Former managing partner of a San Francisco Bay area law firm and president and CEO of a California healthcare system. Received bachelor's degree from Utah State University and law degree from Stanford University. Born Sept. 8, 1940, in Logan, Utah, to J. Vernon and Bernice Kimball Cook. Wife, Mary Gaddie Cook; parents of three children.

Quentin L. Cook

Young Men general president. Sustained to the Second Quorum of the Seventy March 31, 1990, at age 52; called to the First Quorum of the Seventy June 6, 1992, and sustained Oct. 3, 1992. Former president of the Germany Duesseldorf and Germany Munich missions, regional representative, stake president, and bishop. Former president, vice president, and business manager of various universities; has worked for the Salk Institute and was involved with a company that assisted agencies and scientific institutes in the Soviet Union. Born May 10, 1937, in Salt Lake City, Utah, to Frank and Leona Conshafter Dellenbach. Wife, Mary-Jayne Broadbent Dellenbach; parents of three children.

Robert K. Dellenbach

John B. Dickson

Called to the Second Quorum of the Seventy June 6, 1992, at age 48, and sustained Oct. 3, 1992. Sustained to the First Quorum of the Seventy April 1, 1995. Former president of the Mexico Mexico City North Mission, stake president, and stake president's counselor. Was vice president of sawmill and timber company. Received bachelor's degree from Brigham Young University in business administration. Born July 12, 1943, in Tacoma, Wash., to John H. and Helen Baird Dickson. Wife, Delores Jones Dickson; parents of eight children.

Sustained to the First Quorum of the Seventy Oct. 3, 1975, at age 39; called to the Presidency of the Seventy Aug. 15, 1992, and sustained Oct. 3, 1992; served until Aug. 15, 1995. Sunday School general president from 1994-95. Former president of France Switzerland Mission and regional representative; converted to Church in 1957; fluent in five languages, Flemish, French, German, Spanish and English. Received bachelor's degree in economics from University of Liege in Belgium; served as officer in the Belgian Air Force Reserve. Born Oct. 5, 1935, in Ixelles, Belgium, to Andre and Gabrielle Colpaert Didier. Wife, Lucie Lodomez Didier; parents of two children.

Charles Didier

Vaughn J Featherstone

Sustained as second counselor in Presiding Bishopric April 6, 1972, at age 41; sustained to the First Quorum of the Seventy Oct. 1, 1976. Former Young Men general president, president of Texas San Antonio Mission, member of the YMMIA General Board, and stake president; member, Boy Scouts of America National Executive Board, recipient of Silver Antelope and Silver Buffalo awards; former corporate training manager of supermarket chain based in Boise, Idaho. Born March 26, 1931, in Stockton, Utah, to Stephen E. and Emma M. Johnson Featherstone. Wife, Merlene Miner Featherstone; parents of seven children.

John H. Groberg

Second counselor in Sunday School general presidency. Sustained to the First Quorum of the Seventy April 3, 1976, at age 41. Former president of the Tonga Mission, regional representative, and bishop. Has lived in South America, Tonga, Hong Kong and Hawaii while in Church leadership positions. Received bachelor's degree from BYU, master of business administration degree from Indiana University, where he also taught; formerly in real estate, development, and construction; was vice president of Idaho State Real Estate Association. Born June 17, 1934, in Idaho Falls, Idaho, to Delbert V. and Jennie Holbrook Groberg. Wife, Jean Sabin Groberg; parents of 11 children.

Sustained to the First Quorum of the Seventy April 6,1996, at age 55. Former regional representative, counselor in stake presidency and counselor in bishopric. Former president of Ricks College and provost at Brigham Young University. Received bachelor's degree in political science and humanities from Brigham Young University and juris doctorate from University of Utah. Born Oct. 30, 1940, in St. George, Utah, to Orval and Ruth Clark Hafen. Wife, Marie Kartchner Hafen; parents of seven children.

Bruce C. Hafen

Donald L. Hallstrom

Sustained to the First Quorum of the Seventy April 1, 2000, at age 49. Former Area Authority Seventy, regional representative, stake president, and bishop. Former president and owner of real estate economics company. Received bachelor's degree in economics from BYU. Born July 27, 1949, in Honolulu, Hawaii, to James E. and Betty Jo Lambert Hallstrom. Wife, Diane Clifton Hallstrom; parents of four children.

First counselor in Young Men general presidency. Sustained to the Second Quorum of the Seventy April 1, 1989, at age 55; sustained to the First Quorum of the Seventy April 3, 1993. Former president of the Bolivia Cochabamba Mission, stake president, bishop, and worker in the Idaho Falls Temple. Was professor of religion at Ricks College; served eight terms in the Idaho State Legislature and was minority leader for three terms. Born Dec. 19, 1933, in Blackfoot, Idaho, to Floyd Milton and Ruby Hoge Hammond. Wife, Bonnie Sellers Hammond; parents of six children.

F. Melvin Hammond

Sustained to the Second Quorum of the Seventy March 31, 1990, at age 54; sustained to the First Quorum of the Seventy April 6, 1991; called to the Presidency of the Seventy Aug. 15, 1995, and sustained Sept. 30, 1995; served until Aug. 15, 2000. Former Sunday School general president, regional representative, president of the Portugal Lisbon Mission, stake president and counselor. An orthodontist, he has been president of the Rocky Mountain Society of Orthodontists. Born Sept. 1, 1935, in Sugar City, Idaho, to Gordon R. and Florence Evelyn Skidmore Hillam. Wife, Carol Lois Rasmussen Hillam; parents of seven children.

Harold G. Hillam

F. Burton Howard

Sustained to the First Quorum of the Seventy Sept. 30, 1978, at age 45. Former president of Uruguay Montevideo Mission and stake president; was special representative for First Presidency in Latin American affairs. Graduate of Utah State University and received law degree from the University of Utah; former assistant attorney general for Utah, chief counsel for Utah Tax Commission, legal counsel for Mexico in Intermountain Area, and managing partner of Salt Lake law firm. Born March 24, 1933, in Logan, Utah, to Fred P. and Beatrice Ward Howard. Wife, Caroline Heise Howard; parents of five children.

Called to the Second Quorum of the Seventy June 6, 1992, at age 50, and sustained Oct. 3, 1992. Sustained to the First Quorum of the Seventy April 1, 1995. Former president of the Colombia Cali Mission, counselor in the Missionary Training Center presidency, stake president's counselor, and bishop. Formerly director of scripture coordination for the Church Curriculum Department. Received bachelor's, master's, and doctoral degrees in Spanish and history, Church history and doctrine, and education, respectively, from BYU. Born Feb. 5, 1942, in Payson, Utah, to Ruel W. and Ethel Otte Jensen. Wife, Lona Lee Child Jensen; parents of six children.

Jay E. Jensen

Kenneth Johnson

Sustained to the Second Quorum of the Seventy March 31, 1990, at age 49; sustained to the First Quorum of the Seventy April 3, 1993. Former regional representative and stake president; converted to the Church in 1959. Graduated from Norwich City College in England and did graduate work at the City and Guilds of London Institute of Printing; former college instructor and partner in a British insurance brokerage firm. Born July 5, 1940, in Norwich, England, to Bertie A.M. and Ada Hutson Johnson. Wife, Pamela Wilson Johnson; parents of one son.

L. Lionel Kendrick

Sustained to the First Quorum of the Seventy April 2, 1988, at age 56; sustained to the Second Quorum of the Seventy April 1, 1989; sustained to the First Quorum of the Seventy April 6, 1991. Former president of Florida Tampa Mission, regional representative, and stake president; converted to the Church while in the U.S. Air Force in 1954. Received bachelor's, master's, and doctoral degrees of education from Louisiana State University; was professor of health education and director of the Regional Training Center at East Carolina University. Born Sept. 19, 1931, in Baton Rouge, La., to Bonnie Delen and Edna Campbell Forbes Kendrick. Wife, Myrtis Lee Noble Kendrick; parents of four children.

Sustained to the Second Quorum of the Seventy April 6, 1996, at age 60; sustained to First Quorum of the Seventy April 5, 1997. Former president of Texas Dallas Mission, stake president, high councilor, bishop's counselor, and member of Sunday School general board. Was Utah State Commissioner of Higher Education. Received bachelor's degree in agriculture, master's degree in marriage and family relations from Utah State University, and doctorate in educational administration from University of Utah. Born June 29, 1935, in Tremonton, Utah, to Clifton G. and Irene Pack Kerr. Wife, Janeil Raybould Kerr; parents of six children.

Wm. Rolfe Kerr

Yoshihiko Kikuchi

Sustained to the First Quorum of the Seventy Oct. 1, 1977, at age 36; first native-born Japanese called as General Authority. Former president of Hawaii Honolulu Mission, was stake president and counselor to mission president; converted to the Church in 1955. Graduated from Asia University of Tokyo in business psychology and management; former sales manager over Japan for a cookware company, president of a Japanese food storage company. Born July 25, 1941, to Hatsuo and Koyo Ideda Kikuchi in Hokkaido, Japan. Wife, Toshiko Koshiya Kikuchi; parents of four children.

Sustained to the Second Quorum of the Seventy April 6, 1991, at age 57, sustained to the First Quorum of the Seventy April 2, 1994. Former regional representative, president of the New York New York Mission, stake president twice, and bishop. Was managing partner in a law firm. Received bachelor's degree from University of Utah, juris doctorate from the University of Southern California. Born July 11, 1933, in Santaquin, Utah, to Cree Clarence and Melba Nelson Kofford. Wife, Ila Macdonald Kofford; parents of five children.

Cree-L Kofford

John M. Madsen

Second counselor in Young Men general presidency. Sustained to the Second Quorum of the Seventy June 6, 1992, at age 53, Oct. 3, 1992, and sustained to the First Quorum of the Seventy April 5, 1997. Former president of the England Southwest Mission, member of the Melchizedek Priesthood MIA general board and Young Men general board, and regional representative. Was BYU religion professor. Received bachelor's in zoology from Washington State University and master's degree and doctorate in education from BYU. Born April 24, 1939, in Washington, D.C. to Louis L. and Edith Louise Gundersen Madsen. Wife, Diane Dursteler Madsen; parents of six children.

Lynn A. Mickelsen

Sustained to the Second Quorum of the Seventy March 31, 1990, at age 54, and to the First Quorum of the Seventy April 3, 1993. Former president of the Colombia Cali Mission, regional representative, stake president, and bishop. Attended Ricks College and graduated from BYU. Served on a hospital board and in farm associations; formerly self-employed as a farmer and potato shipper. Born July 21, 1935, in Idaho Falls, Idaho, to Lloyd P. and Reva Faye Willmore Mickelsen. Wife, Jeanine Andersen Mickelsen; parents of nine children.

Glenn L. Pace

Sustained as second counselor in the Presiding Bishopric April 6, 1985, at age 45; sustained to the First Quorum of the Seventy Oct. 3, 1992. Former president of the Australia Sydney North Mission, bishop's counselor, stake clerk, and elders quorum president. Received bachelor's and master's degrees in accounting from BYU; chief financial officer for a land development company; former managing director of Church Welfare Services. Born March 21, 1940, in Provo, Utah, to Kenneth LeRoy and Elizabeth A. Wilde Pace. Wife, Jolene Clayson Pace; parents of six children.

Rex D. Pinegar

Sustained to First Council of the Seventy Oct. 6, 1972, at age 41; sustained to First Quorum of the Seventy Oct. 1, 1976, and to the quorum presidency Sept. 30, 1989, where he served until Aug. 15, 1995. Served as counselor in the Young Men general presidency from 1979-85. Former president of North Carolina-Virginia and Virginia Roanoke missions, served on Sunday School general board. Received bachelor's degree from BYU, master's degree from San Francisco State College, and doctorate in education from the University of Southern California. Former chairman of the Educational Psychology Department at BYU. Born Sept. 18, 1931, in Orem, Utah, to John F. and Grace Murl Ellis Pinegar. Wife, Bonnie Lee Crabb Pinegar; parents of six children.

Sustained to the First Quorum of the Seventy Oct. 1, 1977, at age 43, and served in the quorum presidency from Oct. 4, 1986, to Oct. 1, 1989; served twice as general president of the Sunday School, 1979-86 and 1989-92. Former regional representative and president of Pennsylvania Harrisburg Mission. Graduate of University of Utah, former area general agent for insurance company, president of Deseret Foundation of LDS Hospital, was appointed to serve on several governmental boards. Born Jan. 15, 1934, in Salt Lake City, Utah, to Lawrence Sylvester and Florence Boden Pinnock. Wife, Anne Hawkins Pinnock; parents of six children.

Hugh W. Pinnock

Carl B. Pratt

Sustained to the First Quorum of the Seventy April 5, 1997, at age 55. Former area authority, mission president in Spain, regional representative, temple sealer, stake president's counselor, and bishop's counselor. Was law clerk in U.S. 10th Circuit Court of Appeals, and attorney in private practice. Received bachelor's degree from University of Arizona, and juris doctorate from Arizona State University. Born Oct. 30, 1941, in Monterrey, Mexico, to Carl Barton and LaVern Whetten Pratt. Wife, Karen Ann Yeoman Pratt; parents of eight children.

Sustained to the First Quorum of the Seventy April 1, 2000, at age 49. Former president of New York New York North Mission, high councilor, bishop, and and was on the Church Pioneer Sesquicentennial Committee. Was self-employed businessman and previously was president and chief operations officer of Huntsman Chemical Corporation. Attended University of Utah and received an honorary doctorate of business and commerce from Utah Valley State College in Orem, Utah. Born Feb. 6, 1951, in Salt Lake City, Utah, to Rulon Hawkins and Verda Anderson Rasband. Wife, Melanie Twitchell Rasband; parents of five children.

Ronald A. Rasband

Lynn G. Robbins

Sustained to the Second Quorum of the Seventy April 5, 1997, at age 44; sustained to the First Quorum of the Seventy April 1. 2000. Former president of the Uruguay Montevideo Mission, high councilor, bishop, and bishop's counselor. Was co-founder and former senior vice president of Franklin Quest. Received bachelor's degree from Utah State University and master's degree from American Graduate School of International Management. Born Oct. 27, 1952, in Payson, Utah, to Joshua Grant and Evelyn Reed Robbins. Wife, Jan Neilson Robbins; parents of seven children.

Cecil O. Samuelson

Sustained to the First Quorum of the Seventy Oct. 1, 1994, at age 53. Former regional representative and stake president. Received bachelor's, master's, and medical degrees from the University of Utah; was a physician and senior vice president of Intermountain Health Care and former vice president for health sciences and dean of the School of Medicine at the University of Utah; served as director of the Utah Chapter of the American Red Cross and Catholic Heathcare West in San Francisco. Born Aug. 1, 1941, in Salt Lake City, Utah, to Cecil Osborn Sr. and Janet Brazier Mitchell Samuelson. Wife, Sharon Giauque Samuelson; parents of five children.

Dieter F. Uchtdorf

Sustained to the Second Quorum of the Seventy April 2, 1994, at age 53; sustained to the First Quorum of the Seventy April 6, 1996. Former stake president and stake mission president. Was senior vice president for flight operations and chief pilot for Lufthansa German Airlines, and check and training captain for Boeing 747s; received wings as a jet fighter pilot in the German Air Force in 1962. Born Nov. 6, 1940, in Ostrava, Czechoslovakia, to Karl Albert and Hilde Else Opelt Uchtdorf. Wife, Harriett Reich Uchtdorf; parents of two children.

Francisco J. Viñas

Sustained to the Second Quorum of the Seventy April 6, 1996, at age 49; sustained to the First Quorum of the Seventy April 5, 1998. Former area authority in the Europe West Area, president of Argentina Salta Mission, regional representative, stake president and counselor, bishop, and branch president. Was Church Educational System coordinator for Spain. Received bachelor's degree from IAVA. Born Dec. 28, 1946, in Montevideo, Uruguay, to Rafael and Sacramento Serrano de Viñas. Wife, Cristina Helenas Gaminara de Vinas; parents of three children.

Lance B. Wickman

General counsel, office of Legal Services. Sustained to the Second Quorum of the Seventy April 2, 1994, at age 53; sustained to the First Quorum of the Seventy April 1, 2000. Served as regional representative, stake president, and bishop. Received bachelor's degree from University of California at Berkeley and juris doctorate from Stanford University. Former partner in the international law firm of Latham and Watkins in San Diego, Calif. Born Nov. 11, 1940, in Seattle, Wash., to Alton C. and Irene Marilyn Carlson Wickman. Wife, Patricia Farr Wickman; parents of five children.

W. Craig Zwick

Sustained to the First Quorum of the Seventy April 1, 1995, at age 47. Former president of the Chile Santiago South Mission, stake Young Men president, stake mission president's counselor, high councilor, and bishop's counselor. Was executive director of the Utah Department of Transportation, former building contractor. Received bachelor of science degree in business management from the University of Utah. Born June 30, 1947, in Salt Lake City, Utah, to William E. and Audrey McDonough Zwick. Wife, Janet Johnson Zwick; parents of four children.

THE SECOND QUORUM OF THE SEVENTY

Richard D. Allred

Sustained to the Second Quorum of the Seventy April 5, 1997, at age 64. Former president of Guatemala City Temple, director of Missionary Training Center in Guatemala, president of Guatemala Quetzaltenango Mission, regional representative, stake patriarch, stake president, and bishop. Was general manager of Kimball Armor Corp, realtor and chief executive officer of Rios Golden Cut. Retired U.S. Air Force officer. Received bachelor's degree from Utah State University and master of business administration degree from University of Arkansas. Born Aug. 3, 1932, in Salt Lake City, Utah, to Elwood B. and Glendora Malcom Allred. Wife, Gay Banner Allred; parents of three children.

Sustained to the Second Quorum of the Seventy April 4, 1998, at age 65. Former president of Brazil Forteleza Mission, Sao Paulo Temple president, high councilor, branch president and counselor. Was career military officer, secretary to Brazil's Minister of the Army, retired colonel in Army Reserve. Received bachelor's degree from Preparatory Cadet School of Sao Paulo; master's degree from Military Academy of Agulhas Negras; Ph.D. equivalent from Superior War College. Born June 14, 1932, in Rio de Janeiro, Brazil, to Antonio Marques and Maria Carlota Martins Ferreira Amorim. Wife, Maria Alice Pires Ferrao Amorim; parents of two children.

Athos M. Amorim

E Ray Bateman

Sustained to the Second Quorum of the Seventy April 4, 1998, at age 60. Former president of California Carlsbad Mission, multi-region welfare director, stake mission president, bishop, and high councilor. Was sales manager for Bristol-Myers Squibb Co. Served in U.S. Air Force Reserve and Utah National Guard. Attended Brigham Young University and the University of Utah. Born Oct. 20, 1937, in Sandy, Utah, to Marlon Samuel and Mary Armstrong Bateman. Wife, Mira Dorene Odette Bateman; parents of five children.

L. Edward Brown

Sustained to the Second Quorum of the Seventy April 6, 1996, at age 58. Former area authority in the North America Northwest Area, stake president, bishop, and stake mission president. Was area director for Church Educational System; former mayor of Pocatello, Idaho. Received bachelor's degree in English and mathematics from Utah State University, master's degree and doctorate in educational administration from University of Kansas. Born June 18, 1937, in Preston, Idaho, to Lowell and Helen Peterson Brown. Wife, Carol Ewer Brown; parents of eight children.

Douglas L. Callister

Sustained to the Second Quorum of the Seventy April 1, 2000, at age 61. Former Area Authority Seventy, regional representative, president of Minnesota Minneapolis Mission, temple sealer, stake president, and bishop. Received bachelor's degree from BYU; juris doctorate, University of Southern California; and L.L.M. degree (master's of law) from Harvard University. Former tax attorney. Born Feb. 17, 1939, in Glendale, Calif., to Reed Eddington and Norinne Richards Callister. Wife, Jeannette McKibben Callister; parents of six children.

Val R. Christensen

Sustained to the Second Quorum of the Seventy April 4, 1998, at age 62. Former president of Arizona Phoenix Mission, regional representative, stake president, bishop, and high councilor. Was vice president of student services at Utah State University. Served as captain in U.S. Army. Received bachelor's and master's degrees from Utah State University in English and secondary school administration; doctorate in higher education administration from Michigan State University. Born Sept. 27, 1935, in Hooper, Utah, to Leonard and Jennie Lowe Rigby Christensen. Wife, Ruth Ann Wood; parents of five children.

Sustained to the Second Quorum of the Seventy April 1, 2000, at age 64. Former Idaho Falls Temple recorder, president of the Brazil Sao Paulo North Mission, stake president's counselor, high councilor, and bishop. Received bachelor's degree in accounting and business from Idaho State University. Former tax specialist for the Church and served on Idaho Tax Commission. Born Aug. 11, 1935, in Firth, Idaho, to Lars H. and Edith Olive Brough Christenson. Wife, Sandra Joelene Lyon Christenson; parents of four children.

Darwin B. Christenson

Richard E. Cook

Sustained to the Second Quorum of the Seventy April 5, 1997, at age 66. Former president of Mongolia Ulaanbaatar Mission, stake president's counselor, bishop, stake mission president, and stake Young Men president. Was general assistant controller for Ford Motor Co. Served as lieutenant in U.S. Navy. Received bachelor's degree from BYU and master of business administration degree from Northwestern University. Born Sept. 7, 1930, in Pleasant Grove, Utah, to Ernest William and Clara Blackhurst Cook. Wife, Clea Searle Cook, deceased; parents of four children. Married Mary Nielsen Cook.

Sustained to the Second Quorum of the Seventy April 2, 1994, at age 45. Former president of the Brazil Manaus Mission, regional representative, stake president's counselor, and bishop. Graduated from Colegio Pio XII, attended Paulista School of Marketing, Paulista Institute of Gems and Precious Metals. Former Church Educational System associate area director, diamond cutter, manager of jewelry store chain, and finance director of Diversified Almeida Prado Co. Born March 25, 1949, in Santos, Brazil, to Nelson Mendes and Luzia Tassar Simoes Costa. Wife, Margareth Fernandes Morgado Mendes Costa; parents of four children.

Claudio R. M. Costa

Keith Crockett

Sustained to the Second Quorum of the Seventy April 1, 2000, at age 66. Former president of Argentina Buenos Aires South Mission, temple ordinance worker, stake president and counselor, high councilor, and bishop. Received bachelor's degree in music education and master's degree in educational administration and supervision from University of Arizona, and Ed.S. in administration and supervision from Northern Arizona University. Former Church Educational System director and instructor. Born Jan. 15, 1934, in Pima, Ariz., to Wilford Woodruff Crockett III and Jacy Boggs Crockett. Wife, Kathleen McBride Crockett; parents of six children.

Adhemar Damiani

Sustained to the Second Quorum of the Seventy April 3, 1999, at age 59. Former Area Authority Seventy, president of Brazil Curitiba Mission, counselor in Missionary Training Center presidency, regional welfare agent, stake president's counselor, and high councilor. Received bachelor's degree in economics from Sao Paulo University and master's degree in business administration from Fundacao de Getulio Vargas. Retired owner of an accounting, distribution, and billing software company. Born Dec. 18, 1939, in Sao Paulo, Brazil, to Antonio and Maria Damiani. Wife, Walkyria Bronze Damiani; parents of two children.

Duane B. Gerrard

Sustained to the Second Quorum of the Seventy April 5, 1997, at age 58. Former area authority, regional representative, stake president, high councilor, and bishop. Was pilot and administrator for Delta Airlines. Retired U.S. Air Force major. Received bachelor's degree from Utah State University, did graduate work at University of Hawaii and University of Southern California. Born April 22, 1938, in Murray, Utah, to Leonard and Mildred Bird Gerrard. Wife, Kay Bennion Gerrard; parents of eight children.

H. Aldridge Gillespie

Sustained to the Second Quorum of the Seventy April 1, 2000, at age 64. Fomer president of Mexico Tampico Mission, regional representative, stake president, bishop, and branch president. Received bachelor's and master's degrees in civil engineering from Utah State University; doctorate in civil engineering, fracture mechanics, and failure analysis from University of Arizona. Former director of Transportation Safety Institute with U.S. Department of Transportation. Born May 22, 1935, in Riverside, Calif., to Lionel Aldridge and Amelia Eileen Baird Gillespie. Wife, Virginia Ann Larsen Gillespie; parents of five children.

Ronald T. Halverson

Sustained to the Second Quorum of the Seventy April 4, 1998, at age 61. Former Area Authority Seventy, president of the Norway Oslo Mission, regional representative, stake president and counselor, high councilor, and counselor in bishopric. Was president of Halverson Mechanical Inc., Marlowe Plumbing and Heating, H&H Mechanical Inc. Served in Utah House of Representatives and in state Senate. Graduated from Weber State College and attended University of Utah. Born Dec. 18, 1936, in Ogden, Utah, to Marlowe and Hilda Tomlinson Halverson. Wife, Linda Jensen Halverson; parents of five children.

Sustained to the Second Quorum of the Seventy April 5, 1997, at age 65. Former president of the Utah Provo Mission, mission president's counselor, stake president and counselor, high councilor, stake mission president, and bishop. Was vice president and general counsel of Dow Chemical Co., and school teacher. Served as captain in Judge Advocate General Corps, U.S. Air Force. Received bachelor's degree from BYU and juris doctorate from University of Arizona. Born July 16, 1931, in Safford, Ariz., to Wayne M. P. and Phyllis Lines Hancock. Wife, Connie A. Cameron Hancock; parents of eight children.

Wayne M. Hancock

J. Kent Jolley

Sustained to the Second Quorum of the Seventy April 5, 1997, at age 63. Former president of Texas Corpus Christi (later Texas McAllen) Mission, stake president's counselor, high councilor, bishop and counselor, and stake mission president. Was attorney and real estate developer. Served in National Guard. Received bachelor's and juris doctorate degrees from George Washington University. Born Dec. 30, 1933, in Rexburg, Idaho, to William Afton and Mildred Mangum Jolley. Wife, Jill Waldram Leishman Jolley; parents of seven children.

Sustained to the Second Quorum of the Seventy April 5, 1997, at age, 46. Former president of the Mexico Monterrey Mission, stake mission president, high councilor, and counselor in bishopric. Was president of Raymond Production Systems Inc. Received bachelor's degree from BYU, and master's degree from the American Graduate School of International Management. Born Oct. 29, 1950, in Berkeley, Calif., to Stan and Betty Maynes. Wife, Nancy J. Purrington Maynes; parents of four children.

Richard J. Maynes

Dale E. Miller

Sustained to the Second Quorum of the Seventy April 5, 1997, at age 61. Former area authority, president of the Venezuela Caracas Mission, stake president, and bishop. Was business adviser to venture companies, co-founder of Zenger-Miller, and executive in pharmaceutical industry. Received bachelor's degree from BYU and master's in international management from University of Southern California. Born April 2, 1936, in Los Angeles, Calif., to Wade Elliott and Romania Davis Miller. Wife, Laurel Chandler Miller; parents of five children.

Earl M. Monson

Sustained to the Second Quorum of the Seventy April 4, 1998, at age 65. Former stake president, stake mission president, bishop, and high councilor. Was director of Church's Temples and Special Projects Division and former Church international operations and maintenance manager, and consulting structural engineer. Received bachelor's degree in architecture from University of Utah and master's degree in engineering from Iowa State University. Born July 26, 1932, in Salt Lake City, Utah, to Charles Horald and Ortencia Hendricks Merrill Monson. Wife, Donna Mae Hill Monson; parents of five children.

Sustained to the Second Quorum of the Seventy April 4, 1998, at age 62. Former president of the Washington Seattle Mission, stake president and counselor, and bishop and counselor. Was president of medical staff at Utah Valley Regional Medical Center, president of Utah Ophthalmology Society, and had ophthalmology practice. Received bachelor's degree in zoology from Brigham Young University, medical degree from University of Rochester, speciality in ophthalmology from Washington University in St. Louis. Born Jan. 12, 1936, in Twin Falls, Idaho, to Lloyd E. and Stella Harris Oaks. Wife, Josephine Ann Christensen Oaks; parents of nine children.

Merrill C. Oaks

Robert C. Oaks

Sustained to the Second Quorum of the Seventy April 1, 2000, at age 64. Former stake president, mission president's counselor, district president's counselor, high councilor, and bishop's counselor. Received bachelor's degree in military science from Air Force Academy, master's in business administration from Ohio State University, and attended Naval War College. Former senior vice president of operations at U.S. Airways and retired Air Force general. Born Feb. 14, 1936, in Los Angeles, Calif., to Charles E. and Ann Bennett Oaks. Wife, Gloria Unger Oaks; parents of six children.

Sustained to the Second Quorum of the Seventy April 3, 1999, at age 62. Former president of Argentina Buenos Aires South Mission, temple ordinance worker, high councilor, and bishop. Received bachelor's degree in finance and banking from BYU. Former president and owner of a hotel development and management company. Born July 9, 1936, in Grass Valley, Ore., to Merrill M. and Mal Berg Oveson. Wife, Dixie Randall Oveson; parents of six children.

Stephen B. Oveson

Sustained to the Second Quorum of the Seventy April 1, 1995, at age 42. Former stake president's counselor, stake mission president, bishop, and branch president. Was an associate professor of political science at BYU and former executive director of the U.S. Board for International Broadcasting; was research fellow at Harvard University and served as a corporate analyst for the Northrop Corporation, and a staff member of the U.S. Senate Armed Services Committee. Graduated from BYU and earned M.A. and Ph.D. degrees from Harvard University. Born in Albuquerque, N. M., Sept. 18, 1952, to Lyle Kay and Wilma Holmes Porter. Wife, Susan Elizabeth Holland Porter; parents of four children.

Bruce D. Porter

H. Bryan Richards

Sustained to the Second Quorum of the Seventy April 4, 1998, at age 63. Former president of the England Manchester Mission, regional representative; stake president and counselor, high councilor, bishop's counselor, and Young Men president. Was self-employed businessman and former benefits administrator for E-Systems Manufacturing. Received bachelor's degree in business administration from Brigham Young University. Born March 18, 1934, to Horace B. and Carol Bryan Richards in Salt Lake City, Utah. Wife, LynnAnne Taylor Richards; parents of eight children.

Sustained to the Second Quorum of the Seventy April 4, 1998, at age 63. Former president of the Venezuela Barcelona Mission, member of advisory committee in Church Missionary Department, counselor in stake presidency, high councilor, bishop, and temple worker. Was field engineering manager for IBM. Studied electrical and electronic engineering at Weber State College and University of Utah. Born Aug. 5, 1934, to Leonard C. and Ruth Lee Roueche in Salt Lake City, Utah. Wife, JoAnn Sheffield Roueche; parents of five children.

Ned B. Roueche

Dennis E. Simmons

Sustained to the Second Quorum of the Seventy April, 6, 1996, at age 61. Former area authority, president of Washington D.C. North Mission, regional representative, stake president and counselor, high councilor, bishop, and temple sealer. Was senior partner in his own law firm. Received bachelor's degree in music education and English from Utah State University and law degree from George Washington University Law School. Born June 27, 1934, in Beaver Dam, Utah, to Thomas Yates and Sylvia Ericksen Simmons. Wife, Carolyn Thorpe Simmons; parents of six children.

Sustained to the Second Quorum of the Seventy April 5, 1997, at age 65. Former stake president and counselor, high councilor, and bishop's counselor. Was chairman and chief executive officer of Continental Grain Co. Served as first lieutenant in U.S. Air Force. Received bachelor's degree from Utah State University and master's degree and doctorate from the University of Illinois. Born Oct. 19, 1931, in St. George, Utah, to Lafayette and Grace Sullivan Staheli. Wife, Afton Stratton Staheli; parents of four children.

Donald L. Staheli

David R. Stone

Sustained to the Second Quorum of the Seventy April 3, 1999, at age 62. Former president of Dominican Republic Santo Domingo West Mission, regional representative, stake president's counselor, high councilor, and bishop's counselor. Received bachelor's degree in English and economics from BYU. Former president, Housewares Division for Black and Decker. Born June 16, 1936, in Buenos Aires, Argentina, to Hubert J. and Ethel R. Grant Stone. Wife, Rosalie Erekson Stone; parents of six children.

Sustained to the Second Quorum of the Seventy April 3, 1999, at age 61. Former president of England Manchester Mission, area authority, regional representative, stake president, and bishop. Received bachelor's degree in business management from University of Utah. Former executive officer in food distribution and real estate. Born Dec. 1, 1937, in St. George, Utah, to Harvey and Anna Hilda Wittwer Stucki. Wife Cheryl Cox Stucki; parents of six children.

H. Bruce Stucki

Jerald L. Taylor

Sustained to the Second Quorum of the Seventy April 6, 1996, at age 59. Former area authority in the Mexico North Area, president of Chile Santiago South Mission, regional representative, stake president, and bishop. Was rancher, orchardist, and associate of Paquime Fruit Packing Company. Graduated from Brigham Young University in animal husbandry. Born March 22, 1937, in Colonia Dublan, Mexico, to Loren Le Roy and Lillian Hatch Taylor. Wife, Sharon Elizabeth Willis Taylor; parents of six children.

D. Lee Tobler

Sustained to the Second Quorum of the Seventy April 4, 1998, at age 64. Former executive vice president and chief financial officer of BF Goodrich Co. Was Area Authority Seventy, stake president and counselor; bishop, and high councilor. Received bachelor's degree in finance and economics at Brigham Young University and master's degree in business administration from Northwestern University. Born July 25, 1933, in Provo, Utah, to Donald and Louise Shoell Tobler. Wife, Darlene Thueson Tobler; parents of six children.

Sustained to the Second Quorum of the Seventy April 4, 1998, at age 63. Former president of Phillipines Quezon City Mission, regional representative, stake president and counselor, and bishop. Was western regional sales manager for the Glass Division of Ford Motor Co. Received bachelor's degree in education and business administration from Utah State University and master's degree from BYU. Born Feb. 23, 1935, in South Weber, Utah, to Elwood Taylor and Edna Davis Watts. Wife, Connie Welling Watts; parents of four children.

Gordon T. Watts

Stephen A. West

Sustained to the Second Quorum of the Seventy April 4, 1998, at age 63. Former president of Texas San Antonio Mission, member of Church's international advisory group, high councilor, temple sealer, and bishop and counselor. Was senior vice president and general counsel for Marriott International and practiced law. Received bachelor's degree in philosophy from University of Utah and juris doctorate from University of Utah. Born March 23, 1935, in Salt Lake City, Utah, to Allan Morrell and Ferne Page West. Wife, Martha Alice Sears West; parents of three children.

Sustained to the Second Quorum of the Seventy April 4, 1998, at age 54. Former president of Paraguay Asuncion Mission, high councilor, stake mission president's counselor, bishop and counselor. Was vice president of Citibank in New York, Mexico, Argentina, and Uruguay; executive director of Multibanco Comermex in Mexico; and financial consultant. Received bachelor's degree in Spanish and sociology and master of public administration degree from BYU. Born April 12, 1943, in Chuichupa, Chihuahua, Mexico, to Glen A. and Ada May Judd Whetten. Wife, Raquel Lopez Whetten; parents of eight children.

Robert J. Whetten

Richard H. Winkel

Sustained to the Second Quorum of the Seventy April 3, 1999, at age 56. Former president of Spain Madrid Mission, stake president, high councilor, bishop, and seminary teacher. Received bachelor's degree in communications from BYU and master's degree in business administration from Pepperdine University. Retired owner and president of lumber company. Born May 17, 1942, in Oakland, Calif., to Francis Benjamin and Rose Blanche Thompson Winkel. Wife, Karen Hart Winkel; parents of nine children.

Sustained to the Second Quorum of the Seventy April 6, 1996, at age 65. Former regional representative, stake president's counselor, high councilor, and bishop. Was chairman, chief executive officer and founder of Wirthlin Worldwide. Received bachelor's and master's degrees from University of Utah, doctorate from University of California at Berkeley, all in economics. Born March 15, 1931, in Salt Lake City, Utah, to Joseph L. and Madeline B. Wirthlin. Wife, Jeralie Mae Chandler Wirthlin; parents of eight children.

Richard B. Wirthlin

Ray H. Wood

Sustained to the Second Quorum of the Seventy April 4, 1998, at age 66. Former stake president and counselor, high councilor, and bishop and counselor. Was director of tax administration for the Church and partner in Peat Marwick Mitchell in San Jose, Calif. Received bachelor's degree in accounting and juris doctorate from University of Utah. Born July 11, 1931, in Salt Lake City, Utah, to Ray G. and Mary Hunter Wood. Wife, Ann Aylett Wood; parents of six children.

Sustained to the Second Quorum of the Seventy April 3, 1999, at age 62. Former Area Authority Seventy, regional representative, stake president, high councilor, and bishop. Received bachelor's degree in history from Stanford University, master's and doctoral degrees in politcal science from Harvard University. Former Chester W. Nimitz Chair of National Security and Foreign Affairs, U.S. Naval War College. Born Dec. 25, 1936, in Idaho Falls, Idaho, to John Albert (Jack) and Blanche Wood. Wife, Dixie Leigh Jones Wood; parents of four children.

Robert S. Wood

THE THIRD QUORUM OF THE SEVENTY

Area Authority Seventies residing in Europe, Africa, Asia, Australia and the Pacific make up the Third Quorum of the Seventy.

AFRICA SOUTHEAST AREA

Christoffel Golden Jr.

AFRICA WEST AREA

Christopher N. Chukwurah, David W. Eka, Emmanuel O. Opare Sr.

ASIA AREA

Chu-Jen, Chia; Shih An Liang, Su Kiong Tan, Patrick C.H. Wong

ASIA NORTH AREA

Hitoshi Kashikura, Seiji Katanuma, Chong-Youl Kim, Won Yong Ko, Gary Matsuda, Haruyoshi Nakamura

AUSTRALIA/NEW ZEALAND AREA

Victor D. Cave, Robert Malcolm Cowan, Lindsay T. Dil, John A. Grinceri

EUROPE EAST AREA

Johann A. Wondra, Manfred H. Schutze

EUROPE CENTRAL AREA

Franz R. Gaag, Keith K. Hilbig, Ernst Husz, Hans Herbert Mattsson, Wolfgang H. Paul, Holger D. Rakow

EUROPE WEST AREA

Raimondo Castellani, Rowland Edward Elvidge, John Maxwell, Alain A. Petion, Jose A. Teixeira da Silva

PHILIPPINES AREA

Henry F. Acebedo, Modesto M. Amistad Jr., Edison Metra Cabrito, Reynaldo Laguna Cuyong, Fred Cabanos Dimaya, Edgardo E. Fernando, Ruben G. Gapiz, Carlos Condeno S. Revillo, Remus G. Villarete

PACIFIC ISLANDS AREA

Pita F. Hopoate, Jean Alexis Tefan

THE FOURTH QUORUM OF THE SEVENTY

Area Authority Seventies residing in Mexico, Central America and South America make up the Fourth Quorum of the Seventy.

BRAZIL NORTH AREA

Gutenberg G. Amorim, Cesar A. S. Milder, Pedro J. Penha, Iraja B. Soares

BRAZIL SOUTH AREA

Marcos A. Aidukaitis, Paulo C. Amorim, Yatyr Moreira Cesar Filho, Flavio A. Cooper, Silvio Geschwandtner, Paulo A. Grahl, Jairo Mazzagardi, Adelson de Paula Parrella, João R.C. Martins Silva

CENTRAL AMERICA AREA

Julio E. Alvarado, Jose E. Boza Dompe, Enrique R. Falabella, E. Israel Perez

CHILE AREA

Gustavo A. Barrios, John A. Harris, Julio Humberto Jaramillo, Eduardo A. Lamartine, Wilfredo R. Lopez, Julio E. Otay, Jorge A. Pedrero, Claudio D. Signorelli, Hector M. Verdugo, Jorge F. Zeballos

MEXICO NORTH AREA

Juan A. Alvaradejo, Esteban Guevara, Daniel L. Johnson, Rodrigo Obeso, Adrian Ochoa, Tomas Valdes

MEXICO SOUTH AREA

Adolfo Avalos, Marco A. Cardenas, Benjamin De Hoyos, Armando Gaona, Alfonso Landaver Ramos, Guillermo Torres

SOUTH AMERICA NORTH AREA

Horacio P. Araya, Jaime Ferreira, Roberto Garcia, Francisco G. Gimenez, Jose L. Gonzalez Gutierrez, Walter F. Gonzalez

SOUTH AMERICA SOUTH AREA

Jorge O. Abad, Carlos Ernesto Aguero, Antonio Cappi, Jorge L. del Castillo, David Lopez, Jorge W. Ventura, Claudio D. Zivic

SOUTH AMERICA WEST AREA

Jose Aleson, Rene J. Cabrera, Vidal Francisco Chinchay, Mario E. Guzman, Juan Uceda, Willy F. Zuzunaga

THE FIFTH QUORUM OF THE SEVENTY

Area Authority Seventies residing in the United States and Canada make up the Fifth Quorum of the Seventy.

NORTH AMERICA CENTRAL AREA

Blair S. Bennett, Robert K. Bills, Bruce B. Bingham, Kay H. Christensen, Joseph Thomas Hicken, Thomas A. Holt

NORTH AMERICA EAST AREA

David W. Ferrel, Ralph W. Hardy Jr., J. Willard Marriott Jr., James Mitchel Scott, Keith L. Smith, R. Lloyd Smith

NORTH AMERICA NORTHEAST AREA

Lawrence R. Fuller Sr., Ross H. McEachran, Hyde M. Merrill, Lindon Joel Robison

NORTH AMERICA SOUTHEAST AREA

J. Devn Cornish, Dale L. Dransfield, James E. Griffin, Lloyd W. Jones, Spencer V. Jones, Brent H. Koyle, Jesus Nieves

NORTH AMERICA NORTHWEST AREA

Lowell C. Barber, David A. Bednar, Donald Rex Gerratt, C. Scott Grow, Ronald Lee Loveland, Karl E. Nelson, Steven H. Pond, Michael T. Robinson Roland Neil Walker

NORTH AMERICA SOUTHWEST AREA

Harvey L. Gardner, Daryl H. Garn, Larry W. Gibbons, James J. Hamula, J. Michael Moeller, James S. Olson, R. Gordon Porter

NORTH AMERICA WEST AREA

Norman C. Boehm, Craig A. Bullock, Tad Richards Callister, L. Whitney Clayton, Merrill F. Hingham, Michael L. Jensen, William W. Parmley

UTAH NORTH AREA

O. Brent Black, Harold C. Brown, Jess L. Christensen, Ronald J. Hammond, Jon M. Huntsman, Glen Orvil Jenson, Wayne S. Peterson, Dale Gunnar Renlund, Craig T. Vincent

UTAH SOUTH AREA

Carl W. Bacon, Clayton S. Huber, Richard K. Klein, J. Grey Larkin, James Bott McDonald, Ariel Roger Merrill, Glen A. Overton, Steven E. Snow

THE PRESIDING BISHOPRIC

H. David Burton

Called as Presiding Bishop Dec. 27, 1995; sustained April 6, 1996. Sustained as first counselor to Presiding Bishop Robert D. Hales on Oct. 3, 1992, at age 54, and first counselor to Presiding Bishop Merrill J. Bateman on April 2, 1994. Former stake president and temple sealer. Former secretary to the Presiding Bishopric for 14 years. Received bachelor's degree in economics from the University of Utah and master's degree from University of Michigan in business administration. Born April 26, 1938, in Salt Lake City, Utah, to Harold Nelson and Blanche Mabel Swanson Burton. Wife, Barbara Matheson Burton, parents of five children.

Richard C. Edgley

Called as first counselor in the Presiding Bishopric Dec. 27, 1995; sustained April 6, 1996. Sustained as second counselor to Presiding Bishop Robert D. Hales on Oct. 3, 1992, at age 56, and as second counselor to Presiding Bishop Merrill J. Bateman on April 2, 1994. Former stake president and bishop. Was managing director of the Church's Finance and Records Department, board member of various Church-related corporations. Received bachelor's degree in political science from BYU and master's degree in business administration from Indiana University. Born Feb. 6, 1936, in Preston, Idaho, to Phenoi Harrison and Ona Crockett Edgley. Wife, Pauline Nielson Edgley, parents of six children.

Keith B. McMullin

Called as second counselor in the Presiding Bishopric Dec. 27, 1995, at age 54; sustained April 6, 1996. Former president of Germany Frankfurt Mission, stake president, bishop and counselor, and high councilor. Was managing director of Church Welfare Services. Received bachelor's degree in banking and finance from University of Utah. Born Aug. 18, 1941, in St. George, Utah, to Lawrence and Margaret Savage McMullin. Wife, Carolyn Jean Gibbs McMullin, parents of eight children.

HISTORICAL LISTING OF GENERAL AUTHORITIES

PRESIDENTS OF THE CHURCH

1. **Joseph Smith Jr.** — Born Dec. 23, 1805, in Sharon, Windsor Co., Vermont, to Joseph Smith Sr. and Lucy Mack. Married Emma Hale Jan. 18, 1827, seven children. Received the Melchizedek Priesthood (ordained apostle) in May 1829 by Peter, James, and John (D&C 20:2, 27:12); sustained as First Elder of the Church April 6, 1830, at age 24; ordained high priest June 3, 1831, by Lyman Wight, sustained as president of the High Priesthood Jan. 25, 1832, at age 26 at a conference at Amherst, Lorain Co., Ohio; martyred June 27, 1844, at Carthage Jail, Carthage, Hancock Co., Illinois, at age 38.

2. **Brigham Young** — Born June 1, 1801, at Whitingham, Windham Co., Vermont, to John Young and Abigail Howe. Ordained apostle Feb. 14, 1835, at age 33 by the Three Witnesses to the Book of Mormon: Oliver Cowdery, David Whitmer, and Martin Harris; sustained as president of the Quorum of the Twelve Apostles April 14, 1840; sustained as president of the Church Dec. 27, 1847, at age 46; died Aug. 29, 1877, in Salt Lake City, Salt Lake Co., Utah, at age 76.

3. **John Taylor** — Born Nov. 1, 1808, at Milnthorpe, Westmoreland Co., England, to James Taylor and Agnes Taylor. Ordained apostle Dec. 19, 1838, under the hands of Brigham Young and Heber C. Kimball, at age 30; sustained as president of the Quorum of the Twelve Apostles Oct. 6, 1877; sustained as president of the Church Oct. 10, 1880, at age 71; died July 25, 1887, in Kaysville, Davis Co., Utah, at age 78.

4. **Wilford Woodruff** — Born March 1, 1807, at Avon (Farmington), Hartford Co., Connecticut, to Aphek Woodruff and Beulah Thompson. Ordained apostle April 26, 1839, by Brigham Young, at age 32; sustained as president of the Quorum of the Twelve Apostles Oct. 10, 1880; sustained as president of the Church April 7, 1889, at age 82; died Sept. 2, 1898, in San Francisco, San Francisco Co., California, at age 91.

5. **Lorenzo Snow** — Born April 3, 1814, at Mantua, Portage Co., Ohio, to Oliver Snow and Rosetta Leonora Pettibone. Ordained apostle Feb. 12, 1849, by Heber C. Kimball, at age 34; sustained as counselor to President Brigham Young April 8, 1873; sustained as assistant counselor to President Brigham Young May 9, 1874; sustained as president of the Quorum of the Twelve Apostles April 7, 1889; ordained and set apart as president of the Church Sept. 13, 1898, at age 84; died Oct. 10, 1901, in Salt Lake City, Salt Lake Co., Utah, at age 87.

6. **Joseph Fielding Smith** — Born Nov. 13, 1838, at Far West, Caldwell Co., Missouri, to Hyrum Smith and Mary Fielding. Ordained apostle by Brigham Young and named counselor to the First Presidency July 1, 1866, at age 27; set apart as a member of the Quorum of the Twelve Apostles Oct. 8, 1867; released as counselor to the First Presidency at the death of President Young Aug. 29, 1877; sustained as second counselor to President John Taylor Oct. 10, 1880; released at the death of President Taylor

July 25, 1887; sustained as second counselor to President Wilford Woodruff April 7, 1889; sustained as second counselor to President Lorenzo Snow Sept. 13, 1898; sustained as first counselor to Lorenzo Snow Oct. 6, 1901, not set apart to this position; released at the death of President Snow Oct. 10, 1901; ordained and set apart as president of the Church Oct. 17, 1901, at age 62; died Nov. 19, 1918, in Salt Lake City; Salt Lake Co., Utah, at age 80.

7. Heber Jeddy Grant — Born Nov. 22, 1856, in Salt Lake City, Salt Lake Co., Utah, to Jedediah Morgan Grant and Rachel Ridgeway Ivins. Ordained apostle Oct. 16, 1882, by George Q. Cannon, at age 25; became president of the Quorum of the Twelve Apostles Nov. 23, 1916; ordained and set apart as president of the Church Nov. 23, 1918, at age 62; died May 14, 1945, in Salt Lake City, Salt Lake Co., Utah, at age 88.

8. George Albert Smith — Born April 4, 1870, in Salt Lake City, Salt Lake Co., Utah, to John Henry Smith and Sarah Farr. Married Lucy Emily Woodruff May 25, 1892 (she died Nov. 5, 1937); they had three children. Ordained apostle Oct. 8, 1903, by Joseph F. Smith, at age 33; sustained as president of the Quorum of the Twelve Apostles July 1, 1943; ordained and set apart as president of the Church May 21, 1945, at age 75; died April 4, 1951, in Salt Lake City, Salt Lake Co., Utah, at age 81.

9. David Oman McKay — Born Sept. 8, 1873, at Huntsville, Weber Co., Utah, to David McKay and Jennette Eveline Evans. Married to Emma Ray Riggs Jan. 2, 1901 (she died Nov. 14, 1970); they had seven children. Ordained apostle April 9, 1906, by Joseph F. Smith, at age 32; sustained as second counselor to President Heber J. Grant Oct. 6, 1934; sustained as second counselor to President George Albert Smith May 21, 1945; sustained as president of the Quorum of the Twelve Apostles Sept. 30, 1950; sustained as president of the Church April 9, 1951, at age 77; died Jan. 18, 1970, in Salt Lake City, Salt Lake Co., Utah, at age 96.

10. Joseph Fielding Smith — Born July 19, 1876, in Salt Lake City, Salt Lake Co., Utah, to Joseph Fielding Smith and Julina Lambson. Married Louie E. Shurtliff April 26, 1898 (she died March 30, 1908); they had two children. Married Ethel G. Reynolds Nov. 2, 1908 (she died Aug. 26, 1937); they had nine children. Married Jessie Ella Evans April 12, 1938 (she died Aug. 3, 1971). Ordained apostle April 7, 1910, by Joseph F. Smith, at age 33; sustained as acting president of the Quorum of the Twelve Apostles Sept. 30, 1950; sustained as president of the Quorum of the Twelve Apostles April 9, 1951; sustained as counselor in the First Presidency Oct. 29, 1965; ordained and set apart as president of the Church Jan. 23, 1970, at age 93; died July 2, 1972, in Salt Lake City, Salt Lake Co., Utah, at age 95.

11. Harold Bingham Lee — Born March 28, 1899, at Clifton, Oneida Co., Idaho, to Samuel M. Lee and Louisa Bingham. Married Fern Lucinda Tanner Nov. 14, 1923 (she died Sept. 24, 1962); they had two children. Married Freda Joan Jensen June 17, 1963. Ordained apostle April 10, 1941, by Heber J. Grant, at age 42; sustained as president of the Quorum of the Twelve Apostles Jan. 23, 1970; sustained as first counselor to President Joseph Fielding Smith Jan. 23, 1970; ordained and set apart as president of the Church July 7, 1972, at age

73; died Dec. 26, 1973, in Salt Lake City, Salt Lake Co., Utah, at age 74.

12. Spencer Woolley Kimball — Born March 28, 1895, in Salt Lake City, Salt Lake Co., Utah, to Andrew Kimball and Olive Woolley. Married Camilla Eyring on Nov. 16, 1917 (she died Sept. 20, 1987); they had four children. Ordained apostle Oct. 7, 1943, by Heber J. Grant, at age 48; set apart as acting president of the Quorum of the Twelve Apostles Jan. 23, 1970; set apart as president of the Quorum of the Twelve Apostles July 7, 1972; ordained and set apart as president of the Church Dec. 30, 1973, at age 78; died Nov. 5, 1985, in Salt Lake City, Salt Lake Co., Utah, at age 90.

13. Ezra Taft Benson — Born Aug. 4, 1899, at Whitney, Franklin Co., Idaho, to George T. Benson and Sarah Dunkley. Married Flora Smith Amussen Sept. 10, 1926 (she died Aug. 14, 1992); they had six children. Ordained an apostle Oct. 7, 1943, by President Heber J. Grant, at age 44; served as U.S. Secretary of Agriculture, 1953-61. Set apart as president of the Quorum of the Twelve Apostles Dec. 30, 1973; ordained and set apart as president of the Church Nov. 10, 1985, at age 86; died May 30, 1994, in Salt Lake City, Salt Lake Co., Utah, at age 94.

14. Howard William Hunter — Born Nov. 14, 1907, in Boise, Ada Co., Idaho, to John William Hunter and Nellie Marie Rasmussen. Married Clara May (Claire) Jeffs June 10, 1931 (she died Oct. 9, 1983); they had three children (one died in infancy); married Inis Bernice Egan April 12, 1990. Ordained an apostle Oct. 15, 1959, by David O. McKay, at age 51; set apart as acting president of the Quorum of the Twelve Apostles Nov. 10, 1985; set apart as president of the Quorum of the Twelve Apostles June 2, 1988; ordained and set apart as president of the Church June 5, 1994, at age 86; died March 3, 1995, in Salt Lake City, Salt Lake Co., Utah, at age 87.

15. Gordon Bitner Hinckley — See current FIRST PRESIDENCY.

ASSISTANT PRESIDENTS OF THE CHURCH

1. Oliver Cowdery — Born Oct. 3, 1806, at Wells, Rutland Co., Vermont, to William Cowdery and Rebecca Fuller. Received Melchizedek Priesthood (ordained apostle) in May 1829, by Peter, James and John (D&C 20:2, 27:12); sustained as Second Elder of the Church April 6, 1830, at age 23; ordained high priest Aug. 28, 1831, by Sidney Rigdon; ordained assistant president of the High Priesthood Dec. 5, 1834, at age 28; sustained as assistant counselor to the First Presidency Sept. 3, 1837; excommunicated April 11, 1838; rebaptized Nov. 12, 1848; died March 3, 1850, at Richmond, Ray Co., Missouri, at age 43.

2. Hyrum Smith — Born Feb. 9, 1800, at Tunbridge, Orange Co., Vermont, to Joseph Smith Sr. and Lucy Mack. Ordained high priest in June 1831 by Joseph Smith; sustained as assistant counselor to the First Presidency Sept. 3, 1837, at age 37; sustained as second counselor to President Joseph Smith Nov. 7, 1837; given all the priesthood formerly held by Oliver Cowdery (including apos-

tle); ordained Patriarch to the Church and assistant president Jan. 24, 1841, by Joseph Smith, at age 40; martyred June 27, 1844, at Carthage Jail, Carthage, Hancock Co., Illinois, at age 44.

FIRST COUNSELORS IN THE FIRST PRESIDENCY

1. Sidney Rigdon — Born Feb. 19, 1793, at Saint Clair Township, Allegheny Co., Pennsylvania, to William Rigdon and Nancy Bryant. Ordained high priest in June 1831 by Lyman Wight; set apart as first counselor to President Joseph Smith March 18, 1833, at age 40; excommunicated Sept. 8, 1844; died July 14, 1876, at Friendship, Allegany Co., New York, at age 83.

2. Heber Chase Kimball — Born June 14, 1801, at Sheldon, Franklin Co., Vermont, to Solomon Farnham Kimball and Anna Spaulding. Ordained apostle Feb. 14, 1835, under the hands of Oliver Cowdery, David Whitmer, and Martin Harris, at age 33; sustained as first counselor to President Brigham Young Dec. 27, 1847, at age 46; died June 22, 1868, at Salt Lake City, Salt Lake Co., Utah, at age 67.

3. George Albert Smith — Born June 26, 1817, at Potsdam, Saint Lawrence Co., New York, to John Smith and Clarissa Lyman. Ordained apostle April 26, 1839, by Heber C. Kimball at age 21; sustained as first counselor to President Brigham Young Oct. 7, 1868, at age 51; died Sept. 1, 1875, at Salt Lake City, Salt Lake Co., Utah, at age 58.

4. John Willard Young — Born Oct. 1, 1844, at Nauvoo, Hancock Co., Illinois, to Brigham Young and Mary Ann Angell. Ordained apostle Feb. 4, 1864, by Brigham Young. Sustained as counselor to President Brigham Young April 8, 1873, at age 28; sustained as assistant counselor to President Young May 9, 1874; sustained as first counselor to President Young Oct. 7, 1876, at age 32; released at death of President Young Aug. 29, 1877; sustained as a counselor to the Twelve Apostles Oct. 6, 1877; released Oct. 6, 1891; died Feb. 11, 1924, at New York City, New York, at age 79.

5. George Quayle Cannon — Born Jan. 11, 1827, at Liverpool, Lancashire Co., England, to George Cannon and Ann Quayle. Ordained an apostle Aug. 26, 1860, by Brigham Young, at age 33; sustained as counselor to President Young April 8, 1873, at age 46; sustained as assistant counselor to President Young May 9, 1874; released at death of President Young Aug. 29, 1877; sustained as first counselor to President John Taylor Oct. 10, 1880; released at death of President Taylor July 25, 1887; sustained as first counselor to President Wilford Woodruff April 7, 1889; sustained as first counselor to President Lorenzo Snow Sept. 13, 1898; died April 12, 1901, at Monterey, Monterey Co., California, at age 74.

6. Joseph Fielding Smith — See PRESIDENTS OF THE CHURCH, No. 6.

7. John Rex Winder — Born Dec. 11, 1821, at Biddenham, Kent Co., England, to Richard Winder and Sophia Collins. Ordained high priest March 4, 1872, by Edward Hunter; sustained as second counselor to

Presiding Bishop William B. Preston April 8, 1887, at age 65; sustained as first counselor to President Joseph F. Smith Oct. 17, 1901, at age 79; died March 27, 1910, at Salt Lake City, Salt Lake Co., Utah, at 88.

8. Anthon Henrik Lund — Born May 15, 1844, at Aalborg, Jutland, Denmark, to Henrik Lund and Anne C. Andersen. Ordained apostle Oct. 7, 1889, by George Q. Cannon, at age 45; sustained as second counselor to President Joseph F. Smith Oct. 17, 1901, at age 57; sustained as first counselor to President Smith April 7, 1910; sustained as first counselor to President Heber J. Grant Nov. 23, 1918; died March 2, 1921, at Salt Lake City, Salt Lake Co., Utah, at age 76.

9. Charles William Penrose — Born Feb. 4, 1832, at London, Surrey Co., England, to Richard Penrose and Matilda Sims. Ordained apostle July 7, 1904, by Joseph F. Smith, at age 72; sustained as second counselor to President Smith Dec. 7, 1911, at age 79; sustained as second counselor to President Heber J. Grant Nov. 23, 1918; sustained as first counselor to President Grant March 10, 1921; died May 15, 1925, at Salt Lake City, Salt Lake Co., Utah, at age 93.

10. Anthony Woodward Ivins — Born Sept. 16, 1852, at Toms River, Ocean Co., New Jersey, to Israel Ivins and Anna Lowrie. Ordained apostle Oct. 6, 1907, by Joseph F. Smith, at age 55; sustained as second counselor to President Heber J. Grant March 10, 1921, at age 68; sustained as first counselor to President Grant May 28, 1925; died Sept. 23, 1934, at Salt Lake City, Salt Lake Co., Utah, at age 82.

11. Joshua Reuben Clark Jr. — Born Sept. 1, 1871, at Grantsville, Tooele Co., Utah, to Joshua Reuben Clark and Mary Louise Woolley. Sustained as second counselor to President Heber J. Grant, April 6, 1933, at age 61; sustained as first counselor to President Grant, Oct. 6, 1934; ordained apostle Oct. 11, 1934, at age 63, by President Grant; sustained as first counselor to President George Albert Smith May 21, 1945; sustained as second counselor to President David O. McKay April 9, 1951; sustained as first counselor to President McKay June 12, 1959; died Oct. 6, 1961, at Salt Lake City, Salt Lake Co., Utah, at age 90.

12. Stephen L Richards — Born June 18, 1879, at Mendon, Cache Co., Utah, to Stephen Longstroth Richards and Emma Louise Stayner. Ordained apostle Jan. 18, 1917, by Joseph F. Smith, at age 37; sustained as first counselor to President David O. McKay April 9, 1951, at age 71; died May 19, 1959, at Salt Lake City, Salt Lake Co., Utah, at age 79.

13. Joshua Reuben Clark Jr. — See No. 11 above.

14. Henry Dinwoodey Moyle — Born April 22, 1889, at Salt Lake City, Salt Lake Co., Utah, to James H. Moyle and Alice E. Dinwoodey. Ordained apostle April 10, 1947, by George Albert Smith, at age 57; sustained as second counselor to President David O. McKay June 12, 1959, at age 70; sustained as first counselor to President McKay Oct. 12, 1961; died Sept. 18, 1963, at Deer Park, Osceola Co., Florida, at age 74.

15. Hugh Brown Brown — Born Oct. 24, 1883, at Granger, Salt Lake Co., Utah, to Homer Manly Brown and

Lydia Jane Brown. Sustained as Assistant to the Twelve Oct. 4, 1953, at age 69; ordained an apostle April 10, 1958, by David O. McKay, at age 74; sustained as counselor in the First Presidency June 22, 1961; sustained as second counselor to President McKay Oct. 12, 1961; sustained as first counselor to President McKay Oct. 4, 1963; released at death of President McKay Jan. 18, 1970, and resumed position in the Quorum of the Twelve Apostles; died Dec. 2, 1975, at Salt Lake City, Salt Lake Co., Utah, at age 92.

16. Harold Bingham Lee — See PRESIDENTS OF THE CHURCH, No. 11.

17. Nathan Eldon Tanner — Born May 9, 1898, at Salt Lake City, Salt Lake Co., Utah, to Nathan William Tanner and Sarah Edna Brown. Sustained as Assistant to the Twelve Oct. 8, 1960, at age 62; ordained apostle Oct. 11, 1962, at age 64; sustained as second counselor to President David O. McKay Oct. 4, 1963; sustained as second counselor to President Joseph Fielding Smith Jan. 23, 1970; sustained as first counselor to President Harold B. Lee July 7, 1972; sustained as first counselor to President Spencer W. Kimball Dec. 30, 1973; died Nov. 27, 1982, at Salt Lake City, Salt Lake Co., Utah, at age 84.

18. Marion George Romney — Born Sept. 19, 1897, in Colonia Juarez, Mexico, to George Samuel Romney and Teressa Artemesia Redd. Sustained as Church's first Assistant to the Twelve April 6, 1941, at age 43; ordained apostle Oct. 11, 1951, at age 54; sustained as second counselor to President Harold B. Lee July 7, 1972; sustained as second counselor to President Spencer W. Kimball Dec. 30, 1973; sustained as first counselor to President Kimball Dec. 2, 1982; released at the death of President Kimball Nov. 5, 1985, and resumed position in the Quorum of Twelve Apostle; became president of the Quorum of the Twelve Nov. 10, 1985; died May 20, 1988, at Salt Lake City, Salt Lake Co., Utah, at age 90.

19. Gordon Bitner Hinckley — See current FIRST PRESIDENCY.

20. Thomas Spencer Monson — See current FIRST PRESIDENCY.

SECOND COUNSELORS IN THE FIRST PRESIDENCY

1. Frederick Granger Williams — Born Oct. 28, 1787, at Suffield, Hartford, Co., Connecticut, to William Wheeler Williams and Ruth Granger. Called by revelation March 1832 to be a high priest and counselor to President Joseph Smith (D&C 81:1); ordained high priest by Miles H. Jones; set apart as second counselor to President Smith March 18, 1833, at age 45; rejected Nov. 7, 1837; excommunicated March 17, 1839; restored to fellowship April 8, 1840; died Oct. 10, 1842, at Quincy, Adams Co., Illinois, at age 54.

2. Hyrum Smith — See ASSISTANT PRESIDENTS OF THE CHURCH, No. 2.

3. William Law — Born Sept. 8, 1809, at Tyrone Co., North Ireland. Set apart as second counselor to President Joseph Smith Jan. 24, 1841, at age 31; excommunicated April 18, 1844; died Jan. 19, 1892, at Shullsburg, Lafayette Co., Wisconsin, at age 82.

4. Willard Richards — Born June 24, 1804, at Hopkinton, Middlesex Co., Massachusetts, to Joseph Richards and Rhoda Howe. Ordained apostle April 14, 1840, by Brigham Young, at age 35; sustained as second counselor to Pres-

ident Young Dec. 27, 1847, at age 43; died March 11, 1854, at Salt Lake City, Salt Lake Co., Utah, at age 49.

5. Jedediah Morgan Grant — Born Feb. 21, 1816, at Windsor, Broome Co., New York, to Joshua Grant and Athalia Howard. Set apart as one of the First Seven Presidents of the Seventy Dec. 2, 1845, at age 29; ordained apostle April 7, 1854, by Brigham Young, at age 38; sustained as second counselor to President Young April 7, 1854; died Dec. 1, 1856, at Salt Lake City, Salt Lake Co., Utah, at age 40.

6. Daniel Hanmer Wells — Born Oct. 27, 1814, at Trenton, (now Barnveld) Oneida Co., New Jersey, to Daniel Wells and Catherine Chapin. Set apart as second counselor to President Young Jan. 4, 1857, at age 42; released at death of President Young Aug. 29, 1877; sustained as a counselor to the Twelve Apostles Oct. 6, 1877; died March 24, 1891, at Salt Lake City, Salt Lake Co., Utah, at age 76.

7. Joseph Fielding Smith — See PRESIDENTS OF THE CHURCH, No. 6.

8. Rudger Clawson — Born March 12, 1857, at Salt Lake City, Salt Lake Co., Utah, to Hiram Bradley Clawson and Margaret Gay Judd. Ordained apostle Oct. 10, 1898, by Lorenzo Snow, at age 41; sustained as second counselor to President Snow Oct. 6, 1901, at age 44, not set apart to this position; released at death of President Snow Oct. 10, 1901, and resumed position in the Quorum of the Twelve Apostles; sustained as president of the Quorum of the Twelve Apostles March 17, 1921; died June 21, 1943, in Salt Lake City, Salt Lake Co., Utah at age 86.

9. Anthon Henrik Lund — See FIRST COUNSELORS IN THE FIRST PRESIDENCY, No. 8.

10. John Henry Smith — Born Sept. 18, 1848, at Carbunca (now part of Council Bluffs), Pottawattamie Co., Iowa, to George Albert Smith and Sarah Ann Libby. Ordained apostle Oct. 27, 1880, by Wilford Woodruff, at age 32; sustained as second counselor to President Joseph F. Smith April 7, 1910, at age 61; died Oct. 13, 1911, at Salt Lake City, Salt Lake Co., Utah, at 63.

11. Charles William Penrose — See FIRST COUNSELORS IN THE FIRST PRESIDENCY, No. 9.

12. Anthony Woodward Ivins — See FIRST COUNSELORS IN THE FIRST PRESIDENCY, No. 10.

13. Charles Wilson Nibley — Born Feb. 5, 1849, at Hunterfield, Midlothian Region, Scotland, to James Nibley and Jane Wilson. Ordained high priest June 9, 1901, by Joseph F. Smith; sustained as Presiding Bishop of the Church Dec. 4, 1907, at age 58; sustained as second counselor to President Heber J. Grant, May 28, 1925, at age 76; died Dec. 11, 1931, at Salt Lake City, Salt Lake Co., Utah, at age 82.

14. Joshua Reuben Clark Jr. — See FIRST COUNSELORS IN THE FIRST PRESIDENCY, No. 11.

15. David Oman McKay — See PRESIDENTS OF CHURCH, No. 9.

16. Joshua Reuben Clark Jr. — See FIRST COUNSELORS IN THE FIRST PRESIDENCY, No. 11.

17. Henry Dinwoodey Moyle — See FIRST COUNSELORS IN THE FIRST PRESIDENCY, No. 14.

18. Hugh Brown Brown — See FIRST COUNSELORS IN THE FIRST PRESIDENCY, No. 15.

19. Nathan Eldon Tanner — See

FIRST COUNSELORS IN THE FIRST PRESIDENCY, No. 17.

20. Marion George Romney — See FIRST COUNSELORS IN THE FIRST PRESIDENCY, No. 18.

21. Gordon Bitner Hinckley — See current FIRST PRESIDENCY.

22. Thomas Spencer Monson — See current FIRST PRESIDENCY.

23. James Esdras Faust — See current FIRST PRESIDENCY .

OTHER COUNSELORS IN THE FIRST PRESIDENCY

1. Jesse Gause — Born about 1784 at East Marlborough, Chester Co., Virginia, to William and Mary Beverly Gause. Converted from the Shaker sect, he was baptized about the end of 1831. Set apart as counselor to Joseph Smith March 8, 1832; sent on a mission Aug. 1, 1832. Excommunicated Dec. 3, 1832. Died about 1836.

2. John Cook Bennett — Born Aug. 3, 1804, at Fair Haven, Bristol Co., Massachusetts, to J. and N. Bennett. Presented as assistant president with the First Presidency April 8, 1841, at age 36 (See *History of the Church* 4:341); disfellowshipped May 25, 1842; excommunicated latter part of 1842; died Aug. 5, 1867, in Polk City, Polk Co., Iowa.

3. Amasa Mason Lyman — Born March 30, 1813, at Lyman, Crafton Co., New Hampshire, to Roswell Lyman and Martha Mason. Ordained apostle Aug. 20, 1842, by Brigham Young, at age 29; replaced in the Quorum of the Twelve Apostles Jan. 20, 1843, due to reinstatement of Orson Pratt; appointed counselor to the First Presidency about Feb. 4, 1843; retired from the First Presidency with death of Joseph Smith June 27, 1844; returned to the Quorum of the Twelve Apostles Aug. 12, 1844; deprived of apostleship Oct. 6, 1867; excommunicated May 12, 1870; died Feb. 4, 1877, at Fillmore, Millard Co., Utah, at age 63. Blessings restored after death.

4. Joseph Fielding Smith — See PRESIDENTS OF CHURCH, No. 6.

5. Lorenzo Snow — See PRESIDENTS OF CHURCH, No. 5.

6. Brigham Young Jr. — Born Dec. 18, 1836, at Kirtland, Geauga Co., Ohio, to Brigham Young and Mary Ann Angell. Ordained apostle Feb. 4, 1864, by Brigham Young, at age 27; sustained to the Quorum of the Twelve Apostles Oct. 9, 1868; sustained as counselor to President Young April 8, 1873, at age 36; sustained as assistant counselor to President Young May 9, 1874; released at President Young's death Aug. 29, 1877, and resumed position in the Quorum of the Twelve Apostles; sustained as president of the Quorum of the Twelve Apostles Oct. 17, 1901; died April 11, 1903, in Salt Lake City, Salt Lake Co., Utah, at age 66.

7. Albert Carrington — Born Jan. 8, 1813, at Royalton, Windsor Co., Vermont, to Daniel Van Carrington and Isabella Bowman. Ordained apostle July 3, 1870, by Brigham Young, at age 57; sustained as counselor to President Young April 8, 1873, at age 60; sustained as assistant counselor to President Young May 9, 1874; released at death of President Young Aug. 29, 1877; excommunicated Nov. 7, 1885; rebaptized Nov. 1, 1887; died Sept. 19, 1889, at Salt Lake City, Salt Lake Co., Utah, at age 76.

8. John Willard Young — See FIRST COUNSELORS IN THE FIRST PRESI-

DENCY, No. 4.

9. George Quayle Cannon — See FIRST COUNSELORS IN THE FIRST PRESIDENCY, No. 5.

10. Hugh Brown Brown — See FIRST COUNSELORS IN THE FIRST PRESIDENCY, No. 15.

11. Joseph Fielding Smith — See PRESIDENTS OF THE CHURCH, No. 10.

12. Henry Thorpe Beal Isaacson — Born Sept. 6, 1898, at Ephraim, Sanpete Co., Utah, to Martin Isaacson and Mary Jemima Beal. Ordained high priest Oct. 1, 1941, by Charles A. Callis; sustained as second counselor to Presiding Bishop LeGrand Richards Dec. 12, 1946, at age 48; sustained as first counselor to Presiding Bishop Joseph L. Wirthlin April 6, 1952; sustained as Assistant to the Twelve Sept. 30, 1961; sustained as counselor in the First Presidency Oct. 28, 1965, at age 67; released at death of President David O. McKay Jan. 18, 1970; resumed position as Assistant to the Twelve Apostles Jan. 23, 1970; died Nov. 9, 1970, at Salt Lake City, Salt Lake Co., Utah, at age 72.

13. Alvin Rulon Dyer — Born Jan. 1, 1903, at Salt Lake City, Salt Lake Co., Utah, to Alfred R. Dyer and Harriet Walsh. Ordained high priest Oct. 2, 1927, by Joseph Fielding Smith; sustained an Assistant to the Twelve Oct. 11, 1958, at age 55; ordained apostle Oct. 5, 1967, by David O. McKay, at age 64; sustained as counselor in the First Presidency April 6, 1968; released at death of President McKay Jan. 18, 1970; resumed position as Assistant to the Twelve Apostles Jan. 23, 1970; sustained a member of First Quorum of the Seventy Oct. 1, 1976; died March 6, 1977, at Salt Lake City, Salt Lake Co., Utah, at age 74.

14. Gordon Bitner Hinckley — See current FIRST PRESIDENCY.

ASSISTANT COUNSELORS IN THE FIRST PRESIDENCY

1. Oliver Cowdery — See ASSISTANT PRESIDENTS OF THE CHURCH, No. 1.

2. Joseph Smith Sr. — Born July 12, 1771, at Topsfield, Essex Co., Massachusetts, to Asael Smith and Mary Duty. Ordained high priest June 3, 1831, by Lyman Wight; ordained Patriarch to the Church Dec. 18, 1833, at age 62; sustained as assistant counselor to the First Presidency Sept. 3, 1837, at age 66; died Sept. 14, 1840, at Nauvoo, Hancock Co., Illinois, at age 69.

3. Hyrum Smith — See ASSISTANT PRESIDENTS OF THE CHURCH, No. 2.

4. John Smith — Born July 16, 1781, at Derryfield, Hillsboro Co., New Hampshire, to Asael Smith and Mary Duty. Ordained high priest June 3, 1833, by Lyman Wight; sustained as assistant counselor to the First Presidency Sept. 3, 1837, at age 56; released at the death of Joseph Smith June 27, 1844; ordained Patriarch to the Church Jan. 1, 1849, at age 67; died May 23, 1854, at Salt Lake City, Salt Lake Co., Utah, at age 72.

5. Lorenzo Snow — See PRESIDENTS OF THE CHURCH, No. 5.

6. Brigham Young Jr. — See OTHER COUNSELORS IN THE FIRST PRESIDENCY, No. 6.

7. Albert Carrington — See OTHER COUNSELORS IN THE FIRST PRESIDENCY, No. 7.

8. John Willard Young — See FIRST COUNSELORS IN THE FIRST PRESIDENCY, No. 4.

9. George Quayle Cannon — See FIRST COUNSELORS IN THE FIRST PRESIDENCY, No. 5.

THE QUORUM OF THE TWELVE APOSTLES

1. Thomas Baldwin Marsh — Born Nov. 1, 1799, at Acton, Middlesex Co., Massachusetts, to James Marsh and Molly Law. Ordained apostle April 25, 1835, under the hands of Oliver Cowdery, David Whitmer, and Martin Harris, at Kirtland, Ohio, at age 35; sustained as president of the Quorum of the Twelve Apostles May 2, 1835; excommunicated March 17, 1839; rebaptized July 16, 1857; died January 1866, at Ogden, Weber Co., Utah, at age 66.

2. David Wyman Patten — Born Nov. 14, 1799, at Theresa, Jefferson Co., New York, to Benenio Patten and Abigail Cole. Ordained apostle Feb. 15, 1835, under the hands of Oliver Cowdery, David Whitmer, and Martin Harris, at Kirtland, Ohio, at age 35; killed Oct. 25, 1838, at the Battle of Crooked River, Missouri, at age 38.

3. Brigham Young — See PRESIDENTS OF THE CHURCH, No. 2.

4. Heber Chase Kimball — See FIRST COUNSELORS IN THE FIRST PRESIDENCY, No. 2.

5. Orson Hyde — Born Jan. 8, 1805, at Oxford, New Haven Co., Connecticut, to Nathan Hyde and Sally Thorp. Ordained apostle Feb. 15, 1835, under the hands of Oliver Cowdery, David Whitmer, and Martin Harris, at Kirtland, Ohio, at age 30; dropped from Quorum May 4, 1839; restored to Quorum June 27, 1839; sustained as president of the Quorum of the Twelve Apostles Dec. 27, 1847; Brigham Young, on April 10, 1875, took Hyde from his original position in the quorum and placed him in the order he would have been in when he was restored to fellowship had he come into the quorum at that time (See *"Succession in the Priesthood"* by John Taylor, p. 16.); died Nov. 28, 1878, at Spring City, Sanpete Co., Utah, at age 73.

6. William E. M'Lellin — Born Jan. 18, 1806, in Smith Co., Tenn. Ordained apostle Feb. 15, 1835, under the hands of Oliver Cowdery, David Whitmer, and Martin Harris, at Kirtland, Ohio, at age 29; excommunicated May 11, 1838; died April 24, 1883, at Independence, Jackson Co., Missouri, at age 77.

7. Parley Parker Pratt — Born April 12, 1807, at Burlington, Otsego Co., New York, to Jared Pratt and Charity Dickinson. Ordained apostle Feb. 21, 1835, under the hands of Joseph Smith, Oliver Cowdery, and David Whitmer, at Kirtland, Ohio, at age 27; assassinated May 13, 1857, near Van Buren, Crawford Co., Arkansas, at age 50.

8. Luke Johnson — Born Nov. 3, 1807, at Pomfret, Windsor Co., Vermont, to John Johnson and Elsa Jacobs. Ordained apostle Feb. 15, 1835, by Oliver Cowdery, David Whitmer, and Martin Harris, at Kirtland, Ohio, at age 27; excommunicated April 13, 1838; rebaptized in 1846 at Nauvoo, Illinois; died Dec. 9, 1861, at Salt Lake City, Salt Lake Co., Utah, at age 54.

9. William B. Smith — Born March 13, 1811, at Royalton, Windsor Co., Vermont, to Joseph Smith Sr. and Lucy Mack. Ordained apostle Feb. 15, 1835, under the hands of Oliver Cowdery, David Whitmer, and Martin Harris, at Kirtland, Ohio, at age 23; dropped from the quorum May 4, 1839; restored to quorum May 25, 1839; dropped from the quorum Oct. 6, 1845; excommunicated Oct. 19, 1845; died Nov. 13, 1893, at Osterdock, Clayton Co., Iowa, at age

82.

10. Orson Pratt — Born Sept. 19, 1811, at Hartford, Washington, Co., New York, to Jared Pratt and Charity Dickinson. Ordained apostle April 26, 1835, under the hands of Oliver Cowdery, David Whitmer, and Martin Harris, at Kirtland, Ohio, at age 23; excommunicated Aug. 20, 1842; rebaptized Jan. 20, 1843, and ordained to former office in the Quorum of the Twelve Apostles. Brigham Young took him from his original position in the quorum in 1875 and placed him in the order he would have been in when he was restored to fellowship had he come into the quorum at that time; died Oct. 3, 1881, at Salt Lake City, Salt Lake Co., Utah, at age 70.

11. John Farnham Boynton — Born Sept. 20, 1811, at Bradford, Essex Co., Massachusetts, to Eliphalet Boynton and Susannah Nichols. Ordained apostle Feb. 15, 1835, under the hands of Oliver Cowdery, David Whitmer and Martin Harris, at Kirtland, Ohio, at age 23; disfellowshipped Sept. 3, 1837; excommunicated 1837; died Oct. 20, 1890, at Syracuse, Onondaga Co., New York, at age 79.

12. Lyman Eugene Johnson — Born Oct. 24, 1811, at Pomfret, Windsor Co., Vermont, to John Johnson and Elsa Jacobs. Ordained apostle Feb. 14, 1835, under the hands of Oliver Cowdery, David Whitmer and Martin Harris, at Kirtland, Ohio, at age 23; excommunicated April 13, 1838; died Dec. 20, 1856, at Prairie du Chien, Crawford Co., Wisconsin, at age 45.

13. John Edward Page — Born Feb. 25, 1799, at Trenton Township, Oneida Co., New York, to Ebenezer and Rachel Page. Ordained apostle Dec. 19, 1838, under the hands of Brigham Young and Heber C. Kimball at Far West, Missouri, at age 39; disfellowshipped Feb. 9, 1846; excommunicated June 27, 1846; died Oct. 14, 1867, at De Kalb Co., Illinois, at age 68.

14. John Taylor — See PRESIDENTS OF THE CHURCH, No. 3.

15. Wilford Woodruff — See PRESIDENTS OF THE CHURCH, No. 4.

16. George Albert Smith — See FIRST COUNSELORS IN THE FIRST PRESIDENCY, No. 3.

17. Willard Richards — See SECOND COUNSELORS IN THE FIRST PRESIDENCY, No. 4.

18. Lyman Wight — Born May 9, 1796, at Fairfield, Herkimer Co., New York, to Levi Wight and Sarah Corbin. Ordained apostle April 8, 1841, by Joseph Smith, at Nauvoo, Illinois, at age 44; excommunicated Dec. 3, 1848; died March 31, 1858, in Dexter, Texas, at age 63.

19. Amasa Mason Lyman — See OTHER COUNSELORS IN THE FIRST PRESIDENCY, No. 3.

20. Ezra Taft Benson — Born Feb. 22, 1811, at Mendon, Worcester Co., Massachusetts, to John Benson and Chloe Taft. Ordained apostle July 16, 1846, by Brigham Young at Council Bluffs, Iowa, at age 35; died Sept. 3, 1869, at Ogden, Weber Co., Utah, at age 58.

21. Charles Coulsen Rich — Born Aug. 21, 1809, at Campbell Co., Kentucky, to Joseph Rich and Nancy O. Neal. Ordained apostle Feb. 12, 1849, by Brigham Young, at Salt Lake City, Utah, at age 39; died Nov. 17, 1883, at Paris, Bear Lake Co., Idaho, at age 74.

22. Lorenzo Snow — See PRESI-

DENTS OF THE CHURCH, No. 5.

23. Erastus Snow — Born Nov. 9, 1818, at Saint Johnsbury, Caledonia Co., Vermont, to Levi Snow and Lucina Streeter. Ordained apostle Feb. 12, 1849, by Brigham Young, at age 30; died May 27, 1888, at Salt Lake City, Salt Lake Co., Utah, at age 69.

24. Franklin Dewey Richards — Born April 2, 1821, at Richmond, Berkshire Co., Massachusetts, to Phinehas Richards and Wealthy Dewey. Ordained apostle Feb. 12, 1849, by Heber C. Kimball, at age 27; sustained as president of the Quorum of the Twelve Apostles Sept. 13, 1898; died Dec. 9, 1899, at Ogden, Weber Co., Utah, at age 78.

25. George Quayle Cannon — See FIRST COUNSELORS IN THE FIRST PRESIDENCY, No. 5.

26. Joseph Fielding Smith — See PRESIDENTS OF THE CHURCH, No. 6.

27. Brigham Young Jr. — See OTHER COUNSELORS IN THE FIRST PRESIDENCY, No. 6.

28. Albert Carrington — See OTHER COUNSELORS IN THE FIRST PRESIDENCY, No. 7.

29. Moses Thatcher — Born Feb. 2, 1842, at Springfield Sangamon Co., Ill., to Hezekiah Thatcher and Alley Kitchen. Ordained apostle April 7, 1879, by John Taylor, at age 37; dropped from the Quorum of the Twelve Apostles April 6, 1896; died Aug. 21, 1909, at Logan, Cache Co., Utah, at age 67.

30. Francis Marion Lyman — Born Jan. 12, 1840, at Good Hope, McDonough Co., Illinois, to Amasa Mason Lyman and Maria Louisa Tanner. Ordained apostle Oct. 27, 1880, by John Taylor, at age 40; sustained as president of the Quorum of the Twelve Apostles Oct. 6, 1903; died Nov. 18, 1916, at Salt Lake City, Salt Lake Co., Utah, at age 76.

31. John Henry Smith — See SECOND COUNSELORS IN THE FIRST PRESIDENCY, No. 10.

32. George Teasdale — Born Dec. 8, 1831, at London, Middlesex Co., England, to William Russell Teasdale and Harriett H. Tidey. Ordained apostle Oct. 16, 1882, by John Taylor, at age 50; died June 9, 1907, at Salt Lake City, Salt Lake Co., Utah, at age 75.

33. Heber Jeddy Grant — See PRESIDENTS OF THE CHURCH, No. 7.

34. John Whittaker Taylor — Born May 15, 1858, at Provo, Utah Co., Utah, to John Taylor and Sophia Whittaker. Ordained apostle April 9, 1884, by John Taylor, at age 25; resigned Oct. 28, 1905; excommunicated March 28, 1911; died Oct. 10, 1916, at Salt Lake City, Salt Lake Co., Utah, at age 58. Blessings restored May 21, 1965.

35. Marriner Wood Merrill — Born Sept. 25, 1835, at Sackville, Westmoreland Co., New Brunswick, Canada, to Nathan Alexander Merrill and Sarah Ann Reynolds. Ordained apostle Oct. 7, 1889, by Wilford Woodruff, at age 57; died Feb. 6, 1906, at Richmond, Cache Co., Utah, at age 73.

36. Anthon Henrik Lund — See

FIRST COUNSELORS IN THE FIRST PRESIDENCY, No. 8.

37. Abraham Hoagland Cannon — Born March 12, 1859, at Salt Lake City, Salt Lake Co., Utah, to George Quayle Cannon and Elizabeth Hoagland. Sustained as one of the First Seven Presidents of the Seventy Oct. 8, 1882, at age 23; ordained apostle Oct. 7, 1889, by Joseph F. Smith, at age 30; died July 19, 1896, at Salt Lake City, Salt Lake Co., Utah, at age 37.

38. Matthias Foss Cowley — Born Aug. 25, 1858, at Salt Lake City, Salt Lake Co., Utah, to Matthias Cowley and Sarah Elizabeth Foss. Ordained apostle Oct. 7, 1897, by George Q. Cannon, at age 39; resigned Oct. 28, 1905; priesthood suspended May 11, 1911; restored to full membership April 3, 1936; died June 16, 1940, at Salt Lake City, Salt Lake Co., Utah, at age 81.

39. Abraham Owen Woodruff — Born Nov. 23, 1872, at Salt Lake City, Salt Lake Co., Utah, to Wilford Woodruff and Emma Smith. Ordained apostle Oct. 7, 1897, by Wilford Woodruff, at age 24; died June 20, 1904, at El Paso, El Paso Co., Texas, at age 31.

40. Rudger Clawson — See SECOND COUNSELORS IN THE FIRST PRESIDENCY, No. 8.

41. Reed Smoot — Born Jan. 10, 1862, at Salt Lake City, Salt Lake Co., Utah, to Abraham Owen Smoot and Anne Kestine Morrison. Ordained apostle April 8, 1900, by Lorenzo Snow, at age 38; served in the U.S. Senate, 1903-32; died Feb. 9, 1941, at St. Petersburg, Pinellas Co., Florida, at age 79.

42. Hyrum Mack Smith — Born March 21, 1872, at Salt Lake City, Salt Lake Co., Utah, to Joseph Fielding Smith and Edna Lambson. Ordained apostle Oct. 24, 1901, by Joseph F. Smith, at age 29; died Jan. 23, 1918, at Salt Lake City, Salt Lake Co., Utah, at age 45.

43. George Albert Smith — See PRESIDENTS OF THE CHURCH, No. 8.

44. Charles William Penrose — See FIRST COUNSELORS IN THE FIRST PRESIDENCY, No. 9.

45. George Franklin Richards — Born Feb. 23, 1861, at Farmington, Davis Co., Utah, to Franklin Dewey Richards and Nanny Longstroth. Ordained apostle April 9, 1906, by Joseph F. Smith, at age 45; sustained as acting Patriarch to the Church Oct. 8, 1937; released from this position Oct. 3, 1942; sustained as president of the Quorum of the Twelve Apostles May 21, 1945; died Aug. 8, 1950, at Salt Lake City, Salt Lake Co., Utah, at age 89.

46. Orson Ferguson Whitney — Born July 1, 1855, at Salt Lake City, Salt Lake Co., Utah, to Horace Kimball Whitney and Helen Mar Kimball. Ordained apostle April 9, 1906, by Joseph F. Smith, at age 50; died May 16, 1931, at Salt Lake City, Salt Lake Co., Utah, at age 75.

47. David Oman McKay — See PRESIDENTS OF THE CHURCH, No. 9.

48. Anthony Woodward Ivins — See FIRST COUNSELORS IN THE FIRST PRESIDENCY, No. 10.

49. Joseph Fielding Smith — See

PRESIDENTS OF THE CHURCH, No. 10.

50. James Edward Talmage — Born Sept. 21, 1862, at Hungerford, Berkshire Co., England, to James J. Talmage and Susannah Preater. Ordained apostle Dec. 8, 1911, by Joseph F. Smith, at age 49; died July 27, 1933, at Salt Lake City, Salt Lake Co., Utah, at age 70.

51. Stephen L Richards — See FIRST COUNSELORS IN THE FIRST PRESIDENCY, No. 12.

52. Richard Roswell Lyman — Born Nov. 23, 1870, at Fillmore, Millard Co., Utah, to Francis Marion Lyman and Clara Caroline Callister. Ordained apostle April 7, 1918, by Joseph F. Smith, at age 47; excommunicated Nov. 12, 1943; rebaptized Oct. 27, 1954; died Dec. 31, 1963, at Salt Lake City, Salt Lake Co., Utah, at age 93.

53. Melvin Joseph Ballard — Born Feb. 9, 1873, at Logan, Cache Co., Utah, to Henry Ballard and Margaret Reid McNeil. Ordained apostle Jan. 7, 1919, by Heber J. Grant, at age 45; died July 30, 1939, at Salt Lake City, Salt Lake Co., Utah, at age 66.

54. John Andreas Widtsoe — Born Jan. 31, 1872, at Daloe, Island of Froyen, Trondhjem, Norway, to John A. Widtsoe and Anna Karine Gaarden. Ordained apostle March 17, 1921, by Heber J. Grant, at age 49; died Nov. 29, 1952, at Salt Lake City, Salt Lake Co., Utah, at age 80.

55. Joseph Francis Merrill — Born Aug. 24, 1868, at Richmond, Cache Co., Utah, to Marriner Wood Merrill and Mariah Loenza Kingsbury. Ordained apostle Oct. 8, 1931, by Heber J. Grant, at age 63; died Feb. 3, 1952, at Salt Lake City, Salt Lake Co., Utah, at age 83.

56. Charles Albert Callis — Born May 4, 1865, at Dublin, Dublin Co., Ireland, to John Callis and Susanna Charlotte Quillam. Ordained apostle Oct. 12, 1933, by Heber J. Grant, at age 68; died Jan. 21, 1947, in Jacksonville, Duval Co., Florida, at age 81.

57. Joshua Reuben Clark Jr. — See FIRST COUNSELORS IN THE FIRST PRESIDENCY, No. 11.

58. Alonzo Arza Hinckley — Born April 23, 1870, at Cove Fort, Millard Co., Utah, to Ira Nathaniel Hinckley and Angeline Wilcox Noble. Ordained apostle Oct. 11, 1934, by Heber J. Grant, at age 64; died Dec. 22, 1936, at Salt Lake City, Salt Lake Co., Utah, at age 66.

59. Albert Ernest Bowen — Born Oct. 31, 1875, at Henderson Creek, Oneida Co., Idaho, to David Bowen and Annie Schackelton. Ordained apostle April 8, 1937, by Heber J. Grant, at age 61; died July 15, 1953, at Salt Lake City, Salt Lake Co., Utah, at age 77.

60. Sylvester Quayle Cannon — Born June 10, 1877, at Salt Lake City, Salt Lake Co., Utah, to George Quayle Cannon and Elizabeth Hoagland. Sustained as Presiding Bishop of the Church June 4, 1925, at age 47;

sustained as Associate to the Quorum of the Twelve Apostles April 6, 1938; ordained apostle April 14, 1938, by Heber J. Grant; sustained as a member of the Quorum of the Twelve Apostles Oct. 6, 1939, at age 62; died May 29, 1943, at Salt Lake City, Salt Lake Co., Utah, at age 65.

61. Harold Bingham Lee — See PRESIDENTS OF THE CHURCH, No. 11.

62. Spencer Woolley Kimball — See PRESIDENTS OF THE CHURCH, No. 12.

63. Ezra Taft Benson — See PRESIDENTS OF THE CHURCH, No. 13.

64. Mark Edward Petersen — Born Nov. 7, 1900, at Salt Lake City, Salt Lake Co., Utah, to Christian Petersen and Christine M. Andersen. Ordained apostle April 20, 1944, by Heber J. Grant, at age 43; died Jan. 11, 1984, at Salt Lake City, Salt Lake Co., Utah, at age 83.

65. Matthew Cowley — Born Aug. 2, 1897, at Preston, Franklin Co., Idaho, to Matthias Foss Cowley and Abbie Hyde. Ordained apostle Oct. 11, 1945, by George Albert Smith, at age 48; died Dec. 13, 1953, at Los Angeles, Los Angeles Co., California, at age 56.

66. Henry Dinwoodey Moyle — See FIRST COUNSELORS IN THE FIRST PRESIDENCY, No. 14.

67. Delbert Leon Stapley — Born Dec. 11, 1896, at Mesa, Maricopa Co., Arizona, to Orley S. Stapley and Polly M. Hunsaker. Ordained apostle Oct. 5, 1950, by George Albert Smith, at age 53; died Aug. 19, 1978, at Salt Lake City, Salt Lake Co., Utah, at age 81.

68. Marion George Romney — See FIRST COUNSELORS IN THE FIRST PRESIDENCY, No. 18.

69. LeGrand Richards — Born Feb. 6, 1886, at Farmington, Davis Co., Utah, to George Franklin Richards and Alice Almira Robinson. Sustained Presiding Bishop of the Church April 6, 1938, at age 52; ordained apostle April 10, 1952, by David O. McKay, at age 66; died Jan. 11, 1983, at Salt Lake City, Salt Lake Co., Utah, at age 96.

70. Adam Samuel Bennion — Born Dec. 2, 1886, at Taylorsville, Salt Lake Co., Utah, to Joseph Bennion and Mary A. Sharp. Ordained apostle April 9, 1953, by David O. McKay, at age 66; died Feb. 11, 1958, at Salt Lake City, Salt Lake Co., Utah, at age 71.

71. Richard Louis Evans — Born March 23, 1906, at Salt Lake City, Salt Lake Co., Utah, to John A. Evans and Florence Neslen. Sustained as member of the First Council of the Seventy Oct. 7, 1938, at age 32; ordained apostle Oct. 8, 1953, by David O. McKay, at age 47; died Nov. 1, 1971, at Salt Lake City, Salt Lake Co., Utah, at age 65.

72. George Quayle Morris — Born Feb. 20, 1874, at Salt Lake City, Salt Lake Co., Utah, to Elias Morris and Mary L. Walker. Sustained as Assistant to the Quorum of the Twelve Apostles Oct. 6, 1951, at age 77; ordained apostle April 8, 1954, by David O. McKay, at age 80; died April 23, 1962, at Salt Lake City, Salt Lake Co., Utah, at age 88.

73. Hugh Brown Brown — See FIRST

COUNSELORS IN THE FIRST PRESIDENCY, No. 15.

74. Howard William Hunter — See PRESIDENTS OF THE CHURCH, No. 14.

75. Gordon Bitner Hinckley — See current FIRST PRESIDENCY.

76. Nathan Eldon Tanner — See FIRST COUNSELORS IN THE FIRST PRESIDENCY, No. 17.

77. Thomas Spencer Monson — See current FIRST PRESIDENCY.

78. Boyd Kenneth Packer — See current QUORUM OF THE TWELVE.

79. Marvin Jeremy Ashton — Born May 6, 1915, in Salt Lake City, Salt Lake Co., Utah, to Marvin O. Ashton and Rachel Jeremy. Sustained Assistant to the Twelve Apostles Oct. 3, 1969, at age 54; ordained apostle on Dec. 2, 1971, by Harold B. Lee at age 56; died Feb. 25, 1994, at Salt Lake City, Salt Lake Co., Utah, at age 78.

80. Bruce Redd McConkie — Born July 29, 1915, at Ann Arbor, Washtenaw Co., Michigan, to Oscar Walter McConkie and Vivian Redd. Sustained to First Council of the Seventy Oct. 6, 1946, at age 31; ordained apostle Oct. 12, 1972, by Harold B. Lee, at age 57; died April 19, 1985, at Salt Lake City, Salt Lake Co., Utah, at age 69.

81. Lowell Tom Perry — See current QUORUM OF THE TWELVE.

82. David Bruce Haight — See current QUORUM OF THE TWELVE.

83. James Esdras Faust — See current FIRST PRESIDENCY.

84. Neal Ash Maxwell — See current QUORUM OF THE TWELVE.

85. Russell Marion Nelson — See current QUORUM OF THE TWELVE.

86. Dallin Harris Oaks — See current QUORUM OF THE TWELVE.

87. Melvin Russell Ballard Jr. — See current QUORUM OF THE TWELVE.

88. Joseph Bitner Wirthlin — See current QUORUM OF THE TWELVE.

89. Richard Gordon Scott — See current QUORUM OF THE TWELVE.

90. Robert Dean Hales — See current QUORUM OF THE TWELVE.

91. Jeffrey Roy Holland — See current QUORUM OF THE TWELVE.

92. Henry Bennion Eyring — See current QUORUM OF THE TWELVE.

OTHER APOSTLES

1. Joseph Smith Jr. — See PRESIDENTS OF THE CHURCH, No. 1.

2. Oliver Cowdery — See ASSISTANT PRESIDENTS OF THE CHURCH, No. 1.

3. Hyrum Smith — See ASSISTANT PRESIDENTS OF THE CHURCH, No. 2.

4. Amasa Mason Lyman — See OTHER COUNSELORS IN THE FIRST PRESIDENCY, No. 3.

5. Jedediah Morgan Grant — See SECOND COUNSELORS IN THE FIRST PRESIDENCY, No. 5.

6. John Willard Young — See FIRST COUNSELORS IN THE FIRST PRESIDENCY, No. 4.

7. Daniel Hanmer Wells — See SECOND COUNSELORS IN THE FIRST PRESIDENCY, No. 6.

8. Joseph Angell Young — Born Oct. 14, 1834, in Kirtland, Geauga Co., Ohio, to Brigham Young and Mary Ann Angell. Ordained apostle Feb. 4, 1864, by Brigham Young, at age 29; died Aug. 5, 1875, at Manti, Sanpete Co., Utah, at age 40.

9. Brigham Young Jr. — See OTHER COUNSELORS IN THE FIRST PRESIDENCY, No. 6.

10. Joseph Fielding Smith — See PRESIDENTS OF THE CHURCH, No. 6.

11. Sylvester Quayle Cannon — See QUORUM OF THE TWELVE, No. 60.

12. Alvin Rulon Dyer — See OTHER COUNSELORS IN THE FIRST PRESIDENCY, No. 13.

PATRIARCHS TO THE CHURCH

1. Joseph Smith Sr. — See ASSISTANT COUNSELORS IN THE FIRST PRESIDENCY, No. 2.

2. Hyrum Smith — See ASSISTANT PRESIDENTS OF THE CHURCH, No. 2.

William B. Smith — See QUORUM OF THE TWELVE, No. 9. Ordained Patriarch to the Church May 24, 1845, by the Quorum of the Twelve and then gave patriarchal blessings, but was rejected by the Church membership at the General Conference held Oct. 6, 1845.

3. John Smith — See ASSISTANT COUNSELORS IN THE FIRST PRESIDENCY, No. 4.

4. John Smith — Born Sept. 22, 1832, at Kirtland, Geauga Co., Ohio, the eldest son of Hyrum Smith and Jerusha Barden. Ordained Patriarch to the Church Feb. 18, 1855, by Brigham Young, at age 22; died Nov. 5, 1911, at Salt Lake City, Salt Lake Co., Utah, at age 79.

5. Hyrum Gibbs Smith — Born July 8, 1879, at South Jordan, Salt Lake Co., Utah, the eldest son of Hyrum Fisher Smith and Annie Maria Gibbs. Ordained high priest and Patriarch to the Church May 9, 1912, by Joseph F. Smith, at age 32; died Feb. 4, 1932, at Salt Lake City, Salt Lake Co., Utah, at age 52.

(From 1932 to 1937, no Patriarch to the Church was sustained.)

George Franklin Richards — See QUORUM OF THE TWELVE, No. 45. (Served as acting Patriarch.)

6. Joseph Fielding Smith — Born Jan. 30, 1899, at Salt Lake City, Salt Lake Co., Utah, the eldest son of Hyrum Mack Smith and Ida E. Bowman. Ordained high priest and Patriarch to the Church Oct. 8, 1942, by Heber J. Grant, at age 43; released Oct. 6, 1946, due to ill health; died Aug. 29, 1964, in Salt Lake City, Salt Lake Co., Utah, at age 65.

7. Eldred Gee Smith — Born Jan. 9, 1907, at Lehi, Utah Co., Utah, the eldest son of Hyrum Gibbs Smith and Martha Electa Gee. Ordained high priest May 23, 1938, by J. Reuben Clark Jr.; ordained Patriarch to the Church April 10, 1947, by George Albert Smith, at age 40; named emeritus General Authority Oct. 6, 1979.

(No Patriarch to the Church has been sustained since Oct. 6, 1979.)

FIRST COUNCIL OF THE SEVENTY

(Functioned from February 1835 to October 1976)

1. Hazen Aldrich — Chosen and ordained one of the First Seven Presidents Feb. 28, 1835; released April 6, 1837, having previously been ordained high priest.

2. Joseph Young — Born April 7, 1797, at Hopkinton, Middlesex Co., Massachusetts, to John Young and Abigail Howe. Ordained seventy Feb. 28, 1835, under the hands of Joseph Smith, Sidney Rigdon, and Frederick G. Williams; chosen and ordained one of the First Seven Presidents Feb. 28, 1835, at age 37; died July 16, 1881, at Salt Lake City, Salt Lake Co., Utah, at age 84.

3. Levi Ward Hancock — Born April

7, 1803, at Springfield, Hampden, Co., Massachusetts, to Thomas Hancock and Amy Ward. Ordained seventy Feb. 28, 1835, under the hands of Joseph Smith, Sidney Rigdon, and Frederick G. Williams; chosen and ordained one of the First Seven Presidents Feb. 28, 1835, at age 31; released April 6, 1837, having supposedly previously been ordained high priest; restored to former place in the First Council Sept. 3, 1837, as he had not been ordained high priest; died June 10, 1882, at Washington, Washington Co., Utah, at age 79.

4. Leonard Rich — Chosen and ordained one of the First Seven Presidents Feb. 28, 1835; released April 6, 1837, having previously been ordained high priest.

5. Zebedee Coltrin — Born Sept. 7, 1804, at Ovid, Seneca Co., New York, to John Coltrin Jr. and Sarah Graham. Chosen and ordained one of the First Seven Presidents Feb. 28, 1835, at age 30; released April 6, 1837, having previously been ordained high priest; died July 20, 1887, at Spanish Fork, Utah Co., Utah, at age 82.

6. Lyman Royal Sherman — Born May 22, 1804, at Salem, Essex Co., Massachusetts, to Elkanah Sherman and Asenath Hulbert. Chosen and ordained one of the First Seven Presidents Feb. 28, 1835, at age 30; released April 6, 1837, having previously been ordained high priest; died Jan. 27, 1839, at age 34.

7. Sylvester Smith — Chosen and ordained one of the First Seven Presidents Feb. 28, 1835; released April 6, 1837, having previously been ordained high priest.

8. John Gould — Born May 11, 1808. Ordained seventy and set apart as one of the First Seven Presidents April 6, 1837, by Sidney Rigdon and Hyrum Smith, at age 28; released Sept. 3, 1837, to be ordained high priest. Died May 9, 1851, at age 42.

9. James Foster — Born April 1, 1775, at Morgan Co., New Hampshire. Ordained seventy April 6, 1837, under the hands of Sidney Rigdon and Hyrum Smith; set apart as one of the First Seven Presidents April 6, 1837, at age 62; died Dec. 21, 1841, at Morgan Co., Illinois, at age 66.

10. Daniel Sanborn Miles — Born July 23, 1772, at Sanbornton, Belknap Co., New Hampshire, to Josiah Miles and Marah Sanborn. Ordained seventy April 6, 1837, by Hazen Aldrich; set apart as one of the First Seven Presidents April 6, 1837, by Sidney Rigdon and Hyrum Smith, at age 64; died in autumn of 1845, at Hancock Co., Illinois, at age 73.

11. Josiah Butterfield — Born March 13 or 18, 1795, at Saco, York Co., Maine, to Abel and Mary or Mercy Butterfield. Ordained seventy April 6, 1837, under the hands of Sidney Rigdon and Hyrum Smith; set apart as one of the First Seven Presidents April 6, 1837, at age 42; excommunicated Oct. 7, 1844; died in April 1871 at Monterey Co., California, at age 76.

12. Salmon Gee — Born Oct. 16, 1792, at Lyme, New London Co., Connecticut, to Zopher Gee and Esther Beckwith. Ordained seventy April 6, 1837, under the hands of Sidney Rigdon and Hyrum Smith; set apart as one of the First Seven Presidents April 6, 1837, at age 44; fellowship withdrawn March 6, 1838; died Sept. 13, 1845, at Ambrosia, Lee Co., Iowa, at age 52; posthumously reinstated Sept. 14, 1967.

13. John Gaylord — Born July 12, 1797, in Pennsylvania, to Chauncey Gaylord. Ordained seventy Dec. 20, 1836, by Hazen Aldrich; set apart as one of the First Seven Presidents April 6, 1837, at age 39, by Sidney Rigdon and others; excommunicated Jan. 13, 1838; rejoined the Church at Nauvoo, Illinois, Oct. 5, 1839; died July 17, 1878, at age 81.

14. Henry Harriman — Born June 9,

1804, at Rowley, Essex Co., Massachusetts, to Enoch Harriman and Sarah Brocklebank. Ordained seventy March 1835, under the hands of Joseph Smith and Sidney Rigdon; set apart as one of the First Seven Presidents Feb. 6, 1838, by Joseph Young and others, at age 33; died May 17, 1891, at Huntington, Emery Co., Utah, at 86.

15. Zera Pulsipher — Born June 24, 1789, at Rockingham, Windham Co., Vermont, to John Pulsipher and Elizabeth Dutton. Ordained seventy March 6, 1838, under the hands of Joseph Young and James Foster; set apart as one of the First Seven Presidents March 6, 1838, at age 48; released April 12, 1862; died Jan. 1, 1872, at Hebron, Washington Co., Utah, at age 82.

Roger Orton was excommunicated Nov. 30, 1837; returned to the Church; sustained as one of the First Seven Presidents April 7, 1845, but was never set apart and did not function; dropped from this position Oct. 6, 1845.

16. Albert Perry Rockwood — Born June 5, 1805, at Holliston, Middlesex Co., Massachusetts, to Luther Rockwood and Ruth Perry. Ordained seventy Jan. 5, 1839, under the hands of Joseph Young, Henry Harriman, and Zera Pulsipher; set apart as one of the First Seven Presidents Dec. 2, 1845, by Brigham Young and others, at age 40; died Nov. 26, 1879, at Sugar House, Salt Lake Co., Utah, at age 74.

17. Benjamin Lynn Clapp — Born Aug. 19, 1814, at West Huntsville, Madison Co., Alabama, to Ludwig Lewis Clapp and Margaret Ann Loy. Ordained seventy Oct. 20, 1844, under the hands of Joseph Young and Levi W. Hancock; set apart as one of the First Seven Presidents Dec. 2, 1845, by Brigham Young and others, at age 31; excommunicated April 7, 1859; died in 1860 in California, at age 46.

18. Jedediah Morgan Grant — See SECOND COUNSELORS IN THE FIRST PRESIDENCY, No. 5.

19. Horace Sunderlin Eldredge — Born Feb. 6, 1816, at Brutus, Cayuga Co., New York, to Alanson Eldredge and Esther Sunderlin. Ordained seventy Oct. 13, 1844, by Joseph Young; sustained as one of the First Seven Presidents Oct. 7, 1854, at age 38; died Sept. 6, 1888, at Salt Lake City, Salt Lake Co., Utah, at age 72.

20. Jacob Gates — Born March 9, 1811, at Saint Johnsbury, Caledonia Co., Vermont, to Thomas Gates and Patty Plumley. Ordained seventy Dec. 19, 1838, under the hands of Joseph Smith and Sidney Rigdon; sustained as one of the First Seven Presidents April 6, 1860, at age 49; set apart Oct. 8, 1862, by Orson Hyde; died April 14, 1892, at Provo, Utah Co., Utah, at age 81.

21. John Van Cott — Born Sept. 7, 1814, at Canaan, Columbia Co., New York, to Losee Van Cott and Lovinia Pratt. Ordained seventy Feb. 25, 1847, by Joseph Young; sustained as one of the First Seven Presidents Oct. 8, 1862, at age 48; set apart by John Taylor; died Feb. 18, 1883, at Salt Lake City, Salt Lake Co., Utah, at age 68.

22. William Whittaker Taylor — Born Sept. 11, 1853, at Salt Lake City, Salt Lake Co., Utah, to John Taylor and Harriet Whittaker. Ordained seventy

Oct. 11, 1875, by Orson Pratt; sustained as one of the First Seven Presidents April 7, 1880, at age 26; set apart by John Taylor; died Aug. 1, 1884, at Salt Lake City, Salt Lake Co., Utah, at age 30.

23. Abraham Hoagland Cannon — See QUORUM OF THE TWELVE, No. 37.

Theodore Belden Lewis — Born Nov. 18, 1843, at St. Louis, St. Louis Co., Missouri, to Thomas Anderson Lewis and Martha J. O. Belden. Ordained high priest at Nephi, Utah (date not known); sustained as one of the First Seven Presidents Oct. 8, 1882, at age 38; on Oct. 9, when he was to be set apart, he reported that he was already a high priest, so he was not set apart and did not function in this position.

24. Seymour Bicknell Young — Born Oct. 3, 1837, at Kirtland, Geauga Co., Ohio, to Joseph Young and Jane Adeline Bicknell. Ordained seventy Feb. 18, 1857, by Edmund Ellsworth; set apart by Franklin D. Richards as one of the First Seven Presidents Oct. 14, 1882, at age 45; sustained April 8, 1883; died Dec. 15, 1924, at Salt Lake City, Salt Lake Co., Utah, at age 87.

25. Christian Daniel Fjelsted — Born Feb. 20, 1829, at Amagar, Sundbyvester Co., Denmark, to Hendrick Ludvig Fjelsted and Ann Catrine Hendriksen. Ordained seventy Feb. 5, 1859, by William H. Walker; sustained as one of the First Seven Presidents April 6, 1884, at age 55; set apart by Wilford Woodruff; died Dec. 23, 1905, at Salt Lake City, Salt Lake Co., Utah, at age 76.

26. John Morgan — Born Aug. 8, 1842, at Greensburg, Decatur Co., Indiana, to Gerrard Morgan and Ann Eliza Hamilton. Ordained seventy Oct. 8, 1875, by Joseph Young; sustained as one of the First Seven Presidents Oct. 5, 1884, at age 42; set apart by Wilford Woodruff; died Aug. 14, 1894, at Preston, Franklin Co., Idaho, at 52.

27. Brigham Henry Roberts — Born March 13, 1857, at Warrington, Lancashire Co., England, to Benjamin Roberts and Ann Everington. Ordained seventy March 8, 1877, by Nathan T. Porter. Sustained as one of the First Seven Presidents Oct. 7, 1888, at age 31; set apart by Lorenzo Snow; died Sept. 27, 1933, at Salt Lake City, Salt Lake Co., Utah, at age 76.

28. George Reynolds — Born Jan. 1, 1842, at Marylebone, London Co., London, England, to George Reynolds and Julia Ann Tautz. Ordained seventy March 18, 1866, by Israel Barlow; sustained as one of the First Seven Presidents April 5, 1890, at age 48; set apart by Lorenzo Snow; died Aug. 9, 1909, at Salt Lake City, Salt Lake Co., Utah, at age 67.

29. Jonathan Golden Kimball — Born June 9, 1853, at Salt Lake City, Salt Lake Co., Utah, to Heber Chase Kimball and Christeen Golden. Ordained seventy July 21, 1886, by William M. Allred; sustained as one of the First Seven Presidents April 5, 1892, at age 38; set apart by Francis M. Lyman; killed in an automobile accident Sept. 2, 1938, near Reno, Nevada, at age 85.

30. Rulon Seymour Wells — Born July 7, 1854, at Salt Lake City, Salt Lake Co., Utah, to Daniel Hanmer Wells

and Louisa Free. Ordained seventy Oct. 22, 1875, by Brigham Young; sustained as one of the First Seven Presidents April 5, 1893, at age 38; set apart by George Q. Cannon; died May 7, 1941, at Salt Lake City, Salt Lake Co., Utah, at age 86.

31. Edward Stevenson — Born May 1, 1820, at Gibraltar, Spain, to Joseph Stevenson and Elizabeth Stevens. Ordained seventy May 1, 1844, by Joseph Young; sustained as one of the First Seven Presidents Oct. 7, 1894, at age 74; set apart by Brigham Young; died Jan. 27, 1897, at Salt Lake City, Salt Lake Co., Utah, at age 76.

32. Joseph William McMurrin — Born Sept. 5. 1858, at Tooele, Tooele Co., Utah, to Joseph McMurrin and Margaret Leaning. Ordained seventy April 21, 1884, by Royal Barney; sustained as one of the First Seven Presidents Oct. 5, 1897, at age 39; set apart Jan. 21, 1898, by Anthon H. Lund; died Oct. 24, 1932, at Los Angeles, Los Angeles Co., California, at age 74.

33. Charles Henry Hart — Born July 5, 1866, at Bloomington, Bear Lake Co., Idaho, to James Henry Hart and Sabina Scheib. Ordained seventy Aug. 10, 1890, by John Henry Smith; sustained as one of the First Seven Presidents April 9, 1906, at age 39; set apart by Joseph F. Smith; died Sept. 29, 1934, at Salt Lake City, Salt Lake Co., Utah, at age 68.

34. Levi Edgar Young — Born Feb. 2, 1874, at Salt Lake City, Salt Lake Co., Utah, to Seymour Bicknell Young and Ann Elizabeth Riter. Ordained seventy June 18, 1897, by Seymour B. Young; sustained as one of the First Seven Presidents Oct. 6, 1909, at age 35; set apart Jan. 23, 1910, by John Henry Smith; died Dec. 13, 1963, at Salt Lake City, Salt Lake Co., Utah, at age 89.

35. Rey Lucero Pratt — Born Oct. 11, 1878, at Salt Lake City, Salt Lake Co., Utah, to Helaman Pratt and Emeline Victoria Billingsley. Ordained seventy Sept. 23, 1911, by Rulon S. Wells; sustained as one of the First Seven Presidents Jan. 29, 1925, at age 46; set apart April 7, 1925, by Anthony W. Ivins; died April 14, 1931, at Salt Lake City, Salt Lake Co., Utah at age 52.

36. Antoine Ridgeway Ivins — Born May 11, 1881, at St. George, Washington Co., Utah, to Anthony Woodward Ivins and Elizabeth A. Snow. Ordained seventy Dec. 28, 1913, by Fred E. Barker; sustained as one of the First Seven Presidents Oct. 4, 1931, at age 50; ordained high priest June 11, 1961, by David O. McKay; died Oct. 18, 1967, at Salt Lake City, Salt Lake Co., Utah, at age 86.

37. Samuel Otis Bennion — Born June 9, 1874, at Taylorsville, Salt Lake Co., Utah, to John Rowland Bennion and Emma Jane Terry. Ordained seventy March 14, 1904, by Samuel Gerrard; sustained as one of the First Seven Presidents April 6, 1933, at age 58; set apart by Heber J. Grant; died March 8, 1945, at Salt Lake City, Salt Lake Co., Utah, at age 70.

38. John Harris Taylor — Born June 28, 1875, at Salt Lake City, Salt Lake Co., Utah, to Thomas E. Taylor and Emma L. Harris. Ordained seventy

Jan. 24, 1896, by Heber J. Grant; sustained as one of the First Seven Presidents Oct. 6, 1933, at age 58; set apart by Heber J. Grant; died May 28, 1946, at Salt Lake City, Salt Lake Co., Utah, at age 70.

39. Rufus Kay Hardy — Born May 28, 1878, at Salt Lake City, Salt Lake Co., Utah, to Rufus H. Hardy and Annie Kay. Ordained seventy July 2, 1897, by John Henry Smith; sustained to the First Council of the Seventy Oct. 6, 1934, at age 56; set apart Feb. 7, 1935, by Heber J. Grant; died March 7, 1945, at Salt Lake City, Salt Lake Co., Utah, at age 66.

40. Richard Louis Evans — See QUORUM OF THE TWELVE, No. 71.

41. Oscar Ammon Kirkham — Born Jan. 22, 1880, at Lehi, Utah Co., Utah, to James Kirkham and Martha Mercer. Ordained seventy Feb. 26, 1905, by Joseph W. McMurrin; sustained to the First Council of the Seventy Oct. 5, 1941, at age 61; set apart by Heber J. Grant; died March 10, 1958, at Salt Lake City, Salt Lake Co., Utah, at 78.

42. Seymour Dilworth Young — See FIRST QUORUM OF THE SEVENTY, No. 24.

43. Milton Reed Hunter — Born Oct. 25, 1902, at Holden, Millard Co., Utah, to John E. Hunter and Margaret Teeples. Ordained seventy Aug. 31, 1928, by Rulon S. Wells; sustained to the First Council of the Seventy April 6, 1945, at age 42; ordained high priest June 11, 1961, by David O. McKay; died June 27, 1975, at Salt Lake City, Salt Lake Co., Utah, at age 72.

44. Bruce Redd McConkie — See QUORUM OF THE TWELVE, No. 80.

45. Marion Duff Hanks — See PRESIDENCY OF THE SEVENTY, No. 6.

46. Albert Theodore Tuttle — See PRESIDENCY OF THE SEVENTY, No. 4.

47. Paul Harold Dunn — See PRESIDENCY OF THE SEVENTY, No. 7.

48. Hartman Rector Jr. — See FIRST QUORUM OF THE SEVENTY, No. 25.

49. Loren Charles Dunn — See FIRST QUORUM OF SEVENTY, No. 26.

50. Rex Dee Pinegar — See current FIRST QUORUM OF SEVENTY.

51. Gene Raymond Cook — See current FIRST QUORUM OF SEVENTY.

On Oct. 3, 1975, the First Quorum of the Seventy was reconstituted with the sustaining of three members, Elders Charles Didier, William R. Bradford, and George P. Lee. Four additional members, Elders Carlos E. Asay, M. Russell Ballard, John H. Groberg, and Jacob de Jager, were sustained April 3, 1976. On Oct. 1, 1976, the members of the First Council of the Seventy and the Assistants to the Quorum of the Twelve Apostles were released, and sustained to the First Quorum of the Seventy. A Presidency of the First Quorum of the Seventy was sustained, and the members revised.

ASSISTANTS TO THE TWELVE

(Functioned from April 1941 to October 1976)

1. Marion George Romney — See FIRST COUNSELORS IN THE FIRST PRESIDENCY, No. 18.

2. Thomas Evans McKay — Born Oct. 29, 1875, at Huntsville, Weber Co., Utah, to David McKay and Jennette Eveline Evans. Sustained as Assistant to the Quorum of the Twelve Apostles April 6, 1941, and set apart May 23, 1941, by Heber J. Grant, at age 65; died Jan. 15, 1958, at Salt Lake City, Salt Lake Co., Utah, at age 82.

3. Clifford Earl Young — Born Dec. 7, 1883, at Salt Lake City, Salt Lake Co., Utah, to Seymour Bicknell Young and Ann Elizabeth Riter. Sustained as Assistant to the Quorum of the Twelve

Apostles April 6, 1941, and set apart May 23, 1941, by President Grant, at age 57; died Aug. 21, 1958, at Salt Lake City, Salt Lake Co., Utah, at age 74.

4. Alma Sonne — See FIRST QUORUM OF THE SEVENTY, No. 8.

5. Nicholas Groesbeck Smith — Born June 20, 1881, at Salt Lake City, Salt Lake Co., Utah, to John Henry Smith and Josephine Groesbeck. Sustained an Assistant to the Quorum of the Twelve Apostles April 6, 1941; set apart Oct. 1, 1941, by Heber J. Grant, at age 60; died Oct. 27, 1945, at Salt Lake City, Salt Lake Co., Utah, at age 64.

6. George Quayle Morris — See QUORUM OF THE TWELVE, No. 72.

7. Stayner Richards — Born Dec. 20, 1885, at Salt Lake City, Salt Lake Co., Utah, to Stephen Longstroth Richards and Emma Louise Stayner. Sustained as Assistant to the Quorum of the Twelve Apostles Oct. 6, 1951, and set apart Oct. 11, 1951, by David O. McKay, at age 65; died May 28, 1953, at Salt Lake City, Salt Lake Co., Utah, at age 67.

8. ElRay LaVar Christiansen — Born July 13, 1897, at Mayfield, Sanpete Co., Utah, to Parley Christiansen and Dorthea C. Jensen. Sustained as Assistant to the Quorum of the Twelve Apostles Oct. 6, 1951, and set apart Oct. 11, 1951, by Stephen L Richards, at age 54; died Dec. 2, 1975, at Salt Lake City, Salt Lake Co., Utah, at age 78.

9. John Longden — Born Nov. 4, 1898, at Oldham, Lancashire Co., England, to Thomas Johnson Longden and Lizetta Taylor. Sustained as Assistant to the Quorum of the Twelve Apostles Oct. 6, 1951, and set apart Oct. 11, 1951, by J. Reuben Clark Jr., at age 52; died Aug. 30, 1969, at Salt Lake City, Salt Lake Co., Utah, at age 70.

10. Hugh Brown Brown — See FIRST COUNSELORS IN THE FIRST PRESIDENCY, No. 15.

11. Sterling Welling Sill — See FIRST QUORUM OF THE SEVENTY, No. 9.

12. Gordon Bitner Hinckley — See current FIRST PRESIDENCY.

13. Henry Dixon Taylor — See FIRST QUORUM OF THE SEVENTY, No. 10.

14. William James Critchlow Jr. — Born Aug. 21, 1892, at Brigham City, Box Elder Co., Utah, to William James Critchlow and Anna C. Gregerson. Sustained as Assistant to the Quorum of the Twelve Apostles Oct. 11, 1958, and set apart Oct. 16, 1958, by David O. McKay, at age 66; died Aug. 29, 1968, at Ogden, Weber Co., Utah, at age 76.

15. Alvin Rulon Dyer — See OTHER COUNSELORS IN THE FIRST PRESIDENCY, No. 13.

16. Nathan Eldon Tanner — See FIRST COUNSELORS IN THE FIRST PRESIDENCY, No. 17.

17. Franklin Dewey Richards — See PRESIDENCY OF THE SEVENTY, No. 1.

18. Theodore Moyle Burton — See FIRST QUORUM OF THE SEVENTY, No. 12.

19. Henry Thorpe Beal Isaacson — See OTHER COUNSELORS IN THE FIRST PRESIDENCY, No. 12.

20. Boyd Kenneth Packer — See current QUORUM OF THE TWELVE.

21. Bernard Park Brockbank — See

FIRST QUORUM OF SEVENTY, No. 13.

22. James Alfred Cullimore — See FIRST QUORUM OF THE SEVENTY, No. 14.

23. Marion Duff Hanks — See PRESIDENCY OF THE SEVENTY, No. 6.

24. Marvin Jeremy Ashton — See QUORUM OF THE TWELVE, No. 79.

25. Joseph Anderson — See FIRST QUORUM OF THE SEVENTY, No. 15.

26. David Bruce Haight — See current QUORUM OF THE TWELVE.

27. William Hunter Bennett — See FIRST QUORUM OF SEVENTY, No. 16.

28. John Henry Vandenberg — See PRESIDING BISHOPS, No. 9.

29. Robert Leatham Simpson — See FIRST QUORUM OF THE SEVENTY, No. 18.

30. Oscar Leslie Stone — See FIRST QUORUM OF THE SEVENTY, No. 19.

31. James Esdras Faust — See current FIRST PRESIDENCY.

32. Lowell Tom Perry — See current QUORUM OF THE TWELVE.

33. John Thomas Fyans — See PRESIDENCY OF THE SEVENTY, No. 3.

34. Neal Ash Maxwell — See current QUORUM OF THE TWELVE.

35. William Grant Bangerter — See PRESIDENCY OF SEVENTY, No. 8.

36. Robert Dean Hales — See current QUORUM OF THE TWELVE.

37. Adney Yoshio Komatsu — See FIRST QUORUM OF SEVENTY, No. 22.

38. Joseph Bitner Wirthlin — See current QUORUM OF THE TWELVE.

PRESIDENCY OF THE SEVENTY

(From Oct. 1, 1975, to April 1, 1989, served as the Presidency of the First Quorum of the Seventy; from April 1, 1989, to April 1997, served as the Presidency of both the First and Second Quorums of the Seventy; since April 1997, has served as the Presidency of the First, Second, Third, Fourth, and Fifth Quorums of the Seventy.)

1. Franklin Dewey Richards — Born Nov. 17, 1900, in Ogden, Weber Co., Utah, to Charles C. Richards and Louisa L. Peery. Sustained as Assistant to the Quorum of the Twelve Apostles Oct. 8, 1960, at age 59; sustained to First Quorum of the Seventy Oct. 1, 1976; served in Presidency of the First Quorum of the Seventy, Oct. 1, 1976, to Oct. 1, 1983; died Nov. 13, 1987, at Salt Lake City, Salt Lake Co., Utah, at age 86.

2. James Esdras Faust — See current FIRST PRESIDENCY.

3. John Thomas Fyans — Born May 17, 1918, at Moreland, Bingham Co., Idaho, to Joseph Fyans and Mae Farnsworth. Sustained as Assistant to the Quorum of the Twelve Apostles April 6, 1974, at age 55; sustained to First Quorum of the Seventy Oct. 1, 1976; served in Presidency of the First Quorum of the Seventy, Oct. 1, 1976, to Oct. 6, 1985; named emeritus General Authority Oct. 1, 1989.

4. Albert Theodore Tuttle — Born March 2, 1919, in Manti, Sanpete Co., Utah, to Albert M. Tuttle and Clarice Beal. Sustained to First Council of the Seventy April 6, 1958, at age 39; sustained to First

Quorum of the Seventy Oct. 1, 1976; served in Presidency of the First Quorum of the Seventy, Oct. 1, 1976, to Feb. 22, 1980; died Nov. 28, 1986, at Salt Lake City, Salt Lake Co., Utah, at age 67.

5. Neal Ash Maxwell — See current QUORUM OF THE TWELVE.

6. Marion Duff Hanks — Born Oct. 13, 1921, in Salt Lake City, Salt Lake Co., Utah, to Stanley Alonzo Hanks and Maude Frame. Sustained to First Council of the Seventy Oct. 4, 1953, at age 31, and as Assistant to the Quorum of the Twelve Apostles April 6, 1968; sustained to the First Quorum of the Seventy Oct. 1, 1976; served in the Presidency of the First Quorum of the Seventy from Oct. 1, 1976-April 5, 1980, and from Oct. 6, 1984-Aug. 15, 1992; named emeritus General Authority Oct. 3, 1992.

7. Paul Harold Dunn — Born April 24, 1924, at Provo, Utah Co., Utah, to Joshua Harold Dunn and Geneve Roberts. Sustained to First Council of the Seventy April 6, 1964, at age 39; sustained to First Quorum of the Seventy Oct. 1, 1976; served in Presidency of the First Quorum of the Seventy, Oct. 1, 1976, to Feb. 22, 1980; named emeritus General Authority Oct. 1, 1989; died Jan. 9, 1998, at Salt Lake City, Salt Lake Co., Utah, at age 73.

8. William Grant Bangerter — Born June 8, 1918, at Granger, Salt Lake Co., Utah, to William Henry Bangerter and Isabelle Bawden. Sustained as Assistant to the Quorum of the Twelve Apostles April 4, 1975, at age 56; sustained to First Quorum of the Seventy Oct. 1, 1976; served in Presidency of the First Quorum of the Seventy from Sept. 30, 1978, to April 5, 1980, and from Feb. 17, 1985, to Oct. 1, 1989; named emeritus General Authority Oct. 1, 1989.

9. Carlos Egan Asay — Born June 12, 1926, in Sutherland, Millard Co., Utah, to A.E. Lyle Asay and Elsie Egan. Sustained to the First Quorum of the Seventy April 3, 1976, at age 49; served in Presidency of the Seventy from April 5, 1980, to Aug. 15, 1986, and from Oct. 1, 1989, to Aug. 15, 1996; named emeritus General Authority Oct. 5, 1996; died April 10, 1999, in Bountiful, Davis Co., Utah, at age 72.

10. Melvin Russell Ballard Jr. — See current QUORUM OF THE TWELVE.

11. Dean LeRoy Larsen — Born March 24, 1927, at Hyrum, Cache Co., Utah, to Edgar Niels Larsen and Gertrude Prouse. Sustained to First Quorum of the Seventy Oct. 1, 1976, at age 49; served in Presidency of the Seventy, Feb. 22, 1980, to Aug. 15, 1993; named emeritus General Authority Oct. 4, 1997.

12. Royden Glade Derrick — Born Sept. 7, 1915, at Salt Lake City, Salt Lake Co., Utah, to Hyrum H. Derrick and Margaret Glade. Sustained to First Quorum of the Seventy Oct. 1, 1976, at age 61; served in Presidency of the First Quorum of the Seventy, April 5, 1980, to Oct. 6, 1984; named emeritus General Authority Oct. 1, 1989.

13. George Homer Durham — Born Feb. 4, 1911, at Parowan, Iron Co., Utah, to George H. Durham and Mary Ellen Marsden. Sustained to First Quorum of the Seventy

April 2, 1977, at age 66; served in Presidency of the First Quorum of the Seventy, Oct. 1, 1981, until his death Jan. 10, 1985, at Salt Lake City, Salt Lake Co., Utah, at age 73.

14. Richard **Gordon Scott** — See current QUORUM OF THE TWELVE.

15. Marion Duff Hanks — See PRESIDENCY OF THE SEVENTY, No. 6.

16. William Grant Bangerter — See PRESIDENCY OF THE SEVENTY, No. 8.

17. Jack H. Goaslind Jr. — Born April 18, 1928, in Salt Lake City, Utah, to Jack H. Goaslind and Anita Jack. Sustained to the First Quorum of the Seventy Sept. 30, 1978, at age 50; served in the Presidency of the Seventy, Oct. 6, 1985, to Aug. 15, 1987, and from Aug. 15, 1995, to Aug. 15, 1998; named emeritus General Authority Oct. 3, 1998.

18. Robert LeGrand Backman — Born March 22, 1922, in Salt Lake City, Salt Lake Co., Utah, to LeGrand P. Backman and Edith Price. Sustained to the First Quorum of the Seventy April 1, 1978, at age 56; served in the Presidency of the Seventy, Oct. 6, 1985, to Aug. 15, 1992; named emeritus General Authority Oct. 3, 1992.

19. Joseph Bitner Wirthlin — See current QUORUM OF THE TWELVE.

20. Hugh Wallace Pinnock — See current FIRST QUORUM OF THE SEVENTY.

21. James Martin Paramore — Born May 6, 1928, in Salt Lake City, Salt Lake Co., Utah, to James F. Paramore and Ruth C. Martin. Sustained to First Quorum of the Seventy April 2, 1977, at age 48, and served in the Presidency of the Seventy, Aug. 15, 1987, to Aug. 15, 1993; named emeritus General Authority Oct. 3, 1998.

22. John Richard Clarke — Born April 4, 1927, at Rexburg, Madison Co., Idaho, to John Roland Clarke and Nora L. Redford. Sustained as second counselor in Presiding Bishopric Oct. 1, 1976, at age 49, and to the First Quorum of the Seventy, April 6, 1985; served in the Presidency of the Seventy, Oct. 1, 1988, to Aug. 15, 1997; named emeritus General Authority Oct. 4, 1997.

23. Rex Dee Pinegar — See current FIRST QUORUM OF THE SEVENTY.

24. Carlos Egan Asay — See PRESIDENCY OF THE SEVENTY, No. 9.

25. Charles Amand Andre Didier — See current FIRST QUORUM OF THE SEVENTY.

26. Lloyd Aldin Porter — See current PRESIDENCY OF THE SEVENTY.

27. Joe Junior Christensen — Born July 21, 1929, in Banida, Franklin Co., Idaho, to Joseph A. Christensen and Goldie Miles. Sustained to First Quorum of the Seventy April 1, 1989, at age 59; served in the Presidency of the Seventy, Aug. 15, 1993, to Aug. 15, 1999; named emeritus General Authority Oct. 2, 1999.

28. Monte James Brough — See current FIRST QUORUM OF THE SEVENTY.

29. Warren Eugene Hansen — Born Aug. 23, 1928, in Tremonton, Box Elder Co., Utah, to Warren E. Hansen and Ruth Steed. Sustained to the First Quorum of

the Seventy April 1, 1989, at age 60; served in the Presidency of the Seventy, Aug. 15, 1993, to Aug. 15, 1998; named emeritus General Authority Oct. 3, 1998.

30. Jack H Goaslind Jr. — See PRESIDENCY OF THE SEVENTY, No. 17.

31. Harold Gordon Hillam — See current FIRST QUORUM OF THE SEVENTY.

32. Earl Carr Tingey — See current PRESIDENCY OF THE SEVENTY.

33. David Todd Christofferson — See current PRESIDENCY OF THE SEVENTY.

34. Marlin Keith Jensen — See current PRESIDENCY OF THE SEVENTY.

35. David Eugene Sorensen — See current PRESIDENCY OF THE SEVENTY.

36. Benjamin Berry Banks — See current PRESIDENCY OF THE SEVENTY.

37. Dennis Bramwell Neuenschwander — See current PRESIDENCY OF THE SEVENTY.

FIRST QUORUM OF THE SEVENTY

1. Franklin Dewey Richards — See PRESIDENCY OF THE SEVENTY, No. 1.

2. James Esdras Faust — See current FIRST PRESIDENCY.

3. John Thomas Fyans — See PRESIDENCY OF THE SEVENTY, No. 3.

4. Albert Theodore Tuttle — See PRESIDENCY OF THE SEVENTY, No. 4.

5. Neal Ash Maxwell — See current QUORUM OF THE TWELVE.

6. Marion Duff Hanks — See PRESIDENCY OF THE SEVENTY, No. 6.

7. Paul Harold Dunn — See PRESIDENCY OF THE SEVENTY, No. 7.

8. Alma Sonne — Born March 5, 1884, at Logan, Cache Co., Utah, to Niels C. Sonne and Elisa Peterson. Sustained as Assistant to the Quorum of the Twelve Apostles April 6, 1941, at age 57; sustained to First Quorum of the Seventy Oct. 1, 1976; died Nov. 27, 1977, at Logan, Cache Co., Utah, at age 93.

9. Sterling Welling Sill — Born March 31, 1903, at Layton, Davis Co., Utah, to Joseph Albert Sill and Marcetta Welling. Sustained as Assistant to the Quorum of the Twelve Apostles April 6, 1954, at age 51; sustained to First Quorum of the Seventy Oct. 1, 1976; named emeritus General Authority Dec. 31, 1978; died May 25, 1994, in Salt Lake City, Salt Lake Co., Utah, at age 91.

10. Henry Dixon Taylor — Born Nov. 22, 1903, in Provo, Utah Co., Utah, to Arthur N. Taylor and Maria Dixon. Sustained as Assistant to the Quorum of the Twelve Apostles April 6, 1958, at age 54; sustained to First Quorum of the Seventy Oct. 1, 1976; named emeritus General Authority Sept. 30, 1978; died Feb. 24, 1987, at Salt Lake City, Salt Lake Co., Utah, at age 83.

11. Alvin Rulon Dyer — See OTHER COUNSELORS IN THE FIRST PRESIDENCY, No. 13.

12. Theodore Moyle Burton — Born March 27, 1907, at Salt Lake City, Salt Lake Co., Utah, to Theodore T. Burton and Florence Moyle. Sustained as Assistant to the Quorum of the Twelve Apostles Oct. 8, 1960, at age 53; sustained to First

Quorum of the Seventy Oct. 1, 1976; named emeritus General Authority Oct. 1, 1989; died Dec. 22, 1989, at Salt Lake City, Salt Lake Co., Utah, at age 82.

13. Bernard Park Brockbank — Born May 24, 1909, at Salt Lake City, Salt Lake Co., Utah, to Taylor P. Brockbank and Sarah LeCheminant. Sustained as Assistant to the Quorum of the Twelve Apostles Oct. 6, 1962, at age 53; sustained to First Quorum of the Seventy Oct. 1, 1976; named emeritus General Authority Oct. 4, 1980; died Oct. 11, 2000,at Holladay, Salt Lake Co., Utah..

14. James Alfred Cullimore — Born Jan. 17, 1906, at Lindon, Utah Co., Utah, to Albert Lorenzo Cullimore and Luella Keetch. Sustained an Assistant to the Quorum of the Twelve Apostles April 6, 1966, at age 60; sustained to First Quorum of the Seventy Oct. 1, 1976; named emeritus General Authority Sept. 30, 1978; died June 14, 1986, at Salt Lake City, Salt Lake Co., Utah, at age 80.

15. Joseph Anderson — Born Nov. 20, 1889, at Salt Lake City, Salt Lake Co., Utah, to George Anderson and Isabella Watson. Sustained as Assistant to the Quorum of the Twelve Apostles April 6, 1970, at age 80; sustained to First Quorum of the Seventy Oct. 1, 1976; named emeritus General Authority Dec. 31, 1978; died March 13, 1992, at Salt Lake City, Salt Lake Co., Utah, at age 102.

16. William Hunter Bennett — Born Nov. 5, 1910, at Taber, Alberta, Canada, to William Alvin Bennett and Mary Walker. Sustained as Assistant to the Quorum of the Twelve Apostles April 6, 1970, at age 59; sustained to First Quorum of the Seventy Oct. 1, 1976; named emeritus General Authority Dec. 31, 1978; died July 23, 1980, at Bountiful, Davis Co., Utah, at age 69.

17. John Henry Vandenberg — See PRESIDING BISHOPS, No. 9.

18. Robert Leatham Simpson — Born Aug. 8, 1915, at Salt Lake City, Salt Lake Co., Utah, to Heber C Simpson and Lillian Leatham. Sustained as first counselor to Presiding Bishop John H. Vandenberg Sept. 30, 1961, at age 46; sustained as Assistant to the Quorum of the Twelve Apostles April 6, 1972; sustained to First Quorum of the Seventy Oct. 1, 1976; named emeritus General Authority Oct. 1, 1989.

19. Oscar Leslie Stone — Born May 28, 1903, at Chapin, Idaho, to Frank J. Stone and Mable Crandall. Sustained as Assistant to the Quorum of the Twelve Apostles, Oct. 6, 1972, at age 69; sustained to First Quorum of the Seventy, Oct. 1, 1976; named emeritus General Authority Oct. 4, 1980; died April 26, 1986, at Salt Lake City, Salt Lake Co., Utah, at age 82.

20. William Grant Bangerter — See PRESIDENCY OF THE SEVENTY, No. 8.

21. Robert Dean Hales — See current QUORUM OF THE TWELVE.

22. Adney Yoshio Komatsu — Born Aug. 2, 1923, at Honolulu, Honolulu Co., Oahu, Hawaii, to Jizaemon Komatsu and Misao Tabata. Sustained as Assistant to the Quorum of the Twelve Apostles, April 4,1975, at age 51; sustained to the First Quorum of the Seventy Oct. 1, 1976; named emeritus General

Authority Oct. 2, 1993.

23. Joseph Bitner Wirthlin — See current QUORUM OF THE TWELVE.

24. Seymour Dilworth Young — Born Sept. 7, 1897, at Salt Lake City, Salt Lake Co., Utah, to Seymour Bicknell Young Jr. and Carlie Louine Clawson. Sustained to the First Council of the Seventy April 6, 1945, at age 47; sustained to the First Quorum of the Seventy Oct. 1, 1976; named emeritus General Authority Sept. 30, 1978; died July 9, 1981, at Salt Lake City, Salt Lake Co., Utah, at age 83.

25. Hartman Rector Jr. — Born Aug. 20, 1924, at Moberly, Randolph Co., Missouri, to Hartman Rector and Vivian Fay Garvin. Sustained to the First Council of the Seventy April 6, 1968, at age 43; sustained to the First Quorum of the Seventy Oct. 1, 1976; named emeritus General Authority Oct. 1, 1994.

26. Loren Charles Dunn — Born June 12, 1930, in Tooele, Tooele Co., Utah, to Alex F. Dunn and Carol Horsfall. Sustained to the First Council of the Seventy April 6, 1968, at age 37, and to the First Quorum of the Seventy Oct. 1, 1976; named emeritus General Authority Oct. 7, 2000.

27. Rex Dee Pinegar — See current FIRST QUORUM OF THE SEVENTY.

28. Gene Raymond Cook — See current FIRST QUORUM OF THE SEVENTY.

29. Charles Amand Andre Didier — See current FIRST QUORUM OF THE SEVENTY.

30. William Rawsel Bradford — See current FIRST QUORUM OF THE SEVENTY.

31. George Patrick Lee — Born March 23, 1943, at Towaoc, Ute Mountain Indian Reservation, Colorado, to Pete Lee and Mae K. Asdzaatchii. Sustained to First Quorum of the Seventy Oct. 3, 1975, at age 32; excommunicated Sept. 1, 1989.

32. Carlos Egan Asay — See PRESIDENCY OF THE SEVENTY, No. 9.

33. Melvin Russell Ballard Jr. — See current QUORUM OF THE TWELVE.

34. John Holbrook Groberg — See current FIRST QUORUM OF THE SEVENTY.

35. Jacob de Jager — Born Jan. 16, 1923, at The Hague, South Holland, Netherlands, to Alexander Philippis de Jager and Maria Jacoba Cornelia Scheele. Sustained to the First Quorum of the Seventy April 3, 1976, at age 53; named emeritus General Authority Oct. 2, 1993.

36. Vaughn J Featherstone — See current FIRST QUORUM OF THE SEVENTY.

37. Dean LeRoy Larsen — See PRESIDENCY OF THE SEVENTY, No. 11.

38. Royden Glade Derrick — See PRESIDENCY OF THE SEVENTY, No. 12.

39. Robert Earl Wells — Born Dec. 28, 1927, in Las Vegas, Clark Co., Nevada, to Robert Stephen Wells and Zella Verona Earl. Sustained to the First Quorum of the Seventy Oct. 1, 1976, at age 48; named emeritus General Authority Oct. 4, 1997.

40. George Homer Durham — See PRESIDENCY OF THE SEVENTY, No. 13.

41. James Martin Paramore — See PRESIDENCY OF THE SEVENTY, No. 21.

42. Richard Gordon Scott — See current QUORUM OF THE TWELVE.

43. Hugh Wallace Pinnock — See current FIRST QUORUM OF THE SEVENTY.

44. Friedrich Enzio Busche — Born April 5, 1930, in Dortmund, Germany, to Friedrich Busche and Anna Weber. Sustained to the First Quorum of the Seventy Oct. 1, 1977, at age 47; named emeritus General Authority Oct, 7, 2000.

45. Yoshihiko Kikuchi — See current FIRST QUORUM OF THE SEVENTY.

46. Ronald Eugene Poelman — Born May 10, 1928, in Salt Lake City, Salt Lake Co., Utah, to Hendrick Poelman and Ella May Perkins. Sustained to the First Quorum of the Seventy April 1, 1978, at age 49; named emeritus General Authority Oct. 3, 1998.

47. Derek Alfred Cuthbert — Born Oct. 5, 1926, at Nottingham, Derbyshire Co., England, to Harry Cuthbert and Hilda May Freck. Sustained to the First Quorum of the Seventy April 1, 1978, at age 51; died April 7, 1991, at Salt Lake City, Salt Lake Co., Utah, at age 64.

48. Robert LeGrand Backman — See PRESIDENCY OF THE SEVENTY, No. 18.

49. Rex Cropper Reeve Sr. — Born Nov. 23, 1914, at Hinckley, Millard Co., Utah, to Arthur H. Reeve and Mary A. Cropper. Sustained to First Quorum of the Seventy April 1, 1978, at age 63; named emeritus General Authority Oct. 1, 1989.

50. Fred Burton Howard — See current FIRST QUORUM OF THE SEVENTY.

51. Teddy Eugene Brewerton — Born March 30, 1925, at Raymond, Alberta, Canada, to Lee Brewerton and Jane Fisher. Sustained to the First Quorum of the Seventy, Sept. 30, 1978, at age 53; named emeritus General Authority Sept. 30, 1995.

52. Jack H Goaslind Jr. — See PRESIDENCY OF THE SEVENTY, No. 17.

53. Angel Abrea — See current FIRST QUORUM OF THE SEVENTY.

54. John Kay Carmack — See current FIRST QUORUM OF THE SEVENTY.

55. Russell Carl Taylor — Born Nov. 25, 1925, at Red Mesa, Conejos Co., Colorado, to Leo Sanford Taylor and Florence Stella Dean. Sustained to First Quorum of the Seventy April 7, 1984, at age 58; sustained to Second Quorum of the Seventy April 1, 1989; released Oct. 1, 1989.

56. Robert B Harbertson — Born April 19, 1932, at Ogden, Weber Co. Utah, to Brigham Y. Harbertson and Gladys Venice Lewis. Sustained to First Quorum of the Seventy April 7, 1984, at age 51; sustained to Second Quorum of the Seventy April 1, 1989; released Oct. 1, 1989.

57. Devere Harris — Born May 30, 1916, at Portage, Box Elder Co. Utah, to Robert Crumbell Harris and Sylvia Green. Sustained to First Quorum of the Seventy April 7, 1984, at age 67; sustained to Second Quorum of the Seventy April 1, 1989; released Oct. 1, 1989.

58. Spencer Hamlin Osborn — Born July 8, 1921, at Salt Lake City, Salt Lake Co., Utah, to William W. Osborn and Alice M. Hamlin. Sustained to First Quorum of the Seventy April 7, 1984, at age 62;

sustained to Second Quorum of the Seventy April 1, 1989; released Oct. 1, 1989.

59. Phillip Tadje Sonntag — Born July 13, 1921, at Salt Lake City, Salt Lake Co., Utah, to Richard Peter Sonntag and Lena Emma Tadje. Sustained to First Quorum of the Seventy April 7, 1984, at age 62; sustained to Second Quorum of the Seventy April 1, 1989; released Oct. 1, 1989.

60. John Sonnenberg — Born April 11, 1922, at Schneidemuhle, Germany, to Otto Paul Sonnenberg and Lucille Mielke. Sustained to First Quorum of the Seventy Oct. 6, 1984, at age 62; sustained to Second Quorum of the Seventy April 1, 1989; released Oct. 1, 1989.

61. Ferril Arthur Kay — Born July 15, 1916, at Annabella, Sevier Co., Utah, to Samuel Arthur Kay and Medora Hooper. Sustained to First Quorum of the Seventy Oct. 6, 1984, at age 68; sustained to Second Quorum of the Seventy April 1, 1989; released Oct. 1, 1989.

62. Keith Wilson Wilcox — Born May 15, 1921, at Hyrum, Cache Co., Utah, to Irving C. Wilcox and Nancy Mary Wilson. Sustained to First Quorum of the Seventy Oct. 6, 1984, at age 63; sustained to Second Quorum of the Seventy April 1, 1989; released Oct. 1, 1989.

63. Victor Lee Brown — See PRESIDING BISHOPS, No. 10.

64. Harold Burke Peterson — Born Sept. 19, 1923, in Salt Lake City, Salt Lake Co., Utah, to Harold A. Peterson and Juna Tye. Sustained as first counselor in Presiding Bishopric April 6, 1972, at age 48; sustained to the First Quorum of the Seventy April 6, 1985; named emeritus General Authority Oct. 2, 1993.

65. John Richard Clarke — See PRESIDENCY OF THE SEVENTY, No. 22.

66. Hans Benjamin Ringger — Born Nov. 2, 1925, in Zurich, Switzerland, to Carl Ringger and Maria Reif. Sustained to the First Quorum of the Seventy April 6, 1985, at age 59; named emeritus General Authority Sept. 30, 1995.

67. Waldo Pratt Call — Born Feb. 5, 1928, at Colonia Juarez, Chihuahua, Mexico, to Charles Helaman Call and Hannah Skousen. Sustained to First Quorum of the Seventy April 6, 1985, at age 57; sustained to Second Quorum of the Seventy April 1, 1989; released Oct. 6, 1990.

68. Helio da Rocha Camargo — Born Feb. 1, 1926, at Resende, Rio de Janeiro, Brazil, to Jose Medeiros de Camargo and Else Ferreira da Rocha. Sustained to First Quorum of the Seventy April 6, 1985, at age 59; sustained to Second Quorum of the Seventy April 1, 1989; released Oct. 6, 1990.

69. Hans Verlan Andersen — Born Nov. 6, 1914, in Logan, Cache Co., Utah, to Hans Andersen and Mynoa Richardson. Sustained to the First Quorum of the Seventy April 6, 1986, at age 71; sustained to the Second Quorum of the Seventy April 1, 1989; released Oct. 5, 1991; died July 16, 1992, at Orem, Utah Co.,

Utah, at age 77.

70. George Ivins Cannon — Born March 9, 1920, in Salt Lake City, Salt Lake Co., Utah, to George J. Cannon and Lucy Grant. Sustained to the First Quorum of the Seventy April 6, 1986, at age 66; sustained to the Second Quorum of the Seventy April 1, 1989; released Oct. 5, 1991.

71. Francis Marion Gibbons — Born April 10, 1921, in St. Johns, Apache Co., Arizona, to Andrew S. Gibbons and Adeline Christensen. Sustained to the First Quorum of the Seventy April 6, 1986, at age 64; sustained to the Second Quorum of the Seventy April 1, 1989; released Oct. 5, 1991.

72. Gardner Hale Russell — Born Aug. 12, 1920, in Salt Lake City, Salt Lake Co., Utah, to Harry J. Russell and Agnes Gardner. Sustained to the First Quorum of the Seventy April 6, 1986, at age 65; sustained to the Second Quorum of the Seventy April 1, 1989; released Oct. 5, 1991.

73. George Richard Hill III — Born Nov. 24, 1921, in Ogden, Weber Co., Utah, to George Richard Hill Jr. and Elizabeth O. McKay. Sustained to the First Quorum of the Seventy April 4, 1987, at age 65; sustained to the Second Quorum of the Seventy April 1, 1989; released Oct. 3, 1992.

74. John Roger Lasater — Born Dec. 8, 1931, in Farmington, Davis Co., Utah, to Robert B. Lasater and Rowena Saunders. Sustained to the First Quorum of the Seventy April 4, 1987, at age 55; sustained to the Second Quorum of the Seventy April 1, 1989; released Oct. 3, 1992.

75. Douglas James Martin — Born April 20, 1927, in Hastings, New Zealand, to George Martin and Jesse Jamieson. Sustained to the First Quorum of the Seventy April 4, 1987, at age 59; sustained to the Second Quorum of the Seventy April 1, 1989; released Oct. 3, 1992.

76. Alexander Baillie Morrison — Born Dec. 22, 1930, in Edmonton, Alberta, Canada, to Alexander S. Morrison and Christina Wilson. Sustained to the First Quorum of the Seventy April 4, 1987, at age 56; sustained to the Second Quorum of the Seventy April 1, 1989; sustained to the First Quorum of the Seventy April 6, 1991; named emeritus General Authority Oct. 7, 2000.

77. Lloyd Aldin Porter — See current PRESIDENCY OF THE SEVENTY.

78. Glen Larkin Rudd — Born May 18, 1918, in Salt Lake City, Salt Lake Co., Utah, to Charles P. Rudd and Gladys Thomas. Sustained to First Quorum of the Seventy April 4, 1987, at age 68; sustained to the Second Quorum of the Seventy April 1, 1989; released Oct. 3, 1992.

79. Douglas Hill Smith — Born May 11, 1921, in Salt Lake City, Salt Lake Co., Utah, to Virgil H. Smith and Winifred Pearl Hill. Sustained to the First Quorum of the Seventy April 4, 1987, at age 65; sustained to the Second Quorum of the Seventy April 1, 1989; released Oct. 3, 1992.

80. Lynn Andrew Sorensen — Born Sept. 25, 1919, in Salt Lake City, Salt

Lake Co., Utah, to Ulric Andrew Sorensen and Ferny Boam. Sustained to the First Quorum of the Seventy April 4, 1987, at age 67; sustained to the Second Quorum of the Seventy April 1, 1989; released Oct. 3, 1992.

81. Robert Edward Sackley — Born Dec. 17, 1922, in Lismore, New South Wales, Australia, to Cecil James Sackley and Mary Duncan. Sustained to the First Quorum of the Seventy April 2, 1988, at age 65; sustained to the Second Quorum of the Seventy April 1, 1989; died Feb. 22, 1993, near Brisbane, Australia, at age 70.

82. Larry Lionel Kendrick — See current FIRST QUORUM OF THE SEVENTY.

83. Monte James Brough — See current FIRST QUORUM OF THE SEVENTY.

84. Albert Choules Jr. — Born Feb. 15, 1926, in Driggs, Teton Co., Idaho, to Albert Choules and Rula Wilson. Sustained to the First Quorum of the Seventy Oct. 1, 1988, at age 62; sustained to the Second Quorum of the Seventy April 1, 1989; released Oct. 1, 1994.

85. Lloyd Preal George Jr. — Born Sept. 17, 1920, in Kanosh, Millard Co., Utah, to Preal George and Artemesia Palmer. Sustained to the First Quorum of the Seventy Oct. 1, 1988, at age 68; sustained to the Second Quorum of the Seventy April 1, 1989; released Oct. 1, 1994; died May 13, 1996, at Salt Lake City, Salt Lake Co., Utah, at age 75.

86. Gerald Eldon Melchin — Born May 24, 1921, in Kitchener, Ontario, Canada, to Arthur Melchin and Rosetta Willis. Sustained to the First Quorum of the Seventy on Oct. 1, 1988, at age 67; sustained to the Second Quorum of the Seventy on April 1, 1989; released Oct. 1, 1994.

87. Joe Junior Christensen — See PRESIDENCY OF THE SEVENTY, No. 27.

88. Warren Eugene Hansen Jr. — See PRESIDENCY OF THE SEVENTY, No. 29.

89. Jeffrey Roy Holland — See current QUORUM OF THE TWELVE.

90. Marlin Keith Jensen — See current PRESIDENCY OF THE SEVENTY.

91. Earl Carr Tingey — See current PRESIDENCY OF THE SEVENTY.

92. Harold Gordon Hillam — See current FIRST QUORUM OF THE SEVENTY.

93. Carlos Humberto Amado — See current FIRST QUORUM OF THE SEVENTY.

94. Benjamin Berry Banks — See current PRESIDENCY OF THE SEVENTY.

95. Spencer Joel Condie — See current FIRST QUORUM OF THE SEVENTY.

96. Robert Kent Dellenbach — See current FIRST QUORUM OF THE SEVENTY.

97. Henry Bennion Eyring — See current QUORUM OF THE TWELVE.

98. Glenn Leroy Pace — See current FIRST QUORUM OF THE SEVENTY.

99. Floyd Melvin Hammond — See current FIRST QUORUM OF THE SEVENTY.

100. Kenneth Johnson — See current FIRST QUORUM OF THE SEVENTY.

101. Lynn Alvin Mickelsen — See current FIRST QUORUM OF THE SEVENTY.

102. Neil Linden Andersen — See current FIRST QUORUM OF THE SEVENTY.

103. David Todd Christofferson — See current PRESIDENCY OF THE

SEVENTY.

104. Cree-L Kofford — See current FIRST QUORUM OF THE SEVENTY.

105. Dennis Bramwell Neuenschwander — See current PRESIDENCY OF THE SEVENTY.

106. Andrew Wayne Peterson — Born June 8, 1947, in San Francisco, San Francisco Co., Calif., to Wayne Leo Peterson and Virginia Parker. Sustained to First Quorum of the Seventy Oct. 1, 1994, at age 47; named emeritus General Authority Oct. 2, 1999.

107. Cecil Osborn Samuelson Jr. — See current FIRST QUORUM OF THE SEVENTY.

108. John Baird Dickson — See current FIRST QUORUM OF THE SEVENTY.

109. Jay Edwin Jensen — See current FIRST QUORUM OF THE SEVENTY.

110. David Eugene Sorensen — See current PRESIDENCY OF THE SEVENTY.

111. William Craig Zwick — See current FIRST QUORUM OF THE SEVENTY.

112. Merrill Joseph Bateman — See current FIRST QUORUM OF THE SEVENTY.

113. Dallas Nielsen Archibald — Born July 24, 1938, in Logan, Cache Co., Utah, to Ezra Wilson Archibald and Marguerite Nielsen. Called to the Second Quorum of the Seventy June 6, 1992, at age 53, and sustained Oct. 3, 1992; sustained to First Quorum of the Seventy April 6, 1996; drown in a boating accident Dec. 14, 1998, near Concepcion, Chile, at age 60.

114. Dieter Friedrich Uchtdorf — See current FIRST QUORUM OF THE SEVENTY.

115. Bruce Clark Hafen — See current FIRST QUORUM OF THE SEVENTY.

116. Gary Jerome Coleman —See current FIRST QUORUM OF THE SEVENTY.

117. Wm. Rolfe Kerr —See current FIRST QUORUM OF THE SEVENTY.

118. John Max Madsen — See current FIRST QUORUM OF THE SEVENTY.

119. Carl Barton Pratt — See current FIRST QUORUM OF THE SEVENTY.

120. Sheldon Fay Child — See current FIRST QUORUM OF THE SEVENTY.

121. Quentin LaMar Cook — See current FIRST QUORUM OF THE SEVENTY.

122. Francisco Jose Vinas — See current FIRST QUORUM OF THE SEVENTY.

123. Lance Bradley Wickman — See current FIRST QUORUM OF THE SEVENTY.

124. Lynn Grant Robbins — See current FIRST QUORUM OF THE SEVENTY.

125. Donald Larry Hallstrom — See current FIRST QUORUM OF THE SEVENTY.

126. Ronald A. Rasband — See current FIRST QUORUM OF THE SEVENTY.

SECOND QUORUM OF THE SEVENTY

The Second Quorum of the Seventy was created April 1, 1989, in response to the "continued rapid growth of the Church." (*Church News*, April 8, 1989.)

The initial members of the Second Quorum were those General Authorities serving under a five-year call (called from April 1984 to October 1988) in the First Quorum of the Seventy. General Authorities in the Second Quorum are called for five years.

1. Russell Carl Taylor — See FIRST

QUORUM OF THE SEVENTY, No. 55.

2. Robert B Harbertson — See FIRST QUORUM OF THE SEVENTY, No. 56.

3. Devere Harris — See FIRST QUORUM OF THE SEVENTY, No. 57.

4. Spencer Hamlin Osborn — See FIRST QUORUM OF THE SEVENTY, No. 58.

5. Philip Tadje Sonntag — See FIRST QUORUM OF THE SEVENTY, No. 59.

6. John Sonnenberg — See FIRST QUORUM OF THE SEVENTY, No. 60.

7. Ferril Arthur Kay — See FIRST QUORUM OF THE SEVENTY, No. 61.

8. Keith Wilson Wilcox — See FIRST QUORUM OF THE SEVENTY ,No. 62.

9. Waldo Pratt Call — See FIRST QUORUM OF THE SEVENTY, No. 67.

10. Helio Da Rocha Camargo — See FIRST QUORUM OF THE SEVENTY, No. 68.

11. Hans Verlan Andersen — See FIRST QUORUM OF THE SEVENTY, No. 69.

12. George Ivins Cannon — See FIRST QUORUM OF THE SEVENTY, No. 70.

13. Francis Marion Gibbons — See FIRST QUORUM OF THE SEVENTY, No. 71.

14. Gardner Hale Russell — See FIRST QUORUM OF THE SEVENTY, No. 72.

15. George Richard Hill III — See FIRST QUORUM OF THE SEVENTY, No. 73.

16. John Roger Lasater — See FIRST QUORUM OF THE SEVENTY, No. 74.

17. Douglas James Martin — See FIRST QUORUM OF THE SEVENTY, No. 75.

18. Alexander Baillie Morrison — See FIRST QUORUM OF THE SEVENTY, No. 76.

19. Lloyd Aldin Porter — See current PRESIDENCY OF THE SEVENTY.

20. Glen Larkin Rudd — See FIRST QUORUM OF THE SEVENTY, No. 78.

21. Douglas Hill Smith — See FIRST QUORUM OF THE SEVENTY, No. 79.

22. Lynn Andrew Sorensen — See FIRST QUORUM OF THE SEVENTY, No. 80.

23. Robert Edward Sackley — See FIRST QUORUM OF THE SEVENTY, No. 81.

24. Larry Lionel Kendrick — See current FIRST QUORUM OF THE SEVENTY.

25. Monte James Brough — See current FIRST QUORUM OF THE SEVENTY.

26. Albert Choules Jr. — See FIRST QUORUM OF THE SEVENTY, No. 84.

27. Lloyd Preal George Jr. — See FIRST QUORUM OF THE SEVENTY, No. 85.

28. Gerald Eldon Melchin — See FIRST QUORUM OF THE SEVENTY, No. 86.

29. Carlos Humberto Amado — See current FIRST QUORUM OF THE SEVENTY.

30. Benjamin Berry Banks — See current PRESIDENCY OF THE SEVENTY.

31. Spencer Joel Condie — See current FIRST QUORUM OF THE SEVENTY.

32. Floyd Melvin Hammond — See current FIRST QUORUM OF THE SEVENTY.

33. Malcolm Seth Jeppsen — Born Nov. 1, 1924, in Mantua, Box Elder Co., Utah, to Conrad Jeppsen and Laurine Nielsen. Sustained to the Second Quorum of the Seventy April 1, 1989, at age 64; released Oct. 1, 1994.

34. Richard Powell Lindsay — Born March 18, 1926, in Salt Lake City, Salt Lake Co., Utah, to Samuel Bennion Lindsay and Mary Alice Powell. Sustained to the Second Quorum of the Seventy April 1, 1989, at age 63; released Oct. 1, 1994.

35. Merlin Rex Lybbert — Born Jan. 31, 1926, in Cardston, Alberta, Canada, to Charles Lester Lybbert and Delvia

Reed. Sustained to the Second Quorum of the Seventy April 1, 1989, at age 63; released Oct. 1, 1994.

36. Horacio Antonio Tenorio — Born March 6, 1935, in Mexico City, Distrito Federal, Mexico, to Leopoldo Horacio Tenorio and Blanca Otilia Oriza Arenas. Sustained to the Second Quorum of the Seventy April 1, 1989, at age 54; released Oct. 1, 1994.

37. Eduardo Ayala — Born May 3, 1937, in Coronel, Chile, to Magdonio Ayala and Maria Aburto. Sustained to the Second Quorum of the Seventy March 31, 1990, at age 52; released Sept. 30, 1995.

38. LeGrand Raine Curtis — Born May 22, 1924, in Salt Lake City, Salt Lake Co., Utah, to Alexander R. Curtis and Genevieve Raine. Sustained to the Second Quorum of the Seventy March 31, 1990, at age 66; released Sept. 30, 1995.

39. Clinton Louis Cutler — Born Dec. 27, 1929, in Salt Lake City, Salt Lake Co., Utah, to Benjamin Lewis Cutler and Hellie Helena Sharp. Sustained to the Second Quorum of the Seventy March 31, 1990, at age 60; died April 9, 1994, at South Jordan, Salt Lake Co., Utah, at age 64.

40. Robert Kent Dellenbach — See current FIRST QUORUM OF SEVENTY.

41. Harold Gordon Hillam — See current FIRST QUORUM OF THE SEVENTY.

42. Kenneth Johnson — See current FIRST QUORUM OF THE SEVENTY.

43. Helvecio Martins — Born July 27, 1930, in Rio de Janeiro, Brazil, to Honorio Martins and Benedicta Francisca. Sustained to the Second Quorum of the Seventy March 31, 1990, at age 59; released Sept. 30, 1995.

44. Lynn Alvin Mickelsen — See current FIRST QUORUM OF SEVENTY.

45. J Ballard Washburn — Born Jan. 18, 1929, in Blanding, San Juan Co., Utah, to Alvin Lavell Washburn and Wasel Black. Sustained to the Second Quorum of the Seventy March 31, 1990, at age 61; released Sept. 30, 1995.

46. Durrel Arden Woolsey — Born June 12, 1926, at Escalante, Garfield Co., Utah, to Willis A. Woolsey and Ruby Riddle. Sustained to the Second Quorum of the Seventy March 31, 1990, at age 63; released Sept. 30, 1995.

47. Rulon Gerald Craven — Born Nov. 11, 1924, in Murray, Salt Lake Co., Utah, to Gerald and Susie Craven. Called to the Second Quorum of the Seventy Dec. 5, 1990, at age 66, and sustained April 6, 1991; released Oct. 5, 1996.

48. William McKenzie Lawrence — Born Oct. 28, 1926,in Salt Lake City, Salt Lake Co., Utah, to Richard Sterling Lawrence and Thelma McKenzie. Called to the Second Quorum of the Seventy Jan. 1, 1991, at age 64, and sustained April 6, 1991; released Oct. 5, 1996.

49. Julio Enrique Davila — Born May 23, 1932, in Bucaramunga, Colombia, to Julio E. Davila Villamicar and Rita Penalosa de Davila. Sustained to the Second Quorum of the Seventy April 6, 1991, at age 58; released Oct. 5, 1996.

50. Graham Watson Doxey — Born March 30, 1927, in Salt Lake City, Salt Lake Co., Utah, to Graham H. Doxey and Leone Watson. Sustained to the Second Quorum of the Seventy April 6, 1991, at age 64; released Oct. 5, 1996.

51. Cree-L Kofford — See current FIRST QUORUM OF THE SEVENTY.

52. Joseph Carl Muren — Born Feb. 5, 1936, in Richmond, Contra Costa Co., California, to Joseph S. Muren and Alba Maria Cairo. Sustained to the Second Quorum of the Seventy April 6, 1991, at age 55; released Oct. 5, 1996.

53. Dennis Bramwell Neuenschwander — See current PRESIDENCY OF THE SEVENTY.

54. Jorge Alfonso Rojas — Born Sept. 27, 1940, in Delicias, Chihuahua, Mexico, to Rodolfo Rojas and Hilaria Ornelas. Sustained to the Second Quorum of the Seventy April 6, 1991, at age 50; released Oct. 5, 1996.

55. Han In Sang — Born Dec. 10, 1938, in Seoul, Korea, to Han Chang Soo and Lee Do Ho. Called to the Second Quorum of the Seventy June 1, 1991, at age 52, and sustained Oct. 5, 1991; released Oct. 5, 1996.

56. Stephen Douglas Nadauld — Born May 31, 1942, in Idaho Falls, Bonneville Co., Idaho, to Sterling Dwaine Nadauld and Lois Madsen. Called to the Second Quorum of the Seventy June 1, 1991, at age 49, and sustained Oct. 5, 1991; released Oct. 5, 1996.

57. Sam Koyei Shimabukuro — Born June 7, 1925, in Waipahu, Honolulu Co., Oahu, Hawaii, to Kame Shimabukuro and Ushi Nakasone. Called to the Second Quorum of the Seventy July 13, 1991, at age 66, and sustained Oct. 5, 1991; released Oct. 5, 1996.

58. Lino Alvarez — Born July 18, 1944, in Arteaga, Coahuila, Mexico, to Lino Alvarez and Margarita Vasquez. Called to the Second Quorum of the Seventy June 6, 1992, at age 47, and sustained Oct. 3, 1992; released Oct. 4, 1997.

59. Dallas Nielsen Archibald — See FIRST QUORUM OF THE SEVENTY, No. 113.

60. Merrill Joseph Bateman — See current FIRST QUORUM OF THE SEVENTY.

61. Chellus Max Caldwell — Born Dec. 4, 1933, in Salt Lake City, Salt Lake Co., to Chellus M. and Electa J. Caldwell. Called to the Second Quorum of the Seventy June 6, 1992, at age 58, and sustained Oct. 3, 1992; released Oct. 4, 1997.

62. Gary Jerome Coleman — See current FIRST QUORUM OF THE SEVENTY.

63. John Baird Dickson — See current FIRST QUORUM OF THE SEVENTY.

64. John Emerson Fowler — Born Nov. 10, 1944, in Redding, Shasta Co., California, to R. Walter Fowler and Lois Manita Clayton. Called to the Second Quorum of the Seventy June 6, 1992, at age 47, and sustained Oct. 3, 1992; released Oct. 4, 1997.

65. Jay Edwin Jensen — See current FIRST QUORUM OF THE SEVENTY.

66. Augusto Alandy Lim — Born May 4, 1934, in Santa Cruz, Philippines, to Leon B. Lim and Beatriz R. Alandy. Called to the Second Quorum of the Seventy June 6, 1992, at age 58, and sustained Oct. 3, 1992; released Oct. 4, 1997.

67. John Max Madsen — See current FIRST QUORUM OF THE SEVENTY.

68. Victor Dallas Merrell — Born Jan. 25, 1936, in Basalt, Bingham Co., Idaho, to Victor Lybbert Merrell and Beatrice Jensen. Called to the Second Quorum of the Seventy June 6, 1992, at age 56, and sustained Oct. 3, 1992; released Oct. 4, 1997.

69. David Eugene Sorensen — See current PRESIDENCY OF THE SEVENTY.

70. Frank David Stanley — Born Sept. 11, 1935, in Salt Lake City, Salt Lake Co., Utah, to O. Frank Stanley and Winifred Parker. Called to the Second Quorum of the Seventy June 6, 1992, at age 56, and sustained Oct. 3, 1992; released Oct. 4, 1997.

71. Kwok Yuen Tai — Born June 30, 1941, in Hong Kong, to Lung Hing Tai and Yau Yin Chu. Sustained to the Second Quorum of the Seventy June 6, 1992, at age 50, and sustained Oct. 3, 1992; released Oct. 4, 1997.

72. Lowell Dale Wood — Born Jan. 23, 1933, in Cardston, Alberta, Canada, to Wm. Dale Wood and Donna Wolf. Called to the Second Quorum of the Seventy June 6, 1992, at age 59, and sustained Oct. 3, 1992; died March 7, 1997, at Pago Pago, Western Samoa, at age 64.

73. Claudio Roberto Mendes Costa — See current SECOND QUORUM OF THE SEVENTY.

74. William Don Ladd — Born July 14, 1933, in San Mateo, Putnam Co., Fla., to Joseph Donald Ladd and Phyllis Rose Anderson. Sustained to the Second Quorum of the Seventy April 2, 1994, at age 60; released Oct. 7, 2000.

75. James Ostermann Mason — Born June 19, 1930, in Salt Lake City, Salt Lake Co., Utah, to A. Stanton Mason and Neoma Thorup. Sustained to the Second Quorum of the Seventy April 2, 1994, at age 63; released Oct. 7, 2000.

76. Dieter Friedrich Uchtdorf — See current FIRST QUORUM OF THE SEVENTY.

77. Lance Bradley Wickman — See current FIRST QUORUM OF THE SEVENTY.

78. Bruce Douglas Porter — See current SECOND QUORUM OF THE SEVENTY.

79. Lowell Edward Brown — See current SECOND QUORUM OF THE SEVENTY.

80. Sheldon Fay Child — See current FIRST QUORUM OF THE SEVENTY.

81. Quentin LaMar Cook — See current FIRST QUORUM OF THE SEVENTY.

82. Wm. Rolf Kerr — See current FIRST QUORUM OF THE SEVENTY.

83. Dennis Ericksen Simmons — See current SECOND QUORUM OF THE SEVENTY.

84. Jerald Lynn Taylor — See current SECOND QUORUM OF THE SEVENTY.

85. Francisco Jose Vinas — See current FIRST QUORUM OF THE SEVENTY.

86. Richard Bitner Wirthlin — See current SECOND QUORUM OF THE SEVENTY.

87. Richard David Allred — See current SECOND QUORUM OF THE SEVENTY.

88. Eran Abegg Call — Born Dec. 2, 1929, in Colonia Dublan, Mexico, to Anson Bowen Call and Julie Sarah Abegg. Sustained to the Second Quorum of the Seventy April 5, 1997, at age 67; released Oct. 7, 2000.

89. Richard Ernest Cook — See current SECOND QUORUM OF THE SEVENTY.

90. Duane Bird Gerrard — See current SECOND QUORUM OF THE SEVENTY.

91. Wayne Mitchell Hancock — See current SECOND QUORUM OF THE SEVENTY.

92. Joseph Kent Jolley — See current SECOND QUORUM OF THE SEVENTY.

93. Richard John Maynes — See current SECOND QUORUM OF THE SEVENTY.

94. Dale Emerson Miller — See current SECOND QUORUM OF THE SEVENTY.

95. Lynn Grant Robbins — See current FIRST QUORUM OF THE SEVENTY.

96. Donald Lafayette Staheli — See current SECOND QUORUM OF THE SEVENTY.

97. Richard Eyring Turley Sr. — Born Dec. 29, 1930, in El Paso, El Paso Co., Texas, to Edward Vernon Turley and Winifred Louise Roche. Sustained to the Second Quorum of the Seventy April 5, 1997, at age 66; released Oct. 7, 2000.

98. Athos Marques Amorim — See current SECOND QUORUM OF THE SEVENTY.

99. E Ray Bateman — See current SECOND QUORUM OF SEVENTY.

100. Val Rigby Christensen — See current SECOND QUORUM OF THE SEVENTY.

101. Ronald Tomlinson Halverson — See current SECOND QUORUM OF THE SEVENTY.

102. Earl Merrill Monson — See current SECOND QUORUM OF THE SEVENTY.

103. Merrill Clayton Oaks — See current SECOND QUORUM OF THE SEVENTY.

104. Horace Bryan Richards — See current SECOND QUORUM OF THE SEVENTY.

105. Ned Bardeane Roueche — See current SECOND QUORUM OF THE SEVENTY.

106. Don Lee Tobler — See current SECOND QUORUM OF THE SEVENTY.

107. Gordon Taylor Watts — See current SECOND QUORUM OF THE EVENTY.

108. Stephen Allan West — See current SECOND QUORUM OF THE SEVENTY.

109. Robert Jay Whetten — See current SECOND QUORUM OF THE SEVENTY.

110. Raphael Hunter Wood — See current SECOND QUORUM OF THE SEVENTY.

111. Adhemar Damiani — See current SECOND QUORUM OF THE SEVENTY.

112. Stephen Berg Oveson — See current SECOND QUORUM OF THE

SEVENTY.

113. David Rodger Stone — See current SECOND QUORUM OF THE SEVENTY.

114. Harvey Bruce Stucki — See current SECOND QUORUM OF THE SEVENTY.

115. Richard Henry Winkel — See current SECOND QUORUM OF THE SEVENTY.

116. Robert Stephen Wood — See current SECOND QUORUM OF THE SEVENTY.

117. Douglas Lane Callister — See current SECOND QUORUM OF THE SEVENTY.

118. Darwin B. Christenson — See current SECOND QUORUM OF THE SEVENTY.

119. Keith Crockett — See current SECOND QUORUM OF THE SEVENTY.

120. Himan Aldridge Gillespie — See current SECOND QUORUM OF THE SEVENTY.

121. Robert Charles Oaks — See current SECOND QUORUM OF THE SEVENTY.

PRESIDING BISHOPS

1. Edward Partridge — Born Aug. 27, 1793, at Pittsfield, Berkshire Co., Massachusetts, to William Partridge and Jemima Bidwell. Called by revelation to be the First Bishop of the Church Feb. 4, 1831, at age 37 (D&C 41:9); died May 27, 1840, at Nauvoo, Hancock Co., Illinois, at age 46.

2. Newel Kimball Whitney — Born Feb. 5, 1795, at Marlborough, Windham Co., Vermont, to Samuel Whitney and Susanna Kimball. Called by revelation to be the First Bishop of Kirtland (D&C 72:8); sustained as First Bishop of the Church Oct. 7, 1844, at age 49; sustained as Presiding Bishop of the Church April 6, 1847; died Sept. 23, 1850, at Salt Lake City, Salt Lake Co., Utah, at age 55.

George Miller — Born Nov. 25, 1794, at Orange Co., Virginia, to John Miller and Margaret Pfeiffer. Sustained as Second Bishop of the Church Oct. 7, 1844, at age 49; dropped prior to 1847; disfellowshipped Oct. 20, 1848.

3. Edward Hunter — Born June 22, 1793, at Newton, Delaware Co., Pennsylvania, to Edward Hunter and Hannah Maris. Sustained as Presiding Bishop of the Church April 7, 1851, at age 57; died Oct. 16, 1883, at Salt Lake City, Salt Lake Co., Utah, at age 90.

4. William Bowker Preston — Born Nov. 24, 1830, at Halifax, Franklin Co., Virginia, to Christopher Preston and Martha Mitchell Clayton. Sustained as Presiding Bishop of the Church April 6, 1884, at age 53; released due to ill health Dec. 4, 1907; died Aug. 2, 1908, at Salt Lake City, Salt Lake Co., Utah, at age 77.

5. Charles Wilson Nibley — See SECOND COUNSELORS IN THE FIRST PRESIDENCY, No. 13.

6. Sylvester Quayle Cannon — See QUORUM OF THE TWELVE, No. 60.

7. LeGrand Richards — See QUORUM OF THE TWELVE, No. 69.

8. Joseph Leopold Wirthlin — Born Aug. 14, 1893, at Salt Lake City, Salt Lake Co., Utah, to Joseph Wirthlin and Emma Hillstead. Sustained as second counselor to Presiding Bishop LeGrand Richards April 6, 1938, at age 44; sustained as first counselor to Bishop Richards Dec. 12, 1946; sustained as Presiding

Bishop of the Church April 6, 1952, at age 58; released Sept. 30, 1961; died Jan. 25, 1963, at Salt Lake City, Salt Lake Co., Utah, at age 69.

9. John Henry Vandenberg — Born Dec. 18, 1904, at Ogden, Weber Co., Utah, to Dirk Vandenberg and Maria Alkema. Sustained as Presiding Bishop of the Church Sept. 30, 1961, at age 56; sustained as Assistant to the Quorum of the Twelve Apostles April 6, 1972; sustained to First Quorum of the Seventy Oct. 1, 1976; named emeritus General Authority Dec. 31, 1978; died June 3, 1992, at Sandy, Salt Lake Co., Utah, at age 87.

10. Victor Lee Brown — Born July 31, 1914, at Cardston, Alberta, Canada, to Gerald Stephen Brown and Maggie Calder Lee. Sustained as second counselor to Presiding Bishop John H. Vandenberg Sept. 30, 1961, at age 47; sustained as Presiding Bishop of the Church April 6, 1972; sustained to First Quorum of the Seventy April 6, 1985; named emeritus General Authority Oct. 1, 1989; died March 26, 1996, at Salt Lake City, Salt Lake Co., Utah at age 81.

11. Robert Dean Hales — See current QUORUM OF THE TWELVE.

12. Merrill Joseph Bateman — See current FIRST QUORUM OF THE SEVENTY.

13. Harold David Burton — See current PRESIDING BISHOPRIC.

FIRST COUNSELORS TO PRESIDING BISHOPS

1. Isaac Morley — Born March 11, 1786, at Montague, Hampshire Co., Massachusetts, to Thomas Morley and Editha Marsh. Set apart as first counselor to Presiding Bishop Edward Partridge June 6, 1831, at age 45; released at the death of Bishop Partridge May 27, 1840; died June 24, 1865, at Fairview, Sanpete Co., Utah, at age 79.

2. Leonard Wilford Hardy — Born Dec. 31, 1805, at Bradford, Essex Co., Massachusetts, to Simon Hardy and Rhoda Hardy. Sustained as first counselor to Presiding Bishop Edward Hunter Oct. 6, 1856, at age 50; died July 31, 1884, at Salt Lake City, Salt Lake Co., Utah, at age 78.

3. Robert Taylor Burton — Born Oct. 25, 1821, at Amhertsburg, Ontario, Canada, to Samuel Burton and Hannah Shipley. Sustained as second counselor to Presiding Bishop Edward Hunter Oct. 9, 1874, at age 52; sustained as first counselor to Presiding Bishop William B. Preston Oct. 5, 1884; died Nov. 11, 1907, at Salt Lake City, Salt Lake Co., Utah, at age 86.

4. Orrin Porter Miller — Born Sept. 11, 1858, at Mill Creek, Salt Lake Co., Utah, to Reuben G. Miller and Ann Craynor. Sustained as second counselor to Presiding Bishop William B. Preston Oct. 24, 1901, at age 43; sustained as first counselor to Presiding Bishop Charles W. Nibley Dec. 4, 1907, at age 49; died July 7, 1918, at Salt Lake City, Salt Lake Co., Utah at age 59.

5. David Asael Smith — Born May 24, 1879, at Salt Lake City, Salt Lake Co., Utah, to Joseph Fielding Smith and Julina Lambson. Sustained as second counselor to Presiding Bishop Charles W. Nibley Dec. 4, 1907, at age 28; sustained as first counselor to Bishop Nibley July 18, 1918; sustained as first counselor to Presiding Bishop Sylvester Q. Cannon June 4, 1925; released April 6, 1938; died April 6, 1952, at Salt Lake City, Salt Lake Co., Utah, at age 72.

6. Marvin Owen Ashton — Born April 8, 1883, at Salt Lake City, Salt Lake Co., Utah, to Edward T. Ashton and Effie W. Morris. Sustained as first counselor to Presiding Bishop LeGrand Richards April 6, 1938, at age 54; died Oct. 7, 1946, at Salt Lake City, Salt Lake Co., Utah, at age 63.

7. Joseph Leopold Wirthlin — See PRESIDING BISHOPS, No., 8.

8. Henry Thorpe Beal Isaacson — See OTHER COUNSELORS IN THE FIRST PRESIDENCY, No. 12.

9. Robert Leatham Simpson — See FIRST QUORUM OF THE SEVENTY, No. 18.

10. Harold Burke Peterson — See FIRST QUORUM OF THE SEVENTY, No. 64.

11. Henry Bennion Eyring — See current QUORUM OF THE TWELVE.

12. Harold David Burton — See current PRESIDING BISHOPRIC.

13. Richard Crockett Edgley — See current PRESIDING BISHOPRIC.

SECOND COUNSELORS TO PRESIDING BISHOPS

1. John Corrill — Born Sept. 17, 1794, at Worcester Co., Massachusetts. Set apart as second counselor to Presiding Bishop Edward Partridge June 6, 1831, at age 36; released Aug. 1, 1837; excommunicated March 17, 1839.

2. Titus Billings — Born March 25, 1793, at Greenfield, Franklin Co., Massachusetts, to Ebenezer Billings and Esther Joyce. Set apart as second counselor to Presiding Bishop Edward Partridge Aug. 1, 1837, at age 44; released at the death of Bishop Partridge May 27, 1840; died Feb. 6, 1866, at Provo, Utah Co., Utah, at age 72.

3. Jesse Carter Little — Born Sept. 26, 1815, at Belmont, Waldo Co., Maine, to Thomas Little and Relief White. Sustained as second counselor to Presiding Bishop Edward Hunter Oct. 6, 1856, at age 41; resigned summer of 1874; died Dec. 26, 1893, at Salt Lake City, Salt Lake Co., Utah, at age 78.

4. Robert Taylor Burton — See FIRST COUNSELORS IN THE PRESIDING BISHOPRIC, No. 3.

5. John Quayle Cannon — Born April 19, 1857, at San Francisco, San Francisco Co., California, to George Quayle Cannon and Elizabeth Hoagland. Sustained as second counselor to Presiding Bishop William B. Preston Oct. 5, 1884, at age 27; excommunicated Sept. 5, 1886; rebaptized May 6, 1888; died Jan. 14, 1931, at Salt Lake City, Salt Lake Co., Utah, at 73.

6. John Rex Winder — See FIRST COUNSELORS IN THE FIRST PRESIDENCY, No. 7.

7. Orrin Porter Miller — See FIRST COUNSELORS IN THE PRESIDING BISHOPRIC, No. 4.

8. David Asael Smith — See FIRST COUNSELORS IN THE PRESIDING BISHOPRIC, No. 5.

9. John Wells — Born Sept. 16, 1864, at Carlton, Nottinghamshire, England, to Thomas Potter Wells and Sarah

Cook. Sustained as second counselor to Presiding Bishop Charles W. Nibley July 18, 1918, at age 53; sustained as second counselor to Presiding Bishop Sylvester Q. Cannon June 4, 1925; released April 6, 1938, when Bishop Cannon was released; died April 18, 1941, at Salt Lake City, Salt Lake Co., Utah, at age 76.

10. Joseph Leopold Wirthlin — See PRESIDING BISHOPS, No. 8.

11. Henry Thorpe Beal Isaacson — See OTHER COUNSELORS IN THE FIRST PRESIDENCY, No. 12.

12. Carl William Buehner — Born Dec. 27, 1898, at Stuttgart, Wuerttemberg, Germany, to Carl F. Buehner and Anna B. Geigle. Sustained as second counselor to Presiding Bishop Joseph L. Wirthlin April 6, 1952, at age 53; released Sept. 30, 1961; died Nov. 18, 1974, at Salt Lake City, Salt Lake Co., Utah, at age 75.

13. Victor Lee Brown — See PRESIDING BISHOPS, No. 10.

14. Vaughn J Featherstone — See current FIRST QUORUM OF THE SEVENTY.

15. John Richard Clarke — See PRESIDENCY OF THE SEVENTY, No. 22.

16. Glenn Leroy Pace — See current FIRST QUORUM OF THE SEVENTY.

17. Richard Crockett Edgley — See current PRESIDING BISHOPRIC.

18. Keith B McMullin — See current PRESIDING BISHOPRIC.

LENGTH OF SERVICE IN THE FIRST PRESIDENCY AND QUORUM OF THE TWELVE

(As of October 2000)

Name	Date of service, Age at time	Length of service	†Total Years as General Authority
David O. McKay	Apr 1906 (32) - Jan 1970 (96)	63 yrs 9 mos	
Heber J. Grant	Oct 1882 (25) - May 1945 (88)	62 yrs 7 mos	
Joseph Fielding Smith	Apr 1910 (33) - Jul 1972 (95)	62 yrs 3 mos	
Wilford Woodruff	Apr 1839 (32) - Sep 1898 (91)	59 yrs 5 mos	
***Lorenzo Snow**	Feb 1849 (34) - Oct 1901 (87)	52 yrs 8 mos	
Joseph Fielding Smith	Jul 1866 (27) - Nov 1918 (80)	52 yrs 4 mos	
Franklin D. Richards	Feb 1849 (27) - Dec 1899 (78)	50 yrs 10 mos	
Ezra Taft Benson	Oct 1943 (44) - May 1994 (94)	50 yrs 7 mos	
John Taylor	Dec 1838 (30) - Jul 1887 (78)	48 yrs 7 mos	
George Albert Smith	Oct 1903 (33) - Apr 1951 (81)	47 yrs 6 mos	
Orson Pratt	Apr 1835 (23) - Aug 1842		
	Jan 1843 -Oct 1881 (70)	46 yrs 1 mo	
Rudger Clawson	Oct 1898 (41) - Jun 1943 (86)	44 yrs 8 mos	
George F. Richards	Apr 1906 (45) - Aug 1950 (89)	44 yrs 4 mos	
Orson Hyde	Feb 1835 (30) - May 1837		
	Jun 1837 - Nov 1878 (73)	43 yrs 8 mos	
Brigham Young	Feb 1835 (33) - Aug 1877 (76)	42 yrs 6 mos	
Stephen L Richards	Jan 1917 (37) - May 1959 (79)	42 yrs 4 mos	
Spencer W. Kimball	Oct 1943 (48) - Nov 1985 (90)	42 yrs 1 mo	
Reed Smoot	Apr 1900 (38) - Feb 1941 (79)	40 yrs 10 mos	

*George Q. Cannon	Aug 1860 (33) - Apr 1901 (74)	40 yrs 8 mos	
Mark E. Petersen	Apr 1944 (43) - Jan 1984 (83)	39 yrs 9 mos	
Erastus Snow	Feb 1849 (30) - May 1888 (69)	39 yrs 3 mos	
• Gordon B. Hinckley	Oct 1961 (51) - present	39 yrs	42 yrs 6 mos
• Thomas S. Monson	Oct 1963 (36) - present	37 yrs	
Marion G. Romney	Oct 1951 (54) - May 1988 (90)	36 yrs 7 mos	47 yrs 1 mo
George A. Smith	Apr 1839 (21) - Sep 1875 (58)	36 yrs 5 mos	
Francis M. Lyman	Oct 1880 (40) - Nov 1916 (76)	36 yrs 1 mo	
Howard W. Hunter	Oct 1959 (51) - Mar 1995 (87)	35 yrs 5 mo	
Charles C. Rich	Feb 1849 (39) - Nov 1883 (74)	34 yrs 9 mos	
*Brigham Young Jr.	Oct 1868 (31) - Apr 1903 (66)	34 yrs 6 mos	
#Daniel H. Wells	Jan 1857 (42) - Mar 1891 (76)	34 yrs 2 mos	
Heber C. Kimball	Feb 1835 (33) - Jun 1868 (67)	33 yrs 4 mos	
Harold B. Lee	Apr 1941 (42) - Dec 1973 (74)	32 yrs 8 mos	
John A. Widtsoe	Mar 1921 (49) - Nov 1952 (80)	31 yrs 8 mos	
Anthon H. Lund	Oct 1889 (45) - Mar 1921 (76)	31 yrs 5 mos	
John Henry Smith	Oct 1880 (32) - Oct 1911 (63)	31 yrs	
LeGrand Richards	Apr 1952 (66) - Jan 1983 (96)	30 yrs 9 mos	44 yrs 9 mos
• Boyd K. Packer	Apr 1970 (45) - present	30 yrs 6 mos	39 yrs
J. Reuben Clark Jr.	Apr 1933 (61) - Oct 1961 (90)	28 yrs 6 mos	
Delbert L. Stapley	Oct 1950 (53) - Aug 1978 (81)	27 yrs 10 mos	
Anthony W. Ivins	Oct 1907 (55) - Sep 1934 (82)	26 yrs 11 mos	
• L. Tom Perry	Apr 1974 (51) - present	26 yrs 6 mos	28 yrs
Richard R. Lyman	Apr 1918 (47) - Nov 1943 (72)	25 yrs 7 mos	
Amasa M. Lyman	Aug 1842 (29) - Oct 1867 (54)	25 yrs 2 mos	
Orson F. Whitney	Apr 1906 (50) - May 1931 (75)	25 yrs 1 mo	
• David B. Haight	Jan 1976 (69) - present	24 yrs 9 mos	30 yrs 6 mos
George Teasdale	Oct 1882 (50) - Jun 1907 (75)	24 yrs 8 mos	
Ezra T. Benson	Jul 1846 (35) - Sep 1869 (58)	23 yrs 2 mos	
Parley P. Pratt	Feb 1835 (27) - May 1857 (50)	22 yrs 3 mos	
Marvin J. Ashton	Dec 1971 (56) - Feb 1994 (78)	22 yrs 2 mos	24 yrs 4 mos
• James E. Faust	Oct 1978 (58) - present	22 yrs	28 yrs
James E. Talmage	Dec 1911 (49) - Jul 1933 (70)	21 yrs 7 mos	
John W. Taylor	Apr 1884 (25) - Oct 1905 (47)	21 yrs 6 mos	
Charles W. Penrose	Jul 1904 (72) - May 1925 (93)	20 yrs 10 mos	
Melvin J. Ballard	Jan 1919 (45) - Jul 1939 (66)	20 yrs 6 mos	
Joseph F. Merrill	Oct 1931 (63) - Feb 1952 (83)	20 yrs 4 mos	
N. Eldon Tanner	Oct 1962 (64) - Nov 1982 (84)	20 yrs 1 mo	22 yrs 1 mo
• Neal A. Maxwell	Jul 1981 (55) - present	19 yrs 3 mos	26 yrs 6 mos
*#John Willard Young	Apr 1873 (28) - Oct 1891 (47)	18 yrs 6 mos	
Richard L. Evans	Oct 1953 (47) - Nov 1971 (65)	18 yrs 1 mo	33 yrs 1 mo
Hugh B. Brown	Apr 1958 (74) - Dec 1975 (92)	17 yrs 8 mos	22 yrs 2 mos
Moses Thatcher	Apr 1879 (37) - Apr 1896 (54)	17 yrs	
• Russell M. Nelson	Apr 1984 (59) - present	16 yrs 6 mos	
• Dallin H. Oaks	Apr 1984 (51) - present	16 yrs 6 mos	
Henry D. Moyle	Apr 1947 (57) - Sep 1963 (74)	16 yrs 5 mos	
Marriner W. Merrill	Oct 1889 (57) - Feb 1906 (73)	16 yrs 4 mos	
Hyrum Mack Smith	Oct 1901 (29) - Jan 1918 (45)	16 yrs 3 mos	
Albert E. Bowen	Apr 1937 (61) - Jul 1953 (77)	16 yrs 3 mos	

• M. Russell Ballard	Oct 1985 (57) - present	15 yrs	24 yrs 6 mos
Joseph Smith	Apr 1830 (24) - Jun 1844 (38)	14 yrs 2 mos	
• Joseph B. Wirthlin	Oct 1986 (69) - present	14 yrs	25 yrs 6 mos
Willard Richards	Apr 1840 (35) - Mar 1854 (49)	13 yrs 11 mos	
Charles A. Callis	Oct 1933 (68) - Jan 1947 (81)	13 yrs 3 mos	
Bruce R. McConkie	Oct 1972 (57) - Apr 1985 (69)	12 yrs 6 mos	38 yrs 6 mos
• Richard G. Scott	Oct 1988 (59) - present	12 years	23 yrs 6 mos
Sidney Rigdon	Mar 1833 (40) - Jun 1844 (51)	11 yrs 3 mos	
William Smith	Feb 1835 (23) - Oct 1845 (34)	10 yrs 8 mos	
John R. Winder	Oct 1901 (79) - Mar 1910 (88)	8 yrs 5 mos	22 yrs 11 mos
Matthew Cowley	Oct 1945 (48) - Dec 1953 (56)	8 yrs 2 mos	
George Q. Morris	Apr 1954 (80) - Apr 1962 (88)	8 yrs	10 yrs 6 mos
Matthias F. Cowley	Oct 1897 (39) - Oct 1905 (47)	8 yrs	
*Oliver Cowdery	Apr 1830 (23) - Apr 1838 (31)	8 yrs	
Lyman Wight	Apr 1841 (44) - Dec 1848 (52)	7 yrs 8 mos	
John E. Page	Dec 1838 (39) - Feb 1846 (47)	7 yrs 2 mos	
Abraham H. Cannon	Oct 1889 (30) - Jul 1896 (37)	6 yrs 9 mos	13 yrs 9 mos
*Hyrum Smith	Sep 1837 (37) - Jun 1844 (44)	6 yrs 9 mos	
*John Smith	Sep 1837 (56) - Jun 1844 (62)	6 yrs 9 mos	
Abraham O. Woodruff	Oct 1897 (24) - Jun 1904 (31)	6 yrs 8 mos	
Charles W. Nibley	May 1925 (76) - Dec 1931 (82)	6 yrs 7 mos	24 yrs
• Robert D. Hales	Apr 1994 (61) - present	6 yrs 6 mos	25 yrs 6 mos
• Jeffrey R. Holland	Jun 1994 (53) - present	6 yrs 4 mos	11 yrs 4 mos
• Henry B. Eyring	Apr 1995 (61) - present	5 yrs 6 mos	15 yrs 6 mos
Sylvester Q. Cannon	Apr 1938 (60) - May 1943 (65)	5 yrs 1 mo	18 yrs
Adam S. Bennion	Apr 1953 (66) - Feb 1958 (71)	4 yrs 10 mos	
Frederick G. Williams	Mar 1833 (45) - Nov 1837 (50)	4 yrs 8 mos	
*Albert Carrington	Apr 1873 (60) - Aug 1877 (64)	4 yrs 4 mos	
Thorpe B. Isaacson	Oct 1965 (67) - Jan 1970 (71)	4 yrs 3 mos	23 yrs 1 mo
Thomas B. Marsh	Apr 1835 (35) - Mar 1839 (39)	3 yrs 11 mos	
David W. Patten	Feb 1835 (35) - Oct 1838 (38)	3 yrs 8 mos	
William E. M'Lellin	Feb 1835 (29) - May 1838 (32)	3 yrs 3 mos	
William Law	Jan 1841 (31) - Apr 1844 (34)	3 yrs 3 mos	
Luke Johnson	Feb 1835 (27) - Apr 1838 (30)	3 yrs 2 mos	
Lyman E. Johnson	Feb 1835 (23) - Apr 1838 (26)	3 yrs 2 mos	
*Joseph Smith Sr.	Sep 1837 (66) - Sep 1840 (69)	3 yrs	6 yrs 9 mos
Jedediah M. Grant	Apr 1854 (38) - Dec 1856 (40)	2 yrs 8 mos	11 yrs
John F. Boynton	Feb 1835 (23) - Sep 1837 (25)	2 yrs 7 mos	
Alonzo A. Hinckley	Oct 1934 (64) - Dec 1936 (66)	2 yrs 2 mos	
Alvin R. Dyer	Apr 1968 (65) - Jan 1970 (67)	1 yr 9 mos	18 yrs 5 mos

Bold Face denotes Church president.

• Currently serving.

†Includes service in the First Council of the Seventy, Assistants to the Twelve, First Quorum of the Seventy, Presiding Bishopric, or as Church Patriarch.

* Served as assistant counselor in the First Presidency.

Served in the First Presidency under Brigham Young; after his death sustained as counselor to Twelve Apostles.

GENERAL OFFICERS OF THE CHURCH

SUNDAY SCHOOL

Though a few small Sunday School groups met regularly in Latter-day Saint communities before the Saints' westward exodus, Sunday School did not begin as a Church institution until after their arrival in the Salt Lake Valley in 1847.

Richard Ballantyne was a convert to the Church who, as a Presbyterian in his native Scotland, had organized a Sunday School. In Salt Lake City, disturbed by observing the children at play on the Sabbath day, he saw the need for a Sunday School.

In May 1849, he began plans to start a Sunday School. He built a structure on the northeast corner of 100 West and 300 South streets in Salt Lake City to serve both as his home and a place to hold the Sunday School. A monument on that corner today (now 200 West) commemorates the location of the first Sunday School.

On Sunday, Dec. 9, 1849, the first Sunday School was held, involving 50 children. The following year, a meetinghouse was built for the Salt Lake 14th Ward, in which Richard Ballantyne was second counselor in the bishopric. The expanded Sunday School was moved into the new building and divided into a number of smaller classes, with additional teachers and two assistant superintendents.

Other wards in the valley and elsewhere followed the example of Richard Ballantyne and started Sunday Schools. They were somewhat autonomous, devising their own curricula and having their own administration, but functioning under the direction of the ward bishop.

With the coming of Johnston's Army to Utah, the Sunday School movement was suspended as many of the Saints moved south, but with the lessening of tensions in 1860, the Sunday School was resumed. By 1870, more than 200 Sunday Schools had been formed.

On Nov. 11, 1867, the Deseret Sunday School Union was organized by interested Church leaders, including President Brigham Young. Elder George Q. Cannon of the Quorum of the Twelve became the first general superintendent of the Sunday School. Its functions were to determine lesson topics and source materials and to address topics of punctuality, grading, prizes and rewards, recording and increasing attendance, music, elementary catechism, and libraries. The general Sunday School fostered uniformity in the theretofore disparate and independent Sunday Schools in the Church.

In 1866, prior to formation of the general Sunday School, a publication called the *Juvenile Instructor* was founded privately by Elder George Q. Cannon of the Twelve, who served as editor. It featured material on the scriptures, musical compositions and aids to gospel instruction. The publication became the official voice of the Deseret Sunday School Union, which purchased it from the Cannon family in January 1901. In 1929, the name was changed to the *Instructor*. It was discontinued in 1970 when the Church magazine structure was changed.

In early 1877, the sacrament was instituted as part of Sunday School. The practice continued until 1980, when Sunday meetings were consolidated into a three-hour block, with sacrament administered only during sacrament meeting.

The Deseret Sunday School Union continued to grow through the 1900s. Stake Sunday School superintendencies were designated to supervise ward Sunday Schools. General meetings of the Sunday School were held twice a year in connection with general conference. Five new classes for older children and youth were added in the early 1900s, followed shortly by the introduction of adult classes.

A Sunday School general board was introduced in the 1870s. In the 1900s, it was expanded and members traveled extensively to provide advice and support for local Sunday School programs.

An effort in 1971 to correlate all Church functions under priesthood leadership affected the Sunday School. Dynamic changes followed, including centralized curriculum planning and writing, and an eight-year cycle of scripture instruction (later shortened to four years) for adult classes, focusing in turn on the Old Testament and Pearl of Great Price, the New Testament, the Book of Mormon, and the Doctrine and Covenants and Church History. Later, the size of the general board was reduced, and stake boards were discontinued.

On June 25, 1972, during the time that Russell M. Nelson was the presiding officer of the Sunday School, his title was changed from superintendent to president, and the title of his assistants to counselors. The titles were also changed in the YMMIA from superintendent to president and from assistants to counselors.

With the introduction of the consolidated meeting schedule in 1980, children's Sunday School classes were discontinued, that function being filled by the Primary. In recent years, Sunday School curriculum for adults has included a Gospel Doctrine class and additional classes on Gospel Essentials, family history, and family relations.

A modified Church curriculum implemented Jan. 1, 1995, provided that classes for youth ages 14-18 study the scriptures using the Gospel Principles or Gospel Doctrine courses of study. Under the modified plan, youth ages 12-13 on alternate years study presidents of the Church and preparing for exaltation.

Throughout 1999, the Church observed the sesquicentenial of the Sunday School program by opening the 1949 centennial box and putting together a bicentennial box, the latter representative of a global Sunday School program. The new bicentennial box will be opened in 2049. The Museum of Church History and Art held a yearlong exhibit, "Sunday School: 150 Years of Teaching the Gospel," which opened July 6, 1998. Attending the reception were former members of the1949 Deseret Sunday School Union General Board who had watched the centennial box closed 50 years earlier.

Sources: *Encyclopedia of Mormonism*; *Jubilee History of Latter-day Saints Sunday Schools,* published by the Deseret Sunday School Union; *Church News*, July 1, 1972; First Presidency letter to General Authorities and priesthood leaders, April 21, 1994; "Exhibit serves as beginning of Sunday School celebration," by Sarah Jane Weaver, *Church News*, July 11, 1998.

SUNDAY SCHOOL OFFICERS

(As of October 2000)

President

Marlin K. Jensen, 7 Oct 2000-present. See current PRESIDENCY OF THE SEVENTY.

First Counselor

Neil L. Andersen, 7 Oct 2000-present. See current FIRST QUORUM OF THE SEVENTY.

Second Counselor

John H. Groberg, 7 Oct. 2000-present. See current FIRST QUORUM OF THE SEVENTY.

HISTORICAL LISTING OF GENERAL SUPERINTENDENCIES AND PRESIDENCIES OF THE SUNDAY SCHOOL

(Presidents, superintendents pictured)

1. **Superintendent,** George Q. Cannon (as apostle,counselor in First Presidency) - Nov 1867-Apr 1901. See photo, FIRST COUNSELORS IN THE FIRST PRESIDENCY, No. 5.

First Assistants, George Goddard - Jun 1872-Jan 1899; Karl G. Maeser - Jan 1899-Feb 1901.

Second Assistants, John Morgan - Jun 1883-Jul 1894; Karl G. Maeser - Jul 1894-Jan 1899; George Reynolds - Jan 1899-May 1901.

2. **Superintendent**, Lorenzo Snow (as president of the Church) - May 1901-Oct 1901. See photo, PRESIDENTS OF THE CHURCH, No. 5.

First Assistant, George Reynolds - May 1901-Oct 1901.

Second Assistant, Jay M. Tanner - May 1901-Oct 1901.

3. **Superintendent**, Joseph F. Smith (as president of the Church) - Nov 1901-Nov 1918. See photo, PRESIDENTS OF THE CHURCH, No. 6.

First Assistants, George Reynolds - Nov 1901-May 1909, David O. McKay (as apostle) - May 1909-Nov 1918.

Second Assistants, Jay M. Tanner - Nov 1901-April 1906; David O. McKay(as apostle) - Jan 1907-May 1909; Stephen L Richards - May 1909-Nov 1918

4. **Superintendent**, David O. McKay (as apostle) - Dec 1918-Oct 1934. See photo, PRESIDENTS OF THE CHURCH, No. 9.

First Assistant, Stephen L Richards (as apostle) - Dec 1918-Oct 1934.

Second Assistant, George D. Pyper - Dec 1918-Oct 1934.

5. **Superintendent**, George D. Pyper - Oct 1934-Jan 1943.

First Assistant, Milton Bennion - Oct 1934-May 1943.

Second Assistant, George R. Hill - Oct 1934-May 1943.

6. **Superintendent**, Milton Bennion - May 1943-Sep 1949.

First Assistant, George R. Hill - May 1943-Sep 1949.

Second Assistant, Albert Hamer Reiser - May 1943-Sep 1949.

7. **Superintendent**, George R. Hill - Sep 1949-Nov 1966.

First Assistants, Albert Hamer Reiser - Sep 1949-Oct 1952; David Lawrence McKay - Oct 1952-Nov 1966.

Second Assistants, David Lawrence McKay - Sep 1949-Oct 1952; Lynn S. Richards - Oct 1952-Nov 1966.

8. **Superintendent**, David Lawrence McKay - Nov 1966-Jun 1971.

First Assistant, Lynn S. Richards - Nov 1966-Jun 1971.

Second Assistant, Royden G. Derrick - Nov. 1966-Jun 1971.

9. **President**, Russell M. Nelson - Jun 1971-Oct 1979. See photo, current QUORUM OF THE TWELVE. (Note: titles changed from superintendent to

president, and from assistants to counselors on June 25, 1972.)

First Counselors, Joseph B. Wirthlin - Jun 1971-Apr 1975, B. Lloyd Poelman - Apr 1975-Mar 1978; Joe J. Christensen - Mar 1978-Aug 1979; William D. Oswald - Aug 1979-Oct 1979.

Second Counselors, Richard L. Warner - Jun 1971-Apr 1975; Joe J. Christensen - Apr 1975-Mar 1978; William D. Oswald - May 1978-Aug 1979; J. Hugh Baird - Aug 1979-Oct 1979.

(Since Oct. 6, 1979, the presidency of the Sunday School has been composed of members of the Seventy.)

10. **President**, Hugh W. Pinnock - Oct 1979-Aug 1986. See photo, current FIRST QUORUM OF THE SEVENTY.

First Counselors, Ronald E. Poelman - Oct 1979-Jul 1981; Robert D. Hales - Jul 1981-Jul 1985; Adney Y. Komatsu - Jul 1985-Aug 1986.

Second Counselors, Jack H Goaslind Jr. - Oct 1979-Jul 1981; James M. Paramore - Jul 1981-Jan 1983; Loren C. Dunn - Jan 1983-Jul 1985; Ronald E. Poelman - Jul 1985-Aug 1986.

11. **President**, Robert L. Simpson - Aug 1986-30 Sep 1989. See photo, FIRST QUORUM OF THE SEVENTY, No. 18.

First Counselors, Adney Y. Komatsu - Aug 1986-Aug. 1987; Devere Harris - Aug 1987-30 Sep 1989.

Second Counselors, A. Theodore Tuttle - Aug 1986-Nov 1986; Devere Harris - Jan 1987-Aug 1987; Phillip T. Sonntag - Aug 1987-Aug 1988; Derek A. Cuthbert - Aug 1988-30 Sep 1989.

12. **President**, Hugh W. Pinnock - 30 Sep 1989-15 Aug 1992. See photo, current FIRST QUORUM OF THE SEVENTY.

First Counselors, Derek A. Cuthbert - 15 Aug 1988-1 Jan 1991; H. Verlan Andersen - 1 Jan 1991-5 Oct 1991; Hartman Rector Jr. - 5 Oct 1991-15 Aug 1992.

Second Counselors, Ted E. Brewerton - 30 Sep 1989-1 Oct 1990; H. Verlan Andersen - 6 Oct 1990-1 Jan 1991; Rulon G. Craven - 1 Jan 1991-5 Oct 1991; Clinton L. Cutler - 5 Oct 1991-15 Aug 1992.

13. **President**, Merlin R. Lybbert - 15 Aug 1992-15 Aug 1994. See photo, SECOND QUORUM OF THE SEVENTY, No. 35.

First Counselor, Clinton L. Cutler - 15 Aug 1992-April 9, 1994.

Second Counselor, Ronald E. Poelman - 15 Aug 1992-15 Aug 1994.

14. **President**, Charles Didier - 15 Aug 1994-30 Sep 1995. See photo, current FIRST QUORUM OF THE SEVENTY.

First Counselor, J Ballard Washburn - 15 Aug 1994-30 Sep 1995.

Second Counselor, F. Burton Howard - 15 Aug 1994-30 Sep 1995.

15. **President,** Harold G. Hillam, 30 Sep 1995 - 7 Oct 2000. See photo, current FIRST QUORUM OF THE SEVENTY.

First Counselors, F. Burton Howard, 30 Sep 1995 - 4 Oct 1997; Glenn L. Pace, 4 Oct 1997 - 3 Oct 1998; Neil L. Andersen, 3 Oct 1998 - 7 Oct 2000.

Second Counselors, Glenn L. Pace, 30 Sep 1995 - 4 Oct 1997; Neil L. Andersen, 4 Oct 1997 - 3 Oct 1998; John H. Groberg, 3 Oct 1998 - 7 Oct 2000.

YOUNG MEN

The Young Men organization has been significantly streamlined and simplified since its inception in 1875 as the Young Men's Mutual Improvement Association.

The YMMIA was established by President Brigham Young, who called Junius F. Wells to organize Mutual Improvement Associations in wards throughout the Church, under the direction of ward superintendencies. It was intended that the YMMIA help young men develop spiritually and intellectually and provide supervised recreational opportunities. Today, its primary purpose is furthering the work of the Aaronic Priesthood.

On June 10, 1875, Brother Wells called a meeting in the 13th Ward chapel in Salt Lake City and the first ward YMMIA was organized.

In the fall of 1875, John Henry Smith, Milton H. Hardy, and B. Morris Young were called by the First Presidency to assist Brother Wells in visiting the settlements of the Saints and promoting the YMMIA. By April 1876, there were 57 ward YMMIAs in existence with a membership of about 1,200 youth. That same year, a YMMIA central committee was formed with Brother Wells as president. The committee later became the General Board of the YMMIA, which has continued through the years and is now known as the Young Men General Board.

From 1876 to 1905, young men were called to serve YMMIA missions to increase membership and assist local superintendencies. Initially, all of the young men met together regardless of age. Later, the YMMIA adopted four grades or classes: Scouts (ages 12-14), Vanguards (15-16), M Men (17-23), and Adults. As the programs developed and as needs of the youth changed, further refinements were made to the class structure. Today, Young Men classes correspond with the deacons, teachers, and priests quorums in the Aaronic Priesthood.

In October 1879, the monthly *Contributor* was launched with Brother Wells as editor. It served as the publication of the YMMIA until October 1899, at which time the publication of the *Improvement Era* was begun by the General Board.

The YMMIA met separately from the Young Women's Mutual Improvement Association (YWMIA) until around 1900 when the two joined to form the Mutual Improvement Association. (called MIA or Mutual.)

In 1913, the Church formed a formal partnership with Boy Scouts of America and was granted a national charter on May 21 of that year. Scouting exists today as a major component of the Young Men organization to help accomplish the purposes of the Aaronic Priesthood and to complement Sunday quorum instruction. Besides its partnership with BSA, the Church has established affiliations with other national Scouting organizations throughout the world whose programs, values, goals, and ideals are compatible with those of the Church.

In addition to Scouting, YMMIA activities in the early and mid-1900s included sports, dance, drama, and music. Athletics became a major part of the program, and stake tournament winners progressed to the All-Church tournaments in Salt Lake City, which were discontinued in the early 1970s.

In the mid-1900s, the general-level organization consisted of a superintendency of five men and a general board of 60 to 70 men. The general level was supported by a general fund, paid into by stakes based on YMMIA membership, sale of YMMIA materials, and investments. Besides planning and organizing major sports and cultural events, general board members would regularly travel with General Authorities and provide training for local YMMIA leaders.

In the 1960s under priesthood correlation, responsibility for training shifted to local priesthood leaders, the general fund was discontinued, production and sale of materials were centralized, and the size and scope of the general superintendency and board were greatly reduced.

On June 25, 1972, the title of the presiding officers of the YMMIA and Sunday School were changed from superintendent to president, and the title of assistants to counselors "to more closely define the relationship between the two auxiliaries with the functions of the priesthood," according to President Harold B. Lee, then first counselor in the First Presidency.

The Aaronic Priesthood-MIA was organized Nov. 9, 1972, with efforts centering more fully around the Aaronic Priesthood quorums. In June 1974 the name Aaronic Priesthood-MIA was shortened to Aaronic Priesthood and conducted under the direction of the Presiding Bishopric. In May 1977 the name was changed to Young Men and a general presidency was reinstated. In October 1979 it was announced that the Young Men general presidency would be comprised of three members of the Seventy. Since 1989, the general board has been comprised of less than a dozen men who continue to assist the presidency with curriculum development and Aaronic Priesthood and Scouting training.

To commemorate the 1997 Pioneer Sesquicentennial, the young men of the Church participated in a special Aaronic Priesthood Pioneer Sesquicentennial Fireside telecast over the Church's satellite system from the Salt Lake Tabernacle May 18. The fireside, called "Faith in Every Footstep," featured President Gordon B. Hinckley as the main speaker, and was similar to the General Young Women Meeting held in March with the same theme.

Sources: *Encyclopedia of Mormonism*; *Encyclopedic History of the Church* by Andrew Jenson, p. 969; *Church News*, July 1, 1972, May 3, 1997.

YOUNG MEN OFFICERS

(As of October 2000)

President

Robert K. Dellenbach, 3 Oct 1998-present. See photo, current FIRST QUORUM OF THE SEVENTY.

First Counselor

F. Melvin Hammond, 3 Oct 1998-present. See photo, current FIRST QUORUM OF THE SEVENTY.

Second Counselor

John M. Madsen, 3 Oct 1998-present. See photo, current FIRST QUORUM OF THE SEVENTY.

HISTORICAL LISTING OF GENERAL SUPERINTENDENCIES AND PRESIDENCIES OF THE YOUNG MEN'S MUTUAL IMPROVEMENT ASSOCIATION AND YOUNG MEN

(Presidents, superintendents pictured)

1. **Superintendent**, Junius F. Wells - 1876-1880.

First Counselor, M. H. Hardy.

Second Counselor, Rodney C. Badger.

2. **Superintendent**, Wilford Woodruff (as apostle, president of the Church) - 1880-1898. See photo, PRESIDENTS OF THE CHURCH, No. 4.

First Assistant, Joseph F. Smith.

Second Assistant, Moses Thatcher.

3. **Superintendent**, Lorenzo Snow (as president of the Church) - 1898-1901. See photo, PRESIDENTS OF THE CHURCH, No. 5.

First Assistant, Joseph F. Smith.

Second Assistant, Heber J. Grant.

Assistant, B. H. Roberts.

4. **Superintendent**, Joseph F. Smith

(as president of the Church) - 1901-1918. See photo, PRESIDENTS OF THE CHURCH, No. 6.

First Assistant, Heber J. Grant.

Second Assistant, B. H. Roberts.

5. **Superintendent**, Anthony W. Ivins (as apostle) - 1918-1921. See photo, FIRST COUNSELORS IN THE FIRST PRESIDENCY, No. 10.

First Assistant, B. H. Roberts

Second Assistant, Richard R. Lyman.

6. **Superintendent**, George Albert Smith (as apostle — 1921-1935. See photo, PRESIDENTS OF THE CHURCH, No. 8.

First Assistant, B. H. Roberts.

Second Assistants, Richard R. Lyman; Melvin J. Ballard.

7. **Superintendent**, Albert E. Bowen - 1935-1937. See photo, QUORUM OF THE TWELVE, No. 59.

First Assistant, George Q. Morris.

Second Assistant, Franklin West.

8. **Superintendent**, George Q. Morris - 1937-1948. See photo, QUORUM OF THE TWELVE, No. 72.

First Assistants, Joseph J. Cannon; John D. Giles.

Second Assistants, Burton K. Farnsworth; Lorenzo H. Hatch.

9. **Superintendent**, Elbert R. Curtis - 1948-1958.

First Assistant, A. Walter Stevenson.

Second Assistants, Ralph W. Hardy; David S. King.

10. **Superintendent**, Joseph T. Bentley - 2 Jul 1958-6 Oct 1962.

First Assistants, Alvin R. Dyer - 2 Jul 1958-6 Dec 1958; G. Carlos Smith - 6 Dec 1958-9 Jun 1961; Marvin J. Ashton, 9 Jun 1961-6 Oct 1962.

Second Assistants, Marvin J. Ashton - 6 Dec 1958-9 Jun 1961; Verl F. Scott, 9 Jun 1961-4 Oct 1961; Carl W. Buehner, 25 Oct 1961-Oct 1962.

11. **Superintendent**, G. Carlos Smith - 6 Oct 1962-17 Sep 1969.

First Assistant, Marvin J. Ashton - 6 Oct 1962-17 Sep 1969.

Second Assistants, Carl W. Beuhner - 6 Oct 1962-Oct 1967; George R. Hill - 6 Oct 1967-17 Sep 1969.

12. **Superintendent**, W. Jay Eldredge - 17 Sep 1969-25 Jun 1972.

First Assistants, George R. Hill - 17 Sep 1969-24 Jun 1972.

Second Assistant, George I. Cannon - 17 Sep 1969-25 Jun 1972.

13. **President**, W. Jay Eldredge - 25 Jun 1972-9 Nov 1972 (see photo above).

First Counselor, George I. Cannon - 25 Jun 1972-9 Nov 1972.

Second Counselor, Robert L. Backman, 25 Jun 1972-9 Nov 1972.

AARONIC PRIESTHOOD MIA

14. **President**, Robert L. Backman - 9 Nov 1972-23 Jun 1974. See photo, PRESIDENCY OF THE SEVENTY, No. 18.

First Counselor, LeGrand R. Curtis - Nov 1972-23 Jun 1974.

Second Counselor, Jack H Goaslind Jr. - 9 Nov 1972-23 Jun 1974.

Note: On June 23, 1974, the Aaronic Priesthood MIA was dissolved and was replaced by the Aaronic Priesthood and the Young Women directly under the stewardship of the Presiding Bishop. In April 1977, it was renamed the Young Men, and both it and the Young Women came under the direction of the Priesthood Department.

15. **President**, Neil D. Schaerrer - 7 Apr 1977-Oct 1979.

First Counselor, Graham W. Doxey - 7 Apr 1977-Oct 1979.

Second Counselor, Quinn G. McKay - 7 Apr 1977-Oct 1979

(Since Oct. 6, 1979, the presidency of the Young Men has been composed of members of the Seventy.)

16. **President**, Robert L. Backman - Oct 1979-Nov 1985. See photo, PRESIDENCY OF THE SEVENTY, No. 18.

First Counselor, Vaughn J Featherstone - Oct 1979-Nov 1985.

Second Counselor, Rex D. Pinegar - Oct 1979-Nov 1985.

17. **President**, Vaughn J Featherstone - Nov 1985-6 Oct 1990. See photo, current FIRST QUORUM OF THE SEVENTY.

First Counselors, Rex D. Pinegar - Nov 1985-30 Sep 1989; Jeffrey R. Holland - 30 Sep 1989-6 Oct 1990.

Second Counselors, Robert L. Simpson - Nov 1985-15 Aug 1986; Hartman Rector Jr. - 15 Aug 1986-Oct 1988; Robert B Harbertson, Oct 1988-30 Sep 1989; Monte J. Brough, 30 Sep 1989-6 Oct 1990.

18. **President**, Jack H Goaslind - 6 Oct 1990-3 Oct 1998. See photo, PRESIDENCY OF THE SEVENTY, No. 17.

First Counselors, Robert K. Dellenbach - 4 Oct 1997-3 Oct 1998; F. David Stanley - 17 May 1997-4 Oct 1997; Vaughn J Featherstone - 5 Oct 1996-17 May 1997; Stephen D. Nadauld - 3 Oct 1992-5 Oct 1996; Robert K. Dellenbach - 5 Oct 1991-3 Oct 1992; LeGrand R. Curtis -6 Oct 1990-5 Oct 1991.

Second Counselors, F. Melvin Hammond - 4 Oct 1997-3 Oct 1998; Robert K. Dellenbach - 17 May 1997-4 Oct 1997; F. David Stanley - 5 Oct 1996-17 May 1997; Vaughn J Featherstone -15 Aug 1993-5 Oct 1996; L. Lionel Kendrick - 3 Oct 1992-15 Aug 1993; Stephen D. Nadauld - 5 Oct 1991-30 Oct 1992; Robert K. Dellenbach, 6 Oct 1990-5 Oct 1991.

PRIMARY

Noting the rough and careless behavior of the boys in her Farmington, Utah, neighborhood, Aurelia Spencer Rogers asked, "What will our girls do for good husbands, if this state of things continues?" Then she asked, "Could there not be an organization for little boys, and have them trained to make better men?"

The answer was, "Yes." With the approval of President John Taylor, the encouragement of Relief Society general president Eliza R. Snow, and after receiving a calling from her bishop, Sister Rogers began planning for the first meeting of the Primary Association, and it was an overwhelming success. On Sunday, Aug. 25, 1878, she stood at the entrance to the meetinghouse and welcomed 224 boys and girls to Primary. Girls were invited because Sister Rogers thought they could help with the singing that she believed necessary. During the first meeting, Sister Rogers instructed the children to be obedient and to be kind to one another.

Sister Rogers was not only the first Farmington Ward Primary president, but also the first Davis Stake Primary president.

Sister Snow, as well, was actively involved in the organization of the Primary Association. About the time Sister Rogers was holding the first Primary meeting, Sister Snow was in Ogden, Utah, laying the groundwork for the organization there. Upon her return to Salt Lake City, she reported to the Relief Society women there about her activities with the Primary in the northern part of the state.

During the next decade, the Primary Association was organized in almost every LDS settlement. During one trip through Southern Utah, Sister Snow and her first counselor in the Relief Society presidency, Zina Young, organized 35 Primaries.

From its beginning, Primary included songs, poetry, and activities. The boys wore uniforms to the meetings. All the children met together during the first 10 years. After that, they were divided into age groups.

Sister Louie B. Felt was called as the first general president of the Primary in 1880, but the Relief Society continued to take the responsibility for organizing Primaries. Sister Felt and other general officers began taking more responsibility for Primary development after 1890.

Serving as Primary general president for 45 years, Sister Felt oversaw many developments in the organization. In 1902, publication of the *Children's Friend* magazine began. In 1913, the Primary began contributing to pediatric hospital care. That program was culminated in 1952 with the completion of the Primary Children's Hospital in Salt Lake City. Contributions from Primary children helped support the hospital.

Beginning in 1929 when the Primary took over more responsibility for the spiritual training of children, lessons were planned for three weeks of the month and an activity on the fourth week. The Cub Scout program became the responsibility of the Primary in 1952.

Primary meetings were held midweek until the Church instituted the consolidated meeting plan in 1980. Then it replaced Junior Sunday School for providing Sunday religious instruction for children ages 3 to 11. The Primary meets for one hour and forty minutes of the meeting block, dividing the time between group meetings, classroom instruction, and sharing time. Although women continue to serve exclusively in Primary presidencies, men are also called to teach classes. Weekday activities are held on a quarterly basis.

Yearly, usually in September or October, ward and branch Primaries throughout the Church present the Children's Sacrament Meeting Presentation, during which the children share, through song and the spoken word, what they have learned during the year.

Primary also plays a part in the commemoration of Pioneer Day in Salt Lake City. Riding in the annual Days of '47 Youth Parade each year are members of the Church's Primary general presidency.

Sources: *Sisters and Little Saints*, by Carol Cornwall Madsen and Susan Oman; *Encyclopedia of Mormonism*; *Church News*.

PRIMARY GENERAL PRESIDENCY

(As of October 2000)

Sydney S. Reynolds
First Counselor

Coleen K. Menlove
President

Gayle M. Clegg
Second Counselor

President – Coleen Kent Menlove, Oct. 2, 1999-present. Born in Salt Lake City Utah, to Robert D. and Marjorie Moon Kent; received bachelor's degree in elementary education from University of Utah, and master's degree in education curriculum from BYU; former member of Young Women general board, member of Church writing committees, stake Primary president, and ward Young Women president; married Dean Walden Menlove, parents of seven children.

First Counselor – Sydney Smith Reynolds, Oct. 2, 1999-present. Born in Idaho Falls, Idaho, to J. Alvin and Marguerite Rees Smith.; received bachelor's degree in history and political science from BYU; former member of Primary general board, stake and ward Young Women's president, and ward Relief Society president; married Noel B. Reynolds, parents of 11 children.

Second Counselor – Gayle Muhlestein Clegg, Oct. 2, 1999-present. Born in Glendale, Calif., to Grant A. and Lillie Tidwell Muhlestein; received bachelor's degree in history from University of Utah; served with husband when he was president of the Portugal Lisbon Mission; former ward Primary and Young Women president and gospel doctrine teacher; married Calvin Chipman Clegg, parents of five children.

HISTORICAL LISTING OF GENERAL PRESIDENCIES OF THE PRIMARY ASSOCIATION

(Presidents pictured)

1. **President**, Louie Bouton Felt, 19 Jun 1880-6 Oct 1925.

First Counselors, Matilda Morehouse W. Barratt - 19 Jun 1880-Oct 1888; Lillie Tuckett Freeze - Oct 1888-8 Dec 1905; May Anderson - 29 Dec 1905-6 Oct 1925.

Second Counselors, Clare Cordelia Moses Cannon - 19 Jun 1880-4 Oct 1895; Josephine Richards West - 15 Dec 1896-24 Nov 1905; Clara Woodruff Beebe - 29 Dec 1906-6 Oct 1925.

2. **President**, May Anderson - 6 Oct 1925-11 Sep 1939.

First Counselors, Sadie Grant Pack - 6 Oct 1925-11 Sep 1929; Isabelle Salmon Ross - 11 Sep 1929-31 Dec 1939.

Second Counselors, Isabelle Salmon Ross - 6 Oct 1925-11 Sep 1929; Edna Harker Thomas - 11 Sep 1929-11 Dec 1933; Edith Hunter Lambert - 11 Dec 1933-31 Dec 1939.

3. **President**, May Green Hinckley - 1 Jan 1940-2 May 1943.

First Counselor, Adele Cannon Howells - 1 Jan 1940-2 May 1943.

Second Counselors, Janet Murdock Thompson - 1 Jan 1940-May 1942; LaVern Watts Parmley - May 1942-2 May 1943.

4. **President**, Adele Cannon Howells - 29 Jul 1943-14 Apr 1951.

First Counselor, LaVern Watts Parmley - 20 Jul 1943-14 Apr 1951.

Second Counselor, Dessie Grant Boyle - 20 Jul 1943-14 Apr 1951.

5. **President**, LaVern Watts Parmley - 16 May 1951-5 Oct 1974.

First Counselors, Arta Matthews Hale - 16 May 1951-6 Apr 1962; Leone Watson Doxey - 6 Apr 1962-23 Oct 1969; Lucile Cardon Reading - 8 Jan 1970-6 Aug 1970; Naomi Ward Randall - 4 Oct 1970-5 Oct 1974.

Second Counselors, Florence Holbrook Richards - 15 May 1951-11 Jun 1953; Leone Watson Doxey - 10 Sep 1953-6 Apr 1962; Eileen Robinson Dunyon - 6 Apr 1962-3 Jun 1963; Lucile Cardon Reading - 23 Jul 1963-8 Jan 1970; Florence

Reece Lane - 8 Jan 1970-5 Oct 1974.

6. **President**, Naomi Maxfield Shumway - 5 Oct 1974-5 Apr 1980.

First Counselors, Sarah Broadbent Paulsen - 5 Oct 1974-2 Apr 1977; Colleen Bushman Lemmon - 2 Apr 1977-5 Apr 1980.

Second Counselors, Colleen Bushman Lemmon - 5 Oct 1974-2 Apr 1977; Dorthea Christiansen Murdock - 2 Apr 1977-5 Apr 1980.

7. **President**, Dwan Jacobsen Young - 5 Apr 1980-2 Apr 1988.

First Counselor, Virginia Beesley Cannon - 5 Apr 1980-2 Apr 1988.

Second Counselor, Michaelene Packer Grassli - 5 Apr 1980-2 Apr 1988.

8. **President**, Michaelene Packer Grassli - 2 Apr 1988-1 Oct 1994.

First Counselor, Betty Jo Nelson Jepsen - 2 Apr 1988-1 Oct 1994.

Second Counselor, Ruth Broadbent Wright - 2 Apr 1988-1 Oct 1994.

9. **President**, Patricia P. Pinegar - 1 Oct 1994 - 2 Oct 1999.

First Counselor, Anne G. Wirthlin, 1 Oct 1994-2 Oct 199

Second Counselor, Susan L. Warner, 10 Oct 1994-2 Oct 1999.

YOUNG WOMEN

President Brigham Young organized the Young Ladies Department of the Cooperative Retrenchment Association —predecessor to the Young Women program —on the evening of Nov. 28, 1869, in the parlor of the Lion House in Salt Lake City. He encouraged his older daughters, who were the charter members, to"retrench in your dress, in your tables, in your speech, wherein you have been guilty of silly, extravagant speeches and light-mindedness of thought. Retrench in everything that is bad and worthless, and improve in everything that is good and beautiful."

Thus, the Retrenchment Association was organized. Relief Society Gen. Pres. Eliza R. Snow supervised the association; Ella Young Empey was named as president.

News of the organization spread quickly. By the end of 1870, retrenchment associations had been established in several Mormon settlements. In addition, the organization had divided into senior and junior associations.

Not long after the creation of the Young Men's Mutual Improvement Association in 1875, President Young approved a name change to "Young Ladies National Mutual Improvement Association" to correspond to the young men's organization. The two organizations began holding monthly meetings together. In 1904, the word "National" was dropped since the Young Ladies' organization had become international in scope. Throughout the early years of the association's existence, the YLNMIA was directed through local ward efforts. The first stake board was organized in 1878 in the Salt Lake Stake, antedating the appointment of a general board. In 1880, Elmina S. Taylor was called as the first general president. She called as her counselors Margaret (Maggie) Y. Taylor and Martha (Mattie) Horne, with Louie Wells as secretary and Fanny Y. Thatcher as treasurer. That same year, Pres. Taylor presided over the first general conference of the YLNMIA.

Under the new general presidency's direction, the association encouraged the study of gospel principles, development of individual talents, and service to those in need. General, stake, and ward boards were subsequently appointed, lesson manuals were produced, and joint activities were established with the YMMIA. The *Young Woman's Journal* was inaugurated 1889 and soon began printing a series of lessons.

In 1888, the first annual June Conference for young women and young men was held. Leaders provided special training in physical activity, story-telling, and music and class instruction.

Four decades later, in 1929, a new summer camping program was announced at June Conference, and the *Young Woman's Journal* and *The Improvement Era* merged with the November issue. During the 1930s, MIA leaders gave new emphasis to music, dance, and the performing arts, with an annual June Conference dance festival being held.

In the late 1940s and the 1950s, the First Presidency turned over to the YWMIA leaders a girls enrollment incentive program, previously administered by the Presiding Bishopric. It was designed to increase attendance at Church meetings.

In the early 1970s, President Harold B. Lee introduced a correlation program designed to integrate Church programs for youth. From this effort eventually came the Personal Progress program and the Young Womanhood Achievement Awards. During the 1980s, Sunday Young Women classes began meeting at the same time as priesthood meeting for Young Men.

During the tenure of general Pres. Ardeth G. Kapp, who served from 1984-1992, the Young Women motto, "Stand for Truth and Righteousness," was introduced, along with the Young Women logo, represented by a torch with the profile of the face of a young woman. The torch represents the light of Christ, inviting all to "come unto Christ." (D&C 20:59.)

During Pres. Kapp's administration, the Young Women theme and values were also introduced. The values are faith, divine nature, individual worth, knowledge, choice and accountability, good works, and integrity.

A memorable event for the program is the Young Women Worldwide Celebration, held every three years. In 1998, the theme for the celebration was "Turning Hearts to the Family." The celebration was three-fold: reading and studying "The Family: A Proclamation to the World," participating in activities that focus on or strengthen the family, and participating in a culminating activity in local units in November. As of the end of 1997, 548,996 young women ages 12 through 17 in 160 different countries were enrolled in the Young Women program as Beehives, Mia Maids, or Laurels.

Sources: *Encyclopedia of Mormonism*, vols. 3-4; *A Century of Sisterhood; History of the YWMIA*, by Marba C. Josephson; *Deseret News 1993-1994 Church Almanac; Church News*, Jan. 24, 1998, April 4, 1998.

YOUNG WOMEN GENERAL PRESIDENCY

(As of October 2000)

Carol B. Thomas
First Counselor

Margaret D. Nadauld
President

Sharon G. Larsen
Second Counselor

President — Margaret D. Nadauld, Oct 4, 1997-present. Born in Manti, Utah, to R. Morgan and Helen Bailey Dyreng; received bachelor's degree in secondary education in speech and English from BYU, attended Snow College in Ephraim, Utah; served on Relief Society general board, former ward Young Women president and counselor, ward Relief Society president and counselor, ward and stake Primary counselor, and teacher in the auxiliaries; taught English and speech in high schools in the Salt Lake Valley and in the Boston, Mass., area, was founding president of Management Women of Marriott School of Management at BYU; married Stephen D. Nadauld, parents of seven sons.

First Counselor — Carol Burdett Thomas, Oct. 4, 1997-present. Born in Salt Lake City to Karl and Gladys Jacob Burdett; attended the University of Utah; former member of Relief Society general board, stake Relief Society board, Primary president, stake Young Women president, and Relief Society counselor and teacher; married D. Ray Thomas, parents of seven children.

Second Counselor — Sharon Greene Larsen, Oct. 4, 1997-present. Born in Glenwood, Alberta, to Edwin (Ted) Kent and Julia (June) Leavitt Greene; received bachelor's degree in elementary education from BYU; former national vice president and president of Lamba Delta Sigma (women's Church sorority), former member of Young Women General Board and of the general Church writing committee, stake Relief Society president and counselor, stake Young Women president and counselor, ward Relief Society president and counselor, and gospel doctrine teacher; married Ralph T. Larsen, parents of two children.

HISTORICAL LISTING OF GENERAL PRESIDENCIES OF YOUNG WOMEN'S MUTUAL IMPROVEMENT ASSOCIATION AND YOUNG WOMEN

(Presidents pictured)

1. **President**, Elmina Shepherd Taylor - 19 Jun 1880-6 Dec 1904.

First Counselors, Margaret Young Taylor - 19 Jun 1880-1887; Maria Young Dougall - 1887-6 Dec 1904.

Second Counselor, Martha Horne Tingey - 19 Jun 1880-6 Dec 1904.

2. **President**, Martha Horne Tingey - 5 Apr 1905-28 Mar 1929.

First Counselor, Ruth May Fox - 5 Apr 1905-28 Mar 1929.

Second Counselors, Mae Taylor Nystrom - 5 Apr 1905-15 Jul 1923; Lucy Grant Cannon, 15 Jul 1923-28 Mar 1929.

3. **President**, Ruth May Fox - 28 Mar 1929-Oct 1937.

First Counselor, Lucy Grant Cannon - 28 Mar 1929-Oct 1937.

Second Counselor, Clarissa A. Beesley - 30 Mar 1929-Oct 1937.

4. **President**, Lucy Grant Cannon - Nov 1937-6 Apr 1948.

First Counselors, Helen Spencer Williams - Nov 1937-17 May 1944; Verna Wright Goddard - Jul 1944-6 Apr 1948.

Second Counselors, Verna Wright Goddard - Nov 1937-Jul 1944; Lucy T. Anderson - 6 Jul 1944-6 Apr 1948.

5. **President**, Bertha Stone Reeder - 6 Apr 1948-30 Sep 1961.

First Counselor, Emily Higgs Bennett - 13 Jun 1948-30 Sep 1961.

Second Counselor, LaRue Carr Longden - 13 Jun 1948-30 Sep 1961.

6. **President**, Florence Smith Jacobsen - 30 Sep 1961-9 Nov 1972.

First Counselor, Margaret R. Jackson - 30 Sep 1961-9 Nov 1972.

Second Counselor, Dorothy Porter Holt - 30 Sep 1961-9 Nov 1972.

AARONIC PRIESTHOOD MIA (YOUNG WOMEN)

7. **President**, Ruth Hardy Funk - 9 Nov 1972-23 Jun 1974.

First Counselor, Hortense Hogan Child - 9 Nov 1972-23 Jun 1974.

Second Counselor, Ardeth Greene Kapp - 9 Nov 1972-23 Jun 1974.

YOUNG WOMEN

8. **President**, Ruth Hardy Funk - 23 Jun 1974-12 Jul 1978.

First Counselor, Hortense Hogan Child - 23 Jun 1974-12 Jul 1978.

Second Counselor, Ardeth Greene Kapp - 23 Jun 1974-12 Jul 1978.

9. **President**, Elaine Anderson Cannon - 12 Jul 1978-7 Apr 1984.

First Counselor, Arlene Barlow Darger - 12 Jul 1978-7 Apr 1984.

Second Counselor, Norma Broadbent Smith - 12 Jul 1978-7 Apr 1984.

10. **President**, Ardeth Greene Kapp - 7 Apr 1984-4 Apr 1992.

First Counselors, Patricia Terry Holland - 11 May 1984-6 Apr 1986; Maurine Johnson Turley - 6 Apr 1986-4 Apr 1987; Jayne Broadbent Malan - 4 Apr 1987-4 Apr 1992.

Second Counselors, Maurine Johnson Turley - 11 May 1984-6 Apr 1986; Jayne Broadbent Malan - 6 Apr 1986-4 Apr 1987; Elaine Low Jack - 4 Apr 1987-31 Mar 1990; Janette Callister Hales - 31 Mar 1990-4 Apr 1992.

11. **President**, Janette Hales Beckham - 4 Apr 1992-4 Oct 1997.

First Counselor, Virginia Hinckley Pearce - 4 Apr 1992-4 Oct 1997.

Second Counselors, Patricia Peterson Pinegar - 4 Apr 1992-1 Oct 1994; Bonnie Dansie Parkin - 1 Oct 1994-5 Apr 1997; Carol Burdett Thomas - 5 Apr 1997-4 Oct 1997.

RELIEF SOCIETY

In 1842, a small group of women met at the home of Sarah M. Kimball in Nauvoo, Ill., to organize a sewing society to aid Nauvoo Temple workmen. They sought the endorsement of the Prophet Joseph Smith, who praised their efforts but said the Lord had something better in mind for them. It would be an organization under the priesthood after the pattern of the priesthood. He organized the Female Relief Society on March 17, 1842. The Prophet said that the restored Church could not be perfect or complete without it. He charged members with the responsibility to save souls and taught them principles of the gospel. The women elected Emma Smith as their president, and she selected two counselors.

From that original organization stemmed what is now the Relief Society, the official adult women's organization of the Church. Its motto, "Charity Never Faileth," states what has been the objective of society members from the first: to love and nurture one another and minister to the needs of Church members and others. The Female Relief Society of Nauvoo contributed to the Nauvoo Temple and supported moral reform. Members were primarily concerned with helping the poor. In July 1843, a visiting committee of four was appointed in each ward to assess needs and distribute necessities, the beginning of the visiting teaching effort that has been a part of Relief Society since then. By 1844, the society had 1,341 members. The Female Relief Society of Nauvoo ceased to function after March 1844 amid increasing tension and persecution.

Although women carried out charitable works and a few meetings were conducted at Winter Quarters, Neb., there was no formal Relief Society during the Saints' westward trek or for several years thereafter.

In February 1854, 16 women responded to an exhortation of President Brigham Young to form a society of females to make clothing for Indian women and children. This "Indian Relief Society" met until June 1854, when President Young encouraged such organizations in individual wards. Many remained organized to assist the poor within their wards and help provide clothing and bedding for destitute handcart companies. In 1866, President Young reorganized the Relief Society churchwide, appointing Eliza R. Snow to assist bishops in establishing the organization in each ward. By 1880, there was a local unit of the Relief Society in each of 300 wards, caring for the needy within its ward boundaries and using visiting teachers to collect and distribute donations. Ward Relief Societies managed their own finances and many built their own meeting halls. In line with the Church's move for self-sufficiency, the Relief Society sponsored cooperative economic enterprises in the late 1800s, such as making and marketing homemade goods, raising silk worms, storing grain, and financing the medical training of midwives and female doctors.

The Relief Society also promoted women's right to vote and helped organize and nurture the Young Ladies' Retrenchment Association (forerunner to the Young Women) and the Primary.

By the turn of the 20th century, needs of women were changing, and the format of lessons was adapted and standardized to meet the needs. The *Relief Society Magazine*, introduced in 1915, contained lessons for each month on theological, cultural, and homemaking topics. One week a month was spent on each topic, with time left over for charity projects and testimony bearing. The monthly format of rotating topics has remained since then, with the subject matter being varied.

Beginning in 1921, concern over high maternal and infant mortality led to the establishment of health clinics and two stake Relief Society maternity hospitals, one operated in the Snowflake (Arizona) Stake and another in the Cottonwood (Utah) Stake. In 1944, visiting teachers ceased collecting charitable funds.

In 1956, the Relief Society Building in Salt Lake City, built from contributions from LDS women and funds from the Church, was dedicated. Today, the building houses the general offices of the Relief Society, Young Women, and Primary organizations.

After September 1971, all LDS women were automatically included as members of the Relief Society, rather than paying dues.

In the latter 20th Century, Relief Society has become more fully coordinated under the larger Church structure. Reporting and financing systems, magazine and lesson materials, and social services became the responsibility of priesthood leaders and Church departments.

The ward Relief Society president, under the direction of the bishop, has been responsible since 1921 for assessing needs and distributing relief to the needy. Ward Relief Society presidents supervise other charitable work such as caring for the sick, called "compassionate service" to distinguish it from "welfare service."

The Relief Society has promoted scholarly study of women's concerns by helping establish the Women's Research Center at BYU, has rallied members to contribute to the Monument to Women at Nauvoo, Ill., in 1978, and has celebrated its sesquicentennial in 1992. One aspect of this was starting a worldwide effort to improve literacy. The purpose of the Church's Gospel Literacy Effort, implemented in January 1993, was two-fold: to teach basic gospel literacy skills for those who cannot read or write, and to encourage Church members to study the gospel and improve themselves and their families throughout their lives.

On Jan. 1, 1998, a significant modification to the curriculum and gospel study program for the Melchizedek Priesthood and Relief Society went into effect. The new curriculum provided a similar meeting and instruction schedule for both organizations, and, according to a June 1, 1997, letter from the First Presidency, "will allow the opportunity for improved gospel learning in Sunday services and family settings as all adult members study and discuss the same instructional materials."

Under the new curriculum, Relief Society and Melchizedek Priesthood personal study guides are no longer used. Members now follow a common parallel study pattern. On the first Sundays of each month, the purposes of Melchizedek Priesthood and Relief Society are discussed. On second and third Sundays, members study the teachings of presidents of the Church. On the fourth Sundays, lessons or discussions focus on teachings relating to current issues. On the occasional fifth Sunday, topics of local concern are discussed or lessons missed due to stake, regional, or general conferences can be made up. Members of the two organizations continue to meet separately, except on the fifth Sundays when local concerns are discussed.

A declaration reaffirming the roles of Relief Society and the values of women was announced during the General Relief Society Meeting on Sept. 25, 1999, and what had been known as the Relief Society homemaking meeting was renamed "Home, Family, and Personal Enrichment Meeting" with a different focus.

Sources: *Encyclopedia of Mormonism*; *Women of Covenant: The Story of Relief Society*, by Jill Mulvay Derr, Janath Russell Cannon, and Maureen Ursenbach Beecher, Deseret Book, 1992; *Church News*, Jan. 30, 1993; "Strengthening the Work of Melchizedek Priesthood Quorums and Relief Society," by Julie A. Dockstader, *Church News*, Nov. 1, 1997; *Church News*, Oct. 1, 1999.

RELIEF SOCIETY GENERAL PRESIDENCY

(As of October 2000)

Virginia U. Jensen
First Counselor

Mary Ellen W. Smoot
President

Sheri L. Dew
Second Counselor

President — Mary Ellen Wood Smoot, April 5, 1997-present. Born to Melvin and LaVora Smith Wood in Ogden, Utah; attended Utah State University; former director of Church Hosting with husband, Stanley M. Smoot, from 1993 to 1997; served with husband when he presided over the Ohio Columbus and Ohio Akron missions; former member of editorial board of *The Friend* magazine, Relief Society president, and member of the Church Curriculum Writing Committee; she and her husband are the parents of seven children.

First Counselor— Virginia Urry Jensen, April 5, 1997-present. Born to Francis L. and Virginia Carroll Urry in Salt Lake City; attended the University of Utah; serving as director of Church Building Hosting at time of call to the Relief Society general presidency; former counselor in ward Relief Society, Young Women, and Primary presidencies, served on stake boards of those auxiliaries, former Relief Society, Young Women, and Primary teacher, activities committee member; married J. Rees Jensen, parents of four children.

Second Counselor — Sheri L. Dew, April 5, 1997-present. Born to Charles and JoAnn Petersen Dew in Ulysses, Kan.; received bachelor of arts degree from BYU, attended BYU Graduate School; former Relief Society general board member, stake Relief Society president, counselor in stake Relief Society presidency, ward Relief Society president; vice president of publishing, Deseret Book Co., previously director of publishing and associate editor, Deseret Book Co., editor and associate publisher, *This People* magazine, and assistant editor for Bookcraft.

HISTORICAL LISTING OF GENERAL PRESIDENCIES OF THE RELIEF SOCIETY

(Presidents pictured)

1. **President**, Emma Hale Smith - 17 Mar 1842-16 Mar 1844.

First Counselor, Sarah Marietta Kingsley Cleveland - 17 Mar 1842-16 Mar 1844.

Second Counselor, Elizabeth Ann Smith Whitney - 17 Mar 1842-16 Mar 1844.

2. **President**, Eliza Rocxey Snow - 1866-5 Dec 1887.

First Counselor, Zina Diantha Huntington Young - 19 Jun 1880-8 Apr 1888.

Second Counselor, Elizabeth Ann Smith Whitney - 19 Jun 1880-15 Feb 1882.

3. **President**, Zina Diantha Huntington Young - 8 Apr 1888-28 Aug 1901.

First Counselor, Jane Snyder Richards - 11 Oct 1888-10 Nov 1901.

Second Counselor, Bathsheba Wilson Smith - 11 Oct 1888-10 Nov 1901.

4. **President**, Bathsheba Wilson Smith - 10 Nov 1901-20 Sep 1910.

First Counselor, Annie Taylor Hyde - 10 Nov 1901-2 Mar 1909.

Second Counselor, Ida Smoot Dusenberry, 10 Nov 1901-20 Sep 1910.

5. **President**, Emmeline Woodward B. Wells - 3 Oct 1910-2 Apr 1921.

First Counselor, Clarissa Smith Williams - 3 Oct 1910-2 Apr 1921.

Second Counselor, Julina Lambson Smith - 3 Oct 1910-2 Apr 1921.

6. **President**, Clarissa Smith Williams - 2 Apr 1921-7 Oct 1928.

First Counselor, Jennie Brimhall Knight - 2 Apr 1921-7 Oct 1928.

Second Counselor, Louise Yates Robison - 2 Apr 1921-7 Oct 1928.

7. **President**, Louise Yates Robison - 7 Oct 1928-Dec 1939.

First Counselor, Amy Brown Lyman - 7 Oct 1928-Dec 1939.

Second Counselors, Julia Alleman Child - 7 Oct 1928-23 Jan 1935; Kate Montgomery Barker - 3 Apr 1935-31 Dec 1939.

8. **President**, Amy Brown Lyman - 1 Jan 1940-6 Apr 1945.

First Counselor, Marcia Knowlton Howells - Apr 1940-6 Apr 1945.

Second Counselors, Donna Durrant Sorensen, Apr 1940-12 Oct 1942; Belle Smith Spafford, 12 Oct 1942-6 Apr 1945.

9. **President**, Belle Smith Spafford - 6 Apr 1945-3 Oct 1974.

First Counselor, Marianne Clark Sharp - 6 Apr 1945-3 Oct 1974.

Second Counselor, Gertrude Ryberg Garff - 6 Apr 1945-30 Sep 1947; Velma Nebeker Simonsen - 3 Oct 1947-17 Dec 1956; Helen Woodruff Anderson - Jan 1957-Aug 1958; Louise Wallace Madsen - Aug 1958-3 Oct 1974.

10. **President**, Barbara Bradshaw Smith - 3 Oct 1974-7 Apr 1984.

First Counselors, Janath Russell Cannon - 3 Oct 1974-28 Nov 1978; Marian Richards Boyer - 28 Nov 1978-7 Apr 1984.

Second Counselors, Marian Richards Boyer - 3 Oct 1974-28 Nov 1978; Shirley Wilkes Thomas - 28 Nov 1978-24 Jun 1983; Ann Stoddard Reese, 1 Oct 1983-7 Apr 1984.

11. **President**, Barbara Woodhead Winder - 7 Apr 1984-31 Mar 1990.

First Counselor, Joy Frewin Evans - 21 May 1984-31 Mar 1990.

Second Counselor, Joanne Bushman Doxey - 21 May 1984-31 Mar 1990.

12. **President**, Elaine Low Jack - 31 Mar 1990-5 Apr 1997.

First Counselor, Chieko Nishimura Okazaki - 31 Mar 1990-5 Apr 1997.

Second Counselor, Aileen Hales Clyde - 31 Mar 1990-5 Apr 1997.

PROGRESS DURING ADMINISTRATIONS OF THE PRESIDENTS

	At beginning				At end			
	Stakes	Members*	Missions	Temples	Stakes	Members*	missions	Temples
JOSEPH SMITH, 1830-1844	0	280	0	0	2	26,146	3	1
BRIGHAM YOUNG, 1847-1877	2	34,694	4	2	20	115,065	9	3
JOHN TAYLOR, 1880-1887	23	133,628	10	3	31	173,029	13	4
WILFORD WOODRUFF , 1889-1898	32	180,294	13	5	40	267,251	20	6
LORENZO SNOW , 1898-1901	40	267,251	20	6	50	292,931	21	6
JOSEPH F. SMITH, 1901-1918	50	292,931	21	6	75	495,962	22	6
HEBER J. GRANT, 1918-1945	75	495,962	22	6	149	954,004	38	9
GEORGE ALBERT SMITH, 1945-51	149	954,004	38	9	184	1,111,314	43	10
DAVID O. MC KAY, 1951-70	184	1,111,314	43	10	500	2,807,456	89	15
JOSEPH FIELDING SMITH, 1970-72	500	2,807,456	89	15	581	3,218,908	99	17
HAROLD B. LEE, 1972-73	581	3,218,908	99	17	630	3,306,658	109	17
SPENCER W. KIMBALL , 1973-85	630	3,306,658	109	17	1,570	5,920,000	187	38
EZRA TAFT BENSON, 1985-94	1,570	5,920,000	187	38	1,980	8,688,511	295	47
HOWARD W. HUNTER, 1994-95	1,980	8,689,619	295	47	2,029	9,025,914	303	49
						October 2000		
GORDON B. HINCKLEY, 1995 -	2,029	9,025,914	303	49	2,497	11,000,000	333	100

*** Nearest year-end total**

TOTAL MISSIONARIES

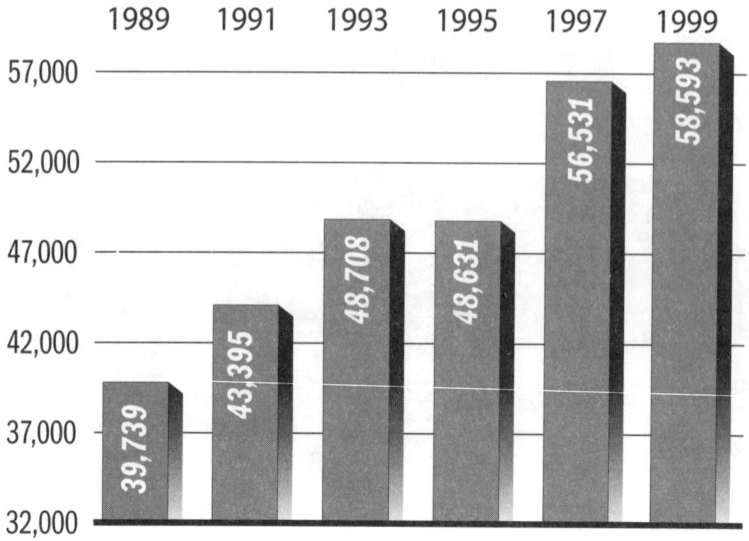

TOTAL MEMBERSHIP

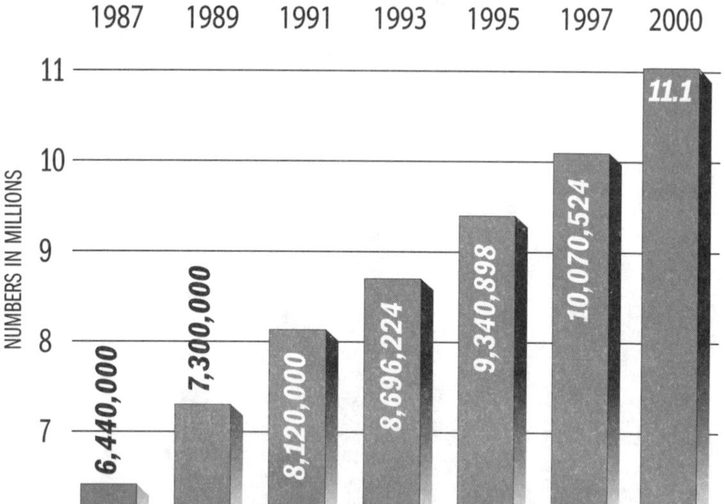

VIEWS OF NAUVOO

NAUVOO — THE CITY OF JOSEPH

President Gordon B. Hinckley's announcement that the Nauvoo Temple will be rebuilt has led to the culminating project following a long effort by the Church and individuals to restore this once-impressive city. The information in this section provides a broad overview of this pivotal period of Church history.

Pre-LDS period

The first whites in the area of Commerce were European explorers. Such well-known figures as Hernando DeSoto, Jacques Marquette, Louis Joliet, and Rene-Robert LaSalle explored the region in the 16th and 17th centuries as a part of a major European effort to explore North America. (From "Commerce," by Donald Q. Cannon, in *Historical Atlas of Mormonism.)*

1800: Sac and Fox Indians lived in the area, which they called Quashquema.

1805:-1819: The first known settler in what is now Nauvoo was Denis Julian.

1818: Illinois is granted statehood.

1819: Rufus Easton of St. Louis uses a license from the U.S. government to teach agriculture to the Sac and Fox Indians. His log house was at or near what is now called the Joseph Smith Homestead.

1824: Treaty with Fox and Sac Indians — they ceded their rights of settlement and hunting to the United States. The tribe then crossed the river to Iowa.

In April, James White and his family settled in the area, and are regarded as the first Anglo settlers.

1829: Hancock County organized.

Venus post office was established at the Nauvoo site.

The Nauvoo Peninsula was located at the head of the Des Moines Rapids, which stretched southward 12 miles to Keokuk, Iowa.

1830: More people began living in the region of the peninsula, which was named "Venus."

1834: Commerce City was founded and various lots and blocks were available to be bought and sold. The entire peninsula was known as Commerce, and the two, Commerce City and Commerce, were distinct entities.

1838: About 350 people had migrated to the peninsula. The region boasted a justice of the peace and a small cemetery. Houses of wood and stone had been erected as well as stores and a tavern (inn). The inhabitants of the peninsula roughly equalled in number the size of the neighboring hamlets of Carthage and Warsaw. It was the largest center of population in Hancock County.

1839: Commerce City remained a mostly paper town as no lots were ever actually sold.

Enhanced image of temple provides most detailed view available. Some questions about the details, however, likely will never be resolved.

The LDS Period

1838-39: Latter-day Saints in the northern part of the state of Missouri are expelled and find refuge in Illinois and what would later become Iowa.

1839: Through the exploration of Israel Barlow in southern Iowa, Joseph Smith learns that lands "at the head of the rapids" in Illinois and across the river in Iowa Territory are available for purchase and concludes these regions should be the main places to gather.

1839: As the Church or its members have little hard money, they have scanty means to purchase properties. However, several arrange to exchange property owned by them in Missouri to the sellers, who accepted the properties in payment. It is not known if the sellers ever collected on the other properties. Joseph Smith and the Church assumed the debt and tried for years to liquidate it. Missionaries are sent to Mormons and non-Mormons in the East and South asking them to exchange their properties and many do so.

1839: The Church makes four purchases of land at the "head of the rapids" in Illinois, totalling nearly 660 acres.

April, 1839: Joseph Smith and his family arrive in what is now Nauvoo in the spring. His home and large yard served as a place for many incoming

Gary Smith painting portrays building effort as temple nears completion.

*"This noble edifice is progressing with great rapidity; strenuous exertions are being made on every hand to facilitate its erection, and materials of all kinds are in a great state of forwardness, and by next fall we expect to see the building enclosed; if not the top stone raised with "shouting of grace—grace unto it." There have been frequently, during the winter, as many as one hundred hands quarrying rock, while at the same time multitudes of others have been engaged in hauling, and in other kinds of labor.... Never since the formation of this church was laid, have we seen manifested a greater willingness to comply with the requisitions of Jehovah;... than there has been since the Lord said, "Let the Temple be built by the tithing of my people." It seemed as though the spirit of enterprise, philanthropy, and obedience rested simultaneously upon young and old; and brethren and sisters, boys and girls, and even strangers, who were not in the church, united with an unprecedented liberality in the accomplishment of this great work; nor could the widow, in many instances, be prevented, out of her scanty pittance, from throwing in her two mites." (*Times and Seasons, *May 2, 1842.)*

saints to live in tents or wagons until more substantial housing could be obtained.

1840: Nauvoo was not immune from the sicknesses that often raged throughout the Mississippi River Valley. Nauvoo sexton records indicate that the children were the chief victims. Deaths by cholera, malaria and even measles were very common.

1840: Nauvoo was basically a wooden town — log cabins, log houses and frame houses to be seen everywhere. But soon brick yards were established. Some brick homes, barns and other out buildings were constructed. An average sized home was 16 by 16 feet square. Dogs, pigs, chickens, flies and mosquitoes roamed at will.

Population jumped to more than 3,000, with citizens coming from every state in the union and Great Britain. Generally, one-third were from Great Britain.

Aug. 14, 1840: Joseph Smith, speaking at the funeral of Seymour Brunson, taught for the first time the doctrine of baptism for the dead.

October 1840: The general conference passed a resolution to begin the construction of a temple at Nauvoo. William Weeks, a self-taught builder, became the architect. Within 10 days, two limestone quarries were located, one in the northwest portion of the city and the other somewhere south of the city. The temple was to be built on land donated by a non-Mormon pre-Nauvoo resident, Daniel H. Wells. As the saints left for the West in 1846, he would join the Church and go with them on the western migration.

December 1840: The Illinois General Assembly passed the Nauvoo Charter, creating Nauvoo, one of five cities in Illinois. The city was an area of roughly six square miles.

Jan. 19, 1841: Joseph Smith received Section 124 of the Doctrine and Covenants, revealing the purpose of temple work.

April 6, 1841: Cornerstones were laid in a grand ceremony.

Construction continued steadily

In the mid-1840s, Nauvoo was a prospering city. By 1847, the city was deserted.
(From *United States Illustrated*, Courtesy Utah State Historical Society.)

Brigham Young Home, in photo taken by B.H. Roberts in 1886, was constructed following the start of brickmaking in Nauvoo.

with limestone rocks blasted from quarry and hauled to temple site by wagon. Workers were obtained as members tithed their time, giving one day in 10 for temple construction. Women provided food and clothing for the workers and also donated precious heirlooms and and coins to fund the construction. Eventual total cost of the building was $750,000.

August 1841: The ten districts that were created earlier in the city to supply workers for the temple were organized into ecclesiastical wards, presided over by bishops, whose main responsibility was welfare.

Nov. 8, 1841: Temporary baptismal font in basement of temple was dedicated. Nov. 21 ordinance work began and 40 people were baptized for their kindred dead.

March 17, 1842: The Relief Society was organized on the second floor of Joseph Smith's Red Brick Store on Water Street. The sisters then joined with the bishops in helping the poor and sick within the city.

Spring, 1842: There were nearly 3,000 people living within the city limits. Many other LDS families, however, lived outside the city both nearby and far away.

The LDS Period, cont.

Aug. 4, 1842: The first rafts carrying high quality wood from Church-operated sawmills in the Black River area of Wisconsin arrived for the temple project.

Oct. 30, 1842: The first official meeting was held in the unfinished temple.

1843: Life continued in a routine of hard work during the week and worship on Sunday. Sunday meetings were really general meetings for the entire community lasting about two hours each, one held in the morning and one held in the evening. They were held in open air groves, one of which was west of the temple, another a few blocks east of the temple.

May-June, 1843: Revelations on celestial marriage were received.

Spring, 1844: They made plans to explore the West, where Latter-day Saints could settle and preach to the Indians.

March and April, 1844: Joseph Smith conferred the keys of temple work upon the Twelve Apostles.

Spring, 1844: The people of Nauvoo nominated Joseph Smith to run for president of the United States and he accepted.

June 27, 1844: Joseph and Hyrum Smith were martyred by a mob in nearby Carthage, Ill.

Aug. 8, 1844: In the grove east of the temple, Brigham Young and the Twelve were sustained to lead the Church.

1845: Population of Nauvoo reached 15,000.

Agriculture played a major role in the economic life of the city, with every family tending at least a household garden. Some cooperated in farming outside the city. Still others owned large farms on the prairie, where they raised wheat, oats, rye, and potatoes. Livestock included cattle, sheep and hogs. More than one-third of the male inhabitants of Nauvoo were farmers, while another third were stonemasons, bricklayers, locksmiths and shoemakers, etc.

Ed Maryon painting of Nauvoo in the 1840s depicts its pastoral possibilities.

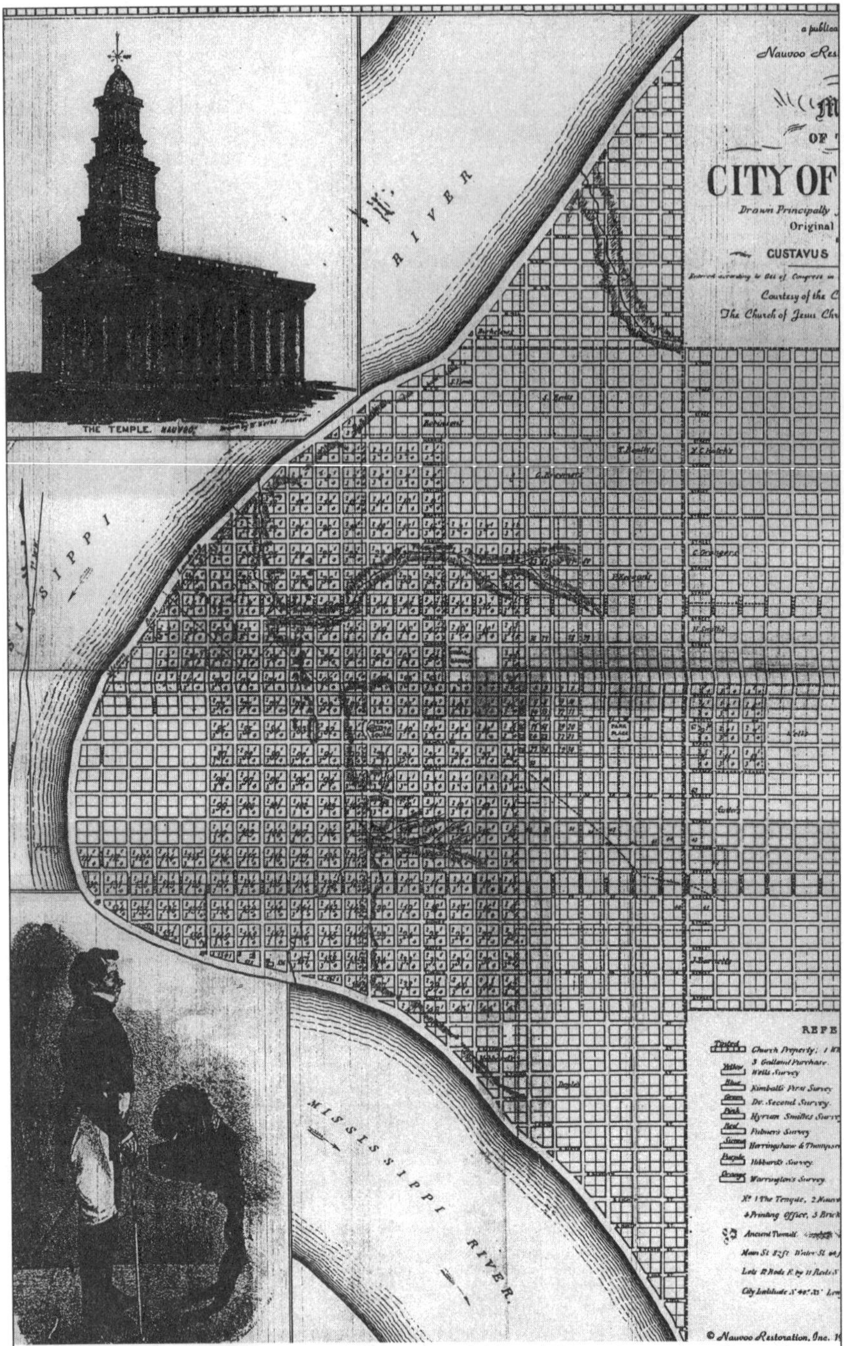

Nauvoo City plat, which did not use previous plats of the same area, allowed room for expected growth.

Exodus of Mormons across the frozen Mississippi River during the winter of 1846 is portrayed by pioneer artist C.C. A. Christensen.

May 24, 1845: Capstone was placed on the Nauvoo Temple.

Sept. 22, 1845: A meeting of antagonists was held in Quincy, Ill., 60 miles to the south, resulting in orders for the Latter-day Saints to leave Nauvoo by the following spring.

Winter of 1845-46: Members tried to sell their homes to get funds to go west. Nauvoo became a city of wagon builders: homes were turned to shops where wagon covers were sewn, wheelwrights worked in several locations and wagonmakers worked long into the night. They planned to leave as soon as "green grass would grow and water would flow."

Nov. 30, 1845: Attic story of the temple was dedicated for endowment work.

Dec. 10, 1845: First full endowment in the Nauvoo Temple given.

December 1845: Gov. Thomas Ford sent a letter suggesting that the U.S. government might not let the Saints go west. As a result, Brigham Young gathered about 1,000 individuals to go west in February of that year. It was a very bitter and snowy

Information for this section was provided by James L. KImball Jr., *Historical Atlas of Mormonism*, edited by S.Kent Brown, Donald Q. Cannon and Richard H. Jackson, *Nauvoo the City of Joseph*, by David E. Miller and Della S. Miller, *Nauvoo the Beautiful,* by E. Cecil McGavin, *Rediscovery of the Nauvoo Temple*, by Virginia S. Harrington and J.C. Harrington and extensive Deseret News files.

Rare daguerreotypes of temple are top, by Louis Rice Chaffin; left, a Mr. Scoville, and right, L.R. Foster.

Mansion House, pictured before the turn of the 20th century, has been restored.

winter, and it took three weeks for this number to cross the Mississippi River, which had frozen.

February-June 1846: After the first group left voluntarily, many others wanted to travel with Brigham Young. Between February and June most of the Mormons who wanted to go west left the city.

May 1, 1846: The temple was dedicated by Orson Hyde and Wilford Woodruff. During the short period of service in the temple, 5,595 endowments were given.

September 1846: The poor and sick who could not leave the city remained behind. At this time a mob came in and the Battle of Nauvoo ensued. Several shots were fired on each side. Some Latter-day Saints were killed and it was at this time that the remaining Saints were forced from Nauvoo.

POST-LDS PERIOD

Sketch by John Schroeder on 1859 map of Hancock County shows city when occupied by French Icarian and German-Swiss residents.

Icarian period: A brief experiment in communal living

Oct. 9, 1848: Arson-caused fire destroyed temple's interior.

March 1849: Etienne Cabet, head of a group of French socialists know as Icarians, brought his group from Texas where they had tried to form a communal society. They moved into the ready-made city, reaching a population of 1,200 at most. They purchased the temple, which had been partially destroyed by fire, and began rebuilding it.

May 27, 1850: A tornado knocked down the walls. The temple stones were used for other buildings around the city.

1856: Dissension split up the Icarians and they moved out in groups. In a few years, the Icarians were gone.

Early 1860s: A group of German settlers took over the city and established a thriving wine industry.

1865: Nauvoo City Council ordered the remaining wall of the Nauvoo Temple taken down

1884: LDS historian B. H. Roberts found the city "withering under a blight from which it cannot recover."

1905: Nearly a hundred members of the Church held a two-day conference. One, Lorin Farr, 86, had helped build the city. He found citizens eager to have the earlier residents return.

Wilford Wood, Bryant S. Hinckley, and J. LeRoy

Wilford Woodruff home, photographed in the late 1800s, was built in1844-46, after he returned in 1841 from a successful mission in England.

Originally intended to be a hotel, Nauvoo House, pictured in 1886, was where bodies of slain Joseph and Hyrum Smith were, for a time, buried in basement.

Kimball would help bring that about.

February 1937: Acting for the Church, Wilford Wood purchased the Nauvoo Temple site for $900.

1938: Bryant S. Hinckley wrote that Nauvoo would rise again and "Annually thousands . . . will visit it."

1954: Dr. J. LeRoy Kimball began first restoration efforts on the home of his great-grandfather, Heber C. Kimball. He envisioned a restored Nauvoo, "a Williamsburg of the Midwest."

1962: The Church founded Nauvoo Restoration Inc., and appointed Dr. Kimball as president to restore the historical importance of the city.

1962-2000: More than a thousand acres have been brought to a park-like appearance with more than two dozen historic buildings restored.

April 4, 1999: President Gordon B. Hinckley, the son of Bryant S. Hinckley, announced plans to rebuild the Nauvoo Temple on its original footprint.

Oct. 24, 1999: More than 5,000 people attended as President Hinckley broke ground for rebuilding the Nauvoo Illinois Temple.

VISITOR'S DESCRIPTION OF NAUVOO TEMPLE

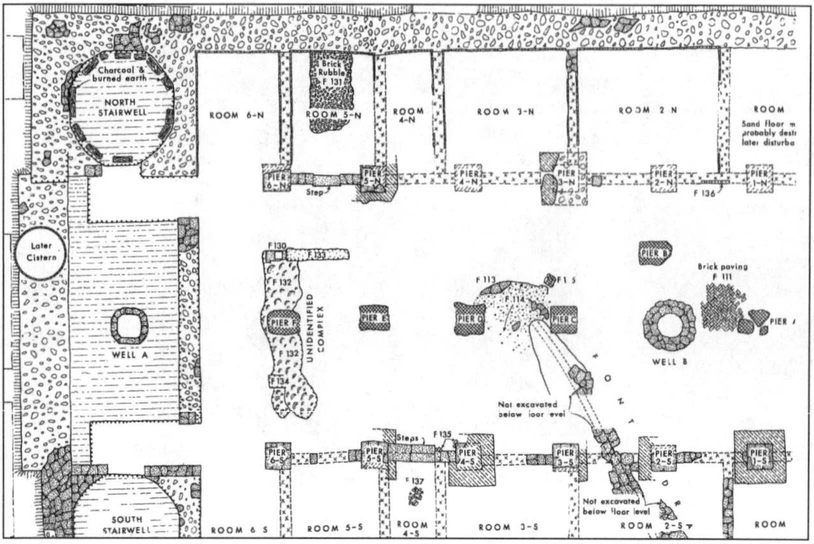

Floor plan of Nauvoo Temple was uncovered during excavation in the 1960s; sketch is from *Rediscovery of the Nauvoo Temple*, by Virginia S. Harrington and J.C. Harrington

The spire of the Nauvoo Temple towered 165 high, dominating the landscape for miles around and was immediately famed up and down the Mississippi River.

Description of the deserted Nauvoo Temple, published in the *Palmyra Courier-Journal* Sept. 22, 1847:

"It is nearly a mile from the landing, the most conspicuous, in fact the only conspicuous object in the city. It is built of white lime-stone. The front is ornamented with sunken square columns of no particular style of architecture, having capitals representing half a man's head. . . . On all sides of the temple are similar columns with similar capitals; the base of each column is heavy, but in good proportion and of a fanciful design, which it would be difficult to describe. There is a basement with small windows. Ten steps lead to the front and only one entrance to the main building. Three arches enable you to enter a sort of vestibule, from which, by doors, you enter the grand hall, and at the sides are the entries to the staircases, to ascend to the upper apartments.

"The front of the temple is apparently three stories high, and is surmounted by an octagonal tower or steeple, which itself is three stories, with a dome and having on four sides a clock next below on the dome. There is a line of circular windows over the arched entrance, ornamented with carved work between each.

Detailed rendering shows how front of Nauvoo Temple may have appeared. However, architectural drawings were not always followed.

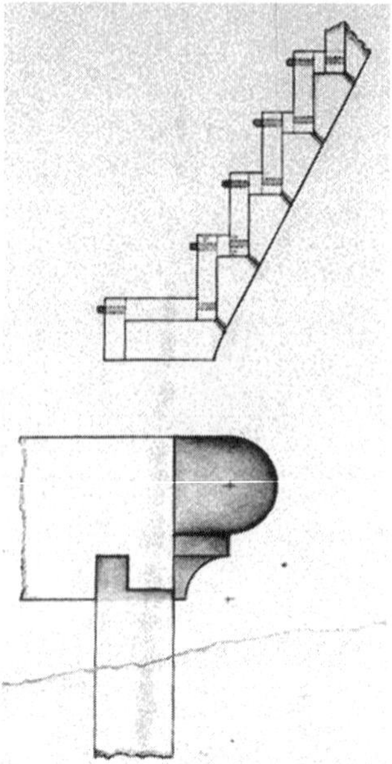

Steps were morticed.

and over that again a line of square entablature, on which is cut the following inscription:

THE HOUSE OF THE LORD
built by THE CHURCH OF JESUS CHRIST OF
LATTER DAY SAINTS
commenced April 6, 1841
HOLINESS TO THE LORD

"A similar entablature is on the front of the interior vestibule, over the doors of the entrance with the same enscription. The letters are gilt. . . .

"We were then taken to the very top of the building, and enjoyed there, for some time, a view of the surrounding country. . . . Coming down, we were ushered into the Council Chamber, which is in a large low room, lighted by one large half circle window at the end and several small sky-lights in the roof. On each side are six ante-chambers, said to have been intended for twelve priests, councilors or elders . . . . The chamber itself is devoid of ornament, and I was unable to ascertain whether it was

Above, pillar tops carried representation of sun; right, sunstone has been restored.

intended to have any, or if it should have been completed.

"In the entry on each side of the door to the Council Chamber, is a room the wardrobe, where the priests were to keep their dresses. On one side was a room intended for a pantry, showing that the priests did not mean to go supperless to bed. Under the Council Chamber was another large hall, with seven windows on each side, and four at the farther end.

"On the lower floor was the grand hall for the assemblage and worship of the people. Over the window at the end was inscribed in gilded capital letters: THE LORD HAS BEHELD OUR SACRIFICE: COME AFTER. This was in a circular line corresponding to the circle of the ceiling. Seats are provided in this hall for the accommodation of thirty-five hundred people, as they are arranged with backs, which are fitted to the seats as in a modern railroad car, so as to allow the spectator to sit and look in either direction, east or west. At the east and west end are raised platforms, composed of a series of pulpits on steps one above another. The fronts of these pulpits are semi-circular and are inscribed

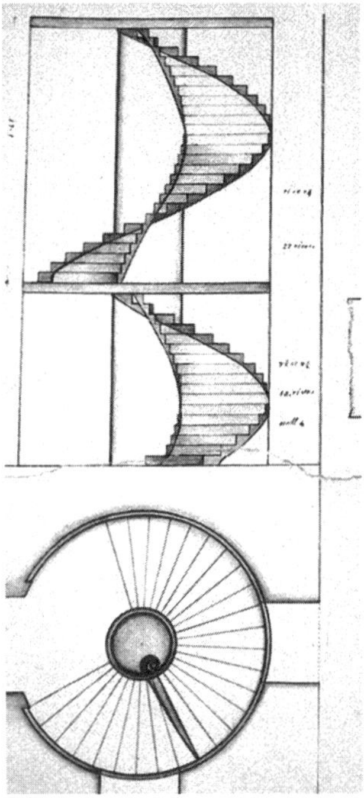

Drawing detail stairways.

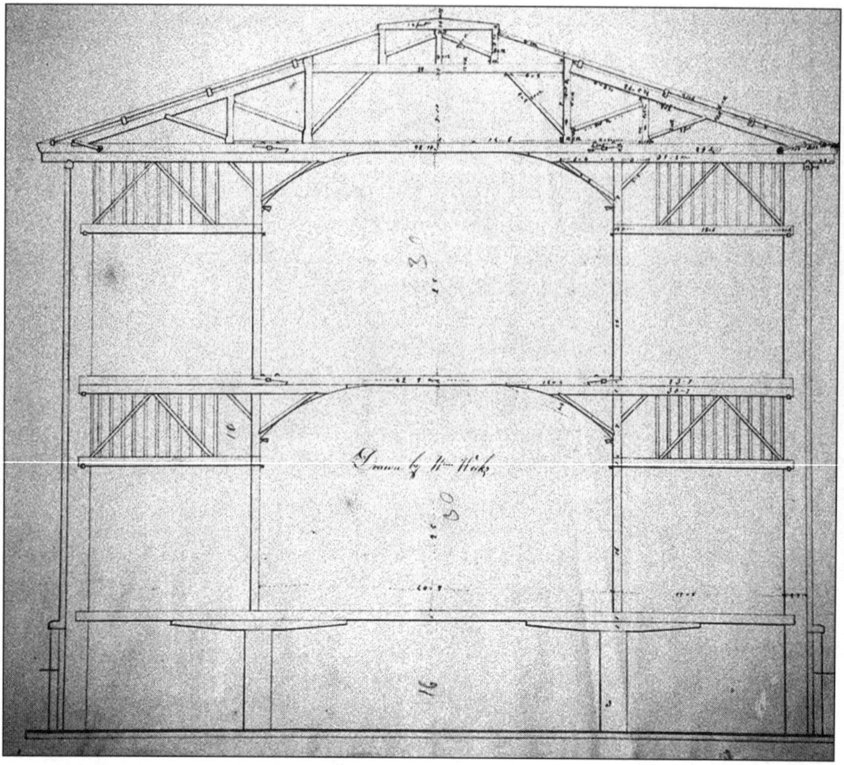

Drawings of details of Nauvoo Temple show high level of craftsmanship that was employed in building the edifice.

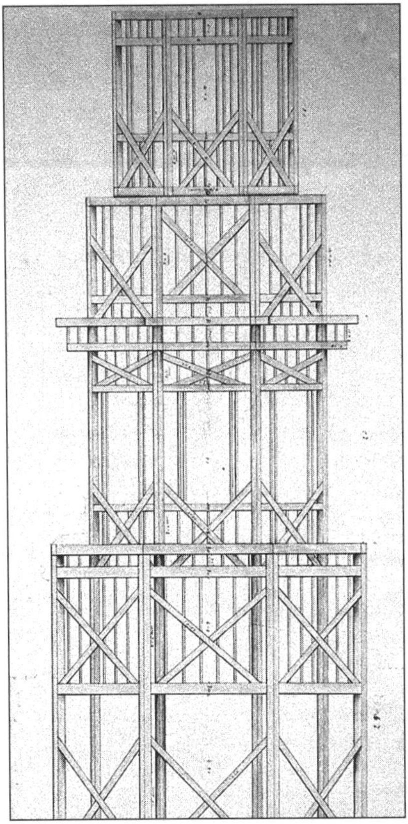

Carefully designed tower rose three stories above imposing temple, immediately dominating the area as a landmark.

in gilded letters on the west side, PAP, PPQ, PTQ, meaning we are informed the uppermost one President of the Aaronic Priesthood; the second, President of the Priests Quorum; the third, President of the Teachers Quorum; and the fourth and lowest, President of the Deacons Quorum. On the east side are pulpits are marked PHP, PSR, PHQ, and the knowledge of our guide was no better than ours as to what these symbolic letters were for. [President of the High Priesthood, President of the Seventies, President of the High Priests Quorum.]

"We next descend to the basement, where is the far-celebrated font. It is in fact the cellar of the building. The font is of white lime-stone, of an oval shape, twelve by sixteen feet in size on the inside and about four and a half feet deep. It is very plain and rests on the back of twelve stone oxen or cows, which stand immersed to their knees in earth. It has two flights of steps, with iron banisters, by which you enter and go out of the font, one at the east end, and the other at the west end. The oxen have tin horns and tin ears, but are otherwise of stone, and a stone drapery hangs like a curtain down from the front, so as to prevent exposure of all back of the forelegs of the beasts." (The *Palmyra Courier-Journal*, Sept. 22, 1847, from *Nauvoo the Beautiful*, by E. Cecil McGavin, 1946.)

Arsonist's confession of burning Nauvoo Temple

By Robert Aveson

Editor's note: The subject of this narrative told this account many times and took some satisfaction in doing so. The reader is advised to consider whether or not it has been thus embellished.

The following article, under the heading "Burning of the Nauvoo Temple," was taken from the *Fort Madison (Iowa) Democrat* many years ago. I herewith reproduce it from my scrapbook.

George H. Rudsill, now of Bowling Green, Florida, but once a Ft. Madison boy, tells of the destruction of the Nauvoo Temple: "Mr. Agnew was in failing health at the time he came to me. He told me that he was going to die soon, which I thought was true. I asked him if he had repented of his wrongdoings and he smiled and said: 'Yes, all but one thing.' I asked what that was and he said it was the burning of the Nauvoo Temple. Says I: Did you do that? And he said: 'Yes, I did it with my own hands. Sit down and I will tell you about it,' which is as follows, as near as I can give it in his own words:

"The reason why I burned it was that there was a continual report in circulation that the Mormons were coming back to Nauvoo and we were afraid they might take it into their heads to do so, and as we had had all the trouble with them we wanted, Judge Sharp of Carthage, Hyrum McCauley of Appanooce, and myself of Pontoosue, determined the destruction of their Temple and by so doing they would not be able ever again to try and come back.

"So on the afternoon of the night that the Temple was burned, in order to make arrangements we three met on the prairie five miles south of Fort Madison, in Illinois, the judge coming from Carthage, the squire from Appanooce, and I from Pentoosue, and we met about where the Mormon Church stood, five miles south of Appanooce, and there we pledged ourselves to destroy the Temple if it cost us our lives. . . . We decided to get the steward to show us through the Temple, and then watch our chance to get in our work. So we hid our horses in the bushes. . .a mile from town and walked in. We looked about town until 4 o'clock in the afternoon, and in the meantime had prepared a bundle of kindling by taking a corn sack and cutting arm holes in it so I could put it on like a coat under my coat. I then stuck in as many tarred rags on sticks as I could carry without being noticed. I then put it on and secured some matches from a store to light my pipe and we were ready. We had but little trouble to find the steward and after laboring with him some time he at last consented to show us through the Temple. We claimed to be strangers in the country and were going away that night and it would be out last chance perhaps of ever having an opportunity to visit the Temple. So on these conditions he would oblige us. . . . So after a good deal of delay the key was at last inserted, it not seeming to fit, but at last the door swung open. We went in with a rush and kept a going, the man being left behind working with the door. He called out for us to stop but we kept on going and I noticed that he left the door with the key in it.

"I stepped back in a side room, and the other two kept on. The man ran on after them, and after he had passed me, I went back to the door and unlocked it and put the key in my pocket and then ran after them. By this time the man had discovered that I was missing, but when I came up to them and explained that I had stopped to look at the crucifixion he seemed to be satisfied but looked suspicious at me, and from that time on he kept close to my side and would not allow us to stop but walked us right on around and out. It was getting dusk and we had no chance for me to light my fire and I saw that it was telling on my companions that they were bitterly disappointed when we were compelled to walk out. I told them to come on in haste, that we were late and would miss our boat that we were going on. So they came along and we stopped behind a house, where I told them what I had done, which made them two of the happiest fellows I ever saw. We had to watch but a few minutes until we saw the steward start away on a run and we knew he was going for a key or someone, and this was our chance, so leaving the judge and squire on guard, I ran back to the Temple.

"I started for the top which I soon gained and found a good place to start my fire where it would get a good start before it would shed any light and be seen from the outside. After seeing it start to success I began to retrace my steps with joy and a light heart, for I was sure that the Temple was as good as burned, with a

"The flames which shot up to the sky. . . threw a lurid glare into the surrounding darkness. Great volumes of smoke and flame burst from the windows, and the crash of the falling timbers was distinctly heard on the opposite side of the river."

Painting courtesy BYU

Pioneer artist C.C.A. Christensen painting depicts destruction of Nauvoo Temple.

chance for me to burn with it, for I had lost my way and did not know which way to turn to get out, although I had been through the Temple a number of times before. I had thought if I would succeed at last in getting out, that I would be sure to get caught by the steward, for he would soon be back and in all probability would have help with him, for I was certain that he would lay the missing key to us. You can imagine my feeling, being left in the burning Temple, and in case I did escape the fire I was sure of an arrest. I ran first one way, then the other, in hopes of gaining some passage that I would know so as to find my way out, but all to no purpose. I was getting worse lost all the time, and I could not tell one direction from another, for it was as dark as an Egyptian night. At last I came to the stairway going up and I took it with the hope that it would lead me back to where I had started the fire and I could then take a new start. After going up two pairs of stairs and through many halls I came to a square turn and a light shone way down the passage in the opposite direction from what I wanted to go, but I thought it best to go and see what it was or who it was, and I soon discovered that it was my fire which was burning at a fearful rate, sending its fiery tongue clear across the hall.

"I drew as near as I could and I happened to see Squire McCauley's bandana handkerchief lying on the floor a short distance from the fire on the opposite side of me. So I knew that my way led through the fire as that room was the end of our trip. Now what was I to do? I knew no other way but through the fire. I became horror stricken. Was I to be burned up by my own hands? O God what shall I do? Not knowing as it were what I did, I threw my coat over my head and made a dive through that hell of fire, striking my full length on the floor and I rolled over and over until I got out of the reach of the fire. When I got to my feet I took off my coat and extinguished the fire that caught in the lining, after which I put it on again. With difficulty I tried to run, for I seriously hurt my arm and one of my legs from my fall on the floor, but was so excited at the time that I did not realize the pain until afterwards. With the assistance of a few matches I had, that I now thought of, I kept striking them along the way, and at last reached the door that I had been going through and found it standing open. The squire had come and thrown it open in hopes I might be able to see a star from without.

"They were satisfied that something had happened on account of my delay. You can imagine our feelings when I stepped through the door. I pulled the door to and locked it and ran away in an easterly direction, the judge and squire following. I was sore, lame and burned and almost choked, not being able to speak and when I came to a well about one hundred yards away, I drank and threw the key down the well. I then told the boys to scatter and to the horses, which they did. They got there long before I did for I was almost beyond going at all. After reaching the horses I told them the job was done and for them to go different directions and get home as soon as possible and avoid meeting anyone. They objected to leaving me as they were afraid I was hurt internally, which I was fearful was the case. I had inhaled the fire and thought my time had come. I told them to go that I would pull through all right. So the squire took the river road up the river to Appanooce ten miles distant; the judge took the road to Carthage, about sixteen miles distant to the south; while I took the prairie road in the direction of Pontoosue, twelve miles distant.

"After going about one-half mile, I looked toward Nauvoo and I saw a flickering light and the next minute flames burst through the roof and lit up the country for miles as light as day. I put my horse into a dead run in the direction of the Missouri timber, which I gained in time without being seen, as the people on the road were all in bed, but I had no sooner jumped my horse over a fence into a field and secreted myself behind some bushes, when along came seven horsemen on their way to the fire, which had by this time been discovered twenty miles around. After they had passed again, I tried to mount my horse, but found it impossible and found my leg had swollen so that I could not walk. I was in a fix, sure enough. What to do I did not know, but I had to do something, so I got down on my hands and knees and crawled on toward a cluster of trees, leading my horse. When I arrived at the timber I fortunately found a large tree which had been cut down, leaving a high stump; crawling upon this stump I managed to get on the back of my horse, and went back, jumping my horse over the fence back into the road.

"I was suffering so terribly that I could but just cling to my saddle. I turned my horse in the direction of Squire McCauley's cabin, where I arrived just before daybreak, and found that the squire had got home nearly two hours before. He was surprised to be called out by me, but after giving him to understand my condition, he cried like a child. He took me in and hid me away for a week, where he and his wife cared for me, as they would for one of their own, until I was able to go about without suspicion. . . .'

"So after nearly fifty years the true history of the burning of the great Mormon Temple is made known. The narrator of this story, as told by Mr. Agnew, was a small boy at the time of the burning of the Temple, living with his mother just west of Ft. Madison, Iowa, and he recollects seeing the light from the burning building on that memorable night. Over twenty years after the destruction of the Temple I became intimately acquainted with all the parties connected with this narrative." — George H. Rudsill, Bowling Green Florida.

(A few years after the burning of the Temple, Elders George A. Smith and Erastus Snow visited Nauvoo, and from Lewis A. Bidamon, landlord of the Nauvoo Mansion, were told that the inhabitants of several of the surrounding settlements — previous to the burning of the sacred edifice — were jealous of Nauvoo, and fearing it would continue to retain its superior influence as a town, and the Mormons be induced to return, they contributed a purse of $500 which they gave to this man Joseph Agnew to perform the diabolical act, and that he was the wretch who set fire to the building. Mr. Bidamon told the brethren that the burning of the Temple did certainly have the effect of diminishing the importance of Nauvoo, for his hotel did not have one-fourth the custom after the burning as it had before the destruction of that magnificent structure.) From "Temples of the Most High," by N. B. Lundwall.

Contemporary sketch shows Nauvoo Temple in 1850 after destructive tornado.

Tornado stops Icarian reconstruction

In 1849, the ruins were purchased by a French group known as the Icarians, whose philosophy and beliefs were based on communal living. They were led by Etienne Cabet, who had first attempted unsuccessfully to found a colony in Texas. After some delay they started work on the temple ruins in the spring of 1850, with the plan of converting the basement area to communal kitchens and dining rooms. They had only made a start on their work before another disaster, a tornado, struck the temple on May 27. Emile Valley describes it:

"The masons began to lay the foundation to rest the columns or pilasters to support the floors. . . At 3 o'clock p.m. a distant report of thunder announced the approach of a storm. At their request I stepped out to ascertain whether it was a severe storm or not. Seeing only an insignificant cloud, I reported no danger. We continued to work. The basement of said temple was divided into small rooms one either side. Two of these rooms had been covered with boards. One on the north side to store green hides. The other on the south side to store tools. Suddenly a furious wind began to blow; four of the masons fearing the nonsolidity of the walls, left to seek shelter elsewhere. Seven of us remained, taking refuge in the tool room on the south side. If there is a Providence it was on our side, for hardly had we taken our position than the tornado began to tear small rocks from the top of the walls and flew in every direction. We became frightened. Some proposed to run away, others opposed it on the ground that it was dangerous, as those loose rocks could fall on our heads and kill us. Before we had decided whether we should stay or run, one of them that was watching exclaimed: 'Friends we are lost, the north wall is caving in!' And so it was. A wall sixty feet high was coming on us, having only forty feet to expand. We fled to the southwest corner, deafened with terror. (History of the Experiment at Nauvoo of the Icarian Settlement, *The Nauvoo Rustler*, Nauvoo, Illinois, n.d., pp. 8-9.)

In addition to toppling the north wall, the tornado did such damage to the east and south walls that they were shortly pulled down as a safety precaution, and the Icarians transferred their efforts to the ground outside. They built a school building of temple stone that is still standing, and several frame apartments on the temple block.

For the next fifteen years the ruined west front stood picturesquely, still considered worthy of note by visitors. Two artists' sketches and a tintype date from this period, and they show the massive masonry remains and the fallen blocks and rubble where the rest of the building had stood. During this time extensive stone salvaging went on, for use in local buildings. Finally the weakened ruin was demolished and the site filled in and leveled. *The Carthage Republican* on February 2, 1865, reported:

"The last remaining vestage (sic) of what the famous Mormon temple was in its former glory has disappeared, and nothing now remains to mark its site but heaps of broken stone and rubbish. The south-west corner, which has braved the blasts of ten or fifteen winters — towering in sad grandeur above the surrounding buildings — a marked object for many miles, the shrine of the pilgrimage of thousands who have annually flocked to gaze in wonder and awe upon the beautiful ruin, — is no more. The eye of the stranger and traveller who approach the classic city of Nauvoo will no more rest upon the towering ruin that first gives notice of their proximity to the sacred soil, where once tread the hurrying feet of thousands of the 'Lord's anointed.'

"The old ruin has been in process of demolition at times during the past winter. One day last week a mine was placed beneath the remaining portion yet standing; and with the blast that followed the last of the famous Mormon temple lay prone and broken in the dust. We understand that the stone, much of which is uninjured, has been sold to parties who contemplate building residences and wine cellars. The facial and other decorations surrounding the columns are reserved by the proprietor, Mr. Dornseiff. Of the large number of decorations, stone carvings, &c., with which the temple was beautified, hundreds have been secured by curiosity seekers in all parts of the country; and numbers have even gone to Europe." (*Carthage Republican*, Feb. 2, 1865, from *Rediscovery of the Nauvoo Temple*.)

In 1886, B.H. Roberts photographed Nauvoo Post Office, once the Icarian House, that was built of stones from Nauvoo Temple

Details from the past provide a blueprint for the future

By Carrie A. Moore / Deseret News religion editor

Like detectives working a major crime scene, they're piecing all the bits of evidence together, sorting through mountains of paperwork and rubble in search of the tiniest clues.

And in the process, the architects, sculptors and engineers charged with reconstructing the Nauvoo LDS Temple are rediscovering much about the dedication of their pioneer forefathers — and their own determination to restore a rich legacy of faith and 19th century craftsmanship.

The challenge is as daunting as it is unusual.

Robert Dewey, former construction manager for the Nauvoo Temple, said when President Gordon B. Hinckley announced in April 1999 that the temple would be rebuilt, "the temple construction department had already prepared some preliminary drawings showing how it could be restored to function like a modern-day temple, but we didn't know we were going to get serious about it until he announced it."

At that point, there were no solid plans, leaving those charged with rebuilding it in a quandary about how they would restore the temple as it was originally. Dewey said they quickly assembled a committee of church members with historical interest and background on the temple to provide suggestions.

"Then we had people calling us with little bits of information, coming up with books now out of print" that provided clues. The accounts by researchers like Don Colvin, who did his master's thesis on the temple, were combined with journal accounts written by the builders themselves, describing what they experienced.

"Once we had that assembled, we started putting the puzzle together," Dewey said. Using bits and pieces of evidence gleaned from hundreds of journal accounts, diaries, letters, archaeological excavations and even a construction materials roster kept by the original builders, architect Roger Jackson, a principal at FFKR Architects in Salt Lake City, has spent the past eight

Worker points to bricks of temple basement floor during 1968 excavation of site.

months deeply immersed in research on how to re-create details of a building that was rarely photographed.

"There is no known photograph on one whole side of the temple," Dewey explained, "and the available photos show only the building's exterior."

Even so, Jackson said the photos that do exist have been invaluable. With vastly enlarged copies of the originals, Jackson and his team are using computer imaging to sketch out intricate architectural plans for 21st century accouterments that weren't even thought of in the 1840s: lighting plans, plumbing fixtures, electrical circuitry, electronic audio and video capacity, heating and cooling.

There were some descriptions of the interior of the building," Jackson says. "As much as we can tell, the inside was very much like" the first temple constructed by Latter-day Saints under the direction of church founder Joseph Smith in Kirtland, Ohio.

Miraculously, Jackson does have the

Aerial photo of temple site before reconstruction looks toward Mississippi River.

original architectural drawings done by William Weeks. (See pages 133-137.)

Dewey said the drawings were retrieved for the church in 1948, when two missionaries knocked at the door of a man who turned out to be the grandson of William Weeks. When he showed them the drawings and offered them, "the missionaries knew what they had, and they (the plans) wound up in the Church archives."

Some 20-30 early sketches including "a framing diagram here, molding details, the corner of a stair section," are part of the cache of original documents that now undergird the project.

As Jackson and his team of 14 work feverishly to finish the plans and drawings, construction is already under way in Nauvoo, making the temple a unique "design-build" project — where builders begin before the plans are entirely finished. While builders plan to reconstruct the temple as much like the original as possible, they are using modern methods and reinforced concrete to make it earthquake and water resistant.

Ron Prince, construction project manager in Nauvoo, said the temple is resting on 67 concrete and steel caissons. Placed at various depths, they range from 2 to 5 feet in diameter and are placed anywhere from 10 to 26 feet deep to rest on limestone bedrock. Originally constructed entirely of limestone, the walls for the new temple will also be of reinforced steel with a thick limestone veneer. Because limestone from the original quarry is not available, Prince visited quarries all over the Midwest and into the Great Lakes region to find stone of the same color, quality and texture as the original. Several stone cutters have been employed fashioning not only the limestone blocks but the same sun-, moon- and star-stones that graced the original temple's exterior.

The unique carvings were one feature that set the building apart from contemporaries of its day and have become a source of fascination for many who know something of the temple, its history and symbolism. Yet for all their mystique, they, too, have had to be reconstructed in exacting detail. They were among the first of the original temple's components to be dismantled and either carried away or defaced and destroyed by vandals, according to researchers who have studied the building's history.

Sculptor and design artist LaVar Wallgren and his partner, James Dell Morris, have researched both the exterior stones and the oxen that support the temple's baptismal font to create patterns of the originals that will be used by the stone-carving craftsmen. The moon stone and star stone were easier to create patterns for because the remains of the originals were mostly intact. The sunstones and the oxen have presented a greater challenge, Wallgren said. Two original sunstones have survived, one of them housed in the Smithsonian, but both have been substantially damaged.

"The church museum had some segments of the stone, and we had photos to work from, but there was no common denominator between the different stones and the different information we had. It was very difficult to use some of the information because it didn't correspond with some of the actual stone fragments."

With the sunstone, "we had to literally recreate this whole pattern from what information we could use and make it acceptable to the architect," he said. Sized to scale and made of fiberglass, the patterns for the exterior stones were crated and shipped to the selected stone quarry. "They'll put them in a big machine and laser scan them to where over 60 percent of the stone can be removed by machine. Then the stone carvers will come in and finish them," Wallgren said.

The pattern for the oxen is still being refined, he said. It was constructed using only four small fragments of stone from the original oxen, coupled with written accounts of what they looked like and enhanced using diagrams of muscle structure and a plethora of photos taken of two bullock oxen at This Is The Place State Park.

The diagrams and photos line one wall above the workbench, where Wallgren has also fashioned removable horn and ear patterns with joint pieces that slip snugly into place, allowing the carvers more flexibility while carving the actual head. Once the horns and ears are carved separately and slipped into place, the joints will be filled with ground-up stone.

When finished, Wallgren said, the twelve oxen will be placed around the oval-shaped baptismal font 18.5 feet long and 12.5 feet wide, to be located in the basement of the structure on the original site.

While the font's placement and other major structural components, such as the circular staircase, are part of the original architectural plans, reconstructing other interior components has posed major challenges, in part because so little is known about the furnishings or interior decor of the building. Newspaper accounts from the mid-1800s describing the building were detailed, but conflicting reports have provided more questions than answers in some cases, Jackson said.

"Newspapers from the east would send these reporters to what was then the wild frontier. The printed versions of it (describing the interior) are all conflicted. There are some puzzles that we've just taken our best educated stab at what they might have been. The frightening part is that some day someone may find things were different based on data they find then that we don't have now."

Another part of the challenge is that the original builders — all relatively new converts with little material wealth— purchased building supplies piecemeal, as they could raise the money to do so. "Window glass, nails and iron pieces were all purchased as they progressed in building, and we have a very careful record of those." The detail comes out of five large rolls of microfilm containing records from construction materials the builders kept. But large items seem to be omitted from the record, Jackson said. "We've been looking for big things that would jump out," but so far, there haven't been any."

A detailed scouring of that record and the accompanying research to find original suppliers would take more than two years to complete — time the architect just doesn't have as walls begin to take shape back in Nauvoo.

Not only are the details missing, but Jackson must now incorporate fixtures and design work into the building that weren't there originally but that would fit well within the Nauvoo period. His biggest challenge is the lighting.

"We're looking at things like light fixtures before there was (electric) light, so we're trying to find things that are close or would at least look close. They had very little light back then. Remember, they were reading by candlelight or a small oil lamp, sometimes in a very large room. Modern man today can't stand those kinds of light levels," and the temple requires an industry standard of lighting in addition to unique lighting levels needed for various rooms in the structure.

"Most of their meetings were held during the day in large assembly rooms with large windows," much like the Kirtland temple looks today. "We're trying to meet the modern requirements within a historically sized and scaled fixture."

Jackson said he has found no evidence of murals or other wall decor in the original temple, and that most of the interior adornment of large public buildings in the Midwest at that time involved "painted woodwork" much like now exists in the St. George temple.

"Millwork details and trim pieces are listed" in written accounts of the interior, "but not in the same terms we would use today. There's so much of it that we don't know."

Another challenge involves electrical outlets and switches, which didn't exist in the original building. Jackson said the design involves disguising outlets in the baseboards around the floor. Unlike modern temples which are carpeted throughout, much of the flooring itself will be oak to match the original. Laid over a concrete floor, the oak will be covered with the same types of rugs that existed during the period, he said.

Plumbing and duct work are also being designed for a building that didn't have them originally. In most areas it can be hidden, he said, but some of the smaller spaces that existed in the original temple had ceilings only 8 feet high, and duct work in such areas would make them even smaller. "So we have to shoehorn all that in."

While the original had large assembly rooms with canvas dividers, the new temple must incorporate smaller ordinance rooms into the design as well. Prince said the temple's celestial room "goes up through two floors."

Other design features have been added to make the building a functioning modern temple, Jackson said, though most components will be as close to the original as possible.

Even the glass for the windows "will be the same" quality and texture as the original, Prince said. The handmade panes are coming from a company in France that's been in business for more than 300 years. "It will have a beautiful shimmering effect as the light hits it," Prince said.

Landscaping around the original building was believed to be virtually nonexistent, Jackson said. "If anything, I think it would have just been swept dirt. They may have tried to plant some native grass, but it wouldn't have been the bluegrass that we love so much."

Jackson said the new building will feature "probably somewhat formal gardens not unlike what the church is already doing at Temple Square."

While much of the material and labor going into the project are funded by the church, the reconstruction is so emotionally tied to the history of the early church that many church members have sought to donate materials and labor to the project, Prince said.

Stan and Mary Hemphill are working in Nauvoo as church service missionaries, coordinating the volunteer goods and services.

"We've had a number of volunteers ... come forward from the time President Hinckley announced the building of the temple," Elder Hemphill said. "This is the first time volunteers have been used in construction of a temple since the Nauvoo temple was originally built."

Skilled craftsmen in all the major building trades are submitting resumes and offering their own time to participate in the project, he said. Each funds his own transportation, food and housing costs, in addition to a physical exam and personal insurance. The volunteers indicate the dates of their availability, and the Hemphills coordinate with the construction managers to schedule them at the appropriate times.

Offers of material donations are screened to insure that the donors "are financially able so we don't bankrupt anybody." They are also screened for quality. "Temple quality is the best you can get, and that's what's going into this building. The people donating materials understand that."

While bids are still being accepted for many of the materials, offers to donate all the carpeting and the labor to install it have been made. "We've also had people offer to donate doors, and another group that says they'll donate all the hardware for the outside doors."

One man has even offered to donate a portion of the roofing materials, plus the labor to install it and a warranty to go with it, Elder Hemphill said. Another has offered all the bark that will be used in the landscaping.

Steve Weber, LDS institute director in Bellevue, Wash., who has worked for 22 years as a contractor and carpenter building homes on the side, is now working as a volunteer at the temple. He left a wife and six sons in Seattle to spend eight weeks in Nauvoo, working on concrete pours by day and sleeping in his tent at a local RV park by night.

His enthusiasm and dedication to the work parallel that of the architects, engineers and designers as they take inspiration from the pioneers of the past in rebuilding what they consider to be a house of God.

Like many of his co-workers — both employees and volunteers — Weber says the project will always be a highlight of his life. "This is very poignant and personal for me." (From *Deseret News*, July 2, 2000.)

Painting "Nauvoo the Beautiful" by Chad Hawkins foretells appearance of rebuilt temple when it is completed.

An imaginative look into the next century

What will the new century and new millennium bring for the Church? Because the progress of the last two decades of the19th Century had such a profound impact on the 20th Century, and the progress of the last two decades of the 20th Century promises an equally significant impact on the 21st Century, it is interesting to look at what the 21st century might bring. Accordingly, the *Deseret News Church Almanac 2001-2002* looks at how the Church might grow and how technology may affect the Church.

Of course, no one really knows. In fact, the hard, cold reality of time's inevitable passage will eventually prove all guessers wrong.

Population projections by sociologist Rodney Stark, University of Washington, published in September of 1984 and updated in 1996, suggest dramatic growth for the Church. In his initial study, Stark suggests that the Church is on its way to becoming a new world religion.

"I shall attempt to demonstrate that The Church of Jesus Christ of Latter-day Saints, the Mormons, will soon achieve a worldwide following comparable to that of Islam, Buddhism, Christianity, Hinduism and other dominant world faiths," he wrote.

"From the beginning the Mormons have excelled in missionary effort — during the first decade of existence they managed to send 597 missionaries, some of them overseas. As a result, by 1837, they had 600 members in Britain. The early success of Mormon foreign missionaries has long been overlooked outside the Mormon community because until well into the 20th century Mormon converts gained abroad were raised on coming to the United States. That prevented the buildup of local congregations and also came to hamper recruitment as converts departed for America before their network ties in the old country could be fully exploited. The Mormon congregations abroad today, especially in Europe, are of relatively recent origins and do not adequately reflect the 19th century response to the Mormon message. . . .

"Mormon missionaries are not paid professionals. Rather each is a young volunteer who pays his (and more frequently today, her) own expenses. The Church pays only the cost of transportation to a mission assignment and back. All other costs needed to serve as a full-time missionary for two years are supplied by the missionary's family, by money saved before going on a mission, or a bank loan. All young Mormon men of good moral standing are encouraged to go on their mission, and today about 40 percent actually do. This has several consequences. First, it provides a steady supply of young, talented, eager missionaries — the best of each generation. Second, converts also tend to be young and talented, since people are most effective in sharing their faith with people like themselves. Third, the missionary experience has immense socialization benefits for the young missionaries and enables the Mormons to rely on a volunteer, unpaid, missionary effort on a scale that would otherwise be inconceivable. The Mormons have nearly as many missionaries in the field as do all the Protestant bodies of North America combined.

"The pattern of growth is not only rapid but since World War II, the rate has been accelerating. For each of the past three decades growth has exceeded 50 percent.

"One reason for Mormon growth is that their fertility is sufficiently high to offset both mortality and defection. But a more important reason is a rapid rate of conversion. Indeed, the majority of Mormons today were not born in the faith, but were converted to it.. . .

"Today [in 1984] there are more than 5 million Mormons on earth. How many will there be in the near future? Projections require assumption. If growth during the next century is like the past, the Mormons will become a major world faith. If, for example, we assume they will grow by 30 percent per decade, then in 2080 there will more than 60 million Mormons. But, since World War II, the Mormon growth rate has been far higher than 30 percent per decade. If we set the rate at 60 percent, then in 2080 there will be 265 million Mormons.

Admittedly, straight-line projections are risky: they assume the future will be like the past. There is no way to be sure that Mormon growth won't suddenly begin to decline. But it would be wise to keep in mind that back in 1880, scholars would have ridiculed anyone who used a straight-line projection to predict that the 160,000 Mormons of that year would number more than 5 million a century hence. But that is now history."

*Stark's Table 1

Actual growth rates and percentage by decade

Year	**Membership**	**% of increase**
1830	62	-
1840	30,000	-
1850	60,000	100
1860	80,000	33
1870	110,000	38
1880	160,000	45
1890	205,000	28
1900	268,331	31
1910	393,437	47
1920	526,032	34
1930	672,488	28
1940	862,664	28
1950	1,111,314	29
1960	1,693,180	52
1970	2,930,810	73
1980	4,638,000	58
1990*	7,761,179	67
2000*	11,300,000	46

* updated

Projected Growth Rates at 30% and 50%

	30%	50 %
1990*	6,029,000	6,957,000
2000	7,837,700	10,435,500
2010	10,189,010	15,653,250
2020	13,245,713	23,479,875
2030	17,219,427	35,219,813
2040	22,385,255	52,829,719
2050	29,100,831	79,244,579
2060	37,831,080	118,866,868
2070	49,180,404	178,300,302
2080	63,934,525	267,450,453
2090	83,114,882	401,175,679
2100	108,049,347	601,763,518

*Projected in 1985

Stark's Table 2, Comparing Projected and Actual Rates of Mormon Growth, 1981-1995

Year	High Estimate	Low estimate	Actual
1981	4,830,000	4,761,000	4,920,000
1982	5,030,000	4,888,000	5,161,000
1983	5,238,000	5,018,000	5,385,000
1984	5,445,000	5,151,000	5,641,000
1985	5,680,000	5,288,000	5,911,000
1986	5,915,000	5,429,000	6,167,000
1987	6,160,000	5,573,000	6,400,000
1988	6,415,000	5,721,000	6,721,000
1989	6,681,000	5,973,000	7,308,000
1990	6,957,000	6,029,000	7,761,000
1991	7,245,000	6,190,000	8,090,000
1992	7,545,000	6,354,000	8,404,000
1993	7,857,000	6,523,000	8,689,000
1994	8,182,000	6,697,000	9,024,000
1995	8,521,000	6,875,000	9,439,000
1996*	8,873,600	7,057,700	9,692,441
1997*	9,240,800	7,245,300	10,071,783
1998*	9,623,200	7,437,900	10,354,24
1999*	10,021,400	7,635.600	10,752,986
2000*	10,436,100	7,838,600	**11,100,000

* updated * *Estimated

In December of 1996, Stark re-visited his projections of 12 years earlier, with the following observations:

"Since that essay appeared, the projections have, from time to time, attracted considerable media attention," he wrote in Review of Religious Research, Vol. 38, No. 2, p.175. "Sometimes this has been prompted by Mormon authorities who, understandably, take considerable satisfaction from my numbers. Some attention has been prompted by Mormon bashers seeking to alarm the world against the impending Mormon takeover. Thankfully, most reporters were simply seeking confirmation of rapid growth."

After looking at the impact of various social conditions, such as war and depression, on the growth rate, he observed:

"In my judgment, these data show two things. First, major environmental disturbances did influence Mormon growth. Secondly, the impact was quite limited — even after 40 years of war and depression the projected number of Mormons wasn't that much in error. The fact is that straight-line projections will be accurate unless or until something basic changes in the process involved. That is unless there is a really dramatic shift in the basis on which current growth rests, the past does reveal the future.

"In all comparisons, the actual rate is substantially higher than the high projection. . . . Granted, there are 85 more years to go, but so far, so good."

PROJECTED GROWTH TO 2050

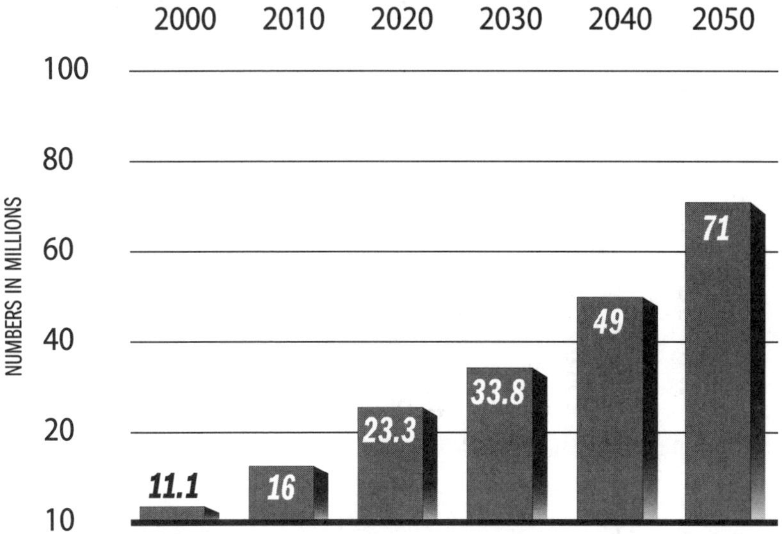

CHURCH ALMANAC PROJECTIONS

Projected Church growth compared with projected world growth

Straight line projections shown as a percentage

	2000	2010	2020	2030	2040	2050
**World census in billions*	*6.08*	*6.82*	*7.52*	*8.14*	*8.67*	*9.10*
		Church pop. in millions				
Almanac projected	11.1	16.0	23.3	33.8	49.0	71
% of world pop.	.18	.23	.31	.41	.56	.77
Stark projected. (low)	11.1	7.8	13.2	17.2	22.4	29.1
% of world pop.	-	.11	.17	.21	.26	.31
Stark projected. (high)	11.1	16.7	23.4	35.1	52.8	78.9
% of world pop.	-	.24	.31	.43	.61	.86

WORLWIDE CHURCH

Above, various designs of temples, and chart below illustrate the phenomena that the year 2000 was in temple building.

TEMPLES DEDICATED

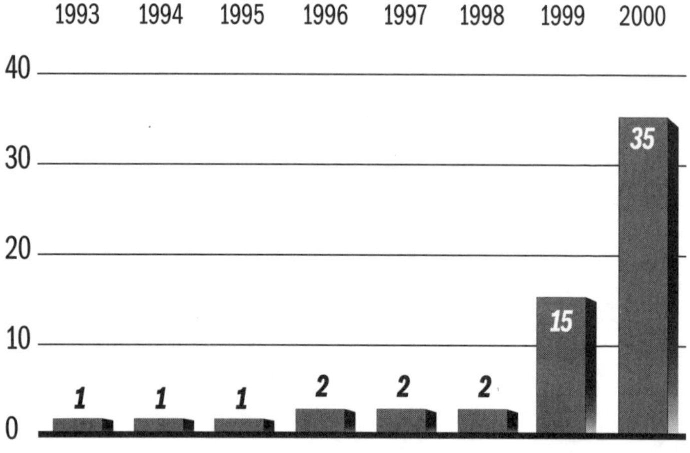

Africa West Area:
Membership, 81,962; Stakes, 20; Wards, 136; Missions, 6; Districts, 24; Branches, 194; Temples , 2 announced; Headquarters, Accra, Ghana.

Africa West Area

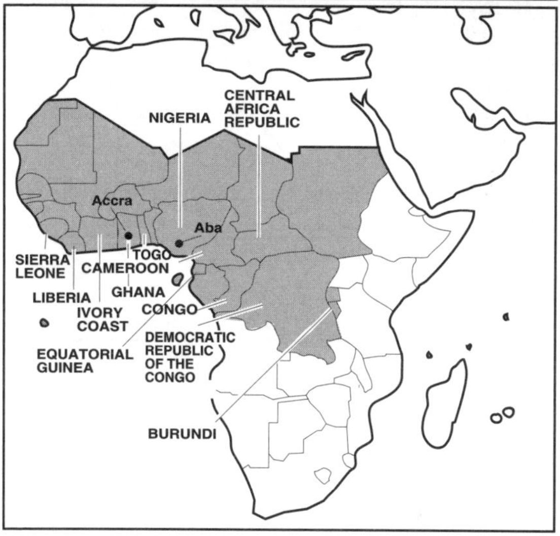

Africa Southeast Area:
Membership, 50,780; Stakes, 10; Wards, 52; Missions, 6; Districts, 9; Branches, 131; Temples, 1; Headquarters, Lonehill, South Africa.

Africa Southeast Area

Asia North Area

Asia North Area: Membership, 182,153; Stakes, 47; Wards, 275; Missions, 13; Districts, 27; Branches, 221; Temples, 3; Headquarters, Tokyo, Japan.

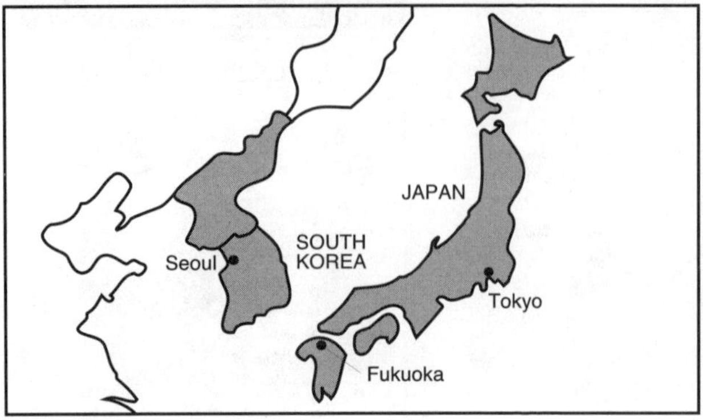

Asia Area

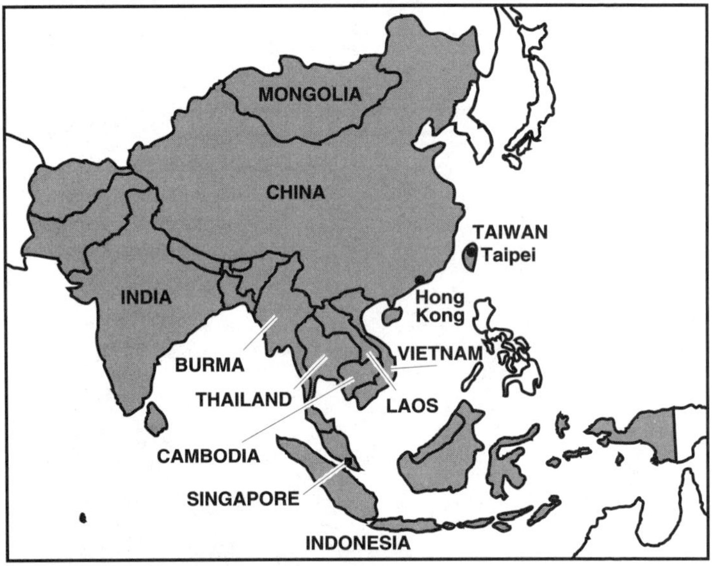

Asia Area: Membership, 75,858; Stakes, 13; Wards, 75; Missions, 10; Districts, 24; Branches, 156; Temples, 2; Headquarters, Hong Kong.

Philippines Area: Membership, 441,359; Stakes, 68; Wards, 414; Missions, 13; Districts, 77; Branches, 637; Temples, 1; Headquarters, Manila, Philippines.

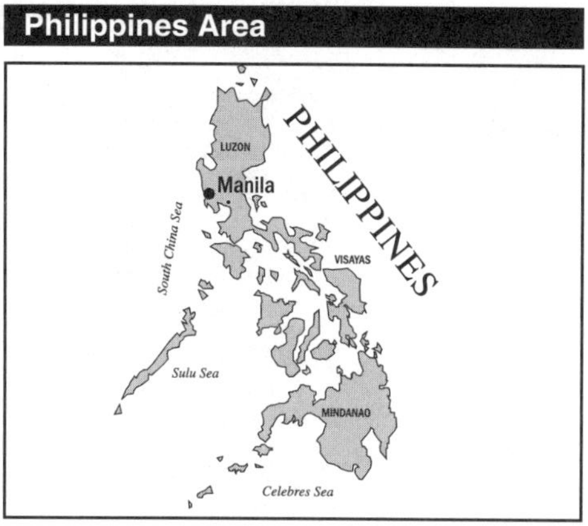

Pacific Islands Area: Membership, 164,311; Stakes, 47; Wards, 315; Missions, 5; Districts, 18; Branches, 189; Temples, 4; Headquarters, Auckland, New Zealand.

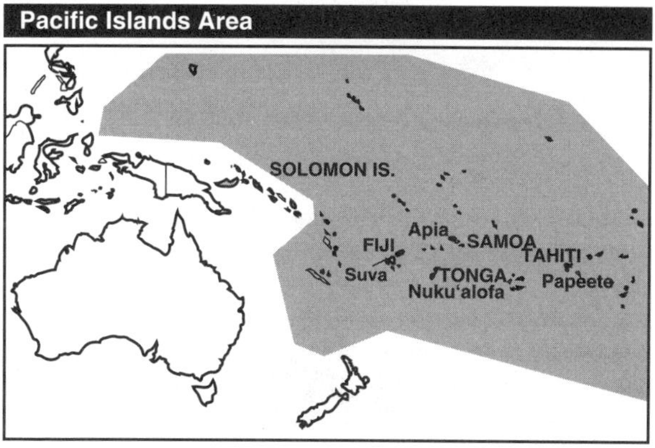

Australia New Zealand Area: Membership, 199,055; Stakes, 57; Wards, 329; Missions, 10, Districts, 20; Branches, 201; Temples, 4, 2 announced; Headquarters, Sydney, Australia.

South America South Area: Membership, 406,762; Stakes, 85; Wards, 515; Missions, 13; Districts, 53; Branches, 587; Temples, 1, 2 announced; Headquarters, Buenos Aires, Argentina.

South America South Area

Chile Area

Chile Area: Membership, 502,082; Stakes, 116; Wards, 744; Missions, 8; Districts, 9; Branches, 349; Temples, 1; Headquarters, Santiago, Chile.

South America West Area: Membership, 446,050; Stakes, 102; Wards, 708; Missions, 10; Districts, 42; Branches, 362; Temples, 2 ; Headquarters, Lima, Peru.

South America West Area

Brazil North Area: Membership, 287,058; Stakes, 60; Wards 411; Missions, 10; Districts, 16; Branches, 204; Temples, 1 announced; Headquarters, Recife, Brazil.

Brazil North Area

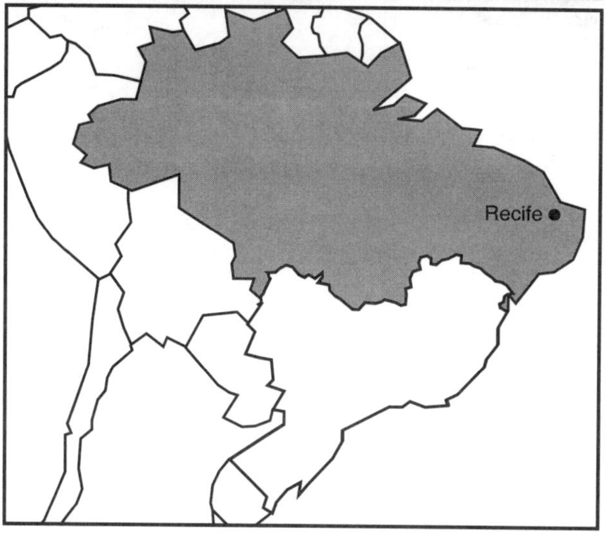

Brazil South Area: Membership, 456,124; Stakes, 126; Wards, 853; Missions, 16; Districts, 26; Branches, 412; Temples, 1, 2 announced; Headquarters, Sao Paulo, Brazil.

Brazil South Area

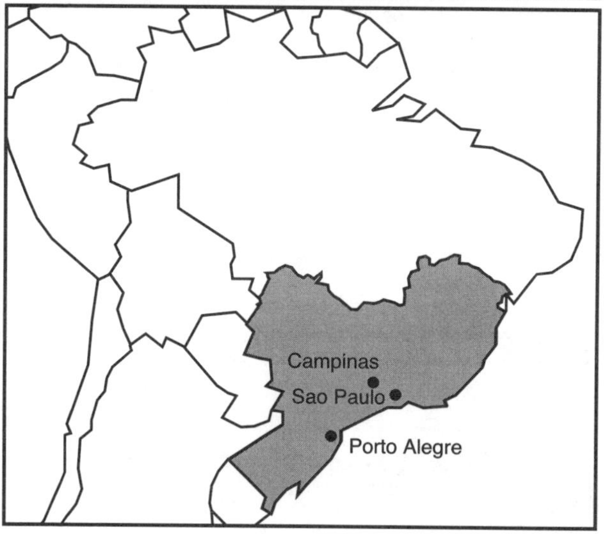

South America North Area: Membership, 365,667; Stakes, 71; Wards, 483; Missions, 11; Districts, 44; Branches, 422; Temples, 3; Headquarters, Quito, Ecuador.

South America North Area

Central America Area: Membership, 454,944; Stakes, 89; Wards, 536; Missions, 12; Districts, 65; Branches, 562; Temples, 2; Headquarters, Guatemala City, Guatemala.

Central America Area

Mexico North Area

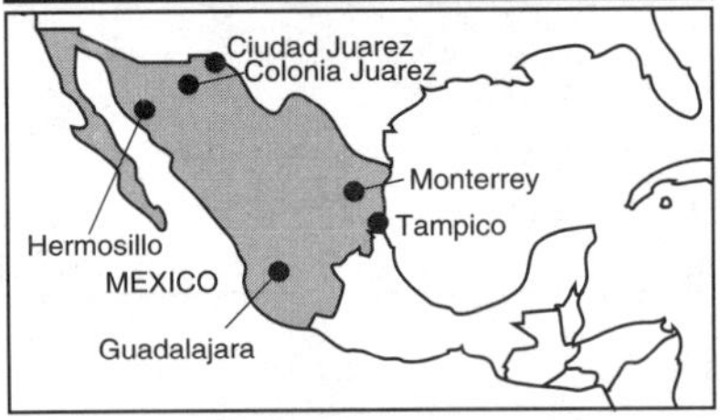

Mexico North Area: Membership, 415,731; Stakes, 80; Wards, 508; Missions, 10; Districts, 29; Branches, 260; Temples, 4; 2 announced; Headquarters, Monterrey, Mexico.

Mexico South Area

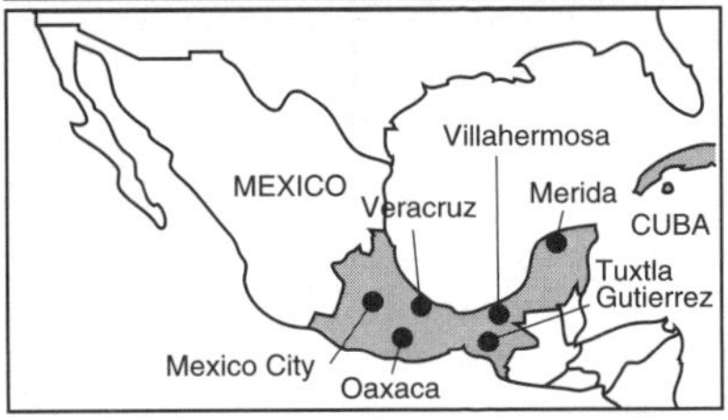

Mexico South Area: Membership, 431,210; Stakes, 99; Wards, 734; Missions, 8; Districts, 11; Branches, 212; Temples, 6; Headquarters, Mexico City, Mexico.

North America Southwest Area: Membership, 782, 340; Stakes, 170; Wards, 1,326; Missions, 15; Branches, 286; Districts, 3;Temples, 7; 2 announced or under construction; Headquarters, Salt Lake City, Utah.

North America Southwest Area

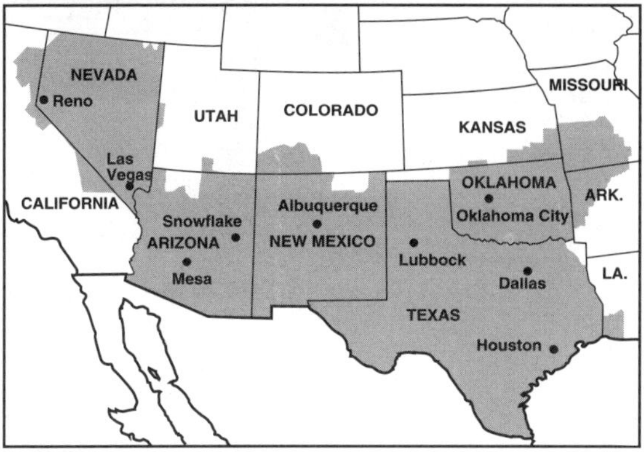

North America Northwest Area: Membership, 733,639; Stakes, 196; Wards, 1,473; Missions, 9; Districts, 2; Branches, 179; Temples, 7, 1 announced; Headquarters, Salt Lake City, Utah.

North America Northwest Area

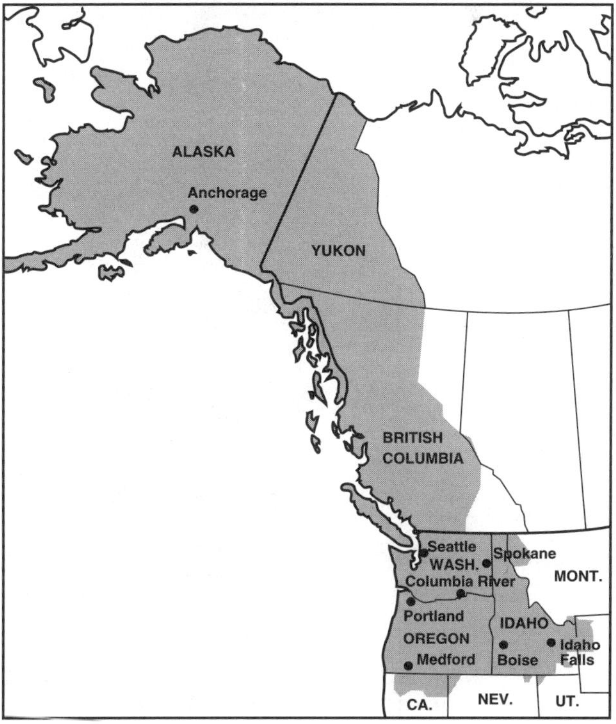

North America West Area: Membership, 797,984; Stakes, 173; Wards, 1,247; Missions, 18; Branches, 156; Temples, 6; Headquarters, Salt Lake City, Utah.

North America West Area

North America Central Area: Membership, 454,075; Stakes, 123; Wards, 852; Missions, 16; Districts, 4; Branches, 356; Temples, 9, 2 announced; Headquarters, Salt Lake City, Utah.

North America Central Area

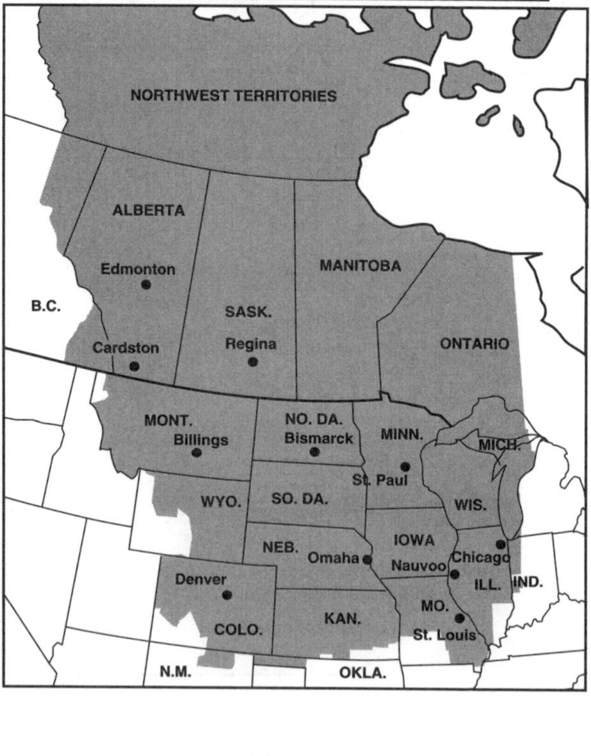

Utah North Area: Membership, 1,088,885; Stakes, 300; Wards, 2,282; Missions, 1; Districts, 1; Branches, 102; Temples, 5; Headquarters, Salt Lake City, Utah.

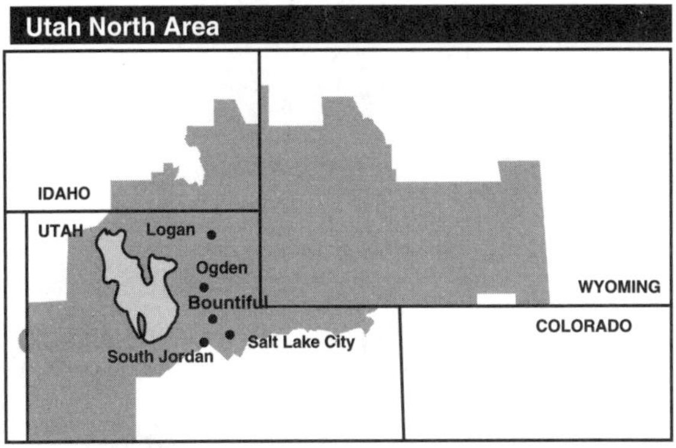

Utah South Area: Membership, 568,428; Stakes, 175; Wards, 1,445; Missions, 1; Branches, 52; Temples, 6; Headquarters, Salt Lake City, Utah.

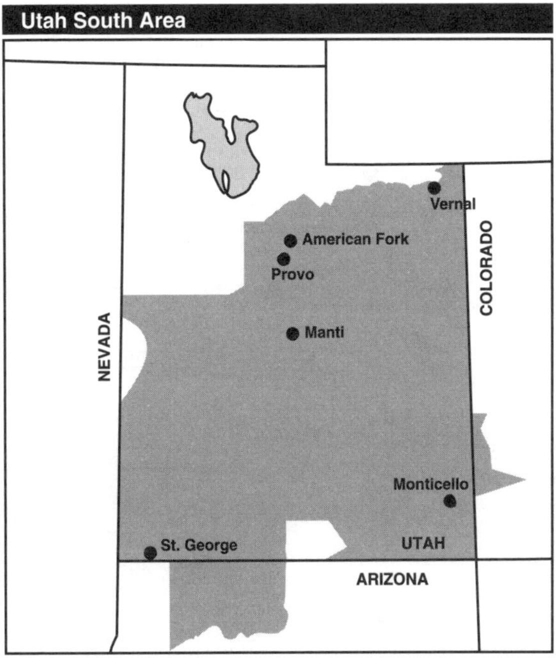

North America Northeast Area: Membership, 277,447; Stakes, 64; Wards, 402; Missions, 18; Districts, 10; Branches, 324; Temples, 6, 1 announced; Headquarters, Salt Lake City, Utah.

North America Northeast Area

North America East Area: Membership, 298,541; Stakes, 71; Wards, 476; Missions, 14, Districts, 1; Branches, 228; Temples, 5; Headquarters, Salt Lake City, Utah.

North America East Area

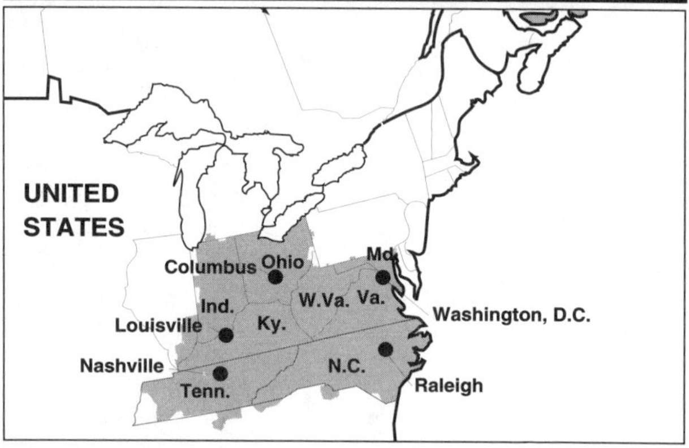

North America Southeast Area: Membership, 389,842; U.S. , 279,352 Caribbean, 110,352 Stakes, 79; Wards, 502; Missions, 19; Districts, 18; Branches, 375; Temples, 7; Headquarters, Salt Lake City, Utah.

North America Southeast Area

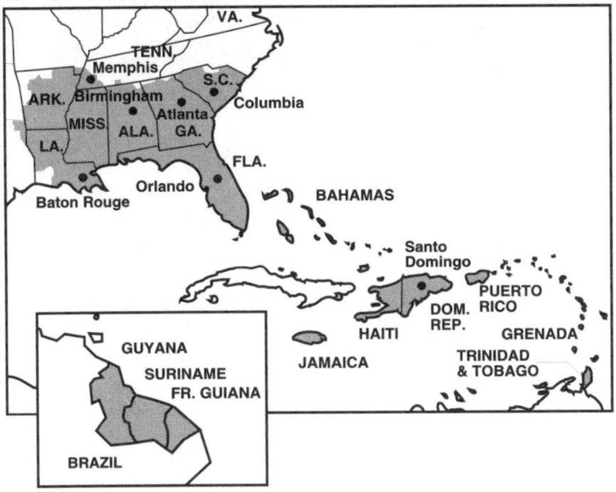

Europe West Area

Europe West Area: Membership, 301,995; Stakes, 69; Wards, 409; Missions, 24; Districts, 54; Branches, 539; Temples, 3; Headquarters, Solihull, England.

Europe Central Area

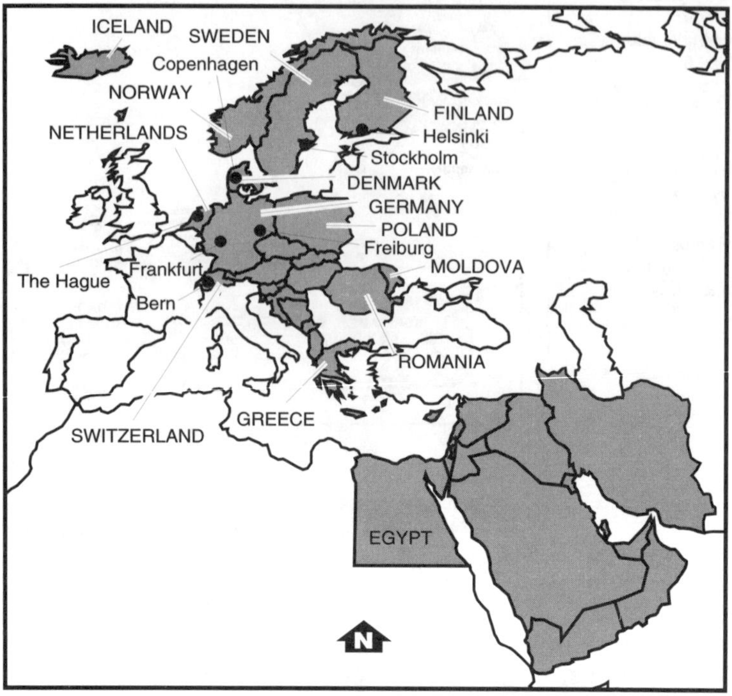

Europe Central Area: Membership, 87,831 Stakes, 32; Wards, 198; Missions, 21; Districts, 21; Branches, 358; Temples, 4, 3 announced; Headquarters, Frankfurt, Germany.

Europe East Area

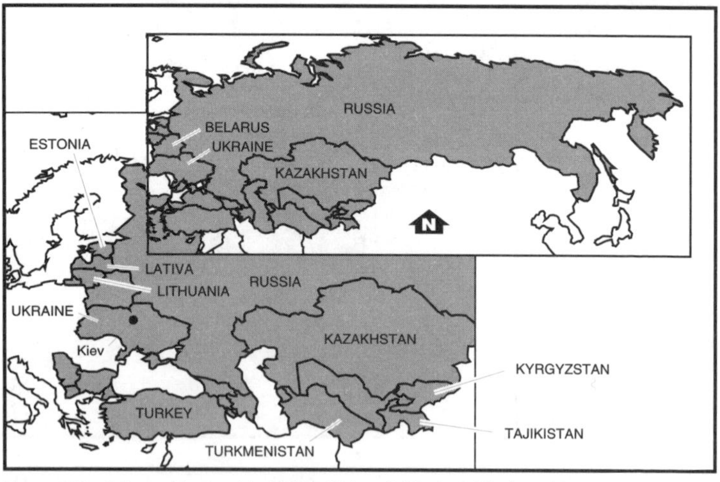

Europe East Area: Membership, 20,872; Stakes, 0; Wards, 0; Missions, 13; Districts, 29; Branches, 191; Temples,1 announced; Headquarters, Moscow, Russia.

Editor's note: Information in this section has been gathered from a variety of sources and is believed to be the best available at the time of publication. Corrections, additional information and further country or state histories will be appreciated. Those with comments or information may write to: Church Almanac Histories, P.O. Box 1257, Salt Lake City, UT 84110.

UNITED STATES OF AMERICA

Year-end 1999: Est. population, 272,691,000; Members, 5,113,409; Stakes, 1,291; Wards, 9,627; Branches, 1,688; Districts, 15; Missions, 99; Temples, 58 in use, under construction or announced; Percent LDS, 1.8, or one in 55.

A few stakes and missions have headquarters in states other than that for which they are named. To simplify this listing, these stakes and missions are listed in the states for which they are named.

Numbers preceding stakes and missions are their chronological numbers assigned at the time of creation. Letters are added if number has been used previously.

* Stake name changed 14 Jan 1974 or as indicated otherwise

‡ Original name

† Transferred to

Alabama

Year-end 1999: Population, 4,370,000; Members, 27,680; Stakes, 6; Wards, 37; Branches, 32; Missions, 1; Temples, 1; Percent LDS, 0.6 or one in 156.

The first missionaries to visit Alabama are said to have preached on the Montgomery County courthouse steps Oct. 7, 1839, but concerted missionary efforts waited until 1842 and 1843 for the work of Elders James Brown and John U. Eldridge. Elder Brown organized branches in Tuscaloosa (the Cybry Branch) and Perry (Bogue-Chitto Branch) counties before Aug. 24, 1842. Elder Eldridge baptized his brother, wife, and mother-in-law, probably in February or March of that year.

Seventeen-year-old John Brown was among the early missionaries. Dressed in ragged clothing, he visited an inn at Tuscumbria, Colbert County, on Aug. 27, 1843. When he asked for lodging as a preacher, he was thought to be a common cotton picker. His host gathered a small group to be entertained at the expense of hearing a supposed cotton picker preach. After he began, however, "they were as motionless as statues of marble." None was baptized, but the young preacher was well-treated afterward.

Elder Brown later baptized a number of people in Tuscaloosa and Perry counties, and, according to some records, baptized some of the first African-Americans to join the Church, two men named Hagar and Jack, on Oct. 24, 1843. Other early missionaries included Peter Haws and Hayden W. Church. Early missionaries frequently passed between Alabama and Mississippi in their work.

In early 1844, three branches, reporting a combined membership of 123, attended a conference. A few months later, in April, seven branches reported a combined membership of 192, although this included some members from Mississippi.

Evidently, most early members immigrated to the West to join the body of the Saints and to avoid persecution. Some Alabama members were among the group of "Mississippi Saints" that emigrated under the leadership of John Brown and William Crosby in 1846.

Missionary work resumed in the South in 1876 with the creation of the Southern States Mission. However, persecution was widespread during the 1880s. As early as 1880, some asked the governor of Alabama to force missionaries from the state. By 1894, the persecution subsided somewhat.

In 1898, John and James Edgar joined the Church in Andalusia, Ala., and that same year immigrated to Texas, where they later founded the LDS colony of Kelsey.

Early convert Olivia Tucker McCoy recalled missionaries coming to Magnolia in 1896, and in May of 1897 a conference was held in Magnolia with 36 elders and Southern States Mission Pres. John Morgan in attendance. Evicted from family property after their conversion, the McCoy family moved from Magnolia to another community and remained faithful.

A Sunday School was organized Aug. 22, 1911, in Montgomery. In the early days, converts were baptized in the Alabama River. In 1930, membership in the state was 2,516, with branches in Bradleyton and Lamison, and Sunday Schools in Bessemer, Birmingham, Camden, Clayton, Decatur, Dothan, Elmont, McCalla, Mobile, Pine Hill, Selma, and Sneed.

Elder Theron W. Borup, district president, recalled that in the mid-1930s, Sunday School groups existed in Elkmont (which had a small chapel), Gadsen, Birmingham, McCalla, and Montgomery. Branches were eventually organized from these Sunday Schools. In 1937, an east-west boundary was drawn through the Alabama District, dividing it into the Alabama and North Alabama districts.

During this period, attitudes held by many people against the Church softened. In 1940, the Montgomery Branch staged a pioneer parade that attracted thousands.

Many LDS servicemen were stationed in the area during World War II, strengthening the branches. After the war, the branches began to grow. One prominent leader at the time was Stance H. Moore, president of the North Alabama District. A chapel was completed in 1955 in Montgomery, and the branch grew more rapidly after that. Alabama's first stake was created in Huntsville in 1968. The military and the National Space and Aeronautics Administration brought in an influx of members during this period. Membership in Alabama in 1974 was about 7,800, increasing to 14,000 in 1980 and to 20,000 in 1989, when the 150th anniversary of missionary work in Alabama was commemorated. One of the speakers at that commemoration was Chief Justice Ernest C. "Sonny" Hornsby of the Alabama Supreme Court.

The Alabama Birmingham Mission was created Jan. 1, 1979. In the 1990s, members served their neighbors in the aftermath of a hurricane, and helped in rebuilding community chapels burned by arsonists. A temple was announced for Birmingham on Sept. 11, 1998, and was dedicated Sept. 3, 2000, by President Gordon B. Hinckley.

Membership in Alabama in 1999 was 27,680.

Sources: *Encyclopedic History of the Church, by* Andrew Jenson; *History of the Southern States Mission, 1831-1861,* by LaMar C. Berrett, a BYU thesis of July 1960; *Sesquicentennial Star,* history published by Montgomery Alabama Stake Oct. 7, 1989, courtesy Frank W. Riggs III, with interviews of Willie Lou Greene and others; "Alabama: The northern Saints of a southern state," April 7, 1988, *Church News*; "Members rally to help hurricane victims," *Church News*, Aug. 12, 1995; "LDS render service in wake of Opal's rage," *Church News*, Oct. 14, 1995; "Helping rebuild burned chapels," *Church News,* Nov. 9, 1996; *Church News*, April 18, 1998, "God is smiling down on us," by Julie A. Dockstader, *Church News,* Sept. 9, 2000.

Stakes — 6

(Listed alphabetically as of Oct. 1, 2000.)

No.	Name	Organized	First President
	North America Southeast Area		
1362	Bessemer Alabama	12 Sep 1982	Robert Henry Shepherdson
678	Birmingham Alabama	2 Feb 1975	Fred M. Washburn
1588	Dothan Alabama	2 Mar 1986	Ned Philip Jenne
452	*Huntsville Alabama ‡Alabama	3 Mar 1968	Raymond D. McCurdy
964	Mobile Alabama	8 Oct 1978	Dean Arthur Rains
717	Montgomery Alabama	2 Nov 1975	Gayle Dorwin Heckel

Mission — 1

(As of Oct. 1, 2000; shown with historical number. See MISSIONS.)

(166a) ALABAMA BIRMINGHAM MISSION
1560 Montgomery Highway, Suite 204
Birmingham, AL 35216

Alaska

Year-end 1999: Est. population, 620,000; Members, 25,340; Stakes, 6; Wards, 38; Branches, 27; Missions, 1; Districts, 1; Temples, 1; Percent LDS, 4, or one in 24.

The first Latter-day Saints in Alaska, John Bigelow and Dr. Edward G. Cannon, were drawn by the gold rush of 1898. They arrived about the turn of the century. Little is known of Bigelow, but Dr. Cannon, a 79-year-old who had been converted in 1871, worked hard to establish the Church. He maintained a "tabernacle which he moved about on wheels from settlement to settlement" in the Seward Peninsula and Nome area.

On June 25, 1902, Dr. Cannon baptized a gold miner, K.N. Winnie, in the Bering Sea near Nome. Winnie reported in 1907 that gospel meetings were being held and quite a number of people were interested, including Eskimos as well as miners and others. Dr. Cannon and Winnie worked together until Dr. Cannon's death in 1910, though they realized little success.

In 1913, a year after Alaska became a territory of the United States, the first two missionaries arrived in Juneau where they worked for a few weeks. The next missionaries,

Elders Heber J. Meeks, Alvin Englestead, James Judd, and Lowell T. Plowman, arrived in Alaska in 1928, under the direction of Pres. William R. Sloan of the Northwestern States Mission.

During the next year, the elders held 105 meetings and placed more than 1,300 copies of the Book of Mormon. They also dealt with a widespread rumor that the Church planned to colonize Alaska. Few people, however, joined the Church, and membership consisted only of a few scattered LDS homesteaders or fortune seekers.

The first branch of the Church in Alaska was organized in Fairbanks on July 10, 1938, with Dr. Murray Shields as president. By 1941, membership in the territory had reached 300. During the next 20 years, other branches were organized so that by 1961, membership was 3,051 with three branches in Anchorage and additional branches in Fairbanks, Palmer, and Juneau. The Alaskan-Canadian Mission was created Jan. 1, 1961, and the first stake in Alaska, the Anchorage Stake, was organized Aug. 13, 1961. In 1964, missionaries working among the native Americans introduced the gospel to many.

A massive earthquake struck Alaska on March 27, 1964, and among those killed were six members of the Valdez Branch. As the area was rebuilt after the earthquake, the construction effort led to a building boom that brought additional members to the state, and the stake grew in membership. A new stake center was dedicated in Anchorage in 1966. In 1970, membership was 6,744. The Alaska Anchorage Mission was organized in 1974 from the Canada Vancouver Mission.

Discovery of oil in the north accelerated growth. Construction of the trans-Alaska oil pipeline created a boom in the number of members in Alaska, but membership dropped after the construction project was completed. Under the leadership of mission President Douglas T. Snarr, special meetinghouses designed for the Arctic were built in 1981 in many of the smaller branches. Membership in 1980 was 14,414, and by 1990 had reached 21,410. In the 1990s, members took part in community service projects that helped improve relationships for the Church.

In June 1995, for the first time in the history of the Church, a prophet visited members of the Church in Alaska. From June 17-23 of that year, President Gordon B. Hinckley spoke at a regional conference, met with missionaries of the Alaska Anchorage Mission, spoke at firesides, and greeted most of the 18 members of the tiny Gustavus Branch.

Anchorage was designated as a site for one of the first three small temples announced in general conference by President Hinckley in October 1997. Ground for the Church's northernmost temple was broken April 17, 1998. The new building, with a stone exterior, art glass windows, and statue of the Angel Moroni, was dedicated by President Hinckley Jan. 9, 1999. Before the temple was dedicated, members had to travel the 1,000 to 2,000-miles to the Seattle or Alberta temples.

In 1999, Alaska had 25,340 members in 65 wards and branches, but many of the units are stretched out over vast areas. The Bush Branch, for example, covers 300,000 square miles in western Alaska, and the branch president, Ed Lindquist, communicates with his 135 members by letters, telephone, and e-mail.

On May 22, 1999, the first seminary building to be constructed in Alaska, located in the Anchorage suburb of Chugiak, was dedicated.

Sources: *Encyclopedic History of the Church, by* Andrew Jenson; *The History of the Mormons in Alaska,* by Barbara Jean Walther; *A Gathering of* Saints *in Alaska,* edited by Patricia B. Jasper and Beverly M. Blasongame; "The Saints in Anchorage, Alaska," *Ensign,* Nov. 1987; "Alaskans: Determined Builders," *Church News,* Feb. 14, 1981; "Refuge facilities improved," *Church News,* Dec. 18, 1993; "Alaskan LDS welcome Pres. Hinckley," *Church News,* July 1, 1995; *Church News,* April 25, 1998; "Northernmost temple dedicated" by Julie A. Dockstader, *Church News,* Jan. 16, 1999; *Church News,* Jan. 23, 1999, June 12, 1999.

Stakes — 6

(Listed alphabetically as of Oct. 1, 2000.)

No.	Name	Organized	First President
	North America Northwest Area		
331	*Anchorage Alaska ‡Alaska	13 Aug 1961	Orson P. Millett
962	Anchorage Alaska North	17 Sep 1978	Wesley R. Grover
1033	Fairbanks Alaska	27 May 1979	Dennis E. Cook
2102	Juneau Alaska	8 Oct 1995	Melvin R. Perkins
1507	Soldotna Alaska	9 Dec 1984	Merrill D. Briggs
1456	Wasilla Alaska	13 Nov 1983	Elbert Thomas Pettijohn

Mission — 1
(As of Oct. 1, 2000; shown with historical number. See MISSIONS.)

(114) ALASKA ANCHORAGE MISSION
12350 Industry Way, Suite 218
Anchorage, AK 99515

Arizona

Year-end 1999: Est. population, 4,778,000; Members, 305,034; Stakes, 71; Wards, 566; Branches, 57; Missions, 3; Temples, 1, (1 announced); Percent LDS, 6.4, or one in 16.

The Mormon Battalion entered the area that is now Arizona in December 1846 and January 1847 during its famous march through the Southwest. As early as 1859, Jacob Hamblin did missionary work among the Navajo and Moqui Indians of the area. The first effort at colonization came in March 1873 when a group of Saints was sent from Utah to the Little Colorado River area, under the direction of Horton D. Haight. Most returned to Utah but a few remained, including John L. Blythe. He and others established farms among the Indians at Moancopi. A second expedition, under the direction of James S. Brown, scouted the Little Colorado River area, preparing the way for a group that later colonized St. Joseph, Sunset, Obed, and Brigham City. These settlers, who came in the spring of 1876, built a fort, dug canals, and constructed dams, then struggled to survive in the arid land. Most practiced the United Order. Settlers on the lower Little Colorado became discouraged after efforts failed to dam the unruly stream.

In 1876, Lot Smith and others established more colonies on the Little Colorado. A year later, Mormon colonizers settled in the Salt River Valley where Lehi and later Mesa were founded. Other colonies, such as Pima and Thatcher, were founded in Gila Valley in 1881. Eventually, some 34 Mormon colonies were started in Arizona.

The Little Colorado Stake was created in 1878, but was discontinued in 1887. The first permanent stake was the Maricopa Stake, created in 1882, followed by the St. Joseph Stake, in 1883.

Members overcame severe hardships in the early years. In the colony of Woodruff, for example, members built 17 successive dams after each previous one was washed out.

Over the years, members gained prominence and were involved in the progress of the state. They earned a good reputation for their industry and integrity. Colonies continued to grow and their influence extended beyond Arizona. Pres. Jesse N. Smith of Snowflake helped locate a site for the Mormon colonies in Mexico. Later, during the members' exodus because of the 1912 revolution in Mexico, Arizona became a place of refuge for the refugees.

The Arizona Temple in Mesa was completed in 1923 and dedicated Oct. 23, 1927. It was the first temple in the Church to be rededicated — on April 15, 1975 — after extensive remodeling and enlarging to accommodate increased membership. A total of 205,248 members and non-members toured the renovated building during an open house held before its rededication. At that time, the temple district included 72 stakes, including 28 Spanish-speaking stakes.

By 1930, Arizona had four stakes with 18,732 members. Two additional stakes were created in the 1930s, and another two in the 1940s; membership in 1940 was 25,272. In 1950, membership was 33,937, and during the decade six more stakes were created. In 1960, membership had nearly doubled to 60,457 and before the decade ended, five more stakes were created. Membership grew to 94,249 by 1970, and 21 new stakes were created in the next 10 years. The Arizona Mission (now Arizona Tempe) was created in 1969, followed by the creation of the Arizona Holbrook Mission in 1974, which was discontinued in 1984 when the Arizona Phoenix Mission was created. The Arizona Tucson Mission was organized in 1990.

President Spencer W. Kimball, who served as president of the Church from 1973-1985, was reared in Thatcher, Ariz., and served as the first president of the Mt. Graham Stake.

The pageant "Jesus the Christ," started in 1938 and presented annually on the Arizona Temple grounds, attracts about 80,000 people each year. Christmas lights on the temple grounds also attract many from the community.

By 1980, membership reached 171,880. By 1990, membership was at 241,000 and had reached 305,000 by 1999. In the past few years, about two new stakes a year have been created in Arizona.

On Sept. 14, 1997, President Gordon B. Hinckley spoke to some 5,000 Native Americans at Window Rock, in the heart of the Navajo Reservation. He was the first Church president to visit the city. On Dec. 13, 1997, the Casa Grande Arizona Stake presented a plaque to officials of the Gila River Indian Community in honor of the kindness shown to the Mormon Battalion by the Pima Indians in this area 150 years earlier.

A second temple for Arizona was announced by President Hinckley in general conference on April 2, 2000, to be built in Snowflake. Ground was broken Sept. 23, 2000.

Sources: *Encyclopedic History of the Church, by* Andrew Jenson; "Early History of Arizona," by Paul Updike, *The Pioneer,* Jan. 1981; *Heart Throbs of the West* by Kate B. Carter; "Mormons in Arizona" by Thomas Edwin Farrish, reprinted in the *Deseret News* Aug. 31, 1918; *Church News,* Dec. 20, 1997; "5,000 Native Americans gather to hear prophet," *Church News* Sept. 20, 1998; *Church News,* April 25, 1997, *Church News,* April 8, 2000.

Stakes — 74

(Listed alphabetically as of Oct. 1, 2000.)

No.	Name	Organized	First President
	North America Southwest Area — 74		
1616	Apache Junction Arizona	16 Nov 1986	Charles Wray Squires
1666	Buckeye Arizona	13 Dec 1987	Charles Roy Rucker
1819	Casa Grande Arizona	13 Oct 1991	Scott J. McEuen
988	Chandler Arizona	3 Dec 1978	Elone Evans Farnsworth
1513	Chandler Arizona Alma	24 Feb 1985	Martin H. Durrant
2255	Chandler Arizona West	20 Oct 1996	Donald Lynn Jones
1773	Chinle Arizona	30 Sep 1990	Edwin I. Tano
888	*Cottonwood Arizona	9 Apr 2000	
	‡Camp Verde Arizona	22 Jan 1978	John Edward Eagar
963	Duncan Arizona	24 Sep 1978	Earl Adair Merrell
1627	Eagar Arizona	25 Jan 1987	Charles D. Martin
232	*Flagstaff Arizona		
	‡Flagstaff	23 Sep 1956	Burton R. Smith
2358	Gilbert Arizona	18 May 1997	John Wootton Lewis
703	*Gilbert Arizona Greenfield	11 Oct 1981	
	‡Gilbert Arizona	24 Aug 1975	Newell A. Barney
2282	Gilbert Arizona Highland	24 Nov 1996	David E. Lesuere
1295	Gilbert Arizona Stapley	11 Oct 1981	Wilburn James Brown
1661	Gilbert Arizona Val Vista	22 Nov 1987	Craig Allen Cardon
612	*Glendale Arizona		
	‡Glendale	6 May 1973	Melvin L. Huber
1236	Glendale Arizona North	15 Feb 1981	Richard Johnson Barrett
650	Globe Arizona	16 Jun 1974	Bennie Joe Cecil
536	*Holbrook Arizona		
	‡Holbrook	22 Nov 1970	Jay Barder Williams
1436	Kingman Arizona	21 Aug 1983	Louis George Sorensen
750	*Lake Havasu City Arizona	11 Feb 1997	
	Blythe California	14 Mar 1976	Jerry Dean Mortensen
161	*Mesa Arizona		
	‡Mesa	8 Dec 1946	L.M. Mecham Jr.
2517	Mesa Arizona Alta Mesa	14 Mar 1999	Donald Milford Erickson
2539	Mesa Arizona Boulder Creek	5 Dec 1999	Russell David Thornock
1265	Mesa Arizona Central	10 May 1981	Clayton H. Hakes
1904	*Mesa Arizona Citrus Heights	7 May 1999	
	‡Mesa Ariz Red Mountain	20 Sep 1992	James Joseph Humula
224	*Mesa Arizona East		
	*Mesa East 29 May 1970		
	‡East Mesa	20 Nov 1955	Donald Ellsworth
1087	Mesa Arizona Kimball	25 Nov 1979	Allen Smith Farnsworth
1741	Mesa Arizona Kimball East	14 Jan 1990	Wayne D. Crismon
1026	Mesa Arizona Lehi	6 May 1979	Otto Stronach Shill Jr.
24	*Mesa Arizona Maricopa		
	‡Maricopa	10 Dec 1882	Alexander F. MacDonald
2544	Mesa Arizona Maricopa North	27 Feb 2000	Jim L. Wright
1628	Mesa Arizona Mountain View	25 Jan 1987	James R. Adair
558	*Mesa Arizona North	27 Feb 2000	
	*Mesa Arizona Maricopa North	15 Mar 1978	
	*Mesa Maricopa North		
	‡Maricopa North	7 Nov 1971	Raymond L. Russell
1479	Mesa Arizona Pueblo	10 Jun 1984	E. Clark Huber
745	Mesa Arizona Salt River	15 Feb 1976	Elden S. Porter
362	*Mesa Arizona South		

	‡Mesa South	18 Nov 1962	Stanley F. Turley
555	*Mesa Arizona West		
	‡Mesa West	10 Oct 1971	Weymouth D. Pew
633	Page Arizona	10 Mar 1974	J Ballard Washburn
1061	Paradise Valley Arizona	9 Sep 1979	James David King
2552	Payson Arizona Stake	9 Apr 2000	J. Fred Hollobaugh
1631	Peoria Arizona	22 Feb 1987	Thomas G. Jones
2545	Peoria Arizona North	27 Jan 2000	Lloyd S. Price
121	*Phoenix Arizona		
	‡Phoenix	27 Feb 1938	James Robert Price
1233	Phoenix Arizona Deer Valley	8 Feb 1981	E. Wayne Pratt
212	*Phoenix Arizona East		
	*Phoenix East	29 May 1970	
	‡East Phoenix	28 Feb 1954	Junius E. Driggs
253	*Phoenix Arizona North		
	‡Phoenix North	19 Jan 1958	Rudger G. Smith
380	*Phoenix Arizona West		
	‡Phoenix West	1 Sep 1963	Keith W. Hubbard
896	*Phoenix Arizona West Maricopa	18 May 1978	
	‡West Maricopa Arizona	5 Mar 1978	DeNelson Jones
1830	Pima Arizona	17 Nov 1991	Stephen Lavar John
2039	Pinetop-Lakeside Arizona	26 Mar 1995	Chester Trent Adams
517	*Prescott Arizona		
	‡Prescott	7 Jun 1970	Edward A. Dalton
137	*St. David Arizona		
	*Arizona South	29 May 1970	
	‡Southern Arizona	2 Mar 1941	A.B. Ballantyne
31	*St. Johns Arizona		
	‡St. Johns(Arizona, N.M.)	23 Jul 1887	David K. Udall
120	*Safford Arizona		
	‡Mount Graham (Arizona, N.M.)	20 Feb 1938	Spencer W. Kimball
1248	*Scottsdale Arizona Camelback	4 Oct 1994	
	‡Phoenix Arizona Camelback	22 Mar 1981	Ernest Widtsoe Shumway
364	Scottsdale Arizona North	4 Oct 1994	
	*Scottsdale Arizona		
	‡Scottsdale	9 Dec 1962	Junius E. Driggs
668	Show Low Arizona	24 Nov 1974	Elbert J. Lewis
1348	Sierra Vista Arizona	6 Jun 1982	C. Lavell Haymore
31a	*Snowflake Arizona		
	‡Snowflake	18 Dec 1887	Jesse N. Smith
1212	Taylor Arizona	30 Nov 1980	Peter Delos Shumway
391	*Tempe Arizona		
	‡Tempe	2 Feb 1964	George Isaac Dana
738	Tempe Arizona South	18 Jan 1976	Fred Dale Markham
1708	Tempe Arizona West	8 Jan 1989	Kent M. Christiansen
25	*Thatcher Arizona		
	‡Saint Joseph	25 Feb 1883	Christopher Layton
2068	Tuba City Arizona	25 June 1995	Edwin I. Tano
238	*Tucson Arizona		
	‡Tucson	2 Dec 1956	Leslie Odell Brewer
878	Tucson Arizona East	6 Nov 1977	Paul Eugene Dahl
477	*Tucson Arizona North		
	‡Tucson North	2 Feb 1969	Don Hakan Peterson
1517	Tucson Arizona Rincon	3 Mar 1985	Ernest G. Blain
2281	Tucson Arizona West	24 Nov 1996	Reed A. Hancock
959	Winslow Arizona	17 Sep 1978	Thomas A. Whipple
263	*Yuma Arizona		
	‡Yuma (Arizona, California)	27 Apr 1958	Marion Turley

Stakes discontinued

22	Eastern Arizona (Arizona, N.M.)	29 Jun 1879	Jesse N. Smith
	Discontinued 18 Dec 1887 †St. Johns (31), Snowflake (31a)		
21	Little Colorado (Ariz., Colo.)	27 Jan 1878	Lot Smith
	Discontinued 18 Dec 1887 †Snowflake (31a)		

562 Tempe University 12 Dec 1971 Leo Rae Huish
Discontinued 28 Apr 1974 †13 Salt River Valley stakes

Missions — 3

(As of Oct. 1, 2000; shown with historical number. See MISSIONS.)

(179c) ARIZONA PHOENIX MISSION
6265 North 82nd St.
Scottsdale, AZ 85250

(87) ARIZONA TEMPE MISSION
1871 East Del Rio Drive
Tempe, AZ 85282-2822

(231) ARIZONA TUCSON MISSION
1840 East River Road, #102
Tucson, AZ 85718

Arkansas

Year-end 1999: Est. population, 2,551,000; Members, 20,077; Stakes, 4; Wards, 28; Branches, 24; Missions, 1; Percent LDS, 0.8, or one in 127.

Elders Wilford Woodruff and Henry Brown arrived as missionaries in Benton County, Ark., on Jan. 28, 1835. They held their first meeting Feb. 1, and preached to an attentive congregation. Later, they were confronted by an apostate, a man who earlier endured severe persecution in Missouri but later turned bitterly against the Church. However, this man died suddenly and Elder Woodruff preached his funeral sermon. Afterward, Elder Woodruff baptized a "Brother and Sister Hubbel."

In 1838, Elder Abraham O. Smoot was called on a five-month mission to Arkansas where he preached frequently with varied results.

Elder Parley P. Pratt of the Quorum of the Twelve was murdered in the town of Van Buren, Ark., on May 13, 1857. Elder Pratt had just been acquitted by a court of charges pressed by the former husband of his wife, Eleanor McLean Pratt. At the trial, she testified that her former husband had frequently physically abused her. Disappointed with the verdict, the enraged accuser assassinated the apostle.

Little, if any, missionary success was realized in Arkansas until 1875 when Elders Henry G. Boyle and J.D.H. McAllister visited a member in Des Arc, Ark. They preached and "baptized a great many of the best citizens of the region," numbering from 80 to 90 people. In 1877, a group of 27 families and 125 people from the Des Arc Branch moved to Utah by wagon train.

Early members and missionaries faced persecution but kept the Church going. In 1897, Elder J.H. Peterson experienced a changed attitude among the people in Arkansas. He reported being treated kindly while serving in Heber, Red River, and Batesville. This change in attitude evidently paved the way for conversions in Marion and Faulkner counties around the turn of the century. In March 1900, several pioneer members were baptized, including Benjamin Franklin Baker and his sister Emoline in Faulkner County; and Rowland William Perry and his family, as well as Mary Chapelle and Martha White, in Marion County.

The Baker family established the nucleus of the Barney Branch, which was a headquarters for missionaries for many years.

Although some of the early converts immigrated to the West, others stayed and reared LDS families. These families were very close and held most of their social activities together. By 1930, membership in Arkansas was 944 with branches at Barney, El Dorado, and Little Rock. New meetinghouses were erected in Little Rock and El Dorado in 1952, in Pine Bluff in 1954, and in Barney and Rolla in 1956.

The first stake in Arkansas was created June 1, 1969, in Little Rock, followed by the Ft. Smith Stake in 1978 and the Jacksonville Stake in 1983. The Arkansas Little Rock Mission was created in 1975.

Membership 9,878 in 1980, increasing to 13,753 and in 1990, and to 20,077 in 1999.

The first full-time Institute of Religion building in Arkansas, a renovated house adjacent to the University of Arkanasa campus in Faytettville, was dedicated Oct. 17, 1999, by Elder James Olsen, an Area Authority Seventy. The first full semester of insitute classes in the new building began with the 1999 fall semester.

Sources: *Encyclopedic History of the Church,* by Andrew Jenson; *History of the Southern States Mission, 1831-1861* a BYU thesis by LaMar C. Berrett, 1960; "History and Genealogy of the Early Mormon Church in Arkansas," by Emogene Tindall; "History of the Church in Marion County Arkansas," by Louise Perry Bird; *Juvenile Instructor,* 15:24; *Millennial Star,* 38:26, 59:15; Early Scenes in

Church History," *Church News*, May 21, 1977; *BYU Studies*, 15:2; "Church members rally to help tornado victims," *Church News*, April 27, 1996; *Church News*, March 8, 1997, June 21, 1997; "Arkansas institute building dedicated," by Alan Gauldin, *Church News*, Nov. 13, 1999.

Stakes — 4

(Listed alphabetically by area as of Oct. 1, 2000.)

No.	Name	Organized	First President
	North America Southeast Area — 4		
484	*Little Rock Arkansas		
	‡Arkansas	1 Jun 1969	Dean C. Andrew
1432	*North Little Rock Arkansas	8 Jun 1993	
	‡Jacksonville Arkansas	19 Jun 1983	Robert Michael McChesney
911	Fort Smith Arkansas	30 Apr 1978	Arthur Donald Browne
1807	Rogers Arkansas	11 Aug 1991	David Allen Bednar

Mission — 1

(As of Oct. 1, 2000; shown with historical number. See MISSIONS.)

(116) ARKANSAS LITTLE ROCK MISSION
University Tower, # 210
1123 South University Ave.
Little Rock, AR 72204-1690

California

Year-end 1999: Est. population, 33,145,000; Members, 740,236; Stakes, 160; Wards, 1,153; Branches, 158; Missions, 17; Temples, 4; Percent LDS, 2.2, or one in 45.

Immigrants on their way to the Great Basin, aboard the ship *Brooklyn*, traveled by way of Cape Horn around the tip of South America, arriving at San Francisco Bay at Yerba Buena July 29, 1846. They were the first Latter-day Saints to set foot in California. They helped build up that community into what became San Francisco. Eventually, most of the members left California and joined the main body of the Church in Salt Lake City.

In January 1847, the Mormon Battalion arrived in San Diego. Battalion members helped to construct a number of buildings and public works in San Diego, and then traveled to Los Angeles where they built a fort and raised the first American flag. Six discharged battalion members were at Sutter's Mill in northern California when gold was discovered Jan. 24, 1848. The diary of battalion veteran Henry W. Bigler is used by historians in determining the actual date for the discovery of gold in California.

In 1850, a Mormon colony, New Hope, was founded in San Joaquin Valley by Mormons who did not go to Utah. They were among California's first farmers, irrigating with a pole-and-bucket method. They built the first LDS chapel in 1850. Apostle Parley P. Pratt presided over the California Mission at San Francisco from 1849-52.

The first colonization from Utah to California came in 1851 when a company of 500 Saints settled in what is now San Bernardino. The colonization effort was to be the western boundary of a string of settlements extending 800 miles from Salt Lake City and to provide a route to the Pacific Coast. Apostles Charles C. Rich and Amasa M. Lyman took charge of the effort. The first stake created in California was the San Bernardino Stake, which was organized July 6, 1851, but was discontinued by 1857. The faithful members in this colony were eventually outnumbered by less-committed members who created considerable dissension. When the troubled colony was dissolved by the Church at the advance of Johnston's army toward Salt Lake City in 1857, some 1,400 — fewer than half the total — returned to Utah to colonize other areas.

The California Mission was discontinued in 1858 and little missionary work took place from then until 1892 when it was reopened. In 1892, Elder John L. Dalton began missionary work in San Francisco and organized branches. Karl G. Maeser presided over the California Mission in 1894, and missionaries then began work in the southern part of the state. The Los Angeles Branch was created Aug. 20, 1895, and a year later in 1896 the Northern California and Southern California conferences were organized. The Sacramento Conference was added in 1898. Most missionary work in California before the turn of the century took place in the larger population centers.

The land boom of the 1920s attracted many members to California. The first stake created in the state in the 20th century was the Los Angeles Stake, which was organized Jan. 21, 1923, but was later discontinued. The first permanent stake (Hollywood Stake, now Los Angeles California Stake) was created May 22, 1927, followed by the creation of the San Francisco Stake also that year on July 10. In 1930, membership in California was 21,254.

On the opening day of the San Francisco World's Fair on Feb. 18, 1939, some 1,400 people visited the Church's exhibit, a miniature Salt Lake Tabernacle.

Eight stakes in the state were created in the 1930s, five in the 1940s, and 30 in the 1950s.

During the 1930s, many members came to California to work in defense industries. Land for California's first temple was purchased in 1937 in Los Angeles and the temple, the second largest temple in the Church with 190,614 square feet of floor space, was dedicated in 1956. The beginning of a higher public profile for the Church and its members in California seemed to come with the completion of the imposing temple, located on a hill near Westwood Village.

On July 28, 1973, a crowd of 55,000, reported to be one of the largest gatherings of Mormons in the history of the Church up to that time, witnessed the Southern California Area Dance Festival in Pasadena's Rose Bowl.

In the past few decades, Latter-day Saints throughout California have reached the highest levels of education, industry, military, medicine, entertainment, science, and government.

President Spencer W. Kimball addressed a Los Angeles Area Conference in the Rose Bowl on May 17-18, 1980, drawing an estimated 75,000 members. Conference talks were simultaneously translated into seven languages. This is believed to be the largest number of members ever gathered for a Church meeting anywhere in the world.

By 1980, membership in the state totaled 541,000. From 1991 to 1993, because of an out-migration of members, membership dropped from 721,000 to 719,000. However, from 1993 to 1995, membership rose to 725,690. The Church is now the second largest religious denomination in California, with a membership of more than 740,000 in 1999.

In July 1996, the sesquicentennial of the arrival of the ship *Brooklyn* was re-enacted on a replica ship that sailed into San Francisco Bay. Members throughout the state commemorated the milestone anniversary with observances that included a special exhibit at the San Francisco Maritime Museum, performances of the Mormon Tabernacle Choir at the Davies Symphony Hall, dedications of plaques honoring the early settlers, and pioneer activities and parades.

In addition to commemorating the arrival of early LDS settlers, as well as their contributions to the development of the state, members throughout California donated many hours of service in community projects sponsored by wards and stakes, including gathering supplies and food for the needy; cleaning parks, beaches, and roadways; painting and repairing homeless shelters; and cleaning up graffiti.

In San Diego's Old Town on Jan. 18, 1997, some 2,400 members re-enacted the arrival of the Mormon Battalion in California 150 years earlier. Other Mormon Battalion celebrations along the coast followed on respective anniversaries. On March 6, 1997, President Gordon B. Hinckley spoke to a record audience of the Los Angeles World Affairs Council, and on March 19 he addressed the World Forum of Silicon Valley. He also spoke at various Church events during the year. A Church-produced video depicting the discovery of gold at Sutter's Mill was donated to the State of California to be shown continuously at Marshall Gold Discovery State Park in Coloma, Calif.

In times of disasters, such as earthquakes, fires and floods, members In California have donated thousands of hours of service, helping communities to recover. In 1997, members in San Diego donated some 40-50 tons of food to eight community agencies for the homeless and needy. Members in the state have also taken leadership roles in moral issues, such as combatting pornography and have cooperated with other congregations in various interfaith endeavors.

California's second temple was dedicated in Oakland in 1964 and a third was dedicated in 1993 in San Diego. After President Hinckley announced in general conference in April 1998 that the Church would construct 30 additional smaller temples, it was announced in January 1999 that another temple in California would be constructed in Fresno. On April 9, 2000, California's fourth temple was dedicated, just over a year after ground was broken for the edifice on March 20, 1999.

At the beginning of the year 2000, California had 17 missions, more than any other state in the United Staters, as missionary work has prospered. In the state's major cities, many minority converts have been taught the gospel in their own language. With burgeoning population increases from Latin America, five Spanish-speaking stakes have been organized, two since 1992. Various Asian and Polynesian wards function as well, and a Tongan stake was created in San Francisco in 1992.

Sources: *Encyclopedic History of the Church,* by Andrew Jenson; "It Started in Yerba Buena," by Richard O. Cowan, *Instructor,* June 1961; "The Church in Early California," by Albert L. Zobell, *Improvement Era,* May 1964; *Deseret News 1974 Church Almanac; Church News, May 24, 1980;* "The Rise and Decline of Mormon San Bernardino," by Edward Leo Lyman, *BYU Studies,* Fall 1989; *Encyclopedia of Mormonism,* edited by Daniel H. Ludlow; multiple sources in *Church News*; "Spanish spoken here," by Julie A. Dockstader, *Church News,* May 15, 1993; articles on *Brooklyn* commemorative activities, *Church News,* July 6, Aug. 3, Aug. 10, Aug. 17, 1996; Jan 25, 1997, March 1, 1997, Dec. 27, 1997, Jan. 31, 1998, March 7, 1998; "Symbol of growth in fertile San Joaquin," by R. Scott Lloyd, *Church News,* April, 22, 2000.

Stakes — 159

(Listed alphabetically by area as of Oct. 1, 2000.)

No.	Name	Organized	First President
North America West Area — 158			
402	*Anaheim California		
	‡Anaheim	14 Mar 1965	Max V. Eliason
1514	Anaheim California East	24 Feb 1985	William E. Perron
1042	Anderson California	10 Jun 1979	Richard Miller Ericson
1263	Antioch California	3 May 1981	Clifford Spence Munns
864	Arcadia California	9 Oct 1977	Cree-L Kofford
1032	Auburn California	27 May 1979	David Oliver Montague
186	*Bakersfield California		
	‡Bakersfield	27 May 1951	E. Alan Pettit
944	Bakersfield California East	18 Jun 1978	William Horsley Davies
1622	Bakersfield California South	14 Dec 1986	Jack Ray Zimmerman
288	*Barstow California		
	‡Mojave	16 Aug 1959	Sterling A. Johnson
763	Camarillo California	8 Aug 1976	Victor Glenn Johnson
337	*Canoga Park California	6 Dec 1992	
	*Los Angeles California Canoga Park		
	‡Canoga Park	8 Oct 1961	Collins E. Jones
309	*Carlsbad California		
	‡Palomar	6 Nov 1960	Wallace F. Gray
1505	Carmichael California	25 Nov 1984	Marc Earl Hall
269	*Cerritos California		
	‡Norwalk	26 Oct 1958	Lewis Milton Jones
565	*Chico California		
	‡Chico	6 Feb 1972	Lloyd Johnson Cope
1072	Chino California	14 Oct 1979	Allen Clare Christensen
770	Chula Vista California	19 Sep 1976	Robert Eugene Floto
1150	Citrus Heights California	22 Jun 1980	James Barnes
378	*Concord California		
	‡Concord	23 Jun 1963	Ted Eugene Madsen
983	Corona California	19 Nov 1978	Darvil David McBride
226	*Covina California (Spanish)		
	‡Covina	26 Feb 1956	Elden L. Ord
502	*Cypress California		
	‡Anaheim West	15 Feb 1970	Hugh J. Sorensen
229	*Danville California	19 Jun 1989	
	*Walnut Creek California		
	‡Walnut Creek	26 Aug 1956	Emery R. Ranker
1151	Davis California	22 Jun 1980	Peter Glen Kenner
1740	Del Mar California	7 Jan 1990	Robert Geoffrey Dyer
279	*Downey California	18 Feb 1986	
	*Huntington Park California		
	‡Huntington Park	19 Apr 1959	Clifford B. Wright
179	*East Los Angeles California (Spanish)	27 Jun 1993	
	*Los Angeles California East		
	*Los Angeles East	29 May 1970	
	‡East Los Angeles (California)	26 Feb 1950	Fauntleroy Hunsaker

261	*El Cajon California	30 Nov 1975	
	*San Diego California El Cajon		
	‡San Diego East	20 Apr 1958	Cecil I. Burningham
1119	*El Centro California Imperial Valley	18 Mar 1997	
	‡El Centro California	16 Mar 1980	Robert Lamoreaux
984	El Dorado California	19 Nov 1978	Harold George Sellers
487	*Elk Grove California	30 Sep 1993	
	*Sacramento California South		
	‡Sacramento South (California)	15 Jun 1969	John Henry Huber
588	*Escondido California		
	‡Escondido	24 Sep 1972	Donald R. McArthur
1847	Escondido California South	9 Feb 1992	Louis L. Rothey
338	*Eureka California		
	‡Redwood		
	(California, Oregon)	22 Oct 1961	David DeBar Felshaw
428	*Fair Oaks California	12 Feb 1967	Harvey Stansell Greer
	‡Fair Oaks		
682	Fairfield California	16 Feb 1975	Byron Gale Wilson
1602	Fontana California	22 Jun 1986	Wayne Hall Bringhurst
425	*Fremont California		
	‡Fremont	11 Dec 1966	Francis B. Winkel
185	*Fresno California		
	‡Fresno	20 May 1951	Alwyn C. Sessions
381	*Fresno California East		
	‡Fresno East	15 Sep 1963	Melvin P. Leavitt
1463	Fresno California North	12 Feb 1984	Stephen L. Christensen
1464	Fresno California West	12 Feb 1984	Gary R. Fogg
707	Fullerton California	21 Sep 1975	Leon Tad Ballard
330	*Garden Grove California		
	‡Garden Grove	25 Jun 1961	James Malan Hobbs
175	*Glendale California		
	‡Glendale	4 Dec 1949	Edwin Smith Dibble
786	Glendora California	14 Nov 1976	William Marshall Raymond
116	*Granada Hills California	8 Apr 1997	
	*Van Nuys California		
	*San Fernando	15 Oct 1939	
	‡Pasadena	19 Apr 1936	David H. Cannon
107	*Gridley California		
	‡Gridley	4 Nov 1934	John C. Todd
442	*Hacienda Heights California	15 Jan 1978	
	*El Monte California		
	‡El Monte	17 Sep 1967	James Cyril Brown
948	Hanford California	6 Aug 1978	Gerald Leo Thompson
228a	*Hayward California		
	‡Hayward	26 Aug 1956	Milton P. Ream
961	Hemet California	17 Sep 1978	Darrel D. Lee
1632	Hesperia California	22 Feb 1987	Larry Dale Skinner
1926	Highland California	14 Mar 1993	Dennis Alvin Barlow
420	*Huntington Beach California		
	‡Huntington Beach	5 Jun 1966	Conway W. Nielsen
802	Huntington Beach California North	16 Jan 1977	Wesley Charles Woodhouse
1477	Huntington Park California West (Sp)	3 Jun 1984	Rafael Nestor Seminario
129	*Inglewood California	21 Feb 1993	
	*Los Angeles California Inglewood		
	‡Inglewood	26 Nov 1939	Alfred E. Rohner
1633a	Irvine California	12 Apr 1987	Jack L. Rushton Jr.
1784	Jurupa California	9 Dec 1990	Lester C. Lauritzen
518	*La Crescenta California		
	‡La Canada	7 Jun 1970	Robert C. Seamons
347	*La Verne California		
	‡Pomona	21 Jan 1962	Vern R. Peel
1354	Laguna Niguel California	20 Jun 1982	Donald H. Sedgwick
794	Lancaster California	28 Nov 1976	Stephen N. Hull
1798	Lancaster California East	19 May 1991	John Milloy Martz

1654	Livermore California	13 Sep 1987	Willis Arthur Sandholtz
822	*Lodi California	3 May 1981	
	‡Stockton California East	10 Apr 1977	Robert Graham Wade
1649	Lompoc California	23 Aug 1987	Billy Ray Williams
117	*Long Beach California		
	‡Long Beach	3 May 1936	John W. Jones
177	*Long Beach California East		
	*Long Beach East	29 May 1970	
	‡East Long Beach	12 Feb 1950	John C. Dalton
704	Los Altos California	24 Aug 1975	W. Kay Williams
98	*Los Angeles California		
	*Los Angeles	19 Nov 1939	
	‡Hollywood	22 May 1927	George W. McCune
188	*Los Angeles California Santa Monica		
	‡Santa Monica (California)	1 Jul 1951	E. Garrett Barlow
1249	Manteca California	22 Mar 1981	David Leon Ward
2108	Menifee California	15 Oct 1995	Timothy Rudd
156	*Menlo Park California		
	‡Palo Alto	23 Jun 1946	Claude B. Petersen
659	Merced California	15 Sep 1974	Robert D. Rowan
826	Mission Viejo California	8 May 1977	Nolan C. Draney
399	*Modesto California		
	‡Modesto	7 Jun 1964	Clifton A. Rooker
716	Modesto California North	26 Oct 1975	Charles Elwin Boice
258	*Monterey California		
	‡Monterey Bay	2 Mar 1958	James N. Wallace Jr.
1656	Moreno Valley California	27 Sep 1987	David Lowell Briggs
831	Morgan Hill California	15 May 1977	Donald Russell Lundell
1693	Murrieta California	20 Mar 1988	Ronald Miguel Peterson
297	*Napa California		
	‡Napa	17 Apr 1960	Harry S. Cargun
652	Newbury Park California	18 Aug 1974	Lavar M. Butler
453	*Newport Beach California		
	‡Newport Beach	31 Mar 1968	Ferren L. Christensen
231	*North Hollywood California	6 Dec 1992	
	*Los Angeles California North Hollywood		
	‡Burbank (California)	16 Sep 1956	James D. Pratt
227a	*Oakland California		
	‡Oakland-Berkeley	26 Aug 1956	O. Leslie Stone
1092	Ontario California	9 Dec 1979	Seth C. Baker
251a	*Orange California		
	‡Santa Ana	8 Dec 1957	Karl C. Durham
441	*Palm Springs California		
	‡Palm Springs	27 Aug 1967	Quinten Hunsaker
459	*Palmdale California		
	‡Antelope Valley	12 May 1968	Sterling A. Johnson
739	Palos Verdes California	18 Jan 1976	Merrill Bickmore
128	*Pasadena California		
	‡Pasadena	1 Oct 1939	Bertram M. Jones
1608	Penasquitos California	21 Sep 1986	Michael Lee Jensen
215	*Placentia California		
	*Fullerton	14 Mar 1965	
	‡Orange County	27 Jun 1954	John C. Dalton
675	Pleasanton California	8 Dec 1974	Dale Edwin Nielsen
2202	Porterville California	16 Jun 1996	Steven E. Tree
1056	Poway California	26 Aug 1979	Paul B. Richardson
1648	Rancho Cucamonga California	13 Aug 1987	
	‡Cucamonga California	28 Jun 1987	Steven Thomas Escher
319	*Redding California		
	‡Redding	13 Dec 1960	Albert C. Peterson
938	*Redlands California	5 May 1987	
	‡San Bernardino California East	4 Jun 1978	Donald L. Hansen
415	*Rialto California		
	‡Rialto	20 Mar 1966	Wayne A. Reeves
521	*Ridgecrest California		

171	*Stockton California		
	‡San Joaquin	25 Apr 1948	Wendell B. Mendenhall
1624	Thousand Oaks California	11 Jan 1987	Grant R. Brimhall
282	*Torrance California		
	‡Torrance	3 May 1959	Roland Earl Gagon
220	*Torrance California North		
	‡Redondo	29 May 1955	Leslie L. Prestwich
1591	Turlock California	23 Mar 1986	Robert Peebles Baker
877	Ukiah California	30 Oct 1977	Robert Vernon Knudsen
583	*Upland California		
	‡Upland	13 Aug 1972	Frank E. Finlayson
1801	Vacaville California	26 May 1991	Edwin Gordon Wells Jr.
1845	Valencia California	2 Feb 1992	Reed E. Halladay
548	*Ventura California		
	‡Ventura	30 May 1971	Joseph F. Chapman
1397	Victorville California	30 Jan 1983	Owen Dean Call
492	*Visalia California		
	‡Visalia	24 Aug 1969	Alva D. Blackburn
967	Vista California	8 Oct 1978	Jack Robert Jones
281	*Walnut California	23 July 1985	
	*La Puente California		
	‡West Covina	3 May 1959	Mark W. Smith
1587a	*Walnut Creek California	17 May 1992	
	‡Walnut Creek California East	16 Feb 1986	Williams F. Matthews
280	*Whittier California		
	‡Whittier	26 Apr 1959	John Collings
1079	Yuba City California	4 Nov 1979	Lowell R. Tingey
1969	Yucca Valley California	9 Jan 1994	Kipton Paul Madsen
North America Southwest Area — 1			
1073	Quincy California	14 Oct 1979	Floyd Eugene Warren

Stakes discontinued

159	Berkeley	13 Oct 1946	W. Glenn Harmon
	Discontinued 26 Aug 1956 †Oakland-Berkeley (227a)		
656	Cerritos California West	8 Sep 1974	Kenneth Laurence Davis
	Discontinued 19 May 1996		
806	Concord California East	23 Jan 1977	Vern W. Clark
	Discontinued 16 Feb 1986 †Walnut Creek California East (1587)		
1107	Lawndale California	17 Feb 1980	Silvon Foster Engilman
	Discontinued 21 Feb 1993		
1683	Long Beach California North	31 Jan 1988	V. Jay Spongberg
	Discontinued 7 Nov 1993		
817	Los Angeles California	13 Mar 1977	Clark Spendlove
	Granada Hills 6 Dec 1992		
88	*Los Angeles South 29 May 1970		
	Discontinued 12 Aug 1973 †Huntington Park (279)		
	*South Los Angeles 19 Nov 1939		
	‡Los Angeles	21 Jan 1923	George W. McCune
109	Oakland	2 Dec 1934	W. Aird Macdonald
	Discontinued 26 Aug 1956 †Oakland-Berkeley (227a)		
247	*Pacifica California		
	Discontinued 21 Feb 1982 †San Francisco California (99)		
	‡San Mateo	15 Sep 1957	Melvin P. Pickering
230	Reseda (California)	16 Sep 1956	Hugh C. Smith
	*Los Angeles California Chatsworth		
	Discontinued 6 Dec 1992		
787	Santa Ana California	14 Nov 1976	Wilbur Orion Jensen
	Discontinued 10 Nov 1996		
4a	San Bernardino	6 Jul 1851	David Seely
	Discontinued 1857		
585	San Jose North (California)	20 Aug 1972	Lloyd M. Gustaveson
	*Santa Clara California		
	Discontinued 10 May 1992		
1584	Fremont California South	12 Jan 1986	Jerry Valient Kirk
	Discontinued 11 Jun 2000		

	‡Mount Whitney	16 Aug 1970	AlDean Washburn
196	*Riverside California		
	‡Mount Rubidoux	26 Oct 1952	Vern Robert Peel
430	*Riverside California West		
	‡Arlington	23 Apr 1967	Clarence Leon Sirrine
1854	Rocklin California	19 Apr 1992	Jay Robert Jibson Jr.
515	*Roseville California		
	‡Roseville	17 May 1970	S. Lloyd Hamilton
108	*Sacramento California		
	‡Sacramento	4 Nov 1934	Mark W. Cram
1691	Sacramento California Antelope	6 Mar 1988	Roger William Mack
1152	*Sacramento California Cordova	11 Jan 1994	
	*Sacramento California Rancho Cordova	17 Sep 1985	
	‡Sacramento California Cordova	22 Jun 1980	Richard W. Montgomery
290	*Sacramento California East		
	‡American River	6 Dec 1959	Austin G. Hunt
219	*Sacramento California North		
	*Sacramento North	30 Sep 1969	
	‡North Sacramento	12 Dec 1954	Austin G. Hunt
111	*San Bernardino California		
	‡San Bernardino	3 Feb 1935	Albert Lyndon Larson
136	*San Diego California		
	‡San Diego	9 Feb 1941	Wallace W. Johnson
736	San Diego California East	30 Nov 1975	Philip Alma Petersen
489	*San Diego California North		
	‡San Diego North	22 Jun 1969	Ray Michael Brown
360	*San Diego California Sweetwater	30 Aug 1988	
	*Lemon Grove California	16 Aug 1983	
	*San Diego California South		
	‡San Diego South	21 Oct 1962	Cecil I. Burningham
1915a	San Fernando California (Spanish)	6 Dec 1992	Jose Gerardo Lombardo
99	*San Francisco California		
	‡San Francisco	10 Jul 1927	W. Aird Macdonald
1863	San Francisco California East (Tongan)	10 May 1992	Sione Fangu
1515	San Francisco California West	24 Feb 1985	Jeremiah I. Alip
202	*San Jose California		
	‡San Jose	30 Nov 1952	Vernard L. Beckstrand
693	San Jose California East	4 May 1975	Leo E. Haney
450	*San Jose California South		
	‡San Jose South (California)	11 Feb 1968	DeBoyd L. Smith
329	*San Leandro California		
	‡San Leandro	21 May 1961	Milton R. Ream
248	*San Luis Obispo California		
	‡San Luis Obispo	22 Sep 1957	Arthur J. Godfrey
462	*San Rafael California		
	‡Marin	23 Jun 1968	Weston L. Roe
1838	Santa Ana California South (Spanish)	5 Jan 1992	Renan Ramos Disner
184	*Santa Barbara California		
	‡Santa Barbara	18 Mar 1951	Arthur J. Godfrey
642	*Santa Clarita California	2 Feb 1992	
	‡Los Angeles California Santa Clarita	19 May 1974	Norman D. Stevensen
823	Santa Cruz California	24 Apr 1977	Edwin Reese Davis
1920	Santa Margarita California	17 Jan 1993	David Michael Daly
384	*Santa Maria California		
	‡Santa Maria	20 Oct 1963	Clayton K. Call
181	*Santa Rosa California		
	‡Santa Rosa	7 Jan 1951	J. LeRoy Murdock
1582	Santee California	8 Dec 1985	Robert Earl Harper
387	*Saratoga California		
	‡San Jose West	10 Nov 1963	Louis W. Latimer
448	*Simi Valley California		
	‡Simi	10 Dec 1967	John Lyman Ballif III

Missions — 17
(As of Oct. 1, 2000; shown with historical number. See MISSIONS.)

(73a) CALIFORNIA ANAHEIM MISSION
501 N. Brookhurst, Ste. 100
Anaheim, CA 92801

(283) CALIFORNIA CARLSBAD MISSION
785 Grand Ave., Ste. 202
Carlsbad, CA 92008

(324)CALIFORNIA LONG BEACH MISSION
2501 Cherry Ave, Ste 255
Long Beach, Ca. 90806

(85)CALIFORNIA OAKLAND MISSION
4945 Lincoln Way
Oakland, CA 94602

(284) CALIFORNIA ROSEVILLE
8331 Sierra College Blvd., Ste. 208
Roseville, CA 95661

(182) CALIFORNIA SAN BERNARDINO
8280 Utica Ave, Ste. 150
Rancho Cucamonga, CA 91730

(297) CALIFORNIA SAN FERNANDO
23504 Lyons Ave, Ste. 107
Santa Clarita, CA 91321

(158a) CALIFORNIA SAN JOSE MISSION
5406 Thornwood Dr., Ste. 145
San Jose, CA 95123

(159) CALIFORNIA VENTURA MISSION
260 Maple Ct., Ste. 120
Ventura, CA 9300-3692

(86) CALIFORNIA ARCADIA MISSION
170 West Duarte Road
Arcadia, CA 91007

(118) CALIFORNIA FRESNO MISSION
2350 West Shaw Ave. Ste. 123
Fresno, CA 93711

(5) CALIFORNIA. LOS ANGELES MISSION
1591 E. Temple Way
Los Angeles, CA 90024-5801

(235) CALIFORNIA RIVERSIDE MISSION
3233 Arlington Ave., Ste. 107
Riverside, CA 92506-3246

(37) CALIFORNIA SACRAMENTO MISSION
9480 Madison Ave., Ste. 2
Orangevale, CA 95662

(113) CALIFORNIA SAN DIEGO MISSION
3322 Sweetwater Springs Blvd., Ste. 203
Spring Valley, CA 91977-3142

(301a) CALIFORNIA SAN FRANCISCO
901 Sneath Lane, Ste. 200
San Bruno, CA 94066

(187a) CALIFORNIA SANTA ROSA MISSION
3510 Unocal Place, 302
Santa Rosa, CA 95403

Colorado

Year-end 1999: Est. population, 4,056,000; Members, 112,232; Stakes, 28; Wards, 204; Branches, 34; Missions, 2; Temples, 1; Percent LDS, 2.7, or one in 36.

In 1846, a group of 43 Saints in 19 wagons traveled to the West from Monroe County, Miss. They expected to meet Brigham Young's wagon train at the Platte River in the Nebraska Territory, and accompany his train west. However, Brigham Young's pioneer train stopped at Winter Quarters, Neb., and did not continue west in 1846. By the time the Mississippi company learned of this, they had reached western Nebraska, too far to return. The Mississippians decided to winter at Fort Pueblo in Colorado in the upper Arkansas River Valley, where they arrived Aug. 7, 1846. During the following winter, three detachments of the Mormon Battalion, including wives and children of battalion members and those who were ill, were sent to join the members in Pueblo.

By the end of winter in 1846, the Pueblo colony had 275 people. It was soon disbanded as some joined Brigham Young's company at Fort Laramie June 3, 1847. Others joined later wagon trains going west and the rest returned east to bring their families. No remains of this settlement exist today; its site is near Blende in metropolitan Pueblo.

In 1858, the S.M. Rooker family, traveling east from Utah, heard of a gold discovery and became the first settlers at the junction of Cherry Creek and the Platte River, which would later become Denver. As the city grew, a few Church members arrived, but the area did not have any ecclesiastical leadership until the Colorado Mission was created Dec. 14, 1896, with Elder John W. Taylor of the Quorum of the Twelve as mission president. The first missionaries in the area were Elders John H. Broshard, Hebert A. White, and William C. Clive. The Denver Branch was created Jan. 3, 1897, and a short time later branches in Colorado Springs were organized.

In 1878, a group of 70 converts from the Southern States Mission, under the leadership of Elder James Z. Stewart, settled in Conejos County, Colo. They, and later immigrants under the direction of Church leaders from Utah, founded the communities of Manassa, Richfield, and Sanford in southwestern Colorado. In 1883, the first stake in Colorado, the San Luis Stake, was created in the area.

In the summer of 1897, Bishop John I. Hart of Manassa was called to live in Pueblo and start a branch there among the handful of members. This branch was organized under the direction of Elder Taylor about mid-January, 1897. The Western States Mission, with headquarters in Denver, was organized in 1907.

Missionaries in this period generally found residents to be hospitable and baptized occasional converts. In 1909, missionaries campaigned against the growing number of saloons in Denver. On Nov. 23, 1911, the Tabernacle Choir gave a concert in Denver, and later another concert in Colorado Springs. Montezuma and La Plata counties in Colorado were included in the Young Stake, with headquarters in New Mexico, when that stake was created in 1912.

In 1930, the Denver, Pueblo, San Luis, and Western Colorado mission districts, and the San Luis Stake and the Colorado portion of Young Stake had a combined membership of 6,435 members. A branch in Fort Collins was started after LDS educators arrived to teach at Colorado State University in the 1930s.

The Denver Stake was organized in 1940. During World War II, a number of former missionaries served at military bases in the Denver area. Denver Stake Pres. Edward E. Drury and former mission Pres. Elbert R. Curtis, who was released at the start of the war, held a special service attended by more than 100 servicemen.

Membership continued to grow after the war, and many buildings were constructed. By 1950, membership was nearly 10,000, increasing to nearly 20,000 in 1960, nearly 40,000 in 1970, and 69,000 by 1980.

A temple in Denver to serve the LDS population in Colorado and nearby states was completed and dedicated Oct. 24, 1986. Released-time seminary began and seminary buildings were erected during this time. Membership grew as jobs increased in areas of high technology and the military. Agriculture continued to be a stable source of livelihood for many.

Indicative of the increasing profile of the Church, Colorado Gov. Roy Romer addressed a Church fireside in Willow Springs March 11, 1990. In August 1993, many LDS volunteers assisted when Pope John Paul II of the Roman Catholic Church visited Denver.

Since 1989, Church members have teamed with community organizations to use the Bishops' Storehouse in Denver for efforts to aid the needy. In 1994, for example, an estimated 100,000 canned items were produced for humanitarian use.

In 1996, President Gordon B. Hinckley addressed about 4,580 youth and young adults in Colorado Springs and Denver. He returned to Colorado Sept. 13, 1997, to speak to 22,000 people in Denver at the centennial of the first branch in Colorado. The sesquicentennial of the Pueblo settlement was observed at the same time.

Members from 19 stakes throughout Colorado organized on July 31, 1999, some 55 service projects on a stake or ward level in a grass-roots "day of service" effort that had been initated by Church members and sanctioned by Gov. Bill Owens. On Sept. 25, 1999, the Colorado Springs Colorado North Stake held "A Day For Covenant People" that resulted in 300 missionary referrals, the placing of 600 copies of the Book of Mormon and 800 videos and tracts, and contact with more than 1,300 people in the Colorado Springs area. In 1999, Colorado's LDS membership was 112,232. Colorado has two missions: the Colorado Denver South Mission, which is an outgrowth of the old Western States Mission, and The Colorado Denver North Mission, created in 1993.

Sources: *Encyclopedic History of the Church,* by Andrew Jenson; "Colorado, Mormons and the Mexican War," by John F. Yurtinus, *Essays in Colorado History,* 1983, No. 1; "A Look at the History of the Church . . . in Pueblo, Colorado," by Gail McHardy; *Comprehensive History of the Church,* by B.H. Roberts; "Pioneer Journeys," *Improvement Era,* July 1910, 802-810; "Mississippi Mormons," by Leonard Arrington, *Ensign,* June 1977; "Denver Saints Claim Spiritual Blessings," *Ensign,* Nov. 1986; *Church News,* Oct. 7,1944; Oct. 20, 1945; Feb. 9, 1974; June 4, 1977; Aug. 24, 1986; March 24, 1990; "LDS among volunteers for papal visit," by Twila Bird, *Church News,* Aug. 21, 1993; *Church News,* Sept 20, 1997; "A grass-roots day of service," by R. Scott Lloyd, *Church News,* Aug. 7, 1999; *Church News,* Nov. 6, 1999.

Stakes — 30

(Listed alphabetically by area as of Oct. 1, 2000.)

No.	Name	Organized	First President
	North America Central Area — 29		

1425	Alamosa Colorado	29 May 1983	Gary Reese Shawcroft
1655	Arapahoe Colorado	27 Sep 1987	Lawry Evans Doxey
287	*Arvada Colorado		
	‡Denver West	21 Jun 1959	Thomas L. Kimball
1318	Aurora Colorado	6 Dec 1981	Lawry Evans Doxey
595	*Boulder Colorado		
	‡Boulder	28 Jan 1973	C. Rodney Claridge
301	*Colorado Springs Colorado		
	‡Pikes Peak		
	(Colorado, New Mexico)	11 Sep 1960	Ralph M. Gardner
1770	Colorado Springs Colorado East	26 Aug 1990	Jack Harmon Dunn
1134	Colorado Springs Colorado North	18 May 1980	Richard Larry Williams
1214	Columbine Colorado	7 Dec 1980	David M. Brown
132	*Denver Colorado		
	‡Denver	30 Jun 1940	Douglas M. Todd Jr.
596	*Denver Colorado North		
	‡Denver North	28 Jan 1973	Gus. F. Ranzenberger
470	*Fort Collins Colorado		
	‡Fort Collins	1 Dec 1968	Raymond Price
2542	Fountain Colorado	12 Dec 1999	Larry M. Lewis
1452	Golden Colorado	6 Nov 1983	John Marshall Simcox
223	*Grand Junction Colorado		
	‡Grand Junction	16 Oct 1955	Loyal B. Cook
1415	Grand Junction Colorado West	24 Apr 1983	Andrew H. Christensen
1528	Greeley Colorado	28 Apr 1985	Gilbert I. Sandberg
1534	*Highlands Ranch Colorado	21 Aug 1998	
	‡Willow Creek Colorado	19 May 1985	Robert K. Bills
394	*Lakewood Colorado		
	‡Denver South	19 Apr 1964	R. Raymond Barnes
625	*Littleton Colorado		
	‡Littleton	2 Sep 1973	Clinton L. Cutler
1778	Longmont Colorado	11 Nov 1990	Lynn Snarr Hutchings
2562	Loveland Colorado	18 Jun 2000	Alan J. Baker
26	*Manassa Colorado 31 May 1983		
	*La Jara Colorado		
	‡San Luis (Colorado, New Mexico)	10 Jun 1883	Silas S. Smith
320	Meeker Colorado		
	‡Craig	15 Jan 1961	Loyal B. Cook
977	Montrose Colorado	5 Nov 1978	Robert M. Esplin
2236	Parker Colorado	15 Sep 1996	William Kenneth Thiess
632	Pueblo Colorado	3 Mar 1974	Louis Edward Butler
2346	Westminster Colorado	27 Apr 1997	David B. Parker
North America Southwest Area — 1			
557	*Durango Colorado		
	‡Mesa Verde	7 Nov 1971	Del A. Talley Sr.

Stakes discontinued

21	Little Colorado	27 Jan 1878	Lot Smith
	Discontinued (Colo., Ariz.) 18 Dec 1887 †Snowflake (31a)		

Missions — 2

(As of Oct. 1, 2000; shown with historical number. See MISSIONS.)

(286) COLORADO DENVER NORTH MISSION
11172 North Huron, Suite 21
Northglenn, CO 80234

(17) COLORADO DENVER SOUTH MISSION
Box 2674
Littleton, CO 80161-2674

Connecticut

Year-end 1999: Est. population, 3,282,000; Members, 12,163; Stakes, 2; Wards, 22; Branches, 12; Missions, 1; Percent LDS, 0.4, or one in 274.

Elders Orson Hyde and Samuel H. Smith began missionary work in Connecticut in 1832 when they preached in the New England states. Evidently they did not have any converts in Connecticut. Other missionaries followed, including Elder Wilford Woodruff, a native of Farmington, Conn. He arranged to have a meeting with his family on July 1, 1838. Earlier on the day of the meeting, he wrote, "Distress overwhelmed the whole household, and all were tempted to reject the work." Later he felt a dramatic change. "Filled with the power of God, I stood in the midst of the congregation and preached unto the people in great plainness the gospel of Jesus Christ." He afterward baptized his father, stepmother, sister, and three others, and organized a small branch in Farmington.

The Eastern States Mission was created in 1839 and branches were established in Hartford, New Haven, and other areas. Missionary work continued in the area until the 1850s when most members left the area, and any further missionary work waited until near the turn of the century. However, at that time missionaries throughout New England encountered prejudice and made little headway.

By 1930, branches existed in Hartford, New Haven, and Springfield. Membership was 198.

In 1932, missionaries reported "striving diligently" in Connecticut and "large attendances" at each meeting of a conference held during the summer.

The New England Mission was created in 1937. On June 16, 1944, a meetinghouse at Bridgeport, which was converted from a home purchased two years earlier, was dedicated at a branch conference.

In 1952, the Hartford Branch meetinghouse was dedicated, the first meetinghouse to be erected in the New England Mission. Mission leaders began seeing some growth in the 1950s and noted that membership increased following 1952, and doubled from 1955 to 1959. During this period, missionwide youth conferences and annual Relief Society gatherings were well-attended by members.

The Hartford Stake was created in 1966 from the Connecticut Valley District, covering most of the state and parts of western Massachusetts. The stake had a membership of nearly 3,000 with wards in Hartford, Manchester, New Haven, New London, and Southington, and branches in Madison and Torrinton in Connecticut, as well as branches and wards in Massachusetts.

The Connecticut Hartford Mission was created in 1979. Membership in 1980 was 6,300. A temple was announced in 1992 for Hartford, but it was announced three years later on Sept. 30, 1995, that two temples would be built, rather than one. The two temples would be built in White Plains, N.Y., and Boston, Mass., both of which had experienced recent growth.

For their youth conference July 5-7, 1995, young men and young women from the New Haven Connecticut Stake volunteered service to the Special Olympics World Games held in and around New Haven. Their service helped make the games a success for 7,000 participants from 140 countries.

During the pioneer sesquicentennial in 1997, 80 youth from New Haven took a five-day handcart trek in Cockaponset State Forest.

Elder Jeffrey R. Holland of the Quorum of the Twelve, a graduate of Yale, returned to the campus in New Haven on April 25, 1997, and spoke to some 800 Latter-day Saints and friends at the famous Battell Chapel on campus. It is believed that Elder Holland was the first Church member to speak at the elegant, century-old edifice. The day next, he dedicated the Wilford Woodruff Center, a multi-purpose facility on campus that serves as an institute of religion for Yale and four other nearby colleges, as well as a meetinghouse for three branches.

In 1999, Elder Donald L. Staheli of the Seventy dedicated a memorial in a park in Avon in honor of President Woodruff, who spent his early years there. That year, there were 12,163 members in Connecticut.

Sources: *Encyclopedic History of the Church,* by Andrew Jenson; *Church News,* July 16, 1932, Sept. 3, 1938, July 22, 1944, Oct. 4, 1952, Sept. 24, 1966, June 11, 1977, Sept. 28, 1986, July 15, 1995, May 3, 1997, July 19, 1997, May 22, 1999.

Stakes — 2

(Listed alphabetically as of Oct. 1, 2000.)

No.	Name	Organized	First President
	North America Northeast Area		
421	*Hartford Connecticut ‡Hartford (Conn., Mass.)	18 Sep 1966	Hugh S. West
1288	New Haven Connecticut	30 Aug 1981	Steven Douglas Colson

Mission — 1

(As of Oct. 1, 2000; shown with historical number. See MISSIONS.)

(169) CONNECTICUT HARTFORD MISSION

P.O. Box 378
Bloomfield, CT 06002

Delaware

Year-end 1999: Est. population, 754,000; Members, 3,730; Stakes, 1; Wards, 7; Branches, 1; Percent LDS: 0.5, or one in 202.

Elder Jedediah M. Grant entered Delaware and began missionary work in 1837. Little is known of his progress or other missionary work during that period. However, Wilmington was an important rendezvous for missionaries of the Eastern States Mission. Wilmington's proximity to Philadelphia and its frontage on the Delaware Intracoastal Waterway made it a likely route of passage for Church leaders, as well as for converts entering the United States.

On Feb. 4, 1901, Elder John E. Baird left Brooklyn, N.Y., to visit missionaries in eastern cities including those in Wilmington. On May 26, 1914, Elders Stanley A. Lawrence and Alphonso W. Taylor reported teaching a woman who had gained a testimony of the Book of Mormon. Two years later, on Nov. 7, 1916, two missionaries reported renting a hall in Wilmington where, beginning the following Sunday, meetings were held during the winter.

A missionary meeting was held Feb. 2, 1925, and in 1926 another meeting was held in a local hall with attendance of about 18 people. In 1931, missionaries broadcast their message over a local radio station. Lack of success resulted in missionaries being withdrawn until 1940 when Wilmington was re-opened.

Block teaching began in 1941 among some 16 LDS families. Meetings began May 4, and the Wilmington Branch was organized Sept. 28, 1941. The branch, with nine adults and 10 children, continued with little growth for the next decade. In 1950, some 63 attended a branch party at the home of the branch president. The Salisbury Branch was organized in 1953.

In 1960, the Philadelphia Stake was created with a ward in Wilmington and branches in Dover and Salisbury in Delaware. In December 1974, the Wilmington Delaware Stake was created. Membership in the state in 1974 was 1,350, increasing to 1,767 in 1980, and to 3,178 in 1990. By 1988, Wilmington was home of three large wards, and Dover, Salisbury, and Elkton each had a large ward. Branches were organized in Cambridge (two) and Smyrna (one). Many members went to Delaware to work for the large chemical companies that have headquarters in this state. Youth in the state participated in a roundtable discussion on challenges on LDS values in May 1998.

In 1999, Delaware had 3,730 members in seven wards and one branch.

Sources: *Encyclopedic History of the Church,* by Andrew Jenson; *Journal History of the Eastern States Mission; The LDS Church in Delaware: A Book of Remembrance,* by Helen Candland Stark, published in Wilmington, Delaware, 1966; "Church grows larger in 2nd smallest state," by Kevin Stoker, *Church News,* Dec. 3, 1988; *Church News,* May 9, 1998.

Stake — 1

(As of Oct. 1, 2000.)

No.	Name	Organized	First President
North America Northeast Area			
673	Wilmington Delaware	8 Dec 1974	Rulon Edward Johnson Jr.

District of Columbia

Year-end 1999: Est. population, 519,000; Members, 1,660; Stakes, 1; Wards, 8; Districts, 1; Branches, 7; Missions, 2; Percent LDS, 0.3, or one in 324.

The Prophet Joseph Smith, accompanied by Elias Higbee, visited the nation's capital in 1839 seeking redress of grievances suffered by the Saints in Missouri. As the coach in which they and others were riding approached the city, the horses began running away. The Prophet heroically saved his fellow passengers. Joseph and Elias stayed in Washington for two weeks and called on President Martin Van Buren, who reportedly said, "Your cause is just, but I can do nothing for you."

The same year, Parley P. Pratt published an address setting forth the principles of the gospel and saw that a copy was presented to the President and each Cabinet member.

On Aug. 16, 1841, Samuel James was appointed to labor in Washington. Apostle John E. Page preached in Washington in 1843, baptizing one convert.

In 1843, Apostles Orson Hyde and Orson Pratt, and later joined by Apostles Heber C. Kimball, William Smith, and Lyman Wight, outlined the plight of the Saints to President John Tyler. Elder Jesse C. Little, while serving as president of the Eastern States Mission, served as the Church's representative in Washington, D.C., and in 1846 negotiated the raising of a 500-man Mormon battalion to be part of the United States' Army of the West during the Mexican War.

Later, Elder Orson Pratt presided over the Saints in the Eastern States and served as a missionary in Washington, D.C. He was joined by Elder Jedediah M. Grant, and together they met with President Millard Fillmore. In Washington, for about 18 months in 1853-54, they published a monthly periodical, *The Seer,* in memory of the Prophet Joseph Smith,

After arriving in the Great Basin, members requested a state government, but were granted territory status instead. In pursuing statehood, members from Utah paid occasional visits to Washington, D.C. Some lived in Washington, D.C., or nearby areas while serving as Utah's delegates to Congress. After the turn of the 20th century, Elder Reed Smoot of the Quorum of the Twelve was elected to the U.S. Senate, and, after four years of well-publicized hearings, was seated. His later powerful leadership in the Senate won admiration for the Church.

During the early years of Senator Smoot's term, a handful of members who lived in Washington met for Church services in his home. In June 1919, a branch was organized, and by 1927, the branch was meeting in an auditorium. Some 150 attended services upstairs while activities, such as circuses and auto shows, went on below.

Later Latter-day Saint leaders, including J. Reuben Clark Jr., Marriner S. Eccles, Edgar Brossard, J. Willard Marriott, and Ezra Taft Benson, gave substantial service to the Church in the nation's capital.

In 1930, the Church began construction on a chapel built of imported Utah marble. The building was completed in 1933 and helped establish the Church's reputation as a permanent institution. It was the only chapel in the Church with a statue of the Angel Moroni atop the building. In 1940, the Washington D.C. Stake was created and Ezra Taft Benson, while he was executive secretary of a federation of cooperative farm groups, was called as president of the stake, only the third stake east of the Mississippi River. After Elder Benson was called as an apostle in 1943, he returned later to the nation's capital as Secretary of Agriculture in the Eisenhower administration from 1953-1961.

In the 1960s, the Tabernacle Choir sang at the inauguration of Lyndon B. Johnson on Jan. 18, 1965, and at Richard M. Nixon's inauguration Jan. 20, 1969. The choir also sang at inauguration festivities for two U.S. presidents in the 1980s, during Ronald Reagan's first inauguration Jan. 20, 1981, and during activities at George Bush's inauguration Jan. 19, 1989.

Membership in the region continued to grow as Latter-day Saints with federal government jobs moved in. Additional stakes were created so by 1970 four stakes covered the area of the original Washington stake. In 1962, a site in suburban Kensington, Md., was purchased for a temple, and the Washington D.C. Temple was dedicated 12 years later in 1974. The imposing edifice immediately became a landmark for the Church in the nation's capital.

Returning from a monthlong South and Central America tour in 1977, President Spencer W. Kimball stopped in Washington, D.C., on March 11 and met with U.S. President Jimmy Carter in the Oval Office in the White House. The visit was requested by President Carter. In 1986, President Ezra Taft Benson visited with President Ronald Reagan at the White House, and on Nov. 13, 1995, President Gordon B. Hinckley met with President Bill Clinton and presented the U.S. president with a copy of the Church's "Proclamation on the Family" and a volume containing six generations of his family history.

By 1985, the four stakes in the greater Washington, D.C., area had increased to 19 stakes and membership jumped from 21,000 to 63,000. In 1986, two wards were created within the city, the Washington DC 1st Ward (Spanish) and the Washington DC 2nd Ward, which met in the National Press Club Building. In 1992 and 1993, several small branches were created. In May 1994, the District of Columbia District was created, and, within a year, two additional branches were added, including the Gallaudet (Deaf) Branch. The new district unified branches that had been under other stakes. By 1997, district membership approached 1,000 members, and in 1999 reached 1,660 in five branches.

Members in the Washington, D.C., area participate in inter-faith food drives, using the resources of the Church cannery, and in other community activities. The Tabernacle Choir performed in the Kennedy Center for the Performing Arts in 1995.

Two annual events in the Washington, D.C., area attract considerable interest and raise the Church's profile not only in the nation's capital but also with ambassadors and diplomats from throughout the world.

The first is the Christmas lighting ceremony, which started in 1978, on the grounds of the Washington, D.C., Temple. In recent years, Washington's diplomatic corps has been invited to the ceremony and each year an ambassador from one of the countries has been selected to participate, with one of the Church's General Authorities, in switching on the lights. In 1996, President Hinckley joined with Brazil's ambassador in turning on the lights. Enhancing the international flavor of the Festival of Lights are the international creche or Nativity scenes exhibit and the international dolls displayed on four Christmas trees in the visitors center. In 1998, 75 countries were represented in the doll display.

The other event is the Western Family Picnic, held each year for ambassadors and embassy officials and their families at the Marriott Farm in rural Hume, Va., designed to acquaint the diplomatic community with the Church's values, history, and heritage. The first picnic was in 1991; by 1994, 40 countries were represented. On Sept. 25, 1999, guests at the picnic participated in one of the Church's humanitarian projects by helping to make quilts for refugees in Kosovo.

Sources: *Encyclopedic History of the Church,* by Andrew Jenson; "History of the Washington Branch," *Church News,* Nov. 4, 1933; "A Little Leavening," by Florian H. Thayn, *BYU Studies,* Spring 1981; "From Colony to Community; the Washington D.C. Saints," by Mary L. Bradford, *Ensign,* August 1974; "Prophet, President Carter confer in D.C.," by Dell Van Orden, *Church News,* March 19, 1977; "Membership triples in Nation's Capital," *Church News,* Dec. 2, 1989; "Pioneer members recall rich memories," *Church News,* July 20, 1991, Oct. 26, 1991, Oct. 23, 1993; Feb. 2, 1994; Dec. 2, 1994, Aug. 12, 1995, Oct. 8, 1995; "White House visit," by Jocelyn Mann Denyer, *Church News,* Nov. 18, 1995; *Church News,* Sept. 28, 1996, Dec. 7, 1996; Correspondence from Kevin P. Riehle, Jan. 26, 1997; *Church News,* Dec. 12, 1998, July 10, 1999, Oct. 16, 1999.

Stake — 1

(As of Oct. 1, 2000. To simplify reference, the stake and missions in the Washington, D.C., area that carry the name of Washington, D.C., are listed in the District of Columbia rather than the state where the mission office is located.)

No.	Name	Organized	First President
North America East Area			
131	*Washington D.C. ‡Washington (D.C., Pa., Md.)	30 Jun 1940	Ezra Taft Benson

Missions — 2

(As of Oct. 1, 2000; shown with historical number. See MISSIONS.)

(188b) WASHINGTON D.C. NORTH MISSION
904 Wind River Lane, Suite 103
North Potomac, MD 20878

(54) WASHINGTON D.C. SOUTH MISSION
5631 Burke Centre Parkway, Suite H
Burke, VA 22015

Florida

Year-end 1999: Est. population, 15,111,000; Members, 108,955; Stakes, 24; Wards, 169; Branches, 32; Missions, 5; Temples 1; Percent LDS, 0.7, or one in 138.

Elders William Brown and Daniel Cathart may have served in Florida in April 1843, but no record exists of them doing so. Possibly the first missionary in Florida was Phineas Young, who reported placing copies of the Book of Mormon during a two-month mission in April to June of 1845 that may have reached into Florida. The first long-term missionary work evidently started before Nov. 1, 1895, when the Florida Conference was organized under the direction of Pres. Elias S. Kimball of the Southern States Mission. Fifteen missionaries were assigned to labor there.

Missionaries started a number of Sunday Schools, the first of which was at Coe Mills, Liberty County, in May 1895. By September 1897, 11 Sunday Schools had been organized. The first branch was created in Jefferson County in 1897. The Sanderson Branch, probably organized Jan. 3, 1898, was the site of a missionary conference in 1898. George P. Canova, a well-to-do landowner and chairman of the Baker County Commission, was the president of the branch. On June 5, 1898, following threats of violence, Pres. Canova was martyred as he returned home from a conference. Missionaries were also temporarily driven out of Tallahassee and Orlando but returned later. They found varying degrees of success in Key West, Sanford, Starke, Peoria, Kissimmee, Tampa, Duck Pond, Lake City, St. Augustin, and Middleburg.

In 1900, Elder William H. Boyle reported the branches in Florida to be "in apple pie order" and that missionaries traveling without purse or scrip were hospitably received.

Growth came slowly, however. In 1906, a meetinghouse was dedicated in Jacksonville, and in 1907, another was completed in Oak Grove.

In 1906, Charles A. Callis, later mission president and a member of the Quorum of the Twelve, became president of the Florida Conference. By 1920, branches in Jacksonville, Sanderson, and Tampa existed. By 1925, branches or Sunday Schools had been added in Miami, Oak Grove, Oldtown, Telogia, Westville, Springfield, and St. Augustine. A larger meetinghouse was completed in Jacksonville in 1926. In 1930, the Florida District had 3,164 members in four branches and eight Sunday Schools. The West Florida District was created about this time, and branches or Sunday Schools increased. By 1935, the Florida District had 22 branches, and the West Florida District had another 13 branches.

The first stake in Florida — and in the South — was created in Jacksonville Jan. 17, 1947, by Elder Charles A. Callis, then of the Quorum of the Twelve, who died there four days later. The new stake had 3,000 members in the Jacksonville, Springfield, Wesconnett, Lake City, Palatka, Axson, (Ga.), and Waycross, (Ga.) wards. Called as the first president of the new stake was Alvin C. Chace, a grandson of early leader George P. Canova.

In 1950, the Church purchased a 300,000-acre area in Central Florida, which became Deseret Ranch.

Membership increased rapidly as members from the West moved into the state, drawn by a strong commerce and the aerospace industry. Additional converts were baptized. When the Florida Mission was created in 1960, four stakes had been organized. Membership in Florida in 1977 was 30,000, increasing to 54,674 in 1980, and to 82,413 in 1990. Creation of the first Spanish-speaking stake in the Southeast in Miami on Jan, 16, 1994, reflected the increase in membership among Latin Americans and immigrants. Another Spanish-speaking stake was created in Hialeah Gardens in 1998.

In February 1990, the First Presidency announced that a temple would be built in the Orlando area. Later, a scenic location in Windermere, five miles southeast of Orlando, was selected for the temple and ground was broken June 20, 1992. The temple was dedicated Oct. 9, 1994.

President Gordon B. Hinckley on Jan. 19, 1997, addressed more than 5,000 members at a conference in Jacksonville, commemorating the stake's 50th anniversary. Today, there are five missions and 24 stakes in Florida, which has an LDS population of 108,955.

Sources: *Encyclopedic History of the Church,* by Andrew Jenson; *History of the Southern States Mission,* a BYU thesis by LaMar C. Berrett, July 1960; A brief summation of the growth of the Church . . . leading to the Florida Stake, by Stanley Clyde Johnson, 1986, unpublished; Church directories, 1919-1935; *Church News,* Jan. 25, 1947, Feb. 22, 1947, Dec. 1, 1956; Oct. 8, 1960; Sept, 14, 1963; March 6, 1976; July 2, 1977; and March 14, 1987; "The first Spanish-speaking stake in Southeast is created in Florida," by Kathleen Ryan, *Church News,* Feb. 19, 1994; *Church News,* May 28, 1994; "Temple is dedicated in Sunshine state, 20,670 attend sessions," by Gerry Avant, *Church News,* Oct. 15, 1994; *Church News,* Jan. 25, 1997.

Stakes — 24

(Listed alphabetically as of Oct. 1, 2000.)

No.	Name	Organized	First President
	North America Southeast Area		
1898	Brandon Florida	23 Aug 1992	James Franklin Henry
879	Cocoa Florida	13 Nov 1977	Cleavy Eugene Waters
2494	De Land Florida	20 Sep 1998	
530	*Fort Lauderdale Florida		
	‡Fort Lauderdale	18 Oct 1970	Stanley C. Johnson
1472	Fort Myers Florida	13 May 1984	John M. Cyrocki
2151	Fort Walton Beach Florida	07 Jan 1996	Charles E. Atkinson Jr.
746	Gainesville Florida	29 Feb 1976	James R. Christianson
2432	Hialeah Gardens Florida (Spanish)	25 Jan 1998	Mario B. Ayaviri
1842	*Homestead Florida 16 Jan 1994		
	‡South Miami Florida	19 Jan 1992	Dean Michael Madsen
465	*Jacksonville Florida East		
	‡Jacksonville	15 Sep 1968	Louis B. Vorwaller
163	*Jacksonville Florida West		
	‡Florida (Florida, Georgia)	19 Jan 1947	Alvin C. Chace
1590	Lake City Florida	16 Mar 1986	Ernest Robert Peacock
1380	*Lake Mary Florida 27 Oct 1987		
	‡Deland Florida	14 Nov 1982	Marvin Knowles

311	*Miami Florida (Spanish)		
	‡Miami	13 Nov 1960	Paul R. Cheesman
257	*Orlando Florida		
	‡Orlando	23 Feb 1958	W. Leonard Duggar
1900	Orlando Florida South	30 Aug 1992	Carl E. Reynolds Jr.
732	*Panama City Florida 4 Feb 1986		
	‡Marianna Florida	16 Nov 1975	Riley Malone Peddie
486	*Pensacola Florida		
	‡Pensacola	15 Jun 1969	S. Elroy Stapleton
1970	Pompano Beach Florida	16 Jan 1994	Richard Merlin Smith
651	St. Petersburg Florida	18 Aug 1974	Bruce Earl Belnap
1190	*Stuart Florida 16 Jan 1994		
	‡West Palm Beach Florida	12 Oct 1980	Donald Wayne Carson
594	*Tallahassee Florida		
	‡Tallahassee	21 Jan 1973	Jay Nicholas Lybbert
289	*Tampa Florida		
	‡Tampa	25 Oct 1959	Edwin H.White
1153	*Winter Haven Florida 10 Oct 1991		
	‡Lakeland Florida	27 Jun 1980	Waymon E. Meadows

Missions — 5

(As of Oct. 1, 2000; shown with historical number. See MISSIONS.)

(178b) FLORIDA FT. LAUDERDALE MISSION
7951 SW 6th St., Ste. 110
Ft. Lauderdale, FL 33324-3211

(326) FLORIDA ORLANDO MISSION
8809 Commodity Cir., Ste. 3
Orlando, FL 32819

(139) FLORIDA TAMPA MISSION
13153 N. Dale Mabry, Ste. 109
Tampa, FL 33618

(197) FLORIDA JACKSONVILLE MISSION
8651 Baypine Road, Ste.105
Jacksonville, FL 32256

(96) FLORIDA TALLAHASSEE MISSION
1535 Killearn Center Blvd., Suite C-4
Tallahassee, FL 32308

Georgia

Year-end 1999: Est. population, 7,788,000; Members, 57,857; Stakes, 14; Wards, 86; Branches, 30; Missions, 2; Temples, 1; Percent LDS, 0.7, or one in 134.

Elder John U. Eldredge briefly opened missionary work in Georgia in 1843. Other missionaries followed to preach and to campaign for Joseph Smith in his presidential bid. When the Prophet was martyred in 1844, the work waned, and was halted in 1846. Missionary work resumed in 1870 in the South, and in 1878 in Georgia. Southern States Mission headquarters were established in Rome, Ga., 60 miles north of Atlanta, in 1879. Pres. John Morgan wrote the pamphlet *Plan of Salvation* in Rome.

Success was realized in Rome and Axson, which was called "Little Utah," by local people. The Douglas Branch was called "Cumorah." One prominent convert, Judge Wyatt N. Williams, was baptized in Buchanan on April 25, 1879, and subsequently donated land and built a chapel in Haralson County at a place called "Mormon Springs," near his mill and cotton gin.

Missionaries were initially treated well upon their return to the South, but before long, their successes led to violent opposition. On July 21, 1879, Elder Joseph Standing was killed by a mob near Varnell's Station, Ga. His companion, Rudger Clawson, later a member of the Quorum of the Twelve, escaped serious injury. Mission leaders were unable to secure protection for missionaries, so Georgia was closed for a decade. In 1884, a small group of members from Georgia joined immigrants who went West by train from Chattanooga, Tenn.

Work resumed cautiously. In 1899, convert Aldora Landrum Yarn was taught in a single meeting held after dark, then baptized. She did not see another missionary for three and a half years.

Disease and persecution slowed the work, the former taking a greater toll than the latter. Ill missionaries were sent to Ohio, which was added to the Southern States Mission in 1899 at the request of Pres. Ben E. Rich so he would have a place where the missionaries could recover.

U.S. Census reports listed 175 Mormons in Georgia in 1890.

By 1908, some 6,800 converts had been baptized throughout the South during Pres. Rich's term. That year, a branch was organized and a meetinghouse constructed in Atlanta. It was replaced in 1915 with a larger building.

Pres. Charles A. Callis succeeded Pres. Rich. Pres. Callis embarked on a 25-year term that saw about 800 to 1,000 converts per year throughout the South. When then-Apostle Heber J. Grant visited Atlanta in 1911, he addressed an overflow congregation in a local Universalist church. He was favorably received.

In 1919, headquarters of the Southern States Mission was moved from Chattanooga, Tenn., to Atlanta, and a new meetinghouse was erected there in 1925.

The first convert in Savannah was Julia Mozell Love, baptized in 1901. The first Sunday School in Savannah was created March 26, 1922, in the home of Arthur B. and Annie Laura Davis. A small meetinghouse, known as the "Little White Chapel," was completed in 1929.

Steady growth continued so that by 1930, the original Southern States Mission had some 50,000 members. The Georgia Conference, in northern Georgia, had 2,626 members in Atlanta, Augusta, Columbus, Macon, and Savannah branches and in Cedar Crossing, Douglas, Empire, Glenwood, Milledgeville, and Thomaston Sunday Schools. The South Georgia District had 1,686 members. The state membership was 4,311.

One of the prominent pioneer leaders in Atlanta was Homer Yarn. In 1916, he became the first local leader of a Sunday School in Atlanta and president of the Atlanta Branch in 1925. When the Georgia District was organized in 1937, he was the first local district president. He served as mission president's counselor from 1939-57.

LeGrand Richards, later a member of the Quorum of the Twelve, served as mission president from 1934-37, and wrote the outline for *A Marvelous Work and a Wonder* while in Atlanta.

In 1957, the first stake in Georgia, the Atlanta Stake (later changed to Tucker Stake) was created. It covered the northern two-thirds of the state and had 3,000 members in wards in Atlanta (2), Columbus, Macon, and Empire, and branches in Buchanan, Athens, Givson, Milledgeville, and Palmetto. Covering the rest of the state was the Georgia-Florida and South Georgia districts. Membership in Georgia was 14,360 in 1974, increasing to 27,210 in 1980, and 41,595 in 1990.

In 1983, the Atlanta Temple was completed and dedicated, giving the South its first temple. In the late 1980s and early 1990s, five branches were established in the central sections of Atlanta among minorities, including Asian and Hispanic people.

North America Southeast Area headquarters in Atlanta include complete temporal and ecclesiastical distribution centers. From Atlanta, supplies have been shipped to many areas of devastation in the South caused by hurricanes and floods, including Hurricane Andrew in 1992, the Albany, Ga., flooding in 1994, and Hurricane Opal in 1995.

In December 1994, the Church donated 158,000 pounds of food through 26 religious and charitable organizations in Atlanta.

In 1996, hundreds of Church members from Georgia gave service during the 1996 Centennial Olympic Summer Games. During the Olympics, Georgia hosted athletes and guests from 198 nations.

Members in Savannah celebrated the 75th anniversary of the first Sunday School in 1997. And part of the Atlanta Temple was rededicated Nov. 14, 1997. President Gordon B. Hinckley again visited Atlanta May 17, 1998, and spoke to more than 13,000 members. In 1999, there were 57,857 members in Georgia.

Sources: *Encyclopedic History of the Church,* by Andrew Jenson; "William L. Nicholls to Preside Over New Altanta Stake," *Church News,* May 11, 1957; *History of the Southern States Mission* by LaMar C. Berrett, a BYU thesis, July 1960; *A Brief History of the Southern States Mission for One Hundred Years 1830-1930,* by DeVon H. Nish, a BYU paper of 1966; Highlights of D. Homer Yarn, by David H. Yarn Jr.;"Georgia enters era of temples," by Gerry Avant, *Church News,* April 24, 1983; "Inner-city district gathers many of diverse cultures into 'gospel net,'" by Mike Cannon, *Church News,* May 29, 1993; "6,000 ease aftermath of flooding," by Gerry Avant, *Church News,* July 30, 1994; "LDS render service in wake of Opal's rage," *Church News,* Oct. 14, 1995; "Through service, members find, share Olympic Spirit," by Sarah Jane Weaver, *Church News,* July 27, 1996; "79 tons of food given to Atlanta's hungry," *Church News,* Dec. 31, 1996; "LDS display touches Olympic visitors," by Richard D. Hall, *Church News,* Aug. 3, 1996; "Savannah," by Gerry Avant, *Church News,* May 5, 1998; *Church News,* Mar. 28, 1998, May 23, 1998.

Stakes — 14

(Listed alphabetically as of Oct. 1, 2000.)

No.	Name	Organized	First President
	North America Southeast Area		
2218	Albany Georgia	11 Aug 1996	Gregory Wayne Widman
2203	Atlanta Georgia	23 Jun 1996	John Devin Cornish
889	*Augusta Georgia 21 Aug 1988		
	‡West Columbia South Carolina	5 Feb 1978	George A. Huff Sr.
886	Columbus Georgia	15 Jan 1978	William F. Meadows Jr.
715	Douglas Georgia	26 Oct 1975	Roswald Mancil
921	*Jonesboro Georgia 29 Jan 1991		
	‡Atlanta Georgia	14 May 1978	Warren Richard Jones
1660	*Kingsland Georgia 13 May 1997		
	‡Jacksonville Florida North	15 Nov 1987	Robert Edwin Bone
241	*Lilburn Georgia 23 Jun 1996		
	*Tucker Georgia 1 Sep 1974		
	*Atlanta Georgia		
	‡Atlanta (Georgia)	5 May 1957	William L. Nicholls
373	*Macon Georgia		
	‡Macon (Georgia, Alabama)	10 Mar 1963	Rayford L. Henderson
1643	Marietta Georgia East	21 Jun 1987	Paul A. Snow
1208	*Powder Springs Georgia 10 Sep 1991		
	‡Marietta Georgia	23 Nov 1980	William K. Farrar Jr.
640	*Roswell Georgia 21 Jun 1987		
	*Sandy Springs Georgia 1 Sep 1974		
	‡Tucker Georgia	12 May 1974	Richard Parry Winder
916	Savannah Georgia	7 May 1978	Robert W. Cowart
1799	Sugar Hill Georgia	26 May 1991	Donald Arthur Cazier

Missions — 2

(As of Oct. 1, 2000; shown with historical number. See MISSIONS.)

(8b) GEORGIA ATLANTA MISSION
1140 Hammond Drive, Ste.B-2110
Atlanta, GA 30328-5338

(239) GEORGIA MACON MISSION
5082 Forsyth Road, Stes. A &B
Macon, GA 31210

Hawaii

Year-end 1999: Est. population, 1,185,000; Members, 55,361; Stakes, 14; Wards, 106; Branches, 5; Missions, 1; Temples, 2; Percent LDS: 4.7, or one in 21.

Sam Brannan and his party of Mormon immigrants aboard the ship *Brooklyn* stopped in Hawaii in 1846, en route to California and the Great Basin via Cape Horn at the southern tip of South America.

Although missionaries had been called in 1843 to the Sandwich Islands, as the islands were then known, they worked instead at Tubuai, one of the southern islands of French Polynesia.

In 1850, gold-mining elders serving in northern California were called to open a mission in Polynesia. They landed in Honolulu Dec. 12, 1850, under the direction of Pres. Hiram Clark. On Feb. 10, 1851, Pres. Clark baptized a 16-year-old Hawaiian young man, the first convert in Hawaii. Other missionaries were not as successful and returned discouraged to the mainland. But Elders George Q. Cannon, James Keeler, William Farrer, Henry W. Bigler, and James Hawkins remained and converted a number of people. Elder Cannon baptized three well-educated Hawaiians, Jonathan Napela, Uaua, and Kaleohano, who later became prominent missionaries for the Church.

On Aug. 6, 1851, the Kula Branch was organized in the village of Kealakou on the island of Maui. At a conference on Aug. 18, four more branches were organized and membership reached 220. The first meetinghouse on the islands was built in 1852 in Pulehu on the island of Maui and still stands today. More missionaries arrived and by 1854, a colony and plantation were started at Lanai, a designated gathering place.

The Book of Mormon was published in Hawaiian in 1855. In 1857, missionaries were called home because of the coming of Johnston's army.

In 1861 a self-appointed leader, Walter Murray Gibson, usurped Church leadership in the absence of missionaries. A recent convert called on a mission to the South Pacific, he took over the Church organization and property. Leading Hawaiian elders notified the Church of Gibson and President Young sent Apostles Ezra T. Benson and Lorenzo Snow to investigate. They immediately excommunicated Gibson.

Defrauded of its property in Lanai, the Church purchased 6,000 acres at Laie, on the main island of Oahu, on Jan. 26, 1865, where a colony and sugar factory were started. Schools have been part of the colony since 1874.

Later, many of the Hawaiians wanted to gather to Utah to receive their temple blessings. So the Church purchased a ranch in Skull Valley, near Tooele, Utah, and the Hawaiian Saints founded the colony of Iosepa (Joseph) in 1889. By 1910 the colony was disbanded and the colonists returned to Hawaii.

The Church subsequently built a temple in Laie, which was dedicated Nov. 27, 1919. The temple was extensively remodeled in the 1970s and rededicated on June 13, 1978.

In 1913, missionaries calculated that 22 percent of the Hawaiian population was LDS. Membership in Hawaii in 1920 was 11,078, increasing to 14,433 by 1930. In 1940, membership dropped to 9,789 but increased again in 1950, following World War II, to 11,855. By 1960, membership grew to 18,327 and to 23,377 in 1970.

The Oahu Stake, the first stake in Hawaii, was created June 30, 1935, by Pres. Heber J. Grant. While there, the former missionary to Japan felt a need for a mission to the many Japanese people in Hawaii. On Feb. 24, 1937, the Japanese Mission (later called the Central Pacific Mission) in Hawaii was organized. Over the next dozen years, nearly 700 Japanese-Americans were converted in this effort, including Elder Adney Y. Komatsu, who served as a General Authority from 1975 to 1993. Many of the missionaries and converts helped open and continue missionary work in Japan after World War II. Hawaiian members also opened the door for missionary work in South Pacific islands.

The Church College of Hawaii opened in Laie Sept. 26, 1955. Many members from the South Pacific and Asia have been educated at the school, now called BYU-Hawaii. On Oct. 12, 1963, the Polynesian Cultural Center, a cluster of villages representing various South Pacific cultures, was opened. It quickly became one of Hawaii's top attractions. In recent years the center has been host to a number of heads of state, including those of China.

In 1992, major renovations were made to three LDS buildings at the Kalaupapa leprosy settlement on the island of Molokai. The buildings include a chapel, cultural hall, and a "mission house," used for visiting General Authorities and mission presidents. A branch has existed here since the 19th century when early Church convert Kitty Napela contracted Hansen's disease and, with her husband, Jonathan, moved to the leprosy settlement in 1872. Jonathan became assistant superintendent of the colony and was later set apart as an LDS branch president. The chapel on the island today is the third chapel, and a small branch existed until recently.

In 1994, President Howard W. Hunter installed Eric B. Shumway as the eighth president of BYU-Hawaii — the first time a prophet had done so since the college was founded.

A Church president once again noted "the spirit of aloha" when President Gordon B. Hinckley spoke to some 13,500 members from nine Oahu stakes Feb. 18, 1996, during two regional conference sessions at the BYU-Hawaii Cannon Activities Center. During the prophet's Feb. 17-19 visit to the islands, he also met with two Catholic leaders who are members of a Hawaiian grassroots coalition opposed to same-gender marriage, legalized prostitution, and casino gambling.

On Oct. 10, 1997, President Hinckley spoke at the dedication of a statue honoring early Hawaiian convert Jonathan Napela and missionary George Q. Cannon. In another tribute to the early Church, Elder David E. Sorensen of the Seventy rededicated on Jan. 18, 1998, the refurbished Honolulu Tabernacle, originally dedicated in 1941.

Hawaii's LDS membership in 1999 was 55,361.

A small temple for the city of Kailua-Kona on the island of Hawaii, was announced May 7, 1998, by the First Presidency. The temple, the second in Hawaii and the 70th operating temple in the Church, was dedicated Jan. 23, 2000, the sesquicentennial year of the establishment of the Church in the tropical Hawaiian islands. While in Hawaii, President Hinckley addressed 15,000 members on Jan. 22, gathered at two regional meetings in Laie,

Sources: *Encyclopedic History of the Church,* by Andrew Jenson; *Unto the Isles of the Sea,* by R. Lanier Britsch; *Guide to Mormon History Travel,* by William C. and Eloise Anderson; *Church News,* June 25, 1988, June 20, 1992, Sept. 19, 1992, Oct. 3, 1992, Nov. 26, 1994, Feb. 24, 1996, Feb. 2, 1997, Oct. 18, 1997, Jan. 24, 1998, Feb. 2, 1998, May 23, 1998; "Second sacred edifice in Hawaiian Islands," by Julie A. Dockstader, *Church News,* Jan. 29, 2000.

Stakes — 14

(Listed alphabetically as of Oct. 1, 2000.)

No.	Name	Organized	First President

North America West Area — 14

807	*BYU-Hawaii 1st	22 Nov 1981	
	‡BYU-Hawaii	23 Jan 1977	Eric B. Shumway
1313	BYU-Hawaii 2nd	22 Nov 1981	Herbert Kamaka Sproat
473	*Hilo Hawaii		
	‡Hilo	15 Dec 1968	Rex Alton Cheney
222	*Honolulu Hawaii		
	‡Honolulu (Hawaii, Guam)	28 Aug 1955	J. A. Quealy Jr.
348	*Honolulu Hawaii West		
	‡Pearl Harbor (Hawaii)	4 Feb 1962	George Q. Cannon
729	Kahului Hawaii	9 Nov 1975	Evan Allan Larsen
560	*Kaneohe Hawaii		
	‡Kaneohe (Hawaii)	21 Nov 1971	Robert H. Finlayson
851	Kauai Hawaii	24 Jul 1977	Garner Dalton Wood
669	Kona Hawaii	24 Nov 1974	Haven J. Stringham
113	*Laie Hawaii		
	‡Oahu	30 Jun 1935	Ralph E. Wooley
1395	Laie Hawaii North	16 Jan 1983	Willard Kaaihue Kekauoha
2291	Makakilo Hawaii	8 Dec 1996	Robert J. K. Paet
1103	Mililani Hawaii	3 Feb 1980	Kotaro Koizumi
566	*Waipahu Hawaii		
	‡Pearl Harbor West (Hawaii)	20 Feb 1972	William E. Fuhrmann

Mission — 1

(As of Oct. 1, 2000; shown with historical number. See MISSIONS.)

(9) HAWAII HONOLULU MISSION
1500 S. Beretania St., Suite 410
Honolulu, HI 96826

Idaho

Year-end 1999: Est. population, 1,252,000; Members, 343,489; Stakes, 105; Wards, 791; Branches, 41; Missions, 2; Temples, 2; Percent LDS, 27.4, or one in 4.

On April 7, 1855, 26 men were called by Brigham Young to establish a settlement among the Bannock and Shoshone Indians on the Salmon River in central Idaho. They founded Fort Lemhi on June 15, 1855, but problems with Indians led to the abandonment of the settlement in 1858.

On April 14, 1860, a party of colonizers arrived at what is now Franklin in northern Cache Valley near the present Utah-Idaho border in southeastern Idaho. Franklin is both Idaho's oldest and the Church's oldest permanent settlement in the state. Preston Thomas became the first bishop of a ward created there in June of that year. The settlers battled deep snows and extreme cold in the winter, but dug canals and began irrigating in the summer. Eventually, during the next 18 years, 16 settlements were founded in this region.

Across the mountains to the east, another colonization effort began in the fall of 1863 when a party under the direction of Apostle Charles C. Rich explored Bear Lake Valley and established the community of Paris. Originally, it was believed by settlers that both Bear Lake Valley and northern Cache Valley were in Utah, but a survey in 1872 showed they were in Idaho.

About 110 people wintered in Bear Lake Valley the first year. In 1864, 700 more settlers arrived and established the towns of Ovid, Liberty, Montpelier, Bloomington, St. Charles, Fish Haven, and Bennington. Nine other settlements were established in the region within 13 years. Bear Lake Stake, the first stake in Idaho and the first permanent stake outside of Utah, was created June 20, 1869.

Members generally got along well with Indians and received permission from Indian leaders to settle. They preached the gospel to Native Americans, taught them agriculture, and shared their supplies with them. Shoshone Chief Washakie, the most prominent chief during the early colonization effort, was baptized by Amos Wright, an early Idaho missionary.

A third colonization movement began in 1875 when LDS families settled in Oakley, Dayton, Elba, and Almo in southcentral Idaho.

In the late 1870s, the Utah Northern Railroad line from Utah to Montana, which ran through Idaho, was completed. Many members were employed in the construction of the rail line. From their favorable reports of the Upper Snake River Valley in southeast

Idaho, settlers soon began colonizing there, beginning in 1879. Under the leadership of Thomas E. Ricks, they established Rexburg in 1883 and 14 other communities. Basic to their success was their expertise in irrigating, and by 1910, more than 100 canals had been dug in the Upper Snake River Valley.

The Bannock Stake, Idaho's second stake, with headquarters in Rexburg, was organized Feb. 4, 1884, and four months later, on June 1, the Oneida Stake was created with headquarters in Preston.

Church leaders encouraged members to continue to settle in Idaho. Many — mostly farmers — migrated to already established communities in southeastern Idaho, and on the western side in the Boise-Payette area.

By 1890, when Idaho was granted statehood, about one-fifth of the state was LDS. Some historians suggest that without the Mormon population, Idaho's land would had been annexed to adjoining states and it never would had become a state. Despite the contributions of Mormons, however, anti-Mormon sentiment in Idaho grew during the last quarter of the 19th century. Mormon women led the statewide effort for women suffrage that was attained in 1896.

Idaho U.S. Senator William E. Borah, though not a member of the Church, helped neutralize anti-Mormon sentiment after the turn of the century.

The Church's worldwide institute of religion program started at the University of Idaho at Moscow in 1926. The first religious education class on the college level had an enrollment of 25 students. From this small beginning, there are more than 2,000 institutes of religion throughout the world today.

in 1900, membership in the "Gem State" was 29,421 in seven stakes. Membership increased to 79,887 by 1925; to 137,250 in 1950; to 213,106 in 1975; to 272,670 in 1980; and to 296,782 in 1990. By 1999, Idaho's LDS population had reached 343,489 in 106 stakes. Idaho's 100th stake, the Rexburg Idaho South Stake, was created Nov. 17, 1996.

Idaho's first temple, the Idaho Falls Temple, was built on the banks of the Snake River and dedicated Sept. 23, 1945. A second temple was built in Boise nearly 40 years later and dedicated May 25, 1984.

On June 5, 1976, the earth-filled Teton Dam in southeastern Idaho burst, sending a huge wall of water between 12 and 20 feet high onto Rexburg, Sugar City, Wilford, and other mostly LDS towns. About 40,000 people, most of them LDS, were driven from their homes. Massive volunteer efforts by members of neighboring stakes in Idaho and Utah speeded the cleanup of debris in the stricken towns. It was described as "a shining example of the priesthood in action." President Spencer W. Kimball visited the devastated area on June 13, 1976, and spoke to 8,000 members at Ricks College, bringing new hope and spirit to the disaster-torn flood victims.

In 1990, members were among the some 20,000-25,000 gathered in Franklin to celebrate Idaho's statehood centennial.

During flooding in the northwestern United States early in 1996, members in northern Idaho were among thousands evacuated from their homes. Members there were also among thousands who reached out in relief efforts — both to LDS and non-LDS. Floods again in 1997 and 1998 brought concerted relief efforts by members to assist those made homeless by the disasters.

Three Church presidents were born in Idaho. President Harold B. Lee was born in Clifton in 1899 and served as president of the Church from 1972-73; President Ezra Taft Benson was born in Whitney, also in 1899, and was Church president from 1985-94; and President Howard W. Hunter was born in Boise in 1907, and was president of the Church from 1994-95.

Ricks College in Rexburg, founded in 1888 as a stake academy, was one of many stake academies throughout the Church. While most of the academies were later closed, Ricks Academy survived and later became a junior college and renamed Ricks College. However, for seven years, from 1949 to 1956, Ricks was a four-year school, and then reverted back to a junior college. On June 21, 2000, President Gordon B. Hinckley made a surprise announcement at a news conference in Salt Lake City that Ricks College would once again become a four-year college and would be renamed Brigham Young University-Idaho. President Hinckley said the change would be "phased in over a period of time and accomplished in such a way as to preserve the school's autonomy and identity." As part of the change, Ricks' intercollegiate athletics program would be phased out, replaced by a year-around activity and intramural athletic program. In June 2000,

8,628 students were enrolled at Ricks College.

Sources: *Encyclopedic History of the Church*, by Andrew Jenson; *Treasures of Pioneer History*, Daughters of the Utah Pioneers, 1955; "Idaho Members Fight Flood," by David Croft, *Church News*, June 12, 1976; "Flood Victims Get New Hope," by Dell Van Orden, *Church News*, June 19, 1976; "Idaho vote spells 'finish' to old feud," by Arnold Irvine, *Church News*, Nov. 13, 1982; "Idaho — A shining Gem since 1855," by Golden A. Buchmiller, *Church News*, May 8, 1983; "Centennials preserving heritage," *Church News*, May 26, 1990; "Centennial celebrations bring festivities to nation's 43rd state," *Church News*, July 7, 1990; "Mormondom in Centennial Idaho," by Leonard J. Arrington, *This People*, Fall 1990; "First LDS Bishop in Idaho: A Pioneer for Gospel's Sake," by Elinor G. Hyde, *Church News*, Dec. 15, 1990; "Paris Tabernacle," by Dean Ward, published locally; "A wake of disaster, a wave of volunteers," *Church News*, Feb. 17, 1996; *Church News*, Jan. 18, 1997, Feb. 21, 1998, Jan. 23, 1999; "4-year status for Ricks," by Carrie Moore, *Deseret News*, June 21, 2000; *Church News*, June 24, 2000.

Stakes — 105

(Listed alphabetically by area as of Oct. 1, 2000.)

No.	Name	Organized	First President
North America Northwest Area — 94			
170	*American Falls Idaho		
	‡American Falls	1 Feb 1948	George R. Woolley
1481	Arimo Idaho	17 Jun 1984	Douglas Sorensen
695	Ashton Idaho	18 May 1975	Horace E. Hess
52	*Blackfoot Idaho		
	‡Blackfoot	31 Jan 1904	Elias S. Kimball
1391	Blackfoot Idaho East	12 Dec 1982	Franklin D. Transtrum
914	Blackfoot Idaho Northwest	30 Apr 1978	Reijo Laverne Marcum
214	*Blackfoot Idaho South		
	*Blackfoot South	1 Mar 1970	
	‡South Blackfoot	20 Jun 1954	Lawrence T. Lambert
504	*Blackfoot Idaho West		
	‡Blackfoot West	1 Mar 1970	Alan F. Larsen
66	*Boise Idaho		
	‡Boise	3 Nov 1913	Heber Q. Hale
1460	Boise Idaho Central	5 Feb 1984	R. Clair Miles
1041	Boise Idaho East	10 Jun 1979	Cecil Frank Olsen
409	*Boise Idaho North		
	*Boise North Jan 1966		
	‡North Boise	26 Sep 1965	L. Aldin Porter
701	Boise Idaho South	17 Aug 1975	Grant Ruel Ipsen
1856	Boise State University	24 Apr 1992	Robert Reed Boren
218	*Boise Idaho West		
	*Boise West	29 May 1970	
	‡West Boise	7 Nov 1954	David Keith Ricks
77	*Burley Idaho		
	‡Burley	27 Jul 1919	David R. Langlois
1421	Burley Idaho West	22 May 1983	Walter Ray Petersen
564	*Caldwell Idaho		
	‡Caldwell	30 Jan 1972	Talmadge C. Blacker
1446	Caldwell Idaho North	9 Oct 1983	Gerald Leland Jensen
78	*Carey Idaho	31 Oct 1977	
	*Richfield Idaho		
	‡Blaine	3 Aug 1919	William Lennox Adamson
960	*Chubbuck Idaho	8 Sep 1987	
	‡Pocatello Idaho Chubbuck	17 Sep 1978	Errol Smith Phippen
359	*Coeur d'Alene Idaho		
	‡Coeur d'Alene	14 Oct 1962	Gerald E. Browning
69	*Declo Idaho		
	*Cassia East	15 Jun 1969	
	‡Raft River	27 Apr 1915	John A. Elison
50	*Driggs Idaho		
	‡Teton (Wyoming, Idaho)	2 Sep 1901	Don Carlos Driggs
1840	Eagle Idaho	12 Jan 1992	Gary Wayne Walker
661	Emmett Idaho	22 Sep 1974	David Lee Morton
1147	Filer Idaho	15 Jun 1980	Karl E. Nelson
655	Firth Idaho	8 Sep 1974	Dale Lavar Christensen
2511	Hayden Lake Idaho	07 Feb 1999	Ronald Bruce McIntire
36	*Idaho Falls Idaho		
	*Idaho Falls	16 Aug 1925	

	‡Bingham	9 Jun 1895	James E. Steele
343	*Idaho Falls Idaho Ammon		
	‡Ammon	26 Nov 1961	Harold W. Davis
825	Idaho Falls Idaho Ammon West	1 May 1977	Boyd Rencher Thomas
1448	Idaho Falls Idaho Central	16 Oct 1983	Paul Roger DeMordaunt
1665	Idaho Falls Idaho Eagle Rock	13 Dec 1987	Michael D. Crapo
285	*Idaho Falls Idaho East		
	*Idaho Falls East	29 May 1970	
	‡East Idaho Falls	7 Jun 1959	Charles P. Birzee
1149	Idaho Falls Idaho Lincoln	22 Jun 1980	Cleon Y. Olson
112	*Idaho Falls Idaho North		
	*Idaho Falls North	29 May 1970	
	‡North Idaho Falls	12 May 1935	David Smith
157	*Idaho Falls Idaho South		
	*Idaho Falls South	29 May 1970	
	‡South Idaho Falls	30 Jun 1946	Cecil E. Hart
2183	Idaho Falls Idaho Taylor Mountain	17 Mar 1996	J Rodney Hayes
602	*Idaho Falls Idaho West		
	‡Idaho Falls West	4 Mar 1973	Terry L. Crapo
607	*Iona Idaho		
	‡Iona	15 Apr 1973	Joseph Dudley Tucker
192	*Jerome Idaho		
	‡Gooding	9 Mar 1952	Ross C. Lee
1015	Kimberly Idaho	15 Apr 1979	David LaVere Carter
2029	Kuna Idaho	26 Feb 1995	Kenneth Arthur Roetto
268	*Lewiston Idaho		
	‡Lewiston (Idaho, Wash.)	19 Oct 1958	Golden Romney
72	*McCammon Idaho	19 Feb 1983	
	*Arimo Idaho		
	‡Portneuf	15 Aug 1915	George T. Hyde
1125	Menan Idaho	30 Mar 1980	Garth Victor Hall
580	*Meridian Idaho		
	‡Meridian	11 Jun 1972	J. Richard Clarke
847	Meridian Idaho East	12 Jun 1977	Leonard E. Graham Jr.
1401	Meridian Idaho South	20 Feb 1983	Wenden Wayne Waite
2299	Meridian Idaho West	12 Jan 1997	Loun G. Easthope
79	*Moore Idaho		
	‡Lost River	18 Aug 1919	William N. Patten
2553	Moscow Idaho University Stake	23 Apr 2000	Jack Evan McPhie
641	Mountain Home Idaho	19 May 1974	Kenneth Herbert Johns
125	*Nampa Idaho		
	‡Nampa	27 Nov 1938	Peter E. Johnson
874	Nampa Idaho South	30 Oct 1977	Dean Ezra Beus
32	*Oakley Idaho		
	‡Cassia (Idaho, Utah)	19 Nov 1887	Horton D. Haight
587	*Paul Idaho		
	‡Minidoka West	24 Sep 1972	Keith C. Merrill Jr.
278	*Pocatello Idaho		
	‡Pocatello	19 Apr 1959	Roland K. Hart
40	*Pocatello Idaho Alameda	17 Jun 1984	
	*Pocatello Idaho East		
	*Pocatello East	29 May 1970	
	*East Pocatello	19 Apr 1959	
	‡Pocatello	7 Aug 1898	William C. Parkinson
1484	Pocatello Idaho Central	17 Jun 1984	Thomas William Ranstrom
971	*Pocatello Idaho East	17 Jun 1984	
	‡Pocatello Idaho South	22 Oct 1978	John Burl McNabb
377	*Pocatello Idaho Highland	17 Jun 1984	
	*Pocatello Idaho Alameda		
	‡Alameda	12 May 1963	Homer S. Satterfield
207	*Pocatello Idaho North		
	*Pocatello North	29 May 1970	
	‡North Pocatello	21 Jun 1953	Jared O. Anderson
1444	Pocatello Idaho Tyhee	25 Sep 1983	Eugene Lester Hancock

406	*Pocatello Idaho University 1st		
	‡Idaho State University	9 May 1965	Robert E. Thompson
2458	Pocatello Idaho University 2nd	3 May 1998	Earl L. Christison III
149	*Pocatello Idaho West		
	*Pocatello West	29 May 1970	
	‡West Pocatello	6 May 1945	Twayne Austin
28	*Rexburg Idaho		
	*Rexburg	23 Jun 1935	
	*Fremont	6 Aug 1898	
	‡Bannock	4 Feb 1884	Thomas E. Ricks
1369	Rexburg Idaho Center	24 Oct 1982	Ronald Curtis Martin
697	Rexburg Idaho East	1 Jun 1975	Keith Lester Peterson
153	*Rexburg Idaho North		
	*Rexburg North	29 May 1970	
	‡North Rexburg	28 Oct 1945	Orval O. Mortensen
2270	Rexburg Idaho South	17 Nov 1996	Garth S. Olsen
405	*Ricks College	1st 7 Nov 1989	
	*Rexburg Idaho College 1st		
	*Ricks College 1st	1 Jun 1969	
	‡Ricks College	7 May 1965	J. Wendell Stucki
480	*Ricks College 2nd	7 Nov 1989	
	*Rexburg Idaho College 2nd		
	‡Ricks College 2nd	27 Apr 1969	Loren Homer Grover
690	*Ricks College 3rd	7 Nov 1989	
	‡Rexburg Idaho College 3rd	13 Apr 1975	Ray Wendell Rigby
1689	*Ricks College 4th	7 Nov 1989	
	‡Rexburg Idaho College 4th	6 Mar 1988	Jay Lufkin Risenmay
1836	Ricks College 5th	8 Dec 1991	R. Brent Kinghorn
2454	Ricks College 6th	19 Apr 1998	Jud Earl Miller
56	*Rigby Idaho		
	‡Rigby	3 Feb 1908	Don Carlos Walker
158	*Rigby Idaho East		
	*Rigby East	29 May 1970	
	‡East Rigby	7 Jul 1946	James E. Ririe
1140	Ririe Idaho	25 May 1980	Arlo J. Moss
606	*Roberts Idaho		
	‡Jefferson	25 Mar 1973	Edwin Cutler Adamson
91	*Rupert Idaho		
	‡Minidoka	11 May 1924	Richard C. May
1476	Rupert Idaho West	3 Jun 1984	Carl B. Garner
60	*Saint Anthony Idaho		
	‡Yellowstone	10 Jan 1909	Daniel G. Miller
211	*Salmon Idaho		
	‡Salmon River	18 Oct 1953	Earl Stokes
952	Sandpoint Idaho	20 Aug 1978	Richard William Goldsberry
67	*Shelley Idaho		
	‡Shelley	16 Aug 1914	Joseph H. Dye
1180	Shelley Idaho South	14 Sep 1980	Kenneth P. Fielding
1129	Sugar City Idaho	4 May 1980	Ferron W. Sonderegger
76	*Twin Falls Idaho		
	‡Twin Falls	26 Jul 1919	Lawrence Gomer Kirkman
490	*Twin Falls Idaho West		
	‡Twin Falls West	17 Aug 1969	Joel A. Tate
1156	Ucon Idaho	29 Jun 1980	Joseph Dudley Tucker
126	*Weiser Idaho		
	‡Weiser	27 Nov 1938	Scott B. Brown
1005	Wendell Idaho	25 Feb 1979	Orlo William Stevens

Utah North Area — 9

1419	*Franklin Idaho	17 Nov 1985	
	‡Preston Idaho East	15 May 1983	Eudean Hawkins Gunnell
39	*Grace Idaho		
	‡Bannock	25 Jul 1898	Lewis S. Pond
32a	*Malad Idaho		

	‡Malad (Idaho, Utah)	12 Feb 1888	Oliver C. Hoskins
75	*Montpelier Idaho		
	‡Montpelier (Idaho, Wyoming)	23 Dec 1917	Edward C. Rich
1020	Montpelier Idaho South	22 Apr 1979	Leonard H. Matthews
8a	*Paris Idaho		
	‡Bear Lake (Idaho, Utah)	20 Jun 1869	David P. Kimball
29	*Preston Idaho North		
	‡Oneida	1 Jun 1884	William D. Hendricks
81	*Preston Idaho South		
	‡Franklin	6 Jun 1920	Samuel W. Parkinson
73	*Soda Springs Idaho		
	‡Idaho	19 Nov 1916	Nelson J. Hogan

Stakes discontinued

70	Curlew (Idaho, Utah)	17 May 1915	Jonathan C. Cutler
	Discontinued 11 Feb 1940 †Malad (32), Pocatello (40)		
1273	Soda Springs Idaho North	31 May 1981	Cleston Murrie Godfrey
	Discontinued 27 Apr 1986 †Montpelier Idaho (75), Soda Springs Idaho (73)		

Missions — 2

(As of Oct. 1, 2000; shown with historical number. See MISSIONS.)

(111) IDAHO BOISE MISSION
2710 Sunrise Rim Road, Suite 220
Boise, ID 83705

(264) IDAHO POCATELLO MISSION
Horizon Plaza
1070 Hiline Road, Suite 320
Pocatello, ID 83201

Illinois

Year-end 1999: Est. population, 12,128,000; Members, 46,135; Stakes, 12; Wards, 82; Branches, 33; Missions, 3; Temples, 1 (1 under construction); Percent LDS, 0.4, or one in 263.

The first missionaries to Illinois were Oliver Cowdery, Parley P. Pratt, Peter Whitmer Jr., Richard Ziba Peterson, and Frederick G. Williams, who visited in the fall of 1830 while on a mission to Native Americans. In 1834, Zion's Camp passed through southern Illinois, en route from Kirtland, Ohio, to Missouri. As a result of missionary work, a few branches were established in Illinois prior to 1839.

When the Saints were driven from Missouri in 1838, they began to gather in Illinois, in Quincy, Springfield, and other locations where they were generally received on friendly terms. One refugee, Israel Barlow, found his way to Commerce, Ill., where he laid the groundwork for the Church to purchase 660 acres of property that later became Nauvoo. The city was platted and lots were sold. As members poured in, the swampy land was drained and buildings were erected. Converts from Canada and Europe arrived by the thousands. The city of Nauvoo received a charter from the state of Illinois in 1840, and had a militia for self-defense. Members built music and cultural halls, as well as meeting halls for priesthood groups. Ten revelations of the Doctrine and Covenants were received in the Nauvoo area.

Joseph Smith planned or established in the area a network of 17 settlements, foreshadowing the colonization of the West by Brigham Young. These included Ramus, Lima, Quincy, Mount Hope, Freedom, Geneva, and Pleasant Vale.

In 1840, on a high bluff overlooking the city, a site was selected for the Nauvoo Temple. Portions of the temple were dedicated and used as soon as completed. A public dedication of the finished building was held on May 1, 1846.

The Church's first auxiliary, the Relief Society, was organized in Nauvoo March 17, 1842.

At its peak in 1845-46, Nauvoo grew to some 15,000 residents.

In 1844, Joseph and Hyrum Smith were arrested on trumped-up charges and taken from Nauvoo to jail in nearby Carthage, Ill., where they were martyred by a mob on June 27. Antagonism against the Mormons increased. Members in Nauvoo and surrounding communities, driven by mobs from their homes in 1846, crossed the Mississippi River and traveled across Iowa to establish a temporary residence at Winter Quarters, Neb., some 300 miles away.

The Saints left behind in Nauvoo their beloved temple, wherein the pattern was set for the sacred ordinances of salvation. Baptisms for the dead were performed in Nauvoo prior to January 1841 and temple endowments were first received in 1842 in Nauvoo. The first endowments in the Church's second temple were received Dec. 10, 1845, and by the time the last endowment was given in the temple on Feb. 7, 1846, a total of 5,595 persons had received the sacred ordinance. After the Mormons were driven from Nauvoo, the temple was destroyed in 1848 by a suspected arson's fire, and then leveled two years later by a tornado.

The Church presence ended in Illinois for a time. After an interlude following the Saints' migration west, missionaries returned to Illinois in the 1870s. Most converts, however, migrated west. Illinois was included in the Northwestern States Mission, created in May 1878. On July 20, 1889, the mission headquarters were established in Chicago, and the name of the mission was changed to the Northern States Mission. By 1890, the mission extended into 22 states and Canada.

Following the conversions of Scandinavian settlers in Minnesota and other nearby states, Elder Christian D. Fjeldsted found success among the Scandinavians in Chicago in 1895-96.

A number of branches were created. By 1930, three conferences were organized: the Chicago, North Illinois, and South Illinois. In Chicago, meetinghouses were built for the Logan Square and University branches. In 1930, membership in the state was 2,281. In June 1933, when the Century of Progress World's Fair was held in Chicago, the Church sponsored an exhibit in the Hall of Religions, which drew an estimated 10,000 people a day.

The first stake in Illinois after the Nauvoo era was organized in Chicago in 1936, followed in 1962 by the Illinois Stake (now Champaign).

In 1954, Dr. J. LeRoy Kimball purchased the Nauvoo home of his great-grandfather, Heber C. Kimball. Dr. Kimball's efforts to restore the home were well-received. This led to the beginning in 1962 of the Church's Nauvoo Restoration Inc., which included the Kimball home. Dr. Kimball served as the project's first president. The Church has since re-purchased some 1,000 acres, built a two-story visitors center, and restored 25 homes and buildings. It has also acquired the pioneer cemetery, where many of the inhabitants of the 1840s' Nauvoo are buried.

In 1979, the 1,000th stake in the Church was organized in Nauvoo by President Ezra Taft Benson of the Quorum of the Twelve. In 1985, the Chicago Illinois Temple was completed in the Chicago suburb of Glenview, and four years later an addition to the temple was dedicated in 1989.

Membership in 1974 was about 18,000, increasing to 29,000 in 1980 and to 38,000 in 1990. In 1999, membership in Illinois was 46,135. In recent years, membership has increased within Chicago's multi-ethnic neighborhoods.

Since 1992, students from Ricks College in Rexburg, Idaho, have traveled to the Chicago area for three weeks each summer to conduct camps for inner-city youth. The Urban Studies program of the college sponsors the camps in cooperation with the Inner City Youth Charitable Foundation, a non-profit organization sponsored by Church members in Chicago.

Members were quick to respond to assist others in the 1993 Mississippi River flooding that damaged many areas in the state and resulted in the cancellation that year of the Nauvoo pageant. Attention of residents throughout the state was drawn to Nauvoo and Carthage in June 1994, when the Church commemorated the 150th anniversary of the martyrdom of the Prophet Joseph Smith. President Howard W. Hunter, in his first scheduled public appearance since becoming president of the Church, spoke at three meetings in connection with the observance. This included an outdoor meeting at Carthage Jail Square that was telecast over the Church's satellite system.

Nationwide attention was focused on Nauvoo on Feb. 4-5, 1996, when the sesquicentennial of the Saints' 1846 exodus was commemorated. In 1995 and 1996, tourist visitation to Nauvoo and news media coverage of the historic city significantly increased. Illinois Gov. Jim Edgar visited Carthage Jail, Nov. 8, 1996, believed to be the first time a governor had been to the jail since Gov. Thomas Ford went there in 1844.

Evidence of the continuing progress of the Church came July 1, 1997, with the re-creation of the Illinois Chicago South Mission — the third mission in the state and the second in Chicago. It had previously existed from 1980-83. For the first time in 24 years, a stake was named after Chicago when the Chicago Illinois Stake was created Jan. 25, 1998, by Elder Hugh W. Pinnock of the Seventy. The new stake is cosmopolitan in nature. The first Chicago stake was re-named the Wilmette Illinois Stake.

At general conference on April 4, 1999, President Gordon B. Hinckley announced that the Nauvoo Temple would be rebuilt on the original temple site, which the Church had reacquired Feb. 20, 1937, when Wilford C. Wood, representing the Church, purchased the property. President Hinckley's announcement was received with considerable joy, especially for those watching the conference proceedings via the Church satellite system at the Nauvoo Illinois Stake center. Groundbreaking ceremonies for the rebuilding of the temple were held Oct. 24, 1999, as 5,000 people crowded onto the site to witness President Hinckley break ground, symbolically signaling the beginning of construction.

Sources: *Encyclopedic History of the Church,* by Andrew Jenson; "Spokes on the Wheel," by Donald Q. Cannon, *Ensign,* Feb. 1986; "Harvest of Faith on Chicago's South Side," by Linda Hoffman Kimball, *Ensign,* Feb. 1986; "He saved old Nauvoo from the ruin of time," *Church News,* Jan. 31, 1987; "Bittersweet memories of Ramus," by Calvin N. Smith and Joseph T. Woolley, *Church News,* Aug. 12, 1989; "A time to remember, honor, respect," by Dell Van Orden, *Church News,* July 2, 1994; "Commemorating 1846 exodus," *Church News,* Feb. 10, 1996; "Led by Spirit, not knowing beforehand," both by R. Scott Lloyd, *Church News,* Sept. 7, 1996; *Church News,* Nov. 30, 1996, March 1, 1997, Jan. 31, 1998; "Historic Nauvoo Temple to be rebuilt," by R. Scott Lloyd, *Church News,* April 10, 1999; "Rebuilding of magnificent temple," by Greg Hill, *Church News,* Oct. 30, 1999; *Church News,* Nov. 27, 1999.

Stakes — 12

(Listed alphabetically by area as of Oct. 1, 2000.)

No.	Name	Organized	First President
North America Central Area			
1672	*Buffalo Grove Illinois	21 May 1991	
	‡Long Grove Illinois	24 Jan 1988	William David Johnston
370	*Champaign Illinois		
	‡Illinois	17 Feb 1963	Ross A. Kelly
2433	Chicago Illinois	25 Jan 1998	A. Clair Jensen
2112	Joliet Illinois	22 Oct 1995	Douglas J. Fredin
368	*Naperville Illinois		
	‡Chicago South (Ill., Ind.)	3 Feb 1963	Lysle R. Cahoon
1000	Nauvoo Illinois	18 Feb 1979	Gene Lee Roy Mann
749	*O'Fallon Illinois 1 Jun 1993		
	‡Fairview Heights Illinois	14 Mar 1976	John Odeen Anderson
1163	Peoria Illinois	3 Aug 1980	Clive Edwin Ashton
1334	Rockford Illinois	11 Apr 1982	Brent L. Horsley
1094	Schaumburg Illinois	20 Jan 1980	Owen D. West Jr.
2280	Springfield Illinois	24 Nov 1996	Alonzo J. Mackelprang
118	*Wilmette Illinois		
	‡Chicago (Ill., Ind., Wis.)	29 Nov 1936	William A. Matheson

Stakes discontinued

4	Crooked Creek [Ramus] Discontinued 4 Dec 1841	4 Jul 1840	Joel Hills Johnson
8	Freedom Discontinued 24 May 1841	27 Oct 1840	Henry W. Miller
9	Geneva Discontinued 24 May 1841	1 Nov 1840	William Bosley
5	Lima Discontinued 1845	22 Oct 1840	Isaac Morley
7	Mount Hope Discontinued 24 May 1841	27 Oct 1840	Abel Lamb
2a	Nauvoo Discontinued 1846	5 Oct 1839	William Marks
6	Quincy Discontinued 24 May 1841	25 Oct 1840	Daniel Stanton
10	Springfield Discontinued 24 May 1841	5 Nov 1840	Edwin P. Merriam

Missions —3

(As of Oct. 1, 2000; shown with historical number. See MISSIONS.)

(9c) ILLINOIS CHICAGO MISSION
1319 Butterfield Road, Suite 522
Downers Grove, IL 60515

(313) ILLINOIS CHICAGO NORTH
3295 N. Arlington Heights Road, Ste. 108
Arlington Heights, IL 60004

(176a) ILLINOIS PEORIA MISSION
4700 North Sterling, Suite 100
Peoria, IL 61615

Indiana

Year-end 1999: Est. population, 5,943,000; Members, 33,058; Stakes, 10; Wards, 57; Branches, 31; Missions, 1; Percent LDS, 0.5, or one in 180.

Missionaries Samuel H. Smith and Reynolds Cahoon preached in the Indiana cities of Unionville, Madison, and Vienna during the summer of 1831. Other missionaries came shortly thereafter, including Parley P. and Orson Pratt. The first branches were organized in September 1831, and the first conference was held Nov. 29, 1831. Joseph Smith spent four weeks in Greenville, Ind., in the spring of 1832.

In 1834, Zion's Camp, from Kirtland, Ohio, to Missouri, crossed Indiana. Although trouble was predicted by their enemies, members of the group passed through Indiana peacefully. In 1838, the Kirtland Camp, a group of seventies, also crossed Indiana. It is believed that a number of people in Indiana joined the Church in the early days.

In 1882, Indiana became part of the Northwestern States Mission, which had been organized in 1878. The name was changed to the Northern States Mission in 1889. Among early converts after the turn of the century were Edward and Anna Faulting of Indianapolis, in whose home meetings were held until 1910. At that time, a home was rented for Church services. Membership grew from 13 people to 10 families by 1913. The first branch was organized that year with John L. Thomas as branch president, and the branch met in a rented hall. In 1920, a larger hall was rented that served until a meetinghouse was erected in 1927. This meetinghouse was dedicated by President Heber J. Grant.

In 1939, a second branch was organized in Indianapolis.

The first stake in Indiana, the Indianapolis Stake, was created from the Central Indiana District on May 17, 1959. In the stake, with a membership of 2,287, were two wards in Indianapolis and other wards in Bloomington, Columbus, Muncie, Purdue, and Richmond, and branches in Kokomo, Anderson, and Connersville.

The Great Lakes Mission, created in 1949 from the Northern States Mission, was renamed the Indiana Indianapolis Mission in 1974. That year the state had 14,787 members, increasing to 20,738 in 1980, to 26,169 in 1990, and to 33,058 in 1999.

In 1998, Indiana members responded with relief supplies for those in North Dakota who had suffered devastation from flooding.

Sources: *Encyclopedic History of the Church,* by Andrew Jenson; *Church News,* May 23, 1959; Indianapolis Stake Center Dedication Program, Nov. 26, 1967; "Zions Camp, Across Swamplands," *Church News,* Sept. 5, 1970, and "Zions Camp, the First Prairie," *Church News,* Sept. 12, 1970; *Discovering Mormon Trails,* by Stanley B. Kimball, Deseret Book Co., 1979; *Church News,* Feb. 21, 1998.

Stakes — 10

(Listed alphabetically as of Oct. 1, 2000.)

No.	Name	Organized	First President
North America East Area — 9			
1078	Bloomington Indiana	4 Nov 1979	Hollis Ralph Johnson
712	Evansville Indiana	19 Oct 1975	Frank R. Fults Jr.
352	*Fort Wayne Indiana ‡Fort Wayne (Indiana, Ohio)	4 Mar 1962	Howard W. Thompson
283	*Indianapolis Indiana ‡Indianapolis	17 May 1959	Phillip F. Low
624a	*Indianapolis Indiana North ‡Indianapolis North	19 Aug 1973	David Val Glover
1417	Lafayette Indiana	15 May 1983	Koy Eldridge Miskin
2159	Muncie Indiana	4 Feb 1996	Michael W. Ellis
1368	New Albany Indiana	24 Oct 1982	Henry Harvey Griffith
873	South Bend Indiana	30 Oct 1977	Kenneth Bryan Fugal
North America Central Area — 1			
646	*Valparaiso Indiana ‡Chicago Heights Illinois	2 Jun 1974	Robert E. Nichols

Mission — 1

(As of Oct. 1, 2000; shown with historical number. See MISSIONS.)

(46) INDIANA INDIANAPOLIS MISSION
3333 Founders Rd., Ste 101
Indianapolis, IN 46268

Iowa

Year-end 1999: Est. population, 2,869,000; Members, 17,465; Stakes, 6; Wards, 32; Branches, 17; Missions, 1; Percent LDS, 0.6, or one in 168.

Following the expulsion of the Saints from Missouri in 1838, Iowa Gov. Robert Lucas expressed sympathy for their plight and offered them refuge. Although Joseph Smith instead chose to go to what became Nauvoo in Illinois, members also settled across the Mississippi River in Lee County, Iowa, and resided in Montrose, Augusta, Keokuk, and other areas. They founded Ambrosia and started a settlement named Zarahemla. A stake was organized in Lee County in 1839, but was discontinued three years later in 1842.

When the Saints were driven from Nauvoo in February 1846, they crossed southern Iowa. En route, they planted grain and established Garden Grove, which today remains a farming community. Farther west, the refugees again farmed at a place they called Mount Pisgah. Noah Rogers, returning from a mission in Tahiti, died and was buried there. Eventually 2,000 Saints lived in Mount Pisgah, which was disbanded in 1852. A cemetery remains with a monument erected by the Church in 1888.

They reached the eastern bluffs of the Missouri River (at Kanesville, which later became Council Bluffs) on June 14, 1846. It was in Kanesville on July 13, 1846, that 500 men from the "Camp of Israel" were mustered in for military service during the Mexican War, and comprised what history has come to call the Mormon Battalion. Thereafter, most the Saints moved across the Missouri River into Nebraska where they established Winter Quarters, but in 1848, the U.S. government required the Mormons to move off Indian Territory in Nebraska. Winter Quarters was abandoned and members moved back across the river to the Iowa side. After 1848, Kanesville became an important staging area for thousands of Mormon and non-Mormon overland travelers. An estimated 8,000 members lived in Iowa at this time.

In a log tabernacle in Kanesville, Brigham Young was formally sustained as president of the Church on Dec. 27, 1847. Three weeks earlier, the Quorum of the Twelve had reorganized the First Presidency on Dec. 5 in Kanesville. The same month, President Young sent the highly influential general epistle calling upon members all over the world to gather in the Great Basin of the Rocky Mountains.

Before the Saints left the Middle Missouri Valley in the 1850s, some 70 temporary settlements had been established in the region. The settlements were abandoned as the pioneers moved west.

In 1856-57, many handcart pioneers started their trek to the West from Iowa City, Iowa, then the terminus of the railroad. Of the 2,500 handcart pioneers who crossed the plains, 200 to 300 died on the trail. A marker was dedicated in 1980 by Elder Mark E. Petersen of the Quorum of the Twelve at the site from where most of the handcart pioneers left, which now is on the University of Iowa campus in Iowa City.

Missionary work in Iowa began in 1869 with Elders Israel Evans and Nymphus C. Murdock. A branch was re-created in Keokuk in 1875 and in Council Bluffs in 1878. When the Northwestern States Mission was organized in 1878, Iowa became a part of that mission.

In 1880, Elder B.H. Roberts began his missionary work in Iowa. On one occasion, he secured a school for preaching in West Fork, Iowa, and word spread in the community that three preachers would "tie the young Mormon with questions." Elder Roberts, though, nearly missed the appointment because of being stranded behind a washed-out bridge some distance away. He waded the stream, walked 10 miles, and arrived to find a standing-room-only crowd and the three preachers. He spoke eloquently and no one contradicted him.

In 1887, the mission headquarters was moved to Council Bluffs, where it remained until 1889, when it was transferred to Chicago, Ill., and the name was changed to the Northern States Mission. By 1930, Iowa had branches in Ames, Boone, Sioux City, and Davenport. The Davenport Branch had a meetinghouse. Membership in the state then was 560.

The first permanent stake in Iowa, the Cedar Rapids Stake, was created in 1966 with 2,000 members in the Cedar Falls, Cedar Rapids, Davenport, Iowa City, and Rock Island wards and the Fayette, Muscatine, and Washington branches. Membership in the state in 1974 was 6,111. It increased to about 9,000 in 1980, 11,000 in 1990, and to 17,465 in 1999.

Appreciation for the contributions of the early members increased in the state as local Latter-day Saints cooperated with many interested residents to preserve early Church sites and the Mormon Trail during the late 1980s and 1990s. In 1996, those efforts resulted in the sesquicentennial observation of the Iowa portion of the Saints' exodus from Nauvoo to Council Bluffs, Iowa. A wagon-train re-enactment, many community celebrations, and a symposium in Des Moines commemorated the 1846 trek across Iowa. The observance was capped July 12-13, 1996, in Council Bluffs with a "Grand Encampment," a celebration that took its name from the huge pioneer encampment on the eastern banks of the Missouri River in 1846. Sesquicentennial events included the re-enactment of the Mormon Battalion mustering; the dedication by President Gordon B. Hinckley of the reconstructed Kanesville Tabernacle; and an address by President Hinckley at an outdoor devotional, attended by 12,500 people,

On Dec. 5, 1997, the Orson Hyde Park in historic Kanesville was dedicated, and three weeks later, on Dec 27, 1997, Church members and other community residents re-enacted in the reconstructed log tabernacle the sustaining of Brigham Young as second president of the Church.

Sources: *Encyclopedic History of the Church,* by Andrew Jenson; "A meeting in Iowa," *Church News,* Nov. 24, 1973; "The LDS Legacy in Southwestern Iowa," by Gail Geo. Holmes, *Ensign,* Aug. 1988; "Handcart camp dedicated in Iowa as historic site," *Church News,* Aug. 9, 1980; "Middle Missouri Valley, 1846-1992," by Gail Geo. Holmes, *Church News,* July 18, 1992; "Iowans honor Saints' trek across 12 of their counties," by R. Scott Lloyd, *Church News,* March 30, 1996; "Tabernacle of log replicated, dedicated," "Mormon Battalion Mustering," and "Devotional honors epic pioneer saga," all by Dell Van Orden, *Church News,* July 20, 1996; *Church News,* Dec. 13, 1997; "1847 sustaining re-enacted in Iowa," by R. Scott Lloyd, *Church News,* Jan. 10, 1998; *Church News,* June 26, 1999.

Stakes — 6

(Listed alphabetically as of Oct. 1, 2000.)

No.	Name	Organized	First President
North America Central Area			
2053	Ames Iowa	21 May 1995	Robert Blaine Schafer
419	Cedar Rapids Iowa		
	‡Cedar Rapids (Iowa, Illinois)	29 May 1966	Richard F. Hagland
2525	Council Bluffs Iowa	25 Apr 1999	Maury Wintle Schooff
902	Davenport Iowa	9 Apr 1978	James Earl Campbell
525	*Des Moines Iowa		
	‡Des Moines	6 Sep 1970	Donald G. Woolley
2157	Sioux City Iowa	21 Jan 1996	David W. Roper

Stakes discontinued

3a	Iowa [Zarahemla] Discontinued 6 Jan 1842	5 Oct 1839	John Smith

Mission — 1

(As of Oct. 1, 2000; shown with historical number. See MISSIONS.)

(140) IOWA DES MOINES MISSION
8515 Douglas Ave., Ste.19
Des Moines, IA 50322

Kansas

Year-end 1999: Est. population, 2,654,000; Members, 27,232; Stakes, 6; Wards, 45; Branches, 24; Districts, 1; Percent LDS, 1.0, or one in 98.

In 1831, Oliver Cowdery and Parley P. Pratt taught Shawnee and Delaware Indians in what is now Kansas. In July 1846, the Mormon Battalion was equipped at Fort Leavenworth, Kan., for its long infantry march across the Southwest to California. The immigration of 1854 passed through eastern Kansas. In 1855, what is now Atchison, Kan., was chosen as a layover site for immigrants who came up the Mississippi and Missouri rivers. They needed a more healthful place to disembark to avoid the ravages of cholera. A camp called Mormon Grove was established and more than 100 acres were cultivated and crops planted for future immigrants. The camp only lasted one summer, but fulfilled its purpose.

Missionary work in Kansas began anew in 1882 when Elders Joseph F. Doxford, Marcus L. Shepherd, and James Mellor labored in Dickinson, Clay, Ottawa, and Saline counties. In May 1882, they organized the Meridian Branch, located on the U.S. meridian that is a border between Dickinson and Saline counties. Ten converts from the branch immigrated to Utah. Others followed, but soon a mob ordered the missionaries to leave. In 1887, Pres. William M. Palmer of the Northern States Mission began laboring with the

"Bickertonites," a group that had earlier splintered from the Church. His success led to the transfer of Kansas to the Northern States Mission from the Southern States Mission so missionaries, whose headquarters was now closer, would have better access to continue their work.

In 1898, Kansas was transferred to the Indian Territory Mission. Among the earliest branches was one in Kansas City, Kan. By 1930, Kansas included branches in Blau, Kansas City, Leavenworth, St. John, Topeka, and Wichita, with a membership of 2,063.

The Kansas City Stake, with headquarters in Missouri, was organized Oct. 21, 1956, and included three wards and three branches in Kansas — Kansas City 1st, 2nd, and Topeka wards, and the Leavenworth, Hiawatha, and Lawrence branches. The first stake with headquarters in Kansas was in Wichita, organized June 24, 1962.

In 1974, the Church acquired its first institute of religion building in Kansas on a historic estate across from Kansas State University. In that year, membership in the state reached 8,134. In 1980, membership grew to 12,246, and in 1990, to 18,169.

On Aug. 3, 1996, at Fort Leavenworth, 500 men from six stakes in the Kansas City area re-enacted part of the Mormon Battalion march. Membership in Kansas continued to grow faster than the general population and at year-end 1997, for the first time, comprised 1 percent of the state population. Membership in 1999 was 27,232.

Sources: *Encyclopedic History of the Church,* by Andrew Jenson; "Martin V. Witbeck, Former Utahn, called to preside over new unit," *Church News,* Oct. 27, 1956; "Estate home now building for institute," *Church News,* Sept. 7, 1974; "Mormon Grove," by Dean L. May, *Church News,* Aug. 20, 1977; "Battalion commemorated at historic military post," by R. Scott Lloyd, *Church News,* Aug. 10, 1996.

Stakes — 6

(Listed alphabetically as of Oct. 1, 2000.)

No.	Name	Organized	First President
	North America Central Area		
2442	Derby Kansas	8 Mar 1998	Brent Edward Nelsen
1994	Lenexa Kansas	16 Oct 1994	Donald D. Deshler
1610	Olathe Kansas	19 Oct 1986	Clifton D. Boyack Jr.
1696	Salina Kansas	29 May 1988	Thomas R. Coleman
747	Topeka Kansas	29 Feb 1976	Vahl W. Bodily
355	*Wichita Kansas		
	‡Wichita (Kansas, Oklahoma)	24 Jun 1962	Lee R. Meador

Kentucky

Year-end 1999: Est. population, 3,961,000; Members, 22,952; Stakes, 5; Wards, 32; Branches, 32; Missions, 2; Temples, 1; LDS, 0.6, or one in 172.

The first missionaries known to have visited Kentucky were Samuel H. Smith and Reynolds Cahoon. On their way to Missouri from Kirtland, Ohio, they passed through the northern part of Kentucky in late June 1831. However, it is unlikely they preached there. About the same time, the Prophet Joseph Smith and several of the brethren, traveling by steamer on the Ohio River, stopped at Louisville for three days. Because of his practice of frequently preaching, the Prophet Jospeh likely was the first to preach in Kentucky, though no record of converts exists. The Prophet also stopped in Louisville in 1832.

After this beginning, missionary work was done in Ballards, Carlisle, McCracken, Graves, Calloway, Jefferson, Boone, Kenton, and Campbell counties, and a few branches were organized. The first was in Licking River, started before May 1834 by Robert Gulbertson, a convert from Indiana. In April 1835, Wilford Woodruff and Warren Parrish crossed into Kentucky and found that several branches had been formed by earlier missionaries in the region. A typical diary entry indicated that they "preached on the gospel of Jesus Christ, the authenticity of the Book of Mormon, and the scattering and gathering of the House of Israel." From July 1835 on, Elder Woodruff labored alone.

In 1835, James Emmett and Peter Dustin baptized 22 people including Benjamin and David Lewis. Benjamin Lewis was killed in 1838 in the massacre at Haun's Mill in Missouri.

The first conference of the Church in Kentucky was held Feb. 26, 1836, at the home of Lewis Clapp in Calloway County.

The first company of Kentucky members to gather with the Saints in Missouri left in September 1836. This started what became a 50-year movement of the Saints from the Southern States area. Missionary work continued until the end of 1839, then began again in 1842. In July 1843, Brigham Young and Wilford Woodruff visited Kentucky on a missionary swing through the East. Converts were still being baptized a year later when the Prophet Joseph Smith was martyred and missionaries were called back to Illinois.

In 1868, Jesse W. Crosby Jr. and Owen Dix worked in Kentucky "with some success." However, post-Civil War circumstances in the South were difficult and Church growth was very slow. The Saints had settled in the West and no missionary work was being done in the Southern States. Persecution dogged missionaries and members through the 1880s, but by the mid-1890s, toleration of the Church and its members improved. By 1900, there were some 1,170 members in Kentucky, which was placed briefly in the Middle States Mission in 1903.

In 1907, Elders M. P. Stinson and Kossnth Dyal visited the tiny community of Jonah, Ky., several miles east of Lebanon, and baptized Alfred Crews and his wife, Fannie. In late 1908 or early 1909, the Jonah Fork Branch of the Kentucky Conference was organized. One of the first Church buildings in Kentucky was completed at Jonah and dedicated in 1910.

With the advent of the automobile and improved roads, Bradfordsville, six miles west of Jonah and seven or eight miles south of Lebanon, became the gathering place for Saints from the surrounding communities. As missionary activity in the region continued, meetings were held in homes and the outdoors into the 1920s and 1930s, One annual tradition was a July 4th fish fry, attended by up to 200 people, including many non-members of the Church. Fiddle and banjo music accompanied the meal, which was followed by preaching by the elders.

Membership in the state in 1930 was 2,879 in the Kentucky and East Kentucky districts, with a total of six branches that had meetinghouses: Grant's Leek, Kentenia, Martin, Owingsville, Louisville, and Larkin.

In 1971, the first stake in Kentucky, the Louisville Stake, was formed with wards in Fort Knox, Louisville (three), and New Albany, and branches in Lebanon, Salem, and Sulphur Well.

Membership in the state was 13,956 in 1980 and 17,000 in 1990. In 1990, Dan Kelly was elected state senator, the first LDS member in Kentucky to be elected to a state office. Membership in Kentucky in 1999 was 22,952 in 64 wards and branches.

A temple was announced for Louisville on March 17, 1999, and dedicated almost one year to the date on March 19, 2000.

Sources: *Encyclopedic History of the Church,* by Andrew Jenson; *History of the Southern States Mission,* a BYU thesis by LaMar C. Berrett, July 1960; *Church News,* Jan. 30, 1971; "His first fruits," by Ronald G. Watt, *Church News,* Aug. 27, 1977; "My Old Kentucky Home," by Mike Cannon, *Church News,* Feb. 22, 1992, March 25, 2000.

Stakes —5

(Listed alphabetically by area as of Oct. 1, 2000.)

No.	Name	Organized	First President
	North America East Area		
926	Hopkinsville Kentucky	21 May 1978	Robert Laurence Fears
571	*Lexington Kentucky ‡Lexington	23 Apr 1972	Philip M. Moody
540	*Louisville Kentucky ‡Louisville	17 Jan 1971	Henry H. Griffith
1375	*Owingsville Kentucky	30 May 1995	
	‡Huntington West Virginia	7 Nov 1982	Grant Earl Jenson
2253	Paducah Kentucky	29 Oct 1996	Larry Wayne Watkins

Mission — 1

(As of Oct. 1, 2000; shown with historical number. See MISSIONS.)

(29) KENTUCKY LOUISVILLE MISSION
1325 Eastern Pkwy.
Louisville, KY 40204

Louisiana

Year-end 1999: Est. population, 4,372,000; Members, 24,143; Stakes, 7; Wards, 37; Branches, 26; Missions, 1; Temples, 1; Percent LDS, 0.5, or one in 182.

Elder Parley P. Pratt considered going to New Orleans in 1837, hoping to establish a mission there, but felt impressed to instead remain in New York. In 1841, the Prophet Joseph Smith received a letter from Elam Luddington (later the first missionary to Thailand) and Eli G. Terrill of New Orleans who indicated they had a group of members and requested an elder to assist them. "Send us Peter, or an Apostle to preach unto us

Jesus," they wrote, and enclosed $10 to help defray expenses. The group may have been among those from the sailing ship *Isaac Newton,* which arrived from London on Dec. 21, 1840 — the first vessel to carry Saints to New Orleans,

Elder Harrison Sagers was sent to New Orleans, arriving March 28, 1841. He preached to large crowds but was troubled by mobs, and was once defended by a group of courageous women who circled him in defense. He baptized several people and ordained Terrill an elder.

In November 1841, New Orleans became the principal port of arrival for members from Europe, 17,463 of whom immigrated via the Gulf of Mexico port through the years. A branch functioned in New Orleans from 1844 until 1855, when New York became the port of arrival for the Church immigrants.

In 1896, missionaries returned to Louisiana, which was part of the Southern States Mission. Elder Joseph A. Cornwall arrived in Louisiana on Sept. 10 of that year, laboring on the Red River in North Louisiana with little results. In 1897, he and his companions baptized their first converts. The Red Rock Branch was organized in 1898. That year, 24 missionaries labored in Louisiana. A sawmill owner, John R. Jones, befriended the missionaries and protected them from opposition. Alexander Colman Wagley, first president of the Red Rock Branch, was baptized Sept. 4, 1898. By June 16, 1899, Elder David A. Broadbent, president of the Louisiana District from 1898 to 1899, reported that 110 people had been baptized. Pres. Wagley and missionaries were held hostage by mobs but were unharmed. When a mob threatened a missionary under the medical care of Jane Holt Clark, a midwife, she confronted the mob with a shotgun and said, "I brought a good many of you into the world and I can take you out again just as easily." The mob left.

In 1915, a wagon train of members from Pride, La., traveled to Corleyville where they settled and erected a meetinghouse in 1920. Other prominent branches were the Hardytown and Many branches. The Many Branch, which eventually absorbed the Hardytown Branch, was organized in 1933 and a meetinghouse was built in 1942.

Missionaries labored in New Orleans for 20 years before a branch was again organized in the city. Howard and Marian Bennion arrived in Louisiana in the 1920s and a branch was organized in their apartment in 1924. By 1926 the branch began meeting in a public hall. The branch faltered in the early 1930s, but members joined missionaries and, contacting through radio, newspapers, and street meetings, helped the branch grow. Some 100 people celebrated the branch's centennial in 1944. In 1948, the branch had grown to 300 members, due in part to an influx of LDS servicemen who came during World War II. A meetinghouse was begun in January 1951 and dedicated about two years later. That same year, meetinghouses were dedicated in Hammond, Williamson, and Lake Charles, and an addition on the Many Branch meetinghouse was dedicated.

The first stake organized in Louisiana was the New Orleans Stake, created in 1955. In 1964, a new stake center was completed. Membership in the area that the former New Orleans branch once covered was about 2,500 in 1973.

Since World War II, Louisiana has been included in the Texas-Louisiana, the Gulf States, and the Louisiana Shreveport missions. The Louisiana Baton Rouge Mission was organized in 1975.

President Spencer W. Kimball visited Baton Rouge in 1977 and addressed 12,000 people from the surrounding regions. Membership in Louisiana in 1980 was about 16,000, increasing to 22,000 in 1990, and 24,143 in 1999.

Elder L. Lionel Kendrick of the First Quorum of the Seventy is a native of Louisiana, and was a professor of health education at the time of his call as a General Authority in 1988.

A temple was announced for Baton Rouge, Louisiana's capital, on Oct. 14, 1998, to serve about 23,000 members in Louisiana and Mississippi. The temple, located near a wetlands nature reserve, was dedicated July 16, 2000.

Sources: *Encyclopedic History of the Church,* by Andrew Jenson; "Boats on the Mississippi are still reminder of part of LDS History," by J Malan Heslop, *Church News,* Dec. 24, 1977; "From Red Rock to Denham Springs," by Carol Ann Wagley Burnham, *Ensign,* April 1983; Branch Notes 100th Anniversary, *Church News,* Jan. 22, 1944; *Church News,* Dec. 6, 1952, Jan. 20, 1973, Sept. 13, 1975, Sept. 3, 1977, May 21, 1977, Oct. 24, 1998; "Baton Rouge temple: 'a house of refuge' " by Sarah Jane Weaver, *Church News,* July 22, 2000.

Stakes — 7

(Listed alphabetically as of Oct. 1, 2000.)

No.	**Name**	**Organized**	**First President**

North America Southeast Area		
954 Alexandria Louisiana	27 Aug 1978	Jeffie Jackson Horn
476 *Baton Rouge Louisiana ‡Baton Rouge	26 Jan 1969	Harmon Cutler
1254 Denham Springs Louisiana	19 Apr 1981	Stephen H. Cutler
1550 Monroe Louisiana	18 Aug 1985	John Robert Falk
221 *New Orleans Louisiana ‡New Orleans	19 Jun 1955	Clive M. Larson
254 *Shreveport Louisiana ‡Shreveport (Louisiana, Texas)	26 Jan 1958	J. Milton Belisle
1575 Slidell Louisiana	17 Nov 1985	Joseph T. Kuchin

Mission — 1

(As of Oct. 1, 2000; shown with historical number. See MISSIONS.)

(31) LOUISIANA BATON ROUGE MISSION
12025 Justice Ave.
Baton Rouge, LA 70816

Maine

Year-end 1999: Est. population, 1,253,000; Members, 8,569; Stakes, 2; Wards, 15; Branches, 11; Percent LDS, 0.7, or one in 147.

On Sept. 19, 1832, two years after the Church was organized, Elders Orson Hyde and Samuel H. Smith crossed the Piscataqua River in a canoe into Maine. They went from door to door in search of converts and soon started a branch in Saco, York County. One of their first converts was Timothy Smith, baptized about Oct. 31, 1832. Other missionaries followed. In 1833, additional branches were organized, including one in York County that included converts from a mass conversion of 30 people. The Maine Conference was created in 1835 with about 317 members.

In 1837, Elders Wilford Woodruff and Jonathan H. Hale found missionary success on the Fox Islands, where several branches were organized among some 100 converts. The converts, however, gathered to Nauvoo a short time later.

Little missionary work was done in Maine after the martyrdom of the Prophet Joseph Smith in 1844. In 1850, Brigham Young requested all the Saints in Maine to gather in the West. In 1855, Elder E.B. Tripp found members in the town of Mexico, Maine, and organized a branch that remained until 1869. Little activity occurred thereafter until after the turn of the century.

In 1904, missionaries began work in Portland, but the work proceeded very slowly. The Maine Conference was reorganized in 1909, and missionaries found "practically a new field for missionary work." They visited homes near Litchfield in 1908, and met Percy E. and Annie Louise Rowe Lane. Five years later, on July 4, 1913, missionaries baptized Sister Lane and her daughter, Mildred, and the rest of the family afterward. Missionaries started a Sunday School in their home.

After 1925, when Maine was placed in the Canadian Mission, the northern part of the state was visited more often by missionaries. Bangor became a Church center for missionary work. Some 275 people, including eight converts, attended a conference in Bangor on Oct. 14, 1930.

Scattered branches continued into the 1950s before significant growth occurred. The first meetinghouse was dedicated in 1957 in Portland. Another building was dedicated in Bangor the same year. The first stake was the Maine Stake, created in Augusta in 1968 with 2,208 members. Members from the West added to the membership. In 1974, membership was 3,851; in 1980 it was 4,664; in 1990, 7,253; and in 1999, 8,569.

Sources: *Encyclopedic History of the Church,* by Andrew Jenson; "A Partial History of Litchfield," by Percy E. Lane, unpublished; "Wilford Woodruff's Mission to Maine," by Donald Q. Cannon, *Improvement Era,* September., 1970; "Old Mormon Palmyra and New England," by Richard Neitzel Holsapfel and T. Jeffery Cottle; *The Narrative of the* Saints *in Maine from 1831 to the 1990s,* an unpublished manuscript by Paul Edward Damron.

Stakes — 2

(Listed alphabetically as of Oct. 1, 2000.)

No. Name	**Organized**	**First President**
North America Northeast Area		
461 *Augusta Maine		

	‡Maine	23 Jun 1968	Olie W. Ross
1595	Bangor Maine	20 Apr 1986	Paul Herald Risk II

Maryland

Year-end 1999: Est. population, 5,172,000; Members, 34,113; Stakes, 7; Wards, 50; Branches, 11; Missions, 1; Temples, 1; Percent LDS, 0.5, or one in 169.

Elders Jedediah M. Grant, Erastus Snow, William Bosley, and John F. Wakefield began missionary work in Maryland in the summer of 1837. Elders Snow and Bosley worked in Washington County between May and October and organized a branch. Elder Snow reported preaching in Greencastle and engaging in a formal debate with a Campbellite minister that lasted 10 hours in Leitersburgh, Washington County. He afterward baptized 11 people. He also baptized seven people in Leitersburgh. In 1838, Elder Benjamin Winchester preached in the same vicinity, traveling with Elder Snow. On this journey, Elder Snow baptized an 89-year-old man after cutting through ice 18 inches thick.

An LDS newspaper, the *Mormon Expositor,* was begun in 1842 in Baltimore but was discontinued. Elders Heber C. Kimball and Lyman Wight traveled to Baltimore in 1844 where they received information about the martyrdom of the Prophet Joseph Smith.

After the exodus west and the gathering of the Saints, little work was done in Maryland near the turn of the 20th century. The Maryland Conference was reorganized June 30, 1899, with Charles A. Hardy as president. At that time, mission leadership wanted to increase the conference size, so they requested an additional four Virginia counties from the Southern States Mission. Southern States Mission Pres. Ben E. Rich humorously agreed to yield the Virginia counties on the condition that they would take six, not four.

By 1900, the conference included the Pratt and Mount Savage branches, but in 1905, the Maryland Conference was absorbed into the Eastern Pennsylvania Conference. That year, a tiny group of members in Baltimore organized a Book of Mormon class that lasted several years. Sunday Schools were organized in Baltimore in 1907 and reorganized in 1917.

Missionary work picked up in 1915 as work proceeded in Havre de Grace, Baltimore, Frederick and Salisbury. In 1918, street meetings in Baltimore brought interest. Work in Annapolis began in 1920. Branch meetings in Washington and Baltimore, presided over by missionaries, and Sunday Schools and Relief Societies in other areas, were held in rented halls. One small frame meetinghouse in Capitol Heights accommodated a membership of mostly Westerners — students or those in government employment.

The Washington Stake was created June 30, 1940, with Ezra Taft Benson as president. This stake included parts of Maryland where the Chesapeake stake, the first Maryland stake was later created in 1970. Maryland membership in 1980 was 17,617.

A site for the Washington D.C. Temple was selected in Kensington, Md., in 1962. The 160,000 square-foot temple, with the statue of the Angel Moroni rising 288 feet above ground, was dedicated in 1974 and has become a prominent landmark along the Belt Route circling the nation's capital. The temple grounds have become a popular place for national leaders and foreign diplomats to visit on special occasions, such as during the Christmas season. At the 15th anniversary of the temple in 1988, it was noted that membership around the nation's capital had increased by some 200 percent since the temple's construction, and numbered some 63,000 members in 19 stakes.

The Maryland Baltimore Mission was created in 1994 from a division of the Washington D.C. North and Washington D.C. South missions. In 1999, Maryland had an LDS population of 34,113.

Sources: *Encyclopedic History of the Church,* by Andrew Jenson; *History of the Southern States Mission,* by LaMar C. Berrett, BYU thesis, July 1960; mission and ward histories; *Church News,* Sept. 19, 1970, Sept. 14, 1974, Sept. 17, 1977.

Stakes — 7

(Listed alphabetically as of Oct. 1, 2000.)

No.	Name	Organized	First President
North America East Area			
1429	*Annapolis Maryland 13 Nov 1988		
	‡Columbia Maryland	12 Jun 1983	Stephen P. Shipley
674	Baltimore Maryland	8 Dec 1974	Kyle W. Petersen
1825	Columbia Maryland	10 Nov 1991	Cecil Brent Bargeron
1390	Frederick Maryland	12 Dec 1982	Earl J. Wahlquist
1566	Seneca Maryland	27 Oct 1985	David Warne Ferrel

526	*Silver Spring Maryland		
	‡Chesapeake (Maryland)	13 Sep 1970	June B. Thayn
1051	Suitland Maryland	19 Aug 1979	Thomas Bailey Kerr

Mission — 1

(As of Oct. 1, 2000; shown with historical number. Washington, D.C., missions are listed in District of Colombia. See MISSIONS.)

(298) MARYLAND BALTIMORE MISSION
4785 Dorsey Hall Drive, Suite 105
Ellicott City, MD 21042-7728

Massachusetts

Year-end 1999: Est. population, 6,175,000; Members, 21,106; Stakes, 4; Wards, 34; Branches, 15; Missions, 1; Temples, 1 under construction; Percent LDS, 0.2, or one in 380.

The first missionaries in Massachusetts are believed to be Elders Orson Hyde and Samuel H. Smith, who arrived in Boston June 22, 1832. They baptized four people, and, by the end of the year, had organized two branches. These branches were short-lived, however.

In 1838, Brigham Young and his brother Joseph baptized 17 people in Boston as they preached the gospel. The Eastern States Mission was created in 1839 with John P. Greene as president. (Greene was the reverend who received a copy of the Book of Mormon during Samuel H. Smith's first missionary journey in New York in 1830). By February 1843, some 14 branches in the Boston area had been organized. Joseph Smith and others visited Boston in December 1839. They were en route to Washington, D.C., seeking redress for the injustices in Missouri.

In 1843, Elder George J. Adams preached nightly to an enthusiastic audience of some 1,200 in Charlestown. Later, eight members of the Quorum of the Twelve attended a Boston conference as part of an effort they were making to press missionary work forward in New England. Their work ended after the martyrdom of Joseph Smith in 1844. A year later the Boston Branch had some 300-400 members. In 1849, Mission Pres. William Appleby led a company of 79 members to St. Louis and on to the Great Basin. Many died of cholera.

Work slowed in 1850, and stopped in 1857 when all missionaries were recalled to Utah because of the approaching Johnston's Army. Until 1893, most of New England, including Massachusetts, saw little progress in the development of the Church.

The Eastern States Mission reopened in 1893 and missionaries sought out members. After a year, membership numbered 96. Despite emphasis on public relations, missionaries encountered substantial hostilities. Highly publicized U.S. Senate hearings on Apostle and Senator-elect Reed Smoot in Washington, D.C., fanned anti-LDS sentiments. Police often refused to allow missionaries to conduct open-air meetings. President Joseph F. Smith addressed a large gathering at Deacon's Hall in Boston in 1905 on a return trip from dedicating a monument at Joseph Smith's birthplace in Vermont.

A Mutual Improvement Association was started in Boston on Jan. 5, 1908, and a branch in Lynn, Mass., was started in 1910. The Church began to grow about 1917 but the onset of World War I halted efforts.

After the war, missionaries resumed serving in Massachusetts and the membership began to increase. On April 18, 1930, missionaries took part in a radio broadcast. At that time, membership in the Massachusetts District numbered about 356. Longtime member Naomi B. Cranney recalled that membership in the 1930s included only about 10 permanent families in the area. Returned missionaries who were students at Harvard University provided great strength, she said. The Great Depression and World War II again slowed growth. But the war also brought couples from Utah to work at the Massachusetts Institute of Technology in Cambridge. In 1947, missionaries were sent to rural areas, where they found some success.

The first meetinghouses were completed in the early 1950s. An exceptional piece of Church property was the Longfellow estate in Cambridge, Mass., that was purchased by Elder Levi Edgar Young. It later became headquarters for the New England Mission that had been organized in 1937. A meetinghouse was dedicated on this site in 1956.

When mission Pres. Truman G. Madsen began serving in 1962, missionaries baptized about 1,000 per year for two years. The same year the Church purchased the shortwave radio station WRUL to beam Church-related information to Europe, Africa, and Latin

America. The station had studios in New York City and a transmitter in Boston.

In 1963, some 2,200 members met in a conference in Boston, the largest LDS gathering in New England history.

The Boston Stake, the first in New England, was created in 1962. It included parts of New Hampshire and Rhode Island. During the 1960s, a number of meetinghouses were constructed with beneficial effects on membership. Members enjoyed a higher profile during the next years with improved relations with government and educational figures. The Massachusetts Boston Mission was organized in 1974, an outgrowth of the New England Mission. Additional stakes in Massachusetts were created in Hingham in 1981 and in Springfield in 1987. Membership in 1974 was 5,628, increasing to 8,174 in 1980, and 13,931 in 1990. In 1999, membership in the state was 21,106.

Shortly after he was sustained president of the Church in 1995, President Gordon B. Hinckley spoke to 7,500 members at the Boston Massachusetts Regional Conference April 23. He also spoke to leaders and missionaries during the trip, and visited historical sites. On Sept. 30, 1995, in general conference, President Hinckley announced a temple would be built in Boston.

The Peabody Essex Museum in Salem, Mass., held a major exhibit about the Church during the summer of 2000, titled "From New England to the Great Salt Lake: The Mormon Legacy of Faith." The exhibit featured the Prophet Joseph Smith's Essex County ties. The Prophet went to Salem in 1836 to research his family roots and preach in a city that was steeped in theological debate and missionary activity.

The Boston Massachusetts Temple was dedicated Oct. 1, 2000 — the 100th operating temple in the Church. Dedication of the temple came just 2 1/2 years after President Hinckley announced ambitious plans in general conference in April 1998 to have 100 temples in service by the year 2000. At the time of the announcement, 51 temples were in operation.

Sources: "Yankee Saints: The Church in New England in the Twentieth Century," by Richard O. Cowan, *Regional Studies in Latter-day Saint History,* New England; Highlights in the History of The Church of Jesus Christ of Latter-day Saints, a paper by J. D. Williams, Cambridge Branch; *Church News,* April 29, 1995, April 1, 2000, July 22, 2000, Oct. 7, 2000.

Stakes — 4

(Listed alphabetically as of Oct. 1, 2000.)

No.	Name	Organized	First President
	North America Northeast Area		
354	*Boston Massachusetts ‡Boston (Mass., N.H., R.I.)	20 May 1962	Wilbur W. Cox
2497	Cambridge Massachusetts	18 Oct 1998	Lloyd S. Baird
1287	Hingham Massachusetts	30 Aug 1981	Brent W. Lambert
1646	Springfield Massachusetts	28 Jun 1987	David O. Sutton

Mission — 1

(As of Oct. 1, 2000; shown with historical number. See MISSIONS.)

(35) MASSACHUSETTS BOSTON MISSION
385 Concord Ave., Suite 100
Belmont, MA 02178

Michigan

Year-end 1999: Est. population, 9,864,000; Members, 36,888; Stakes, 8; Wards, 59; Branches, 44; Missions, 2; Districts, 2; Temples, 1; Percent LDS, 0.4, or one in 266.

Visiting her relatives in Pontiac, Lucy Mack Smith arrived in Michigan in the spring of 1831. With her was her niece, Almira Mack of Pontiac, who had been baptized in New York in 1830. They visited Lucy Mack Smith's brother, Col. Stephen Mack, considered the founder of Pontiac.

Preaching in Pontiac, she warned one unfriendly pastor that one third of his flock would soon be members of the LDS Church, including the deacon. After she returned to Kirtland, Ohio, the Prophet Joseph Smith sent Jared Carter and Joseph Wood to Pontiac where they arrived Jan. 7, 1833, and baptized 22 people from the pastor's congregation, including the deacon, Samuel Bent.

In 1834, Joseph Smith visited Pontiac with his father and brother Hyrum, the three witnesses to the Book of Mormon, Frederick G. Williams, and Robert Orton. Missionary work continued in Michigan, although no records exist of how many people were converted because converts often soon gathered with the body of the Church.

Parley P. and Orson Pratt visited Detroit in the fall of 1839 where they preached to crowded houses. Parley published a pamphlet, *History of the Late Persecution by the State of Missouri upon the Mormons.*

Elder Mephibosheth Serrine was a leader of the Church in southeastern Michigan. In the early 1840s, branches were in Oakland, Lapeer, Wayne, Livingston, Washtenaw, and Lenawee counties. Converts from Jared Carter's efforts of 1833 continued to spread the gospel to most of western Michigan. On Jan. 12, 1844, Elder Serrine reported that in the previous six months, more than 100 converts had left to gather in Nauvoo. Visiting Church authorities created more branches in June 1844. The martyrdom of Joseph and Hyrum Smith on June 27 ended the early period of the Church in Michigan. Many members accepted the leadership of Brigham Young and joined the westward movement. Apostate James J. Strang claimed to be the successor of the Prophet and attracted a group who later settled on Beaver Island in Lake Michigan before disbanding. Other splinter groups resided in Michigan as well.

In 1876, William M. Palmer served a mission in Michigan. He soon organized several branches despite serious persecution. The Northwestern States Mission was organized in 1878 with Cyrus H. Wheelock as president. Faithful converts migrated steadily to Utah. In 1889, the Northern States Mission was organized and included Michigan. After the turn of the 20th century, the first branch in Michigan was created by German E. Ellsworth in Detroit on April 21, 1915. By 1930, membership in the East Michigan and West Michigan districts, created that year, had a combined membership of 972.

The first meetinghouse in Detroit was erected and dedicated in December 1928. In 1939, 25 missionaries who had been recalled from foreign areas because of World War II formed a chorus that performed public concerts. By 1945, some 7,183 members resided in branches in Detroit (3), Ann Arbor, Battle Creek, Grand Rapids, Jackson, Muskegon, Flint, Lansing, Pontiac, and Saginaw. Michigan's first stake was created Nov. 9, 1952, in Detroit, with later-to-be Michigan Gov. George W. Romney as president. Additional stakes were created in 1962 (Lansing), 1969 (Dearborn) and 1979 (Kalamazoo).

The Great Lakes Mission was created in 1949, and the Indiana-Michigan Mission in 1970. In 1973, the Michigan Mission (changed later to Michigan Lansing) was created. The Michigan Dearborn (later renamed Michigan Detroit) Mission was created in 1978. In 1980, Michigan had a membership of 22,607, and in 1990, 28,245.

President Spencer W. Kimball spoke to 14,500 Saints from Michigan and parts of Indiana, Ohio, and Pennsylvania at an area conference in Ann Arbor, Mich., Sept. 20, 1980.

On July 26, 1995, longtime national and Church leader, and Michigan's most prominent citizen in the 1960s, George W. Romney, died. He was the governor of Michigan from 1962 until he resigned in 1969 to join President Richard Nixon's cabinet as secretary of Housing and Urban Development. He also was a candidate for president of the United States in 1964. In April 1998, BYU's Institute of Public Management was named after George Romney.

A temple in the Detroit suburb of Bloomfield Hills was announced Aug. 29, 1998, and dedicated 14 months later on Oct. 23, 1999. The roadway in front of the temple was originally built by the Prophet Joseph Smith's uncle, Stephen Mack, who had figured prominently in the early history of the Detroit area.

In 1999, 36,888 members resided in Michigan.

Sources: *The Michigan Mormons,* written and compiled by Hilda Faulkner Browne; "The Saints Come to Michigan," by John and Audrey Cumming, *Michigan History,* March 1965; "The Mormon Era in Detroit," by John Cumming, *Detroit Historical Society Bulletin,* March 1968; *Encyclopedic History of the Church,* by Andrew Jenson; "LDS influence felt in much of Michigan history," by Frank C. Davis, *Church News,* Nov. 15, 1980, Dec. 11, 1983, July 29, 1995, April 25, 1998, Aug. 29, 1998; "A temple in their midst," by Greg Hill, *Church News,* Oct. 30, 1999.

Stakes — 8

(Listed alphabetically as of Oct. 1, 2000.)

No.	Name	Organized	First President
North America Northeast Area			
854	Ann Arbor Michigan	14 Aug 1977	Duane Marvin Laws
197	*Bloomfield Hills Michigan ‡Detroit (Michigan, Ohio, Canada)	9 Nov 1952	George W. Romney
940	Grand Blanc Michigan	11 Jun 1978	Trent Pickett Kitley

684	Grand Rapids Michigan	2 Mar 1975	Glenn Goodwin
1091	Kalamazoo Michigan	9 Dec 1979	Donald Lee Lykins
349	*Lansing Michigan		
	‡Lansing	18 Feb 1962	Sylvan H. Wittwer
469	*Midland Michigan		
	‡Mid-Michigan	1 Dec 1968	E. Richard Packham
474	*Westland Michigan 14 Aug 1978		
	*Dearborn Michigan		
	‡Dearborn (Michigan)	12 Jan 1969	Carl S. Hawkins

Missions — 2

(As of Oct. 1, 2000; shown with historical number. See MISSIONS.)

(164) MICHIGAN DETROIT MISSION
33505 State St., Suite 101
Farmington, MI 48335

(104) MICHIGAN LANSING MISSION
1500 Abbott Rd., Suite 110
East Lansing, MI 48823

Minnesota

Year-end 1999: Est. population, 4,776,000; Members, 22,941; Stakes, 6; Wards, 38; Branches, 25; Missions, 1; Temples, 1; Percent LDS, 0.5, or one in 208.

In 1854, a Mormon elder, Ralph Joung, "preached at Spring Grove," according to a Minnesota county newspaper.

In 1857, missionaries baptized Minnesota settler Robert Pope and his wife, Sarah Leduc Pope, along with Edwin Theodore Pope and his wife, whose name was not recorded, in Morristown in southern Minnesota. These converts soon gathered with the Saints in Utah.

The next missionary to Minnesota was Elder Silas Hoyt, who labored in the state in September 1868. In 1870, Ariah C. Brower and Eli Whipple worked in Minnesota and adjoining states. They were received with enthusiasm, but gained few converts. In 1875, Elder Bengt P. Wulffenstein, who spoke Swedish, German, and Danish, began a systematic and successful effort to teach the many Scandinavians who had settled in Minnesota.

In 1875, Elder Wulffenstein organized Minnesota's first branch, a small group of converts in Freeborn County. By 1877, five more branches were organized, and in February 1882, mission history records indicate that Minnesota had 74 members. The town of Monticello became a center for the work as Deborah Houghton Riggs, the wife of its founder, Ashley C. Riggs, joined the Church.

Work in Minnesota was incorporated into the Northwestern States Mission in 1878, when nine missionaries served in this state. The missionaries located LDS members or those who had heard the gospel preached in their homeland. Missionaries were often the target of eggs, stones, and threats as they made arduous journeys across the sparsely populated region. With few exceptions, their efforts were rewarded only with a handful of converts. During this period, several small companies of members immigrated to Utah from Minnesota, the largest being a party of 70 from Monticello.

In 1886, some 227 members belonged to the Minnesota Conference, then including Wisconsin, the Dakotas, and Iowa.

Missionary work halted from 1891 until 1896. However, following the Manifesto of 1890, public opinion improved as people began to realize that the Mormons had been maligned. In 1899, a conference was attended by Apostle Heber J. Grant. By the turn of the 20th century most Minnesota converts had left for Zion. The handful of members who remained worked as a very small minority to build a Mormon presence.

Minnesota Conference headquarters were established in Minneapolis in 1900. A Sunday School was organized May 20, 1900, in Minneapolis. Another was organized in St. Paul on Aug. 5. The Sunday Schools were combined in 1902, and the new unit had an average attendance of 50. Mission Pres. German E. Ellsworth served from 1904-1919, and under his leadership the mission made steady progress. More Sunday Schools were started, and branches were organized and divided. The first Church-owned building in Minnesota was purchased May 9, 1914, for the St. Paul Branch, and a baptismal font installed in its basement was used for baptismal services for converts from the entire state.

By 1919, membership had increased to 4,000 in 30 branches, and possibly hundreds of others migrating west. A large meetinghouse was erected and dedicated in 1924. By 1930, there were three districts in the state: the North, South and Lake districts. Over the next

20 years, many branches were established. The first stake in the state, the Minnesota Stake, was organized in Minneapolis Nov. 29, 1960, with six wards and five branches, and a membership of 2,600. By 1970, its membership had reached 4,800. The Minnesota-Manitoba Mission was created in 1970, and the Minnesota-Wisconsin Mission in 1973. When the name of the Minnesota Stake was changed to the Minneapolis Minnesota Stake in 1974, it had 4,936 members. In 1976, the St. Paul Stake was created, and the same year the Minnesota Minneapolis Mission was created. Membership was 11,755 in 1980, 16,741 in 1990, and 22,941 in 1999.

Members in western Minnesota assisted the community during floods in 1997 and 1998.

A temple was announced July 29, 1998, for the Minneapolis-St. Paul area. The temple, built in St. Paul, was dedicated in a misting rain and unusually high temperatures for the season on Jan. 9, 2000, the first of 35 temples expected to be completed in 2000.

Sources: *Encyclopedic History of the Church,* by Andrew Jenson; *Minnesota Mormons, a History of the Minneapolis Minnesota Stake,* by Fayone B. Willes; The Church in Minnesota, unpublished, no author listed; *Mormon Missionaries and Minnesota Scandinavians,* by Kenneth O. Bjork, *Minnesota History,* published by the Minnesota Historical Society; *Church News,* Dec. 3, 1960; May 3, 1997; Aug. 15, 1998; "First temple in the year 2000," by Janet Kruckenberg, *Church News,* Jan. 15, 2000.

Stakes — 6

(Listed alphabetically as of Oct. 1, 2000.)

No.	Name	Organized	First President
	North America Central Area		
1562	Anoka Minnesota	20 Oct 1985	Lyle T Cottle
2192	Burnsville Minnesota	28 Apr 1996	Matthew Artell Smith
1939	Duluth Minnesota	9 May 1993	John G. Hancock
317	*Minneapolis Minnesota		
	‡Minnesota (Minn., Wis.)	29 Nov 1960	Delbert F. Wright
910	Rochester Minnesota	30 Apr 1978	Lee McNeal Johnson
744	St. Paul Minnesota	15 Feb 1976	Thomas Albert Holt

Mission — 1

(As of Oct. 1, 2000; shown with historical number. See MISSIONS.)

(26a) MINNESOTA MINNEAPOLIS MISSION
5931 West 96th St.
Bloomington, MN 55438

Mississippi

Year-end 1999: Est. population, 2,769,000; Members, 17,578; Stakes, 4; Wards, 26; Branches, 15; Missions, 1; Percent LDS, 0.6, or one in 158.

Missionary work in Mississippi evidently began when Elder John D. Hunter and Benjamin L. Clapp arrived in Tishomingo County in 1839. They baptized 13 people in Tishomingo County. In 1840, Elder Norvel M. Head said he visited a branch in the same county. Elders Daniel Tyler and R. D. Sheldon began work in Copiah, Miss., and baptized five people in 1841. A group of 80 to 90 members in 40 wagons, escaping persecution, arrived in Nauvoo from Mississippi in April 1842. A small branch was organized in Monroe County in 1843, where other converts, including plantation owner James M. Flake, were converted and baptized by Elder Clapp. Several branches were created and membership continued to increase.

In 1846, a company of emigrants left Monroe County expecting to join the main body of Saints that was then planning to travel to the Rocky Mountains. Instead, the Mississippi Saints became the first group of Mormons to cross the plains, wintering with fur trappers in Pueblo, Colo., that year. These members made significant contributions. They were the first to establish a religious colony in the West since the Spanish priests of 1769. They later founded the second colony in Salt Lake Valley at Cottonwood (once called the Mississippi Ward) and Holladay (named after a Mississippian), helped found San Bernardino, Calif., and years later were involved in other colonies along the Little Colorado in Arizona. (Snowflake, Ariz., was originally named Snow Flake after Erastus Snow and James M. Flake.) One of the children of these early pioneers from Mississippi was Alice Rowan, who taught school in Riverside, Calif., among the first African-American women to teach at a public school in the nation.

Missionary work is believed to have continued in Mississippi until the Civil War. It resumed in the 1870s. In 1880, enemies of the Church tried but failed to enlist the governor of Mississippi in forcing missionaries to leave the state.

A colony of African-American converts may have created a township in 1891 called Republican Square near the Mississippi Gulf Coast, but all traces of this community subsequently vanished.

Persecution increased and missionaries were often abused. Elder Alma P. Richards was murdered in 1888, though a Church investigation committee concluded the motive likely was robbery, not religious persecution.

The U.S. Census listed 123 members in Mississippi in 1890. By 1906, that number had increased to 1,018.

A meetinghouse in Quitman, Miss., was completed in 1908, and the branch had 11 members but grew to 30 members in 10 years.

By 1930, the Mississippi Conference had a membership of 2,170 in the Darburn and Red Star branches and the Sunday Schools in Bay St. Louis, Meadville, Raytown, Red Hill, Sarah, and Smithville. New buildings were completed for the Senatobia, McNeill, and Jackson branches in 1943, and in Biloxi in 1954.

The first two stakes in Mississippi were created in 1965. The first, Jackson, had 2,245 members in two Jackson wards and wards in Meridian, Natchez, Columbus, Vicksburg, and Red Star and a branch in Greenville. The second stake in Biloxi included 2,515 members in the Biloxi, Columbia, Gulfport, Hattiesburg, Liberty, and Pascagoula wards and the Bayou La Croix, Darbun, Laurel, McNiell, Sant Hill, and Seminary branches.

Membership grew slowly, reaching 6,527 in 1970, 10,403 in 1980 and 13,000 in 1990. The Kosciusko Branch in the Jackson Mississippi Stake, won the "best religious entry" award in the local Christmas parade in Kosciusko, Miss., in 1993 and 1994. In May 1996, members in Monroe County, Miss., honored early pioneers from Mississippi, known as the Mississippi Saints, by dedicating a monument at Mormon Springs where many of the early converts were baptized. Also during that year, a program was held commemorating the temporary colony in Pueblo, Colo., established by the Mississippi Saints.

A total of 17,578 members resided in Mississippi in 1999.

Sources: *Encyclopedic History of the Church,* by Andrew Jenson; "Anniversary Noted for Old Backwoods Chapel," *Church News,* Aug. 9, 1958; *History of the Southern States Mission 1831-1861,* by LaMar C. Berrett, BYU thesis, July 1960; "Gulf States Get New Stake," *Church News,* May 8, 1965, and July 3, 1965; *A Brief History of the Southern States Mission for One Hundred Years, 1830-1930,* by DeVon H. Nish, a BYU paper, August 1966; "Orthodoxy Versus Nonconformity: The Mormon Experience in Tennessee and Mississippi, 1875-1905," a University of Chicago paper by Mary Elizabeth Stovall, March 1976; "Mississippi Mormons," by Leonard Arrington, *Ensign,* June 1977; "Branch wins parade honor for second consecutive year," *Church News,* Dec. 24, 1994; "Mississippi Saints headed west in 1846," *Church News,* July 13, 1996, Sept. 20, 1997.

Stakes — 4

(Listed alphabetically as of Oct. 1, 2000.)

No.	Name	Organized	First President
North America Southeast Area			
1364	Gulfport Mississippi	10 Oct 1982	John Sibbald Scott II
408	*Hattiesburg Mississippi ‡Hattiesburg	27 Jun 1965	Edwin White
404	*Jackson Mississippi ‡Jackson	2 May 1965	Neil J. Ferrell
1801	Tupelo Mississippi	9 Jun 1991	Thomas Evan Nebeker

Mission — 1

(As of Oct. 1, 2000; shown with historical number. See MISSIONS.)

(171) MISSISSIPPI JACKSON MISSION
5200 Keele St.
Jackson, MS 39206

Missouri

Year-end 1999: Est. population, 5,468,000; Members, 51,187; Stakes, 13; Wards, 96; Branches, 25; Missions, 2; Temples, 1 ; Percent LDS, 0.9, or one in 107.

Oliver Cowdery, Parley P. Pratt, Peter Whitmer Jr. and Ziba Peterson, joined by Frederick G. Williams, a convert from their stopover in Ohio, arrived in Missouri on Jan. 13, 1831. They preached to Delaware and Shawnee Indians in the adjacent Indian Territory. Indian agents soon asked them to leave. The next year, in 1832, Joseph Smith received a revelation (D&C 84), indicating that the "New Jerusalem," would be built in

Independence, Jackson County, Mo.

This revelation led to an immediate influx of members, some of whom were ill-prepared for settling and less obedient to Church instructions. This influx laid the groundwork for what became, in essence, a battle for turf between old settlers and Mormon colonists with their strikingly different economic, political, and spiritual values. By June 1833, 1,200 members in 12 branches lived in Jackson County. On July 30, 1833, nearly 500 Missourians ordered the Mormons from Jackson County. Church leaders tried to seek protection through the courts but failed. Mormons seeking to defend themselves were disarmed and mobs drove them out.

The first LDS publication, the *Evening and Morning Star,* was issued June 1, 1832, in Independence.

In 1834, Joseph Smith and a group of 150-200 armed men, called Zion's Camp, arrived from Kirtland, Ohio, to protect the members. A violent storm prevented confrontation and undoubtedly preserved the group that was subsequently disbanded at the Prophet's direction.

The Jackson County LDS refugees found safety in adjacent Clay County for two years and then, amid growing adversity, moved to western, uninhabited Caldwell and Daviess counties. By 1838, Far West, the principal settlement in Caldwell County, became Church headquarters and had more than 100 homes, hotels, a printing house, and a school. A temple site was dedicated here and cornerstones were placed on July 4, 1838. Joseph F. Smith, president of the Church from 1901-18, was born in Far West in 1838.

It was revealed to Joseph Smith on May 19, 1838, that Adam-ondi-Ahman, in Daviess County, was where Adam "shall come to visit his people," as spoken by Daniel the prophet. (D&C 116.) Twenty revelations of the Doctrine and Covenants were received in Missouri.

Apostasy fueled internal problems in 1838. Several prominent leaders were excommunicated, and unwise rhetoric against them incited Missourians once again against the Church.

Violence erupted on Aug. 6, 1838, when Church members were prevented from voting at Gallatin, Mo. Mob raids began and the Mormons organized, armed themselves, and fought against the attacks as their county charter allowed. Apostle David W. Patten, who was ahead of Brigham Young in seniority in the Quorum of the Twelve, was killed Oct. 25. Hearing exaggerated reports of Mormon armies, Missouri Gov. Lilburn W. Boggs, who refused to aid the Saints or quell violence, signed the infamous order on Oct. 27 to drive out or exterminate the Mormons. Seventeen men and boys were killed at Haun's Mill on Oct. 30 by the unauthorized Livingston County Militia. On Oct. 31, Joseph Smith was arrested and the next day sentenced to death. His life was saved by Brig. Gen. A.W. Doniphan, who refused to carry out the order. On Nov. 2, the militia plundered Far West and drove out the Saints. The thousands LDS refugees from Missouri settled on the Mississippi River in Illinois where they established Nauvoo.

During this period, some members found shelter in the more tolerant city of St. Louis, where citizens once raised funds for their aid. In 1844, a branch was started in St. Louis by Momon refugees. Shiploads of LDS immigrants used St. Louis as a port of debarkation. After the exodus from Nauvoo in 1846, more members came to St. Louis. By 1849, a district was formed with 3,000-4,000 members. The St. Louis Stake was organized in 1854. Many pioneer supplies were imported to Utah through St. Louis. The so-called "Utah War" of 1857 brought the end of the St. Louis Stake when Brigham Young called all members to Utah.

With the members gone, little missionary work occurred in Missouri until later in the century. The state became part of the Northern States Mission and in 1900 was transferred to the Southwestern States Mission, which became the Central States Mission in 1904. A branch in St. Louis was reorganized in 1898, and the Church placed an exhibit in the 1904 World's Fair at St. Louis. In 1915, as a missionary, Elder Spencer W. Kimball became president of the district and helped purchase a meetinghouse.

Mission headquarters were moved to Independence in 1907 and a meetinghouse was erected in 1913.

By 1930, eight branches functioned in Independence, Joplin, Kansas City, St. Louis, Sedalia, St. Joseph, Springfield, and Webb City. In June 1939, Wilford Wood, in behalf of the Church, purchased the old Liberty Jail where the Prophet Joseph Smith and others were incarcerated during the winter of 1838-39.

The first modern stake in Missouri was the Kansas City Stake, created Oct. 21, 1956. It included the Kansas City, Independence, Liberty Ward, and St. Joseph wards; the Rock

Hill Branch; and the Albany and Chillicothe Sunday Schools.

The St. Louis Stake was organized once again on June 1, 1958, and additional stakes followed in the 1970s. On June 25, 1976, Gov. Christopher S. Bond signed an executive order rescinding the extermination order issued in 1838 by Gov. Boggs.

The Missouri St. Louis Mission, the second mission headquartered in Missouri, was created in 1977. Membership in the state in 1974 was 13,796; in 1980, 25,243; and in 1990, 35,084.

On Dec. 29, 1990, the First Presidency announced plans for a temple in St. Louis. As the temple was being constructed, community leaders enthusiastically supported the effort. The temple's location at the intersection of two major freeways raised awareness of the Church.

President Gordon B. Hinckley visited St. Louis in April 1995 to conduct his first regional conference since becoming Church president. He later returned June 1, 1997, to dedicate the temple, the 50th operating temple in the Church.

In Independence, local members took part in inter-faith activities and in recent years presented an annual Church pageant in June. The visit of the Tabernacle Choir in 1992, performing in the RLDS Church's Auditorium, helped solidify friendships as well. In 1997-98, Church members volunteered to process and microfilm probate records in Independence. Also, an old log home in Far West was studied by local and LDS archaeologists, who believed that it was built by later-Apostle Charles C. Rich. An exhibit at Missouri's capitol, Jefferson City, "Mormon Experience in Missouri," was shown during the summer of 1998.

In 1999, there were 51,187 members living in Missouri.

Sources: *Encyclopedic History of the Church,* by Andrew Jenson; "Martin V. Witbeck, Former Utahn, Called to Preside over New Unit," *Church News,* Oct. 27, 1956; *Encyclopedia of Mormonism,* edited by Daniel H. Ludlow; "Missouri's Impact on the Church," by Max H Parkin, *Ensign,* April 1979; "Saints in Independence," by Janet Brigham, *Ensign,* June 1979; "The Saints in Saint Louis," by Violet Kimball, *Ensign,* March 1988; "Missouri Past Forgotten, Church Gains," by Hal Knight, *Church News,* Oct. 20, 1979; "Growth continues in river port where Church thrived in 1850s," by John L. Hart, *Church News,* Jan. 20, 1990; *Church News,* Nov. 6, 1993; *Church News,* Jan. 8, 1994; "Pres. Hinckley Greets Saints in St. Louis," *Church News,* April 22, 1995, *Church News,* June 7, 1997, May 2, 1998, April 17, 1999.

Stakes — 13

(Listed alphabetically by area as of Oct. 1, 1998.)

No.	Name	Organized	First President
North America Central Area — 9			
1563	Cape Girardeau Missouri	20 Oct 1985	David E. Payne
511	*Columbia Missouri ‡Columbia	19 Apr 1970	Samuel D. Richards
544	*Independence Missouri ‡Independence	25 Mar 1971	Melvin James Bennion
234	*Kansas City Missouri ‡Kansas City (Missouri, Kansas)	21 Oct 1956	Martin V. Witbeck
1071	Liberty Missouri	14 Oct 1979	Dell Earl Johnsen
2323	Platte City Missouri	9 Mar 1997	Ronald Blaine Stapley
265	*St. Louis Missouri ‡St. Louis (Missouri, Illinois)	1 Jun 1958	Roy W. Oscarson
634	St. Louis Missouri North	15 Mar 1987	Neal C. Lewis
1118	St. Louis Missouri South	16 Mar 1980	Verner Lorenzo Stromberg Jr.
North America Southwest Area — 4			
859	Joplin Missouri	28 Aug 1977	Kenneth Rae Martin
2356	St. Robert Missouri	18 May 1997	Gary Wayne Pulsipher
610	*Springfield Missouri ‡Ozark	29 Apr 1973	Carroll S. Claybrook
2052	Springfield Missouri South	21 May 1995	Robert Charles Brusman

Stakes discontinued

2	Clay-Caldwell Discontinued 1839	3 Jul 1834	David Whitmer
3	Adam-Ondi-Ahman Nov 1838	28 Jun 1838	John Smith
6a	St. Louis	4 Nov 1854	Milo Andrus

1858, reinstated as 265

Missions — 2

(As of Oct. 1, 2000; shown with historical number. See MISSIONS.)

(14b) MISSOURI INDEPENDENCE MISSION
517 West Walnut
Independence, MO 64050

(153) MISSOURI ST. LOUIS MISSION
745 Craig Road, Suite 306
Creve Coeur, MO 63141

Montana

Year-end 1999: Est. population, 883,000; Members, 39,842; Stakes, 11; Wards, 72; Branches, 42; Missions, 1; Districts, 1; Temples, 1; Percent LDS, 4.5, or one in 22.

A Mormon, E.W. Van Etten, traded with Flathead Indians in Montana in the late 1850s, and a Mormon woman, Minnie Miller, wife of Henry G. Miller, was the first white woman to live in western Montana. When the Church established the Fort Lemhi settlement on the Salmon River in Idaho, which lasted only from 1855 to 1858, it familiarized members with the trail to Montana that became an important trading route, known as the Montana Trail.

Some members left Utah and moved to Montana when Col. Albert Sidney Johnston's army approached Utah in 1857.

After the discovery of gold in the 1860s and the subsequent gold rush, Mormon freighters hauled food and goods along the Montana Trail for substantial profit. The overland railway was completed in 1869 and afterward a Utah company was formed by Mormon leaders that constructed a narrow gauge railway from Ogden, Utah, to Butte, Mont., and the Northern Pacific Railway at Garrison, Mont., in 1884. Although some members went to Montana during the gold rush and stayed, no Church units were organized. Evidently, all of these members fell away. In 1896, the Montana Mission was organized and efforts were made to find those members who had moved to Montana earlier. However, Church leaders did not encourage members to go to Montana to live.

While exploring for a site for a settlement in the mid-1880s, Charles Ora Card traveled through Montana. He met Duncun McDonald, a Montana explorer who told him of the vast prairies east of the Rocky Mountains in Canada. After Card led a colony to these prairies, the colonists often purchased supplies from Montana. Two areas in Montana were once considered for settlements by the Saints: northern Montana and the valleys west of the Rocky Mountains.

When the Montana Mission was created in 1896, Phineus Tempest was called as president. He soon organized a branch in Lima. On Oct. 27, 1897, Pres. Tempest's successor, Franklin S. Bramwell, and three missionaries met with Montana Gov. John E. Rickards and received the promise of religious freedom. Four converts were baptized near Gregson Springs on March 31, 1897. A meeting of 75 people was held in Anaconda, and a gathering of 300 met in Butte later that spring. The mission was dissolved into the Northwestern States Mission in 1898, after 71 converts had been baptized and the way paved for the establishment of the Church.

By 1930, the Church had grown to 10 branches and a membership of 1,181 with meetinghouses in Anaconda, Butte, Allendale, Dillon, Great Falls, and Sun River. Membership increased to 5,210 in 1940 and 6,416 in 1950. In 1950, the West Central States Mission was created, with headquarters in Billings, Montana, and covered all of Montana and areas of Wyoming and North and South Dakota.

Montana's first stake was created in Butte on June 28, 1953, and the first wards were created in Butte, Anaconda, Dillon, Bozeman, and Helena. Stake population was about 3,500.

Additional stakes were created June 16, 1957, in Great Falls and Missoula. The Great Falls Stake had about 2,500 members and the Missoula Stake had 3,085 members. At that time, Montana had 14,223 members, increasing to 23,890 in 1960. In 1980, membership was 30,784 and in 1990, 34,401.

Church members in Montana have been active in community affairs. "Project Good Turn" began in the late 1980s as an annual event led by LDS Scouts and Scouters in Montana to clean up the state's highways. Also, Church members have led a fight against pornography.

A major event occurred in August 1996 with the announcement that the Church's 64th operating temple would be built in Billings. Within the temple district are 17 federally recognized Indian reservations. The temple's groundbreaking March 28, 1998, was attended by 4,800 members from 12 states and two Canadian provinces, despite a heavy spring snowstorm. The temple was dedicated Nov. 20, 1999.

Montana's LDS population was 39,842 in 1999.

Sources: *Mormonism in Montana,* thesis in 1969 at Montana State University by Don Cornelius; *Encyclopedic History of the Church,* by Andrew Jenson; *Church News,* Feb. 2, 1991, Aug. 31, 1996; correspondence from Dean Snelling, Oct. 3, 1996; "Temple Ground Made White and Pure," by David G. Hein, *Church News,* April 4, 1998, Nov. 27, 1999.

Stakes — 11

(Listed alphabetically as of Oct. 1, 2000.)

No.	Name	Organized	First President
North America Central Area			
369	*Billings Montana		
	‡Billings (Montana, Wyoming)	10 Feb 1963	Howard C. Anderson
849	Billings Montana East	12 Jun 1977	Wynn J. Ferrell
1066	Bozeman Montana	16 Sep 1979	Frank Wilbert Coil
208	*Butte Montana		
	‡Butte	28 Jun 1953	Edgar T. Henderson
2349	Glendive Montana	4 May 1997	Larry Norman Wolf
244	*Great Falls Montana		
	‡Great Falls	16 Jun 1957	Victor Bowen
976	Great Falls Montana East	5 Nov 1978	Howard Merle Hennebry
464	*Helena Montana		
	‡Helena	8 Sep 1968	Ronald Rex Dalley
535	*Kalispell Montana		
	‡Kalispell	20 Nov 1970	Roy K. Deming
243	*Missoula Montana		
	‡Missoula	16 Jun 1957	Grant K. Patten
1074	Stevensville Montana	21 Oct 1979	Robert H. Sangster

Mission — 1

(As of Oct. 1, 2000; shown with historical number. See MISSIONS.)

(43a) MONTANA BILLINGS MISSION
1848 Rimrock Road
Billings, MT 59102
Phone: (406) 245-6146

Nebraska

Year-end 1999: Est. population, 1,666,000; Members, 18,613; Stakes, 4; Wards, 33; Branches, 21; Missions, 1; Temples, 1; Percent LDS, 1.0, or one in 90.

After the Saints were driven from Nauvoo, Ill., in February 1846, they traveled 300 miles across southern Iowa before crossing the Missouri River into what is now Nebraska. The first settlement in Nebraska was at Cutler's Park, organized on Indian lands in 1846 with about 2,500 Latter-day Saints, and which served as headquarters camp for the Church. Months later, the settlers moved the camp three miles northeast to higher ground and established Winter Quarters. Eventually, Winter Quarters, which later became Florence, was laid out into 41 blocks of some 1,000 dwellings, schools, mills, and shops.

The saints created a city government, schools, ferries, bridges, developed trades — especially those to make and outfit wagons — and established a mail service, and took time for dances and concerts. A stockade and water-powered gristmill were added later.

It was from Winter Quarters, Neb., that the first pioneer train under Brigham Young left on April 5, 1847. Nine other trains followed that year.

When Brigham Young returned from Utah in October, 1847, he received word that the Indian agent wanted the members off the Indian Territory. So in the spring of 1848 the remaining members crossed back over the Missouri River and founded Kanesville in Iowa. They left Winter Quarters as a ghost settlement, which was burned in a prairie fire in the 1850s.

In 1854, the Florence Land Company, which included some Mormons, was organized to occupy the old Winter Quarters site, and from 1856 to 1864 Florence became an important Mormon pioneer staging area. An estimated 60,000 Mormon pioneers crossed the plains before the transcontinental railroad was completed in 1869. Many were outfitted in Florence. Today, Florence is part of greater Omaha. Only the pioneer cemetery and a gristmill remain from the Winter Quarters era.

In the 1850s, Brigham Young hoped to establish settlements along the pioneer trail and started Genoa, or the "Nebraska Mission," in May 1857, as well as several other colonies. The so-called "Utah War" of 1857-58 led to the migration west of most of these settlers, although those in Genoa remained until Indian agents forced them from the land in 1859.

In 1875 James Little served a short-term mission in Nebraska, bringing John Carlile and his family back to Utah as active members where they had once lived. Missionary work resumed in 1877 when Ferdinand F. Hintze and Anders Frandsen baptized 11 people and created a branch in Fremont, Dodge County.

The area was included in the Northwestern States Mission (later the Northern States Mission) until it became part of the Colorado Mission (later Western States Mission) in 1900. By this time the Omaha and Lincoln branches had been organized. A conference of missionaries was held April 21, 1901, for those serving in Nebraska. In 1916, about 40 people attended a Sunday School in Lincoln. In 1921, a conference numbering from 75 to 200 was "the largest ever held by missionaries of this conference." Some 23 people were baptized under the direction of Elder Amasa Lyman. Progress was also made in Columbus, despite some opposition.

By 1930, the first meetinghouse had been erected, and districts functioned in East and West Nebraska with a total of 1,052 members. Nebraska's first stake was organized in Omaha, called Winter Quarters, on Dec. 11, 1960, with the Omaha 1st and 2nd, Bellevue, and Lincoln wards in Nebraska, and the Fremont, Grand Island, Kearney, and Hastings branches. On July 1, 1993, the Nebraska Omaha Mission was created from the Missouri Independence Mission. Membership in Nebraska in 1980 was 8,406, increasing to 13,089 in 1990, and to 18,613 in 1999.

A new Church visitors center was constructed at historic Winter Quarters and dedicated April 18, 1997, by President Gordon B. Hinckley. Nebraska Gov. E. Benjamin Nelson also spoke at the dedicatory services. In cooperation with state governments in Iowa and Nebraska and the city of Omaha, signs have been installed on interstate highways directing travelers to the Mormon Trail Center at Winter Quarters. A wagon train re-enactment traversed the state in 1997, commemorating the sesquicentennial of the 1847 trek of the Saints to the Salt Lake Valley. The sesquicentennial wagon train rolled out of Omaha on a cold, damp, and foggy morning on April 21, 1997. Among Nebraskans to see them off was Gov. Nelson.

On April 1, 1999, the city of Omaha deeded to the Church the pioneer cemetery at Winter Quarters, which contains the remains of some 600 Latter-day Saints from the 1846-47 period. The Church had leased the cemetery from the city for $1 a year since the mid-1930s.

On June 14, 1999, the First Presidency announced that a temple would be built in north Omaha adjacent to the Winter Quarters cemetery, the third early-Church historic area where a temple will be erected. The other two sites, both announced in 1999, are Palmyra, N.Y., and Nauvoo, Ill. Ground for Nebraska's first temple was broken Nov. 28, 1999, by Elder Hugh W. Pinnock of the Seventy.

Sources: *Liahona, The Elder's Journal,* June 21, 1921; *Encyclopedic History of the Church,* by Andrew Jenson; "Winter Quarters, Nebraska," by E. Widtsoe Shumway, *Nebraska History,* June, 1954; "Proposed New Stake has Historic Setting," *Church News,* Dec. 10, 1960, and Dec. 17, 1960; "After Winter Quarters and Council Bluffs: The Mormons in Nebraska Territory, 1854-1867," by Michael W. Homer, *Nebraska History,* Winter 1984; "Mormons, Nebraska, and the Way West," by A. R. Mortensen, *Nebraska History,* Dec. 1965; *Mormons at the Missouri,* 1846-1852, by Richard E. Bennett, University of Oklahoma Press, 1987; "Reflections on Winter Quarters," by Gail Geo. Holmes, unpublished; "Seven-year epic flowed along Missouri River with tragedy, triumph," by Gail Geo. Holmes, *Church News,* July 18, 1992; *Church News,* July 20, 1996; "Wagonmaster declares: 'Wagons, ho' " and "Visitors center memoralizes early pioneers," both by Dell Van Orden, *Church News* April 26, 1997; *Church News,* April 17, 1999; "Historic Winter Quarters now site for temple," *Church News,* June 26, 1999; "New temple to stand on sanctified soil," *Church News,* Dec. 4, 1999, both by R. Scott Lloyd.

Stakes — 4

(Listed alphabetically as of Oct. 1, 2000.)

No.	Name	Organized	First President
North America Central Area			
1803	Kearney Nebraska	16 Jun 1991	Arthur Haymore Taylor
663	*Lincoln Nebraska 2 Nov 1986		
	‡Bellevue Nebraska	27 Oct 1974	Leonard Leroy Gregory
318	*Omaha Nebraska		
	‡Winter Quarters (Nebraska, Iowa)	11 Dec 1960	William D. Hardy
161	*Omaha Nebraska Papillion 3 Dec 1996		
	‡Papillion Nebraska	2 Nov 1986	Wayne Leon Mangelson

Mission — 1

(As of Oct. 1, 2000; shown with historical number. See MISSIONS.)

(289) NEBRASKA OMAHA MISSION
11930 Arbor Street, Suite 203
Omaha, NE 68144-2998

Nevada

Year-end 1999: Est. population, 1,809,000; Members, 143,372; Stakes, 30; Wards, 249; Branches, 30; Missions, 2; Temples, 2; Percent LDS, 8.0, or one in 13.

Samuel Brannan and his party became the first Latter-day Saints to set foot in what is now Nevada as they crossed from the West Coast to Utah in 1847 to report the safe arrival of the Brannan party in San Francisco. They had traveled by ship around the tip of South America.

Three years later, after the discovery of gold in California, 13 members joined 65 non-LDS overlanders and crossed Nevada from Utah toward California. Seven men dropped out of the party near what is now Genoa and founded a trading post. These men included Abner Blackburn, a former member of the Mormon Battalion, who had found a little gold near the area on an earlier trip. They traded profitably during the summer but sold out and returned to Utah. A year later, in 1851, John Reece came with others and provisions in 13 wagons and established a trading post that became known as Mormon Station, located two miles south of the original trading post. The Reece station became a profitable trading post and the site of Nevada's first colony, Genoa. Member and non-member settlers soon followed. Apostle Orson Hyde became president of the Carson Valley Stake, organized in 1856. Elder Hyde hoped to maintain the station for the assistance of immigrants coming to Utah via the West Coast, and did much to establish it. The LDS presence in the promising colony ended and the stake was dissolved when the settlers were recalled at the approach of Johnston's army to Salt Lake City in 1857.

In 1855, during the same time colonists were sent to Genoa, a group of 30 men was sent to establish an Indian mission at the Meadows in southern Nevada at what is now Las Vegas. The party, under the direction of William Bringhurst, arrived June 15, 1855, and soon built a fort. They found farming difficult in the hot region, but discovered a lead mine and made friendships with the many Indians who lived nearby and on the Muddy River, a fertile area in a valley to the northwest.

Another mission was sent to mine the lead, which which included silver, and years later became a prosperous silver mine. This metal, made into bullets by the settlers, was the basis for a legend that Mormons used silver bullets. Both missions were recalled at the advance of Johnston's army. The abandoned fort was then named Fort Baker, placed on U.S. Army maps, and served strategic purposes during the Civil War, although uninhabited. It later became a ranch headquarters and foundation for Las Vegas, now Nevada's largest city.

On May 6, 1864, colonists from St. George, Utah, under the direction of Francis C. Lee, arrived at what is now Panaca, a site earlier considered an alternative place of settlement should the Saints be driven from Salt Lake City by Johnston's army. The Lee party made a prosperous settlement, the oldest continuous Mormon colony in the state. In December 1864, Anson Call and a group established Call's landing on the Colorado River, about 12 miles above the present Hoover Dam. This settlement briefly became an important inland dock for boats that navigated the Colorado River from the Pacific Ocean with goods for Utah settlers and the U.S. Army in Arizona. The settlement continued until 1867.

The Muddy River area north of Las Vegas, known to the Church ever since the Bringhurst mission to the Meadows in 1855, was settled, beginning May 22, 1865, under the direction of Joseph Warren Foote. The long growing season and fertile land helped the settlers survive the difficulties of that frontier. Several colonies began but were eventually abandoned when the land became part of Nevada, and Nevada officials demanded back taxes. The United Order was practiced for a time at Bunkerville, which was founded in 1877 near the Arizona border.

The area was re-settled in the 1880s and the Overton Branch was reorganized in 1883. Overton became headquarters of Nevada's first permanent stake, the Moapa Stake, in 1912.

In 1897, the government offered the Church 15,000 acres in the White Pine area in remuneration for Church livestock that the government confiscated and lost following the 1882 Edmunds Act. Here, the present-day communities of Lund and Preston were founded.

Completion of the railroad from Salt Lake to Los Angeles in 1905 began steady growth in Nevada. The first Sunday School in Las Vegas was organized by Newell Leavitt in 1914 and became a ward in 1925. In the 1920s, many Utahns moved to Nevada in search of better economic conditions. Membership in the state increased from 2,328 in 1920, to 5,319 in 1930 and to 9,139 by 1940.

Construction of the Hoover Dam in the 1940s brought an influx of people, and that same decade gambling, legalized in 1931, was widely promoted. Members did not support the move, but, as a minority, avoided confrontation. The Las Vegas Stake was created in 1954.

Substantial membership also grew in the Humboldt (Elko) and Ely areas, though these communities were not founded by Mormons. Eastern Nevada reflects a great deal of Utah culture. Members have increasingly greater strength today in this area where colonization efforts failed during Brigham Young's day. Members also gathered in western Nevada, in Reno and nearby Sparks. Growth in "the Silver State" has been steady.

The Las Vegas Nevada Temple was dedicated in 1989 as "an oasis of peace and light." On Nov. 14, 1993, a regional welfare complex was dedicated in Las Vegas near the site of the original fort. Nevada membership in 1950 was 14,223; in 1960, 23,890; in 1970, 44,282; in 1980, 71,462; in 1990, 110,060; and in 1999, 143,372.

A second temple in Nevada was announced April 12, 1999. Built in Reno, the temple was dedicated on Easter Sunday, April 23, 2000.

Sources: *Encyclopedic History of the Church,* by Andrew Jenson; "The Mormons in Nevada: an Historical Portrait," by Leonard J. Arrington, *Las Vegas Sun; The Old Fort,* compiled by the Daughters of the Utah Pioneers; History of the Las Vegas First Ward, compiled by Marion B. Earl; "Panaca: Mormon Outpost Among Mining Camps, The Afterlife of St. Mary's County; or, Utah's Penumbra in Eastern Nevada," by James W. Hulse, *Utah Historical Quarterly,* Vol. 55, (1987); "Regional Welfare Center with multiple facilities dedicated in Las Vegas," by Ashley Hall, *Church News,* Nov. 20, 1993; *Church News,* April 25, 1998, April 29, 2000.

Stakes — 30

(Listed alphabetically as of Oct. 1, 2000.)

No.	Name	Organized	First President
North America Southeast Area			
906	Carson City Nevada	9 Apr 1978	Edgar Gilbert Carlson
143	*Elko Nevada East 19 Mar 1995		
	*Elko Nevada		
	‡Humboldt	31 May 1942	Rodney S. Williams
2038	Elko Nevada West	19 Mar 1995	Kurt Glenn Alleman
96	*Ely Nevada		
	‡Nevada	19 Sep 1926	Carl K. Conrad
500	*Fallon Nevada		
	‡Fallon	18 Jan 1970	G. Verl Hendrix
1650	Fallon Nevada South	30 Aug 1987	Robert Floyd Weed
605	*Henderson Nevada Black Mountain	10 Mar 1992	
	*Henderson Nevada West		
	‡Lake Mead West	11 Mar 1973	Joseph Dee Reese
228	Henderson Nevada Lake Mead	2 Mar 1993	
	*Henderson Nevada		
	‡Lake Mead		
	(Nevada, Arizona, Calif.)	19 Aug 1956	James I. Gibson
216	*Las Vegas Nevada		
	‡Las Vegas	10 Oct 1954	Thomas Gay Myers
451	*Las Vegas Nevada Central		
	‡Las Vegas Central	18 Feb 1968	Samuel M. Davis
915	Las Vegas Nevada East	30 Apr 1978	Kendall E. Jones
1519	Las Vegas Nevada Green Valley	3 Mar 1985	Roger Lee Hunt
1542	Las Vegas Nevada Lakes	23 Jun 1985	Dennis E. Simmons
1775	Las Vegas Nevada Lone Mountain	4 Nov 1990	Scott Keith Higginson
1406	*Las Vegas Meadows 4 Nov 1990		
	‡Las Vegas Nevada West	20 Mar 1983	Terry Dale Rogers
401	*Las Vegas Nevada Paradise 30 Apr 1978		
	*Las Vegas Nevada East		

	‡Las Vegas East	24 Jan 1965	Rulon A. Earl
855	Las Vegas Nevada Redrock	14 Aug 1977	E. LeGrande Bindrup
1776	Las Vegas Nevada Sandstone	4 Nov 1990	Keith R. Edwards
509	*Las Vegas Nevada South ‡Las Vegas South	29 Mar 1970	Erval L. Bindrup
1576	Las Vegas Nevada Sunrise	17 Nov 1985	Norman Wellington Gates
2137	Las Vegas Nevada Tule Springs	3 Dec 1995	Scott Keith Higginson
1777	Las Vegas Nevada Warm Springs	4 Nov 1990	Roger Lee Hunt
64	*Logandale Nevada ‡Moapa	9 Jun 1912	Willard L. Jones
1974	Mesquite Nevada	13 Feb 1994	Elwin J. Whipple
308	*North Las Vegas Nevada ‡Las Vegas North	6 Nov 1960	William L. Taylor
2019	Panaca Nevada	29 Jan 1995	Robert Jay Matthews
135	*Reno Nevada ‡Reno (Nevada, California)	9 Feb 1941	Nathan T. Hurst
635	Reno Nevada North	24 Mar 1974	Wilford Darrell Foote
339	*Sparks Nevada ‡Reno North (Nevada, California)	22 Oct 1961	Vern Waldo
1296	Winnemucca Nevada	11 Oct 1981	Kenneth H. Lords

Stakes discontinued

7a	Carson Valley Discontinued 1858	4 Oct 1856	Orson Hyde

Mission — 2

(As of Oct. 1, 2000; shown with historical number. See MISSIONS.)

(127) NEVADA LAS VEGAS MISSION
3910 Pecos-McLeod, Suite 900
Las Vegas, NV 89121-3815

(314) NEVADA LAS VEGAS WEST
6655 W Sahara Ave., Ste. A-218
Las Vegas, NV 89146

New Hampshire

Year-end 1999: Est. population, 1,201,000; Members, 7,296; Stakes, 3; Wards, 12; Branches, 8; Missions, 1; Percent LDS, 0.6, or one in 167.

Elders Orson Pratt and Lyman E. Johnson arrived in New Hampshire in 1832. During their 26-day stay they baptized 20 people in Bath, N.H., among whom were Amasa M. Lyman and Hazen Aldrich, who later became General Authorities. Elders Orson Hyde and Samuel H. Smith baptized others later in 1832. A branch of 15 members was created in July 1833, at Dalton, Coos County. Other branches were created in New Rowley and Lyman, Grafton County. The latter was organized in 1835 by Erastus Snow, then 17 years old. A conference held in Nashua, N.H., on Dec. 15, 1840, was attended by 55 people.

In 1841, Zadock Parker wrote that the Grafton County Branch met regularly and that he baptized 13 more people. Some 20-30 members continued to meet in the Gilsum Branch. Eli P. Maginn wrote that he could not "fill from one to twenty of the calls for preaching; there is the greatest excitement in the country."

The Peterborough Branch was created, and by 1843, it had 115 members. Most of the members "removed" to the West following the martyrdom of the Prophet Joseph Smith. In 1856, Solomon Mack headed the membership in New Hampshire. This state was part of the Eastern States Mission, but little work was done during the next few years. The mission was discontinued from 1869 to 1893, when New Hampshire was placed in the New England Conference. The New Hampshire Conference was created in 1909, combined with Maine from 1913-1925, with Vermont, 1925-1928, and in 1928, included in the Canadian Mission. In 1930, the New Hampshire District was headquartered at Nashua, evidently under the direction of a missionary. A branch was organized in Nashua by September 1937, the date of the creation of the New England Mission, but later dissolved. A branch in Concord was created in 1945. In 1951, Sunday Schools were held in Keene and Portsmouth.

Additional branches and Sunday Schools were subsequently organized. In 1970, the Merrimack (Nashua) Stake was created with wards in Keene, Laconia, Manchester, Portsmouth, and Concord, with two wards and a branch in Massachusetts and a branch in Maine.

Wards and branches continued to be organized. A branch in Peterborough was formed in 1980. The New Hampshire Manchester Mission was created in 1987. Membership in New Hampshire was 4,237 in 1980, increasing to 6,383 in 1990 and 7,296 in 1999.

Sources: *Encyclopedic History of the Church,* by Andrew Jenson; Church directories, 1920-1980; "4 new stakes are organized," *Church News,* April 4, 1970; "The gospel net," *Church News,* Nov. 19, 1977; "She helped nurture fledgling Church during life of service," by J Malan Heslop, *Church News,* Jan. 23, 1993.

Stakes — 3

(Listed alphabetically as of Oct. 1, 2000.)

No.	Name	Organized	First President
North America Northeast Area			
1289	Concord New Hampshire	6 Sep 1981	John Tucker Hills
1290	*Exeter New Hampshire ‡Portland Maine	6 Sep 1981	J. Barton Seymour
507	*Nashua New Hampshire 9 May 1980 *Manchester New Hampshire ‡Merrimack	22 Mar 1970	William A. Fresh

Mission — 1

(As of Oct. 1, 2000; shown with historical number. See MISSIONS.)

(195) NEW HAMPSHIRE MANCHESTER
6 Bedford Farms
Bedford, NH 03110-6532

New Jersey

Year-end 1999: Est. population, 8,143,000; Members, 25,945; Stakes, 5; Wards, 31; Branches, 24; Districts, 1; Missions, 2; Percent LDS, 0.3, or one in 313.

The first missionaries to work in New Jersey were Elders Orson Pratt and Lyman E. Johnson, who arrived in the state in 1832. In 1837, Elders Parley P. Pratt, Benjamin Winchester, and Jedediah M. Grant preached and converted people in New Jersey. Elder Winchester preached in Toms River, Ocean County, and baptized 11. By 1840, the branch had 90 members. Several missionaries labored in New Jersey during the next few years. At a conference in New York on Oct. 19, 1842, branches were represented from Patterson, Lodi Print Works, Wacake, Newark, and Mead's Basin in New Jersey. Converts often joined the westward movement. On April 22, 1844, William Smith arrived in Illinois from New Jersey with a group of 40 or 50.

Other branches were organized so that by 1848, 21 dotted the New Jersey map. After the exodus from Nauvoo, missionary work slowed. Branches in Toms Corner and Hornerstown existed in 1857. Many others had "gathered" previously.

Little work was performed until well after the trek West. In 1879, B.F. Cummings reported meeting some "old-time Saints" in Perth Amboy, N. J., whom he tried to inspire with the spirit of gathering. Ten members from there migrated to Utah in 1896.

In the 1920s, Ernest L. Wilkinson, who later became president of Brigham Young University, was among the presidents of the Newark Branch. A branch also functioned in Metuchen in the 1930s with Robert H. Daines as branch president. When the New Jersey Stake was created in 1960, it included the Montclair, North Jersey and Short Hills wards and the New Brunswick, Trenton, Monmouth and Lakehurst branches.

In 1974, membership was 6,799, reaching 10,512 in three stakes in 1980 and 16,000 in 1990. The New Jersey Morristown Mission was created in 1987. Local and state dignitaries took part in the Church's sesquicentennial in New Jersey, which was celebrated in 1988.

Inner city branches and wards in Newark were started with the Spring Garden Branch in 1990, and continue to develop with a diverse membership. At a 1997 pioneer sesquicentennial service project, Scouts in East New Brunswick built a barge to carry people and equipment to a small island at the Quail Hill Scout Reservation in Manalapan. Membership in 1999 was 25,945 in 60 wards and branches.

Sources: Eastern States Mission history; *Deseret News,* Jan. 7, 1879, and Jan. 8, 1896; *Encyclopedic History of the Church,* by Andrew Jenson; "New stake created by division of New York," *Church News,* March 5, 1960; "Neighborliness: Daines Style," by Orson Scott Card, *Ensign,* April 1977; "New Jersey – Church members celebrate 100 years," *Church News,* Sept. 17,1988; "Gospel fosters unity, peace in inner city," by Clawson Cannon, Church News, Dec. 28, 1996; *Church News,* July 19, 1997.

Stakes — 5

(Listed alphabetically as of Oct. 1, 2000.)

No.	Name	Organized	First President
North America Northeast Area			
1252	Caldwell New Jersey	12 Apr 1981	Weldon Courtney McGregor
1084	*Cherry Hill New Jersey 23 Sep 1986		
	‡Pitman New Jersey	18 Nov 1979	Victor Warren Hammond
429	*East Brunswick New Jersey		
	‡New Jersey Central		
	(N.J., Penn.)	26 Mar 1967	Robert H. Daines
292	*Morristown New Jersey 26 Feb 1976		
	*Caldwell New Jersey		
	‡New Jersey	28 Feb 1960	George H. Mortimer
2235	Scotch Plains New Jersey	15 Sep 1996	Andrew Kim Smith

Missions — 2

(As of Oct. 1, 2000; shown with historical number. See MISSIONS.)

(304a) NEW JERSEY CHERRY HILL MISSION
100 Century Parkway, Suite 160
Mt. Laurel, NJ 08054

(202) NEW JERSEY
MORRISTOWN MISSION
1719 Rte 10, Ste. 309
Parsippany, NJ 07054

New Mexico

Year-end 1999: Est. population, 1,740,000; Members, 57,807; Stakes, 12; Wards, 84; Branches, 37; Districts, 1; Missions, 1; Temples, 1; Percent LDS, 3.3, or one in 30.

In 1831, just one year after the organization of the Church, Oliver Cowdery preached to Indians in Missouri and, from that experience, reported to Joseph Smith of a civilized "Navashoes" (Navajo) tribe living 300 miles west of Santa Fe. Leaders once discussed sending a delegation to Santa Fe in 1844 to begin exploration for a possible colonization site. In 1846, the Mormon Battalion crossed what is now New Mexico during its historic march to the Pacific Coast from Fort Leavenworth, Kan. The first part of the battalion arrived in Santa Fe Oct. 9, 1846. At Santa Fe, the battalion sent a detachment of sick to winter in Colorado.

Missionary work among the Indians perhaps began as early as the 1860s when Jacob Hamblin and James S. Brown may have traveled to New Mexico in their labors. Missionaries called to Mexico in 1875 included Ammon M. Tenney and Robert H. Smith, who found success while laboring among the Zuni Indians on the Little Colorado River in New Mexico, baptizing more than 100. In 1876, a colony was established among the converts. It succeeded until smallpox decimated the Indian population. Two years later, at an adjacent site, LDS settlers founded what is now Ramah. In 1878, the settlement of Burnham (originally called Fruitland) was founded, followed in 1883 by the community of Luna. The settlers at Luna had clear title to their land, but had trouble with a cattle baron who claimed the area. The San Juan Stake in Utah, comosed of settlers from the "Hole-in-the-Rock" expedition of 1879-80, included members in the New Mexico settlements of Kirtland and Waterflow. During this period, New Mexico settlements were troubled by outlaws. A severe drought from 1900-04 seriously affected settlers, but eliminated the outlaws.

Nearly all of the Mormon settlements in New Mexico absorbed some refugees from the Mormon colonies in Mexico during the Mexican Revolution of 1912. Other refugees founded the town of Virden, near the Mexican border.

The Young Stake in Farmington, the first stake in New Mexico, was created in 1912. Other New Mexico wards and branches were included in Arizona and Utah stakes. By 1930, membership in New Mexico was 1,643. The Albuquerque Stake was created in 1957. Membership increased during the 1960s and 1970s. The New Mexico Albuquerque Mission was organized in 1975.

In the 1980s, H. Vern Payne, president of the Santa Fe New Mexico Stake, served as chief justice of the New Mexico Supreme Court. A number of LDS scientists worked at the U.S. research facility at Los Alamos. In September 1996, more than 700 Church members in New Mexico joined with government officials in rededicating a monument built to honor members of the Mormon Battalion, who had passed through the state 150 years earlier.

Membership in the state in 1980 was 36,881; in 1990, 48,000; and in 1999, 57,807. Members have learned to interact with patience and understanding in a state where three cultures meld — American Indian, Hispanic, and Anglo.

The First Presidency announced on April 3, 1997, that a temple would be build in Albuquerque, the first in New Mexico. Serving 55,000 members of the Indian, Hispanic and Anglo cultures in three states, the temple was dedicated March 5, 2000.

Sources: *Encyclopedic History of the Church,* by Andrew Jenson; "New Mexico and the Mormons," by Robert Thomas Devitt, *Southwest Heritage,* Vol. 6, Spring 1976; *Do You Remember Luna? 100 Years of Pioneer History,* published by the Luna Ward, Adobe Press, 1983; *Church News,* July 24, 1983; June 27, 1998; "Temple melding members of three cultures," by Sarah Jane Weaver, *Church News,* March 11, 2000.

Stakes — 14

(Listed alphabetically as of Oct. 1, 2000.)

No.	Name	Organized	First President
North America Southwest Area			
250	*Albuquerque New Mexico		
	‡Albuquerque	27 Oct 1957	William J. Wilson
422	*Albuquerque New Mexico East		
	‡Albuquerque East	25 Sep 1966	George Van Lemmon
2556	Albuquerque New Mexico North	21 May 2000	Lane S. Sego
	Albuquerque New Mexico West	21 May 2000	Lane S. Sego
742	*Bloomfield New Mexico 19 Sep 1982		
	‡Farmington New Mexico East	1 Feb 1976	Marlo L. Webb
63	*Farmington New Mexico		
	‡Young (N.M., Colo.)	21 May 1912	David Halls
687	Gallup New Mexico	16 Mar 1975	Donald C. Tanner
1298	Grants New Mexico	18 Oct 1981	Elbert Leon Roundy
1363	Kirtland New Mexico	19 Sep 1982	John Scot Fishburn
654	Las Cruces New Mexico	25 Aug 1974	Harold A. Daw
1353	*Los Lunas New Mexico		
	‡Albuquerque New Mexico South	20 Jun 1982	Ivan Gary Waddoups
816	Roswell New Mexico	13 Mar 1977	J. Allen Levie
1219	Santa Fe New Mexico	4 Jan 1981	H. Vern Payne
1409	Silver City New Mexico	17 Apr 1983	Hal Butler Keeler

Mission — 1

(As of Oct. 1, 2000; shown with historical number. See MISSIONS.)

(128) NEW MEXICO ALBUQUERQUE MISSION
6100 Seagull Lane, N.E., #109
Albuquerque, NM 87109

New York

Year-end 1999: Est. population, 18,197,000; Members, 60,516; Stakes, 14; Wards, 66; Branches, 95; Missions, 4; Temples, 1, (1 announced); Districts, 3; Percent LDS, 0.3, or one in 300.

In 1820, Joseph Smith received "the glorious vision which marked the ushering in of the Dispensation of the Fullness of Times" in a grove of trees, now known as the Sacred Grove, near Palmyra, N.Y. Later, young Joseph received a visit from the Angel Moroni who revealed the existence of a sacred record written on gold plates hidden in the nearby Hill Cumorah. Four years later, the records were obtained by Joseph Smith, translated in Pennsylvania and Fayette, N.Y., into the Book of Mormon, and printed by Egbert Grandin in Palmyra in early 1830. On April 6, 1830, the Church was organized at the home of Peter Whitmer Sr. in Fayette, with some 50 people present. As required by law, six were named "incorporators" of the new church. In late June of that year, Samuel H. Smith began a missionary journey to neighboring communities. By year's end, membership had reached more than 100 with members from Colesville to Canandaigua. Many, however, moved in 1831 to Kirtland, Ohio.

Twenty-five revelations in the Doctrine and Covenants were received in New York.

Among successful later missionaries were Martin and Emer Harris, who baptized 100 people in Chenango Point, N.Y., in 1832. During the next few years, missionaries organized several branches as well as the Freedom and Black River conferences. In July 1837, Parley P. Pratt was the first missionary to preach in New York City, and he organized a branch there. Branches were also organized in Long Island and Brooklyn. While there, he published his *Voice of Warning* pamphlet, the first tract published for missionary use in the Church. In 1839, John P. Greene became the first president of the Eastern States Mission, headquartered in New York City.

A group of 41 LDS emigrants arrived from England on the ship *Britannia* July 20, 1840, the first of an estimated 50,000 to arrive between 1840 and 1890.

A newspaper, *The Prophet,* began publication in 1844 in New York. On Feb. 4, 1846, Samuel Brannan headed a company of Saints aboard the sailing ship *Brooklyn* that sailed from New York harbor, around the tip of South America, to California. They also carried the press to California that was formerly used to print *The Prophet. The Mormon,* a weekly newspaper, was printed by John Taylor in 1855. Because of the so-called "Utah War" in 1857, most missionaries were withdrawn from New York. The Civil War also hindered the work; little progress was realized until the 1880s. By 1890, the New York Conference was organized. New York was returned to the Eastern States Mission in 1893, and in January, Elder Job Pingree was set apart to re-open the work in New York City. Mission headquarters at the time were established in Brooklyn. By 1900, the mission had a total membership of 975 in eight conferences within three states and Canada. When the radio came into use in the 1920s, missionaries were quick to take advantage of the new media to promote the gospel cause. By 1930, branches had been organized in Albany, Brooklyn, Erie, Hudson, Rochester, and Susquehanna (including parts of Pennsylvania).

In 1907, the Church purchased the Joseph Smith Sr. farm and Sacred Grove.

The first Book of Mormon pageant was produced in 1928 on the Hill Cumorah, which the Church had purchased that year. The first Hill Cumorah pageant near Palmyra was a forerunner to the present pageant, "America's Witness for Christ," started in July 1937 and which has attracted as many as 100,000 people during its annual seven-night run.

The New York Stake was created in 1934 and took part in special Church events, including an exhibit in 1936 on the centennial of the coming of Elijah and in the 1946 observance of the centennial of the sailing ship *Brooklyn.* LDS servicemen and leaders of businesses headquartered in New York helped strengthen the stake.

On Oct. 10, 1962, the Church purchased a short wave radio station, WRUL, with studios in New York City and a transmitter in Boston. The station was used to transmit Church broadcasts to Europe and South America. In 1964, the Church's pavilion at the World's Fair pioneered media technology and drew a large response to the specially made film "Man's Search for Happiness." This paved the way for future use of technology in spreading the gospel message.

Membership in New York in 1974 reached 17,000, increasing to 26,000 by 1980, and 40,000 in 1990. By 1999, it had topped 60,000.

On April 6, 1980, for the first time in its history, the Church held general conference simultaneously in two different locations — in Salt Lake City and Fayette, N.Y., which were linked by satellite, the first time that that had been done in the Church. Portions of the April 6 sessions originated from Fayette where so many important events in early Church history took place. With this conference, the Church entered the satellite age, and soon satellite receivers dotted the landscape of hundreds of meetinghouses in the United States and Canada, mushrooming to some 3,500 by the 1990s. Highlight of the Fayette portion of the sesquicentennial conference was the dedication of the reconstructed Peter Whitmer farmhouse by President Spencer W. Kimball and a "proclamation to the nations" that was read from the farmhoiuse by Elder Gordon B. Hinckley of the Quorum of the Twelve.

After he became president of the Church, President Hinckley visited New York on Nov. 13, 1995, and again July 12, 1996. During the first trip he spoke to a group of corporate executives, representatives of the national media, and heads of charitable organizations at a reception and luncheon in New York City. During the second trip, he visited Palmyra where he spoke to the cast, crew and staff of the Hill Cumorah Pageant before the opening performance. On Sept. 30, 1995, President Hinckley announced in general conference that a temple would be built in New York.

Some 20,000 members from area states gathered at Madison Square Garden April 26, 1998, to hear President Hinckley speak at the first such conference in the famed arena. President Hinckley also dedicated a replica of the Smith family home near Palmyra, and the restored Grandin Building in Palmyra where the Book of Mormon was printed.

On Oct. 23, 1999, the Plainview New York Stake center, which was originally dedicated in 1970 by President Harold B. Lee, was rededicated after extensive renovations. Included in the construction of the meetinghouse were 36 concrete panels that comprised the walls of the Church's Mormon Pavilion at the New York World's Fair in the mid-1960s.

A seven-year project, involving the copying of inscriptions from cemetery headstones in 14 towns of rural Rensselaer County, was completed in the spring of 2000 by members of the Latham Ward, a project spearheaded by Donald and Clare Radz. In all, more than 600 cemeteries were surveyed, resulting in 93,274 names being recorded. The names were complied into books and each town was provided a copy of the headstone information found in their respective cemeteries.

On Feb. 9, 1999, the First Presidency announced that a temple would be built in the Palmyra area, often referred to as "the Cradle of the Restoration." The announcement brought to 100 the number of temples in operation, under construction, or in planning stages worldwide. Just a little more than a year later, the temple, built on land overlooking the Sacred Grove and other historic sites, was dedicated by President Hinckley on April 6, 2000, exactly 170 years after the Church was organized in nearby Fayette.

Overwhelming interest in the Palmyra area prompted Church leaders to telecast the first dedicatory session to the Tabernacle in Salt Lake City and to some 1,300 stake centers and other selected Church facilities in the United States and Canada. An estimated 1.3 million members participated in either the live telecast in the morning, or during a rebroadcast in the evening. The telecast, aired in 12 languages and in six time zones, was the first encrypted broadcast of a temple dedication on the Church satellite system to multiple settings on such a grand scale.

Sources: *Encyclopedic History of the Church,* by Andrew Jenson; *Church News,* May 16, 1936 and Jan. 19, 1946; "The Church in New York City," by William Woolf, *Improvement Era,* Dec. 1938; "Fayette links past, present of Church," by Dell Van Orden, *Church News,* April 12, 1980; *Palmyra — a Bicentennial Celebration,* edited by Betty Troskosky, published by Historic Palmyra Inc., 1989; "LDS history unfolded in New York and Ohio," *Church News,* Jan. 7, 1989; "Legacy of the Mormon Pavilion," by Brent L. Top, *Ensign,* Oct. 1989; *Church News,* Nov. 18, 1995; July 20, 1996; April 4, 1998; Feb. 20, 1999; May 2, 1998, July 10, 1999, Dec. 4, 1999; "A day of sacred significance," by Shaun D. Stahle, *Church News,* April 15, 2000; "Cemetery project keeps data from crumbling away," by Jason Swensen, *Church News,* May 6, 2000.

Stakes — 13

(Listed alphabetically as of Oct. 1, 2000.)

No.	Name	Organized	First President
	North America Northeast Area		
485	*Albany New York		
	‡Hudson River	8 Jun 1969	Thomas Lorin Hicken
2501	Brooklyn New York	22 Nov 1998	Alejandro Ernesto Soffiantini
657	Buffalo New York	15 Sep 1974	Ronald Glen Vincent
1592	*Jamestown New York	16 May 1995	
	‡Erie Pennsylvania	23 Mar 1986	Philip Dale Baker
2315	Newburgh New York	2 Mar 1997	Gary R. Ricks Jr.
110	*New York New York		
	‡New York (N.Y., Connecticut)	9 Dec 1934	Fred G. Taylor
483	*Owego New York 9 Oct 1990		
	*Ithaca New York		
	‡Susquehanna	25 May 1969	Harold R. Capener
439	*Plainview New York		
	‡Long Island	20 Aug 1967	Gordon E. Crandall
346	*Rochester New York		
	‡Cumorah	21 Jan 1962	Bryant W. Rossiter
1543	Rochester New York Palmyra	30 Jun 1985	Kay R. Whitmore
711	Syracuse New York	19 Oct 1975	George Dale Weight
2152	Utica New York	14 Jan 1996	Dallas Williams Jones
2409	Westchester New York	9 Nov 1997	Douglas Romney Jackson
909	*Yorktown New York 28 Aug 1978		
	‡Kitchiwan New York	30 Apr 1978	Victor B. Jex

Stakes discontinued

1574	New York New York East Discontinued 19 May 1991	17 Nov 1985	Mark Eliot Butler

Missions — 4

(As of Oct. 1, 2000; shown with historical number. See MISSIONS.)

(290)NEW YORK NEW YORK NORTH MISSION
700 White Plains Road, Ste. 34
Scarsdale, NY 10583

(2) NEW YORK NEW YORK SOUTH MISSION
55 Northern Blvd., Ste. 206
Great Neck, NY 11021

(77)NEW YORK ROCHESTER MISSION
P.O. Box 92580
Rochester, NY 14692

(299) NEW YORK UTICA MISSION
P.O. Box 220
New Hartford, NY 13413-0220

North Carolina

Year-end 1999: Est. population, 7,651,000; Members, 56,261; Stakes, 12; Wards, 86; Branches, 30; Missions, 2; Temples, 1; Percent LDS, 0.7, or one in 136.

Evidently the first missionary to enter North Carolina was Jedediah M. Grant. On May 18, 1838, he reported that he had preached for six months in Stokes, Surrey, and Rockingham counties and baptized four people. In 1840, two additional missionaries joined Elder Grant, and they baptized another six or eight people. Missionaries also began work in other parts of the state. Writing in 1844, Elder John Eldridge said meetings he held "caused the greatest stirs imaginable. . . . I never thought that one poor mortal could make such a stir." He mentioned "some" baptisms and also located earlier converts, whom he encouraged to gather to Zion.

Elder Grant wrote in 1845 that before he left North Carolina, he had organized a conference of 200 members in seven branches, and 150 more had joined after he left.

Following the exodus of the main body of the Church from Nauvoo, Ill., in 1846, little work was done for some time in North Carolina. In 1868, a Southern convert, Elder Henry G. Boyle, wrote that he had held 40 public meetings, baptized 30 members and organized the Surrey County Branch. This branch (soon changed to Pilot Mountain) was dissolved following the migration to the West in 1870.

The Southern States Mission was created in 1875 and the Pilot Mountain Branch was reorganized in 1876. The Mount Airy Branch was organized July 28, 1879, and the Burke County Branch followed in 1885. Continuation of these branches was sporadic as converts migrated to the West. Membership in 1894 was 128, with 35 immigrating to the West during the previous three years. Some 1,000 members from surrounding areas attended a conference held in Bradford Cross Roads on Nov. 21, 1894. After 1895, members were encouraged to remain in North Carolina.

Anti-Mormon sentiment in North Carolina was strong, but the majority of citizens remained above mob actions. In 1906, however, a newly completed meetinghouse on Harker's Island was burned and missionaries driven out by a mob. The meetinghouse was replaced in 1936 and the island's members remained faithful.

Occasional mobs gathered in various other locations, but after the turn of the century, public attitudes generally improved and missionaries were offered more freedom to preach.

During the next 30 years, many local leaders presided over branches and Sunday Schools, forming a strong base of experience. In 1921, Andrew Jenson, visiting as Church historian, reported three branches and 15 Sunday Schools in North Carolina. Meetinghouses were built in Mount Airy, Hampstad, Union Ridge, Wilmington, Goldsboro, and Gilreath by 1930. Membership in the state then was 2,725.

North Carolina was divided into the East and West districts in 1935. James L. Bennett Sr. was the first local member to be district president, sustained on March 26, 1939. The Central District was created July 11, 1948. A large building program was started in 1947 and 16 buildings were subsequently constructed.

On Aug. 29, 1961, the North Carolina Stake, the first in the state, was created in Kinston from the East District, and the Central District was organized into the Greensboro Stake the next month.

Membership in the state was 29,512 in 1980, 45,960 in 1990, and 56,261 in 1999.

The First Presidency announced Sept. 3, 1998, that a temple would be built in the Raleigh-Durham area. In 1999, the Raleigh North Carolina Temple was dedicated on Dec. 18 in the surburban community of Apex.

Sources: *Encyclopedic History of the Church,* by Andrew Jenson; *History of The Church of Jesus Christ of Latter-day Saints in North Carolina,* by Wallace R. Draughon; "A Christmastime 'offering' to the Lord," by R. Scott Lloyd, *Church News,* Dec. 25, 1999.

Stakes — 12

(Listed alphabetically as of Oct. 1, 2000.)

No.	Name	Organized	First President

North America East Area

1086	Asheville North Carolina	25 Nov 1979	Luther Andrew Goad
1606	Charlotte North Carolina Central	21 Sep 1986	Kenneth Larson
591	*Charlotte North Carolina South	21 Sep 1986	
	*Charlotte North Carolina ‡Charlotte	19 Nov 1972	Byron Cole Williams
1637	Durham North Carolina	3 May 1987	James L. Bennett Jr.
698	Fayetteville North Carolina	8 Jun 1975	Leland Reid Fillmore
1344	Goldsboro North Carolina	30 May 1982	James William Dixon
335	*Greensboro North Carolina ‡Greensboro	13 Sep 1961	Eugene A. Gulledge
1371	Hickory North Carolina	31 Oct 1982	Gordon M. Thornton
332	*Kinston North Carolina ‡North Carolina	27 Aug 1961	Cecil E. Reese
363	*Raleigh North Carolina ‡Raleigh	9 Dec 1962	William V. Bartholomew
574	*Wilmington North Carolina ‡Wilmington	21 May 1972	Dean Bevin Powell Jr.
881	*Winston-Salem North Carolina	25 Nov 1979	
	‡Statesville North Carolina	20 Nov 1977	Michael Stephen Bullock

Missions — 2

(As of Oct. 1, 2000; shown with historical number. See MISSIONS.)

(105) NORTH CAROLINA CHARLOTTE MISSION
6425 Idlewild Rd., Suite 104
Charlotte, NC 28212

(186) NORTH CAROLINA RALEIGH MISSION
6508 Falls of Neuse, Suite 100
Raleigh, NC 27615-6845

North Dakota

Year-end 1999: Est. population, 634,000; Members, 5,070; Stakes, 2; Wards, 7; Branches, 8; Temples, 1; Percent LDS, 0.8, or one in 127.

Four missionaries first arrived in North Dakota in 1885. There were reportedly three Church members in the Dakotas at that time. The four elders labored from house to house across the scattered farmland. The missionaries made friends in the "northern part, [in] Johnstown [Grand Forks County] especially. . . . The Elders are bound to leave those paths through the winter season, so as not to be exposed to the cold, which is a drawback to the Mission."

South and North Dakota were organized into separate conferences on July 5, 1898, and Charles A. Haacke was appointed president of the North Dakota Conference. "The Lord has seen fit to carry the Gospel to this northern state," a report in the *Deseret News* noted. Two pairs of missionaries started in Fairmont, but found little success so they planned to go north. Before leaving they held a prayer meeting in a grove of box elder trees near the train station. Afterward, one pair of elders traveled to Wahpeton and one to Fargo. In Fargo, missionaries were warned by the mayor that he would do everything he could to obstruct them. Local newspapers were more accommodating, however, and published favorable reports of the missionaries. In 1899, the missionaries transferred to South Dakota "as very little good was being done in North Dakota."

In 1900, North Dakota was taken from the Central States Mission and placed in the Colorado Mission (changed in 1907 to the Western States Mission). After the turn of the 20th century, a convert from Montana named Sitting Eagle moved to North Dakota and explained the gospel to many people. Chief Moses White Horse corresponded with the missionaries and received a copy of the Book of Mormon. When Elders Lewis Roberts and Russell Woolf first visited Shell Village in the summer of 1914, they taught 108 Indians and baptized seven converts. Within a few years the Sully Lake Branch, under Indian leadership, included 40 members from the Fort Berthold Reservation. This branch comprised the majority of membership in the state for many years.

In 1919, the first LDS meetinghouse in the state was completed in Sully Lake, and the first services in the new building were held on Christmas Day that year. By 1930, a second meetinghouse had been completed in Grand Forks. Membership in 1930 was 145. In 1943, member Dorothy Hanks recalled that the Fargo Branch consisted of five to 10 people attending meetings in the basement of the YMCA building. In the late 1940s, the Church purchased a Quonset-style building in the New Town area to serve as a meetinghouse.

After 1950, the Church organizations began to increase with converts and members moving in. A branch was organized in Bismarck, the capital city, on Aug. 22, 1954, with 13 members. Buildings were erected and leaders began traveling more to nurture small branches. In the 1970s, more professionals moved in and continued strengthening the branches.

Church history was made Aug. 7, 1977, when North Dakota became the final state in the United States to have a stake within its boundaries. Covering the eastern half of the state, the Fargo North Dakota Stake had a membership of 2,000 living in four wards and seven branches. Church membership in the state in 1980 was 3,495 and in 1990, 4,570. The second stake in North Dakota, in Bismarck, was created in 1996 and covered the western half of the state. In the 1990s, the Church became better known as members took part in many service projects in their communities. In 1997, 400 members in Grand Forks were among those displaced by floods, and some were displaced by fires that followed the floods.

Members in North Dakota were elated with the announcement Aug. 15, 1998, that a small temple would be built in Bismarck. The temple was dedicated Sept. 19, 1999. The temple dedication trip was the first time that President Gordon B. Hinckley, who has logged millions of miles in his travels since being called as a General Authority in 1958, had ever been in North Dakota.

North Dakota has the fewest number of Church members of any state that has a temple. In 1999, membership in the state was 5,070. Serving an area upwards of 200,000 square miles spread out over four states, the temple shortened considerably the vast distances members in this part of the country have to travel to attend a temple. However, it is still an eight-hour drive to the temple from the Marshall, Minn., Branch on the eastern end of the temple district. President Gordon B. Hinckley said after the dedication that, "Even with the temple [in Bismarck] some will still have to travel a very long distance, but it will be much shorter than it was before."

On July 2, 2000, in conjuction with the 125th anniversary of the founding of the Fargo (N.D.)-Moorhead (Minn.) community, members of the Fargo 1st and 2nd wards joined with other groups — Jewish, Islam, Baha'i, Quakers, Hindu, Moslem, Protestant, and Roman Catholic — in a Festival of Faiths.

Sources: *Church News*, Aug. 13, 1977, Dec. 24, 1977; March 11, 1989; *Encyclopedic History of the Church*, by Andrew Jenson; *Deseret News*, 57:273; Northern States Mission history; *Church News*, April 26, 1997, Aug. 15, 1998; "Shortening the vast distances," by Dell Van Orden, *Church News*, Sept. 25, 1999; "Red River Valley members participate in Festival of Faiths," by Janet Kruckenberg, *Church News*, July 8, 2000.

Stakes — 2

(As of Oct. 1, 2000.)

No.	Name	Organized	First President
North America Central Area			
2243	Bismarck North Dakota	22 Sep 1996	Richard A. Adsero
852	Fargo North Dakota	7 Aug 1977	John R. Price

Ohio

Year-end 1999: Est. population, 11,257,000; Members, 47,437; Stakes, 10; Wards, 77; Branches, 38; Missions, 2; Temples, 1; Percent LDS, 0.4, or one in 239.

One month after Parley P. Pratt was baptized in New York on Sept. 1, 1830, he began his first missionary journey. In the company of Oliver Cowdery, Peter Whitmer Jr., and Ziba Peterson, he returned to Ohio, where he previously homesteaded, on a mission to the Native Americans. En route to their destination, however, they taught the gospel to Sidney Rigdon, who was then a preacher, and to his congregation in Painesville, near Kirtland, Ohio. Within a week, a nucleus for the Church was established in Kirtland. In a few weeks they had baptized 127 people including Rigdon and Frederick G. Williams. Later the missionaries preached to Wyandot Indians in Sandusky, Ohio, and to Delaware Indians in Missouri.

In December 1830, Joseph Smith was instructed by revelation to gather in Ohio (D&C 37), the first commandment in this dispensation concerning a gathering. He made the trip in February, and met Newel K. Whitney at the Gilbert and Whitney store in Kirtland. He and his wife, Emma, lived with Whitney for a time. Members soon gathered to Kirtland, and in June, 1831, Joseph received the revelation (D&C 52:42) to assemble in Missouri, "the land of your inheritance." From 1831 to 1838, Kirtland was headquarters of the Church, with the first stake in the Church created here in 1834. Some 46 revelations were received in the Whitney store, and an additional 16 at the John Johnson farm in nearby Hiram, Ohio. In all, 65 revelations of the Doctrine and Covenants were received in Ohio, including the vision of the three degrees of glory (D&C 76) in February 1832, the revelation and prophecy on war (D&C 87) in December 1832, and the Word of Wisdom (D&C 89) in February 1833. The Quorum of the Twelve was organized here, as directed by revelation (D&C 18), on Feb. 14, 1835, and the First Quorum of the Seventy was organized two weeks later on Feb. 28. In Ohio, newspapers were started by the Church, and missionaries were sent to other areas in the United States, Canada, and Great Britain. Lorenzo Snow, president of the Church from 1898 to 1901, was born in Ohio in 1814.

Construction of the Kirtland Temple began June 5, 1833, and was dedicated by the Prophet Joseph Smith on March 27, 1836. The dedicatory prayer was given to the Prophet by revelation (D&C 109). The temple was the site of several heavenly visitations a week later on April 3, including the visit of the Savior and restoration of priesthood keys by Moses, Elias, and Elijah (D&C 110). The second edition of the Book of Mormon was printed in Kirtland in 1837. This edition was planned to contain both the Book of Mormon and Doctrine and Covenants, but proved too cumbersome.

In its prime, Kirtland had some 3,200 members. The Saints left Kirtland and surrounding areas for Missouri, mostly completing the exodus in 1838. Apostle Lyman Wight returned to Kirtland in 1842 and rebaptized some 200 members. The temple was acquired in the late 1800s by the Reorganized Church of Jesus Christ of Latter Day Saints and opened for tours.

Ohio was part of the Northern States Mission until 1899, when it was included in the Southern States Mission as a place where ill missionaries could go to recover. In 1926, it was returned to the Northern States Mission.

In 1930, Ohio had two conferences with branches in Akron, Cincinnati, Cleveland, Columbus, Dayton, Middleton, Portsmouth, Springfield, and Toledo. The Cincinnati and Dayton branches had their own meetinghouses. Membership was 697.

In 1949, Ohio became part of the Great Lakes Mission. The Ohio Mission was created in 1967 and renamed the Ohio Columbus Mission in 1974.

In 1954, a branch meetinghouse was dedicated in Cleveland by President David O. McKay. Work prospered in Cincinnati, Columbus, and Cleveland where stakes were organized in 1958, 1961, and 1963, respectively.

Full-time missionaries returned to Kirtland in 1977, the same year the Kirtland Ward was created. In 1979, the Church acquired the Newel K. Whitney store, and it has since become a well-visited historic site. Additional missions were organized in Ohio in 1977, with headquarters in Cleveland; and in 1998, with headquarters in Cincinnati

In 1980, membership in the state reached 28,000, and in 1990, 38,000. In 1999, membership was 47,437.

The Tabernacle Choir visited Kirtland July 24, 1992, and sang hymns in the Kirtland Temple. In 1996, Kirtland was the site of a large group of young single adults from several states and Canada for the "Zion's Camp Conference."

President Gordon B. Hinckley visited Columbus, Ohio, April 25, 1998, and as he addressed some 6,800 members, announced that a temple would be built in that city. The temple, the 60th operating temple in the Church, was dedicated a year-and-a-half later on Sept. 4, 1999.

On April 17, 2000, the Church announced plans to restore or reconstruct six facilities in Kirtland that were prominent in Church history in the 1830s. At a press conference in Kirtland, Elder Loren C. Dunn, of the Seventy and president of the North America East Area and executive director of the Church Historical Department, said the new or restored facilities would include: Construction of a new visitors center resembling a 19th century gristmill used by Samuel Whitney, restoration of the Newel K. Whitney home, the building of a replica of the John Johnson Inn on its original foundation, and the restoration of a tannery, ashery, and school house.

Restoration of the historic sites will begin in 2001 with completion expected by the end of 2002. Dedication ceremonies are projected for the spring of 2003.

Another important project in Ohio is the renovation of the John Johnson home in Hiram, which is to be completed in 2001.

Sources: *Encyclopedic History of the Church,* by Andrew Jenson; "Kirtland: The Crucial Years," by Milton V. Backman Jr., *Ensign,* Jan. 1979; "Kirtland Today," by Janet Brigham, *Ensign,* Feb. 1979; "Kirtland stirs once again as Church grows in Ohio," by Hal Knight, *Church News,* Sept. 22, 1979; *Ohio History,* by Joseph H. Young, unpublished manuscript, Dec. 21, 1979; *Church News,* Nov. 29, 1958, Nov. 3, 1979, March 18, 1979, Jan. 7, 1989, Aug. 1, 1992, June 8, 1996; Jan. 10, 1998, May 9, 1998, Sept. 11, 1999, April 1, 2000, April 22, 2000; "Plans announced to renovate six major Kirtland structures," by

Shaun Stahle, *Church News*, April 29, 2000.

Stakes — 11

(Listed alphabetically as of Oct. 1, 2000)

No.	Name	Organized	First President
North America East Area			
696	Akron Ohio	25 May 1975	Carmen J. Libutti
270	*Cincinnati Ohio		
	‡Cincinnati (Ohio, Kentucky)	23 Nov 1958	Thomas Blair Evans
1523	Cincinnati Ohio North	17 Mar 1985	William B. Wallis
336	*Cleveland Ohio		
	‡Cleveland (Ohio, Penn.)	20 Sep 1961	E. Doyle Robison
351	*Columbus Ohio		
	‡Columbus	25 Feb 1962	James L. Mortensen
793	Columbus Ohio East	28 Nov 1976	Paul Frank Eastman
1609	Columbus Ohio North	19 Oct 1986	D. Richard McFerson
516	*Dayton Ohio		
	‡Dayton	24 May 1970	Joseph M. McPhie
1029	Dayton Ohio East	27 May 1979	Melvin Elwin Gourdin
1447	Kirtland Ohio	16 Oct 1983	Zane F. Lee
1204	Toledo Ohio	2 Nov 1980	Ronald Rufus Burke

Stakes discontinued

1	Kirtland	17 Feb 1834	Joseph Smith Jr.
	Discontinued 24 May 1841 (Reinstated as No. 1447)		

Missions — 3

(As of Oct. 1, 2000; shown with historical number. See MISSIONS.)

(328) OHIO CINCINNATI MISSION
3940 Olympic Blvd, Ste. 370
Erlanger, KY 41018

(154) OHIO CLEVELAND MISSION
23550 Center Ridge Rd. Ste 2
West Lake, OH 44145

(77a) OHIO COLUMBUS MISSION
5025 Arlington Centre Blvd., Ste. 310
Columbus, OH 43220

Oklahoma

Year-end 1999: Est. population, 3,358,000; Members, 33,721; Stakes, 7; Wards, 48; Branches, 27; Missions, 2; Temples,1; Percent LDS, 1.0, or one in 100.

In the late 1840s, George Miller, a former bishop who delayed going to the West, traveled from Winter Quarters, Neb., to visit his son in Texas. He and two other members with him, Joseph Kilting and Richard Hewitt, found construction work available in the Cherokee Nation. They arrived in Tahlequah on July 9, 1847, and began to build houses. They also began to teach others about the Church, but antagonism forced Miller to leave in December. Hewitt and Kilting remained to work.

In 1855, Orson Spencer and James McGaw visited the Indian Territory from St. Louis, Mo., and on April 8, 1855, five more missionaries were sent from Salt Lake City and four from St. Louis. The Indian Territory Mission was created and placed under the leadership of Henry W. Miller on June 26, 1855. The missionaries met and re-converted followers of Lyman Wight. One of these was Jacob Croft, who had met missionaries earlier and started for Utah, but met another apostate group that told the Croft party untruths about conditions in Utah. The discouraged Croft party had then settled in Indian Territory and built a gristmill.

As early as July, 1835, the missionaries preached to some 400 Indians, and the Cherokee Branch was started at Croft's Spavinaw Creek mill. This became mission headquarters. Croft later led a party of 56, including other former followers of Wight and some re-converted "Strangites" (followers of James J. Strang) to Utah.

Later in the year missionaries were sent from St. Louis to southern portions of the Cherokee Nation. In 1856, the Princess Creek Branch was organized. The Lehi and Nephi branches were organized in 1858.

Illness was a problem in this mission for many years. At least four missionaries died from the effects of serving in Indian Territory, including Orson Spencer. Many suffered the effects of malaria afterward.

In 1858-59, the remaining groups immigrated to Utah and by 1860 all the missionaries but John A. Richards, who had married an Indian wife, returned to Utah and the mission was discontinued. The Civil War ended what was left of the Church in the Indian Territory. Members and leaders were scattered.

When Elders Matthew Dalton and John Hubbard returned in 1877, they found John Richards was still faithful, and they received hospitality from him. Elder Hubbard died later that year and work stopped until 1883 when the next missionaries, Elder Dalton and Elder George Teasdale of the Quorum of the Twelve, came and the mission was reopened. Tracts in the Cherokee language were printed. Plagued with ill health, these missionaries persevered and found converts in Arkansas.

Andrew Kimball, the father of President Spencer W. Kimball, presided over the mission in 1885. Although he contracted malaria, he carried on the work and was assisted by John Richards and later by additional full-time missionaries. In 1892, the first meetinghouse was erected in Manard, Cherokee County. Another was erected at Massey, Choctaw Nation.

Converts during this period whose descendants became stalwarts in the local branches included the families of former minister John W. Davis, Simon Peter Hubler, William Edward Roberts, and George Washington Aaron, to name a few.

In 1898, the mission became part of the Southwestern States Mission, and in 1904 was included in the Central States Mission. By 1921, a branch was established at Gore, Okla., with 113 members but was later dissolved. A Sunday School began in Bartlesville in 1924. Membership increased but many converts went West.

Membership began to increase in the 1950s and 1960s. In 1960, two stakes were created in Oklahoma, the Tulsa Stake on May 1 and the Oklahoma City Stake on Oct. 23. Additional stakes followed in 1970, 1977, 1978, and three in the 1980s. Membership in the state in 1974 was 10,105; in 1980, 20,819; and in 1990, 26,596. The Oklahoma Mission was created in 1970 and renamed the Oklahoma Tulsa Mission in 1974. A second mission in Oklahoma, headquartered in Oklahoma City, was created in 1990.

The LDS community reached out to those in need after a terrorist bomb ripped apart the nine-story Alfred P. Murrah Federal Building in downtown Oklahoma City April 19, 1995. President Gordon B. Hinckley met July 14, 1996, with 1,900 youth and leaders gathered in the auditorium of the Union High School in Tulsa.

In 1999, membership was 33,721.

On March 17, 1999, the First Presidency announced that a temple would be built in Oklahoma City. The temple, the Church's 95th temple in operation, was dedicated July 30, 2000.

Sources: *A History of The Church of Jesus Christ of Latter-day Saints in Eastern Oklahoma, from Oklahoma and Indian Territories to 1980* by Lynetta K. Bingham, Bonnie Lee Blamires, Clara Laster and Lenet Read, published by the Tulsa Oklahoma Stake; *Mormon Indian Missions — 1855,* a BYU thesis by Wesley R. Law, 1959; "The Cherokee Nation," by A.W. Miller, *Millennial Star,* Oct. 6, 1855, p. 637; "Faith, courage rise from the rubble," *Church News*, April 29, 1995; "Church leader visits 5 states in 4 days," *Church News*, July 20, 1996; *Church News*, Aug. 5, 2000.

Stakes — 7

(Listed alphabetically as of Oct. 1, 2000.)

No.	Name	Organized	First President
North America Southeast Area			
777	Lawton Oklahoma	31 Oct 1976	Ralph E. Siebach
531	*Norman Oklahoma ‡Oklahoma South	18 Oct 1970	H. Aldridge Gillespie
305	*Oklahoma City Oklahoma ‡Oklahoma	23 Oct 1960	James A. Cullimore
1381	Oklahoma City Oklahoma South	14 Nov 1982	Lawrence Andrew Jackson
1277	Stillwater Oklahoma	14 Jun 1981	C. Jay Murray
298	*Tulsa Oklahoma ‡Tulsa (Okla., Ark., Kan.)	1 May 1960	Robert N. Sears
912	Tulsa Oklahoma East	30 Apr 1978	Raleigh L. Huntsman
Stakes discontinued			
1418	Muskogee Oklahoma Discontinued 11 Aug 1991	15 May 1983	Samuel J. Hughes

Missions — 2

(As of Oct. 1, 2000; shown with historical number. See MISSIONS.)

(248) OKLAHOMA OKLAHOMA CITY MISSION
1236 SW 89th St. Suite C
Oklahoma City, OK 73139

(88) OKLAHOMA TULSA MISSION
5215 East 71st St., Suite 300
Tulsa, OK 74136

Oregon

Year-end 1999: Est. population, 3,316,000; Members, 134,438; Stakes, 35; Wards, 238; Branches, 36; Missions, 2; Temples, 2; Percent LDS, 4.0, or one in 25.

In 1838, Joseph Smith visited Washington, D.C., where, on one occasion Henry Clay, "the great compromiser," suggested the Prophet take the Mormons to the Oregon Territory. The Prophet did not take the suggestion seriously. Oregon, however, was one of several locations considered for possible settlement after difficulties in Illinois in the early 1840s. At the time, Oregon was claimed by both Great Britain and the United States. Saints in both countries offered to settle there with their government's support, but the offers were declined.

As early as Sept. 25, 1850, Elder R. Boyd Stewart, who lived in a settlement on the Sacramento River in California, was called to serve in Oregon. Additional missionaries served in 1854 and later, but were called back with their converts at the coming of Johnston's army to Utah in 1857. The exodus to Utah began March 6, 1858.

After Oregon became a state in 1858, a more favorable attitude toward members developed. During the 1860s, Mormons found work as loggers in Oregon. A few settled, but any significant Mormon presence did not occur until 1887 when LDS businessmen from Utah, David Eccles and Charles Nibley (joined in 1889 by John Stoddard), built a lumber mill on North Powder River and persuaded LDS families to migrate to Oregon. The Baker Branch was organized in 1893.

The Northwestern States Mission, with headquarters in Portland, was organized for the second time July 26, 1897, under the direction of George C. Parkinson. (The first Northwestern States Mission was organized in 1878 with headquarters in Chicago.) Early convert Jens (James) Christensen Westergaard became the first branch president in Portland after his baptism in 1898.

Around the turn of the 20th century, another LDS movement into Oregon occurred when ranches in eastern Oregon were purchased and divided into sugar beet farms. The Eccles partnership supported this migration effort. By June 9, 1901, enough members had migrated that the first stake in the state, the Union Stake in LaGrande was created. Two years later, the five original wards had increased to 12, "all in excellent working order." Completion of the Oregon Shortline Railroad led more members to migrate to the Northwest.

Both World War I and World War II defense industry efforts led to more members moving to Oregon. In 1929, a meetinghouse was completed in Portland. By 1930, membership in the state was 3,226, with wards at Baker, Imbler, LaGrande (two), Mt. Glen, and Union, and branches in Bend, Eugene, Klamath Falls, Medford, Portland, Hood River, and Salem.

Another stake was organized in Portland in 1938. Many members also moved into Oregon in the post-World War II boom and four more stakes were created in the 1950s.

In 1961 or earlier, the Church purchased property near Portland for eventual use for a junior college in Portland. However, the location was later selected as the site for the Portland Oregon Temple, which was dedicated Aug. 19, 1989. More than 300,000 people toured the temple during its open house.

One evidence of the growing LDS population in the state was a dance festival held in July 1989 in which some 10,000 youth participated.

Members continued to support missionary work, and in 1990, a second mission in the state, with headquarters in Eugene, was created. Membership in 1980 was 94,093, increasing to 113,774 in 1990, and to 134,438 in 1999.

In early 1996, devastating floods struck the Northwest, including parts of Oregon. Several homes of LDS families were flooded and damaged, while some 300 other LDS families were evacuated because of potential dike failure. Members outside stricken areas joined relief efforts, including clean-up projects and working with county officials to match victims with relief crews. In 1997, members in Beaverton shared their pioneer heritage with the community by joining the state's third largest parade, and pushing handcarts and wearing pioneer clothing.

A second temple in Oregon, located in Medford, was announced March 17, 1999, and was dedicated April 16, 2000.

Sources: *Encyclopedic History of the Church,* by Andrew Jenson; *Mormon Migration to Oregon's Grande Ronde Valley: A Portent of Future Mormon Expansion,* by Kenneth Gerald Dull, master's thesis, Utah State University, 1981; "Enterprising beet farmers," by Bruce D. Blumell, *Church News,* Jan. 14, 1978; *Church News,* July 22, 1989, Jan. 27, 1990; *History of the Church in the Pacific Northwest,* by Leonard J. Arrington, Task Papers in LDS History, No. 18; "A wake of disaster, a wave of volunteers,"

Church News, Feb. 17, 1996, *Church News*, July 19, 1997, March 27, 1999, April 22, 2000.

Stakes — 35

(Listed alphabetically by area as of Oct. 1, 2000.)

No.	Name	Organized	First President
	North America Northwest Area		
386	*Beaverton Oregon		
	‡Portland West (Oregon)	10 Nov 1963	C. Carlile Carlson
2124	Beaverton Oregon West	12 Nov 1995	William Stanley Richardson
472	*Bend Oregon		
	‡Bend	15 Dec 1968	Norman K. Whitney
1373	Cedar Mill Oregon	31 Oct 1982	Edgar Lee Stone
1325a	Central Point Oregon	7 Mar 1982	Michael T. Robinson
493	*Coos Bay Oregon		
	‡Oregon West	12 Sep 1969	Edward Harold Sypher
385	*Corvallis Oregon		
	‡Corvallis	3 Nov 1963	Hugh F. Webb
191	*Eugene Oregon		
	‡Willamette	2 Dec 1951	Ralph B. Lake
1410	Eugene Oregon Santa Clara	17 Apr 1983	Terrel B. Williams
767	Eugene Oregon West	12 Sep 1976	Robert W. Hill
779	Grants Pass Oregon	31 Oct 1976	Darwin Jay Wright
643	Gresham Oregon	26 May 1974	Wilford Smith Stevenson Jr.
1365	Gresham Oregon South	10 Oct 1982	Max B. Holbrook
1200	Hermiston Oregon	26 Oct 1980	Allen D. Alder
710	Hillsboro Oregon	12 Oct 1975	H. Keith Buhler
743	*Keizer Oregon	4 Apr 1984	
	*Salem Oregon Keizer	25 Oct 1981	
	‡Salem Oregon North	8 Feb 1976	Jay Gerald Nelson
205	*Klamath Falls Oregon		
	‡Klamath (Oregon, California)	22 Mar 1953	Carroll William Smith
49	*La Grande Oregon		
	‡Union	9 Jun 1901	Franklin S. Bramwell
1469	Lake Oswego Oregon	29 Apr 1984	Thomas Dean Cottle
1102	Lebanon Oregon	3 Feb 1980	Henry Boyd Walthuis
1300	McMinnville Oregon	25 Oct 1981	Thomas Babb III
400	*Medford Oregon		
	‡Medford (Oregon, California)	23 Aug 1964	Dennis R. Hassell
999	Milwaukie Oregon	11 Feb 1979	Thomas Dean Cottle
1171	*Monmouth Oregon	21 May 1996	
	*Dallas Oregon	25 Sep 1990	
	‡Salem Oregon East	24 Aug 1980	William Paul Hyde
176	*Nyssa Oregon		
	‡Nyssa (Oregon, Idaho)	8 Jan 1950	Arvel L. Child
1504	Ontario Oregon	18 Nov 1984	Reed Neils Dame
563	*Oregon City Oregon		
	‡Oregon City	16 Jan 1972	James Hayward Bean
123	*Portland Oregon		
	‡Portland	26 Jun 1938	Monte L. Bean
190	*Portland Oregon East		
	‡Columbia River (Ore., Wash.)	2 Dec 1951	R. Spencer Papworth
1852	Ranier Oregon	8 Mar 1992	Marion Royal Johnstun
1239	*Redmond Oregon	18 Feb 1986	
	‡Prineville Oregon	1 Mar 1981	Heber D. Perrett
830	Roseburg Oregon	15 May 1977	Gary Richards Lowe
321	*Salem Oregon		
	‡Salem	22 Jan 1961	Hugh F. Webb
850	The Dalles Oregon	26 Jun 1977	Wayne B. Bush
1895	Tualatin Oregon	16 Aug 1992	Paul Walker Roberts

Missions — 2

(As of Oct. 1, 2000; shown with historical number. See MISSIONS.)

(249) OREGON EUGENE MISSION (18) OREGON PORTLAND MISSION

55 W 29th Ave, Ste A
Eugene, OR 97405

13635 NW Cornell Rd., Suite 100
Portland, OR 97229

Pennsylvania

Year-end 1999: Est. population, 11,994,000; Members, 37,749; Stakes, 10; Wards, 65; Branches, 37; Missions, 3; Districts, 1; Percent LDS, 0.3, or one in 318.

Joseph Smith and his wife, Emma, moved to Harmony, Pa., in December 1827, and first lived in the home of Isaac Hale, the Prophet's father-in-law. A few weeks later, he moved to a small cabin on an adjacent farm where he eventually translated most of the Book of Mormon. First he acted as his own scribe, but later his wife, Martin Harris, and Oliver Cowdery each served as scribes during the period of translation in Pennsylvania. At the nearby Susquehanna River, Joseph Smith and Oliver Cowdery were ordained to the Aaronic Priesthood by John the Baptist on May 15, 1829. (See D&C 13.) The ordinance of baptism was then performed for the first time in this dispensation as Joseph Smith baptized Oliver Cowdery and afterward Oliver baptized Joseph. Later Peter, James, and John appeared to Joseph and Oliver and conferred upon them the Melchizedek Priesthood. Fifteen of the revelations in the Doctrine and Covenants were received in Harmony. The first child of Joseph and Emma, a son who died in infancy, is buried at this farm site. The farm was purchased by the Church Feb. 7, 1947, and a historical marker has been erected.

Orson Hyde, Samuel H. Smith, and a number of others began missionary work in Pennsylvania shortly after the Church was organized in New York in 1830. By 1831, a branch had been created in Columbia, Bradford County. Additional branches were organized in Pittsburgh in 1832 and in Springfield and Elk Creek in 1833. A total of 12 branches were created in the 1830s, although these branches were of short duration as members gathered to Ohio, or later to Missouri and Illinois, with the body of the Saints.

From 1839 to 1846, missionary work in the Church was focused mostly in the cities of Philadelphia, Boston, and New York. The Philadelphia Branch was created in 1839 after initial efforts by Elders Jedediah M. Grant, Joshua Grant, and Benjamin Winchester, and sustained efforts by Elders Samuel and Lewis James. By 1840, more than 200 were members of the branch and 8 to 10 were baptized weekly.

Converts from Philadelphia included Edward Hunter, a wealthy landowner who later became Presiding Bishop of the Church, and John Neff, a well-to-do businessman. Both contributed generously of their means to sustain the members during later privations brought about by persecution.

Following the martyrdom of Joseph Smith in 1844, Sidney Rigdon and James J. Strang, among others, claimed leadership of the Church and established apostate groups from among Church members who had not "gathered," including those in Pennsylvania. However, many were later reclaimed. Apostate leader William Bickerton drew away members in western Pennsylvania who became known as the Bickertonites.

On March 26, 1850, Col. Thomas L. Kane delivered a landmark address, "History of the Persecutions of the Latter-day Saints," to the Historical Society of Pennsylvania. During the 1850s, Philadelphia was a port of entry for many LDS emigrants from Europe.

Missionary work continued sporadically. In 1878, the Northwestern States Mission (which at the time included the Eastern states) was created, becoming the Northern States Mission in 1889. During this time, the Redstone and New England (later called Wilson) branches were organized in May 1886. Pennsylvania was transferred to the Eastern States Mission in 1897, and the East and West Pennsylvania districts were created.

By 1930, the East District included one branch in Philadelphia with 284 members. The West District, with a membership of 510, included branches in Pittsburgh, which had its own meetinghouse, and in Wilson.

During World War II, membership in Pennsylvania increased and additional branches were created. Missionaries arrived in Lancaster, near Harrisburg, in 1941, and their first converts were Lester D. Ross and his wife, Mary Eleanor. A branch was organized in 1943, with 10-14 members. However, as the branch grew, its members often moved to the West.

The state's first stake, the Philadelphia Stake, was created Oct. 16, 1960, with 2,000 members in the Pennsylvania wards of Philadelphia, Valley Forge, and Wyncote, and branches in Allentown, Chester, and Reading.

The Pittsburgh Stake was created May 11, 1969, with 2,258 members in four wards in Pittsburgh, and others in Beaver Valley, Butler, Punxsutawney, and Washington, and branches in Greensburg and Monongahela. The next year, Pennsylvania's third stake, the Gettysburg (now York) Stake, was organized April 19, 1970.

On July 1, 1970, Pennsylvania's first mission (now Pennsylvania Harrisburg Mission) was created, followed by the creation of the Pennsylvania Pittsburg Mission in 1975 and the Pennsylvania Philadelphia Mission in 1977. Membership in Pennsylvania in 1980 was 22,211, increasing to 28,976 in 1990.

President Gordon B. Hinckley spoke to priesthood leaders, missionaries, and members during a trip to Pittsburgh April 27-28, 1996. About 5,000 members attended Sunday's meeting in the Sewell Center of Pittsburgh's Robert Morris College.

On June 28, 1997, the property of Edward Hunter in Chester County, near Philidelphia, was dedicated with a plaque honoring the early Church presiding bishop and pioneer, who led the third company of pioneers into Salt Lake Valley. The dedication was under the leadership of the Philadelphia Pennsylvania Stake.

Sources: *Encyclopedic History of the Church,* by Andrew Jenson; *A Study of the Origins of the Church in the States of New York and Pennsylvania, 1816-1831,* a BYU dissertation by Larry C. Porter, August 1971; *Church News,* Oct. 22, 1960, May 17, 1969, Nov. 30, 1986; *Missionary Activities and Church Organizations in Pennsylvania, 1830-1840,* a BYU thesis by V. Alan Curtis, 1976; "The Hospitable Squire," by William Hartley, *Church News,* Jan. 21, 1978; *The Church in Pennsylvania (1830-1854),* an East Stroudsburg State College thesis by Paul Zilch Rosenbaum, December 1982; Neff History, unpublished; Interview with Lester D. Ross by Julie Dockstader, *Church News,* Oct. 19, 1991; *Church News,* May 4, 1996, July 12, 1997.

Stakes — 10

(Listed alphabetically as of Oct. 1, 2000.)

No.	Name	Organized	First President
North America Northeast Area			
946	*Altoona Pennsylvania 31 Oct 1982		
	‡State College Pennsylvania	23 Jul 1978	Robert Armstrong Wood Sr.
1047	Harrisburg Pennsylvania	12 Aug 1979	Charles A. Cooper
304	*Philadelphia Pennsylvania		
	‡Philadelphia		
	(Penn., Del., Md., N.J.)	16 Oct 1960	Bryant F. West
481	*Pittsburgh Pennsylvania		
	‡Pittsburgh	11 May 1969	William P. Cook
985	*Pittsburgh Pennsylvania North 18 Feb 1992		
	‡Pittsburgh Pennsylvania East	26 Nov 1978	Garth Harrison Ladle
1372	Reading Pennsylvania	31 Oct 1982	Hugh G. Daubek
1044	Scranton Pennsylvania	2 Aug 1979	Frederick Adelman Alderks
2512	Valley Forge Pennsylvania	14 Feb 1999	Robert Blaine Smith
2337	Williamsport Pennsylvania	13 Apr 1997	Russell James Stankiewicz
510	*York Pennsylvania 12 Aug 1979		
	*Gettysburg Pennsylvania		
	‡Gettysburg (Pennsylvania)	19 Apr 1970	Laurence L. Yager

Missions — 3

(As of Oct. 1, 2000; shown with historical number. See MISSIONS.)

(91a) PENNSYLVANIA HARRISBURG MISSION
3903 Hartzdale Dr., Ste. 303
Camp Hill, PA 17011

(156) PENNSYLVANIA PHILADELPHIA MISSION
300 West State St., Ste.107
Media, PA 19063

(129) PENNSYLVANIA PITTSBURGH MISSION
2589 Washington Road, Ste. 410
Pittsburgh, PA 15241-2596

Rhode Island

Year-end 1999: Est. population, 991,000; Members, 3,214; Stakes, 1; Wards, 5; Branches, 2; Percent LDS, 0.3, or one in 319.

Elders Orson Hyde and Samuel H. Smith arrived in Rhode Island on July 13, 1832, baptizing their first convert on July 18. They baptized another person before persecutors drove them from the state a few days afterward.

Four years later, records note the existence of a Rhode Island Branch represented by Brigham Young at a conference in Newry, Maine. The Newport Branch was organized in 1844, or earlier, with 21 members.

Elder John Druce worked as an engraver and missionary in Pawtucket, R.I., in 1846, where he also preached and baptized many converts. A branch was organized June 7, 1857, in Providence, but discontinued as the members moved to the West. Druce immigrated to the West in 1861, but returned in 1876 to resume his missionary work.

In 1873, Elder Henry G. Bywater organized another branch in Providence with 25 members, and predicted many would soon emigrate. In 1876, Elder Erastus Snow wrote that he and Elder Benjamin F. Cummings met with the Saints in Pawtucket who were on their way to the Great Basin from England. A year later, Elder Cummings preached to an attentive audience in a school house in Pawtucket. In 1896, Elder Joseph A. Anderson reported illness after sleeping outside in the rain for some 12 days as he traveled in Rhode Island without purse or scrip. A conference of the Eastern States Mission was held March 22, 1899, in Providence and received favorable publicity in the *Providence Journal* and the *Telegram.* Missionaries also reported that residents treated them kindly.

The Providence Branch was organized in 1905, and by 1917 increased to about 20 people. Membership in the nation's smallest state continued to increase gradually. In 1938, a private library was purchased for the Providence Branch, which was remodeled into a meetinghouse by the members. The facility was dedicated by Elder John A. Widtsoe of the Quorum of the Twelve on June 14, 1944. The branch often dwindled when members moved to the West to be closer to the Church. However, the branch was bolstered by converts introduced to the Church by LDS servicemen stationed at nearby military bases. The library meetinghouse was sold and another site purchased in 1960. A new building was dedicated in 1966.

The Providence Stake was created March 20, 1977, the 49th state to receive its first stake. Rhode Island wards in the stake then included those in Newport and Providence, and the Davisville Branch. Also in the stake were two wards and two branches in Massachusetts and two wards in Connecticut. Membership in Rhode Island in 1974 was 799, increasing to 1,052 in 1980, and 1,701 in 1990.

On July 5-7, 1995, young men and young women from the Providence Rhode Island Stake turned their youth conference into a service project. They helped make the Special Olympics World Games a success for 7,000 participants from 140 countries by helping with activities such as food services and cleanup and by cheering the athletes on in their competitions.

In 1999, LDS membership in Rhode Island was 3,214 in five wards and two branches.

Sources: *Encyclopedic History of the Church,* by Andrew Jenson; Journal History of the Church, Aug. 14, 1836, Oct. 22, 1843, July 30, 1844, March 10, 1873, March 13, 1876, Feb. 5, 1977; *Deseret News,* March 31, 1877, July 12, 1877, Oct. 9, 1878, Aug 11, 1896, April 1, 1899, Dec. 3, 1932; *Church News,* March 31, 1945, March 26, 1977; "Missionary Printer," by Ronald G. Watt, *Church News,* Jan. 28, 1978; *Church News,* July 15, 1996.

Stake — 1

(As of Oct. 1, 1998.)

No.	Name	Organized	First President
	North America Northeast Area		
818	Providence Rhode Island	20 Mar 1977	Morgan W. Lewis Jr.

South Carolina

Year-end 1999: Est. population, 3,886,000; Members, 27,399; Stakes, 4; Wards, 35; Branches, 20; Missions, 1; Temples, 1; Percent LDS, 0.7, or one in 141.

While missionary work in the Southern States began as early as 1831, the first member in South Carolina is believed to have been Emmanual Masters Murphy, who was baptized in Tennessee in 1836. When Elder Lysander M. Davis arrived in South Carolina about the first of November in 1839, he found the Murphys had people prepared for baptism. Seven of these were baptized.

Opposition arose and Elder Davis was briefly jailed, but progress continued with additional conversions. Murphy reportedly later visited Joseph Smith in Carthage Jail shortly before the Prophet's martyrdom. The Prophet reminded him of the prophecy that soon war would begin in South Carolina, and exhorted Murphy to warn the people of his home state.

Elder Abraham O. Smoot preached in Charleston and upstate in 1841, but failed to gain any converts. However, an "unknown missionary" traveled to Charleston earlier that year and baptized three ministers and eight others. Another missionary, Elder John Eldredge, preached in South Carolina in 1842-43.

The next missionary activity in the state began in the 1870s. The South Carolina Conference was organized in July 1882. Among the earliest branches were at King's Mountain (1882), Gaffney (1883), and among the Catawba Indian community (1885). Conference headquarters were established at the plantation of John Black, a man who remained unbaptized in order to provide refuge to the Church. Many converts, including Indians, moved onto his plantation to escape persecution. The Catawbas also shielded missionaries from persecutors. Most of the Catawbas joined the Church and remained faithful.

Stalwart missionaries braved such adversities as floggings, jailings, disease (12 missionaries died from illness from 1895-1900 in the Southern States Mission), and frequent exposure to the elements. They walked hundreds of miles, often missing meals, and endured other privations. But they continued to find converts and organize branches. From 1880 to 1888, 2,238 converts were baptized throughout the South, and 1,169 converts migrated to Utah.

Mission leaders of the 1880s and later included Henry G. Boyle, John Morgan, William Spry, J. Golden Kimball, Elias S. Kimball, and Benjamin E. Rich. Later, Ephraim H. Nye, Charles A. Callis, and LeGrand Richards were prominent mission leaders.

In the 1890s, progress and persecution continued. Mobs often gathered to punish and banish missionaries. But the members and missionaries persevered. Branches were organized in Society Hill, Columbia, Charleston, and Fairfield, to name a few. About 350 members attended a conference in Society Hill in 1897. However, as converts migrated to the West, branches dwindled and some were reorganized later with new converts.

At the turn of the century, membership in the state was 1,200. That membership increased to 3,343 by 1930. The conference included six branches (four with meetinghouses) and 10 Sunday Schools. In the 1930s, mission president LeGrand Richards introduced "systematic teaching," a forerunner of today's missionary discussions. By 1937, membership in the entire Southern States Mission had increased to 18,000.

South Carolina's first stake was created in Columbia in 1947. It included the entire state with wards in Columbia, Greenville, Charleston, Gaffney, Hartsville, Ridgeway, and Spartanburg, and branches in Augusta (Ga.), Sumter, Society Hill, Winnsboro, and Darlington. Membership totaled about 1,900 members.

Additional stakes were added in 1963, 1968, and 1972. The South Carolina Columbia Mission was organized from the Georgia Atlanta Mission July 1, 1975. Church membership in South Carolina in 1974 was 10,775, increasing to 17,012 in 1980, 23,731 in 1990, and to 27,399 in 1999.

In November 1996, Church leaders met with South Carolina Gov. David Beasley to thank him for his efforts in organizing a foundation, "Putting Families First." LDS students from Camden, Columbia, and Lugoff provided significant service at an elementary school in July 1998.

South Carolina was the third of the original American colonies to have a temple, Maryland was first, followed by Georgia. On Sept. 11, 1998, it was announced that a temple would be built in Columbia, the capital of South Carolina. Thirteen months later, the temple, which serves some 40,000 Latter-day Saints in South Carolina and portions of Georgia, North Carolina, and Tennessee, was completed and dedicated on Oct. 16, 1999.

Sources: *Encyclopedic History of the Church,* by Andrew Jenson; *Columbia South Carolina Stake Fortieth Anniversary, Oct. 19, 1947 to 1987,* compiled under direction of stake Pres. Gary L. Fish; *History of the Southern States Mission 1831-1861,* a BYU thesis by LaMar C. Berrett, July 1960; *Brief History of the Southern States Mission for One Hundred Years, 1830-1930* by DeVon H. Nish, a BYU paper, August 1966; "Stake Birthday Notes Growth of Church in South Carolina," *Church News,* Dec. 9, 1972; *Southern States Mission and the Administration of Ben E. Rich, 1898-1908,* a thesis for BYU by Ted S. Anderson, April 1976; "Persecutor converted," by Richard L. Jensen, *Church News,* Feb. 4, 1978; *Church News,* Nov. 16, 1996; Aug. 1, 1998; "New temple in a 'place of history,' " by R. Scott Lloyd, *Church News,* Oct. 23, 1999.

Stakes — 4

(Listed alphabetically as of Oct. 1, 2000.)

No.	Name	Organized	First President
North America Southeast Area			
584	*Charleston South Carolina ‡Charleston	20 Aug 1972	Fred Ittner Harley
169	*Columbia South Carolina ‡South Carolina (S.C., Georgia)	19 Oct 1947	W. Wallace McBride
454	*Florence South Carolina 5 Feb 1978 *Columbia South Carolina East ‡South Carolina East (South Carolina)	21 Apr 1968	Clyde Elmer Black Sr.
366	*Greenville South Carolina *Greenville 19 Nov 1972 ‡South Carolina West (S.C., N.C.)	27 Jan 1963	Ivan A. Larsen

Mission — 1

(As of Oct. 1, 2000; shown with historical number. See MISSIONS.)

(130) SOUTH CAROLINA COLUMBIA MISSION
1345 Garner Lane, Suite #307
Columbia, SC 29210-8362

South Dakota

Year-end 1999: Est. population, 733,000; Members, 8,077; Stakes, 2; Wards, 9; Branches, 24; Missions, 1; Districts, 1; Percent LDS, 1.0, or one in 91.

In the 1840s, Church leaders seeking a refuge in the West considered various locations for settlement, including the Indian country of the Dakotas. An area was chosen in 1845 for settlement by a group of volunteer colonizers under maverick leader James Emmett. The group, which evidently communicated with Brigham Young but did not have his full approval, penetrated deep into South Dakota's Indian country and established a settlement at Fort Vermillion on the Missouri River. They arrived at the fort June 17, 1845, and immediately began building cabins and planting crops. They preached to the Sioux Indians and befriended them, but the threat of attack was constant. The colony was nearly attacked when Emmett unwisely interfered in a horse-trading deal between the Indians and traders and an argument ensued.

Emmett, who had lost some favor with Church leaders after the death of Joseph Smith, returned to Nauvoo the summer of 1845 and sought to regain favor with the Church. He was accepted in full fellowship, and on his return to Fort Vermillion, he was accompanied by two other leaders, Henry G. Sherwood and John S. Fullmer, who rebaptized the settlers. In the spring of 1846, the group received word from Brigham Young to join the Saints in the westward trek. The settlement was abandoned as most members complied with President Young's direction.

Missionary work in South Dakota began May 3, 1883, when, at a conference in Kirkhaven, Minn., Charles N. Nielsen and N.L. Lund were appointed to "open the Gospel door in the states of Dakota." Elder Nielsen arrived at Big Stone, Dakota Territory, on June 5, 1883, staying only one day. In 1885, the Dakota Conference membership was listed at "four souls," including two elders from Utah. The same year, Elder Soren Christiansen reported that he received both hospitality and threats backed up by guns as he traveled in Dakota. Missionaries reported in 1887 that Dakota was a "worn-out" territory. Missionary work continued in 1888, and in 1898, missionaries from North Dakota were transferred to the Southern Dakota Conference. The Dakotas were placed in the Colorado Mission in 1900. The mission name was renamed the Western States Mission in 1907. Missionary work continued with another organization of the South Dakota Conference in 1925, and yet another re-opening in 1931.

The South Dakota Conference was organized for western South Dakota, and a Sunday School was organized in Sioux Falls on Aug. 17, 1930, which became a branch June 19, 1949. Another branch existed in Gettysburg. By 1950, Sunday Schools were organized at Mitchell, Aberdeen, Brookings, Ft. Thompson, and Huron. That same year, ground was broken for a meetinghouse in Sioux Falls. A number of meetinghouses were completed in the 1970s. The Rapid City South Dakota Stake, the first in the state, was created in 1973, the same year that the Dakota-Manitoba Mission was organized. The following year, in 1974, the South Dakota Rapid City Mission was created.

Membership in South Dakota in 1980 was 6,121, which grew to 7,657 in 1990. Members, often meet in small units and drive long distances to attend services. In 1999, there were

8,077 members living in South Dakota.

Sources: *Encyclopedic History of the Church,* by Andrew Jenson; The Church in South Dakota, no author listed; *Church News,* July 8, 1944; "An Early Mormon Settlement in South Dakota," by Gerald E. Jones, *South Dakota State Historical Society Quarterly,* Spring of 1971; "Mormon Renegade: James Emmett at the Vermillion, 1846," by Richard E. Bennett, *South Dakota History,* Fall of 1985; "The Church in the Dakotas," by R. Janet Kruckenberg, *Church News,* Nov. 30, 1996; *Church News,* June 6, 1998.

Stakes — 2

(Listed alphabetically as of Oct. 1, 2000.)

No.	Name	Organized	First President
	North America Central Area		
592	*Rapid City South Dakota ‡Rapid City	10 Dec 1972	Briant LeRoy Davis
1085	Sioux Falls South Dakota	18 Nov 1979	Russell Lloyd Harward

Mission — 1

(As of Oct. 1, 2000; shown with historical number. See MISSIONS.)

(78)SOUTH DAKOTA RAPID CITY MISSION
2525 West Main, Suite 311
Rapid City, SD 57702

Tennessee

Year-end 1999: Est. population, 5,484,000; Members, 31,104; Stakes, 9; Wards, 51; Branches, 22; Missions, 2; Temples 2; Percent LDS, 0.6, or one in 176.

Apostle David W. Patten and Elder Warren Parrish arrived in Tennessee shortly before Oct. 11, 1834, where they preached at a large Campbellite meeting and baptized seven. Another 24 were baptized later. A small branch was organized by the end of the year. Missionary efforts took place in Henry, Benton, and Humphreys counties. In 1835, Elder Parrish worked alone after Elder Patten returned to Kirtland, Ohio. Elder Parrish continued to baptize converts and was unable to fill all the requests for preaching. One of his converts was Abraham O. Smoot, who later became a prominent Church leader in Salt Lake City.

On March 27, 1835, Wilford Woodruff, then a priest, came to assist Elder Parrish. He arrived at a tavern covered with mud and identified himself as a preacher. In jest, the innkeeper urged him to preach and gathered 500 people to hear him. Elder Woodruff told the rowdy congregation individually of "their wicked deeds and the reward they would obtain." One by one, the people left until he was alone. During the next three months, he and Elder Parrish baptized 20 converts.

When Elder Parrish was called as a seventy in July 1835, he ordained Elder Woodruff an elder and placed him in charge of the work in Tennessee. At that time, membership in the district was 86 members in six branches (one in Kentucky). Elder Woodruff continued the work, reporting at year's end that he had traveled 3,248 miles, baptized 43 people, three of whom were Campbellite preachers, and had three mobs rise against him. Mob activity temporarily forced missionaries from Benton County in 1836. However, work progressed well, and by 1839, 12 branches existed in Tennessee. Work continued through 1844 as missionaries promoted Joseph Smith's short-lived candidacy for president of the United States.

By 1846, missionaries had preached in 26 counties in Tennessee. Following the exodus to the West, little work was done in Tennessee. Missionaries visited the state in 1857 to call the Saints to gather in the West.

In 1870, Elder Hayden Church resumed missionary work in Tennessee. The Southern States Mission was formally organized in 1875 with headquarters in Nashville, which were moved to Chattanooga in 1882 and remained there until 1919, when Atlanta, Ga., became mission headquarters.

Elder Henry G. Boyle had established a branch at Shady Grove, Tenn., in 1875. Mob activity increased significantly in 1879. Some converts in the South left their homes and immigrated to the West in 1883. In 1884, members were fired upon in separate incidents. The worst massacre of Church members in the South occurred on Aug. 10, 1884, when mobbers shot to death missionaries William S. Berry and John H. Gibbs, and local members Martin Condor and John Riley during Church services near Cane Creek, Lewis County, Tenn. Mission Pres. B.H. Roberts heroically donned a disguise, traveled to the tense area and retrieved the bodies of the slain missionaries. During this period, missionaries faced down many mobs and sometimes suffered violence. Occasionally, non-members courageously defended the missionaries. In 1888, a group of 177 Saints left Chattanooga for Colorado and Utah.

By the 1890s, public opinion became more tolerant. U.S. Census records list 136 members in Tennessee in 1890. By 1906, membership had increased to 841.

The oldest existing meetinghouse in the Southeast was dedicated in Northcutts Cove in 1909. By 1919, branches were listed in Chattanooga and Memphis.

By 1930, some 2,832 members lived in the Middle and East Tennessee districts in the Chattanooga, Memphis, and Nashville branches, and Sunday Schools in Brighton, Pope, Short Creek, Silver Point, and Turkey Creek.

On April 18, 1965, Tennessee,'s first stake, the Memphis Stake, was created with two wards in Memphis and another in Jackson, plus wards in Mississippi and Arkansas.

The Tennessee Nashville Mission was created in 1975 and in 1993, the Tennessee Knoxville Mission was organized. Membership in Tennessee in 1980 was 15,839, increasing to 23,007 in 1990 and to 31,104 in 1999.

In 1996, more than 150 Church members participated in the three-mile "'96 Walk for the Homeless" in downtown Nashville. More than 6,500 people, 66 percent of the nearest four stakes, attended a meeting where President Gordon B. Hinckley spoke in the Knoxville Civic Coliseum March 15-16, 1997.

On Nov. 12, 1994, a letter sent to priesthood leaders announced plans to build a temple in Nashville. However, after three years of trying to gain approvals, Church leaders announced on April 25, 1998, they would move ahead with plans to build a temple somewhere else in the Nashville area, and said the temple would be substantially smaller. That fall, on Sept. 17, 1998, the First Presidency announced that a second temple would be built in Tennessee, this one in Memphis. The Memphis Tennessee Temple, in the suburb of Bartlett, was dedicated April 23, 2000, a little more than 165 years after Wilford Woodruff brought the gospel message to western Tennessee. The next month, on May 21, 2000, the Nashville Tennessee Temple, in the suburb of Franklin, was dedicated.

Sources: Southern States Mission directories, 1919-1935; *Encyclopedic History of the Church,* by Andrew Jenson; *History of the Southern States Mission,* a BYU thesis by LaMar C. Berrett, July 1960; *Orthodoxy Versus Nonconformity: The Mormon Experience in Tennessee and Mississippi, 1875-1905,* a University of Chicago paper by Mary Elizabeth Stovall, March 12, 1976; *Church News,* April 24, 1965, March 22, 1975, Nov. 9, 1986; "Chattanooga: LDS in Tennessee build on a firm foundation," by R. Scott Lloyd, *Church News,* May 25, 1991; "150 Church members serve the homeless," *Church News,* May 18, 1996; *Church News,* March 22, 1997, April 25, 1998, Oct. 24, 1998, April 29, 2000, May 27, 2000.

Stakes — 9

(Listed alphabetically as of Oct. 1, 2000.)

No.	Name	Organized	First President
North America East Area — 7			
927	Chattanooga Tennessee	21 May 1978	Earl Eugene Callens Jr.
1089	Franklin Tennessee	2 Dec 1979	Buryl Gene McClurg
1093	Kingsport Tennessee	13 Jan 1980	William Keith Clay
581	*Knoxville Tennessee ‡Knoxville	25 Jun 1972	Eugene H. Perkins
2269	Knoxville Tennessee Cumberland	17 Nov 1996	Richard Edwin Riggs
1810	McMinnville Tennessee	18 Aug 1991	Gary Wayne Bradford
537	*Nashville Tennessee ‡Nashville	6 Dec 1970	Robert N. Brady
North America Southeast Area — 2			
403	*Memphis Tennessee ‡Memphis (Tenn., Mo., Ark., Miss.)	18 Apr 1965	Richard Stoddard
1179	Memphis Tennessee North	14 Sep 1980	Edward Victor Martin

Missions — 2

(As of Oct. 1, 2000; shown with historical number. See MISSIONS.)

(294) TENNESSEE KNOXVILLE MISSION
P.O. Box 22730
Knoxville, TN 37933-0730

(131) TENNESSEE NASHVILLE MISSION
P.O. Box 1287
Brentwood, TN 37024

Texas

Year-end 1999: Est. population, 20,044,000; Members, 210,892,000; Stakes, 42; Wards, 324; Branches, 117; Districts, 2; Missions, 7; Temples, 2, 1 announced; Percent LDS, 1.0, or one in 95.

The Church's first missionary to Texas was William C. Steffey in 1843. In 1844, Joseph Smith considered Texas as an alternate location for the saints should they be driven from Illinois. The Church negotiated with Sam Houston and considered purchasing a large tract of land in western Texas. However, the martyrdom of Joseph Smith cut short these tentative plans. Lyman Wight, an apostle who lost faith after the martyrdom, proceeded on his own to lead a colony of 100 people into central Texas, leaving Nauvoo March 25, 1845, and arriving in the spring of 1846. Although he was excommunicated in 1848, Wight and his followers pioneered in five counties in Texas and generally left a good reputation for Mormons in the area.

Among the first successful missionaries to Texas was Preston Thomas who visited the Wight colonies in 1849 and rebaptized some of them. He also baptized his brother, Daniel. Preston Thomas led the first company of Texas converts to Salt Lake City in April 1853. He served six missions to Texas and led several companies to Utah.

In 1853, Thomas A. Martindale and James McGaw labored in Harris, Grimes, and Montgomery counties. Two years later, Elder Benjamin L. Clapp labored in Freestone County. The Texas Conference was organized Dec. 25, 1855. Work also went forward in Washington, Milam, McLennan, and Ellis counties. From 1854 to 1857, several hundred converts immigrated to Utah. Many privations accompanied some of these immigrants. Edward Wallace and Wilmirth Greer East, converts from Port Sullivan, Texas, lost four of their six young children as well as her father and brother from cholera on an 1855 trek to the West.

While records of missionary work after this period are scarce, some 276 members in Texas were on Church records after the Civil War ended. However, harsh attitudes against the members existed for many years and little growth was realized. Elder J. Golden Kimball entered the mission field in 1892, and in 1897, he reported that public opinion was by then more favorable toward the Church. The Texas Conference was reorganized June 17, 1893, and membership began a slow but steady increase. The Texas Conference was divided into several conferences in 1898, and local leaders were called.

On Dec. 31, 1898, John and James Edgar purchased property that eventually became the Mormon colony of Kelsey, where 300 members lived. In 1906, the settlements at Kelsey, Poynor, Williamson, and Spurger were the largest places of LDS worship, and membership throughout the state reached 1,000. Missionaries began tracting the areas, though some were overwhelmed by the 1901 oil boom in Beaumont that brought in thousands of people.

Until 1917, members in Houston met in rented halls while branches at Williamson and Josey built their own meetinghouses. By 1930, the state had 14 branches and an additional 11 independent Sunday Schools with a total membership of 3,837. A non-member donated her home to the Houston Branch for a meetinghouse, and it was remodeled and dedicated in 1933.

For about the next 20 years, membership in Texas continued to grow slowly and local members assumed more and more leadership roles. During World War II "home missions" were instituted.

The first stake in the state was the El Paso Stake, which was created Sept. 21, 1952, and in 1953, stakes were organized in Houston and Dallas, followed by a stake in San Antonio in 1958.

Growth of the Church in Texas continued and by 1977, membership totaled more than 50,000. The Dallas Texas Temple was dedicated Oct. 19, 1984. The temple district at the time included 46 stakes and 120,000 members in Texas and nearby states. In 1990, membership in Texas was 154,000. On Oct. 14, 1993, Richard A. Searfoss of League City, Texas, became the first Latter-day Saint to pilot a flight of a space shuttle. In 1998, he became the first Latter-day Saint to command a space shuttle flight,

President Gordon B. Hinckley addressed 3,600 members of the Church at the Corpus Christi Texas multi-stake conference Jan. 7, 1996. He also addressed 14,000 members at two different regional conference in Northeast Texas March 16-17, 1996.

Members in Texas help advance the work. In December 1997 in San Antonio, they promoted the Christian nature of the Church by displaying more than 600 creche scenes. At the same time, members in Beaumont held a celebration of National Family Week with a fair, giving information on how to strengthen families. In Amarillo, Violet Burk extended an outreach to the Laotian community. And in Laredo, Luciano Duarte, who served in a branch presidency or a bishopric continuously for 50 years, became well-known in the community as a Church member and promoter of Latin Tejano music.

On June 13, 1998, ground was broken for a second temple in the state in Houston, the fourth largest city in the United States. Two years later, the temple was dedicated on Aug. 26, 2000. A third temple in Texas was anounced in general conference by President Hinckley on April 2, 2000, to be built in Lubbock.

Today, there are seven missions in Texas, with headquarters in Houston (3), Dallas, San Antonio, Fort Worth, and McAllen. In 1999, 210,892 members lived in Texas.

Sources: *Encyclopedic History of the Church,* by Andrew Jenson; Church in Texas, by Ruby Denton; *A History of the Mormon Church in Texas 1843-1906,* by Bonnie Means Durning, a master's thesis for East Texas State College; *The Houston First Ward: From Stopover to Ward in One Hundred and Ten Years,* by Robert C. Petersen, a BYU paper, 1971; "Mormon Grove Trail beset with travails," by Chris Miasnik, *Church News,* July 24, 1993; "Shuttle pilot fulfilling childhood dream," by Julie A. Dockstader, *Church News,* Sept. 18, 1993; "Read Book of Mormon, prophet admonishes," *Church News,* Jan. 13, 1996; "Pres. Hinckley addresses 14,000," *Church News,* March 23, 1996; *Church News,* Dec. 20, 1997, April 18, 1998, April 25, 1998, June 6, 1998, June 20, 1998, April 8, 2000.

Stakes — 42

(Listed alphabetically as of Oct. 1, 2000.)

No.	Name	Organized	First President
North America Southwest Area			
1262	Abilene Texas	3 May 1981	William E. Seegmiller
1272	Amarillo Texas	31 May 1981	Donald Eugene Pinnell
1594	Arlington Texas	13 Apr 1986	Richard S. Pickering
626	Austin Texas	14 Oct 1973	Amos Luther Wright
1835	Austin Texas Oak Hills	1 Dec 1991	Gary Scott Robinson
1818	Bay City Texas	13 Oct 1991	Joseph Nathanial Cannon Jr.
333	*Beaumont Texas		
	‡Beaumont (Texas, Louisiana)	3 Sep 1961	Alden C. Stout
1076	*College Station Texas 10 Oct 1989		
	‡Conroe Texas	28 Oct 1979	Nylen Lee Allphin Jr.
2338	Colleyville Texas	13 Apr 1997	Randy J. Vest
398	*Corpus Christi Texas		
	‡Corpus Christi	31 May 1964	Clarence Cottam
1451	Cypress Texas	6 Nov 1983	Bruce A. Nelson
210	*Dallas Texas		
	‡Dallas	18 Oct 1953	Ervin W. Atkerson
828	Dallas Texas East	15 May 1977	Arthur Eugene Gabriel
1860	Denton Texas	3 May 1992	James Boyd Martino
194	*El Paso Texas		
	‡El Paso (Texas, New Mexico)	21 Sep 1952	Edward V. Turley Sr.
1359	El Paso Texas Mount Franklin	29 Aug 1982	Gerald Merrell Pratt
443	*Fort Worth Texas		
	‡Fort Worth (Texas)	24 Sep 1967	John Kelly Jr.
843	Friendswood Texas	29 May 1977	Newell Kenneth Hill
1394	Gilmer Texas	16 Jan 1983	Von Webber Freeman
1247	Harlingen Texas	22 Mar 1981	Leonard Moore
209	*Houston Texas (Spanish)		
	‡Houston (Texas, Louisiana)	11 Oct 1953	Jack Byron Trunnell
456	*Houston Texas East		
	‡Houston East (Texas)	5 May 1968	Martell A. Belnap
733	Houston Texas North	16 Nov 1975	Harold Elison DeLaMare
1211	Houston Texas South	30 Nov 1980	Leo C. Smith
784	*Hurst Texas	12 Apr 1981	
	‡Fort Worth Texas North	14 Nov 1976	Richard W. Ragsdale
1834	Katy Texas	1 Dec 1991	Collins Wise Steward
986	Killeen Texas	26 Nov 1978	Stephen Brian Hutchings
1337	Kingwood Texas	18 Apr 1982	Robert Lee Ezell
1253	Lewisville Texas	12 Apr 1981	Richard W. Ragsdale
496	*Longview Texas		
	‡Texas East	9 Nov 1969	Gerald C.F. Knackstedt
446	*Lubbock Texas		
	‡Texas North	26 Nov 1967	Franklin S. Gonzalez
692	McAllen Texas	4 May 1975	Daniel Birch Larsen
1991	McKinney Texas	11 Sep 1994	Robert C. Packard
471	*Odessa Texas		

	‡Texas West	15 Dec 1968	Roland Lamar Hamblin
1360	Orange Texas	29 Aug 1982	Bernard E. Packard
616	*Plano Texas 12 Apr 1981		
	*Dallas Texas North		
	‡Dallas North	27 May 1973	Ivan Leslie Hobson Jr.
1396	Richardson Texas	30 Jan 1983	Larry Wayne Gibbons
2531	Round Rock Texas	6 Jun 1999	Howard J. Nicholas
252	*San Antonio Texas		
	‡San Antonio	19 Jan 1958	Roland C. Bremer
758	San Antonio Texas East	30 May 1976	Archie M. Brugger
2401	San Antonio Texas North	19 Oct 1997	Frank J. Dittmar
1426	San Antonio Texas West	5 Jun 1983	Jan M. Sterneckert

Missions — 7

(As of Oct. 1, 2000; shown with historical number. See MISSIONS.)

(60) TEXAS DALLAS MISSION
13747 Montfort Drive, Ste.120
Dallas, TX 75240-4454

(189) TEXAS FORT WORTH MISSION
1331 Airport Freeway, Ste. 305
Euless, TX 76040.

(142) TEXAS HOUSTON MISSION
16623 Hafer Road
Houston, TX 77090

(254) TEXAS HOUSTON EAST MISSION
2815 W Lake Houston Pky, Ste. 109
Kingwood, TX 77339

(316) TEXAS HOUSTON SOUTH MISSION
4627 Austin Pky.
Sugarland, TX 77479-2146

(224) TEXAS MC ALLEN MISSION
3825 North 10th St., Ste E
McAllen, TX 78501

(233) TEXAS SAN ANTONIO MISSION
404 E. Ramsey Rd., Ste. 105
San Antonio, TX 78216

Utah

Year-end 1999: Est. population, 2,130,000; Members, 1,604,686; Stakes, 458; Wards, 3,599; Branches, 148; Missions, 5; Districts, 1; Temples, 11; Percent LDS, 75.3, or one in 1.3.

Apostle Orson Pratt and Erastus Snow were the first to enter the Great Basin, arriving in what is now Salt Lake City July 21, 1847, followed by the advance party, and on July 24 by Brigham Young and the rest of the group of 148 Saints. They had left Winter Quarters, Neb., 3 1/2 months earlier, on April 5 — the beginning of fulfillment of Joseph Smith's 1842 prophecy that the Saints would be driven to the Rocky Mountains and there "become a mighty people." The Saints found a habitable but unsettled place where they hoped to live in peace. They planted crops and explored, and on July 28, Brigham Young selected the site where the Salt Lake Temple now stands. Within a month, the city had been surveyed, 80 acres of land planted, 29 log houses built, nearby valleys explored, a bowry built, an adobe fort constructed, Indians befriended, and trade shops started.

Other pioneer companies followed, starting a flood of immigration into the Great Basin that continued through the turn of the 20th century and afterward.

On Sept. 26, 1847, Perregrine Sessions established a settlement in what is now Bountiful. Nearby Farmington was founded the same year by Hector C. Haight. In 1848, Captain James Brown of the Mormon Battalion purchased the land rights of early settler Miles Goodyear and built Brown's Fort in what is now Ogden. Centerville was established in 1848, as were many Salt Lake-area settlements, such as East Millcreek and Sugar House. About 4,500 people were in the Salt Lake Valley before the harsh winter of 1848. Many subsisted on roots of sego lilies and boiled rawhide.

On Oct. 3, 1847, the first stake in the new territory was created. A year-and-a-half later, on Feb. 22, 1849, the original 19 wards in what was then known as Great Salt Lake City were organized.

Provo was founded in 1849, along with Kaysville, Granger, Tooele, and Manti. By 1850, Iron City in southern Utah and 28 other setlements had been started. That year, Salt Lake City had a population of more than 11,000 people and the essentials of a successful commerce.

Before 1900, up to 500 settlements had been founded within the state and in the adjoining states of Idaho, Nevada, California, Arizona, New Mexico, Colorado, and Wyoming. Most of the first settlers were members from the Nauvoo period, primiarly American or British converts. Later emigrants came from Scandinavia, Europe, and a variety of lands such as Australia, India, South Africa, and even Hawaii. At least 236 parties or companies of pioneers crossed the plains to Utah with wagon freighters, handcart companies, and various Mormon wagon companies. Many were assisted by the Church's Perpetual Emigrating Fund. An estimated 60,000 Mormon pioneers crossed the plains before the coming of the railroad in 1869. Of these, some 3,000 came with handcart companies in 1856-60. Two companies, the late-starting Willie and Martin companies of 1856, however, met with tragedy in Wyoming in an unseasonably early winter, and 200 died from exposure and starvation. The majority of the people in these two handcart companies, some 875, were rescued through heroic efforts of the Saints in Utah.

Members generally got along well with the Indians, and the most prominent local leader, Ute Chief Walker, was friendly and was baptized in 1850, though he led a brief resistance movement in 1853. Members traded with Indians and shared food with them, and the Indians helped members survive. Indian farms were established in the 1850s, but troubles between the Mormons and the government discouraged most of the Indians.

On Feb. 14, 1853, ground was broken for the granite, six-spired Salt Lake Temple. The edifice was constructed of stone quarried 20 miles away. The stone was hauled from the quarry by ox-drawn wagons until 1869 when the railroad was completed.

In 1857, responding to false reports of insurrection, President James Buchanan sent an army under Col. Albert Sidney Johnston to put down the rebellion and install a new governor in Utah. In Utah, members considered it another act of persecution (see New York, Ohio, Missouri, and Illinois histories) and prepared to protect themselves. If attacked, the Saints would not fight but would burn their homes to the ground, leaving their persecutors nothing but "scorched earth," said Brigham Young. However, partly through intercession of friends of the Church, particularly Col. Thomas L. Kane, war was averted and Johnston's army passed peacefully through Salt Lake City. At the height of the war-time hysteria, a group of 120 members of the Baker-Fancher Wagon Train, most of them from Arkansas, were killed in 1857 at Mountain Meadows while passing through southern Utah.

Difficulties between federal appointees and citizens continued until Utah was granted statehood in 1896. A major obstacle to statehood was the practice of plural marriage, which ended when the Manifesto was issued by President Wilford Woodruff on Sept. 24, 1890.

Three years later in 1893, the 253,015 square-foot Salt Lake Temple — the largest in the Church — was dedicated. The temple, with its gilded statue of an angel and trumpet (see Rev. 14:6) on the highest spire, has become the most recognized worldwide symbol of the Church. Before the completion of the Salt Lake Temple, three other temples in Utah, in St. George in 1877, in Logan in 1884, and Manti in 1888, were built and dedicated. Three of the four pioneer temples have been extensively remodeled and rededicated — the St. George Temple in 1975, the Logan Temple in 1979, and the Manti Temple in 1985.

While the Salt Lake Temple was being construction, a companion building on Temple Square, the Tabernacle, was built from 1863-67 and dedicated in 1875. It is among the largest timber-roofed buildings in the world, and from its impressive interior emanates the weekly broadcast of the Tabernacle Choir, the longest continuous broadcast program in the United States.

During the pioneer period and shortly after the turn of the century, many of the larger outlying communities also erected tabernacles, ornate meetinghouses built for large gatherings. Several of these still stand today, an outstanding example of pioneer craftsmanship.

Completion of the overland railroad in 1869 brought many changes, including more extensive mining interests. The state's population, which reached 40,273 in 1860, jumped to 210,779 in 1890. By 1900, the population was 276,749, and Utah had 27 stakes.

The first seminary program in the Church was started in Salt Lake City in 1912 when 70 LDS teenagers, all members of the Granite Stake, began gathering for daily religious instruction in a small red brick building near Granite High School. News of the Granite Seminary program spread. By 1918, seminaries had been established in Brigham City, Mt. Pleasant, American Fork, Lehi, and Blanding in Utah; Mesa, Ariz.; and Star Valley, Wyo. Little did they know that they were part of a historic event that would by the end of the 20th century, reach 144 nations of the world. Today, more than 379,000 youth attend seminary.

Granite Stake is also credited with starting the family home evening program, which was begun by stake Pres. Frank Y. Taylor and, in 1915, adopted Churchwide.

During the Depression of the 1930s, the Church founded Deseret Industries in Salt Lake City, and on Jan. 14, 2000, the system's newest store was opened in Centerville, Utah, making a total of 47 Deseret Industries stores in Utah, Idaho, Nevada, Arizona, California, Washington, and Oregon.

At the beginning of the 20th century, more than half the new stakes being created were in Utah. From 1900 to 1910, 23 stakes were created in the Church with 16 of them in Utah. In 1950, Utah gained 28 new stakes and 46 were created elsewhere. By 1992, about one stake in five was in Utah.

Converts from other nations and states continued to migrate to Utah. Many non-members also came to the state. Utah officially became a mission field with its own headquarters in 1975 when the Utah Salt Lake City Mission was organized. Previously, full-time missionaries worked in parts of Utah under the leadership of missions headquartered in other states. The mission proved to be successful and has been divided twice. Utah's four missions, according to mission leaders, are among the most successful in the United States.

On Oct. 26, 1978, the Missionary Training Center in Provo, previously the Language Training Mission, began training all missionaries.

In the 1970s and 1980s, three other temples were erected and dedicated, in Ogden and Provo in 1972, and South Jordan (Jordan River Temple) in 1981. These were followed by the Bountiful Utah Temple in 1995, and the Mount Timpanogos Utah Temple in American Fork in 1996. In 1997, the Vernal Utah Temple was dedicated, which was the first temple in the Church constructed from an existing building, the Vernal Tabernacle. After the announcement that smaller temples would be built, the first of such temples completed and dedicated was in Monticello, Utah, in the remote southeast corner of state. The temple, the 11th temple in Utah, was dedicated on July 26, 1998, only eight months after ground was broken for the edifice.

Temple Square in Salt Lake City is visited annually by nearly 5 million people and ranks among the top tourist attractions in the nation.

Over the years, the Utah membership supplied the Church with many missionaries and leaders, and has taken a pivotal role in supporting the expansion of the Church.

On Jan. 4, 1996, Utahns celebrated 100 years of statehood with dancing in the streets, parades, speeches, fireworks, and music. "I think it fair to say," said President Gordon B. Hinckley during a special program, "that no other community of citizens worked longer and harder for statehood or were more grateful when it was finally granted."

In 1997, during the celebration of the sesquicentennial of the arrival of the 1847 pioneers, a wagon train re-enacted the original trek. Media coverage of the re-enactment trek reached monumental proportions not only in the United States but also throughout the world, and undoubtedly was the most publicized event in Church history. When the wagon train arrived in Salt Lake City on July 22, some 50,000 people, including all three members of the First Presidency, welcomed the train at This Is the Place monument at the mouth of Emigration Canyon. President Hinckley addressed the huge crowd. Multiple other celebrations were held, including a spectacular celebration at BYU's football stadium and a day of service in communities throughout Utah.

Membership and Church activity continued to increase in Utah in 1998. In 1999, Utah's LDS membership topped 1.6 million in 458 stakes.

On Sept. 11, 1999, President Hinckley spoke to 1,000 people gathered in a remote corner of southwestern Utah and dedicated a monument, memorializing the victims of the Mountain Meadows Massacre. "It is time to leave the entire matter in the hands of God who deals justly in all things," said President Hinckley.

The Beaver Utah Stake, originally organized in 1869 as the seventh stake in pioneer Utah, was divided for the first time on Jan. 31, 2000. It was the oldest stake in the Church that had never been divided.

In October 1999, the last general conference in the Tabernacle on Temple Square was held, ending an era of holding conferences in the famed pioneer building, which dated back to 1867. Six months later, on April 1-2, 2000, the first general conference in the nearly completed 21,000-seat Conference Center, across the street north of Temple Square, was held. Plans for the Conference Center were announced by President Hinckley in general conference in April 1996, and four years later the center was far enough along so that conference could be held in the building. Granite for the exterior of the new center came from the same area in Little Cottonwood Canyon east of Salt Lake City as did the granite for the Salt Lake Temple more than 100 years earlier. The April 2000 general conference was the largest conference gathering in the 170-year history of the Church. The Conference Center was dedicated at the 170th Semiannual General Conference Oct. 8, 2000, by President Hinckley.

Sources: *Utah's Heritage*, by S. George Ellsworth; *Utah's History*, Richard D. Poll, general editor, BYU Press; *Pioneer Companies that Crossed the Plains*, by Melvin S. Bashore; *Encyclopedic History of the Church*, by Andrew Jenson; *Deseret News 1991-1992 Church Almanac*; multiple sources in *Church News* through 1998; "Let the book of the past be closed," by John L. Hart, *Church News*, Sept. 18, 1999; *Church News*, Jan. 23, 1999; "First wards in Utah created 150 years ago," by R. Scott Lloyd, *Church News*, Feb. 6, 1999; *Church News*, Sept. 18, 1999, Jan. 22, 2000, Feb. 12, 2000, April 8, 2000.

Stakes — 469

(Listed alphabetically by area as of Oct. 1, 2000.)

No.	Name	Organized	First President
Utah North Area — 288			
664	Bennion Utah	27 Oct 1974	John Labrum
1459	Bennion Utah East	29 Jan 1984	Jack L. Green
1482	*Bennion Heights Utah 28 Aug 1988		
	‡Bennion Utah Central	17 Jun 1984	Glen Alvin Weight
875	Bennion Utah West	30 Oct 1977	Glenn A. Weight
918	Benson Utah	7 May 1978	Dale Morgan Rindlisbacher
1521	Bluffdale Utah	10 Mar 1985	Michael Van Jeppson
193	*Bountiful Utah		
	‡Bountiful	23 Mar 1952	Thomas Amby Briggs
539	*Bountiful Utah Central		
	‡Bountiful Center	10 Jan 1971	Steven S. Davis
383	*Bountiful Utah East		
	‡Bountiful East	29 Sep 1963	Rendell N. Mabey
546	*Bountiful Utah Heights		
	‡Bountiful Heights	16 May 1971	Jesse Earl Godfrey
1127	Bountiful Utah Mueller Park	27 Apr 1980	Duane Bowring Welling
260	*Bountiful Utah North		
	‡Bountiful North	20 Apr 1958	Henry E. Peterson
1206	Bountiful Utah North Canyon	9 Nov 1980	Robert Heiner Garff
71	*Bountiful Utah Orchard		
	*Davis South 29 May 1970		
	‡South Davis	20 Jun 1915	James H. Robinson
262	*Bountiful Utah South		
	‡Bountiful South	20 Apr 1958	Ward C. Holbrook
1269	Bountiful Utah Stone Creek	24 May 1981	Richard S. Lemon
501	*Bountiful Utah Val Verda		
	‡Val Verda	25 Jan 1970	Milton W. Russon
382	*Brigham City Utah		
	‡Brigham City	22 Sep 1963	Lawrence C. Taylor
148	*Brigham City Utah Box Elder		
	*Box Elder 30 Aug 1959		
	‡South Box Elder	12 Nov 1944	Abel S. Rich
147a	*Brigham City Utah North		
	*Box Elder North 29 May 1970		
	‡North Box Elder	12 Nov 1944	John P. Lillywhite
375	*Brigham City Utah South		
	*Box Elder South	29 May 1970	
	‡South Box Elder	28 Apr 1963	LeGrande Tea
1242	Brigham City Utah West	8 Mar 1981	Lowell Sherratt Jr.
575	*Centerville Utah		
	‡Centerville	21 May 1972	Joseph A. Kjar
1798	Centerville Utah Canyon View	12 May 1991	Bruce Garrett Pitt
1335	Centerville Utah North	11 Apr 1982	Richard C. Edgley
903	Centerville Utah South	9 Apr 1978	Robert A. Trump
277	*Clearfield Utah		
	‡Clearfield	12 Apr 1959	George Smith Haslam
966	Clearfield Utah North	8 Oct 1978	Alfred Clyde Van Wagenen
2308	Clearfield Utah South	9 Feb 1997	Phillip Michael Hardison

728	Clinton Utah	9 Nov 1975	Albert DeMar Mitchell
1467	Clinton Utah North	15 Apr 1984	Jay Barr Snelgrove
18	*Coalville Utah		
	‡Summit	9 Jul 1877	William W. Cluff
142	*Draper Utah		
	‡Mount Jordan	3 May 1942	Stanley A. Rasmussen
2422	Draper Utah Corner Canyon	7 Dec 1997	Brent Reynolds Bonham
2273	Draper Utah Crescent View	17 Nov 1996	Craig Eugene Middleton
1319	*Draper Utah Eastridge 25 Aug 1991		
	‡Draper Utah North	6 Dec 1981	Richard D. Alsop
152	*Farmington Utah		
	‡Davis	14 Oct 1945	Leroy H. Duncan
1342	Farmington Utah North	16 May 1982	Richard J. White
1769	Farmington Utah Oakridge	19 Aug 1990	Jerry L. King
1750	Farmington Utah South	13 May 1990	John Leon Sorenson
1531	Fielding Utah	12 May 1985	Mark H. Jensen
1568	Fruit Heights Utah	27 Oct 1985	Newell John Law
59	*Garland Utah		
	‡Bear River	11 Oct 1908	Milton H. Welling
147	*Grantsville Utah		
	‡Grantsville	16 Jan 1944	Paul E. Wrathall
1069	Grantsville Utah West	23 Sep 1979	Don Henning Johnson
1494	Harrisville Utah	23 Sep 1984	Robert Lynn Nielsen
2486	Herriman Utah	28 Jun 1998	Carmen Ray Freeman
141	*Hooper Utah		
	‡Lakeview	22 Mar 1942	John Child
924	Huntsville Utah	14 May 1978	Marlin K. Jensen
1559	Hyde Park Utah	22 Sep 1985	Vincent Eugene Erickson
46	*Hyrum Utah		
	‡Hyrum	30 Apr 1901	William C. Parkinson
1046	Hyrum Utah North	5 Aug 1979	J. Spencer Ward
106	*Kamas Utah		
	*Summit South 29 May 1970		
	‡South Summit	8 Jul 1934	Zach J. Oblad
1635	Kanesville Utah	19 Apr 1987	Roland B. Hadley
350	*Kaysville Utah		
	‡Kaysville	18 Feb 1962	Alan B. Blood
2101	Kaysville Utah Central	24 Sep 1995	Wesley H. Wilcox
1027	Kaysville Utah Crestwood	13 May 1979	Wallace Eldean Holliday
568	*Kaysville Utah East		
	‡Kaysville East	27 Feb 1972	Lawrence E. Welling
1010	Kaysville Utah South	11 Mar 1979	Newell John Law
255	*Kearns Utah		
	‡Kearns	2 Feb 1958	Merrill A. Nelson
1055	Kearns Utah Central	26 Aug 1979	Garth D. Mecham
990	Kearns Utah East	10 Dec 1978	Earl M. Monson
256	*Kearns Utah North		
	‡Kearns North	2 Feb 1958	Volma W. Heaton
653	Kearns Utah South	25 Aug 1974	Garth D. Mecham
1462	Kearns Utah West	12 Feb 1984	Rodney W. Bushman
1258	Kearns Utah Western Hills	26 Apr 1981	Clarence Myron White
203	*Layton Utah		
	‡Layton	25 Jan 1953	I. Haven Barlow
449	*Layton Utah East		
	‡Layton East	4 Feb 1968	Robert F. Bitner
957	Layton Utah Holmes Creek	3 Sep 1978	K. Roger Bean
2062	Layton Utah Kays Creek	11 Jun 1995	Stephen George Handy
2196	Layton Utah Layton Hills	19 May 1996	S. Clair Bankhead
1529	Layton Utah North	5 May 1985	Lorin Winslow Hurst Jr.
1657	Layton Utah Northridge	11 Oct 1987	Samuel Clair Bankhead
1629	Layton Utah South	8 Feb 1987	William C. Barney Jr.
1948	Layton Utah Valley View	27 Jun 1993	Floyd Stenquist
858	Layton Utah West	21 Aug 1977	William C. Barney Jr.
80	*Logan Utah		
	‡Logan	4 Jun 1920	Oliver H. Budge

13	*Logan Utah Cache		
	‡Cache	21 May 1877	Moses Thatcher
1422	Logan Utah Cache West	22 May 1983	Miles Peter Jensen
1241	Logan Utah Central	8 Mar 1981	Thad August Carlson
164	*Logan Utah East		
	*Cache East 29 May 1970		
	‡East Cache	2 Feb 1947	J. Howard Maughan
160	*Logan Utah Mount Logan		
	‡Mount Logan	17 Nov 1946	A. George Raymond
1347	Logan Utah South	6 Jun 1982	Ronald Skeen Peterson
259	*Logan Utah University 1st		
	‡Utah State University	13 Apr 1958	Reed Bullen
427	*Logan Utah University 2nd		
	‡Utah State University 2nd	12 Feb 1967	Reynold K. Watkins
785	Logan Utah University 3rd	14 Nov 1976	LaGrande C. Larsen
1719	Logan Utah University 4th	7 May 1989	Russell Miles Warren
2069	Logan Utah University 5th	25 Jun 1995	Bartell Cowley Jensen
2488	*Logan Utah University 6th	11 Sep 1998	
	*Logan University 6th	2 Aug 1998	Hyrum Grant Vest Jr.
2519	Logan Utah University 7th	21 Mar 1999	Steven Lee Stowers
90	*Magna Utah		
	‡Oquirrh	3 Jun 1923	George A. Little
1013	Magna Utah Central	8 Apr 1979	Charles Robert Canfield
410	*Magna Utah East		
	‡Oquirrh East	17 Oct 1965	William B. Martin
1510	Magna Utah South	20 Jan 1985	Hendrick Dorenbosch
2416	Mendon Utah	23 Nov 1997	Edwin Hyrum Jenson
246	*Midvale Utah		
	‡Midvale	30 Jun 1957	Reed H. Beckstead
457	*Midvale Utah East		
	*Midvale East 29 May 1970		
	‡East Midvale	5 May 1968	R. Kent King
1561	Midvale Utah North	13 Oct 1985	Grant Leon Pullan
96a	*Midvale Utah Union Fort		
	*Midvale Utah Fort Union		
	*Fort Union 17 Jun 1973		
	*Jordan East 9 May 1970		
	‡East Jordan	8 May 1927	Heber J. Burgon
2509	Midvale Utah Union Park	24 Jan 1999	David D. Cerva
16	*Morgan Utah		
	‡Morgan	1 Jul 1877	Willard G. Smith
1240	Morgan Utah North	8 Mar 1981	Robert Warner Poll
183	*Murray Utah		
	‡Murray	11 Feb 1951	Oral J. Wilkinson
543	*Murray Utah Little Cottonwood	8 Jan 1989	
	*Murray Utah East		
	‡Little Cottonwood	21 Feb 1971	James S. McCloy
1009	Murray Utah North	11 Mar 1979	John Mace Johnson
1849	Murray Utah Parkway	1 Mar 1992	Dan Alan Anderson
240	*Murray Utah South		
	‡Murray South	28 Apr 1957	Donald W. Challis
468	*Murray Utah West		
	‡Murray West	24 Nov 1968	Robert H.M. Killpack
528	*North Logan Utah		
	‡Cache North	11 Oct 1970	Charles L. Hyde
2244	North Logan Utah		
	Green Canyon	22 Sep 1996	Jerry Allen Wilson
146	*North Ogden Utah		
	‡Ben Lomond	21 Nov 1943	William Arthur Budge
956	North Ogden Utah Ben Lomond	27 Aug 1978	Calvin J. Heiner
1804	North Ogden Utah Coldwater	23 Jun 1991	Eugene Jensen Low
2566	North Ogden Utah East	13 Aug 2000	Carl L. Grunander
1016	North Salt Lake Utah	15 Apr 1979	Clare Anderson Jones
1333	*North Salt Lake Utah Parkway	14 Nov 1999	
	‡Woods Cross Utah East	21 Mar 1982	Wayne A. Beers

57	*Ogden Utah		
	‡Ogden	19 Jul 1908	Thomas B. Evans
998	Ogden Utah Burch Creek	4 Feb 1979	J. Kirk Moyes
1133	Ogden Utah Canyon View	18 May 1980	Luan Holly Ferrin
199	*Ogden Utah East		
	*Ogden East 29 May 1970		
	‡East Ogden	23 Nov 1952	Scott B. Price
198	*Ogden Utah Lorin Farr		
	‡Lorin Farr	16 Nov 1952	Elton W. Wardle
140	*Ogden Utah Mound Fort	23 Sep 1984	
	*Ogden Utah Farr West		
	‡Farr West	18 Jan 1942	Wilmer J. Maw
1157	Ogden Utah Mount Lewis	29 Jun 1980	Kenneth J. Alford
87	*Ogden Utah Mount Ogden		
	‡Mount Ogden	21 May 1922	Robert I. Burton
314	*Ogden Utah North		
	‡Ben Lomond South	20 Nov 1960	Robert M. Yorgason
458	*Ogden Utah University Stake	18 Oct 1998	
	*Weber State University Stake	21 Aug 1990	
	*Ogden Utah College		
	‡Weber State College	12 May 1968	E. LaMar Buckner
520a	*Ogden Utah Weber		
	‡Weber	16 Aug 1970	Nathan C. Tanner
272	*Ogden Utah Weber Heights		
	‡Weber Heights	30 Nov 1958	Keith W. Wilcox
58	*Ogden Utah Weber North		
	*Weber North 29 May 1970		
	‡North Weber	19 Jul 1908	James Wotherspoon
1191	*Ogden Utah West 23 Nov 1993		
	‡Ogden Utah Weber South	12 Oct 1980	Allan T. Clarke
1520	Park City Utah	10 Mar 1985	B. Douglas Glad
876	Plain City Utah	30 Oct 1977	Kent W. Calvert
559	*Pleasant View Utah		
	‡Ben Lomond West	21 Nov 1971	Jay Herbert Rhees
561	*Providence Utah		
	‡Providence	12 Dec 1971	Asa L. Beecher
1351	Providence Utah South	13 Jun 1982	Lanny J. Nalder
47	*Richmond Utah		
	‡Benson	1 May 1901	William H. Lewis
201	*Riverdale Utah		
	*Ogden Utah Riverdale 14 Mar 1995		
	‡Riverdale	30 Nov 1952	Rudolph L. VanKampen
303	*Riverton Utah		
	‡Riverton	18 Sep 1960	J. Harold Berrett
2573	Riverton Utah Central	17 Sep 2000	William Charles Mills
2564	Riverton Utah Copperview	25 Jun 2000	Ronald L. Larsen
1067	Riverton Utah North	23 Sep 1979	Keith LeRoy Bergstrom
2262	Riverton Utah South	3 Nov 1996	David Blaine Brown
1843	Riverton Utah Summerhill	19 Jan 1992	L. Chad Campbell
328	*Roy Utah		
	‡Roy	26 Mar 1961	Henry Adolph Matis
1485	Roy Utah Central	24 Jun 1984	Mark Lee Angus
2567	Roy Utah Midland	13 Aug 2000	Grant L. Morgan
438	*Roy Utah North		
	‡Roy North	11 Jun 1967	Walter D. Bingham
1673	Roy Utah South	24 Jan 1988	Alonzo C Heiner
942	Roy Utah West	11 Jun 1978	Lewis R. Child
1a	Salt Lake	3 Oct 1847	John Smith
576	*Salt Lake Big Cottonwood		
	‡Big Cottonwood	28 May 1972	Robert B. Barker
115	*Salt Lake Bonneville		
	‡Bonneville	27 Oct 1935	Joseph L. Wirthlin
603	*Salt Lake Brighton		
	‡Butler South	4 Mar 1973	Alvin Don Nydegger
361	*Salt Lake Butler		

	‡Butler	18 Nov 1962	James C. Taylor
418	*Salt Lake Butler West		
	‡Butler West	8 May 1966	Sherman M. Crump
204	*Salt Lake Cannon		
	‡Cannon	1 Mar 1953	Fred H. Peck
237	*Salt Lake Canyon Rim		
	‡Canyon Rim	28 Oct 1956	Verl F. Scott
291	*Salt Lake Central		
	‡University West	7 Feb 1960	Lemonte Peterson
133	*Salt Lake Cottonwood		
	*Cottonwood 11 Feb 1951		
	‡Big Cottonwood	20 Oct 1940	Irvin T. Nelson
936	Salt Lake Cottonwood Heights	28 May 1978	R. Gordon Porter
1607	Salt Lake Eagle Gate	21 Sep 1986	W. Herbert Klopfer
150	*Salt Lake East Mill Creek		
	‡East Millcreek	17 Jun 1945	L.B. Gunderson
996	Salt Lake East Millcreek North	28 Jan 1979	Joel R. Garrett
129a	*Salt Lake Emigration		
	‡Emigration	10 Mar 1940	George A. Christensen
55	*Salt Lake Ensign		
	‡Ensign	1 Apr 1904	Richard W. Young
249	*Salt Lake Foothill		
	‡Monument Park West	29 Sep 1957	Frank Carl Berg
266	*Salt Lake Granger		
	‡Granger	8 Jun 1958	Wm. Grant Bangerter
491	*Salt Lake Granger East		
	‡Granger East	24 Aug 1969	David D. Lingard
324	*Salt Lake Granger North		
	‡Granger North	26 Feb 1961	Frankland J. Kennard
764	Salt Lake Granger South	22 Aug 1976	Gordon W. Evans
497	*Salt Lake Granger West		
	‡Granger West	4 Jan 1970	Dwayne T. Johnson
42	*Salt Lake Granite		
	‡Granite	28 Jan 1900	Frank Y. Taylor
1457	Salt Lake Granite Park	4 Dec 1983	Robert T. Fitt
92	*Salt Lake Grant		
	‡Grant	25 May 1924	Joseph J. Daynes
114	*Salt Lake Highland		
	‡Highland	8 Sep 1935	Marvin O. Ashton
154	*Salt Lake Hillside		
	‡Hillside	13 Jan 1946	Casper Hugh Parker
227	*Salt Lake Holladay		
	‡Holladay	18 Mar 1956	G. Carlos Smith Jr.
891	Salt Lake Holladay North	12 Feb 1978	John A. Larsen
460	*Salt Lake Holladay South		
	‡Holladay South	16 Jun 1968	Marvin L. Pugh
390	*Salt Lake Hunter		
	‡Hunter	5 Jan 1964	E. Verne Breeze
982	Salt Lake Hunter Central	19 Nov 1978	Evans T. Doxey
1533	Salt Lake Hunter Copperhill	12 May 1985	Stanley Martin Kimball
839	Salt Lake Hunter East	22 May 1977	Merrill Dimick
1539	Salt Lake Hunter South	9 Jun 1985	Morris L. Terry
582	*Salt Lake Hunter West		
	‡Hunter West	13 Aug 1972	Evans T. Doxey
863	Salt Lake Jordan	9 Oct 1977	Robert B. Arnold
162	*Salt Lake Jordan North		
	*Jordan North 29 May 1970		
	‡North Jordan	12 Jan 1947	John D. Hill
53	*Salt Lake Liberty		
	‡Liberty	26 Feb 1904	Hugh J. Cannon
2298	Salt Lake Little Cottonwood	5 Jan 1997	John L. Halverson
68	*Salt Lake Millcreek		
	*Millcreek 11 Feb 1951		
	‡Cottonwood	29 Nov 1914	Uriah G. Miller
187	*Salt Lake Monument Park		

	‡Monument Park	24 Jun 1951	George L. Nelson
1832	Salt Lake Monument Park North	24 Nov 1991	B. Lloyd Poelman
393	*Salt Lake Mount Olympus		
	‡Mount Olympus	12 Apr 1964	Orin R. Woodbury
904	Salt Lake Mount Olympus North	9 Apr 1978	William Schaubel Partridge
267	*Salt Lake Olympus		
	‡Olympus	29 Jun 1958	Heber E. Peterson
145	*Salt Lake Park		
	‡Park	24 Oct 1943	J. Percy Goddard
273	*Salt Lake Parleys		
	‡Parleys	7 Dec 1958	Walter J. Eldredge Jr.
54	*Salt Lake Pioneer		
	‡Pioneer	24 Mar 1904	William McLachlan
130	*Salt Lake Riverside		
	‡Riverside	24 Mar 1940	John B. Matheson
222a	*Salt Lake Rose Park		
	‡Rose Park	9 Oct 1955	Joseph F. Steenblik
412	*Salt Lake Rose Park North		
	‡Rose Park North	28 Nov 1965	Joseph L. Lundstrom
345	*Salt Lake South Cottonwood		
	‡South Cottonwood	10 Dec 1961	James S. McCloy
144	*Salt Lake Sugar House		
	‡Sugar House	16 May 1943	Thomas M. Wheeler
178	*Salt Lake University 1st		
	*University 1st 30 Apr 1967		
	‡University	12 Feb 1950	J. Quayle Ward
433	*Salt Lake University 2nd		
	‡University 2nd	30 Apr 1967	Oscar W. McConkie Jr.
1488	Salt Lake University 3rd	19 Aug 1984	James S. Jardine
1857	Salt Lake University 4th	26 Apr 1992	John C. Pingree
1934	Salt Lake University 5th	18 Apr 1993	Kem C. Gardner
2466	Salt Lake University 6th	17 May 1998	Harold Roger Boyer
236	*Salt Lake Valley View		
	‡Valley View	28 Oct 1956	Lamont B. Gundersen
1928	Salt Lake Utah (Tongan)	28 Mar 1993	Pita Masaku Kinikini
1111	Salt Lake Wasatch	24 Feb 1980	Richard G. Peterson
105	*Salt Lake Wells		
	‡Wells	31 Dec 1933	Thomas E. Towler
182	*Salt Lake Wilford		
	‡Wilford	11 Feb 1951	George Z. Aposhian
274	*Salt Lake Winder		
	‡Winder	25 Jan 1959	M. Elmer Christensen
706	Salt Lake Winder West	21 Sep 1975	Wayne O. Ursenbach
1489	Sandy Utah Alta View	19 Aug 1984	G. Scott Dean
611	*Sandy Utah Canyon View 31 Jul 1990		
	*Sandy Utah North		
	‡Sandy North (Utah)	29 Apr 1973	Eugene D. Tenney
955	Sandy Utah Central	27 Aug 1978	Charles Alma Jones
968	Sandy Utah Cottonwood Creek	15 Oct 1978	John Robert Ruppel
627	*Sandy Utah Crescent		
	‡Crescent Utah	21 Oct 1973	Allen Eugene Hilton
1110	Sandy Utah Crescent North	24 Feb 1980	Gerald Leigh Gunnell
1639	Sandy Utah Crescent Park	17 May 1987	Brad Jensen Sheppard
981	Sandy Utah Crescent South	19 Nov 1978	Marlin Alma Fairborn
775	Sandy Utah Crescent West	24 Oct 1976	John Burton Anderson
365	*Sandy Utah East		
	‡Sandy East	13 Jan 1963	Orren J. Greenwood
972	Sandy Utah Granite	22 Oct 1978	William Stanley Bush
1367	Sandy Utah Granite South	17 Oct 1982	Charles Winston Dahquist II
1612	Sandy Utah Granite View	26 Oct 1986	Alan Snelgrove Layton
1812	Sandy Utah Hidden Valley	25 Aug 1991	Mark James Pendleton
811	Sandy Utah Hillcrest	13 Feb 1977	Arnold Christensen
2339	Sandy Utah Lone Peak	13 Apr 1997	Byron Dale Jorgenson
1278	*Sandy Utah Midvalley 9 Oct 1988		
	‡Midvale Utah Fort Union South	14 Jun 1981	Kenneth William Kraudy

	Union South		
276	*Sandy Utah Mount Jordan 11 Aug 1998		
	*Sandy Utah		
	‡Sandy	12 Apr 1959	Stanley A. Rasmussen
579	*Sandy Utah West		
	‡Sandy West	11 Jun 1972	Reed Neff Brown
623	*Sandy Utah Willow Creek		
	‡Willow Creek	17 Jun 1973	Wayne E. Saunders
119	*Smithfield Utah		
	‡Smithfield	9 Jan 1938	Alfred W. Chambers
1384	Smithfield Utah North	21 Nov 1982	W. Noble Erickson
482	*South Jordan Utah		
	*South Jordan 30 Nov 1970		
	*Jordan South 29 May 1970		
	‡South Jordan	18 May 1969	Theron B. Hutchings
2087	South Jordan Utah Country Park	13 Aug 1995	Calvin H. Newbold
1192	*South Jordan Utah Glenmoor 19 Sep 1993		
	‡South Jordan Utah West	12 Oct 1980	Calvin George Osborne
2532	South Jordan Utah Highland	13 Jun 1999	Roger Glen Christensen
1956	South Jordan Utah Parkway	19 Sep 1993	Roger Glen Christensen
1491	*South Jordan Utah River 18 Dec 1990		
	‡South Jordan Utah East	9 Sep 1984	Charles Elmo Turner
2128	South Jordan Utah River Ridge	19 Nov 1995	William H. Webb
139	*South Ogden Utah		
	‡South Ogden	7 Dec 1941	William J. Critchlow
138	*South Salt Lake 31 May 1979		
	*Salt Lake South		
	‡South Salt Lake	2 Sep 1941	Axel J. Andresen
1705	South Weber Utah	27 Nov 1988	LeRoy Horace Poll
2514	Stansbury Park Utah	21 Feb 1999	Douglas Brent Rose
424	*Sunset Utah		
	‡Sunset	11 Dec 1966	John L. Nicholas
70a	*Syracuse Utah		
	*Davis North 29 May 1970		
	‡North Davis	20 Jun 1915	Henry H. Blood
1858	Syracuse Utah South	26 Apr 1992	Wesley Miller White
2555	Syracuse Utah West	30 Apr 2000	David Lawrence Cook Jr.
217	*Taylorsville Utah		
	‡Taylorsville	10 Oct 1954	Wayne C. Player
598	*Taylorsville Utah Central		
	‡Taylorsville Central	4 Feb 1973	Richard A. Barker
629	Taylorsville Utah North	28 Oct 1973	LeVere Elihu Brady
1473	Taylorsville Utah North Central	13 May 1984	Floyd Keith Rupp
1461	Taylorsville Utah South	5 Feb 1984	Clinton D. Topham
809	*Taylorsville Utah Valley Park 4 Dec 1988		
	‡Taylorsville Utah West Central	6 Feb 1977	Floyd Keith Rupp
411	*Taylorsville Utah West		
	‡Taylorsville West	31 Oct 1965	Richard A. Barker
15	*Tooele Utah		
	‡Tooele	24 Jun 1877	Francis M. Lyman
2536	Tooele Utah East	15 Aug 1999	Kim Albert Halladay
206	*Tooele Utah North		
	*Tooele North 29 May 1970		
	‡North Tooele	29 Mar 1953	Orland T. Barrus
928	Tooele Utah South	21 May 1978	Joel James Dunn
173	*Tremonton Utah		
	*Bear River South 29 May 1970		
	‡South Bear River	1 May 1949	Clifton G.M. Kerr
1004	Tremonton Utah South	25 Feb 1979	Boyd Lee Cullimore
371	*Washington Terrace Utah		
	‡Washington Terrace	24 Feb 1963	Ernest B. Wheeler
798	*Washington Terrace Utah South 3 Dec 1996		
	Ogden Utah Terrace View	12 Dec 1976	Leo Neeley Harris
1043	Wellsville Utah	17 Jun 1979	Donald Joseph Jeppesen Jr.

578	*West Bountiful Utah 9 Oct 1984		
	*Bountiful Utah West		
	‡Bountiful West	11 Jun 1972	Clarence D. Samuelson
97	*West Jordan Utah		
	‡West Jordan	8 May 1927	Joseph M. Holt
1511	*West Jordan Utah Bingham Creek	29 Nov 1988	
	‡West Jordan Utah Southeast	27 Jan 1985	Frederick James Haydock
2475	West Jordan Utah Copper Hills	7 Jun 1998	David Russell Murray
735	West Jordan Utah East	30 Nov 1975	Dale P. Bateman
929	*West Jordan Utah Heritage	9 Oct 1990	
	‡West Jordan Utah West	21 May 1978	Robert B. Rowley
2155	West Jordan Utah Jordan Oaks	14 Jan 1996	Jerrald M. Jensen
1099	*West Jordan Utah Mountain Shadows 6 Dec 1994		
	‡West Jordan Utah Central	27 Jan 1980	M. Curtis Jewkes
614	*West Jordan Utah Mountain View	21 Feb 1989	
	*West Jordan Utah South		
	‡Jordan River	20 May 1973	Max Curtis Jewkes
1311	West Jordan Utah Oquirrh	22 Nov 1981	Johannes Gerald Erkelens
1686	West Jordan Utah Prairie	7 Feb 1988	J. Kim Christensen
1443	West Jordan Utah River	18 Sep 1983	Dennis Arthur Hope
2496	West Jordan Utah River Oaks	20 Sep 1998	Martin Dean Hill
1509	West Jordan Utah Welby	20 Jan 1985	Russell Jean Abney
1512	*West Jordan Utah Westbrook 16 May 1989		
	‡West Jordan Utah North	3 Feb 1985	Henry Keonaona Chai II
2557	West Jordan Utah Westland	21 May 2000	Stephen Brown Allen
1128	West Point Utah	27 Apr 1980	Vern L. Thurgood
636	*West Valley Utah	17 Jan 1989	
	‡Salt Lake Granger Central	31 Mar 1974	Norman H. Bangerter
1506	Willard Utah	25 Nov 1984	Robert Kent Lund
498	*Woods Cross Utah		
	‡Woods Cross	4 Jan 1970	D. Hatch Howard

Stakes discontinued

20	Box Elder	19 Aug 1877	Oliver G. Snow
	Discontinued 12 Nov 1944		
	†North Box Elder (147), South Box Elder (148)		
14	Davis	17 Jun 1877	William R. Smith
	Discontinued 20 Jun 1915 †North Davis (70), South Davis (71)		
41	Jordan	21 Jan 1900	Orrin P. Miller
	Discontinued 8 May 1927 †East Jordan (96), West Jordan (97)		
275	*Salt Lake Granite Park		
	Discontinued 31 May 1979 †South Salt Lake (138)		
	‡Granite Park	22 Feb 1959	Rolf Christiansen
155	*Salt Lake Temple View		
	Discontinued 24 June 1979 †Salt Lake Wells (105), Salt Lake Liberty (53)		
	*Temple View 14 Apr 1946		
	‡Temple	13 Jan 1946	Adiel F. Stewart
2b	Weber	26 Jan 1851	Lorin Farr
	Discontinued 14 Jun 1970 †Mount Ogden (87)		

Utah South Area — 181

44	*Alpine Utah		
	‡Alpine	13 Jan 1901	Stephen L. Chipman
2206	Alpine Utah North	23 Jun 1996	Terry L. Brown
1526	Altamont Utah	21 Apr 1985	Everett Dee Roberts
376	*American Fork Utah		
	‡American Fork	12 May 1963	Stanley D. Roberts
2042	American Fork Utah Central	23 Apr 1995	Paul Joseph Rasband
1022	American Fork Utah East	29 Apr 1979	Dale Orville Gunther
2154	American Fork Utah Hillcrest	14 Jan 1996	Craig B. Terry
624	*American Fork Utah North		
	‡American Fork North	17 Jun 1973	Leland Forbes Priday
1218	American Fork Utah West	14 Dec 1980	Brent Lindsay Milne
7b	*Beaver Utah		
	‡Beaver	12 Mar 1869	John R. Murdock
897	Blanding Utah	5 Mar 1978	Fred Eugene Halliday

1283	Blanding Utah West	12 Jul 1981	Preston Gardner Nielson
1690	Bloomington Utah	6 Mar 1988	Steven Howard Peterson
225	*Brigham Young University 1st		
	‡Brigham Young University	8 Jan 1956	Antone K. Romney
295	Brigham Young University 2nd	17 Apr 1960	Bryan W. Belnap
296	Brigham Young University 3rd	17 Apr 1960	William Noble Waite
395	Brigham Young University 4th	3 May 1964	William R. Siddoway
396	Brigham Young University 5th	3 May 1964	A. Harold Goodman
397	Brigham Young University 6th	3 May 1964	Wayne B. Hales
431	Brigham Young University 7th	30 Apr 1967	Dean A. Peterson
432	Brigham Young University 8th	30 Apr 1967	David H. Yarn
478	Brigham Young University 9th	27 Apr 1969	Carl D. Jones
479	Brigham Young University 10th	27 Apr 1969	Ivan J. Barrett
688	Brigham Young University 11th	13 Apr 1975	Gregory E. Austin
689	Brigham Young University 12th	13 Apr 1975	Charles Verl Clark
973	Brigham Young University 13th	29 Oct 1978	Leo Preston Vernon
974	Brigham Young University 14th	29 Oct 1978	Curtis Nicholas VanAlfen
1605	Brigham Young University 15th	31 Aug 1986	H. Donl Peterson
1688	Brigham Young University 16th	21 Feb 1988	Donald J Butler
1722	Brigham Young University 17th	21 May 1989	Stanley Armond Taylor
1889	Brigham Young University 18th	28 Jun 1992	Clark D. Webb Jr.
2489	Brigham Young University 19th	9 Aug 1998	Thomas Edwin Myers
2535	Brigham Young University 20th	15 Aug 1999	Ed Jolley Pinegar
2543	Brigham Young University 21st	6 Feb 2000	James M. Harper
23	*Castle Dale Utah		
	‡Emery	Aug 1880	Christen G. Larsen
413	*Cedar City University 1st	30 Apr 1995	
	*Southern Utah University	13 Dec 1990	
	*Cedar City Utah College		
	*Southern Utah State College	12 Oct 1969	
	‡College of Southern Utah	6 Jan 1966	Robert B. White Jr.
2045	Cedar City University 2nd	30 Apr 1995	Warren Morrill Woolsey
2520	Cedar City University 3rd	21 Mar 1999	Russell Grant Bulloch
172	*Cedar City Utah		
	‡Cedar	2 May 1948	David L. Sargent
2170	Cedar City Utah Canyon View	18 Feb 1996	Robert Browning Platt
901	Cedar City Utah North	19 Mar 1978	Robert L. Blattner
316	*Cedar City Utah West		
	‡Cedar West	27 Nov 1960	Franklin D. Day
65	*Delta Utah		
	‡Deseret	11 Aug 1912	Alonzo A. Hinckley
1068	Delta Utah West	23 Sep 1979	Glen Wilford Swalberg
62	*Duchesne Utah		
	‡Duchesne	14 Sep 1910	William H. Smart
2546	Eagle Mountain Utah	27 Feb 2000	Carl B. Faulkner
1564	Enoch Utah	20 Oct 1985	Robert Louis Blattner
134	*Enterprise Utah		
	‡Uvada (Utah, Nevada)	15 Dec 1940	David J. Ronnow
1524	Ephraim Utah	24 Mar 1985	Joseph C. Nielsen
1525	*Ephraim Utah College 1st	25 Jun 1999	
	*Snow College Utah 1st	28 Apr 1996	
	‡Snow College Utah	24 Mar 1985	Allen P. Jacobson
2193	*Ephraim Utah College 2nd	25 Jun 1999	
	Snow College Utah 2nd	28 Apr 1996	Richard Wheeler
83	*Escalante Utah		
	‡Garfield	29 Aug 1920	Charles E. Rowan Jr.
1336	Ferron Utah	11 Apr 1982	Jerry D Mangum
6b	*Fillmore Utah		
	‡Millard	9 Mar 1869	Thomas Callister
2523	Goshen Utah	18 Apr 1999	David Byron Allen
89	*Gunnison Utah		
	‡Gunnison	6 May 1923	Allen E. Park
19	*Heber City Utah		
	‡Wasatch	15 Jul 1877	Abraham Hatch

649	Heber City Utah East	16 Jun 1974	Robert F. Clyde
1170	Helper Utah	24 Aug 1980	Robert E. Olsen
1167	Highland Utah	10 Aug 1980	Merlin B. Larson
1827	Highland Utah East	10 Nov 1991	Stephen Mark Studdert
871	Huntington Utah	23 Oct 1977	Ira Wallace Hatch
104	*Hurricane Utah		
	‡Zion Park	8 Dec 1929	Claudius Hirschi
2180	Hurricane Utah West	10 Mar 1996	Scott W. Colton
2165	Ivins Utah	11 Feb 1996	Bruce Lynn Gubler
11	*Kanab Utah		
	‡Kanab (Utah, Arizona)	18 Apr 1877	L. John Nuttall
1638	*Kanab Utah Kaibab 20 Aug 1991		
	‡Kanab Utah South	3 May 1987	Nils G. Bayles
1294	*La Verkin Utah 30 Nov 1984		
	‡Hurricane Utah North	11 Oct 1981	Floyd Leon Lewis
100	*Lehi Utah		
	‡Lehi	1 Jul 1928	Anchor C. Schow
2556	Lehi Utah East	7 May 2000	Douglas C. Muir
637	Lehi Utah North	5 May 1974	Francis Russell Hakes
2169	Lehi Utah South	18 Feb 1996	James Earl Smith
1416	Lehi Utah West	8 May 1983	Boyd Sabey Stewart
1392	Lindon Utah	12 Dec 1982	Noel Thomas Greenwood
2091	Lindon Utah West	20 Aug 1995	James La Verle Hacking
34	*Loa Utah		
	‡Wayne	27 May 1893	Willis E. Robison
43	*Manti Utah		
	*Sanpete South 29 May 1970		
	‡South Sanpete	9 Dec 1900	Canute Peterson
714	Mapleton Utah	19 Oct 1975	Jay M. Smith Jr.
2371	Mapleton Utah North	8 Jun 1997	Kenneth Harold Jones
1407	Midway Utah	27 Mar 1983	Wayne Watkins Probst
2543	Milford Utah	30 Jan 2000	Gary M. Jensen
553	*Moab Utah		
	‡Moab	19 Sep 1971	Leland D. Teeples
85	*Monroe Utah		
	*Sevier South	29 May 1970	
	‡South Sevier	30 Jan 1921	John E. Magleby
27	*Monticello Utah		
	‡San Juan (Utah, Colorado)	23 Sep 1883	Platte D. Lyman
102	*Moroni Utah		
	‡Moroni	16 Jun 1929	James Louis Nielsen
42a	*Mount Pleasant Utah		
	*Sanpete North 29 May 1970		
	‡North Sanpete	9 Dec 1900	Christian N. Lund
2330	Mount Pleasant Utah North	16 Mar 1997	Warren Lynn Benincosa
5b	*Nephi Utah		
	*Juab 1871		
	‡Nephi	20 Sep 1868	Jacob G. Bigler
1538	Nephi Utah North	9 Jun 1985	James Randy McKnight
166	Orem Utah		
	‡Orem	13 Apr 1947	Walter R. Holdaway
1668	Orem Utah Aspen	10 Jan 1988	Ross Steve Wolfley
1518	*Orem Utah Canyon View	1 Mar 1988	
	‡Orem Utah Northeast	3 Mar 1985	Jerry C. Washburn
2230	Orem Utah Cascade	8 Sep 1996	Richard Bryant Brady
271	*Orem Utah Cherry Hill	15 Apr 1988	
	*Orem Utah Sharon West		
	*Sharon West	29 May 1970	
	‡West Sharon	30 Nov 1958	Clyde M. Lunceford
1490	*Orem Utah College	25 Jun 1999	
	*Orem Utah Student	8 Jan 1991	
	Orem Utah College	26 Aug 1984	Charles E. Peterson
751	Orem Utah East	21 Mar 1976	Mirl Blake Hymas

251	*Orem Utah Geneva Heights	5 Apr 1988	
	*Orem Utah West		
	‡Orem West	3 Nov 1957	Edward C. Bunker
2272	Orem Utah Heatheridge	17 Nov 1996	Wayne Thomas Watson
1581	*Orem Utah Hillcrest	27 Nov 1988	
	‡Orem Utah Sharon South	1 Dec 1985	Wynn Howard Hemmert
867	*Orem Utah Lakeridge	1 Mar 1988	
	‡Orem Utah South Central	16 Oct 1977	Gordon Max Thomas
2204	Orem Utah Lakeridge North	23 Jun 1996	Spencer Floyd Mack
1184	Orem Utah Lakeview	28 Sep 1980	Merrill Gappmayer
533	*Orem Utah North		
	‡Orem North	1 Nov 1970	Eli Karl Clayson
1682	Orem Utah Northridge	31 Jan 1988	Larry V. Perkins
1176	Orem Utah Park	7 Sep 1980	Richard S. Johns
103	*Orem Utah Sharon		
	‡Sharon	15 Sep 1929	Arthur V. Watkins
812	*Orem Utah Sharon Park 20 Dec 1988		
	‡Orem Utah Central	13 Feb 1977	Clifton M. Pyne
862	*Orem Utah Suncrest 1 Mar 1988		
	‡Utah West Central	18 Sep 1977	James Edwin Mangum
554	*Orem Utah Sunset Heights 19 Apr 1988		
	*Orem Utah South		
	‡Orem South	19 Sep 1971	Richard P. Shumway
1048	Orem Utah Timpview	12 Aug 1979	Carl Crawford
905	Orem Utah Windsor	9 Apr 1978	Dennis LeRoy Hill
12	*Panguitch Utah		
	‡Panguitch	23 Apr 1877	James Henrie
5a	*Parowan Utah		
	‡Parowan	May 1852	John C.L. Smith
	13 Jan 1901	Jonathan S. Page Jr.	
45	*Payson Utah	25 Mar 1997	
	*Payson Utah	Nebo 18 Mar 1997	
	‡Nebo	13 Jan 1901	Jonathan S. Page Jr.
634	*Payson Utah Mountain View 9 Aug 1994		
	‡Payson Utah East	24 Mar 1974	David R. Mangelson
1297	*Payson Utah South	25 Mar 1997	
	*Payson Utah Mount Loafer	18 Mar 1997	
	‡Payson Utah South	18 Oct 1981	Joe Lynn Spencer
1310	*Payson Utah West	25 Mar 1997	
	*Payson Utah Spring Creek 18 Mar 1997		
	‡Payson Utah West	22 Nov 1981	Gerald M. Finch
529	*Pleasant Grove Utah		
	‡Pleasant Grove	11 Oct 1970	Leon R. Walker
894	Pleasant Grove Utah East	26 Feb 1978	Evan Mack Palmer
2551	Pleasant Grove Utah Garden	9 Apr 2000	Rex Lewis Barrington
1958	Pleasant Grove Utah		
	Grove Creek	24 Oct 1993	David Wesley Dickerson
1124	Pleasant Grove Utah Manila	23 Mar 1980	Grant Kay Fugal
2426	Pleasant Grove Utah North Field	11 Jan 1998	Daniel Boyd Fugal
101	*Pleasant Grove Utah Timpanogos		
	‡Timpanogos	1 Jul 1928	Wilford W. Warnick
61	*Price Utah		
	‡Carbon	8 May 1910	Gustave A. Iverson
2247	Price Utah College	13 Oct 1996	Michael A. Harrison
151	*Price Utah North		
	*Carbon North 29 May 1970		
	‡North Carbon	24 Jun 1945	Cecil Broadbent
127	*Provo Utah		
	‡Provo	19 Feb 1939	Charles E. Rowan Jr.
1437	Provo Utah Bonneville	28 Aug 1983	Norman Dean Anderson
3b	*Provo Utah Central		
	*Utah 1855		
	‡Provo	19 Mar 1851	Isaac Higbee

165	*Provo Utah East		
	*Provo East 29 May 1970		
	‡East Provo	13 Apr 1947	Charles E. Rowan
541	*Provo Utah Edgemont		
	‡Edgemont	17 Jan 1971	Richard A. Call
1692	Provo Utah Edgemont North	20 Mar 1988	Clayton S. Huber
899	Provo Utah Edgemont South	19 Mar 1978	Keith Hale Hoopes
1209	Provo Utah Grandview	23 Nov 1980	Laren R. Robison
2271	Provo Utah Grandview East	17 Nov 1996	John Melvin Beck Jr.
547	Provo Utah Grandview South	13 June 2000	
	*Provo Utah North		
	‡Provo North	30 May 1971	Wayne Alvin Mineer
2187	Provo Utah North Park	21 Apr 1996	Brent A. Gines
821	Provo Utah Oak Hills	10 Apr 1977	John R. Christiansen
200	*Provo Utah Sharon East		
	*Sharon East 29 May 1970		
	‡East Sharon	23 Nov 1952	Henry D. Taylor
1090	Provo Utah South	2 Dec 1979	Moorlan Wayne Snow
1424	Provo Utah Sunset	29 May 1983	Glen Howard Snyder
167	*Provo Utah West		
	*Utah West 29 May 1970		
	‡West Utah	4 May 1947	J. Earl Lewis
10a	*Richfield Utah		
	‡Sevier	24 May 1874	Joseph A. Young
848	Richfield Utah East	12 Jun 1977	Warren T. Harward
82	*Roosevelt Utah		
	‡Roosevelt	26 Jun 1920	William H. Smart
1458	Roosevelt Utah East	11 Dec 1983	Earl V. Allred
685	Roosevelt Utah West	2 Mar 1975	Alvin Leonard Bellon
9a	*St. George Utah		
	‡Saint George (Utah, Arizona)	7 Nov 1869	Joseph W. Young
1623	*St. George Utah		
	Bloomington Hills	20 Nov 1994	
	Bloomington Hills Utah	4 Jan 1987	James Grey Larkin
759	*Saint George Utah College 1st	25 June 1998	
	‡St. George Utah College	30 May 1976	Peter A. Nyberg
2492	Saint George Utah College 2nd	16 Aug 1998	Charles Jeffrey Morby
322	*St. George Utah East		
	‡St. George East	5 Feb 1961	Rudger C. Atkin
1813	St. George Utah Green Valley	25 Aug 1991	La Rell David Muir
1999	St. George Utah Morningside	20 Nov 1994	James Grey Larkin
1625	*St. George Utah Pine View 12 Dec 1989		
	‡Washington Utah West	18 Jan 1987	H. Carlyle Stirling
1814	*St. George Utah Snow Canyon	9 Mar 1999	
	St. George Utah Dixie Downs	25 Aug 1991	Thomas Randy Judd
895	St. George Utah West	5 Mar 1978	Dale Gubler
686	*Salem Utah 8 Dec 1976		
	‡Spanish Fork Utah Salem	9 Mar 1975	Kent Blaine Hansen
2565	St. George Utah		
	Washington Fields	25 Jun 2000	Terry L. Wade
2205	Salem Utah West	23 Jun 1996	Stanley W. Green
84	*Salina Utah		
	*Sevier North 29 May 1970		
	‡North Sevier	30 Jan 1921	Moroni Lazenby
1361	Santa Clara Utah	29 Aug 1982	Dale Gubler
74	*Santaquin Utah		
	*Santaquin-Tintic 2 Apr 1939		
	‡Tintic	22 Apr 1917	Erastus Franklin Birch
233	*Spanish Fork Utah		
	‡Spanish Fork	30 Sep 1956	Joseph Y. Toronto

2179	Spanish Fork Utah East	10 Mar 1996	Allen Dredge Ward
94	*Spanish Fork Utah Palmyra		
	‡Palmyra	23 Nov 1924	Henry A. Gardner
1115	Spanish Fork Utah South	9 Mar 1980	Wilbur Angus Stephenson
900	Spanish Fork Utah West	19 Mar 1978	Clair O. Anderson
235	*Springville Utah		
	‡Springville	21 Oct 1956	Leo A. Crandall
1483	Springville Utah Hobble Creek	17 Jun 1984	Donald Blaine Hadley
93	*Springville Utah Kolob		
	‡Kolob	23 Nov 1924	George R. Maycock
705	*Springville Utah Spring Creek	21 Jun 1988	
	‡Springville Utah North	31 Aug 1975	F. Calvin Packard
2311	Springville Utah Spring Creek South	23 Feb 1997	Don D. Bloxham
239	*Vernal Utah Ashley		
	‡Ashley	2 Dec 1956	William Budge Wallis
1434	Vernal Utah Glines	19 Jun 1983	Gayle F. McKeachnie
913	Vernal Utah Maeser	30 Apr 1978	Venil P. Johnson
30	*Vernal Utah Uintah 10 Jun 1986		
	*Vernal Utah		
	‡Uintah	11 Jul 1886	Samuel R. Bennion
991	Washington Utah	7 Jan 1979	Lorel Wynn Turek
2368	Washington Utah Buena Vista	1 Jun 1997	Leo G.Richardson
1193	Wellington Utah	12 Oct 1980	Charles V. Bradshaw

Stakes discontinued

122	Moon Lake	24 Apr 1938	Edwin L. Murphy
	Discontinued 10 Nov 1957 †Duchesne (62)		
17	Sanpete	4 Jul 1877	Canute Peterson
	Discontinued 9 Dec 1900 †North Sanpete (42), South Sanpete (43)		

Missions — 6

(As of Oct. 1, 2000; shown with historical number. See MISSIONS.)

(132) UTAH OGDEN MISSION
2133 Washington Blvd
Ogden, UT 84401

(222) UTAH PROVO MISSION
2500 N. University Ave., Ste.100
Provo, UT 84604

(187) UTAH SALT LAKE CITY MISSION
2120 S. 1300 E., Ste. 102
Salt Lake City, UT 84106

(331) UTAH SALT LAKE CITY SOUTH MISSION
7001 S. 900 E., Ste. 250
Midvale, UT 84047-1746

(304) UTAH SLC TEMPLE SQUARE MISSION
50 W. North Temple St.
Salt Lake City, UT 84150-1006

MISSIONARY TRAINING CENTER
2005 North 900 East
Provo, UT 84604

Vermont

Year-end 1999: Est. population, 594,000; Members, 3,759; Stakes, 1; Wards, 6; Branches, 6; Percent LDS, 0.6, or one in 156.

The Prophet Joseph Smith was born in Sharon, Vt., on Dec. 23, 1805. Other prominent leaders born in this state include Brigham Young, Oliver Cowdery, Heber C. Kimball, and Erastus Snow. In all, about a dozen of the early Church leaders were born in Vermont.

Jared Carter was the first to preach the restored gospel in Vermont. He arrived in Benson, Rutland County, Vt., about Oct. 25, 1831, and after preaching, baptized 27 converts. Elders Orson Pratt and Lyman E. Johnson are believed to have preached in Vermont in early 1832. Other missionaries followed, and most of the newly baptized members remained faithful, migrating to be with the body of the Saints in 1833.

By 1835, branches were organized in St. Johnsbury, Danville, Charleston, Andover, and Benson. Additional branches were organized in Irasburg in 1836, Addison in 1840, and Woodstock in 1843. Elders Erastus Snow and William Hyde were laboring in Woodstock in 1844 when they heard of the martyrdom of the Prophet Joseph Smith.

Members of these branches dispersed in large numbers to join the westward movement of the Saints, and missionary work did not resume until many years later. Membership in the mostly rural state, which is the second least populated in the United States, has remained sparse. In 1905, the Church purchased the Joseph Smith birthplace in Vermont, and on Dec. 23, 1905, the centennial of the Prophet's birth, a 100-ton granite shaft 38 feet 6 inches (one foot for each year of the Prophet's life) high, was dedicated at the site by President Joseph F. Smith. Community members supported the construction and the dedication was well-attended. The monument has been a frequent site for missionary conferences through the years.

The Eastern States Mission, which was discontinued in 1869, reopened in 1893. The Vermont Conference was organized in 1909, though no branches were organized. In 1916, 30 people attended a conference at Barre. The Morrisville Branch was in existence by 1924. In 1927, Vermont was transferred to the Canadian Mission, which had been organized in 1919. In 1930, a small branch was functioning at Burlington, organized in 1927 or after. Responsibility for the state was placed with the New England Mission when it was created in 1937. Its first conference was held at the Joseph Smith Monument in July 1938 with 60 missionaries in attendance. Beginning in 1987, lights were placed around the Joseph Smith Monument during the Christmas season, attracting thousands of visitors. About 70,000 visitors, including those at Christmastime, come to the site annually.

The majority of the state's LDS live in the Montpelier area, where the the state's first and only stake, the Montpelier Vermont Stake, was created, April 11, 1976, with a membership of 2,116 members (two of its wards were in New Hampshire). In 1980, statewide membership was 2,196 and had increased to 2,758 by 1990.

Church membership today is composed almost entirely of converts, and a large percentage of them are natives of Vermont. The birthplace of Joseph Smith has become a spiritual center for members here. "Camp Joseph" has been constructed at the birthplace of the Prophet where groups can stay in cabins when they come to visit. During the sesquicentennial of the Mormon pioneers in 1997, members re-enacted a handcart trek, starting at the Joseph Smith Monument, and traveling for three days while wearing authentic pioneer clothing.

Few, however, visit the birthplace of Brigham Young, located at Whitingham in a remote corner of southern Vermont. A 12-foot granite monument, dedicated by President George Albert Smith in 1950, and a small display in a local museum memorialize the place where the great colonizer was born.

Vermont's LDS population was 3,759 in 1999.

Sources: "Proceedings at the Dedication of the Joseph Smith Memorial Monument," distributed at the dedication Dec. 23, 1905; *Encyclopedic History of the Church,* by Andrew Jenson; "The Benson Exodus of 1833: Mormon Converts and the Westward Movement," by Erik Barnouw, Summer, 1986, *Vermont Journal History;* "Gospel Brothers," by James L. Kimball, *Church News,* March 11, 1978; "Yankee Saints: The Church in New England during the Twentieth Century," by Richard O. Cowan, 1988, "Members reflect spirit of pioneers in state rich in Church history," by Sheridan R. Sheffield, *Church News,* Dec. 21, 1991; *Regional Studies in Latter-day Saint History,* BYU; *Church News,* Dec. 18, 1993, July 26, 1997, July 25, 1998; "Brigham Young's birthplace," by Dell Van Orden, *Church News,* Sept. 5, 1998.

Stake — 1

(Listed alphabetically as of Oct. 1, 2000.)

No.	Name	Organized	First President
	North America Northeast Area		
753	Montpelier Vermont	11 Apr 1976	C. Lynn Fife

Virginia

Year-end 1999: Est. population, 6,873,000; Members, 66,622; Stakes, 17; Wards, 109; Branches, 32; Missions, 1; Percent LDS, 0.9, or one in 106.

In 1837, Jedediah M. Grant preached where no Mormon elder had preached before, in Patrick County, Va., establishing a small branch there. In 1838, Elder George A. Smith preached in Montgomery County and realized some success. Francis Gladden Bishop labored in various locations in Virginia from 1838-39 and baptized many converts. Other missionaries also worked in Wythe and Nelson counties.

Elder Grant returned to Virginia in 1840 and preached successfully in Smyth, Washington, and Tazewell counties. He was in high demand as a preacher and had three invitations for every one he could fill. He frequently read Joseph Smith's prophecy of the Civil War. His listeners gave him a horse, clothing, and funds to assist him in preaching in more locations.

Elder Grant was later joined by his brother Joshua in the work, and in 1841 it was reported that there were 80 members in the state, including a branch of 25 in Rich Valley, Smyth County. After the Grant brothers left in 1842, Elder R.H. Kinnamon traveled to nine counties and baptized more than 100 persons. Prominent Southern States missionary and mission president, Henry G. Boyle, was among those converted from Tazewell County. He preached in his home state in 1844-45 and baptized a number of converts.

Work progressed well until the martyrdom of the Prophet Joseph Smith, when some elders returned to Nauvoo, Ill. Membership at the time was probably in excess of 350. Most of these faithful early members migrated west.

Missionary work resumed with some success in 1870. In 1879, when Elders Mathias F. Cowley and Frank A. Benson preached in Tazewell, Bland, and Smyth counties. They baptized a few children and grandchildren of those who first heard the gospel preached by Elder Grant. Some of these people recalled the prophecy of the Civil War that was fulfilled 30 years after it was given.

In 1886, the Virginia Conference was divided and the West Virginia Conference was created. In 1902, Virginia was briefly placed in the Middle States Mission until the next year when it was returned to the Southern States Mission.

By 1919, branches existed in Danville, Petersburg, Portsmouth, and Richmond. In 1929, the state was transferred to the East Central States Mission. In 1930, the Virginia Conference had a membership of 2,267 in the Danville, Norfolk, Richmond, and Roanoke branches, and Sunday Schools in Mt. Lake, Petersburg, Portsmouth, Scholfield, Vinton, and Oilville. The Virginia East District was created in 1944. The Virginia Stake, the first in the stake, was created June 30, 1957, with about 1,600 members in the Dutch Gap, Petersburg, Newport News, Norfolk, Richmond, and Portsmouth wards, and the Franklin Branch

In 1977, members of the Church were involved in an anti-pornography effort that resulted in the removal of all sexually explicit magazines from juvenile access in Fairfax County in the Washington, D.C. area.

Commemorating the 500th anniversary of Columbus' voyage to the Americas, the Mormon Tabernacle Choir performed in the Mosque Theater in Richmond, July 20, 1992. The Virginia Richmond Mission was created in 1992, an outgrowth of the old Central Atlantic States Mission that was created in 1947.

The increasing numbers of members in the state was evident May 3, 1997, when President Gordon B. Hinckley spoke at a conference of the Potomac Virginia Region, attended by some 13,500 members. An annual western-style barbecue and picnic for ambassadors is held each year at the Mariott Ranch in rural Hume, Va., and has become increasingly popular among Washington's diplomatic corp. (See District of Columbia history.)

In 1998, members of the Waynesboro Virginia Stake distributed nearly 300 copies of the Church's Proclamation on the Family to people from all walks of life in an effort to promote the Church and strengthen families.

Through the years, missionary work and an influx of members working in military and industrial fields have accounted for increased membership in the state, which by 1999 had reached 66,622. Growth has also come as members have assumed roles in governmental agencies headquartered in nearby Washington, D.C.

Sources: *Encyclopedic History of the Church,* by Andrew Jenson; Southern States Mission, manuscript history; *Church News,* July 6, 1957; *History of the Southern States Mission,* a BYU thesis by LaMar C. Barrett, July 1960; *Church News,* Jan. 14, 1978; "Church blossoms where history's roots run deep," by Mike Cannon, *Church News,* April 21, 1990; "Choir launches tour in historic Virginia," by Gerry Avant, *Church News,* July 25, 1992; *Church News,* May 3, 1997, *Church News,* Oct. 25, 1997, Jan. 16, 1999.

Stakes — 17

(Listed alphabetically as of Oct. 1, 2000.)

No.	Name	Organized	First President

North America East Area

512	*Annandale Virginia ‡Mount Vernon	26 Apr 1970	Allen Claire Rozsa
2530	Buena Vista Virginia	6 Jun 1999	Edwin Allen Sexton
740	*Centreville Virginia ‡Fairfax Virginia	29 Jan 1995 1 Feb 1976	Ed Mordue Hayward
1671	Chesapeake Virginia	17 Jan 1988	Joseph Craig Merrell
1198	Fredericksburg Virginia	26 Oct 1980	Douglas Lynn Marker
1325	McLean Virginia	14 Feb 1982	Earl John Roueche
1583	Mount Vernon Virginia	5 Jan 1986	Keith Alan Gulledge
846	Newport News Virginia	12 Jun 1977	Kirk Thomas Waldron
372	*Oakton Virginia ‡Potomac (Virginia, D.C., Md.)	3 Mar 1963	Miller F. Shurtleff
922	Pembroke Virginia *New River Virginia 24 Oct 1989 *Bluefield Virginia	6 Jun 1999 14 May 1978	Norman Perry Tyler Jr.
245	*Richmond Virginia ‡Virginia (Va., N. C.)	30 Jun 1957	Cashell Donahoe Sr.
1450	Richmond Virginia Chesterfield	30 Oct 1983	John Leonard Ruckart Jr.
499	*Roanoke Virginia ‡Roanoke	11 Jan 1970	Russell B. Maddock
392	*Virginia Beach Virginia 21 Jun 1994 *Norfolk Virginia ‡Norfolk (Virginia, North Carolina)	12 Apr 1964	Walter H. Hick
2018	Warrenton Virginia	29 Jan 1995	Richard L. Brown
934	*Waynesboro Virginia 16 Dec 1982 ‡Charlottesville Virginia	28 May 1978	Wilford John Teerlink
837	Winchester Virginia	22 May 1977	Harold S. Harrison

Mission — 1

(As of Oct. 1, 2000; shown with historical number. See MISSIONS. Washington D.C. missions, though headquarters are located in Virginia and Maryland, are listed under District of Columbia.)

(42) VIRGINIA RICHMOND MISSION
9327 Midlothian Tpk, Suite 1-B
Richmond, VA 23235

Washington

Year-end 1999: Est. population, 5,756,000; Members, 226,411; Stakes, 53; Wards, 425; Branches, 45; Missions, 3; Temples, 2 (1 announced); Percent LDS, 4.0, or one in 25.

In 1854, four missionaries serving in California, Elders John Hughes, Clark Faben, Alfred Bybee, and Silas Harris, were sent to labor in the Washington and Oregon territories. Elder Hughes converted enough people to start a branch on the Lewis River, near Portland and the Oregon border, but generally a spirit of intense persecution impeded the work.

One early convert who remained in Washington despite persecution was Louisa A. Johns Bozarth. She was faithful throughout her life. When she died in 1911, animosity against the Church was still so pronounced that her grave was dedicated secretly at night.

Many Mormons worked on the construction of the Northern Pacific and Oregon Short Line railroads in the 1880s and a few later moved into the Northwest.

In 1886, a mission effort was organized under the direction of George C. Parkinson, president of the Oneida Stake in southeastern Idaho. He wanted to search for the members of his stake who had moved into Washington, Oregon, and Montana. The first full-time missionaries were active in Spokane by 1896. A second Northwestern States Mission was created in that city July 26, 1897. (The first Northwestern States Mission, created in 1878, had its headquarters in Chicago, Ill.

A meeting held in a Church facility in Colfax, Wash., on Jan. 3, 1898, had an attendance of 65 people. Missionaries began working in Walla Walla on Jan. 17, 1898.

A year later, an Eastern Washington Conference was held with one elder and 20 members in attendance. On Sept. 9, 1906, a Sunday School was organized in Spokane, and a branch was organized on March 12, 1916. A milestone was reached when President

Melvin J. Ballard reorganized the Spokane Brance entirely with local members. A meetinghouse was built for the branch in 1920. In Seattle, a Sunday School was started in 1915, and a branch organized Sept. 12, 1920. A building for this branch was purchased in 1927.

In 1930, membership in the state was 1,855 in eight branches, with chapels in Everett, Spokane, Seattle, and Olympia. The first stake in Washington, the Seattle Stake, was created July 31, 1938. In 1940, membership in the state reached 5,000, and during World War II a great influx of members came to Washington to work in defense industries.

The completion of the Grand Coulee Dam on the Columbia River in the early 1940s opened the way for additional farming in the Columbia River Basin, and many members flocked to the state to farm. By 1960, membership had increased to 11,000.

The Pacific Northwest Mission was created from the Northwestern States Mission in 1968, and was renamed the Washington Mission in 1970 and the Washington Seattle Mission in 1974. Two other missions in the state were created in 1978, with headquarters in Spokane, and in 1990, with headquarters in Tacoma.

By 1970, membership in the state had increased to 67,203 and to 138.000 by 1980. The Seattle Temple was dedicated that year on Nov. 17. By 1990, membership reached 189,000, and in 1992, Washington became the fifth state in the United States with at least 50 stakes.

By 1999, membership in Washington had reached 226,411, and the second temple in the state, in the Spokane suburb of Opportunity, was dedicated Aug. 21, 1999. The temple district covers eastern Washington, northern Idaho, and western Montana. Today, some 1,000 people are baptized annually in the Washington Spokane Mission.

A third temple for the state was announced in general conference on April 2, 2000, by President Gordon B. Hinckley. The temple will be built in the tri-cities area of Richland, Kennewick, and Pasco, the Columbia River Washington Temple.

Sources: *Encyclopedic History of the Church,* by Andrew Jenson; *Latter-day Saints in the Great Northwest,* by J. Arthur Horne, published by Graphic Arts Press, Seattle, Wash.; *History of the Church in the Pacific Northwest,* by Leonard J. Arrington, task papers in LDS History, No. 18; *Church News,* Aug. 28, 1999, April 8, 2000,

Stakes — 53

(Listed alphabetically as of Oct. 1, 2000.)

No.	Name	Organized	First President
North America Northwest Area			
1388	Auburn Washington	28 Nov 1982	Alan Warner Bolles
388	*Bellevue Washington ‡Seattle East	1 Dec 1963	Raymond W. Eldredge
1266	Bellingham Washington	10 May 1981	Eugene Clifford Hatch
1312	Bothell Washington	22 Nov 1981	Arnold R. Parrott
299	*Bremerton Washington ‡Puget Sound	19 Jun 1960	Herbert S. Anderson
958	Centralia Washington	10 Sep 1978	Frank Edward Berrett
1299	Colville Washington	18 Oct 1981	Garnett Russell Port
1438	Elma Washington	28 Aug 1983	Lou Elwin Green
1148	Ephrata Washington	15 Jun 1980	Robert A. Hammond
532	*Everett Washington ‡Cascade South	25 Oct 1970	Wesley K. Duce
883	Federal Way Washington	20 Nov 1977	Jack Lynn Smith
776	Kennewick Washington	24 Oct 1976	Elton Elias Hunt
1374	Kennewick Washington East	31 Oct 1982	Donald LeRoy Brunson
1495	Kent Washington	14 Oct 1984	Owen Edvin Jensen
1855	Kirkland Washington	19 Apr 1992	Peter Gideon Condie
2397	Lacey Washington	14 Sep 1997	Ralph W. Smith Jr.
1565	Lakewood Washington	20 Oct 1985	James Rolland Ely
599	*Longview Washington ‡Columbia River West	4 Feb 1973	Walter Lee Robinson

925	Lynnwood Washington	14 May 1978	Robert C. Barnard
2448	Maple Valley Washington	22 Mar 1998	Larry J. Thomas
1251	Marysville Washington	29 Mar 1981	Verle George Call
213	*Moses Lake Washington ‡Grand Coulee	18 Apr 1954	Elmo J. Bergeson
379	*Mount Vernon Washington ‡Cascade	30 Jun 1963	Robert E. Jones
440	*Olympia Washington ‡Olympia	27 Aug 1967	Herbert S. Anderson
1049	Othello Washington	12 Aug 1979	Jay L. Christensen
437	*Pasco Washington ‡Pasco (Washington, Oregon)	21 May 1967	David K. Barber
1848	Port Angeles Washington	23 Feb 1992	Richard Ernest Shaw
638	Pullman Washington	5 May 1974	John Leo Schwendiman
542	*Puyallup Washington ‡Mount Rainier	17 Jan 1971	Owen H. Dickson
1389	Puyallup Washington South	28 Nov 1982	Dennis Tripp Sampson
844	Redmond Washington	29 May 1977	Arnold R. Parrott
514	*Renton Washington ‡Renton	3 May 1970	Harris A. Mortensen
1244	Renton Washington North	15 Mar 1981	Denzel Nolan Wiser
180	*Richland Washington ‡Richland (Washington, Oregon)	25 Jun 1950	James V. Thompson
124	*Seattle Washington ‡Seattle	31 Jul 1938	Alex Brown
242	*Seattle Washington North *Seattle North 29 May 1970 ‡North Seattle	19 May 1957	Wilford H. Payne
1496	Seattle Washington Shoreline	14 Oct 1984	Brent Isaac Nash
1023	*Selah Washington 31 Aug 1982 ‡Yakima Washington North	29 Apr 1979	Robert Atwood Hague
1057	Silverdale Washington	26 Aug 1979	David Junior Jones
1890	Snohomish Washington	28 Jun 1992	Craig L. Morrison
168	*Spokane Washington ‡Spokane	29 Jun 1947	Albert I. Morgan
556	*Spokane Washington East ‡Spokane East	17 Oct 1971	James B. Cox
992	Spokane Washington North	7 Jan 1979	Dwaine E. Nelson
1841	Spokane Washington West	12 Jan 1992	Elroy C. McDermott
195	*Tacoma Washington ‡Tacoma	28 Sep 1952	Elvin E. Evans
1052	Tacoma Washington South	19 Aug 1979	James Rolland Ely
389	*Vancouver Washington *Columbia River North 29 May 1970 ‡North Columbia	1 Dec 1963	Wallace V. Teuscher
2467	Vancouver Washington East	17 May 1998	Thomas H. Jensen
1570	Vancouver Washington North	3 Nov 1985	Bruce A. Schreiner
979	Vancouver Washington West	5 Nov 1978	Earl Clifford Jorgensen
1011	Walla Walla Washington	11 Mar 1979	David L. Hafen
426	*Wenatchee Washington 7 Dec 1978 *Quincy Washington ‡Grand Coulee North	29 Jan 1967	Leslie H. Boyce
284	*Yakima Washington ‡Yakima	24 May 1959	F. Edgar Johnson

Missions — 3

(As of Oct. 1, 2000; shown with historical number. See MISSIONS.)

(78a) WASHINGTON SEATTLE MISSION
13353 Bel-Red Road, Suite 103
Bellevue, WA 98005-2329
Phone: (425) 641-5050

(166) WASHINGTON SPOKANE MISSION
P.O. Box 14808
Spokane, WA 99214-0808
Phone: (509) 924-8932

(255) WASHINGTON TACOMA MISSION
4007-D Bridgeport Way W.
University Place, WA 98466-4330
Phone: (253) 566-5480

West Virginia

Year-end 1999: Est. population, 1,807,000; Members, 12,290; Stakes, 2; Wards, 17; Branches, 19; Missions, 1; Percent LDS, 0.7, or one in 147.

Missionaries entered what is now West Virginia in 1832 when Luke S. Johnson and William W. M'Lellin preached in Cabell County, which lies just over the Ohio River from Ohio on the western tip of West Virginia. The Prophet Joseph Smith visited Wheeling, W.V., on April 4, 1832, and purchased paper for the Church's press that was then in Jackson County, Mo. The paper was used to publish the *Book of Commandments,* which was later mostly scattered by a mob. That same year, Elder Amasa M. Lyman and an Elder Johnson baptized 40 converts in West Virginia. In 1836, Elders Lorenzo D. Barnes and Samuel James baptized enough converts to start a branch in Shinnston, Harrison County. In 1837, some 1,200 (mostly non-members) attended a meeting there. Elder George A. Smith taught a grammar school at or near Shinnston, which had 75 members.

One convert was Bathsheba Wilson Bigler Smith, who later became the wife of Apostle George A. Smith. She was baptized Aug. 21, 1837, along with a number of other family members including parents, brothers and sisters. "The spirit of gathering with the Saints in Missouri came upon me . . . ," she wrote in her autobiography. "About this time my father sold his farm in West Virginia and we started for Far West." She later served as Relief Society general president from 1901-1910.

Others felt the same spirit and immigrated to Missouri with the Saints, and the branches were discontinued.

Missionary work did not resume until 1881 when Elders John E. Carlisle and Joseph L. Townsend served in McDowell County and baptized three adults.

Laboring in Logan County in June 1884, Elder Andrew W. Spence and an Elder Vickers were served with a warrant for suspicion of being part of a band of robbers. The pair opened their satchels and not only convinced the officers that they were innocent, but also distributed tracts that opened the way for the missionaries to teach at the courthouse. From this opening, a branch of 26 people was organized. The West Virginia Conference was organized Sept. 18, 1886. A year later, missionaries from the Northern States Mission searched out and taught "Bickertonites" (see Pennsylvania history), but failed to make any headway among them. In 1889, a local newspaper wrote of the "serious" success of the missionaries among other residents in the Wheeling area.

West Virginia was placed in the Eastern States Mission in 1897. It became part of the Middle States Mission in 1902, but was soon after reunited with the Eastern States Mission.

In 1906, Elder George D. Ward and a companion completed a small chapel for the Franklin Branch. One of the early converts in this branch was William Perry Hartman. Nearly 100 of his descendants joined the Church. Three branches were later developed from his family's influence.

The West Virginia Conference was divided and the West Virginia North and South conferences were created. In 1930, the North conference had 888 members and the South conference 1,397 members, for a statewide total of 2,285.

The membership built up gradually and the first stake was created in 1970 in Charleston, with a membership of 3,966. Units in West Virginia included the Asheland, Charleston, Charleston 2nd, Huntington, and Parkersburg wards and the Beckley, Logan, Portsmouth, Ripley, Point Pleasant, and Webster Spring branches. The West Virginia Charleston Mission was organized in 1980. Additional stakes were created in Fairmont in 1979 and Huntington in 1982. Membership in West Virginia in 1974 was 9,149, growing to 9,734 in 1980, 10,000 in 1990, and 12,290 in 1999. Humanitarian service was performed as the Church donated food and clothing to residents in underpriviledged areas of West Virginia in the late 1990s.

Sources: *Encyclopedic History of the Church,* by Andrew Jenson; *Autobiography,* Bathsheba Wilson Bigler Smith; Southern States, Eastern States and Northern States Missions histories; *Church News,* Sept. 5, 1970; "West Virginia and Mormonism's Rarest Book" by Lisle G. Brown, *West Virginia History,* January/April 1978, Vol. 39;"'Bell-snickeled' builders," by Richard L. Jensen, *Church News,* April 1,

1978; "West Virginia," by Mike Cannon, *Church News,* Oct. 2, 1989; *Church News,* Sept. 5, 1992, Aug. 21, 1993, March 28, 1998.

Stakes — 2

(Listed alphabetically as of Oct. 1, 2000.)

No.	Name	Organized	First President
North America East Area			
522	*Charleston West Virginia ‡West Virginia (W. Va., Ky.)	23 Aug 1970	David L. Atkinson
1025	Fairmont West Virginia	6 May 1979	David Glen Williams

Mission — 1

(As of Oct. 1, 2000; shown with historical number. See MISSIONS.)

(188) WEST VIRGINIA CHARLESTON MISSION
Oakwood Centre
888 Oakwood Rd, Ste. 310
Charleston, WV 25314

Wisconsin

Year-end 1999: Est. population, 5,250,000; Members, 19,282; Stakes, 5; Wards, 35; Branches, 22; Missions, 1; Percent LDS, 0.4, or one in 273.

Settlement of the Saints in Wisconsin was suggested as early as 1836 at a citizens meeting in Liberty County, Mo. The suggestion, however, was not acted upon. Moses and Aaron Smith established Wisconsin's first LDS congregation in 1837 in what is now Burlington, about 40 miles southwest of Milwaukee. and attempted to persuade Church leaders to send missionaries to the state. Missionary work in Wisconsin began in 1841. That year, Elder Elisha H. Groves opened a small branch in Vienna, Dane County, and Elder William O. Clark baptized 17 people at Mineral Point, Lafayette County. Amasa Lyman also labored in Wisconsin that year.

A group of 14 members was sent to the Wisconsin Territory in 1841 from Nauvoo, Ill., to obtain lumber from the pine forests along the Black River to be used in the construction of the temple and other buildings in Nauvoo. Workers in this "pinery expedition" floated logs some 600 miles from Church-operated sawmills in Wisconsin to Nauvoo. By 1843, the camp at Black River had more than 150 people, but members learned then that they were on Indian territory. Bishop George Miller met with Menominee Indian Chief Oshkosh and reached an agreement to pay for the wood. He also preached to the Indians.

After the 1847 exodus from Nauvoo, little missionary work was done in Wisconsin until 1877 when Cyrus H. Wheelock, laboring in Fond du Lac, Wis., was called to organize a mission. The Northwestern States Mission was organized the next year in 1878. During the next decade, some converts likely were gained, but work proceeded slowly in the early 1890s with few or no missionaries serving. The Milwaukee Conference was organized in Madison in 1896, but soon after, the conference headquarters were established in Milwaukee and missionaries were assigned to labor there. The Milwaukee Branch was created on April 16, 1899, with seven members and e Sunday School enrollment of 17. Christopher Leonard Rueckert, a former missionary in Wisconsin, was assigned by the Church in 1904 to return to Milwaukee with his family and head the new branch. On March 23, 1907, a branch chapel was dedicated. Pres. Rueckert oversaw the growth of the Church in Milwaukee from 1904 to 1914, when he unexpectedly died.

By 1930, membership in Wisconsin was 932 in the Eleva, La Crosse, Milwaukee, and Racine branches. When the Chicago (Illinois) Stake was organized in 1936, the Milwaukee Ward was created and included in that stake. This ward was divided in 1958. The Milwaukee Stake was created in 1963, and a stake center was dedicated in 1967. Membership in 1974 was more than 6,000. On July 1, 1978, the Wisconsin Milwaukee Mission was created. In 1980, Wisconsin had 9,855 members, and in 1990, 13,159 members. In 1999, membership was 19,282 in 35 wards and 22 branches.

Efforts in recent years to enhance the visibility of the Church in Wisconsin have included a three-year exhibit beginning in 1995 at the Sun Prairie Historical Library and Museum. Assembled by the Sun Prairie Ward, Madison Wisconsin Stake, exhibit highlights Church history and doctrine.

Sources: *Encyclopedic History of the Church,* by Andrew Jenson; "Brief History of the Milwaukee

Stake," published at the dedication of the Milwaukee Stake Center, Aug. 27, 1967; "The Pinery Expedition," by Jill Mulvay Derr, *Church News*, April 8, 1978; "Minnesota Mormons," by Fayone B. Willes, published by the Minnesota Stake, 1990; "Exhibit Acquaints Visitors with Church," *Church News*, July 15, 1995; "Mormons in Milwaukee," by R. Scott Lloyd, *Church News*, Dec. 5, 1998.

Stakes — 5

(Listed alphabetically as of Oct. 1, 2000.)

No.	Name	Organized	First President
North America Central Area			
1597	Appleton Wisconsin	11 May 1986	Nevin Richard Limburg
2335	Green Bay Wisconsin	23 Mar 1997	Ronald S. Godfrey
702	*Madison Wisconsin	11 Apr 1982	
	‡Beloit Wisconsin	24 Aug 1975	Arval Lewis Erikson
367	*Milwaukee Wisconsin		
	‡Milwaukee	3 Feb 1963	DeWitt C. Smith
2261	Wausau Wisconsin	3 Nov 1996	Robert Thomas Growcock

Mission — 1

(As of Oct. 1, 2000; shown with historical number. See MISSIONS, p. 286.)

(167) WISCONSIN MILWAUKEE MISSION
5651 Broad St.
Greendale, WI 53129-1889

Wyoming

Year-end 1999: Est. population, 480,000; Members, 54,425; Stakes, 16; Wards, 125; Branches, 18; Percent LDS, 11.3, or one in 9.

In 1846, a group of Mississippi converts came West hoping to join the Saints en route to the Great Basin. However, they stopped a few miles below Fort Laramie in July 1846. There, they learned that the Saints had waited a year at Winter Quarters, Neb., so the Mississippians decided to winter in Pueblo, Colo. Some of these Mississippi members joined Brigham Young's pioneer wagon train the next year, which entered Wyoming May 31, 1847, near Fort Laramie. The Mississippi group included members of the Mormon Battalion sick detachments as well. On June 28, 1847, the combined company under Brigham Young met famed mountainman Jim Bridger in southwestern Wyoming, who gave them a generally optimistic appraisal of the Great Basin area.

Most emigrant companies crossed Wyoming without incident, but the Willie and Martin Handcart companies of 1856 were trapped in early winter snows before reaching South Pass, Wyo., and about 200 of the 1,075 in the two companies died. The rest were saved by rescue parties from Utah.

Fort Supply was erected near Fort Bridger and a colony was started in 1853. It provided supplies for wagon companies coming from the East. This flourishing colony was abandoned and burned at the advance of Johnston's army in 1857. Fort Bridger, which the Church had purchased in 1855, was partially burned at the same time. The army subsequently camped at Fort Bridger before a peaceful settlement was reached in Utah the following summer.

In 1877, Moses Thatcher and William Preston, seeking areas to colonize, went to western Wyoming, then known as Salt River Valley. Thatcher re-named the area Star Valley. Apostle Brigham Young Jr. visited the area the following year and dedicated it as a gathering place. The first settlers from Bear Lake Valley, Idaho, stayed the winter of 1879-80 near what is now Auburn, Wyo. In the 1880s, the settlements of Grover, Afton, Freedom, Smoot, Thayne, Bedford, and Fairview were established. Others followed. Wyoming's first stake was organized in 1892 in Star Valley, which today is still primarily composed of LDS communities.

Later, Church members were involved in other colonizing efforts in Wyoming. The Big Horn Basin in northcentral Wyoming was settled in 1900 after Wyoming Gov. DeForrest Richards sent a request to President Lorenzo Snow for settlers. The first settlement of Burlington was founded by LDS members from Uintah County, Utah, and organized under Apostle Abraham O. Woodruff. Also founded around the turn of the 20th century were the Big Horn Basin communities of Byron, Cowley, Lovell, and others. The settlers dug a 37-mile canal to provide irrigation water only to find that irrigation lifted underground alkali to the surface. Settlers persevered, however, and the problem abated.

In 1930, about 12,000 members lived in Wyoming, primarily in the western part of the state and the Big Horn Basin, but members began moving into other areas as well. By 1980, membership in the state reached 47,314, increasing to 51,692 in 1990.

During the observance of Wyoming's state centennial in 1990, the LDS heritage of the state, including the Mormon Trail, were included in commemorations.

In 1992, as part of Riverton Wyoming Stake's "second rescue" program, three monuments were erected in central Wyoming in memory of the Willie and Martin handcart pioneer companies. The monuments were dedicated Aug. 15, 1992, by President Gordon B. Hinckley, then first counselor in the First Presidency. During the "second rescue," members of the stake researched family histories and performed temple ordinances for those handcart pioneers whose work had not previously been done. Later purchased by the Church was the site surrounding a monument at the mouth of Sweetwater Canyon where 21 people perished in one night, and was dedicated in 1994 by President Hinckley.

Wyoming played a large part in the re-enactment wagon train during the 1997 pioneer sesquicentennial. Members and non-members participated in and welcomed the train throughout the portion of the trail running through Wyoming. On May 3, 1997, President Hinckley dedicated a new visitors center near the 6,100-foot elevation Martin's Cove in central Wyoming in memory of the Willie and Martin handcart companies. President Thomas S. Monson also traveled to Wyoming to greet the travelers. The train provided a situation to re-enact the 1858 raid by Lot Smith on Johnston's army. A wall built by Mormons at Fort Bridger was dedicated, and Wyoming Gov. Jim Geringer welcomed the train at Evanston.In 1999, Wyoming had an LDS population of 54,425.

Sources: *Encyclopedic History of the Church,* by Andrew Jenson; "Star Valley and Its Communities," by Lee Roland Call, Afton, Wyo., *Star Valley Independent,* 1970; *Lovell, Our Pioneer Heritage,* by Rosa Vida Bischoff Black; "Fort Supply: Brigham Young's Green River Experiment," by Frederick R. Gowans and Eugene E. Campbell, BYU, 1976; *Wyoming Place Names,* by Mae Urbanek, Mountain Press Publishing Co., 1988; *Church News,* May 26, 1990, Dec. 15, 1990, Dec. 22, 1990; "Mormon Settlers helped make Wyoming a state," *Church News,* May 26, 1990; "'Second rescue' of handcart pioneers," by Dell Van Orden, *Church News,* Aug. 22, 1992; "Project stands as reminder of legacy," by Julie A. Dockstader, *Church News,* July, 30, 1994; *Church News,* May 9, 1997, July 12, 1997, July 19, 1997.

Stakes — 16

(Listed alphabetically by area as of Oct. 1, 2000.)

No.	Name	Organized	First President
	North America Central Area — 8		
357	*Casper Wyoming ‡Casper	14 Oct 1962	W. Reed Green
286	*Cheyenne Wyoming ‡Cheyenne (Wyo., Colo.)	21 Jun 1959	Archie R. Boyack
593	*Cody Wyoming ‡Cody	7 Jan 1973	Parley J. Livingston
1158	Gillette Wyoming	29 Jun 1980	Marion A. Dalene
1420	Laramie Wyoming	15 May 1983	Philip Munro Hoyt
48	*Lovell Wyoming ‡Big Horn	26 May 1901	Byron Sessions
358	*Riverton Wyoming ‡Wind River	14 Oct 1962	J. Rex Kocherhans
1194	Worland Wyoming	12 Oct 1980	David Harris Asay
	Utah North Area — 8		
33	*Afton Wyoming ‡Star Valley	14 Aug 1892	George Osmond
38	*Evanston Wyoming ‡Woodruff (Wyoming, Utah)	5 Jun 1898	John M. Baxter
1493	Evanston Wyoming South	23 Sep 1984	Harold Sidney Stock
660	Green River Wyoming	23 Sep 1984	Ronald Clyde Walker
708	Kemmerer Wyoming	12 Oct 1975	Merrill R. Anderson
790	Lyman Wyoming	21 Nov 1976	Ronald C. Walker
95	*Rock Springs Wyoming ‡Lyman (Wyoming, Utah)	18 Jul 1926	H. Melvin Rollins
975	Thayne Wyoming	29 Oct 1978	Marlow C. Bateman

TOTAL CONVERTS

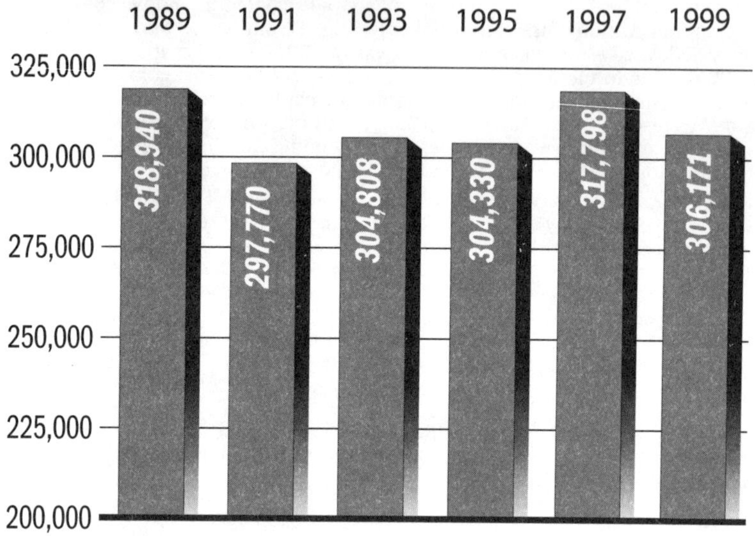

WORLDWIDE CHURCH

Territories or possessions are listed under the name of the administering country.

Numbers preceding stakes and missions are their chronological numbers assigned at the time of creation. A letter means number was used previously.

* Name changed 14 Jan 1974 unless another date indicates otherwise

‡Original name

†Transferred to

ALBANIA

Year-end 1999: Est. population, 3,414,000; Members, 789; Branches, 7; Missions, 1; Percent LDS, .82, or one in 4,327; Europe Central Area.

Albania is a small mountainous country in southeastern Europe's Balkan Peninsula where the Albanian- and Greek-speaking people are 70 percent Sunni Muslim, with 20 percent Greek Orthodox and 10 percent Roman Catholic.

Elder Hans B. Ringger of the Seventy and president of the Europe Area, accompanied by Austria Vienna Mission Pres. Kenneth D. Reber, visited Albania in 1991. In June 1992, four full-time missionaries arrived in Albania: Elders Matthew Wirthlin, Mark Slabaugh, Paul McAlister, and Jonathan Jarvis. In addition, Elder George Niedens and Sister Nancy Niedens were transferred to Albania from Austria to assist in agriculture.

Elder Dallin H. Oaks of the Quorum of the Twelve visited Albania in April 1993 and spoke to a gathering of 78 people, including 55 Albanian members. In 1994, Albania was among eastern European nations receiving shipments of food and other humanitarian relief supplies from the Church.

Albania was once part of the Switzerland Zurich Mission. The Albania Tirana Mission was created in July 1996. Missionaries were withdrawn from Albania from March to September of 1997 following a government collapse and civil unrest, and from summer to fall of 1998. The Albania Tirana District, comprised of six branches in three cities, was created in May 1999. The first Albanian family was sealed in the Frankfurt Germany Temple in April 2000.

Sources: *Church News*, June 22, 1992, June 12, 1993; March 16, 1996; *The Universal Almanac* 1996, Andrew's and MS Meel, a Universal Press Syndicate Company; *Church News*, Aug. 29, 1998; correspondence Sept. 20, 2000, from Pres. Stephen C. Lenker, Albania Tirana Mission.

AMERICAN SAMOA

Year-end 2000: Est. population, 57,000; Members, 12,883; Stakes, 4; Wards, 29; Branches, 5; Percent LDS, 22.5, or one in 4; Pacific Islands Area, Samoa Apia Mission.

Located in the South Pacific, American Samoa is a U.S. territory. The people are Protestant, 50 percent; LDS, 25 percent; and Roman Catholic, 20 percent.

In 1863, two missionaries from Hawaii, Kimo Pelia and Samuela Manoa, arrived in Samoa. However, they had been sent by an unauthorized leader, Walter Murray Gibson, who had been excommunicated by the Church. The pair labored faithfully for nearly 20 years without the knowledge or support of the Church. They baptized a few people on Tutuila, which is now American Samoa. Later, after Elder Joseph H. Dean and his wife, Florence, arrived in Samoa in 1888, missionaries were again sent to Tutuila. The first branch was started in Pago Pago on May 27, 1893, and before the turn of the 20th century, 11 branches had been organized on the island.

On April 27, 1900, the U.S. flag was raised over Tutuila and conflict between the German and U.S. governments that had hindered missionary work was largely resolved.

An LDS village with a school and a supporting plantation was founded at Mapusaga May 10, 1903. On Nov. 26, 1906, a Relief Society was organized at Mapusaga, and 14 members were enrolled. A Primary was organized May 24, 1908.

In 1938, the Boy Scout organization was started at Mapusaga.

Missionaries were recalled from American Samoa in 1940 prior to World War II because of troubled conditions in the Pacific, and local members assumed more leadership. After the war, the work quickened considerably. The first stake in American Samoa, the Pago Pago Stake, was created in 1969.

In 1989, Eni F. [Hunkin Jr.] Faleomavaega, former lieutenant governor of American

Samoa, was elected as a non-voting member of 101st U.S. Congress, the first Samoan LDS member to do so. He was still serving in 2000.

Hurricanes in February 1990 and December 1991 caused major damage and members suffered considerably, but local units responded well in dealing with the devastation. Membership in 1990 was 7,500, increasing to 12,833 in 1999. President Gordon B. Hinckley was welcomed by a proclamation from the governor during a visit to American Samoa on Oct. 13, 1997, where he addressed 7,900 people, the largest crowd ever assembled in the newly opened Veteran's Memorial Stadium in Pago Pago.

President Hinckley returned to American Samoa during a six-nation tour of Asia and the South Pacific in 2000 and spoke again in Veteran's Memorial Stadium to 5,000 people on June 17. Before the meeting, he was greeted by the governor, Tauese Sunia.

Sources: *Encyclopedic History of the Church,* by Andrew Jenson; *Unto the Isles of the Sea,* by R. Lanier Britsch; *Samoa Apia Mission History, 1888-1983,* published by R. Carl Harris, president of the Samoa Apia Mission; *Church News,* Feb. 25, 1989, Feb. 17, 1990, Dec. 21, 1991; "Church responds swiftly to Samoa disaster," *Church News,* Dec. 28, 1991; "Prophet goes to islands of Pacific," by Gerry Avant; *Church News,* Oct. 25, 1997; *Church News,* July 1, 2000.

Stakes — 4

(Listed alphabetically as of Oct. 1, 2000.)

No.	Name	Organized	First President
Pacific Islands Area			
488	*Pago Pago Samoa		
	‡Pago Pago	15 Jun 1969	Patrick Peters
1972	Pago Pago Samoa Central	6 Feb 1994	Beaver T. Ho Ching
2324	Pago Pago Samoa Mapusaga	9 Mar 1997	Eugene Reid
1169	Pago Pago Samoa West	24 Aug 1980	William T. Geleai

ANDORRA

Year-end 1999: Est. Population: 66,000; Members, 64; branches, 1; Percent LDS, .9, or one in 1,031; Europe West Area; Spain Barcelona Mission.

A principality in the high Pyrenees mountains on the border of France and Spain, Andorra joined the European Common market in 1991. Its people speak Catalan and French and Spanish. The first to be baptized in Andorra was Marlize Gomez Lima, on April 11, 1992. The Andorra Branch was created in August 1993, and the first branch presidents were Javier Ortega and Jose Luis Bota, who did not live in the branch boundaries. Pres. Javier Agulced Jerez, baptized with his wife and two daughters in March 1998, became the first branch president to live in the branch.

Source: Correspondence from the Spain Barcelona Mission, Oct. 4, 1998.

ANGOLA

Year-end 1999: Est. population, 10,070,000; Members, 502; Branches, 2; Percent LDS, 0.05, or one in 20,060; Africa Southeast Area.

A country on the southwest coast of Africa, the People's Republic of Angola has a population of about 11 million. The nation's official language is Portuguese, although the majority of black Angolans speak a language that belongs to the Bantu language group. About 90 percent of the people are Christians, mostly Roman Catholic, with the remainder practicing mainly indigenous beliefs. Some three-fourths of the people of Angola live in rural areas, mainly as farmers and herders.

Latter-day Saints had been living in Angola since 1985. However, many had been baptized while living for a short time in France or Portugal. After their return to Angola, they formed the nucleus of the Church. Records indicate that some 400 members baptized in Europe since the early 1980s had returned to cities in Angola.

The Church was officially recognized in Angola in 1993, with the first branch being created in 1996 in Luanda, the capital city. Some 86 members and investigators attended the branch meeting, with Elder J. Richard Clarke of the Seventy, then president of the Africa Area, presiding. Called as the first branch president was Tshaka Mbenza Vuamina, a professor at the University of Angola. Elder Clarke praised the members for their faith while living in an area burdened by civil war. Until the branch was organized, members had been meeting as a group in the homes of priesthood holders.

Sources: *World Book Encyclopedia,* published by World Book, Inc., 1993, vol. 1, pp. 464-65; *Church News,* Sept. 7, 1996.

ANTIGUA AND BARBUDA

Year-end 1999: Est. population, 65,000; Members, 115; Branches, 1; Percent LDS, .18, or one in 565; North America Southeast Area; West Indies Mission.

These eastern Caribbean islands are a constitutional monarchy with a British type of parliament. The population speaks English and is mostly members of the Church of England.

Missionary work began in St. John's, Antigua, on May 19, 1984, when President Kenneth Zabriskie of the West Indies Mission visited the governor of Antigua and received permission to station missionaries on the island.

The first missionaries, Elder Ralph and Sister Aileen Tate arrived on July 28, 1984, under the direction of President Zabriskie. They were followed in late August by Elders Gill W. Halford, Jay R. Schroeder, Carl Read, and Russell T. Hansen. The first baptism was Evelyn Shaw on Sept. 15, 1984. On Dec. 2, Ezzard Weston received the Aaronic Priesthood, the first to receive the priesthood on Antigua.

Elder Rex B. Blake, serving a mission with his wife, Ruth, was the first president of the St. John's Branch, which was organized Jan. 6, 1985, in a rented conference room of a bank. The Church slowly grew to about 70 members in 1995 and to 150 in 1999.

Sources: Journal of Pres. Kenneth L. Zabriskie and his wife, LeOra; interview with Rex and Ruth Blake; *Church News*, Dec. 11, 1993, Sept. 30, 1995; unpublished St. John's Branch history.

ARGENTINA

Year-end 1999: Est. population, 34,293,000; Members, 288,865; Stakes, 64; Wards, 389; Branches, 412; Missions, 10; Districts, 37; Temples, 1; Percent LDS, .84, or one in 119.

Located in southern South America, the Republic of Argentina has a Spanish-speaking population that is about 92 percent Roman Catholic.

Church members Wilhelm Friedrichs and Emil Hoppe and their families emigrated from Germany to Argentina about 1923. Brother Friedrichs was particularly missionary-minded and began announcing gospel messages in local newspapers. He also sent letters to the First Presidency requesting missionaries.

In response, Elder Melvin J. Ballard of the Quorum of the Twelve and Elders Rulon S. Wells (who spoke German) and Rey L. Pratt (who spoke Spanish) were sent to Argentina, arriving in Buenos Aires Dec. 6, 1925. On Dec. 13, they baptized six persons who had been taught by Brother Friedrichs: Anna and Jacob Kullick and their adopted daughter, Herta; Ernst and Maria Biebersdorf and their daughter, Maria. On Dec. 25, Elder Ballard dedicated South America for the preaching of the gospel. He later prophesied that "the work will go forth slowly just as the oak grows from an acorn. . . . [But] the South American Mission will become a power in the Church."

Reinhold Stoof arrived in 1926 as the first mission president to preside over the South American Mission. The mission was divided into the Brazilian and Argentine missions in 1936. A decade later, after a slowing of activity during World War II, membership in Argentina was 800. Branches had been established, ranging from 500 miles south of Buenos Aires to 700 miles to the north and west.

The Argentine Mission was divided in 1962. The first stake in Argentina, the Buenos Aires Stake, was organized in Nov. 20, 1966, with Angel Abrea, now a member of the First Quorum of the Seventy, as stake president. By 1978, membership had reached about 40,000 members.

On Oct. 28-29, 1978, President Spencer W. Kimball addressed 11,200 members at an area conference in Buenos Aires, the second area conference in Argentina in three years. While in Buenos Aires for the 1978 conference, President Kimball visited the president of Argentina, Jorge Rafael Videla. Because of the emphasis the Church places on home and family, President Kimball was hosted at the Argentina president's home rather than his government office.

The Buenos Aires Argentina Temple was announced in 1980, and dedicated Jan. 17, 1986.

Buenos Aires was designated headquarters of the South America South Area in 1984. Three new missions in 1990 — Mendoza, Resistencia, and Trelew — and one in 1992, the Buenos Aires West, reflected the continuing growth in the early 1990s in Argentina. By 1997, there were 10 missions in Argentina.

President Gordon B. Hinckley visited Argentina on Nov. 12, 1996, and spoke to some 30,000 gathered in Buenos Aires. Members donated thousands of service hours during the pioneer sesquicentennial in 1997, and honored their pioneer members as well.

Membership in 1990 was 171,000, growing to 235,000 in 1995, and 288,865 in 1999. Argentina, with 64 stakes, was one of seven countries in the world in 1999 with more than 50 stakes. In 2000, members celebrated the 75th anniversary of the arrival of missionaries in South America and dedication of the continent for missionary work.

Sources: *Encyclopedic History of the Church,* by Andrew Jenson; *From Acorn to Oak Tree,* by Frederick S. Williams and Frederick G. Williams; *LDS Beginnings in South America, A Look at Argentina,* BYU paper by Denise H. Williams; "Emotions swell as meetings ends," by Dell Van Orden, *Church News,* Nov. 11, 1978; *50 Anos de la Iglesia en Argentina — Cronologia,* by Nestor Curbelo, seminary system, 1986; "Argentina: Bright and Joyous Day," by Judy C. Olsen, *Ensign,* Feb. 1998; *Church News,* Nov. 16, 1996, May 30, 1998.

Stakes — 64

(Listed alphabetically as of Oct. 1, 2000.)

No.	Name	Organized	First President
South America South Area			
1097	Bahia Blanca Argentina	23 Jan 1980	Daniel Humberto Fucci
2117	Bahia Blanca Argentina Villa Mitre	5 Nov 1995	Jorge Horacio Cizek
2172	Bariloche Argentina	25 Feb 1996	Miguel Angel Reginato
2259	Buenos Aires Argentina Adrogue	3 Nov 1996	Enrique Manuel Garcia
1797	*Buenos Aires Argentina Aldo Bonzi	2 Jun 1996	
	‡Buenos Aires Argentina Ezeiza	12 May 1991	Carlos Ernesto Aguero
2239	Buenos Aires Argentina Avellaneda	22 Sep 1996	Oscar Altera
920	Buenos Aires Argentina Banfield	14 May 1978	Heber Omar Diaz
1992	Buenos Aires Argentina Belgrano	18 Sep 1994	Nestor Esteban Curbelo
1143	Buenos Aires Argentina Castelar	8 Jun 1980	Jorge H. Michalek
2502	Buenos Aires Argentina Congreso	6 Dec 1998	Oscar Alberto Ormeno
2295	Buenos Aires Argentina Escobar	15 Dec 1996	Andres Bernardo Martin
2200	Buenos Aires Argentina Gonzalez Catan	2 Jun 1996	Pedro Emilio Ayala
423	*Buenos Aires Argentina Liniers	10 Dec 1998	
	*Buenos Aires Argentina East		
	‡Buenos Aires	20 Nov 1966	Angel Abrea
1178	Buenos Aires Argentina Litoral	12 Sep 1980	Jorge Fernandez
2276	Buenos Aires Argentina Marcos Paz	24 Nov 1996	Ismael Hector Segovia
950	Buenos Aires Argentina Merlo	13 Aug 1978	Enrique Alfredo Ibarra
1824	Buenos Aires Argentina Monte Grande	10 Nov 1991	Hugo Vicente Riccinti
1405	Buenos Aires Argentina Moreno	20 Mar 1983	Carlos Domingo Marapodi
995	Buenos Aires Argentina North	28 Jan 1979	Tomas Federico Lindheimer
1946	Buenos Aires Argentina Sarmiento	27 Jun 1993	Carlos Antonio Moure
639	Buenos Aires Argentina West	12 May 1974	May Hugo Angel Catron
1975	Comodoro Rivadavia Argentina	20 Feb 1994	Jorge EstebanDetlefsen
1021	Cordoba Argentina North	29 Apr 1979	Juan Aldo L.
1959a	Cordoba Argentina Sierras	7 Nov 1993	Roberto Jose Echegaray
569	*Cordoba Argentina South	20 Jun 1996	
	*Cordoba Argentina		
	‡Cordoba	28 Feb 1972	Arturo Palmieri
2228	Cordoba Argentina West	8 Sep 1996	Ruben B. Luis Spitale
1951	Florencio Varela Argentina	22 Aug 1993	Jorge Luis del Castillo
2059	General Roca Argentina	4 Jun 1995	Ruben Sabatino Tidei
1036	Godoy Cruz Argentina	6 Jun 1979	Salvador Molt'o
1978	Guaymallen Argentina	17 Apr 1994	Angel Licursi

1642	Jujuy Argentina	7 Jun 1987	Pedro Horacio Velazquez
1207	La Plata Argentina	23 Nov 1980	Hector Alejandro Olaiz
2284	La Plata Argentina Villa Elvira	1 Dec 1996	Angel Daniel Gatica
2058	Maipu de Cuyo Argentina	4 Jun 1995	Luis Wachman
997	Mar del Plata Argentina	31 Jan 1979	Hector Luis Catron
2049	Mar del Plata Argentina North	21 May 1995	Eduardo Bautista Ferrari
570	*Mendoza Argentina ‡Mendoza	1 Mar 1972	Mario A. Rastelli
1918	Neuquen Argentina	20 Dec 1992	Ruben Sabatino Tidei
2210	Neuquen Argentina West	7 Jul 1996	Sergio Marcelo Redaelli
2460	Pergamino Argentina	10 May 1998	Daniel Oscar Banuls
1902	Posadas Argentina	20 Sep 1992	Manuel Aristides Franco
694	Quilmes Argentina	15 May 1975	Hugo Nestor Salvioli
1237	Resistencia Argentina	17 Feb 1981	Leopoldo Oscar Fuentes
2266	Resistencia Argentina South	17 Nov 1996	Oscar Daniel Fernandez
2160	Rio Cuarto Argentina	11 Feb 1996	Esteban Eliseo Colaberardino
636a	Rosario Argentina	5 May 1974	Hugo Ruben Gazzoni
1177	Rosario Argentina North	10 Sep 1980	Daniel Arnoldo Moreno
2055	Rosario Argentina West	28 May 1995	Esteban Gabriel Resek
1260	Salta Argentina	29 Apr 1981	Victor Hugo Machado
2104	Salta Argentina West	15 Oct 1995	Angel Eleodoro Caceres
2166	San Juan Argentina Chimbas	18 Feb 1996	Ruben Dario Romeu
1871	San Juan Argentina Nuevo Cuyo	24 May 1992	Jorge Eduardo Chacon
1001	San Nicolas Argentina	22 Feb 1979	Deolindo Antonio Resek
2023	San Rafael Argentina	19 Feb 1995	Armando Hector Scorziello
1161	Santa Fe Argentina	20 Jul 1980	Raimundo Eduardo Rippstein
2085	Santa Fe Argentina North	13 Aug 1995	Pedro Manuel Zapata
2252	Santa Rosa Argentina	20 Oct 1996	Nicholas Arturo Paradiso
1945	Santiago Del Estero Argentina	20 Jun 1993	Jose Badami
1727	*Trelew Argentina North ‡Trelew Argentina	8 Dec 1996 11 Jun 1989	Oscar Daniel Filipponi
2288	Trelew Argentina South	8 Dec 1996	Juan Carlos Pino
1095	Tucuman Argentina	21 Jan 1980	Ronaldo Juan Walker
2004	Tucuman Argentina West	18 Dec 1994	Ricardo Ismael Rodriguez
2208	Zapala Argentina	30 Jun 1996	Humberto Nakad Saade
2385	Zarate Argentina	27 Jul 1997	Jose A. Gutierrez

Stakes discontinued

1250 Parana Argentina — 29 Mar 1981 — Carlos Arturo Sosa
Discontinued 15 Apr 1990

1096 San Juan Argentina — 22 Jan 1980 — Ricardo N. Ontiveros
Discontinued 30 Jul 1989 †Argentina Cordoba Mission

Missions — 10

(As of Oct. 1, 2000; shown with historical number. See MISSIONS.)

(180) ARG. BAHIA BLANCA MISSION
Casilla de Correo 70
8000 Bahia Blanca, Buenos Aires
Argentina

(32) ARG. BUENOS AIRES NO. MISSION
Ituzaingo 355, 1 Piso, C.C. 46
1642 San Isidro
Buenos Aires, Argentina

(112) ARG. BUENOS AIRES SO. MISSION
Italia 26, 4 Piso
1832 Lomas de Zamora
Buenos Aires, Argentina

(269) ARG. BUENOS AIRES W. MISSION
Casilla de Correo 92
1702 Cuidadela
Buenos Aires, Argentina

(73) ARG. CORDOBA MISSION
Casilla de Correo 17 - Suc. 9
5009 Cordoba
Argentina

(228) ARG. MENDOZA MISSION
Casilla de Correo 631
5500 Mendoza
Argentina

(230) ARG. NEUQUEN MISSION
Casilla de Correo, Suite 321
8300 Neuquen, Neuquen
Argentina

(229) ARG. RESISTENCIA MISSION
Casilla de Correo #1
3500 Resistencia - CHACO
Argentina

(100) ARG. ROSARIO MISSION
Casilla de Correo 341
2000 Rosario, Santa Fe
Argentina

(206) ARG. SALTA MISSION
Casillo de Correo 429
4400 Salta
Argentina

ARMENIA

Year-end 2000; Est. population, 3,422,000; Members, 500; Branches, 4; Districts 1; Europe East Area; Armenia Yerevan Mission.

Missionaries worked among Armenian people in Turkey and Syria as early as the 1880s. However, units established among the Armenians were discontinued following unsettled conditions in 1909. Some converts immigrated to the United States.

In modern times, the Church provided assistance in Armenia following the devastating earthquake of 1988 that killed 55,000 people and left half a million people homeless.

The Church and LDS industrialist Jon Huntsman worked together to help provide housing. Huntsman's company built a factory to build cement panels for homes. In response, Armenia donated property where the Church built a multipurpose building for factory workers.

In 1992, Utah farmers donated tons of milk for Armenian children. In 1993, the Europe East Area presidency invited BYU's International Folk Dance Ensemble to perform in Armenia. In 1995, missionary couples helped to distribute food to 200,000 people that was donated by the Jon Huntsman family of Salt Lake City. Humanitarian missionaries helped members in a crop and canning project in the summer of 1998. The Armenia Yerevan Mission was created in March 16, 1999. At year-end 1999, membership in Armenia was 656 in five branches.

Sources: *Church News,* April 28, 1981, July 4, 1981, July 6, 1991, Sept. 28, 1991, April 2, 1992, Aug. 29, 1998.

Mission — 1

(As of Oct. 1, 2000; shown with historical number. See MISSIONS.)

(332) ARMENIA YEREVAN MISSION
Teryan U1. #62 Kb 35
Yerevan 375009
Armenia

AUSTRALIA

Year-end 1999: Est. population, 18,322,000; Members, 99,121; Stakes, 31; Wards, 177; Branches, 98; Missions, 7; Districts, 12; Temples, 3; (2 announced) Percent LDS, 0.5, or one LDS in 185.

In the southwest South Pacific, the island-continent of Australia is a democratic federal state in the British commonwealth. Australia's population speaks English, and is Anglican, 26 percent; other Protestant, 25 percent; and Roman Catholic, 25 percent.

In 1840, William Barratt was called at age 17 from England to serve a mission in Australia. He found circumstances difficult, but evidence suggested that he baptized converts, including Robert Beauchamp, who later became an influential mission president in Australia. Historians believe Barratt was unable to contact the Saints in England or the United States after the martyrdom of Joseph Smith, and so married and remained in Australia until his death in 1891. The next missionary was Andrew Anderson, a Scottish immigrant to Australia who had been baptized by Orson Pratt in Scotland and given license to preach before sailing to Australia. He and his family arrived in 1841. He found converts and by the end of 1844, organized a branch in the private township of Montefiores, some 220 miles northwest of Sydney. Elder James Wall also served and baptized converts about this time, but information about his work is largely unknown.

Missionaries from Utah, Elders John Murdock and Charles Wandell, arrived Oct. 31, 1851, in Sydney, which became mission headquarters. They published tracts, began preaching and found a few converts among a people very distracted by a gold rush. A year later, 47 members were in the mission when Elder Murdock left because of ill health. On April 6, 1853, Elder Wandell left with a company of Saints. A few days later, another 10 missionaries arrived under the direction of Elder Augustus Farnham to continue the work. More branches were established but emigrations of converts continued, and at least two voyages involved serious mishaps. The most serious ship accident among all the LDS emigrants occurred Oct. 3, 1855, when the bark *Julia Ann*, carrying 350 tons of coal, in addition to 28 Saints, broke up on shoals near the Scilly Islands. Five people were drowned, but the rest managed to survive. In 1856, among the emigrants was Joseph Ridges, who brought with him components for the first of the Tabernacle organs in Salt Lake City.

Work continued in the 1860s and 1870s with a great emphasis on emigrating to Utah.

During one period, mission headquarters were moved to New Zealand and little work was done in Australia. On Jan. 1, 1898, the Australasian Mission was divided, forming a mission in Australia and a mission in New Zealand, and work resumed. At the time, membership in Australia was about 200.

The first LDS meetinghouse in the country was completed in Brisbane in 1904. Emigrating members continually depleted numbers and upset the Australian government, who in 1918 forbade "emigration propaganda."

The Church grew slowly, and the lack of buildings was a serious hindrance. In 1920, membership was about 1,000, and in 1940, 2,000. World War II particularly slowed the work. However, activity resumed in 1950-55, as President David O. McKay visited in 1955 and authorized building of many more meetinghouses. The mission was divided in 1955, with a second mission in Melbourne. The new meetinghouses provided the base for further growth. Membership reached 7,071 in 1960, 25,063 in 1970, and 40,000 in 1980.

Australia's first stake was organized in Sydney March 27, 1960. Additional missions were created in 1958 (Adelaide), 1973 (Brisbane), and 1975 (Perth). The Sydney Australia Temple was dedicated Sept. 20, 1984. Membership in 1990 was 76,000.

Members in Brisbane helped computerize government genealogy records in 1992, and Australia's sixth mission was created that year in Sydney. Elder Robert E. Sackley, who served in the First and then Second Quorum of the Seventy from 1988 until his death in 1993, was a native of Australia. In 1994, a group of 40 aborigine members gathered in Sydney to do temple work and enjoy their culture. In 1996, the Australian National Maritime Museum in Sydney announced that it would prepare an exhibit to feature the 1855 shipwreck of the *Julia Ann,* with its load of Mormon emigrants. President Gordon B. Hinckley visited the museum in May 1997 and loaned additional artifacts during his visit to Australia, which took him to the cities of Sydney, Brisbane, Adelaide, Melbourne, and Perth.

In 1998, the First Presidency announced that two more temples would be built in Australia, one in Brisbane and the other in Melbourne. A year later, the First Presidency announced another two temples for Australia, to be built in Adelaide and Perth.

In 1999, there were 99,121 members in Australia.

On a tour of the Pacific and Asia in January 2000, President Hinckley spoke to 625 members in the city of Cairns, located in the northeast corner of Australia. He returned to Australia later in the year, during an extended tour of Asia and the South Pacific, to dedicate the Adelaide Australia Temple on June 15, 2000, and the Melbourne Australia Temple the next day of June 16. Prior to the dedications, President Hinckley visited members in Darwin, Australia, on June 14, where 250 members greeted him at the airport. Members assisted as volunteers with the 2000 summer Olympic Games

Sources: *History of the Church,* Vol. 4, p. 154; *Encyclopedic History of the Church,* by Andrew Jenson; *Unto the Islands of the Sea,* by R. Lanier Britsch; *Church News,* Feb. 12, 1955, Dec. 27, 1958, Oct. 28, 1967, July 29, 1978; "The Church in Australia," by Garry P. Mitchell, *Ensign* February 1976, pp.13-19; "Australia Today: And Now the Harvest," by Michael Otterson, *Ensign,* October 1986; "Pioneering in the Gospel," by Marjorie A. Newton, *Ensign,* October 1986; *Church News,* Aug. 15, 1992; *Church News,* Nov. 29, 1992; *Church News,* Feb. 27, 1993; *Church News,* Jan. 15, 1994; "Aborigines gather for temple work," *Church News,* Feb. 5, 1994; *Church News,* March 26, 1994, May 4, 1996, Dec. 23, 1996, May 24, 1997, May 31, 1997; "Australia's Pioneer Saints," by Marjorie B. Newton, *Ensign,* February 1997; *Church News,* Feb. 12, 2000, June 24, 2000.

Stakes — 31

(Listed alphabetically as of Oct. 1, 2000.)

No.	Name	Organized	First President
Australia/New Zealand Area			
2129	Adelaide Australia Firle	26 Nov 1995	Philip F. Howes
414	*Adelaide Australia Marion	6 Jan 1982	
	*Adelaide Australia Payneham	23 Apr 1978	
	*Adelaide Australia		
	‡Adelaide	23 Feb 1966	Dudley Russell Tredrea
907	Adelaide Australia Modbury	23 Apr 1978	Douglas E. Hann
306	*Brisbane Australia		
	‡Brisbane	23 Oct 1960	William E. Waters
1684	Brisbane Australia North	7 Feb 1988	Douglas Walter Hill
2022	Canberra Australia	19 Feb 1995	Peter John Moir
2141	Devonport Australia	10 Dec 1995	John Robert Hargreaves
892	*Eight Mile Plains Australia	10Dec 1995	
	‡Brisbane Australia South	19 Feb 1978	John D. Jeffrey
2140	Gold Coast Australia	10 Dec 1995	Robert Gordon

860	Hobart Tasmania Australia	14 Sep 1977	John Douglas Jury
1279	*Ipswich Australia	6 May 1986	
	‡Brisbane Australia West	21 Jun 1981	John D. Jeffrey
	Launceton Tasmania		
2498	Liverpool Australia	25 Oct 1998	Maa Junior Maa
1988	Sydney Australia Campbelltown	28 Aug 1994	Ma'a Ma'a Jr.
551	*Melbourne Australia Braeside	5 Apr 1994	
	*Melbourne Australia Dandenong	18 Mar 1986	
	*Melbourne Australia Moorabbin		
	‡Melbourne South	22 Aug 1971	Bruce James Opie
1175	*Melbourne Australia Deer Park	18 Mar 1986	
	*Melbourne Australia		
	‡Fairfield West	7 Sep 1980	Edward Anderson
307	*Melbourne Australia Heidelberg	2 Jul 1995	
	*Melbourne Australia Fairfield		
	‡Melbourne	30 Oct 1960	Boyd C. Bott
1617	*Melbourne Australia Maroondah	2 Jul 1995	
	‡Melbourne Australia Waverly	7 Dec 1986	Ian Frank Davenport
2070	Melbourne Australia Pakenham	2 Jul 1995	J. Murray Lobley
2478	Melbourne Australia West	21 Jun 1998	Russell Bruce John Bielenberg
2264a	Nambour Australia	17 Nov 1996	Michaael Douglas Keily
1106	*Newcastle Australia	15 Jul 1986	
	‡Sydney Australia Newcastle	15 Feb 1980	Peter R. Barr
2450	Penrith Australia	19 Apr 1998	Jeffrey D. Cummings
447	*Perth Australia Dianella	6 Jul 1980	
	*Perth Australia		
	‡Perth	28 Nov 1967	Donald W. Cummings
2292	Perth Australia Rockingham	15 Dec 1996	Adrian Shane Palm
1159	Perth Australia Southern River	6 Jul 1980	Roy B. Webb
2033	Perth Australia Warwick	12 Mar 1995	Peter Fletcher Meurs
293	*Sydney Australia Greenwich		
	‡Sydney	27 Mar 1960	Dell C. Hunt
1105	Sydney Australia Hebersham	15 Feb 1980	Peter J. Moir
2303	Sydney Australia Hyde Park	2 Feb 1997	Patrick R. Ormond Jr.
435	*Sydney Australia Mortdale	2 Jun 1992	
	*Mortdale Australia	31 Mar 1992	
	*Sydney Australia Mortdale	15 Feb 1980	
	*Sydney Australia South		
	‡Sydney South	14 May 1967	John Daniel Parker
495	*Sydney Australia Parramatta	2 Jun 1992	
	*Parramatta Australia	31 Mar 1992	
	*Sydney Australia Parramatta	15 Feb 1980	
	*Parramatta Australia		
	‡Parramatta (Australia)	2 Nov 1969	Stanley Owen Gray

Missions — 7

(As of Oct. 1, 2000; shown with historical number. See MISSIONS.)

(82) AUSTRALIA ADELAIDE MISSION
P.O. Box 97
Marden, South Australia 5070
Australia

(106) AUSTRALIA BRISBANE MISSION
P.O. Box 348
Hamilton, Brisbane
Queensland 4007, Australia

(43c) AUSTRALIA MELBOURNE MISSION
1216 Old Burke Road
North Balwyn, Victoria 3104
Australia

(319) AUSTRALIA MELBOURNE WEST
PO Box 354
Niddrie, VIC 3040
Australia

(117) AUSTRALIA PERTH MISSION
P.O. Box 185
Tuart Hill, Western Australia 6939
Australia

(278) AUSTRALIA SYDNEY NORTH MISSION
P.O. Box 60
Epping, New SouthWales 1710
Australia

(10) AUSTRALIA SYDNEY SOUTH MISSION
P.O. Box 403
Mortdale, NSW 2223
Australia

AUSTRIA

Year-end 1999: Est. population,7,987,000; Members, 3,889; Stakes, 2; Wards, 12; Branches, 10; Missions, 1; Percent LDS, .05, or one in 2,054.

Austria, which is 98 percent German-speaking, is in south-central Europe. Some 85 percent of the people in the parliamentary democracy are Roman Catholic.

Elder Orson Pratt of the Quorum of the Twelve and Elder William W. Ritter arrived in Austria on Jan. 18, 1865, but were soon banished. The first Austrian convert was Joseph A. Oheim, baptized Jan. 22, 1870, in Munich, Germany. The first convert in Austria was Paul Haslinger, who was baptized Nov. 25, 1883. That same year, Elders Thomas Biesinger and Paul E. B. Hammer arrived and baptized a few converts. These elders were also expelled. By 1901 a branch was established in the Haag am Hausruck. A second branch was established in Vienna in 1909. Government restrictions then stopped work for a time.

The Church began to grow at the end of World War I when religious freedom was allowed. Missionaries were withdrawn during World War II and local members carried on. Missionary work began again in 1946 when Elder Ezra Taft Benson, then of the Quorum of the Twelve and president of the European Mission, established the Austrian District of the Swiss Austrian Mission. The Austrian government officially recognized the Church in 1955. In 1965, the centennial of the Church in Austria was celebrated. President Benson created Austria's first stake in Vienna on April 20, 1980.

In the late 1980s and early 1990s, the Austria mission supervised developing areas in Eastern Europe. During the subsequent difficult economic times in various countries, including the conflict in the former Yugoslavia, members donated food and clothing for relief. In October 1992, members began receiving general conference live via satellite.

The Church's 2,300th stake was created in Salzburg Jan. 19, 1997.

In 1999, there were 3,889 members in Austria, compared to 3,700 in 1990, 2,756 in 1979, and 2,675 in 1972.

Enthusiasm for family history research in Austria was high in 2000, thanks to the efforts of the national directors of Public Affairs for the Church, Freddy and Elisabeth Pletsch. In September 1999, they authored a newspaper article following the announcement of the creation of the Church's FamilySearch web site. That mushroomed into a major campaign requiring telephone hotlines, mail correspondence, and a link on the newspaper's home page accessing the FamilySearch web site. The newspaper announced the family history campaign in a 12-article feature package on Sept. 19, 1999, and the program began three days later. It developed into an continuing effort as Austrians have shown a great interest to search out their ancestors.

Sources: *Encyclopedic History of the Church,* by Andrew Jenson; "Austria gains 1st new stake," *Church News,* May 3, 1980; "Humanitarian relief in Europe," *Church News,* Feb. 29, 1992; *Church News,* Oct. 3, 1992; "The Church in Austria: Sounds of gospel ring in Salzburg," *Church News,* March 15, 1997; "Austrians join in search for their roots," *Church News,* Feb. 19, 2000, both by Shaun D. Stahle.

Stakes — 2

(As of Oct. 1, 1998.)

No.	Name	Organized	First President
Europe Central Area			
2300	Salzburg Austria	19 Jan 1997	Gerold Roth
1126	Vienna Austria	20 Apr 1980	Johann Anton Wondra

Mission — 1

(As of Oct. 1, 2000; shown with historical number. See MISSIONS.)

(53) AUSTRIA VIENNA MISSION
Fuerfanggasse 4
A-1190 Vienna, Austria

BAHAMAS

Year-end 1999: Est. population, 257,000; Members, 503; Branches, 2; Percent LDS, 0.2, or one in 511; North America Southeast Area; Florida Ft. Lauderdale Mission.

A Caribbean commonwealth, the Bahamas is made up of nearly 800 islands. Its English-speaking population includes Baptist, 29 percent; Anglican, 23 percent; and Roman Catholic, 22 percent.

Two LDS families, Larry and Margery McCombs and Albert and Karen Ballard, moved to Nassau in the summer of 1979. Missionaries arrived in December of that year but were refused visas and were asked to leave, which they did the following May. Full-time missionaries were allowed to return in March 1985. Alexandre Paul, consul general from Haiti to the Bahamas, and his wife were baptized Jan. 6, 1980. Some 48 investigators and members attended the first branch conference Sept. 12, 1981. A missionary couple, Dr. Thomas E. and Donna Bauman, arrived Dec. 11, 1982. A number of members from the Bahamas have served full-time missions.

A new meetinghouse was dedicated May 8, 1988, but within a few weeks the Soldiers Road and Nassau branches began to outgrow the building. The Soldiers Road Branch is made up of French Creole-speaking Haitians. In 1992, a collection of LDS books was donated to the College of the Bahamas library.

In 1999, membership in the Bahamas was 503 in two branches.

Sources: Personal journal, Margery McCombs; *Church News,* April 22, 1984, Nov. 9, 1986, March 19, 1988, June 18, 1988, Dec. 5, 1992.

BANGLADESH

Year-end 1999: Est. population, 127,000,000; Members, fewer than 100; Branches, 1; Asia Area.

Located on the northern coast of the Bay of Bengal, the People's Republic of Bangladesh is a parliamentary republic and member of the commonwealth of nations. Its people are Islam, 83 percent, and Hindi, 16 percent.

Among the first members in Bangladesh were Kenneth and Beatrice Nielsen, an LDS couple working for the Canadian government in 1985. A year or two later, the Nielsens' former cook, Bono Barua, and his family were baptized, the first converts in the country. Also baptized was Roseline Gomes, a young woman who later became the first of her nationality to serve a full-time mission. She left her homeland at age 19 to live in Canada with Church members who had lived in Bangladesh.

In 1999, there was one branch in Dhaka.

Sources: "Welcome mat is out in several countries," by Sheridan R. Sheffield, *Church News,* Oct. 23, 1993; *Church News,* May 15, 1993.

BARBADOS

Year-end 1999: Est. population, 256,000; Members, 568; Branches, 3; Percent LDS, 0.22, or one in 451; North America Southeast Area; West Indies Mission.

A Caribbean independent sovereign state of Great Britain, English-speaking Barbados is made up of one island where some 70 percent are Anglican.

The first branch in Barbados was the Christ Church Branch, created Oct. 20, 1979, followed by the organization of the Black Rock Branch on Aug. 24, 1983. Among the first LDS in Barbados were John and Norman Namie, who served as presidents of the Black Rock and Christ Church branches. The island was in the Puerto Rico San Juan Mission and transferred to the West Indies Mission when that mission was created in 1983. In 1994, headquarters of the West Indies Mission were transferred from Barbados to Tobago.

BELARUS

Year-end 1999: Est. population, 10,437,000; Members, 372, Districts, 1; Branches, 1; Europe East Area; Lithiania Vilnius Mission.

Formerly Byelorussia (also spelled Belorussia) or White Russia, Belarus is a hilly lowland with forests, rivers and lakes. It is bordered by Latvia, Lithuania, Ukraine, Russia, and Poland. Its people speak Russian and Belarusian and are mostly Russian Orthodox.

Belarus is part of the Lithiania Vilnius Mission, which was created July 1, 1993. The country was visited by Church leaders in May 1993. Two branches, the Minsk Pushkinsky and the Minsk Tsentralny, were created in January 1994. A missionary couple, John and Shirley Hess, headed a potato farm project from 1998-00 that has quadrupled productivity. A group of Ricks College dancers performed in Belarus in May 1997. The Church sponsors a humanitarian project, Charity Society Sophi, that operates in Belarus.

Sources: *Church News,* June 12, 1993, June 14, 1997; correspondence from the Lithuania Vilnius Missioon, Dec. 2, 1999.

BELGIUM

Year-end 1999: Est. population, 10,082,000; Members, 5,771; Stakes, 2; Wards, 11; Branches, 18; Missions, 1; Percent LDS, .06, or one in 1,747.

Located in northwest Europe on the North Sea, Belgium is a parliamentary democracy under a constitutional monarch. Its population speaks Flemish, 55 percent; French, 33 percent; and minority languages. About 75 percent of the population is Roman Catholic.

Mischa Markow, a Hungarian converted in Turkey, is believed to be the first member to have come to Belgium. Markow, baptized in Turkey in 1887, visited Antwerp in 1888. He preached to a family named Esselman, and baptized the mother, Henreite, and her oldest son, Frederick, on Oct. 17, 1888. Four other members of the family were baptized later.

Three missionaries from the Swiss and German Mission were then sent, and within two months they had baptized 80 people and organized branches in Liege, Brussels. and Antwerp. In 1891, Belgium became part of the Netherlands Mission.

Opposition was manifest in 1896 when a mob estimated at nearly 500 people threatened to kill Elder John Ripplinger in Liege. The mob stormed the home where he was staying, but was dispersed by police. However, he remained in the city and eventually baptized some 10 people.

Several French-speaking branches were transferred to the French Mission in 1924, with the Flemish-speaking branches remaining in the Netherlands Mission.

Work stopped during World War I, and by 1930, just a few scattered members remained in the country. However, by World War II, six branches were functioning and members remained active during the German occupation of Belgium. But when the Flemish section of Belgium was re-opened in January 1948 by the Netherlands Mission, there were no known members in Antwerp. Work progressed slowly, and in 1963 the Franco-Belgian Mission was organized, which is now the Belgium Brussels Mission. Ten years later, there were some 3,500 members in three districts in Belgium.

The first stake in the country was the Brussels Belgium Stake, organized Feb. 20, 1977.

The Belgium Antwerp Mission was organized in 1975, discontinued in 1982, and reorganized in 1990 and discontinued again in 1994.

Elder Charles Didier of the Seventy is a native of Ixelles, Belgium. Members in Brussels received a boost with the visit of President Gordon B. Hinckley in June 1996, the first president in some 40 years to visit the city. In Charleroi on Aug. 23, 1997, members presented what they called "the largest parade in Belgium's history," featuring pioneer wagons and handcarts in commemoration of the Mormon Pioneer sesquicentennial. About 6,000 spectators watched the parade. In June 1998, the Tabernacle Choir performed in Brussels, and a group of 40 singers performed at the U.S. Embassy. The public concert in Brussels was filmed by the State Radio and Television Network for re-broadcast. Belgium is in the new The Hague Netherlands temple district.

In 1999, membership in Belgium was 5,771.

Sources: *Encyclopedic History of the Church,* by Andrew Jenson; *Ensign,* Aug. 1973; *Church News* Oct. 22, 1977; "Anti-LDS Boomerang," by William Hartley, *Church News,* Aug. 12, 1978; "Missionary to the Balkans: Mischa Markow," by William Hale Kehr, *Ensign,* June 1980; *Church News,* Jan. 10, 1981; June 22, 1996, Aug. 30, 1997; "Choir tours under spotlight of European media," by Gerry Avant, *Church News,* June 27, 1998.

Stakes — 2

(As of Oct. 1, 1998.)

No.	Name	Organized	First President
Europe West Area			
1993	Antwerp Belgium	16 Oct 1994	Johan A. Buysse
813	Brussels Belgium	20 Feb 1977	Joseph Scheen

Mission — 1

(As of Oct. 1, 2000; shown with historical number. See MISSIONS.)

(76) BELGIUM BRUSSELS MISSION
87, Blvd. Brand Whitlock
1200 Bruxelles, Belgium

BELIZE

Year-end 1999: Est. population, 214,000; Members, 2,605; Districts, 3; Branches, 16; Percent LDS, 1.2, or one in 82; Central America Area; Guatemala Guatemala City North Mission.

Located on the eastern coast of Central America, Belize formerly was known as British

Honduras, it has a parliamentary government and a population that speaks English, Spanish, and Creole. They are Roman Catholic, 60 percent; Protestant, 40 percent. Belize received independence from Great Britain in 1981.

Missionary work opened in Belize on May 5, 1980, when President Samuel Flores of the Honduras Tegucigalpa Mission and Elder Robert Henke arrived to prepare for 10 additional missionaries coming the following day. On the day of their arrival, Elder Merlin Mikkelson was set apart as president of a newly organized branch, and the first Sunday meeting was held May 11, 1980. Elders Larry Pinnock and Scott Harries baptized Ernesto Alay on June 1, 1980.

The Belize District was organized April 17, 1983, with Harold Smith as president. Meetinghouses were completed in Orange Walk in August of 1987, and in San Ignacio in September 1987. By 1987, some 1,000 members in seven branches comprised the Belize District. On July 1, 1990, the Honduras Tegucigalpa Mission was divided, and Belize was placed in the new Honduras San Pedro Sula Mission. Hilberto Cassanova was the first missionary from Belize, and served in the Honduras Tegucigalpa Misssion from 1987-89.

Elder Russell M. Nelson of the Quorum of the Twelve visited and dedicated a meetinghouse in December 1992, at which some 289 members attended.

Some 1,200 members gathered in Belize City on Nov. 13, 1997, to hear President Gordon B. Hinckley, the largest gathering of members in the country.

Sources: Honduras Tegucigalpa Mission history; *Church News,* Feb. 16, 1990; *Church News,* Dec. 19, 1992; Correspondence from Ralph D. and Dawnetta A. Erickson, Nov. 30, 1994; *Church News,* Nov. 22, 1997, Feb. 7, 1998.

BOLIVIA

Year-end 1999: Est. population, 7,896,000; Members, 112,222; Stakes, 21; Wards, 151; Districts, 9; Branches, 81; Missions, 3; Temples, 1; Percent LDS, 1.4, or one in 70.

Bolivia, located in central South America, is a republic with a population that speaks Spanish, Quechua, and Aymara. Some 95 percent are Roman Catholic.

Three LDS members who lived in Bolivia in 1963 — Duane Wilcox and Dube Thomas in La Paz, and Norval Jesperson in Cochabamba — helped the Church gain legal status. On Nov. 24, 1964, missionaries arrived from the Andes Mission. The first branch meeting in Cochabamba was held Nov. 22, 1964, in a little house that was on a site occupied in 2000 by the Diplomat Hotel. Nineteen people attended that first meeting. Missionaries baptized Victor Walter Vallejos at Cochabamba just before Christmas in 1964. In two years, branches opened in Oruro and Santa Cruz. The first Bolivian to serve a mission was Desiderio Arce Cano. While pursuing a singing career in Argentina, he was called on April 25, 1967, to return to his native land. The first missionary called from Bolivia was Carlos Pedraja, baptized May 30, 1965, and called to the Andes South Mission in 1968. He later served as stake and mission president.

In 1968, there were about 350 members in Bolivia. That number increased to 9,700 by 1977. Church education, including seminary, helped prepare many young people for leadership positions. The Andes South Mission, later named the Bolivia La Paz Mission, was organized in 1966. In 1977, the Bolivia Santa Cruz Mission was organized, and was renamed the Bolivia Cochabamba Mission in 1982. Some 4,373 members attended an area conference in La Paz on March 3, 1977, with President Spencer W. Kimball, who also met with the head of state, President Hugo Bonzer Suarez.

The Santa Cruz Bolivia Stake, the first stake in Bolivia, was organized Jan. 14, 1979.

In recent years, a number of Church-sponsored humanitarian projects have improved the health of members and non-members in various rural areas. Membership in 1990 was 64,000, and in 1999, it was 112,222.

In 1998, a new Bolivia Santa Cruz Mission was created.

Bolivian leader Jorge Leano was called as president of the Lima Peru Temple in 1995, the same year that a temple was announced for Cochabamba, Bolivia. Ground for the Bolivia temple was broken on Nov. 10, 1996, and some 4,000 members witnessed the ceremony in a pouring rainstorm. The temple was dedicated by President Gordon B . Hinckley on April 30, 2000, following a five-day openhouse in which 65,570 people visited, resulting in 2,232 referrals.

Sources: *Improvement Era,* Jan. 1965; "Bolivia," *Ensign,* Feb. 1977; "Love, respect and emotion end area conference series," by Dell Van Orden, *Church News,* March 12, 1977; *Church News,* Jan. 27, 1979, Feb. 24, 1990, May 26, 1990, June 8, 1991; *Church News,* Nov. 23, 1996; "Pioneering in the Andes,"

Ensign, Jan. 1997; "Worthy of the heart of a people," by Jerry Johnston, *Church News*, May 13, 2000.

Stakes — 21

(Listed alphabetically as of Oct. 1, 2000.)

No.	Name	Organized	First President
South America West Area			
1465	Cochabamba Bolivia Cobija	19 Feb 1984	Guillermo Rivero Paz Soldan
2143	Cochabamba Bolivia Jaihuayco	10 Dec 1995	Ivan Jorge Gutierrez
1940	Cochabamba Bolivia Los Alamos	16 May 1993	Jose Ruben Rivero Zeballos
1062	*Cochabamba Bolivia Universidad	19 Feb 1984	
	‡Cochabamba Bolivia	11 Sep 1979	Carlos L. Pedraja
1831	El Alto Bolivia	24 Nov 1991	Edmundo Chavez Vasquez
1227	*El Alto Bolivia Satelite	6 Mar 1992	
	‡La Paz Bolivia El Alto	18 Jan 1981	Victor Hugo Saravia R.
2207	La Paz Bolivia Alto San Pedro	30 Jun 1996	Juan Carlos Mogrovejo Rocabado
1112	*La Paz Bolivia Constitucion	18 Jan 1981	
	‡La Paz Bolivia West	24 Feb 1980	Victor Hugo Saravia R.
1007	*La Paz Bolivia Miraflores	18 Jan 1981	
	‡La Paz Bolivia	11 Mar 1979	Jorge Leano
1670	La Paz Bolivia Sopocachi	17 Jan 1988	Eduardo Gabarret I.
2120	Montero Bolivia	12 Nov 1995	Hugo Walter Sandoval Pinto
1213	Oruro Bolivia	1 Dec 1980	J. Adrian Velasco C.
2277	Oruro Bolivia Agua de Castilla	24 Nov 1996	Johnny Chambi Joaniquina
2063	Potosi Bolivia	18 Jun 1995	Edgar Medardo Lopez Loayza
993	*Santa Cruz Bolivia Canoto	15 Feb 1981	
	‡Santa Cruz Bolivia	14 Jan 1979	Noriharu Ishigaki Haraguichi
2434	Santa Cruz Bolivia El Bajio	1 Feb 1998	Jose Martin Tellez T.
1782	Santa Cruz Bolivia Equipetrol	2 Dec 1990	Antonio Rolando Oyola
1235	Santa Cruz Bolivia Paraiso	15 Feb 1981	Erwin Birnbaumer
1981	Santa Cruz Bolivia Piray	19 June 1994	Rolando A. Oyola Suarez
2191	Sucre Bolivia	28 Apr 1996	Esteban Portillo Rios
2184	Tarija Bolivia	24 Mar 1996	Juan Garcia Vargas

Missions — 3

(As of Oct. 1, 2000; shown with historical number. See MISSIONS.)

(150) BOLIVIA COCHABAMBA MISSION
Casilla de Correo 1375
Cochabamba, Bolivia

(75a) BOLIVIA LA PAZ MISSION
Casilla de Correo 4789
La Paz, Bolivia

(320) BOLIVIA SANTA CRUZ
Casilla de Correo 2042
Zona Central, Santa Cruz
Bolivia

BOTSWANA

Year-end 1999: Est. population, 1,392,000; Members, 700; Wards, 1; Branches, 2; Percent LDS, .05, or one in 1,989 ;Africa Southeast Area; South Africa Johannesburg Mission.

Located north of South Africa, Botswana is a parliamentary democracy with a population that speaks English and Setswana. The majority follow indigenous beliefs, and 15 percent are Christian.

Missionary work in Botswana began in 1990 with the arrival in Gabarone of Pres. R.J. Snow of the South Africa Johannesburg Mission, followed by occasional visits by Elder Karl and Sister Marjorie Jenkins. The first missionaries assigned to Botswana were Elder Bruce Midgley and his wife, Patricia, who established a group in Gabarone on June 24, 1990, with Elder Midgley as the presiding elder.

Members living in Botswana at the time included two returned missionaries who had become Peace Corps workers, Patricia Lutz of Levittown, Pa., in Molepolole, and Javotte Pickering of Enterprise, Utah, stationed in Kang. The Maurice Mzwinila and Anthony

Mogare families, who had joined the Church while studying in the United States, were later located through a newspaper article.

In September 1990, a baptismal service was held. Among the converts was Kwasi Agyare Dwomoh, an architect from Ghana working for the Botswana government. When the Church registration was filed in August 1991 and the first branch was organized, Brother Dwomoh was called as its first president. By March 1992, the fast-growing branch was ready to be divided into two branches, and Brother Dwomoh was called as the first district president in Botswana. He also was the first member in Botswana to receive his endowments at the Johannesburg South Africa Temple.

By August 1992, membership had grown to 160, with a number of baptisms planned for the city of Lobatse. A third unit was added to the district in 1992.

On Feb. 18, 1996, members from Botswana were among the 5,000 people who gathered for the Johannesburg South Africa Regional Conference at Soweto. An open house sponsored in January 1997 by the Roodeport South Africa Stake was well-attended.

Sources: Correspondence from Pres. R.J. and Sister Marilyn M. Snow; "Missionary work begins in Botswana," by Elder Darwin and Sister Maureen Cook, *Church News*, Sept. 15, 1990; "Four nations in central, southern Africa," by Mary Mostert and Gerry Avant, *Church News*, Sept. 26, 1992; *Church News*, March 2, 1996; "Open houses in Africa show rapid growth," by Hiram McDonald, *Church News*, Feb. 15, 1997.

BRAZIL

Year-end 1999: Est. population, 160,737,000; Members, 743,182; Stakes, 186; Wards, 1,264; Branches, 615; Missions, 26; Districts, 42; Temples, 1 (3 announced); Percent LDS, .5, or one in 216.

Brazil, a federal republic, covers almost half the continent of South America, and has a population that speaks Portuguese and is 89 percent Roman Catholic.

The first Church members in Brazil were German immigrants, Augusta Kuhlmann Lippelt and her four children. Her husband, Roberto, was baptized several years later. They arrived in Brazil in 1923. The first missionaries were Elders William Fred Heinz and Emil A.J. Schindler, accompanied by Pres. Rheinold Stoof of the South American Mission in Buenos Aires, Argentina. Pres. Stoof first visited Brazil in 1927, and returned with the elders to begin proselyting among German-speaking people in September 1928. Bertha Sell and her children, Theodore, Alice, Seigfried, and Adell, were the first converts, baptized April 14, 1929. The first Church-owned meetinghouse in South America was dedicated Oct. 25, 1931, in Joinville.

A mission was created and headquartered in Brazil on May 25, 1935. At first, missionaries taught only in German. However, the Book of Mormon was translated into Portuguese in 1937, and missionaries began teaching in Portuguese a year later. By 1940, there were still fewer than 200 members in the country. Missionary work progressed very slowly during World War II. More than a decade later, in 1957, the Church had reached about 1,000 members.

In the next decade, however, the work began to accelerate. By 1959, membership was 3,700. The Sao Paulo Stake, the first in South America, was organized May 1, 1966. Ten years later, Brazil had 10 stakes, and a temple had been announced for Sao Paulo. President Spencer W. Kimball presided over a cornerstone ceremony for the temple March 9, 1977, at which 3,000 people attended.

The Sao Paulo Temple was dedicated Oct. 30, 1978. The Brazil Area was created in August 1987, and divided in August of 1998 to form the Brazil North and South areas.

On Feb. 2, 1986, Brazil became the third country outside the United States to have 50 stakes, with the creation of the Campinas Brazil Castelo Stake. With the creation of the Sao Leopoldo Stake Dec. 5, 1993, Brazil reached 100 stakes, the second country outside the United States to do so. Elder Helio A. Camargo, who served in the Seventy from 1985-1990, was the first Brazilian to serve as a General Authority. Other Brazilians called as General Authorities as members of the Seventy have been Helvecio Martins, released in 1995, and Claudio R.M. Costa. Membership in 1990 was 368,000.

In October 1993, construction began on Brazil's missionary training center, the Church's second largest. With 23 missions in 1996, Brazil has the largest number of missions outside the United States. A temple for Recife was announced Jan. 21, 1995, and President Gordon B. Hinckley broke ground for the temple Nov. 15, 1996. He also visited members in Porto Alegre, Campinas, Sao Paulo, and Manaus during his visit. In March of 1997, Brazil passed Mexico to become second only to the United States in number of stakes.

Temples were also announced for Campinas and Porte Alegre, and ground was broken for them by President James E. Faust, second counselor in the First Presidency on May 1 and 2, 1998. While President Faust was in Brazil, he was made an honorary citizen of Sao Paulo.

In 1998, members in the south donated substantial amounts of food and clothing to lessen the effects of a serious drought in the north. On April 21, 1999, about 3,000 youth from two missions and 11 stakes took part in "Project Clean Wave" on the world-famous Copacabana Beach, north of Rio de Janeiro, in part in commemoration of the 500th anniversary of the founding of Brazil.

A new seven-story Brazilian Missionary Training Center in Sao Paulo, capable of accommodating 750 missionaries was dedicated May 18, 1997, by Elder Russell M. Nelson of the Quorum of the Twelve. In October 1988, North American missionaries called to Brazil began receiving nearly half of their training at the Brazilian training center. The program to send North American missionaries to Brazil for four weeks of training enabled them to be immersed in the Brazilian culture and Portuguese language in a controlled environment. The program was so successful that on April 22, 2000, the first 22 North American missionaries were sent to Brazil for their full eight weeks of training. The group was the first of four pilot groups to enter the Brazilian center during the summer of 2000 to be entirely trained in another language at a missionary training center in another country. The pilot training program ended in August 2000, and, afterward, an average of 33 North American missionaries began their full training in the Brazil center each week.

As the 1990s came to a close, the missionaries in Brazil were baptizing enough converts monthly to fill a stake center. Membership in Brazil in 1999 was 743,182 in 186 stakes and 26 missions.

Sources: *From Acorn to Oak Tree,* by Frederick S. Williams and Frederick G. Williams; *Deseret News,* Nov. 14, 1935; "Brazil, A new frontier for the Restored Gospel," by Rulon S. Howells, *Improvement Era,* May 1936 and Sept. 1938; "Brazilian Missions," *Improvement Era,* May 1963; "Sao Paulo Temple cornerstone laid by President Romney," by Dell Van Orden, *Church News,* March 19, 1977; "Gospel story in Brazil begun by German Family," by Jason Souza Garcia, *Church News,* May 31, 1980; *Church News,* Sept. 18, 1993, Feb. 19, 1994, Feb. 22, 1997, May 14, 1997, June 14, 1997, May 9, 1998; "Tudo Ben in Brazil," by Don L. Searle, *Ensign,* March 1997; *Church News,* March 20, 1999, May 22, 1999; "Missionaries receive full training in Brazil," by Shaun D. Stahle, *Church News,* Aug. 12, 2000.

Stakes — 185

(Listed alphabetically as of Oct. 1, 2000.)

No.	Name	Organized	First President
Brazil North Area - 58			
2383	Anapolis Brazil	29 Jun 1997	Cassio Barbosa Piazzarola
2078	*Aracaju Brazi North	27 Feb 2000	
	‡Aracaju Brazil Cidade Nova	23 Jul 1995	Raulino Gairao LIma Jr.
1851	*Aracaju Brazil South	27 Feb 2000	
	*Aracaju Brazil Bela Vista	23 Jul 1995	
	‡Aracaju Brazil	8 Mar 1992	Manuel Durval Andrade Neto
2100	Arapiraca Brazil	17 Sep 1995	Antonio de A. de Banos
1837	Belem Brazil	29 Dec 1991	Luiz Carlos Silva De Franca
2067	Belem Brazil Cabanagem	25 Jun 1995	Jaime Carneiro Costa
2381	Belem Brazil Cidade Nova	22 Jun 1997	Wenceslau W. da C. Coelho
1189	Brasilia Brazil	12 Oct 1980	Daniel Alberta da Gloria
1393	*Brasilia Brazil Alvorada	22 Mar 1983	
	‡Alvorada Brazil	9 Jan 1983	Manoel Francisco Clavery G.
2418	Brasilia Brazil North	30 Nov 1997	Joao A. Machado de Lima
2147	Brasilia Brazil Taguatinga	17 Dec 1995	Jose Claudio de Almeida
1984	Camaragibe Brazil	24 Jul 1994	Altair Roque da Silva
1442	Campina Grande Brazil	18 Sep 1983	Jose Francisco Barbosa
2032	Cuiaba Brazil	5 Mar 1995	Ildemar Ferreira Vilas Boas
2231	Feira de Santana Brazil	15 Sep 1996	Vaguiner Cruciol Tobias
1284	Fortaleza Brazil	19 Jul 1981	Orville Wayne Day Jr.

1828	Fortaleza Brazil Bom Sucesso	17 Nov 1991	Manoel A. De Carvalho Filho
1935	Fortaleza Brazil Ceara	2 May 1993	Jose Vieira de Matos Filho
2380	Fortaleza Brazil Litoral	22 Jun 1997	Miguel Alves dos Santos
1454	Fortaleza Brazil Montese	13 Nov 1983	Fernando J. Duarte D.
2386	Fortaleza Brazil South	17 Aug 1997	David Garcia Fernandes
1578	Fortaleza Brazil West	24 Nov 1985	Antenor Silva Junior
2048	Garanhuns Brazil	21 May 1995	Jose C. Furtado Campos
1641	Goiania Brazil	24 May 1987	Antonio Casado Rodriguez
2294	Goiania Brazil East	15 Dec 1996	Jose Renato Ungarelli
2256	Itabuna Brazil	27 Oct 1996	Jose M. Sepulveda da Costa
1891	*Jaboatao Brazil Dos Guararapes	15 May 1994	
	‡Recife Brazil Jaboatao	26 Jul 1992	Jose Antonia da Silva
1979	Jaboatao Brazil Litoral	15 May 1994	Domingos Savio Linhares
1185	Joao Pessoa Brazil	2 Oct 1980	Jose Francisco Barbosa
1896	Joao Pessoa Brazil Rangel	23 Aug 1992	
1322	Maceio Brazil	21 Jan 1982	Abelardo Rodrigues Camara
1923	Maceio Brazil Litoral	7 Feb 1993	Gilberto C. da Silva Moraes
2030	Maceio Brazil Pajucara	5 Mar 1995	Jose Domingues Silva
1700	Manaus Brazil	16 Oct 1988	Eduardo A. Soares C.
2116	Manaus Brazil Cidade Nova	5 Nov 1995	Walter Braga De Souza
2447	Manaus Brazil Rio Amazonas	22 Mar 1998	Jose A. Viana Guimaraes
1941	Manaus Brazil Rio Negro	30 May 1993	Divino Presenca
2319	Manaus Brazil Solimoes	9 Mar 1997	Jose A. Viana Guimaraes
2145	Maracanau Brazil	17 Dec 1995	Raimundo Vieira de Oliveira
1894	Natal Brazil	16 Aug 1992	Ricardo Gueiros
2470	Natal Brazil Potengi	31 May 1998	Jorge Borges DeLira
1282	Olinda Brazil	12 Jul 1981	Reinhold Kraft
2020	*Olinda Brazil Paulista	22 Aug 1995	
	‡Paulista Brazil	5 Feb 1995	Reginaldo de Morais Junior
2479	Petrolina Brazil	21 June 1998	Nilo Manuel de Sa
2287	Porto Velho Brazil	8 Dec 1996	Jose S. Paulino de Lacerda
1201	Recife Brazil	31 Oct 1980	Iraja Bandeira Soares
1332	*Recife Brazil Boa Viagem	26 Jul 1992	
	*Boa Viagem Brazil	21 Mar 1982	Iraga Bandeira Soares
2379	Recife Brazil Caxanga	22 Jun 1997	Altair Rogue da Silva
2135	Recife Brazil Imbiribeira	3 Dec 1995	Marcone Magalhaes Santos
1811	*Recife Brazil Jardim Sao Paulo	10 May 1994	
	‡Recife Brazil Southwest	25 Aug 1991	Herbert Otto Homolka
2136	Rio Branco Brazil	3 Dec 1995	Tarciso Barboza Friere
1862	Salvador Brazil	10 May 1992	Carlos Shunji Obata
1934a	Salvador Brazil North	2 May 1993	Sandro Silva Quatel
2227	Santa Rita Brazil	1 Sep 1996	Jose Joel Alves Fernandes
2071	Sao Luis Brazil	2 Jul 1995	Jose Benicio Pereira
1960a	Teresina Brazil	28 Nov 1993	Alexandre J. Gomes da Cruz
2490	Uberaba Brazil	16 Aug 1998	Jorge Ribeiro Barbosa
2017	Uberlandia Brazil	29 Jan 1995	Raimundo Walter Tavares A.
2375	Vitoria da Conquista Brazil	15 Jun 1997	Octavio Santos Sousa Neto

Brazil South Area-126

1292	Alegrete Brazil	20 Sep 1981	Waldomiro Siegfried Radtke
2066	Americana Brazil	25 Jun 1995	Donizetti de Paul Tavares
1886	Aracatuba Brazil	14 June 1992	Paulo Henrique Itinose
970	Araraquara Brazil	22 Oct 1978	Marcio Rodrigues Galhardo
1959	Bage Brazil	31 Oct 1993	Cecer R. Loureiro Dutra
2402	Barueri Brazil	26 Oct 1997	Marcos Antony Aidukaitis
1893	Bauru Brazil	2 Aug 1992	Lazaro Beteto

1234	*Belo Horizonte Brazil	6 Mar 1990	
	*Belo Horizonte Brazil De Siao	10 Jan 1989	
	‡Belo Horizonte Brazil	15 Feb 1981	Ernani Teixeira
2570	Belo Horizonte Brazil Pampulha	3 Sep 2000	Rodrigo De Lima E. Myrra
1963a	Belo Horizonte Brazil West	12 Dec 1993	Rodrigo de Lima e Myrrha
2074	Birigui Brazil	9 Jul 1995	Sebastiao Henrique Neto
621	*Campinas Brazil		
	‡Campinas	9 Jun 1973	Nelson de Genaro
1586	Campinas Brazil Castelo	2 Feb 1986	S. Lourenco de Oliveira
1897	Campinas Brazil Flamboyant	23 Aug 1992	Luiz Antonio Cairo
1805	Campo Grande Brazil	30 Jun 1991	Ricardo Kasimerczak
2412	Campos Brazil	23 Nov 1997	Jarbas Pereira de Souza Filho
1962	Canoas Brazil	5 Dec 1993	Raul Anibal Proenca Krieger
2341	Cascavel Brazil	20 Apr 1997	Luiz C. Bernardino da Silva
1963	Caxias Do Sul Brazil	5 Dec 1993	Alvacir Luiz Siedschlag
1942	Contagem Brazil	6 June 1993	Evandro Chevitarese Parada
552	*Curitiba Brazil		
	‡Curitiba	12 Sep 1971	Jason Garcia Souza
2446	Curitiba Brazil Boa Vista	22 Mar 1998	Ozair de Jesus Ribeiro Filho
1243	*Curitiba Brazil Boqueirao	14 Mar 1989	
	‡Curitiba Brazil East	15 Mar 1981	Francisco Reguim
1468	Curitiba Brazil Iguacu	29 Apr 1984	Waldemar de Lima
2438	Curitiba Brazil Luz	15 Feb 1998	Luiz Antonio Cruzato
1974a	Curitiba Brazil Novo Mundo	29 Feb 1994	Valdemiro Skraba
893	*Curitiba Brazil Portao	14 Mar 1989	
	‡Curitiba Brazil South	26 Feb 1978	Albina Bruno Schmeil
1302	*Curitiba Sao Lourenco		
	‡Curitiba Brazil Bacacheri	1 Nov 1981	Casemiro Antunes Gomes
2073	Curitiba Brazil Taruma	9 Jul 1995	Ildefonso de C. Dues Neto
2249	Diadema Brazil	20 Oct 1996	Adelson de Paula Parrella
1569	Florianopolis Brazil	3 Nov 1985	Cesar A. Seiguer Milder
1952	Franca Brazil	5 Sep 1993	Donizete Pugliesi Braz
2142	Gravatai Brazil	10 Dec 1995	Fabiano Ribeiro Barreto
2310	Guaratingueta Brazil	23 Feb 1997	Pedro G. L. de C. Bruno
2221	Guaruja Brazil	18 Aug 1996	Carlos Roberto Couto E. Silva
2480	Itatiba Brazil	21 June 1998	Eliseli Colleoni
2342	Itu Brazil	20 Apr 1997	Valoir Teixeira Arantes
1338	Joinville Brazil	21 Apr 1982	Heins Dorival Halter
2275	Juiz De Fora Brazil	24 Nov 1996	Eraldo Luis dos Santos
1833	Jundiai Brazil	1 Dec 1991	Domingos Fatobene Jr.
2257	Lajes Brazil	27 Oct 1996	Sebastiao C. de Lima Dias
1821	Livramento Brazil	27 Oct 1991	Clademir Elton Trage
1080	Londrina Brazil	11 Nov 1979	Carlos Roberto Moeller
2251	Londrina Brazil Tiradentes	20 Oct 1996	Amancio Marques do Santos
1449	Marilia Brazil	23 Oct 1983	Wilson de Souza Novelli
2095	Maringa Brazil	27 Aug 1995	Dirceu Freire
2065	Mogi Mirim Brazil	25 Jun 1995	Milton Cenko
1964	Monte Cristo Brazil	19 Dec 1993	Adelson de Paula Parrella
2325	Nova Iguacu Brazil	16 Mar 1997	Carlos M. Figueireda Patriota
987	Novo Hamburgo Brazil	3 Dec 1978	Paulo R. Grahl
1932	Osasco Brazil	18 Apr 1993	Marcos Anthony Aidu Kaitis
2471	Paranagua Brazil	31 May 1998	
1604	Passo Fundo Brazil	10 Aug 1986	Helio Rodrigues Severo
1658	Pelotas Brazil	18 Oct 1987	Marco Antonio Rais
2080	Pelotas Brazil North	23 Jul 1995	Victor A. Asconavieta da Silva
1377	Petropolis Brazil	14 Nov 1982	Antonio Jose Mendoza

2012	Piracicaba Brazil	22 Jan 1995	Marcos T. Michailuca Nolli
1182	Ponta Grossa Brazil	30 Nov 1997	
	*Ponta Grossa Brazil Parana	7 Apr 1992	
	‡Ponta Grossa Parana Brazil	22 Sep 1980	Silvina Mendes de Jesus
2419	Ponta Grossa Brazil Campos Gerais	30 Nov 1997	Gilberto P. Lucas de Farias
2423	Ponta Pora Brazil	14 Dec 1997	Rubens Paim Quadros
601	*Porto Alegre Brazil		
	‡Porto Alegre	13 Feb 1973	Miguell Sorrentino
1858	Porto Alegre Brazil Moinhos De Vento	3 May 1992	Claudio Weihert
1256	Porto Alegre Brazil North	21 Apr 1981	Silvio Geschwasdtner
1793	Porto Alegre Brazil Partenon	5 May 1991	Ulisses Pereira Filho
2283	Porto Alegre Brazil South	1 Dec 1996	Hilario Olmar da Silva
2436	Praia Grande Brazil	8 Feb 1998	Fernando da Silva E Souza
1916a	Ribeiro Pires Brazil	13 Dec 1992	Guilherme Tell Peixoto
1645	Ribeirao Preto Brazil	28 Jun 1987	Moises Barreiro Damasceno
1888	Ribeirao Preto Brazil Centro	21 Jun 1992	Augusto Martinez Perez
1953	Ribeirao Preto Brazil Ipiranga	5 Sep 1993	Jose Alberto Borges da Silva
1954	Ribeirao Preto Brazil Quintino	5 Sep 1993	Euclides Jose Maggio
1135	Rio Claro Brazil	21 May 1980	Marcio Rodriques Galhardo
589	*Rio de Janeiro Brazil		
	‡Rio de Janeiro	22 Oct 1972	Veledmar Cury
1028	Rio de Janeiro Brazil Andarai	20 May 1979	Nelson Gennari
2293	Rio de Janeiro Brazil Campo Grande	15 Dec 1996	Jackson Alves do Santos
2445	Rio De Janeiro Brazil Jacarepagua	22 Mar 1998	Claudio Jose Hottum Da Silva
1378	Rio de Janeiro Brazil Madureira	14 Nov 1982	Atilio Pinto Maio
769	Rio de Janeiro Brazil Niteroi	19 Sep 1976	Joao Eduardo Kemeny
2079	Rio Grande Brazil	23 Jul 1995	Carlos W. Ramires de Oliveira
2031	Rosario Do Sul Brazil	5 Mar 1995	Jean Jaques
1922	Santa Maria Brazil	31 Jan 1993	Aires Luciano
1136	Santo Andre Brazil	23 May 1980	Ademar Leal
620	*Santos Brazil		
	‡Santos	8 Jun 1973	Jose Gonzalez Lopes
523	*Sao Bernardo Brazil	23 May 1980	
	*Sao Paulo Brazil South		
	‡Sao Paulo South	6 Sep 1970	Saul Messias de Oliveira
2491	Sao Bernardo Brazil Rudge Ramos	16 Aug 1998	Valdir Antunes
1909a	Sao Carlos Brazil	15 Nov 1992	Justino Carlos Atchiza Peres
2081	Sao Joao da Boa Vista Brazil	30 Jul 1995	Izaias Pivato Nogueira
1965	Sao Jose Brazil	19 Dec 1993	Jose Jorge Cordeiro Campos
1917	Sao Jose Do Rio Preto Brazil	13 Dec 1992	Guilherme Tell Peixoto
1516	Sao Jose Dos Campos Brazil	3 Mar 1985	Eric Brito Correa
2396	Sao Jose Dos Pinhais Brazil	14 Sep 1997	Nata Cruciol Tobias
1961	Sao Leopoldo Brazil	5 Dec 1993	Valmir Severo Dutra
417	*Sao Paulo Brazil		
	‡Sao Paulo	1 May 1966	Walter Spat
1846	Sao Paulo Brazil Campo Limpo	9 Feb 1992	Dejanir Hadleck de Castro
2369	Sao Paulo Brazil Grajau	8 Jun 1997I	Dario Marcolino dos Santos
2367	Sao Paulo Brazil Guarapiranga	1 Jun 1997	Caio Bezerra da Silva
1868	Sao Paulo Brazil Guarulhos	24 May 1992	Gilmar Silva Diasta
1536	Sao Paulo Brazil Interlagos	26 May 1985	Walter Guedes de Queiroz
1137	Sao Paulo Brazil Ipiranga	25 May 1980	Demar Staniscia

1869	Sao Paulo Brazil Itaquera	24 May 1992	Vanderlei Zanchetta
2198	Sao Paulo Brazil Jacana	02 Jun 1996	Jorge Luiz de Oliveira
1870	Sao Paulo Brazil Mogi Das Cruzes	24 May 1992	Gilberto Vicente da Silva
815	Sao Paulo Brazil North	20 Feb 1977	Jorge Flavio de Moraes
2395	Sao Paulo Brazil Parque Bristol	14 Sep 1997	Ricardo Vieira
2318	Sao Paulo Brazil Parque Pinheiros	9 Mar 1997	Mario Helio Emerick
467	*Sao Paulo Brazil Penha	24 May 1992	
	*Sao Paulo Brazil East		
	‡Sao Paulo East	24 Nov 1968	Helio da Rocha Camargo
1138	Sao Paulo Brazil Perdizes	25 May 1980	Oswaldo Silva Camargo
1913	Sao Paulo Brazil Piratininga	6 Dec 1992	Luiz Carlos Coronetti
2359	Sao Paulo Brazil Pirituba	25 May 1997	Pedro Pereira do Santos
2076	*Sao Paulo Brazil Raposo Taveres	14 Jan 1997	
	‡Sao Paulo Brazil Cotia	16 Jul 1995	Ulisses Soares
1082	Sao Paulo Brazil Santo Amaro	12 Nov 1979	Wilson Sanchez Netto
1823	Sao Paulo Brazil Sao Miguel Paulista	10 Nov 1991	Gilberto V. Da Silva
1441	Sao Paulo Brazil Taboao	18 Sep 1983	Octavio Baptists de Carvalho
1921	Sao Paulo Brazil Vila Sabrina	24 Jan 1993	Jose Olimpio Fabrizio
622	*Sao Paulo Brazil West		
	‡Sao Paulo West	10 Jun 1973	Jose Benjamin Puerta
1291	Sao Vincente Brazil	20 Sep 1981	Vicente Verta Jr.
2462	Sete Lagoas Brazil	17 May 1998	Edson D. Goncalves Ribeiro
989	Sorocaba Brazil	10 Dec 1978	Nelson de Genaro
1892	Sorocaba Brazil Barcelona	26 Jul 1992	Mauro Junot De Maria
2146	Sorocaba Brazil Trujillo	17 Dec 1995	Valdimir Fernandes Tasso
2441	Teresopolis Brazil	8 Mar 1998	Valter Queiroz Pinheiro
1966	Tubarao Brazil	19 Dec 1993	Gelson Januario
1912	Uruguaiana Brazil	29 Nov 1992	Saul E. Seiguer Milder
2250	Vale do Itajai Brazil	20 Oct 1996	Joni Luiz Koch
2094	Vila Velha Brazil	27 Aug 1995	Washington Luiz Lima
1630	Vitoria Brazil	15 Feb 1987	Pedro J. da Cruz Penha
2366	Volta Redonda Brazil	1 Jun 1997	Paulo da Silva Santos

Stakes discontinued

1030	Curitiba Brazil North	27 May 1979	Alfredo Heliton de Lemos
	Discontinued 30 Apr 1989 †Curitiba Brazil Iguacu (No. 1468)		
2077	Aracaju Brazil America	23 Jul 1995	Valdeilson de Oliveira
	Discontinued 27 Feb 2000		

Missions — 26

(As of Oct. 1, 2000; shown with historical number. See MISSIONS.)

(294a) BRAZIL BELEM MISSION
Avenida Nazare, 532 Sala 412
Royal Trade Center
66035-170 Belem, PA
Brazil

(213) BRAZIL BELO HORIZONTE MISSION
Rua Sao Paulo, 1781, 10 Andar
Edif. 17 de Maio, Sala 1001Barrio Lourdes
30170-132 Belo Horizonte MT,
Brazil

(295a) BRAZIL BELO HORIZONTE EAST MISSION
Rua Paraiba, 1174, Sala 401-B
Savassi
30130-141 Belo Horizonte MG
Brazil

(185a) BRAZIL BRASILIA MISSION
SAS Quadra 5, Bloco N
ED. OAB, Salas 201-204
70438-900 Brasilia DF
Brazil

(190) BRAZIL CAMPINAS MISSION
Rua 10 de Setembro, N. 38
Cambui
13023-100 Campinas SP, Brazil

(181) BRAZIL CURITIBA MISSION
Caixa Postal 9501
Portao
80613-991 Curitiba - PR, Brazil

(281) BRAZIL FLORIANOPOLIS MISSION
Caixa Postal 361
88010-970 - Florianapolis SC
Brazil

(321) BRAZIL GOIANIA MISSION
Rua 18, No. 110, Salas 1105 a 1107
ED. Business Center, Setor Oeste
74120-080 Goiania GO, Brazil

(302a) BRAZIL LONDRINA MISSION
Rua Higienpolis, 1100, Sala 61
Centro
Londrina PR 8686020-911, Brazil

(233) BRAZIL MANAUS MISSION
Caixa Postal No 3461
69042-010 Manaus, AM
Brazil

(48) BRAZIL PORTO
ALEGRE SOUTH MISSION
Caixa Postal 20251
90620-970 - Porto Alegre RS,
Brazil

(279) BRAZIL RIBEIRAO PRETO MISSION
Caixa Postal 388
14001-970 Ribeirao Preto - SP
Brazil

(280) BRAZIL RIO
DE JANEIRO NORTH MISSION
Rua Dois de Dezembro, 78 Sala 703
22220-040 Catete, Rio de Janeiro - RJ,
Brazil

(296) BRAZIL SALVADOR SOUTH MISSION
Caiza Postal 7384
Pituba
41811-970 - Salvador - BA , Brazil

(257) BRAZIL SAO PAULO
EAST MISSION
Caixa Postal 13339
Mooca
03198-970 - Sao Paulo - SP
Brazil

(101) BRAZIL SAO PAULO NORTH
MISSION
Caixa Postal 26095
05513-970 - Sao Paulo - SP
Brazil

(200) BRAZIL FORTALEZA MISSION
Rua Barao de Aracati, 1145
Aldeota, 60115-081 Fortaleza - CE
Brazil

(322) BRAZIL JOAO PESSOA MISSION
Rua Jose Mariz, 515
Tambauzinho
58042-020 Joao Pessoa PB, Brazil

(102) BRAZIL MACEIO MISSION
Av. Dom Antonio Brandao 333/402
Edificio Work Center/Farol
57021-190 Maceio AL, Brazil

(256a) BRAZIL PORTO ALEGRE
NORTH MISSION
Caixa Postal 20256
90620-970 Porto Alegre - RS,
Brazil

(167a) BRAZIL RECIFE MISSION
RuaGeneral Joaquim Inacio 412 sala 1202
Ilha de Leite
50070-270 Recife PE
Brazil

(80) BRAZIL RIO
DE JANEIRO MISSION
Av. das Americas, 1155, salas 502/503,
Barra da Tijuca
22631-000 Rio de Janeiro - RJ, Brazil

(234) BRAZIL SALVADOR MISSION
Caixa Postal 6946
Pituba
41811-970 - Salvador, BA,
Brazil

(323) BRAZIL SANTA MARIA MISSION
Caixa Postal 13339
Santa Maria RS, 97001-970
Brazil

(258) BRAZIL SAO PAULO
INTERLAGOS MISSION
Caixa Postal 55.031
Santo Amaro
04799-970 Sao Paulo - SP
Brazil

(102) BRAZIL SAO PAULO
SOUTH MISSION
Caixa Postal 26504
04311-990 - Sao Paulo - SP
Brazil

BULGARIA

Year-end 1999; Est. population, 8,240,000; Members, 1,367; Branches, 12; Missions, 1; Districts, 1; persent LDS, .02, or one in 6,027.

Located on the eastern Balkan peninsula on the Black Sea, Bulgaria has a population, with an Orthodox background in religion, that speaks Bulgarian, Turkish, and Greek.

Mischa Markow, prominent early missionary to the Balkans, visited Bulgaria in about 1900 when he registered with the police and received permission to preach. Soon he was challenged by a Protestant minister, which had the effect of bringing in many more curious people. He preached to many, but was soon banished by the police.

The first missionaries to Bulgaria in recent times were two couples and two sister missionaries, who arrived Sept. 10, 1990. The first missionary couples were Elder Delbert and Sister Marilyn Fowler who taught English in the town of Pravets, and Elder Morris and Sister Annetta Mower who served in Sofia. Sisters Judy Gubler and Rose Marie Daigle were the first sister missionaries. They taught English in the city of Smolyan. The first elders arrived Nov. 13, 1990, from the Austria Vienna East Mission. The elders also took part in charitable endeavors.

Elder Russell M. Nelson of the Quorum of the Twelve and Elder Hans B. Ringger of the Seventy visited government officials Feb. 13, 1990. Following their visit, the Bulgaria Sofia Mission was created July 1, 1991, at which time there were about 50 members, mostly in Sofia. The first president of the mission was Kiril P. Kiriakov of Manassas, Va., a native of Bulgaria.

Missionaries were also brought from Yugoslavia because they spoke Serbo-Croatian, a language similar to Bulgarian, which helped them overcome the language barrier. The Lamanite Generation from BYU toured the country in 1991.

In 1993, pediatricians, ophthalmologists, audiologists, and others, working through the Europe Area presidency and Church Humanitarian Services, went to Bulgaria to help train doctors and nurses in efforts to improve health care of children. Other LDS volunteers served in hospitals and educational institutions. Also, through Church Humanitarian Services, educators went to Bulgaria to help strengthen special education programs, and two Bulgarian school administrators were brought to Utah and Idaho for a tour of training facilities. In May 1993, Elder M. Russell Ballard of the Quorum of the Twelve and Elder Dennis B. Neuenschwander of the Seventy visited Church humanitarian projects in Sofia. That year, seminary programs in the country began for youth.

In 1999, the first youth conference in Bulgaria was held in Batak, where 106 youth attended workshops and meetings, and participated in games and a talent show. Membership in 1999 was 1,367.

The first LDS building in Bulgaria, which includes a meetinghouse, offices for the Bulgaria Sofia Mission, and a home for the mission president and his wife, was dedicated in Sofia June 18, 2000, by Elder Charles Didier of the Seventy and president of the Europe East Area. The day before, on June 17, ground was broken for a second meetinghouse in Bulgaria, in Plovdiv.

In 2000, 20 missionaries from Bulgaria were serving in Russia, England, France, and in other areas of the world.

Sources: "Missionary to the Balkans, Mischa Markow," by William Hale Kehr, *Ensign,* June 1980; *Church News,* May 18, 1991, June 5, 1993, May 31, 1997, May 22, 1999; "LDS Bulgarians come together for historic dedication," by Esther McFarlane, *Church News,* July 8, 2000.

Mission — 1

(As of Oct. 1, 2000; shown with historical number. See MISSIONS.)

(259) BULGARIA SOFIA MISSION
Marin Drinov 21
1504 Sofia, Bulgaria

BURUNDI

Year-end 1999: Est. population, 6,262,000; Members, 28; Branches, 1; Africa West Area; DR Congo Kinshasa Mission.

About the size of Maryland, Burundi is a republic bordered by Tanzania, Zaire, and Rwanda. Its people speak Kirundi and French, the official language, and are 62 percent Roman Catholic, 5 percent Protestant and 32 percent indigenous beliefs.

The Church established a branch in the capital city of this East Central African country following Burundi's adoption of a new constitution in 1992. After its first six months of organization, the Bujumbura Branch in Burundi continued to flourish with 36 members and four full-time missionaries.

The first branch president, Pres. Egide Nzojibwami, was set apart by Elder J Ballard Washburn of the Africa Area presidency and a member of the Seventy on Nov. 27, 1992. The first branch meeting was held two days later with 39 in attendance. Pres. Homer M. LeBaron of the Zaire Kinshasa Mission and his wife, Aleene, met with the Nzojibwami family and arranged for the organization. Pres. Nzojibwami and his wife, Beatrice, were baptized in Liege, Belgium, in 1984, while pursuing studies in that country. He was dean of the school of Geological Engineering at the University of Burundi.

Soon after the branch was organized, missionaries from the Ivory Coast Abidjan Mission (formerly Cameroon Yaounde Mission) arrived and began teaching the pool of investigators. These missionaries were Elders Francois Boue, Felix Gnamba, Aime Cesar Kipre, and Bassin Kouhon. In 1998, Burundi was transferred to the Africa West Area.

Source: *Church News*, Aug. 21, 1993, July 4, 1998.

CAMBODIA

(Kampuchea)

Year-end 1999: Est. population, 10,561,000; Members, 1,018; Branches, 5; Districts, 1; Missions, 1; Asia Area.

Many Cambodian refugees in the United States joined the Church in the 1970s following the Vietnam War. Cambodian branches were also established in a number of metropolitan centers in other countries.

On March 6, 1994, President Gordon B. Hinckley, first counselor in the First Presidency, announced that the government of Cambodia had granted legal recognition to the Church two days earlier on March 4. Missionary couples serving there do not proselyte but perform Christian service work.

On May 28-29, 1996, President Hinckley visited Cambodia, traveling with his wife, Marjorie, and Elder Joseph B. Wirthlin of the Quorum of the Twelve and his wife, Elisa, and Elder John H. Groberg of the Seventy and his wife, Jean. On the evening of May 28, President Hinckley spoke at a fireside attended by 439 people — more than half were investigators — at the Cambodiana Hotel in Phnom Penh. Three branches, two for Cambodians and one for Vietnamese, are in Phnom Penh. Before departing Cambodia the morning of May 29, President Hinckley and his party went to a hillside overlooking the Mekong River where President Hinckley offered a prayer. Seminary began for LDS youth in Cambodia in 1996.

Source: *Church News*, March 12, 1994, June 8, 1996, May 31, 1997.

Mission — 1

(As of Oct. 1, 2000; shown with historical number. See MISSIONS.)

(318) CAMBODIA PHNOM PENH MISSION
11 A Tou Samut
Noradom Blvd.
Phnom Penh, Cambodia

CAMEROON

Year-end 1999: Est. population, 13,521,000; Members, 194; Branches, 1; Africa West Area; DR Congo Kinshasa Mission.

Located on the western coast of Africa on the Gulf of Guinea, Cameroon is a republic where the people speak French and English, and Bamileke and Fulani. The people follow Animist, Christian, and Moslem beliefs.

A few members lived in Cameroon, representing various health organizations in the 1980s and earlier. Cameroon Pres. Paul Biya approved the Church's request for legal recognition on Sept. 9, 1993. At the time, two missionary couples, Elder Gerard and Sister Georgette Gagne of Montreal, Quebec, and Elder Ken and Sister Bea Nielsen from Calgary, Alberta, were serving in the French-speaking country. Up to the time the government granted recognition, about 30 people had been baptized, and another 60 investigators were attending Sunday meetings.

The Cameroon Yaounde Mission was created on July 1, 1992. The mission headquarters were moved to Abidjan, Ivory Coast, on May 18, 1993, which is also French-speaking. That same year, seminary classes began for the youth in Cameroon.

Representatives from Cameroon have participated in widely publicized LDS events. On Oct. 8, 1994, Cameroon was among 40 nations represented at the fourth annual "Western Family Picnic" at the Marriott Farm in Hume, Va. In addition, the Cameroon ambassador attended the Christmas season lighting ceremony for the Festival of Lights at the Washington Temple Visitors Center in 1995. The African nation was among some 50 nations represented at the ceremony.

In 1996, a Church group was created in Duoala. It was transferred to the Democratic Republic of Congo on Jan. 14, 1999.

Sources: *Church News,* Feb. 2, 1992; *Church News,* Jan. 22, 1994; *Church News* Oct. 15, 1994; *Church News,* Dec. 9, 1995; correspondence from Elder James O. Mason of the Seventy and president of the Africa Area, Sept. 26, 1996; *Church News,* May 31, 1997.

CANADA

Year-end 1999: Est. population, 28,435,000; Members, 156,575; Stakes, 42; Wards, 270; Branches, 163; Missions, 7; Districts, 7; Temples, 7; Percent LDS, .5, or one in 182.

At the northern end of North America, Canada is a confederation with a parliamentary democracy. It includes 10 provinces and two territories. Its population speaks English and French, and is Roman Catholic, 46 percent; and Protestant, 41 percent.

ALBERTA

Year-end 1999: Est. population, 2,794,000; Members, 63,866; Stakes, 21; Wards, 150; Branches, 42; Missions, 2; Temples, 2; Percent LDS, 2.30, or one in 44.

Mormon railway crews from northern Utah helped lay track for the Canadian Pacific Railway as early as 1883 and were familiar with southern Alberta, and supported later colonization efforts. In 1886, Charles O. Card, president of the Cache Valley Stake in Logan, Utah, explored southern Alberta, seeking a location to colonize in Canada. In March 1887, he left with a small advance party, arrived at Lee's Creek on June 3, and started a settlement that later became Cardston. The Cardston Ward was organized in 1888. Others welcomed the opportunity for land away from the burgeoning population of the Great Basin. Soon settled were Mountain View and Aetna (1890); Beazer (1891); Leavitt (1893); Kimball (1897); Caldwell, Taylorville, Magrath, and Stirling, (1898); and, after the turn of the century, Woolford, Welling, Orton, Raymond, Barnwell, Welling, Taber, Frankburg, Glenwood, and Hill Spring.

Completion of some 115 miles of irrigation canal by 1900, contracted to the Church by C.A. McGrath, and considerable investment from Utahn Jesse Knight in starting a sugar beet industry facilitated development of the prairie.

The Alberta Stake was created in 1895, the Taylor Stake in 1903, and the Lethbridge Stake in 1921. By 1914, more than 10,000 members lived in the vicinity. In 1913, ground was broken in Cardston for the Alberta Temple, which was dedicated in 1923. In 1920, membership was 8,896, increasing to 10,067 in 1930.

The Edmonton Branch began in 1933. By the 1940s, fewer that 100 branch members gathered each week in the Old Fellows Hall for Church services. Headquarters of the Western Canadian Mission was established in Edmonton in September 1941. In 1951, the first meetinghouse in Edmonton was dedicated.

Membership in Alberta in 1940 was 11,343, and in 1950, 14,583.

Members began gathering in population centers, including Calgary, Alberta, the province of British Columbia, and eastern Canada, where they continued to provide stability and leadership. The Calgary Stake was created in 1953. Over the next decades, membership increased to 19,985 in 1960, to 27,989 in 1970. and to 41,444 in 1981. By 1990, membership had reached 56,000 and in 1999, it was more than 63,000. Nathan Eldon Tanner, who served as a counselor in the First Presidency from 1963-1982, was a resident of Alberta at the time of his calling as a General Authority. Other General Authorities from Alberta have included Presiding Bishop Victor L. Brown, and Elders Ted E. Brewerton, Alexander B. Morrison, and Lowell D. Wood of the Seventy. In addition, former Young Women Gen. Pres. Ardeth Kapp and Relief Society Gen. Pres. Elaine Jack were born in Alberta.

One of the northernmost stakes of the Church was created April 12, 1998, at Grand Prairie, 300 miles north of Edmonton, and includes the northwest corner of Alberta and the northeast corner of British Columbia.

Members in Edmonton received a spiritual boost in 1998 with the creation of the Canada Edmonton Mission July 1, 1998; the visit of President Gordon B. Hinckley Aug. 2, 1998, when he spoke to some 10,000 members and to Parliament members; and the announcement of Alberta's second temple, in Edmonton, on Aug. 11. President Hinckley also visited Lethbridge on Aug. 2. On Aug. 10, 1998, 14 wagons and 90 people left Logan, Utah, re-enacting the 735-mile trip of a century ago. They arrived in Cardston Sept. 25.

The Edmonton Alberta Temple, which serves 14,800 members in five northern Alberta stakes, was dedicated Dec. 11, 1999.

Sources: *Encyclopedic History of the Church*, by Andrew Jenson; *A History of the Mormon Church in Canada*, compiled and published by the Lethbridge Stake in 1968; "Canada," by Richard E. Bennett, *Ensign*, Sept. 1988; "The Alberta Settlements, 1887-1925," chapters by Brigham Y. Card and Leonard Arrington, *The Mormon Presence in Canada*, published by the University of Alberta Press, 1990; *Church News*, April 18, 1998; "Temple dedicated in 'hub of the north,' " by Sarah Jane Weaver, *Church News*, Dec. 18, 1999; *Church News*, Feb. 19, 2000.

Stakes — 21

(Listed alphabetically as of Oct. 1, 2000.)

North America Central Area

No.	Name	Organized	First President
211a	*Calgary Alberta		
	‡Calgary	15 Nov 1953	N. Eldon Tanner
1924	Calgary Alberta East	14 Feb 1993	Geoffrey Bryan Grunewald
2540	Calgary Alberta Foothills	5 Dec 1999	John N. Craig
416	*Calgary Alberta North		
	‡Calgary North	17 Apr 1966	Gerald E. Melchin
1101	Calgary Alberta South	3 Feb 1980	Clarence Lee Robertson
1031	Calgary Alberta West	27 May 1979	Lynn Albert Rosenvall
35	*Cardston Alberta		
	‡Alberta	9 Jun 1895	Charles O. Card
1455	Cardston Alberta West	13 Nov 1983	Brent L. Nielson
655	*Edmonton Alberta Bonnie Doon	6 Nov 1983	
	‡Edmonton Alberta East	3 Nov 1974	Bryant L. Stringham
1453	Edmonton Alberta Millwoods	6 Nov 1983	Kenneth O. Higginbotham
312	*Edmonton Alberta Riverbend	6 Nov 1983	
	*Edmonton Alberta		
	‡Edmonton	15 Nov 1960	Leroy Rollins
1560	Fort Macleod Alberta	29 Sep 1985	Heber James Beazer
2449	Grande Prairie Alberta	12 Apr 1998	Lenard R. Shaw
189	*Lethbridge Alberta		
	*Lethbridge	15 Nov 1953	
	‡East Lethbridge	28 Oct 1951	Grant G. Woolley
667	Lethbridge Alberta East	24 Nov 1974	Bryce C. Stringham
2405	Lethbridge Alberta West	26 Oct 1997	David Paul Koegler
1199	Magrath Alberta	26 Oct 1980	James Dickson Bridge
1998	Medicine Hat Alberta	20 Nov 1994	Robert Albin Gehmlich
51	*Raymond Alberta		
	‡Taylor	30 Aug 1903	Heber S. Allen
1350	Red Deer Alberta	13 Jun 1982	Dennis William Guenther
302	*Taber Alberta		
	‡Taber	11 Sep 1960	Ray B. Evenson

Stakes discontinued

No.	Name	Organized	First President
86	Lethbridge	10 Nov 1921	Hugh B. Brown

Discontinued 15 Nov 1953 †Calgary (No. 211a), Lethbridge (No. 189)

Missions — 2

(As of Oct. 1, 2000; shown with historical number. See MISSIONS.)

(36a) CANADA CALGARY MISSION
6940 Fisher Road SE, Suite 122
Calgary, Alberta T2H 0W3
Canada

(325) CANADA EDMONTON MISSION
8925 51st Avenue, Suite 305
Edmonton, Alberta T6E 5J3
Canada

BRITISH COLUMBIA

Year-end 1999: Est. population, 4,010,700; Members, 27,564; Stakes, 8; Wards, 48; Branches, 32; Missions, 1; Districts, 1; Percent LDS, .7, or one in 145.

Vancouver Island was one of several locations Brigham Young considered as a western settlement site for the Saints. In a letter to the members published Nov. 1, 1845, he mentioned the island as "one of many good locations for settlement on the Pacific." The letter sparked a petition by the members in England to Queen Victoria to support the Mormons in settling the island. However, the petition was ignored, and no LDS immigrants settled on the island until 1875. That year William Francis and Maria Judson Copley and their three children settled at Shawigan. For the next 15 years they were the only members there. The first convert on the island was Anthony Maitland Stenhouse, a member of the legislative assembly of British Columbia who chose to resign from the assembly and be baptized in 1887. He became a vigorous defender of the faith, living in Cardston, Alberta, and eventually returning to his homeland of Great Britain.

On March 15, 1902, most of British Columbia was placed in the Northwestern States Mission. On May 13, 1903, seven missionaries, led by mission Pres. Nephi Pratt, arrived. The Victoria Conference was organized the next day. Their first converts were unbaptized members of the Copley family. By 1918 membership on the island was 21. A Sunday School was organized on Vancouver Island, but later dissolved when several families moved away. It was resumed in 1937.

World War II brought members to the island, and a branch was started in Victoria. A second group began meeting in Nanaimo in 1946. Missionaries arrived following the war, and additional branches were started. Membership over the years has increased. In 1920, British Columbia had 200 members, 584 in 1930 and 455 in 1940.

Work in Vancouver City on the mainland began in 1904 when Pres. Pratt visited and located an LDS family, that of Edward Neill. A conference with 12 in attendance was held in 1909 and a branch was organized on Feb. 12, 1911. By 1925 the branch had a chapel. The branch was made a ward and was included in the new Seattle Stake in 1938. The Vancouver District of the new Western Canadian Mission was created in 1948. From then on, the area grew significantly as members moved in and more converts joined the Church. Membership in the province grew to 1,582 in 1950, 4,104 in 1960, and 10,123 in 1970.

On Nov. 21, 1960, the Vancouver Stake was created with wards in Vancouver (two), North Shore, New Westminister, Fleetwood, Richmond, White Rock, Langley, and Chilliwack. A new stake center was started in 1966. A growth spurt during this period came when a number of LDS professors were hired at the University of Victoria, as well as others who came to this area. The Canada Vancouver Mission was organized June 20, 1974, an outgrowth of the Alaska-Canada Mission that had been created in 1960.

Membership in Vancouver has grown increasingly international. Membership in British Columbia was 15,494, in 1981, and reached 24,000 in 1990 and 27,564 in 1999. President Gordon B. Hinckley spoke to about 2,000 members during a visit to Victoria July 31, 1998, and the next day to 6,000 in Vancouver and 1,600 in Prince George.

Sources: *A History of the Mormon Church in Canada,* compiled and published by the Lethbridge Stake in 1968; "The Church of Jesus Christ of Latter-day Saints and Vancouver Island: The Establishment and Growth of the Mormon Community," by Robert J. McCue, *BC Studies,* Summer 1979; "No One Is an Island," by Giles H. Florence Jr., *Ensign,* August 1990; "LDS roots run deep in community," by Julie A. Dockstader, *Church News,* Aug. 22, 1998.

Stakes — 8

(Listed alphabetically as of Oct. 1, 2000.)

No.	Name	Organized	First President
North America Northwest Area — 7			
1980	Abbottsford British Columbia	12 Jun 1994	Andrew Howard Rattray
2406	Nanaimo British Columbia	26 Oct 1997	William Bert Nilsson
1905	Prince George British Columbia	26 Sep 1992	A. Brice Gurney
315	*Vancouver British Columbia		
	‡Vancouver	21 Nov 1960	Ernest E. Jensen
1014	*Surrey British Columbia	12 Jun 1994	
	‡Vancouver B.C. South	8 Apr 1979	Richard Bulpitt

709	Vernon British Columbia	12 Oct 1975	James Ronald Burnham
679	Victoria British Columbia	9 Feb 1975	Howard Lowell Biddulph
North America Central Area – 1			
994	Cranbrook British Columbia	14 Jan 1979	Brian James Erickson

Mission — 1

(As of Oct. 1, 2000; shown with historical number. See MISSIONS.)

(58) CANADA VANCOUVER MISSION
8440 Williams Rd
Richmond, B.C. V6Y 2X4, Canada

MANITOBA

Year-end 1999: Est. population, 1,159,000; Members, 3,866; Stakes, 1; Wards, 5; Branches, 7; Missions, 1; Percent LDS, .3, or one in 313.

A request from John Sherman, a member who lived in Souris, Manitoba, to Pres. Charles O. Card of the Canadian Mission led to missionaries coming to Manitoba. Elder Niels Hansen supervised six other missionaries who arrived in Manitoba in 1897 and made progress in spreading the gospel. Soon another dozen elders arrived to help. Several converts immigrated to Alberta. In 1899, Manitoba was placed in the Northern States Mission. A conference organized in 1901 was later discontinued but re-opened in 1906. That year, missionaries vigorously sold copies of the Book of Mormon, with eight missionaries selling 308 copies. A year later their efforts bore fruit, and five in the province were baptized. Many of the converts later moved to LDS centers in other areas.

In 1910, the Winnipeg Sunday School was organized with 37 members. The branch was organized in 1922.

Membership in the district in 1930 was 197, including the Winnipeg and Bergland, Ontario, branches. The Brandon Branch was created in 1955, and a second branch in Winnipeg was created in 1961. Other branches were organized in Portage La Prairie (for U.S. Air Force personnel in 1951), Kenora (1955), Thompson (1963), Dauphin (a Sunday School in 1957). Membership in the province in 1966 was 1,368.

The Canada Winnipeg Mission was created in 1976 with about 4,200 members in four districts, including those in Saskatchewan and western Ontario. The Winnipeg Manitoba Stake was created Nov. 12, 1978. A new stake center was dedicated in 1988, and stake membership reached 2,500. Membership in Manitoba was 2,136 in 1981, 3,700 in 1990, and 3,866 in 1999.

At one of the largest gatherings ever in Manitoba on Aug. 4, 1998,, President Gordon B. Hinckley, accompanied by President Boyd K. Packer, acting president of the Quorum of the Twelve, addressed some 1,500 members of the Winnipeg Stake and Fort Francis Ontario District. Among them was a choir of 170 youth.

Sources: *Encyclopedic History of the Church,* by Andrew Jenson; Northern States Mission, manuscript history, 1899-1908; *A History of the Church of Jesus Christ of Latter-day Saints in Canada, 1830-1963,* a BYU dissertation by Melvin S. Tagg, May 1963; *A History of the Mormon Church in Canada,* compiled by the Lethbridge Stake, 1968; "North Star Harvest," by Carol Cornwall Madsen, *Church News,* May 13, 1978; "Thompson Saints Sink Roots in Manitoba Soil," by Bruce Northcott, *Ensign,* August 1986; "In Winnipeg: An Exciting Time to be a Member," by Raman Job, *Ensign,* May 1989; *Church News,* May 17, 1997, Aug. 15, 1998, and Aug. 22, 1998.

Stake — 1

(As of Oct. 1, 2000.)

No.	Name	Organized	First President
North America Central Area			
980	Winnipeg Manitoba	12 Nov 1978	Lorne Leslie Clapson

Mission — 1

(As of Oct. 1, 2000; shown with historical number. See MISSIONS.)

(136) CANADA WINNIPEG MISSION
1661 Portage Avenue, #306
Winnipeg, Manitoba R3J 3T7

NEW BRUNSWICK

Year-end 1999: Est. population, 764,700; Members, 2,060; Stakes, 1; Wards, 5; Branches, 2; Percent LDS, .3, or one in 371; Canada Halifax Mission.

Missionary work in the Maritime provinces began in 1833 when Lyman E. Johnson and James Heriot began proselyting in Nova Scotia and New Brunswick. Elder Johnson preached in Saint John, New Brunswick, in the spring of 1836 and later in Sackville, where he baptized 18 people and organized the first branch in the Maritimes.

Among those baptized in Sackville was Marriner W. Merrill, who later preached extensively in Canada and eventually become a member of the Quorum of the Twelve.

In 1920, a branch was organized in Saint John, New Brunswick. The branch was discontinued, and then reorganized and has been continuous since 1948. A meetinghouse was completed in 1954. The Fredericton Branch was organized in 1940, later discontinued and started again in 1957, and completed a meetinghouse in 1963. The Moncton Branch, created in 1966, included the Sackville area where the first branch of the Church in the Maritimes was created. Membership in this branch reached 160 in 1974. The Saint John New Brunswick Stake was created in 1988. Growth of the Church in the Maritimes has fluctuated over time, but the work of missionaries and members has pushed efforts along in the 1990s. Membership in 1990 was 2,100. New Brunswick is in the temple district of the Halifax Nova Scotia Temple, which was dedicated Nov. 14, 1999.

Sources: *Encyclopedic History of the Church,* by Andrew Jenson; *A History of the Mormon Church in Canada,* published in 1968 by the Lethbridge Alberta Stake under the direction of Dr. Melvin S. Tagg; "Portrait of a New Mission," by Jack E. Jarrard, *Church News,* Sept. 22, 1973; "The Saints in Canada's Maritime Provinces," by Eleanor Knowles, *Ensign,* June 1974; and "LDS in Canada — Growth through faithfulness," *Church News,* Oct. 23, 1983; "Maritime provinces," by Sheridan R. Sheffield, *Church News,* Oct. 24, 1992; *Church News,* May 23, 1998, Nov. 20, 1999.

Stake — 1

(As of Oct. 1, 2000.)

No. Name	Organized	First President
North America Northeast Area		
1698 Saint John New Brunswick	26 Jun 1988	Blaine E. Hatt

NEWFOUNDLAND

Year-end 1999: Est. population, 544,500; Members, 585; Branches, 3; Percent LDS, .1 or one in 930; North America Northeast Area; Canada Halifax Mission.

The St. John's Branch in Newfoundland was created Feb. 7, 1957, and in 10 years grew to 92 members. Other branches in the province include Corner Brook and Gander.

About half of the converts in this area are immigrants, often from eastern European countries. Retention of converts in the area is extremely high. Unemployment and economic difficulties are challenges that hamper growth. Newfoundland is in the Halifax Nova Scotia Temple district.

Sources: *Encyclopedic History of the Church,* by Andrew Jenson; *A History of the Mormon Church in Canada,* published in 1968 by the Lethbridge Alberta Stake under the direction of Dr. Melvin S. Tagg; "Portrait of a New Mission," by Jack E. Jarrard, *Church News,* Sept. 22, 1973; "The Saints in Canada's Maritime Provinces," by Eleanor Knowles, *Ensign,* June 1974; and "LDS in Canada — Growth through faithfulness," *Church News,* Oct. 23, 1983; "Maritime provinces," by Sheridan R. Sheffield, *Church News,* Oct. 24, 1992. *Church News,* May 23, 1998.

NOVA SCOTIA

Year-end 1999: Est. population, 957,900; Members, 4,268; Stakes, 1; Wards, 6; Branches, 12; Missions, 1; Temples, 1; Percent LDS, .4, or one in 222.

Lyman E. Johnson and James Heriot began proselyting in the Maritime Provinces in 1833 when they arrived in Nova Scotia and New Brunswick. Two missionaries were sent to Nova Scotia by Joseph Smith in 1843. A conference was attended by 18 members under the direction of district Pres. Robert Dixon. The Halifax Branch was created Nov. 14, 1843, and smaller branches began in Preston, Popes Harbour, and Onslow.

In 1845, John Sherry, a member from Nova Scotia, preached on Prince Edward Island. Branches were organized at Beddeque and Charlottetown. Persecution followed the members and most left for the West by 1855. One group of 50, most of the Halifax Branch, traveled with their branch president, John A. Jost, aboard the ship *Barque Halifax,* which left May 12, 1855, and took them the first leg of their journey around Cape Horn to San Francisco. This exodus ended organized branches in the Maritimes until work resumed under the Canadian Mission in 1920. Membership in the area after this time was often depleted when converts moved to be closer to the established Church.

After missionary work resumed, missionaries presided over groups in Halifax, Windsor, and New Glasgow in Nova Scotia. The Halifax Branch in Nova Scotia was organized in July 1947 by mission Pres. S. Dilworth Young. A meetinghouse was completed in 1959. Another branch, in Sydney, was created in 1958,

In 1959, converts were baptized in Bridgewater, Nova Scotia. The branch, created in 1961, grew to 135 in 1967. A meetinghouse was completed in 1966. Membership in Nova Scotia is among the most rapidly growing in Canada. With 250 members in 1972, it increased more than 800 percent in 10 years, reaching 2,331. In 1974, the Halifax and Dartmouth branches numbered about 750.

The Canada-Maritimes Mission was created from the New England Mission on July 26, 1973, and its name was changed to the Canada Halifax Mission the next year on June 20, 1974.

The Dartmouth Nova Scotia Stake was created in 1985. The Dartmouth/Halifax area in Nova Scotia continues to serve as the center of Church activity in the Maritimes. Membership in Nova Scotia was 3,800 in 1990 and 4,268 in 1999,

President Gordon B. Hinckley visited Halifax on Feb. 12, 1998, and addressed some 2,000 members who had come from throughout the Maritime provinces.

Three months later, on May 7, 1998, a temple was announced for Halifax to serve the members in the Maritime provinces, a land renowned for towering white lighthouses. For the first time in Church history, two temples were dedicated on the same day — Nov. 14, 1999. Both were in Canada. The Halifax Nova Scotia Temple, located in the Cole Harbour area of the city of Dartmouth, across the harbor from Halifax, was dedicated by President Hinckley, and the Regina Saskatchewan Temple was dedicated by President Boyd K. Packer, acting president of the Quorum of the Twelve. They were the 64th and 65th operating temples in the Church.

Sources: *Encyclopedic History of the Church,* by Andrew Jenson; *A History of the Mormon Church in Canada,* published in 1968 by the Lethbridge Alberta Stake under the direction of Dr. Melvin S. Tagg; "Portrait of a New Mission," by Jack E. Jarrard, *Church News,* Sept. 22, 1973; "The Saints in Canada's Maritime Provinces," by Eleanor Knowles, *Ensign,* June 1974; and "LDS in Canada — growth through faithfulness," *Church News,* Oct. 23, 1983; "Maritime provinces," by Sheridan R. Sheffield, *Church News,* Oct. 24, 1992; *Church News,* Feb. 7, 1998, May 23, 1998; "Historic Sabbath in Canada," by Shaun D. Stahle and Janet Kruckenberg,*Church News,* Nov. 20, 1999.

Stake — 1

(As of Oct. 1, 2000.)

No.	Name	Organized	First President
North America Northeast Area			
1530	Dartmouth Nova Scotia	12 May 1985	Terry Lee Livingstone

Mission — 1

(As of Oct. 1, 2000; shown with historical number. See MISSIONS.)

(107) CANADA HALIFAX MISSION
202 Brownlow Ave., Unit F, Bldg F
Dartmouth, Nova Scotia B3B 1T5
Canada

ONTARIO

Year-end 1999: Est. population, 11,519,300; Members, 40,289; Stakes, 9; Wards, 57; Branches, 35; Missions, 2; Districts, 2; Temples, 1; Percent LDS, .35, or one in 285.

Seeking ways to finance the publication of the Book of Mormon, the first Mormons to enter Canada were Hiram Page and Oliver Cowdery, who crossed the border from New York in the winter of 1829-30, even before the Church was organized. In 1830, Phinehas Young traveled to Earnestown. Though unbaptized, he preached about the Book of Mormon.

Joseph Smith Sr. and Don Carlos Smith entered Canada briefly in September 1830, visiting a few villages north of the St. Lawrence River. Early in June 1832, Phinehas Young returned to Canada, this time as an ordained elder in the company of five others. Before the last of these missionaries left Canada, four branches had been organized. Other missionaries soon followed, including Joseph Smith, who traveled to Brantford and Mt. Pleasant in October 1833 and visited Toronto in July 1837. Two of the most successful missionaries were John E. Page and Parley P. Pratt. Elder Page baptized almost a thousand converts. Elder Pratt brought in such future Church leaders as John Taylor, who later became president of the Church; and Isaac Russell, John Snider, John Goodson, and

Joseph Fielding. These four opened the highly successful work in Great Britain. Missionaries organized a district in Toronto that was placed under the direction of John Taylor.

Between 1830 and 1850, an estimated 2,500 Canadians, mostly from Ontario, joined the Church. Most of these who remained faithful gathered with the Saints in the Great Basin in the West. By 1861, the Ontario census lists only 74 members.

Little work took placed in eastern Canada until the Canadian Mission was organized in 1919, with conferences in Toronto and Ottawa. That same year, branches were organized in Toronto and Hamilton. Other branches were organized in Kitchener in 1923, in Ottawa in 1926, and in St. Catherines in 1933. The Oshawa Branch began in 1947 after functioning off and on as a Sunday School since 1944. Membership in all of eastern Canada reached 1,974 in 1950.

The first meetinghouse in eastern Canada was dedicated in Toronto in 1939, and the first stake in eastern Canada was organized in 1960, also in Toronto, while President Thomas S. Monson, now first counselor in the First Presidency, was mission president. In attendance at the conference when the stake was created were 2,249 members, which constituted 92 percent of the new stake's membership. The Toronto Temple was announced April 7, 1984, and dedicated Aug. 25, 1990. Membership in Ontario 1981 was 16,138, and in 1990, 28,000.

On July 1, 1993, Toronto's second mission was created. Missionaries may potentially work with people from upwards of 100 nations who come to the Toronto area in hopes of immigrating. From Toronto, efforts to increase the profile of the Church through the media led to a prime-time television series across Canada in 1994.

On June 22, 1986, President Monson and Elder M. Russell Ballard of the Quorum of the Twelve created the Kitchener Ontario Stake, the 1,600th stake in the Church. They returned on May 5, 1996, to create the Sudbury Ontario Stake. President Monson and Elder Ballard had previously been based in Toronto while presiding over Canadian missions.

In 1997, a marker was placed in Bath by the Napese Branch in honor of the first branch in Canada. President Monson dedicated the marker Aug. 9 of that year.

President Gordon B. Hinckley, accompanied by President Boyd K. Packer, acting president of the Quorum of the Twelve, visited Sudbury, on Aug. 5, 1998, where President Hinckley spoke to 850 members; on the same day in Ottawa he spoke to 3,000, and in Hamilton, on Aug. 8, he spoke to 12,000 people.

In commemoration of the 40th anniversary of the creation of the Toronto Canada Stake and of the 10th anniversary of the Toronto Canada Temple, President Monson returned to Ontario on Aug. 19, 2000, to dedicate a historical monument. The monument commemorates the contributions of early missionaries and members who served and lived in Upper Canada.

Ontario's LDS population in 1999 was 40,289.

Sources: *Encyclopedic History of the Church,* by Andrew Jenson; *A History of the Mormon Church in Canada,* compiled and published by the Lethbridge Stake, 1968; "Canada: From Struggling Seed, The Church Has Risen to Branching Maple," by Richard E. Bennett, *Ensign,* Sept. 1988; "Toronto, A Growing Light in the East," by Richard Robertson, *Ensign,* Sept. 1988; "Plucking not Planting," by Richard E. Bennett, *The Mormon Presence in Canada,* published by the University of Alberta Press, 1990; " 'Our treasure,' a new temple is dedicated," and "Past legacy builds today's faith," both by Dell Van Orden, *Church News,* Sept. 1, 1990; *Church News,* March 13, 1993; "Church begins series on TV across Canada," by William B. Smart, *Church News,* Feb. 5, 1994; *Church News,* May 18, 1996, Aug. 16, 1997, Jan. 24, 1998, Aug. 8, 1998, Aug. 15, 1998; "LDS stalwarts in Upper Canada are remembered," by Gerry Avant, *Church News,* Aug. 26, 2000.

Stakes — 9

(Listed alphabetically as of Oct. 1, 2000.)

No.	Name	Organized	First President
North America Northeast Area			
1222	Brampton Ontario	11 Jan 1981	Cecil Malcolm Warner
524	*Hamilton Ontario		
	‡Niagara	6 Sep 1970	Eldon C. Olsen
1600	Kitchener Ontario	22 Jun 1986	Graeme K. Hingston
752	London Ontario	11 Apr 1976	Harold Crookell
1907	Mississauga Ontario	18 Oct 1992	Lawrence R. Fuller
761	*Oshawa Ontario	22 Jun 1986	
	‡Toronto Ontario East	13 Jun 1976	John Bruce Smith

796	Ottawa Ontario	12 Dec 1976	Boyden E. Lee
2194	Sudbury Ontario	05 May 1996	G. Boyd McGinn
300	*Toronto Ontario		
	‡Toronto	14 Aug 1960	William M. Davies

Missions — 2

(As of Oct. 1, 2000; shown with historical number. See MISSIONS.)

(285) CANADA TORONTO EAST MISSION
2025 Sheppard Avenue East, Suite 2300
Willowdale, Ontario M2J 1V7
Canada

(23a) CANADA TORONTO WEST MISSION
197 Country Court Blvd Ste 203
Brampton, Ontario L6W 4P6
Canada

PRINCE EDWARD ISLAND

Year-end 1999: Est. population, 140,200; Members, 391; Branches, 3; Percent LDS, .28, or one in 358; North America Northeast Area; Canada Halifax Mission.

The first missionary to preach in the province was John Sherry, who came to Prince Edward Island in 1845. Branches were organized in Bedeque and Charlottetown, but were disbanded in 1850 when all members immigrated to Utah.

The first modern presence of the Church on Prince Edward Island came in 1964 when Ralph and Gerda Waugh, converts from New York, returned to the land of Brother's Waugh's birth. They contacted another member and began holding Sunday School.

At the time, Elder Boyd K. Packer, then an Assistant to the Twelve, was president of the New England Mission, which included Prince Edward Island. Elder Packer visited the Waugh home with missionaries in July 1966. About two weeks later full-time missionaries were transferred to the island and missionaries have been here since then.

Brother Waugh was called as the first president of the Summerside Branch on Dec. 21, 1969. In 1974 the branch was divided and the Charlottetown Branch was formed.

The Church continued to grow on the island, and in 1982 the Prince Edward Island District was formed. The island's first meetinghouse was completed in Summerside on June 18, 1983. A second meetinghouse in Charlottetown was started in 1983 and completed on July 14, 1984. The Montague Branch was formed in November 1985 and a meetinghouse was completed in June 1988. The three branches became part of the Saint John New Brunswick Stake on June 26, 1988.

One of the most popular tourist locations in the Maritimes, Prince Edward Island is home to the smallest number of members of any province in Canada. Membership in 1999 was 391. Prince Edward Island is within the Halifax Nova Scotia Temple district.

Sources: *A History of the Mormon Church in Canada,* published in 1968 by the Lethbridge Alberta Stake under the direction of Dr. Melvin S. Tagg; "The Saints in Canada's Maritime Provinces," by Eleanor Knowles, *Ensign,* June 1974; "Prince Edward Island: Members find peace in 'little land' where 'you find your soul,' " by Sheridan R. Sheffield, *Church News,* July 10, 1993; *Church News,* May 23, 1998.

QUEBEC

Year-end 1999: Est. population, 7,559,000; Members, 8,500; Stakes, 2; Wards, 12; Branches, 15; Missions, 1; Districts, 1; Temples, 1; Percent LDS, 0.11, or one in 889.

Early missionaries in the 1830s frequently traveled through but found little success in Lower Canada, as the province of Quebec was then called. They found proselyting difficult among its largely French-speaking people. In 1836, however, Hazen Aldrich and Winslow Farr labored in Stanstead County and baptized a number of people. Twenty-three of these emigrated on July 20, 1837. Converts also came from the community of Eardley, north of Ottawa. After the 1840s, missionary work experienced an interlude until the 20th century.

The Canadian Mission was organized in 1919. By 1930, an English-speaking branch began meeting in Montreal. A meetinghouse for this branch was purchased from another faith in 1942 and served the branch until the late 1970s.

The Ottawa-Montreal District was created in 1953 as part of the Canadian Mission. The same year a mission district was created in Quebec. In 1961, then-Mission Pres. Thomas S. Monson sent six French-speaking missionaries into the area around Quebec. The missionaries found investigators who joined the Church and established a base that attracted LDS French-speaking immigrants. From this effort, missionaries entered

Quebec City where a branch was started in 1969. The Quebec (later changed to the Canada Montreal) Mission was created in 1972, and by 1974, a French-speaking district was created. By 1987, membership among the French-speaking people was 2,753, some 65 percent of the total membership in the province. These converts tended to stay in Quebec where their roots were instead of moving to the West as did many of their English-speaking counterparts.

The Tung Fong Branch was created in 1975 for the many Chinese people in the Montreal area.

The Montreal Quebec Stake, considered the first French-speaking stake in North America, was created in 1978. Called as a high councilor was Kitchner Young, one of the first French-speaking missionaries.

French-speaking members from Quebec have made contributions as missionaries in French-speaking countries in West Africa and other developing nations of the world.

The Quebec District consists of the Quebec (1969), Alma (1984), Chicoutimi (1976), and Rimouksi (1979) branches. In 1975, membership in this district was 977 members.

In 1980, the English-speaking Montreal Mount Royale Quebec Stake was created. In addition, many Hispanics have immigrated to Montreal, and in 2000, there were two Spanish-speaking wards in the city.

Membership in Quebec reached 3,246 in 1981 and 6,800 in 1990. In 1999, membership was 8,500.

President Gordon B. Hinckley addressed some 3,000 members in Montreal Aug. 6, 1998, and while there, announced that a temple would be built in this city. The temple, the sixth in Canada, was dedicated June 4, 2000.

Sources: *Encyclopedic History of the Church,* by Andrew Jenson; *The Mormon Church in Canada,* compiled and published by the Lethbridge Stake, 1968; "History of the Church in Quebec and Ontario," *Culture for Missionaries,* Missionary Training Center, 1977; "Converts in Quebec," *Church News,* by Maureen Ursenbach Beecher, June 24, 1978; *Church News,* July 8, 1978; "Canada, From Struggling Seed, the Church has Risen to Branching Maple," by Richard E. Bennett, *Ensign,* Sept. 1988; "Canadian Mormon Identity and the French Fact," by Dean R. Louder, in *The Mormon Presence in Canada,* published by the University of Alberta Press, 1990; *Church News,* June 5, 1993, Aug. 15, 1998, June 10, 2000.

Stakes — 2

(Listed alphabetically as of Oct. 1, 2000.)

No.	Name	Organized	First President
North America Northeast Area			
943	Montreal Quebec	18 Jun 1978	Gerard C. Pelchat
1160	Montreal Quebec Mount Royal	6 Jul 1980	Ian Gillespie Wilson

Mission — 1

(As of Oct. 1, 2000; shown with historical number. See MISSIONS.)

(99a) CANADA MONTREAL MISSION
1320 Blv. Graham, Suite 310
Ville Mont-Royal, Quebec H3P 3C8
Canada

SASKATCHEWAN

Year-end 1999: Est. population, 1,030,000; Members, 4,794; Stakes, 1; Wards, 5; Branches, 13; Districts, 1; Temples, 1; percent LDS, .5, or one in 214; Canada Winnipeg Mission; North America Central Area.

In the early 1920s, G. Gordon Whyte of Moose Jaw acquired a copy of the Book of Mormon, accepted it as being true and requested baptism. He was baptized Aug. 17, 1923, in Moose Jaw and later lived in Regina. His membership was kept in the Raymond 1st Ward, under the direction of Bishop John G. Allred. That same year, Bishop Allred, who later served as president of the North Central States Mission from 1925-29, and Brother Whyte held a street meeting in Regina where they placed 16 copies of the Book of Mormon.

The first missionaries in Saskatchewan were Elders Leo E. Nielsen and John A. Ward in Saskatoon and Elders Reuben T. Reynolds and Raymond L. Allen in Regina, who arrived in 1925. The North Saskatchewan and South Saskatchewan conferences were organized Aug. 6 of that year, but were combined by 1930 and had a membership of 145.

Progress was slow, but a Sunday School was organized May 8, 1927, in Regina, which became a branch on May 27, 1934. That year, LDS farmers in southern Alberta and their non-LDS neighbors donated two boxcars of vegetables and food to 200 families in Saskatchewan suffering from the effects of a severe drought. Among them were 20 families in the Regina Branch. A meetinghouse was dedicated for the Regina Branch in 1939.

Saskatchewan became part of the Western Canadian Mission Dec. 6, 1942, and a mission home was purchased in Saskatchewan on Dec. 9. At that time, the district had 173 members, including 79 in the Regina Branch.

During this time, Brother Whyte continued to do missionary work among various Indians on nearby reserves. An Indian seminary program began in 1965 with 45 Lamanite children on the Piapot, Carry-the-Kettle and Cowesses reserves east of Regina.

In 1949, the Saskatoon Branch functioned for a short time with no actual membership as members had moved away and investigators held positions. Later, missionary work and baptisms led to the normalization of the branch.

By 1961, branches in Regina (1934), Moose Jaw (a Sunday School functioned from 1929 until a branch was organized in 1945), Saskatoon (1944), Swift Current (1952), Prince Albert (1959), and Silver Park (re-named Melfort; organized in 1947) were included in the Saskatchewan District, with a total of about 600 members. On Sept. 3, 1961, the district was divided into the North and South districts. The Yorktown and Carry-the-Kettle branches were organized in 1966.

The only stake in Saskatchewan was created in Saskatoon Nov. 5, 1978, combining two districts, with 2,101 members. At that time, Saskatoon and Regina had two wards each. Membership in Saskatchewan in 1980 was 2,857, increasing to 4,200 in 1990.

President Gordon B. Hinckley, accompanied by President Boyd K. Packer, acting president of the Quorum of the Twelve, visited Regina Aug. 3, 1998, and addressed 1,400 members in a meetinghouse. While there, President Hinckley announced that a temple would be built in Regina. The Regina Saskatchewan Temple was dedicated Nov. 14, 1999, by President Packer, the same day that President Hinckley dedicated the Halifax Nova Scotia Temple, the first time in the history of the Church that two temples were dedicated on the same day.

In 1999, there were 4,794 members of the Church in Saskatchewan.

Sources: *Encyclopedic History of the Church,* by Andrew Jenson; *Liahona,* Oct. 20, 1925, p. 182; North Central States Mission Manuscript History, 1925-40; *History of the Western Canadian Mission,* by Wilbur Gordon Hackney, a BYU thesis, May 17, 1950; *A History of the Mormon Church in Canada,* compiled and published by the Lethbridge Stake, 1968; "The Christian Way," by Carol Cornwall Madsen, *Church News* July 1, 1978; *Church News,* Feb. 10, 1945, Feb. 2, 1949, July 5, 1950, Nov. 18, 1978, Oct. 23, 1983; *Church News* Aug. 8, 1998, Aug. 15, 1998; "Historic Sabbath in Canada," by Shaun D. Stahle and Janet Kruckenberg,*Church News,* Nov. 20, 1999.

Stakes — 1

(As of Oct. 1, 2000.)

No.	Name	Organized	First President
North America Central Area			
978	Saskatoon Saskatchewan	5 Nov 1978	Noel W. Burt

NORTHWEST TERRITORIES & NUNAVUT

Year-end 1999: Est. population, 67,500; Members, 200; Branches, 1; percent LDS, .29, or one in 337; North America Central Area; Canada Edmonton Mission.

Nunavut became a territory in 1999. The Yellowknife Branch in the Northwest Territories covers half a million square miles and is called the largest branch in area in the Church. Half the members live in Yellowknife and half are scattered in the communities of Hay River, Fort Smith, Coppermine, Inuvik, Rankin Inlet, and Iqaluit. Members occasionally travel hundreds of miles for socials and meetings.

Sources: *A History of the Mormon Church in Canada,* published in 1968 by the Lethbridge Alberta Stake under the direction of Dr. Melvin S. Tagg; "Northern Hospitality," by Ronald G. Watt, *Church News,* July 8, 1978; "Largest Branch in the World," *Ensign,* September 1988.

YUKON TERRITORY

Year-end 1999: Est. population, 31,070; Members, 204; Branches, 1; percent LDS, .6, or one in 152; North America Northwest Area; Alaska Anchorage Mission.

A branch was created in Whitehorse, Yukon Territory, on Oct. 15, 1963, and meetings were held in rented quarters with a mostly 100 percent attendance of the 35 members.

The branch now has a meetinghouse. A highlight in branch history came in 1968 when Apostle LeGrand Richards visited and witnessed the baptism of four people. His was the first known visit of a General Authority to the branch. The temple in Anchorage, Alaska, serves members of the Yukon Territory.

Sources: *A History of the Mormon Church in Canada*, published in 1968 by the Lethbridge Alberta Stake; *Church News*, April 25, 1998.

CAPE VERDE

Year-end 1999: Est. population, 436,000; Members, 3,893; Districts, 3; Branches, 18; percent LDS, .88 or one in 112; Europe West Area; Portugal Lisbon South Mission.

The Republic of Cape Verde is made up of 10 main islands, 400 miles west of Senegal off the African coast. The people, who are mostly Roman Catholics influenced by indigenous beliefs, speak Portuguese and Criuolo.

Spain Canary Islands Mission Pres. Marion K. Hamblin opened the Cape Verde area when he visited the islands in November 1988. He sent Elders Christopher Lee and Ken Margetts there a short time later to create the Praia/Lajes Branch on Cape Verde. The ambassador of Cape Verde attended the lighting ceremony of the Washington Temple in 1993. In September 1994, Elder Dallin H. Oaks visited the islands and made courtesy visits to the president of the republic, Antonio Mascarenhas, and Praia mayor Jacinto Santos.

By September 1994, some 50 members from Cape Verde had been called to serve full-time missions.

On a return trip from the African continent in 1998, President Gordon B. Hinckley stopped in Cape Verde, where he addressed 780 members, many of whom had come on expensive boat rides from distant areas to see the prophet.

Sources: Spain Canary Islands Mission correspondence; *Church News*, Dec. 7, 1991, Dec. 11, 1993, Sept. 24, 1994, March 7, 1998.

CENTRAL AFRICA REPUBLIC

Year-end 1999: Est. population, 3,210,000; Members, 135; Branches, 1; Africa West Area; Ivory Coast Abidjan Mission.

Located in Central Africa along the northern border of Zaire, the Central Africa Republic is a republic with a population that speaks French and local dialects. The population is Protestant, 25 percent; Catholic, 25 percent; tribal beliefs, 24 percent; and other beliefs.

The first known member living in Central Africa Republic was Carol Forrest of the U.S. Peace Corps, a returned missionary and one of the medical personnel who arrived in June 1991. She shared the gospel with many of her associates and in September 1991 was set apart as a district missionary. Elder J Ballard Washburn of the Seventy and a counselor in the Africa Area presidency visited Sister Forrest and a group of investigators in September 1992.

Traveling with Elder Washburn was Pres. Robert L. Mercer of the Cameroon Yaounde Mission. On Sept. 19, 1992, 20 people were baptized and two branches were organized. Celestin N'Gakondou was called as president of the Bangui 1st Branch, and Gaspard Lapet was called to preside over the Bangui 2nd Branch.

A French couple, Elder Raymond and Sister Christianne Fourtina, arrived in January of 1993.

An ambassador from the Central Africa Republic attended the Christmas lighting ceremony at the 1995 Festival of Lights at the Washington Temple Visitors Center. The African republic was among some 50 nations represented at the widely publicized event.

Youth in the Central Africa Republic began seminary classes in 1995.

Sources: "Medical officer ministers to souls," by Mary Mostert, *Church News*, Dec. 5, 1992; Correspondence from the Ivory Coast Abidjan Mission, March 1994; *Church News*, Dec. 9, 1995, May 5, 1997.

CHILE

Year-end 1999: Est. population, 14,161,000; Members, 502,153; Stakes, 116; Wards, 744; Branches, 207; Missions, 8; Districts, 9; Temples, 1; Percent LDS, 3.6 or one in 28.

On the west coast of South America, the Republic of Chile has a Spanish-speaking population that is 89 percent Roman Catholic.

Parley P. Pratt, his wife, Phebe, and Elder Rufus C. Allen traveled to Chile, arriving Nov. 8, 1851, but remained only five months. Their inability to speak the language and their meager funds, along with continuing civil turbulence in the country, proved to be insurmountable obstacles. The next LDS presence began with LDS families living in Santiago in the early 1950s. President David O. McKay visited the William Fotheringham family in Santiago on Feb. 8, 1954. On May 26, 1956, Chile became part of the Argentine Mission. At that time, Elders Joseph Bentley and Verle Allred crossed the Andes from Argentina and arrived in Chile June 23, 1956, beginning missionary work in Chile. They stayed with the Fotheringhams and on July 5, the first branch was organized. A few months later they baptized Ricardo and Perla Garcia and others on Nov. 2, 1956. It became part of the Andes Mission in 1956. Six more branches were created by 1959.

When Elder Spencer W. Kimball, then of the Quorum of the Twelve, visited in 1959, the country had about 450 members. In October of that year, 45 more people were baptized, a 10 percent increase in one month. The Chile Mission was organized Oct. 8, 1961, with 1,100 members. When the first stake was organized in Santiago 11 years later in 1972, membership had grown to more than 20,000 members.

By Feb. 28, 1977, when President Spencer W. Kimball visited Chile, there were approximately 30,000 members in the country. After arriving in Santiago, President Kimball flew by helicopter 60 miles to the national summer palace to visit Chilean president, Augusto Pinochet Ugarte.

On March 1, 1977, President Kimball addressed nearly 7,000 members in an area conference. At the same gathering, Elder Bruce R. McConkie of the Quorum of the Twelve predicted that in the future, the Church would become the most powerful influence in the nation and said that the day would come when a temple would be built in Chile. This was during the time when there was no temples in all of South America, although the Sao Paulo Temple in Brazil had been announced. Four years later, President Kimball returned to Santiago on May 30, 1981, to break ground for a temple; the ceremony was attended by 6,000 people who waited in the rain for several hours.

The temple was completed in 1983, and dedicated on Sept. 15. At that time, the country had 140,400 members in 27 stakes. On Oct. 29, 1988, Chile became the fourth country in the world to reach 50 stakes. Chile has strong local leadership, a high percentage of local missionaries, and a number of local mission and temple presidents.

Chile's first General Authority was Elder Eduardo Ayala of the Seventy. Membership in 1990 was 298,000, and increased to 502,153 in 1999. At the commemoration of the 10th anniversary of the temple in 1994, it was noted that Chile, with the fastest growing membership in South America, had doubled membership and the number of stakes during the decade. Continued growth, including the creation of 26 stakes from 1994-96, led to the creation of the Chile Area in 1996.

On Nov. 11, 1996, President Gordon B. Hinckley visited Santiago and spoke to some 48,000 members, one of the largest gatherings of Saints in South America. He returned April 25, 1999, and spoke to 57,500 members at a regional conference in Santiago.

On March 9, 1997, Chile joined an elite group of four nations that have 100 or more stakes. This milestone came only 25 years after the first stake was created. Chile's eight mission was created in Santiago July 1, 1997. A new temple patron housing complex with 168 units was dedicated March 22, 1998, by Elder Dallas N. Archibald, president of the Chile Area.

Severe flooding in July 1997 damaged 26 meetinghouses.

On the Juan Fernandez archipelago, also known as Robinson Crusoe Islands, which is owned by Chile, the first member was Ricardo Ponce, who came with his family in the 1970s. Missionaries came in 1982 and baptized a family by the name of Lopez. About 60 members lived on the islands, as of 1998.

There are also members on Easter Island, which is part of Chile.

Sources: *Encyclopedic History of the Church,* by Andrew Jenson; "Chile," by Steven J. Iverson, *New Era,* February 1977; "Growth predicted for Chile," *Church News,* March 12, 1977; "Love, respect and emotion end area conference series," by Dell Van Orden, *Church News,* March 12, 1977; *Los Mormones in Chile,* by Rodolfo Acevedo Acevedo, published in Santiago, Chile, 1989; *Church News,* Sept. 25, 1993, *Church News,* June 15, 1996, and *Church News,* Aug. 13, 1996, by Nestor Curbelo; *Church News,* Nov. 11, Nov. 23, 1996; March 1, 1997, "Chile 4th Nation with 100 stakes," by Rodolfo Acevedo, *Church News,* March 22, 1997; "Branch on Robinson Crusoe Island," by Nestor Curbelo, *Church News,* July 12, 1997; *Church News,* July 19, 1997, April 4, 1998, May 8, 1999, Sept. 11, 1999.

Stakes — 115

(Listed alphabetically as of Oct. 1, 2000.)

No.	Name	Organized	First President
Chile Area			
2005	Angol Chile	18 Dec 1994	Juan Carlos Morales Vasquez

1165	Antofagasta Chile	10 Aug 1980	Octavio Araya Y.
1501	*Antofagasta Chile Caliche 24 June 1997		
	‡Caliche Chile	4 Nov 1984	Ricardo Manuel Palma F.
1955	Antofagasta Chile		
	La Portada	5 Sep 1993	Miguel A. Gonzalez Romero
1100	Arica Chile	29 Jan 1980	Jose Ulloa C.
2035	Arica Chile Azapa	12 Mar 1995	Arnando Ernesto Perez M.
1598	Arica Chile El Morro	18 May 1986	Sergio Alberto Funes
2026	Buin Chile	26 Feb 1995	Jorge H. Herrera Carmona
1522	Calama Chile	17 Mar 1985	Ivan Gonzalez Castillo
1398	Chillan Chile	13 Feb 1983	Sergio Rios S.
2278	Chillan Chile Nuble	24 Nov 1996	Carlos C. Ortiz Rubilar
808	Concepcion Chile	30 Jan 1977	Claudio Signorelli G.
1075	*Concepcion Chile Andalien 25 June 1998		
	‡Andalien	28 Oct 1979	Pedro E. Arias
2463	*Concepcion Chile Baquedano 25 Jun 1998		
	‡Andalien Chile		
	Baquedano	17 May 1998	Hernan D. Ferreira P.
2006	*Concepcion Chile Chiguayante 24 Jun 1997		
	‡Chiguayante Chile	18 Dec 1994	Carlos Andres Puig Iguat
2481	Concepcion Chile		
	Hualqui	21 Jun 1998	Carlos Andres Puig Iguat
1929	Copiapo Chile	11 Apr 1993	Sergio Orlando Mora Oviedo
2348	Copiapo Chile East	4 May 1997	Leonardo Esteban Lufi Mazuela
1960b	Coquimbo Chile	5 Dec 1993	Marco Oyarzun Vera
2334	Coronel Chile	23 Mar 1997	Juan Bautista Pereira A.
2167	Coyhaique Chile	18 Feb 1996	Feberico Sanchez G.
1264	Curico Chile	10 May 1981	Jose Luis Ferreira P.
2400	Curico Chile		
	Rauquen	12 Oct 1997	Nelson Adolfo Vasquez Carrasco
1931	El Belloto Chile	11 Apr 1993	Hugo L. Garrido Gonzalez
1621	Iquique Chile	14 Dec 1986	Nelson C. Mondaca I.
2320	Iquique Chile South	9 Mar 1997	Ruperto Arnoldo Reyes Tello
1702	La Serena Chile	23 Oct 1988	Ricardo Thomas Rubina
2196a	La Union Chile	26 May 1996	Lautaro Roberto Sanchez Cerda
2313	Lebu Chile	23 Feb 1997	
1694	Linares Chile	24 Apr 1988	Alberto Ariosto Alveal V.
1949	Los Andes Chile	4 Jul 1993	Vicente E. Zuniga Figueroa
1599	*Los Angeles Chile North 1 Dec 1996		
	‡Los Angeles Chile	1 Jun 1986	Mario Carlos Escobar
2285	Los Angeles Chile		
	South	1 Dec 1996	Mario A. Gutierrez Castillo
1950	Melipilla Chile	18 Jul 1993	Natanael Toro Navarrete
1267	Osorno Chile	17 May 1981	Raul Hernan Paredes P.
2362	Osorno Chile Rahue	25 May 1997	Jose Luis Valderas Saldivia
1976	Ovalle Chile	20 Feb 1994	Wilson B. Nunez Castillo
1320	*Penaflor Chile 18 Jul 1993		
	*Santiago Chile Penaflor 10 Apr 1990		
	‡Penaflor Chile	10 Dec 1981	Sergio Venegas Pacheo
1268	Penco Chile	24 May 1981	Abel Poblete Flores
1339	Puerto Montt Chile	25 Apr 1982	Juan Carlos Lopez L.
2321	Puerto Varas Chile	9 Mar 1997	Gerardo J. Wilhelm Kretschmar
1478	Punta Arenas Chile	10 Jun 1984	Luis Elqueda C.
1275	Quillota Chile	7 Jun 1981	Maximo Ananias Iribarren I.
791	Quilpue Chile	28 Nov 1976	Eduardo Lamartine A.
2353	Quilpue Chile		

	Marga Marga	18 May 1997	Ivan Robinson Letelier C.
1285	Rancagua Chile	26 Aug 1981	Hector Verdugo Radrigan
1930	Rancagua Chile Tupahue	11 Apr 1993	Juan Carlos Fredes Duran
1731	San Antonio Chile	2 Jul 1989	Sergio Enrique Gonzalez S.
2384	San Felipe Chile	6 Jul 1997	Alejandro E. Asete Figueroa
1703	San Fernando Chile	30 Oct 1988	Jose Luis Ferreira P.
1286	San Pedro Chile	30 Aug 1981	Juan Cuevas I.
2290	Santa Cruz Chile	8 Dec 1996	Rodolfo E. Herrera Mejias
2089	Santiago Chile Alicahue	20 Aug 1995	Patricio R. Ortega H.
1960	Santiago Chile Cerro Navia	7 Nov 1993	Juan David Huaiguinir Castro
1038	Santiago Chile Cinco de Abril	10 Jun 1979	Poblibio Gonzalez Gutierrez
1077	Santiago Chile Conchali	4 Nov 1979	Juan Castro Duque
2036	Santiago Chile Cordillera	19 Mar 1995	Jorge Andres Pedero
1216	Santiago Chile El Bosque	14 Dec 1980	Eduardo Ayala Aburto
2410	Santiago Chile Estacion Central	16 Nov 1997	Cesar Manuel Escobar Perez
2352	Santiago Chile Fermin Vivaceta	8 May 1997	Leopoldo S. Parra Suco
2289	Santiago Chile Gabriela	8 Dec 1996	Rene Esteban del Pino Carcia
1933	Santiago Chile Gran Avenida	18 Apr 1993	Andres Maja Basaez
1024	Santiago Chile Independencia	6 May 1979	Wilfredo Lopez G.
1902	Santiago Chile Javiera Carrera	20 Sep 1992	Patricio LaTorre Orellana
2075	Santiago Chile La Bandera	9 Jul 1995	Felix Reinaldo Cofre Quezada
672	*Santiago Chile La Cisterna	18 Apr 1976	
	‡Santiago Chile South	8 Dec 1974	Eduardo Ayala
1039	Santiago Chile La Florida	10 Jun 1979	Carlos G. Zuniga Campusano
1899	Santiago Chile La Granja	30 Aug 1992	Arturo del C. Jorquera M.
1947	Santiago Chile La Reina	27 June 1993	Santiago Vicente Vera Barrera
2090	Santiago Chile Las Araucarias	20 Aug 1995	Luis Enrique Moya Basaez
1402	Santiago Chile Las Condes	12 Mar 1983	E. Gustavo Flores Carrasco
2086	Santiago Chile Lo Blanco	13 Aug 1995	Eric A. Nunez Yevenes
2024	Santiago Chile Lo Espejo	19 Feb 1995	David Ormeno Parra
2178	Santiago Chile Lo Prado	10 Mar 1996	Raul Alfredo Dote
2082	Santiago Chile Los Cerrillos	30 Jul 1995	Renato Alejandro Ruz Leon
2121	Santiago Chile Los Manantiales	12 Nov 1995	Luis A. Inostroza Gomez
1915	Santiago Chile Maipu	6 Dec 1992	Julio Cesar Valdivia Marin
792	Santiago Chile Nunoa	28 Nov 1976	Gustavo Alberto Barrios C.
2126	Santiago Chile Ochagavia	19 Nov 1995	Gerardo Gabezas Leyton
1919	Santiago Chile O'Higgins	20 Dec 1992	Victor A. Cifuentes Droguett
2500	Santiago Chile Olimpo	22 Nov 1998	Alberto Octavio Gonzalez G.
2487	Santiago Chile Penalolen	26 Jul 1998	Santiago V. Vera Barrera
2345	Santiago Chile Progreso	27 Apr 1997	Patricio Latorre O.
1403	Santiago Chile Pudahuel	13 Mar 1983	Enrique Espinoza
1548	Santiago Chile Puente Alto	18 Aug 1985	Jorge A. Pedrero Martinez
1205	*Santiago Chile Quilicura	13 Dec 1988	
	‡Santiago Chile Huechuraba	9 Nov 1980	Juan Humberto Body B.
590	*Santiago Chile Quinta Normal	10 Jan 1980	
	*Santiago Chile Providencia	18 Apr 1976	
	*Santiago Chile		
	‡Santiago (Chile)	19 Nov 1972	Carlos A. Cifuentes
1492	Santiago Chile Renca	16 Sep 1984	Eduardo Cabezas O.
754	Santiago Chile Republica	18 Apr 1976	Julio Jaramillo
1003	Santiago Chile San Bernardo	25 Feb 1979	Hugo Balmaceda
2451	Santiago Chile San Joaquin	19 Apr 1998	Nicanor Teuquil A.
1549	Santiago Chile San Miguel	18 Aug 1985	Hector G. Carvajal Arenas

1927	Santiago Chile Vicuna Mackenna	21 Mar 1993	Jorge A. Pedrero Martinez
1379	*Santiago Chile Zapadores	13 Dec 1988	
	‡Santiago Chile Las Canteras	14 Nov 1982	Juan Castro Duque
2421	Talagante Chile	7 Dec 1997	Juan Carlos Mena Carreno
2060	Talca Chile El Mirador	11 Jun 1995	Gaston A. Rocha Fernandez
1083	*Talca Chile Lircay	11 Jun 1995	
	‡Talca Chile	17 Nov 1979	Emilio Diaz
866	Talcahuano Chile	16 Oct 1977	Claudio Daniel Signorelli G.
2047	Talcahuano Chile Colon	7 May 1995	Daniel Marcelo Canoles M.
1146	*Talcahuano Chile Hualpen	7 May 1995	
	*Hualpen Chile	26 Jul 1988	
	‡Talcahuano Chile Hualpen	15 Jun 1980	Fernando Aguilar
2133	Temuco Chile Cautin	26 Nov 1995	Hector L.F. Sandoval
1245	*Temuco Chile Nielol	26 Nov. 1995	
	‡Temuco Chile	18 Mar 1981	Eleazar F. Magnere D.
1667	Valdivia Chile	10 Jan 1988	Armando Ambrosio Linco P.
2413	Valdivia Chile Calle Calle	23 Nov 1997	Jaime Enrique Gonzalez Caro
882	Valparaiso Chile	20 Nov 1977	Abel Correa Lopez
2014	Valparaiso Chile Oriente	22 Jan 1995	Sergio Ignacio Padovani T.
2013	Valparaiso Chile Playa Ancha	22 Jan 1995	Bernardo Felix Gallegos B.
1230	Valparaiso Chile South	1 Feb 1981	Juan Rios R.
1037	Villa Alemana Chile	8 Jun 1979	Eduardo Adrian LaMartine
2212	Villa Alemana Chile West	14 Jul 1996	M. Gonzalo Sepulveda Moya
671	Vina del Mar Chile	5 Dec 1974	Jose Leyton
1499	*Vina del Mar Achupallas	25 Jun 1998	
	‡Achupallas Chile	28 Oct 1984	Luis Alino Pereira P.
2016	Vina del Mar Chile Agua Santa	22 Jan 1995	Dinar Michael Reyes Barbe
2015	Vina del Mar Chile Forestal	22 Jan 1995	Edgardo Ramon Salina H.
1967	*Vina Del Mar Chile Miraflores		
	‡Miraflores Chile	19 Dec 1993	Jorge Bernardo Toro

Stakes discontinued

1995	Santiago Chile Jose Miguel Carrera Discontinued 23 Apr 2000	6 Nov 1994	Patricio G. Latorre O.

Missions — 8

(As of Oct. 1, 2000; shown with historical number. See MISSIONS.)

(214) CHILE ANTOFAGASTA MISSION
Casilla 70
Antofagasta
Chile

(119) CHILE CONCEPCION MISSION
Casilla 2210
Concepcion
Chile

(151) CHILE OSORNO MISSION
Casilla 7-0
Osorno, X Region
Chile

(311) CHILE SANTIAGO EAST MISSION
Pedro de Valdivia 1423
Casilla 47, Providencia
Santiago 29, Chile

(148) CHILE SANTIAGO NORTH MISSION
Casilla 172,
Providencia
Santiago 29, Chile

(67) CHILE SANTIAGO SOUTH MISSION
Casilla 137,
Providencia
Santiago 29, Chile

(303) CHILE SANTIAGO WEST
Casilla 73,
Santiago 29, Chile

(168) CHILE VINA DEL MAR MISSION
Casilla 24-D
Vina del Mar, Chile

CHINA

Encompassing most of east Asia, the People's Republic of China has a population that speaks Mandarin Chinese, Yue, Wu Minbei, Minnan, and Xiang. Population inlcudes atheists, and traditional Confucians, Buddhists, and Taoists.

In 1853, Hosea Stout, James Lewis, and Chapman Duncan were called to teach the gospel to the Chinese. They arrived in Hong Kong April 27, 1853, and stayed only four months, finding access to the country impossible. They may have baptized one convert. On a world tour, Elder David O. McKay, then of the Quorum of the Twelve, visited China in January 1921.

In more recent times, annual visits by BYU performing groups beginning in 1979 have led to warmer relations. The Chinese ambassador, Chai Zemin, visited Church headquarters Jan. 9-11, 1981. His visit was followed by a visit to the Polynesian Cultural Center by Premier Zhao Ziyang Jan. 7, 1984. President Li Xiannian visited the cultural center July 31, 1985.

Further exchanges were made as Elder Russell M. Nelson of the Quorum of the Twelve was named an honorary professor in 1985 by a Chinese medical college in appreciation for his earlier work in China.

As cultural exchanges continued, a few expatriate LDS families began living in China. For these families and Chinese people who joined the Church while living abroad, branches were established in Beijing and Shanghai.

Elder Nelson and Elder Dallin H. Oaks of the Quorum of the Twelve continued discussions with Chinese leaders in the late 1980s.

A group of high-ranking Chinese educators visited Elder Oaks in his office in the Church Administration Building in Salt Lake City Nov. 10, 1989, and received a set of LDS books to be placed in their institutions' libraries. On Feb. 21, 1990, on behalf of the First Presidency, Elder Nelson presented to the Chinese ambassador to the United States a check for $25,000 to help in reconstruction efforts after a major earthquake caused extensive damage in China.

While in Beijing Jan. 19-23, 1990, Elder Oaks was invited by the Chinese Academy of Social Sciences to deliver an hour-and-a-half lecture about the Church.

David Hsiao Hsin Chen, a professor at BYU-Hawaii who was born and raised in China, was set apart as the first traveling elder in China at the Beijing Branch Jan. 21, 1990, by Beijing Branch Pres. Timothy Stratford. Elder Chen's responsibility was to go to China several times a year to train LDS Chinese leaders and to oversee the Church's membership in China.

Most of the LDS members in China are foreign teachers, foreign businessmen or diplomats and their families, and Chinese members who have returned to their homeland after having studied or worked in North America, Europe, or other parts of the world.

President Gordon B. Hinckley visited Shenzhen May 27-28, 1996, becoming the first Church president to go to China. With him were President Thomas S. Monson, first counselor in the First Presidency; Elders Neal A. Maxwell and Joseph B. Wirthlin of the Quorum of the Twelve; and Elder Kwok Yuen Tai of the Seventy. Sisters Marjorie Hinckley, Frances Monson, Colleen Maxwell, Elisa Wirthlin, and Hui Hua Tai accompanied their husbands to China. The invitation to visit China was arranged through the Church-owned Polynesian Cultural Center in Hawaii, which helped officials in China establish a similar cultural center in Shenzhen. The Church extended aid to China for flooding relief in September, 1998.

Hong Kong became part of China in 1997. Macau, which has one branch, became part of China in 1999. On Aug. 29, 1999, the Church donated $20,000 to the Chinese ambassador in Washington, D.C. , for flood relief in China's central province, Hubei.

Sources: *Encyclopedic History of the Church,* by Andrew Jenson; *Church News,* Jan. 17, 1981, Jan. 15, 1984, Nov. 18, 1989, Feb. 3, 1990; "President Hinckley visits China," *Church News,* June 1, 1996; *Church News,* Sept. 4, 1999.

HONG KONG

Year-end 1999: Est. population,6,000,000; Members, 20,256; Stakes, 5; Wards, 29; Branches, 10; Missions, 1; Temples, 1; percent LDS, .3, or one in 296

At the mouth of the Canton River on the southern coast of mainland China, Hong Kong was a British Crown Colony, acquired in 1841, which reverted to China in 1997. Its people speak Cantonese and English, and are mostly Buddhists and Taoists, although small groups of Christians, Hindus, and Jews also live in Hong Kong.

In 1852, Hosea Stout, James Lewis, and Chapman Duncan were called to teach the gospel to the Chinese. They arrived in Hong Kong April 27, 1853. They stayed only four months and may have baptized one convert. However, because of internal problems in China, a mission was not opened in Hong Kong until 1949. Hilton A. Robertson was president of the new China Mission.

The first two missionaries, H. Grant Heaton and William K. Paalani, arrived Feb. 25, 1950, and later their ranks were increased to eight. Three converts were baptized Dec. 31, 1950. Soon, an average of 30 people attended weekly meetings. Work in Hong Kong was interrupted by the Korean War and did not reopen until 1955, when Grant Heaton returned as mission president of the new Southern Far East Mission. Leaders emphasized language training and translation. By November of that year, two branches were opened. On April 26, 1956, 11 converts were baptized.

Four years later, there were 91 full-time foreign and 12 full-time local missionaries serving in Hong Kong, with eight branches and a membership of about 1,700.

Membership grew to 3,000 over the next five years, but continuing emigration took a heavy toll on both membership and leadership. A district was established in 1965. That same year, the Book of Mormon was printed in Chinese, and work began to increase. The first meetinghouse was completed in 1966. President Spencer W. Kimball participated in area conferences in Hong Kong in 1975 and 1980. The Hong Kong Stake was organized April 25, 1976, with a membership of 3,410. Membership remained at that number for about five years, but by 1986 had jumped to 12,200 members in four stakes.

On May 26, 1996, the Hong Kong Temple was dedicated. There were seven dedicatory sessions attended by 5,000 members of the Church. The temple in Kowloon Tong on the Kowloon Peninsula serves more than 20,000 members in Hong Kong, Macao, and Singapore. The temple occupies the top three floors of the building and the baptismal font is in the basement. A meetinghouse, mission office, apartments for the temple president and the mission president, and a small outlet of Beehive clothing are located on the other floors.

On April 23, 1997, President James E. Faust, second counselor in the First Presidency, met with Mr. Tung Chee-hwa, chief executive of the Hong Kong special administrative region of the People's Republic, who assured him that "religious freedom will remain here."

In 1999, LDS membership in Hong Kong was more than 20,000.

Sources: *The Church Encounters Asia,* by Spencer J. Palmer, Deseret Book, 1970; Hong Kong, Pearl of the Orient, by Jay A. Parry, *Ensign,* August 1975; *Church News,* May 15, 1976; *Culture for Missionaries, Taiwan, Hong Kong,* Missionary Training Center, 1980; "Saints throng to area meetings in the Far East," by Dell Van Orden, *Church News,* Nov. 1, 1980; "Pearls of the Orient," by Kellene Ricks, *Ensign,* Sept. 1991; *Church News,* Feb. 5, 1994; *Church News,* May 25, 1996; "Hong Kong Temple dedicated," by Gerry Avant, *Church News,* June 1, 1996; *Church News,* May 3, 1997.

Stakes — 5

(Listed alphabetically as of Oct. 1, 2000.)

No.	Name	Organized	First President
Asia Area			
756	*Hong Kong Island 29 May 1980		
	‡Hong Kong	25 Apr 1976	Shiu-Tat Sheldon Poon
1141	Hong Kong Kowloon East	20 Mar 1994	
	*Hong Kong Kowloon 11 Nov 1984		
	‡Kowloon Hong Kong	29 May 1980	Patrick Chung-hei Wong
1977	Hong Kong Kowloon West	20 Mar 1994	Poon Yin Sang Peter
1503	Hong Kong New Territories	11 Nov 1984	Johnson Ma
1502	*Hong Kong Tolo Harbour	20 Mar 1994	
	*Hong Kong Kowloon North	11 Nov 1984	Fu Man Yau

Mission — 1

(As of Oct. 1, 2000; shown with historical number. See MISSIONS.)

(44a)CHINA HONG KONG MISSION
2 Cornwall Street, Kowloon Tong, Kowloon, Hong Kong

COLOMBIA

Year-end 1999: Est. population, 36,200,000; Members, 129,105; Stakes, 23; Wards, 150; Branches, 159; Missions, 4; Districts, 21; Temples, 1; percent LDS, .4, or one in 280.

Located in the northwest corner of South America, Colombia is a republic with a Spanish-speaking population that is predominantly Roman Catholic.

In early 1966, some 45 members, mostly North Americans, were meeting in branches in Bogota and Cali. Elders Randall Harmsen and Jerry Broome of the Andes Mission were assigned to Bogota in May of that year. Elders Harmsen and Broome soon rented a facility, a former residence of a military general, for the first Church meetinghouse. Among the first converts was Antonio Vela. Aura Ivars was the first convert in Cali. The Colombia-Venezuela Mission was created in 1968, and by 1971, 27 branches had been established in 10 cities, and the Venezuela Mission was divided from Colombia, where the mission headquarters were in Bogota. In 1975, the Colombia Cali Mission was created. President Spencer W. Kimball visited Colombia and addressed a gathering of 4,600 at an area conference on March 5, 1977. That year, the first stake in Colombia was created in Bogota on Jan. 23.

Seminaries and institutes were begun in 1972, and by 1976, 900 students were taking part in the educational programs, and membership reached 6,178. By 1986, membership mushroomed to 45,800.

A temple was announced for Colombia on April 7, 1984, and a site for the temple was announced in 1988. However, construction was delayed pending government approvals.

In September 1989, internal political difficulties led to a temporary withdrawing of North American missionaries. Despite these problems, missionary work continued to progress. The Colombia Barranquilla Mission was formed in 1988. Since then, three other stakes have been created in Barranquilla. Membership in Colombia in 1990 was 83,000 and by 1999 had reached 129,105. The first General Authority from Colombia was Julio Davila, who was called to the Second Quorum of the Seventy in 1991.

Following countrywide fasts of Latter-day Saints, government approvals were received and the long-awaited construction of the Bogota Colombia Temple was started in late spring of 1995. Significant growth continued in the country as the number of stakes doubled in about two years. President Gordon B. Hinckley visited Bogota Nov. 8, 1996, spoke to some 7,100 members, and toured the temple construction project while there. After 15 years, the temple was dedicated April 24, 1999, in what President Hinckley called "the greatest event in the history of Colombia." He said many factors contributed to the long period of time — the location, the site, trying to get property — but "finally it has happened."

In 1999, a devastating earthquake struck the mountain community of Armenia Colombia, on Jan. 25, and the Church responded immediately with relief supplies. The day after the earthquake, which killed 920 people including three Church members, a truck from the stakes in Bogota arrived in Armenia with food, clothing, and water. Two trucks arrived later from Cali, and another from the two stakes in Medellin and nearby districts.

Sources: "Church in Colombia moving ahead," by Jack E. Jarrard, *Church News* Feb. 1, 1969; "The Saints in Colombia," by Colleen J. Heninger, *Ensign*, October, 1976; "Colombia," *Ensign*, February 1977; "Love, respect and emotion end area conference series," by Dell Van Orden, *Church News*, March 12, 1977; *Church News*, Oct. 23, 1976, March 19, 1988; *Church News*, June 3, 1995, Nov. 16, 1996, Feb. 6, 1999; "Greatest event in history of Colombia," by John L. Hart, *Church News*, May 1, 1999.

Stakes — 22

(Listed alphabetically as of Oct. 1, 2000.)

No.	Name	Organized	First President
South America North Area			
1537	*Barranquilla Colombia El Carmen	30 May 1992	
	‡Barranquilla Colombia	30 May 1985	Libardo Rodriguez
1879	Barranquilla Colombia Hipodromo	31 May 1992	Donaldo A. Osorio P.
1880	Barranquilla Colombia Paraiso	31 May 1992	Jose Peralbo Aparicio
805	Bogota Colombia	23 Jan 1977	Julio E. Davila P.
1113	Bogota Colombia Ciudad Jardin	2 Mar 1980	Miguel Oswaldo Porras
1659	Bogota Colombia El Dorado	18 Oct 1987	Humberto Lopez S.
2326	Bogota Colombia El Salitre	16 Mar 1997	Orlando Moscoso P.

2336	Bogota Colombia Granada	13 Apr 1997	Hector Hernandez Malaver
1008	Bogota Colombia Kennedy	11 Mar 1979	Miguel A. Vargas
2327	Bogota Colombia Suba	16 Mar 1997	Juan Alfonso Cerquera
2382	Bogota Colombia Tunjuelito	22 Jun 1997	David Fabian Saavedra L.
1308	Bucaramanga Colombia	22 Nov 1981	Horacio Julio Insignarez
937	Cali Colombia	4 Jun 1978	Luis Alfonso Rios
1054	Cali Colombia Americas	24 Aug 1979	Libber A. Montoya O.
2391	Cali Colombia Jardin	7 Sep 1997	Nestor Antonio Lopez
2306	Cali Colombia Versalles	9 Feb 1997	Arnold Porras Martinez
2377	Cartagena Colombia	15 Jun 1997	Rafael A. Ulloque Barrios
1697	Medellin Colombia	5 Jun 1988	Arnold Porras Martinez
2213	Medellin Colombia Belen	14 Jul 1996	Harold Cristian Cruz Arango
2363	Neiva Colombia	25 May 1997	Carlos Julio Cubillos Mora
2161	Pasto Colombia	11 Feb 1996	Jose L.Santacruz Fernandez
1968	Pereira Colombia	19 Dec 1993	Jose Luis Gonzalez

Stakes discontinued

1878	Barranquilla Colombia Cevillar	31 May 1992	Carlos M. Lopez M.
	Discontinued	1 Nov 1998	
2245	Ibague Colombia	13 Oct 1996	Cesar Hernando Bravo Parra
	Discontinued 21 May 2000		

Missions — 4

(As of Oct. 1, 2000; shown with historical number. See MISSIONS.)

(215) COLOMBIA BARRANQUILLA MISSION
Apartado Aereo 50710
Barranquilla Atlantico
Colombia

(79a) COLOMBIA BOGOTA
NORTH MISSION
Apartado Aereo 90746
Bogota 8, D.C., Colombia

(270) COLOMBIA BOGOTA SOUTH MISSION
Apaartado Aereo #77604
Santafe de Bogota 2 D.C.
Colombia

(120) COLOMBIA CALI MISSION
Apartado Aereo 4892
Cali, Valle
Colombia

REPUBLIC OF CONGO

Year-end 1999: Est. population, 2,505,000; Members, 1,602; Branches, 6; Districts, 1; Percent LDS, .06, or one member in 1,564; Africa West Area; Ghana Accra Mission.

Congo is a West African republic, where the people speak French and Kongo. A slight majority of the population is Christian but many follow tribal beliefs.

Congo granted the Church formal recognition Dec. 23, 1991. Missionaries were subsequently assigned to Congo from the Zaire Kinshasa Mission. Branches have been established in the capital city of Brazzaville.

For a period in 1992, missionaries to the Congo were withdrawn because of political turmoil.

Source: *Church News,* Dec. 28, 1991, Dec. 18, 1993.

COOK ISLANDS (RAROTONGA)

Year-end 1999: Est. population, 19,000; Members, 880; Districts, 1; Branches, 6; Percent LDS, 4.63, or one in 22; Pacific Islands Area; New Zealand Auckland Mission.

Located in the South Pacific, about 400 miles southwest of French Polynesia, the Cook Islands are self-governing, and 75 percent of the population are Protestants. The islands maintain close ties with New Zealand.

The first missionaries arrived in 1899, but failed to gain converts. Elder Osborne J.P. Widtsoe and a companion, Elder Mervin Davis, arrived in Rarotonga May 23, 1899, becoming the first LDS missionaries in the Cook Islands. During World War II, Matthew Cowley, then president of the New Zealand Mission, assigned Fritz Bunge Kruger, a New Zealand baker who owned a business at Avarua, Rarotonga, to help establish the Church on the Cook Islands. He and his family subsequently moved to Rarotonga, and their first convert was Samuel Glassie and his family, baptized May 12, 1942.

In 1946, Elder Trevor and Sister Mildred Hamon, and later Elders Donlon DeLaMar and John L. Sorenson were sent to Avarua. By 1949, 160 Cook Islanders had joined the Church.

During the next decades, the Cook Islands were transferred to several missions in an attempt to maintain better communication with the remote location. The islands were part of the Samoan Mission (1954), New Zealand North Mission (1966), Fiji Mission (1971), and the Tahiti Papeete Mission (1975). The Islands are now part of the New Zealand Auckland Mission.

President David O. McKay visited in 1955. A Rarotonga Mission was created Nov. 20, 1960, but was discontinued in 1966, and Rarotonga became part of the New Zealand Mission. In the early 1960s, the Book of Mormon was translated into Cook Island Maori. In 1979, there were 718 members in 10 branches in the Cook Islands.

President Spencer W. Kimball visited Rarotonga in February 1981 during a trip to the South Pacific, and held a short service with members there in an airport hangar.

In 1990, the government issued a series of stamps featuring the first missionaries to the Cook Islands of various denominations. The LDS stamp featured a painting of Elder Widtsoe in the foreground and a drawing of an LDS meetinghouse in the background. On Sept. 4-7, 1996, Church members celebrated the 50th anniversary of the Church in the Cook Islands. During the four-day celebration, members participated in dances, exhibits, sporting events, district conference, and a special fireside. A celebration in Hawaii attended by President Gordon B. Hinckley Oct. 7, 1997, honored pioneers of the Pacific, including those from the Cook Islands.

Sources: *Unto the Islands of the Sea,* by R. Lanier Britsch; "New day dawns for temples in Pacific," by Dell Van Orden, *Church News,* Feb. 28, 1981; "Island stamp honors LDS elder," *Church News,* June 23, 1990; interview with Fritz Kruger; *Church News,* Feb. 28, 1991; Aug. 29, 1992; interview with Mere Fiore; *Church News,* Nov. 23, 1996, Oct. 18, 1997.

COSTA RICA

Year-end 1999: Est. population, 3,419,000; Members, 30,118; Stakes, 5; Wards, 35; Branches, 43; Missions, 1; Districts, 6; Temples, 1; percent LDS, .88, or one in 114.

A Central American democratic republic, Costa Rica has a population that speaks Spanish, and is 95 percent Roman Catholic.

Pres. Arwell L. Pierce of the Mexican Mission was authorized by the First Presidency to add Costa Rica to the Mexican Mission on July 8, 1946. He visited the country on Sept. 12 of that year.

Elders Robert B. Miller and David D. Lingard arrived in Costa Rica about Sept. 10, 1946. They presented the president of the republic with a copy of the Book of Mormon. The missionaries left to avoid being in the nation during a revolution in 1948, but Elder Lingard and Elder Jack M. Farnsworth returned in 1949 and enjoyed a Pioneer Day celebration with the members on July 24. The first conference was held in Costa Rica June 7, 1950, and about 70 attended. A branch was organized Aug. 25, 1950, and property for a meetinghouse was purchased in 1951.

During the 1950s, the Church in Costa Rica grew slowly. General Authorities visited several times. The Central American Mission was organized from the Mexican Mission Nov. 16, 1952. When the Guatemala-El Salvador Mission was created in 1965, it included Costa Rica. The first district conference was held in August 1968, with 296 people in attendance. Six years later, the Costa Rica Mission was organized June 20, 1974.

Costa Rica's first stake, the San Jose Costa Rica Stake, was created Jan. 20, 1977. A month later, President Spencer W. Kimball spoke at an area conference in San Jose that was part of his seven-nation Latin America tour. At that time, there were 3,800 members in the country. By 1986, Costa Rica had 7,100 members. Eight years later, by 1995, this number had reached 25,000. President Gordon B. Hinckley visited Costa Rica on Jan. 20, 1997, and spoke to about 7,000 members. He also visited Costa Rica President Jose Maria Figueres at his office in San Jose.

In 1999, there were 30,118 members in Costa Rica.

The San Jose Costa Rica Temple, the first temple in southern Central America, was dedicated June 4, 2000, just 15 months after it was announced March 17, 1999.

Sources: San Jose Branch manuscript history; Address by Pres. Manuel Najera at San Jose, Costa Rica, area conference, Feb. 23, 1977; *Church News,* Feb. 1, 1997, June 10, 2000.

Stakes — 5

(Listed alphabetically as of Oct. 1, 2000.)

No.	Name	Organized	First President
Central America Area			
1783	*Alajuela Costa Rica	20 Jun 1995	
	‡San Jose Costa Rica Alajuela	9 Dec 1990	Milton Perez Ruiz
1826	San Jose Costa Rica La Paz	10 Nov 1991	Max Enrique Urena Fallas
917	San Jose Costa Rica La Sabana	7 May 1978	Jorge Arturo Solano Castillo
803	*San Jose Costa Rica Los Yoses	10 Nov 1991	
	‡San Jose Costa Rica	20 Jan 1977	Manuel Najera G.
2524	San Jose Costa Rica Toyopan	25 Apr 1999	Rodrigo Bernal Soto Bolanos

Mission — 1

(As of Oct. 1, 2000; shown with historical number. See MISSIONS.)

(43b) COSTA RICA SAN JOSE MISSION
Apartado Postal 2339-1000
San Jose, Costa Rica C.A.

CROATIA

Year-end 1999: Est. Population, 4,666,000; Members, 299; Branches, 4; Districts, 1; Percent LDS, .01, or one member in 15,605; Europe Central Area; Austria Vienna Mission.

Located on the Balkan Peninsula in southeast Europe, Croatia is a republic made up of what was a northern internal division of Yugoslavia.

In the early 1970s, a few Latter-day Saints were living in Yugoslavia, some of whom had joined the Church while working or studying abroad. The first testimony meeting in the capital city of Zadar was held Sept. 11, 1972.

In early 1975, the Church was recognized as a legal entity in Yugoslavia and a branch was organized in Zadar.

Among those who joined the Church while studying abroad was Kresimir Cosic, a BYU basketball star who returned to play on and coach the Yugoslavia Olympic team. He served as president of the Yugoslavia District. Following the dissolution of Yugoslavia, he persuaded the United States to send a representative to Croatia, and he was appointed deputy ambassador to the United States from Croatia in 1992.

Humanitarian relief has been provided to Croatia by the Church and Church members in the United States and Europe. Thousands of tons of food, clothing, bedding and medical supplies were shipped between 1993-98. Since 1995, the Church has participated in a pig project that helps refugee farmers return to their lands and begin life again. Youth from Croatia, Serbia, Bosnia, and Slovenia participated in a youth conference, with the theme, "Love one another" on July 23, 1998. Membership in Croatia in 1999 was 299, meeting in four branches.

Sources: Yugoslavia manuscript history; "Missionary to the Balkans, Mischa Markow," by William Hale Kehr, *Ensign*, June 1980; Zagreb Branch history, published by the branch at dedication of meetinghouse, Oct. 30, 1985; "Tears of joy," by Richard L. Jensen, *Church News*, Dec. 8, 1979; "Yugoslavia's bright future," *Church News*, March 2, 1986; Sept. 26, 1992; Feb. 26, 1993; April 24, 1994; Dec. 3, 1994; and Feb. 25, 1995; Church News, March 28, 1998, Aug. 29, 1998; "Members aid peacekeeping mission," by Lt. Col. James H. Comish, *Church News*, Sept. 5, 1998; *Church News*, June 5, 1999.

CYPRUS

Year-end 1999: Est. population, 737,000; Members, 99; Branches, 2; Percent LDS, .01 , or one member in7,444; Europe Central Area; Greece Athens Mission.

Located in the Mediterranean Sea off the Turkish coast, the republic has groups speaking Greek and Turkish, and follow the Greek Orthodox and Muslim religions.

The Cyprus LDS group was organized in 1962 among member families living in Cyprus on government service. The group, also called the Nicosia Branch, was dissolved in 1969, reorganized in 1971, temporarily dissolved in 1980 and later reorganized. The members are part of an English-speaking community residing in Cyprus, and they occasionally meet with other religious denominations for interdenominational meetings. On Sept. 14, 1993, Elder Joseph B. Wirthlin of the Quorum of the Twelve and Elder Hans B.

Ringger of the Seventy and their wives, Elisa Wirthlin and Helen Ringger, met with a small group of members at Larnaca.

Sources: *Church News*, Nov. 27, 1993, Oct. 4, 1997.

CZECH REPUBLIC

Year-end 1999: Est. population, 10,433,000; Members, 1,654; Branches, 20; Missions, 1; Districts, 4; Branches, 19; Percent LDS, .02, or one member in 6,308; Europe Central Area.

In east-central Europe, the Czech Republic's people speak Czech and Slovak, both of which are official languages. Some 65 percent of the population is Roman Catholic.

Elder Thomas Biesinger, the first missionary to enter what was then Austria, arrived in 1884. However, he was imprisoned and banished following a trial. After his release and before his departure, he baptized and confirmed Anthon Just, one of his previous investigators and a witness at his trial, on June 21, 1884.

After Elder Biesinger left, the work awaited his return in 1928, at the age of 84. On his second attempt, he obtained legal permission for the Church. The Czechoslovakia Mission was organized July 24, 1929, by Elder John A. Widtsoe, president of the European Mission. Arthur Gaeth, one of the elders in the German-Austrian Mission, was chosen to preside over the new mission. At that time, there were seven members in the nation. Among them were Franziska Brodil, a widow whose two daughters, Frances and Jane, were baptized in Czechoslovakia in 1921.

Lectures on the Church were delivered over radio, and at a cultural fair in 1931 missionaries handed out more than 150,000 tracts. The Book of Mormon was translated in 1933, and additional materials were later translated and published. A shortage of missionaries during the Great Depression slowed the work. With the approach of World War II in the fall of 1938, missionaries were recalled from the country. The mission was left under the direction of a young convert, Josef Roubicek. During the war, Pres. Roubicek kept the Saints together, added 28 members, and published a mission circular letter. Missionary work resumed in 1946 and continued until April 6, 1950, when the mission was closed. Roubicek immigrated to America in 1949.

The Czechoslovakia District was organized Feb. 3, 1982. Local missionaries began having success after about 1985. After the democratization of the nation in 1989-90, the first full-time missionaries arrived in 1990. About that time, the Church applied for recognition. According to President Thomas S. Monson, then second counselor in the First Presidency, "The government leaders had said to us, 'Don't send an American, a German, or a Swiss. Send us a Czech.'" Acknowledging Church leadership during the prohibition of religion was tantamount to imprisonment. Pres. Jiri Snederfler, Czechoslovakia district president, answered the call and faced this risk as he applied to the government for recognition.

Pres. Snederfler met in Prague on Feb. 6, 1990, with Deputy Prime Minister Josef Hromadka, and recognition that was first granted to the Church in 1928 was officially renewed on Feb. 21, 1990. The Czechoslovakia Prague Mission was reorganized July 1, 1990, from a division of the Austria Vienna East Mission, with Richard W. Winder as president. He had served a mission in Czechoslovakia 40 years earlier. By 1990, there were more than 200 members. The Tabernacle Choir performed in Prague in 1991. In 1993, Czech broadcasters visited Salt Lake City and broadcast a nationwide feature on the Church.

BYU International Folk Dancers visited Kladno, Czech Republic, in August 1997, and their performance was taped for broadcast. In 1999, 1,654 LDS members lived in the Czech Republic.

Sources: *Encyclopedic History of the Church*, by Andrew Jenson; *Church News*, Feb. 22, 1936, Feb. 29, 1936, March 7, 1936, March 14, 1936; Feb. 14, 1951, March 3, 1990; "A Missionary's Two Months in Jail," by William G. Hartley, *New Era*, Nov. 1982; "Prayed for a mission," by Davis Bitton, *Church News*, Oct. 28, 1978; Swiss Mission history, May 8, 1968; "Czech broadcasters see Church close-up," by R. Scott Lloyd, *Church News*, May 22, 1993; Correspondence from Kahlile Mehr, Dec. 29, 1992; *Church News*, Aug. 30, 1997.

Mission — 1

(As of Oct. 1, 2000; shown with historical number. See MISSIONS.)

(236) CZECH PRAGUE MISSION
Milady Horakove 85/95
170 00 PRAGUE 7 - Holesovice, Czech Republic

DEMOCRATIC REPUBLIC OF CONGO

Year-end 1999: Est. population, 44,061,000; Members, 8,197; Stakes, 3; Wards, 20; Districts, 1; Branches, 13; Missions, 1; Percent LDS, .02, or one member in 5,375; Africa West Area.

Formerly Belgian Congo in central Africa, the country became an independent republic in 1960 and was renamed Zaire in 1971, and Congo in 1997. The people speak French and Bantu dialects, and are Christian, 70 percent, and Muslim, 10 percent.

Elder R. Bay and Sister Jean Hutchings arrived in Kinshasa in February 1986, when the Church received legal status through the efforts of David M. Kennedy, special representative of the First Presidency. Pres. Hutchings was soon called as president of the Zaire Kinshasa Mission, created July 1, 1987. Meetings were first held in the home of Michael C. Bowcutt, an employee of the U.S. Embassy, and later at the home of Nkita Bungi Mbuyi, a returned missionary from England, who was converted in Belgium. The Church purchased a villa and had it remodeled into a meetinghouse in September 1986. At the first meeting in the 200-seat facility, 208 attended. The first baptisms in Zaire were Banza Jr. and Philippe Muchioko, sons of Banza Muchioko, who were converted in Switzerland seven years earlier.

Many young men and young families were converted in the first year. In July 1987, membership reached 300. Some 20 of the new converts were called as local missionaries to extend the work.

The first full-time missionaries from Zaire were Banza Muchioko Jr., Diamany Ngalamulume, Mutombo Nkadi Thomas, and Maly-malu Kanda, who began serving in their homeland before April 1991.

Church Educational System missionaries Phyll and Betty Hansen introduced seminary in Zaire in late 1991. Elder Hansen instructed Kabwika Natambwe, a member of the Zaire mission presidency, who carried the work forward throughout the country.

The Lubumbashi Democratic Republic of Congo Stake was created on Sept. 7, 1997.

Membership in the country in 1999 was 8,197.

Sources: *Church News,* April 25, 1987; "Zaire's people, thirsty for the gospel," *Church News,* July 18, 1987; "A new day dawns on African nations," by Dell Van Orden and Gerry Avant, *Church News,* Oct. 17, 1987; *Church News,* April 25, 1992, Sept. 9, 1992; Church News, Oct. 4, 1997.

Stakes —3

(Listed alphabetically as of Oct. 1, 2000.)

No.	Name	Organized	First President
2258	*Kinshasa Democratic Republic of Congo	12 Aug. 1997	
	‡Kinshasa Zaire	3 Nov 1996	Mulielegwa Musithi
2527	Kinshasa Democratic Republic of Congo Masina	2 May 1999	Kola Kapumba Tusey
2390	Lubumbashi Democratic Republic of Congo	7 Sep 1997	Nzembelenge Kefa Milambo

Mission — 1

(As of Oct. 1, 2000; shown with historical number. See MISSIONS.)

(198) DR CONGO KINSHASA MISSION
9-11 Ave. Lemarinel (Ngabi)
Sofide Building, Zone de la Gombe
BP 20.572 KIN XV CCIZ, Kinshasa
DR Congo

DENMARK

Year-end 1999: Est. population, 5,199,000; Members, 4,527; Stakes, 2; Wards, 14; Branches, 11; Missions, 1; Temples, 1 under construction; Percent LDS, .09 , or one in 1,148.

Located in northern Europe on the Baltic Sea, Denmark is a constitutional monarchy with a population that speaks Danish, 90 percent of whom are Evangelical Lutherans.

Elder Erastus Snow was called in October 1849 to open the work in Scandinavia. He and Elders John E. Forsgren and George P. Dykes traveled to Denmark, arriving in Copenhagen June 14, 1850. Another member, Peter O. Hansen, had arrived about a month earlier.

The first baptism took place Aug. 12, 1850, and within two months, the elders had established the headquarters of the mission in Copenhagen and baptized 15 people. The first branch was organized Sept. 15, 1850, in Copenhagen. Elder Dykes opened a second branch in Aalborg Nov. 25, 1850.

The Book of Mormon was translated into Danish in 1851, the first non-English language in which the book was translated

Work continued to progress as the elders pushed into every corner of Denmark, but heavy persecution was waged against members. In Aalborg in 1851, a mob vandalized the hall where the Saints were meeting. Soon conferences (districts) were established in eight areas to accommodate the multiplying branches. The first converts to emigrate left Jan. 31, 1852. Of about 26,000 people who were converted during this early period, 13,984 converts immigrated to the United States by 1930.

The Danish Mission was organized April 1, 1920. Convert baptisms varied from 50 to 200 a year between 1966 and 1974. In 1971, the Church membership in Denmark consisted of about 4,193 people in three districts. Although members were limited in number, they took part in home seminary, served missions, and attended the Swiss Temple after it was dedicated in 1955.

The Copenhagen Denmark Stake, the first in the country, was created in 1974. In 1983, membership totaled 4,097, and in 1990, 4,200.

On Jan. 25, 1975, it was reported that the Church had been classified as a Christian religion by the Danish Library Committee on Classification, opening the way for the Church to enjoy the privileges of other Christian churches in Denmark.

Church presidents visited the country several times in later years. President Spencer W. Kimball addressed 3,800 members at an area conference in Copenhagen in August 1976. President Gordon B. Hinckley visited on June 14, 1996, and challenged the Saints to double their membership in five years. President Thomas S. Monson, first counselor in the First Presidency, visited Copenhagen on June 7, 1998, and offered a prayer of rededication for missionary work in Denmark. Richard Swett, a Church member and two-term Congressman, was sworn in as the U.S. ambassador to Denmark on Sept. 5, 1998.

A temple, to be constructed from an existing building for only the second time in the history of the Church, was announced for Denmark in 1999. Site dedicatory services for the Copenhagen Denmark Temple were held April 24, 1999, by Elder Spencer J. Condie of the Seventy at the Church's Priorvej Chapel in downtown Copenhagen. The chapel was originally dedicated by Elder John A. Widtsoe of the Quorum of the Twelve June 14, 1931.

LDS population in Denmark in 1999 was 4,527.

The 150th anniversary of the Church in Scandinavia was celebrated in Denmark during the first week of July 2000, with a series of firesides, dances, reunions, and the unveiling of two statues. The first statue, unveiled July 4 in Denmark's only national park in the hills of Rebild, is titled "The Family," and symbolizes a Mormon family as they prepare to make the voyage to Utah in the late 1800s. The second statue was unveiled July 6 in the harbor area of Copenhagen, where many of the Saints boarded sailing ships for the journey to America.

Sources: *Encyclopedic History of the Church,* by Andrew Jenson; *History of the Danish Mission, 1850; Deseret News 1976 Church Almanac; Church News,* June 22, 1996, June 13, 1998, Sept. 5, 1998, May 29, 1999, July 15, 2000; *Ensign,* September 2000.

Stakes — 2

(Listed alphabetically as of Oct. 1, 2000.)

No.	Name	Organized	First President
Europe Central Area			
945	Aarhus Denmark	2 Jul 1978	Knud Bent Andersen
648	Copenhagen Denmark	16 Jun 1974	Johan Helge Benthin

Mission — 1

(As of Oct. 1, 2000; shown with historical number. See MISSIONS.)

(23b) DENMARK COPENHAGEN MISSION
Borups Alle 128, 1, tv.
DK-2000 Frederiksberg Denmark

GREENLAND

Year-end 1999: Population, 58,000; Members, 14; Branches, 1; Percent LDS, .02, or one member in 4,143;North America Northeast Area; Denmark Copenhagen Mission.

This very large island, slightly larger than Mexico, in the North Atlantic between Canada and Iceland is a province of Denmark under home rule. Greenland has a parliamentary government with a population that speaks Danish and Greenlandic, and most are members of the Evangelical Lutheran Church.

A branch of LDS servicemen was organized in 1953 and functioned for at least five years. The branch was discontinued in 1989, but a military group continues to meet at Thule Air Base, although the staffing of this base has been greately reduced. A Church group of the Danish family of Kim Hvistendahl, and one other member, meets weekly in Nuuk, under the direction of Greenland Branch president, who is also the Denmark Copenhagen Mission president.

Sources: *Church News,* April 19, 1958; Jan. 9, 1960; correspondence from Kim Hvistendahl, May 13, 1998.

DOMINICAN REPUBLIC

Year-end 1999: Est. population,7,511,000; Members, 69,466; Stakes, 11; Wards, 60; Branches, 111; Missions; 3; Districts, 11; Temples, 1; percent LDS, .92, or one in 108.

On the island of Hispanolia, Dominican Republic is about the size of Vermont and New Hampshire combined, but has nearly five times their combined populations. The Dominican Republic is a representative democracy. Its population speaks Spanish, and is mostly Roman Catholic.

The Eddie and Mercedes Amparo family arrived in the Dominican Republic on June 9, 1978, the day the revelation was announced that allowed all worthy men to hold the priesthood. They and another newly arrived family, John and Nancy Rappleye, began doing missionary work. An associate of the Amparos, Rodolfo Bodden, was the first convert, baptized in August 1978. Among the first missionaries were John A. and Ada Davis of Provo, Utah. The Dominican Republic Santo Domingo Mission was organized Jan. 1, 1981. At that time, membership was at 2,500. A highlight came March 8-9, 1981, when President Spencer W. Kimball visited.

Membership increases have been rapid. In 1979, 354 people were baptized. By 1986, membership reached 11,000. The Santo Domingo Dominican Republic Stake was organized March, 23, 1986. A second mission was organized in Santiago on July 1, 1987, when the country's membership was about 13,000. A second stake was organized Oct. 16, 1988, and a third on Nov. 5, 1989. Membership in 1990 was 31,000. In 1992, the Dominican members received satellite transmissions of general conference.

The first temple in the Caribbean was announced for Santo Domingo, Dominican Republic on Dec. 4, 1993. More than 4,000 Church members gathered Aug. 18, 1996, to witness the temple groundbreaking by Elder Richard G. Scott of the Quorum of the Twelve. The temple was dedicated Sept. 17, 2000, seven years after it was announced.

Sources: *Church News,* Dec. 6, 1980; March 21, 1981; "Dominican Growth: From Zero to Thousands since 1978," *Ensign,* January 1987; "2 families bring gospel to a nation," by William B. Smart, *Church News,* July 11, 1981; *Church News,* Aug. 25, 1985; July 15, 1989; Jan 26, 1986; "Rendering Service to Others," an address by Pres. Spencer W. Kimball, *Ensign,* May 1981; Conversion account of Eric Olivero delivered May 26, 1991, and conference report by Elder Stan Bradshaw; "Dominican Republic, a Second Decade for Dominican Saints," by Elizabeth and Jed VanDenBerghe, *Ensign,* October 1990; *Church News,* Dec. 4, 1993; "Ground broken for Caribbean's first temple," *Church News,* Aug. 24, 1996; *Church News,* Oct. 3, 1998, Sept. 23, 2000.

Stakes — 11

(Listed alphabetically as of Oct. 1, 2000.)

No.	Name	Organized	First President
North America Southeast Area			
2480	La Vega Dominican Republic	21 Jun 1998	Juan E. Almonte
2360	San Cristobal Dominican Republic	25 May 1997	Juan Paciano Felipe
1800	San Francisco de Macoris Dominican Republic	26 May 1991	Eric Edison Olivero P.
2009	Santiago Dominican Republic North	8 Jan 1995	Roberto Antonio Rodriguez
1786	*Santiago Dominican Republic South	8 Jan 1995	
	Santiago Dominican Republic	17 Feb 1991	Ramon Matias Lantigua
1593	Santo Domingo	23 Mar 1986	Jose Delio Ceveno

	Dominican Republic		
1906	Santo Domingo Dominican Republic Independencia	18 Oct 1992	Felix Sequi-Martinez
1735a	*Santo Domingo Dominican Republic Oriental 2 Feb 1992		
	*Oriental Dominican Republic 29 Oct 1991		
	*Santo Domingo Dominican Republic Oriental 24 Sep 1991		
	‡Santo Domingo Dominican Republic East	5 Nov 1989	Pedro Arturo Abreu C.
1844	Santo Domingo Dominican Republic Ozama	2 Feb 1992	Jose Andres Taveras Arias
1701	*Santo Domingo Dominican Republic San Geronimo 18 Oct 1992		
	‡San Geronimo Dominican Republic	16 Oct 1988	Victor Alejandro Navarro M.
2182	Santo Domingo Dominican Republic Villa Mella	17 Mar 1996	Domingo Antonio Aybar A.

Missions — 3

(As of Oct. 1, 2000; shown with historical number. See Missions.)

(196) DOMINICAN REPUBLIC SANTIAGO MISSION
Apartado 1240
Santiago,
Dominican Republic

(259)DOMINICAN REPUBLIC SANTO DOMINGO EAST MISSION
Padre Boil #1
Gazcue
Santo Domingo, Dominican Republic

(188a)D.R. SANTO DOMINGO WEST MISSION
Edificio Manuel Arsenio Urena,
27 de Febrero No. 514
Esq. Calle La Plaza, Santo Domingo
Dominican Republic

ECUADOR

Year-end 1999: Est. population, 10,891,000; Members, 146,420; Stakes, 32; Wards, 219; Branches, 154; Missions, 3; Districts, 11; Temples, 1; Percent LDS, 1.3, or one in 74.

Located on the equator on the Pacific Coast side of South America, the Republic of Ecuador is divided into three zones by two ranges of Andes mountains. Its Spanish- and Quechua-speaking population is 95 percent Roman Catholic.

A telephone call from Elder Spencer W. Kimball, then of the Quorum of the Twelve, to Pres. J. Averil Jesperson of the Andes Mission in Lima, Peru, on Sept. 22, 1965, directed the opening of missionary work in Ecuador. Elders Craig Carpenter, Bryant R. Gold, Joel Lindon Robinson, and Paul O. Allen were sent to Quito, and on Oct. 9, Elder Kimball visited the city. Within the month of Elder Kimball's visit, the first nine persons were baptized in Alangasi de la Merced, located about 50 miles southeast of Quito, on Oct. 31, 1965. Missionary work progressed rapidly. Guayaquil was opened up to missionary work on Jan. 28, 1966, and when the Ecuador Mission, with headquarters in Quito, was created Aug. 1, 1970, membership was 1,000.

Some of the first proselyting was done among the Otavalo Indians near Quito, among whom the first all-Lamanite stake in South America was organized in 1981.

Others in Ecuador eagerly accepted the gospel. By the end of 1975, membership had tripled to 3,226. Ecuador's first stake was organized in Guayaquil June 4, 1978, under the leadership of Pres. Lorenzo Garaycoa. Gustavo Maruri was called as the first bishop in Ecuador. A second mission in the country was organized in Guayaquil, on July 1, 1978. Membership at the beginning of 1979 was 19,000, reaching 43,000 in 1986. In 1989, the headquarters for the South America North Area was moved from Lima, Peru, to Quito, Ecuador.

A temple was announced for Guayaquil on March 31, 1982. Ground was broken for the temple 14 years later by Elder Richard G. Scott of the Quorum of the Twelve on Aug. 10, 1996. During this time, members continued to prepare family names for temple work.

President Gordon B. Hinckley visited Ecuador Aug. 11-12, 1997, the first time a Church president had been in this land. He spoke to 15,000 members in two meetings and toured the temple under construction, and told how he had been impressed to find the site several years earlier. The temple was dedicated Aug. 1, 1999. The evening before, at a regional conference on July 31, President Hinckley spoke to nearly 22,000 members gathered at the Estadio Modelo and told them, in contemplation of the temple dedication, "This is a day to be remembered by Latter-day Saints for many years to come."

Membership in 1999 approached 150,000 in 32 stakes.

Sources: *The Improvement Era,* May 1966; "Ecuador", *Ensign,* February 1977; "Language no barrier," *Church News,* Nov. 11, 1978; "Tip your Panama hat, this is Ecuador," by Gerry Avant, *Church News,* Feb. 14, 1981; *Church News,* July 8, 1978; "In the Andes, Lehi's children grow strong in the gospel," by Elayne Wells, *Church News,* Feb. 17, 1990; *Church News,* June 25, 1994, Aug. 23, 1997, Aug. 29, 1998, Aug. 10, 1999; "Burst of zeal opens work in Ecuador," by John L. Hart, *Church News,* Nov. 6, 1999.

Stakes — 32

(Listed alphabetically as of Oct. 1, 2000.)

No.	Name	Organized	First President
South America North Area			
2144	Ambato Ecuador	10 Dec 1995	Jorge Humberto Verde
2414	Cuenca Ecuador	23 Nov 1997	Wilson Arcesio Pulla Quito
1882	Duran Ecuador North	31 May 1992	Mark Roy Kent
1883	Duran Ecuador South	31 May 1992	Jimmy Winston Olvera
2110	Esmeraldas Ecuador	22 Oct 1995	Jorge Miguel Arroyo Jacombe
2162	Guayaquil Ecuador Alborada	11 Feb 1996	Henry Alejandro Mora
1808	Guayaquil Ecuador Centenario	18 Aug 1991	Luis Guillermo Granja G.
1809	Guayaquil Ecuador East	18 Aug 1991	Jimmy Winston Olvera C.
2163	Guayaquil Ecuador El Cisne	11 Feb 1996	Melvin Merchan
939	*Guayaquil Ecuador El Salado	11 Feb 1996	
	‡Guayaquil Ecuador West	22 Mar 1987	
	‡Guayaquil Ecuador	4 Jun 1978	Lorenzo Garaycoa
1716a	*Guayaquil Ecuador Garcia Moreno	11 Feb 1996	
	‡Guayaquil Ecuador Central	30 Apr 1989	Gonzalo Eduardo Alvarado R.
1916	Guayaquil Ecuador Huancavilca	6 Dec 1992	Jose Eladio Paredes Garcia
2370	Guayaquil Ecuador Pascuales	8 Jun 1997	Luis Fernando Ramirez C.
1117	*Guayaquil Ecuador Prosperina	11 Feb 1996	
	‡Guayaquil Ecuador North	22 Mar 1987	
	‡Guayaquil Ecuador Febres Cordero	16 Mar 1980	Douglas Alarcon Arboleda
2394	Guayaquil Ecuador Puerto Liza	7 Sep 1997	Luis E. Romo Martinez
1006	*Guayaquil Ecuador South	22 Mar 1987	
	‡Guayaquil Ecuador Centenario	4 Mar 1979	Vincente de la Cuadra S.
1853	Machala Ecuador	22 Mar 1992	Manuel Andres Galan Pereira
2173	Manta Ecuador	25 Feb 1996	Wilson Marino Chinga H.
1796	Milagro Ecuador	5 May 1991	Alberto W. Guillen Fuentes
1316	Otavalo Ecuador	6 Dec 1981	Luis Alfonso Morales C.
2301	Otavalo Ecuador Imbabura	19 Jan 1997	Juan J. Munoz Otavalo
1224	Portoviejo Ecuador	13 Jan 1981	Jorge Vicente Salazar H.
1259	*Quevedo Ecuador Bellavista	7 Sep 1997	
	‡Quevedo Ecuador	27 Apr 1981	Pedro Jose Cantos J.
2392	Quevedo Ecuador Guayacan	7 Sep 1997	Jose Meliton Vera Lopez
2393	Quevedo Ecuador San Camilo	7 Sep 1997	Angel Cristobal Garcia M.
2453	Quito Ecuador Calderon	19 Apr 1998	Jorge Gonzalo Montoya
2050	Quito Ecuador Chillogallo	21 May 1995	Eduardo Calderon Poveda
1053	*Quito Ecuador Colon	15 Jan 1981	
	‡Quito Ecuador	22 Aug 1979	Ernesto Franco
1839	Quito Ecuador Inaquito	12 Jan 1992	Horacio Araya Olivares
2431	Quito Ecuador La Ofelia	25 Jan 1998	Olvin Enrique Mora B.
1225	Quito Ecuador Santa Ana	15 Jan 1981	Cesar Hugh Cacuango C.
2096	Santo Domingo Ecuador	3 Sep 1995	Wilson Alcides Echanique Cueve

Stakes discontinued

2279 Esmeraldas Ecuador San Rafael 24 Nov 1996 Cesar O. Intriago Argandena
Discontinued 14 Mar 1999

1116 Guayaquil Ecuador Duran 16 Mar 1980 Lorenzo Augusto Garaycoa
Discontinued 22 Mar 1987 †Guayaquil Ecuador West (939), Guayaquil Ecuador South (1006), Guayaquil Ecuador North (1117)

1221 Guayaquil Ecuador Kennedy 11 Jan 1981 Fausto Montalvan Morla
22 Mar 1987 †Guayaquil Ecuador West (939), Guayaquil Ecuador South (1006), Guayaquil Ecuador North (1117)

(As of Oct. 1, 2000; shown with historical number. See MISSIONS.)

(261) ECUA. GUAYAQUIL NORTH MISSION
Casilla de Correo 16160
Guayaquil
Ecuador

(160) ECUA. GUAYAQUIL SOUTH MISSION
Casilla 8750
Guayaquil
Ecuador

(93) ECUADOR QUITO MISSION
Casilla 17-03-078
Quito
Ecuador

EGYPT

Year-end 1999: Est. population, 66,050,000; Members, fewer than 100; Branches, 1; District 1; Europe Central Area.

Located in the northeast corner of Africa, the republic has a population that speaks Arabic and English, and is 94 percent Sunni Muslim.

The Cairo Branch functioned from 1971-74 as part of the Switzerland Mission. In 1974, two students arrived in Cairo for intensive study of Arabic. Dilworth B. Parkinson and John Sharp met with Carol Azeltine, a teacher at an international school in suburban Digla, and began holding LDS meetings in the garden area of the American University in downtown Cairo.

From 1974 to 1987, the branch was in the International Mission until the mission was dissolved and the branch was placed in the Austria Vienna East Mission. Membership of the branch is made up of about 100 expatriates, most of whom are in the country on U.S. or other government service projects, or for BYU's ongoing archaeology studies. Beginning in 1980, a continual string of couples has gone to Egypt specifically to serve as special Church representatives, who make friends for the Church but do not proselyte. The members met in each other's homes until 1982, when a villa was rented in Maadi. On Feb. 1, 1985, the branch began meeting in a larger, two-story villa in the same community. They hold outings in historic places, and participate in camel rides and boating on the Nile.

Among those who helped make significant contributions in Egypt in recent years are members who have worked on mechanization for small farms, modern drip irrigation methods, various farm production projects, dental service projects, medical technology training, and a significant on-going BYU archaeology excavation performed under the direction of Dr. C. Wilfred Griggs.

Sources: *Church News,* Nov. 26, 1988; "Benson Institute improves lives," *Church News,* Nov. 18, 1989; "Branch in land of pyramids is 'home away from home,'"by Edwin O. Haroldsen, *Church News,* June 12, 1993.

EL SALVADOR

Year-end 1999: Est. population, 5,870,000; Members, 84,683; Stakes, 16; Wards, 96; Branches, 56; Missions, 2; Districts, 2; Percent LDS, 1.4, or one in 69.

El Salvador, in Central America, is a republic with a Spanish, and some Nahuatl-speaking population of mostly Roman Catholics.

On Aug. 20, 1948, Pres. Arwell L. Pierce of the Mexican Mission visited El Salvador and explored the possibility of proselyting. On May 26, 1949, he assigned Elders Glenn Whipple Skousen and Omer Farnsworth to go to El Salvador and open the work. A conference was held at San Salvador on Feb. 16, 1951, attended by Elder Albert E. Bowen of the Quorum of the Twelve, at which 63 people were present. A short time later, on March 2, 1951, Ana Villasenor became the first person baptized in the country. Elder Vance Whipple performed the baptism at Apulo Beach at Lake Ilopango. Eleven others were baptized at the same time.

The country was transferred from the Mexican Mission on Nov. 16, 1952, when the new Central America Mission was created. The San Salvador District was organized in January 1965, and was soon followed by the Guatemala-El Salvador Mission. Membership then numbered 4,200. On June 3, 1973, the district was organized into the San Salvador Stake, which had a membership of 5,600. The El Salvador San Salvador Mission was organized July 1, 1976, at which time the nation had 4,745 members. Ten years later in 1986, membership had climbed to 15,100, and the number of stakes increased to six. The nation reached self-sufficiency in local missionaries in 1989. In 1990, the El Salvador San Salvador East Mission was created and membership in the country was 38,000, nearly doubling in five years to 64,000 in 1995.

In the first visit of a Church president to Central America since 1977, President Gordon B. Hinckley visited San Salvador on Jan. 23, 1997, and spoke to some 10,000 members. Membership in 1999 was 84,683.

Sources: El Salvador San Salvador Mission history, year ending Dec. 31, 1976; *El* Salvador District Manuscript History; *Church News*, Feb. 3, 1990, Feb. 1, 1997.

Stakes — 16

(Listed alphabetically as of Oct. 1, 2000.)

No.	Name	Organized	First President
Central America Area			
1817	Ahuachapan El Salvador	22 Sep 1991	Juan Antonio Merlos V.
2254	Apopa El Salvador	20 Oct 1996	Julio Alberto Reyes Vargas
2219	Atiquizaya El Salvador	11 Aug 1996	Jose Salvador Molina Linares
2114	Chalchuapa El Salvador	20 Oct 1995	Jose Salvador Molina
2122	Juayua El Salvador	12 Nov 1995	Oswaldo Rodriguez Villata
1223	San Miguel El Salvador	11 Jan 1981	Carlos Antonio Hernandez
618	*San Salvador El Salvador		
	‡San Salvador (El Salvador)	3 Jun 1973	Mario Edmundo Scheel
1035	San Salvador El Salvador Cuzcatlan	3 Jun 1979	Franklin Henriquez Melgar
741	*San Salvador El Salvador Ilopango	3 Jun 1979	
	‡San Salvador El Salvador East	1 Feb 1976	Alfonso Octavio Diaz
2111	San Salvador El Salvador La Libertad	22 Oct 1995	H. Edgardo Alvarado Renderos
2241	San Salvador El Salvador Layco	22 Sep 1996	E. Leonardo Rivera Herrera
1745a	San Salvador El Salvador Los Heroes	8 Apr 1990	Cristobal A. Hernandez
1744	San Salvador El Salvador Soyapango	8 Apr 1990	Rene Francisco Esquivel G.
1217	Santa Ana El Salvador Modelo	14 Dec 1980	Jorge Alberta Benitez M.
1088	*Santa Ana El Salvador Molino	14 Dec 1980	
	‡Santa Ana El Salvador	2 Dec 1979	Elmer Barrientos
1816	Sonsonate El Salvador	22 Sep 1991	Rolando Arturo Rosales H.

Missions — 2

(As of Oct. 1, 2000; shown with historical number. See MISSIONS)

(137a) EL SALVADOR SAN SALVADOR EAST MISSION
Apartado Postal #3362
San Salvador
El Salvador, C.A.

(181a) EL SALVADOR SAN SALVADOR WEST MISSION
Apartado Postal 367
San Salvador
El Salvador, C.A.

ENGLAND

(See United Kingdom)

EQUATORIAL GUINEA

Year-end 1999: Est. population, 454,000; Members, 339; Africa West Area; Ivory Coast Abidjan Mission; percent LDS, .07 or one in 1,339.

Located near the equator on the west coast of Africa, Equatorial Guinea is a unitary republic with a population that is mostly Roman Catholic.

Equatorial Guinea was included in the Ivory Coast Abidjan Mission when it was created Feb. 1, 1992.

ESTONIA

Year-end 1999: Est. population, 1,625,000; Members, 300; Districts, 1; Branches, 3; Percent LDS, .02 , or one in 4,794;Europe East Area; Lithuania Vilnius Mission.

The first contacts in recent times in Estonia were established by Finnish members who worked in Tallinn, Estonia. Among these were Valtteri Rotsa and Enn Lembit, who were baptized in Helsinki, Finland.

LDS Finnish businessman Pekka Uusituba, who was visiting in Estonia, taught the gospel to a group of 10 investigators at Lembit's home in November 1989. The first Estonians baptized in Estonia were Alari Allik, Eva Reisalu, Jaana Lass, and Kristi Lass, on Dec. 17, 1989. Later, Jaanus Silla from Tallinn, was baptized Jan. 6, 1990. He was the first missionary from Estonia, and was called to the Utah Salt Lake City Mission. At that time, the branch had an attendance of some 50 people.

In May 1991, the Estonian and Russian branches (both in Tallinn) had 130 members. Humanitarian relief was supplied to members in Estonia from Europe and the United States during 1990-92. During the summer of 1993, BYU's Young Ambassadors toured Estonia and other Eastern European countries, helping raise the Church's profile.

In July 1993, Estonia was placed in the newly created Latvia Riga Mission, relocated in Lithuania Vilnius in 1996.

During a summer tour in 1995, members of BYU's women's volleyball team attended Church in Tallinn. Estonia was one of the countries featured in a sesquicentennial lecture series about pioneers of the Church. The first meetinghouse was dedicated in Estonia and the Baltic Countries Nov. 7, 1999, by Elder Johann Wondra. The Book of Mormon in Estonian was published and available in January 2000.

Sources: Interview and records of Elder Jaanus Silla; correspondence from Mission Pres. Gary L. Browning; correspondence from Kahlile Mehr, Dec. 29, 1992; "Y. troupe tours Russia, Baltic states," *Church News,* July 17, 1993; "Growth of Church in 'that vast empire' " by Gary L. Browning, *Church News,* Nov. 6, 1993; *Church News,* March 6, 1993; "European trip unites BYU volleyball team," *Church News,* Sept. 23, 1995, *Church News,* Nov. 8, 199; Correspondence from the Lithuania Vilnius Mission.

ETHIOPIA

Year-end 1999: Est. population, 55,979,000; Members, 257; Branches, 1; Africa Southeast Area; Kenya Nairobi Mission.

In east central Africa, Ethiopia has a population that speaks Amharic, English, Orominga, and Tigrigna and who are primarily Ethiopian Orthodox, Islam, and animist (a belief of conscious life within objects).

The first members in Ethiopia were expatriates attached to embassies who held Church meetings in homes in Addis Ababa. In March 1985, Elders M. Russell Ballard and Glenn L. Pace visited Addis Ababa with LDS relief supplies. They held a sacrament meeting in the home of Harry Hadlock, an expatriate airline consultant, on March 17, 1985. The Church donated some $2.8 million for famine relief and irrigation development in Ethiopia and neighboring countries, such as Sudan.

After the Kenya Nairobi Mission was created in 1991, Robert DeWitt, serving with the American embassy, and his wife arrived and stayed for two years. The first official meeting was held in the DeWitt home in August 1992 with Brother Dewitt presiding. The Church was legally registered Sept. 16, 1993, in Addis Ababa. The first missionaries were Elder Eugene and Sister Ruth Hilton, who arrived Feb. 28, 1993. The first convert was Binyam Negash. The Addis Ababa Branch was created Jan. 5, 1994.

The first Ethiopian branch president was Girma Denisa, who was baptized while attending Ricks College in Idaho in 1973. He was also the first missionary from Ethiopia, serving in Kenya.The seminary program was instituted in Ethiopia in 1995. In addition, later in the year, a representative from Ethiopia attended the Christmas lighting ceremony for the 1995 Festival of Lights at the Washington Temple Visitors Center. Ethiopia was among some 50 nations represented at the widely publicized event. Members from Ethiopia traveled to Nairobi, Kenya, to see President Gordon B. Hinckley when he visited there Feb. 17, 1998.

Source: Correspondence from Larry K. Brown, president of the Kenya Nairobi Mission, April 12, 1994; *Church News,* Dec. 9, 1995; *Church News,* March 9, 1996, Feb. 28, 1998; correspondence with Eugene and Ruth Hilton, July 17, 1998.

FIJI

Year-end 1999: Est. population, 773,000; Members, 11,998; Stakes, 4; Wards, 23; Branches, 18; Missions, 1; Districts, 2; Temples, 1; Percent LDS, 1.6 or one in 64.

Located in western South Pacific, the republic of Fiji has a population speaking English, Hindustani, and Fijian. The archipelago has 322 islands, of which 106 are inhabited.

In the 1950s, LDS Tongan and Samoan families, including Cecil B. Smith and Mele Vea Ashley and their families, held Church meetings in Suva, Fiji. When the first missionaries, Elders Boyd L. Harris and Sheldon L. Abbott, arrived, they began working with this group and organized the Suva Branch Sept. 5, 1954.

Work proceeded slowly. Missionaries were limited by the multiple languages spoken in Fiji and by restrictions of only two missionary visas at a time. In January 1955, President David O. McKay had a airplane layover in Suva, and he met the missionaries and attended services at the Smith home. Twenty-eight people attended that day. He urged missionaries to proceed and to purchase property for a meetinghouse. The meetinghouse that was later built was a nearly normal-sized stake center, anticipating future growth. Fiji was placed in the Tonga Mission on Jan. 15, 1958, and 93 people attended the conference that day. Later in 1958, 300 attended dedicatory services for the new meetinghouse. About that time, the quota of missionaries was increased by six. Gideon Dolo was the first Fijian to serve a mission, leaving in February 1959.

Growth continued in the 1960s. In 1966, 150 attended district conferences in Suva. Three years later, the attendance at conference reached 500, and the district was divided. The Fiji Mission was created July 23, 1971. In 1972, Mission Pres. Eb L. Davis expanded the mission into several new areas. By 1972, the meetinghouse was filled with Fijians, Indians, Rotumans, Tongans, Samoans, New Zealanders, Australians, Europeans, and Americans.

Educational efforts were also strengthened. In 1969, a Church school was held in the meetinghouse, and in 1973, it had more than 100 students. In 1975, the LDS Fiji Technical College was opened. By 1984, 372 students were enrolled at the college.

The Suva Fiji Stake was organized June 12, 1983, the first stake in the island nation. At year-end 1983, membership in Fiji was 2,722. By 1995, membership was 11,000. A milestone was reached June 15, 1997, when the 100th stake in the Pacific, the Suva Fiji North Stake, was organized. Some 2,800 members, more than 57 percent of the members in Suva, gathered for the event.

On Oct. 15, 1997, President Gordon B. Hinckley visited Fiji and spoke to 10,000 people in the National Stadium in Suva.

Membership in Fiji in 1999 was 11,998.

Because of political unrest in Suva, all missionaries serving in or near the city were transferred in May 2000 to the west side of the island as a precautionary measure. Later, because of continuing civil unrest, missionaries and mission leaders who were not Fijian citizens were temporarily relocated to New Zealand, leaving missionaries native to Fiji to continue the work.

Because of the political unrest, only a small dedicatory service was held when the Suva Fiji Temple was dedicated on June 18, 2000. Only 60 people were invited to attend the dedication of the temple, which was announced two years earlier on May 7, 1998. The Suva Fiji Temple district is a large district, covering Fiji, New Caledonia, Vanuatu, Kiribati, Nauru, and Tuvalu.

Sources: *Unto the Isles of the Sea,* by R. Lanier Britsch; *Church News,* Sept. 14, 1991; "Fiji: Church gaining prominence in isle cultures," *Church News,* Nov. 2, 1991; *Church News,* July 19, 1997, Oct. 16, 1997, May 23, 1998, June 3, 2000, June 24, 2000, July 29, 2000.

Stakes — 4

(As of Oct. 1, 1998.)

No.	**Name**	**Organized**	**First President**
Pacific Islands Area			
2216	Lautoka Fiji	11 Aug 1996	Jone Sovasova
2040	*Nausori 15 Jun 1997		
	‡Nasinu Fiji	16 Apr 1995	Vilikesa Ravia
1428	Suva Fiji	12 Jun 1983	Inosi Naga
2372	Suva Fiji North	15 Jun 1997	Josefa N.T. Sokia

Mission — 1

(As of Oct. 1, 2000; shown with historical number. See MISSIONS.)

(99) FIJI SUVA MISSION
GPO Box 215
Suva, Fiji Islands

FINLAND

Year-end 1999: Est. population, 5,149,000; Members, 4,403; Stakes, 2; Wards, 13; Branches, 17; Missions, 1; Districts, 3; Temples, 1 announced.

Located in northern Europe, the Republic of Finland has a population that speaks Finnish and Swedish, and 90 percent are Lutherans.

The first Latter-day Saints in Finland were Finnish emigrants who had been baptized in Sweden in the early 1870s. The first missionaries were Swedish brothers Carl A. and John E. Sundstrom. They preached in Vaasa and found converts in 1876. During the first decade in Finland, the missionaries worked among Swedish-speaking Finns, and by 1886 had baptized 25 people. Because Finnish law forbade "getting up and preaching," missionaries learned to preach while sitting.

In 1903, Elder Francis M. Lyman of the Quorum of the Twelve visited Finland.

Efforts were made to establish branches in several areas, but the branches were not permanent. When Anders and Lovis Stromberg were converted in Larsmo, a permanent branch eventually grew up around them. Membership in the country was 35 in 1930. As late as 1941, all Church members in Finland had their records in Larsmo.

In 1946, seven missionaries from Sweden were sent to Finland, the first being Mark E. Anderson. In 1947, Henry A. Matis, an American with Finnish roots, was called as president of the Finnish Mission. Membership in Finland was 129 when he arrived. During the seven years that he served, the Church gained legal status (July 1, 1948), began microfilming Finnish church records (December 1948-November 1955) and translated and published the Book of Mormon in Finnish (December 1954). Missionaries taught English, played basketball, and did everything they could to raise the Church's profile.

After 1954, local Finnish members served missions. A building program was started and more people were converted. By 1957, membership was 904. The first temple trip to Switzerland was made in June 1960.

In August 1976, President Spencer W. Kimball spoke to nearly 2,000 members at an area conference in Helsinki. The next year, the Helsinki Stake, the first in Finland, was organized Oct. 16, 1977. At that time there were 3,642 members. Ten years later, it had increased to 4,100.

Finnish members were the first to introduce the gospel to Estonia and parts of Russia (see Estonia history). The Helsinki East Mission was created in 1990 to serve members in Leningrad and other areas in the Soviet Union. It was discontinued with the creation of the Russia missions in 1991, although Finnish leaders were among those called to serve in Russia. Membership in 1990 was 4,200. Nearly half the members in Finland attended the commemoration of the 50th anniversary of the Finnish Mission, held in September of 1997. Among those who attended were previous mission presidents Henry A. Matis, 1947-54; Phileon Robinson, 1954-58; Mark E. Anderson, 1961-64; and Malcolm Asplund, 1964-67. Members held Pres. Matis, 92, in high esteem. He spoke for nearly an hour and observed how deeply into the Finnish culture the gospel had permeated.

Finland's LDS population in 1999 was 4,403.

Advances in technology through the internet and satellite have brought Finnish members in close contact with Church headquarters.

In general conference on April 2, 2000, President Gordon B. Hinckley announced that a temple would be built in Helsinki.

Sources: *Ensign,* May 1973; *Church News,* Aug. 14, 1976; "A man worth the wait," by John L. Hart, *Church News,* Nov. 14, 1987; *Church News,* Nov. 16, 1991; "Finland," *Church News,* Feb. 15, 1992, Oct. 5, 1996, April 11, 1998, Sept. 27, 1998, April 8. 2000.

Stakes — 2

(Listed alphabetically as of Oct. 1, 2000.)

No. Name	Organized	First President
Europe Central Area		
865 Helsinki Finland	16 Oct 1977	Kari Juhani Aslak Haikkola
1408 Tampere Finland	17 Apr 1983	Kari Juhani Aslak Haikkola

Mission — 1

(As of Oct. 1, 2000; shown with historical number. See MISSIONS.)

(41) HELSINKI MISSION
Neitsytpolku 3 A 4
00140 Helsinki, Finland

FRANCE

Year-end 1999: Est. population, 58,109,000; Members, 30,541; Stakes, 7; Wards, 44; Branches, 84; Missions, 3; Districts, 7; Percent LDS, .05 , or one in1,903.

In western Europe, France has a population that speaks French, and includes minorities who speak Breton, Alsatian, German, Flemish, Italian, Basque, and Catalan. The population of France is mostly Roman Catholic.

A Welsh member named William Howells arrived in Le Havre, France, in July 1849, and on July 30, 1849, baptized Augustus Saint d'Anna. After a short detour to the Island of Jersey, Howells returned to France and baptized a man named Pebble and a young woman, Anna Browse. The Boulogne-sur-Mer Branch with six members was organized April 5, 1850. On June 18, Apostle John Taylor and Elder Curtis E. Boulton arrived. The party traveled to Paris, and on Dec. 8, 1850, a branch of eight members was organized in that city. The Book of Mormon was translated and published in French in January 1852. By July 24, 1853, nine branches had been organized, with 337 members including 289 from the Channel Islands.

Government restrictions by French Emperor Louis Napoleon prohibited gathering of any more than 20 people, making it difficult for missionaries to hold meetings. Louis Bertrand, a member of the original branch in Paris, published a periodical and tried to extend missionary work. In 1859, Pres. Bertrand was called to preside over the mission but in 1864, the work in France was closed. The work re-opened in 1912 when the French Mission was reorganized. Sixty-two converts joined that year, but World War I halted the work until 1923 when the French Mission was re-established. In 1924, the first year of mission activity, some 200 converts joined. By 1930, there were two meetinghouses in the Belgian sector of the French Mission, and missionaries were working in 33 cities in the two countries.

Missionaries worked hard to build the Church's image and some helped by singing in groups while others played on successful basketball teams. During World War II, a local leader, Leon Fargier, conducted the affairs of the Church. After World War II, missionary work resumed. The Tabernacle Choir visited in 1955. In 1959, membership reached 1,909 members. The first meetinghouse in France was constructed in Nantes in 1962. In 1974, 29 French members were serving full-time missions. The Paris France Stake, the first stake in France, was created Nov. 16, 1975. At that time, membership in the nation was about 10,000. A decade later, it had grown to 16,500 in three stakes. By 1996, 28,454 members were organized into seven stakes. President Spencer W. Kimball spoke to 4,200 members at an area conference in Paris in 1976.

The France Bordeaux Mission was created in 1989, and the France Marseille Mission was created July 1, 1991. On Aug. 15, 1992, the Europe Mediterranean Area was created and headquarters were established in Thoiry, France, later tranferred to Frankfurt, Germany, when the area boundaries were changed.

The Tabernacle Choir performed in Strasbourg, June 11, 1991, and returned to perform in Marseille the same month in 1998. President Gordon B. Hinckley visited and spoke in Versailles and in Paris on June 4, 1998. Membership in 1999 was 30,541.

Sources: "Moments in History," *Church News,* July 31, 1971; "Church in Europe," *Ensign,* August, 1973; "Church's Second Generation Growth is Strong in France," by J Malan Heslop, *Church News,* Dec. 1, 1973; *Church News* Feb., 25, 1989; "His Faith Wouldn't Go Underground," by Alain Marie, *Ensign,* Sept. 1991; *Church News,* Sept. 7, 1991; Church News, June 20, 1998, July 11, 1998, July 18, 1998.

Stakes — 7

(Listed alphabetically as of Oct. 1, 2000.)

No.	Name	Organized	First President
Europe West Area			
1867	Bordeaux France	24 May 1992	Jacquie Simonet
1669	Lille France	17 Jan 1988	Dominique Degrave
1772	Lyon France	9 Sep 1990	Pierre-Marie Brenders
1413	Nancy France	24 Apr 1983	John Keith Bishop
1130	Nice France	14 May 1980	Joseph Michel Paya
731	Paris France	16 Nov 1975	Gerard Giraud-Carrier
1850	Paris France East	8 Mar 1992	Dominique Calmels

Missions — 3

(As of Oct. 1, 2000; shown with historical number. See MISSIONS.)

(221a) FRANCE BORDEAUX MISSION
5, Place des Quinconces
33000 BORDEAUX
France

(262) FRANCE MARSEILLE MISSION
48, Av Robert Schumann
F-13090 Aix-en-Provence,
France

(6) FRANCE PARIS MISSION
23, rue du Onze Novembre

78110 Le Vesinet
France

FRENCH GUIANA

Year-end 1999: Est. population, 145,000; Members, 209; Branches, 2; Percent LDS, .14, or one in 694; North America Southeast Area; West Indies Mission.

French Guiana is an overseas department of France located in northern South America. Charles Fortin, a native of French Guiana, was baptized in France and returned to his homeland. Rosiette Fauvette, also baptized in France, returned to French Guiana July 8, 1981, and sacrament meetings with the two were held at Brother Fortin's home in Cayenne. Brother Fortin introduced the Church to many people before his death in April 1986. By then several other members were attending services including Gerard Charpentier, who later became branch president. Meetings were then held in the home of the Masinski family until January 1987 when the meetings were moved to Sister Fauvette's home in Kourou, which had a special room added for the meetings.

Elder Charles Didier of the Seventy visited on March 4, 1988, and organized a group. On Nov. 5, 1988, Serge and Christie Bonnoit of France became the first converts in French Guiana. On June 26, 1989, the Kourou Branch was divided and the Cayenne Branch created. On July 1, 1989, Michaela Papo, the first native Guyanaise convert, was baptized.

The first missionary couple was Elder Wilbur and Sister Jacqueline Wortham, followed in November 1989 by Elder A. Edward and Sister Louise P. Schmidt. The newly organized branch in Cayenne had about 23 members in 1989.

Source: "History of the Church in French Guiana," supplied by Pres. Elden L. Wood, 1994; Interview with Elder and Sister A. Edward and Louise P. Schmidt.

FRENCH POLYNESIA
(Tahiti)

Year-end 1999: Est. population, 220,000; Members, 16,230; Stakes, 6; Wards,45; Branches, 28; Missions, 1; Districts, 3; Temples, 1; Percent LDS, 7.38, or one in 14.

Located in the South Pacific midway between South America and Australia, the French Polynesia archipelago is a French overseas territory. Tahiti's population speaks French and Tahitian. Most of the French Polynesians are Protestants.

Elders Benjamin F. Grouard, Addison Pratt, Noah Rogers, and Knowlton F. Hanks were sent by Joseph Smith to the Pacific Islands. They boarded the whaling ship *Timoleon* Oct. 10, 1843, and sailed around the Cape Horn. During the voyage, Elder Hanks died of tuberculosis and was buried at sea. When the ship reached Tubuai, an island about 500 miles south of Tahiti, on April 30, 1844, Elder Pratt disembarked and remained to preach. He is considered the first missionary to a foreign-language area in modern Church history. He baptized many people and established a branch.

Elders Grouard and Rogers went on to Tahiti, where initially they found proselyting difficult. Elder Rogers returned to the United States, while Elder Grouard visited the Tuamotu Islands and was successful, though at great personal sacrifice and effort. He was later joined by Elder Pratt, and their converts numbered in the hundreds. Elder Pratt returned to United States in 1848, but came back to Tahiti with his family in 1850. This promising start for the Church was halted when French government restrictions led to the mission being closed in May 1852.

The work was re-opened in 1892, with Elders Joseph W. Damron and William A. Seegmiller, who found that most of the early members had fallen away. They started branches again among those who had remained stalwart, and built meetinghouses that helped speed the work.

Completion of the New Zealand Temple in 1958 was a blessing for the Tahitian Saints, who proved to be faithful attenders.

On May 23, 1963, in the worst-recorded sea disaster for Latter-day Saints in the South Pacific, 15 members of the Maupiti Branch, about 160 miles northwest of Tahiti, lost their lives when the boat in which they were returning from a meetinghouse dedication cracked up on the Maupiti reef. Elder Gordon B. Hinckley, then of the Quorum of the Twelve, visited the bereaved branch members to offer solace and comfort.

In 1964, the Church constructed an elementary school in Tahiti, and in 1972 the Tahiti Stake was organized, the first in Tahiti. The Papeete Tahiti Temple was dedicated Oct. 27, 1983. Tahiti's second stake was created in 1982, and its third stake in 1990.

In 1991, a group of members from the Maupiti Branch, many of them aged, made their first trip to the new Papeete Temple.

In 1991, Saints in Takaroa in the Tuamotu islands observed the 100th anniversary of a meetinghouse built by early members, the oldest meetinghouse in the South Pacific. The imposing building took 20 years to complete and has withstood tropical storms. On Jan 6, 1991, the Takaroa Branch was divided, with a total membership of more than 300. Some of the members are descendants of those converted in the 19th century.

In 1994, members celebrated the 150th anniversary of the missionaries arriving in their islands. Closer relations with other religions resulted as Elder Russell M. Nelson of the Quorum of the Twelve was formally introduced to the territory's president and full cabinet. President Gaston Flosse and other top government leaders attended several events. President Gordon B. Hinckley was welcomed to French Polynesia by President Flosse Oct. 15, 1997. President Hinckley addressed some 7,000 people in Papeete that evening.

The first meetinghouse in the Marqueses, which are in the Tahiti Papeete Mission, was dedicated May 11, 1998, by Pres. Tekehu Mananui of the Tahiti Papeete Mission. Rudolphe Etienne and Marie Hana Teura Tua served a mission on the Marqueses in 1989 and were able to bring in four large families, including Robert O'Conner who became the first branch president on the islands. His wife, Ziella Vivish O'Conner, was the first member on the island who welcomed the Tuas. The first missionaries to these islands arrived in 1961, but were unsuccessful. Others returned in the 1980s with more success.

Members in Papeete took it upon themselves in 1997 to donate food to a crew of Russians on board a vessel stranded in the harbor when their company went bankrupt.

In 1999, there were 16,230 members in French Polynesia.

On Jan. 11, 2000, the president of the Territory of French Polynesia, Gaston Flosse; vice president Edward Fritche; and 15 government ministers attended a dinner at the mission home in Papeete, hosted by Mission Pres. Ralph T. Andersen and local stake and district presidents.

Sources: *Encyclopedic History of the Church,* by Andrew Jenson; *Histoire de l'Eglise Mormone en Polynesie Francaise de 1844 a 1982,* by Yves R. Perrin; "A bright new future dawns for Polynesian atoll and 100-year-old meetinghouse," by Kathleen C. Perrin, *Church News,* Feb. 2, 1991; "Temple Blessings broaden view of paradise," by Kathleen C. Perrin, *Church News,* Aug. 24, 1991; "150th year of Church in Tahiti," by Kathleen C. Perrin, *Church News,* May 7, 1994; "LDS note 150 years in French Polynesia," by John L. Hart, *Church News* May 14, 1994; "Sesquicentennial: 'Spiritual feast,'" by John L. Hart, *Church News,* May 21, 1996, , Feb. 18, 1995; Feb. 2, 1997; "Prophet goes to islands of the Pacific," by Gerry Avant, *Church News,* Oct. 25, 1997; *Church News,* Dec. 13, 1997, Feb. 26, 2000.

Stakes —6

(Listed alphabetically as of Oct. 1, 2000.)

No.	Name	Organized	First President
Pacific Islands Area			
573	*Arue Tahiti 28 May 1995		
	*Papeete Tahiti		
	‡Tahiti	14 May 1972	Raituia Tehina Tapu
2398	Faaa Tahiti	21 Sep 1997	Benajmin Tauraa Sinjoux
1747	Paea Tahiti	15 Apr 1990	Jean Alexis Tefan
2054	*Papeari Tahiti 21 Sep 1997		
	‡Punaauia Tahiti	28 May 1995	Tetuanui Marama Tarati
1355	*Papeete Tahiti		
	‡Pirae Tahiti	20 Jun 1982	Lysis G. Terooatea
1962a	*Raromatai Tahiti 7 Jan 1994		
	‡Uturoa Tahiti Raiatea	5 Dec 1993	Michel Just Doucet

Mission — 1

(As of Oct. 1, 2000; shown with historical number. See MISSIONS.)

(3) TAHITI PAPEETE MISSION
B.P. 93
Papeete, Tahiti
French Polynesia

GUADELOUPE

Year-end 1999: Est. population, 403,000; Members, 195; Branches, 2; Percent LDS, .05, or one in 2,067; North America Southeast Area; West Indies Mission.

The Caribbean Island of Guadeloupeis a department of France. Andre Condoris, a young man baptized in France while serving in the military, returned to his homeland Aug. 9, 1980. He encouraged Mission Pres. Kenneth L. Zabriskie of the West Indies Mission to send missionaries. French-speaking Elders Mark Richards, Stan Jones, and David Simons were transferred from missions in Paris, France, and Brussels, Belgium, to open the work in Guadeloupe. Among the first converts in Guadeloupe were the Claire Dinane family, who soon moved to the the small island of St. Martin.

MARTINIQUE

Year-end 1999: Est. population, 395,000; Members, 143; Branches, 2; Percent LDS, .04 or one in 2,762; North America Southeast Area; West Indies Mission.

The Caribbean island of Martinique is a department of France. Martinique is the northernmost of the windward islands. Joell Joseph-Agathe, a young woman baptized in France, returned to Martinique and also welcomed missionaries to the country. They arrived May 4, 1984, and held the first meeting May 6. The branch first met in Case Pilote, then Ducos and then in Chateau Boef. The branch now meets in Lamentin.

By 1994, the branch in Martinique had 80 members.

ST. MARTIN

The island of St. Martin in the Caribbean, with an area of 20 square miles, was part of the France Toulouse Mission when the St. Martin Branch was organized Jan. 9, 1979. The mission was discontinued a short time later, and work resumed under the West Indies Mission in 1983. Elders Thad Ariens and Victor Quarty began working in St. Martin, the administration of which is divided between two governments, French and Dutch. The Claire Dinane family, which was baptized on Guadeloupe, moved to St. Martin and helped re-open the St. Martin Branch on Jan. 31, 1984. In September 1995 Hurricane Luis and Hurricane Marilyn struck the island of St. Martin, destroying at least 80 percent of the homes on the island. Members, many who lost their homes and jobs because of damage done by the hurricanes, rallied to help each other.

Sources: Journal of Pres. Kenneth and Sister LeOra Zabriskie; "A religion, the Mormons," by Albert Albicy, *France-Antilles*, Jan. 27, 1994, courtesy Pres. J. Richard Toolson; *Manuscript history of France Toulouse Mission*, "Extensive hurricane damage, but LDS safe," Church News, Sept. 30, 1995.

NEW CALEDONIA

Year-end 1999: Est. population, 185,000; Members, 1,449; Branches,9; Districts, 1; percent LDS, .78, or one in 128; Pacific Islands Area; Fiji Suva Mission.

An overseas territory of France, New Caledonia is a group of islands in the South Pacific.

Church activity in New Caledonia began in the 1950s as a few Tahitian members migrated to work in a nickel smelter. They were organized into the Noumea Branch on Oct. 21, 1961. However, visas for missionaries were not obtained until 1967. On July 15, 1968, the first two missionaries arrived, Harold and Jeannine Richards, and their daughter, Jacquelina.

In June 1975, administration over the island group was transferred to the Fiji Suva Mission, and the work continued to progress. The Noumea Branch was divided, and the small meetinghouse was enlarged. In July 1978, the Tontouta Branch was organized. In 1990, there were 382 members in New Caledonia.

Membership in New Caledonia in 1999 was 1,449 in nine mission branches.

President Gordon B. Hinckley visited Noumea June 17, 2000, as part of a six-nation tour of Asia and the South Pacific. About 1,000 members crowded into the local meetinghouse to hear the Church leader, and many more gathered outside in tents, where the proceedings of the meeting was relayed via video feed.

Source: *Unto the Islands of the Sea,* by R. Lanier Britsch; *Church News,* July 1, 2000.

REUNION

Year-end 1999: Est. population, 666,000; Members, 695; Districts, 1; Branches, 4; Percent LDS, .1, or one in 958; Africa Southwest Area; Madagascar Antananarivo Mission.

A volcanic island in the Indian Ocean, Reunion is a department of France.

Missionary work began in Reunion in 1979 under the direction of the International

Mission. Among the first members in Reunion were Alain and Danielle Chion-Hock, converted in France. On Nov. 4, 1979, Chion-Hock baptized his sister, Rose Tahi Soui Tchong, the first convert on Reunion.

Elder Joseph T. and Sister Ruth Edmunds were the first modern missionaries on the islands in 1979. They were joined by Elder Theo and Sister Nita Verhaarens. The first branch was established on Dec. 30, 1979. In 1986, the islands were transferred to the South Africa Johannesburg Mission. The Mascarene Islands Mission was created July 1, 1988, at which time there were 400 members on the islands with three branches in Reunion and two on the nearby island of Mauritius, which is included in the same district. Headquarters of the mission was transferred to Durban, South Africa, in January 1992. Seminary classes for the youth began in 1993. On July 1, 1998, Reunion was placed in the newly created Madagascar Antananarivo Mission.

In 1999, membership in Reunion was 695 in four mission branches.

Sources: *Church News*, Sept. 21, 1986; Feb. 7, 1987; Oct. 24, 1987; March 19, 1988; Nov. 5, 1987; Dec. 17, 1988; "Tropical Isles receive best news as mission opens," by Allen W. Palmer, *Church News*, Nov. 5, 1988; "At Home on the Island of Mauritius," by Lori Palmer, *Ensign*, March, 1991, Feb. 1986, March 1989; *Church News*, May 31, 1997, Jan. 10, 1998.

GABON

Year-end 1999: Est. population, 1,200,000; Members, fewer than 100; Africa West Area; Ivory Coast Abidjan Mission.

Gabon is a republic on the Atlantic coast of west central Africa where the people speak French and Bantu dialect, and follow tribal beliefs, although some are Christians. Some 100,000 expatriate Europeans, as well as Africans, live in Gabon, including about 18,000 of French ancestry.

Jerome Obounou-Mbogo, a diplomat of the the Embassy of Gabon, traveled to Utah and had a favorable visit with Elder Neal A. Maxwell of the Quorum of the Twelve and Elder Richard P. Lindsay of the Seventy in their offices as part of his visit Aug. 4-6, 1990. The Church received permission to enter the country in 1992.

Jean Mickouma, a member of the Church from Gabon, accompanied Obounou to Salt Lake City. Mickouma joined the Church several years previous while working in Washington, D.C.

Gabon was included in the Cameroon Yaounde Mission, which was created on Feb. 1, 1992, and later transferred to the Ivory Coast Abidjan Mission.

Sources: *Church News,* Aug. 25, 1990; correspondence with Elder James O. Mason of the Seventy and president of Africa area, Sept. 26, 1996.

GERMANY

Year-end 1999: Est. population, 81,338,000; Members, 36,303; Stakes, 14; Wards, 91; Branches, 97; Missions, 6; Districts, 1; Temples, 2.

A central European nation divided following World War II and reunited in October 1990, Germany is composed of Catholics, 45 percent, and Protestants, 44 percent.

The first Latter-day Saint in Germany was James Howard, a British convert working in there in 1840. He tried to preach but was unsuccessful. Elder Orson Hyde spent 10 months in Germany in 1841-42, but was unsuccessful in preaching, although he did study German and introduce the language to the Prophet Joseph Smith. He oversaw the translation of a tract into German.

Another missionary, Johan Greenig, is often credited with having established the first German branch, in Darmstadt, Germany, in 1843.

In 1849, apostles and other missionaries were sent to Scandinavia, Italy, and France. Each of these mission efforts also reached into Germany. George P. Dykes, assigned to the Scandinavian Mission, went to Schleswig-Holstein, which, at that time, was under Danish rule, and may have baptized the first two German converts on Sept. 15, 1851. Elder John Taylor, assigned to France, went to Hamburg in October 1851, where he joined Elder Dykes and supervised translation of the Book of Mormon into German.

Daniel Carn was called by Brigham Young to be the first mission president in Germany. Pres. Carn arrived in Hamburg April 3, 1852. By Aug. 1, he had baptized 12 and organized the Hamburg Branch. Pres. Carn was exiled but continued to supervise the German Saints, and strengthened Danish branches as well. Five additional missionaries from the United States arrived, but within four months went to England, discouraged by constantly being called before the police.

The first converts to emigrate left Germany Aug. 13, 1852. In 1854, apostates and police halted missionary work as the missionaries were imprisoned and exiled. Most of the local faithful converts emigrated and the branch was dissolved.

A prominent convert of this period from Dresden was Karl G. Maeser, who was attracted to the Church by an anti-Mormon tract. He was taught by Elder William Budge, a native of Scotland, who later became president of the Logan Temple. On Oct. 21, 1855, the Dresden Branch was established with Maeser as president. The branch lasted until 1857, when opposition led to the emigration of most members of the branch, including its president.

Southern Germany's first branch was organized in Karlsruhe in 1860, under the direction of the Swiss-German Mission. During the next seven years, missionaries were halted by rigid law and frequently prevented from effective proselyting. The faltering mission was boosted in 1867 by the return of Karl G. Maeser as a missionary. More than 600 people joined the Church in the next three years. However, for the next decades, work proceeded slowly amid opposition, but by 1898 branches had been established in Saargemuend, Frankfurt-on-the-Main, Leipzig, Hamburg, and Cologne. As the Church seemed poised for progress, World War I began. Nearly 200 missionaries left some 60 branches in Switzerland and Germany. Despite the war, most branches remained intact. By 1925, the German Mission was divided, leaving 6,125 members in the German-Austrian Mission, and 5,305 members in the Swiss-German Mission.

In 1937, President Heber J. Grant made an extensive tour of Europe and visited 11 countries, including Germany. In spite of war clouds hovering over the country, President Grant said the Church was at liberty to hold meetings even though many other denominations were prohibited from preaching there.

On Sept. 16, 1939, the First Presidency directed all missionaries to be evacuated from Germany and move to neutral countries. Later, the missionaries were instructed to return to the United States.

During World War II, more than 600 German Saints were killed, 2,500 were missing, and 80 percent were homeless.

Relief efforts by the Church, supervised by Elder Ezra Taft Benson, then of the Quorum of the Twelve, and members from neighboring countries, including the Dutch, helped sustain German members during the difficult post-war period. Missionaries returned in 1947. In the next 20 years, five stakes were organized, three missions created, and European headquarters were established for the Church in Frankfurt.

Membership in Germany in 1975 was 13,829. In 1985, it had increased to 29,900. A temple in Frankfurt was announced in 1981, and was dedicated Aug. 28, 1987. Following the publicity of the dedication and an increased missionary effort, missionary work increased in the late 1980s. The Germany Dusseldorf Mission started in 1961 but was dissolved in 1982 and then re-organized in July 1990.

The German Democratic Republic (East Germany), which existed following World War II until reunification in 1990, was the home of many faithful members cut off from the rest of the Church. The history of the Church in East Germany following the end of the war is a legacy of devout members quietly living their faith. Despite many difficulties, these members continued in faithfulness, strengthening each other through fellowship. "The war cost us everything," said one. "But there was something they couldn't take — our testimonies."

Among the leaders to visit in the 1960s was Elder Thomas S. Monson, then of the Quorum of the Twelve, who promised the Saints they would eventually have every blessing of members elsewhere. A patriarch was ordained, and plans for a meetinghouse were made and completed. The first stake in the GDR was organized in Freiberg in 1982, followed by a second stake, in Leipzig, in 1984. Later, following prayers and fasting of the members, German Democratic Republic leaders gave permission for a temple to be built in Freiberg. After the temple was completed, 89,789 people toured the public open house. It was dedicated June 29, 1985. Government approval was later given for missionary work to begin. On March 30, 1989, foreign missionaries arrived in the country, and on May 28, 1989, missionaries from the German Democratic Republic entered the Missionary Training Center in Provo, Utah, to begin foreign missions.

The Berlin Wall separating East and West Berlin for 28 years fell Nov. 9, 1989, and the two Germanys were reunified on Oct. 3, 1990. When American military personnel was withdrawn in 1993, overall membership was reduced. In October of that year, the first official broadcast of general conference to Germany was received.

Elder F. Enzio Busche of the First Quorum of the Seventy was called as a General Authority on Oct. 1, 1977, and Elder Dieter F. Uchtdorf was sustained to the Second Quorum of the Seventy on April 2, 1994, and later to the First Quorum of the Seventy.

On Aug. 27, 1995, President Monson, first counselor in the First Presidency, dedicated the Goerlitz Branch meetinghouse in what had been East Germany.

President Gordon B. Hinckley presided at a Berlin Regional Conference in June 1996 as part of a five-country tour. Member participation was high with an estimated 50 percent of the members in the former German Democratic Republic attending.

Retired U.S. Air Force Col. Gail S. Halvorsen "the Candy Bomber," who initiated dropping candy from airplanes to children during the 1948 Berlin blockade, was the guest of honor in Berlin in 1998, and was welcomed by a crowd of 7,000 people.

In 1999, Elder Uchtdorf of the Seventy presented $100,000, as a gift from the German Saints, to the German Red Cross to help refugees in Kosovo. By 1999, membership in Germany reached 36,303, the greatest number of members of any country in continental Europe.

Sources: *Encyclopedic History of the Church*, by Andrew Jenson; *Mormonism in Germany*, by Gilbert W. Scharffs, Deseret Book, 1970; "Memories of West German Evacuation," by J. Richard Barnes, unpublished; interview with Emil Fetzer; correspondence from Tim T. Brosnahan Jr., June 15, 1985; multiple newspaper sources, 1989-91; *Church News*, Oct. 2, 1993, April 9, 1994, Sept. 2, 1995, June 22, 1996; "Candy Bomber returns to German base," by Shaun Stahle, *Church News*, May 23, 1998; *Church News*, April 17, 1999, June 5, 1999, Jan. 22, 2000, Aug. 5, 2000.

Stakes — 14

(Listed alphabetically as of Oct. 1, 2000.)

No.	Name	Organized	First President
Europe Central Area			
334	*Berlin Germany ‡Berlin	10 Sep 1961	Rudi Seehagen
768	Dortmund Germany	19 Sep 1976	Klaus Fritz K. Hasse
1358	*Dresden Germany 21 Oct 1990 ‡Freiberg German D. R.	29 Aug 1982	Frank Herbert Apel
577	*Duesseldorf Germany ‡Duesseldorf	4 Jun 1972	Frerich Jakob Emil Goerts
766	Frankfurt Germany	12 Sep 1976	Magnus R. Meiser
342	*Hamburg Germany ‡Hamburg	12 Nov 1961	Michael Panitsch
845	*Hannover Germany 4 Nov 1996 *Hanover Germany 25 Jan 1993 ‡Hannover Germany	12 Jun 1977	Michael Schulze
466	*Kaiserslautern Germany Military ‡Servicemen Stake Europe (W. Germany)	30 Oct 1968	Herbert B. Spencer
1475	*Leipzig Germany 21 Oct 1990 ‡Leipzig German Democratic Republic	3 Jun 1984	Hermann M. Schutze
1324	Mannheim Germany	7 Feb 1982	Baldur H.H. Stoltenberg
870	Munich Germany	23 Oct 1977	August Schubert
1305	*Neumuenster Germany 9 Apr 1985 ‡Hamburg Germany North	8 Nov 1981	Karl-Heinz Danklefsen
1651	*Nuremberg Germany 4 Nov 1996 Nuerenberg Germany Servicemen	6 Sep 1987	Jon Paul Baker
340	*Stuttgart Germany ‡Stuttgart	26 Oct 1961	Hermann Moessner

Stakes discontinued

824	Frankfurt Germany Servicemen Discontinued 20 Feb 1994	1 May 1977	Kenneth Alvin Nessen
765	Stuttgart Germany Servicemen Discontinued 15 Nov 1992	12 Sep 1976	Gary K. Spencer

Missions — 6

(As of Oct. 1, 2000; shown with historical number. See MISSIONS.)

(263) GERMANY BERLIN MISSION
Zerbster Str. 42
12209 Berlin
Germany

(240) GERMANY DUSSELDORF MISSION
Morsenbroicher Weg 184 A
40470 Dusseldorf
Germany

(35a) GERMANY FRANKFURT MISSION
Kurfuerstenstrasse 60
60486 Frankfurt am Main
Germany

(36) GERMANY HAMBURG MISSION
Rugenbarg 7A
22549 Hamburg
Germany

(225) GERMANY LEIPZIG MISSION
Springerstrasse 16
04105 Leipzig
Germany

(49) GERMANY MUNICH MISSION
Lommel Strasse #7
D-81479 Munich
Germany

GHANA

Year-end 1999: Est. population, 17,763,000; Members, 17,278; Stakes, 5; Wards, 32; Branches, 28; Missions, 1; Districts, 4; Temples, 1 announced; percent LDS, .1, or one in 1,028.

A republic, Ghana is located on the south central west coast of Africa and has a population of 52 percent Christian, 30 percent tribal, and 13 percent Muslim.

In the 1950s, various pamphlets about the Church somehow found their wa to Ghana, and were read by Ghanaians, believed, and used as the basis to start their own, but unauthorized, LDS congregations. As early as 1960, President David O. McKay attempted to have leaders visit these sincere congregations, but the leaders were unable to obtain visas. Ghanaians also learned of the Church as they visited other countries. Pricilla Sampson-Davis, for example, received a copy of the Book of Mormon from missionaries during a visit to the Netherlands in 1963, from which she gained a testimony. In 1964, Joseph W. B. Johnson gained a testimony of the Book of Mormon and began organizing congregations.

In August 1978, just two months after the revelation on the priesthood, Merrill J. Bateman (now a member of the Seventy and BYU president) and Edwin Q. "Ted" Cannon were sent by the Church to West Africa on a fact-finding trip. Three months later, on Nov. 8, 1978, Elder Cannon, with his wife, Janath, and Rendell N. and Rachel Mabey arrived in Nigeria as Church representatives. They entered Ghana Dec. 9, 1978, and baptized Abraham Frank Mensah; Brother Johnson and his 10-year-old son, Brigham Young Johnson; Pricilla Sampson-Davis, and many in Brother Johnson's congregations. In all 89 people were baptized that day.

A building program was started in 1979.

Within a year, more than 400 people had been baptized and branches were organized. The first president of the Africa West Mission, which was organized in 1980 and included Ghana, was Pres. Bryan Espenschied. He and his successsor, Pres. Sylvester Cooper, saw to it that converts were taught the gospel in their own language and trained in leadership skills. By 1981, seven branches functioned in Ghana.

One of the early converts was Dr. Emmanuel Abu Kissi, a physician who established a clinic supported by friends of the Church. Several humanitarian projects were completed by the Church in Ghana in the 1980s.

Growth continued and by 1983, the number of branches increased to 28. The Ghana Accra Mission was organized July 1, 1985. By 1987, membership had reached 5,500.

On June 14, 1989, the Ghana government expelled the missionaries and banned the Church. Members were permitted to hold services in the privacy of their homes, however. On Dec. 1, 1990, the government permitted Church activities to resume. (Sacrament meetings resumed Dec. 9.) The government announcement expressed satisfaction that the Church teaches members to be obedient to government laws and promotes racial harmony. By year-end 1990, membership was more than 9,000.

In the 1990s, humanitarian efforts have focused on member self-reliance. A number of projects have been undertaken through local initiative by members in districts and stakes. Some 90 percent of the meetinghouses in Ghana have some form of gardening activity going on. A gari-processing project, using locally manufactured machinery, automates parts of the processing so it requires less time and effort. (Gari is a West African staple food made from the starchy root vegetable cassava.) Through this project, families can produce more food for themselves and extra to sell.

A gathering of 6,000 members welcomed President Gordon B. Hinckley Feb. 16, 1998, on the first visit of the Church president to West Africa. During the visit, President Hinckley announced that the first temple in West Africa would be built in Ghana. He also met with Ghana Pres. Jerry Rawlings.

In 1999, some 30 missionaries from the Ghana Accra Mission helped greet and assist more than 6,000 political and business leaders from throughout the world as they converged in Accra for a six-day African-African/American summit.

In 1999, membership in Ghana reached 17,278.

Sources: *Church News,* Dec. 22, 1979, Sept. 30, 1984, Oct. 17, 1987, June 24, 1989, Dec. 8, 1990; "Nigeria and Ghana," by Janet Brigham, *Ensign,* Feb. 1980; "Pioneers in Africa," by E. Dale LeBaron, *Church News,* Sept. 21, 1991; *Church News,* Oct. 23, 1994, Feb. 11, 1995, June 3, 1995, April 27, 1996; "Pres. Hinckley announces plans for first temple in West Africa," by Steve Fidel, *Deseret News,* Feb. 16, 1998; *Church News,* Aug. 28, 1999.

Stakes — 5

(Listed alphabetically as of Oct. 1, 2000.)

No.	Name	Organized	First President
Africa West Area			
2407	Accra Ghana Christiansborg	9 Nov 1997	Emmanuel Ohene Opare
1792	*Accra Ghana Lartebiokorshie	9 Nov. 1997	
	‡Accra Ghana	21 Apr 1991	Emmanuel Ohene Opare
1791	Cape Coast Ghana	21 Apr 1991	Kweku Prah Ghartey
2499	Kumasi Ghana	22 Nov 1998	Kwaku Annoh
2351	Takoradi Ghana	18 May 1997	Kenneth Kobena Andam

Mission — 1

(As of Oct. 1, 2000; shown with historical number. See MISSIONS.)

(183a) GHANA ACCRA MISSION
P.O. Box 2585 Main
Accra, Ghana

GREECE

Year-end 1999: Est. population, 10,648,000; Members, 479; Missions, 1; Branches, 5; Europe Central Area.

Located on the southern end of the Balkan Peninsula in southeast Europe, Greece is a presidential parliamentary republic. About 98 percent of the Greek-speaking population belong to the Greek Orthodox Church.

A letter to Church leaders in Salt Lake City, Utah, from Rigas Profantis, a printer in Athens, requesting more information about the Church led missionaries to Greece around the turn of the 20th century. He and a friend, Nicholas Malavetis, had started a search for truth in 1895 that led them to write to Church headquarters. Pres. Ferdinand F. Hintze of the Turkish Mission visited the pair in April 1899, and taught them about the Church. In 1905, Profantis wrote requesting baptism, and noted that he had translated a pamphlet into Greek and that three other people were awaiting baptism as well. They were baptized Oct. 22, 1905, by J. Wilford Booth of the Near East Mission.

The group continued until 1909 or 1910, after which missionaries were withdrawn.

Little activity by the Church in Greece occurred until the 1950s. The Church donated wheat seed to Greece for humanitarian purposes in November 1947. In Salt Lake City in the 1950s, LDS Greek-Americans formed the Hellenic Latter-day Saint Society to retain their heritage and maintain ties with their homeland.

The Athens Branch was created in 1965 and reorganized in 1967 at a conference presided over by Pres. Rendell N. Mabey of the Swiss Mission. Many of those in attendance were expatriates stationed with the military in Greece.

A number of diplomatic exchanges were made during the next decades, including a visit to Greece by President Ezra Taft Benson in 1979, and a visit to Salt Lake City Oct. 14, 1980, by the Greek ambassador to the United States, John A. Tzounis.

The Greece Athens Mission was created from a division of the Austria Vienna East Mission on July 1, 1990. On Feb. 9, 1992, the Thessaloniki Branch was created with 32 in attendance, including 12 non-LDS investigators. Ground was broken for the first meetinghouse in Greece on Sept. 20, 1997, by Elder Wayne M. Hancock of the Seventy as 73 members, friends, and missionaries observed. Members and missionaries also helped in service projects as they cleaned debris from Mars Hill, and missionaries joined a fire-watch service project, and spent time cleaning the forest.

The first LDS meetinghouse in Greece was dedicated in Athens May 30, 1999, by Elder Charles Didier of the Seventy. An estimated 20 percent of the 200 who attended the services were investigators of the Church.

Sources: Swiss Mission manuscript history; *Church News,* March 3, 1990, March 3, 1991, May 18, 1991; "Branch begins in historic city," *Church News,* May 9, 1992, Oct. 4, 1997, Nov. 15, 1997, June 12, 1999.

Mission — 1

(As of Oct. 1, 2000; shown with historical number. See MISSIONS.)

(241) GREECE ATHENS MISSION
Panayias Eleftherotrias 9
145 63 Kifissia
Athens, Greece

GREENLAND
(See Denmark)

GRENADA

Year-end 1999: Est. population, 94,000; Members, 109; Branches, 1; Percent LDS, .12, or one in 862; North America Southeast Area; West Indies Mission.

Composed of three Caribbean mountainous islands, Grenada is an independent state with a parliamentary democracy. Its population is 64 percent Roman Catholic and 22 percent Anglican.

Although LDS members lived in Grenada attending medical school, little permanent missionary work started until after the 1983 coup and subsequent invasion of Grenada by U.S. and United Nations forces. Under the direction of Pres. Kenneth L. Zabriskie of the West Indies Mission, Elders Robert W. Hoffmaster and Leonard G. Gill arrived in Grenada in May 1985. They met with a medical student, Tom Nuttal, and his wife, Julie, and their children. A branch was established in St. George on Sept. 3, 1985.

Sources: *Church News,* Nov. 20, 1983, Nov. 6, 1983; Kenneth and LeOra Zabriskie journals.

GUAM
(See also Micronesia)

Year-end 1999: Est. population, 153,000; Members, 1,476; Branches, 4; Missions, 1; Districts, 1; Percent LDS, .96, or one in 105; Philippines/Micronesia Area.

The largest of the Mariana islands in the South Pacific, the self-governing U.S. territory of Guam has a population that is mostly Roman Catholic.

The first LDS members on Guam probably came as members of the armed forces during World War II. Branches of from 50 to 300 servicemen began on Guam in 1944, functioning under the Far East Mission. In 1945, four groups were organized on the island. On one occasion, they dedicated graves of fallen LDS servicemen.

In 1951, fund-raising events by the members raised enough money to purchase land and two quonset huts, which they used for a chapel and classrooms. The facilities were dedicated in 1953 and Guam became a dependent branch of the Oahu Hawaii Stake.

In 1952, Ethel T. Kurihara, a native of Guam, became the first local Relief Society president.

Elders Danny Gallego and Paul Ray arrived on Aug. 25, 1955, and served for a year and a half.

As more LDS military personnel arrived, land for another meetinghouse was purchased. A new meetinghouse in Barrigada was dedicated March 10, 1970, and the Guam Branch became a ward. Open houses were frequently held, but few joined the Church. In May 1976, the Guam Ward was divided. The first Chamorro couple to join the Church, Don Calvo and his wife, Maria, were baptized in May 1977. The Agat Branch was created in 1978. And in 1979, Herbert J. Leddy, the first missionary of Chamorro lineage, was called to the Tennessee Nashville Mission.

The Micronesia Guam Mission was created April 1, 1980. In June, the Guam District was created with four branches.

In 1989, selections of the Book of Mormon were translated into Chamorro, and the same year, Herbert J. Leddy became the first Chamorro member to be called as district president. Membership in 1995 was 1,400.

President Gordon B. Hinckley visited Guam Jan. 31, 2000, on a tour of Pacific Rim countries. He was welcomed to Agana by Carl Gutierrez, governor of Guam, and 684 members. His address was carried to a meetinghouse on the island of Saipan where a congregation had gathering in a meetinghouse.

Sources: "A Brief History of the Micronesia-Guam Mission, 1980-1990," published by the Micronesia Guam Mission, 1990; *Unto the Islands of the Sea,* by R. Lanier Britsch; *Church News,* Feb. 12, 2000.

Mission — 1

(As of Oct. 1, 2000; shown with historical number. See MISSIONS.)

(178) MICRONESIA GUAM MISSION
673 Chalan San Antonio
Perezville
Tamuning GU 96921

GUATEMALA

Year-end 1999: Est. population, 10,999,000; Members, 174,784; Stakes, 40; Wards, 236; Branches, 213; Missions, 4; Districts, 24; Temples, 1; Percent LDS, 1.59, or one in 63.

The northernmost isthmus country in Central America, the Republic of Guatemala has people who speak Spanish and various Indian dialects, and are mostly Roman Catholics.

John F. O'Donnal, a member of the Church from the Mormon colonies in Mexico moved to Central America in 1942 as an agricultural adviser of the U.S. government. He paved the way for the arrival of the first missionaries in 1947. Pres. A. L. Pierce of the Mexican Mission assigned Elders Seth G. Mattice, Earl E. Hansen, Robert B. Miller, and David D. Lingard, who arrived in Guatemala on Sept. 4, 1947. They held a sacrament meeting, and with the assistance of Brother O'Donnal, visited several government leaders. A year later, on Aug. 12, Brother O'Donnal was set apart as district president. Some 66 people attended the first meeting in a rented building on Aug. 22, 1948. On Nov. 13, 1948, Pres. O'Donnal baptized his wife, Carmen, the first convert in Guatemala.

On Nov. 16, 1952, Elder Spencer W. Kimball, then of the Quorum of the Twelve, visited and organized the Central American Mission. By 1956, three branches with a membership of about 250 had been established. The Guatemala-El Salvador Mission was created Aug. 1, 1965.

When the Church received official recognition in November 1966, there were 10,000 members. On May 21, 1967, the Guatemala City Stake was organized, the first in the country. The stake was divided in 1972, and the mission was divided in 1976, creating separate missions in Guatemala and El Salvador.

President Spencer W. Kimball visited Guatemala Feb. 22, 1977, and met with Guatemalan President Kjell Eugenio Laugerud-Garcia. He also spoke at an area conference at the National Gymnasium to members from Guatemala and El Salvador, and was given the key to the city from Mayor Leonel Ponciano Leon.

By 1977, the mission had been divided again with the creation of the Guatemala Quetzaltenango Mission, with John F. O'Donnal as president. Four stakes had been established and membership was more than 17,000. A temple was announced for Guatemala City in 1981, and completed and dedicated Dec. 14-16, 1984. Called as president of the temple was Brother O'Donnal. At that time, membership was 40,000 in eight stakes and 13 districts. A third mission, the Guatemala City North, was created Jan. 1, 1988. The fourth, Guatemala Central, was created July 1, 1993. Membership in 1990 was 125,000, increasing to 148,000 in 1995 and to 174,784 in 1999.

On April 1, 1989, Elder Carlos H. Amado, former temple committee chairman, was called to the Second Quorum of the Seventy, becoming the first Guatemalan General Authority.

On Jan. 22, 1994, Elder Boyd K. Packer of the Quorum of the Twelve dedicated a new 36,400-square-foot missionary training center. President Gordon B. Hinckley visited this nation Jan. 26, 1997, and addressed about 20,000 members from 17 stakes and districts in the morning and another 15,000 from another 12 stakes in the evening.

Sources: Guatemala Branch manuscript history; *Encyclopedic History of the Church* by Andrew Jenson; *Church News*, Aug. 20, 1966, Sept. 10, 1966, Nov. 10, 1966, March 5, 1977, Jan. 13, 1979, June 30, 1985, Nov. 27, 1993, Feb. 12, 1994, Feb. 1, 1997.

Stakes — 40

(Listed alphabetically as of Oct. 1, 2000.)

No.	Name	Organized	First President
Central America Area			
2843	Amatitlan Guatetmala	28 Jun 1998	Vicente Bernardo Rodriguez C.
1611	*Chimaltenango Guatemala	22 Mar 1988	
	Guat. Chimaltenango		
	‡Guatemala City	26 Oct 1986	Mario Salazar Moran
1738	Coatepeque Guatemala	10 Dec 1989	Ricardo Rolando Morales
2115	Coban Guatemala	29 Oct 1995	Jorge Rafael Cabrera Galindo
436	*Guatemala City Guatemala		
	‡Guatemala City	21 May 1967	Udine Falabella
2506	Guatemala City Guatemala	10 Jan 1999	Luis Javier Rabanales

	Alameda		
1618	Guatemala City Guatemala Atlantico	7 Dec 1986	Luis Alvarez Ovando
2105	Guatemala City Guatemala Bosques De San Nicolas	15 Oct 1995	Cesar Antonio de Leon
1619	Guatemala City Guatemala Central	7 Dec 1986	Armando G. Diaz L.
1768	Guatemala City Guatemala El Molino	19 Aug 1990	Jose Julio Aguilar
1620	Guatemala City Guatemala Florida	7 Dec 1986	Miguel A. Gomez L.
2510	Guatemala City Guatemala La Esperanza	30 Jan 1999	Erwin Reynaldo Rosales Chigua
1704	Guatemala City Guatemala La Laguna	27 Nov 1988	Carlos Estrado Mouna M.
778	Guatemala City Guatemala Las Victorias	31 Oct 1976	Carlos Enrique Soto D.
1040	Guatemala City Guatemala Mariscal	10 Jun 1979	Samuel Ramirez Abrego
1745	Guatemala City Guatemala Milagro	15 Apr 1990	Victor Manuel Canenguez P.
2484	Guatemala City Guatemala Monte Maria	28 Jun 1998	Gerardo Soto U.
2106	Guatemala City Guatemala Monserrat	15 Oct 1995	Sam Mino Galvez Orellana
1733	Guatemala City Guatemala Nimajuyu	9 Jul 1989	Rene Humberto Oliva L.
2010	Guatemla City Guatemala Palmita	15 Jan 1995	Carlos Francisco Arredondo C.
699	*Guatemala City Guatemala Utatlan 31 Oct 1976		
	‡Guatemala City Guatemala West	8 Jun 1975	Mario Antonio Lopez
2043	Guatemala City Guatemala Villa Hermosa	30 Apr 1995	Bruno Emilio Vasquez R.
1982	Huehuetenango Guatemala Calvario	19 Jun1994	Victor M. Rodas Corado
1706	*Huehuetenango Guatemala Zachuteu 19 Jun 1994		
	Huehuetenango Guatemala	4Dec 1988	Edgar Leonardo Fuentes P.
1937	Jalapa Guatemala	9 May 1993	Luis Daniel Aragon Aquino
1938	Malacatan Guatemala	9 May 1993	Edilzar Joel Barrios Rodriguez
1737	Mazatenango Guatemala	10 Dec 1989	Mario Antonio de Leon S.
2505	Mazatenango Guatemala East	13 Dec 1998	Armando Gonzalez Figueroa
2195	Momostenango Guatemala	12 May 1996	Francisco de J. Rosales Santiago
2263	Patzicia Guatemala	10 Nov 1996	Carlos Antonio Guit Ajiquichi
713	Quetzaltenango Guatemala	19 Oct 1975	Jorge Herminio Perez C.
1996	Quetzaltenango Guatemala El Bosque	6 Nov 1994	Melvin Enrique Recinos D.
1497	Quetzaltenango Guatemala West	24 Oct 1984	Amilcar Raul Robles A.
1168	Retalhuleu Guatemala	17 Aug 1980	Manuel Efrain Barrios F.
2514	Retalhuleu Guatemala Las Palmas	28 Feb 1999	Moises Gomez Guzman
1955a	San Felipe Guatemala	19 Sep 1993	Mario A. Monterroso Gonzalez
1498	San Marcos Guatemala	24 Oct 1984	Abraham Raymundo Juarez C.
2469	San Pedro Guatemala	24 May 1998	Arnoldo O. Gonzalez G.
1785	Villa Nueva Guatemla	27 Jan 1991	Luis Gomez Garcia
2153	Zacapa Guatemala	14 Jan 1996	Arnulfo Franco Martinez

Stakes discontinued

1681	*Escuintla Guatemala 3 Apr 1990 Discontinued 12 Jun 1994		
	‡Guatemala City Guatemala Escuintla	31 Jan 1988	Enrique Leveron L.

Missions — 4

(As of Oct. 1, 2000; shown with historical number. See MISSIONS.)

(287) GUATEMALA GUATEMALA CITY CENTRAL MISSION
Apartado Postal 921-A
Guatemala City
Guatemala, C.A.

(76a) GUATEMALA GUATEMALA CITY SOUTH MISSION
Apartado Postal340-A
Guatemala City 01909
Guatemala, C.A.

(205a) GUATEMALA GUATEMALA CITY NORTH MISSION
Ave. Las Americas 7-30
Edificio Los Arcos- Nivel 5- Zona 13
Guatemala, Guatemala, C.A.

(152) GUATEMALA QUETZALTENANGO MISSION
8a. Calle 6-31, Zona 2
Quetzaltenango 09001
Guatemala

GUYANA

Year-end 1999: Est. population,1,026,000; Members, 700; Branches, 3; percent LDS, .06 or 1 in 1,465; North America Southeast Area; West Indies Mission.

On the northern coast of South America, Guyana is a republic in the United Kingdom commonwealth of nations. Its population is 57 percent Christian and 37 percent Hindu, and speaks English and Amerindian dialects.

Elder Benjamin Hudson and his wife, Ruth, entered Guyana Aug. 19, 1988, and held a sacrament meeting in September 1988. Among those who attended was the Majid Abdulla family, which had been baptized previously in Canada. The first convert was Indra Sukhdeo, who was baptized Oct. 23, 1988, by Brother Abdulla.

The Church gained recognition in February 1989, and a small branch in Georgetown was organized in March with about 23 in attendance.

In February 1990, Elder M. Russell Ballard of the Quorum of the Twelve visited the branch, and, along with missionary couples Carvel G. and Lois N. Jackson and Joseph W. and Florence B. Allen, attended services with 45 members and investigators.

Kenrick Latchmansingh was called as the first local branch president in 1990.

On Sept. 15, 1992, President Desmond Hoyte, Guyana's head of state, was a special guest at a luncheon hosted by Elder Stephen D. Nadauld of the Seventy and a member of the North America Southeast Area presidency, and Pres. J. Richard Toolson of the Trinidad Tobago Mission.

Sources: History, personal histories, other information submitted by Joseph and Florence Allen, Benjamin and Ruth Hudson, and Carvel and Lois Jackson; "Taking root in 'Land of Waters,'" *Church News*, May 18, 1991; *Church News*, Nov. 7, 1992.

HAITI

Year-end 1999: Est. population, 6,540,000; Members, 8,157; Stakes, 1; Wards, 7; Branches, 12; Missions, 1; Percent LDS, .12 , or one in 802; North America Southeast Area.

On the west side of Hispaniola Island in the West Indies, Haiti has a people who speak Hatian and Creole. Eighty percent are Roman Catholic and 10 percent are Protestant; voodoo is influential.

The first LDS member in Haiti was Alexandre Mourra, who traveled to Florida from his home to be taught and baptized by the missionaries on June 30, 1977. Earlier, he had read a pamphlet and the Book of Mormon in Haiti.

On July 2, 1978, 22 Haitians were baptized in Hatte-Maree, near Port-au-Prince. In September of that year, J. Frederick Templeman of the Canadian embassy arrived. He and Alexandre Mourra worked to start the first branch, which was created in October 1980 in Port-au-Prince.

Missionary work opened in Haiti in May 1980 under the direction of Pres. Glen E. Stringham of the West Indies Mission. In 1982, 12 missionaries were serving in Haiti.

A branch was created in Petionville on March 31, 1981, with Alexandre Mourra as president, and divided in 1982. At that time, the Haiti District was created and four missionaries were sent to open the city of Cap Hatien. Called as president was Ludner Armand. Missionaries had more referrals than they could teach. In August 1981, Fritzner Joseph, called to Puerto Rico, was the first Haitian to serve a full-time mission. In 1992, he was called as the first Haitain mission president, serving in the Haiti mission.

Selections of the Book of Mormon were translated into Haitian Creole in 1983, and that year, Haitian convert Luckner Huggins translated several hymns into Creole. Year-end membership was 485. The Haitian mission was created Aug. 4, 1984. By 1986, membership reached 1,500, and by 1988 it was 2,200. At a Port-au-Prince District conference in May 1989, 1,200 of the total 3,000 members attended district conference, and 49 men were ordained elders. Due to troubled internal conditions, foreign missionaries were temporarily removed from Haiti on Oct. 25, 1991. Haitian members rejoiced when ground was broken Aug. 18, 1996, for a temple in Dominican Republic, a more accessible location. In August 1998, Jeffrey G. Randle, a physician and returned missionary to Haiti, took a team of 14 medical professionals to Port-au-Prince and treated individuals with special needs.

Sources: *Church News,* June 10, 1989, April 22, 1984, July 10, 1983, May 22, 1983, Nov. 29, 1980; Kenneth and LeOra Zabriskie journals; "Haitian Saints See Hope in Gospel," by Elizabeth and Jed VandenBerge, *Ensign,* March 1991; correspondence from Margene Stringham, Oct. 9, 1991; correspondence from Dr. Michael T. Johnson, Feb. 16, 1993; *Church News,* June 27, 1992 and March 26, 1994; "Ground broken for Caribbean's first temple," *Church News,* Aug. 24, 1996, Sept. 12, 1998.

Stake — 1

(Listed alphabetically as of Oct. 1, 2000.)

No. Name	Organized	President
2399 Port-au-Prince Haiti	21 Sep 1997	Reynolds Antoine Saint-Louis

Mission — 1

(As of Oct. 1, 2000; shown with historical number. See MISSIONS.)

(180a) HAITI PORT-AU-PRINCE MISSION
Boite Postale 15319
Petionville,
Haiti, F.W.I.

HONDURAS

Year-end 1999: Est. population, 5,460,000; Members, 95,750; Stakes, 20; Wards, 127; Branches, 89; Missions, 3; Districts, 11; Percent LDS, 1.8 or one in 57.

In Central America between Nicaragua and Guatemala, Honduras has a population that speaks Spanish and Indian dialects, and most are Roman Catholic.

Elders Spencer W. Kimball and Marion G. Romney, then of the Quorum of the Twelve, were instrumental in promoting missionary work in Central America. On Nov. 17, 1952, they visited and left a tract and a copy of the Book of Mormon with a hotel waiter, Jose Santos Ortega Flores, who was later baptized. Missionary work in Honduras began Dec. 10, 1952, a month after the Central America Mission was opened in Guatemala City, Guatemala. Elders James T. Thorup and George W. Allen, the first two missionaries in Honduras, baptized Jose Ortega, Alicia Castanado, Corina de Bustamonte, Mario A. de Chotria, and Carmen B. Corina on March 21, 1953. They organized a branch in Tegucigalpa March 22, 1953. Missionaries opened San Pedro Sula on Oct. 4, 1954, and a branch was organized there in 1955. The San Pedro Sula District was organized June 4, 1961.

The first stake in Honduras was created in San Pedro Sula April 10, 1977. The Honduras Mission was created Jan. 1, 1980, with 6,300 members in the country. By the end of 1987, membership had increased to 23,000. The mission was divided July 1, 1990, and the country's ninth stake was created in September 1990. Membership in 1995 was 65,000, ten times what it was just 15 years earlier.

The Church responded with extensive food and clothing following the devastation of Hurricane Mitch in November and December, 1998. President Gordon B. Hinckley visited Nov. 19-21 and promised the members they would not be forgotten.

Sources: *Church News,* Sept. 28, 1974, April 23, 1977, Oct. 27, 1979, July 20, 1986, Nov. 30, 1986, Oct. 3, 1987, April 16, 1988, Feb. 3, 1990; *Ensign,* Aug. 1977, June 1990; Honduras Tegucigalpa manuscript history.

Stakes — 20

(Listed alphabetically as of Oct. 1, 2000)

No. Name	Organized	President

Central America Area

2051	Choluteca Honduras	21May 1995	Edwin Raul Ferman Zelaya
2150	Comayagua Honduras	17 Dec 1995	Carlos Armando Zepeda H.
1383	Comayaguela Honduras	21 Nov 1982	Jorge Alberto Sierra B.
2097	Comayaguela Honduras Country	3 Sep 1995	Carlos Martin Velasquez Aceituno
1990	Comayaguela Honduras Torocagua	4 Sep 1994	Luis Gustavo Duarte Fonseca
2027	Danli Honduras	26 Feb 1995	Rodolfo Diaz Ortiz
1757	El Merendon Honduras	17 Jun 1990	Jose Francisco Funes R.
2061	Fesitranh Honduras	11 June 1995	Victor Guillermo Sierra Barahona
1647	La Ceiba Honduras	28 Jun 1987	Luis Alfredo Salazar V.
1601	La Lima Honduras	22 Jun 1986	Rodolfo Arguello A.
2224	San Pedro Honduras El Progresso	25 Aug 1996	Sami G. Medrano Ramiriz
820	San Pedro Sula Honduras	10 Apr 1977	Samuel Ben-Zion Ventura
2168	Satelite Honduras	18 Feb 1996	Marvin Ivan Gudiel Castillo
947	Tegucigalpa Honduras	30 Jul 1978	Jose Miguel Dominguez C.
1709	Tegucigalpa Honduras Guaymuras	29 Jan 1989	Armando Antonio Sierra
2099	Tegucigalpa Honduras La Esperanza	10 Sep 1995	Jose Benigno Triminio Rodriguez
1771	*Tegucigapa Honduras Toncontin	4 Sep 1994	
	‡Toncontin Honduras	2 Sep 1990	Ricardo Valladares B.
2197	Tegucigalpa Honduras Uyaca	26 May 1996	Moises Abraham Molina Guillen
1732	Valle de Sula Honduras	2 Jul 1989	Solomon Jaar Welchez
2322	Villa Nueva Honduras	9 Mar 1997	Aaron Fernandez Amaya

Missions — 3

(As of Oct. 1, 2000; shown with historical number. See MISSIONS.)

(312) HONDURAS COMAYAGUELA MISSION
Apartado Postal 2625 y/o 3688
Tegucigalpa, Honduras C.A.

(177) HONDURAS TEGUCIGALPA MISSION
Apartado Postal 556 o 3539
Tegucigalpa, Honduras, C.A.

(242) HONDURAS SAN PEDRO SULA MISSION
Apartado Postal 1970
San Pedro Sula, Honduras

HUNGARY

Year-end 1999: Est. population, 10,319,000; Members: 3,191; Branches, 19; Missions, 1; Districts, 2; Percent LDS, .03, or one in 3,234; Europe Central Area.

In east central Europe, Hungary has a population that speaks Hungarian (Magyar), and is Roman Catholic, 67 percent, and Protestant, 25 percent.

The first missionary effort into Hungary was made by Elders Thomas Biesinger and Paul E.B. Hammer in Vienna, in what was then in the dual sovereignty of Austria-Hungary. Elder Biesinger labored in Prague, but was eventually banished from the country.

Mischa Markow, a native of Hungary who was converted near Constantinople, Turkey, in 1887, preached the gospel in Belgium, Hungary, Romania, Bulgaria, Germany, Turkey, Russia, and Serbia, which later became part of Yugoslavia. He visited Hungary the year of his baptism to preach to his parents, but they were not converted. He immigrated to America, and returned as a missionary in about May 1899 and preached in Serbia until banished to Hungary three months later. In about July 1899, he was banished from Hungary after being imprisoned in solitary confinement. He went to Temesvar, Hungary, Sept. 3, 1900. He and his companion, Elder Hyrum Lau, were soon ordered to surrender their passports. In the few days afterward, while they could legally remain in the country, they worked feverishly, and the day before they were banished they baptized 12 people and ordained leaders to watch over a branch of 31 people.

Missionaries worked among German-speaking Hungarians in 1908, and the Church received legal recognition in 1911. However, missionary work among Hungarian-speaking people was not successful, and the area was closed by March 10, 1913.

The Book of Mormon was translated into Hungarian in 1933, but selections were not published until 1979.

In modern times, the Church received legal recognition from Hungary on June 24, 1988. A fireside on that day was attended by Elder Russell M. Nelson of the Quorum of the Twelve, as well as a congregation of 85 people. Two converts were baptized the next day. The first meetinghouse in Hungary was dedicated Oct. 17, 1989, by President Thomas S. Monson, then second counselor in the First Presidency.

Yuri and Ludmilla Terebenin and their daughter Anna of Leningrad, then in the Soviet Union, heard about the Church during a trip to Budapest, Hungary, where they were baptized on July 1, 1989. They were were among the first converts in Russia. One of Lithuania's first converts, Irute Meskiene of Vilnius, also heard the gospel preached in Szeged, Hungary, where she was later baptized.

The Hungary Budapest Mission was created from the Austria Vienna East Mission on June 1, 1990. At the time there were some 75 members in one district. The Tabernacle Choir performed in Budapest's elegant Opera House in June 1991 to an enthusiastic audience, which gave it eight curtain calls.

On May 17-20, 1992, Elder Dallin H. Oaks of the Quorum of the Twelve participated in a major international consultation on religious liberty and ethnic rights. Held in Budapest, Hungary, the consultation brought together 72 participants to discuss problems and share ideas pertaining to church-state issues in east-central European nations that were once part of the communist bloc, particularly Albania, Bulgaria, Czechoslovakia, Hungary, Latvia, Poland, Romania, Croatia, Slovenia, and Russia. The consultation helped emphasize religious freedom in many countries.

Seminary in Hungary began in 1993.

In June 1996, Elder Jeffrey R. Holland of the Quorum of the Twelve and Elder Dennis B. Neuenschwander of the Seventy met with nearly 1,000 members in an all-mission conference in Budapest. The two General Authorities were interviewed by Hungarian national television. They met with LDS service personnel in Taszar.

Sources: *Millennial Star,* March 13, 1913; "Hungary — Then and Now," by Kahlile Mehr, *Ensign,* June 1990; German and Swiss mission manuscript histories; *Church News,* June 22, 1991, May 30, 1992, June 27, 1992, Aug. 24, 1996, May 31, 1997.

Mission — 1

(As of Oct. 1, 2000; shown with historical number. See MISSIONS.)

(243) HUNGARY BUDAPEST MISSION
Kinizsi Pal Utca 37
1029 Budapest, Hungary

ICELAND

Year-end 1999: Est. population, 266,000; Members, 248; Branches, 2; Districts, 1; Percent LDS, .09 , or one in 1,073; Europe Central Area; Denmark Copenhagen Mission.

Located between Scandinavia and Greenland, the constitutional Republic of Iceland has a people who speak Icelandic and who are 95 percent Evangelical Lutheran.

Converted in Denmark while learning trades, Thorarinn Thorason and Gudmund Gudmundson of Iceland were baptized in 1851. They returned to Iceland that year and began preaching on Westmann Island. A number believed, and Benedikt Hanson and his wife were among the first baptized by Thorason. Unfortunately, Thorason drowned a short time later and Gudmundson, who had been ordained a teacher, was not authorized to baptize. He continued his work, but it wasn't until 1853 that other missionaries received permission to enter the country and assist him. Missionaries and members endured severe persecution. Johan P. Lorentzen arrived and ordained Gudmundson an elder, baptized several more converts and organized a branch June 19, 1853. Soon after, nearly all the members immigrated to America.

In 1873, Elders Magnus Bjarnason and Loptur Johnson of the Scandinavian Mission returned to Westmann Island and baptized a few more converts and reorganized a branch. In 1874, 11 converts immigrated to America. Missionary work continued in 1875 with the return of Samuel Bjarnason and Thordar Dedikson. In 1879, a pamphlet was translated, printed in Denmark, and distributed in Iceland. Small emigrating companies left Iceland throughout the early 1880s. Many of the Icelandic members settled in Spanish Fork, Utah. An Icelandic Mission was organized for a short time, from about 1894 until after 1900. Proselyting in Iceland was discontinued in 1914.

Missionary work, under the direction of the Denmark Copenhagen Mission, resumed in Iceland in 1975, building on the efforts of LDS servicemen who had been stationed in Iceland. A branch was organized on a military base at Keflavik with 130 servicemen and their families. Byron and Melva Geslison, with their twin sons, returned missionaries David and Daniel, were called from Utah to re-open the work. In two years, some 40 Icelanders were baptized and a branch was organized at Reykjavik Aug. 8, 1976, with about 10 members. A year later, it had grown to 40 members. A meetinghouse was dedicated in 1981 by Elder David B. Haight of the Quorum of the Twelve.

The Book of Mormon was translated into Icelandic in 1980, and the other standard works followed. By 1986, membership had reached 180.

Iceland's president, Olafur Ragnar Grimsson and his wife, Guorun Katrin Thorbergsdottir, visited Spanish Fork, Utah, July 23-29, 1997, at the invitation of the Icelandic Association of Utah. The president and his wife were guests of honor and visited Church headquarters and he spoke at a fireside attended by some 2,000 people. Spanish Fork is the oldest Icelandic community in the United States.

In 1999, there were two branches with 248 members in Iceland.

Ground was broken March 6, 1999, in the Reykjavik suburb of Garoabaer by Elder Wm. Rolfe Kerr of the Seventy for the first meetinghouse, built for that purpose, in Iceland, to house the two branches. After the groundbreaking, Elder Kerr, along with Pres. Byron A. Rasmussen of the Denmark Copenhagen Mission and Pres. Olafur Einarsson of the Iceland District, visited the president of Iceland, Olafur Grimsson. A year later, on July 4, 2000, the meetinghouse was dedicated by Elder Kerr. The day before, on July 3, a museum, part of the new Icelandic Emigration Center and devoted to LDS Church history focusing on the Mormon emigration, was opened in Hofsos, Iceland. Iceland's president participated in both events.

In addition, on June 30, 2000, a monument, honoring 410 Icelanders who immigrated to America from 1854 to 1914, was dedicated June 30, 2000, near "Mormon Pond," a tide pool on the rocky coast of Westmann Islands, where many of the early Icelander converts were baptized. Mormon Pond has retained its name for 145 years since the days of the early baptisms.

Sources: *Encyclopedic History of the Church,* by Andrew Jenson; Denmark Mission manuscript history, "Fire and Ice," by Flint J. Stephens, *New Era,* Dec. 1981; correspondence from D.B. Timmins; "Gospel touches remote Iceland," by Tod Harris, *Church News,* Aug. 6, 1994; "Iceland president visits Utah," by Gerry Avant, *Church News,* Aug. 2, 1997; *Church News,* March 2, 1999, July 15, 2000.

INDIA

Year-end 1999: Est. population, 936,546,000; Members, 2,435; Missions, 1; Districts, 4; Branches, 18; percent LDS, .0003, or one in 384,618; Asia Area.

Occupying the Indian subcontinent in south Asia, India is a federal republic with a population that speaks 16 languages including the official language, Hindi, and associate official, English, and is 83 percent Hindu; 11 percent Muslim; 3 percent Christian; and 2 percent Sikh.

Church members Benjamin Richey and George Barber, British sailors converted in 1849, visited Calcutta, India, in 1850 and shared their testimonies. They were followed in 1851 by Elder Joseph Richards, who also preached in Calcutta. He baptized James Patrick Meik, Mary Ann Meik, Matthew McCune, and Maurice White, and set them apart as missionaries. Soon after, White was appointed to preside over the branch, and he baptized Anna, a native. The little branch was depleted by emigration, but additional missionaries arrived and baptized a few more people, and a small meetinghouse was built.

In 1853, additional missionaries took the gospel message to Madras, Bombay, Rangoon, Karatchi, Poona, and other areas, and several small branches were established.

However, when these missionaries returned to Utah in 1858, some of the converts also emigrated. Although other missionaries and conversions followed, the India Mission was not considered a successful one. At least one branch existed through 1903. Missionaries were not successful in learning the Hindustani, Tamil, Telugu, or other native languages.

In 1954, S. Paul Thiruthuvadoss, an accountant for a cement company in Coimbatore in southern India, found an LDS tract, and through it was introduced to the Church. He was not baptized until Feb. 7, 1965, when missionaries from the Southern Far East Mission visited. His baptism was performed by mission Pres. Jay A. Quealy Jr., grandson of early India convert Matthew McCune.

Thiruthuvadoss held schools for underprivileged children, and shared the message of the gospel with many people. In 1967, Pres. G. Carlos Smith of the Singapore Mission visited and baptized 24 of the people prepared by Thiruthuvadoss. As of 1980, the Coimbatore branch had 225 members and regular services were conducted in Tamil.

In Delhi, northern India, Baldwin Das was baptized by Charles Redford in 1968, and was joined by the Roshan Juriel family. In 1972, Maureen Das was the first to serve a mission from India. In 1981, government regulations allowed a missionary couple, Horace and Edna Hayes, to establish a branch. A visit by the BYU Young Ambassadors in 1983, and the arrival of LDS families involved in diplomatic service strengthened the branch. Later, the branch was divided for Indian and American members. By 1987, a congregation of 50 met in the Indian branch with all the auxiliaries functioning.

In 1977, Edwin and Elsie Dharmaraju of Hyderabad, India, living in Samoa, were converted to the Church. They received permission to return to India and teach the gospel to their family. They arrived in December 1978, and on Dec. 27, eighteen members of their family were baptized. A branch was organized with Victor David as president. In 1981, the Dharmarajus delivered to the Church, a 700-page manuscript, the Book of Mormon translated into Telegu by her father, the Rev. P. Sreenivasam. This translation of the Book of Mormon was printed in 1982, as was another full translation in Hindi and translated selections of the Book of Mormon in Tamil.

In the 1980s, the Church microfilmed genealogical records in India. In December 1992, Elaine L. Jack, Relief Society general president, visited branches in Bangalore and reported that members met in homes three times a month and in a rented building on the fourth Sunday.

The India Bangalore Mission was created Jan. 1, 1993. Gucharan Singh Gill, a native of India, was called as mission president. At that time, India had 1,150 members in 13 branches.

In 1999, 18 branches, with 2,435 members, was functioning in India.

Sources: *Encyclopedic History of the Church* by Andrew Jenson; Church History in North India, report by Baldwin Das and Douglas Rose, Aug. 1987; Testimony of S. Paul Thiruthuvadoss; *The Church in Asia,* by J. Spencer Palmer, Deseret Book, 1970; "India fills genealogy link," by William B. Smart, *Church News*, Jan. 9, 1988; *Church News,* Dec. 19, 1992; "Asia Area: Welcome mat is out in several countries," by Sheridan R. Sheffield, *Church News*, June 19, 1993; Feb. 2, 1998.

Mission — 1

(As of Oct. 1, 2000; shown with historical number. See MISSIONS.)

(277) INDIA BANGALORE MISSION
1117, 13th Cross
Indiranagar, Stage II
Bangalore 560 038
India

INDONESIA

Year-end 1999: Est. population, 203,584,000; Members, 5,339; Missions, 1; Districts, 3; Branches, 21; percent LDS, .003 or one in 38, 131; Asia Area.

An archipelago of more than 13,500 islands, including Java, one of the world's most densely populated areas, Indonesia is a republic whose population speaks Bahasa, Indonesian (the official language), Javanese, and up to 100 other Austronesian languages.

Six missionaries entered Indonesia on Jan. 5, 1970, and began work on Jan. 20. The Jakarta Branch was organized Feb. 15, 1970, and the first converts were baptized March 29, 1970. Door-to-door tracting was halted by the government in April 1970, but it resumed in May after the Church was granted clearance. The Church was officially recognized Aug. 11, 1970.

The first missionaries to the city of Solo in Central Java arrived on June 27, 1972. After only a few weeks, they had more than 100 people in attendance at their English classes and were also teaching English on radio, but proselyting was limited due to government regulations.

During the next few years, branches were organized throughout Java where the work was performed. The Indonesia Jakarta Mission was organized July 1, 1975. By 1977, when the Book of Mormon was published in Indonesian, membership had reached 1,200 and local missionaries carried on the work.

However, difficulties with missionary visas and government limitations continued to restrict missionaries. Indonesia's difficult internal religious conflicts and activities by others against missionary work made progress difficult.

On Aug. 1, 1978, the government issued restrictions on proselyting.

The mission was discontinued Jan. 1, 1981. In 1982, some 30 local missionaries maintained efforts and were finding success. An Indonesian, Effian Kadarusman, was called as mission president and the mission was reopened July 1, 1985. A new mission home was dedicated July 24, 1988, but all foreign missionaries were restricted from the country on Nov. 26, 1988, and the Indonesia Mission was consolidated with the Singapore Mission on July 1, 1989.

In 1993, Dr. Dean and Sister Elan Belnap entered Indonesia to work with the medical school in Jakarta, and help with the local branches. Their service helped raise the Church's profile. The Indonesia Jakarta Mission was re-opened July 1, 1995, with districts in Jakarta, Surabaya, and Kurakarta.

Highly illustrated cloth batiks created by Indonesian members have been regularly contributed to art displays at the Museum of Church History and Art in the 1990s.

In January 2000, President Gordon B. Hinckley, on a Pacific Rim tour, met with the president of Indonesia, Abdurranhman Wahid, at a dinner on Jan. 27 in the presidential palace in Jakarta. The two had met the previous year in Salt Lake City. While in Jakarta, President Hinckley spoke at a fireside Jan. 28, 2000, to 1,800 members, the largest congregation of Church members ever to assemble in Indonesia.

Later in the year, the Church, as a result of political turmoil in East Tumor, provided hundreds of thousands of pounds of rice and 20,000 hygiene kits, along with eight 38,000-pound containers of warm-weather clothing to assist refugees who fled conflict in their homeland. The hygiene kits were assembled by Church members in Jakarta, employees of the Indonesian government's Ministry of Foreign Affairs and local volunteers from the Bina Bingsa Foundation. On May 3, 2000, in a meeting with Church leaders in Jakarta, the Indonesian minister for foreign affairs, Alwi Shihab, expressed appreciation to the Church for the relief supplies.

In 1999, there were 5,339 Church members live in Indonesia.

Sources: *Spreading the Gospel in Indonesia: Organizational Obstacles and Opportunities,* a university paper by Garth N. Jones, Winter 1982; *Church News,* Aug. 3, 1991; "Asia Area: Welcome mat is out in several countries," by Sheridan R. Sheffield, *Church News,* June 19, 1993; *Deseret News,* May 27, 1996; *Church News,* Feb. 5, 2000, Feb. 12, 2000, May 6, 2000.

Mission — 1

(As of Oct. 1, 2000; shown with historical number. See MISSIONS.)

(306) INDONESIA JAKARTA MISSION
Jalan Senopati 115
Kebayoran Baru
Jakarta 12190, Indonesia

IRELAND

(See also Northern Ireland, under United Kingdom)

Year-end 1999: Est. population, 3,550,000; Members, 2,341; Stakes, 1; Wards, 4; Branches, 9; Missions, 1; Districts, 1; Percent LDS, .07, or one in 1,516; Europe West Area.

The island of Ireland lies in the Atlantic Ocean, west of Great Britain. It is a parliamentary republic where English is the dominant language, but Irish (Gaelic) is also spoken. The population is Roman Catholic, 95 percent, and Anglican, 3 percent. Northern Ireland, part of the United Kingdom, has a population of 1.6 million, of whom about half are Protestant.

The first missionary to Ireland was Reuben Hedlock, who arrived in Belfast in May 1840, but stayed only three days before sailing to Paisley. He was followed on July 28 by Apostle John Taylor, who was accompanied by James McGuffie and William Black, a native Irishman. A non-member Irishman, Thomas Tait (or Tate), also accompanied them. More than 600 people heard Elder Taylor preach that evening in Newry. On July 31, as the party walked between towns and arrived at a lake called Loughbrickland, Tait was baptized, becoming Ireland's first convert.

Two months later, Elder Theodore Curtis arrived in Ireland and established a branch of 35 in Hillsborough. A second branch, organized in Crawfordsburn, had 22 members by July 21, 1841.

In 1842, many of the 71 members in Ireland emigrated. Membership declined over the next years, despite renewed efforts in 1843. The 1845-47 famine prompted the emigration of most of the remaining 51 members.

Early missionaries remarked that proselyting was slowed by opposition, particularly that of landholders who threatened sharecroppers with expulsion if they welcomed LDS missionaries. However, historians believe that a good number of the British converts during the 1840s and '50s were expatriated Irish.

In the early 1850s, missionaries established a few branches, but in 1853 most missionaries left for America. Another group arrived in 1854, found new converts and saw membership increase from some 20 to 210 in 1855, and to nearly 300 in 1856. However, the 1857 "Utah War" led to the recall of the missionaries and the branches were unsupervised for four years. Missionary work was discontinued in 1867.

In 1884, a few native Irish members were called as missionaries in their homeland. They found some success despite opposition and established a branch in Belfast that by the end of 1884 had 50 members. Political unrest prompted most of the converts to emigrate. By 1900, about 90 had left Ireland for Utah.

However, a branch grew up in Dublin after 1900, made up of Germans. By 1920, there were about 225 members in the Belfast Conference (District) and 60 in and around Dublin.

In 1949, the Emerald Isle was divided amid continued unrest, into an independent Ireland and Northern Ireland, which remained under the British government.

The Ireland Dublin Mission was created in 1976, an outgrowth of the Irish Mission, created in 1962.

As part of the 150th anniversary of the Church in the British Isles in 1987, markers were dedicated at the site of the first baptism and at the birthplace in Dublin of Elder Charles A. Callis of the Quroum of the Twelve, once president of the Irish Conference while a missionary about 1894. Membership in 1990 was 1,800, increasing to 2,341 in 1999.

Indicative of the strength of the Church, Pres. Van F. Dunn noted in 1994 that seven missionaries from Ireland were serving at the same time in the England London South Mission.

President Gordon B. Hinckley visited Ireland Sept. 1-2, 1995, the first Church president to do so since President David O. McKay in August 1953. He spoke to members from the newly created Dublin Ireland Stake, Cork Ireland District, and Belfast Northern Ireland Stake.

Sources: *Encyclopedic History of the Church,* by Andrew Jenson; "Emerald Isle Hosts Beauty, Friendliness," by Gerry Avant, *Church News,* Feb. 25, 1978; "The Saints in Ireland," by Orson Scott Card, *Ensign,* Feb. 1978; *Church News,* July 6, 1974, Dec. 1, 1985; "Markers tell where history was made," by Dell Van Orden and Gerry Avant, *Church News,* Aug. 1, 1987, and *Church News,* Aug. 8, 1987; *Church News,* Aug. 27, 1994; "Visit to Ireland caps 'whirlwind trip' " by Mike Cannon, *Church News,* Sept. 9, 1995.

Stakes — 1

(Listed alphabetically as of Oct. 1, 2000.)

No.	Name	Organized	First President
Europe West Area			
2034	Dublin Ireland	12 Mar 1995	Liam Gallagher

Mission — 1

(As of Oct. 1, 2000; shown with historical number. See MISSIONS.)

(70) IRELAND DUBLIN MISSION
The Willows, Finglas Road
Glasnevin, Dublin 11, Ireland

ITALY

Year-end 1999: Est. population, 58,262,000; Members, 18,599; Stakes, 3; Wards, 16; Branches, 117; Missions, 4; Districts, 15; Percent LDS, .03, or one in 3,133.

In southern Europe jutting into the Mediterranean Sea, the boot-shaped Republic of Italy has a population that speaks Italian, and is nearly all Roman Catholic.

The first missionaries in Italy were Elders Lorenzo Snow of the Quorum of the Twelve, and Joseph Toronto and Thomas B.H. Stenhouse. They arrived in Genoa, Italy, on June 25, 1850. They traveled to the Piedmont Valley to work among a group of Protestants of French origin called the Waldenses. They were joined there by Elder Jabez Woodard.

On Oct. 27, 1850, Elder Snow baptized Jean Antoine Box at La Tour. Other baptisms followed and three branches of the Church were organized in Angrogne, St. Germain, and St. Bartholomew, all in Piedmont. Tracts were published in the French language for the Waldenses. The Book of Mormon was published in 1852. By 1855, 50 members had immigrated to America and membership was 64.

Proselyting outside the Piedmont Valley was very difficult, due to a great deal of anti-Mormon activity. Missionaries labored with little success in Italy, departing for Switzerland in 1857. Elder Daniel B. Hill Richards tried to re-open the work in 1900, but was refused legal permission.

In 1965, the Church was given legal status and missionary work resumed. The first modern convert of Italy was Leopoldo Larcher, who later served as the first Italian mission president and as regional representative. On Aug. 2, 1966, the Italian Mission was re-established.

By that time, there were two Italian branches and seven combined servicemen and Italian branches, and a membership of 66. By 1978, membership had increased to 7,271, and the nation had four missions. Italy's first stake was created June 7, 1981, in Milan.

Local missionaries and leaders contributed to increased growth in the 1980s. By mid-1985, membership increased to 12,000 and to 14,000 in 1990.

A milestone was reached May 12, 1993, when Italy formally granted legal status to the Church for the first time. The application to have the Italian government officially recognize the Church was filed four to five years earlier, underwent several reviews and an investigation, and was signed by Italy's president, Oscar Luigi Scalfaro, on Feb. 22, 1993. Italian law does not require legal status for proselyting.

On Dec. 19, 1993, a group of 50 missionaries was invited to sing on Vatican Radio from St. Peter's Basilica at the Vatican.

During May 1996, the District of Turin celebrated the 30-year anniversary of the Church being organized in the northwestern area of Italy with an emphasis on missionary work. Activities included opening and closing ceremonies and a presentation by the BYU Lamanite Generation. In a unique celebration of the Church's pioneer sesquicentennial in 1997, members in Italy took horse-drawn wagons down the streets of Rome. The members borrowed five wagons from a movie company, which were followed by a folk ensemble, a blue grass band from Ricks College, and other performers. The parade received extensive coverage in the Italian media.

The Tabernacle Choir, during a tour of Europe, sang in Turin June 20, 1998, and in Rome at the Accademia Santa Caecilia near the Vatican on June 22. The choir was widely acclaimed for it performances. One of the many doors opened by the Tabernacle Choir after its performances in 1998 was to the office of Oscar Luigi Scalfaro, president of the Italian Republic. Later in the year, Elder Dieter F. Uchtdorf of the Seventy and president of the Europe West Area met with the Italian president and presented him with a leatherbound, inscribed copy of the Book of Mormon and a porcelain statue of the family.

Membership in Italy in 1999 was 18,599. Four missions are headquartered in the country today.

In 2000, the Church was featured every three to four months on national television on a program of general interest, which was aired by satellite across Europe, and which generated a considerable number of missionary referrals. The first program in which the Church participated covered key points of doctrine, missionary work, the Book of Mormon, and an introduction to the Church. Later programs covered the Church's FamilySearch website and the Church Educational System.

Sources: *Millennial Star*, Dec. 15, 1850; *Encyclopedic History of the Church*, by Andrew Jenson; *The Scriptural Allegory*, by Dr. Daniel B. Richards, Magazine Publishing Company, Salt Lake City, Utah, April 1931; *History of the French Mission of the Church, 1850-1960*, by Gary Ray Chard, master's thesis at Utah State University, 1965; *Church News*, June 12, 1993, Jan. 15, 1994, July 19, 1997; "Concert is artistic treasure in Rome's cultural landscape," by Gerry Avant, *Church News*, June 27, 1998; *Church News*, Jan. 9, 1999, July 29, 2000.

Stakes —3

(Listed alphabetically as of Oct. 1, 2000.)

No.	Name	Organized	First President

Europe West Area

1274	Milan Italy	7 Jun 1981	Mario Vaira
2317	Puglia Italy	9 Mar 1997	Giovanni Carlo DiCarlo
1556	Venice Italy	15 Sep 1985	Claudio E. Luttmann

Missions — 4

(As of Oct. 1, 1998 shown with historical number. See MISSIONS.)

(158) ITALY CATANIA MISSION
Via Corsaro, 84 (Parco Inglese)
95030 S. Agata Li Battiati CT, Italy

(98) ITALY MILAN MISSION
Via Gramsci 13/4
20090 Opera (MI), Italy

(244) ITALY PADOVA MISSION
Via Caldonazzo, 10
35030 Selvazzano Dentro PD, Italy

(7) ITALY ROME MISSION
C.P. 11/282 MONTESACRO
I-00141 Rome, Italy

CÔTE D'IVOIRE (IVORY COAST)

Year-end 1999: Est. population, 14,791,000; Members, 5,402; Stakes, 1; Wards, 11; Missions, 1; Branches, 3; Percent LDS, .04, or one in 2,738; Africa West Area.

Located on the Gulf of Guinea on the west coast of Africa next to Ghana, Ivory Coast has a population that speaks tribal languages and French, and belongs to tribal religions and Islam.

Isolated LDS families lived in Ivory Coast in the 1970s and earlier, including Baernard and Cherry Silver and Terry and Bobby Broadhead.

Lucien Yapi Affoue and his wife, Agathe, joined the Church in 1980 in Lyon, France, where he was a student. They were sealed in the Swiss Temple and served in the Bordeaux Branch. They returned to Abidjan in March 1984, and eventually helped establish four branches. They were joined in 1986 by Philippe Assard and his wife, Anelise Noetzel Assard, and their two children. Brother Assard, an engineer, felt impressed to help establish the Church in his homeland, even though he was without a job for year. There were 16 members in the country in 1987.

In 1988, the Church donated $60,000 to Rotary International for polio vaccinations of children in Ivory Coast.

The Affoue family moved to Bouake, where another branch was established on Oct. 4, 1988. The Abidjan Branch was created on June 1, 1989, with Brother Assard as branch president.

The first missionaries to Ivory Coast were Elder Barnard Stewart Silver and his wife, Cherry, who arrived in April 1988. Elder Robert M. and Sister Lola Walker arrived in 1988, and introduced the gospel to some 100 members. A U.S. expatriate, Douglas Arnold, was called as the first district president in October 1989.

The first district conference was held March 10-11, 1990, in Abidjan with about 200 people from the branches of Abidjan and Boauke. At the time, local records indicated a membership of 350. Two missionary couples from the Ghana Accra Mission continued baptizing about 30-35 a month. The Plateau Dokui Branch, Ivory Coast's fourth, was organized at the conference. At the time, 35 men held the Melchizedek Priesthood.

The Church received legal recognition on April 19, 1991.

Eighteen local elders were called to serve in the mission in December 1991. On June 30, 1992, Ivory Coast was transferred from the Ghana Accra Mission to the Cameroon Yaounde Mission. Mission Pres. Robert L. Mercer moved the Cameroon Yaounde Mission headquarters to Ivory Coast and this became the Ivory Coast Abidjan Mission on May 1993.

The mission concentrated its resources in the Abidjan area to establish a center of the Church here for French-speaking Africa.

In 1993, Mayor Alan Dawson of Midrand, South Africa, a Church member, initiated a sister city partnership with Yamoussoukro, Ivory Coast. In 1995, Sister Jennie Kallunki, wife of mission Pres. J. Thomas Kallunki, directed a sister missionaries' training conference, the first-ever such conference in Ivory Coast, which included workshops on community service, strengthening branches, and teaching about the Book of Mormon.

Early in 1996, the symbolic "first stone," a ceremonial start of construction, was held for the first meetinghouse in Ivory Coast. More than 60 members and friends gathered for the ceremony for the Yopugon meetinghouse, which was to house two branches and the offices of the Abidjan District presidency. Ivory Coast reached a milestone when its first stake was created in August of 1997.

In 1999, 5,402 members were living in Ivory Coast.

Sources: "When a Woman Is Alone," by Cherry Silver, *Ensign*, June 1978; *Church News*, Oct. 17, 1987, June 25, 1988, June 10, 1989, April 28, 1990; correspondence from Chirley Roundy Arnold, April 19-23, 1991; *Church News*, Dec. 4, 1993; correspondence from the Ivory Coast Abidjan Mission, March 1994; *Church News*, Dec. 30, 1995; Feb. 24, 1996; Jan. 1, 1997, Sept. 27, 1997; "Pioneers in Ivory Coast," by Robert L. Mercer, *Ensign*, September 1997.

Stakes—2

(Listed alphabetically as of Oct. 1, 2000.)

No.	Name	Organized	First President
2387	Abidjan Ivory Coast	17 Aug 1997	Cyr Philippe Assard
2569	Abobo Ivory Coast	27 Aug 2000	Kalogo Norbert Ounleu

Mission — 1

(As of Oct. 1, 2000; shown with historical number. See MISSIONS.)

(271) IVORY COAST ABIDJAN MISSION
06 B.P. 1077
Abidjan 06
Cote d'Ivoire
West Africa, Ivory Coast

JAMAICA

Year-end 1999: Est. population, 2,574,000; Members, 4,240; Districts, 2; Branches, 16; Missions, 1; percent LDS, .16, or one in 607; North America Southeast Area.

Located in the West Indies, south of Cuba, Jamaica is an independent state where English and Jamaican Creole are spoken, and 70 percent of the people are Protestants.

The first LDS elder on Jamaica was Harrison Sager, who preached here briefly in 1841. Twelve years later, Elders James Brown, Aaron F. Farr, Alfred B. Lambson, Darwin Richardson, and Elijah Thomas returned to preach the gospel, but found a great deal of antagonism and stayed only six weeks.

In modern times, two LDS families, the John L. Whitfields and Jay P. Bills families, began holding meetings in Mandeville, and the Mandeville Branch was created March 22, 1970. One of the first converts was Victor Nugent and his family, who were baptized Jan. 20, 1974. As new converts, the Nugents remained faithful when the branch's priesthood leaders moved away. They introduced the gospel to soccer star Errol Tucker and his family, who helped them maintain the branch. Full-time missionaries began work again in Jamaica in November 1978, under the direction of Pres. Richard L. Millett of the Florida Ft. Lauderdale Mission. By 1983, membership had increased to 300, and by 1985, to 520.

The first Jamaican branch president was Victor E. Nugent, who was also the first elder ordained on the island. Brother Tucker was his counselor. Vaughn and Mary Soffe microfilmed the statistical records of Jamaica in 1982. Seminary began in Jamaica in the mid-1980s and by 1989, 141 students were taking seminary. Membership in 1990 was 1,900 and continued to increase. With improvements in technology, Jamaican members are able enjoy the programs included on the Church satellite system.

Sources: *Millennial Star*, April 2, 1853; *Encyclopedic History of the Church*, by Andrew Jenson; "A Trusted Friend," by Ronald W. Walker, *Church News*, March 17, 1979; Kenneth and LeOra Zabriskie journals; "Jamaicans nurture new gospel tradition," by Wanda Kenton Smith, *Church News*, Jan. 29, 1984; *Church News*, Aug. 28, 1976, Nov. 29, 1980, April 22, 1984, Nov. 24, 1985, May 27, 1989, April 11, 1998.

Mission — 1

(As of Oct. 1, 2000; shown with historical number. See MISSIONS.)

(186a) JAMAICA KINGSTON MISSION
PO Box 2316
Kingston 8, Jamaica, West Indies

JAPAN

Year-end 1999: Est. population, 126,506,000; Members, 110,987; Stakes, 30; Wards,

170; Branches, 147; Missions, 8; Districts, 20; Temples, 2; Percent LDS, .09, or one in 1,140.

Off the eastern coast of Asia, Japan is a parliamentary democracy with people who are primarily Buddhists and Shintoists.

The history of the Church in Japan dates back to the turn of the 20th century when Elder Heber J. Grant of the Quorum of the Twelve, and missionaries Horace S. Ensign, Louis A. Kelsch, and Alma O. Taylor arrived in the country Aug. 12, 1901.

Under Elder Grant's direction, the first Church mission in Asia was established, with headquarters in Tokyo. The first baptism came March 8, 1902, when Elder Grant baptized Hijime Nakazawa, a former Shinto priest, in Tokyo Bay. A second baptism came on March 10, 1902, when Saburo Kikuchi was baptized.

Elder Taylor began translating the Book of Mormon into Japanese in 1904, and continued that work for more than five years, while he served as president of the Japanese Mission. The book was printed in October 1909.

Missionary work came to a halt in 1924 when President Heber J. Grant, then president of the Church, closed the mission to await a more "favorable time." Fujiya Nara was one of the converts who saw the missionaries off, later being appointed presiding elder over the small group that remained. He published a newsletter, "Shuro" (Palm). In 1926, the MIA was organized. The Japan Mission was re-opened in 1937 with headquarters in Honolulu, Hawaii. Hilton Robertson was named president. In 1947, Edward L. Clissold was called to preside over the Japan Mission, and in 1948 was given permission to return to Japan to do missionary work. He found a group of about 50 meeting with Brother Nara each Sunday. The first five missionaries arrived in June that year.

During the time the mission was closed, LDS servicemen had prepared the way for proselyting by baptizing Tatsui Sato on July 7, 1946. His wife, Chiyo, and son, Yasuo, were also baptized. Sister Sato was baptized by Boyd K. Packer, later of the Quorum of the Twelve, who was in the military service in Japan at the time. This was the first baptism of local members in Japan in more than 20 years and was the beginning of a new era for the Church in the Far East.

Brother Sato re-translated the Book of Mormon, the Doctrine and Covenants, the Pearl of Great Price, and other important works. The work went forward, and the Japanese Mission was divided in July 1955 to form the Northern Far East and the Southern Far East missions.

The first meetinghouse in Asia, housing the Tokyo North Branch, was dedicated by Elder Gordon B. Hinckley, then of the Quorum of the Twelve, on April 26, 1964.

Hawaii native Adney Y. Komatsu was called as mission president in 1965, the first mission president of Japanese ancestry. Ten years later, in April 1975, he was called to be the first General Authority of Japanese ancestry. The first General Authority from Japan was Elder Yoshihiko Kikuchi, who was called to the First Quorum of the Seventy in 1977.

The first stake of the Church in Asia, the Tokyo Stake, was organized on March 15, 1970. The Japan Nagoya Mission was formed from the Japan Mission and the Japan Central Mission in 1973.

Plans for the Tokyo Temple were announced in August 1975. The edifice, the first temple in the Orient and the first in a non-Christian country, was dedicated Oct. 27, 1980, in what was described as "the most significant and important event in the history of Asia." Following the dedication, President Spencer W. Kimball participated in area conferences on Oct. 30-31 in Tokyo, which was attended by 10,000 members, and Nov. 1 in Osaka, attended by 6,387 members. The message of the conferences was clear: "Japan is a place where the Church has a tremendous future."

The Japan Okinawa Mission was created in 1985. In 1991, the Asia North Area was created and the area offices were established in Tokyo.

The Church provided extensive assistance after a major earthquake devastated the Kobe/Osaka area in the predawn hours of Jan. 17, 1995. The Kobe Ward meetinghouse and adjoining Japan Kobe Mission Home were used as shelters for members and others. One member of the Church died in the earthquake and 35 LDS families were left homeless.

President Hinckley spoke at six meetings in Japan May 17-21, 1996, during an extended visit to Asia. It was the first visit of a Church president to Japan in 16 years. He spoke to members and missionaries in Tokyo, Osaka, Fukuoka, and Naha, Okinawa. He also met with the U.S. ambassador to Japan, Walter Mondale, and with the media. On May 7, 1998, a temple was announced for Fukuoka in southern Japan. Two years later, on June 11,

2000, the temple was dedicated. A week before the dedication, an open house was held and among the 4,800 who attended was the United States ambassador to Japan, Tom Foley.

Sources: *Encyclopedic History of the Church,* by Andrew Jenson; "Dedication of temple called historic event," "'Tremendous' future for Church in Japan," both by Dell Van Orden, *Church News,* Nov. 8, 1980; *A History of the Church in Japan from 1948 to 1980,* by Terry G. Nelson, a BYU thesis August 1986; "Kyoto, the cultural center of Japan," by Sheridan Sheffield, *Church News,* June 22, 1991; "Growth reflected in Asia areas," by Sheridan Sheffield, *Church News,* Nov. 16, 1991; "The Blossoming of the Church in Japan," by R. Lanier Britsch, *Ensign,* October 1992; "Fujiya Nara, Twice a Pioneer," by Yukikon Konn, *Ensign,* April 1993; *Church News,* Jan. 28, 1995; "President Hinckley visits Japan for a fast-paced three days," by Gerry Avant, *Church News,* May 25, 1996; *Church News,* May 28, 1998; "Church members rejoice over temple in southern Japan," by Greg Hill, *Church News,* June 17, 2000.

Stakes — 30

(Listed alphabetically as of Oct. 1, 2000.)

No.	Name	Organized	First President
Asia North Area			
1901	Abiko Japan	13 Sep 1992	Shigejiro Akamatsu
2493	Asahikawa Japan	20 Sep 1998	Katsuo Fuji
1018	Fukuoka Japan	20 Apr 1979	Yoshizawa Toshiro
2508	Ginowan Japan	24 Jan 1999	Yoshitaka Asato
1271	Hiroshima Japan	31 May 1981	Satoshi Nishihara
2547	Kanazawa Japan	5 Mar 2000	Motokazu Arata
1120	Kobe Japan	19 Mar 1980	Keiichi Mizuno
2350	Kumamoto Japan	18 May 1997	Mitsunori Sumiya
1874	*Kyoto Japan	25 Apr 1993	
	‡Kyoto Japan North	31 May 1992	Kaatsuichiro Fukuyama
1197	Machida Japan	26 Oct 1980	Koichi Aoyagi
919	Nagoya Japan	10 May 1978	Masaru Tsuchida
1203	Nagoya Japan West	2 Nov 1980	Take Shi Nakamura
1195	Naha Okinawa Japan	23 Oct 1980	Kensei Nagamine
1404	Okayama Japan	20 Mar 1983	Akira Watanabe
2498a	Okazaki Japan	8 Nov 1998	Toshihide Tsukahara
586	*Osaka Japan		
	‡Osaka (Japan)	12 Sep 1972	Noboru Kamio
1873	Osaka Japan East	31 May 1992	Ryochi Tanaka
872	Osaka Japan North	30 Oct 1977	Noboru Kamio
1328	Osaka Japan Sakai	17 Mar 1982	Hiroshi Takayoshi
949	Sapporo Japan	13 Aug 1978	Geiji Katanuma
1154	Sapporo Japan West	29 Jun 1980	Bin Kikuchi
1202	Sendai Japan	2 Nov 1980	Shigenori Funayama
1255	Shizuoka Japan	21 Apr 1981	Tadachika Seno
1164	Takasaki Japan	10 Aug 1980	Masataka Kitamura
505	*Tokyo Japan		
	‡Tokyo	15 Mar 1970	Kenji Tanaka
1121	Tokyo Japan East	23 Mar 1980	Ryotaro Kanzaki
869	Tokyo Japan North	23 Oct 1977	Ryo Okamoto
1270	Tokyo Japan South	30 May 1981	Kazutoshi Ono
1329	Tokyo Japan West	21 Mar 1982	Koichi Aoyagi
662	Yokohama Japan	27 Oct 1974	Hitoshi Kashikura
2455	Yokohama Japan South	19 Apr 1998	Seiji Saijo

Stakes discontinued

No.	Name	Organized	First President
1875	Kyoto Japan South	31 May 1992	Kenichiro Kimura
	Discontinued 25 Apr 1993		
1257	Takamatsu Japan	23 Apr 1981	Takejiro Kanzaki
	Discontinued 2 June 1991		

Missions — 8

(As of Oct. 1, 2000; shown with historical number. See MISSIONS.)

(91) JAPAN FUKUOKA MISSION
46 Hiao Josui Machi
Chuo-ku
Fukuoka-shi, Fukuoka-ken 810-002
Japan

(83) JAPAN KOBE MISSION
6-28 4-Chome
Shinohara Honmachi
Nada Ku, Kobe, T 657
Japan

(90) JAPAN SAPPORO MISSION
Kita 2 Jo Nishi 24 Chome 1-25
Chuo-ku, Sapporo-Shi
Hokkaido 064-0822
Japan

(82a) JAPAN TOKYO NORTH MISSION
4-25-12 Nishi Ochiai
Shinjuku-ku
Tokyo 161-0031, Japan

(144) JAPAN HIROSHIMA MISSION
1-11-26 Hikari-machi
Higashi-ku
Hiroshima-shi 732-0052
Japan

(108) JAPAN NAGOYA MISSION
1-304 Itakadai
Meito-ku, Nagoya-shi, T 465-0028
Japan

(109a) JAPAN SENDAI MISSION
Yagiyama Minami 3 Chome 1-5
Taihaku-k
Sendai-Shi, Miyagi-ken 982-0807
Japan

(162) JAPAN TOKYO SOUTH MISSION
1-7-7 Kichijoji-Higashi Machi
Musashino-shi
Tokyo T 180-0002, Japan

KENYA

Year-end 1999: Est. population, 28,817,000; Members, 4,039; Missions, 1; Districts, 2; Branches, 17; Percent LDS, .01 , or one member in 7,135; Africa Southeast Area.

American USAID employees and their families serving in Kenya in the 1970s held Church services in their own homes. The first African converts in Kenya, Elizaphan Osaka and his wife, Ebisiba, and their two oldest children, Margaret and Jairo, were baptized Oct. 21, 1979. Brother Osaka, a former minister, was ordained a priest the same day. The first missionaries were Elder Farrell and Sister Blanch McGhie of Palo Alto, Calif., who arrived Sept. 6, 1980.

The Kenya District, with two branches in Nairobi and Kiboko, was created May 10, 1981. The first Kenyan called as a full-time missionary was Benson Kasue, who served in the Los Angeles, Calif., area from 1983-85.

In 1988, the Church donated funds that were collected on special fasts to bring water to 15 Kenyan villages, located 100 miles from Nairobi. The water systems were installed by 1989. The first branch was organized in Nairobi March 15, 1989.

The Church received official recognition in Kenya Feb. 25, 1991, through the efforts of local members. The Kenya Nairobi Mission, which includes Kenya, Uganda, and Tanzania, was created in July 1991. In February 1992, more than 200 members and investigators from five branches attended a district conference in Nairobi, in the Parklands Branch meetinghouse. The meeting was conducted by district Pres. Joseph Sitati. Pres. Sitati, a convert since 1985, and his wife, Gladys, and their children were the first Kenyans to go through the temple. More than 30 missionaries served during the first year of the mission.

In 1992, the Church provided food staples to Somalian and Kenyan refugees affected by severe drought conditions. On Oct. 21, 1992, a six-acre plot of Church land was planted under the direction of LDS agronomist Joel K. Ransom, and the self-help project expanded later to members' own property and saw vital crops harvested.

By 1994, four districts had been created and large congregations attended many of the meetings. The first meetinghouse was completed in July 1994 for the Langata Branch in Nairobi.

Church humanitarian projects have blessed the lives of Kenyans, including a community water project in 1994 that provided personal water taps to hundreds of families. Members throughout eastern Africa received a boost with the visit of President Gordon B. Hinckley to Nairobi on Feb. 17, 1998. He spoke to about 900 members, who had gathered from Kenya, Uganda, Tanzania, Ethopia, and Somalia, and promised them the work would continue to grow in eastern Africa. President Hinckley was the first Church president to visit eastern Africa.

In 1997, LDS membership in Kenya was about 2,800. By 1999, it had increased to 4,039.

Sources: *Church News*, March 18, 1989, March 23, 1991, April 25, 1992, Sept. 26, 1992, Nov. 21, 1992, Feb. 11, 1995; Journals and correspondence of Kirk P. Lovenbury, June 10, 1993; correspondence from Pres. Larry K. Brown, Kenya Nairobi Mission, April 12, 1994; "This work will grow and grow in this land," by John L. Hart, *Church News*, Feb. 28, 1998.

Mission — 1

(As of Oct. 1, 2000; shown with historical number. See MISSIONS.)

(265) KENYA NAIROBI MISSION
P.O. Box 39634
Nairobi, Kenya

KIRIBATI

Year-end 1999: Est. population, 79,000; Members, 7,877; Stakes, 1; Wards, 10; Districts, 1; Branches, 13; Percent LDS, 9.97, or one in 10; Pacific Islands Area; Fiji Suva Mission.

Made up of 36 Micronesian islands in the mid-Pacific where the equator and international dateline meet, Kiribati is a republic that became independent in 1979. The islands' population speaks Gilbertese and English. About half of the population is Protestant and half is Roman Catholic.

The Church was introduced to Kiribati when Waitea Abiuta, a school teacher and headmaster of a school, asked to have graduates from his school attend the Church-owned Liahona High School in Tonga. Fijian mission Pres. Eb L. Davis visited Kiribati in September 1972, and approved 12 students to come to the Church school. Students were converted at the high school and they began serving as missionaries in Kiribati on Oct. 19, 1975.

Among those who joined the Church were Waitea Abuita and several of the staff and students of the school. However, when opposition to the Church arose, enrollment at the school declined. In August 1976, Grant and Pat Howlett, LDS educators at Liahona High, were called to teach at the Kiribati school. Through their efforts, enrollment increased and government relations improved. Later, the Church purchased the school and renamed it Moroni Community School, and other teachers arrived from Tonga as enrollment continued to increase. In 1984, the student body reached 240, and has remained at that number.

In 1982, a new meetinghouse was completed, and Buren Ratieta, Gilbertese branch president, held services in February of that year. Among the 250 who attended the dedicatory services was the president of the Kiribati Republic, Ieremia T. Tabai. He said government leaders at first feared the Church would divide the people, but when he saw the great social contribution the Church made, he became happy to cooperate with the Church. Since that time, missionary work has expanded to more distant islands in Kiribati. Selections of the Book of Mormon were translated into Gilbertese in 1988.

In the fall of 1993, a group of first-time basketball players from Moroni High School, the age of U.S. high school sophomores and juniors, won the championship of Kiribati in their division. They also defeated the 20-30-year-olds division champions.

In 1994, Teatao Teanaki, president of the Republic, was the main speaker at the graduation ceremonies at Moroni High School. Elder L. Tom Perry of the Quorum of the Twelve dedicated the Church's high school Aug. 9, 1996. Two days later, on Aug. 11, he created the Tarawa Kiribati Stake, the first stake in the country. Seminary began for LDS youth on Kiribati in March 1997.In 1999, the president of the Republic, Teburoro Tito, visited Moroni High School, and spoke to the students, commenting on the spirit of cooperation among Church members and the rapid growth of the Church in Kiribati. Membership in 1999 was 7,964, up from 2,300 in 1990.

On Jan. 26, 2000, President Gordon B. Hinckley, on a tour of Pacific Rim countries, stopped at Tarawa, Kiribati, and was met by 1,500 members. Among those who gathered was Kataotiki Teeke, minister of Environment and Social Development, who represented the president of Kiribati in welcoming President Hinckley and his group. Minister Teeke, whose brother Timea Teeke was one of the first missionaries to serve in Kiribati, expressed appreciation for Moroni High School and for humanitarian aid the island nation has received from the Church.

Sources: *Unto the Isles of the Sea*, by R. Lanier Britsch; interviews with various missionaries; *Church News*, Oct. 23, 1993, Feb. 5, 1994; "Elder Perry creates first Kiribati stake, dedicates islands," *Church News*, Sept. 21, 1996; *Church News*, May 3, 1997, July 3, 1999, Feb. 12, 2000.

Stake — 1

(Listed alphabetically as of Oct. 1, 2000.)

No.	Name	Organized	First President
Pacific Islands Area			
2215	Tarawa Kiribati	8 Aug 1996	Atunibeia Mote

CHRISTMAS ISLAND

Year-end 1999: Est. population, 4,000; Members, 100; Branches, 1; percentage of LDS, .25 or one in 400; North America West Area; Hawaii Honolulu Mission.

Situated among the Line Islands in the South Pacific, Christmas Island, a 140-square mile atoll, is a part of the Republic of Kiribati with a population that speaks Gilbertese and English. It is about 2,000 miles from Tarawa

The first branch on Christmas Island was organized by Pres. H. Ross Workman of the Hawaii Honolulu Mission on May 23, 1999, in the village of London. Located some 1,500 miles south of Hawaii, Christmas Island previously was in the Fiji Suva Mission, but was transferred to the Hawaii mission in 1998.

The first president of the branch was Timei Kaitaua, who, early in 1999, had contacted Pres. Workman about the possibility of a branch on Christmas Island.

Most of the 117 members of the branch were converted elsewhere, many attending Moroni High School on Tarawa, the capital of the Republic of Kiribati, and/or BYU Hawaii, and then either returning or moving to Christmas Island for one reason or another.

Source: "New branch created on Pacific isle," by Julie A. Dockstader, *Church News*, July 3, 1999,

KOREA

Year-end 1999: Est. population, 45,554,000; Members, 71,166; Stakes, 17; Wards,105; Branches, 70; Missions, 4; Districts, 6; Temples, 1; percent LDS, .16, or one in 640.

In northern east Asia, the Republic of Korea, or South Korea, has a population that speaks Korean and principally follows Buddhism, Confucianism, and Christianity.

LDS servicemen performed the first missionary work during the Korean War in 1951. Among the first Korean members was Ho Jik Kim, converted while earning a doctorate in the United States. He became an influential leader in the Korean government and paved the way for missionaries to enter Korea. His children, Tai Whan and Young Sook, were among the first four baptized on Aug. 3, 1952. He died of a stroke in 1959.

The first missionaries, Elders Richard L. Detton and Don G. Powell, arrived in Korea in 1954. At that time, membership in Korea was 64. The missionaries learned to speak Korean and taught many young students.

The Korean Mission was created on July 8, 1962, with Gail C. Carr, one of the early missionaries to Korea, as president. The new mission had seven branches, in Seoul, Pusan, and Taegu. By 1964, membership had reached 1,800. The Book of Mormon was printed in Korean in 1967. By 1968, significant increases in membership began to develop. From 1974 to 1977, a girls choir in an orphanage operated by LDS member Whang Keun-Ok was promoted on national media, increasing the percent of those who recognized the name of the Church from 10 to 70 percent. The first stake in Korea — and he first stake on mainland Asia — was created in Seoul on March 8, 1973. The Church's first visitors center in Korea was opened Oct. 7, 1974, in Kwang Ju, the provincial capital in southwestern Korea. Membership increased to 9,000 in 1975, and by 1983, it had reached 28,795. In 1990, membership was 59,000, increasing to 62,000 the next year.

President Spencer W. Kimball visited Korea on Oct. 26, 1980, and spoke to 6,000 members in two sessions of an area conference. One session was held outdoors with a stiff wind sending the wind chill factor to many degrees below the freezing mark.

A temple was announced for Seoul, Korea, on April 1, 1981, and was dedicated Dec. 14, 1985.

When the 1988 summer Olympic Games were held in Korea, the BYU Folk Dancers performed at opening ceremonies, viewed by an estimated audience of 1 billion worldwide.

Elder In Sang Han, called to the Second Quorum of the Seventy on June 1, 1991, was the first Korean General Authority. In 1992, a record of the testimonies of the early Korean converts was published by Spencer J. and Shirley Palmer.

In May 1996, President Gordon B. Hinckley conducted meetings for members and missionaries in Seoul and Pusan during an extended visit to Asia. He also attended a press conference and luncheon with members of the media in Korea. When a worker for world peace from South Korea went to Atlanta, Ga., members there presented the woman, Dr. Hak Ja Han Moon, with a framed copy of the Proclamation on the Family.

Membership in 1999 was 71,166.

Sources: *History of the Church in Korea,* by John D. Nash; *The Church Encounters Asia,* by Spencer J. Palmer, Deseret Book, 1970; "Saints throng to area meetings in the Far East," by Dell Van Orden, *Church News,* Nov. 1, 1980; *Ensign,* Nov. 1985; *Church News,* Oct. 1, 1988; *Church News,* Feb. 5, 1992; "Whang Keun-Ok: Caring for Korea's Children," by Shirleen Meek Saunders, *Ensign,* Oct. 1993; "Renewing ties with Asian lands, peoples," by Gerry Avant, *Church News,* June 8, 1996; *Church News,* Aug. 29, 1998; "Pioneering in South Korea," by Spencer J. Palmer, *Ensign,* October 1997.

Stakes — 17

(Listed alphabetically as of Oct. 1, 2000.)

No.	Name	Organized	First President
Asia North Area			
1865	Anyang Korea	24 May 1992	Young Hwan Lee
1385	*Chong ju Korea 23 Sep 1986		
	‡Seoul Korea Chong Ju	28 Nov 1982	Chung Yul Hwang
1306	Inchon Korea	12 Nov 1981	Chea Huo
1596a	Jeon Ju Korea	27 Apr 1986	Ju In Pak
1196	Kwang Ju Korea	25 Oct 1980	Bjong Kyu Pak
1382	*Ma San Korea	13 Apr 1995	
	‡Pusan Korea West	20 Nov 1982	Gil Whe Do
1059	Pusan Korea	6 Sep 1979	Chaewhan Chang
604	*Seoul Korea		
	‡Seoul	8 Mar 1973	Ho Nam Rhee
1412	Seoul Korea		
	Dong Dae Mun	24 Apr 1983	Son Awunf Ju
1017	Seoul Korea East	18 Apr 1979	Won Yong Ko
1386	Seoul Korea Kang Seo	28 Nov 1982	Do Hwan Lee
1060	Seoul Korea North	9 Sep 1979	Moo Kwang Hong
834	Seoul Korea West	22 May 1977	Chang Sun Kim
1387	Seoul Korea Yung Dong	28 Nov 1982	Jae Am Park
1866	Suwon Korea	24 May 1992	Yong Hwan Lee
1435	*Tae Gu Korea	29 Jun 1993	
	*Dae Gu Korea	3 Dec 1990	
	‡Daegu Korea	24 Jun 1983	Chan Tae Kwon
2440	Taejeon Korea	8 Mar 1998	Song Yoom-heon

Missions — 4

(As of Oct. 1, 2000; shown with historical number. See MISSIONS.)

(124) KOREA PUSAN MISSION
Tongnae P.O. Box 73
Pusan 607-600, Korea

(71) KOREA SEOUL MISSION
Kwang Hwa Mun, PO Box 210
Seoul 110-602, Korea

(170) KOREA SEOUL WEST MISSION
Song Pa PO Box 31
Seoul, 138-600, Korea

(191) KOREA TAEJON MISSION
Taejon PO Box 38
Taejon, 300-600, Korea

LATVIA

Year-end 1999: Est. population, 2,763,000; Members, 178; Districts, 1; Branches, 4; Percent LDS, .01 , or one in 15,522; Europe East Area; Lithuania Vilnius Mission.

Latvia is a republic on the eastern shore of the Baltic Sea.

Mischa Markow, a Hungarian who had previously pioneered missionary work in Serbia, Hungary, Romania, and Bulgaria, was the first to preach in Latvia. Elder Markow registered with the district court and then preached to Germans in Riga, Latvia, on Oct. 9, 1903, and three families requested baptism. However, when he was summoned to court, he chose to comply with instructions from Pres. Francis M. Lyman of the European Mission: leave the country if he were summoned to court.

In modern times, Elder Dallin H. Oaks of the Quorum of the Twelve addressed Latvian and other leaders at a major international consultation on religious liberty and ethnic rights held in Budapest, Hungary, May 17-20, 1992.

Recent missionary work in Lativa began June 17, 1992, with the arrival of four missionaries serving under the direction of Pres. Charles H. Creel: Elders Dale Franklin, Dennon Ison, Matthew H. Lyman, and Michael G. Van Patten. They were followed on June 30 by the arrival of a missionary couple, Elder Boris A. and Sister Liselotte Schiel. The first convert in Latvia, Gunars Kavals, was baptized July 25, 1992.

In March 1993, Latvia was visited by Elder James E. Faust of the Quorum of the Twelve, and at that time, some 40 Latvian members comprised the membership of the Church in this land. LDS humanitarian assistance has been given to Latvia.

The Latvia Riga Mission was created July 1, 1993, and included Latvia, Lithuania, and Estonia. On April 16, 1996, the mission was transferred and the name changed to the Lithuania Vilnius Mission. More than 200 youth from Estonia, Latvia, Lithuania and Belarus participated in youth conferences in Riga, Latvia. Membership in 2000 was 450.

Source: "Missionary to the Balkans: Mischa Markow" by William Hale Kehr, *Ensign,* June 1980; *Church News,* Nov. 16, 1991, June 27, 1992, March 6, 1993, June 12, 1993. Correspondence from the Lithuania Vilnius Mission.

LESOTHO

Year-end 1999: Est. population, 1,993,000; Members, 411; Branches, 1; Percent LDS .02, or one in 4,849; Africa Southeast Area; South Africa Johannesburg Mission.

Completely surrounded by South Africa, Lesotho is a mountainous kingdom where the people speak English and Sotho, and are primarily Roman Catholic, 38 percent, and Protestant, 42 percent.

Scattered LDS families from the United States lived in Lesotho during the 1980s. In July 1988 at a meeting attended by 15 people, the Maseru Branch was organized by Pres. R. J. Snow of the South Africa Johannesburg Mission at the home of expatriates Garry and Mary Massey. Brother Massey was called as president. John and Elaine Scott later moved to Lesotho from Swaziland. The Church was registered July 6, 1989, and the first missionaries, Elders Marc Modersitzki of Bancroft, Idaho, and Bradley Saunderson of Durban, South Africa, entered in September. They baptized Paul Khobutle and Lawrence van Tonder Dec. 17 of that year. As the branch grew, facilities were rented in a local school. A home was purchased and remodeled into a meetinghouse, and the first meeting in it was held Jan. 2, 1994.

A seminary program functioned in the country as early as 1991. On July 31, 1993, six converts traveled to the Johannesburg South Africa Temple. The first full-time missionary from Lesotho was Patrick Molapo, who began serving in the Durban South Africa Mission Dec. 21, 1993.

A second branch was created July 4, 1993, at Mazenod, which functioned for a short time before being disbanded because facilities for meetings were not available.

On Feb. 18, 1996, members from Lesotho were among some 5,000 who attended the Johannesburg Regional Conference — the largest LDS gathering assembled in South Africa up to that point. They also participated when President Gordon B. Hinckley visited in 1998. Elder Henry B. Eyring of the Quorum of the Twelve visited Nov. 13, 1999, for a priesthood leadership meeting for members from the Baltic area.

Sources: Correspondence from R.J. Snow; *Church News,* Dec. 12, 1989, March 10, 1990, Dec. 15, 1990, Jan. 26, 1991, April 25, 1992, March 2, 1996; Lesotho historical information, by Peter Daubney, May 1994.

LIBERIA

Year-end 1999: Population, 2,772,000; Members, 2,694; Districts, 1; Branches,12; Africa West Area; Ghana Accra Mission.

On the southwest coast of West Africa, the republic has a marshy coastline that gives way to low mountains and plateaus; the interior is forested. It is 20 percent Muslim, 20 percent Christian, and 60 percent tribal beliefs.

Among the early Church members in Liberia were Joan Raily, baptized in New Jersey in 1986, and expatriates Steven P. and Barbara Wolf, who were in Liberia on a military assignment. Meetings were held in their home in 1986. A year earlier, Thomas Peihopa of New Zealand began teaching a Sunday School class for Joe Jawloh, a school principal in

New Kru Town. Peihopa brought some 80 investigators to a social in the Wolf home. Bihise "Biz" Kajunju and his family, converts from Zaire, also joined the group.

Missionary couples opened missionary work in Liberia in 1987. Among the early couples were J. Duffy and Jacelyn Palmer, who arrived July 3, 1987, and Philander and Juanita Smartt. The first convert was John Tarsnoh, who was baptized Aug. 22, 1987. The missionaries baptized 47 people Aug. 27, 1987, in a lagoon. A decade later, only five from that group were less-active. The New Kru Town and Congo Town branches were organized that day. On Feb. 21, 1988, Joseph Forkpah became the first Liberian branch president. The Liberia Monrovia Mission was created March 1, 1988. Missionary couples were then working with some 133 members in Congo Town and New Kru Town.

Under the direction of Pres. Miles Cunningham, a handful of newly converted young men served full-time missions in 1990. At the beginning of 1990, the mission had one district and 8 branches.

The mission was closed in April 1991 because of civil war that started Dec. 24, 1989. Missionaries from Liberia were transferred to Freetown, Sierra Leone, on May 8, 1990. Da A. Tarr, then first counselor in the Monrovia District, was left in charge. During that time, about 400 members remained, another 400 fled to neighboring countries and another 400 were unaccounted for. Pres. Sando of the Monrovia District even dragged an unexploded bomb from his home during the peak of the fighting in Monrovia. When the war began to abate, some of the members returned. While conditions remained unsettled, no missionaries were assigned to Liberia. Church leaders instructed the members to meet in homes and not to hold large gatherings. Members suffered greatly during the war, but were provided for.

In October 1992, a second outbreak of serious hostilities occurred. Members regrouped, however, and by the spring of 1993, seven of the eight branches had been reorganized. With a renewal of hostilities, members in Liberia experienced additional hardships and suffering. Even though missionary work was halted in Liberia, 43 young men and women from Liberia served in missions in other countries.

In 1996, one of the residents owned a radio station that frequently broadcast music from the Tabernacle Choir. After the fighting, all the equipment had been taken but the transmitter, and it had been shot four times. However, the owner, Charles Snetter Jr., repaired the transmitter and began broadcasting the choir music without any announcements or interruptions.

In the late 1990s, members were optimistic that a brighter future awaited Liberia. The Church continues to grow in the country. In 1993, membership was 1,400, but six years later in 1999, membership had increased to 2,694.

At least partial fulfillment of a brighter future in Liberia came June 11, 2000, with the creation of the first stake in Liberia, the Monrovia Liberia Stake, by Elder H. Bruce Stucki of the Seventy. Included in the new stake were eight wards and one branch: Caldwell, Congo Town, Gardnersville, Logan Town, New Kru Town, Paynesville, Point Four, and Sinkor wards, and the Duala Branch.

Sources: Interview with Miles Cunningham, correspondence from James C. Palmer, Bill K. Jarkloh, June, 1994, and information from Da A. Tarr; *Church News*, July 9, 1994, March 9, 1996, April 27, 1996; correspondence with Richard Woolley, Aug. 17, 1998; *Church News*, July 22, 2000.

Stakes — 1

(Listed alphabetically as of Oct. 1, 2000.)

No.	Name	Organized	First President
Africa West Area			
2562	Monrovia Liberia	11 Jun 2000	Toby Wleboe Tweh Sr.

LITHUANIA

Year-end 1999: Est. Population, 3,876,000; Members, 499; Missions, 1; Districts, 1; Branches, 3; Percent LDS, .01, or one in 7,768; Europe East Area.

Lithuania is a republic on the eastern shore of the Baltic Sea. Its residents are mostly Lithuanian with a large Polish minority.

One of the first converts in modern Lithuania was Irute Meskiene of Vilnius. She heard the gospel preached in Szeged, Hungary, and was baptized in 1988 in Hungary. Robert and Ruth Rees, retired literature and music teachers, respectively, were called to Lithuania as missionaries in October 1992.

BYU's Young Ambassadors performed in Lithuania and stayed three nights with host families from the Neamanus Folk Ensemble in Kaunas.

In late 1993 and 1994, Lithuanian media presented Church-produced programs and also focused on missionaries and their work. In November 1994, Elder Marek Vasilkov of Vilnius became the first native Lithuanian to be called on a mission. He served in the Utah Salt Lake City Mission.

By November 1995, the Church in Lithuania had grown enough to create three branches, two in Vilnius and one in Kaunas. In 1996, the Latvia Riga Mission was relocated and renamed the Lithuania Vilnius Mission.

Source: *Church News,* June 12, 1993, and July 17, 1994; correspondence from Elder Robert A. Rees and Gabriele Sirtl, May 2, 1994.

Mission — 1

(As of Oct. 1, 2000; shown with historical number. See MISSIONS.)

(288) LITHUANIA VILNIUS MISSION
A/D 3016
2026 Vilnius, Lithuania

LUXEMBOURG

Year-end 1999: Est. population, 405,000; Members, 155; Branches, 1; Percent LDS, .04 , or one in 2,613; Europe West Area; Belgium Brussels Mission.

Located in western Europe, the Grand Duchy of Luxembourg's population speaks French, German, and Luxembourger. The people are 97 percent Roman Catholic.

On Nov. 19, 1963, Elders Hyrum M. Smith and Gerald E. Malmrose of the Franco-Belgian Mission went into the city of Luxembourg to help new missionaries there get started in their labors. They were there four days and left several missionaries to continue the work.

A branch was formed in the mid-1960s, and in 1965 Sunday meetings were conducted in the Hotel Kons. Attendance varied from one to three members and six missionaries. The branch remained small and struggled until it was discontinued in 1971.

The city and country of Luxembourg became part of the newly created Belgium Brussels Mission June 20, 1974, and continues as part of that mission today.

In late 1989 more than 1,000 people from 23 countries attended a nine-day exhibition titled "The Origin of Man" at the Luxembourg municipal hall. The event was hosted by area Church members and full-time missionaries. Of the 1,000 guests, nearly 200 signed the visitors book, leading to the placement of 190 copies of the Book of Mormon. In June 1994, Luxembourg became part of the newly created Metz France District, which was divided from the Nancy France Stake.

Sources: *Church News,* Jan. 6, 1990; Belgian Mission manuscript history; *Church News,* July 9, 1994.

MADAGASCAR

Year-end 1999: Est. population, 13,862,000; Members, 1,349; Missions, 1; Districts, 1; Branches, 6; Percent LDS, .01, or one in 10,276; Africa Southeast Area.

Located in the Indian Ocean off Mozambique, Madagascar is the world's fourth largest island. Its population speaks Malagasy and French, and 52 percent follow traditional beliefs, while 41 percent are Christian, and 7 percent are Islam.

The first member in Madagascar was Razanapanala Rameandricso, who was baptized in Bordeaux, France. He at first was loud in his opposition to the missionaries, but experienced a change of heart and was baptized Nov. 1, 1986. He returned to Madasgascar in 1989 and began teaching the gospel to a small group of people in his home. He contacted Pres. Girard Giraud-Carrier of the Mascarene Islands Mission, who visited. The first five converts were baptized upon his visit, near the end of 1990.

The first missionaries to Madagascar were Elder Fred L. and Sister Eileen Forsgren, who arrived March 3, 1991. The Antananarivo Branch was organized in February 1991 in a restaurant in Antananarivo. Called as the first branch president was Razanapanala Rameandricso. When the second missionary couple, Elder Marvyn and and Sister LaVeeta Hogenson, arrived in May 1991, the branch had 33 members. During their stay, the Church continued to grow. They completed their mission in September of 1992 and there were more than 130 attending meetings.

The first young full-time missionaries, Elders Jason Tarbet and Jeffry Gifford, arrived Sept. 25, 1992. The Hogensons returned for a second mission, and served from December 1993 to August 1994. During that period, seminary was started and the auxiliaries began to function.

The Church received legal status in Madagascar on July 13, 1993. At the end of August 1994, membership was at 375. A boost to the Church in Madagascar came with the creation of the Madagascar Antananarivo Mission July 1, 1998. Progress is being made on translation of the Book of Mormon into Malagasy. By 1999, membership had climbed to 1,349 in six branches. On May 9, 1999, the first Church building in Madagascar, in the capital city of Antananarivo, was dedicated by Elder Dennis E. Simmons of the Seventy to serve as a mission home for the Madagascar Antananarivo Mission, mission office, and meetinghouse facilities for two branches in Antananarivo.

Source: Journal of Eileen Forsgren, interview with LaVeeta Hogensen and journal of Elder Jason Tarbet; "Rich harvest of souls on island of Madagascar," by Marvyn and La Veeta Hogenson, *Church News*, Feb. 4, 1995; *Church News*, Jan. 10, 1998, June 5, 1999.

Stakes — 1

(As of Oct. 1, 2000.)

No.	Name	Organized	First President
2572	Antananarivo Madagascar	17 Sep 2000	Dominique L. Andriamanantoa

Mission — 1

(As of Oct. 1, 2000; shown with historical number.)

(327) MADAGASCAR ANTANANARIVO MISSION
B.P. 5094
Antananarivo 101
Madagascar

MALAWI

Year-end 1999: Est. population, 10,000,000; Members, 250 est.; Branches, 2; Africa Southeast Area; Zimbabwe Harare Mission.

A f ormer British protectorate that was granted independence in 1964, Malawi is a multiparty democracy with a population of 55 percent Protestant, 20 percent Roman Catholic, 20 percent Muslim and indigenous beliefs.

Elder Richard P. Lindsay of the Seventy visited Lilongwe, Malawi, on Jan 12-14, 1991, and after meeting with American LDS expatriates, set apart Jerry Mills as lead elder. The first baptism was the daughter of Elder Mills. Elder Lindsay met with McFarlane N. Phiri, who had been investigating the Church for 12 years after reading a copy of *Jesus the Christ*, by Elder James E. Talmage. Elder Lindsay also met with Christopher Samuel, another investigator. In 1993, James and Diane Griggs visited Malawi and were assigned to care for the members in this country. However, a severe drought impacted the nation and the resultant unrest slowed progress. The Church received legal recognition in April 25, 1995. Expatriate James Palmer, in Malawi with his family, was the presiding elder in Lilongwe in 1997. In May of 1999, Elder Dennis E. Simmons and Frank D. Bagley visited the Sitima Village Branch in central Malawi, home of McFarlane Phiri, who was sustained as branch president. Pres. Phiri had gathered a large group of villagers who had joined the Church. Six were ordained elders. Later a branch was created in Blantyre. Elder and Sister Dan and Berylene Frampton served there from 1999-2000.

Source: Interview with James Palmer, oral interviews provided by Matt Heiss, Family and Church History Department.

MALAYSIA

Year-end 1999: Est. population, 19,724,000; Members, 1,141; Districts, 2; Branches, 12; Percent LDS, .01, or one in 17,287; Asia Area; Singapore Mission.

On the southeast tip of Asia and the northern half of the island of Borneo, Malaysia is a federal parliamentary democracy with a constitutional monarch. Its people speak Malay, Chinese, English, and Indian languages, and practice primarily Muslim, Hindu, Buddhist, Confucian, Taoist, and local religions.

When the Singapore Mission opened in 1974, with Malaysia a part of the mission, missionaries were rotated in and out of the country on 30-day tourist visas to comply with the law of the land. The first missionaries came to Kuala Lumpur, the capital of Malaysia, on June 27, 1972.

Elder and Sister Werner Kiepe of Salt Lake City, Utah, special representatives of the International Mission, were sent to Malaysia shortly after the government granted the Church recognition status in 1977. They helped acquire the first property owned by the

Church in Malaysia in a suburb of Kuala Lumpur. Church membership was small, with many members being Americans and Australians temporarily working in the country, as well as some Chinese members living in the country.

In 1981, a milestone was reached when two native Malaysian elders were called to serve as missionaries in the Singapore Mission. A district was organized in Malaysia.

In 1986, the seminary and institute program was established with groups of young people attending in Pinang, Ipoh, and Kuala Lumpur.

On Oct. 20, 1990, King Syed Putra Jamallai, the rajah of Perlis state in Malaysia, was honored during a visit at the Polynesian Cultural Center in Laie, Hawaii.

Elder Halvor P. Hansen, serving in the Singapore Mission with his wife, Colleen, presented a copy of the *Encyclopedia of Mormonism* to the National Library of Malaysia in 1993.

Elder Monte J. Brough of the Seventy, then Asia Area president, reported in 1993 that while proselyting is not allowed, members and leaders were very devoted to the Church.

In 1994, local Church leaders were invited to dine with the Tenth King and Queen of Malaysia, Tuanku Ja'afar and Tuanku Najihah, in the royal couple's coronation events. The meeting in the dining hall of the Royal Palace in Kuala Lumpur was arranged by Vincent and Sandra Gordacan of Las Vegas, Nevada, close personal friends of the king and queen.

Sources: *The Church Encounters Asia,* by Spencer J. Palmer, Deseret Book, 1970; *Church News,* May 23, 1981; Aug. 14, 1982; Dec. 9, 1984; March 10, 1985; "Specific Prayers led him to specific answers," by Gerry Avant, *Church News,* Jan. 20, 1985; *Church News,* May 11, 1986, Nov. 3, 1990; *Church News,* Aug. 21, 1993; "Welcome mat is out in several countries," by Sheridan R. Sheffield, *Church News,* June 19, 1993; "Members dine with royalty," *Church News,* Dec. 17, 1994.

MALTA

Year-end 1999: Est. population, 370,000; Members, 120; Branches, 1; Percent LDS, .03, or one in 3,083; Europe West Area; Italy Catania Mission.

Located in the Mediterranean Sea, Malta is a republic with a population that speaks Maltese and English, and is mostly Roman Catholic. For the third time in recent history, the gospel is being taught in Malta.

When Apostle Lorenzo Snow was in charge of missionary work in Italy in the early 1850s, he saw the island as a possible point of beginning for carrying the gospel to other countries in the region.

After a visit to Malta in 1852, he left Elders Jabez Woodard and Thomas Obray in charge of missionary efforts here. Between 1852 and 1856, some proselyting progress was made, and a branch of about 25 people came into existence. But there was intense opposition to the work, and when the Crimean War scattered most of the British military personnel who had joined the Church, missionary efforts on the island ceased.

More than a century later, in 1979, a second effort on Malta was undertaken when the Italy Catania Mission sent Elders Victor Bonnici (of Maltese descent) and Paul Anderson to the island. They had good contacts among the island's nearly 350,000 inhabitants, but because of visa problems were unable to stay long enough to establish a branch.

Then in early 1988, Elder Rodger and Sister Helen Gunn were sent as a missionary couple to Malta. Assisted by two elders from the mission, they baptized several Maltese people, established a branch and sponsored cultural evenings and a family history seminar.

The branch, under the direction of early convert Pres. Emanuel d'Emanuele, met in an old villa near Naxxar. Another milestone in 1993 came when the Malta Branch held its first branch conference, presided over by Pres. G. Robert Dewitt of the Italy Catania Mission.

Sources: *Encyclopedic History of the Church,* by Andrew Jenson; *Church News,* Jan. 12, 1974; "Soldier converts," by Ronald W. Walker, *Church News,* April 21, 1979; "A Valiant Little Band: LDS Soldiers in the Crimean War," by Wilford Hill LeCheminant, *Ensign,* Jan. 1981; *A History of the Discontinued Mediterranean Missions of the Church,* by Ralph L. Cottrell Jr., a BYU master's thesis, 1983; *Church News,* Dec. 3, 1993.

MARSHALL ISLANDS

Year-end 1999: Est. population, 56,000; Members, 3,369; Districts, 2; Branches, 10; Percent LDS, 6, or one in 17; Philippines/Micronesia Area; Micronesia Guam Mission.

A republic, the Marshall Islands are made up of two atoll chains in the South Pacific.

MAJURO

Elders William Wardel and Steven Cooper arrived in Majuro Feb. 3, 1977, and they baptized Misao Lokeijak, who had been introduced to the Church in Hawaii. By the end of 1977, there were 27 converts on the island. The Laura Branch was created May 11, 1978, with Misao Lokeijak as president. By the end of 1979, there were 177 members. Meetinghouses for the Laura and Rita branches were started in September 1984 and dedicated Jan. 13-14, 1986, respectively. By 1987, Majuro had a district with five branches. By 1990, Majuro had 1,100 members.

In May 1992, BYU and the Republic of Marshall Islands agreed to have BYU give special training for government administrators and teachers.

KWAJALEIN/EBEYE

The Kwajalein Island Branch in the Marshall Islands was organized in 1978, made up entirely of U.S. citizens serving in the military or as civil service personnel. Missionaries opened the island of Ebeye on May 16, 1989, and Elders Kepiloni Foliaki and Michael Steele baptized Mary Kekuhuna on Jun 11, 1989.

ARNO AND MILI

Arno and Mili, located at the eastern end of Micronesia, some 2,200 miles west of Hawaii, are part of the 28-island Marshall group. In 1994, the Church had four branches in the Marshall Islands and three Church-owned meetinghouses.

Source: *Brief History of the Micronesia-Guam Mission,* published by the Micronesia Guam Mission, 1990, Lewis V. Nord, president.

MAURITIUS

Year-end 1999: Est. population, 1,127,000; Members, 277; Branches, 1; Percent LDS, .02, or one in 4,069; Africa Southeast Area; South Africa Durban Mission.

East of Madagascar in the Indian Ocean, Mauritius is a subtropical island with a parliamentary democracy, whose population speaks English, French, Creole, Hindi, Urdu, Hakka. and Bojpoori, and is 51 percent Hindu, 30 percent Christian,and 16 percent Muslim.

Elder George Kershaw, an LDS settler in South Africa, served two months in Mauritius in 1856. His only known converts were an army private and seven or eight members of the crew of the ship on which he arrived.

In modern times, missionary work began in the Mascarenes in 1979 under the direction of the International Mission. In 1986, the islands were transferred to the South Africa Johannesburg Mission.

Elder Joseph T. and Sister Ruth Edmunds, and Elder Theo and Sister Nita Verhaarens visited the island briefly. The first branch was established on Feb. 25, 1982, by Elder Preston and Sister Isabelle Gledhill, the first full-time missionaries on the island. The Mascarene Islands Mission was created July 1, 1988, at which time there were 400 members on the islands in three branches in Reunion and two in Mauritius. Headquarters of the mission was transferred to Durban, South Africa, in January 1992.

Sources: *Church News*, Sept. 21, 1986, Feb. 7, 1987, Oct. 24, 1987, Nov. 5, 1987, March 19, 1988, Dec. 17, 1988; "Tropical Isles receive best news as mission opens," by Allen W. Palmer, *Church News*, Nov. 5, 1988; "At Home on the Island of Mauritius," by Lori Palmer, *Ensign*, March, 1991; *Church News*, Jan 1, 1998.

MEXICO

Year-end 1999: Est. population, 93,9863,000; Members, 846,931; Stakes, 179; Wards, 1,242; Branches, 472; Missions, 18; Districts, 40; Temples, 10 (2 under construction); percent LDS, .9 or one in 111.

In southern North America, Mexico is a federal republic with a Spanish-speaking population that is 97 percent Roman Catholic.

In 1874, Daniel W. Jones and Henry Brizzee were called by Brigham Young to translate the Book of Mormon into Spanish. They struggled in the process until a convert, Meliton G. Trejo, arrived in Salt Lake City to assist them. They printed "Trozos Selectos del Llibro de Mormon[Short Selections from the Book of Mormon]." In 1875, seven missionaries were sent to Mexico. On the way, they preached to Indians and sent a favorable report that led to founding Mesa, Ariz. Rebuffed in Mexico at first in 1876, the missionaries divided into two groups. The first, Daniel W. Jones, James Z. Stewart, Helaman Pratt, Anthony W. Ivins and Wiley Jones, traveled to Chihuahua, where they were well-received. There, they scouted settlement sites and mailed pamphlets containing translated sections of the Book of Mormon to 500 influential leaders throughout Mexico. They found many listeners among the mountain villages and among the Indians, but did not baptize. Helaman Pratt and George Terry attempted to preach to the Yaqui Indians, but were not allowed. However, Louis Garff and Meliton G. Trejo traveled to Hermosillo, Sonora, where they baptized the first five members in Mexico and returned home.

Dr. Plotino C. Rhodakanaty of Mexico City received a tract from the original Jones expedition and began corresponding with Meliton Trejo. Rhodakanaty claimed a group of 20 believers and asked for missionaries to baptize them. Apostle Moses Thatcher and Elders Trejo and James Z. Stewart were sent to Mexico City, where on Nov. 20, 1879, they baptized Rhodakanaty and Silviano Arteaga, organized a branch and placed Rhodakanaty over it. By 1880, more literature had been translated. Political difficulties in Utah and changing moods in Mexico resulted in less success in Mexico City. Missionaries left Mexico City, and found converts in the small rural town of Ozumba. Additional missionaries arrived, and despite setbacks, the work moved forward in the states of Hidalgo, Mexico, and Morelos.

In 1885, a group of nearly 400 colonists from Utah arrived at the northern Mexico Casas Grandes River and acquired property. In 1887, members from central Mexico arrived at the colonies but found circumstances difficult and returned to their homes. Missionary efforts among the local population was closed in mid-1889. Mexico's first stake was created in Colonia Juarez among the English-speaking colonists in 1895. In 1901, Ammon M. Tenney became president of the Mexican Mission. Visiting village branches in Mexico, he found the early members still faithful. Branches were re-organized and by 1911, membership in the region reached 1,000. By 1912, more than 4,000 members had settled in Chihuahua and Sonora.

The Mexican Revolution halted much of the Church's progress, as Latter-day Saint colonists in the north left Mexico in 1912 to avoid the conflict, and members in central Mexico were left without leaders and were abused by conflicting armies. Two local leaders, Rafael Monroy and Vicente Morales, were executed because of their faithfulness to the Church.

When Rey L. Pratt returned to central Mexico in November 1917, he found the members had remained faithful despite extreme hardship. Work again progressed, but in 1926 all foreign clerics were expelled from Mexico. Local Mexican leaders again maintained stability and expanded the work, calling six local missionaries in 1930. In 1936, however, a group called the Third Convention broke away from the Church for a period, but was reunited under the leadership of mission Pres. Arwell Pierce. In 1946 President George Albert Smith visited the members. Membership then was more than 5,300.

During the next two decades membership increased as local priesthood holders were called to more leadership positions, and the missionary zeal of the Mexican members was manifest.

On June 10, 1956, the Mexican Mission was divided and the Northern Mexico Mission was created. On Dec. 3, 1961, the Mexico Stake was created, the first Spanish-speaking stake in the Church. Six years later, Agricol Lozano became the first local stake president in Mexico. Membership then in the country was about 25,000.

Church schools were established in 1959; the capstone of these was the large preparatory school, Benemerito in Mexico City, which was started in 1963, and its first class was graduated Nov. 27, 1966. This educational flagship of the Church in Mexico helped the Church advance in leadership and reputation.

In the late 1960s, membership began to expand rapidly. By 1972, it reached 100,000. In February 1977, President Spencer W. Kimball spoke at area conferences in Monterrey and Mexico City, Mexico, as part of a monthlong seven-nation tour that took him 13,000 miles. Nearly 25,000, the largest congregation ever to attend an area conference during the 10 years they were held from 1971-80, participated in the Mexico City conference. While in Mexico City, President Kimball visited with President Jose Lopez Portillo at the national palace, built on the site of the Aztec emperor Montezuma's headquarters.

On April 3, 1976, a temple was announced for Mexico City and was dedicated Dec. 2, 1983. At that time, membership in Mexico was conservatively placed about 240,000. Mexico was the first country outside the United States to reach 100 stakes. When the 100th stake was created at Tecalco July 25, 1989, membership in Mexico was estimated to be more than half a million. In 1992, Mexico made Church history when it became the first nation outside the United States to be divided into two areas, Mexico North and Mexico South.

Elder Waldo Call was called to the Seventy in 1985 from the original Mexican colonies, the first Mexican General Authority. He was followed in 1989 by Elder Horacio Tenorio, the first of Mexican ancestry to be called as a General Authority.

A historic and significant event occurred June 29, 1993, when the Mexican government formally registered the Church, allowing it to own property. The recognition was granted at a ceremony presided over by Patrocinio Gonzalez Garrido, Secretary of Government. Instrumental in gaining the recognition for the Church was Agricol Lozano H., the Church's legal counsel in Mexico, who bore his testimony at the ceremony. The effort was under the direction of Elders F. Burton Howard and Angel Abrea of the Seventy, presidents of the Mexico North and Mexico South areas.

President Howard W. Hunter visited Mexico to create the Church's 2,000th stake, the Mexico City Contreras Stake, on Dec. 11, 1994. A second temple was announced for Mexico, in Monterrey, in December 1995. President Gordon B. Hinckley visited Veracruz Jan. 27-28, 1996, for a regional conference and addressed 9,000 members. He returned to Mexico frequently to address members. He visited the Mormon colonies June 5, 1997, and spoke at the centennial observance of Juarez Academy in Colonia Juarez. Returning to El Paso, Texas, to catch a flight back to Salt Lake City, President Hinckley conceived the plan for the small temples that he announced at general conference in October 1997.

President Hinckley returned to Mexico Nov. 8-13, 1997, and spoke to 54,000 members in Mexico City, Puebla, Villahermosa, Cancun, and Merida. During the trip, he met with Mexico President Dr. Ernesto Zedillo and foreign minister Jose Angel Gurria at the president's Los Pinos residence. The next year, shortly after a long trip to Africa, President Hinckley once again went to Mexico March 9-15, 1998, and visited the cities of Hermosillo, Ciudad Obregon, Culiacan, Guadalajara, Torreon, Leon, Ciudad Victoria, Monterrey, Chihuahua, and Ciudad Juarez in northern Mexico.

Flooding in Tapachula, Guasave, and Ciudad Acuna affected many LDS families in September 1998, and relief and assistance were provided by members of other stakes nearby. Flooding hit the southeast coastal area on Mexico in October 1999, forcing 3,500 members in eight stakes to temporarily evacuate from their homes. The Church provided 20,000 food boxes, enough to feed 100,000 people for a week, as well as clothing and emergency supplies.

Mexico, with 846,931 members in 1999, has the second largest LDS population of any country in the world, behind only the United States.

After the Church-wide announcement of small temples, temples were announced for Colonia Juarez in October 1997, Ciudad Juarez in May 1998, Hermosillo and Tampico in July 1998, Merida in September 1998, Villahermosa in October 1998, Oaxaca and Tuxtla Gutierrez in Feburary 1999, and Guadalajara and Veracruz in April 1999.

The temple in Colonia Juarez was dedicated March 6, 1999. The year 2000 was a milestone year for temple dedications in Mexico with eight temples dedicated during the year. The temple in Ciudad Juarez was dedicated Feb. 26, 2000, and in Hermosillo, Feb. 27, 2000. The Hermosillo temple was the 50th temple dedicated or rededicated by President Gordon B. Hinckley. Other temple dedications during 2000 in Mexico were Oaxaca, March 11, 2000; Tuxtla Gutierrez, March 12, 2000; Tampico, May 20, 2000; Villahermosa, May 21, 2000; Merida, July 8, 2000; and Veracruz, July 9, 2000.

"This has been a spiritual 'watershed' year in Mexico," said Elder Lynn A. Mickelsen of the Seventy and president of the Mexico North Area.

Sources: *Historia Del Mormonismo en Mexico,* by Agricol Lozano; Tecalco history, unpublished history by "Ixta" and "Popo" wards; extensive selections from journals, publications and histories courtesy Gerry R. Flake; multiple other published and unpublished papers and books and *Church News* articles; "Emotional farewell in Mexico,"*Church News,* Feb. 19, 1977; "Prophet Meets Latin Leaders," *Church News,* March 5, 1977, both by Dell Van Orden; "Mexico formally registers Church," *Church News,* July 17, 1993; *Church News,* Dec. 17, 1994, Feb. 3, 1996, June 14, 1997, Nov. 15, 1997; "Los Primeros: Mexico's Pioneer Saints," by F. LaMond Tullis, *Ensign,* July 1997. Corrections by El Museo de Historia del Mormonismo en Mexico, A.C.; *Church News,* March 14, 1998, March 21, 1998, Aug. 1, 1998, Oct. 16, 1999, Oct. 30, 1999. March 4, 2000, March 18, 2000, May 27, 2000, July 15, 2000; "New temples in Mexico are making eternal impact in thousands of lives," by Jason Swensen, *Church News,* Aug. 12, 2000.

Stakes — 182

(Listed alphabetically by area as of Oct. 1, 2000.)

No.	Name	Organized	First President
Mexico North Area — 81			
1640	Aguascalientes Mexico	17 May 1987	Jose Luis Rios A.
2472	Aguascalientes Mexico Jardines	31 May 1998	

941	Celaya Mexico	11 Jun 1978	Armando Gaona
782	Chihuahua Mexico	13 Nov 1976	Gustavo Ulises Cortez S.
1633	*Chihuahua Mexico Chuviscar	14 Nov 1989	
	‡Chihuahua Mexico East	1 Mar 1987	Humberto Enrique Serna G.
1736a	Chihuahua Mexico Tecnologico	26 Nov 1989	Arturo Galindo Rubalcava
1109	Ciudad Juarez Mexico East	24 Feb 1980	Armando Arzate Saldana
2264	Ciudad Juarez Mexico	10 Nov 1996	Jesus Octavio Seanez Flores
	La Cuesta		
1699	Ciudad Juarez Mexico North	9 Oct 1988	Luis Carlos Gomez M.
783	*Ciudad Juarez Mexico South	9 Oct 1988	
	‡Ciudad Juarez Mexico	14 Nov 1976	Sergio Armando de la Mora M.
1301	*Ciudad Mante Mexico	25 Jan 1982	
	‡Mante Mexico	1 Nov 1981	Humberto Noriega F.
772	Ciudad Obregon Mexico	10 Oct 1976	Jorge Mendez I.
1712	Ciudad Obregon Mexico Nainari	19 Feb 1989	Jesus Angulo Montoya
1500	Ciudad Obregon Mexico Yaqui	28 Oct 1984	Jorge Mendez Ibarra
797	Ciudad Victoria Mexico	12 Dec 1976	Jesus Martinez T.
1742	Colonia Dublan Mexico	25 Feb 1990	Carl L. Call
37	*Colonia Juarez Mexico		
	‡Juarez	9 Dec 1895	Anthony W. Ivins
838	Culiacan Mexico	22 May 1977	Federico Fragoza Diaz
1710	Culiacan Mexico Humaya	12 Feb 1989	Jose Exaltacion Astorga E.
1644	Culiacan Mexico Tamazula	21 Jun 1987	Rosario Lobo
1707	Delicias Mexico	18 Dec 1988	Sergio Trejo L.
1228	Durango Mexico	21 Jan 1981	Ernesto Padilla Lozano
2057	Durango Mexico Del Valle	28 May 1995	Miguel Angel Martinez Macias
1761	*Ensenada Mexico	8 Aug 1990	
	‡Tijuana Mexico Ensenada	24 Jun 1990	Jose Pedroza A.
935	Gomez Palacio Mexico	28 May 1978	Ruben Martinez A.
1749	Gomez Palacio Mexico	6 May 1990	Magdaleno Sanchez S.
	La Laguna		
1183	Guadalajara Mexico	27 Sep 1980	Felipe Covarrubias S.
	Independencia		
2474	Guadalajara Mexico Lomas	7 Jun 1998	Sergio Miguel Anaya
2495	Guadalajara Mexico Mirador	20 Sep 1998	Jose Romero Gutierrez
2457	Guadalajara Mexico	3 May 1998	Americo Garcia Soto
	Moctezuma		
1753	Guadalajara Mexico Reforma	3 Jun 1990	Jose Saavedra T.
2482	Guadalajara Mexico		
	Tlaquepaque	21 Jun 1998	Rogelio Martinez
683	*Guadalajara Mexico Union	28 Sep 1980	
	‡Guadalajara Mexico	23 Feb 1975	Emilio Garcia L.
2044	Guadalajara Mexico Victoria	30 Apr1995	Luis Ruben Castrejon Bonilla
1779	Guaymas Mexico	18 Nov 1990	Ruben A. Palestino
771	Hermosillo Mexico	8 Oct 1976	Hector Ceballos L.
1636	Hermosillo Mexico Pitic	26 Apr 1987	Carlos Pineda O.
1232	*Irapuato Mexico	24 Mar 1992	
	‡Leon Mexico	8 Feb 1981	Armando Gaona J.
1734b	*La Paz Mexico	30 Jan 1990	
	‡Finisterra Mexico	10 Sep 1989	Antonio Aguilar V.
2220	Leon Mexico	11 Aug 1996	Alberto Galo de Jesus Romo Gonzalez
1139	Los Mochis Mexico	25 May 1980	Victor Manuel Soto
1714	Los Mochis Mexico El Fuerte	5 Mar 1989	Ezequiel Fernando Ramirez Q.
795	Madero Mexico	11 Dec 1976	Gabriel Raymundo Saldivar F.
1131	Matamoros Mexico	18 May 1980	Luciano Ramirez
1718	Mazatlan Mexico	7 May 1989	Jose Alberto Holcombe I.
819	Mexicali Mexico	20 Mar 1977	Eduardo Del Rio P.
1626	Mexicali Mexico Los Piños	18 Jan 1987	Jose de Jesus Ruelas U.
644	Monclova Mexico	26 May 1974	Francisco Aragon Garza
774	Monterrey Mexico Anahuac	17 Oct 1976	Lehi Gracia L.
2571	Monterrey Mexico Andalucia	3 Sep 2000	Francisco Rivera Davila
572	*Monterrey Mexico Libertad	17 Oct 1976	
	*Monterrey Mexico East		
	‡Monterrey East	7 May 1972	Jose Humberto Gonzalez
1765	Monterrey Mexico Los Angeles	22 Jul 1990	Carlos Charles Plata

508	*Monterrey Mexico Mitras	8 Jun 1980	
	*Monterrey Mexico		
	‡Monterrey	22 Mar 1970	Guillermo G. Garza
1114	Monterrey Mexico Moderna	9 Mar 1980	Mauro Garcia Herrera
1144	Monterrey Mexico Morelos	8 Jun 1980	Carlos R. Merino D.
908	Monterrey Mexico Paraiso	23 Apr 1978	Alfredo Gallegos L.
773	Monterrey Mexico Roma	16 Oct 1976	Jose Humberto Gonzalez G.
1615	Monterrey Mexico Valle Verde	2 Nov 1986	Jose F. Torres M.
2425	Morelia Mexico	4 Jan 1998	Juan Alberto Gonzalez S.
2443	Nuevo Laredo Mexico	15 Mar 1998	Santiago Vazquez Davalos
1716	Papantla Mexico	23 Apr 1989	Antonio Casino C.
857	Piedras Negras Mexico	21 Aug 1977	Fidencio Guzman Lugo
730	Poza Rica Mexico	13 Nov 1975	Jose Luis Pichardo M.
799	Poza Rica Mexico Palmas	15 Jan 1977	Angel Valle G.
1132	Reynosa Mexico	18 May 1980	Noe Flores Silva
1767	Saltillo Mexico Miravalle	12 Aug 1990	Edmundo Rodriguez Pena
1155	Saltillo Mexico Republica	29 Jun 1980	Roberto Teodoro Guzman R.
1231	San Luis Potosi Mexico	1 Feb 1981	Guillermo G. Soubervielle R.
2214	*San Luis Potosi Benito Juarez	27 Aug 1996	
	Benito Juarez Mexico	4 Aug 1996	Victor Joaquin Herrejon Faburrieta
2268	San Nicolas Mexico	17 Nov 1996	Abelardo Morales Mendez
567	*Tampico Mexico		
	‡Tampico	27 Feb 1972	Guillermo Garmendia
2123	Tampico Mexico Bosque	12 Nov 1995	Luis Eduardo de Leon de Leon
2296	Tepic Mexico	15 Dec 1996	Jose A. Prida Herrma
757	Tijuana Mexico	23 May 1976	Carlos Mendez S.
2248	Tijuana Mexico Insurgentes	13 Oct 1996	Jorge Mendez Ibarra
1587	*Tijuana Mexico La Mesa	15 Apr 1986	
	‡La Mesa Mexico	9 Feb 1986	Angel Luevano Cordova
781	Torreon Mexico	12 Nov 1976	David Limon Miranda
1532	Torreon Mexico Jardin	12 May 1985	Rafael Leon Miranda
1736	Torreon Mexico Reforma	15 Oct 1989	Miguel Angel Rivera C.
628	*Valle Hermosa Mexico		
	‡Valle Hermosa	28 Oct 1973	Benjamin Morales
2553	Zacatecas Mexico	16 Apr 2000	Jesus Antonio Madera L.
2242	Zamora Mexico	22 Sep 1996	Juan Lopez Tejeda

Mexico South Area — 101

735	Acapulco Mexico	24 Sep 1989	Francisco Javier Torres G.
2328	Acayucan Mexico	16 Mar 1997	Leonardo Hoyes Montiel
2485	Amecameca Mexico	28 Jun 1998	Cuauhtemoc Sanchez Pineda
1971	Atlixco Mexico	16 Jan 1994	Hector Garcia Ceballos
1474	Campeche Mexico	27 May 1984	Gabriel Francisco Ramos G.
2056	Cancun Mexico	28 May 1995	Victor Sebastian Roca Gomez
2456	Cancun Mexico Kabah	26 Apr 1998	Victor S. Roca Gomez
2343	Cardenas Mexico	20 Apr 1997	Raymundo Morales Barrera
722	Chalco Mexico	9 Nov 1975	Ruben Valenzuela G.
1822	Chetumal Mexico	27 Oct 1991	Raul Gaspar Rodriguez F.
2364	Chilpancingo Mexico	25 May 1997	Jesus Antonio Torrijos Acevedo
2518	Civac Mexico	21 Mar 1999	Saul Figueroa Lopez
1043a	Coatzacoalcos Mexico	1 Jul 1979	Raymundo Madris Carbajal
1766	Coatzacoalcos Mexico Puerto	29 Jul 1990	Raul Munoz Z.
721	Cuautla Mexico	9 Nov 1975	Juan Angel Alvaradejo
1983	*Cuautla Mexico Palmas	23 Jan 1996	
	‡Cuautla Mexico Aguahedionda	19 Jun 1994	Luis F. Rodriguez Trejo
2526	Cuautla Mexico Zapata	25 Apr 1999	Hugo Alberto Sanchez Morales
1427	Cuernavaca Mexico	5 Jun 1983	Sergio Rojas Espinoza
2107	Iguala Mexico	15 Oct 1995	Alberto Saucedo Roa
1589	Jalapa Mexico	2 Mar 1986	Jorge Sanchez
1764	Juchitan Mexico	22 Jul 1990	Gerardo Castellanos A.
2415	Juchitan Mexico Las Flores	23 Nov 1997	Wilfrido Orozco Ramirez
804	Merida Mexico	22 Jan 1977	Abel R. Ordaz R.
1728	Merida Mexico Centro	11 Jun 1989	Joaquin Eduardo Carrillo V.
1754	Merida Mexico Itzimna	10 Jun 1990	Mauro Jose Luis Gil P.

923	Merida Mexico Lakin	14 May 1978	Benigno Pena Pech
1603	Mexico City Mexico Anahuac	29 Jun 1986	Luis Manuel Angel B.
617	*Mexico City Mexico Aragon		
	‡Mexico City Aragon	27 May 1973	Agricol Lozano H.
658	Mexico City Mexico Arbolillo	15 Sep 1974	Guillermo Torres
1317	Mexico City Mexico Azteca	6 Dec 1981	Juan Alberta Ramos B.
719	Mexico City Mexico Camarones	8 Nov 1975	Jorge Rojas O.
2420	Mexico City Mexico Centenario	30 Nov 1997	Dominguez G. D. Rodriguez I.
1357	Mexico City Mexico Chapultepec	27 Jun 1982	Jose Ismael Ruiz G.
716a	Mexico City Mexico Churubusco	8 Nov 1975	Juan Casanova C.
2000	Mexico City Mexico Contreras	11 Dec 1994	Victor Manuel Salinas G.
1752	Mexico City Mexico Cuautepec	20 May 1990	Salvador Aguirre Osorio
1763	Mexico City Mexico Cuautitlan	8 Jul 1990	Victor M. Cardenas L.
1759	Mexico City Mexico Culturas	17 Jun 1990	Octavio Saul Morales A.
1663	Mexico City Mexico Ecatepec	6 Dec 1987	Juan Manuel Rodriguez C.
718	Mexico City Mexico Ermita	8 Nov 1975	Aurelio Valdespino O.
723	Mexico City Mexico Industrial	9 Nov 1975	Juan Roberto Alva
2403	Mexico City Mexico Iztapalapa	26 Oct 1997	Daniel Delgado Rios
1760	Mexico City Mexico La Perla	24 Jun 1990	Pedro Espinosa C.
965	Mexico City Mexico Linda Vista	8 Oct 1978	Fernando R. Dorantes T.
2522	Mexico City Mexico Lomas Verdes	18 Apr 1999	Omar Villalobos Saunders
2267	Mexico City Mexico Los Reyes	17 Nov 1996	I. Pedro Espinosa Cruz
1070	*Mexico City Mexico Meyehualco	11 Dec 1994	
	*Mexico City Mexico Iztapalapa	14 Oct 1979	Aurelio Valdespino
726	Mexico City Mexico Moctezuma	9 Nov 1975	Filiberto Ledezma M.
727	Mexico City Mexico Netzahualcoyotl	9 Nov 1975	Jaime Garay M.
1433	Mexico City Mexico Oriental	19 Jun 1983	Felipe Gerardo Ramirez N.
2404	Mexico City Mexico Pantitlan	26 Oct 1997	Luis R. Rosales Gonzalez
2307	Mexico City Mexico Prados	9 Feb 1997	Guillermo Velasco Coronado
717a	Mexico City Mexico Tacubaya	8 Nov 1975	Roman Gomez I.
2286	Mexico City Mexico Tecamac	1 Dec 1996	Francisco C. Salazar Sanchez
2477	Mexico City Tepalcapa	14 Jun 1998	Rafael Eduardo Ramos R.
720	*Mexico City Mexico Tlalnepantla	10 Oct 1978	
	‡Mexico City Mexico Satelite	9 Nov 1975	Horacio Tenorio O.
1356	Mexico City Mexico Tlalpan	27 Jun 1982	Jose Alberto Rasales G.
1579	Mexico City Mexico Valle Dorado	28 Nov 1985	Arturo Lopez G.
1980	Mexico City Mexico Vergel	15 May 1994	Ernesto Rosas Vazquez
724	Mexico City Mexico Villa de las Flores	9 Nov 1975	Juan Manuel Cedeno R.
2357	Mexico City Mexico Xalostoc	18 May 1997	Jose Luis Escobar Maya
715a	Mexico City Mexico Zarahemla	8 Nov 1975	Bonaerges Rubalcava E.
829	Minatitlan Mexico	15 May 1977	Ignacio Cruz S.
2329	Minatitlan Mexico Tecnologico	16 Mar 1997	Gabriel Garcia Gomez
1280	Oaxaca Mexico	21 Jun 1981	M. Ociel Bengoa Vargas
2209	Oaxaca Mexico Mitla	30 Jun 1996	Jose Luis Alonso Trejo
1685	Oaxaca Mexico Monte Alban	7 Feb 1988	Valentin Cruz B.
801	Orizaba Mexico	16 Jan 1977	Humberto Sanchez R.
1466	*Pachuca Mexico	13 Nov 1990	
	‡Mexico City Mexico Pachuca	18 Mar 1984	Alejandro Chavez Rodriguez
2158	Pachuca Mexico Centro	28 Jan 1996	Ismael Mendoza Regino
2225	Puebla Mexico Amalucan	25 Aug 1996	Jose Manuel de la Rosa Rojas
898	*Puebla Mexico Cholula	25 Sep 1997	
	Puebla Mexico Popocateptl	12 Mar 1978	Zeferino Tlatelpa
1293	Puebla Mexico Fuertes	11 Oct 1981	Francisco Pineda Salazar
2424	Puebla Mexico La Libertad	14 Dec 1997	Zeniff Mejia Mora
680	Puebla Mexico La Paz	16 Feb 1975	Santiago Mejia M.
2543	Puebla Mexico Mayorazgo	27 Feb 2000	Edgar Flores P.
1758	Puebla Mexico Nealtican	17 Jun 1990	Marcelino Osorio P.

681	Puebla Mexico Valsequillo	16 Feb 1975	Ramiro Goana M.
2037	Queretaro Mexico	19 Mar 1995	Glendon Lyons Castillo
2550	Queretaro Mexico Los Arcos	12 Mar 2000	Jose Cruz Pineda C.
2021	Salina Cruz Mexico	5 Feb 1995	Jose Ceferino Castillo Cupil
951	Tapachula Mexico	20 Aug 1978	Jorge David Arrevilla M.
1762	Tapachula Mexico Izapa	8 Jul 1990	Guillermo Sanchez R.
1730	Tecalco Mexico	25 Jun 1989	Felipe Hernandez L.
2521	Tehuacan Mexico	18 Apr 1999	Demesio de Jesus Rueda J.
2516	Teziutlan Mexico	7 Mar 1999	Alejandro Perez Alvarez
2439	Tizimin Mexico	1 Mar 1998	Samuel Ayala P.
2164	Tlaxcala Mexico	11 Feb 1996	Mosiah Saul Delgado Gonzalez
1829	Toluca Mexico	17 Nov 1991	Gilberto Lopez D'Antin
725	Tula Mexico	9 Nov 1975	Silvino Mera U.
1943	Tuxtepec Mexico	6 Jun 1993	Marcelo Valis Medina
1174	Tuxtla Gutierrez Mexico	31 Aug 1980	Enrique Sanchez Casillas
2515	Tuxtla Gutierrez Mexico Centro	28 Feb 1999	Mario Alberto Morales Z.
2028	Tuxtla Gutierrez Mexico Grijalva	26 Feb 1995	Moises Ulloa Solis
1653	Valle del Mezquital Mexico	13 Sep 1987	Joel Gandara Salazar
700	Veracruz Mexico	15 Jun 1975	Leon Lopez Alavez
1751	Veracruz Mexico Mocambo	20 May 1990	Fernando Lagunez V.
800	Veracruz Mexico Reforma	16 Jan 1977	Leon Lopez A.
2119	Veracruz Mexico Villa Rica	5 Nov 1995	Marco A. Carrillo Bogard
1166	Villahermosa Mexico	10 Aug 1980	Jose Luis Madrigal N.
1746	*Villahermosa Mexico Gaviotas	5 Oct 1993	
	‡Villahermosa Mexico Las Gaviotas	15 Apr 1990	Joaquin Gonzalez L.

Stakes discontinued

344 ‡Mexico City Mexico
Discontinued 8 Nov 1975 †Mexico City Mexico Churubusco (716a), Mexico City Mexico, Tacubaya (717a), Mexico City Mexico Ermita (718), Mexico City Mexico Chapultepec (No. 1357)

	*Mexico City	May 1967	
	‡Mexico	3 Dec 1961	Harold Brown
534	*Mexico City Mexico East	15 Nov 1970	Agricol Lozano

Discontinued 8 Nov 1975 †Chalco Mexico (No. 722), Mexico City Mexico Villa de las Flores (No. 724), Mexico City Mexico Moctezuma (726), Mexico City, Mexico Netzahualcoyotl (727)
‡Mexico City Mexico East

434	*Mexico City Mexico North		
	‡Mexico City North	7 May 1967	Agricol Lozano

Discontinued 8 Nov 1975 †Tampico Mexico (No. 567), Mexico City Mexico Camarones (No. 719), Mexico City Mexico Satelite (No. 720)

Missions — 18

(As of Oct. 1, 2000; shown with historical number. See MISSIONS.)

(208) MEXICO CHIHUAHUA MISSION
Sucursal 3 de Correos
Apartado Postal 3-41
Chihuahua, Chihuahua C.P. 31250, Mexico

(201) MEXICO CULIACAN MISSION
A.P. 645 Rio Mocorito 251 Ote.
Colonia Guadalupe
Culiacan, Sinaloa C.P. 80000, Mexico

(125) MEXICO GUADALAJARA MISSION
Apartado Postal 22-3
C.P. 44290
Guadalajara, Jalisco Mexico

(56) MEXICO HERMOSILLO MISSION
Apartado Postal 557
Hermosillo, Sonora, C.P. 83000
Mexico

(222a) MEXICO LEON MISSION
Apartado Postal 1-1125
Leon, Gto 37000
Mexico

(126) MEXICO MERIDA MISSION
Apartado Postal 26 y 27
CAP Terminal
Merida, Yucatan C.P. 97003
Mexico

(193) MEXICO MEXICO CITY
EAST MISSION
Fuente de Piramides No. 1, Piso 1,
Lomas de Tecamachalco
Naucalpan, Edo. de Mexico C.P. 53950
Mexico

(20) MEXICO MEXICO CITY
SOUTH MISSION
Monte Caucaso 1110
Lomas de Chapultepec
Mexico D.F., C.P. 11000, Mexico

(209) MEXICO TUXTLA GUTIERREZ MIS.
Apartado 278
Tuxtla Gutierrez, Chiapas CP 29000
Mexico

(276) MEXICO MONTERREY SOUTH
MISSION
Calle Chiapas #2202
Colonia Roma Sur,
Monterrey, Nuevo Leon, 64700, Mexico

(217) MEXICO PUEBLA MISSION
Calle 25 Sur # 907
Col. La Paz
Puebla, Puebla 72160
Mexico

(247) MEXICO TIJUANA MISSION
PMB 157 POB 439056
San Diego,
CA 92143-9056

(163) MEXICO MEXICO CITY
NORTH MISSION
Fuente de Piramides #1, Piso 1
Lomas de Tecamachalco,
Edo. de Mexico C.P. 53950
Mexico

(45)
MEXICO MONTERREY NORTH MISSION
Calle Cerralvo 134
Colonia Libertad
Cd. Guadelupe, Nuevo Leon, CP 67130,
Mexico

(75) MEXICO VERACRUZ MISSION
Apartado Postal 103
Veracruz, Veracruz CP 91700
Mexico

(246) MEXICO OAXACA MISSION
Huerta de los Olivos #100
Fracc. Trinidad de las Huertas
Oaxaca,
Oaxaca, C.P. 68120
Mexico

(218) MEXICO TAMPICO MISSION
Apartado Postal 241
Cd. Madero, Tamaulipas C.P. 89460
Mexico

(81) MEXICO TORREON MISSION
Apartado Postal 792
Torreon, Coahuila C.P. 29000
Mexico

MICRONESIA

Year-end 1999: Est. population, 123,000; Members, 3,008; Districts, 4; Branches, 18; Percent LDS, 2.45, or one in 41; Pacific Islands Area; Micronesia Guam Mission.

Extending along the 1,800-mile Caroline Islands archipelago in the Pacific east of the Philippines, the Federated States of Micronesia has a culturally diverse population that speaks eight island dialects.

CHUUK

In Chuuk (Truk), two missionaries, Elders Don Baldwin and Torlik Tima, arrived, July 7, 1977. They baptized T. M. Conrad Mailo and his wife, Nisor Cerly David, on Oct. 22, 1977. The first Trukese missionary was Happiness Ichin, the second convert on the island. By 1980, membership reached 170, and on May 31, 1981, the Truk-Pohnpei District was created. A meetinghouse was dedicated April 24, 1983. By 1990, the district had been divided, and two meetinghouses dedicated.

A visit to Micronesia by Michaelene P. Grassli, Primary general president, and Virginia H. Pearce, board member, in June 1991, included stops in Chuuk, Pohnpei, Kosrae, and Kwajalein.

KOSRAE

Work in Kosrae began in March 1985, but missionaries found little success. They worked hard to break down public opinion against the Church. The first Kosraen, Isidro Abraham, was baptized April 26, 1986. By October 1989 when a branch conference was held at Lela, 72 people attended. Kosrae became a district on March 14, 1990. The first seminary graduation took place on Aug. 1, 1990. Ground was broken for the Malem meetinghouse on Dec. 21, 1989, and the facility was dedicated Dec. 3, 1992. The Lelu meetinghouse was dedicated in January 1993.

POHNPEI

Pohnpei Island was opened to missionary work on Oct. 23, 1976, when Elders George

L. Mortensen and Aldric Porter arrived. The first baptism on the island, however, did not occur until Feb. 7, 1981. Missionary work progressed steadily and the Pohnpei District was created Nov. 22, 1985. In 1990, membership was 464. In late 1993, 18 young women in the Pohnpei District held their first camp on the island of Madolenihmn.

YAP

The Church came to Yap in 1977, when Charles Keliikipi, under contract to organize a police department on the island, was assigned to organize the Church here. The first missionaries, Elders David S. Ige and Douglas Andrews, came that year as well. The first convert was baptized in March 1978, and afterwards several families came into the Church. The first missionary couple was Elder Claude W. and Sister Ada I. Stuart, who arrived Aug. 2, 1979. A meetinghouse was completed Jan. 13, 1981. By 1990, membership on the island was 150. The first seminary graduation on Yap was held Aug. 16, 1990.

Sources: *Church News,* Jan 9, 1952; *Unto the Isles of the Sea,* by R. Lanier Britsch; *Church News,* March 4, 1989; *Brief History of the Micronesia-Guam Mission,* published by the Micronesia Guam Mission, 1990, Lewis V. Nord, president; "Visit to area reveals growing gospel roots," by Sheridan R. Sheffield, *Church News,* June 22, 1991; *Church News,* Nov. 13, 1993.

MONGOLIA

Year-end 1999: Est. population, 2,494,000; Members, 1,850; Missions, 1; Districts, 1; Branches, 9; Percent LDS, .74, or one in 1,348, Asia Area.

In east central Asia between Russia and China, Mongolia is a republic with a population that speaks Mongolian and traditionally follows Lama Buddhist beliefs.

Elder Monte J. Brough of the Asia Area presidency met with top government officials and the directors of five universities in May and August 1992. Afterward, six missionary couples were sent to assist the country's higher education program and to teach others about the Church. The first couples arrived Sept. 16, 1992, and lived in Ulaanbaatar, the capital city, which is home to half the population of Mongolia. Elder Kenneth H. Beesley, former president of LDS Business College in Salt Lake City, Utah, and his wife, Donna, headed the couples. The first sacrament meeting was held Sept. 20, 1992, in Elder and Sister Beesley's apartment. The Ulaanbaatar Branch was organized in 1993. The first converts were Lamjav Purevsuren and Tsendkhuu Bat-Ulzii, who were baptized Feb. 6, 1993.

The first six missionary couples to arrive included the Beesleys, Royce P. and Mary Jane Flandro, Richard G. and Anna M. Harper, Stanley B. and Marjorie Smith, C. DuWayne and Alice C. Schmidt, and Gary and Barbara L. Carlson. The first full-time elders were Bart Jay Birch, Duane Lee Blanchard, Brett Andrew Hansen, Jared K. Meier, Curtis Dee Mortensen, and Bradley Jay Pierson.

On April 15, 1993, Elder Neal A. Maxwell of the Quorum of the Twelve and Elder Kwok Yuen Tai of the Seventy visited Mongolia. Fifty government officials attended a reception that evening hosted by the Church.

A foundation representing the Church was legally registered Jan. 17, 1994, and efforts continue to have the Church fully recognized.

By March 1, 1996, attendance at the branch averaged between 85 and 110. Among the early converts were a professor at Mongolian University of Art, editor of an English-language newspaper, a veterinarian, a physician, and a computer operator. The Mongolia Ulaanbaatar Mission was created July 1, 1995, with Richard E. Cook (who was called to the Second Quorum of the Seventy in 1997) serving as president.

Seminary and institute classes for the youth in Mongolia began in 1996. Missionaries from Mongolia served on Temple Square in Salt Lake City and helped translate the scriptures into Mongolian.

On June 6, 1999, a well-known building in Ulaanbaatar, was dedicated by Elder Cook as the first LDS meetinghouse in Mongolia. A historical landmark, the building, before it was remodeled into a meetinghouse, was most widely known as the "Children's Cinema," and had been featured on postage stamps and in magazines.

In 1999, membership in Mongolia was 1,850 in nine branches.

Mongolian government leaders made an appeal in 2000 for international assistance, after a severe winter, followed by the worst drought in 60 years. In response, the Church sent three shipping containers of clothing and quilts, in addition to 8,000 food boxes.

Source: *Church News,* Sept. 19, 1992; correspondence from Elder Kenneth H. Beesley to Asia Area presidency, Feb. 24, 1994; *Church News,* May 31, 1997; "Testimonies burn brightly: Mongolia," by Sarah Jane Weaver, *Church News,* Feb. 22, 1997; "Well-known building is first meetinghouse in Mongolia," by Mary N. Cook, *Church News,* July 3, 1999; *Church News,* May 27, 2000.

Mission — 1

(As of Oct. 1, 2000; shown with historical number. See MISSIONS.)

(307) MONGOLIA ULAANBAATAR MISSION
Box #258
Ulaanbaatar 210644
Mongolia

Church Pouch for letters
POB 30150
Salt Lake City, UT84130-0150

MOZAMBIQUE

Year-end 1999: Est. population, 18,115,000; Members, 311, Branches, 3; Africa Southeast Area.

A country on the southeast coast of Africa, Mozambique covers 309,496 square miles and has a population of more than 18 million. Almost all Mozambicans are Africans and speak one of the Bantu languages, although fewer than 1 percent of the population are minorities. The country's official language is Portuguese.

About 55 percent of the people practice tribal African religions. About 30 percent are Christians, mostly Roman Catholics. Many are Muslims.

The Church was legally recognized in Mozambique in 1996. But prior to that, people in Mozambique benefited from Church humanitarian aid. A deadly drought, the worst in 100 years, caused great suffering in Mozambique and in neighboring countries. In 1992, the Church shipped 1 million pounds of food and relief items for victims of the drought in this area.

Sources: World Book Encyclopedia, vol. 13, pp. 904-905; 1996 correspondence from Elder James O. Mason, Africa Area president and member of the Seventy; "Deadly drought," *Church News,* Sept. 26, 1992.

NAMIBIA

Year-end 1999: Est. population, 1,652,000; Members, 261; Branches, 1; Africa Southeast Area; South Africa Cape Town Mission; percentage LDS .002, or one in 6,329

The Republic of Namibia in Southern Africa became an independent nation March 20, 1990, and has a population that speaks Afrikaans, English, and indigenous languages. Namibians are 50 percent Lutheran and 30 percent other Christian.

Namibia, which prior to independence was known as South West Africa, did not have a formal LDS Church organization until 1973, when Otto Krauss was called as the presiding elder. The first Church meeting had been held in the Krauss home in April 1972. The first missionaries in Namibia were Elders Daniel Gustafson and Douglas Stone, who arrived in 1978. The first baptism was Vernon Collett, and the first branch was organized in Windhoek in 1983, with Dieter Greiner as the first branch president. The first missionary called from Namibia was Andre Van der Merwe, who began serving in the South Africa Johannesburg Mission in 1992. The first district was formed in 1991, with Elder A. Eugene Hilton as the first district president. However, the district was dissolved in 1992.

A few weeks before Namibia gained its independence, four elders and one couple began proselyting in Windhoek. At the time there were fewer than 20 members in the entire country. Namibian President-elect Sam Nujoma had stated at the time of independence that missionaries were welcome in his country.

Converts were steadily added to the Windhoek and Rehoboth branches, and about 100 people attended each branch, as of October 1991.

Leaders reported that the branches frequently have more people attending than are on the records. A Scouting program was organized in Windhoek that provides wholesome activities for the young men. Relief Society sisters took part in an educational program for less-fortunate women during a service project in 1992-93.

In 1995, the seminary program was begun. On Feb. 18, 1996, members from Namibia joined some 5,000 other Latter-day Saints for the Johannesburg Regional Conference — the largest such gathering in South Africa.

Sources: Brief history of Namibia prepared in 1994 by Elder Darol D. Allred, executive secretary of the Windhoek Branch and full-time missionary with his wife, Beth; "Gospel springs forth in harsh desert land of new Africa nation," by Mark Newman and Greg Hagen, *Church News,* Oct. 5, 1991; "Four nations in central, southern Africa," by Mary Mostert and Gerry Avant, *Church News* Sept. 26, 1992, *Church News,* March 2, 1996, March 9, 1996.

NAURU

Year-end 1999: Est. population, 10,000; Members, 96; Branches, 1; Pacific Islands Area; Fiji Suva Mission.

A republic in the west Pacific Ocean just south of the Equator and near the Solomon Islands, Nauru is an island of 8.2 square miles bearing rich phosphate deposits. Its residents are mostly Christian who speak Nauruan. The Church arrived in Nauru in 1995 when Taoki Buautoa of Kiribati was set apart to preside over a branch when he traveled to Nauru to work for the phosphate company here. Other members from Kiribati also went to work for the company. A missionary couple, Elder Raymond Joseph and Sister Lorraine Kay Schmedes, traveled to Nauru in the summer of 1998 and helped establish seminary, and noted that the branch has recently called a Relief Society, Primary, Young Women and elders quorum presidents. They also interviewed and baptized eight people, including the wife of branch Pres. Takai Raieta. He and his counselor, Papua Ulisese, both returned missionaries, were given special permission to give the missionary lessons.

Source: Correspondence from Elder and Sister Schmedes and the Fiji Suva Mission, Sept. 28, 1998.

NETHERLANDS

Year-end 1999: Est. population, 15,453,000; Members, 7,627; Stakes, 3; Wards, 17; Branches, 26; Missions, 1; Temples, 1 announced; Percent LDS, .05, or one in 2,026.

In northwest Europe on the North Sea, The Netherlands, also known as Holland, is a constitutional monarchy with a Dutch-speaking population that is 36 percent Roman Catholic and 19 percent Dutch Reformed.

The Church's presence in The Netherlands goes back to 1841, when Elder Orson Hyde, while on a missionary journey to Jerusalem, spent more than a week in Rotterdam and Amsterdam explaining the gospel to Jewish rabbis.

The first missionaries assigned to labor in The Netherlands, Elders Paul Schettler and A.W. Vander Woude, arrived Aug. 5, 1861. By May 10, 1862, they had baptized 14 people in Amsterdam, and organized the first branch there.

For the first three years, the area was part of the Swiss-German Mission. The Netherlands Mission was established Nov. 1, 1864 and has been functioning ever since. The mission also serves the Flemish-speaking northern half of Belgium.

For many years, the Church was not allowed to own property in The Netherlands, and it remains difficult to obtain permits to purchase land for meetinghouses. Official recognition of the Church was received in August 1955, after nearly 20 years of petitioning. This was considered a major breakthrough, since legal recognition gives the Church the right to hold property, exempt from taxation, and a certain degree of stature.

The first non-English-speaking stake in the Church was organized in The Hague March 12, 1961. President Spencer W. Kimball spoke to 2,305 members at an area conference in Amsterdam Aug. 6-8, 1976, and met with the Dutch media at a press conference.

In the first 100 years of the Church in The Netherlands, some 4,500 missionaries served here, and more than 14,000 people were baptized. A large percentage of those converts immigrated to the United States. However, after more temples were constructed in Europe, few members emigrated, and today there are many second-, third-, and even fourth-generation members in the 17 wards and 26 branches. Elder Jacob de Jager, an emeritus member of the Seventy, was the first General Authority born in Holland.

More than 2,000 people attended the first regional conference held in The Netherlands in June 1984.

In 1990, Church members organized a food drive that resulted in the shipment of 12 large truckloads of food to Romania. LDS member Jeane Henny Kirschbaum received a royal golden medal of honor from the burgomaster of Heemstede in 1993 for her community service.

During the summer of 1995, members organized displays, offered workshops, and presented theme-centered entertainment for 650 visitors interested in learning to deal with youth problems, different lifestyles, and pressures affecting children. The purpose was to educate parents and increase their influence with their children while acquainting them with the Church.

The First Presidency announced Aug. 16, 1999, that a temple would be built in The Hague, the second smaller temple announced for continental Europe; the first smaller temple in Europe was announced in 1998 for Kiev, Ukraine.

In 1999, membership in The Netherlands was 7,627.

Sources: *Encyclopedic History of the Church,* by Andrew Jenson; *Church News,* March 11 and 25,

1961; *History of the Netherlands Mission 1861-1966,* by Keith C. Warner, a BYU thesis, August 1967; "Netherlands," *Ensign,* August, 1973; "Visits Bless Lands of World," by Dell Van Orden, *Church News,* Aug. 14, 1976; *Church News,* June 24, 1984, March 17, 1990, Nov. 20, 1993, July 29, 1995, Aug. 28, 1999.

Stakes — 3

(Listed alphabetically as of Oct. 1, 2000.)

No.	Name	Organized	First President
Europe Central Area			
1720	Apeldoorn Netherlands	14 May 1989	Max Henning Van Der Put
933	*Rotterdam Netherlands	16 Oct 1994	
	Utrecht Netherlands	28 May 1978	Eugene M. Engelbert
326	*The Hague Netherlands	12 Aug 1976	
	*The Hague Holland		
	‡Holland	12 Mar 1961	Johan Paul Jongkees

Mission — 1

(As of Oct. 1, 2000; shown with historical number. See MISSIONS.)

(8a) NETHERLANDS AMSTERDAM MISSION
Noordse Bosje 16
1211 BG Hilversum, Netherlands

NETHERLANDS ANTILLES

Year-end 1999: Est. population, 206,000; Members, fewer than 100; North America Southeast Area; West Indies Mission.

Made up of two groups of islands in the Caribbean, the Netherlands Antilles are considered part of The Netherlands. Work was opened and closed on Curacao in 1978-79 by the Venezuela Caracas Mission. However, a branch was created on Curacao Oct. 31, 1979. The branch was divided in April 1987, but was rejoined in January 1988. A meetinghouse was dedicated in August 1988.

Sources: Venezuela Caracas Mission manuscript history; "Book of Mormon now in 80 Languages," *Ensign,* March 1988; *Church News,* April 2, 1988.

ARUBA

Year-end 1999: Est. population, 66,000; Members, 230; Branches, 2; Percent LDS, .35, or one in 287; North America Southeast Area; West Indies Mission.

An autonomous member of The Netherlands, Aruba lies 18 miles off the coast of Venezuela. A branch was organized on Aruba Aug. 13, 1986, and missionaries were sent in January 1987. Selections of the Book of Mormon were translated into Papiamento in 1987, and coupled with activity by missionaries, brought a successful reactivation effort.

Sources: Venezuela Caracas Mission manuscript history; "Book of Mormon now in 80 Languages," *Ensign,* March 1988; *Church News,* April 2, 1988.

ST. MAARTEN

Year-end 1999: Est. population, 4,500; Members, 39; Branches, 1; Percent LDS, .35, or one in 283; North America Southeast Area; West Indies Mission.

The Island of St. Maarten in the Caribbean, with 20 square miles and an estimated population of 4,500, was part of the France Toulouse Mission when the St. Maarten Branch was organized Jan. 9, 1979. The mission was discontinued and work resumed with the West Indies Mission. Elders Thad Ariens and Victor Quarty began working in St. Maarten, the administration of which is divided between the Dutch and French governments. The Claire Dinane family, which was baptized on Guadeloupe, moved to St. Maarten and helped re-open the St. Maarten Branch on Jan. 31, 1984.

Source: Manuscript History of the France Toulouse Mission.

NEW CALEDONIA

(See FRANCE)

NEW ZEALAND

Year-end 1999: Est. population, 3,407,000; Members, 89,952; Stakes, 25; Wards, 145; Branches, 66; Missions, 2; Districts, 5; Temples, 1; Percent LDS, 2.64, or one in 38.

Located in the South Pacific in the Tasman Sea, New Zealand has a parliamentary government. Its English-speaking population is Anglican, 29 percent; Presbyterian, 18 percent; and Roman Catholic, 15 percent.

Augustus Farnham, president of the Australian Mission, accompanied by William Cooke, arrived in New Zealand Oct. 27, 1854, and preached for two months with little success in Auckland and Nelson. Elder Cooke then remained alone and in March 1855, baptized 10 people, and organized a branch at Karori in April. A few other missionaries followed, and a handful of converts immigrated to Utah. Persecution arose, and in 1871 the New Zealand parliament briefly considered the "Mormon invasion."

At first, missionary work centered among Europeans. At the end of 1880, seven branches had been established with 133 members. However, at this time President Joseph F. Smith of the First Presidency instructed missionaries to concentrate on the indigenous Maori people.

Mission Pres. William F. Bromley subsequently assigned Elders Alma Greenwood and Ira N. Hinckley Jr. to teach Maoris in the southern tip of the North Island.

Prior to the arrival of the missionaries to the Maoris, at least five Maori leaders, some of whom were Tohungas (spiritual leaders) while others were tribal wise men, had told of a "true religion" that would come. Because many beliefs of the Maoris and missionaries were similar, a number of Maoris were converted. The first conversions came in the Waikato region, but others soon followed. The first Maori baptized was Ngataki, on Oct. 18, 1881.

By the end of 1884, membership included 265 Europeans and 811 Maoris. Membership among the Maoris increased to nearly 4,000 in 79 branches by the turn of the 20th century, an almost all-Maori membership.

The Book of Mormon was translated into Maori in April 1889. The New Zealand Mission was created Jan. 1, 1898. In 1907, the First Presidency authorized a secondary school to add to the primary educational program that was previously established. The Maori Agricultural College was completed in 1913. It operated until 1931, when it was damaged beyond repair by an earthquake. Elder Matthew Cowley of the Quorum of the Twelve made many contributions to the Church as he served as missionary, mission president, and supervising General Authority of New Zealand.

By the mid-1930s, the Church had grown to 8,600. After World War II ended, the Church expanded beyond its primarily Maori membership, as many of European ancestry joined.

In 1948, Elder Cowley announced plans for a new school, and in February 1955, the First Presidency announced plans for a temple near Hamilton. Both facilities were largely constructed by labor missionaries. Dedicated in 1958 were the newly built temple on April 20, and the Church College of New Zealand on April 26. The first stake in New Zealand was created in Auckland May 18 of the same year. Membership at the time was 17,000 but grew to 26,000 during the next eight years. In 1968-70, the seminary program was established. Some 13,000 members attended an area conference in Temple View in 1976, at which President Spencer W. Kimball spoke. Three years later, President Kimball addressed 11,600 in area conferences in Auckland and Wellington Nov. 24-25, 27, 1979.

In 1987, Elder Douglas J. Martin, a former stake president from Hamilton, was called to the Second Quorum of the Seventy. Membership was 76,000 in 1990 and 89,952 in 1999.

President Gordon B. Hinckley spoke at a regional conference in Hamilton May 10-11, 1997, and addressed some 10,000 members in Auckland May 11. In Auckland, a cast of 220 from 10 stakes presented a sesquicentenntial production for some 8,000 people. A weeklong celebration was held in May in honor of the 40th anniversary of the Church College of New Zealand. Members also commemorated the 40th anniversary of the creation of the first stake outside North America, the Auckland Stake which was created in 1958.

Sources: *Zion in New Zealand* by Brian W. Hunt; *Encyclopedic History of the Church,* by Andrew Jenson; Origin of the Maori People in New Zealand, by Stewart Meha; *Church News*, Jan. 18, 1964, p. 6; *Church News,* May 9, 1936, p. 1; The Church in New Zealand, by Mervyn Dykes, *Ensign*, February 1976; *Church News*, May 17, 1997, Dec. 20, 1997, May 30, 1998, July 18, 1998.

Stakes — 25

(Listed alphabetically as of Oct. 1, 2000.)

No.	Name	Organized	First President
Australia/New Zealand Area			
630	Auckland N. Z. Harbour	4 Nov 1973	Kenneth M. Palmer
1304	Auckland N. Z. Henderson	8 Nov 1981	Alan Robert Patterson
861	Auckland N. Z. Manukau	18 Sep 1977	Oscar Westerlund
455	*Auckland New Zealand Manurewa		
	‡Auckland South	5 May 1968	Geoffrey R. Garlick

264	*Auckland New Zealand Mount Roskill ‡Auckland	18 May 1958	George R. Biesinger
1973	Auckland N. Z. Panmure	13 Feb 1994	Stephen Aubrey Keung
2222	Auckland N. Z. Papakura	25 Aug 1996	Moses Christopher Armstrong
2223	Auckland N.Z. Papatoetoe	25 Aug 1996	Ephraim Cooper
1664	Auckland N.Z. Tamaki	13 Dec 1987	Clark W. Palmerston Larkins
2305	Auckland N.Z. Waterview	9 Feb 1997	Panama Leauanae
953	Christchurch New Zealand	27 Aug 1978	Bardia Pine Taiapa
1104	Gisborne New Zealand	14 Feb 1980	William Pakimana Taurima
310	*Hamilton New Zealand ‡Hamilton	13 Nov 1960	Wendell H. Wiser
2001	Hamilton New Zealand Glenview	18 Dec 1994	Richard Saxon Ball
313	*Hastings New Zealand ‡Hawkes Bay	20 Nov 1960	Joseph Alvin Higbee
2103	Hastings N.Z. Flaxmere	15 Oct 1995	Lawrence Victor Maxwell
475	*Kaikohe New Zealand ‡New Zealand North (New Zealand)	19 Jan 1969	Stanley J. Hay
1012	Palmerston North N.Z.	18 Mar 1979	James Dunlop
2302	Porirua New Zealand	26 Jan 1997	Michael John Fermanis
884	Rotorua New Zealand	27 Nov 1977	Paul Robert Thomas
2304	Tauranga New Zealand	9 Feb 1997	Robert Solomon
445	*Temple View New Zealand ‡Hamilton South	19 Nov 1967	Harry S. Peckham
853	Upper Hutt New Zealand	14 Aug 1977	Trevor A. Beatson
407	*Wellington New Zealand ‡Wellington	12 May 1965	Keith A. Harrison
2002	Whangarei New Zealand	18 Dec 1994	Hira Paea Nepia Christy

Missions — 2

(As of Oct. 1, 2000; shown with historical number. See MISSIONS.)

(20) NEW ZEALAND AUCKLAND MISSION
P.O. Box 33-840
Takapuna, Auckland 9
New Zealand

(143) NEW ZEALAND WELLINGTON MISSION
P.O. Box 50448
Porirua
New Zealand

NICARAGUA

Year-end 1999: Est. population, 4,206,000; Members, 31,747; Stakes, 1; Wards, 7; Missions, 1; Districts, 11; Branches, 70; percent LDS, .75, or one in 132; Central America Area.

Located in Central America, the Republic of Nicaragua has a Spanish-speaking population that is 95 percent Roman Catholic.

Elder Spencer W. Kimball, then of the Quorum of the Twelve, promoted work in Central America that led to the opening of the Central America Mission in 1952. Two missionaries from that mission, Elders Manuel Arias and Archie R. Mortensen, entered Nicaragua in 1953. They encountered difficulties at first, but on April 11, 1954, baptized Jose D. Guzman. Other conversions followed. The Nicaraguan District was organized in 1959. The Managua Stake was organized March 22, 1981, but was discontinued on Oct. 15, 1989.

Missionary work was interrupted in September 1978, as internal conflicts and a civil war led to missionaries being withdrawn. Work continued under local missionaries, and full-time work resumed in the late 1980s. During the periods when few outside leaders entered the country, the local members continued faithfully. In the summer of 1987, members of the Managua Stake received government permission and traveled by bus to the Guatemala City Temple to do temple work.

When the Nicaragua Managua Mission was organized Oct. 15, 1989, following normalization of the government, membership was 3,453. By December 1990, membership had increased to 8,000 members, and by 1995, to 18,000. The members had 100 percent home teaching in the last three months of 1990, and 800 men were ordained to the Melchizedek Priesthood, reported Elder Ted E. Brewerton of the Seventy and area president. President Gordon B. Hinckley visited Nicaragua Jan. 21, 1997, and spoke to some 2,400 members. This was the first visit to Nicaragua of a Church president since 1954. An auto accident occurred there when a truck carrying unsecured aluminium beams stopped suddenly and the beams slid forward through the windows of the car carrying President and

Sister Hinckley. They were not injured.

The Managua stake was re-organized on June 21, 1998. In 1999, membership in Nicaragua was 31,747.

Sources: "LDS Scene," *Ensign*, November, 1978; "Church Continues to Progress in Nicaragua," *Ensign*, Feb. 1979; "A Prayer Answered," by William Hale Kehr, *Church News* May 19, 1979; "Nicaraguans eager to learn, improve lives through gospel," by Gerry Avant, *Church News*, Nov. 22, 1980; "Church Denies Charges in Nicaragua," *Ensign*, Oct. 1982; "Work is booming as members eagerly share their testimonies with friends," *Church News*, Feb. 16, 1991, Feb. 1, 1997.

Stake — 2

(Alphabetically as of Oct. 1, 1998.)

No.	Name	Organized	First President
2563	Chinandega Nicaragua	25 Jun 2000	Jose Ernesto Maravilla
2481	Managua Nicaragua	21 Jun 1998	Pedro Jose aviles Zapata

Stakees discontinued

1246 Managua Nicaragua 22 Mar 1981 Jose R. Armando Garcia A.
Discontinued 15 Oct 1989 †Nicaragua Managua Mission

Mission — 1

(As of Oct. 1, 2000; shown with historical number. See MISSIONS.)

(227) NICARAGUA MANAGUA MISSION
Apartado Postal 3527
Managua, Nicaragua C.A.

NIGERIA

Year-end 1999: Est. population, 101,232,000; Members, 42,746; Stakes, 11; Wards, 73; Branches, 112; Missions, 3; Districts, 13; temples, 1 announced; percent LDS, .4, or one in 2,368.

On the west coast of Africa bordering the Gulf of Guinea, the Federal Republic of Nigeria has a military government with a population that speaks English, Hausa, Yoruba, and Ibo. Three-fourths of the population is Muslim, with a large number of Christians in the southern half.

The restored gospel took root spontaneously in Nigeria two decades before it was formally preached in the country. Letters came to Church headquarters from Nigeria inquiring about the Church as early as 1946. From the late 1950s on, some Nigerians learned about the Church through magazine articles and acquired Church literature. Groups of people began meeting unofficially in the Church's name, and through the years some of them wrote to Church headquarters requesting missionaries. These groups had boards of directors and were legally registered. Glen G. Fisher, returning from serving as president of the South Africa Mission, visited Nigeria in 1960 and reported that the groups were sincere, and recommended sending missionaries. However, attempts to send missionaries were thwarted because visas were unavailable. LDS Sunday Schools were organized in 1966.

The historic revelation on the priesthood, announced June 9, 1978, was the catalyst for the start of missionary work in Nigeria. In August of that year, Merrill Bateman and Edwin Q. Cannon were sent to Nigeria on a fact-finding trip. In November, two couples — Elder and Sister Rendell N. Mabey and Elder and Sister Edwin Q. Cannon Jr. — were sent to Nigeria and Ghana as special representatives of the Church's International Mission. They arrived Nov. 9, and soon searched out and taught the gospel to people who had been meeting in the Church's name and praying for the coming of Church representatives. Although a number of Nigerians had been baptized abroad and later returned to Nigeria, the first to be baptized in Nigeria was Anthony Ozodimma Obinna, one of those who had waited many years for the coming of the missionaries. He was baptized Nov. 21, 1978, followed by a number of others. The first branch, the Aboh Branch, was created the same day. Brother Obinna was called as branch president, his brothers Francis and Raymond as counselors, and Sister Fidelia Obinna, Anthony's wife, was set apart by him as the branch Relief Society president. By early 1980, more than 1,700 converts were baptized in the Nigeria and Ghana.

The Africa West Mission was organized July 1, 1980, with Bryan Espenschied as president. He performed a valuable service in anchoring the gospel and ensuring that the Church culture in Africa was the same as it was in the rest of the world. The mission name was changed to Nigeria Lagos Mission July 1, 1985.

Less than 10 years after the Church's establishment in Nigeria, membership approached 10,000 in 1987. Twin milestones occurred in 1988, with the creation of the Aba Nigeria Stake May 15, under the direction of Elder Neal A. Maxwell of the Quorum of the Twelve. On July 1, the Nigeria Lagos Mission was divided to create the Nigeria Aba Mission. The Jos and Ilorin missions, with Nigerian mission presidents, Ato Kwamina Dadson and John Agbonkonkon Ehanire, respectively, were organized July 1, 1992, but discontinued a year later. In the local branches, self-help was emphasized.

By 1994, Nigeria had three stakes and 12 districts. Church programs continue to bless the lives of Nigerian Saints, such as young women in the Port Harcourt 2nd Ward, who held their first Young Women in Excellence program. In addition, Relief Society sisters in Port Harcourt participated in the Church's Gospel Literacy Effort to increase spiritual and temporal self-reliance. Saints in this African country are faithful despite challenges. Benin City Nigeria Stake members do home teaching though few families have cars or telephones. Sacrament meeting attendance is high despite political turmoil and frequent transportation disruptions.

The creation of five stakes in two years is evidence of the faithfulness of the members in Nigeria. Their faith was rewarded Feb. 14, 1998, when President Gordon B. Hinckley visited the country and addressed 1,150 priesthood leaders and more than 12,000 members in a regional conference in Port Harcourt. He also visited Aba, where members lined the streets to welcome him. While speaking to members in Ghana on the same trip, President Hinckley announced that a temple would be built in Accra, more accessible to the Nigerians. Two years later in general conference on April 2, 2000, President Hinckley announced that a temple would be built in Aba, Nigeria.

In 1999, membership in Nigeria was 42,746, the most of any country in Africa.

Sources: Swiss Mission manuscript history; "Nigeria and Ghana", by Janet Brigham, *Ensign*, Feb. 1980; *Brother to Brother*, by Rendell N. Mabey and Gordon T. Allred, Bookcraft, 1984; "Nigeria marks twin milestones," *Church News*, May 21, 1988; *All Are Alike unto God*, edited by E. Dale LeBaron, Bookcraft, 1990; *Church News*, Oct. 8, 1994, Dec. 2, 1995, June 1, 1996, Sept. 7, 1996, Feb. 2,1998; "Nigeria needs gospel in hearts of its people," by John L. Hart, *Church News*, Feb. 21, 1998; *Church News*, April 8, 2000.

Stakes — 11

(Listed alphabetically as of Oct. 1, 2000.)

No.	Name	Organized	First President
Africa West **Area**			
1695	Aba Nigeria	15 May 1988	David William Eka
1957	*Benin City Nigeria East 2 Mar 1997		
	Benin City Nigeria	24 Oct 1993	Alexander Afamefuna Odume
2314	Benin City Nigeria South	2 Mar 1997	Godpower Etinosa Uwadiae
2211	*Eket Nigeria 31 Dec 1996		
	Qua River Nigeria	14 Jul 1996	Udo David Umoh
2237	Etinan Nigeria	22 Sep 1996	Emmanuel Sunday Ekaete
2534	Ikot Akpaden Nigeria	27 Jun 1999	Idem Adiaha Etuk
2309	Lagos Nigeria	23 Feb 1997	Adesina Joshua Olukanni
2538	Nsit Ubium Nigeria	19 Sep 1999	Etim Thomas Ekong
2476	Owerri Nigeria	14 Jun 1998	Stephen Chukwuma Ejielo
1781	Port Harcourt Nigeria	25 Nov 1990	Ephriam Sobere Etete
2238	Umuahia Nigeria	22 Sep 1996	Godwin E. Woko

Missions —3

(As of Oct. 1, 2000; shown with historical number. See MISSIONS.)

(275) NIGERIA ENUGU MISSION
83 Ogui Road
P.O. Box 4133
Enugu, Enugu State Nigeria

(179) NIGERIA LAGOS MISSION
P.O. Box 9028
Ikeja, Lagos State
Nigeria

(221) NIGERIA PORT HARCOURT MISSION
P.O. Box 7116, Trans-Amadi
Port Harcourt, Rivers State,
Nigeria

NIUE

Year-end 1999: Est. population, 2,000; Members, 230; Districts, 1; Branches, 4; Percent LDS, 11.5, or one in 9; Pacific Islands Area; New Zealand Auckland Mission.

Niue, located in the South Pacific about 300 miles south of the Samoan Islands, is a self-governing island nation under New Zealand protection. Most residents speak Niuean, and belong to the London Missionary Society religion. The island has a -6 percent growth rate.

The first LDS members in Niue were Fritz Bunge-Kruger and his family from Samoa, who arrived in 1952 on business. He was set apart to do missionary work on Niue before arriving. A cinematographer, he traveled about the island and showed movies, and then, with the contacts he made, started a home Sunday School. It soon grew to an attendance of 80. They moved to a local dance hall for meetings, and on May 29, 1952, a Mutual Improvement Association was organized. At Brother Kruger's recommendation, full-time missionaries were sent to the island. The first baptisms took place Aug. 14, 1952, when 26 people were baptized by Elder Thayne Christensen. Other baptismal services followed, and a total of 65 were baptized the first year. Because of persecution during open air meetings, activities were held quietly at first, but at times entire villages attended. The first Niuean missionary was Sionemologa Tagavaitau.

On Feb. 12, 1955, work commenced on the Alofi Chapel with a handful of members raising money and doing much of the building by hand. They were assisted by labor missionaries. The building was completed in 1958. Additional Church buildings were erected later.

About a third or more of the Niuean members have moved to New Zealand. Members in Niue, particularly the youth, have often distinguished themselves in island competitions.

Despite early opposition and persecution of Church members, LDS membership in 1999 was 11 percent of the island population and many members were holding key governmental positions. As of 1999, they included Veve Jacobsen, a member of the National Assembly and Minister of Health and Education; and Lagavalu Haioti, senior magistrate of the court, responsible for 50 land commissioner judges and six justices of the peace. He was also serving in 1999 as president of the Alofi Niue District of the Tonga Nuku'Alofa Mission and directing the translation of LDS publications into Niuean.

Sources: *History of the Church in Niue* by Sister Relva R. Price, May 1973; *Unto the Islands of the Sea,* by R. Lanier Britsch; correspondence from Adelia Shumway from Niue Island, Aug. 24, 1990; interview with Fritz Kruger, 1991; *Church News,* Aug. 29, 1992; "Church grows prominent on coral atoll of Pacific," by Douglas W. Banks, *Church News,* Sept. 18, 1999.

NORTHERN IRELAND

(See United Kingdom)

NORTHERN MARIANA ISLANDS

Year-end 1999: Est. population, 51,000; Members, 870; Branches, 1; Percent LDS, 1.71, or one in 59; Philippines/Micronesia Area; Micronesia Guam Mission.

The Northern Mariana Islands are a commonwealth administered by the United States. Its population is primarily of Chamorro people.

SAIPAN

Among the first Church members to Saipan were American servicemen in 1944, including L. Tom Perry, later a member of the Quorum of the Twelve. Missionary work in Saipan began in the early 1970s, but was stopped because of local hostility. In February 1975, Elders Jeff Frame and Callis Carlton began full-time missionary work. One of the first group meetings on the island was held July 24, 1975.

LDS member Alfred "Mustang" Gonzalez became construction manager of the new airport, arriving July 16, 1975, and brought his family the following October. They utilized a small vacant quonset hut that had been abandoned in the jungle and used it for a meetinghouse. After this building was too small, meetings were held in the elders' kitchen and living room. Sunday School classes were held outside under the coconut trees. A small building was completed in 1983. Brad T. Nago and his wife, Jean, were converted in Saipan and baptized Jan. 24, 1976. He became president of Saipan's Chalan Laulau Branch after the Gonzalez family returned to Hawaii. At the time the Micronesia Guam Mission was created in 1980, the Saipan Branch had 85 members.

President Gordon B. Hinckley and Elder Joseph B. Wirthlin visited briefly with 10 missionaries and met with about 60 of Saipan's 300 members during a refueling stop en route home from Asia June 1, 1996.

ROTA — TINIAN

Elders Stephen Jones and Kamealoha Kaniho were assigned to open Rota, an island in the Northern Marianas, for proselyting on Sept. 5, 1986. Work was opened on Tinian Aug. 14, 1992, by Elder James Adamson and Elder Ryan C. McCune.

Source: *Brief History of the Micronesia-Guam Mission,* published by the Micronesia Guam Mission, 1990, Lewis V. Nord, president; unpublished "History of the Chalan Laulau Branch of the Guam Micronesia Mission"; *Church News,* June 8, 1996.

NORWAY

Year-end 1999: Est. population, 4,331,000; Members, 4,120; Stakes, 1; Wards, 7; Branches, 18; Missions, 1; Districts, 3; percent LDS, .1, or one in 1,051.

In western Scandinavia on the Norwegian Sea, the kingdom of Norway is a hereditary constitutional monarchy. Its people speak Norwegian and Lappish, and 94 percent are Evangelical Lutheran.

Missionary work in Norway grew out of the effort in Denmark. Hans F. Petersen, one of the first converts in Denmark, was sent as a missionary to Norway in September 1851. Other elders followed, and the first baptisms took place at Osterrisor on Nov. 26, 1851. A branch was organized there July 16, 1852, and another in Frederikstad July 25, 1852.

Church units in Norway were part of the Scandinavian Mission until 1905, when the Danish-Norwegian Mission was organized. Norway was separated from Denmark into a mission of its own in 1920.

Elder John A. Widtsoe, who served in the Quorum of the Twelve from 1921-52, was born in Norway.

In the early days, many missionaries in Norway were arrested and imprisoned because of their preaching. By 1930, 8,555 baptisms had been performed in Norway, with about 3,500 converts immigrating to Zion. Members remained under local leadership during World War II, and some missionary work was done. Many Church members immigrated to the United States after the war.

Until 1950, members and missionaries in Norway used the Danish translation of the Book of Mormon. That year, a Norwegian translation was published, and Norwegian translations of the Doctrine and Covenants and the Pearl of Great Price followed in 1954 and 1955, respectively.

Norway's only stake was created in Oslo on May 22, 1977.

In the 1980s, member-missionary work proceeded. Pres. Stein Pedersen called 30 stake missionaries to assist missionaries of the Norway Oslo Mission. Membership in 1990 was 3,700. At the same time, stake public affairs director Rigmor Heistoe helped improve relationships between university professors and the Church. In 1988, Elder Russell M. Nelson of the Quorum of the Twelve presented Kjell Eliassen, Norwegian ambassador to the United States, with a book containing his family history.

In the 1990s, work also progressed in the Tromso District, made up of four small branches: Tromso, Alta/Hammerfest, Bodo and Harstad/Narvik, headquartered in the largest city in the part of Norway above the Arctic Circle. In June 1998, Svein Ludvigsen, a member of the Norwegian Parliament, was baptized.

LDS membership in Norway in 1999 was 4,120.

Sources: *Encyclopedic History of the Church,* by Andrew Jenson; "Norway Saints Note Anniversary," *Church News,* July 1950; "Beyond the Arctic Circle," by Elder Dennis Mead, *Church News,* Jan. 17, 1959; *The Mormon Migration from Norway,* a University of Utah thesis by Helge Slejaas, August 1972; "Norway," *Ensign,* July 1974; "First Stakes for Norway. . ." *Church News,* June 11, 1977; "Norway — Land of the Blue Fjords," *Relief Society Course of Study,* 1979-80; *Church News,* Jan. 16, 1988; " 'Field is white' in Norway's Arctic region," by R. Scott Lloyd, *Church News,* March 16, 1991; "Inner peace can come during time of war," by John Floisand, *Church News,* Feb. 26, 1994; *Church News,* Oct. 17, 1998.

Stake — 1

(As of Oct. 1, 2000.)

No.	Name	Organized	First President
	Europe Central Area		
835	Oslo Norway	22 May 1977	Osvald Bjareng

Mission — 1

(As of Oct. 1, 2000; shown with historical number. See MISSIONS.)

(24) NORWAY OSLO MISSION
Postboks 145
1355 BPT, Norway

PALAU (BELAU)

Year-end 1999: Est. Population, 17,000; Members, 370; Branches, 1; Percent LDS, 2.18, or one in 46; Pacific Islands Area, Micronesia Guam Mission.

Palau is a republic in the West Pacific Ocean whose residents speak English and Palauan, and are mostly Roman Catholic and Protestant. Missionary work began when Elders Ron Brown and Stanton Akana arrived in Palau on July 8, 1978, from the Hawaii Honolulu Mission. They were accompanied by Pres. Heber Butler, counselor in the Hawaii mission. At the first meeting was James Moikeha, a member who was manager of a local hotel. The missionaries first baptized Brother and Sister Ronnie Oei and their eight children on Sept. 15, 1978. The Oeis are of New Guinean ancestry and they had moved to Palau from The Netherlands. On Dec. 1, 1978, the Sakuma family was baptized, the first Palauans, who became a strength to the group. Another early convert was Ben Roberto, who was baptized Dec. 19, 1980. He felt "the strange but refreshing feeling" that he should serve full-time, which he did. When the Mayuns Branch was organized in 1987, Brother Roberto was called as branch president. Later, the Airai and Koror Topside branches were organized. A district was organized in March 1989.

Pres. Roberto has since been elected to the senate of the Federated States of Micronesia. Sister Sakuma was named "Teacher of the Year," and traveled to Washington, D.C. to meet the U.S. president.

Source: Correspondence from the Micronesia Guam Mission, Sept. 28, 1998.

PANAMA

Year-end 1999: Est. population, 2,681,000; Members, 35,257; Stakes, 7; Wards, 35; Branches,75; Missions, 1; Districts, 8; Percent LDS,1.32, or one in 76.

Located in southern Central America, the Republic of Panama has a population that speaks Spanish and some English. The country is 93 percent Roman Catholic.

The first members in Panama were LDS servicemen associated with the Panama Canal. In 1941, the first branch in Panama was organized for the military personnel. The branch reached a membership of 100 in its first year. Servicemen, including Eran A. Call, later a member of the Second Quorum of the Seventy, and Ladd Black, taught some of the San Blas Indians in 1953 who were employed at the base. They also taught the San Blas chief, Iguanigdipipi, who gave permission for his people to join the Church. The first of these baptized was his son-in-law, Jose Coleman. Coleman was personally interviewed for baptism by President David O. McKay, who had stopped in Panama Feb. 13, 1954, while returning from a three-continent tour. The young man was baptized April 18, 1954. The first missionaries to Panama were Elders Guthrie and Parker, who came in the early summer of 1954. Elder Marion G. Romney of the Quorum of the Twelve visited the chief on the San Blas island. In 1961, Elder Romney presented a copy of the Book of Mormon to the president of the republic, Roberto F. Chiari. Because the Panamanian government did not recognize the Church until 1965, missionary work was limited until that time. When the Church was officially recognized, missionary work increased in Panama.

In 1965, Central America Mission Pres. Ted E. Brewerton visited San Blas and started full-time missionary work. Because the people there had traditions that corresponded closely with Book of Mormon events, many joined the Church. The first meetinghouse, completed in April 1970, was built on the island of Ustopo. The Panama Stake, the first in the country, was created Nov. 11, 1979, with Nelson L. Altamirano as president.

The Panama Panama City Mission was created July 1, 1989. At the time, some 10,400 members lived in Panama. Most North American missionaries were withdrawn from the country in 1988, but local leaders and missionaries continued the work.

Cuna Indians from the San Blas Islands have regularly contributed outstanding molas, or fabric paintings, to the Church's international art competitions.

President Gordon B. Hinckley visited Panama Jan. 20, 1997, and spoke at the Analayami Atlapa Convention Center in Panama City to some 3,000 members.

Sources: "Elder Romney sets busy schedule in Canal Zone," *Church News*, Dec. 2, 1961; "San Blas Indians," by Ronald K. Esplin, *Church News*, June 2, 1979; "Panama gains first stake from Costa Rica mission," *Church News*, April 25, 1970, Dec. 22, 1979; "New Missions," *Church News*, Feb. 25, 1989; *Church News*, Aug. 8, 1993, Feb. 1, 1997; information from Elder Eran A. Call, Oct. 3, 1998.

Stakes — 7

(Listed alphabetically as of Oct. 1, 2000.)

No.	Name	Organized	First President
Central America Area			
2118	Colon Panama	5 Nov 1995	Eugenio Antonio Rodriguez Jacclos
1634a	David Panama	19 Apr 1987	Manuel Salvador Arauz

1734	*La Chorrera Panama	5 Nov 1995	
	*Bella Vista Panama	25 Jan 1993	
	‡Bellavista Panama	23 Jul 1989	Gustavo Brandaris Vergara
1081	Panama City Panama	11 Nov 1979	Nelson Altamirano Lopez
2464	San Isidro Panama	17 May 1998	
1596	San Miguelito Panama	20 Apr 1986	Domingo Estribi
2465	Tocumen Panama	17 May 1998	Eliezar Navarro O.

Missions — 1

(As of Oct. 1, 2000; shown with historical number. See MISSIONS.)

(226) PANAMA PANAMA CITY MISSION
Apartado Postal 55-0036
Paitilla, Panama

PAPUA NEW GUINEA

Year-end 1999: Est. population, 4,295,000; Members, 8,954; Stakes, 1; Wards, 7; Missions, 1; Districts, 2; Branches, 20; percent LDS, .21, or one in 480.

On the eastern half of the island of New Guinea in the Coral Sea and spreading across hundreds of smaller islands, Papua New Guinea is a parliamentary democracy. Its population speaks up to 700 village languages. They are 63 percent Protestant and 31 percent Roman Catholic.

Members visited Papua New Guinea long before the first missionaries arrived in 1980. The Port Moresby Branch was organized Oct. 10, 1979, with Athol Pike as branch president. Attending the branch were mostly expatriates of Australia. Elder L. Douglas and Sister Eva Johnson of the Australia Brisbane Mission arrived Aug. 15, 1980. On Oct. 19, 1980, Maria Biai, Komara Nana, Sarah Nana, and Rhoda Baka were baptized. Some 63 investigators attended services the following Sunday. Elder Douglas and Sister Nita Campbell succeeded the Johnsons, and during their service, property was obtained for a mission home and meetinghouse. Membership at that time had grown to 280. By October 1982, membership had reached 475 in three branches. Many of those converted had heard of the Church by word of mouth and contacted the missionaries to learn more.

By 1983, five branches had been organized under the direction of mission Pres. Dennis D. Flake. A meetinghouse was completed in 1984. That year, two Papuans, Elders George Mauhi and Robert Goisisi, were called as full-time missionaries.

Despite opposition, membership continued to increase. By March 1987, there were 1,450 members in nine branches. As the Church grew, more and more contacts were made in remote villages where many were interested in learning about the gospel. For example, residents of the Daru Village asked for missionaries, who arrived in July 1990. Just three months later, the Daru Branch had 160 members. During this short time, two full-time missionaries, Elders Brian Mott of Washington and Benjamin Lish of Ohio, were involved in the conversion of approximately 100 of the new branch members.

District Pres. Valba Rome, one of the early converts, led some 138 Papuans to the Sydney Australia Temple in late 1991.

The Papua New Guinea Port Moresby Mission was created Feb. 13, 1992, and includes the Solomon Islands. The Relief Society continues to make contributions to the branches. Some sisters learned to read the scriptures through the Relief Society's gospel literacy effort. And in a Relief Society service project in the 1990s, sisters in the Popondetta Branch completed a service project of donating bandages for the hospital in their city. On Oct. 21, 1995, Elder V. Dallas Merrell of the Seventy created the Papua New Guinea Port Moresby Stake, the first stake on the island. The stake had 2,200 members in six wards and one branch.

A devastating tidal wave destroyed a village July 17, 1998, but no members or Church facilities were involved. Mission Pres. Mosese Fehoko Naeata visited the damaged areas to help provide Church assistance. Most of the members live in or near Port Moresby, said Pres. Naeata.

Sources: Manuscript History of Church in Papua New Guinea; *Unto the Islands of the Sea,* by R. Lanier Britsch; "Light and Truth pouring into nation 10 years following Church's arrival," by Carol West, *Church News,* Sept. 16, 1989; *Church News,* Feb. 2, 1992; "Literacy opened 'whole new world' for her," *Church News,* Feb. 6, 1993; *Church News,* May 15, 1993; "Faith leads to first Papua New Guinea stake," by Sarah Jane Weaver, *Church News,* Nov. 11, 1995, July 25, 1998.

Stake — 1

(Listed alphabetically as of Oct. 1, 2000.)

No.	Name	Organized	First President

Australia/New Zealand Area			
2109	Port Moresby Papua New Guinea	22 Oct 1995	Valba Rome

Mission — 1

(As of Oct. 1, 2000; shown with historical number. See MISSIONS.)

(275) PAPUA NEW GUINEA PORT MORESBY MISSION
P.O. Box 6947
Boroko, NCD.
Papua New Guinea

PARAGUAY

Year-end 1999: Est. population, 5,358,000; Members, 44,632; Stakes, 6; Wards, 34; Branches, 89; Missions, 2; Districts, 10; Temples, 1 announced; percent LDS, .83, or one in 120.

The Republic of Paraguay in central South America has a population that speaks Spanish and Guarani. They are 87 percent Roman Catholic.

Among the first Latter-day Saints to visit Paraguay was Frederick S. Williams, president of the Argentine Mission, who came in 1939. Samuel J. Skousen, a former missionary in Argentina working for the U.S. government in Rio de Janeiro and later in Asuncion, Paraguay, introduced the gospel to Carlos Alberto Rodriguez and his wife, Mafalda. Rodriguez was baptized in Asuncion Aug. 21, 1948, and his wife, awaiting the birth of their baby, followed Jan. 15, 1949. A branch with Brother Skousen as president was organized in Asuncion on July 26, 1948. The first missionaries arrived Jan. 9, 1950. Their efforts proceeded slowly, but by 1951 two branches had been organized. Their first baptism was Clara Ans de Krisch.

The Paraguay Mission was organized July 1, 1977, with a membership of 2,063, and the first stake was organized in Asuncion Feb. 25, 1979. Membership then was about 2,900.

An interesting development occurred in 1980 when a colony of 200 Nivacle Indians, who returned to their ancestral homeland in the Gran Chaco, joined the Church. The colony, under its own leadership for 10 years, continued to progress into the 1990s.

The Church in the population centers continued to progress, indicated by the creation of the Asuncion Paraguay North Stake in late 1992. Membership in 1990 was 12,000, and increased to 24,000 in 1995. In 1999, membership was 44,632. The recent increases have come from expanding missionary work into the interior, with missionaries speaking Spanish, Portuguese and Guarani.

President Gordon B. Hinckley visited Asuncion on Aug. 10, 1997, the first Church president to visit members in Paraguay. He addressed 7,000 members, some of whom had traveled up to nine hours on buses, and asked them to be helpful in retaining new converts in activity.

A second mission for Paraguay was created July 1, 1998, reflecting the growth of the Church in the nation where the number of converts baptized in 1996 was double the number baptized in the previous five years.

In general conference on April 2, 2000, President Hinckley announced that a temple would be built in Asuncion.

Sources: *From Acorn to Oak Tree,* by Frederick S. Williams and Frederick G. Williams; "The Church in Uruguay and Paraguay," *Ensign,* Feb. 1975; "Unexpected Welcome," by William Slaughter, *Church News,* June 9, 1979; *Church News,* Nov. 27, 1983; "Chulupi colony, Mistolar, thrives deep in interior," by Nestor Curbelo, *Church News,* June 2, 1990; *Church News,* Jan. 2, 1993, "'Heart' of South America opening to the gospel," by Nestor Curbelo, *Church News,* May 27, 1995; *Church News,* Aug. 23, 1997, Jan. 10, 1998. April 2, 2000.

Stakes — 6

(Listed alphabetically as of Oct. 1, 2000.)

No.	Name	Organized	First President
South America South Area			
1002	Asuncion Paraguay	25 Feb 1979	Carlos Ramon Espinola
1911	Asuncion Paraguay North	22 Nov 1992	Gregorio Figueredo Servian
2199	Ciudad Del Este Paraguay	2 Jun 1996	Juan Ramon Ocampos Gonzalez
1142	Fernando de la Mora Paraguay	1 Jun 1980	Guillermo M. Riveros A.
2376	Fernando De La Mora Paraguay South	15 Jun 1997	Humberto Canete Castorino
1997	San Lorenzo Paraguay	20 Nov 1994	Jorge Daniel Colina

Mission — 1

(As of Oct. 1, 2000; shown with historical number. See MISSIONS.)

(155) PARAGUAY ASUNCION MIS.
Casilla de Correo 818
Asuncion, Paraguay

(329) PAR. ASUNCION NORTH MISSION
Casilla de Correo 1871
Asuncion 1831, Paraguay

PERU

Year-end 1999: Est. population, 24,087,000; Members, 333,828; Stakes, 81; Wards, 557; Branches, 281; Missions, 7; Districts, 33; Temples, 1; Percent LDS, 1.39, or one in 72.

Located on the Pacific Coast side of South America, Peru is a constitutional republic with a population that speaks Spanish, Quechua, and Aymara. Some 90 percent are Roman Catholic.

Prior to 1956, LDS families living in Peru held group meetings, but no organized missionary work was done. A Peruvian copper mine owned by a member from Salt Lake City, Utah, Alfred W. McCune, also brought a few members to Peru. On Jan. 1, 1956, Frederick S. Williams, a former mission president in Argentina and Uruguay, and his family moved to Peru and contacted Church headquarters for permission to organize a branch and begin missionary work. A branch was organized July 8, 1956, by Elder Henry D. Moyle of the Quorum of the Twelve. Elders Darwin Thomas, Edward T. Hall, Donald L. Hokanson, and Shirrel M. Plowman arrived Aug. 7, 1956, and began proselyting. A building for branch meetings was purchased Nov. 30 of that year. At the first branch conference held Feb. 24, 1957, 44 attended, 22 of whom were investigators. Missionaries were sent to Arequipa later in the year. The Andes Mission, headquartered in Lima, was established Nov. 1, 1959. At the time, there were five branches and 300 members.

The mission was divided Oct. 1, 1961. After the division, the Chile and Andes missions (comprising Bolivia and Peru) each had 12 branches and more than 2,000 members. The number of members in Peru increased to 6,391 in 1965. When the first stake was organized in Lima on Feb. 22, 1970, membership in Peru was 10,771. Called as president was Roberto Vidal, an early convert. That same year, the mission was divided and renamed the Peru Mission.

Growth continued as local leaders assumed priesthood leadership, and by 1977 there were 17,000 members in Peru. At an area conference in Lima, which was presided over by President Spencer W. Kimball, on Feb. 26-27, 1977, 7,900 attended. Four years later in 1981, President Kimball announced a temple for Lima, which was completed and dedicated Jan. 10, 1986.

On Jan. 30-31, 1988, just 32 years after missionary work started in Peru, seven stakes in Lima were created in one weekend by Elder M. Russell Ballard of the Quorum of the Twelve, and Lima had the second largest number of stakes of any metropolitan area outside the United States.

In July, 1993, Peru's sixth mission was created, the Peru Chiclayo, which includes the highland Andes bordering Ecuador, where many of Lamanite descent live. Seven additional stakes were created from October 1992 to October 1994, and 18 from October 1994 to October 1996. A seventh mission in Peru was created July 1, 1994. President Gordon B. Hinckley visited Lima Nov. 8-9, 1996, and addressed some 35,000 people. A new area, the South American West Area, was created Aug. 15, 1998, and comprising only Peru and Bolivia, with headquarters in Lima.

A new mission training center, with capacity for 150 missionaries and room for expansion, was dedicated Sept. 3, 1998, by Elder Russell M. Nelson of the Quorum of the Twelve. In 1999, there were 353,828 members in Peru.

Sources: Andes Mission manuscript history; Peru, *Ensign,* February 1977; *From Acorn to Oak Tree,* by Frederick S. Williams and Frederick G. Williams; *Church News,* Jan. 19, 1986; "Resourceful people of Lima making Church 'blossom'," by Lee Warnick, *Church News,* Feb. 6, 1988; *Church News,* Jan. 28, 1996, Nov. 16, 1996, July 4, 1998, Sept. 12, 1998.

Stakes — 80

(Listed alphabetically as of Oct. 1, 2000.)

No.	Name	Organized	First President
South America West Area			
1815	Arequipa Peru Central	15 Sep 1991	Cesar Leoncio Gamarra G.
2361	Arequipa Peru Hunter	25 May 1997	Alberto Enrique Mansilla Luque
1540	Arequipa Peru Manuel Prado	20 Jun 1985	Efrain Jorge Rodriguez M.
1985	Arequipa Peru Selva Alegre	24 Jul 1994	Elias A. Rebaza Rado

1108	*Arequipa Peru Umacollo	20 Jun 1985	
	‡Arequipa Peru	21 Feb 1980	Victor H. Gamero
2312	Arequipa Peru Zamacola	23 Feb 1997	Federico A. Rosas Molina
2189	Ayacucho Peru	21 Apr 1996	Job Edwin Quintanilla Pretel
2246	Cajamarca Peru	13 Oct 1996	German Maximo
2156	Cerro de Pasco Peru	21 Jan 1996	Bernardo Cristocal Santiago
1145	Chiclayo Peru	8 Jun 1980	Jorge Humberto del Carpio M.
1567	Chiclayo Peru Central	27 Oct 1985	Franklin D. Orroyo S.
1820	*Chiclayo Peru Eldorado	29 Oct 1995	
	‡Chiclayo Peru North	20 Oct 1991	Javier Delgado Torres
2260	Chiclayo Peru La Victoria	3 Nov 1996	Erasmo Delgado Rivera
2113	Chiclayo Peru Latina	29 Oct 1995	Oswaldo Tello Mier y Teran
1122	Chimbote Peru	23 Mar 1980	Carlos Santos Lopez O.
1790	Chimbote Peru South	17 Mar 1991	Julio Arturo Leiva P.
1527	Cuzco Peru	28 Apr 1985	Jose U. Coacalla
1910	Cuzco Peru Inti Raymi	15 Nov 1992	Miguel A. Vallenas Frisancho
1725	Huacho Peru	4 Jun 1989	Carlos Manuel Zapata P.
1471	Huancayo Peru	6 May 1984	Moises Sanchez T.
1756	Huanuco Peru	17 Jun 1990	Raul Rodriguez S.
2148	Huanuco Peru Amarilis	17 Dec 1995	Jesus Antonio Epinoza Solorzano
1739	Ica Peru	17 Dec 1989	Alexander Alfonso Nunez T.
2041	Ilo Peru	23 April 1995	Miguel Fernando Neyra M.
1162	Iquitos Peru	3 Aug 1980	Carlos Rojas Romero
2132	Iquitos Peru Nueve de Octubre	26 Nov 1995	Johnny Padilla Bustos
1864	Iquitos Peru Punchana	23 May 1992	Alfonso Frederico Rojas R.
2007	Juliaca Peru	18 Dec 1994	Jesus Mario Barreda Ponze
1924a	Lima Peru Bayovar	7 Mar 1993	Augusto R. Ordinola Salva
1063	Lima Peru Callao	16 Sep 1979	Manuel Paredes
2355	Lima Peru Campoy	18 May 1997	Carlos Roberto Cabrera Rondon
1743	*Lima Peru Canto Grande	7 Mar 1993	
	‡Canto Grande Peru	18 Mar 1990	Augusto Ordinalo S.
2181	Lima Peru Carabayllo	17 Mar 1996	Johnny Enrique Tunque Carrasco
789	Lima Peru Central	21 Nov 1976	Oscar H. Aguayo U.
1679	Lima Peru Chorrillos	31 Jan 1988	Israel Antonio Gonzalez B.
1794	Lima Peru Chosica	5 May 1991	Ricardo Enrique Lazo T.
1675	Lima Peru Comas	31 Jan 1988	Grover Pinto R.
1680	Lima Peru El Olivar	31 Jan 1988	Antero Miguel Sanchez M.
788	Lima Peru Lamanita	21 Nov 1976	Rafael de la Cruz
2297	Lima Peru La Molina	5 Jan 1997	Abel T. Gonzales Rebaza
1677	Lima Peru Las Flores	31 Jan 1988	Miguel Fernando Rojas A.
1674	Lima Peru Las Palmeras	31 Jan 1988	Albina Isidro Chagua C.
2354	Lima Peru Las Violetas	18 May 1997	Elras Humberto Alcantara
503	*Lima Peru Limatambo	21 Nov 1976	
	*Lima Peru		
	‡Lima	22 Feb 1970	Roberto Vidal
670	*Lima Peru Magdalena	21 Nov 1976	
	‡Lima Peru West	1 Dec 1974	Manuel Paredes L.
1678	Lima Peru Maranga	31 Jan 1988	Benedicto S. Pacheco M.
1486	Lima Peru Palao	1 Jul 1984	Rene Loli
2201	Lima Peru Rimac	16 Jun 1996	Gustavo Guillermo Andrade Brouseet
1439	Lima Peru San Felipe	11 Sep 1983	Mauro Luis Artica Q.
2185	Lima Peru San Gabriel	24 Mar 1996	Juan Carlos Mercado Briceno
1064	Lima Peru San Juan	16 Sep 1979	Jorge Salazar
1440	Lima Peru San Luis	11 Sep 1983	Philippe J. Kradolfer
1065	Lima Peru San Martin	16 Sep 1979	Rene Loli
2149	Lima Peru Santa Anita	17 Dec 1995	Jose Humberto Naupori Velez
2378	Lima Peru Santa Isabel	15 Jun 1997	Gerardo R. Jillar Quevedo
2186	Lima Peru Surco	24 Mar 1996	Alejandro Julian Llanos Morales
1795	Lima Peru Tahuantinsuyo	5 May 1991	Albino Isidro Chagua C.
1553	Lima Peru Villa Maria	25 Aug 1985	Juan Maguina Colquis
1881	Lima Peru Villa Salvador	31 May 1992	Victor Nicolas Anicama
1676	Lima Peru Vitarte	31 Jan 1988	Luis E. Stiglich S.
1734a	Mantaro Peru	30 Jul 1989	Manuel Moises Sanchez T.
2008	Moquegua Peru	18 Dec 1994	Claudio Luis Zeballos Flores
1925	Pisco Peru	13 Mar 1993	Marcelo P. Munante Salguero

1755	Piura Peru Castilla	17 Jun 1990	Oscar Alfredo Galvez C.
1400	*Piura Peru Central	10 Mar 1996	
	‡Piura Peru	16 Feb 1983	Pedro Puertas Rojas
2177	Piura Peru Miraflores	10 Mar 1996	Jose Alberta Castillo Saldarriaga
1961a	Pucallpa Peru	5 Dec 1993	Ferrando Vela Lopez
2130	Puno Peru Bellavista	26 Nov 1995	Pedro Tito Huanca
1872	*Puno Peru Central	10 Mar 1998	
	*Puno Peru Titicaca	26 Nov 1995	
	‡Puno Peru	28 May 1992	Adan Bravo Mathens
1399	Tacna Peru	13 Feb 1983	Abraham La Torre Parades
2233	Tacna Peru Alameda	15 Sep 1996	Roger Valdivia
1914	Tacna Peru Arias Araguez	6 Dec 1992	Derliz Guzman Tejadi
1987	Trujillo Peru Central	14 Aug 1994	Pedro Gerardo Rodriguez H.
1802	Trujillo Peru East	16 Jun 1991	Raymundo Aponte Garcia
2428	Trujillo Peru Esperanza	18 Jan 1998	Laureano Gaspar Arrellano L.
2429	Trujillo Peru Laureles	18 Jan 1998	Luis Yvan Sanchez
1487	Trujillo Peru Palermo	12 Aug 1984	Jose Neyra
2452	Trujillo Peru Porvenir	19 Apr 1998	Wilson Americo Moreno U.
887	*Trujillo Pero Primavera	23 Feb 1998	
	*Trujillo Peru North	19 Aug 1984	
	Trujillo Peru	22 Jan 1978	Teofilo Puertas Vega
2229	Ventanilla Peru	8 Sep 1996	Luis Arnaldo Alvarado Zegarra

Stakees discontinued

2131	Iquitos Peru Mi Peru	26 Nov 1995	Roger Braga Llerena
	Discontinued21 Jun 1998		
1541	Iquitos Peru Sachachorro	23 Jun 1985	Jorge Diaz Suarez
	Discontinued	21 Jun 1998	
2234	Tacna Peru Los Angeles	15 Sep 1996	Rolando Melchor
	Discontinued	6 Feb 2000	
1860	Chincha Peru	8 May 1992	Alfonso Eduardo Ormeno Villa
	Discontinued	26 Sep 1999	

Missions — 7

(As of Oct. 1, 2000; shown with historical number. See MISSIONS.)

(165) PERU AREQUIPA MISSION
Casilla 1884
Arequipa,Peru

(291) PERU CHICLAYO MISSION
Casilla de Corrreo 630
Chiclayo, Peru

(302) PERU LIMA CENTRAL MISSION
Av. Jorge Basadre 592
Oficina 604-B, Casilla 11-0129
San Isidro, Lima 27, Peru

(210) PERU LIMA EAST MISSION
Casilla de Correo 14-0196
Lima 14, Peru

(149) PERU LIMA NORTH MISSION
Casilla de Correo 11-0123
Lima 11, Peru

(50) PERU LIMA SOUTH MISSION
Casilla de Correo 14-0293
San Isidro, Lima 14, Peru

(184a) PERU TRUJILLO MISSION
Casilla de Correo 10
Urbanizacion California
Trujillo, Peru

PHILIPPINES

Year-end 1996: Est. population, 73,266,000; Members, 441,359; Stakes,68; Wards, 414; Branches, 637; Missions, 13; Districts, 77; Temples, 1; percent LDS, .6, or one in 166.

An archipelago off the southeast coast of Asia, the Republic of the Philippines has a population that speaks Tagalog and English. They are Roman Catholic, 83 percent; Protestant, 9 percent; and Muslim, 5 percent.

The Church was introduced in the Philippines during the Spanish-American War in 1898. Two artillery batteries from Utah were sent to the Philippines, and Willard Call and George Seaman were set apart as missionaries, making them the first elders to preach the gospel among the people of the Philippine islands. Beginning in 1955, the

Philippines became part of the Southern Far East Mission, servicemen baptized some converts. Pres. H. Grant Heaton and Filipino missionaries visited and conducted missionary work.Following World War II, Maxine Grimm, wife of a U.S. Army colonel, serving in the American Red Cross in the Philippines, introduced the gospel to Aniceta Pabilona Fajardo, the first Filipino to join the Church in the islands. Sister Fajardo was baptized in 1945. Dean Franklin Clair, a U.S. Army medic who married Leona H. Seno of the Philippines, was another stalwart in the Philippines.

The Church experienced a growth spurt in the area in 1953 during the Korean War when the Luzon Servicemen's District was organized.

On April 28, 1961, Elder Gordon B. Hinckley, then an Assistant to the Twelve, met with a small group of local servicemen, American residents, Filipino members, and their families at the American War Memorial Cemetery to offer a prayer for the islands and open the islands for missionary work. The first missionaries, Elders Ray Goodson, Harry Murray, Kent Lowe and Nestor Ledesma, arrived in Manila on June 5, 1961.

The first two to be baptized by the missionaries were Jose Gutierez Sr. and Lino Brocka. By the end of 1961, there had been eight baptisms.

In 1967, the Philippine Mission was organized with Paul S. Rose as president. Two years later the Church had spread to eight major islands of the country and the mission had the highest number of baptisms in the Church.

The Philippines Mission was divided into two missions in 1974, creating the Philippines Manila Mission, under the leadership of Pres. Raymond L. Goodson, and the Philippines Cebu City Mission, under the direction of Pres. Carl D. Jones. In the next 12 years, seven more missions were created.

President Spencer W. Kimball spoke to 18,000 members at an area conference Oct. 18-19, 1980, and met with Philippines president Ferdinand E. Marcos during a 30-minute meeting in the presidential palace on Oct. 18.

The Manila Missionary Training Center was established in 1983 to train missionaries, and in September 1984 the Manila Philippines Temple was dedicated. At that time, membership was 76,000.

In 1987, the Philippines/Micronesia Area was created with headquarters in Manila. Nine more missions were created in the Philippines between 1986-92.

During 1990-91, members experienced volcanic eruptions, earthquakes, flooding, and conflicts between insurgent and government forces. Church relief efforts were sent to help in the recovery of the natural disasters. Membership continued to grow, reaching 237,000 in 1990.

The first Filipino General Authority, Elder Augusto A. Lim, was called to the Second Quorum of the Seventy June 6, 1992. The Church became more prominent as Christmas lights on the temple grounds attracted more people, and its youth became involved in more service projects.

President Hinckley returned to this land once again on May 30-June 1, 1996, where he had first visited 36 years ago. The trip was part of an eight-nation tour that included the dedication of the Hong Kong Temple. His visit to the Philippines served to renew long-time acquaintances. Many traveled great distances to hear the prophet. Members of the Bacolod Philippines North Stake joined others to celebrate the Philippines centennial in 1998, and presented a musical with historical highlights that was well-attended.

In 1999, membership reached 441,359.

Sources: "The Philippines," *The Improvement Era,* March 1964; *History of the Church in the Philippines,* compiled by the Luzon District, 1965; "Philippines: the Land of Joyous Service," *Ensign,* August 1975; "Missionaries in Khaki," by Carol Cornwall Madsen, *Church News,* June 23, 1979; "Saints throng to area meetings in the Far East," by Dell Van Orden, *Church News,* Nov. 1, 1980; "Gospel flourishes in soil of Filipino faith," by Francis M. Orquiola, *Ensign,* September 1984; "Dateline Philippines," *Tambuli,* April 1991; *Church News,* Dec. 25, 1993, Oct. 4, 1997, Aug. 1, 1998.

Stakes — 76

(Listed alphabetically as of Oct. 1, 2000.)

No.	Name	Organized	First President
Philippines/Micronesia Area			
2537	Agoo Philippines	22 Aug 1999	Ricardo Castillo Lopez
1226	Angeles Philippines	18 Jan 1981	Orlando D. Aquilar
2388	Antipolo Philippines	31 Aug 1997	Arnulfo T. Roda
1281	Bacolod Philippines	5 Jul 1981	Remus G. Villarete
1323	Bacolod Philippines North	7 Feb 1982	Rufino Alvarez Villaneuva Jr.
2559	Bacolod Philippines South	4 Jun 2000	Avelino N. Santillan

1573	Baguio Philippines	17 Nov 1985	Carlos F. Chavez
1806	Balanga Philippines	7 Jul 1991	Torbio Nuguid Santos
2331	Batac Philippines	23 Mar 1997	Nathaniel Oasan Berroidan
2411	*Bauang Phillippines	22 Aug 1999	
	‡Aringay Philippines	23 Nov 1997	Buenaventura Soriano Obscena
2374	Bayambang Philippines	15 Jun 1997	Jose Mirafelix Balajadia
1788	Binalbagan Philippines	3 Mar 1991	Jose Vicente Pioquinto
1711	Butuan Philippines	19 Feb 1989	Henry Ferrer Acebedo
1340	Cabanatuan Philippines	9 May 1982	Arsenio A. Pacaduan
1884	Cabuyao Philippines	7 June 1992	Tomas S. Merdegia Jr.
1572	Cadiz Philippines	10 Nov 1985	Carmelino M. Cawit
1535	Cagayan De Oro Philippines	26 May 1985	Loreto Balanta Libid
1748	Cagayan de Oro Philippines East	6 May 1990	Danilo D. De La Vega
2528	Cagayan de Oro Philippines West	16 May 1999	Harry Waga Tenestrante
2427	Cainta Philippines	18 Jan 1998	Ramon De La Cruz Rodriguez
1807	Camiling Philippines	14 Jul 1991	Celso Arenzana Nicolas
1545	Cavite Philippines	24 Oct 1989	
	‡Makiling Philippines	18 Aug 1985	Jose Trinidad Aguilar
1220	Cebu City Philippines	11 Jan 1981	Jacob Torres Lopez
2568	Cebu Philippines Central	27 Aug 2000	Paul Johnson Reyes Codina
2538a	Cebu Philippines Liloan	17 Oct 1999	Allen Sagario Velasco
2554	Daet Philippines	30 Apr 2000	Aquilino Zapanta Aloc
1229	Dagupan Philippines	25 Jan 1981	Bernardo G. Reamon
2504	Dasmarinas Philippines	13 Dec 1998	Remegio Evangelista Meim Jr.
1307	Davao Philippines	15 Nov 1981	George S. Lavarino
1544	Davao Philippines Buhangin	18 Aug 1985	Patrick Hartford M. Clair
1876	Digos Philippines	31 May 1992	Paul Farinas Bunoan
2561	Fairview Philippines	11 Jun 2000	Raul Antonio V. Jose
2461	Gapan Philippines	17 May 1998	Roger Young Salvador
2084	General Santos Philippines	6 Aug 1995	Fabian L. Simamban
2558	Goa Philippines	28 May 2000	Edgar Pia Pesimo Sr.
1908	Iligan Philippines	18 Oct 1992	William C. Garife
1508	Iloilo Philippines	20 Jan 1985	Hannibal Delgado D.
2316	Iloilo Philippines North	9 Mar 1997	Eusebio B. Sollesta
2548	Kalibo Philippines	5 Mar 2000	Winston Bantigue Del Rosario
1238	*Kalookan Philippines	17 Feb 1996	
	‡Caloocan Philippines	22 Feb 1981	Godofredo Hilario Esguerra
1547	La Carlota Philippines	18 Aug 1985	Antonio V. Custodio
1715	Laoag Philippines	23 Apr 1989	Jose Miguel Tumaneng
1555	Las Pinas Philippines	15 Sep 1985	Delfin T. Justiniano
1551	Legazpi Philippines	19 Aug 1985	Jose P. Leveriza
1557	Lingayen Philippines	22 Sep 1985	Oberlito R. Cantillo
2503	Lucena Philippines	13 Dec 1998	David D. Sanglap
841	Makati Philippines	29 May 1977	Ruben Moscaira Lancanienta
1726	Malolos Philippines	11 Jun 1989	Rogelio C. Coronel
1735b	Mandaue Philippines	19 Nov 1989	Cesar Abina Perez Jr.
1789	*Mangaldan Philippines	22 Aug 1999	
	‡San Fabian Philippines	17 Mar 1991	Loreto D. Querimit
613	*Manila Philippines		
	‡Manila	20 May 1973	Augusto Alandy Lim
1210	Marikina Philippines	30 Nov 1980	Augusto Alandy Lim
2560	Montalban Philippines	4 Jun 2000	Hernelio Alos Baradi
1546	Naga Philippines	18 Aug 1985	Avelino S. Babia Sr.
2332	Narvacan Philippines	23 Mar 1997	William R. Beralta Sr.
2389	Novaliches Philippines	7 Sep 1997	Bartolme M. Baldenor
2533	Ormoc Philippines	27 Jun 1999	Reynaldo Saligo Delante Sr.
2340	Oroquieta Philippines	20 Apr 1997	Arturo Bugas Macalisang
1309	Paranaque Philippines	22 Nov 1981	Ruben M. Lacanienta
2430	Pasay Philippines	25 Jan 1998	Eleazer Salipot Collado
1554	Pasig Philippines	15 Sep 1985	Macario Molina Yasona Jr.
842	Quezon City Philippines	29 May 1977	Augusto Alandy Lim
2417	Quezon City Phillippines South	30 Nov 1997	Manuel Mendoza Agustin

2176	Rosales Philippines	10 Mar 1996	Emmanuel Vallejos Damasco
2549	Roxas Philippines	12 Mar 2000	Francisco D. Dariagan
1315	San Fernando La Union Phil.	6 Dec 1981	Angel B. Salanga Jr.
2459	San Jose Philippines	10 May 1998	Gavino Penales Apao Jr.
1552	San Pablo Philippines	20 Aug 1985	Cleofas S. Canoy
1875	Santa Cruz Philippines	31 May 1992	Rolando Pramis Nueva
2444	Santiago Philippines	22 Mar 1998	Efren M. Lamoglia
1330	*Talisay Philippines 10 Aug 1989		
	‡Cebu City Philippines South	21 Mar 1982	Bienvenido Pangilinan Flores
1321	Tarlac Philippines	13 Dec 1981	Mario de Jesus
1721	Tuguegarao Philippines	21 May 1989	Quirino Sumabat Donato
1558	Urdaneta Philippines	22 Sep 1985	Felino Caparas Ocampo
2435	Valenzuela Philippines	8 Feb 1998	Godofredo Hilario Esguerra
1571	Zamboanga Philippines	10 Nov 1985	Catalino A. Dugupan Sr.

Stakes discontinued

1877	Kidapawan Philippines	31 May 1992	Rodolfo Bergado Estrella
	Discontinued	19 Feb 1995	
1577	Munoz Philippines	24 Nov 1985	Juanito Wytangooy Tanedo
	Discontinued	31 May 1992	
1713	Olongapo Philippines	5 Mar 1989	Richard Noboru Kivabu
	Discontinued	5 Sep 1993	
1780	Ozamiz Philippines	25 Nov 1990	Wilfredo Tumampos Romero
	Discontinued	7 Nov 1993	

Missions — 13

(As of Oct. 1, 2000; shown with historical number. See MISSIONS.)

(268) PHILIPPINES ANGELES MISSION
1827 Gumain Street
Redwood Villas
Clark Field, Pampamga 2009
Philippines

(110) PHILIPPINES BACOLOD MISSION
P.O. Box 660, Bacolod City
6100 Negros Occidental
Philippines

(172) PHILIPPINES BAGUIO MISSION
P.O. Box 380
2600 Baguio City, Benguet
Philippines

(211) PHILIPPINES CAGAYAN DE ORO
P.O. Box 0400
Cagayan de Oro City 9000
Philippines

(194) PHILIPPINES CEBU MISSION
P.O. Box 338
Cebu City 6000
Philippines

(157) PHILIPPINES DAVAO MISSION
P.O. Box 80741
8000 Davao City,
Philippines

(256) PHILIPPINES ILAGAN MISSION
PO Box 78
Tuguegarao, Cagayan 3500
Philippines

(76b) PHILIPPINES MANILA MISSION
P.O. Box 1997
Makati Central Post Office
Makati, Metro Manila 1200
Philippines

(223) PHILIPPINES NAGA MISSION
P.O. Box 8857
Camarines Sur
4400 Naga City,
Philippines

(219) PHLIPPINES OLONGAPO MIS.
11 Sander Street
Gordon Heights
Olongapo City 2200,
Philippines

(192) PHILIPPINES QUEZON CITY MISSION
P.O. Box 13873
1600 Pasig
Metro Manila, Philippines

(250) PHILIPPINES SAN PABLO MISSION
Mabini Street Extension
P.O. Box 38
San Pablo City, Laguna 4000
Philippines

(251) PHILIPPINES TACLOBAN MISSION
P.O. Box 69
6500 Leyte, Tacloban City
Philippines

POLAND

Year-end 1999: Est. population, 38,792,000; Members, 1,094; Missions, 1; Branches, 11; Europe Central Area; percent LDS, .003 or one in 35,438.

On the Baltic Sea in east central Europe, Poland has a population that speaks Polish, and is mostly Roman Catholic.

In 1928, the Selbongen Branch meetinghouse was erected in Germany. After World War II, the town of Selbongen was part of the area ceded to Poland, and its name was changed to Zelbak.

Ezra Taft Benson, then a member of the Quorum of the Twelve, was the first priesthood leader to visit Zelbak after the war. Upon his arrival, more than 100 members and friends gathered in a quickly convened a meeting to bear their testimonies, sing and pray, and receive his counsel.

While the branch struggled to stay alive during the subsequent years, the spirit of the Saints did not falter. In 1947, government officials ordered the Zelbak meetings discontinued on the grounds that only the Polish language could be spoken in public meetings of any kind. Three years later, the branch was re-opened. The branch continued until 1978, when priesthood leaders made the decision to discontinue the branch. The meetinghouse there still stands, but is no longer used for LDS functions.

President Spencer W. Kimball visited Poland Aug. 24, 1977, after official recognition of the Church by the Polish government that was received May 30, 1977.

A number of couple missionaries served in Poland following 1977. The first elders arrived in January 1988. Sister Urzula Adamska, the first Polish missionary, was called in 1989.

On June 15, 1989, ground was broken for a meetinghouse in Warsaw. The ceremony was attended by more than 200 people, including government and religious leaders of different faiths. Elder Russell M. Nelson of the Quorum of the Twelve presided over and addressed the groundbreaking ceremony. The day after the groundbreaking, Elder Nelson and other Church leaders met with Poland's minister of religious affairs, who shared copies with them of a new law guaranteeing freedom of conscience and belief. The meetinghouse was dedicated June 22, 1991, in a service attended by more than 400 people, including government leaders. At the time work on the Warsaw meetinghouse was begun, Poland was part of the Austria Vienna East Mission. The Poland Warsaw Mission was created July 1, 1990.

Church Welfare Service workers served in a non-denominational consulting company helping Poland modernize its agriculture. The Church donated medical supplies, clothing, and bedding to Poland in 1991. The Tabernacle Choir performed in Warsaw June 22, 1991 and seminary classes began in Poland in 1994. In 1995, members of BYU's women's volleyball team participated in a fireside in Warsaw. In 1999, 1,094 LDS members lived in Poland.

Sources: Swiss Mission manuscript history; *Church News,* July 13, Aug. 17, and Aug. 24, 1946; "New Branch Organized in Red Poland," *Church News,* Oct. 1, 1966; "The Branch that Wouldn't Die," by Gilbert W. Scharffs, *Ensign,* 1971; *Church News,* Sept. 17, 1977; "Zelwagi survives," by Richard L. Jensen, *Church News,* June 30, 1979; "Church in Poland: Small but Strong," *Ensign,* August 1979; "The Book of Mormon in Polish," by Kerril Sue Rollins, *Ensign,* June 1982; "Reunion revives spirit of Selbongen," *Church News,* Oct. 14, 1989; *Church News,* July 1, 1989, July 6, 1991, Sept. 23, 1995, May 31, 1997, Nov. 22, 1997.

Mission — 1

(As of Oct. 1, 2000; shown with historical number. See MISSIONS.)

(252) POLAND WARSAW MISSION
ul. Wolska 142
P1-01-258 Warsaw, Poland

PORTUGAL

Year-end 1999: Est. population, 10,562,000; Members, 35,248; Stakes, 5; Wards, 28 Branches, 77; Missions, 3; Districts, 12; percent LDS, .33, or one in 300.

At the southwest corner of Europe, the Republic of Portugal is a parliamentary democracy. Its population is 97 percent Roman Catholic.

The first members of the LDS Church in Portugal were members in the U.S. Armed Forces stationed in the country in the early 1970s. The first known regularly held Church meetings were conducted by military personnel John C. Peterson and Steven Lindsey, who in the spring of 1974 visited the Spain Madrid Mission to see if missionary work could begin in Portugal. However, the Church was not recognized by the government in Portugal so missionary work could not proceed. In May 1974, a revolution led to a new government, which gave recognition to religious entities. Shortly thereafter, David M. Kennedy, special representative of the First Presidency, visited Portugal, and received assurances that the Church could enter the country.

In August 1974, Church member Ray E. Caldwell was assigned by the Canadian government to be first secretary of the Canadian embassy in Lisbon. He stopped en route in Salt Lake City, Utah, and was set apart as the group leader over any members he might find.

Church meetings were soon held in the Caldwell home. In November 1974, Pres. Wm. Grant Bangerter, later of the Presidency of the Seventy, arrived in Lisbon to preside over the newly created Portugal Lisbon Mission. Four missionaries were transferred from a mission in Brazil to begin the work, and they found many people who were interested in the gospel. By July 1975, there were 100 Portuguese members.

From those beginnings, the Church reached its first thousand members by July 1978. The Lisbon Portugal Stake, the first in Portugal, was created July 10, 1981. The Portugal Porto Mission was formed from the Portugal Lisbon Mission in July 1987. The Lisbon mission was further divided in 1989 to create the Lisbon North and Lisbon South missions. The visit and performance of the Tabernacle Choir in Lisbon July 1, 1998, raised the profile of the Church.

In 1999, there were 35,248 members in Portugal, second only to Germany in continental Europe, as the country with the most LDS members.

Sources: Culture for Missionaries: Portugal, 1984; "Discovering Gospel Riches in Portugal," by Don L. Searle, *Ensign,* Oct. 1987; *Church News,* Feb. 16, 1989; "Brotherly Love," *Ensign,* August 1989; *Church News,* July 4, 1998, July 18, 1998.

Stakes — 5

(Listed alphabetically as of Oct. 1, 2000.)

No.	Name	Organized	First President
Europe West Area			
1276	Lisbon Portugal	10 Jun 1981	Jose Manuel da Costa Santos
1729	Lisbon Portugal Oeiras	25 Jun 1989	Vitor Manuel Pereira M.
1613	Porto Portugal	2 Nov 1986	Alcino Pereira Da Silva
1723	*Porto Portugal South	10 Nov 1998	
	*Matosinhos Portugal	28 May 1989	Alexandre Rocha Benidio
1652	Setubal Portugal	6 Sep 1987	Octavio Da Silva Melo

Missions — 3

(As of Oct. 1, 2000; shown with historical number. See MISSIONS.)

(253) PORTUGAL LISBON NORTH MISSION
Rua Jorge Barradas 14B
1500 Lisbon, Portugal

(115) PORTUGAL LISBON SOUTH MISSION
Largo Com. Augusto Madureira, 7-B
1495 Alges, - Lisbon
Portugal

(203) PORTUGAL PORTO MISSION
Rua Amalia Luazes, No. 23 - Sala 1
4200 Porto
Portugal

AZORES AND MADEIRA ISLANDS

The Azores Islands, located 800 miles off the coast of Portugal in the North Atlantic, includes nine main islands that are populated.

Both archipelagos are Portuguese territories where Portuguese is spoken. The first branch was organized in Funchal on Sept. 4, 1983. In 1991 a group of Boy Scouts from Madeira took part in the Church's first Boy Scout encampment in Portugal. One district with four branches has been established in the Madeira Islands, as well as two districts in the Azores.

Sources: French Mission correspondence; Portugal Lisbon North Mission; *Church News,* March

19,1988; *Church News*; Oct. 5, 1991.

PUERTO RICO

Year-end 1999: Est. population, 3,813,000; Members, 23,223; Stakes, 4; Wards, 23; Districts, 4; Branches, 32; Missions, 1; percent LDS, .61, or one in 164.

The easternmost island of the Greater Antilles in the east Caribbean Sea, Puerto Rico is a U.S. commonwealth with a population that speaks Spanish. Most of the people are Roman Catholic.

Gardner H. Russell (who served in the Seventy from 1986-71) began holding Church meetings with his family and LDS servicemen at Guajataca in 1947, and later in San Juan. For the first few years, those who attended the meetings were LDS servicemen. Later, other members moved to Puerto Rico. In 1953, Reginald R. Dorff, military group leader, presided at the baptism of Dorothy Tate.

Florida Mission Pres. Ned Winder visited Puerto Rico in October 1963 on a routine visit and felt inspired to send missionaries. In January 1964, Elders Verl Tolbert and Dwight K. Hunter arrived in Puerto Rico. They visited several branches in the Puerto Rico District, which had been organized earlier for military personnel. They baptized a serviceman, Dennis Wayne Hart, on Feb. 8, 1964. The first Puerto Rican baptized was Ilka Josephina Frau, who was baptized at the Naval Beach on March 2, 1964.

The next mission president was Pres. Glen L. Rudd (who served in the Seventy from 1987-92), who sent Spanish-speaking missionaries to the island. The first Spanish-speaking branch was organized in 1970. On March 8 of that year, the first meetinghouse in the Caribbean District of the Florida Mission was dedicated in San Juan. On Oct. 17, home seminary was started. The Spanish branch became an independent branch a year later. Members' spirits were lifted March 8, 1981, by a visit from President Spencer W. Kimball.

The Puerto Rico San Juan Mission was created in 1979 with a membership of 1,892. The first stake was created in San Juan on Dec. 14, 1980, by President Ezra Taft Benson, then of the Quorum of the Twelve, at a meeting attended by 81 percent of the membership.

New stakes were added in 1982, 1984, and 1985. President Benson visited again on April 12, 1987, and noted that membership had increased to more than 12,000. Four stakes were discontinued in December 1993 following the reduction of military personnel stationed in Puerto Rico. In 1996, two stakes were reinstated because of the increase in local members. The advance of technology provides Puerto Rico access to all the Church programs on the Church's satellite network, including general conference.

The Church's administrative office in Puerto Rico sent relief supplies to help hurricane victims in the Caribbean. Hurricane Luis and Hurricane Marilyn both hit the area in September 1995 and Hurricane Georges, which struck in September 1998, destroyed considerable property, including that of members. In 1999, there were 23,223 members in Puerto Rico.

Sources: "Puerto Rico organizes two branches," by Elder Delbert Goates, *Church News*, June 25, 1955; Florida Mission manuscript history; "The Saints in Puerto Rico," by Orson Scott Card, *Ensign*, March 1978; "Caribbean beginnings," by Gordon Irving, *Church News*, April 22, 1978; "First Puerto Rican stake organized," *Church News*, Dec. 27, 1980; "History is made: prophet visits Caribbean islands," by Gerry Avant, *Church News*, March 21, 1981; "President Benson visits Puerto Rico," by Gerry Avant, *Church News*, April 18, 1987; "Outline of Historical Events . . . in Caribbean Nations," *VASAA Newsletter*, by Virgil N. Kovalenko; "Extensive hurricane damage, but LDS safe," *Church News*, Sept. 30, 1995; *Church News*, April 11, 1998, Oct. 3, 1998.

Stakes — 4

(Listed alphabetically as of Oct. 1, 2000.)

No.	Name	Organized	First President
North America Southeast Area			
2217	Mayaguez Puerto Rico Reinstated from No. 1580	11 Aug 1996	Tomas Olmo
2240	Ponce Puerto Rico Reinstated from No. 1349	22 Sep 1996	Rafael Ortiz
2347	San Juan Puerto Rico Reinstated from No. 1215	4 May 1997	William A. Burk
2473	Toa Baja Puerto Rico	7 Jun 1998	Jorge Miguel Alvarado
	Stakes discontinued		
1480	Carolina Puerto Rico Discontinued	17 Jun 1984 5 Dec 1993	Jesus Nieves
1580	Mayaguez Puerto Rico	1 Dec 1985	Heriberto Hernandez Vera

	Discontinued	5 Dec 1993	
1349	Ponce Puerto Rico	13 Jun 1982	Noah Jefferson Burns
	Discontinued	5 Dec 1993	
1215	San Juan Puerto Rico	14 Dec 1980	Herminio De Jesus
	Discontinued	5 Dec 1993	

Mission — 1

(As of Oct. 1, 2000; shown with historical number. See MISSIONS.)

(157) PUERTO RICO SAN JUAN MISSION
Urb. Villa Andalucia
A-14 Ronda Street Ste. 201
San Juan, PR 00926

ROMANIA

Year-end 1999: Est. population, 23,198,000; Members, 1,545; Missions, 1; Districts, 2; Branches, 17; Percent LDS, .01, or one in 15,015; Europe Central Area.

Romania is a republic in southeast Europe located on the Black Sea. Its people are Romanian with a Hungarian minority. Most are Romanian Orthodox with a small percentage of Protestant and Roman Catholics.

In July 1899, Mischa Markow, a prominent missionary to the Balkans, arrived in Constanta, Romania, with a Bulgarian companion, Argir Dimitrov, whom he baptized on Aug. 30, 1899. The pair traveled to Bucharest where they baptized another person. They made no further progress until Elder Markow had a dream about meeting a mother and daughter who would hear the gospel. The dream was realized in every detail and the mother and daughter were eventually baptized. Five others were later baptized as well and a branch organized.

Elder Markow was arrested a short time later. During his trial, Elder Markow defended the gospel and a dispute about the apostasy broke out in the courtroom. Elder Markow was confined to a jail for few days and banished.

In modern times, Elder Russell M. Nelson of the Quorum of the Twelve and Elder Hans B. Ringger of the Seventy met with the ministers of justice, health, and religion, and other dignitaries, including the mayor of Bucharest and members of the district council on Feb. 8-9, 1990. Following this meeting, the Church began assisting with the Romanian orphanages and supplying medical supplies to the country.

Romania became part of the Austria Vienna East Mission in 1990, where it remained until the mission was discontinued in 1992. Missionaries serving in Romania provided humanitarian services under the Hungary Budapest Mission until the Romania Bucharest Mission was created July 1, 1993.

Assistance to Romania continued from European stakes through the early 1990s. Members in Romania were blessed with the announcement on Aug. 8, 1998, that a temple would be built in the nearby Ukraine.

The six branches that comprise the Romania Bucharest District met June 30, 2000, for an evening of roadshow-like skits enacting key events of the Book of Mormon. The evening was in commemoration of the translation of the Book of Mormon into Romanian a year-and-a-half before.

The first youth conference in Romania since the Romania Bucharest Mission was organized in 1993 was held July 13-15, 2000. About 70 youth from 17 branches participated in the conference, held on a mountain top overlooking verdant farmlands below.

Sources: "Began with one," by William Slaughter, *Church News*, July 21, 1979; "Mischa Markow, Missionary to the Balkans," by William Hale Kehr, *Ensign*, June 1980; *Church News*, Aug. 18, 1990; Aug. 17, 1991, Dec. 7, 1991, Jan. 11, 1992, correspondence from Kahlile Mehr, Dec. 29, 1992; "Pioneering in Russia," by Gary Browning, *Ensign*, June 1997; *Church News*, Aug. 8, 1998, Aug. 12, 2000, Aug. 19, 2000.

Mission — 1

(As of Oct. 1, 2000; shown with historical number. See MISSIONS.)

(292) ROMANIA BUCHAREST MISSION
C.P. 42-54
Bucharest
Romania

RUSSIA

Year-end 1999: Est. population, 159,909,000; Members, 11,092; Missions, 8; Districts,

11; Branches, 103; Percent LDS, .01, or one in 14,417; Europe East Area.

Russians speak nearly 100 languages, the most widespread of which is Russian. Non-religious or atheists make up 51 percent of the population, with Russian Orthodox 31 percent, and Muslim, 11 percent.

As early as 1843, Russia was considered a prospective mission field. Orson Hyde and George J. Adams were called to go to Russia by the Prophet Joseph Smith, but their mission was aborted by the Prophet's martyrdom a year later.

In 1895, Elder August Joel Hoglund, a native of Sweden, was sent to St. Petersburg where he arrived June 9. He met with the Johan M. Lindelof family and baptized Johan and his wife, Alma, on June 11 in the river Neva. The Lindelof family was visited periodically and in 1903, Elder Francis M. Lyman of the Quorum of the Twelve and then president of the European Mission, accompanied by Joseph J. Cannon, visited the family in St. Petersburg. The Lindelof family later left Russia during the revolution of 1918, went to Finland, and remained faithful.

On April 27, 1919, Andrew Hasberg, a member of the U.S. Expeditionary Forces during World War I, was baptized in a lake about four miles south of Vladivostok, Russia's easternmost port city, by Thomas E. Hunsaker.

In 1959 Elder Ezra Taft Benson of the Quorum of the Twelve, then U.S. Secretary of Agriculture, visited the Central Baptist Church in Moscow and preached to an attentive congregation.

Missionary work resumed tentatively in 1989, two years before the Soviet Union broke up. Among the first to be baptized were Yuri, Ludmilla, and Anna Terebenin, who heard about the Church and were baptized during a trip to Budapest, Hungary. Olga Smolyanova, then 18, was baptized in Italy. Others were baptized by Finnish member-missionaries. One of these was Leena Laitinen, who taught a group of investigators in her home in Leningrad. During this period, visits were made to Leningrad and Moscow by Elder Hans B. Ringger of the Seventy and mission presidents Steven R. Mecham of the Finland Helsinki Mission and Dennis B. Neuenschwander (called to the Seventy in April 1991) of the Austria Vienna East Mission. In September of 1989, Pres. Neuenschwander authorized U.S. Embassy worker Dohn Thornton to begin holding group meetings in his apartment. Two missionaries, Elders David S. Reagan and Kevin A. Dexter, arrived in Leningrad on Jan. 26, 1990. They taught Sister Laitinen's investigators and baptized Anton Skripko on Feb. 3, 1990, the first member baptized in Russia in modern times. He later became the first to serve a full-time mission from Russia, arriving at the Missionary Training Center, in Provo, Utah, on July 26, 1991, and serving in the Utah Ogden Mission.

The first missionaries stationed in Leningrad were Elder Reagan and Elder Burt Dover. The Vyborg Branch was created in February 1990.

Elders Russell M. Nelson and Dallin H. Oaks of the Quorum of the Twelve visited a number of times and continued efforts to strengthen the Church in Russia and its neighboring countries.

By mid-summer 1990, the Leningrad Branch, which had been created Dec. 3, 1989, numbered 100 members, and the Vyborg Branch had 25 members. In September 1990, the St. Petersburg Branch was recognized by the government and in October, a religious freedom law was passed.

In June 1991, the Tabernacle Choir received publicity "beyond its wildest expectations" as it performed in the Bolshoi Theater in Moscow and in Leningrad (now St. Petersburg), and recorded songs that were later broadcast to a potential audience of 339 million. The Church was officially recognized by Russia on May 28, 1991, and announcement of this was made at a dinner following the Choir's Moscow performance on June 24, 1991.

The Russia Moscow and Russia St. Petersburg missions were created Feb. 3, 1992, with the membership of Russia numbering about 750. The first Russian branch president was Andrei Petrov, sustained in March 1991. A year later, the Moscow Branch was divided into six branches, and in 1993, these became 15 branches. At that time, there were as many members in the Moscow area as in the whole of Russia a year earlier. A third mission, Russia Samara, was created July 1993, and two additional missions, Russia Novosibirsk and Russia Rostov, were created July 1, 1994. The sixth mission, Russia Yekaterinburg, was created in July 1995, followed by the creation of the Russia Moscow South Mission in 1997. The eighth mission, Vladivostok, was created in 1999.

During 1991 and afterward, humanitarian relief to Russia was supplied by members from Europe and the United States. Tons of food and clothing were distributed to members and non-members, including shipments to Kommi and Ossetia regions in the fall of 1994; 160,000 pounds of food and 40,000 pounds of winter clothing were sent to

Partizansk in December 1994.

On May 14, 1998, a certificate of registration was issued to the Church, allowing the Church to continue to provide humanitarian and missionary work, and have places for its members to meet. The new approval was needed following passage of a law requiring re-registration. New visa regulations, issued in August 1998, required foreign clerics to leave the country four times a year to renew their visas. At the time, the Church had 800 missionaries in Russia.

Count Nikolai Tolstoy-Miloslavsky loaned relics from his family, once owned by Count Leo Tolstoy, for display at the Church museum in Salt Lake City, Utah. Members of the Tolstoy family and Church members have corresponded over the years.

When a powerful thunderstorm swept through Moscow June 13, 1998, and caused serious damage, missionaries from the Russia Moscow Mission were among the volunteers to clean up the damage.

The Church's first organized institute class in Siberia was started in the fall of 1998, when Elena Evanova and Olga Tolomyeva, both recent converts, began teaching 21 students who gathered in a small apartment in Krasnoyarsk, Russia. Seminary and institute programs also began in the fall of 1998 in Novosibirsk, Yekaterinburg, and Odessa.

LDS membership in Russia in 1999 was 11,092 in 103 branches in eight missions, the eighth of which, Vladivostok, was created in 1999.

On May 12-14, 2000, more than 200 young single adults participated in a Chuch conference in Zvenigorod, Russia, coming from Moscow, St. Petersburg, Samara, Saratov, Volograd, Rostov, Zelenograd, Voronezh, Nizhny Novgorod, and Podolsk. Young adults from Belarus and Armenia also attended.

Sources: *Times and Seasons,* 4:218; *Millennial Star,* Aug. 27, 1903; *Improvement Era,* November, 1903; "Mischa Markow, Missionary to the Balkans," by William Hale Kehr, *Ensign,* June 1980; *Journal of Mormon History,* Vol. 13, 1986-87; *Ezra Taft Benson, A Biography*; "Choir leaves trail of joyful tears," by Gerry Avant, *Church News,* July 7, 1991; *Church News,* Oct. 12, 1991; "Converts pioneer frontier in Russia," by Steve Fidel, *Church News,* Sept. 19, 1992; "Many families in Russia are blessed by relief effort," *Church News,* Jan. 28, 1995; and "Victims of hardship 'full of gratitude,' " *Church News,* April 27, 1996; "1989-90, The Curtain Opens," by Kahlile Mehr, *Ensign,* Dec. 1993 and correspondence from Kahlile Mehr, Dec. 29, 1992; "Growth of the Church in 'that vast empire,'" an address by Gary L. Browning, *Church News,* Nov. 6, 1993, May 23, 1998, July 4, 1998; "Finding hope in gospel message," by Sarah Jane Weaver, *Church News,* Jan. 19, 1999; *Church News,* June 3, 2000.

Missions — 8

(As of Oct. 1, 2000; shown with historical number. See MISSIONS.)

(272) RUSSIA MOSCOW MISSION
Glavpochtampt a/ia 257
Moscow 101000
Russia

(301) RUSSIA NOVOSIBIRSK MISSION
Mochishchenskaya Shosse 18, 2 etazh
Pochtamt a/ai 208
630123 Novosibirsk
Russia

(293) RUSSIA SAMARA MISSION
Glavpochtamt a/ia 3007
443099 Samara
Russia

(333) RUSSIA VLADIVOSTOK MISSION
Mordovtseva 3-304
Vladivostok 690000
Russia

(315) RUSSIA MOSCOW SOUTH
International PO Box 148
131000 Moscow
Russia

(302) RUSSIA ROSTOV NA DONU MISSION
Glavpochamp A/Y 96
344008 g. Rostov-na-Donu
Russia

(273) RUSSIA ST. PETERSBURG
Nab. Reki Moiki 11-11
St. Petersburg, 191065
Russia

(305) RUSSIA YEKATERINBURG MISSION
Glavpochtamt a/ya 250
620151 Yekaterinburg
Russia

SAMOA

(See American Samoa or Western Samoa)

ST. KITTS AND NEVIS
(ST. CHRISTOPHER-NEVIS)

Year-end 1999: Est. population, 41,000; Members, 95; Branches, 1; Percent LDS, .23, or one in 432; North America Southeast Area; West Indies Mission.

Located in the Eastern Caribbean in the Leeward Islands, St. Kitts and Nevis has a population that speaks English and is mostly Protestant.

In 1983, Pres. Kenneth Zabriskie of the West Indies Mission and his wife, LeOra, were introduced to the deputy prime minister of St. Kitts through a mutual acquaintance, Kutaba Alghanin, who sailed about the Caribbean in his yacht and employed two returned missionaries as tutors to his children.

In July 1984, Elders Douglas Myers and Robert J. Molina arrived on St. Kitts and were soon followed by Reuel and Alice Lambourn on Oct. 20, 1984. They adapted a home into a meetinghouse and the St. Kitts-Nevis Branch was organized on Sept. 10, 1985, with Elder Lambourn as the first president. On Feb. 2, 1985, Dianna Ermintude Johnson was baptized, the first convert on the island. A weekly open house was held on Thursdays where the newly baptized members and investigators could study together.

A local member, Carol Pamela Heather Thomas, became the first missionary from the islands when she was called June 14, 1991, to serve in the New Jersey Morristown Mission. Three other missionaries served from St. Kitts and Nevis in the next two years. In 1994, the branch had about 70 members taking part in all the programs, including seminary. Two choirs regularly participate in the meetings. In February 1995, a small group of Church members went to the government and asked permission to clean up a park in the center of town. This act help change many people's attitudes about the Church. Terry Lewellyn Hanley became the first native branch president to serve on St. Kitts in early 1996.

Sources: Kenneth and LeOra Zabriskie journals; correspondence from West Indies Mission, 1994; "Caribbean members plan to celebrate achievements of pioneers — those on island and of 1847 trek," *Church News*, June 22, 1996; *Deseret News*, Sept. 21, 1998.

ST. VINCENT AND THE GRENADINES

Year-end 1999: Est. population, 117,000; Members, 342; Branches, 1; percent LDS, .29, or one in 342; North America Southeast Area; West Indies Mission.

In the eastern Caribbean and part of the Windward Island chain, the Grenadines are a parliamentary democracy. Most of the population speaks English. Religious adherents are primarily Methodist, Anglican, and Roman Catholic.

The Grenadines were part of the Puerto Rico San Juan Mission until 1983, when the islands were placed in the West Indies Mission. The Kingstown Branch was organized Oct. 22, 1980. Under the direction of Pres. Edmund Israel the branch developed. Missionaries cleared the land for a meetinghouse and a site dedication was held June 16, 1985, and a building was subsequently constructed. A former prime minister of St. Vincent, Ebeneezer Joshua, joined the Church and served in the branch presidency. Sharon Nichols was the first local member called on a full-time mission in 1983.

When Brother Joshua died in 1991, from 30,000 to 40,000 people, including top government officials, viewed or attended his televised funeral in the Kingstown meetinghouse and learned of the plan of salvation.

Sources: Kenneth and LeOra Zabriskie journals; correspondence from Pres. A. Dean Jeffs, West Indies Mission; *Church News*, March 30, 1991.

SCOTLAND

(See United Kingdom)

SIERRA LEONE

Year-end 1999: Est. population, 4,753,000; Members, 3,564; Districts, 3; Branches, 16; Percent LDS, .07, or one in 1,334; Africa West Area; Ghana Accra Mission.

On the west coast of West Africa, the Republic of Sierra Leone has a population that speaks English and tribal languages, and is Muslim, 30 percent; Animist, 30 percent; and Christian, 10 percent.

Michael Samura was baptized in Holland in 1981, and later returned to Freetown, Sierra Leone, where he stayed until 1984. He later returned to Sierra Leone. Elizabeth

Bangura and Monica Orleans were baptized in Ghana and formed a study group in Freetown in January 1988. Christian George was baptized outside the country and returned to preside over the first approved meeting, held Jan. 18, 1988, at Goderich, a suburb of Freetown. In May 1988, Elder and Sister Clair Fisher, and Elder and Sister Erwin Waite arrived and took part in a service on June 11, 1988, where the first 14 converts were baptized.

The Liberia Monrovia Mission, which included Sierra Leone, was created on March 1, 1988. The Goderich Branch was organized Aug. 7, 1988, with Brother Samura as a counselor in the branch presidency. On Oct. 6, 1989, Abu H. Conteh was called as the first full-time missionary and assigned to serve in Sierra Leone.

The Freetown District was created December 1990 by Elder Robert E. Sackley of the Seventy and a member of the Africa Area presidency. Seminary was introduced into the country by 1991, and two more districts, Bo and Wellington, were created Aug. 25 of that year.

The Liberia mission offices were moved to Freetown, Sierra Leone, in May 1990 because of the unrest in Liberia. Later, as civil war developed, the Liberia Monrovia Mission was discontinued on April 22, 1991, and the area was transferred to the Ghana Accra Mission. In May and August 1992, two missionary couples were temporarily removed from Sierra Leone because of unrest.

By year-end 1993, 89 Sierra Leonians were serving full-time missions, including 41 from the six branches of the Freetown District.

In 1994, quilts from young women of the Frederick Maryland Stake were shipped to Sierra Leone through the Church's Washington, D.C., welfare complex. With each quilt was a letter, signed by the young women, that explained that individual pieces of the quilt represent acts of love and service.

In 1994, an artist from Sierra Leone, Abu Hassan Conteh, entered a textile in the Third International Art Competition sponsored by the Museum of Church History and Art in Salt Lake City, and his work was singled out for display. His work was again exhibited in the museum in 1995 among other award-winning entries from the competition.

LDS in Sierra Leone in 1999 numbered 3,564.

Sources: Pres. Miles Cunningham of the Liberia Monrovia Mission; *Church News*, Jan. 26, 1991; correspondence from Pres. Christopher N. Chukwurah, Ghana Accra Mission, March 14, 1994; *Church News*, Jan. 8, 1994, April 2, 1994, Feb. 4, 1995.

SINGAPORE

Year-end 1999: Est. population, 2,890,000; Members, 2,099; Stakes, 1; Wards, 6; Branches, 2; Missions, 1; Percent LDS, .07, or one in 1,377.

On the tip of the Malay Peninsula in southeast Asia, Singapore is a parliamentary democracy. Its population speaks Chinese, Malay, Tamil, and English (all are official languages). The people are Buddhist, Christian, Islam, Taoist, and Hindu.

In 1960, the First Presidency gave Elder Gordon B. Hinckley of the Quorum of the Twelve responsibility for the work of the Church in Asia. Among the millions of residents, only four members of the Church, all expatriates, could be found in Singapore.

Members in the British military and Chinese members who moved from Hong Kong began holding meetings in Singapore in 1963. On March 19, 1968, four missionaries from the Southern Far East Mission arrived in Singapore. A branch was organized Oct. 13, 1968, with John McSweeney as president and Sheila Hsia, a member from Hong Kong, as Relief Society president. The Southeast Asia Mission was created Nov. 1, 1969.

About a year later the branch membership numbered approximately 100.

In 1970, the government restricted tracting and visas, and work progressed through the local members. By 1976, membership was 309. The Singapore Mission was re-opened Jan. 1, 1980. In 1985, membership increased to 960. Three meetinghouses were completed in 1990.

In August 1992, a returned missionary from Taiwan, Jon Huntsman Jr., was sworn in as U.S. ambassador to Singapore. The youngest-ever U.S. ambassador to Singapore and the first to speak Mandari, he served until June 15, 1993.

By mid-1993, membership had increased to 1,750 members in seven branches, and to 2,099 in one stake in 1999. The stake was created from the Singapore District on Feb. 25, 1995, by Elder Neal A. Maxwell of the Quorum of the Twelve.

On a Pacific Rim tour in 2000, President Hinckley addressed 1,450 members at a fireside Jan. 30 in Singapore.

Sources: LDS Scene, *Improvement Era,* June 1969; "Help from members," *Church News,* Aug. 18, 1979; March 10, 1985; address by Elder Marion D. Hanks, Salt Lake Institute devotional April 5, 1981; *Church News,* Nov. 17, 1973, Nov. 16, 1991, Sept. 5, 1992, June 5, 1993; "Asia area: Welcome mat is out in several countries," by Sheridan R. Sheffield, *Church News,* June 19, 1993; "New Stakes," *Church News,* April 27, 1995; *Church News,* Feb. 12, 2000.

Stake — 1

(Listed alphabetically as of Oct. 1, 2000.)

No. Name	Organized	First President
Asia Area		
2025 Singapore Singapore	26 Feb 1995	Woo Hoi Seng Leonard

Mission — 1

(As of Oct. 1, 2000; shown with historical number. See MISSIONS.)

(89) SINGAPORE MISSION
253 Bukit Timah Road, Floor 4
259690
Singapore

SLOVAK REPUBLIC

Year-end 1999: Est. Population, 5,432,000; Members, fewer than 100; Branches, 3; Europe Central Area; Czech Republic Prague Mission.

The east side of the former state of Czechoslovakia, Slovak Republic is a federal republic with a population that speaks Slovak, Czech, and Hungarian, and which is mostly Roman Catholic, Protestant, and Orthodox Jewish.

The first member in Slovak Republic was Valerie Ruzena Frantiska Zizkova, born to members in the Czech Republic and baptized July 1939, just before the missionaries departed prior to World War II. She regained contact with missionaries for a brief period after the war, and then, from the pressure of the Communist government, lost contact with the Church. She later married and moved to Central Slovakia and remained faithful, renewing contact with the Church in 1992. Other members baptized as expatriates included Alzbeta Domotorova, who had been baptized in Germany in 1977; and Pavel Pirovits, who had requested political asylum in Germany prior to the fall of the Communist regime. Other influential converts were Peter and Hanka Vaclav. Brother Vaclav had been baptized in March 1991 stemming from contact with members in Moravia. His wife joined several months later following an accident, after which she began to have a deeper interest in God. The first Church meeting held in modern times in Slovakia was at the home of Brother and Sister Vaclav. The meeting was held in October 1991 with visiting missionaries from the Czech Republic presiding. The family interest led to the establishment of the first branch in Slovakia, the Trencin Branch. This branch was created under the direction of Pres. Richard W. Winder of the Czechslovakia Prague Mission on Jan. 24, 1993. A group of members began meeting in Bratislava, and a second branch was created there later in the year.

Elders David Backman and Christopher Williams arrived to work in Trencin on March 29, 1992, and they baptized Martin and Zuzana Blaskova on July 25, 1992, in Trencin.

In 1993, producer Radim Smetana and reporter Premysl Cech of Czechoslovak Television visited Salt Lake City to make a documentary featuring the Church for broadcast in the Czech Republic and Slovak Republic. Mr. Smetana came in contact with the Church in June 1991 when the Tabernacle Choir performed in Prague; his contact then led to subsequent programs featuring the Church.

On April 30, 1994, a translation team with Elder Marcello de Oliveira as coordinator began translating basic Church materials into Slovak.

Sources: Unpublished history of the Church in Slovakia, courtesy Pres. Phil J. Bryson; "Czech broadcasters see Church close up," *Church News,* May 22, 1993.

SLOVENIA

Year-end 1999: Est. Population, 2,051,000; Members, 200; Districts, 1; Branches, 3; Missions, 1; Europe Central Area.

Located on the Balkan Peninsula in southeast Europe, Slovenia is a republic made up of what was the northernmost internal division of Yugoslavia.

By the early 1970s, a few Latter-day Saints were living in Yugoslavia, some of whom had joined the Church while working or studying abroad.

In early 1975, Neil D. Schaerrer, president of the Austria Vienna Mission, established the Church as a legal entity in Yugoslavia. He met with members in Ljubljana, a major city in central Slovenia, during the following months. However, the Church is relatively new in Slovenia, with most of the members joining the Church since independence was declared after the collapse of communism. In 1993, Elder Matjaz Juhart became the first full-time missionary called from the Republic of Slovenia. He was called to the Utah Salt Lake City Mission.

Boza Gardner, 22, and Albin Lotric, 24, president of the Ljubljana Branch, were the first couple to marry in the temple from Slovenia. They even found a wedding dress for her among clothing donated from members in other countries. The two were married in the Frankfurt Germany Temple July 8, 1992.

The presence of BYU's men's basketball team, on a European tour in 1994, led to many referrals for the 20 missionaries and 60 members residing in Slovenia. Team members, seven of whom were returned missionaries, attended sacrament meeting in a hotel in Ljubjana.

Members in Slovenia were among those who placed their testimonies in a book that accompanied a handcart taken across Russia in honor of the pioneer sesquicentennial in 1997. Leon Bergant, a timed trial bicycle champion, and a promising member of the Slovene National Bike Team, left the team in 1997 to serve a full-time mission in Croatia. Two main newspapers carried major stories about the young man's decision.

At a youth conference in Ljubljana in July 1998, 55 young members from Croatia, Serbia, Bosnia, and Slovenia met together on the theme "Love One Another," and set an example for others as they lived up to the theme. Headquarters of the Austria Vienna South Mission was relocated in Ljublana in March of 1999, and re-named the Slovenia Ljubljana Mission. In 1999, membership in Slovenia was 199.

Sources: Yugoslavia, manuscript history; "Missionary to the Balkans, Mischa Markow," by William Hale Kehr, *Ensign*, June 1980; Zagreb Branch history, published by the branch at dedication of meetinghouse, Oct. 30, 1985; *Church News*, Sept. 26, 1992; "Cinderella story: A dress for bride-to-be," *Church News*, Feb. 6, 1993; *Church News*, Jan 22, 1994, Sept. 10, 1994, June 28, 1997; "Bike champion gives up racing to serve mission," *Church News*, Feb. 14, 1998, "Youth forget barriers, join in conference of friendship," *Church News*, Aug. 29, 1998, both by Shaun D. Stahle.

Mission — 1

(As of Oct. 1, 2000; shown with historical number. See MISSIONS.)

(309) SLOVENIA LJUBLJANA
Molekova U1. 3
1211 Ljubljana
Slovenia

SOLOMON ISLANDS

Year-end 1999: Est. population: 399,000; Members, 148; branches, 1; Percent LDS, .37, or one in 2,696; Papua New Guinea Mission.

The Solomon Islands lie in the West Pacific Ocean east of Papua New Guinea and its people speak English and Papuan, and are Anglican, 34 percent; Roman Catholic, 19 percent; and other Christian.

The first members on the Solomon Islands were Imo Ta'asi, who had been baptized in 1986 at BYU, and Peter Joseph Salaka, a member of Parliament who had been baptized in England. On March 10, 1987, Elder James E. Faust of the Quorum of the Twelve visited the island for missionary purposes. The first missionaries were Elder E. Crawford Jones and his wife, Sister Judith Jones, who arrived in February 1995. President John Gibson of the Papua New Guinea Mission sent two missionaries, Elders Glenn R. Cockburn and Sa Francis Togia. These two began preaching the gospel to the people of the Solomon Islands. The first sacrament meetings were held in Honaira on Feb. 5, 1995, with four in attendance. On April 26, 1995, Pres. Gibson met with Prime Minister Solomon Mamaloni and gave him a copy of the Book of Mormon.

The first baptism on the island was Eddie Misi on May 21, 1995. He later became the first branch president. The Honiara Branch was created Feb. 4, 1996. Sixty-two people were in attendance that day, including 17 members. Since that time, membership has increased to 148 people.

In June 2000, because of political unrest, eight missionaries — six elders and one senior couple — were temporarily relocated from the Solomon Islands and sent to the Australia Brisbane Mission.

Source: Brief "Church History in the Solomon Islands," by Christopher Cooper, public affairs officer for the Pacific Area. He cites: Letter from James E. Faust, July 31, 1995; *Church News*, April 15, 1995; *Ensign*, June 1995; *Church News*, June 17, 2000.

SOMALIA

Year-end 1999: Est. population, 6,842,000; Members, fewer than 100; Africa Southeast Area.

The easternmost country in Africa, the Somalia Democratic Republic covers more than 246,000 square miles. Almost all Somalians speak the Somali language and are Sunni Muslims.

Somalia gained its independence in 1960. Prior to that, Great Britain ruled the northern section and Italy ruled the southern.

There are fewer than 100 members in the country and, as of 1998, no official Church group. In 1992, the Church shipped 1 million pounds of food and relief supplies to Somalia and neighboring countries to help alleviate suffering from drought. A large portion of Church aid went to Somalians, victims of not only the drought, but also of civil war. Several members traveled from Somalia to Nairobi, Kenya, to hear President Gordon B. Hinckley when he spoke at a member meeting Feb. 17, 1998.

Sources: World Book Encyclopedia, vol. 18, p. 588; Church membership records; "Deadly drought," *Church News*, Sept. 26, 1992, Feb. 28, 1998.

SOUTH AFRICA

Year-end 1999: Est. population, 45,095,000; Members, 29,220; Stakes, 9; Wards,36; Branches, 51; Missions, 3; Districts, 2; Temples, 1; percent LDS, .06, or one in 1,543.

At the southern end of the continent of Africa, the Republic of South Africa is a tricameral parliament. Its people speak Afrikaans, English, and Bantu, and are mainly Christian, with Hindu and Muslim minorities.

Elders Jesse Haven, Leonard L. Smith, and William H. Walker began missionary labors in Cape Town, South Africa, on April 19, 1853. On May 23, 1853, the trio officially organized the Church in the Cape of Good Hope. Elder Haven was appointed the first mission president of the South African Mission. Despite immediate, heavy persecution, they baptized Henry Stringer, the first convert, on June 15, 1853.

On Aug. 16, 1853, the first branch of the Church in South Africa was organized at Mowbray, four miles from Cape Town. A second branch was organized Sept. 7, 1853, at Newlands, six miles from Cape Town. A third branch was organized Feb. 23, 1854, at Beaufort, Cape Colony. These branches later formed the the Cape Conference. At a conference held in Port Elizabeth on Aug. 13, 1855, the "Church in the Cape of Good Hope" (South African Mission) was reported to consist of three conferences, six branches, and 126 members.

Due to proselyting restrictions and lack of knowledge of the Afrikaans language, the South African Mission was closed from 1865 to 1903. Elder Warren H. Lyon reopened and presided over the mission. The first LDS meetinghouse in South Africa was built in 1916-17 as an addition to the first mission home at Mowbray. In 1950, missionary work was extended to Rhodesia, where several branches of the Church were established.

The first stake in South Africa, the Transvaal Stake, was organized on March 22, 1970. The Afrikaans translation of the Book of Mormon was first introduced to the South African Saints on May 14, 1972.

The first area conference in South Africa was held in Johannesburg Oct. 23-24, 1978, attended by 3,450 of the subcontinent's 7,200 members living in South Africa, Rhodesia (now Zimbabwe), and South West Africa (now Namibia). Five General Authorities attended the conference, the first time ever that more than one General Authority was in South Africa at the same time.

The Johannesburg South Africa Temple was completed and dedicated in 1982 and has been visited by members throughout the southern part of the continent.

The South African Mission was divided on July 1, 1984, creating the South Africa Johannesburg and South Africa Cape Town missions. The South Africa Durban Mission was created in 1988, an outgrowth of the Mascarene Mission.

Work in townships and other areas in South Africa progressed significantly in the 1980s. At a regional conference held Feb. 8-9, 1992, in Johannesburg, attendance reached 4,200, including a choir of 140 youths from three area stakes. Membership in the Soweto township continued to grow as members and missionaries worked closely together. Following the abolition of aparthied (apartness), members of all origins worked together to overcome cultural barriers.

Among Church or Church-affiliated programs active in South Africa is the Scouting organization. In 1996, some 5,000 gathered for the Johannesburg Regional Conference — the largest such LDS gathering in South Africa up to that time. However, the visit of President Gordon B. Hinckley on Feb. 19, 1998, attracted 5,500 members in Johannesburg, making it the largest gathering of Church members in South Africa; 1,800 in Durban; and 1,500 in Cape Town. Leaders in South Africa worked to increase membership in townships and at the same time reassure their longtime members of a bright future in South Africa.

In 1999, there were 29,220 LDS members in South Africa.

Sources: *Encyclopedic History of the Church,* by Andrew Jenson; "South Africa,", *Relief Society Magazine,* June 1969; "Mission Opening — 117 Years Ago," by Jack E. Jarrard, *Church News,* June 20, 1970; "The Saints in South Africa," by Lawrence E. Cummins, *Ensign,* March 1973; "South Africans greet prophet at conference," by Dell Van Orden, *Church News,* Nov. 4, 1978;"Early Mormon Imprints in South Africa", by David J. Whittaker, *Brigham Young University Studies,* spring 1980; Saints in South Africa, by Marjorie E. Woods, September 1986; *Church News,* Feb. 29, 1992, Sept. 26, 1992; "South Africa: Land of Good Hope," by R. Val Johnson, *Ensign,* February 1993; *Church News,* Nov. 11, 1995, March 2, 1996; "Members urged to build up homeland," by John L. Hart and Steve Fidel, *Church News,* Feb. 28, 1998; *Church News,* June 6, 1998.

Stakes — 9

(Listed alphabetically as of Oct. 1, 2000.)

No.	Name	Organized	First President
Africa Southwest Area			
2437	Bedfordview South Africa	15 Feb 1998	Neil P. Fourie
1662	Benoni South Africa	29 Nov 1987	Jan G. Hugo
1470	Cape Town South Africa	6 May 1984	Otto Wilhelm Miessner
1314	Durban South Africa	29 Nov 1981	Percy E.A. Winstanley
2529	Hillcrest South Africa	16 May 1999	Garith Charles Hill
506	*Johannesburg South Africa		
	‡Transvaal (South Africa)	22 Mar 1970	Louis P. Hefer
969	*Pretoria South Africa 29 Nov 1987		
	‡Sandton South Africa	22 Oct 1978	Johannes P. Brummer
2046	Roodepoort South Africa	7 May 1995	Christoffel Golden Jr.
2516a	Soweto South Africa	14 Mar 1999	Robert Eppel

Missions — 3

(As of Oct. 1, 2000; shown with historical number. See MISSIONS.)

(177a) S. AFRICA CAPE TOWN MISSION
P.O. Box 217
Howard Place
7450 Pinelands
Republic of South Africa

(216) S. AFRICA DURBAN MISSION
8 Windsor Ave.
Westville, 3630
Republic of South Africa

(14) SOUTH AFRICA JOHANNESBURG MISSION
Private Bag X 7
Weltevreden Park 1715
Republic of South Africa

TRANSKEI

Year-end 1999: Est. population, 3,500,000; Members, fewer than 100; Branches, 1; Africa Southeast Area; South Africa Cape Town Mission.

Transkei is on the southwest coast of South Africa. In March 1988, a member, Dr. Emmanuel Danso and his wife, Akosua Seiwa, moved to Port Saint Johns, where they met with missionaries and she was baptized. The Umtata Branch was organized with Dr. Danso as branch president on April 8, 1990. The branch is part of the East London South Africa District and part of the South Africa Cape Town Mission.

Sources: South Africa Johannesburg Mission manuscript history; "Gospel takes root in Africa's Wild Coast," by Jay H. Buckley, *Church News,* June 16, 1990.

SPAIN

Year-end 1999: Est. population, 39,404,000; Members, 30,439; Stakes, 7; Wards, 37; Branches, 107; Missions, 5; Districts, 16; Temples, 1; percent LDS, .08, or one in 1,295.

Located in southwest Europe, Spain is a constitutional monarchy. Its people speak Spanish, Catalan, Galician, and Basque, and 90 percent are Roman Catholic.

Regular Church services began in Spain among LDS servicemen after World War II when the United States established relations with that country. Two American branches were functioning in 1966, and a district presidency operated under the French Mission. One of the first converts in Spain, Jose Maria Oliveira, was baptized in France on March 12, 1966, because it was illegal for other churches to perform ordinances in Spain. Before the Spanish Religious Liberty Law was passed in 1967, Elders Howard W. Hunter and Gordon B. Hinckley of the Quorum of the Twelve traveled to Spain and met with the Spanish Minister for Religious Affairs and then instructed local Church leaders, assisted by David B. Timmins, head of the economic section of the U.S. Embassy, to apply for registration of the Church. Passage of the religious liberty law paved the way for the organization of the Madrid Branch on the first Sunday in February 1968. Some 40 attended, including Spanish wives of American servicemen, other Spanish-speaking members, and investigators.

Official recognition for the Church in Spain was formalized on Oct. 22, 1968. The first missionaries arrived in Spain in 1969, and the Spain Mission was organized July 11, 1970. During this period, many Spanish-speaking members were transferred by their businesses to Spain and this helped to strengthen the new branches. By 1974, 17 branches, with a total membership of 619, were operating in Spain.

Elder Hinckley, accompanied by Elder Neal A. Maxwell of the Presidency of the First Quorum of the Seventy, visited King Juan Carlos de Bourbon in August 1978.

Spain's first stake was created in Madrid on March 14, 1982. Additional stakes followed. When the Seville Spain Stake was created in 1988, one area within the stake reported 98 percent activity among Melchizedek Priesthood holders, and noted that 54 members of the stake were serving full-time missions.

President Hinckley visited King Juan Carlos I and Queen Sofia March 9, 1992, and presented the couple with a personalized, leather-bound copy of the Book of Mormon. About that time, Spain was among the countries to receive satellite broadcasts of general conference. At the April 1993 general conference, as first counselor in the First Presidency, President Hinckley announced that the Church was acquiring property for a temple in Spain, the Church's fifth in continental Europe.

President Hinckley returned to Spain on June 11, 1996, as the first president of the Church to visit Spain, to break ground for the Madrid Spain Temple in Moratalez section of Madrid.

The Tabernacle Choir performed in three cities in Spain in June 1998. On June 28, the choir's performance in El Escorial, a famed basilica near Madrid, was "a melding of cultures and histories, of shared hopes and dreams from divergent pasts." The choir also performed in Barcelona on June 26 and in Madrid on June 29.

In 1999, President Hinckley returned to Spain to dedicate the Madrid Spain Temple on March 19. The day before, President Hinckley, along with his first counselor, President Thomas S. Monson, and Elder Jeffrey R. Holland of the Quorum of the Twelve, visited King Juan Carlos and Queen Sofia at the royal palace in Madrid and presented them with a Lladro figurine of the "Christus," especially created in commemoration of the opening of the first temple in Spain. It was the third time that President Hinckley had met with the king.

Membership in Spain in 1999 was 30,439.

Sources: *Encyclopedic History of the Church*, by Andrew Jenson; "The Church Grows in Spain," by J Malan Heslop, *Church News*, Oct. 30, 1971; "Spain," *Ensign*, August 1973; "This is Spain," by Betty Ventura, *Ensign*, April 1975; "The Restored Church in Spain," unpublished history and correspondence Jan. 16, 1997, by David B. Timmins; "Relief Society Offers New Outlook for Spanish Women," by Gerry Avant, *Church News*, May 17, 1975; "Mormons meet king of Spain," *Church News*, Oct. 14, 1978; "Lead their own," by Jill Mulvay Derr, *Church News*, Sept. 1, 1979; *Church News*, March 20, 1982; March 28, 1992, June 22, 1996; "Spectacular: best word to describe look, sound of choir," by Gerry Avant, *Church News*, July 4, 1998; *Church News*, March 20, 1999, March 27, 1999.

Stakes — 7

(Listed alphabetically as of Oct. 1, 2000.)

No.	Name	Organized	First President
Europe West Area			
1370	Barcelona Spain	31 Oct 1982	Jose Lara Straube
2022a	Cadiz Spain	19 Feb 1995	Cristobal Rodriguez Vasquez
2408	Elche Spain	9 Nov 1997	Manuel Parreno Ruiz
2365	Hospitalet Spain	1 Jun 1997	Vicenc Lacambra
2507	Madrid Spain East	17 Jan 1999	Jose Leopoldo Reina A.
1327	*Madrid Spain West	17 Jan 1999	
	Madrid Spain	14 Mar 1982	Jose Maria Oliveira Aldamiz
1687	Seville Spain	14 Feb 1988	Jesus Manuel Benitez S.

Missions —5 (See Las Palmas Mission below)

(As of Oct. 1, 2000; shown with historical number. See MISSIONS.)

(137) SPAIN BARCELONA MISSION
Calle Calatrava, 10-12, bajos
08017 Barcelona, Spain

(199) SPAIN BILBAO MISSION
c/Bidearte 6, 4o Dcha
48930 Las Arenas (Vizcaya), Spain

(92) SPAIN MADRID MISSION
Calle San Telmo, 26
28016 Madrid
Spain

(141) SPAIN MALAGA MISSION
Edf. Ofisol
Avda. Jesus Santos Rein 4, 3 D-E
29640 Fuengirola, Malaga
Spain

CANARY ISLANDS

Year-end 1999: Est. population, 1,343,000; Members, 3,500; Districts, 3; Branches, 18; percent LDS, .26, or one in 384; Europe West Area; Spain Las Palmas Mission.

The Canary Islands, two provinces of Spain in the South Atlantic off the coast of Africa, are rugged, volcanic mountainous islands with rich soil and long beaches where sand from the western Sahara Desert has drifted.

The first converts on the Canary Islands were Francisco Dominguez Pena; his wife, Francisca; and their son, Javier, who were baptized June 13, 1979. They were introduced to the Church by Jesus Gomez y Vega, a resident of the islands who had moved to Spain and had been baptized in 1973. Meetings were subsequently held in their home. The first missionaries were Elders David L. Gill and Scott C. Jensen.

The first branch was organized in Las Palmas on Jan. 29, 1980. The first district, Las Palmas Gran Canarias, was organized Oct. 2, 1984, with eight branches. The second district, Santa Cruz de Tenerife Canaria, was organized Aug. 8, 1989, with six branches. The Spain Las Palmas Mission, with headquarters in the Canary Islands, was created July 1, 1988, under the leadership of Pres. Marion K. Hamblin.

President Gordon B. Hinckley stopped in Las Palmas on Feb. 13, 1998, on his way to Nigeria, and spoke to 775 members.

Sources: The Beginings of the Church in the Canary Islands, by Maria Torio de Gomez Vega, unpublished; Spain Las Palmas Mission history; *Church News*, Nov. 10, 1990, *Church News*, March 7, 1998.

(220) SPAIN LAS PALMAS MISSION
Calle Venegas 27, 1A
35003 Las Palmas de Gran Canaria
Spain

SURINAME

Year-end 1999: Est. population, 430,000; Members, 454; Branches, 1; Percent LDS, .11, or one in 947; North America Southeast Area; West Indies Mission.

Located on the Atlantic Coast at the top of South America, the Republic of Suriname has a population that speaks Dutch, Creole, and English. They are Hindu, 27 percent; Muslim, 23 percent; and Christian, 25 percent.

Elder John Limburg and his wife, Beverly, arrived in Paramaribo in October 1988 and started the Paramaribo Branch. By the beginning of 1989, some 16 people were attending services. The first convert was baptized March 26, 1989, in services attended by about 25 people.

By 1990, attendance at the branch averaged about 100 people. Meetings were also held in the rural communities of Lelydorp and Uitkijk. In 1999, there were 454 members in Suriname.

Sources: Interview with John M. and Beverly Limburg; manuscript history of Suriname; *Church News*, April 29, 1989, March 10, 1990; "Work flourishing among a people without guile," by Elayne Wells, *Church News*, Dec. 1, 1990.

SWAZILAND

Year-end 1999: Est. population, 967,000; Members, 798; Wards, 1; Branches, 2; Percent LDS, .08, or one in 1,212; Africa Southeast Area; South Africa Johannesburg Mission.

The second smallest country in Africa, Swaziland is a mountainous kingdom located in southern Africa near the Indian Ocean. The people speak Siswati and English, and 57 percent are Christian while 43 percent have indigenous beliefs.

A group of LDS non-Africans living in Swaziland in 1984 included the Herman Van Thiel Berghuijs, George Gardner, and John Scott families. The Mbabane Branch was organized Nov. 5, 1985, with Brother Gardner as president. The Church was recognized by the government in February 1987, and Elder Kenneth Edwards and his wife, Betty, the first missionaries, arrived that year and converts came into the Church.

The first called on a mission from Swaziland was Elder Paulo Cipriano Zandamela, a Mozambican, who was baptized July 31, 1988. Sister Fikile Dlamini was the first Swazi to serve a full-time mission. By 1990, converts were serving full-time missions and of the 115 members, only Branch Pres. Larry Brown and his family were non-Africans.

On Feb. 24, 1991, three more branches were organized under local priesthood leadership. By then, several members from Swaziland had been through the temple, and seven local missionaries had been called. Swaziland's first meetinghouse was dedicated July 18, 1993, in a ceremony attended by government representatives, and presided over by Elder Richard P. Lindsay of the Seventy and president of the Africa Area. At the time, in Swaziland, there were 650 members in five branches. Other branches have been established in Ezulwini, Manzini, and Nhlangano.

Members and residents here have benefited from both giving and receiving service. In 1993, young adults from the Johannesburg South Africa Stake spent three days giving service to orphans at the Swaziland Government Hospital, cleaning the local meetinghouse and training prospective elders. Full-time missionaries in the Mbabane Swaziland District served at the SOS Children's Village for Orphans. In 1996, members from Swaziland joined some 5,000 others at the Johannesburg Regional Conference, and in 1998, joined 5,500 in Johannesburg to hear President Gordon B. Hinckley speak.

From January 1997-April 1998, missionaries built a concrete home for a woman whose home had caved in from heavy rains.

Sources: Manuscript history of South Africa Johannesburg Mission; correspondence from mission Pres. R.J. and Marilyn M. Snow; *Church News* Jan. 27, 1990, March 10, 1990; Sept. 25, 1993, Nov. 13, 1993, March 2, 1996, July 11, 1998.

SWEDEN

Year-end 1999: Est. population, 8,822,000; Members, 8,587; Stakes, 4; Wards, 22; Branches, 28; Missions, 1; Districts, 2; Temples, 1; percent LDS, .1, or one in 1,027.

In northern Europe on the east side of the Scandinavian Peninsula, the kingdom of Sweden is a constitutional monarchy; its population speaks Swedish and Finnish, and is 95 percent Lutheran.

The first missionary to Sweden was John E. Forsgren, a Swedish seaman who joined the Church in Boston, Mass., and then moved to Nauvoo, Ill., to be with the Saints.

After migrating to the Salt Lake Valley with the pioneers, he answered a mission call to Sweden. He went first to his hometown of Gavle, where his brother, Peter, was healed by the power of the priesthood. He then baptized Peter on July 26, 1850, as the first convert to the Church in Sweden.

After baptizing a few more converts, Elder Forsgren was arrested and banished from the country for preaching. Thereafter, missionaries occasionally visited Sweden from Denmark. In 1853, successful missionary operations were commenced in southern Sweden by Anders W. Winberg and others.

On April 24, 1853, the first branch of the Church was organized in Skonaback by Elder Winberg, and another branch was soon started in Malmo. From there, the Church extended northward, with many converts immigrating to the United States.

In 1905, Sweden was taken from the Scandinavian Mission and the Swedish Mission was organized.

Notable events of the Church in Sweden in recent times include the first Nordic area conference Aug. 16-18, 1974, in Stockholm and organization of stakes in Stockholm on April 20, 1975, and in Goteborg Nov. 20, 1977. On March 17, 1984, ground was broken for a temple near Stockholm, which was dedicated July 2, 1985.

On March 24, 1988, President Thomas S. Monson, then second counselor in the First Presidency, took part in Sweden's observance of the 350th anniversary of the first Swedish settlement in the United States. President Monson and his wife, Frances, exchanged greetings with King Carl XVI Gustaf and Queen Silvia. Also taking part was Gregory J. Newell, the U.S. ambassador to Sweden, a member of the Church.

As Eastern Europe opened to the preaching of the gospel, the temple in Sweden offered an opportunity for the Swedish members to host many visitors. The first group of Russian Saints to come to the temple arrived Aug. 30, 1993.

On Aug. 23, 1995, King Carl XVI Gustaf and Queen Silvia were hosted on a visit to the Stockholm Temple grounds by President Monson, first counselor in the First Presidency.

Sweden's LDS population in 1999 was 8,587.

The 150th anniversary of the first baptism in Sweden was observed July 25-26, 2000, in a series of events in Gavle, Sweden, that was covered by two newspapers and a television station. In addition to local media coverage, about 35 newspaper articles were printed around the country, and a 40-minute national radio report was broadcast.

Sources: *Encyclopedic History of the Church,* by Andrew Jenson; *History of the Church in Sweden 1850-1905,* by A. Dean Wengreen, a BYU dissertation, August 1968; *History of the Swedish Mission of the Church, 1905-1973,* by Carl-Erik Johansson, a BYU thesis August 1973; *Church News,* Nov. 21, 1987; *Church News,* Nov. 20, 1993; "Royal couple visits at Swedish temple with Pres. Monson" by Gerry Avant, *Church News,* Sept. 2, 1995; "Sweden festivities note 150-year anniversary," Aug. 19, 2000.

Stakes — 4

(Listed alphabetically as of Oct. 1, 2000.)

No.	Name	Organized	First President
Europe Central Area			
880	*Goeteborg Sweden 7 Jan 1991		
	‡Goteborg Sweden	20 Nov 1977	Arne Lennart Hedberg
2226	Malmoe Sweden	1 Sep 1996	C. Urban Girhammar
691	Stockholm Sweden	20 Apr 1975	Evert W. Perciwall
2088	Stockholm Sweden South	20 Aug 1995	Ulf Arne Gilhammer

Mission — 1

(As of Oct. 1, 2000; shown with historical number. See MISSIONS.)

(145) SWEDEN STOCKHOLM MISSION

Box 2087

S-183 02 Taby, Sweden

SWITZERLAND

Year-end 1999: Est. population, 7,085,000; Members, 7,043; Stakes, 3; Wards, 20; Branches, 20; Missions, 2; Temples, 1; percent LDS, .10, or one in 1,006.

In central Europe, Switzerland is a federal republic with a population that speaks German, 65 percent; French, 18 percent; Italian, 12 percent; and Romansch, 1 percent. The Swiss people are 49 percent Roman Catholic and 48 percent Protestant.

Missionary work began in Switzerland on Nov. 24, 1850, as an outgrowth of the work in Italy. Elder Lorenzo Snow of the Quorum of the Twelve, laboring in Italy, set apart Thomas B.H. Stenhouse as the first president of the Swiss Mission. The mission has been functioning ever since. The *Millennial Star* reported that 20 converts were baptized in 1851 in Switzerland.

In August 1914 and again in September 1938, missionaries were evacuated from Switzerland due to World War I and World War II, respectively, and during both wars, local priesthood holders in Switzerland were placed in leadership of the missions, branches, and districts .

After World War I, as many Church publications and manuals were translated into languages spoken by the Swiss people, programs of the Church steadily developed in Switzerland. Although in the 1920s, members throughout the world were encouraged to build up the Church in their own nations, emigration from Switzerland continued until the early 1950s.

President David O. McKay visited in 1952 and a building site for the Swiss Temple was selected in Zollikofen, near Bern. The temple was dedicated Sept. 11, 1955, and served Church members in Western Europe and the Nordic countries, as well as Switzerland. The Swiss Temple was the first temple in the Church to use a film presentation. Today, the audiovisual presentation is used in nearly every temple in the Church.

The first stake in Switzerland was organized Oct. 28, 1961, in Zurich. A second mission in Switzerland, headquartered in Geneva, was created in 1974. The first General Authority from Switzerland was Elder Hans B. Ringger, who served in the Seventy from 1985-1995.

After refurbishment of the Swiss Temple, European Saints from many countries attended the rededication Oct. 23, 1992.

President Howard W. Hunter visited Switzerland Aug. 8-16, 1994, the first country he visited as Church president. He spoke to members and missionaries and attended to matters at the recently rededicated temple. President Gordon B. Hinckley spoke to 4,200 members in Geneva on June 6, 1998. About two weeks later, on June 18, the Tabernacle Choir visited Geneva.

Two General Authorities and two Church auxiliary general presidents, as well as several Church members, participated Nov. 14-17, 1999, in the second World Congress of Families in Geneva. Elder Bruce C. Hafen of the Seventy; Sister Mary Ellen Smoot, Relief Society general president; and Sister Margaret D. Nadauld, Young Women general president, all presented speeches calling for a return to moral values. Elder Charles Didier of the Seventy and president of the Europe East Area also participated. Richard G. Wilkins of the World Family Policy Center at BYU, was general secretariat for the congress.

In 1999, Switzerland had a LDS population of 7,043.

Sources: *Encyclopedic History of the Church,* by Andrew Jenson; *Church News,* Nov. 11, 1961; *History of the Church in Switzerland,* by Dale Z. Kirby, a BYU thesis, May 1971; "Switzerland," *Ensign,* April 1973; "Switzerland: land of peace, precision and great progress," by Gerry Avant,*Church News,* Dec. 22, 1979; "Thousands tour London and Swiss temples," and "LDS officials rededicate Swiss Temple," by Gerry Avant, *Church News,* Oct. 24, 1992; *Church News,* Aug. 20, 1994, June 13, 1998, June 27, 1998, Nov. 20, 1999, Nov. 27, 1999.

Stakes — 3

(Listed alphabetically as of Oct. 1, 2000.)

No.	Name	Organized	First President
Europe Central Area			
1261	Bern Switzerland	3 May 1981	Peter Lauener
1352	Geneva Switzerland	20 Jun 1982	Denis Bonny
341	*Zurich Switzerland ‡Swiss (Switzerland, Germany)	28 Oct 1961	Wilhelm Friedrich Lauener

Missions — 2

(As of Oct. 1, 2000; shown with historical number. See MISSIONS.)

(59) SWITZERLAND GENEVA MISSION
8, chemin William Barbey
CH-1292 Chambesy (GE)
Switzerland

(8)SWITZERLAND ZURICH MISSION
Pilatusstrasse 11
CH-8032 Zurich
Switzerland

TAHITI

(See French Polynesia under FRANCE)

TAIWAN

Year-end 1999: Est. population, 21,501,000; Members, 26,805; Stakes, 6; Wards, 35; Branches, 36; Missions, 3; Districts, 5; Temples, 1; percent LDS, .12, or one in 802.

Off the southeast coast of China, the Republic of China has a population that speaks Mandarin Chinese, and Taiwan and Hakka dialects. They mostly adhere to Buddhism, Taoism, and Confucianism.

An American servicemen's group was functioning in Taipei when the first four missionaries departed in June 1956 from Hong Kong to open the work in Taiwan (then called Formosa). They were Elders Weldon J. Kitchen, Keith Madsen, Duane W. Dean, and Melvin C. Fish. Progress was slow at first, and anti-American riots hindered the work in 1957. However, by the end of 1957 almost 50 people had been baptized. After another year, nearly 200 had been converted and 31 missionaries were working in six cities. By the end of 1959, eight branches had been organized. Two large meetinghouses were completed in the 1960s in Taipei and Kaohsiung. Translation of the Book of Mormon into Chinese in 1965 also helped the work. Local leadership presided over most of the branches. In 1975, 30 branches in three districts were functioning, with a membership of 7,000. Church educational programs were established, and many young people grew up taking seminary and institute classes. Some 2,500 members attended an area conference held in Taipei Aug. 13-14, 1975. On Oct. 22-23, 1980, another area conference was held in Taipei and attended by 2,550. While in Taipei, President Spencer W. Kimball was visited by two top leaders of the country, the president, Chiang Ching-kuo, and prime minister, Sun Y.S., during a 45-minute meeting.

The Taipei Taiwan Stake was created April 22, 1976. A temple was announced for Taipei in April 1982 and was dedicated Nov. 17, 1984. At the time, membership numbered about 13,000. Membership in 1990 was 18,000. Missionaries performing service projects in the 1990s have earned favorable publicity for the Church.

In 1993, some 20,300 members were in 57 units, three stakes, and three districts in two missions. In December 1994, Chien-nien Chen, a pharmacist and former branch president, became the first elected LDS magistrate for Taitung County government. President Gordon B. Hinckley addressed more than 3,000 members at a meeting May 23, 1996, in the Taipei International Convention Center. June 4, 1996, marked the 40-year anniversary of the Church in Taiwan.

The re-creation of the Taiwan Kaohsiung Mission, the third in Taiwan, placed a mission headquarters on the south end of the island, making Kaohsiung the third of Taiwan's large cities to have a mission. More than 90 percent of the eligible students enrolled in institute in 1998 as members worked hard, despite harsh economic demands, to fulfill their Church callings.

In 1999, LDS membership in Taiwan reached more than 26,000.

The Church donated $25,000 to the Taipei Economics & Cultural Representative Office for the United States to assist in relief efforts in Taiwan following a destructive earthquake Sept. 21, 1999.

Sources: "Mormon Missionaries Now Labor in Formosa," *Church News*, June 23, 1956; China and the Restored Church, by William Heaton, *Ensign*, August 1972; "My Sheep Know My Voice," *Church News*, April 28, 1973; "Taiwan: Steep Peaks and Towering Faith," by Janice Clark, *Ensign*, August 1975; "Relative Freedom of Taiwan Allows Growth of Church," by Gerry Avant, *Church News*, Dec. 6, 1975; "Saints throng to area meetings in the Far East," by Dell Van Orden, *Church News*, Nov. 1, 1980; "First Temple in Chinese Realm," by Gerry Avant, *Church News*, Nov. 25, 1984; *Church News*, July 9, 1994, June 8, 1996," June 22, 1996; "Taiwan: Four Decades of Faith," by Christopher K. Bigelow, *Ensign*, September 1998; *Church News*, Oct. 2, 1999.

Stakes —6

(Listed alphabetically as of Oct. 1, 2000.)

No.	Name	Organized	First President
Asia Area			
1303	Kaohsiung Taiwan	6 Nov 1981	Ho Tung Hai
2003	Taichung Taiwan	18 Dec 1994	Chou, Wen Tsung
2373	Tainan Taiwan	15 Jun 1997	Hsin-chin Chen
2468	Taipei Taiwan Central	24 May 1998	Shuei-Tyan Konrad Tzeng
1326	Taipei Taiwan East	14 Mar 1982	Yuan-Hu Yen
755	*Taipei Taiwan West 14 Mar 1982		
	‡Taipei Taiwan	22 Apr 1976	I-Ch'ing Chang

Missions —3

(As of Oct. 1, 2000; shown with historical number. See MISSIONS.)

(330) TAIWAN KAOHSIUNG MISSION
38 Hsin Kwang Road
25th Floor #6
Kaohsiung 802
Taiwan, R.O.C.

(146) TAIWAN TAICHUNG MISSION
498-11 Wu Chuan Road
Taichung 40415
Taiwan, R.O.C.

(94) TAIWAN TAIPEI MISSION
Floor 4, No. 24, Lane 183
Chin Hua Street
Taipei 106-06, Taiwan ROC

TANZANIA

Year-end 1999: Est. population, 28,701,000; Members, 406; Branches, 1; Percent LDS, .001 or one in 70,692; Africa Southeast Area; Kenya Nairobi Mission.

On the east coast of Africa, Tanzania is a republic with its people speaking Swahili and English. The people are Muslim, 35 percent; Christian, 30 percent; and the remainder follow tribal beliefs.

One of the first families to hold Church meetings was D.E. Tapie Rohm Jr. from Los Angeles, Calif., a Fulbright scholar assigned to Dar es Salaam from 1988-1989. In August 1991, Bruce Wilson and his family from Smith Falls, Ontario, Canada, arrived in Dar es Salaam. He was employed by International Development Co. The Wilson family began holding meetings in September 1991.

The Kenya Nairobi Mission, which includes Kenya, Uganda, and Tanzania, was created in July 1991. Application for legal recognition was made March 15, 1992, and was approved Oct. 8, 1992. This recognition was assisted by a visit to Tanzania by Chief Judge J. Clifford Wallace of the U.S. Court of Appeals in San Diego, Calif. Robert Muhile, a Tanzanian, was baptized in Cairo, Egypt, before the arrival of the missionaries. On Dec. 15, 1992, the Dar es Salaam Branch was created, and Brother Muhile was called as its president on March 13, 1994.

A missionary couple, Elder Lervae and Sister Joyce Cahoon, arrived in February, 1992. The first converts were Projest S. Captain, Dickson and Japhet Kiiza, Dishon Z. Makunge and Mariam Mohamed-Chui, all baptized March 15, 1992. Members from Tanzania were among those to travel to Nairobi, Kenya, Feb. 17, 1998, to hear President Gordon B. Hinckley, speak.

Sources: *Church News,* March 23, 1991; correspondence from Pres. Larry K. Brown, Kenya Nairobi Mission, April 12, 1994, Church News, Sept. 6, 1997, Feb. 28, 1998.

THAILAND

Year-end 1999: Est. population, 60,271,000; Members,10,808; Stakes, 1; Wards, 5; Branches, 24; Districts, 5; Missions, 1; Percent LDS, .02, or one in 5,577.

On the Indochinese and Malay Peninsula, Thailand is a constitutional monarchy. The Thai-speaking population is 95 percent Buddhist and 4 percent Muslim.

Elder Elam Luddington arrived in Bangkok, Thailand, April 6, 1854, as the first missionary to preach the gospel in the Asian country. Four elders had been assigned to preach the gospel in Thailand, then known as Siam, but only Elder Luddington reached the country. After laboring under difficult circumstances, he was able to baptize a ship's captain, James Trail, and his wife. When Elder Luddington left Thailand four months later, missionary work came to a halt for more than a century.

Six missionaries were transferred to Thailand from the Taiwan and Hong Kong zones of the Southern Far East Mission on Feb. 2, 1968. Thanks to the help of Anan Eldredge, a Thai who had been adopted by an American family and subsequently baptized, the elders were able to learn the language and teach the people the gospel. Brother Eldredge was the first Thai to hold the priesthood, the first to be a full-time missionary, and the first to be called as a mission president on July 1, 1988.

Thailand continued to grow as an important part of the Southern Far East Mission, which was divided Nov. 1, 1969. The new Southeast Asian Mission included Thailand with G. Carlos Smith as president. Under his direction, construction began on the country's first meetinghouse, located in Bangkok, which was dedicated Oct. 19, 1974, by Elder David B. Haight of the Quorum of the Twelve. Church leaders spent several years overcoming challenges and finally, on July 19, 1973, Thailand became its own mission with Paul D. Morris as president of the Thailand Bangkok Mission. The first sister missionaries arrived in the country in 1974.

In 1987, three new meetinghouses were dedicated for the Bangnaa, Thonburi, and Chiang Mai branches. The Church in Thailand noted a milestone in June 1990, when 201 Thai members went to the Manila Temple to receive their endowments or to be sealed to their families.

In 1993, long-term visas were extended to the Church by the government of Thailand.

Missionaries in the mission translated for the Utah Army National Guard in providing volunteer medical and dental services to residents near Ubon, Thailand, in 1993.

In July 1994, the Church's Thailand Bangkok office purchased and sent rice by a three-truck caravan over the Mekong River to Vientiane, Laos, as humanitarian service. The Church also contributed cash to aid in distribution of the rice, and agreed to send a shipment of clothing.

On June 18, 1995, Elder Neal A. Maxwell of the Quorum of the Twelve created the first stake in Thailand, the Bangkok Thailand Stake. Wards in the stake at the time of its creation were Asoke, Bangkapi, Bangkhan, Bangnaa, and Thonburi; and the branches were Bangkok (English), Chonburi, and Lopburi. In July 1997, some 20 LDS couples began teaching English to public school teachers in a program established by Bangkok's governor. By 2000, 100 members had served in the program, and had taught more than 300,000 teachers and students.

In 1999, membership in Thailand was 10,808.

President Gordon B. Hinckley visited Thailand in 2000, during a six-nation tour of Asia and the South Pacific, and met with Prime Minister Chuan Leepkai and Governor Bhichit Rattakul. It was the first visit of a Church president to Thailand. A pre-birthday celebration on June 12 (President Hinckley turned 90 years old on June 23, 2000), hosted by the deputy prime minister, was held in President Hinckley's honor. At a member meeting the next day on June 13, President Hinckley addressed more than 2,600 members, some traveling 18 hours by bus to attend the meeting. After the meeting, the Church president greeted Srilaksana Suntarhut, 78, a pioneer of the work in Thailand and the principal translator of the LDS standard works into the Thai language. She was baptized in 1968, the year the mission was opened in Thailand.

Sources: *Encyclopedic History of the Church,* by Andrew Jenson; Culture for Missionaries: *The Church Encounters Asia,* by Spencer J. Palmer, Deseret Book, 1970; "Thailand," prepared by Language Training Mission, 1978; *Church News,* Jan. 16, 1988, Feb. 13, 1988, July 16, 1988; Sept. 3, 1988, May 23, 1993; "Asia Area: Welcome mat is out in several countries," by Sheridan R. Sheffield, *Church News,* June 19, 1993; *Church News,* July 26, 1997, July 1, 2000.

Stake — 1

(Listed alphabetically as of Oct. 1, 2000.)

No.	Name	Organized	First President
Asia Area			
2064	Bangkok Thailand	18 Jun 1995	Thipparad Kitsaward

Mission — 1

(As of Oct. 1, 2000; shown with historical number. See MISSIONS.)

(109) THAILAND BANGKOK MISSION
50/829-832 Muang Thong Thani
Chaengwatana Rd., T. Ban Mai, A. Pakkret
Nonthaburi 11120
Thailand

TONGA

Year-end 1999: Est. population, 106,000; Members, 44,819; Stakes, 16; Wards, 100; Districts, 1; Branches, 47; Missions, 1; Temples, 1; Percent LDS, 42.28, or one in 2.

In the western South Pacific, the kingdom of Tonga is a constitutional monarchy whose population speaks Tongan and English. Tongans are Free Wesleyan, LDS, Roman Catholic, Church of Tonga, and Free Church of Tonga.

The first missionaries to Tonga were Brigham Smoot and Alva J. Butler, sent by Samoan Mission Pres. William O. Lee. The missionaries arrived July 15, 1891, and soon visited King Jiaoji (George) Tubou and received permission to preach. They acquired property and erected a mission home and school, and also purchased a boat to travel between islands. The first convert was Alipate, who was baptized July 15, 1892. The mission made some progress, but was closed in 1897.

In 1907, the Tonga Mission was re-opened by Elders William O. Facer and Heber J. McKay. They opened a school in Nieafu on the island of Vava'u and by 1908, there were 28 day students and 13 night students. Elder Facer later was stationed in Ha'alaufuli where he found success, organizing a branch with 32 converts. Missionary work opened on the main island of Tongatapu on March 17, 1911, and by December 1912, a meetinghouse and school had been completed and a conference organized. A mission in Tonga was organized July 8, 1916, and more missionaries began serving.

Relationships with the government became strained as more people joined the Church. In 1921, Elder David O. McKay, then of the Quorum of the Twelve, visited, but was quarantined on a nearby island for 11 days before he was allowed to enter the country. Later, visas were denied to missionaries for two years. Local missionaries were called to do the work and served in positions of leadership.

All foreign missionaries were called home during World War II, but many LDS servicemen were stationed near Tonga and attended local meetings. After the war, foreign missionaries were once again restricted, with the exception of the mission president and his family. Publication of the Book of Mormon in 1946 also helped strengthen the Church. Membership in Tonga in 1946 was 2,422. From among them, mission presidents called local missionaries in what became one of the most successful local missionary programs in the Church.

Much of the progress on the islands has been through Church schools. The establishing of schools in 1892 and 1908 proved significant, and led to other schools starting. The Makeke School was opened Feb. 20, 1926, and it was the principal method of advancing the Church for many years. A new educational complex, the Liahona High School, was opened in 1952. Its building in 1949 was the beginning of the Church's labor missionary program and probably the catalyst for expansion of the Church in Tonga.

In 1968, a jubilee celebration was held under the direction of mission Pres. John H. Groberg, now of the Seventy. Tonga's first stake was created Sept. 5, 1968. After that, the Church in Tonga was led almost exclusively by local members, including its mission, many of the schools, and the stakes.

Membership reached 10,000 in 1967, increased to 14,355 in 1970, 18,484 in 1980, and 27,400 in 1985.

President Spencer W. Kimball visited Tonga in February 1976 and spoke to 10,600 members at an area conference in Nuku'alofa.

A highlight came Aug. 9-11, 1983, when the Tonga Nuku'alofa Temple was dedicated. In 1991, LDS and other Tongans joined in celebrating the centennial of the Church in Tonga. Among the most significant parts of the lengthy celebration was a dance festival in which 3,000 youths performed for King Taufa'ahau Topou IV.

President Gordon B. Hinckley visited Nuku'alofa Oct. 14, 1997, spoke to some 11,400 people and met with Tonga's King Taufa'ahau Topou IV. That night, a strong earthquake struck but did little damage, nor did it slow the Church president who resumed his journey.

Tonga has the highest percentage of LDS members of any country in the world. Nearly one out of every two persons in the island nation is a member of the Church. In 1999, the Church had 44,819 members in Tonga.

Sources: *Unto the Islands of the Sea,* by R. Lanier Britsch; *Mighty Missionary of the Pacific,* by David W. Cummings, Bookcraft, 1961; *Church News,* Feb. 21, 1976; *Tongan Saints, Legacy of Faith,* translated and edited by Eric B. Shumway, Institute for Polynesian Studies, Laie, Hawaii; *From Tonga to Zion,* prepared by Ella Mae Judd from journals of Fa'aki K. A. Richter; "Celebrating 100 years in Tonga," *Church News,* Aug. 31, 1991, "Prophet goes to islands of the Pacific," by Gerry Avant, *Church News,* Oct. 25, 1997.

Stakes — 16

(Listed alphabetically as of Oct. 1, 2000.)

No.	Name	Organized	First President
Pacific Islands Area			
2174	Eua Tonga	26 Feb 1996	Tuifio Finau
1430	Ha'apai Tonga	14 Jun 1983	Fanongonongo Vaitai
737	Neiafu Vava'u Tonga	4 Dec 1975	Mosese Hetau Langi
1172	Neiafu Vava'u Tonga North	27 Aug 1980	Mosese Hetau Langi
2092	Neiafu Vava'u Tonga West	27 Aug 1995	Tukia'i Vava'u Havea
463	*Nuku'alofa Tonga ‡Nuku'alofa	5 Sep 1968	Orson Hyde White
1986	Nuku'alofa Tonga Central	31 Jul 1994	Filimone Fie'eiki
550	*Nuku'alofa Tonga East ‡Nuku'alofa East	21 Jul 1971	Viliami Pele Folau
2175	Nuku'alofa Tonga Ha'akame	10 Mar 1996	Sosaia Lehonitai Mateaki
2083	Nuku'Alofa Tonga Halaliku	3 Aug 1995	Staleki Tonga Faemani
1173	Nuku'alofa Tonga Liahona	31 Aug 1980	Vaikalafi Lutui
2188	Nuku'alofa Tonga Mu'a	21 Apr 1996	J. William Harris
1445	Nuku'alofa Tonga North	9 Oct 1983	Sione Moala Fineanganofa
519	*Nuku'alofa Tonga South ‡Nuku'alofa South	26 Jul 1970	Tevita Folau Mahuinga
1431	Nuku'alofa Tonga Vaini	15 Jun 1983	Samuela Iloa
520	*Nuku'alofa Tonga West ‡Nuku'alofa West	26 Jul 1970	Orson H. White

Mission — 1

(As of Oct. 1, 2000; shown with historical number. See MISSIONS.)

(22c) TONGA NUKU'ALOFA MISSION
P.O. Box 58
Nuku'Alofa, Tonga

TRINIDAD & TOBAGO

Year-end 1999: Est. population, 1,117,000; Members, 1,581; Districts, 1; Branches, 6; Missions, 1; percent LDS, .05, or one in 1,857; North America Southeast Area; West Indies Mission.

Off the east coast of Venezuela in the Caribbean Sea, Trinidad & Tobago is a parliamentary democracy where the people speak English as the official language. The major religions are Roman Catholic, 32 percent; Protestant, 29 percent; and Hindu, 25 percent.

Among the first converts to the Church were Basil D. and Felicia Borde, baptized in 1977 by Elder Daniel Rector. A branch in Port of Spain was organized June 5, 1980, as part of the Venezuela Caracas Mission. The area was transferred to the West Indies Mission in September 1983. The first missionaries from the West Indies Mission were Elders Chris Doty, Doug Mathews, Randy Clark, and David Roos, who helped organized a citywide cross-country race that raised the Church's profile. In 1991, Elder Newell Anderson and his wife, Cora Gene, taught agriculture and developed ways to grow row crops of vegetables. Sister Anderson taught sewing classes.

On Sept. 2-5, 1991, LDS basketball players Danny Ainge, Greg Kite, Jeff Chatman and Scott Runia held a series of basketball clinics on both islands. They also appeared on television talk shows to discuss family values. The Trinidad Tobago Mission was created July 1, 1991, but discontinued in 1994. That year, however, the West Indies Mission was headquartered in Trinidad.

Sources: Kenneth and LeOra Zabriskie journals; *Church News*, March 6, 1983, July 10, 1983, March 10, 1990, Sept. 21, 1991; March 26, 1994.

Mission — 1

(As of Oct. 1, 2000; shown with historical number. See MISSIONS.)

(178a) WEST INDIES MISSION
P.O. Bag 543
Valsayn
Trinidad, West Indies

UGANDA

Year-end 1999: Est. population, 19,573,000; Members, 2,375; Districts, 2; Branches, 12; Percent LDS, .01, or one in 8,241; Africa Southeast Area; Kenya Nairobi Mission.

Uganda, in east central Africa, has a military government and a population that speaks Luganda, Acholi, Lango, and other languages. English is the official language and is understood by about 70 percent of the population. Its people are Christian, 63 percent; Muslim, 6 percent, and tribal beliefs.

Expatriate Latter-day Saints lived in Uganda and held meetings as early as the 1960s. The first Ugandan to join the Church was Charles Osinde, who was baptized in Scotland, and returned to his homeland. Guy Denton and his wife, Peggy, arrived in Uganda in March 1990 as part of a USAID program. The Dentons held meetings in their home and Osinde and others joined them. The first Ugandan baptized in Uganda was Mugisa James Collins, baptized Aug. 25, 1990, by Brother Denton.

A branch was soon created in Kampala and the people met in the Osinde's home. In December 1990, the first missionaries, Elder Lark and and Sister Arlea Washburn of Mesa, Ariz., arrived in Uganda. By March 1991, an average of 30 to 35 people attended branch meetings.

The Kenya Nairobi Mission, which includes Kenya, Uganda, and Tanzania, was created in July 1991.

Church humanitarian efforts have benefited Ugandans through such projects as delivering clothing to the Kitgum District in Northern Uganda for victims of fighting between political factions. Senior missionary couples and elders working in Uganda are bringing progress.

Sources: History provided by LuDean Worthen; *Church News*, March 30, 1991, Feb. 11, 1995, Sept. 6, 1997.

UKRAINE

Year-end 1999: Est. population, 51,868,000; Members, 6,369; Missions, 2; Districts, 8; Branches, 59; Temples, 1 announced; Percent LDS, .01, or one in 8,144; Europe East Area.

Bordering the Black Sea, Ukraine is a member of the Commonwealth of Independent States.

Missionary work began in October 1991 in Ukraine under the direction of Pres. Gary L. Browning of the Finland Helsinki East Mission. The Ukraine Kiev Mission was created Feb. 3, 1992, under the direction of Pres. Howard L. Biddulph, formerly president of the Austria Vienna East Mission. The mission, with 35 missionaries in 1992, served the entire Ukraine population.

On Sept. 12, 1991, Elders Boyd K. Packer and Dallin H. Oaks of the Quorum of the Twelve visited Ukraine and met with about 40 people, including members, missionaries and investigators. The Kiev Branch was organized in June 1991.

Humanitarian assistance to people in Kiev was offered by members in Germany and the United States, who shipped thousands of pounds of food and clothing in 1991, 1992 and 1993. In July 1993, Ukraine received its second mission in Donetsk as work moved rapidly forward. Membership increased from 1,700 in 1993 to 3,100 in 1995. By 1999, membership was 6,369.

Members in Ukraine joined with Russian members to commemorate the pioneer sesquicentennial in 1997 by taking a handcart, filled with dolls and journals with testimonies, across the land, from city to city. The handcart later joined the re-enactment wagon train in Utah and was pulled the last few miles by Tamara Visir from Ukraine, and former missionaries from Russia and Ukraine.

In October 1997, seminary and institute classes were established in Ukraine.

History was made July 20, 1998, with the announcement that a temple would be built in Ukraine, the first in eastern Europe. Just two weeks before that, the first meetinghouse in Ukraine was dedicated in Donetsk by Elder Wayne M. Hancock of the Seventy.

Sources: *Church News,* Feb. 15, 1992, Feb. 29, 1992, July 7, 1997, July 25, 1998, Aug. 8, 1998, Jan. 16, 1999.

Missions — 2

(As of Oct. 1, 2000; shown with historical number. See MISSIONS.)

(295) UKRAINE DONETSK MISSION
P.O. Box 3494
340050 Donetsk
Ukraine

(274) UKRAINE KIEV MISSION
P.O. Box 144
252001 Kiev
Ukraine

UNITED KINGDOM

Year-end 1999: Est. population, 59,390,000; Members, 176,493; Stakes, 44; Wards, 264; Branches, 106; Missions, 8; Temples, 2; percent LDS, .29, or one in 336.

The United Kingdom consists of England, Scotland, Wales, and Northern Ireland, and is located off the northwest coast of Europe. The population speaks English, Welsh, and Gaelic. Most belong to the Church of England or are Roman Catholics.

Sources: *Truth Will Prevail,* editors V. Ben Bloxham, James R. Moss and Larry C. Porter; A History of the Church in Cambridgeshire, unpublished history by Leonard Reed; *Church News,* July 6, 1974, Dec. 1, 1985; "Church celebrates its British history," "Markers tell where history was made," both by Dell Van Orden and Gerry Avant, *Church News,* Aug. 1, 1987, Aug. 8, 1987; *Church News,* Nov. 24, 1990; "Temples rededicated, lives renewed," by Gerry Avant, *Church News,* Oct. 31, 1992; "Ground broken for Preston temple," by Bryan J. Grant, *Church News,* June 18, 1994; "Prophet returns to beloved England" by Mike Cannon, *Church News,* Sept. 2, 1995; *Church News,* June 13, 1998, June 20, 1998, June 27, 1998, May 15, 1999, Sept. 11, 1999, April 22, 2000, May 6, 2000.

ENGLAND

Year-end 1999: Est. population, 46,293,000; Members, 135,748; Stakes, 36; Wards, 219; Branches, 71; Missions, 6; Temples, 2; percent LDS, .29, or one in 341.

On July 1, 1837, seven Canadian and American missionaries set sail for England on the packet ship *Garrick.* The seven, Elders Heber C. Kimball and Orson Hyde of the Quorum of the Twelve; and Willard Richards, Joseph Fielding, John Goodson, Isaac Russell, and John Snider, arrived July 19, 1837. They preached in Preston on Sunday, July 23, and on July 30 — only 11 days after their arrival — a baptismal service was held at nearby River Ribble that was viewed by some 8,000 curious onlookers. Nine converts were baptized by Elder Kimball, the first of whom was George D. Watt. A week later, the number of converts reached 50. The first conference was held on Christmas. Missionaries began working in Alston and Bedford, where branches were established, but the greatest work was done in the Preston area. Opposition began to mount through ministers and the press, but within nine months, more than a thousand had been baptized.

From 1840-41, seven members of the Quorum of the Twelve labored in England, finding significant success. Some 800 converts emigrated during the apostles' stay. The flow of British converts was life-sustaining for the struggling Church in America. In 1840, efforts began in Liverpool to print other editions of the Book of Mormon. Brigham Young obtained the British copyright and saw the first European edition of the book printed in 1849. Liverpool remained the headquarters of Church printing for 30 years.

By 1850, 42,316 people had been baptized, and 6,832 had emigrated; from 1851-60, 37,215 converts were baptized, and 12,972 had emigrated; from 1861-70, 14,977 had joined and 10,094 emigrated.

The Church faced considerable opposition during the next several decades and the work was slowed. Missionary work increased after the turn of the 20th century. With the onset of World War I, local sisters took over missionary work. The Relief Society was particularly active during the war. After the war, missionary work increased and anti-Mormon activity waned. Membership increased and in the mid-1930s, a large building program began and local leadership and missionaries became stronger. Members were urged to stay in England rather than emigrate.

World War II again interrupted missionary work, and British Saints took charge of their affairs. Despite difficulties finding leaders, they persisted in "home missionary work." When American leadership resumed in 1944, the number of branches had increased from 68 to 75, although they were later consolidated into 29. After the war, the missionary force was bolstered and conversions increased, but many members immigrated to America. The Genealogical Society of Utah began microfilming European records after the war, with the first microfilming in England in 1945.

The announcement on Aug. 1, 1953, that a temple would be built in London, along with visits of authorities and the Tabernacle Choir during the next few years, lifted members' spirits. Many aspects of the Church were strengthened during this period. More than 12,000 members attended the dedication of the London Temple Sept. 7-9, 1958. On March 27, 1960, the first stake in England was created in Manchester, and the British Mission was divided on the same day, creating the North British Mission. Growth continued, more missions were created, and a large building program was started. By 1971, membership was nearly 70,000, increasing to 91,000 in 1980.

The first-ever area conference in the Church was held in 1971 in Manchester. Fourteen General Authorities, including President Joseph Fielding Smith, participated in the Aug. 27-29 conference. After the Church discontinued holding large area conferences and replaced them with more localized regional conferences, the first-ever regional conference was also held in England, in London on Oct. 13, 1983.

With a "supreme consciousness of history," Latter-day Saints throughout the British Isles participated in three days of celebration July 24-26, 1987, in commemoration of the 150th anniversary of the first missionary work in Great Britain. Thirteen General Authorities, including President Ezra Taft Benson and his first counselor, President Gordon B. Hinckley, four apostles, and seven members of the First Quorum of the Seventy participated in the events. Former Prime Minister Edward Heath attended the anniversary dinner in London, which featured a videotaped message from U.S. President Ronald Reagan.

Conferences were held in six cities in the British Isles and nine public markers were dedicated at various sites of importance to the Church. Five of the markers were dedicated in England: in Avenham Park along the banks of the River Ribble where the first converts were baptized July 30, 1837, which was dedicated by President Gordon B. Hinckley; at Benbow Farm in Herefordshire, where Wiflord Woodruff baptized 65 in March 1840, dedicated by Elder Russell M. Nelson of the Quorum of the Twelve; at Hungerford, where Apostle James E. Talmage was born, dedicated by Elder Nelson; at Hyde Park Chapel in London, dedicated by Elder Carlos E. Asay of the Seventy; at Albert Dock in Liverpool, where the first missionaries landed and where the first emigrants sailed from on July 6, 1840; dedicated by Elder Russell C. Taylor of the Seventy.

In November 1990, Terry Rooney of the Bradford 2nd Ward, Huddersfield England Stake, became the first LDS member elected to Parliament.

In October 1991, area president Elder Jeffrey R. Holland, then of the Seventy, presented to the Federation of Family History Societies microfiche containing the 1881 census of the British Isles, which had been placed on microfiche by members.

Natives of England who have been called as General Authorities through the years include John Taylor, president of the Church 1880-87; Elders George Q. Cannon, John R. Winder, George Teasdale, James E. Talmage, John Longden, B. H. Roberts, George Reynolds, Joseph W. McMurrin, and Derek A. Cuthbert. Elder Kenneth Johnson is currently serving in the Seventy.

The London Temple was rededicated Oct. 18, 1992. A second temple in Preston, England, was announced Oct. 19, 1992, and dedicated six years later on June 7, 1998.

On a trip to England and the Republic of Ireland Aug. 24-Sept. 2, 1995, President Gordon B. Hinckley created the Canterbury England Stake, rededicated the Hyde Park Chapel, and met with members, missionaries, and news media in Liverpool and elsewhere. The Tabernacle Choir performed in Royal Albert Hall in London on June 14, 1998, a performance taped by BBC for rebroadcast in September 1998.

Membership in England in 1999 was 135,748.

Following a six-year effort, the rebuilt Gadfield Elm Chapel, the oldest LDS chapel in England where Wilford Woodruff and Brigham Young preached in 1840, was rededicated April 23, 2000, by Elder Holland of the Quorum of the Twelve. The chapel, constructed by members of the United Brethren in 1836, was given to the LDS Church four years later after 600 members of that faith joined the Church en masse, largely due to Elder Woodruff's missionary efforts. In 1842, the chapel was sold to assist the new British converts who were immigrating to America and during the next 152 years the building fell into major disrepair. Six years ago, a group of members from the Cheltenham England Stake, formed a charitable trust to purchase the historic site and restore it.

Church members from seven stakes in England participated in a massive service project in June 2000, preparing shipments of wheat to help feed those threatened with starvation in Ethiopia and Eritrea in Africa.

Stakes — 36

(Listed alphabetically as of Oct. 1, 2000)

No.	Name	Organized	First President
Europe West Area			
1345	Ashton England	6 Jun 1982	Brian Ashworth
760	*Billingham England 10 Jun 1986		
	‡Hartlepool England	13 Jun 1976	Craig Lithgow Marshall
494	*Birmingham England		
	‡Birmingham	14 Sep 1969	Derek A. Cuthbert
609	*Bristol England		
	‡Bristol	29 Apr 1973	Donald V. Norris
2093	Canterbury England	27 Aug 1995	Christopher Brian Munday
1331	Cheltenham England	21 Mar 1982	Warrick N. Kear
1346	Chester England	6 Jun 1982	Peter Furniss Lee
1936	Coventry England	9 May 1993	Thomas William Phillips
856	Crawley England	19 Aug 1977	J.A. Casbon
327	*Huddersfield England		
	‡Leeds	19 Mar 1961	Dennis Livesey
608	*Hull England		
	‡Hull	26 Apr 1973	Ian David Swanney
1423	Ipswich England	29 May 1983	Brian Arthur Frank Watling
780	Leeds England	12 Nov 1976	Douglas Rawson
325	*Leicester England		
	‡Leicester	5 Mar 1961	Derek A. Cuthbert
814	Lichfield England	20 Feb 1977	Robert James Mawle
748	Liverpool England	14 Mar 1976	Michael R. Otterson
928a	London England Hyde Park	28 May 1978	Vance R. Leavitt
	‡London North	20 Sep 1970	Thomas Hill
929a	London England Wandsworth	28 May 1978	John Dodd
930	Maidstone England	28 May 1978	William J. Joliffe III
294	*Manchester England		
	‡Manchester	27 Mar 1960	Robert G. Larson
677	Newcastle-Under-Lyme England	17 Jan 1975	James Kenneth Cork
810	Northampton England	13 Feb 1977	Michael J. Wade
549	*Norwich England 28 May 1978		
	*Ipswich England		
	‡East Anglia	20 Jun 1971	Dennis R. Reeves
597	*Nottingham England		

	‡Nottingham	4 Feb 1973	Ernest Hewitt
885	Plymouth England	27 Nov 1977	Leonard Eden
1343	Poole England	23 May 1982	Peter J. Crockford
600	*Portsmouth England 6 Feb 1990		
	*Southampton England		
	‡Southampton	11 Feb 1973	Reginald V. Littlecott
762	Preston England	17 Jun 1976	Eric Cryer
615	*Reading England		
	‡Thames Valley	24 May 1973	Peter B.C. Brighty
666	Romford England	24 Nov 1974	Arthur James Turvey
932	Saint Albans England	28 May 1978	Roland Edward Elvidge
1376	Sheffield England	14 Nov 1982	Kenneth Jones
931	Staines England	28 May 1978	Peter Benjamin C. Brighty
374	*Sunderland England		
	‡Sunderland	17 Mar 1963	Fred W. Oates
2190	Watford England	28 Apr 1996	Michael John Plant
2274	York England	24 Nov 1996	David Clark Thiriot

Stakes discontinued

323	*London England		
	‡London	26 Feb 1961	Donald W. Hemingway
	Discontinued 28 May 1978 †London England Hyde Park (928a), London England Wandsworth (929a), Staines England (931)		
527	*London England North		
	Discontinued 28 May 1978 †Saint Albans England (932), Romford England (666), Staines England (931), London England Hyde Park (928a)		

Missions — 6

(As of Oct. 1, 2000; shown with historical number. See MISSIONS.)

(183) ENG.BIRMINGHAM MISSION
187 Penns Lane
Sutton Coldfield
West Midlands B76 1JU England

(68) ENGLAND BRISTOL MISSION
Southfield House
#2 Southfield Road, Westbury-on-Trym
Bristol BS9 3BH, England

(52) ENGLAND LEEDS MISSION
Lister House, Listern Hill
Horsforth, Leeds LS18 5AZ
England

(1) ENGLAND LONDON MISSION
64-68 Princes Gate
Exhibition Road, South Kensington
London SW7 2PA, England

(79) ENGLAND LONDON SOUTH MISSION
West Park Road
Newchapel
Surrey RH7 6NB
England

(138) ENG. MANCHESTER MISSION
Trafalgar House
110 Manchester Road
Altrincham, Cheshire WA14 1NU,
England

NORTHERN IRELAND

Year-end 1999: Est. population, 1,600,000; Members, 5,5160; Stakes, 1; Wards, 4; Branches, 6; percent LDS, .34, or one in 290; Ireland Dublin Mission.

Located in the northeast corner of Ireland, Northern Ireland is part of the United Kingdom. About 66 percent of the people are Protestant and 33 percent are Roman Catholic. (See also Ireland history.)

Northern Ireland remained in the United Kingdom when Ireland became an independent republic in 1949. Most of the Church membership is centered in and around Belfast.

When the London Temple was dedicated in 1958, it marked a "new era" for the Saints in Northern Ireland, who then numbered 540 in 10 branches. The Irish Mission was organized July 7, 1962. Twelve years later, June 9, 1974, the Belfast Ireland Stake was organized.

On Sept. 7, 1986, 1,350 people attended a regional conference in Belfast, the largest-ever gathering of Saints in this area. The next year in July 1987, members in Northern Ireland participated in the 150th anniversary of the Church in the British Isles. Elders Marvin J. Ashton and M. Russell Ballard of the Quorum of the Twelve spoke at a conference in Belfast on July 26. The day before, Elder Ashton dedicated a marker at Loughbrickland where John Taylor performed the first baptism in Ireland on July 31, 1840. The marker was one of nine markers erected and dedicated in the British Isles during the sesquicentennial anniversary.

In 1999, LDS membership in Northern Ireland was 5,516.

Stake — 1

(As of Oct. 1, 2000)

No.	Name	Organized	First President
Europe West Area			
1647	*Belfast Northern Ireland	13 Jan 1987	
	‡Belfast Ireland	9 Jun 1974	Andrew Renfrew

SCOTLAND

Year-end 1999: Est. population, 5,205,000; Members, 25,791; Stakes, 5; Wards, 24; Branches, 26; Missions, 1; percent LDS, .52, or one in 194.

Native Scots converted in Canada, Alexander Wright and Samuel Mulliner, were the first missionaries to Scotland, arriving in Glasgow Dec. 20, 1839. Alexander and Jessie Hay were baptized by Elder Mulliner in the River Clyde on Jan. 9, 1840. By May 3, membership had increased to 80. Elder Orson Pratt arrived and organized a branch at Paisley on May 8, and labored in Edinburgh, where he found a number of converts. During this period, he wrote an influential pamphlet, *An Interesting Account of Several Remarkable Visions*. By March 1841, more than 200 had joined the Church in Edinburgh. Another branch had been organized in Glasgow. By 1850, membership had risen to 3,257 in more than 50 branches. By 1855, four conferences had been organized. However, membership began a decline in the 1850s that lasted for many years.

One missionary about the turn of the 20th century was Elder David O. McKay, who experienced little success; membership in the country was 338. Discouraged, he saw engraved in stone the words: "What e'er thou art, act well thy part." The inspiration from this had a great impact on his life, and the future of the Church as well.

Low conversions and frequent emigration reduced Church membership in Scotland. The Scottish-Irish Mission was created in 1961, and re-named Scottish Mission the following year. Scotland's first stake was created in Glasgow Aug. 26, 1962.

Members in Scotland participated in the 150th anniversary of the Church in the British Isles in July 1987. Two markers were dedicated July 25 by Elder David B. Haight of the Quorum of the Twelve, commemorating events in Scotland in early Church history. Elder Haight dedicated a marker on the banks of the River Clyde near Glasgow, where the first converts in Scotland were baptized in January 1840; and a marker in Holyrood Park in Edinburgh where Orson Hyde dedicated Scotland for the preaching of the gospel in 1840. The markers were two of nine erected and dedicated in the British Isles during the sesquicentennial anniversary. Elder Haight also spoke to 3,000 members July 26 at an anniversary conference, the largest-ever conference in Scotland.

Members also celebrated the 150th anniversary of the Glasgow Branch Oct. 21, 1990. Members of five Scotland stakes formed a chorus and took part in Glasgow's prestigious European Year of Culture 1990, receiving a standing ovation for their performance.

Membership in Scotland was 12,000 in 1980, and 22,000 in 1990, 10,000 more than ever joined the Church during the entire 19th century.

In the 1990s, missionary work continued to progress as membership reached 25,791 in 1999.

Stakes — 5

(Listed alphabetically as of Oct. 1, 2000.)

No.	Name	Organized	First President
Europe West Area			
1186	Aberdeen Scotland	12 Oct 1980	William Albert Wilson
734	Dundee Scotland	23 Nov 1975	John Keogh
1187	Edinburgh Scotland	12 Oct 1980	Alexander Mutter Clark
356	*Glasgow Scotland		
	‡Glasgow	26 Aug 1962	Archibald R. Richardson

1188	Paisley Scotland	12 Oct 1980	Alexander Cumming

Mission — 1

(As of Oct. 1, 2000; shown with historical number. See MISSIONS.)

(61) SCOTLAND EDINBURGH MISSION
51 Spylaw Road
Edinburgh, EH10 5BP
Scotland

WALES

Year-end 1999: Est. population, 2947,000; Members, 7,097; Stakes, 2; Wards, 13 Branches, 8; percent LDS, .24, or one in 415; England Bristol Mission.

It is supposed that the first Welshman was converted at the lectures of Wilford Woodruff in Herfordshire in 1840, but records cannot confirm this. Possibly the first member to preach in Wales was James Morgan. The first known missionary was Elder Henry Royle and his companion, Frederick Cook. They met with immediate success. Just three weeks after their arrival, they organized the first branch in Wales on Oct. 30, 1840, at Flintshire in North Wales, with 32 members. In four months, there were two congregations totaling 150 members, but the missionaries experienced active opposition from ministers. Evidently, most of these early converts promptly emigrated.

In South Wales, work proceeded more slowly at first. Elder James Palmer labored there with little success late in 1840. Two years later, 44 Welshmen had been baptized. In 1843, Elder William Henshaw began proselyting in the Merthyr Tydfil area, and a branch of 50 was eventually organized. In 1844, the first Welsh-language materials were printed and work began to progress. A converted Welshman and associate of the Prophet Joseph Smith, Dan Jones, arrived in 1845. After a disappointing year in North Wales, he found success in the south and by 1849, left for America as captain of 300 Saints. He later was called to a second mission in Wales, which he completed in 1856, again leaving with a company, this one with 560 members.

The work slowed considerably afterward, but began to build up in the 1900s. By 1950, there were 1,500 members in two districts. The first stake was created Jan. 12, 1975, in Merthyr Tydfil.

Members in Wales participated in the 150th anniversary of the Church in the British Isles in July 1987. A sesquicentennial anniversary conference was held July 26 in Cardiff, with Elder Russell M. Nelson of the Quorum of the Twelve participating.

Membership in 1990 was 6,500, increasing to 7,097 in 1999. Members in Wales are in the Preston England Temple District. Many members from Wales attended the dedication of the Preston temple, June 7-10, 1998.

Stakes — 2

(Listed alphabetically as of Oct. 1, 2000.)

No.	Name	Organized	First President
Europe West Area			
1341	Cardiff Wales	9 May 1982	Barry Derek Roy Whittaker
676	Merthyr Tydfil Wales	12 Jan 1975	Ralph Pulman

BERMUDA

Year-end 1999: Est. population, 62,000; Members, 101; Branches, 1; Percent LDS, .16 or one in 613; North America Northeast Area; New York New York South Mission.

Bermuda, a United Kingdom dependency, consists of 360 small coral islands, 20 of which are inhabited, located 580 miles east of North Carolina. Most of the residents of are Protestant.

Church members serving in the Air Force and Navy and their families created the first LDS presence in Bermuda. On July 16, 1953, a group of servicemen's wives organized a Relief Society, which was brought under the Eastern States Mission on Oct. 11, 1956. Sacrament meetings and Sunday School were held among the military personnel beginning Oct. 8, 1961,

Arthur L. McMullin and his wife, Melba, arrived April 19, 1966, and received permission to proselyte on May 3, 1966. On May 31, Elders Kenneth R. French and Curt S. Call arrived and began tracting and proselyting. The Bermuda Branch, which had about 50 in attendance, was organized June 25, 1966, by mission Pres. W. Jay Eldredge. This branch was made part of the New York New York Mission in 1974.

Native Bermudans began to join the branch in the 1980s. Vernon Every, converted in 1982, became the first Bermudan priesthood holder, and the first to be called to the branch presidency in 1985. In 1993, Bermuda was placed in the New York New York South Mission. Seminary began here in 1994.

Sources: *Church News*, Dec. 14, 1957; Bermuda Branch manuscript history; "Bermuda Branch sprouts in gentle island climate," by Heidi Waldrop, *Church News*, Aug. 25, 1985; *Church News* March 13, 1993, May 31, 1997.

CAYMAN ISLANDS

Year-end 1999: Est. population, 38,000; members, Fewer than 100; branches, 1; West Indies Mission.

Lying south of Cuba, the Cayman Islands are a British dependency, located in the Caribbean Sea some 400 miles south of Florida, with most of the population on the Grand Cayman Island. In September 1985, missionaries from the West Indies Mission opened the work. A branch, with fewer than 100 members, was created Nov. 25, 1981.

GIBRALTAR

Year-end 1999: Est. population, 32,000; members, Fewer than 100; branches, 1; Cadiz Spain Stake; Spain Malaga Mission.

A British dependency on Spain's southern coast, Gibralter is a narrow isthmus ending with a rock nearly one-fourth of a mile high.

A group was created on Gibraltar Aug. 12, 1991, with Keven Paul Wahnon as the leader. On Feb. 19, 1995, Gibraltar became a part of the Cadiz Spain Stake, created that day by Elder Neil L. Andersen of the Seventy.

URUGUAY

Year-end 1999: Est. population, 3,223,000; Members, 73,194; Stakes, 15; Wards, 92; Branches, 84; Missions, 2; Districts, 6; Temples, 1; Percent LDS, 2.27, or one in 44.

On the eastern coast of South America, the Republic of Uruguay has a people who speak Spanish. Some 66 percent of the population is Roman Catholic.

The first Church contact in Uruguay came in 1940 when Elder Rolf L. Larson of the Argentina Mission starred on the championship Argentine basketball team in games held in Montevideo. His example and the publicity about him led to Uruguayan contacts.

The Montevideo Branch was organized June 25, 1944, by Frederick S. Williams, former president of the Argentine Mission, for his family and a few North Americans living here while on government service. Pres. Williams was called as mission president and opened the Uruguay Mission on Aug. 31, 1947. By the year's end, 24 missionaries were serving in Uruguay, though few spoke Spanish fluently. By the end of 1948 there were 14 branches, all well-attended by investigators.

The first converts in Uruguay were Avelino Juan Rodriguez and his wife, Maria Esther, baptized by Pres. Williams on Nov. 4, 1948. Baptismal services were held regularly after that, and eight new branches were created in 1949. By 1957, the mission was baptizing 500 converts a year. The first stake, the Montevideo Stake, was organized Nov. 12, 1967. At that time, there were 14,800 members in the country. In 1979, membership reached 26,000. On Oct. 26-27, 1978, President Spencer W. Kimball addressed 9,000 members at an area conference in Montevideo. While in Montevideo, President Kimball visited with the president of Uruguay, Dr. Aparicio Mendez, in the House of Government in downtown Montevideo.

In 1990, Elder Luis Alberto Ferrizo, a regional representative, was elected as national deputy in the Uruguayan government, equivalent to a governor in the United States. Membership in Uruguay in 1990 was 52,000, growing to 64,000 in 1995.

On April 6, 1996, Francisco J. Vinas, from an LDS pioneer family in Uruguay, was the first General Authority called from Uruguay.

Church members in Uruguay gave many hours of service in July 1997 in honor of the worldwide celebration of the pioneer sesquicentennial. They painted schools, cleaned parks, and provided repairs to many facilities, efforts that were covered by local media.

President Gordon B. Hinckley visited Montevideo and spoke at a regional conference Aug. 9-10, 1997, to some 11,000 members. His visit was in conjunction with the 50th anniversary of the Uruguay Mission. In the visit, it was noted that Uruguay also gained its second mission, the Montevideo West mission, which was created July 1, 1997. A temple was announced for Uruguay on Nov. 2, 1998. The Montevideo Uruguay Temple was expected to be dedicated in December 2000.

Membership in 1999 was 73,194.

In 2000, the 100th meetinghouse in Uruguay, which housed the Real Branch of the Colonia Uruguay Stake, was dedicated.

Sources: *From Acorn to Oak Tree,* by Frederick S. Williams and Frederick G. Williams; "Emotions swell as meetings end," by Dell Van Orden, *Church News,* Nov. 11, 1978; *50 Anos de la Iglesia in Argentina — Cronologia,* by Nestor Curbelo, seminary system, 1986; *Church News,* Nov. 9, 1986, March 17, 1990, Aug. 24, 1995, April 6, 1996, Aug. 23, 1997, Sept. 6, 1997, June 17, 2000.

Stakes — 15

(Listed alphabetically as of Oct. 1, 2000.)

No.	Name	Organized	First President
South America South Area			
1123	Artigas Uruguay	23 Mar 1980	Luis Gonzalez
1098	Durazno Uruguay	25 Jan 1980	Luis Alberto Ferrizo
2072	Las Piedras Uruguay	2 Jul 1995	Gustavo Eduardo Sarasua
2232	Maldonado Uruguay	15 Sep 1996	Louise Laurito
1033a	Melo Uruguay	2 June 1979	Santiago Gonzalez
1944	Mercedes Uruguay	20 Jun 1993	Milton Jose Airala Perez
1058	Montevideo Uruguay Cerro	2 Sep 1979	Nester Rivera M.
631	Montevideo Uruguay East	17 Feb 1974	Ariel A. Fedrigotti
2265	Montevideo Uruguay Flores	17 Nov 1996	Miguel H. D'Amore Tavani
1034	Montevideo Uruguay Maronas	3 Jun 1979	Jorge Washington Ventura
890	Montevideo Uruguay North	12 Feb 1978	Ariel Omar Fedrigotti
444	*Montevideo Uruguay West	17 Feb 1974	
	*Montevideo Uruguay		
	‡Montevideo	12 Nov 1967	Vincente C. Rubio
2344	Paysandu Uruguay	27 Apr 1997	Jorge Bautista Scarpiny Inda
832	Rivera Uruguay	20 May 1977	Ormesindo Correa
1019	Salto Uruguay	22 Apr 1979	Atilio Silveiro
	Stakes discontinued		
836	Minas Uruguay	22 May 1977	Alberto E. Hernandez
	Discontinued	12 Nov 1989	
833	Paysandu Uruguay	21 May 1977	Atilio Silveira
	Discontinued	22 Oct 1989 †Uruguay Montevideo Mission;	
	reinstated 27 Apr 1997		
840	Santa Lucia Uruguay	23 May 1977	Hector Julio Vigo
	Discontinued 20 Aug 1989 †Uruguay Montevideo Mission		

Missions — 2

(As of Oct. 1, 2000; shown with historical number. See MISSIONS.)

(40) URUGUAY MONTEVIDEO MISSION
C.C. 18939, Dist. 9
Carrasco, Montevideo 11.500
Uruguay

(317) URU. MONTEVIDEO WEST
Casilla de Correo 18962, Distrito 9
Carrasco, Montevideo C.P. 18962
Uruguay

VANUATU

Year-end 1999: Est. population, 174,000; Members, 1,121; Districts, 2; Branches, 8; .64 percent LDS, or one in155; Pacific Islands Area; Fiji Suva Mission.

Formerly known as the New Hebrides, Vanuatu is an archipelago of 80 islands in the southwest Pacific that became an independent republic in 1980. Vanuatu is populated by mostly Melanesians who speak Bislama, French, and English, and who are mostly Protestants.

Missionary work began in Vanuatu in 1974 after several LDS Tongan families had moved there earlier. Pres. Ebbie L. Davis of the Fiji Suva Mission organized the Port Vila Branch on July 15, 1973, with Lanipoto Fehoko as president. The first missionaries were Tongans and members of the British Commonwealth, Elders Mokofisi and Malohifo'ou. Other missionaries came, but restrictions slowed the work. By 1978, membership reached 83 and by 1984, 120.

In 1989, Elders Fred Massing and Timothy Proveau, both of Vanuatu, were the only two missionaries on the island. They found success and baptized more than 40 people, including several family members. The Port Vila District was created Oct. 19, 1996.

Additional branches were organized in the 1990s on other islands: Efate, 4; Espiritu Santo, 1; Tanna, 1; and Ambae, 2. By the summer of 1998, Vanuatu had eight branches.

As of October, 1998, 28 missionaries served on the islands, including the first couple from Vanuatu to serve, and four local missionaries. A seminary class was in each branch, and an institute class in each district. The Luganville District was organized Sept. 27, 1998. In 1999, membership was 1,121.

Source: *Church News* archives; correspondence from the Fiji Suva Mission, Oct. 8, 1998.

VENEZUELA

Year-end 1999: Est. population: 22,803,000; Members, 89,484; Stakes, 16; Wards, 114; Branches, 105; Missions, 4; Districts, 13; Temples, 1; percent LDS, .43, or one in 235.

On the Caribbean coast of South America, Venezuela is a federal republic where the people speak Spanish and Indian languages, and are 96 percent Roman Catholic.

A group of members, mostly expatriates working in Venezuela, held Church meetings in the home of Carl C. Wilcox in 1966, and perhaps earlier. On Nov. 2, 1966, a branch of 45 members was organized by Elder Marion G. Romney, then of the Quorum of the Twelve. Pres. Wilcox, a top financial officer of Del Monte Corp., was called as branch president. Pres. Ted E. Brewerton (who served in the First Quorum of the Seventy from 1978 to 1995) of the Costa Rica Mission sent four missionaries to open Venezuela for missionary work. The first missionaries were Elders Floyd Baum, Neil Gruwell, David Bell, and Fred Podlesny. Maracaibo was opened July 7, 1967, by Elders Baum and Bell and Elders Steve Jensen and Stephen Edmunds.

Work progressed very slowly as missionaries at first sought converts who had leadership ability, and tried to introduce the Church through the media and the family home evening program. On Feb. 12, 1967, Elders Fred Podlesny and David Bell baptized Hernan Sepulveda, the first convert. Though initial converts were few, work progressed to the point where the Colombia-Venezuela Mission was created in 1968. Soon the Caracas 1st, 2nd, and 3rd branches in the Caracas District were organized with 150 members. Other small branches began in Merida, San Cristobal, and Maracaibo in the Venoc District. The first district conference was held Oct. 15, 1968, with 28 missionaries then serving in Caracas and Maracaibo.

When the Venezuela Mission was created July 1, 1971, membership had reached 1,259, and the Church entered a new phase. Under the leadership of mission Pres. Clark D. Webb, the mission began to average 40 converts a month. Emphasis was placed on bringing in entire families, which greatly strengthened local branches.

The Church Educational System started in Venezuela in 1972, under the direction of Alejandro Portal Campos, and has involved many youth since then

In 1977, some 4,000 members were in 23 branches in five districts. Successive mission presidents emphasized building programs and leadership preparation. President Spencer W. Kimball visited Venezuela in January 1975.

On May 15, 1977, Venezuela's first stake, Caracas Venezuela Stake, was created, followed by the creation of the Maracaibo Venezuela Mission in 1979. Membership that year was 5,000, increasing to 23,516 by 1986 in five stakes, two missions, and eight districts. By 1999, membership had reached 89,484 in 16 stakes, four missions, and 13 districts.

A temple for Venezuela was announced in general conference on Sept. 30, 1995, by President Gordon B. Hinckley, and later confirmed for Caracas. Some 1,000 members in Caracas had the opportunity to hear that conference announcement live at the Caurimare meetinghouse in Caracas. Five years later, the temple was dedicated on Aug 20, 2000.

President Hinckley traveled to Valencia on Aug. 13, 1997, where he addressed 11,000 members in two meetings. He returned to Venezuela in 1999 and spoke to 5,000 members in Marcaibo on Aug. 3, 1999.

Sources: "Venezuela,", *Ensign* 1977; "Perseverance pays," *Church News*, Nov. 10, 1979; *La Historia de la Iglesia en Venezuela 1966 a 1986*, published by the Church Educational System in Venezuela *Church News*, Oct. 7, 1995 and Nov. 4, 1995; *Church News*, Aug. 23, 1997, Aug. 14, 1999, Aug. 26, 2000.

Stakes — 16

(Listed alphabetically as of Oct. 1, 2000.)

No.	Name	Organized	First President
South America North Area			
1724	Barcelona Venezuela	4 Jun 1989	Angel Luis Fajardo C.
1989	Barquisimeto Venezuela	28 Aug 1994	Julio Ramon Davila Duran
827	Caracas Venezuela	15 May 1977	Adolfo F. Mayer G.

1887	Caracas Venezuela Palo Verde	14 June 1992	Edgardo Angulo de la Paua
1717	Caracas Venezuela Urdaneta	7 May 1989	Hector Manuel Arraez R.
1787	Ciudad Ojeda Venezuela	24 Feb 1991	Juan Silfrido Carrizo C.
1585	Guayana Venezuela	15 Jan 1986	Luis A. Aguilar Guevara
1181	Maracaibo Venezuela	15 Sep 1980	Francisco Giminez S.
1862	Maracaibo Venezuela Centro	17 May 1992	Ruben Dario Blanco Valles
1414	Maracaibo Venezuela South	24 Apr 1983	Omar Alvarez
1774	Maracay Venezuela	4 Nov 1990	Jairo R. Herrera
2333	Merida Venezuela	23 Mar 1997	Freddy V. Herrera Molma
1885	Puerto La Cruz Venezuela	7 June 1992	Luis Jose Gonzalez
2127	San Cristobal Venezuela	19 Nov 1995	Javier Ibanez Leon
1050	*Valencia Venezuela Los Sauces	19 Nov 1995	
	Valencia Venezuela	19 Aug 1979	Teodoro Hoffman
2125	Valencia Venezuela Candelaria	19 Nov 1995	Gamaliel de Jesus Osorno Flores

Missions — 4

(As of Oct. 1, 2000; shown with historical number. See MISSIONS.)

(303) VENEZUELA BARCELONA MISSION
Apdo. Postal 295
Barcelona 6001,
Venezuela

(95) VENEZUELA CARACAS MISSION
Apartado 69204
Caracas 1060-A
Venezuela

(174) VENEZUELA MARACAIBO MISSION
Apartado 10020 Bella Vista
Maracaibo, Estada Zulia CP 4002A
Venezuela

(267) VENEZUELA VALENCIA MISSION
Ave. Bolivar Norte, Centro Professional
Norte, Piso 3, Oficina 3-1
Apdo 1249, Valencia, Edo Carabobo
Venezuela

VIETNAM

Year-end 1999: Est. population, 76,236,000; Members, 100; Branches, 2; Percent LDS, .0001 or one in 762,360; Asia Area.

LDS servicemen arrived in Vietnam in the early 1960s in sufficient numbers to establish groups. An LDS serviceman's group was organized as part of the Southern Far East Mission on June 30, 1962, by mission Pres. Robert D. Taylor with Cecil Cavender as president.

On Nov. 3, 1962, U.S. Air Force Capt. John T. Mullennex was baptized in Saigon by Maurice H. Lee of the Saigon Group presidency. Converts Nguyen Thi Thuy and Duong Thuy Van, baptized in early 1963 by Capt. Loring B. Bean, were the first Vietnamese to join the Church.

The size of the LDS group began to grow as the Vietnam War became more intense and more servicemen arrived. Other groups were added, and several General Authorities visited. A small meetinghouse was erected at Bien Hoa Air Base. By 1971, three districts had been organized under the Hong Kong Mission.

When the cease-fire was reached Jan. 27, 1973, the Saigon Branch numbered about 100 under branch Pres. Nguyen Van The. Elders were sent to Vietnam immediately afterward. Elders Colin B. Van Orman, James L. Christensen, David T. Posey, and Richard C. Holloman were transferred to Saigon from Hong Kong, arriving April 6, 1973.

These elders and those who came later found success, but on April 30, 1975, South Vietnam was defeated in war. Many of the members in Vietnam were able to leave and were relocated in America by the Church. Some 83 members were assigned to sponsors in the United States and Canada by Church refugee workers, along with 672 of their relatives and friends. Following the relocation, many refugees joined the Church and a number of full-time missionaries came from their ranks.

LDS veterans from that period helped locate many former branch members and reunify families.

At the end of 1991, the Church donated medical equipment that enabled Vietnamese surgeons to use microsurgery. Presenting the gift was Elder Merlin R. Lybbert of the Seventy, the first General Authority to enter Vietnam since 1975.

A year later, two LDS couples entered Hanoi on Jan. 6, 1993, to teach English. The couples, Elder James L. and Sister Helen Ream Bateman and Elder Stanley G. and Sister

Mavis Lynnette Steadman, were warmly welcomed in ceremonies at Tran Hung Dao Hospital and at the Children's Palace. The couples taught English to many people and also set up the first-ever presentation of Handel's Messiah in Vietnam, an unusual event partly funded by professional Vietnamese musicians who donated 70 cents at each rehearsal.

President Gordon B. Hinckley and his wife, Marjorie; Elder Joseph B. Wirthlin of the Quorum of the Twelve and his wife, Elisa; Elder John H. Groberg of the Seventy and his wife, Jean; visited Ho Chi Minh City (formerly Saigon) and Hanoi on May 29, 1996.

Sources: *Church News,* March 30, 1963; history by Virgil N. Kovalenko; "Church donates medical gift to Vietnam," *Church News,* Jan. 11, 1992; "Asia Area: Welcome mat is out in several countries," by Sheridan R. Sheffield, *Church News,* June 19, 1993; "Vietnam: Musicians perform 'Messiah'" *Church News,* Dec. 4, 1993; "Pres. Hinckley dedicates Cambodia — Gives addendum to prayer during his visit to Vietnam," *Church News,* June 8, 1996.

VIRGIN ISLANDS
(British and U.S.)

Year-end 1999: Est. population,110,000; Members,293; Branches, 3; North America Southeast Area; Puerto Rico San Juan Mission.

The Virgin Islands are made up of three large and 50 small islands located 70 miles east of Puerto Rico. The residents, who are U.S. citizens, speak English and have a republican form of government.

The first missionaries to St. Croix were Elders Thomas Williams, Eric Leach, Gregory Collier, and Kurtis Gibbons, who arrived Jan. 28, 1981. They held meetings in the home of a member, Jack Cluett, with about 15 attending. A branch was organized Feb. 8, 1981, with Stephen L. Whitmer as the first president. Missionaries baptized several converts the first year. A meetinghouse was later built on the island. Branches have also been established on St. John and St. Thomas.

On St. Thomas, various expatriate families lived on the island. In 1969, one of these was the Earl Keele family. He arrived May 1969, and his wife, Celia, and two children followed in August. The family held a home Sunday School as part of the San Juan Branch in Puerto Rico. In 1970 another family, James and Carolyn Boykin, joined the group. Debra Rybacki met with the family and received permission to be baptized in Brewer's Bay in January 1976. Other families arrived and the St. Thomas Branch was created Dec. 13, 1977. The first missionaries, Elders John Sorensen and D.E. Blomquist, came in June 1978. They baptized the supervisor of Sister Rybacki, Aubrey Nelthropp, and his wife, Carol, on July 16, 1978. The first branch meetinghouse was used July 16, 1978.

A devastating hurricane, Hugo, struck St. Croix in September 1989, destroying the homes of many members. A shipment of food from the mainland and use of the branch meetinghouse helped alleviate emergency conditions. Damage to the islands was reported repaired within a year. Hurricane Georges, which struck Sept. 20-21, 1998, devastated many of the islands but no members were lost.

Sources: Kenneth and LeOra Zabriskie journals; *Church News,* Sept. 9, 1989; *Ensign,* November 1989; unpublished historical sketch of the Church in St. Thomas, by Celia Keele, *Deseret News,* Sept. 21, 1998.

WALES

(See United Kingdom)

WESTERN SAMOA

Year-end 1999: Est. population, 209,000; Members, 58,477; Stakes, 16; Wards, 108; Branches, 22; Missions, 1; Districts, 1; Temples, 1; Percent LDS, 27.98, or one in 4.

Located in the South Pacific, Western Samoa is a parliamentary democracy. The people are Protestant, 45 percent; LDS, 28 percent; and Roman Catholic, 20 percent.

In 1863, two missionaries from Hawaii arrived in Samoa. The two, Kimo Pelia and Samuela Manoa, however, had been sent by an unauthorized leader, Walter Murray Gibson, who had been excommunicated by the Church. The pair labored faithfully for nearly 20 years without the support of the Church.

Elder Joseph H. Dean and his wife, Florence, arrived June 21, 1888. The mission was organized June 17, 1888. The Deans found that Pelia had died but Manoa was still very supportive. He was re-baptized and re-ordained. The same day, Elder Dean baptized a woman named Malaea, who is considered his first convert. Within four months 40 others had joined, and Elder Dean received additional help as more missionaries arrived. Missionaries visited all the islands and baptized converts. A local member, Polonga, was called as the first local missionary.

By 1896, investigators began to join in greater numbers. Missionaries also helped educate youths in small chapel schools. As local members filled leadership positions, they were assigned to distant branches, a pattern unique to Samoa. Local members also served missions and contributed toward the growth of the Church.

Proselyting continued, but was made difficult by internal political conflicts. In 1899, the Samoan islands were divided up between Germany and the United States. Western Samoa became a German colony. Soon, the Germans banned English-language schools, an act that temporarily slowed missionary work. The German control ended in 1914.

In the early 1900s, President Joseph F. Smith authorized the establishment of Sauniatu, in the mountains near the capital city of Apia, as a refuge for converts expelled from their villages for joining the Church. Today, it encompasses a small LDS primary school and the Sauniatu Agriculture Center, a program designed to promote family self-reliance based on gospel principles and training in agriculture and entrepreneurship.

By June 1903, the Book of Mormon had been translated into Samoan. At the end of 1920, membership numbered 3,500, about 5 percent of the total population of the islands.

A visit by Elder David O. McKay, then of the Quorum of the Twelve, in May 1921, had great impact upon the membership. Conversions increased afterward and some entire villages joined the Church.

By 1950, membership had grown to more than 7,000, and by 1961, to more than 16,000. By 1974, the country had six stakes and became the first country of the world to be entirely covered by stakes.

On Oct. 15, 1977, a temple was announced to be built in Apia, Western Samoa, and was dedicated Aug. 5, 1983. At that time, membership had reached an estimated 40,000, about 20 percent of the population of the islands. In 1980, membership was 27,000, increasing to 41,000 in 1990.

Members suffered considerable property losses and one member died during tropical storms in 1991. However, local units responded well to dealing with the disaster. A number of former missionaries to Samoa helped in preserving a 30,000-acre rain forest in Falealupo, and in restoring and preserving the historic home of Robert Louis Stevenson. In June 1995, Tufuga Samuelu Atoa of the Pesega 5th Ward, Pesega Samoa Stake, was awarded the Western Samoa Order of Merit by Head of State Malietoa Tanumafili II for his service to the Samoan Olympic team. Lester W. B. Moore, president of the Polynesian Cultural Center in Hawaii, received a princely title May 10, 1997, from his highness Malietoa Tanumafili II, head of state for Western Samoa, the first non-Samoan to be so honored.

Six new stakes were created in Western Samoa from 1994-96.

President Gordon B. Hinckley visited Savai'i on Oct. 12, 1998, where he spoke to 4,000 members and met with Samoa's Prime Minister Tofilau Eti Alesana. In the afternoon, he addressed another 10,000 members in Apia Park on Upulo. LDS members in Western Samoa numbered 58,477 in 1999.

Sources: *Encyclopedic History of the Church,* by Andrew Jenson; *Unto the Isles of the Sea,* by R. Lanier Britsch; *Samoa Apia Mission History, 1888-1983,* published by R. Carl Harris, president of the Samoa Apia Mission; "Samoan rain forest reprieved from ruin," *Church News,* Aug. 19, 1989; *Deseret News,* Oct. 14, 1990; "Stevenson's historic home and grave to get a face lift," *Deseret News,* July 24, 1994; "Member is honored by government leader," *Church News,* July 22, 1995, June 7, 1997, "Prophet goes to islands of Pacific," by Gerry Avant, *Church News,* Oct. 25, 1997; *Church News,* Feb. 19, 2000.

Stakes — 16

(Listed alphabetically as of Oct. 1, 2000.)

No.	Name	Organized	First President
Pacific Islands Area			
353	*Apia Samoa		
	‡Apia	18 Mar 1962	Percy John Rivers
2134	Apia Samoa Navu	3 Dec 1995	Tigi Manumaluena
513	*Apia Samoa West		
	‡Apia West	26 Apr 1970	Percy J. Rivers
2138	Fagamalo Samoa	4 Dec 1995	Rama Endemann

2011	Pesega Samoa	22 Jan 1995	Meliula Meafou Fata
538	*Savai'i Samoa		
	‡Savai'i	8 Jan 1971	Amuia W. Hunt
2098	Savai'i Samoa Sagone	10 Sep 1995	Paulo Sofeni Matofai
1366	Savai'i Samoa South	17 Oct 1982	Malina Ropeti Ti'a
619	*Savai'i Samoa West		
	‡Savai'i West	3 Jun 1973	Fa'afoi Tuitama
1045	Upolu Samoa Aleisa	10 June 2000	
	Apia Samoa East	5 Aug 1979	Daniel Afamasaga Betham
868	Upolu Samoa East	23 Oct 1977	Kovana Pauga
2171	Upolu Samoa Faleasiu	25 Feb 1996	Pouono Lameko
1909	Upolu Samoa North	25 Oct 1992	Sofeni Pilimai
2139	Upolu Samoa Saleilua	5 Dec 1995	Polesi Avauli Salani
645	Upolu Samoa South	1 Jun 1974	William Richard Schwalger
545	*Upolu Samoa West		
	‡Upolu West	25 Apr 1971	Tua'ifaiva O. Aiono

Mission — 1

(As of Oct. 1, 2000; shown with historical number. See MISSIONS.)

(13c) SAMOA APIA MISSION
P.O. Box 1865
Apia, Samoa

YUGOSLAV FEDERATION

(SERBIA, MONTENEGRO)

Year-end 1999: Est. population, 10,526,000; Members, 100; Districts, 1; Branches, 3; Europe East Area; Austria Vienna Mission.

Located on the Balkan Peninsula in southeast Europe, Serbia is a republic made up of the easternmost internal division of Yugoslavia.

Mischa Markow, a Hungarian who had immigrated to Salt Lake City, Utah, arrived as a missionary in Belgrade, Serbia, in June 1899. He was taken to court where he preached. Even his arresting officer pled his case. But one judge was so irate that he reportedly said the missionary should be "thrown into the Danube to drown." Elder Markow was banished to Hungary. He wrote that he shed tears of joy that he was privileged to testify before a magistrate and a high court.

In modern times, missionary work has proceeded slowly. A few members live in Belgrade, where a branch was organized in 1988.

The Church provided members and non-members in Serbia with humanitarian supplies in 1992, which included food, clothing, blankets and medical supplies. Also, from 1996-98, the Church contributed through the American Red Cross more than $1 million in cash and commodities, including clothing, food, soap, milk, medical supplies, and blood donor bags, to Serbia.

On July 23-26, 1998, youth from Serbia joined others from Croatia, Bosnia, and Slovenia in a Balkan States LDS youth conference at Ljubljana, Slovenia. They met with the theme, "Love One Another," and lived up to it, said Pres. John A. Wondra, president of the Austria Vienna South Mission, which includes the Balkan states.

Sources: "Tears of joy," by Richard L. Jensen, *Church News,* Dec. 8, 1979; Yugoslavia, manuscript history; "Missionary to the Balkans, Mischa Markow," by William Hale Kehr, *Ensign,* June 1980; Zagreb Branch history, published by the branch at dedication of meetinghouse, Oct. 30, 1985; *Church News,* Sept. 26, 1992, June 6, 1998, Aug. 29, 1998.

ZAMBIA

Year-end 1999: Est. population, 9,446,000; Members, 711; Branches, 3; Percent LDS, .01, or one in 13,286; Africa Southeast Area; Zimbabwe Harare Mission.

A republic in south-central Africa, Zambia has a population that speaks English and local dialects. Most of the population follows Christian beliefs, with smaller numbers who have indigenous and Muslim beliefs.

In the 1960s, a meetinghouse was built in Kwekwe, Rhodesia (now Zimbabwe), for a branch composed almost totally of expatriates working in northern Rhodesia in the copperbelt, and farmers from South Africa. Those original members left, presumably across the border into Zambia. However, when none were located, Pres. Vern Marble of the Zimbabwe Harare Mission went to Zambia in 1991 to search for members.

He searched for, but could not find, a man who had been baptized in England, Johnson Makombe, and his wife, Noria. However, a taxi driver in Lusaka offered to find them and deliver a message. When Pres. Marble returned a short time later, Noria Makombe went to the hotel where he was staying. When she met him in the lobby, her first words were, "Where can I pay my tithing?"

The first missionary couple, Elder Dean and Sister Ruth Harrison, were assigned to open the work in Zambia in April 1992, and the Church was formally registered July 10, 1992. When a branch of the Church was organized in Lusaka on July 14, 1992, by Pres. Marble, the congregation of about 50 was almost the same size as when the meetinghouse was built in Kwekwe in the early 1960s.

By 1993, the Church had stored alphabet characters in computers in Bemba, one of Zambia's 70 indigenous languages, in preparation for publishing scriptures in that language.

The seminary program was established in Zambia in 1995, and missionaries from the Zimbabwe Harare Mission continue to serve in Zambia.

Sources: "Four nations in central, southern Africa," by Mary Mostert and Gerry Avant, *Church News*, Sept. 26, 1992; "Alphabets of the world at fingertip," by John L. Hart, *Church News*, May 5, 1993; "Seminary thrives in Africa," by Sarah Jane Weaver, *Church News*, March 9, 1996; *Church News*, Jan. 18, 1997.

ZIMBABWE

Year-end 1999: Est. population, 11,140,000; Members, 8,287; Stakes, 1; Districts, 2; Branches, 23; Missions, 1; percent LDS, .07, or one in 1,344; Africa Southwest Area.

In southern Africa, Zimbabwe is a one-party socialist state where the people speak English (official language), Shona, and Sindebele. Traditional tribal beliefs dominate, with a Christian minority.

Missionary work began in what was then Rhodesia in the early 1930s but soon slowed, continued by only short visits by missionaries from South Africa. In 1950, under the direction of mission Pres. Evan P. Wright, eight missionaries began working in Salisbury and Bulawayo. Hugh Hodgkiss was the first convert, baptized Feb. 1, 1951.

On April 17, 1951, the missionaries distributed 3,000 handbills, and a fairly large crowd attended an introductory meeting. The first services were held in a pre-school building and prospective members sat on tiny chairs. Later, they met in the cloak room of a primary school.

During that period, Sir John Kennedy, governor of Southern Rhodesia, invited the missionaries to teach square dancing. They attended four large dances and made many contacts, but few conversions, as they taught dancing.

In 1980, the government changed and the nation of Zimbabwe was formed. A new mission was established in Zimbabwe in 1987. At the time, membership was 1,014. Missionary work increased as local missionaries began serving full-time missions.

Since 1988, the Church has had an ongoing humanitarian project in Zimbabwe that included funds, a mill for grinding grain, a dam near Masvingo, gardening materials, and two large shipments of new textbooks for Zimbabwe's school children.

On July 26, 1990, mission president George T. Brooks died in a car-truck accident near Kwekwe, Zimbabwe. His wife, Sister Lillis Remington Brooks, was seriously injured.

In 1996, LDS teenagers enjoyed participating in the seminary program. One teacher, Wilson Athgten, walked eight miles every morning to teach seminary, and, when students were involved in evening activites, he walked each home.

President Gordon B. Hinckley, on a five-country tour of Africa, visited Zimbabwe on Feb. 18, 1998, and spoke to some 1,497 members. Several high-level government officials, including the Secretary of Defense and the Social Welfare director, attended the meeting in a rented hall in Harare.

LDS membership in Zimbabwe in 1999 was 8,287.

Sources: A History of the South African Mission, by Evan P. Wright; "Preached by Dancing," *Church News*, July 14, 1979; *Church News*, March 14, 1987, March 23, 1991; "Seminary thrives in Africa," by Sarah Jane Weaver, *Church News*, March 9, 1996; "Zimbabwe pioneers take front row seats at historic occasion," by Steve Fidel, *Church News*, Feb. 28, 1998.

Stakes — 1

(Listed alphabetically as of Oct. 1, 2000.)

No.	Name	Organized	First President
2541	Harare Zimbabwe	12 Dec 1999	Edward Dube

Mission — 1

(As of Oct. 1, 2000; shown with historical number. See MISSIONS.)

(204) ZIMBABWE HARARE MISSION
65 Enterprise Road, Highlands, Harare, Zimbabwe

Editor's note: Information in this section has been gathered from a variety of sources and is believed to be the best available at the time of publication. Corrections, additional information and further country or state histories will be appreciated. Those with comments or information may write to: Church Almanac Histories, P.O. Box 1257, Salt Lake City, UT 84110 or E-mail churchnews@desnews.com

WARDS/BRANCHES

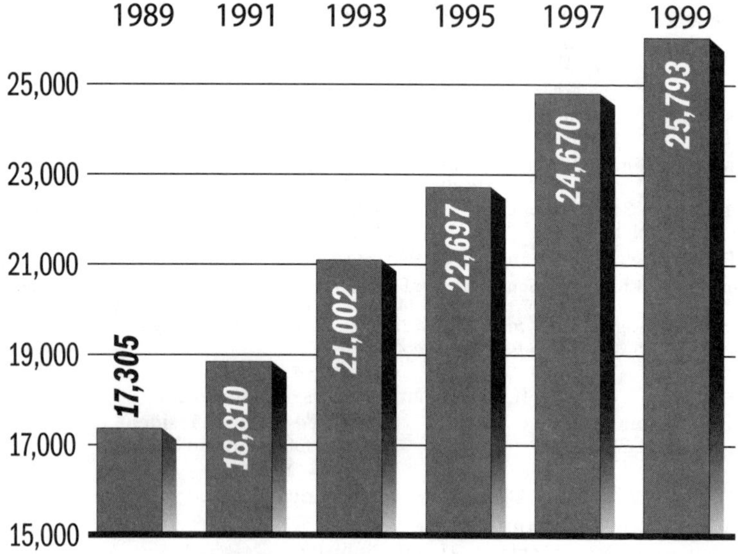

DISTRICTS

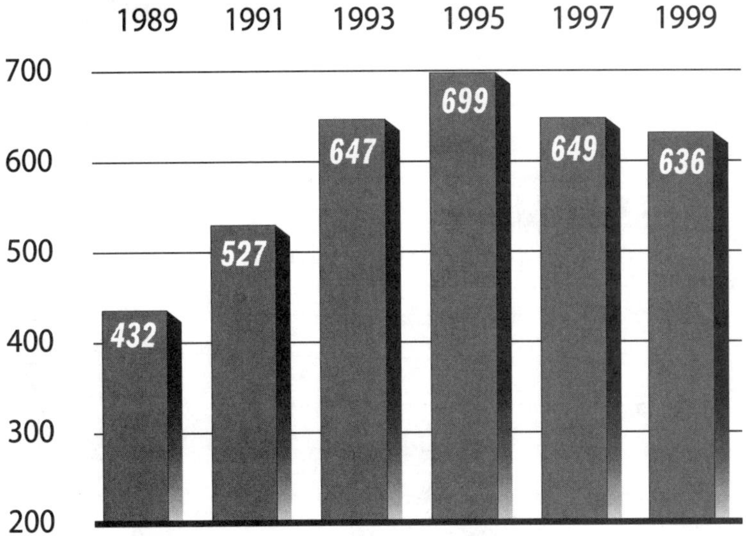

STAKES

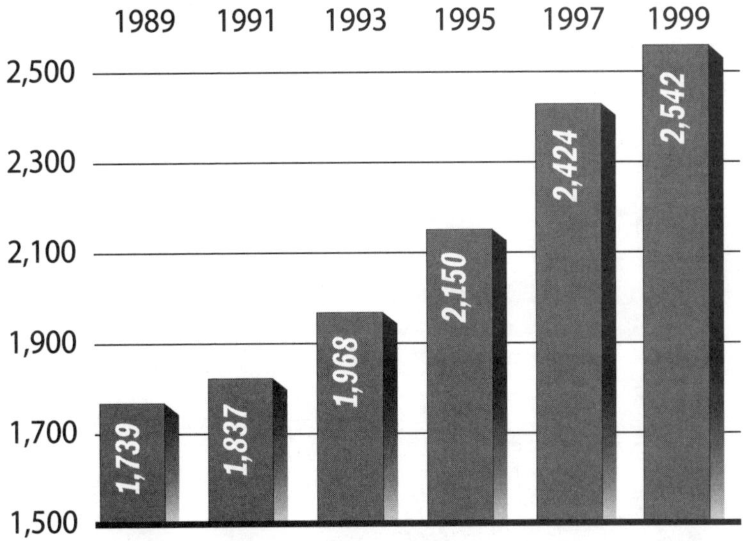

MISSIONS

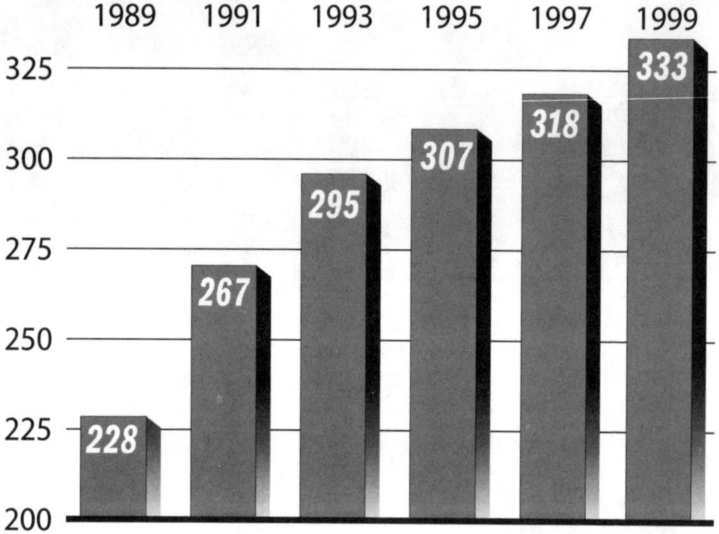
1989
1991
1993
1995
1997
1999
325
300
275
250
225
200
228
267
295
307
318
333

MISSIONS

MISSIONS

FULL-TIME MISSIONS

Missions are listed here in chronological order and according to the name under which they were originally organized. On June 20, 1974, most mission names were changed under the Church's current naming system; these and other name changes are indicated in the "Name" column.

* Denotes a name change; capital letters indicate the mission's new name.

The number immediately preceding the name of the mission indicates the total number of missions in existence at the time of its organization. A letter after the number indicates that the number was reached previously; the letter is added to clarify cross-references. This number is also placed with the mission in the "Worldwide Church" section.

By using this list it is possible to trace the "family tree" of each mission. Included in each mission entry is the number, in parentheses, of the "parent" mission from which it was created and, in the "See also" entry, the numbers of "offspring" missions that were created from divisions of this mission. Also included are the numbers of missions that this mission may have been transferred to when it was discontinued and the number the mission was assigned when it was reopened.

	NAME	ORGANIZED	FIRST PRESIDENT
1	BRITISH *10 Jun 1970 ENGLAND EAST *20 Jun 1974 ENGLAND LONDON See also 4, 52, 62, 68, 79, 161	20 Jul 1837	Heber C. Kimball
2	EASTERN STATES Discontinued Apr 1850 Reopened 1854 (15) Discontinued 1858 Reopened 1865 (9a) Discontinued 1869 Reopened from Northern States Jan 1893 (15b) *20 Jun 1974 NEW YORK NEW YORK *1 JUL 1993 NEW YORK NEW YORK SOUTH See also 23a, 29, 35, 54, 77, 202	6 May 1839	John P. Greene
3	SOCIETY ISLANDS Discontinued 15 May 1852 Reopened 29 Apr 1892 (13d) *1907 TAHITIAN *25 Nov 1959 FRENCH-POLYNESIAN *10 Jun 1970 FRENCH-POLYNESIA *20 Jun 1974 TAHITI PAPEETE	30 Apr 1844	Noah Rogers
4	WELSH Organized from British (1) Discontinued 26 Mar 1854, transferred to British (1)	15 Dec 1845	Dan Jones
5	CALIFORNIA Discontinued 1858 Reopened 23 Aug 1892 (14c) *20 Jun 1974 CALIFORNIA LOS ANGELES See also 37, 73a, 86, 159, 324	31 Jul 1846	Samuel Brannan
5a	SCANDINAVIAN Discontinued 1 Apr 1920, transferred to Danish (23b), Norwegian (24) See also 22a	11 May 1850	Erastus Snow
6	FRENCH Discontinued 1864 Reopened 15 Oct 1912 (22b) Discontinued 18 Sep 1914 Reopened 20 Aug 1923 (26) from Swiss-German (8) *10 Jun 1970 FRANCE *20 Jun 1974 FRANCE PARIS See also 59, 76, 92, 121, 221a	18 Jun 1850	John Taylor
7	ITALIAN Discontinued 1 Jan 1854, transferred to Swiss and Italian (8) Reopened 2 Aug 1966 (74a) from Swiss (8)	1 Nov 1850	Lorenzo Snow

	*10 Jun 1970 ITALY *1 Jul 1971 ITALY SOUTH *20 Jun 1974 ITALY ROME See also 98, 123, 158, 244		
8	SWISS *1 Jan 1854 SWISS AND ITALIAN *1 Jan 1861 SWISS, ITALIAN AND GERMAN *1 Jan 1868 SWISS AND GERMAN *1 Jan 1898 SWISS *22 May 1904 SWISS-GERMAN *1 Jan 1938 SWISS AUSTRIAN *21 Nov 1938 SWISS *25 May 1946 SWISS AUSTRIAN *18 Sep 1960 SWISS *10 Jun 1970 SWITZERLAND *20 Jun 1974 SWITZERLAND ZURICH See also 6, 7, 13, 8a, 19, 26, 30, 53	24 Nov 1850	Thomas B.H. Stenhouse
9	SANDWICH ISLANDS Discontinued 1 May 1858 Reopened 27 Mar 1864 (7a) *1900 HAWAIIAN *1 Apr 1950 HAWAII *20 Jun 1974 HAWAII HONOLULU See also 34, 178	12 Dec 1850	Hiram Clark
10	AUSTRALIAN *1854 AUSTRALASIAN *1 Jan 1898 AUSTRALIAN *10 Jun 1970 AUSTRALIA EAST *20 Jun 1974 AUSTRALIA SYDNEY *1 Jan 1993 AUSTRALIA SYDNEY SOUTH See also 20, 43c, 106	30 Oct 1851	John Murdock
11	EAST INDIAN Discontinued 2 May 1856 Reopened 1 Aug 1884 (12a) Discontinued 10 Jun 1885	1851	Lorenzo Snow
12	MALTA Discontinued 1856	26 Feb 1852	Lorenzo Snow
13	GERMAN Discontinued 1 Jan 1861, transferred to Swiss, Italian and German (8) Reopened 1 Jan 1898 (19) from Swiss and German (8) Discontinued 22 May 1904, transferred to Swiss-German (8) Reopened 23 Aug 1925 as German-Austrian (27) from Swiss-German (8) Discontinued 1 Jan 1938, transferred to West German (35a), East German (36), Swiss Austrian (8) See also 30	3 Apr 1852	Daniel P. Garn
13a	GIBRALTAR Discontinued 5 Jul 1854	7 Mar 1853	Edward Stevenson
14	SOUTH AFRICAN Discontinued 12 Apr 1865 Reopened 25 Jul 1903 (23) *10 Jun 1970 SOUTH AFRICA *20 Jun 1974 SOUTH AFRICA JOHANNESBURG See also 177a, 204, 216, 327	19 Apr 1853	Jesse Haven
15	EASTERN STATES (See 2)	1854	John Taylor
14a	SIAM Discontinued 12 Aug 1854	6 Apr 1854	Elam Luddington
15a	EUROPEAN (Administrative) Discontinued 14 Feb 1950 Reopened 17 Jan 1960 (51) Discontinued 14 Sep 1965 See also 64	28 Jun 1854	Franklin D. Richards
14b	INDIAN TERRITORY Discontinued 23 May 1860	26 Jun 1855	Henry W. Miller

	Reopened Mar 1877 (9b) Discontinued 12 Sep 1877 Reopened 20 Apr 1883 (11a) *29 Mar 1898 SOUTHWESTERN STATES *4 Apr 1904 CENTRAL STATES *10 Jun 1970 KANSAS-MISSOURI *20 Jun 1974 MISSOURI INDEPENDENCE See also 31, 88, 140, 153		
7a	SANDWICH ISLANDS (See 9)	27 Mar 1864	Joseph F. Smith
8a	NETHERLANDS Organized from Swiss, Italian and German (8) *31 Jan 1891 NETHERLANDS-BELGIUM *15 May 1914 NETHERLANDS *20 Jun 1974 NETHERLANDS AMSTERDAM See also 135, 232	1 Nov 1864	Joseph Weiler
9a	EASTERN STATES (See 2)	1865	John Taylor
8b	SOUTHERN STATES *Jun 1971 GEORGIA-SOUTH CAROLINA *20 Jun 1974 GEORGIA ATLANTA See also 22, 29, 55, 130, 166a, 239	Nov 1876	Henry G. Boyle
9b	INDIAN TERRITORY (See 14b)	Mar 1877	Matthew W. Dalton
9c	NORTHWESTERN STATES *20 Jul 1889 NORTHERN STATES *1 Jul 1973 ILLINOIS *20 Jun 1974 ILLINOIS CHICAGO *1 Jul 1980 ILLINOIS CHICAGO NORTH *1 Jul 1983 ILLINOIS CHICAGO *1 JUL 1997 ILLINOIS CHICAGO NORTH See also 23a, 26a, 43a, 46, 97, 167, 184, 313	6 May 1878	Cyrus H. Wheelock
10a	MEXICAN Discontinued Jun 1889 Reopened 8 Jun 1901 (20a) *10 Jun 1970 MEXICO *20 Jun 1974 MEXICO MEXICO CITY *1 Jul 1978 MEXICO MEXICO CITY SOUTH See also 33, 43b, 45a, 75, 125, 163, 193	16 Nov 1879	Moses Thatcher
11a	INDIAN TERITORY (See 14b)	20 Apr 1883	George Teasdale
12a	EAST INDIAN (See 11)	1 Aug 1884	William Willis
13b	TURKISH Discontinued 1 Oct 1909 Reopened 6 Nov 1921 (25) *23 Jan 1924 ARMENIAN *12 Aug 1933 PALESTINE-SYRIAN Discontinued 1939 Reopened 8 Nov 1947 (43) *25 Jan 1950 NEAR EAST Discontinued Jan 1951	30 Dec 1884	Jacob Spori
13c	SAMOAN *10 Jun 1970 SAMOA *20 Jun 1974 SAMOA APIA See also 22c, 57, 99	17 Jun 1888	Joseph H. Dean
13d	SOCIETY ISLANDS (See 3)	29 Apr 1892	Joseph W. Damron
14c	CALIFORNIA (See 5)	23 Aug 1892	John L. Dalton
15b	EASTERN STATES (See 2)	Jan 1893	Job Pingree
16	MONTANA Discontinued 12 Jun 1898, transferred to Northwestern States (18) See also 43a	10 Sep 1896	Phineas Tempest
17	COLORADO *1 Apr 1907 WESTERN STATES *10 Jun 1970 COLORADO-NEW MEXICO *10 Oct 1972 COLORADO *20 Jun 1974 COLORADO DENVER	15 Dec 1896	John W. Taylor

*01 Jul 1993 COLORADO DENVER SOUTH
See also 26a, 33, 43a, 132, 286

18	NORTHWESTERN STATES *10 Jun 1970 OREGON *20 Jun 1974 OREGON PORTLAND See also 26a, 36a, 43a, 78a, 249	26 Jul 1897	George C. Parkinson
19	GERMAN (See 13)	1 Jan 1898	Peter Loutensock
20	NEW ZEALAND Organized from Australasian (10) *10 Jun 1970 NEW ZEALAND NORTH *20 Jun 1974 NEW ZEALAND AUCKLAND See also 47, 99	1 Jan 1898	Ezra F. Richards
20a	MEXICAN (See 10a)	8 Jun 1901	Ammon N. Tenney
21	JAPAN Discontinued 31 Jul 1924 Reopened 6 Mar 1948 as Japanese (44) Discontinued 28 Jul 1955, transferred to Northern Far East (43d), Southern Far East (44a)	12 Aug 1901	Heber J. Grant
22	MIDDLE STATES Organized from Southern States (8b) Discontinued 7 Aug 1903, transferred to Southern States (8b)	28 Jun 1902	Ben E. Rich
23	SOUTH AFRICAN (See 14)	25 Jul 1903	Warren H. Lyon
22a	SWEDISH Organized from Scandinavian (5a) *10 Jun 1970 SWEDEN *20 Jun 1974 SWEDEN STOCKHOLM See also 41, 145	15 Jun 1905	Peter Matson
22b	FRENCH (See 6)	15 Oct 1912	Edgar B. Brossard
22c	TONGAN Organized from Samoan (13c) *10 Jun 1970 TONGA *20 Jun 1974 TONGA NUKU'ALOFA See also 99	8 Jul 1916	Willard L. Smith
23a	CANADIAN Organized from Eastern States (15b), Northern States (9c) *10 Jun 1970 ONTARIO-QUEBEC *1 Jul 1972 ONTARIO *20 Jun 1974 CANADA TORONTO *01 Jul 1993 CANADA TORONTO WEST See also 26a, 35, 99a, 285	1 Jul 1919	Nephi Jensen
23b	DANISH Organized from Scandinavian (5a) *10 Jun 1970 DENMARK *20 Jun 1974 DENMARK COPENHAGEN	1 Apr 1920	Carl E. Peterson
24	NORWEGIAN Organized from Scandinavian (5a) *10 Jun 1970 NORWAY *20 Jun 1974 NORWAY OSLO	1 Apr 1920	Andrew S. Schow
25	TURKISH (See 13b)	6 Nov 1921	Joseph Wilford Booth
26	FRENCH (See 6)	20 Aug 1923	Russell H. Blood
26a	NORTH CENTRAL STATES Organized from Northern States (9c), Western States (17), Northwestern States (18), Canadian (23a) *10 Jun 1970 MANITOBA-MINNESOTA *1 Jul 1973 MINNESOTA-WISCONSIN *20 Jun 1974 MINNESOTA MINNEAPOLIS See also 36a, 43a, 167	12 Jul 1925	John G. Allred
27	GERMAN-AUSTRIAN (See 13)	23 Aug 1925	Fred Tadje
28	SOUTH AMERICAN Discontinued 25 May 1935, transferred to Brazilian (31a), Argentine (32)	6 Dec 1925	Melvin J. Ballard
29	EAST CENTRAL STATES	9 Dec 1928	Miles L. Jones

Organized from Southern States (8b), Eastern States, (15b)
*10 Jun 1970 KENTUCKY-TENNESSEE
*20 Jun 1974 KENTUCKY LOUISVILLE
See also 42, 131, 328

30 CZECHOSLOVAK 24 Jul 1929 Arthur Gaeth
Organized from German-Austrian (27), Swiss (8)
Discontinued 6 Apr 1950
Reopened 1 Jul 1990, see 236
Organized from Austria Vienna East (205)
*2 Mar 1993 CZECH PRAGUE
*26 Aug 1993 CZECH REPUBLIC PRAGUE
*15 May 1995 CZECH PRAGUE

31 TEXAS 11 Jan 1931 Charles Elliott Rowan Jr.
Organized from Central States (11a)
*May 1945 TEXAS-LOUISIANA
*19 Jun 1955 GULF STATES
*20 Jun 1974 LOUISIANA SHREVEPORT
*1 Jul 1975 LOUISIANA BATON ROUGE
See also 60, 116, 171

31a BRAZILIAN 25 May 1935 Rulon S. Howells
Organized from South American (28)
*10 Jun 1970 BRAZIL CENTRAL
Discontinued 17 Oct 1972, transferred to Brazil North Central (101), Brazil South Central (102)
See also 48, 80

32 ARGENTINE 14 Aug 1935 W. Ernest Young
Organized from South American (28)
*10 Jun 1970 ARGENTINA SOUTH
*20 Jun 1974 ARGENTINA BUENOS AIRES NORTH
See also 40, 50, 73, 100, 112, 269

33 SPANISH-AMERICAN 28 Jun 1936 Orlando C. Williams
Organized from Mexican (20a)
Discontinued Dec 1967, transferred to Texas (60), Texas South (77b), Western States (17)
See also 46a, 77b

34 JAPANESE 24 Feb 1937 Hilton A. Robertson
Organized from Hawaiian (7a)
*14 May 1944 CENTRAL PACIFIC
Discontinued 1 Apr 1950, transferred to Hawaii (9)
(Administrative headquarters different from 21)

35 NEW ENGLAND 24 Sep 1937 Carl Eyring
Organized from Eastern States (15b), Canadian (23a)
*20 Jun 1974 MASSACHUSETTS BOSTON
See also 107, 169, 195, 299

35a WEST GERMAN 1 Jan 1938 Philemon M. Kelly
Organized from German-Austrian (27)
*10 Jun 1970 GERMANY WEST
*20 Jun 1974 GERMANY FRANKFURT
See also 49, 63, 240

36 EAST GERMAN 1 Jan 1938 Alfred C. Rees
Organized from German-Austrian (27)
*12 Sep 1957 NORTH GERMAN
*10 Jun 1970 GERMANY NORTH
*20 Jun 1974 GERMANY HAMBURG
See also 65

36a WESTERN CANADIAN 15 Sep 1941 Walter Miller
Organized from North Central States (26a), Northwestern States (18)
*10 Jun 1970 ALBERTA-SASKATCHEWAN
*20 Jun 1974 CANADA CALGARY
See also 58, 136

37 NORTHERN CALIFORNIA 2 Jan 1942 German E. Ellsworth
Organized from California (14c)
*15 Jul 1966 CALIFORNIA NORTH

	*20 Jun 1974 CALIFORNIA SACRAMENTO See also 85, 127, 187a		
38	NAVAJO-ZUNI *1 Jan 1949 SOUTHWEST INDIAN *10 Oct 1972 NEW MEXICO-ARIZONA *20 Jun 1974 ARIZONA HOLBROOK Discontinued 1 Jul 1984, transferred to Arizona Phoenix (179b) See also 78, 128, 132	7 Mar 1943	Ralph W. Evans
39	PACIFIC (Administrative) Discontinued 27 Nov 1948	7 Dec 1946	Matthew Cowley
40	URUGUAY Organized from Argentine Mission (32) *10 Jun 1970 URUGUAY-PARAGUAY *20 Jun 1974 URUGUAY MONTEVIDEO See also 50, 155, 317	31 Aug 1947	Frederick S. Williams
41	FINNISH Organized from Swedish (22a) *10 Jun 1970 FINLAND *20 Jun 1974 FINLAND HELSINKI See also 238	1 Sep 1947	Henry A. Matis
42	CENTRAL ATLANTIC STATES Organized from East Central States (29) *10 Jun 1970 NORTH CAROLINA-VIRGINIA *1 Jul 1973 VIRGINIA *20 Jun 1974 VIRGINIA ROANOKE *25 Feb 1992 VIRGINIA RICHMOND See also 105, 188	26 Oct 1947	Robert J. Price
43	PALESTINE-SYRIAN (See 13b)	8 Nov 1947	Badwagan Piranian
44	JAPANESE (See 21)	6 Mar 1948	Edward L. Clissold
45	CHINESE Discontinued 9 Feb 1953	10 Jul 1949	Hilton A. Robertson
46	GREAT LAKES Organized from Northern States (9c) *10 Jun 1970 INDIANA-MICHIGAN *1 Jul 1973 INDIANA *20 Jun 1974 INDIANA INDIANAPOLIS See also 77a, 104	31 Oct 1949	Carl C. Burton
43a	WEST CENTRAL STATES Organized from North Central States (26a), Northwestern States (18), Western States (17) *10 Jun 1970 MONTANA-WYOMING *20 Jun 1974 MONTANA BILLINGS See also 111	11 Nov 1950	Sylvester Broadbent
43b	CENTRAL AMERICAN Organized from Mexican (20a) *10 Jun 1970 CENTRAL AMERICA *20 Jun 1974 COSTA RICA SAN JOSE See also 76a, 79a, 177, 226	16 Nov 1952	Gordon M. Romney
43c	SOUTH AUSTRALIAN Organized from Australian (10) *Nov 1958 SOUTHERN AUSTRALIAN *1 Aug 1968 AUSTRALIA SOUTH *20 Jun 1974 AUSTRALIA MELBOURNE See also 82, 319	3 Jul 1955	Thomas S. Bingham
43d	NORTHERN FAR EAST Organized from Japanese (44) Discontinued 31 Aug 1968, transferred to Japan (82a), Japan-Okinawa (83) See also 71	28 Jul 1955	Hilton A. Robertson
44a	SOUTHERN FAR EAST Organized from Japanese (44) *1 Nov 1969 HONG KONG TAIWAN *11 Jan 1971 HONG KONG See also 76b, 89, 94	17 Aug 1955	H. Grant Heaton

45a	NORTHERN MEXICAN Organized from Mexican (20a) *10 Jun 1970 MEXICO NORTH *20 Jun 1974 MEXICO MONTERREY *2 Sep 1992 MEXICO MONTERREY WEST *3 Nov 1992 MEXICO MONTERREY NORTH See also 56, 81, 193, 218	10 Jun 1956	Joseph T. Bentley
46a	WEST SPANISH-AMERICAN Organized from Spanish-American (33) *10 Jun 1970 WEST SPANISH AMERICA Discontinued 1 Jul 1970, transferred to California (5) California South (73a), Arizona (87)	8 Mar 1958	Leland M. Perry
47	NEW ZEALAND SOUTH Organized from New Zealand (20) *20 Jun 1974 NEW ZEALAND WELLINGTON Discontinued 1 Jul 1981, transferred to New Zealand Christchurch (143), New Zealand Auckland (20)	1 Sep 1958	Alexander P. Anderson
48	BRAZILIAN SOUTH Organized from Brazilian (31a) *10 Jun 1970 BRAZIL SOUTH *20 Jun 1974 BRAZIL PORTO ALEGRE *25 Jan 1991 BRAZIL PORTO ALEGRE SOUTH See also 80, 181, 256a, 258,	20 Sep 1959	Asael T. Sorensen
49	SOUTH GERMAN Organized from West German (35a) *10 Jun 1970 GERMANY SOUTH *20 Jun 1974 GERMANY MUNICH See also 69, 240	4 Oct 1959	John A. Buehner
50	ANDES Organized from Uruguay (40), Argentine (32) *10 Jun 1970 PERU-ECUADOR *1 Aug 1970 PERU *Feb 1971 PERU ANDES *Apr 1971 ANDES PERU *20 Jun 1974 PERU LIMA *1 Jan 1977 PERU LIMA SOUTH See also 67, 75a, 79a, 93, 149, 165, 300	1 Nov 1959	J. Vernon Sharp
51	EUROPEAN (Administrative) (See 15a)	17 Jan 1960	Alvin R. Dyer
52	NORTH BRITISH Organized from British (1) *10 Jun 1970 ENGLAND NORTH *20 Jun 1974 ENGLAND LEEDS See also 61, 72, 138	27 Mar 1960	Bernard P. Brockbank
53	AUSTRIAN Organized from Swiss Austrian (8) *10 Jun 1970 AUSTRIA *20 Jun 1974 AUSTRIA VIENNA See also 205	18 Sep 1960	W. Whitney Smith
54	EASTERN ATLANTIC STATES Organized from Eastern States (15b) *10 Jun 1970 DELAWARE-MARYLAND *20 Jun 1974 WASHINGTON D.C. *1 Jul 1986 WASHINGTON D.C. SOUTH See also 91a, 188b, 298	16 Oct 1960	George B. Hill
55	FLORIDA Organized from Southern States (8b) *10 Jun 1971 FLORIDA SOUTH *20 Jun 1974 FLORIDA FT. LAUDERDALE Discontinued 20 Jun 1983, transferred to Florida Tampa (139), West Indies (178a) Reopened 1 Jul 1984 (178b) See also 96, 175	1 Nov 1960	Karl R. Lyman
56	WEST MEXICAN Organized from Northern Mexican (45a)	1 Nov 1960	Harold E. Turley

*10 Jun 1970 MEXICO WEST
*20 Jun 1974 MEXICO HERMOSILLO
See also 125, 247

57 RAROTONGA 20 Nov 1960 Joseph R. Reeder
Organized from Samoan (13c)
Discontinued 15 Apr 1966, transferred to New Zealand (20)

58 ALASKAN-CANADIAN 21 Nov 1960 Milton L. Weilenmann
Organized from Western Canadian (36a)
*10 Jun 1970 ALASKA-BRITISH COLUMBIA
*20 Jun 1974 CANADA VANCOUVER
See also 114

59 FRENCH EAST 19 Jan 1961 Henry D. Moyle Jr.
Organized from French (26)
*10 Jun 1970 FRANCE-SWITZERLAND
*20 Jun 1974 SWITZERLAND GENEVA
See also 221a, 262

60 TEXAS 16 Feb 1961 Ralph J. Hill
Organized from Gulf States (31)
*10 Jun 1970 TEXAS NORTH
*20 Jun 1974 TEXAS DALLAS
See also 77b, 189

61 SCOTTISH-IRISH 28 Feb 1961 Bernard P. Brockbank
Organized from North British (52)
*8 Jul 1962 SCOTTISH
*10 Jun 1970 SCOTLAND
*20 Jun 1974 SCOTLAND EDINBURGH
See also 70, 74, 147

62 CENTRAL BRITISH 6 Mar 1961 James A. Cullimore
Organized from British (1)
*10 Jun 1970 ENGLAND CENTRAL
*20 Jun 1974 ENGLAND BIRMINGHAM
Discontinued 1 Jul 1983, transferred to England Coventry (183)

63 CENTRAL GERMAN
Organized from West German (35a)
10 Jun 1970 GERMAN CENTRAL
20 JUN 1974 GERMANY DUSSELDORF
Reopened 1 Jul 1990, Germany, Duesseldorf; from Germany Frankfurt (35a), Germany Munich (49) See 240

64 WEST EUROPEAN (Administrative) 30 Apr 1961 N. Eldon Tanner
Organized from European (51)
Discontinued 14 Sep 1965

65 BERLIN 14 Jul 1961 Percy K. Fetzer
Organized from North German (36)
Discontinued 31 May 1966, transferred to North German (36)

66 SOUTH AMERICA (Administrative) 25 Aug 1961 A. Theodore Tuttle
Discontinued 17 Jul 1965

67 CHILEAN 8 Oct 1961 A. Delbert Palmer
Organized from Andes (50)
*10 Jun 1970 CHILE
*20 Jun 1974 CHILE SANTIAGO
*1 Jan 1977 CHILE SANTIAGO SOUTH
See also 119, 148, 214, 303a, 311

68 SOUTHWEST BRITISH 1 Feb 1962 A. Ray Curtis
Organized from British (1)
*10 Jun 1970 ENGLAND SOUTHWEST
*20 Jun 1974 ENGLAND BRISTOL
See also 79

69 BAVARIAN 4 Mar 1962 Owen Spencer Jacobs
Organized from South German (49)
Discontinued 10 Jun 1965, transferred to South German (49)

70	IRISH Organized from Scottish-Irish (61) *10 Jun 1970 IRELAND *20 Jun 1974 IRELAND BELFAST *11 Sep 1976 IRELAND DUBLIN	8 Jul 1962	Stephen R. Covey
71	KOREAN Organized from Northern Far East (43d) *10 Jun 1970 KOREA *20 Jun 1974 KOREA SEOUL See also 124, 170	8 Jul 1962	Gail Edward Carr
72	NORTHEAST BRITISH Organized from North British (52) Discontinued May 1965, transferred to North British (52)	1 Sep 1962	Grant S. Thorn
73	NORTH ARGENTINE Organized from Argentine (32) *10 Jun 1970 ARGENTINA NORTH *20 Jun 1974 ARGENTINA CORDOBA See also 100, 206, 228	16 Sep 1962	Ronald V. Stone
74	NORTH SCOTTISH Organized from Scottish (61) Discontinued 31 May 1965, transferred to Scottish (61)	24 Nov 1962	William N. Waite
75	SOUTHEAST MEXICAN Organized from Mexican (20a) *10 Jun 1970 MEXICO SOUTHEAST *20 Jun 1974 MEXICO VERACRUZ See also 126, 193	27 Mar 1963	Carl J. Beecroft
76	FRANCO-BELGIAN Organized from French (26) *10 Jun 1970 FRANCE-BELGIUM *20 Jun 1974 BELGIUM BRUSSELS See also 135	1 Oct 1963	Joseph T. Edmunds
77	CUMORAH Organized from Eastern States (15b) *20 Jun 1974 NEW YORK ROCHESTER	26 Jan 1964	N. Lester Petersen
78	NORTHERN INDIAN Organized from Southwest Indian (38) *1 Jul 1973 DAKOTA-MANITOBA *20 Jun 1974 SOUTH DAKOTA RAPID CITY See also 136	8 Apr 1964	Grant Roper Farmer
79	BRITISH SOUTH Organized from British (1), Southwest British (68) *10 Jun 1970 ENGLAND SOUTH *20 Jun 1974 ENGLAND LONDON SOUTH	27 Dec 1964	Don K. Archer
76a	GUATEMALA-EL SALVADOR Organized from Central American (43b) *20 Jun 1974 GUATEMALA GUATEMALA CITY *29 Mar 1988 GUATEMALA GUATEMALA CITY SOUTH See also 137a, 152, 205a, 227	1 Aug 1965	Terrance L. Hansen
73a	CALIFORNIA SOUTH Organized from California (14c) *20 Jun 1974 CALIFORNIA ANAHEIM See also 86, 87, 113, 182, 324	10 Jul 1966	D. Crawford Houston
74a	ITALIAN (See 7)	2 Aug 1966	John Duns Jr.
75a	ANDES SOUTH Organized from Andes (50) *1969 BOLIVIA *20 Jun 1974 BOLIVIA LA PAZ See also 320	14 Nov 1966	Franklin Kay Gibson
76b	PHILIPPINE Organized from Southern Far East (44a) *10 Jun 1970 PHILIPPINES *20 Jun 1974 PHILIPPINES MANILA	28 Jan 1967	Paul S. Rose

See also 110, 172, 194, 250, 268

77a OHIO — 31 Jul 1967 — E. Garrett Barlow
Organized from Great Lakes (46)
*31 Aug 1972 OHIO-WEST VIRGINIA
*20 Jun 1974 OHIO COLUMBUS
See also 154, 188, 179a

77b TEXAS SOUTH — 10 Dec 1967 — Dean L. Larsen
Organized from Texas (60), Spanish-American (33)
*20 Jun 1974 TEXAS SAN ANTONIO
See also 142, 224

78a PACIFIC NORTHWEST — 1 Jan 1968 — Joe E. Whitesides
Organized from Northwestern States (18)
*10 Jun 1970 WASHINGTON
*20 Jun 1974 WASHINGTON SEATTLE
See also 166, 255

79a COLOMBIA-VENEZUELA — 1 Jul 1968 — Stephen L. Brower
Organized from Central American (43b), Andes (50)
*1 Jul 1971 COLOMBIA
*20 Jun 1974 COLOMBIA BOGOTA
*1 Jul 1992 COLOMBIA BOGOTA NORTH
See also 95, 120, 215, 270

80 BRAZILIAN NORTH — 7 Jul 1968 — Hal Roscoe Johnson
Organized from Brazilian (31a), Brazilian South (48)
*10 Jun 1970 BRAZIL NORTH
*20 Jun 1974 BRAZIL RIO DE JANEIRO
See also 167a, 185a

81 MEXICO NORTH CENTRAL — 5 Aug 1968 — Arturo R. Martinez
Organized from Northern Mexico (45a)
*20 Jun 1974 MEXICO TORREON
See also 125, 208

82 AUSTRALIAN WEST — 7 Aug 1968 — Milton J. Hess
Organized from Southern Australian (43c)
*10 Jun 1970 AUSTRALIA WEST
*20 Jun 1974 AUSTRALIA ADELAIDE
See also 117

82a JAPAN — 1 Sep 1968 — Walter R. Bills
Organized from Northern Far East (43d)
*20 Jun 1974 JAPAN TOKYO
*1 Jul 1978 JAPAN TOKYO NORTH
See also 90, 108, 109a, 162

83 JAPAN-OKINAWA — 1 Sep 1968 — Edward Y. Okazaki
Organized from Northern Far East (43d)
*16 Mar 1970 JAPAN CENTRAL
*20 Jun 1974 JAPAN KOBE
See also 91, 108, 144, 185, 245

84 GERMANY DRESDEN — 14 Jun 1969 — J. Henry Burkhart
Discontinued Dec 1978
*12 Mar 1984 GERMANY DEMOCRATIC REPUBLIC DRESDEN
Discontinued 3 Jun 1984
Reopened 1 Jul 1989, see 225
*6 Sep 1990 GERMANY DRESDEN
*13 Jan 1994 GERMANY LEIPZIG
See also 263

85 CALIFORNIA CENTRAL — 1 Jul 1969 — Wilbur Wallace Cox
Organized from California North (37)
*20 Jun 1974 CALIFORNIA OAKLAND
See also 118, 158a, 187a, 310a

86 CALIFORNIA EAST — 7 Jul 1969 — William L. Nicholls
Organized from California South (73a), California (14c)
*20 Jun 1974 CALIFORNIA ARCADIA
See also 182, 297, 324

87 ARIZONA — 1 Aug 1969 — Clark M. Wood

Organized from California South (73a)
*20 Jun 1974 ARIZONA TEMPE
See also 127, 132, 179b, 231

88 SOUTH CENTRAL STATES — 4 Aug 1969 — Albert B. Crandall
Organized from Central States (11a)
*10 Jun 1970 OKLAHOMA
*20 Jun 1974 OKLAHOMA TULSA
See also 116, 248

89 SOUTHEAST ASIA — 1 Nov 1969 — G. Carlos Smith
Organized from Southern Far East (44a)
*20 Jun 1974 SINGAPORE
Discontinued 1 Jul 1978, transferred to Indonesia Jakarta (122)
Reopened 1 Jan 1980 (176)
See also 109

90 JAPAN EAST — 15 Mar 1970 — Russell N. Horiuchi
Organized from Japan (82a)
*20 Jun 1974 JAPAN SAPPORO

91 JAPAN WEST — 18 Mar 1970 — Kan Watanabe
Organized from Japan-Okinawa (83)
*20 Jun 1974 JAPAN FUKUOKA
See also 144

91a PENNSYLVANIA — 1 Jul 1970 — George M. Baker
Organized from Delaware-Maryland (54)
*20 Jun 1974 PENNSYLVANIA HARRISBURG
See also 129, 156

92 SPAIN — 11 Jul 1970 — R. Raymond Barnes
Organized from French (26)
*20 Jun 1974 SPAIN MADRID
See also 137, 141, 199

93 ECUADOR — 1 Aug 1970 — Louis W. Latimer
Organized from Peru-Ecuador (50)
*20 Jun 1974 ECUADOR QUITO
See also 160

94 TAIWAN — 11 Jan 1971 — Malan R. Jackson
Organized from Hong Kong-Taiwan (44a)
*20 Jun 1974 TAIWAN TAIPEI
See also 146, 330

95 VENEZUELA — 1 Jul 1971 — Clark D. Webb
Organized from Colombia-Venezuela (79a)
*20 Jun 1974 VENEZUELA CARACAS
*1 Jul 1991 VENEZUELA CARACAS EAST
*25 Mar 1994 VENEZUELA CARACAS
See also 174, 267, 303

96 ALABAMA-FLORIDA — 1 Jul 1971 — Hartman Rector Jr.
Organized from Florida (55)
*20 Jun 1974 FLORIDA TALLAHASSEE
See also 166a, 197

97 NAUVOO — 1 Jul 1971 — J. LeRoy Kimball
Organized from Northern States (9c)
Discontinued 1 Jul 1974, transferred to Illinois Chicago (9c)

98 ITALY NORTH — 6 Jul 1971 — Dan Charles Jorgensen
Organized from Italy (74a)
*20 Jun 1974 ITALY MILAN
See also 244

99 FIJI — 23 Jul 1971 — Sherman A. Lindholm
Organized from Samoa (13c), New Zealand North (20), Tonga (22c)
*20 Jun 1974 FIJI SUVA
See also 178

99a QUEBEC — 14 Jul 1972 — John K. M. Olsen
Organized from Ontario-Quebec (23a)
*20 Jun 1974 CANADA MONTREAL

100 ARGENTINA EAST — 30 Jul 1972 — Joseph T. Bentley

Organized from Argentina North (73), Argentina South (32)
*20 Jun 1974 ARGENTINA ROSARIO
See also 229

101 BRAZIL NORTH CENTRAL 17 Oct 1972 Leroy A. Drechsel
Organized from Brazil Central (31a)
*20 Jun 1974 BRAZIL SAO PAULO NORTH
See also 190, 257

102 BRAZIL SOUTH CENTRAL 17 Oct 1972 Owen Nelson Baker
Organized from Brazil Central (31a)
*20 Jun 1974 BRAZIL SAO PAULO SOUTH
See also 181, 257

103 INTERNATIONAL 9 Nov 1972 Bernard P. Brockbank
Organized for "unattached" members worldwide
Discontinued 15 Aug 1987
See also 179, 205

104 MICHIGAN 3 Jul 1973 C. Russell Hansen
Organized from Indiana-Michigan (46)
*20 Jun 1974 MICHIGAN LANSING
See also 164

105 NORTH CAROLINA 18 Jul 1973 Charles M. Alexander
Organized from North Carolina-Virginia (42)
*20 Jun 1974 NORTH CAROLINA GREENSBORO
*1 Jul 1980 NORTH CAROLINA CHARLOTTE
See also 186

106 AUSTRALIA NORTHEAST 26 Jul 1973 J. Martell Bird
Organized from Australia East (10)
*20 Jun 1974 AUSTRALIA BRISBANE
See also 275

107 CANADA-MARITIMES 27 Jul 1973 Thurn J. Baker
Organized from New England (35)
*20 Jun 1974 CANADA HALIFAX

108 JAPAN-NAGOYA 1 Aug 1973 Satoru Sato
Organized from Japan (82a), Japan Central (83)
*20 Jun 1974 JAPAN NAGOYA

109 THAILAND 1 Aug 1973 Paul D. Morris
Organized from Southeast Asia (89)
*20 Jun 1974 THAILAND BANGKOK
See also 318

109a JAPAN SENDAI 1 Jul 1974 Walter Teruya
Organized from Japan Tokyo (82a)

110 PHILIPPINES CEBU CITY 1 Jul 1974 Carl D. Jones
Organized from Philippines Manila (76b)
*3 Aug 1984 PHILIPPINES CEBU
*1 Jul 1988 PHILIPPINES BACOLOD
See also 157, 194, 223

111 IDAHO POCATELLO 1 Jul 1974 Ernest Eberhard Jr.
Organized from Montana Billings (43a)
*29 May 1979 IDAHO BOISE
See also 132, 264

112 ARGENTINA BUENOS AIRES SOUTH 22 Jul 1974 Juan Carlos Avila
Organized from Argentina South (32)
See also 180, 269

113 CALIFORNIA SAN DIEGO 1 Aug 1974 Frank M. Bradshaw
Organized from California Anaheim (73a)

114 ALASKA ANCHORAGE 15 Oct 1974 Weston F. Killpack
Organized from Canada Vancouver (58)

115 PORTUGAL LISBON 19 Nov 1974 Wm. Grant Bangerter
* 1 Jul 1990 PORTUGAL LISBON SOUTH
See also 203, 253

116 ARKANSAS LITTLE ROCK 1 Jul 1975 Richard M. Richards
Organized from Louisiana Shreveport (31), Oklahoma Tulsa (88)

117 AUSTRALIA PERTH 1 Jul 1975 Bruce James Opie

Organized from Australia Adelaide (82)

118 CALIFORNIA FRESNO 1 Jul 1975 Robert B Harbertson
Organized from California Oakland (85)

119 CHILE CONCEPCION 1 Jul 1975 Lester D. Haymore
Organized from Chile Santiago (67)
See also 151

120 COLOMBIA CALI 1 Jul 1975 Jay E. Jensen
Organized from Colombia Bogota (79a)

121 FRANCE TOULOUSE 1 Jul 1975 George W. Broschinsky
Organized from France Paris (26)
Discontinued 1 Jul 1982, transferred to France Paris (26), Switzerland Geneva (59)

122 INDONESIA JAKARTA 1 Jul 1975 Hendrik Gout
Organized from Singapore (89)
Discontinued 1 Jan 1981, transferred to Singapore (89)
Reopened 1 Jul 1985 (182b)
Discontinued 1 Jul 1989
Reopened 1 Jul 1995 See 306

123 ITALY PADOVA 1 Jul 1975 John Anthony Grinceri
Organized from Italy Rome (7)
Discontinued 1 Jul 1982, transferred to Italy Milan (98)
Reopened 1 Jul 1990; organized from Italy Milan (98), Italy Rome (7)see 244

124 KOREA PUSAN 1 Jul 1975 Han In Sang
Organized from Korea Seoul (71)
See also 191

125 MEXICO GUADALAJARA 1 Jul 1975 Isauro Gutierrez
Organized from Mexico Mexico City (20a), Mexico Torreon (81),
Mexico Hermosillo (56)
See also 201

126 MEXICO VILLAHERMOSA 1 Jul 1975 Abraham Lozano
Organized from Mexico Veracruz (75)
*1 Jul 1978 MEXICO MERIDA
See also 193, 209

127 NEVADA LAS VEGAS 1 Jul 1975 Ronald M. Patterson
Organized from Arizona Tempe (87), California Sacramento (37)
See also 314

128 NEW MEXICO ALBUQUERQUE 1 Jul 1975 Stanley D. Roberts
Organized from Arizona Holbrook (38)
See also 231

129 PENNSYLVANIA PITTSBURGH 1 Jul 1975 Kenneth W. Godfrey
Organized from Pennsylvania Harrisburg (91a)
See also 188, 326

130 SOUTH CAROLINA COLUMBIA 1 Jul 1975 Ronald L. Knighton
Organized from Georgia Atlanta (8b)
See also 239

131 TENNESSEE NASHVILLE 1 Jul 1975 Emerson Taylor Cannon
Organized from Kentucky Louisville (29)

132 UTAH SALT LAKE CITY 1 Jul 1975 Ernest Eberhard Jr.
Organized from Idaho Pocatello (111), Colorado Denver (17),
Arizona Tempe (87), Arizona Holbrook (38)
*1 Jul 1980 UTAH SALT LAKE CITY NORTH
*1 Jan 1989 UTAH OGDEN
See also 187, 222, 331

133 YUGOSLAVIA ZAGREB 1 Jul 1975 Gustav Salik
Discontinued 1 Jul 1976

134 IRAN TEHRAN 4 Jul 1975 D. Burton Farnsworth
Discontinued 1 Jan 1979

135 BELGIUM ANTWERP 16 Jul 1975 Larry Hyde Brim
Organized from Belgium Brussels (76), Netherlands Amsterdam (8a)
Discontinued 1 Jul 1982, transferred to Netherlands Amsterdam (8a)
Reopened 1 Jul 1990, Organized from Netherlands Amsterdam (8a)
See also 232

136 CANADA WINNIPEG 15 Feb 1976 Howard L. Lund
Organized from Canada Calgary (36a), South Dakota Rapid City (78)

137 SPAIN BARCELONA 8 May 1976 Smith B. Griffin
Organized from Spain Madrid (92)
See also 199

137a EL SALVADOR SAN SALVADOR 1 Jul 1976 Eddy L. Barillas
Organized from Guatemala Guatemala City (76a)
Discontinued 1 Apr 1981, transferred to Guatemala Guatemala City (76a)
Reopened 1 Oct 1984 (181a)
*1 Jul 1990 EL SALVADOR SAN SALVADOR WEST

138 ENGLAND MANCHESTER 1 Jul 1976 O. Louis Alder
Organized from England Leeds (52)

139 FLORIDA TAMPA 1 Jul 1976 A. Sterling Workman
Organized from Florida Ft. Lauderdale (55)
See also 178a, 197

140 IOWA DES MOINES 1 Jul 1976 Erwin E. Wirkus
Organized from Missouri Independence (11a), Illinois Chicago (9c)

141 SPAIN SEVILLE 3 Jul 1976 Hugo A. Catron
Organized from Spain Madrid (92)
12 Jan 1993 SPAIN MALAGA
See also 220

142 TEXAS HOUSTON 3 Jul 1976 George L. Merrill
Organized from Texas San Antonio (77b)
See also 254, 316

143 NEW ZEALAND CHRISTCHURCH 5 Jul 1976 Ivan G. Radman
Organized from New Zealand Wellington (47)
*15 Jan 1991 NEW ZEALAND WELLINGTON

144 JAPAN OKAYAMA 9 Jul 1976 William H. Nako
Organized from Japan Fukuoka (91), Japan Kobe (83)
JAPAN HIROSHIMA 24 Sep 1998

145 SWEDEN GOTEBORG 26 Jul 1976 Paul Kent Oscarson
Organized from Sweden Stockholm (22a)
Discontinued 1 Jul 1982, transferred to Sweden Stockholm (22a)

146 TAIWAN KAOHSIUNG 3 Aug 1976 P. Boyd Hales
Organized from Taiwan Taipei (94)
*28 Sep 1983 TAIWAN TAICHUNG
See also 173, 330

147 SCOTLAND GLASGOW 1 Nov 1976 Roy W. Oscarson
Organized from Scotland Edinburgh (61)
Discontinued 1 Jul 1981, transferred to Scotland Edinburgh (61)

148 CHILE SANTIAGO NORTH 1 Jan 1977 Berkley A. Spencer
Organized from Chile Santiago (67)
See also 168, 214, 303a, 311

149 PERU LIMA NORTH 1 Jan 1977 Jose A. Sousa
Organized from Peru Lima (50)
See also 165, 184a, 210, 300

150 BOLIVIA SANTA CRUZ 1 Jul 1977 DeVere R. McAllister
Organized from Bolivia La Paz (75a)
*1 Feb 1982 BOLIVIA COCHABAMBA
See also 320

151 CHILE OSORNO 1 Jul 1977 Lester D. Haymore
Organized from Chile Concepcion (119)

152 GUATEMALA QUETZALTENANGO 1 Jul 1977 John F. O'Donnal
Organized from Guatemala Guatemala City (76a)

153 MISSOURI ST. LOUIS 1 Jul 1977 Norman W. Olsen
Organized from Missouri Independence (11a)
See also 176a

154 OHIO CLEVELAND 1 Jul 1977 Donald S. Brewer
Organized from Ohio Columbus (77a)
See also 179a

155 PARAGUAY ASUNCION 1 Jul 1977 Mearl K. Bair
Organized from Uruguay Montevideo (40)
See also 329

156 PENNSYLVANIA PHILADELPHIA 1 Jul 1977 Lewis K. Payne
Organized from Pennsylvania Harrisburg (91a)
See also 304a

157 PHILIPPINES DAVAO 1 Jul 1977 Layton B. Jones
Organized from Philippines Cebu City (110)
See also 211

158 ITALY CATANIA 10 Jul 1977 Leopoldo Larcher
Organized from Italy Rome (7)

158a CALIFORNIA SAN JOSE 1 Jul 1978 Lysle R. Cahoon
Organized from California Oakland (85)
See also 310a

159 CALIFORNIA VENTURA 1 Jul 1978 Hyrum S. Smith
Organized from California Los Angeles (14c)
See also 182, 297

160 ECUADOR GUAYAQUIL 1 Jul 1978 William J. Mitchell
Organized from Ecuador Quito (93)
*25 Apr 1991 ECUADOR GUAYAQUIL SOUTH
*16 Jun 1995 ECUADOR GUAYAQUIL
*25 Apr 1996 ECUADOR GUAYAQUIL SOUTH
See also 261, 310

161 ENGLAND LONDON EAST 1 Jul 1978 Carl D. Jones
Organized from England London (1)
Discontinued 1 Jul 1983, transferred to England London (1), England London South (79)

162 JAPAN TOKYO SOUTH 1 Jul 1978 Delbert H. Groberg
Organized from Japan Tokyo (82a)

163 MEXICO MEXICO CITY NORTH 1 Jul 1978 John B. Dickson
Organized from Mexico Mexico City (20a)
See also 193, 218, 222a

164 MICHIGAN DEARBORN 1 Jul 1978 William R. Horton
Organized from Michigan Lansing (104)
* 1 Dec 1989 MICHIGAN DETROIT

165 PERU AREQUIPA 1 Jul 1978 Norval C. Jesperson
Organized from Peru Lima North (149), Peru Lima South (50)

166 WASHINGTON SPOKANE 1 Jul 1978 Norwood C. McKoy
Organized from Washington Seattle (78a)

167 WISCONSIN MILWAUKEE 1 Jul 1978 L. Flake Rogers
Organized from Minnesota Minneapolis (26a), Illinois Chicago (9c)

166a ALABAMA BIRMINGHAM 1 Jan 1979 William J. Attwooll
Organized from Georgia Atlanta (8b), Florida Tallahassee (96)

167a BRAZIL RECIFE 1 Jul 1979 Harry Eduardo Klein
Organized from Brazil Rio de Janeiro (80)
See also 200, 234, 322

168 CHILE VINA DEL MAR 1 Jul 1979 Gerald J. Day
Organized from Chile Santiago North (148)
See also 214

169 CONNECTICUT HARTFORD 1 Jul 1979 Gerald L. Ericksen
Organized from Massachusetts Boston (35)
See also 195, 299

170 KOREA SEOUL WEST 1 Jul 1979 D. Brent Clement
Organized from Korea Seoul (71)

171 MISSISSIPPI JACKSON 1 Jul 1979 Frank W. Hirschi
Organized from Louisiana Baton Rouge (31)

172 PHILIPPINES QUEZON CITY 1 Jul 1979 Robert E. Sackley
Organized from Philippines Manila (76b)
*1 Jan 1981 PHILIPPINES BAGUIO
*11 Feb 1991 PHILIPPINES LA UNION

*22 Aug 1991 PHILIPPINES BAGUIO
See also 192, 219

173 TAIWAN T'AICHUNG — 1 Jul 1979 — Frederick W. Crook
Organized from Taiwan Kaohsiung (146)
Discontinued Jul 1982, transferred to Taiwan Kaohsiung (146), Taiwan Taipei (94)
See also 330

174 VENEZUELA MARACAIBO — 1 Jul 1979 — Alejandro Portal
Organized from Venezuela Caracas (95)

175 PUERTO RICO SAN JUAN — 7 Jul 1979 — Richard L. Millett
Organized from Florida Ft. Lauderdale (55)
See also 178a, 188a

176 SINGAPORE (See 89) — 1 Jan 1980 — J. Talmage Jones
Organized from Indonesia Jakarta (122)

177 HONDURAS TEGUCIGALPA — 1 Feb 1980 — Samuel Flores
Organized from Costa Rica San Jose (43b)
See also 242, 312

178 MICRONESIA GUAM — 1 Apr 1980 — Ferron C. Losee
Organized from Hawaii Honolulu (7a), Fiji Suva (99)

179 AFRICA WEST — 1 Jul 1980 — Bryan Espenschied
Organized from International (103)
*1 Jul 1985 NIGERIA LAGOS
See also 183a, 221, 276

180 ARGENTINA BAHIA BLANCA — 1 Jul 1980 — Allen B. Oliver
Organized from Argentina Buenos Aires South (112)
See also 230

181 BRAZIL CURITIBA — 1 Jul 1980 — Dixon D. Cowley
Organized from Brazil Sao Paulo South (102), Brazil Porto Alegre (48)
See also 302a

182 CALIFORNIA SAN BERNARDINO — 1 Jul 1980 — Howard C. Sharp
Organized from California Anaheim (73a), California Arcadia (86), California Ventura (159)
See also 235, 297

183 ENGLAND COVENTRY — 1 Jul 1980 — Quinn G. McKay
Organized from England Birmingham (62)
*22 Aug 1991 ENGLAND BIRMINGHAM
See also 62

184 ILLINOIS CHICAGO SOUTH — 1 Jul 1980 — Charles E. Petersen
Organized from Illinois Chicago (9c)
Discontinued 1 Jul 1983, transferred to Illinois Chicago (9c)
See also 313

185 JAPAN OSAKA — 1 Jul 1980 — Shigeki Ushio
Organized from Japan Kobe (83)
Discontinued 1 Jul 1995, transferred to Japan Kobe

186 NORTH CAROLINA RALEIGH — 1 Jul 1980 — Joel N. Gillespie
Organized from North Carolina Greensboro (105)

187 UTAH SALT LAKE CITY SOUTH — 1 Jul 1980 — Jonathan W. Snow
Organized from Utah Salt Lake City (132)
*1 Jan 1989 UTAH SALT LAKE CITY
See also 222, 304, 331

188 WEST VIRGINIA CHARLESTON — 1 Jul 1980 — O. Rex Warner
Organized from Ohio Columbus (77a), Virginia Roanoke (42), Pennsylvania Pittsburgh (129)

188a DOMINICAN REPUBLIC SANTO DOMINGO — 1 Jan 1981 — John A. Davis
Organized from Puerto Rico San Juan (175)
*1 Jul 1991 DOMINICAN REPUBLIC SANTO DOMINGO WEST
See also 178a, 196, 260

178a WEST INDIES — 20 Jun 1983 — Kenneth L. Zabriskie
Organized from Florida Tampa (139), Dominican Republic Santo Domingo (188a), Puerto Rico San Juan (175)
See also 180a, 186a, 266

176a ILLINOIS PEORIA — 1 Jul 1983 — Brent Reed Rigtrup

Organized from Missouri St. Louis (153)

177a SOUTH AFRICA CAPE TOWN 1 Jul 1984 G. Philip Margetts
Organized from South Africa Johannesburg (23)

178b FLORIDA FT. LAUDERDALE (See 55) 1 Jul 1984 Claud Darwin Mangum
See also 326

179a OHIO AKRON 1 Jul 1984 Stanley M. Smoot
Organized from Ohio Columbus (77a)
Discontinued 1 Jul 1989, transferred to Ohio Cleveland (154)

179b ARIZONA PHOENIX 1 Jul 1984 Francis M. Bay
Organized from Arizona Holbrook (38), Arizona Tempe (87)
See also 231

180a HAITI PORT-AU-PRINCE 1 Aug 1984 James S. Arrigona
Organized from West Indies (178a)

181a EL SALVADOR SAN SALVADOR 1 Oct 1984 Manuel Antonio Diaz
See also 137a, 237

182b INDONESIA JAKARTA (See 122) 1 Jul 1985 Effian Kadarusman
Organized from Singapore (89)

183a GHANA ACCRA 1 Jul 1985 Miles H. Cunningham
Organized from Africa West (179)

184a PERU TRUJILLO 1 Jul 1985 Roberto Vidal
Organized from Peru Lima North (149)

185a BRAZIL BRASILIA 1 Jul 1985 Demar Staniscia
Organized from Brazil Rio de Janeiro (80), Brazil Recife (167)
See also 200, 213, 233, 321

186a JAMAICA KINGSTON 1 Jul 1985 Richard L. Brough
Organized from West Indies (178a)

187a CALIFORNIA SANTA ROSA 1 Jul 1985 Robert C. Witt
Organized from California Sacramento (37), California Oakland (85)
See also 310a

188b WASHINGTON D.C. NORTH 1 Jul 1986 Dennis E. Simmons
Organized from Washington D.C. (54)
See also 298

189 TEXAS LUBBOCK 1 Jul 1986 Lyle L. Wasden
Organized from Texas Dallas (60)
*20 Jan 1988 TEXAS FT. WORTH

190 BRAZIL CAMPINAS 1 Jul 1986 Sheldon R. Murphy
Organized from Brazil Sao Paulo North (101)
See also 213, 302a

191 KOREA TAE JON 1 Jul 1986 Moo-Kwang Hong
Organized from Korea Pusan (124)

192 PHILIPPINES QUEZON CITY 1 Jul 1986 Joel E. Leetham
Organized from Philippines Baguio (172)
See also 219, 256, 268

193 MEXICO MEXICO CITY EAST 1 Jan 1987 Enrique Moreno
Organized from Mexico Mexico City North (163), Mexico Mexico City South (20a), Mexico Monterrey (45a), Mexico Merida (126), Mexico Veracruz (75)
See also 217

194 PHILIPPINES CEBU EAST 1 Jul 1987 C. Elliott Richards
Organized from Philippines Cebu (110), Philippines Manila (76b)
*1 Jul 1988 PHILIPPINES CEBU
See also 251

195 NEW HAMPSHIRE MANCHESTER 1 Jul 1987 Lynn E. Thomsen
Organized from Massachusetts Boston (35), Connecticut Hartford (169)

196 DOMINICAN REPUBLIC SANTIAGO 1 Jul 1987 Michael D. Stirling
Organized from Dominican Republic Santo Domingo (188a)

197 FLORIDA JACKSONVILLE 1 Jul 1987 Douglas W. DeHaan
Organized from Florida Tampa (139), Florida Tallahassee (96)

198 ZAIRE KINSHASA 1 Jul 1987 R. Bay Hutchings
Organized from International Mission (103)

12 Aug 1997 DEMOCRATIC REPUBLIC OF CONGO KINSHASA

199 SPAIN BILBAO 1 Jul 1987 Garth J. Wakefield
Organized from Spain Madrid (92), Spain Barcelona (137)

200 BRAZIL FORTALEZA 1 Jul 1987 Helvecio Martins
Organized from Brazil Recife (167a), and Brazil Brazilia (185a)
See also 233

201 MEXICO MAZATLAN 1 Jul 1987 Samuel Lara M.
Organized from Mexico Guadalajara (125)
*21 Feb 1995 MEXICO CULIACAN

202 NEW JERSEY MORRISTOWN 1 Jul 1987 Dan J. Workman
Organized from New York New York (15b)
See also 304a

203 PORTUGAL PORTO 1 Jul 1987 Dan Copeland
Organized from Portugal Lisbon (115)
See also 220

204 ZIMBABWE HARARE 1 Jul 1987 Joseph Hamstead
Organized from South Africa Johannesburg (23)

205 *AUSTRIA VIENNA EAST 1 Jul 1987 Dennis B. Neuenschwander
Organized from Austria Vienna (53), International (103)
*3 Feb 1992 UKRAINE KIEV
See also 236, 241, 243, 252, 259, 274

205a GUATEMALA GUATEMALA CITY NORTH1 Jan 1988 Gordon W. Romney
Organized from Guatemala Guatemala City South (76a)

206 ARGENTINA SALTA 8 Jan 1988 Francisco Jose Vinas
Organized from Argentina Cordoba (73)

207 BOLIVIA LA PAZ (See 75a) 8 Jan 1988 Steven R. Wright
See also 320

208 MEXICO CHIHUAHUA 8 Jan 1988 Victor M. Cerda
Organized from Mexico Torreon (81)

209 MEXICO TUXTLA GUTIERREZ 8 Jan 1988 Alberto D. Gamboa
Organized from Mexico Merida (126)
See also 246

210 PERU LIMA EAST 8 Jan 1988 Douglas K. Earl
Organized from Peru Lima North (149)
See also 300

211 PHILIPPINES CAGAYAN DE ORO 8 Jan 1988 Rufino A. Villanueva Jr.
Organized from Philippines Davao (157)

212 LIBERIA MONROVIA 1 Mar 1988 J. Duffy Palmer
Discontinued 12 Feb 1991, transferred to Ghana Accra (183a)

213 BRAZIL BELO HORIZONTE 1 Jul 1988 Nivio Varella Alcover
Organized from Brazil Brasilia (185a), Brazil Campinas (190)
*2 Aug 1994 BRAZIL BELO HORIZONTE EAST
See also 295a, 321

214 CHILE ANTOFAGASTA 1 Jul 1988 Carlos Ramon Espinola
Organized from Chile Santiago North (148), Chile Santiago South (67), Chile Vina del Mar (168)

215 COLOMBIA BARRANQUILLA 1 Jul 1988 Frank Berrett
Organized from Colombia Bogota (79a)

216 MASCARENE ISLANDS 1 Jul 1988 Gerard Giraud-Carrier
Organized from S. Africa Johannesburg (23)
*22 Apr 1991 SOUTH AFRICA DURBAN
See also 327

217 MEXICO PUEBLA 1 Jul 1988 George G. Sloan
Organized from Mexico Mexico City East (193)

218 MEXICO TAMPICO 1 Jul 1988 Hector Ceballos
Organized from Mexico Mexico City North (163), Mexico Monterrey (45a)
*2 Sep 1992 MEXICO MONTERREY EAST
*3 Nov 1992 MEXICO TAMPICO

219 PHILIPPINES QUEZON CITY WEST 1 Jul 1988 Robert J. Kennerley

Organized from Philippines Baguio (172), Philippines Quezon City (192)
*1 Jul 1991 PHILIPPINES SAN FERNANDO
*7 Jun 1994 PHILIPPINES OLONGAPO

220 SPAIN LAS PALMAS 1 Jul 1988 M. K. Hamblin
Organized from Spain Seville (141), Portugal Porto (203)

221 NIGERIA ABA 1 Jul 1988 Arthur W. Elrey Jr.
Organized from Nigeria Lagos (179)
*1 May 1995 NIGERIA PORT HARCOURT
See also 277

222 UTAH PROVO 1 Jan 1989 George E. Magnusson
Organized from Utah Salt Lake City South (187)
See also 331

221a FRANCE BORDEAUX 1 Jul 1989 Neil L. Andersen
Organized from France Paris (6), Switzerland Geneva (59)
See also 262

222a MEXICO QUERETARO 1 Jul 1989 Scott T. Lyman
Organized from Mexico Mexico City North (163)
*24 Mar 1992 MEXICO LEON

223 PHILIPPINES NAGA 1 Jul 1989 Augusto A. Lim
Organized from Philippines Cebu (110)

224 TEXAS CORPUS CHRISTI 1 Jul 1989 S. Gibbons Frost
Organized from Texas San Antonio (77b)
*24 Feb 1994 TEXAS MCALLEN

225 GERMAN DEM. REPUBLIC DRESDEN 1 Jul 1989 Wolfgang Paul
Reopened, see 84

226 PANAMA PANAMA CITY 1 Jul 1989 Pedro E. Abularach
Organized from Costa Rica San Jose (43b)

227 NICARAGUA MANAGUA 15 Oct 1989 Luis A. Alvarez O.
Organized from Guatemala Guatemala City South (76a)

228 ARGENTINA MENDOZA 1 Jul 1990 Charles W. Eastwood
Organized from Argentina Cordoba (73)

229 ARGENTINA RESISTENCIA 1 Jul 1990 Wilfredo R. Lopez G.
Organized from Argentina Rosario (100)

230 ARGENTINA TRELEW 1 Jul 1990 Antonio Cappi
Organized from Argentina Bahia Blanca (180)
*25 May 1993 ARGENTINA NEUQUEN

231 ARIZONA TUCSON 1 Jul 1990 James E. Mangum
Organized from Arizona Tempe (87), Arizona Phoenix (179b), New Mexico Albuquerque (128)

232 BELGIUM ANTWERP 1 Jul 1990 R. Bruce Barrett
Discontinued 1 Jul 1995, Transferred to Netherlands Amsterdam (8a)
See 135

233 BRAZIL MANAUS 1 Jul 1990 Claudio R. Mendes C.
Organized from Brazil Brasilia (185a), Brazil Fortaleza (200)
See also 294a

234 BRAZIL SALVADOR 1 Jul 1990 Jairo Massagardi
Organized from Brazil Recife (167a)
See also 296

235 CALIFORNIA RIVERSIDE 1 Jul 1990 Jerry M. Hess
Organized from California San Bernardino (182)

236 CZECHOSLOVAKIA PRAGUE 1 Jul 1990 Richard W. Winder
Organized from Austria Vienna East (205)
See 30

237 EL SALVADOR SAN SALVADOR EAST 1 Jul 1990 Ramon E. Turcios D.
Organized from El Salvador San Salvador (181a)

238 FINLAND HELSINKI EAST 1 Jul 1990 Gary L. Browning
Organized from Finland Helsinki (41)
*2 Jan 1992 RUSSIA MOSCOW
See also 272, 273, 293, 315

239 GEORGIA MACON 1 Jul 1990 John H. Cox
Organized from South Carolina Columbia (130), Georgia Atlanta (8)

240 GERMANY DUESSELDORF 1 Jul 1990 Edgar Wolferts
Reopened, see 63; organized from Germany Frankfurt (35a), Germany Munich (49)

241 GREECE ATHENS 1 Jul 1990 R. Douglas Phillips
Organized from Austria Vienna East (205)
See also 308

242 HONDURAS SAN PEDRO SULA 1 Jul 1990 Lehi Gracia
Organized from Honduras Tegucigalpa (177)

243 HUNGARY BUDAPEST 1 Jul 1990 James L. Wilde
Organized from Austria Vienna East (205)

244 ITALY PADOVA 1 Jul 1990 Vicenzo Conforte
Reopened, see 123

245 JAPAN OKINAWA 1 Jul 1990 Evan Allan Larsen
Organized from Japan Kobe (83)
Discontinued 1 Jul 1996

246 MEXICO OAXACA 1 Jul 1990 Miguel Hidalgo N.
Organized from Mexico Tuxtla Gutierrez (209)

247 MEXICO TIJUANA 1 Jul 1990 Arturo de Hoyos
Organized from Mexico Hermosillo (56)

248 OKLAHOMA OKLAHOMA CITY 1 Jul 1990 Duane Beazer
Organized from Oklahoma Tulsa (88)

249 OREGON EUGENE 1 Jul 1990 Lloyd M. Rasmussen
Organized from Oregon Portland (18)

250 PHILIPPINES SAN PABLO 1 Jul 1990 Dean O. Peck
Organized from Philippines Manila (76b)

251 PHILIPPINES TACLOBAN 1 Jul 1990 Leonardo S. Mina
Organized from Philippines Cebu (194)

252 POLAND WARSAW 1 Jul 1990 Walter Whipple
Organized from Austria Vienna East (205)

253 PORTUGAL LISBON NORTH 1 Jul 1990 Vitor Martins
Organized from Portugal Lisbon (115)

254 TEXAS HOUSTON EAST 1 Jul 1990 Allen S. Farnsworth
Organized from Texas Houston (142)
See also 316

255 WASHINGTON TACOMA 1 Jul 1990 Sidney R. Henderson
Organized from Washington Seattle (78)

256 PHILIPPINES ILAGAN 1 Sep 1990 Reynaldo Ibanez Vergara
Organized from Philippines Quezon City (192)

256a BRAZIL PORTO ALEGRE NORTH 1 Jul 1991 Joseph Larry Memmott
Organized from Brazil Porto Alegre (48)
See also 323

257 BRAZIL SAO PAULO EAST 1 Jul 1991 Willis C. Fails
Organized from Brazil Sao Paulo North (101) , Brazil Sao Paulo South (102)

258 BRAZIL SAO PAULO INTERLAGOS 1 Jul 1991 Frederick G. Williams
Organized from Brazil Sao Paulo South (102)

259 BULGARIA SOFIA 1 Jul 1991 Kiril P. Kiriakov
Organized from Austria Vienna East (205)

260 DOM. REPUBLIC SANTO DOMINGO EAST1 Jul 1991 Mark Allen Jarman
Organized from Dominican Republic Santo Domingo (188a)

261 ECUADOR GUAYAQUIL NORTH 1 Jul 1991 Daniel L. Johnson
Organized from Ecuador Guayaquil (160), Ecuador Quito (93)
Discontinued 16 Jun 1995
Reopened 1 Jul 1996 (310)

262 FRANCE MARSEILLE 1 Jul 1991 Richard W. Thatcher
Organized from Switzerland Geneva (59), France Bordeaux (221a)

263 GERMANY BERLIN 1 Jul 1991 Manfred H. Schutze

	Organized from Germany Dresden (84)		
264	IDAHO POCATELLO Organized from Idaho Boise (111)	1 Jul 1991	Wayne W. Probst
265	KENYA NAIROBI	1 Jul 1991	Larry King Brown
266	TRINIDAD TOBAGO Organized from West Indies (178a) Discontinued 1 Jul 1994, transferred to West Indies (178a)	1 Jul 1991	J. Richard Toolson
267	VENEZUELA CARACAS WEST Organized from Venezuela Caracas (95) Venezuela Maracaibo (174) *25 Mar 1994 VENEZUELA VALENCIA See also 303	1 Jul 1991	Charles M. Hunter
268	*PHILIPPINES ANGELES 16 Apr 1999 PHILIPPINES CABANATUAN Organized from Philippines Quezon City (192),Philippines Manila (76b) Philippines San Fernando (219)	1 Jan 1992	Martin D. Openshaw
269	ARGENTINA BUENOS AIRES WEST Organized from Buenos Aires North (32) Buenos Aires South (112)	27 Jan 1992	Lloyd H. Richmond
270	COLOMBIA BOGOTA SOUTH Organized from Colombia Bogota (79a)	27 Jan 1992	Jerry P. Cahill
271	CAMAROON YAOUNDE *1 June 1993 IVORY COAST ABIDJAN	1 Jul 1992	Robert L. Mercer
272	RUSSIA ST. PETERSBURG Organized from Russia Moscow (238, 272)	3 Feb 1992	Thomas S. Rogers
273	PAPUA NEW GUINEA PORT MORESBY Organized from Australia Brisbane Mission (106)	13 Feb 1992	Joseph Jones Grigg
274	NIGERIA ILORIN *Organized from Nigeria Lagos (179) 2 Aug 1993 NIGERIA IBADAN Discontinued 1 Jul 1995	1 Jul 1992	John A. Ehanire
275	NIGERIA JOS Organized from Nigeria Aba (221) *14 Dec 1993 NIGERIA ENUGU	1 Jul 1992	Ato Kwamina Dadson
276	MEXICO MONTERREY SOUTH Organized from Mexico Monterrey East (218)	3 Nov 1992	Garry R. Flake
277	INDIA BANGALORE Organized from Singapore (89)	1 Jan 1993	Gurcharan Singh Gill
278	AUSTRALIA SYDNEY NORTH Organized from Australia Sydney (10)	1 Jan 1993	Glenn L. Pace
279	BRAZIL RIBEIRO PRETO Organized from Brazil Campinas See also 321	1 Feb 1993	Cesar A. Seiquer Milder
280	BRAZIL RIO DE JANEIRO NORTH Organized from Brazil Rio de Janeiro (80)	1 Feb 1993	Moises B. Damasceno
281	BRAZIL FLORIANOPOLIS Organized from Brazil Curitiba (181)	1 Jul 1993	Jose Benjamin Puerta
282	BRAZIL RECIFE SOUTH BRAZIL MACEIO Organized from Brazil Recife (167a) See also 322	1 Jul 1993 19 May 1998	Jorge Moreira
283	CALIFORNIA CARLSBAD Organized from California San Diego (113)	1 Jul 1993	Merlyn K. Jolley
284	CALIFORNIA ROSEVILLE Organized from California Sacramento (37)	1 Jul 1993	John Hoybjerg
285	CANADA TORONTO EAST Organized from Canada Toronto (23a)	1 Jul 1993	Harold Roger Boyer
286	COLORADO DENVER NORTH Organized from Colorado Denver (17)	1 Jul 1993	Lynn M. Paulson
287	GUATEMALA CITY GUATEMALA CENTRAL Organized from Guatemala City North (205a), Guatemala City South (294), Guatemala Quetzaltenango (152)	1 Jul 1993	Denis R. Morrill
288	LATVIA RIGA MISSION Organized from Russia St. Petersburg (272)	1 Jul 1993	Robert W. Blair

*16 Apr 1996 LITHUANIA VILNIUS
289 NEBRASKA OMAHA 1 Jul 1993 Reed B. Maw
See also 332
Organized from Missouri Independence (14b)
290 NEW YORK NEW YORK NORTH 1 Jul 1993 Parley L. Howell
Organized from New York New York (2)
291 PERU CHICLAYO 1 Jul 1993 Rene Loli
Organized from Peru Trujillo (184a) and Peru Lima North (149)
292 ROMANIA BUCHAREST 1 Jul 1993 John Rolph Morrey
Organized from Hungary Budapest (243)
293 RUSSIA SAMARA 1 Jul 1993 Arlo R. Nelson
Organized from Russia Moscow (238)
See also 305
294 TENNESSEE KNOXVILLE 1 Jul 1993 Richard Karl Sager
Organized from Tennessee Nashville (131)
295 UKRAINE DONETSK 1 Jul 1993 Leo Merrill
Organized from Ukraine Kiev (205)
294a BRAZIL BELEM 1 Jul 1994 Pedro J. D. Penha
Organized from Brazil Manaus (233)
295a BRAZIL BELO HORIZONTE SOUTH 1 Jul 1994 Thomas P. Smith
BRAZIL BELO HORIZONTE EAST 2 Aug 1994
Organized from Brazil Belo Horizonte (213)
296 BRAZIL SALVADOR SOUTH 1 Jul 1994 Marcos A.C. Prieto
Organized from Brazil Salvador (234)
297 CALIFORNIA SAN FERNANDO 1 Jul 1994 Steven E. Snow
Organized from California Arcadia (86), California San Bernardino (182), California Ventura (159)
298 MARYLAND BALTIMORE 1 Jul 1994 Bruce M. Ballard
Organized from Washington D.C. North (188b), Washington D.C. South (54)
299 NEW YORK UTICA 1 Jul 1994 Robert Noel Hatch
Organized from Connecticut Hartford (169), Massaschusetts Boston (35)
300 PERU LIMA CENTRAL 1 Jul 1994 Carlos A. Cuba Q.
Organized from Peru Lima North (149), Peru Lima East (210), Peru Lima South (50)
301 RUSSIA NOVOSIBIRSK 1 Jul 1994 Jerald C. Sherwood
See also 305
302 RUSSIA ROSTOV NA DONU 1 Jul 1994 Vladimir Siwachok
*24 Apr 1995 RUSSIA ROSTOV
303 VENEZUELA BARCELONA 1 Jul 1994 Ned B. Roueche
Organized from Venezuela Caracas East (95), Venezuela Caracas West (267)
304 UTAH SALT LAKE CITY TEMPLE SQUARE 5 Apr 1995 Robert C. Witt
Organized from Utah Salt Lake City (187)
302a BRAZIL MARILIA 1 Jul 1995 Gutenberg G. Amorim
Organized from Brazil Campinas (190)
*BRAZIL LONDRINA 23 Sep 1999
303a CHILE SANTIAGO WEST 1 Jul 1995 Ronald N. Walker
Organized from Chile Santiago North (148), Chile Santiago South (67)
304a NEW JERSEY CHERRY HILL 1 Jul 1995 John Glen Sanford
Organized from New Jersey Morristown (202), Pennsylvania Philadelphia (156)
305 RUSSIA YEKATERINGBURG 1 Jul 1995 Vyacheslav I. Efimov
Organized from Russia Samara (293), and Russia Novosibirsk (301)
306 INDONESIA JAKARTA (See 122) 1 Jul 1995 Vern M. Tueller
307 MONGOLIA ULAANBATAAR 1 Jul 1995 Richard E. Cook
308 ALBANIA TIRANA 1 Jul 1996 Laurel L. Holman
Organized from Greece Athens (241)
309 AUSTRIA VIENNA SOUTH 1 Jul 1996 Johann A. Wondra
*SLOVENIA LJUBLJANA 1 Jul 1999

Organized from Austria Vienna (53)

310 ECUADOR GUAYAQUIL NORTH (see 261) 1 Jul 1996 B. Renato Maldonado

310a CALIFORNIA SAN FRANCISCO 1 July 1997 Robert E. Sorenson Jr.
Organized from Calif. Oakland (85), Calif. San Jose (158a), Calif. Santa Rosa (187a)

311 CHILE SANTIAGO EAST 1 July 1997 D. Kelly Ogden
Organized from Chile Santiago North (148), Chile Santiago South (67)

312 HONDURAS COMAYAGUELA 1 July 1997 Roberto Ocampo
Organized from Honduras Tegucigalpa (177)

313 ILLINOIS CHICAGO NORTH 1 Jul 1997 Dallas H. Bradford
Organized from Illinois Chicago (9c, 184)

314 NEVADA LAS VEGAS WEST 1 Jul 1997 Grant E. Starley
Organized from Nevada Las Vegas (127)

315 RUSSIA MOCOW SOUTH 1 Jul 1997 G. Lowell Wright Jr.
Organized from Russia Moscow (238)

316 TEXAS HOUSTON SOUTH 1 Jul 1997 Brent K. Pratt
Organized from Texas Houston (142), Texas Houston East (254)

317 URUGUAY MONTEVIDEO WEST 1 Jul 1997 Kevin E. Monson
Organized from Uruguay Montevideo (40)

318 CAMBODIA PHNOM PENH 1 Jul 1998 Leland D. White
Organized from Thailand Bangkok (109)

319 AUSTRALIA MELBOURNE WEST 1 Jul 1998 Gary Lynn Brenchley
Organized from Australia Melbourne (43c)

320 BOLIVIA SANTA CRUZ 1 Jul 1998 Wilford D. Shumway
Organized from Bolivia Cochabamba (150), Bolivia La Paz (75a, 207)

321 BRAZIL GOIANIA 1 Jul 1998 Antonio Casado R.
Organized from the Belo Horizonte (213), Brasilia (185A) , and Ribeirao Preto (279)

322 BRAZIL JOAO PESSOA 1 Jul 1998 Wilson Roberto Gomes
Organized from Brazil Recife (167a), Brazil Recife South (282)

323 BRAZIL SANTA MARIA 1 Jul 1998 Duane Herman Zobrist
Organized from Brazil Porto Alegre North (256a), Brazil Porto Alegre South (48)

324 CALIFORNIA LONG BEACH 1 Jul 1998 Grant L. Pullan
Organized from Calif. Los Angeles (5), Calif. Arcadia (86), Calif. Anaheim (73a)

325 CANADA EDMONTON 1 Jul 1998 Richard M. Andrus
Organized from Canada Calgary (36a)

326 FLORIDA ORLANDO 1 Jul 1998 Wayne Mark Reilly
Organized from Florida Fort Lauderdale (178b), Florida Tampa (139)

327 MADAGASCAR ANTANANARIVO 1 Jul 1998 R. Chris Fee South
Organized from South Africa Durban (216), South Africa Johannesburg (14)

328 OHIO CINCINNATI 1 Jul 1998 Roger Kirkby Wilson
Organized from Kentucky Louisville (29)

329 PARAGUAY ASUNCION NORTH 1 Jul 1998 Lavorn G. Sparks Jr.
Organized fromParaguay Asuncion (155)

330 TAIWAN KAOHSIUNG 1 Jul 1998 Robert Dean Murdock
Organized from Taiwan Taipei (94), Taiwan T'aichung (173, 146)

331 UTAH SALT LAKE CITY SOUTH 1 Jul 1998 James Albert Stephens
Organized from Utah Salt Lake City (187, see also 132, 222)

332 ARMENIA YEREVAN 16 Mar 1999 Robert H. Sangster
Organized from Russia Rostov Mission (302)

333 RUSSIA VLADIVOSTOK 16 Mar 1999 Alvin H. Price

334 ILLINOIS NAUVOO MISSION 1 Nov 2000 Richard K. Sager
Organized from the Illinois Peoria Mission (176a)

FIRST STAKE IN EACH STATE OF THE UNITED STATES

STATE	NAME OF STAKE	DATE ORGANIZED	CURRENT NAME
ALABAMA	Alabama (452)	3 Mar 1968	Huntsville Alabama
ALASKA	Alaska (331)	13 Aug 1961	Anchorage Alaska

ARIZONA	Little Colorado (21)	27 Jan 1878	‡18 Dec 1887
	*Maricopa (24)	10 Dec 1882	Mesa Arizona Maricopa
ARKANSAS	Arkansas (484)	1 Jun 1969	Little Rock Arkansas
CALIFORNIA	San Bernardino (4a)	6 Jul 1851	‡By 1857
	*Hollywood (98)	22 May 1927	Los Angeles California
COLORADO	San Luis (26)	10 Jun 1883	Manassa Colorado
CONNECTICUT	Hartford (421)	18 Sep 1966	Hartford Connecticut
DELAWARE	Wilmington Delaware (673)	8 Dec 1975	Same
DIST. OF COLUMBIA	Washington (131)	30 Jun 1940	Washington D.C.
FLORIDA	Florida (163)	19 Jan 1947	Jacksonville Florida West
GEORGIA	Atlanta (241)	5 May 1957	Tucker Georgia
HAWAII	Oahu (113)	30 Jun 1935	Laie Hawaii
IDAHO	Bear Lake (8a)	20 Jun 1869	Paris Idaho
ILLINOIS	Nauvoo (2a)	5 Oct 1839	‡By 1846
	*Chicago (118)	29 Nov 1936	Wilmette Illinois
INDIANA	Indianapolis (283)	17 May 1959	Indianapolis Indiana
IOWA	Iowa (3a)	5 Oct 1839	‡6 Jan 1842
	*Cedar Rapids (419)	29 May 1966	Cedar Rapids Iowa
KANSAS	Wichita (355)	24 Jun 1962	Wichita Kansas
KENTUCKY	Louisville (540)	17 Jan 1971	Louisville Kentucky
LOUISIANA	New Orleans (221)	19 Jun 1955	New Orleans Louisiana
MAINE	Maine (461)	23 Jun 1968	Augusta Maine
MARYLAND	Chesapeake (526)	13 Sep 1970	Silver Spring Maryland
MASSACHUSETTS	Boston (354)	20 May 1962	Boston Massachusetts
MICHIGAN	Detroit (197)	9 Nov 1952	Bloomfield Hills Michigan
MINNESOTA	Minnesota (317)	29 Nov 1960	Minneapolis Minnesota
MISSISSIPPI	Jackson (404)	2 May 1965	Jackson Mississippi
MISSOURI	Clay-Caldwell (2)	3 Jul 1834	‡By 1839
	*Kansas City (234)	21 Oct 1956	Kansas City Missouri
MONTANA	Butte (208)	28 Jun 1953	Butte Montana
NEBRASKA	Winter Quarters (318)	11 Dec 1960	Omaha Nebraska
NEVADA	Carson Valley (7a)	4 Oct 1856	‡By 1858
	*Moapa (64)	9 Jun 1912	Logandale Nevada
NEW HAMPSHIRE	Merrimack (507)	22 Mar 1970	Nashua New Hampshire
NEW JERSEY	New Jersey (292)	28 Feb 1960	Morristown New Jersey
NEW MEXICO	Young (63)	21 May 1912	Farmington New Mexico
NEW YORK	New York (110)	9 Dec 1934	New York New York
NORTH CAROLINA	North Carolina (332)	27 Aug 1961	Kinston North Carolina
NORTH DAKOTA	Fargo North Dakota (852)	7 Aug 1977	Same
OHIO	Kirtland (1)	17 Feb 1834	‡24 May 1841
	*Cincinnati (270)	23 Nov 1958	Cincinnati Ohio
OKLAHOMA	Tulsa (298)	1 May 1960	Tulsa Oklahoma
OREGON	Union (49)	9 Jun 1901	La Grande Oregon
PENNSYLVANIA	Philadelphia (304)	16 Oct 1960	Philadelphia Pennsylvania
RHODE ISLAND	Providence R.I. (818)	20 Mar 1977	Same
SOUTH CAROLINA	South Carolina (169)	19 Oct 1947	Columbia South Carolina
SOUTH DAKOTA	Rapid City (592)	10 Dec 1972	Rapid City South Dakota
TENNESSEE	Memphis (403)	18 Apr 1965	Memphis Tennessee
TEXAS	El Paso (194)	21 Sep 1952	El Paso Texas
UTAH	Salt Lake (1a)	3 Oct 1847	Same
VERMONT	Montpelier Vermont (753)	11 Apr 1976	Same
VIRGINIA	Virginia (245)	30 Jun 1957	Richmond Virginia
WASHINGTON	Seattle (124)	31 Jul 1938	Seattle Washington
WEST VIRGINIA	West Virginia (522)	23 Aug 1970	Charleston West Virginia
WISCONSIN	Milwaukee (367)	3 Feb 1963	Milwaukee Wisconsin
WYOMING	Star Valley (33)	14 Aug 1892	Afton Wyoming

( ) Chronological number of stake; ‡ Discontinued; * First permanent stake

FIRST STAKE ORGANIZED IN COUNTRIES OF THE WORLD

COUNTRY	NAME OF STAKE	DATE ORGANIZED	CURRENT NAME
AMERICAN SAMOA	Pago Pago (488)	15 Jun 1969	Pago Pago Samoa
ARGENTINA	Buenos Aires (423)	20 Nov 1966	Buenos Aires Argentina East
AUSTRALIA	Sydney (293)	27 Mar 1960	Sydney Australia Greenwich
AUSTRIA	Vienna Austria (1126)	20 Apr 1980	Same

BELGIUM	Brussels Belgium (813)	20 Feb 1977	Same
BOLIVIA	Santa Cruz Bolivia (993)	14 Jan 1979	Santa Cruz Bolivia Canoto
BRAZIL	Sao Paulo (417)	1 May 1966	Sao Paulo Brazil
CANADA	Alberta (35)	9 Jun 1895	Cardston Alberta
CHILE	Santiago (590)	19 Nov 1972	Santi. Chile Quinta Normal
CHINA	Hong Kong (756)	25 Apr 1976	Hong Kong Island
COLOMBIA	Bogota Colombia (805)	23 Jan 1977	Same
COSTA RICA	San Jose Costa Rica (803)	20 Jan 1977	Same
DEMOCRATIC REPUBLIC OF CONGO	Kinshasa Zaire (2258)	3 Nov. 1996	Kinshasa Dem. Rep. Congo
DENMARK	Copenhagen Denmark (648)	16 Jun 1974	Same
DOMINICAN REPUBLIC	Santo Domingo Dominican Republic (1593)	23 Mar 1986	Same
ECUADOR	Guayaquil Ecuador (939)	11 Jun 1978	Guayaquil Ecuador West
EL SALVADOR	San Salvador (618)	3 Jun 1973	San Salvador El Salvador
ENGLAND	Manchester (294)	27 Mar 1960	Manchester England
FIJI	Suva Fiji (1428)	12 Jun 1983	Same
FINLAND	Helsinki Finland (865)	16 Oct 1977	Same
FRANCE	Paris France (731)	16 Nov 1975	Same
GERMANY	Berlin (334)	10 Sep 1961	Berlin Germany
GHANA	Accra Ghana (1791)	21 Apr 1991	Same
GUATEMALA	Guatemala City (436)	21 May 1967	Guatemala City Guatemala
HAITI	Port-au-Prince Haiti (2399)	21 Sep 1997	Same
HONDURAS	San Pedro Sula Honduras (820)	10 Apr 1977	Same
IRELAND	Dublin Ireland (2034)	12 Mar 1995	Same
ITALY	Milan Italy (1274)	7 Jun 1981	Same
IVORY COAST	Abidjan Ivory Coast (2387)	17 Aug 1997	Same
JAPAN	Tokyo (505)	15 Mar 1970	Tokyo Japan
KOREA	Seoul (604)	8 Mar 1973	Seoul Korea
KIRIBATI	Tarawa Kiribati (2215)	8 Aug 1996	Same
LIBERIA	Monrovia Liberia (2562)	11 Jun 2000	Same
MADAGASCAR	Antananarivo Madagascar (2572) 17 Sep 2000	Same	
MEXICO	Juarez (37)	9 Dec 1895	Colonia Juarez Mexico
NETHERLANDS	Holland (326)	12 Mar 1961	The Hague NetherlandsNEW
NEW ZEALAND	Auckland (264)	18 May 1958	Auckland N.Z. Mt. Roskill
NICARAGUA	Managua Nicaragua (1246)	22 Mar 1981	‡15 Oct 1989; Reinstated 21 Jun 1998
NIGERIA	Aba Nigeria (1695)	15 May 1988	Same
NORTHERN IRELAND	Belfast Ireland (647)	9 Jun 1974	Belfast Northern Ireland
NORWAY	Oslo Norway (835)	22 May 1977	Same
PANAMA	Panama City Panama (1081)	11 Nov 1979	Same
PAPUA NEW GUINEA	Port Moresby Papua New Guinea (2109)	22 Oct 1995	Same
PARAGUAY	Asuncion Paraguay (1002)	25 Feb 1979	Same
PERU	Lima (503)	22 Feb 1970	Lima Peru Limatambo
PHILIPPINES	Manila (613)	20 May 1973	Manila Philippines
PORTUGAL	Lisbon Portugal (1276)	10 Jun 1981	Same
PUERTO RICO	San Juan Puerto Rico (1215)	14 Dec 1980	Same
SCOTLAND	Glasgow (356)	26 Aug 1962	Glasgow Scotland
SINGAPORE	Singapore Singapore (2025)	26 Feb 1995	Same
SOUTH AFRICA	Transvaal (506)	22 Mar 1970	Johannesburg South Africa
SPAIN	Madrid Spain (1327)	14 Mar 1982	Same
SWEDEN	Stockholm Sweden (691)	20 Apr 1975	Same
SWITZERLAND	Swiss (341)	28 Oct 1961	Zurich Switzerland
TAHITI	Tahiti (573)	14 May 1972	Papeete Tahiti
TAIWAN	Taipei Taiwan (755)	22 Apr 1976	Taipei Taiwan West
THAILAND	Bangkok Thailand (2064)	18 Jun 1995	Same
TONGA	Nuku'alofa (463)	5 Sep 1968	Nuku'alofa Tonga
UNITED STATES	Kirtland (1)	17 Feb 1834	‡24 May 1841
	*Salt Lake (1a)	3 Oct 1847	Same
URUGUAY	Montevideo (444)	12 Nov 1967	Montevideo Uruguay West
VENEZUELA	Caracas Venezuela (827)	15 May 1977	Same
WALES	Merthyr Tydfil Wales (676)	12 Jan 1975	Same
WESTERN SAMOA	Apia (353)	18 Mar 1962	Apia Samoa
ZIMBABWE	Harare Zimbabwe (2541)	12 Dec 1999	Same

( ) Chronological number of stake; ‡ Discontinued; * First permanent stake

TEMPLES

Temples of the world

Oct. 1, 2000

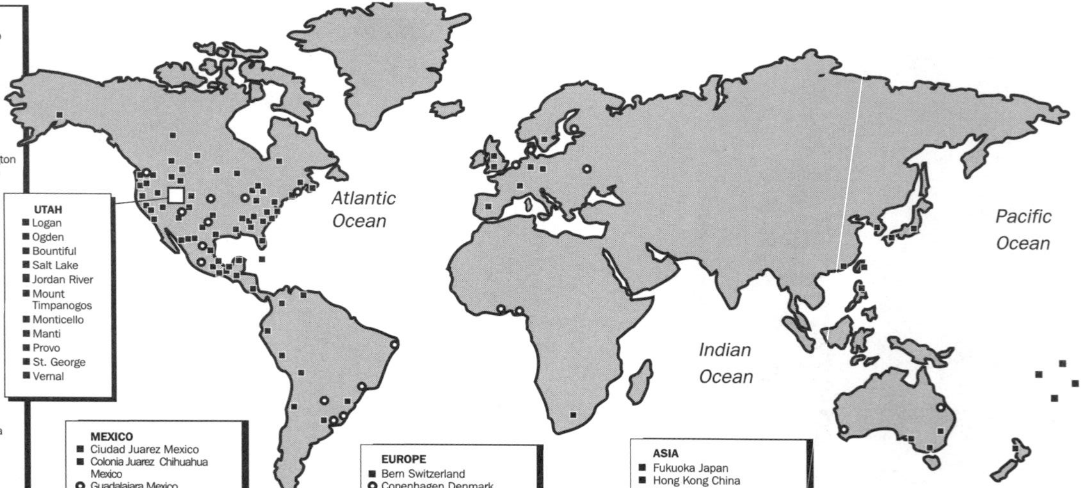

○ Planned
■ In operation

UNITED STATES
■ Albuquerque New Mexico
■ Anchorage Alaska
■ Atlanta Georgia
■ Baton Rouge Louisiana
■ Billings Montana
■ Birmingham Alabama
■ Bismarck North Dakota
■ Boise Idaho
■ Boston Massachusetts
■ Chicago Illinois
○ Columbia River, Washington
■ Columbia South Carolina
■ Columbus Ohio
■ Dallas Texas
■ Denver Colorado
■ Detroit Michigan
■ Fresno California
■ Houston Texas
■ Idaho Falls
■ Kona Hawaii
■ Laie Hawaii
■ Las Vegas Nevada
■ Los Angeles California
■ Louisville Kentucky
○ Lubbock Texas
■ Medford Oregon
■ Memphis Tennessee
■ Mesa Arizona
■ Nashville Tennessee
○ Nauvoo Illinois
○ New York New York
■ Oakland California
■ Oklahoma City Oklahoma
■ Orlando Florida
■ Palmyra New York
■ Portland Oregon
■ Reno Nevada
■ St Louis Missouri
■ St. Paul Minnesota
■ Raleigh North Carolina
■ San Diego California
■ Seattle Washington
○ Snowflake Arizona
■ Spokane Washington
■ Washington D.C.
○ Winter Quarters Nebraska

CANADA
■ Cardston Alberta
■ Edmonton Alberta
■ Halifax Nova Scotia
■ Montreal Quebec
■ Regina Saskatchewan
■ Toronto Ontario

UTAH
■ Logan
■ Ogden
■ Bountiful
■ Salt Lake
■ Jordan River
■ Mount Timpanogos
■ Monticello
■ Manti
■ Provo
■ St. George
■ Vernal

MEXICO
■ Ciudad Juarez Mexico
■ Colonia Juarez Chihuahua Mexico
○ Guadalajara Mexico
■ Hermosillo Sonora Mexico
■ Merida Mexico
■ Mexico City Mexico
○ Monterrey Mexico
■ Oaxaca Mexico
■ Tampico Mexico
■ Túxtla Gutierrez Mexico
■ Veracruz Mexico
■ Villahermosa Mexico

CENTRAL/SOUTH AMERICA
○ Asunción Paraguay
■ Bogota Colombia
■ Buenos Aires Argentina
○ Campinas Brazil
■ Caracas Venezuela
■ Cochabamba Bolivia
■ Guatemala City Guatemala
■ Guayaquil Ecuador
■ Lima Peru
○ Montevideo Uruguay
○ Porto Alegre Brazil
○ Recife Brazil
■ San Jose Costa Rica
■ Santiago Chile
■ Santo Domingo DR
■ Sao Paulo Brazil

EUROPE
■ Bern Switzerland
○ Copenhagen Denmark
■ Frankfurt Germany
■ Freiberg Germany
○ Helsinki Finland
○ Kiev Ukraine
■ London England
■ Madrid Spain
■ Preston England
■ Stockholm Sweden
○ The Hauge Netherlands

AFRICA
○ Aba Nigeria
○ Accra Ghana
■ Johannesburg South Africa

ASIA
■ Fukuoka Japan
■ Hong Kong China
■ Seoul Korea
■ Taipei Taiwan
■ Tokyo Japan

PACIFIC/AUSTRALIA
■ Adelaide Australia
■ Apia Samoa
○ Brisbane Australia
■ Hamilton New Zealand
■ Manila Philippines
■ Melbourne Australia
■ Nuku'alofa Tonga
■ Papeete Tahiti
○ Perth Australia
■ Suva Fuji
■ Sydney Australia

TEMPLES OF THE CHURCH

Listed in order of completion

	TEMPLE	LOCATION	DEDICATED	BY WHOM
	Kirtland*	Kirtland, Ohio	27 Mar 1836	Joseph Smith
	Nauvoo**	Nauvoo, Ill.	30 Apr 1846	Joseph Young (private)
			1 May 1846	Orson Hyde (public)
1	St. George Utah	St. George, Utah	6 Apr 1877	Daniel H. Wells
	Rededicated after remodeling		11 Nov 1975	Spencer W. Kimball
2	Logan Utah	Logan, Utah	17 May 1884	John Taylor
	Rededicated after remodeling		13 Mar 1979	Spencer W. Kimball
3	Manti Utah	Manti, Utah	17 May 1888	Wilford Woodruff (private)
			21 May 1888	(His prayer read by Lorenzo Snow; public)
	Rededicated after remodeling		14 Jun 1985	Gordon B. Hinckley
4	Salt Lake	Salt Lake City, Utah	6 Apr 1893	Wilford Woodruff
5	Laie Hawaii	Laie, Oahu, Hawaii	27 Nov 1919	Heber J. Grant
	Rededicated after remodeling		13 Jun 1978	Spencer W. Kimball
6	Cardston Alberta	Cardston, Alberta, Canada	26 Aug 1923	Heber J. Grant
	Portions rededicated after remodeling		2 Jul 1962	Hugh B. Brown
	Rededication after remodeling		22 Jun 1991	Gordon B. Hinckley
7	Mesa Arizona	Mesa, Ariz.	23 Oct 1927	Heber J. Grant
	Rededicated after remodeling		15 Apr 1975	Spencer W. Kimball
8	Idaho Falls Idaho	Idaho Falls, Idaho	23 Sep 1945	George Albert Smith
9	Bern Switzerland	Zollikofen, near Bern, Switzerland	11 Sep 1955	David O. McKay
	Rededicated after remodeling		23 Oct 1992	Gordon B. Hinckley
10	Los Angeles California	Los Angeles, Calif.	11 Mar 1956	David O. McKay
11	Hamilton New Zealand	Hamilton, New Zealand	20 Apr 1958	David O. McKay
12	London England	Newchapel, Surrey,	7 Sep 1958	David O. McKay
	Rededicated after remodeling		18 Oct 1992	Gordon B. Hinckley
13	Oakland California	Oakland, Calif.	17 Nov 1964	David O. McKay
14	Ogden Utah	Ogden, Utah	18 Jan 1972	Joseph Fielding Smith
15	Provo Utah	Provo, Utah	9 Feb 1972	Joseph Fielding Smith (His prayer read by Harold B. Lee)
16	Washington D.C.	Kensington, Md.	19 Nov 1974	Spencer W. Kimball
17	Sao Paulo Brazil	Sao Paulo, Brazil	30 Oct 1978	Spencer W. Kimball
18	Tokyo Japan	Tokyo, Japan	27 Oct 1980	Spencer W. Kimball
19	Seattle Washington	Bellevue, Wash.	17 Nov 1980	Spencer W. Kimball
20	Jordan River Utah	South Jordan, Utah	16 Nov 1981	Marion G. Romney
21	Atlanta Georgia	Sandy Springs, Ga.	1 Jun 1983	Gordon B. Hinckley
22	Apia Samoa	Apia, Western Samoa	5 Aug 1983	Gordon B. Hinckley
23	Nuku'alofa Tonga	Nuku'alofa, Tonga	9 Aug 1983	Gordon B. Hinckley
24	Santiago Chile	Santiago, Chile	15 Sep 1983	Gordon B. Hinckley
25	Papeete Tahiti	Pirae, Tahiti	27 Oct 1983	Gordon B. Hinckley
26	Mexico City Mexico	Mexico City, Mexico	2 Dec 1983	Gordon B. Hinckley
27	Boise Idaho	Boise, Idaho	25 May 1984	Gordon B. Hinckley
28	Sydney Australia	Carlingford, Australia	20 Sep 1984	Gordon B. Hinckley
29	Manila Philippines	Quezon City, Philippines	25 Sep 1984	Gordon B. Hinckley
30	Dallas Texas	Dallas, Texas	19 Oct 1984	Gordon B. Hinckley
31	Taipei Taiwan	Taipei, Taiwan	17 Nov 1984	Gordon B. Hinckley
32	Guatemala City Guatemala	Guatemala City, Guat.	14 Dec 1984	Gordon B. Hinckley
33	Freiberg Germany	Freiberg, Germany	29 Jun 1985	Gordon B. Hinckley
34	Stockholm Sweden	Vasterhaninge, Sweden	2 Jul 1985	Gordon B. Hinckley
35	Chicago Illinois	Glenview, Ill.	9 Aug 1985	Gordon B. Hinckley
36	Johannesburg South Africa	Johannesburg, South Africa	24 Aug 1985	Gordon B. Hinckley
37	Seoul Korea	Seoul, Korea	14 Dec 1985	Gordon B. Hinckley
38	Lima Peru	Lima, Peru	10 Jan 1986	Gordon B. Hinckley
39	Buenos Aires Argentina	Buenos Aires, Argentina	17 Jan 1986	Thomas S. Monson
40	Denver Colorado	Littleton, Colo.	24 Oct 1986	Ezra Taft Benson
41	Frankfurt Germany	Friedrichsdorf, Germany	28 Aug 1987	Ezra Taft Benson
42	Portland Oregon	Lake Oswego, Ore.	19 Aug, 1989	Gordon B. Hinckley
43	Las Vegas Nevada	Las Vegas, Nev.	16 Dec 1989	Gordon B. Hinckley
44	Toronto Ontario Canada	Brampton, Ontario,	25 Aug 1990	Gordon B. Hinckley
45	San Diego California	San Diego, Calif.	25 Apr 1993	Gordon B. Hinckley
46	Orlando Florida	Windermere, Fla.	9 Oct. 1994	Howard W. Hunter

47	Bountiful Utah	Bountiful, Utah	8 Jan. 1995	Howard W. Hunter
48	Hong Kong China	Hong Kong	26 May 1996	Gordon B. Hinckley
49	Mount Timpanogos Utah	American Fork, Utah	13 Oct. 1996	Gordon B. Hinckley
50	St. Louis Missouri	Town and Country, Mo.	1 June 1997	Gordon B. Hinckley
51	Vernal Utah	Vernal, Utah	2 Nov 1997	Gordon B. Hinckley
52	Preston England	Chorley, England	7 July 1998	Gordon B. Hinckley
53	Monticello Utah	Monticello, Utah	26 July 1998	Gordon B. Hinckley
54	Anchorage Alaska	Anchorage, Alaska	Jan. 9, 1999	Gordon B. Hinckley
55	Colonia Juarez Chihuahua Mexico	Colonia Juarez	March 6, 1999	Gordon B. Hinckley
56	Madrid Spain	Moratalaz, Spain	March 19, 1999	Gordon B. Hinckley
57	Bogota Colombia	Bogota, Colombia	April 24, 1999	Gordon B. Hinckley
58	Guayaquil Ecuador	Guayaquil, Ecuador	Aug. 1, 1999	Gordon B. Hinckley
59	Spokane Washington	Opportunity, Wash.	Aug. 21-23, 1999	Gordon B. Hinckley
60	Columbus Ohio	Columbus, Ohio	Sept. 4-5, 1999	Gordon B. Hinckley
61	Bismarck North Dakota	Bismarck, N.D.	Sept. 19, 1999	Gordon B. Hinckley
62	Columbia South Carolina	Columbia, S.C.	Oct. 16, 1999	Gordon B. Hinckley
63	Detriot Michigan	Bloomfield Hills, Mich.	Oct 23-24, 1999	Gordon B. Hinckley
64	Halifax Nova Scotia	Dartmouth, Nova Scotia	Nov. 14, 1999	Gordon B. Hinckley
65	Regina Saskatchewan	Regina, Saskatchewan	Nov. 14, 1999	Boyd K. Packer
66	Billings Montana	Billings, Mont.	Nov. 20-21, 1999	Gordon B. Hinckley
67	Edmonton Alberta	Edmonton, Alberta	Dec. 11-12, 1999	Gordon B. Hinckley
68	Raleigh North Carolina	outside Raleigh, N.C.	Dec. 18-19, 1999	Gordon B. Hinckley
69	St. Paul Minnesota	Oakdale, Minn.	Jan. 9, 2000	Gordon B. Hinckley
70	Kona Hawaii	Kailua-Kona, Hawaii	Jan. 23, 2000	Gordon B. Hinckley
71	Ciudad Juarez Mexico	Ciudad Juarez, Mexico	Feb. 26, 2000	Gordon B. Hinckley
72	Hermosillo Sonora Mexico	Hermosillo, Mexico	Feb. 27, 2000	Gordon B. Hinckley
73	Albuquerque New Mexico	Albuquerque, N. M.	March 5, 2000	Gordon B. Hinckley
74	Oaxaca Mexico	Oaxaca, Mexico	March 11, 2000	James E. Faust
75	Tuxtla Gutierrez Mexico	Tuxtla Gutierrez, Mexico	March 12, 2000	James E. Faust
76	Louisville Kentucky	Pewee Valley, Ky.	March 19, 2000	Thomas S. Monson
77	Palmyra New York	Palmyra Village, N. Y.	April 6, 2000	Gordon B. Hinckley
78	Fresno California	Fresno, Calif.	April 9, 2000	Gordon B. Hinckley
79	Medford Oregon	Central Point, Ore.	April 16, 2000	James E. Faust
80	Memphis Tennessee	Bartlett, Tenn.	April 23, 2000	James E. Faust
81	Reno Nevada	Reno, Nev.	April 23, 2000	Thomas S. Monson
82	Cochabamba Bolivia	Cochabamba, Bolivia	April 30, 2000	Gordon B. Hinckley
83	Tampico Mexico	Ciudad Madero, Mexico	May 20, 2000	Thomas S. Monson
84	Nashville Tennessee	Franklin, Tenn.	May 21, 2000	James E. Faust
85	Villahermosa Mexico	Villahermosa, Mexico	May 21, 2000	Thomas S. Monson
86	Montreal Quebec	Longueuil, Quebec	June 4, 2000	Gordon B. Hinckley
87	San Jose Costa Rica	San Antonio, Costa Rica	June 4, 2000	James E. Faust
88	Fukuoka Japan	Fukuoka, Japan	June 11, 2000	Gordon B. Hinckley
89	Adelaide Australia	Marden, South Australia	June 15, 2000	Gordon B. Hinckley
90	Melbourne Australia	Wantirna, Victoria, Aus.	June 16, 2000	Gordon B. Hinckley
91	Suva Fiji	Suva, Fiji	June 18, 2000	Gordon B. Hinckley
92	Merida Mexico	Merida, Mexico	July 8, 2000	Thomas S. Monson
93	Veracruz Mexico	Veracruz, Mexico	July 9, 2000	Thomas S. Monson
94	Baton Rouge Louisiana	Baton Rouge, La.	July 16, 2000	Gordon B. Hinckley
95	Oklahoma City Oklahoma	Yukon, Okla.	July 30, 2000	James E. Faust
96	Caracas Venezuela	Caracas, Venezuela	Aug. 20, 2000	Gordon B. Hinckley
97	Houston Texas	Klein, Texas	Aug 26-27, 2000	Gordon B. Hinckley
98	Birmingham Alabama	Gardendale, Ala.	Sept. 3, 2000	Gordon B. Hinckley
99	Santo Domingo Dominican Republic	Santo Domingo, Dominican Republic	Sept. 17, 2000	Gordon B. Hinckley
100	Boston Massachusetts	Belmont, Mass.	Oct. 1, 2000	Gordon B. Hinckley
101	Recife Brazil	Recife, Brazil	Dec. 14, 2000***	
102	Porto Alegre Brazil	Porto Alegre, Brazil	Dec. 16, 2000***	
103	Montevideo Uruguay	Montevideo, Uruguay	Dec. 17, 2000***	

* No longer in use by the Church **No longer stands *** Announced dates

Temples announced or under construction:

Aba Nigeria
Accra Ghana
Asuncion Paraguay
Brisbane Australia
Campinas Brazil
Columbia River Washington
Copenhagen Denmark
Guadalajara Mexico
Helsinki Finland
Kiev (Kyiv) Ukraine
Lubbock Texas
Montevideo Uruguay
Monterrey Mexico
Nauvoo Illinois
New York New York
Perth Australia
Porto Alegre Brazil
Recife Brazil
Snowflake Arizona
The Hague Netherlands
Winter Quarters Nebraska

TEMPLES OF THE CHURCH

(Listed alphabetically as of Oct. 15, 2000)

ABA NIGERIA TEMPLE

Announced: April 3, 2000. **Status:** Awaiting groundbreaking.

ACCRA GHANA TEMPLE

Announced: Feb. 16, 1998. **Status:** Awaiting groundbreaking.

ADELAIDE AUSTRALIA TEMPLE

Announced: March 17, 1999.

Location: 53-59 Lower Port Bush Road, Marden, South Australia.

Site: 6.94 acres.

Exterior finish: Snow white granite

Temple design: Traditional.

Architects: Simon Drew.

Project manager: Graham Sully.

Contractor: Balderstone-Hornibrook.

Number of rooms: Celestial room, two endowment rooms, two sealing rooms and baptistry.

Total floor area: 10,700 square feet.

Dimensions: 144 feet by 77 feet.

District: Adelaide Firle, Adelaide Marion, Adelaide Modbury stakes and Mildura Australia, Northern Territory Australia and Woomera, Australia districts.

Groundbreaking, site dedication: May 29,

1999, by Elder Vaughn J. Featherstone of the Seventy and president of the Australia/New Zealand Area.

Dedicated: June 15, 2000, by President Gordon B. Hinckley; 4 sessions.

Dedicatory prayer excerpt: "*We are grateful for this nation of Australia, where there is freedom of worship, freedom of assembly, and freedom to take upon ourselves the name of our Divine Redeemer, and to keep sacred the covenants which we make with Him.*"

ALBUQUERQUE NEW MEXICO TEMPLE

Announced: April 4, 1997.

Location: 10301 San Francisco Dr. NE, Albuquerque, N.M.

Site: 8.5 acres.

Exterior finish: Cast stone / granite.

Temple design: Classic modern.

Architects: Fanning Bard & Tatum.

Project manager: James Aulestia and Lloyd Hess.

Contractor: Okland Construction Co.

Number of rooms: Celestial room, baptistry, three sealing rooms, two ordinance rooms.

Total floor area: 34,000 square feet.

Dimensions of building: 145 feet by 133 feet.

District: 15 stakes and one district in New Mexico, part of Arizona and Colorado.

Groundbreaking, site dedication: June 20, 1998, by Elder Lynn A. Mickelsen of the Seventy and president of the North America Southwest Area.

Dedicated: March 5, 2000, by President Gordon B. Hinckley; 4 sessions.

Dedicatory prayer excerpt: "*Let it be a sanctuary of peace, a refuge from the noise of the world. May it be a house of quiet contemplation concerning the eternal nature of life and of Thy divine plan for Thy sons and daughters as they walk the road of immortality and eternal life.*"

ANCHORAGE ALASKA TEMPLE

Announced: Oct. 4, 1997.

Location: 13111 Brayton Drive, Anchorage, Alaska.

Site: 5.54 acres, including adjoining meetinghouse.

Exterior finish: Granite.

Temple design: Classic modern.

Architects: McCool, Carlson & Green Architects and Church A&E Services.

Project manager: Cory Karl.

Contractor: H. Watt & Scott.

Number of rooms: 21 rooms.

Total floor area: 6,800 square feet.

Dimensions: 79 by 108 feet.

District: Alaska and Yukon.

Groundbreaking, site dedication: April 17, 1998, by Elder F. Melvin Hammond of the Seventy and president of the North America Northwest Area.

Dedication: Jan. 9, 1999, by President Gordon B. Hinckley; 7 sessions.

Dedicatory prayer excerpt: "*May this great work of temple building go forward across the earth to bless Thy people wherever they may be found. May all who come with hope and high expectation, leave with satisfaction and gratitude, having tasted of the sweet things of Thy divine work.*"

APIA SAMOA TEMPLE

Location: Near the school and mission home in Pesega.

Site: 1.7 acres.

Exterior finish: "R-wall" exterior finish and insulation system on concrete block; split cedar shake shingles on roof.

Temple design: Modern.

Architect: Emil B. Fetzer, Church architect.

Construction advisers: Dale Cook and Richard Rowley.

Contractor: Utah Construction and Development.

Number of rooms: Three sealing rooms, two ordinance rooms.

Total floor area: 13,020 square feet.

Dimensions: 142.88 feet by 115.32 feet; statue of Angel Moroni on top spire, 75 feet high.

District: Western Samoa and American Samoa.

Groundbreaking, site dedication: Feb. 19, 1981, by President Spencer W. Kimball, assisted by the head of state, Malieotoa Tanumafil II. Nearly 4,000 people attended.

Dedication: Aug. 5-6, 1983, by President Gordon B. Hinckley; 7 sessions.

Dedicatory prayer excerpt: *"We pray for Thy blessings upon those who govern these islands and the people who dwell here that principles of peace and equity may prevail and that the citizens of these islands may have cause to rejoice in the liberty that is theirs."*

ASUNCION PARAGUAY TEMPLE

Announced: April 3, 2000 **Status:** Awaiting groundbreaking

ATLANTA GEORGIA TEMPLE

Location: In Sandy Springs, on the northeastern outskirts of Atlanta.

Site: 5.9 acres.

Exterior finish: Pre-cast stone walls, built-up roof.

Temple design: Modern.

Architect: Emil B. Fetzer, Church architect.

Construction adviser: Michael Enfield and Ronald Prince.

Contractor: Cube Construction Company.

Number of rooms: Five sealing rooms, four ordinance rooms.

Total floor area: 27,360 square feet.

Dimensions: 187 feet 8 inches by 166 feet 3 inches; statue of Angel Moroni on top spire.

District: Georgia, Alabama, and districts in Jamaica and Trinidad.

Groundbreaking, site dedication: March 7, 1981, by President Spencer W. Kimball, attended by 10,000 people.

Dedication: June 1-4, 1983, by President Gordon B. Hinckley; 11 sessions.

Dedicatory prayer excerpt: *"May the very presence of this temple in the midst of Thy people become a reminder of the sacred and eternal covenants made with Thee. May they strive more diligently to banish from their lives those elements which are inconsistent with the covenants they have made with Thee.*

"May all who enter these holy precincts feel of Thy spirit and be bathed in this marvelous, sanctifying influence. May they come . . . in a spirit of love and dedication."

BATON ROUGE LOUISIANA TEMPLE

Announced: Oct. 14, 1998.

Location: 10339 Highland Road, Baton Rouge, La.

Site: 6.3 acres, including adjoining meetinghouse.

Exterior finish: Imperial Danby White marble.

Temple design: Classic modern.

Architect: Paul Tessier of Paul Tessier & Associates, and Church A&E Services.

Project managers: Leon Rowley.

Contractor: Layton Construction Co., Construction Management Co.; Cangelosi Ward, general contractor.

Number of rooms: Celestial room, baptistry, two ordinance rooms, two sealing rooms.

Total floor area: 10,700 square feet.

Dimensions: 144 by 77 feet.

District: Nine stakes in Louisiana and Mississippi.

Groundbreaking, site dedication: May 8, 1999, by Elder Monte J. Brough of the Seventy and president of the North America Southeast Area.

Dedicated: July 16, 2000, by President Gordon B. Hinckley; 4 sessions.

Dedicatory prayer excerpt: *"We thank Thee for this nation in which this temple stands. It was established by men whom Thou didst raise up unto this very purpose. Thou hast spoken concerning the Constitution of its government. Surely it is a choice land and a favored nation."*

BERN SWITZERLAND TEMPLE

Location: In a northern suburb of Bern in a setting with the Alps on the south, and the Jura Mountains on the west and north; Tempelstrasse 4, Ch - 3052 Zollikofen, Switzerland.

Site: 7 acres, selected July 1952, by President David O. McKay and President Samuel E. Bringhurst of the Swiss-Austrian Mission.

Exterior finish: Reinforced concrete with a creamish gray terra cotta facing trimmed in white. Tower is white base and spire is gold-colored.

Temple design: Modern-contemporary, but similar to lines of early Church temples.

Architect: Edward O. Anderson, Church architect. Re-drawn into German specifications by Wilhelm Zimmer of Bercher and Zimmer Architects.

Contractor: Hans Jordi of Bern.

Number of rooms: Four ordinance rooms, seven sealing rooms.

Total floor area: Originally 34,750 square feet; now 39,063 square feet.

Dimensions: 152 feet by 84 feet; top of tower rises 140 feet.

District: Stakes in Switzerland, Austria, southern France, Italy, and districts in Israel (ex-patriot), Albania.

Groundbreaking, site dedication: Aug. 5, 1953, by President David O. McKay.

Dedication: Sept. 11-15, 1955, by President David O. McKay; 10 sessions, Tabernacle Choir participated. Rededicated Oct. 23-25, 1992, by President Gordon B. Hinckley; 10 sessions.

Dedicatory prayer excerpt: *"Increase our desire, O Father, to put forth even greater effort towards the consummation of Thy purpose to bring to pass the immortality and eternal life of all thy children."*

BILLINGS MONTANA TEMPLE

Announced: Aug. 31, 1996.

Location: 3100 Rim Point Drive in Billings, Mont.

Site: 10 acres.

Exterior finish: Wyoming white dolomite precast concrete.

Temple design: Classic modern.

Architects: CTA Architects Engineers.

Project manager: Cory Karl.

Contractor: Jacobson Construction Inc.

Number of rooms: 91 total rooms.

Total floor area: 33,800 square feet.

Dimensions: 170 feet by 182 feet.

District: 13 stakes in Montana and Wyoming.

Groundbreaking, site dedication: March 28, 1998, by Elder Hugh W. Pinnock of the Seventy, president of the North America Central Area.

Dedicated: Nov. 20, 1999, by President Gordon B. Hinckley; 8 sessions.

Dedicatory prayer excerpt: *"Those of this area who are called to teach the gospel to the world will first come here to be endowed with power from on high. Lead them in their ministry to those who will accept their testimony of the divinity of Thy restored work."*

BIRMINGHAM ALABAMA TEMPLE

Announced: Sept. 11. 1998.

Location: 1925 Mount Olive Road, Gardendale, Ala.

Site: 5.6 acres, adjoining including meetinghouse.

Exterior finish: Imperial Danby White Marble.

Temple design: Classic modern

Architects: Robert Waldrip of Joyce, Prout and Associates, and Church A&E Services.

Project manager: Leon Rowley.

Contractor: Layton Construction Co., Construction Management Co. Gary C. Wyatt, Inc., general contractor.

Number of rooms: Celestial room, baptistry, two ordinance rooms; two sealing rooms.

Total floor area: 11,000 square feet.

Dimensions: 144 by 77 feet.

District: Members in Alabama and Mississippi.

Groundbreaking, site dedication: Oct. 9, 1999, by Elder Stephen A. West of the Seventy and second counselor in the North America Southeast Area presidency.

Dedication: Sept. 3, 2000, by President Gordon B. Hinckley: 4 sessions.

Dedicatory prayer excerpt: *"May the influence of this Thy house be felt throughout this great temple district. May the Church grow and prosper here. May those in government be friendly to Thy people."*

BISMARCK NORTH DAKOTA TEMPLE

Announced: July 29, 1998.

Location: 2930 Cody Drive in northwest Bismarck, N.D.

Site: 1.6 acres.

Exterior finish: White marble.

Temple design: Classic modern.

Architects: Ritterbush-Ellig-Hulsing, and Church A&E Services.

Project manager: Cory Karl.

Contractor: Capital City Construction.

Number of rooms: Celestial room, two ordinance rooms, two sealing rooms, baptistry.

Total floor area: 10,700 square feet.

Dimensions: 144 by 77 feet..

District: Four stakes, one district in North Dakota, South Dakota, western Minnesota and northern Nebraska.

Groundbreaking, site dedication: Oct. 17, 1998; Elder Kenneth Johnson of the Seventy and first counselor in the North America Central Area.

Dedication: Sept. 19, 1999, by President Gordon B. Hinckley; 3 sessions.

Dedicatory prayer excerpt: *"We thank Thee for the faith of Thy sons and daughters in the vast area of this temple district, men and women who love Thee and love their Redeemer, and have stood steadfast as Thy people. They have felt much alone. They are out on the frontier of the Church. Their numbers are still not large. But they are entitled to every blessing which the Church has to offer."*

BOGOTA COLOMBIA TEMPLE

Announced: April 7, 1984.

Location: Carrera 37 # 125A-45 in Niza section of northern Bogota.

Site: 3.71 acres.

Exterior finish: granite, Asa Branca.

Temple design: Classic modern.

Architects: Cuellar, Cerrano y Gomez, S.A. and Church A&E Services.

Project manager: Cesar Davila.

Contractor: Cuellar, Cerrano y Gomez, S.A.

Number of rooms: Celestial room, baptistry, four ordinance rooms and three sealing rooms.

Total floor area: 53,500 square feet.

Dimensions: 76 feet by 186 feet.

District: Countries of Colombia and Panama.

Groundbreaking, site dedication: June 26, 1993, by Elder William R. Bradford of the Seventy and president South America North Area.

Dedication: April 24, 1999, by President Gordon B. Hinckley; 11 sessions.

Dedicatory prayer excerpt: *"The faithful Saints of Colombia have given generously of their means to this cause."*

BOISE IDAHO TEMPLE

Location: Just off Interstate 84 on South Cole Road in the west end of Boise.

Site: 4.8 acres.

Exterior finish: Faced with light colored marble and has a slate roof. It is surrounded by three detached towers on each end; 8-foot statue of the Angel Moroni tops highest spire.

Temple design: Modern adaptation of six-spire design.

Architects: Church architectural staff, with assistance from Ron Thurber & Associates of Boise.

Construction adviser: Jerry Sears.

Contractor: Comtrol Inc. of Midvale, Utah.

Number of rooms: Four ordinance rooms, three sealing rooms.

Total floor area: 32,269 square feet, following 1987 addition.

Dimensions: 236 feet by 78 feet; statue of Angel Moroni on top spire.

District: Western Idaho and eastern Oregon.

Groundbreaking, site dedication: Dec. 18, 1982, by Elder Mark E. Petersen of the Quorum of the Twelve.

Dedication: May 25-30, 1984, by President Gordon B. Hinckley; 24 sessions. Addition dedicated by Elder James E. Faust of the Quorum of the Twelve, May 29, 1987.

Dedicatory prayer excerpt: *"May Thy faithful Saints of this and future generations look to this beautiful structure as a house to which they will be made welcome . . . for the making of eternal covenants with Thee, for inspiration and sanctification, as they serve unselfishly."*

BOSTON MASSACHUSETTS TEMPLE

Announced: Sept. 30, 1995.

Location: 86 Frontage Rd., Belmont, Mass.

Site: 8 acres.

Exterior finish: Granite.

Temple design: Classic Modern.

Architect: Tsoi/Kobus & Associates and Church A&E Services.

Project manager: William Treu.

Contractor: Barr & Barr.

Number of rooms: 84 rooms.

Total floor area: 69,000 square feet.

Dimensions: 90 feet by 190 feet.

District: Connecticut, Maine, New Hampshire, Vermont, Rhode Island, Massachusetts and New York.

Groundbreaking, site dedication: June 13, 1997, by Elder Richard G. Scott of the Quorum of the Twelve.

Dedication: Oct. 1, 2000, by President Gordon B. Hinckley, 4 sessions.

Dedicatory prayer excerpt: *"We are assembled to dedicate this Thy holy house. It is a special occasion. This temple becomes the 100th operating temple of Thy Church.*

We have looked forward to this occasion. We have prayed for this day. We extend our gratitude to all who have labored so faithfully and diligently, often in the face of serious opposition, to bring to pass the miracle of the completion of this temple.

To us it is indeed a miracle. The ground on which it stands, the circumstances of its preservation for this use, and the decision to build it here — all are miracles unto those who have been a part of this process."

BOUNTIFUL UTAH TEMPLE

Location: In the Bountiful foothills on east bench, 640 S. Bountiful Blvd, Bountiful, Utah. (1650 East.)

Site: 9 acres.

Exterior finish: Bethel white granite.

Temple design: Modern, with single spire.

Architect: Church architectural staff.

Contractor: Okland Construction Co.

Construction adviser: Michael Enfield.

Number of rooms: Four endowment rooms, eight sealing rooms.

Total floor area: 104,000 square feet.

Dimensions: 195 feet by 157 feet; statue of Angel Moroni on top spire; 176 feet high.

District: Central and south Davis County, Utah.

Groundbreaking, site dedication: May 2, 1992, by President Ezra Taft Benson.

Dedication: Jan. 8-14, 1995, by President Howard W. Hunter; 28 sessions.

Dedicatory prayer excerpt: *"May this house provide a spirit of peace to all who observe its majesty, and especially to those who enter for their own sacred ordinances and to perform the work for their loved ones beyond the veil. Let them feel of Thy divine love and mercy. May they be privileged to say, as did the Psalmist of old, 'We took sweet counsel together, and walked unto the house of God in company.' "*

BRISBANE AUSTRALIA TEMPLE

Announced: July 20, 1998. **Status:** Awaiting groundbreaking

BUENOS AIRES ARGENTINA TEMPLE

Location: On southwest outskirts of Buenos Aires; Autopista Richieri y Puente 13, 1778 Ciudad Evita, Buenos Aires, Argentina. Telephone: (011-54-1) 487-1520.

Site: 3 acres.

Exterior finish: Light gray native granite.

Temple design: Modern adaptation of earlier six-spire design.

Dimensions: 178 by 71 feet. Angel Moroni statue is atop tallest spire, 112 feet.

Architects: Church architectural staff; local architect Ramon Paez.

Construction adviser: Gary Holland.

Contractor: Benito Roggio and Sons.

Number of rooms: Four ordinance rooms, three sealing rooms.

Total floor area: 11,980 square feet.

District: Argentina.

Groundbreaking, site dedication: April 20, 1983, by Elder Bruce R. McConkie of the Quorum of the Twelve.

Dedication: Jan. 17-19, 1986, by President Thomas S. Monson; 11 sessions.

Dedicatory prayer excerpt: *"We remember that it was in this very city of Buenos Aires, on Christmas Day in the year 1925, just 60 years ago, that Elder Melvin J. Ballard, an apostle of the Lord, dedicated all of South America for the preaching of the gospel. What a fulfillment to an inspired prayer is evident today."*

CAMPINAS BRAZIL TEMPLE

Announced: April 3, 1997.

Location: Campinas, Brazil.

Site: 6.18 acres.

Exterior finish: Granite, Asa Branca.

Temple design: Classic modern.

Architect: JCL Arquitetos Ltd., and Church A&E Services.

Project manager: Raul Lins.

Contractor: Hochtief do Brazil.

Number of rooms: Four ordinance rooms, three sealing rooms, celestial room, baptistry; 67 total rooms.

Total floor area: 49,100 square feet.

Dimensions: 142 feet by 163 feet.

District: Southern Brazil.

Groundbreaking, site dedication: May 1, 1998, by President James E. Faust of the First Presidency.

Status: Under construction.

CARACAS VENEZUELA TEMPLE

Announced: Sept. 30, 1995.

Location: Caracas, Venezuela.

Site: .5 acre.

Exterior finish: Granite.

Temple design: Classic modern.

Architect: Taller de Arquitectura and Church A&E Services.

Project manager: Duane Cheney.

Contractor: Jahn

Number of rooms: Two ordinance rooms, two sealing rooms, celestial room, baptistry.

Total floor area: 15,327 square feet.

Dimensions: 79 feet by 125 feet.

District: Venezuela.

Groundbreaking, site dedication: Jan. 10, 1999, by Elder Francisco J. Vinas of the Seventy and president of the South America North Area.

Dedication: Aug. 20, 2000, by President Gordon B. Hinckley; 4 sessions.

Dedicatory prayer excerpt: *"We pray for this great nation of Venezuela. May it hold its place among the sovereign nations of the earth. May its people be blessed and prospered. May they enjoy freedom to worship Thee without molestation of any kind. Bless the leaders of the nation with wisdom and understanding, and a great desire to serve the needs of the people."*

CARDSTON ALBERTA TEMPLE

Location: Cardston, about 140 miles south of Calgary in southern Alberta; 348 3rd St. West, Cardston, Alberta. Telephone: (403) 653-3552.

Site: In 1887, eight-acre site laid out and given to the Church by Charles Ora Card. It was then called the Tabernacle Block. In the mid-1950s the area was increased to more than 10 acres.

Exterior finish: White granite quarried near Kootenai Lakes in Nelson, British Columbia. Each stone was hand-hewn at the quarry or temple site. Additions of artificial precast granite.

Temple design: Octagonal design has Grecian massiveness and a Peruvian touch of Aztec influence with pyramid silhouette.

Architects: Hyrum C. Pope and Harold W. Burton of Salt Lake City.

Number of rooms: Approximately 40 in original structure; now 80, including four ordinance, five sealing rooms.

Total floor area: Originally 29,471 square feet, now 89,405 square feet.

Dimensions: 118 feet square, height, 85 feet; footprint now 165 by 311 feet.

District: Central and southern Alberta, southeastern British Columbia, northern Montana.

Groundbreaking, site dedication: July 27, 1913, President Joseph F. Smith dedicated site in the presence of about 1,500 people. Ground broken Nov. 9, 1913, by Daniel Kent Greene of Glenwood, Alberta.

Dedication: Aug. 26-29, 1923, by President Heber J. Grant; 11 sessions. Rededicated after remodeling July 2, 1962, by President Hugh B. Brown of the First Presidency; closed for remodeling May 1988-June 1991; toured by 101,000 people during an open house June 6-15, 1991. Rededicated by President Gordon B. Hinckley June 22-24, 1991; 12 sessions.

Rededicatory prayer excerpt: "*Bless the Latter-day Saints of Canada that they may be good citizens of the nation, men and women of integrity worthy of the respect of the people of this nation, and contributing of their talents and strength to its well-being.*"

CHICAGO ILLINOIS TEMPLE

Location: 20 miles north of Chicago; 4151 West Lake Ave., Glenview, IL.

Site: 13 acres.

Exterior finish: Gray buff marble, gray slate roof.

Temple design: Modern adaptation of earlier six-spire design.

Architects: Church architectural staff; local architect, Wight & Co.

Construction adviser: Virgil Roberts.

Contractor: Pora Construction Co., Des Plaines, Ill., with Utah Construction and Development Co.

Number of rooms: Five ordinance rooms, three sealing rooms.

Total floor area: Originally 17,850 square feet; 37,060 square feet following addition.

Dimensions: 236 feet by 78 feet; seven-foot-tall Angel Moroni statue is atop tallest spire, 112 feet high.

District: Illnois, Iowa, Wisconsin, Indiana, Michigan, South Dakota.

Groundbreaking, site dedication: Aug. 13, 1983, by President Gordon B. Hinckley.

Dedication: Aug. 9-13, 1985, by President Gordon B. Hinckley; 19 sessions.

Dedicatory prayer excerpt: *"We are mindful that thy Prophet Joseph and his brother Hyrum were martyred in Carthage, Ill., at a time of terrible conflict and persecution. May there now be peace and goodwill in the land. Bless the officers of this state and nation that they shall stand firmly for those principles of freedom and equity which were written into the Constitution of the United States under thine inspiration."*

CIUDAD JUAREZ MEXICO TEMPLE

Announced: May 7, 1998.

Location: Paraguay 290, on the corner of Paraguay and Jose Barunda, in Colonia Partido Romero.

Site: 1.64 acres.

Exterior finish: White marble veneer.

Temple design: Classic modern.

Architect: Alvaro Iñigo and Church A&E Services.

Project manager: David Wills.

Contractor: Granay Montero / Jacobsen Construction.

Number of rooms: Two ordinance rooms, two sealing rooms, celestial room, baptistry.

Total floor area: 8,600 square feet.

Dimensions: 84 feet by 150 feet.

District: Serves 36,150 members in 10 stakes and one district.

Groundbreaking, site dedication: Jan. 9, 1999, by Elder Eran A. Call of the Seventy and president of the Mexico North Area.

Dedication: Feb. 26-27, 2000, by President Gordon B. Hinckley; 6 sessions.

Dedicatory prayer excerpt: *"Bless this great nation of Mexico that it may rise and shine among the nations of the earth. Lift the burden of poverty from the backs of the people. Bless the leaders of government that they may welcome Thy servants, and may the message brought by Thy servants take root in the hearts of many souls."*

COCHABAMBA BOLIVIA TEMPLE

Announced: Jan. 13, 1995.

Location: Northern side of Cochabamba at Melchor Urquidi Street 1500.

Site: 6.67 acres.

Exterior finish: Blend of hand-hewn Comanche granite and plaster.

Temple design: Classic modern.

Architects: BSW and Church A&E Services.

Project manager: Javier Mendieta.

Contractor: CBI.

Number of rooms: Two ordinance rooms, three sealing rooms, celestial room, baptistry.

Total floor area: 35,500 square feet.

Dimensions: 137 feet by 102 feet.

District: Bolivia.

Groundbreaking, site dedication: Nov. 10, 1996, by President Gordon B. Hinckley.

Dedicated: April 30, 2000, by President Gordon B. Hinckley; 4 sessions.

Dedicatory prayer excerpt: *"Our hearts are filled with thanksgiving on this historic day when we meet to dedicate this Thy holy house in Bolivia. How thankful we are for it. It is the fulfillment of our dreams, our hopes, our prayers, our faith. Father, it is beautiful to look upon."*

COLONIA JUAREZ CHIHUAHUA MEXICO TEMPLE

Announced: Oct. 4, 1997.

Location: On a hill behind Juarez Academy in Colonia Juearez, Chihuahua, Mexico.

Site: 2.56 acres.

Exterior finish: White marble.

Temple design: Classic modern.

Architects: Alvaro Iñigo and Church A&E Services.

Project manager: David Wills.

Contractor: Jacobsen Construction Co.

Number of rooms: One ordinance room, sone sealing room.

Total floor area: 10.700 square feet.

Dimensions: 102 by 76 feet.

District: Northern Mexico.

Groundbreaking, site dedication: Mar. 7, 1998, by Elder Eran A. Call of the Seventy and president of the Mexico North Area.

Dedication: Mar. 6, 1999, by President Gordon B. Hinckley; 4 sessions.

Dedicatory prayer excerpt: *"It was here in Northern Mexico, that Thou didst reveal the idea and the plan of a smaller temple, complete in every necessary detail, but suited in size to the needs and circumstances of the Church membership in this area of Thy vineyard. That revelation came of a desire and a prayer to help Thy people of these colonies who have been true and loyal during the century and more that they have lived here. They are deserving of this sacred edifice in which to labor for themselves and their forebears."*

COLUMBIA RIVER WASHINGTON TEMPLE

Announced: April 3, 2000 **Status:** Awaiting groundbreaking

COLUMBIA SOUTH CAROLINA TEMPLE

Announced: Sept. 11, 1998.

Location: Corner of Trotter Road and Caughman Road in the southeastern outskirts of Columbia, S.C.

Site: 6.55 acres, including adjoining meetinghouse.

Exterior finish: Imperial Danby Vermont marble.

Temple design: Traditional.

Architects: Mike Watson of Watson-Tate Architects Inc.

Project manager: Bruce Catanzaro.

Contractor: Walbridge Aldinger.

Number of rooms: Celestial room, two ordinance rooms, two sealing rooms and baptistry.

Total floor area: 10,700 square feet.

Dimensions: 144 by 77 feet.

District: South Carolina, North Carolina, Georgia, and Tennessee.

Groundbreaking, site dedication: Dec. 5, 1998, by Elder Gordon T. Watts of the Seventy and first counselor in the North America Southeast Area presidency.

Dedicated: Oct. 16-17, 1999, by President Gordon B. Hinckley; 6 sessions.

Dedicatory prayer excerpt: *"We rejoice in the presence of this house in this great state of South Carolina which has hosted Thy messengers of eternal truth. They have been coming here for generations, and there has been established a great body of faithful Latter-day Saints. We pray that the very presence of this Thy house will have a sanctifying influence upon the people of this area, and particularly upon those who enter its portals."*

COLUMBUS OHIO TEMPLE

Announced: April 25, 1998.

Location: Corner of Wilson and Gateway Blvd., Columbus, Ohio.

Site: 1.35 acre.

Exterior finish: Imperial Danby Vermont marble.

Temple design: Traditional.

Architects: Firestone Jaros Mullin.

Project manager: Bruce Catanzaro.

Contractor: Corna/Kokosing Construction Co.

Number of rooms: Celestial room, baptistry, two ordinance rooms, two sealing rooms.

Total floor area: 10,700 sq. feet.

Dimensions: 144 feet by 77 feet.

District: Northern and central Ohio, western West Virginia.

Groundbreaking, site dedication: Sept. 12, 1998, by Elder John K. Carmack of the Seventy and president of North America East Area.

Dedicated: Sept. 4, 1999, by President Gordon B. Hinckley; 6 sessions.

Dedicatory prayer excerpt: *"We are assembled to dedicate this Thy house. It is now 163 years since a temple was dedicated in the state of Ohio. We are reminded today of the dedication of the Kirtland Temple and of the prayer given on that occasion which Thy prophet declared was revealed unto him.*

We, too, as Saints of this day, seek Thine inspiration in the words which we direct in prayer to Thee, our Father and our God."

COPENHAGEN DENMARK TEMPLE

Announced: March 17, 1999. Status: Meetinghouse being remodeled; Site dedicated April 24, 1999

DALLAS TEXAS TEMPLE

Location: 12 miles north of the downtown area, at 6363 Willow Lane, Dallas, TX.

Site: 6 acres.

Exterior finish: Light-colored marble tile walls, dark gray slate roof.

Temple design: Modern adaptation of earlier six-spire design.

Architects: Church architectural staff, with assistance from West & Humphries of Dallas.

Construction adviser: Virgil Roberts.

Contractor: Comtrol Inc. of Midvale, Utah.

Number of rooms: Five ordinance rooms, three sealing rooms.

Total floor area: Originally 17,850 square feet; 42,383 square feet following addition.

Dimensions: 236 by 78 feet; tower, 95 feet; statue of Angel Moroni on top spire.

District: Texas and Louisiana and parts of Arkansas.

Groundbreaking, site dedication: Jan. 22, 1983, by President Gordon B. Hinckley.

Dedication: Oct. 19-24, 1984, by President Gordon B. Hinckley; 23 sessions.

Dedicatory prayer excerpt: *"May this beautiful temple, standing in this community, become a declaration to all who shall look upon it of the faith of thy Saints in the revealed things of eternity, and may they be led to respect that which is sacred unto us, thy people."*

DENVER COLORADO TEMPLE

Location: In Littleton, a suburban community in Arapahoe County, about 20 miles south of Denver, at County Line Road and South University Boulevard; 2001 E. Phillips Circle, Littleton, CO.

Site: 7.5 acres.

Exterior finish: Modern design; precast stone walls and built-up roof.

Dimensions: 187 by 160 feet; single 90-foot spire capped with statue of Angel Moroni.

Temple design: Modern.

Architects: Church architectural staff.

Supervising architect: Local architect, Bobby R. Thomas.

Construction adviser: Michael Enfield.

Contractor: Langley Constructors.

Number of rooms: Four ordinance rooms, six sealing rooms.

Total floor area: 29,117 square feet.

District: Colorado, eastern Wyoming, Nebraska, western South Dakota and part of Kansas.

Groundbreaking, site dedication: May 19, 1984, by President Gordon B. Hinckley.

Dedication: Oct. 24-28, 1986, by President

Ezra Taft Benson; 18 sessions.

Dedicatory prayer excerpt: *"Touch the hearts of Thy people that they may look to this temple as a refuge from the evil and turmoil of the world. May they ever live worthy of the blessings here to be found. May they be prompted to seek the records of their forebears and to serve here in their behalf, under that plan which thou hast revealed for the salvation and exaltation of Thy children of all generations."*

DETROIT MICHIGAN TEMPLE

Announced: Aug. 10, 1998.

Location: 425 N. Woodward Ave., in Bloomfield Hills, Mich.

Site: 6.34 acres, including adjoining meetinghouse.

Exterior finish: Imperial Danby Vermont marble.

Temple design: Traditional.

Architect: John Coakley of Bernath—Bernath-Coakley Associates.

Project manager: Bruce Catanzaro.

Contractor: Walbridge-Aldinger.

Number of rooms: Celestial room, baptistry, two ordinance, two sealing.

Total floor area: 10,700 square feet.

Dimensions: 144 feet by 77 feet.

District: Michigan.

Groundbreaking, site dedication: Oct. 10, 1998, by Elder Jay E. Jensen of the First Quorum of the Seventy and president of the North America Northeast Area.

Dedication: Oct. 23, 1999, by President Gordon B. Hinckley; 6 sessions.

Dedicatory prayer excerpt: *"May the work that will go forward in this sacred edifice please Thee and bring untold blessings to Thy sons and daughters on both sides of the veil. May the sacred covenants entered into in Thy house become an eternal binding element between Thee and Thy children."*

EDMONTON ALBERTA TEMPLE

Announced: Aug. 11, 1998.

Location: 14325 53rd Ave., Edmonton, Alberta.

Site: 1 acre, temple only.

Exterior finish: Light gray granite quarried in Quebec.

Temple design: Classic modern.

Architect: Robert Bennett of Bennett Architect, Inc. and Church A&E Services.

Project manager: Cory Karl.

Contractor: Binder Construction Limited.

Number of rooms: 2 ordinance rooms, 2 sealing rooms.

Total floor area: 10,700 square feet.

Dimensions: 144 by 77 feet.

District: Northern Alberta and northwest territories.

Groundbreaking, site dedication: Feb. 27, 1999, by Elder Yoshihiko Kikuchi of the Seventy and second counselor in the North America Central Area presidency.

Dedication: Dec. 11-12, 1999, by President Gordon B. Hinckley; 7 sessions.

Dedicatory prayer excerpt: *"Let Thy providence be felt in this great nation of Canada that it shall continue to be a land where Thy sons and daughters enjoy the precious boon of freedom of assembly and worship. Bless those who govern that they shall look with favor upon Thy people, and may Thy work grow in numbers, in majesty, and in strength in this good land."*

FRANKFURT GERMANY TEMPLE

Location: In the center of Friedrichsdorf, a small town nine miles north of Frankfurt; Talstrasse #10, D-61381 Friedrichsdorf/TS, Germany.

Site: 5.2 acres.

Exterior finish: White granite, copper roof.

Architects: Church architectural staff; local architect, Borchers-Metzner-Kramer; project architect, Hanno Luschin.

Construction adviser: Henry Haurand.

Contractor: Hochtief AG.

Number of rooms: Four ordinance rooms, five sealing rooms.

Total floor area: 24,757 square feet.

Dimensions: 93 feet by 232 feet; statue of Angel Moroni on top spire, 82 feet high.

District: Belgium, the Netherlands, Luxembourg, northern France, much of Germany, and a small part of Austria.

Groundbreaking, site dedication: July 1, 1985, by President Gordon B. Hinckley.

Dedication: Aug. 28-30, 1987, by President Ezra Taft Benson; 11 sessions.

Dedicatory prayer excerpt: *"The presence of this house, on the soil of this nation, is an answer to the prayers of thy people."*

FREIBERG GERMANY TEMPLE

Location: In Freiberg, about 120 miles south of Berlin; Hainchener Strasse 64, 009599 Freiberg, Germany.

Site: 1 acre.

Exterior finish: Exterior white German stucco over 24-inch thick brick walls, blue gray slate stone slab roof.

Temple design: Modern design with German influence; two high arches, reminicent of Gothic style, are parallel with front of building and bisected by two similar arches to form a single spire.

Architect: Emil B. Fetzer.

Government construction adviser: Dr. Dieter Hantzche, architect director of Bauakademie of Dresden.

Number of rooms: One ordinance room, two sealing rooms.

Total floor area: 7,840 square feet.

Dimensions: 98 feet by 98 feet.

District: Eastern Germany and most of eastern Europe.

Groundbreaking, site dedication: April 23, 1983, by Elder Thomas S. Monson of the Quorum of the Twelve.

Dedication: June 20-30, 1985, by President Gordon B. Hinckley; 7 sessions.

Dedicatory prayer excerpt: *"On this day of dedication our hearts turn to Thee. We thank Thee for this holy temple in this land and nation. We thank Thee for all who have made possible its building — the officers of the government who have given encouragement and made available land and materials, the architects and the builders, and all who have made possible this glorious day of dedication."*

FRESNO CALIFORNIA TEMPLE

Announced: Jan. 8, 1999.

Location: Northwest Fresno at 6290 N. Valentine, near intersection of Valentine and Sierra avenues.

Site: 2.34 acres.

Exterior finish: Sierra white granite

Temple design: Traditional.

Architects: Paul Stommel.

Project manager: Amos and Gloria Wright.

Contractor: Jacobsen Construction Co.

Number of rooms: Celestial room, baptistry, two ordinance rooms, two sealing rooms.

Total floor area: 10,850 square feet.

Dimensions: 144 feet by 77 feet.

District: Serves 27,000 members in eight stakes.

Groundbreaking, site dedication: March 20, 1999, by Elder John B. Dickson of the Seventy and president of the North America West Area.

Dedicated: April 9, 2000, by President Gordon B. Hinckley; 4 sessions.

Dedicatory prayer excerpt: *"May the work in this house unlock the prison doors beyond the veil that those who there receive the gospel may rejoice in the vicarious work performed here in their behalf."*

FUKUOKA JAPAN TEMPLE

Announced: May 7, 1998.

Location: 47-2 Hiral Josui, Machi, Chao-Ku, Fukuoka, Japan.

Site: 1.25 acres.

Exterior finish: Two granites: Empress White and Majestic Grey granite from China.

Temple design: Traditiional.

Architect: Kanji Moriya and Church A&E Services.

Project manager: Jerry Sears.

Contractor: Taisei Construction Co.

Number of rooms: Celestial room, two endowment rooms, two sealing rooms and a baptistry.

Total floor area: 10,800 square feet.

Dimensions: 144 feet by 77 feet.

District: Fukuoka, Hiroshima, Kumamoto, Okayama stakes and Kagoshima, Matsuyama, Nagasaki, Takamatsu and Yamaguchi districts.

Groundbreaking, site dedication: March 20, 1999, by Elder L. Lionel Kendrick of the Seventy and president of the Asia North Area.

Dedication: June 11, 2000, by President Gordon B. Hinckley; 4 sessions.

Dedicatory prayer excerpt: *"Bless Thy Saints of this great nation. Magnify them, inspire them, bless them among the millions of this land that by the virtue of their lives they may stand as a city upon a hill whose light cannot be hid. Prosper them in their labors. May they never lack for food upon their tables or clothing on their backs or a shelter over their heads."*

GUADALAJARA MEXICO TEMPLE

Announced: April 14, 1999. **Groundbreaking:** June 12, 1999.

GUATEMALA CITY GUATEMALA TEMPLE

Location: At the base of hills in southeastern Guatemala City; 24 Avenida 2-20, Zona 15, Vista Hermosa 1, Guatemala City, Guatemala.

Site: About 1.4 acres.

Exterior finish: Natural white Guatemala marble.

Temple design: Modern adaptation of earlier six-spire design.

Architects: Church archectural staff, assisted by Jose Asturias, Guatemala City.

Construction adviser: David Judd.

Contractor: Isa Constructors Aires Y Cia Ltd.

Number of rooms: Four ordinance rooms, three sealing rooms.

Total floor area: 11,610 square feet.

Dimensions: 178 feet by 72 feet, six spires; statue of Angel Moroni tops 126-foot spire.

District: Guatemala, Nicaragua, El Salvador, Honduras, Belize.

Groundbreaking, site dedication: Sept. 12, 1982, by Elder Richard G. Scott of the First Quorum of the Seventy.

Dedication: Dec. 14-16, 1984, by President Gordon B. Hinckley; 10 sessions.

Dedicatory prayer excerpt: *Bless our land, O Father, this nation of Guatemala where stands thy holy house. May those who govern do so in righteousness. . . . Bless them as they act to preserve the liberties . . . and enhance the prosperity of the people. May there be peace in the land."*

GUAYAQUIL ECUADOR TEMPLE

Announced: March 31, 1982.

Location: El Principado de Las Lomas de Urdesa North in Guayaquil.

Site: 6.2 acres.

Exterior finish: Granite (Asa Branca).

Temple design: Classic modern.

Architects: Rafael Velez Calisto, Architects & Consultants and Church A&E Services.

Project manager: Roger Sears.

Contractor: Inmomariuxi.

Number of rooms: Celestial room, baptistry, four ordinance rooms, three sealing rooms.

Total floor area: 45,000 square feet.

Dimensions: 154 feet by 76 feet.

District: Ecuador, 32 stakes.

Groundbreaking, site dedication: Aug. 10, 1996, by Elder Richard G. Scott of the Quorum of the Twelve.

Dedicated: Aug. 1, 1999, by President Gordon B. Hinckley; 8 sessions.

Dedicatory prayer excerpt: *"We thank Thee for the inspiration given Thy servant in selecting this property on which to construct this sacred building. Thy guiding hand was evident in the circumstances when this site was found and determined upon."*

HALIFAX NOVA SCOTIA TEMPLE

Announced: May 7, 1998.

Location: Near intersection of Cole Harbour Road and Cumberland Dr., in Dartmouth.

Site: 2 acres.

Exterior finish: White Bethel Granite.

Temple design: Classic modern.

Architects: L.A. Beaubien and Associates, and Church A&E Services.

Project manager: William Treu.

Contractor: Dineen Construction.

Number of rooms: Two ordinance rooms, two sealing rooms; celestial room and bap-

tistry; 44 total rooms.

Total floor area: 10,850 square feet.

Dimensions of building: 144 by 77 feet.

District: Nova Scotia, New Brunswick, New Glasgow District and Newfoundland.

Groundbreaking, site dedication: Oct. 12, 1998, by Elder Jay E. Jensen of the Seventy.

Dedication: Nov. 14, 1999, by President Gordon B. Hinckley; 3 sessions.

Dedicatory prayer excerpt: *"We dedicate the ground which surrounds this temple and upon which it stands. In the season of summer it will be beautiful with Thy wondrous*

HAMILTON NEW ZEALAND TEMPLE

Location: At site of Church College of New Zealand in Temple View, outside of Hamilton, New Zealand. Private Bag 3003, Hamilton, New Zealand.

Site: Temple site and college grounds, 86 acres.

Exterior finish: Reinforced concrete block, manufactured at site, structural steel; painted white.

Temple design: Modern-contemporary.

Architect: Edward O. Anderson, Church architect.

Construction chairman: Wendell B. Mendenhall.

Construction supervisor: E. Albert Rosenvall and George R. Biesinger.

Number of rooms: One ordinance room, three sealing rooms.

Total floor area: 34,000 square feet.

Dimensions: 159 feet by 84 feet; total height of tower, 215 feet above highway, 157 feet above ground line.

District: New Zealand and nearby South Pacific islands.

Groundbreaking, site dedication: Dec. 21, 1955. First sod turned by Ariel Ballif, Wendell B. Mendenhall, and George R. Biesinger.

Dedication: April 20, 1958, by President David O. McKay.

Dedicatory prayer excerpt: *"We invoke Thy blessing particularly upon the men and women who have so willingly and generously contributed their means, time and effort to the completion of this imposing and impressive structure. Especially we mention all those who have accepted calls as labor missionaries and literally consecrated their all upon the altar of service."*

HELSINKI FINLAND TEMPLE

Announced: April 3, 2000 **Status:** Awaiting groundbreaking

HERMOSILLO SONORA MEXICO TEMPLE

Announced: July 20, 1998.

Location: Garcia Conde y Juan Jose Rios in Colonia Pitic.

Site: 1.54 acres, including adjoining meetinghouse.

Exterior finish: White marble veneer.

Temple design: Classic modern.

Architect: Alvaro Iñigo and Church A&E Services.

Project manager: David Wills.

Contractor: Grana y Montero / Jacobsen Construction Co.

Number of rooms: Two ordinance rooms, two sealing rooms, celestial room, baptistry.

Total floor area: 12,469 square feet.

Dimensions of building: 84 feet by 150 feet.

District: Serves 46,200 members in 11 stakes and six districts.

Groundbreaking, site dedication: Dec. 5, 1998, by Elder Eran A. Call of the Seventy and counselor in the Mexico South Area presidency.

Dedication: Feb. 27, 2000, by President Gordon B. Hinckley, 4 sessions.

Dedicatory prayer excerpt: *"May [this temple] be a structure of beauty, a crowning gem in this great city. We are grateful that the officials of government have permitted its construction, and that it is now completed and ready to be presented to Thee."*

HONG KONG CHINA TEMPLE

Location: Cornwall Street, Kowloon Tong on the Kowloon Peninsula. 2 & 4a Cornwall St., Kowloon Tong, Kowloon, Hong Kong.

Announced: Oct. 3, 1992.

Site: .3 acres.

Exterior finish: Polished granite.

Temple design: Hong Kong colonial.

Architects: Liang Peddle Thorpe Architects.

Number of rooms: 2 ordinance rooms, two sealing rooms.

Total floor area: 22,600 square feet.

Dimensions of building: 70 feet by 92 feet; statue of Angel Moroni is 135 feet above main floor.

District: Hong Kong and Macau.

Groundbreaking, site dedication: Jan. 22, 1994 by Elder John K. Carmack of the First Quorum of the Seventy and Asia Area president.

Dedication: May 26-27, 1996; by President Gordon B. Hinckley; 7 sessions.

Dedicatory prayer excerpt: *"Thy Church in this area now comes to full maturity with the dedication of this sacred temple. We pray that this harvest of souls may continue, that in the future as in the present, thy people may be free and secure in their worship and that none shall hinder the service of missionaries called to this area. We pray that Thy work may grow and prosper in the great Chinese realm, and may those who govern be ever receptive to those called and sent as messengers of revealed truth."*

HOUSTON TEXAS TEMPLE

Announced: Sept. 30, 1997.

Location: 11725 Champions Forrest Drive, Klein, Tx.

Site: 11 acres.

Exterior finish: Cast stone / granite.

Temple design: Classic modern.

Architect: Spencer Partnership Architects and Church A&E Services.

Project manager: Leon Rowley.

Contractor: SpawGlass Const.

Number of rooms: Two endowment rooms, three sealing rooms, celestial room, baptistry.

Total floor area: 35,345 square feet.

Dimensions of building: 145 feet by 133 feet.

District: Portions of Texas, Louisana

Groundbreaking, site dedication: June 13, 1998, by Elder Lynn A. Mickelsen of the Seventy and president of the North America Southwest Area.

Dedication: Aug. 26-27, 2000, by President Gordon B. Hinckley; 8 sessions.

Dedicatory prayer excerpt: *"How glorious and complete is Thy plan for the salvation and exaltation of Thy children of all generations. How tremendous is our obligation to carry forward this great vicarious work in their behalf. . . ."*

IDAHO FALLS IDAHO TEMPLE

Location: In northwestern Idaho Falls on the banks of the Snake River; 1000 Memorial Drive, Idaho Falls, ID.

Site: 7 acres.

Exterior finish: Built of reinforced concrete. A mixture of white quartz aggregate and white cement called cast stone covers the 16-inch thick exterior walls in slabs two inches thick.

Temple design: Modern-contemporary.

Architects: Church board of temple architects: Edward O. Anderson, Georgius Y. Cannon, Ramm Hansen, John Fetzer, Hyrum C. Pope, Lorenzo S. Young.

Construction adviser: Arthur Price.

Contractor: Birdwell Finlayson of Pocatello, Idaho.

Number of rooms: 1 ordinance room, 9 sealing rooms; total of 38 rooms in original plans.

Total floor area: 86,972 square feet.

Dimensions: 175 feet by 190 feet; tower 148 feet high. Two annexes added 7,700 square feet. A 12-foot statue of Angel Moroni was added to the tower Sept. 5, 1983.

District: Eastern Idaho, western Wyoming.

Groundbreaking, site dedication: Dec. 19, 1939, ground broken by David Smith, North Idaho Falls Stake president. Site dedicated Oct. 19, 1940, by President David O. McKay of the First Presidency.

Dedication: Sept. 23-25, 1945, by President George Albert Smith.

Dedicatory prayer excerpt: *"We pray that Thou wilt accept this temple as a freewill offering from Thy children, that it will be sacred unto thee."*

JOHANNESBURG SOUTH AFRICA TEMPLE

Location: 2 miles north of city center; 7 Jubilee Rd., Parktown, Johannesburg, 2193, South Africa.

Site: One acre.

Exterior finish: Masonry exterior.

Temple design: Modern adaptation of earlier six-spire design.

Architects: Church architectural staff; local architect, Halford & Halford.

Construction adviser: Stanley G. Smith.

Contractor: Tiber Bonvac.

Number of rooms: Four ordinance rooms, three sealing rooms.

Total floor area: 13,025 square feet.

Dimensions: 178 feet by 71 feet; Angel Moroni statue is atop tallest spire at 112 feet.

District: Africa south of the Sahara.

Groundbreaking, site dedication: Nov. 27, 1982, by Elder Marvin J. Ashton of the Council of the Twelve.

Dedication: Aug. 24-25, 1985, by President

Gordon B. Hinckley; 4 sessions.

Dedicatory prayer excerpt: *"Almighty God, wilt thou overrule for the blessing and safety of Thy faithful Saints. We pray for peace in this troubled land. Bless this nation which has befriended Thy servants. May those who rule in the offices of government be inspired to find a basis for reconciliation among those who now are in conflict one with another. May the presence of Thy house on the soil of this land bring blessings to the entire nation."*

JORDAN RIVER UTAH TEMPLE

Location: About 15 miles south of Salt Lake City in South Jordan, Utah, 10200 South 1300 West, South Jordan, UT.

Site: 15 acres, announced Feb. 3, 1978, by the First Presidency.

Exterior finish: Cast stone containing white marble chips. Tower appears same as the rest of the building, but in order to reduce weight it contains fiberglass in a product called cemlite.

Temple design: Modern.

Architect: Emil B. Fetzer, Church architect.

Resident project inspector: Jerry Sears.

Construction superintendent: Lawrence O. Dansie for Layton Construction Co.

Number of rooms: Six ordinance rooms, 17 sealing rooms.

Total floor area: 153,641 square feet.

Dimensions: Basement and main floor, 211 by 218 feet; two upper levels, 140 by 166 feet. Height to square is 58 feet, to top of tower, 199 1/2 feet. Tower topped with a 20-foot figure of the Angel Moroni.

District: Southern Salt Lake County, Utah.

Groundbreaking, site dedication: June 9, 1979, by President Spencer W. Kimball.

Dedication: Nov. 16-20, 1981, by President Marion G. Romney; 15 sessions.

Dedicatory prayer excerpt: *"May all who enter have clean hands and pure hearts, and may they participate with faith in the ordinances to be given herein."*

KIRTLAND TEMPLE*

*No longer in use by the Church.

Location: Kirtland, Ohio, 25 miles east of Cleveland, on a hill west of the Chagrin River.

Site: Selected March 1833; deed recorded Aug. 4, 1834.

Exterior finish: Sandstone covered with stuccoed plaster.

Temple design: Adaptation of Federal Georgian and New England Colonial.

Architect: Joseph Smith.

Building committee: Hyrum Smith, Reynolds Cahoon and Jared Carter.

Master builder: Artemis Millett.

Number of rooms: Originally 15.

Total floor area: Approximately 15,000 square feet.

Dimensions: 79 feet by 59 feet; walls 50 feet high; tower height above ground, 110 feet.

Start of work: Hauling of sandstone to site began June 5, 1833.

Cornerstones: July 23, 1833.

Dedication: March 27, 1836, by President Joseph Smith.

Dedicatory prayer excerpt: *"And we ask Thee, Holy Father, that Thy servants may go forth from this house, armed with thy power and that thy name may be upon them. . . ."*

KIEV UKRAINE TEMPLE

Announced: July 20, 1998. **Status:** Awaiting groundbreaking.

KONA HAWAII TEMPLE

Announced: May 7, 1998.

Location: 75-230 Kalani Road, Kailua-Kona, Hawaii.

Site: 7.02 acres, including adjoining meetinghouse.

Exterior finish: White marble veneer.

Temple design: Traditional.

Architect: Jon Pharis of Pharis & Associates.

Project manager: Jerry Sears.

Contractor: Bud Bailey Construction.

Number of rooms: Celestial room, baptistry, two ordinance rooms, two sealing rooms.

Total floor area: 10,700 square feet.

Dimensions: 144 by 77 feet.

District: Serves more than 11,000 members in the Kona and Hilo Hawaii stakes, and the Kahului Hawaii Stake, with members on the islands of Maui, Molokai and Lanai.

Groundbreaking, site dedication: Mar. 13, 1999, by Elder John B. Dickson of the Seventy and president of the North America West Area.

Dedication: Jan. 23, 2000, by President Gordon B. Hinckley; 4 sessions.

Dedicatory prayer excerpt: *"Now we have this second temple, here on the big island. May the work increase. May there come into the hearts of the people a growing desire to come to the House of the Lord, here to taste the sweet refreshment of the Holy Spirit."*

LAIE HAWAII TEMPLE

Location: In Laie, on the northeast side of the island of Oahu, formerly a 6,000-acre plantation purchased by the Church in 1865, 32 miles from Honolulu.

Site: 11.4 acres, a portion of original property purchased by Church.

Exterior finish: Built of concrete made of the crushed lava rock of the area, reinforced with steel. After hardening, it was dressed on the exterior by pneumatic stone cutting tools that produced a white cream finish.

Temple design: The first of three temples built with no tower; shaped like a Grecian cross and suggestive of the ancient temples found in South America.

Architects: Hyrum C. Pope and Harold W. Burton.

General superintendent: Samuel E. Woolley. Much of the work on this temple was done by the Polynesian Saints.

Number of rooms: Three ordinance rooms, six sealing rooms; total rooms after remodeling, 163.

Total floor area: 10,500 square feet originally; approximately 40,971 square feet after remodeling.

Dimensions of building: 140 feet by 282 feet, rising to a height of 50 feet above the upper terrace. Very similar "cubical contents" as ancient temple of Solomon.

District: Oahu and some central islands.

Groundbreaking, site dedication: June 1,

1915, site dedicated by Pres. Joseph F. Smith.

Dedication: Thanksgiving Day, Nov. 27, 1919, by President Heber J. Grant.

Rededicated June 13-15, 1978, by President Spencer W. Kimball after extensive remodeling; nine sessions.

Dedicatory prayer excerpt: *"May all who come upon the grounds which surround this temple, in the years to come, whether members of the Church or not, feel the sweet and peaceful influence of this blessed hallowed spot."*

LAS VEGAS NEVADA TEMPLE

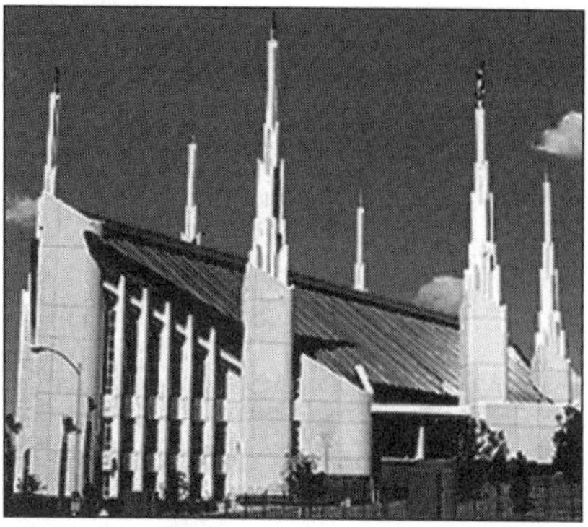

Location: On the east side of Las Vegas at edge of a residential area on the slope of Frenchman Mountain, 827 Temple View Drive, Las Vegas, NV.

Site: 10.3 acres; announced April 7, 1984.

Exterior finish: White precast stone walls and copper roof and detailing.

Temple design: Six spires

Architects: Tate & Snyder.

Construction adviser: Gary Holland

Contractor: Hogan & Tingey.

Number of rooms: Four ordinance rooms, six sealing rooms.

Total floor area: 80,900 square feet.

Dimensions: 260 feet by 127 feet; statue of Angel Moroni on top spire, 119 feet.

District: Southern Nevada, parts of Arizona and California.

Groundbreaking, site dedication: Nov. 30, 1985, by President Gordon B. Hinckley.

Dedication: Dec. 16-18, 1989, by President Gordon B. Hinckley; 11 sessions.

Dedicatory prayer excerpt: *"Within its walls are to be tasted the refreshing waters of living and eternal truth. For all who enter the portals of Thy house may this be an oasis of peace and life and light, in contrast with the clamor and evil and darkness of the world."*

LIMA PERU TEMPLE

Location: Southwest part of Lima, in the Molina district; Avenida Javier Prado Este y Av. Los Ingenieros, La Molina, Lima, Peru.

Site: 4.5 acres.

Exterior finish: Local granite, Oriental design.

Temple design: Modern adaptation of earlier six-spire design.

Dimensions: 178 by 71 feet. Angel Moroni statue is atop tallest spire at 112 feet.

Architects: Church architectural staff; local architect Jose Asturias.

Construction adviser: Sergio Gomez.

Number of rooms: Four ordinance rooms, three sealing rooms.

Total floor area: 10,052 square feet.

District: Peru.

Groundbreaking, site dedication: Sept. 11, 1982, by Elder Boyd K. Packer of the Quorum of the Twelve.

Dedication: Jan. 10-12, 1986, by President Gordon B. Hinckley; 11 sessions.

Dedicatory prayer excerpt: *"We are particularly mindful this day of the sons and daughters of Lehi. They have known so much of suffering and sorrow in their many generations. They have walked in darkness and in servitude. Now thou hast touched them by the light of the everlasting gospel. The shackles of darkness are falling from their eyes as they embrace the truths of thy great work."*

LOGAN UTAH TEMPLE

Location: On eastern bench overlooking Cache Valley; 175 N. 300 East, Logan, UT.

Site: 9 acres, selected by Brigham Young, May 15, 1877.

Exterior finish: Dark-colored, siliceous limestone, extremely hard and compact in texture, was used for the major portion of the temple. Buff-colored limestone, more easily carved, was used wherever intricate shaping was necessary.

Temple design: Castellated style.

Architect: Truman O. Angell.

Construction heads: Superintendent of construction, Charles O. Card; master mason, John Parry; plastering foreman, William Davis. Labor needs met by 25,000 people who worked on Logan Temple.

Number of rooms: Four ordinance rooms, 11 sealing rooms; five stories.

Total floor area: Originally 59,130 square feet; 115,507 square feet after remodeling.

Dimensions : 171 feet by 95 feet; 86 feet high. The east tower is 170 feet high; west tower, 165 feet high; four octagonal towers, each 100 feet high.

District: Northern Utah, southeastern Idaho.

Groundbreaking, site dedication: May 17, 1877; site dedicated by Elder Orson Pratt, ground broken by President John W. Young of the First Presidency.

Dedication: May 17-19, 1884, by President John Taylor; 3 sessions.

On March 13-15, 1979, after extensive remodeling, the temple was rededicated by President Spencer W. Kimball; 9 sessions.

Dedicatory prayer excerpt: *"We ask that in this house a more full knowledge of thee and Thy laws may be developed.... And, as all wisdom dwells with thee, and, as all light, truth and intelligence ... we humbly seek unto thee for thy learning under Thy guidance, direction and inspiration."*

LONDON ENGLAND TEMPLE

Location: 25 miles south of London, formerly an Elizabethan farm; Newchapel, Nr. Lingfield, Surrey, England.

Site: In June 1952, President David O. McKay and Elder Stayner Richards, president of the British Mission, selected site at Newchapel. Purchased several months later in 1953; 32 acres.

Exterior finish: Reinforced concrete and structural steel skeleton, walls of brick masonry faced with cut Portland limestone, white in color. Spire sheathed in lead-coated copper.

Temple design: Modern-contemporary.

Architect: Edward O. Anderson, Church architect.

Supervising architects: T.T. Bennett and Son, London.

Contractor: Kirk and Kirk, Ltd., London.

Number of rooms: four ordinance rooms, seven sealing rooms.

Total floor area: Originally 34,000 square feet; now 42,652 square feet.

Dimensions: 84 feet wide, 159 feet long, 56 feet to the square. The tower rises 156 feet 91/2 inches from ground level, spire 33 feet above that.

District: 20 stakes in England and two in Wales.

Groundbreaking, site dedication: Aug. 10, 1953; site dedicated by David O. McKay, who broke ground on Aug. 27, 1955.

Dedication: Sept. 7-9, 1958, by President David O. McKay; 6 sessions. Rededicated Oct. 18-20, 1992, by President Gordon B. Hinckley; 10 sessions.

Dedicatory prayer excerpt: *"With humility and deep gratitude we acknowledge Thy nearness, Thy divine guidance and inspiration. Help us, we pray Thee, to become even more susceptible in our spiritual response to Thee.*

"Temples are built to Thy holy name as a means of uniting Thy people, living and dead, in bonds of faith, of peace and of love throughout eternity."

LOS ANGELES CALIFORNIA TEMPLE

Location: Atop a hill near Westwood Village, two miles west of Beverly Hills, 10777 Santa Monica Blvd., Los Angeles, CA.

Site: On 13 of the original 24.23 acres purchased from the Harold Lloyd Motion Picture Company on March 23, 1937, by President Heber J. Grant.

Exterior finish: The exterior is covered with 146,000 square feet of Mo-Sai stone facing, a mixture of crushed quartz and white Portland cement quarried in Utah and Nevada. Wainscot around exterior is Rockville granite from Minnesota.

Temple design: Modern.

Architect: Edward O. Anderson, Church architect. (Millard F. Malin, sculptor of 15-foot statue of Angel Moroni on spire.)

Superintendent: Vern Loder.

Contractor: Soren N. Jacobsen.

Number of rooms: Four ordinance rooms, 10 sealing rooms.

Total floor area: 190,614 square feet, or approximately 4.5 acres.

Dimensions: 364 feet by 241 feet; overall height is 257 feet 1 1/2 inches.

District: Southern California.

Groundbreaking, site dedication: Sept. 22, 1951, by President David O. McKay.

Dedication: March 11-14, 1956, by President David O. McKay; 8 sessions.

Dedicatory prayer excerpt: *"May all who come within these sacred walls feel a peaceful, hallowed influence. Cause, O Lord, that even people who pass the grounds, or view the temple from afar, may lift their eyes from the groveling things of sordid life and look up to Thee and Thy providence."*

LOUISVILLE KENTUCKY TEMPLE

Announced: March 17, 1999.

Location: 7114 West Highway 22, Pewee Valley, Ky.

Site: 3 acres, including adjoining meetinghouse.

Exterior finish: Danby Vermont marble.

Temple design: Traditional.

Architects: Firestone Jaros Mullin — Mike Karpinski Architect.

Project manager: Bruce Catanzaro.

Contractor: Corna/Kokosing Construction Co.

Number of Rooms: Celestial room, baptistry, two ordinance rooms, two sealing rooms.

Total floor area: 10,700 square feet.

Dimensions: 144 feet by 77 feet.

District: Serves 36,500 members in 10 stakes.

Groundbreaking, site dedication: May 29, 1999, by Elder John K. Carmack of the Seventy and president of the North America East Area.

Dedicated: March 19, 2000, by President Thomas S. Monson first counselor in the First Presidency; 4 sessions.

Dedicatory prayer excerpt: *"May those in the life beyond who are helpless to move forward rejoice in the completion of this sacred building."*

LUBBOCK TEXAS TEMPLE

Announced: April 3, 2000 **Status:** Awaiting groundbreaking

MADRID SPAIN TEMPLE

Announced: Country announced at general conference on April 4, 1993, by President Gordon B. Hinckley; city announced at groundbreaking of Mt. Timpanogos Utah Temple on Oct. 9, 1994.

Location: Barrio of Moratalez, corner of Hacienda DePauches and Valdebernando.

Site: 3.5 acres.

Exterior finish: Camaro Marble from Italy.

Temple design: Modern Classic.

Architects: Arquitechior Langdon, SA.

Project manager: Ralph Cluff.

Contractor: JOSTSA Construction Co.

Number of rooms: Four ordinance; four sealing.

Total floor area: 45,800 square feet.

Dimensions of building: 116 feet by 138 feet.

District: Spain, Portugal.

Groundbreaking, site dedication: June 11, 1996, by President Gordon B. Hinckley.

Dedication: March 19-21, 1999, by President Gordon B. Hinckley; 10 sessions.

Dedicatory prayer excerpt: *"We thank thee for this great kingdom of Spain which has been hospitable to Thy Saints. Bless this land. We are mindful that it was from these shores that Columbus sailed to discover America as foretold in the Book of Mormon."*

MANILA PHILIPPINES TEMPLE

Location: In Quezon City; 13 Temple Drive, Greenmeadows Subdivision, Quezon City, Metro Manila, Philippines.

Site: About 3.5 acres.

Exterior finish: Ceramic tile.

Temple design: Modern adaptation of earlier six-spire design.

Architect: Church architectural staff, with assistance from Felipe M. Mendoza & Partners, Manila.

Construction adviser: Wayne Tuttle.

Contractor: A. C. K. Construction of Manila.

Number of rooms: Four ordinance rooms, three sealing rooms.

Total floor area: 19,388 square feet.

Dimensions of building: 200 feet by 75 feet, six spires; tallest is 115 feet high, including statue of Angel Moroni.

District: Philippines, Micronesia, Indonesia, Singapore, Thailand, India, and part of Burma.

Groundbreaking, site dedication: Aug. 25, 1982, by President Gordon B. Hinckley. Despite the threat of a typhoon, 2,000 members attended groundbreaking.

Dedication: Sept. 25-27, 1984, by President Gordon B. Hinckley; 9 sessions.

Dedicatory prayer excerpt: *"Lift the blight of poverty from which so many suffer. Particularly bless thy faithful Saints who live honestly with Thee in the payment of their tithes and offerings. Bless them that neither they nor their generations after them will go hungry, nor naked, nor without shelter from the storms that beat about them.*

"We thank Thee for this beautiful edifice and for all who have worked to make it possible. May it stand as a pillar of truth and as an invitation to all who look upon it to learn of the purposes for which it has been created."

MANTI UTAH TEMPLE

Location: Hill above U.S. Highway 89 in Sanpete Valley in Manti, Utah, 120 miles south of Salt Lake City; Temple Hill, Manti, UT.

Site: 27 acres. "Manti Stone Quarry" had been prophesied as site for a temple since area's settlement in 1849. President Brigham Young on June 25, 1875, announced the temple would be built there. It then became known as "Temple Hill."

Exterior finish: Fine-textured, cream-colored oolite limestone obtained from quarries in hill upon which it is built.

Temple design: The castellated style reflecting influence of Gothic Revival, French Renaissance Revival, French Second Empire and colonial architecture.

Architect: William H. Folsom.

Construction heads: William H. Folsom from Oct. 15, 1877, to Aug. 7, 1888, when Daniel H. Wells took his place as supervisor; master mason, Edward L. Parry.

Number of rooms: Four floors including basement, one ordinance room and eight sealing rooms.

Total floor area: 86,809 square feet.

Dimensions of building: 171 feet by 95 feet; 86 feet high. The east tower is 179 feet high, west tower 169 feet high, building at ground level 60 feet above highway below.

District: Central Utah.

Groundbreaking, site dedication: April 25, 1877, by President Brigham Young.

Dedication: May 17, 1888, private dedication held; dedicated by President Wilford Woodruff. Three public dedicatory services held May 21-23, 1888; Elder Lorenzo Snow, then of the Quorum of the Twelve, read prayer.

Rededicated June 14-16, 1985, by President Gordon B. Hinckley; 9 sessions.

Dedicatory prayer excerpt: *"May this holy temple be to them as one of the gates of heaven, opening into the straight and narrow path that leads to endless lives and eternal dominion."*

MEDFORD OREGON TEMPLE

Announced: March 17, 1999.

Location: 3900 Grant Road, in Central Point, Ore.

Site: 2 acres.

Exterior finish: Granite.

Temple design: Traditional.

Architects: Dan Park and Church A&E Services.

Project manager: Amos and Gloria Wright.

Contractor: Corey Vitas Construction.

Number of rooms: Celestial room, baptistry, two ordinance rooms, two sealing rooms.

Total floor area: 10,700 square feet.

Dimensions: 144 by 77 feet.

District: Serves more than 28,600 members in nine stakes in Oregon and Northern California.

Groundbreaking, site dedication: May 20, 1999, by Elder D. Lee Tobler of the Seventy and first counselor in the North America Northwest Area presidency.

Dedicated: April 16, 2000, by President James E. Faust, second counselor in the First Presidency; 4 sessions.

Dedicatory prayer excerpt: *"Bless the youth of the Church, dear Father. Lead them in paths of righteousness and truth. Protect them from the alluring and seductive calls of the adversary."*

MELBOURNE AUSTRALIA TEMPLE

Announced: Oct. 30, 1998.

Location: Corner of Cathies Road and Pumps Lane, Wantirna, Victoria.

Site: 5.98 acres, including adjoining meetinghouse.

Exterior finish: Snow white granite.

Temple design: Traditional.

Architect: Warwick Tempany and Church A&E Services.

Project manager: Graham Sully.

Contractor: Probuild.

Number of rooms: Celestial room, two endowment rooms, two sealing rooms and a baptistry.

Total floor area: 10,700 square feet.

Dimensions: 144 feet by 77 feet.

District: Melbourne Braeside, Melbourne Deer Park, Melbourne Heidelberg, Melbourne Maroondah, Melbourne Pakenham, Melbourne West, and Devonport Australia, and Hobart Australia stakes, and the Albury New South Wales District.

Groundbreaking, site dedication: March 20, 1999, by Elder P. Bruce Mitchell, Area Authority Seventy and second counselor in the Austrialia/New Zealand Area presidency.

Dedicated: June 16, 2000, by President Gordon B. Hinckley; 4 sessions.

Dedicatory prayer excerpt: *"We are grateful for this nation of Australia, where we may worship Thee in peace, without molestation or fear or threat. Bless this land that is may remain ever strong, a nation of peace and progress among the nations of the earth."*

MEMPHIS TENNESSEE TEMPLE

Announced: Sept. 17, 1998.

Location: 4199 Kirby Whitten Road, Bartlett, Tenn.

Site: 6.35 acres, including adjoining meetinghouse.

Exterior finish: Imperial Danby White marble.

Temple design: Classic modern.

Architect: Dusty Driver of Bounds & Gillespie Architects and Church A&E Services.

Project manager: Leon Rowley.

Contractor: Layton Construction Co., Construction Management Company; Rentenbach Construction, general contractor.

Number of rooms: Celestial room, baptistry, two ordinance rooms, two sealing rooms.

Total floor area: 10,700 square feet.

Dimensions: 144 by 77 feet.

District: Five stakes in Memphis, Tenn., and Little Rock, Ark.

Groundbreaking, site dedication: Jan. 16, 1999, by Elder Gordon T. Watts of the Seventy and first counselor in the North America Southeast Area presidency.

Dedication: April 23, 2000, by President James E. Faust, second counselor in First Presidency; 4 sessions.

Dedicatory prayer excerpt: *"We are grateful for this nation whose Constitution and laws protect us in our worship. May these precious liberties never be lost to the people. May they be safeguarded and kept secure from those who would destroy the precious boon of freedom of worship."*

MERIDA MEXICO TEMPLE

Announced: Sept. 25, 1998.

Location: Calle 70 #527 X65-67, centro, Merida.

Site: 1.53 acres.

Exterior finish: Guardiano white marble.

Temple design: Classic modern.

Architect: Alvaro Iñigo and Church A&E Services.

Project manager: Dean Fife.

Contractor: PyCSA / Okland Construction Co.

Number of rooms: Celestial room, baptistry, two ordinance rooms, two sealing rooms.

Total floor area: 12,469 square feet.

Dimensions: 84 feet by 150 feet.

District: Nine stakes, two districts and three unaffiliated branches.

Groundbreaking, site dedication: Jan. 16, 1999, by Carl B. Pratt of the Seventy and president of the Mexico South Area.

Dedication: July 8, 2000, by Thomas S. Monson, first counselor in the First Presidency; 4 sessions.

Dedicatory prayer excerpt: *"Help us this day to rededicate our lives to the advancement of Thy cause and kingdom."*

MESA ARIZONA TEMPLE

Location: In Mesa, 16 miles east of Phoenix, in central Arizona's Valley of the Sun. Mesa's Main Street passes the site on the north; 101 S. LeSueur, Mesa, AZ.

Site: 20-acre site selected Feb. 1, 1920, by President Heber J. Grant, Apostles David O. McKay and George F. Richards. Purchased in 1921.

Exterior finish: Concrete reinforced with 130 tons of steel. Exterior is faced with a terra cotta glaze that is egg-shell in color and tile-like in finish.

Temple design: Modification of the classic style, suggestive of pre-Columbian temples and even the Temple of Herod.

Architects: Don C. Young and Ramm Hansen.

Construction supervisor: Arthur Price.

Construction chairman: Executive building committee: J.W. LeSueur, chairman; O.S. Stapley, John Cummard, Andrew Kimball.

Number of rooms: Four ordinance, nine sealing rooms.

Total floor area: 72,712 square feet.

Dimensions: 128 feet by 184 feet, and 50 feet in height above the foundation.

District: Most of Arizona.

Site dedication, groundbreaking: Site dedicated Nov. 28, 1921; ground broken April 25, 1922, by President Heber J. Grant.

Dedication: Oct. 23, 1927, by President Heber J. Grant; services broadcast by radio. Rededicated after extensive remodeling April 15-16, 1975, by President Spencer W. Kimball; 8 sessions.

Dedicatory prayer excerpt: *"Accept the dedication of this house, and these grounds, which we have dedicated unto thee by virtue of the Priesthood of the Living God which we hold."*

MEXICO CITY MEXICO TEMPLE

Location: Near Aragon public park and zoological gardens, bounded by Calle Ignacio Allende and Calle Emiliano Capata; Avenida 510 #90, Col. San Juan de Aragon, Mexico.

Site: 7 acres.

Exterior finish: White cast stone, ornate with adaptations of ancient Mayan designs, especially on upper portion of the structure.

Temple design: Modern adaptation of ancient Mayan architecture.

Architect: Emil B. Fetzer, Church architect.

Resident project inspector: Ricardo Espiriti.

Construction superintendent: Jose Ortiz for Urbec Construction Co.

Number of rooms: Four ordinance rooms, 11 sealing rooms.

Total floor area: 117,133 square feet.

Dimensions Basement and first floors, 178 by 214.5 feet; two upper levels, 119.5 by 157 feet. Height to square, 70 feet; to top of tower, 152 feet. Statue of Angel Moroni stands on top tower.

District: 128 stakes in Mexico.

Groundbreaking, site dedication: Nov. 25, 1979, by Elder Boyd K. Packer of the Quorum of the Twelve, 10,000 people attended.

Dedication: Dec. 2-4, 1983, by President Gordon B. Hinckley; 9 sessions.

Dedicatory prayer excerpt: *"Bless Thy Saints in this great land and those from other lands who will use this temple. Most have in their veins the blood of Father Lehi. Thou hast kept thine ancient promises."*

MONTERREY MEXICO TEMPLE

Announced: Dec. 21, 1995. **Status:** Awaiting groundbreaking

MONTEVIDEO URUGUAY TEMPLE

Announced: Nov. 2, 1998.

Location: Calle San Carlos de Bolivar, entre Horacio Quiroga y Bologna, Montevideo.

Site: 1.59 acres.

Exterior finish: Granite.

Temple design: Classic modern.

Architect: Edvardo Signorelli

Project manager: Javier Mendieta

Contractor: Luis Maranges S.A.

Number of rooms: Two ordinance, two sealing, celestial room, baptistry.

Total floor area: 11,232 square feet

Dimensions of building: 144 feet by 79 feet

District: Uruguay

Groundbreaking, site dedication: April 27, 1999, by Elder Richard G. Scott of the Quorum of the Twelve.

Dedication: December 2000.

MONTICELLO UTAH TEMPLE

Announced: Oct. 4, 1997.

Location: 347 North 200 West, Monticello, Utah.

Site: 1.33 acres.

Exterior finish: White marble.

Temple design: Classic modern.

Architects: Church Architectural Services

Construction adviser: Bob Dewey, Ron Prince

Contractor: Jacobsen Construction Co.

Number of rooms: Celestial room, one ordinance room, one sealing room, baptistry.

Total floor area: 7,000 square feet.

Dimensions: 78 feet by 110 feet, 55 feet high to the top of 6-foot statue of Angel Moroni.

District: Southeastern Utah and southwestern Colorado.

Groundbreaking, site dedication: Nov. 17, 1997, by Elder Ben B. Banks of the Seventy and president of the Utah South Area.

Dedication: July 26-27, 1998, by President Gordon B. Hinckley; 8 sessions.

Dedicatory prayer excerpt: *"Bless the children that there may grow in their hearts a desire to serve Thee all the days of their lives."*

MONTREAL QUEBEC TEMPLE

Announced: Aug. 6, 1998.

Location: 1450 Boulevard Marie-Victorin, Longueuil on the south shore of the St. Lawrence River across from Montreal.

Site: 2.4 acres.

Exterior finish: Bethel white granite.

Temple design: Classic modern.

Architect: Andrij Serbyn, Sichten Soiferman and Church A&E Services.

Project manager: William Treu.

Contractor: Opron Inc.

Number of rooms: Celestial room, two endowment rooms, two sealing rooms and a baptistry.

Total floor area: 10,700 square feet.

Dimensions: 144 by 77 feet.

District: Montreal Quebec Stake, Montreal Quebec Mount Royal Stake, Ottawa Ontario Stake, Quebec Quebec District and Montpelier Vermont Stake.

Groundbreaking, site dedication: April 9, 1999, by Elder Gary J. Coleman of the Seventy.

Dedication: June 4, 2000, by President Gordon B. Hinckley; 4 sessions.

Dedicatory prayer excerpt: *"On this historic day we sing Thy praises, dear Father. We speak words of thanksgiving....*

"May all who enter the portals of Thy house be worthy to come as Thy guests and enjoy Thy rich and bounteous blessings. This is a house of salvation and exaltation for the living and the dead, made possible through the Atonement of the Savior of the world. Every ordinance performed herein, every blessing granted will be eternal in its consequences."

MOUNT TIMPANOGOS UTAH TEMPLE

Location: 742 North 900 East, American Fork, Utah.

Announced: Oct. 3, 1992, by President Gordon B. Hinckley and President Thomas S. Monson.

Site: 16.7 acres, part of a larger parcel of land that was once a welfare farm.

Exterior finish: Sierra white granite clad temple with art glass windows and bronze doors.

Temple design: Traditional, with a single spire.

Architects: Church physical facilities staff.

Contractor: Okland Construction Company.

Number of rooms: Four ordinance, eight sealing.

Total floor area: 104,000 square feet.

Dimensions: 195 feet by 157 feet; 190 foot spire, including statue of Angel Moroni.

District: Northern Utah County and Wasatch County.

Groundbreaking, site dedication: Oct. 9, 1993, by President Gordon B. Hinckley.

Dedication: Oct. 13-19 1996, by President Gordon B. Hinckley; 27 sessions.

Dedicatory prayer excerpt: *"May it be a beacon of peace and a refuge to the troubled. May it be an holy sanctuary to those whose burdens are heavy and who seek Thy consoling comfort."*

NASHVILLE TENNESSEE TEMPLE

Announced: Originally announced Nov. 9, 1994. Revised plans announced April 25, 1998.

Location: Franklin, Tenn., about 15 miles south of Nashville, at 1150 Gray Fox Lane near Mack Hatcher Parkway.

Site: 6.86 acres, including adjoining meetinghouse.

Exterior finish: White Imperial Danby marble.

Temple design: Classic modern.

Architect: Robert Waldrip of Joyce Prout & Associates and Church A&E Services.

Project manager: Leon Rowley.

Contractor: Layton Construction Co., construction management company; MPact Construction Group, general contractor.

Number of rooms: Celestial Room, two endowment rooms, two sealing rooms and a baptistry.

Total floor area: 10,700 square feet.

Dimensions: 144 by 77 feet.

District: Parts of Kentucky and Tennessee.

Groundbreaking, site dedication: March 13, 1999, by Elder John K. Carmack of the Seventy and president of the North America East Area.

Dedication: May 21, 2000, by President James E. Faust, second counselor in the First Presidency; 4 sessions.

Dedicatory prayer excerpt: *"Bless all who come into the Church that they may look forward with eagerness to the day when they may enter this Thy holy house and receive the higher ordinances of the gospel."*

NEW YORK NEW YORK TEMPLE

Announced: April 30, 1995. **Status:** Awaiting groundbreaking

NAUVOO ILLINOIS TEMPLE

Announced: April 4, 1999. **Groundbreaking:** Oct. 24, 1999.

NAUVOO TEMPLE

No longer stands; burned by arson fire in 1848 after Nauvoo exodus; walls later destroyed by a tornado.

Location: In Nauvoo, Ill., on a high bluff on the east side of the Mississippi River. Temple block bounded by Woodruff, Mulholland, Knight and Wells streets.

Site: Selected in October 1840 by Joseph Smith on property known as the Wells addition, slightly less than four acres.

Exterior finish: Light gray limestone quarried to the north and south of the city.

Temple design: Incorporated several types of architecture, no single style dominating.

Architect: William Weeks.

Temple building committee: Alpheus Cutler, Elias Higbee and Reynolds Cahoon. After the death of Elias Higbee in 1843, Hyrum Smith replaced him until his own death.

Number of rooms: Approximately 60.

Total floor area: Approximately 50,000 square feet.

Dimensions: Approximately 128 feet by 88 feet; 65 feet high, with the tower and spire reaching to 165 feet.

Cornerstones: April 6, 1841, President Joseph Smith presiding.

Dedication: Portions of the temple were dedicated and used as soon as completed. To avoid possible violence, a private dedication was held April 30, 1846, with Orson Hyde and Joseph Young officiating. The temple was dedicated publicly May 1-3, 1846, with the dedicatory prayer offered by Orson Hyde.

Dedicatory prayer excerpt: *"We thank Thee that Thou hast given us strength to accomplish the charges delivered by Thee. Thou hast seen our labors and exertions to accomplish this purpose. By the authority of the Holy Priesthood now we offer this building as a sanctuary to Thy worthy name. We ask thee to take the guardianship into Thy hands and grant Thy spirit shall dwell here and may all feel a sacred influence on their hearts that His Hand has helped this work."*

NUKU'ALOFA TONGA TEMPLE

Location: At site of Church's Liahona College, several miles outside of Nuku'alofa; Loto Rd., Tongatapu, Nuku'alofa, Tonga.

Site: 5 acres.

Exterior finish: "R-wall" exterior finish and insulation system on concrete block; split cedar shake shingles on roof.

Temple design: Modern.

Architect: Emil B. Fetzer, Church architect.

Construction adviser: Richard Westover and Richard Rowley.

Contractor: Utah Construction & Development.

Number of rooms: Three sealing rooms, two ordinance rooms.

Total floor area: 13,020 square feet.

Dimensions: 142.88 feet by 115.32 feet; statue of Angel Moroni on top spire, 75 feet high.

District: Tongan islands.

Groundbreaking, site dedication: Feb. 18, 1981, by President Spencer W. Kimball with Tonga's King Taufa'ahau Tupou IV. Nearly 7,000 people attended.

Dedication: Aug. 9-11, 1983, by President Gordon B. Hinckley; 13 sessions.

Dedicatory prayer excerpt: *"We ask that Thou wilt accept this temple as the gift of Thy people presented unto Thee with love for the accomplishments of Thy holy purposes with reference to Thy children. It is Thy house. It is the house of Thy Son. May it always be held in reverence by Thy people."*

OAKLAND CALIFORNIA TEMPLE

Location: On hill overlooking Oakland, Berkeley, San Francisco and the Bay, near intersection of Lincoln Avenue and Warren Freeway; 4700 Lincoln Ave., Oakland, CA.

Site: Inspected and approved by President David O. McKay in 1942; 14.5 acres purchased Jan. 28, 1943; additional land acquired later to make 18.3 acres.

Exterior finish: Reinforced concrete faced with Sierra white granite from Raymond, Calif.

Temple design: Modern, with an Oriental motif.

Architect: Harold W. Burton. Resident architect supervisor, Arthur Price.

Construction chairman: W. B. Mendenhall.

Construction supervisor: Robert C. Loder. Contractors: Leon M. Wheatley Co., Palo Alto, Calif., and Jacobsen Construction Co., Salt Lake City.

Number of rooms: Four ordinance rooms, 7 sealing rooms.

Total floor area: 82,417 square feet.

Dimensions: Temple proper, 210 feet by 190 feet with a central tower rising 170 feet; other towers 96 feet.

District: Northern California.

Groundbreaking, site dedication: May 26, 1962, by President David O. McKay.

Dedication: Nov. 17-19, 1964, by President David O. McKay, 6 sessions.

Dedicatory prayer excerpt: *"This temple is a monument testifying to the faith and loyalty of the members of thy Church in the payment of their tithes and offerings. We thank Thee for every effort that has been put forth by the members, from every sacrifice that has been made by the young boys and girls who have given of their dimes and dollars, to the millionaire who gave of his thousands."*

OAXACA MEXICO TEMPLE

Announced: Feb. 23, 1999.

Location: Avenida Universidad, Fracc. Real de Candiani, esquina Hacienda de Candiani.

Site: 1.87 acres, including adjoining meetinghouse.

Exterior finish: White marble.

Temple design: Classic modern.

Architects: Alvaro Iñigo and Church A&E Services.

Project manager: Jay Erekson.

Contractor: Impulsa / Okland Construction Co.

Number of rooms: Celestial room, baptistry, two ordinance rooms, two sealing rooms.

Total floor area: 12,469 square feet.

Dimensions: 84 feet by 150 feet.

District: Serves 26,000 members in 10 stakes, one district, four branches.

Groundbreaking, site dedication: March 13, 1999, by Elder Carl B. Pratt of the Seventy and president of the Mexico South Area.

Dedicated: March 11, 2000, by President James E. Faust, second counselor in the First Presidency; 4 sessions.

Dedicatory prayer excerpt: *"We pray for this nation of Mexico that its people may be blessed of Thee, that the poverty of the past may be lifted from their shoulders, that freedom and peace and prosperity might be enjoyed."*

OGDEN UTAH TEMPLE

Location: In downtown Ogden, between Grant Avenue and Washington Boulevard; 350 22nd Street, Ogden, UT.

Site: Approved by President David O. McKay and announced Aug. 14, 1967; 18.3 acres.

Exterior finish: White cast stone with a fluted appearance, gold anodized aluminum grillwork, gold directional glass windows.

Temple design: Modern and functional.

Architect: Emil B. Fetzer, Church architect.

Construction chairman: Mark B. Garff, with Fred A. Baker, vice chairman.

Contractor: Okland Construction Company.

Number of rooms: Six ordinance rooms, 11 sealing rooms, four floors.

Total floor area: 115,000 square feet.

Dimensions: 200 feet by 184 feet; tower 180 feet above ground level; single tower of 180 feet.

District: Part of northeastern Utah, southwestern Wyoming.

Groundbreaking, site dedication: Sept. 8, 1969, President N. Eldon Tanner conducted; prayers given by President Alvin R. Dyer and President Joseph Fielding Smith; ground broken by President Hugh B. Brown.

Dedication: Jan. 18-20, 1972, by President Joseph Fielding Smith; 6 sessions.

Dedicatory prayer excerpt: *"It has been our privilege, as guided by the whisperings of Thy Spirit, to build unto Thee this temple, which we now present unto Thee as another of Thy holy houses."*

OKLAHOMA CITY OKLAHOMA TEMPLE

Announced: March 14, 1999.

Location: 12030 North Mustang Road, Yukon, Okla.

Site: 1 acre.

Exterior finish: Imperial Danby White Marble.

Temple design: Classic modern.

Architects: Richard Lueb of the Architectural Partnership and Church A&E Services.

Project manager: Leon Rowley.

Contractor: Arnell-West Inc.

Number of rooms: Celestial room, baptistry, two ordinance rooms, two sealing rooms.

Total floor area: 10,700 square feet.

Dimensions: 144 feet by 77 feet.

District: Members in Oklahoma, Texas, Kansas, Arkansas and Missouri.

Groundbreaking, site dedication: July 3, 1999, by Elder Rex D. Pinegar of the Seventy and president of the North America Southwest Area.

Dedication: July 30, 2000, by President James E. Faust, second counselor in the First Presidency; 4 sessions.

Dedicatory prayer excerpt: *"We pray for Thy cause and kingdom, that it may grow ever stronger in this community. May all who have favored Thy cause be blessed for that which they have done. May many continue to seek for knowledge concerning Thy work until they have embraced Thy restored gospel."*

ORLANDO FLORIDA TEMPLE

Location: On a knoll overlooking Butler chain of lakes at Apopka-Vineland Road on the edge of Orlando suburb of Windermere, five miles southwest of Orlando near Florida Turnpike and Interstate 4; 9000 Windy Ridge Road, Windermere, FL.

Site: 13 acres.

Exterior finish: White precast concrete with marble chips.

Temple design: Classic modern with one spire.

Architects: Scott Partnership Architects.

Church project manager: Ralph Cluff.

Contractor: Brice Building Company.

Number of rooms: Four ordinance rooms, five sealing rooms.

Total floor area: 70,000 square feet.

Dimensions: 180 feet by 182 feet; tower with statue of Angel Moroni is 165 feet high.

District: Florida, part of southern Georgia.

Groundbreaking, site dedication: June 20, 1992, by Elder James E. Faust of the Quorum of the Twelve.

Dedication: Oct. 9-11, 1994, by President Howard W. Hunter; 12 sessions.

Dedicatory prayer excerpt: *"To all who look upon it, including those who reside in this area, may it ever present a picture of peace and beauty, a structure partaking of Thy divine nature."*

PALMYRA NEW YORK TEMPLE

Announced: Feb. 21, 1999, temple was 100th to be announced.

Location: 2720 Temple Road, Palmyra Village, New York.

Site: 5 acres.

Exterior finish: Bethel White granite.

Temple design: Classic modern.

Architects: Dave A. Richards and Church A&E Services.

Project manager: William Treu.

Contractor: Okland Construction Co.

Number of rooms: Specially designed art glass windows inside the temple depict First Vision. Cherrywood moldings are used throughout endowment rooms and hallways. Celestial room; baptistry; two endowment rooms; two sealing rooms.

Total floor area: 10,944 sq. feet.

Dimensions: 144 by 77 feet.

District: Serving 18,000 members in seven stakes of upper New York.

Groundbreaking, site dedication: May 25, 1999, by President Gordon B. Hinckley.

Dedicated: April 6, 2000, by President Gordon B. Hinckley, exactly 170 years after the organization of the Church by Joseph Smith in nearby Fayette, New York; 4 sessions.

Dedicatory prayer excerpt: *"This is the anniversary of the organization of Thy restored Church. One hundred and seventy years ago it was established in nearby Fayette.*

But it was here, on this land which the Smiths once farmed, it was here in the Grove below and to the west that Thou, the Almighty God of the universe, and Thy Beloved Son, the resurrected Lord, appeared to the boy Joseph Smith. This wondrous event parted the curtain that had been closed for centuries."

PAPEETE TAHITI TEMPLE

Location: In Pirae, adjacent to Papeete, on Rua de Pierri Loti, Titioro; B.P. 5682, (Allee Pierre Loti, Titioro) Pirae, Tahiti, French Polynesia.

Site: 5 acres.

Exterior finish: Stucco, using imported white sand.

Temple design: Shows some European elements of French influence as well as Polynesian culture.

Architect: Emil B. Fetzer, Church architect; adapted by Temples and Special Projects Architecture.

Construction adviser: George Bonnet.

Contractor: Comtrol Inc., a Midvale, Utah, construction firm.

Number of rooms: Two ordinance rooms, two sealing rooms.

Total floor area: 10,658 square feet.

Dimensions of building: 125 feet by 105 feet, with an eight-foot statue of Angel Moroni on a 66-foot spire.

District: French Polynesia.

Groundbreaking, site dedication: Feb. 13,

1981, by President Spencer W. Kimball, who also offered a prayer of dedication that the temple would be "a light to all in these islands."

Dedication: Oct. 27-29, 1983, by President Gordon B. Hinckley; 6 sessions.

Dedicatory prayer excerpt: *"We ask that Thou wilt preserve [the temple]... as Thy house. May it be protected by Thy power from any who would defile it. May it stand against the winds and the rains."*

PERTH AUSTRALIA TEMPLE

Announced: June 11, 1999.

Temple design: Classic modern.

Architects: Church A&E Services.

Total floor area: 10,944 sq. feet.

Dimensions: 144 by 77 feet.

Groundbreaking, site dedication: Nov. 20, 1999, by Elder Kenneth Johnson, first counselor in the Australia/New Zealand Area Presidency.

Status: Under construction

PORTLAND OREGON TEMPLE

Location: In a wooded suburb about 10 miles southwest of downtown Portland, in the northwest corner of Oswego, adjacent to Interstate 5; 13600 SW Kruse Oaks Blvd., Lake Oswego, OR 97035.

Site: The land was purchased by the Church in mid-1960s for a junior college, but 7.3 acres was later chosen as a temple site.

Exterior finish: White marble walls and slate roof.

Temple design: Six spires.

Architects: Leland A. Gray, architect; Lee/Ruff/Waddle, site and local architects.

Construction adviser: Michael Enfield

Contractor: Zwick Construction Co.

Number of rooms: Four ordinance, fourteen sealing rooms.

Total floor area: 65,000 square feet.

Dimensions: 270 feet by 183 feet, four towers 124 feet tall; statue of Angel Moroni on east spire, 169 feet tall.

District: Most of Oregon and parts of Washington.

Groundbreaking, site dedication: Sept. 20, 1986, by President Gordon B. Hinckley.

Dedication: Aug. 19-21, 1989, by President Gordon B. Hinckley; 11 sessions.

Dedicatory prayer excerpt: *"May a spirit of solemnity rest upon all who enter herein. Open to their vision a glimpse of Thy great and everlasting designs."*

PORTO ALEGRE BRAZIL TEMPLE

Announced: Oct 4, 1997.

Location: Porto Alegre, Brazil.

Site: 2 acres.

Exterior finish: Granite

Temple design: Classic modern.

Architects: Bross Associates and Church A&E Services.

Project manager: Raul Lins.

Contractor: Ernesto Woebcke.

Number of rooms: Two ordinance rooms, two sealing rooms, celestial room, baptistry.

Total floor area: 13,325 square feet.

Dimensions: 162 feet by 82 feet.

District: Southern Brazil.

Groundbreaking, site dedication: May 2, 1998, by President James E. Faust, second counselor in the First Presidency.

Dedication: December 2000.

PRESTON ENGLAND TEMPLE

Announced: Oct. 19,1992.

Location: A6/M61 Link road, Hartwood Green, Chorley; Lancashire.

Site: 15 acres or 6 hectares.

Exterior finish: Olympia white granite from Sardinia.

Temple design: Modern.

Architects: Church physical facilities staff.

Project manager: Hanno Luschin.

Contractor: John Laing Construction, Ltd.

Number of rooms: Four ordinance rooms; four sealing rooms.

Total floor area: 70,033 square feet (6482.53 square meters).

Dimensions: 102.3 feet by 174.9 feet (31 meters by 53 meters); 155 foot high spire (47 meters), including statue of Angel Moroni.

District: Northern England, Scotland, Ireland, and Northern Ireland.

Groundbreaking, site dedication: June 12, 1994, by President Gordon B. Hinckley.

Dedication: June 7-10, 1998, by President Gordon B. Hinckley; 15 sessions.

Dedicatory prayer excerpt: "*This magnificent temple has been reared in this beautiful area where thy chosen servants, in the days of their deep poverty and great sacrifice, first preached the restored gospel. Through 161 years of history this land of England, together with Scotland, Wales, and Ireland, has yielded a harvest of converts who have blessed and strengthened thy Church.*"

PROVO UTAH TEMPLE

Location: At the entrance of Rock Canyon on the east bench of Provo; 2200 Temple Hill Drive, Provo, UT.

Site: 17 acres. Announced by President David O. McKay on Aug. 14, 1967.

Exterior finish: White cast stone, gold anodized aluminum grills, bronze glass panels, and single spire finished in gold and anodized aluminum; similar to Ogden Temple.

Temple design: Modern and functional.

Architect: Emil B. Fetzer, Church architect.

Construction chairman: Mark B. Garff, with Fred A. Baker, vice chairman.

Construction supervisor: Hogan and Tingey, general contractors.

Number of rooms: Six ordinance, 12 sealing rooms.

Total floor area: 115,000 square feet.

Dimensions: 200 by 184 feet; 175 feet high with a 118-foot spire on top of the building.

District: Central and eastern Utah.

Groundbreaking, site dedication: Sept. 15, 1969, ground broken by President Hugh B. Brown.

Dedication: Feb. 9, 1972; dedicatory prayer written by President Joseph Fielding Smith and read by President Harold B. Lee; 2 sessions.

Dedicatory prayer excerpt: "*We dedicate this temple to thee, the Lord. We dedicate it as a house of baptism, a house of endowment, a house of marriage, a house of righteousness for the living and the dead.*"

RALEIGH NORTH CAROLINA TEMPLE

Announced: Sept. 3, 1998.

Location: 574 Bryan Dr., Apex, N.C. (off State Highway 55 about 10 miles SW of Raleigh).

Site: 12 acres.

Exterior finish: Danby white marble with art glass windows.

Temple design: Traditiional.

Architects: Dan Dills of Dills and Ainscuff.

Project manager: Bruce Catanzaro.

Contractor: Walbridge Aldinger.

Number of rooms: Celestial room, baptistry, two ordinance rooms, two sealing rooms; 44 total rooms.

Total floor area: 10,700 square feet

Dimensions: 144 by 77 feet.

District: Eight stakes of Winston-Salem, Durham, Greensboro, Raleigh, Goldsboro, Kinston, Fayetteville and Wilmington.

Groundbreaking, site dedication: Feb. 6, 1999, by Elder Loren C. Dunn of the Seventy, first counselor in the North America East Area.

Dedication: Dec. 18, 1999, by President Gordon B. Hinckley; 7 sessions.

Dedicatory prayer excerpt: *"May all who come as patrons to this temple know that they are dealing with the things of eternity, and that the relationships here entered into are everlasting."*

RECIFE BRAZIL TEMPLE

Announced: Jan. 13, 1995.

Location: Recife, Brazil.

Site: 5.59 acres.

Exterior finish: Granite (Asa Branca).

Temple design: Classic modern.

Architects: J&P Arquitetos Ltd. and Church A&E Services.

Project manager: Raul Lins.

Contractor: Hochtief do Brasil SA.

Number of rooms: Celestial room, baptistry, two ordinance rooms and three sealing rooms.

Total floor area: 37,200 square feet.

Dimensions: 108 feet by 157 feet.

District: Northern Brazil.

Groundbreaking, site dedication: Nov. 15, 1996, by President Gordon B. Hinckley.

Dedication: December 2000.

REGINA SASKATCHEWAN TEMPLE

Announced: Aug. 3, 1998.

Location: 11 Wascana Gate North, Regina, Saskatchewan.

Site: 1 acre.

Exterior finish: Light gray granite.

Temple design: Classic modern.

Architect: Roger B. Mitchell of Banadyga Mitchell Partnership and Church A&E Services.

Project manager: Cory Karl.

Contractor: Graham Construction and Engineering, Ltd.

Number of rooms: Celestial room, baptistry, two ordinance rooms, two sealing rooms.

Total floor area: 10,700 square feet.

Dimensions: 144 by 77 feet.

District: Serves 3,500 members in two stakes and one district.

Groundbreaking, site dedication: Nov. 14, 1998, by Elder Hugh W. Pinnock of the Seventy and president of the North America

Central Area.

Dedication: Nov. 14, 1999, by President Boyd K. Packer, acting president of the Quorum of the Twelve; 3 sessions.

Dedicatory prayer excerpt: *"May all who come within these walls be clean of hands and pure of mind as they engage in Thy sacred work. Bless them with joy in this service."*

RENO NEVADA TEMPLE

Announced: April 12, 1999.

Location: 2000 Beaumont Parkway, Reno, Nev.

Site: 7.9 acres.

Exterior finish: Granite.

Temple design: Traditional.

Architects: Church A&E Services.

Project manager: Amos and Gloria Wright

Contractor: Jacobsen Construction Co.

Number of rooms: Celestial room, baptistry, two ordinance rooms, two sealing rooms.

Total floor area: 10,700 square feet.

Dimensions: 144 feet by 77 feet.

District: Serves 25,474 members in eight stakes in western Nevada and eastern California.

Groundbreaking, site dedication: July 24, 1999, by Elder Rex D. Pinegar of the Seventy and president of the North American Southwest Area.

Dedicated: April 23, 2000, by President Thomas S. Monson, first counselor in the First Presidency; 4 sessions.

Dedicatory prayer excerpt: *"Bless all who enter the portals of this structure that they may be worthy to come here as Thy Saints. May they do so with reverence and with a desire to promote Thy work in behalf of Thy children of all generations. May the youth who come to be baptized in behalf of those who have passed beyond the veil of death feel of Thy Holy Spirit and never forget the importance of the sacred work which they perform. May it have a beneficent effect upon their lives."*

ST. GEORGE UTAH TEMPLE

Location: near the center of St. George; 250 E. 400 South, St. George, UT.

Site: 6 acres, selected by Brigham Young in 1871.

Exterior finish: Native red sandstone quarried north of the city was used for the temple which was then plastered white.

Temple design: Castellated Gothic style.

Architect: Truman O. Angell.

Construction superintendent: Miles P. Romney; Edward L. Parry, head stone mason.

Number of rooms: Three ordinance rooms; eight sealing rooms, 64 rooms in original structure.

Total floor area: 56,062 square feet in original building; 110,000 square feet after remodeling completed in 1975.

Dimensions: 142 feet by 96 feet. To the top of the buttresses, the height is 80 feet, and to the top of the vane, 175 feet.

District: Southwestern Utah, small part of Nevada and Arizona.

Groundbreaking, site dedication: Nov. 9, 1871, by President Brigham Young; site dedication prayer by George A. Smith.

Dedication: Jan. 1, 1877, completed portions were dedicated. Final dedication, April 6-8, 1877, President Brigham Young presiding, and Daniel H. Wells offered prayer.

On Nov. 11-12, 1975, after extensive remodeling, the temple was rededicated by President Spencer W. Kimball; 5 sessions.

Dedicatory prayer excerpt: *"We implore Thy blessings upon the various congregations of Thy people who may assemble in this house from time to time."*

ST. LOUIS MISSOURI TEMPLE

Location: 12555 North Forty Drive, Town and Country, MO.

Exterior finish: Cast stone and Bethal white granite with thermal finish.

Temple design: Modern.

Architects: Chiodini Associates.

Project manager: Gary Holland.

Contractor: BSI Constructors Inc.

Number of rooms: Four ordinance rooms, four sealing rooms.

Total floor area: 58,749 square feet.

Dimensions of building: 88 feet by 189 feet.

District: Missouri, Illinois, Iowa, Kansas, Nebraska.

Groundbreaking, site dedication: Oct. 30, 1993, by President Gordon B. Hinckley.

Dedication: June 1-5, 1997, by President Gordon B. Hinckley; 19 sessions.

Dedicatory prayer excerpt: *"Today thy Church basks in the sunlight of good will. Hundreds of thousands of visitors have come to view this thy holy house. They have left with respect and appreciation."*

ST. PAUL MINNESOTA TEMPLE

Announced: July 29, 1998.

Location: 2140 North Hadley, Oakdale, Minn., east of St. Paul. Exit off Interstate 694, at 10th Street, drive south to Hadley Street, then west.

Site: 7.5 acres, including adjoining meetinghouse.

Exterior finish: Light gray granite veneer.

Temple design: Classic modern.

Architect: Ed Kodet, Jr. of Kodet Architect Group Ltd., and Church A&E Services.

Project manager: Cory Karl.

Contractor: Walbridge Aldinger.

Number of rooms: Celestial room, baptistry, two ordinance rooms, two sealing rooms.

Total floor area: 10,700 square feet.

Dimensions: 144 by 77 feet.

District: Minnesota, parts of Wisconson and Manitoba.

Groundbreaking, site dedication: Sept. 26, 1998, by Elder Hugh W. Pinnock of the Seventy and president of the North America Central Area.

Dedication: Jan. 9, 2000, by President Gordon B. Hinckley; 4 sessions.

Dedicatory prayer excerpt: *"And that all people who should enter upon the threshold of the Lord's house may feel thy power, and feel constrained to acknowledge that thou hast sanctified it, and that it is thy house, a place of thy holiness." (D&C 109:12-13.)*

"May the wonder and the majesty of that great act of atonement enter the minds and hearts of all who serve here in behalf of those beyond the veil of death."

SALT LAKE TEMPLE

Location: On Temple Square in the center of Salt Lake City; 50 W. North Temple St., Salt Lake City, UT.

Site: 10 acres. Selected July 28, 1847, by Brigham Young.

Exterior finish: Granite from Little Cottonwood Canyon, 20 miles to the southeast of Salt Lake City. The chapel and office annex are reinforced concrete faced with Utah granite.

Temple design: Suggestive of Gothic and other classical styles, but unique and distinctive.

Architect: Truman O. Angell, Church architect, worked out plans under direction of Brigham Young. During Angell's illness, William Folsom temporarily filled his post. After Angell's death in 1887, Don Carlos Young completed work on the temple.

Construction supervisor: Daniel H. Wells supervised construction; "Public Works," was organized Jan. 26, 1850, to provide labor and materials.

Number of rooms: One ordinance room, four sealing rooms.

Total floor area: 253,015 square feet in the temple, including the annex.

Dimensions: 118 feet 6.75 inches by 181 feet 7.25 inches. At east end of the building, the height of the center pinnacle is 210 feet. The center of the three towers on the west end is 204 feet high.

District: Tooele County and part of Salt Lake and Summit counties in Utah.

Groundbreaking, site dedication: Feb. 14, 1853, President Brigham Young broke ground and Heber C. Kimball dedicated the site.

Dedication: April 6-24, 1893, by President Wilford Woodruff; 31 sessions.

On April 5, 1893, more than 600 non-LDS residents of Salt Lake City toured the temple, which had taken more than 40 years to complete.

Dedicatory prayer excerpt: "*When Thy people... are oppressed and in trouble... we beseech thee, to look down from Thy holy habitation in mercy and tender compassion.*"

SAN DIEGO CALIFORNIA TEMPLE

Location: In the northern part of city of San Diego near the suburb of La Jolla on a ridge above the San Diego Freeway; 7474 Charmant Dr., San Diego, CA 92122. Telephone: (619) 622-0991.

Site: 7.2 acres.

Exterior finish: Marble chips in plaster.

Temple design: Modern, with two major towers.

Architects: Deems, Lewis & McKinnley-William Lewis, and Hyndman & Hyndman.

Project representative: Stanley G. Smith.

Contractor: Okland Construction Co.

Number of rooms: Four ordinance and eight sealing rooms.

Total floor area: 82,447 square feet.

Dimensions: 165 feet by 194 feet; roof 62 feet high; statue of Angel Moroni on top spire, 200 feet high.

Groundbreaking, site dedication: Ground broken Feb. 27, 1988, by President Ezra Taft Benson; site dedicated the same day by President Thomas S. Monson of the First Presidency.

District: Parts of Southern California and northwestern Mexico.

Dedicated: April 25-30, 1993, by President Gordon B. Hinckley in 23 sessions.

Dedicatory prayer excerpt: *"We thank Thee that hundreds of thousands of men and women of various faiths and philosophies have had the opportunity of walking through this sacred house prior to this time of dedication. May an attitude of respect and reverence grow within them. May very many of them be stirred to seek and learn the truths of Thy restored work that they too might become eligible to enjoy the blessings offered herein. May any voices of criticism be stilled and any words of disrespect be silenced."*

SAN JOSE COSTA RICA TEMPLE

Announced: March 17, 1999.

Location: Half mile west of Hotel Marriott in San Antonio, a suburb of San Jose.

Site: 1.93 acres.

Exterior finish: Blanco Guardiano white marble.

Temple design: Classic modern.

Architect: Alvaro Iñigo and Church A&E Services.

Project manager: Duane Cheney.

Contractor: Galvez y Volio.

Number of rooms: Celestial room, two endowment rooms, two sealing rooms, baptistry.

Total floor area: 12,469 square feet.

Dimensions: 150 feet by 84 feet.

District: Costa Rica, Panama.

Groundbreaking, site dedication: April 24, 1999, by Elder Lynn G. Robbins of the Seventy and first counselor in the Central America Area presidency.

Dedicated: June 4, 2000, by President James E. Faust, second counselor in the First Presidency; 4 sessions.

Dedicatory prayer excerpt: *"We thank Thee for him through whom Thou hast revealed the ordinances of this house, even the Prophet Joseph Smith. May we ever hold him in sacred remembrance as Thy servant in initiating Thy work in this season when Thou hast moved again to build Thy kingdom and to roll it forth as a small stone cut from the mountain without hands rolls forth to fill the earth."*

SANTIAGO CHILE TEMPLE

Location: At site of former Church school headquarters in Santiago suburb of Providencia on Pedro de Valdivia 1423; Pocuro #1940 Providencia, Santiago, Chile.

Site: 2.61 acres.

Exterior finish: Stucco on concrete block.

Temple design: Modern.

Architect: Emil B. Fetzer, Church architect.

Construction adviser: Gary Holland.

Contractor: H. Briones Y Cia & The Church of Jesus Christ of Latter-day Saints.

Number of rooms: Two ordinance rooms, three sealing rooms; 31 total rooms.

Total floor area: 13,020 square feet.

Dimensions: 142.88 feet by 115.32 feet; statue of Angel Moroni on top spire, 76.5 feet high.

District: Chile.

Groundbreaking, site dedication: May 30, 1981, by President Spencer W. Kimball, in a cold rain, attended by 6,000 members.

Dedication: Sept. 15-17, 1983, by President Gordon B. Hinckley; 10 sessions.

Dedicatory prayer excerpt: *"Bless thy work upon this great continent of South America which is part of the land of Zion. Bless thy work in this nation of Chile. May all that has been done in the past be but a prologue to a far greater work in the future. May thy people be recognized for the virtue of their lives."*

SANTO DOMINGO DOMINICAN REPUBLIC TEMPLE

Announced: Nov. 16, 1993.

Location: Avenidz Bolivar and Avenida Genesis.

Site: 6.42 acres.

Exterior finish: Granite, regina white.

Temple design: Classic modern.

Architects: Scott Partnership and Church A&E Services.

Project manager: Robert Prina.

Contractor: Caralva.

Number of rooms: Four ordinance rooms and four sealing rooms, celestial room, baptistry.

Total floor area: 74,000 square feet.

Dimensions: 88 feet by 190 feet.

District: Caribbean.

Groundbreaking, site dedication: Aug. 18, 1996, by Elder Richard G. Scott of the Quorum of the Twelve.

Dedication: Sept. 17, 2000, by Gordon B. Hinckley; 4 sessions.

Dedicatory prayer excerpt: *"Dear Father, please look down with love upon Thy sons and daughters in this island nation and in surrounding lands. Prosper them in their labors that they may have food upon their tables and shelter over their heads. As they look to Thee, reward their faith and open Thy hand of providence toward them. May they find peace in the midst of conflict, and faith amidst the stress of the world. Open the windows of heaven, as Thou hast promised, and let blessings flow down upon them. May they be strengthened in their love one for another. May they find happiness in their association together as Thy faithful Saints."*

SAO PAULO BRAZIL TEMPLE

Location: In the Butanta section of Sao Paulo; Av. Prof. Francisco Morato 2390, CEP 05512-300, Sao Paulo, Brazil.

Exterior finish: Reinforced concrete faced with cast stone composed of quartz and marble aggregates set in special white-base cement.

Temple design: Modern design with Spanish influence.

Architect: Emil B. Fetzer, Church architect.

Construction chairman: Christiani Nielsen, general contractor.

Construction supervisor: Ross Jensen and James Magleby.

Number of rooms: Two ordinance rooms, four sealing rooms.

Total floor area: 51,279 square feet.

Dimensions: 116 feet by 256 feet, with tower reaching 101 feet, 4 inches.

District: Brazil, Paraguay.

Groundbreaking, site dedication: March

20, 1976, by Elder James E. Faust, then an Assistant to the Twelve; attended by 2,000 Church members.

Dedication: Oct. 30-Nov. 2, 1978, by President Spencer W. Kimball; 10 sessions.

Dedicatory prayer excerpt: *"Our Father, may peace abide in all the homes of Thy saints. May holy angels guard them. May prosperity shine upon them and sickness and disease be rebuked from their midst. May their land be made fruitful. May the waters be pure and the climate tempered to the comfort and well-being of thy people.*

"Bless the poor of Thy people, that the cry of want and suffering may not ascend unto thy saints."

SEATTLE WASHINGTON TEMPLE

Location: Across from Bellevue Community College, near the Eastgate Interchange on Interstate 90; 2808 148th Ave. SE, Bellevue, WA.

Site: 23.5 acres, selected June 1975.

Exterior finish: Reinforced concrete faced with white marble aggregate and cast stone.

Temple design: Modern.

Architect: Emil B. Fetzer, Church architect.

Project representative: Michael Enfield.

Construction superintendent: Kent Carter for Jacobsen Construction Co. of Salt Lake City.

Number of rooms: Four ordinance rooms, 12 sealing rooms.

Total floor area: 110,000 square feet.

Dimensions: Ground level is 142 feet by 194 feet; upper levels are 117 feet by 163 feet. Height to square is 70 feet; to top of the Angel Moroni, 179 feet.

District: Western Washington, British Columbia.

Groundbreaking, site dedication: May 27, 1978, by President Marion G. Romney of the First Presidency.

Dedication: Nov. 17-21, 1980, by President Spencer W. Kimball; 13 sessions.

Dedicatory prayer excerpt: *"Bless, we pray Thee, the presidency of this temple and the matron and all the officiators herein. Help them to create a sublime and holy atmosphere so that all ordinances may be performed with love and a sweet, spiritual tone that will cause the members to greatly desire to be here, and to return again and again."*

SEOUL KOREA TEMPLE

Location: 500-23 Chang Chun-dong, Seodaemun-Ku, Seoul, Korea 120-180.

Site: 1 acre.

Exterior finish: Granite exterior.

Temple design: Modern adaptation of earlier six-spire design.

Dimensions: 178 feet by 71 feet; Angel Moroni statue is atop tallest spire at 112 feet.

Architects: Church architectural staff; local architect, Komerican Architects.

Construction adviser: Calvin Wardell.

Contractor: Woo Chang.

Number of rooms: Four ordinance rooms, three sealing rooms.

Total floor area: 12,780 square feet.

District: South Korea.

Groundbreaking, site dedication: May 9, 1983, by Elder Marvin J. Ashton of the Quorum of the Twelve.

Dedication: Dec. 14-15, 1985, by President Gordon B. Hinckley; 6 sessions.

Dedicatory prayer excerpt: *"This is the first such house of the Lord ever constructed on the mainland of Asia, this vast continent where through the generations of the past have lived unnumbered hosts whose lives have not been touched by the saving principles of the gospel."*

SNOWFLAKE ARIZONA TEMPLE

Announced: April 3, 2000.

Groundbreaking, site dedication: Sept. 23, 2000, by Elder Rex D. Pinegar of the Seventy.

Status: Under construction.

SPOKANE WASHINGTON TEMPLE

Announced: Aug. 13, 1998.

Location: Highway 27 and Belle Terre in Opportunity, a suburb of Spokane.

Site: 2 acres.

Exterior finish: Granite.

Temple design: Traditional.

Architect: Church A&E Services.

Contractor: Arnell-West Inc.

Number of rooms: Two ordinance rooms, two sealing rooms.

Total floor area: 10,700 square feet.

Dimensions: 144 feet by 77 feet

District: 10 stakes in eastern Washington and parts of northern Idaho and western Montana.

Groundbreaking, site dedication: Oct. 10, 1998, by F. Melvin Hammond of the Seventy and president of the North America Northwest Area.

Dedication: Aug. 21, 1999, by President Gordon B. Hinckley; 11 sessions.

Dedicatory prayer excerpt: *"Touch the hearts of the people in this temple district that the spirit of Elijah may rest upon them, that their hearts may turn to their fathers, and that they may be motivated to search out their forebears and do a great vicarious work in their behalf. May they experience the joy of totally unselfish service as they so labor, emulating the great vicarious sacrifice of our Redeemer."*

STOCKHOLM SWEDEN TEMPLE

Location: Vasterhaninge, about 13 miles southeast of Stockholm; Box 153, (Tempelvagen 5) S-13732 Vasterhaninge, Sweden.

Exterior finish: Masonry exterior, copper roof.

Temple design: Modern adaptation of earlier six-spire design.

Architects: Church architectural staff; local architect, John Sjostrom.

Construction adviser: Henry Haurand.

Contractor: Johnson Construction Co.

Number of rooms: Four ordinance rooms; three sealing rooms.

Total floor area: 14,508 square feet.

Dimensions: 178 feet by 71 feet; Angel Moroni statue is atop tallest spire at 112 feet.

District: Sweden, Finland, Denmark, Norway.

Groundbreaking, site dedication: March 17, 1984, by Elder Thomas S. Monson of the Quorum of the Twelve.

Dedication: July 2-4, 1985, by President Gordon B. Hinckley; 11 sessions.

Dedicatory prayer excerpt: *"Bless this nation where is found Thy temple, and its sister nations. . . .*

"Save these nations from war and oppression, and may their people look to Thee and open their doors and hearts to thy messengers of eternal truth."

SUVA FIJI TEMPLE

Announced: May 7, 1998.

Location: Corner of Princes Road and Lakeba Street, Suva, Fiji.

Site: 4.7 acres.

Exterior finish: Granite.

Temple design: Traditional.

Architects: Conway Beg of Architects Pacific.

Project manager: Jerry Sears.

Contractor: Fletcher Construction Co.

Number of rooms: Celestial room, two endowment rooms, two sealing rooms, baptistry.

Total floor area: 10,700 square feet.

Dimensions: 144 feet by 77 feet.

District: Lautoka Fiji, Nausori Fiji, Suva Fiji, Suva Fiji North and Tarawa Kiribati stakes; and Labasa Fiji, Tavueni Fiji, Luganville Vanuatu, Port Vila Vanuatu, Noumea New Caledonia and Tarawa Gilbert Islands districts.

Groundbreaking, site dedication: May 8, 1999, by Elder Earl M. Monson of the Seventy and second counselor in the Pacific Islands Area presidency.

Dedication: June 18, 2000, by President Gordon B. Hinckley; 1 session.

Dedicatory prayer excerpt: *"We are grateful for this day of dedication, that Thou hast favored us with a temple in this island nation. No longer will we have to travel far across the seas to do that work which Thou hast established as sacred and necessary for Thy Saints in this latter-day dispensation. Thou hast heard our prayers and hearkened to our entreaties that this blessing might come to us."*

SYDNEY AUSTRALIA TEMPLE

Location: In suburban Carlingford, 15 miles northwest of downtown Sydney; Pennant Hill Road & Moseley Street, Carlingford, NSW Australia.

Area of site: 3 acres.

Exterior finish: Precast panels, white quartz finish, terra cotta roof tiles.

Temple design: Modern.

Architect: Emil B. Fetzer, Church architect, and R. Lindsay Little.

Construction adviser: D. Crosbie and Richard Rowley.

Contractor: J.P. Cordukes Pty. Ltd.

Number of rooms: Three sealing rooms, two ordinance rooms.

Total floor area: 13,020 square feet.

Dimensions: 145.11 feet by 115.14 feet; statue of Angel Moroni added to top spire.

District: Southern Australia and Papua New Guinea.

Groundbreaking, site dedication: Aug. 13, 1982, by Elder Bruce R. McConkie of the Quorum of the Twelve.

Dedication: Sept. 20-23, 1984, by President Gordon B. Hinckley; 14 sessions.

Dedicatory prayer excerpt: *"May this temple with its grounds be a place of beauty to all who look upon it. May they be touched by Thy spirit."*

TAIPEI TAIWAN TEMPLE

Location: In the Taipei business district; 256 Ai Kuo East Road, Taipei, Taiwan, R.O.C.

Site: 0.5 acres.

Exterior finish: White ceramic tile.

Temple design: Modern adaptation of earlier six-spire design.

Architect: Church architectural staff with assistance from Philip Fei & Associates of Taipei.

Construction adviser: Harold Smith.

Contractor: I. Cheng Construction & Development Corp.

Number of rooms: Four ordinance rooms, three sealing rooms.

Total floor area: 16,214 square feet.

Dimensions: 178 feet by 72 feet, six spires; statue of Angel Moroni rises to height of 126 feet.

District: Taiwan.

Groundbreaking, site dedication: Aug. 27, 1982, by President Gordon B. Hinckley.

Dedication: Nov. 17-18, 1984, by President Gordon B. Hinckley; 5 sessions.

Dedicatory prayer excerpt: *"We thank Thee for the firm foundation on which Thy Church is now established in this part of the earth. We thank Thee for this day when those who will use this temple may turn their hearts to their fathers, participating in this Thy holy house in those ordinances which will make it possible for their deceased forebears to move forward on the way that leads to eternal life."*

TAMPICO MEXICO TEMPLE

Announced: July 20, 1998.

Location: Ejercito Mexicano 74, Colonia Loma de Gallo, Tamaulipas, Mexico.

Site: 2.96 acres, including adjoining meetinghouse.

Exterior finish: Blanco Guardiano white marble.

Temple design: Classic modern.

Architects: Alvaro Iñigo and Church A&E Services.

Project manager: Rodolfo Avalos.

Contractor: PyCSA / Okland Const. Co.

Number of rooms: Celestial room, baptistry, two ordinance rooms, two sealing rooms.

Total floor area: 12,469 square feet.

Dimensions: 84 feet by 150 feet.

District: Eight stakes and three districts with 38,600 members.

Groundbreaking, site dedication: Nov. 28, 1998, by Elder Eran A. Call of the Seventy and counselor in the Mexico South Area presidency.

Dedication: May 20, 2000, by President Thomas S. Monson, first counselor in the First Presidency; 4 sessions.

Dedicatory prayer excerpt: *"On this historic day, may a new sense of dedication come into our hearts that we may serve Thee more diligently and walk before Thee more faithfully.*

THE HAGUE NETHERLANDS TEMPLE

Announced: Aug. 16, 1999. **Status:** Awaiting construction.

TOKYO JAPAN TEMPLE

Location: Opposite the Arisugawa Park; 5-8-10 Minami Azabu, Minato-Ku, Tokyo, Japan 106.

Site: 18,000 square feet (about 0.5 acre).

Exterior finish: Structural steel and reinforced concrete faced with 289 panels of precast stone, having the appearance of light gray granite.

Architect: Emil B. Fetzer, Church architect. Architect's local representative, Masao Shiina.

Resident engineer: Sadao Nagata.

Construction superintendent: Yuji Morimura for the Kajima Corporation.

Number of rooms: Two ordinance rooms, five sealing rooms.

Total floor area: 58,000 square feet.

Dimensions: Ground floor is 103 feet by 134 feet; upper levels are 103 by 105 feet. Height to square is 70.5 feet, to top of tower, 178.5 feet.

Design: Modern, one spire.

District: Northern Japan and Vladivostok, Russia.

Groundbreaking, site dedication: Neither was held.

Dedication: Oct. 27-29, 1980, by President Spencer W. Kimball.

Dedicatory prayer excerpt: *"Kind Father, bless all those who come to this temple, that they may do so with humble hearts, in cleanliness, and honor, and integrity. We are grateful for these Saints, for their devotion and their faith, for their worthiness and their determination to be pure and holy."*

TORONTO ONTARIO TEMPLE

Location: On the outskirts of Brampton, about 20 miles west of Toronto; 10060 Bramalea Rd, Brampton, Ontario, Canada L6R 1A1.

Site: Announced April 15, 1984; 13.4 acres.

Exterior finish: White cast stone.

Temple design: Modern.

Architects: Allward-Gouinlock Inc.

Supervising architects: Alfred T. West Jr. and Dagmar Wertheim.

Construction adviser: Jerry Sears

Contractor: Milne & Nicholls Ltd.

Number of rooms: Four ordinance rooms, six sealing rooms.

Total floor area: 56,000 square feet.

Dimensions: 154 feet by 208 feet; spire, 105 feet high with 11-foot statue of Angel Moroni.

District: Ontario.

Groundbreaking, site dedication: Oct. 10, 1987, by President Thomas S. Monson of the First Presidency..

Dedication: Aug. 25-27, 1990, by President Gordon B. Hinckley; 11 sessions.

Dedicatory prayer excerpt: *"This nation has become a gathering place for people from scores of other lands. In their veins flows the blood of Israel. Many have hearkened to the testimony of thy servants and been favored*

with a knowledge of the principles and ordinances of thine everlasting gospel.'

TUXTLA GUTIERREZ MEXICO TEMPLE

Announced: Feb. 25, 1999.

Location: Carretero a Chicoasen, km. 14, casi esquina Avenida Pasea de la Rosetta.

Site: 1.56 acres, including adjoining meetinghouse.

Exterior finish: White marble.

Temple design: Classic modern.

Architects: Alvaro Iñigo and Church A&E Services

Project manager: Bryan Hutchings and John Webster.

Contractor: Impulsa / Okland Construction Co.

Number of rooms: Celestial room, baptistry, two ordinance rooms, two sealing rooms.

Total floor area: 12,469 square feet.

Dimensions: 84 feet by 150 feet.

District: Serves 18,300 members in five stakes one district and three missions.

Groundbreaking, site dedication: March 20, 1999, by Elder Richard E. Turley Sr. of the Seventy.

Dedicated: March 12, 2000, by President James E. Faust, second counselor in the First Presidency; 4 sessions.

Dedicatory prayer excerpt: *"We invoke Thy blessings upon this nation of Mexico where so many of the sons and daughters of Father Lehi dwell. Bless these Thy children. Lift them out of the depths of poverty. Bring new light and understanding into their minds. Cause them to rejoice at Thy watchcare over them."*

VERACRUZ MEXICO TEMPLE

Announced: April 14, 1999.

Location: Av. Ejercito Mexicano, Esq Michoacan CP 94290, Boca del Rio, Veracruz

Site: 3.39 acres, including future meetinghouse site.

Exterior finish: Blanco Guardiano white marble.

Temple design: Classic modern.

Architect: Alvaro Iñigo and Church A&E Services.

Project manager: Rodolfo Avalvos.

Contractor: Impulsa / Okland Const. Co.

Number of rooms: Celestial room, baptistry, two ordinance rooms, two sealing rooms.

Total floor area: 12,469 square feet.

Dimensions: 84 feet by 150 feet.

District: Nine stakes, two districts and two unaffiliated branches.

Groundbreaking: May 29, 1999, by Elder Carl B. Pratt of the Seventy and president of the Mexico South Area.

Dedicated: July 9, 2000, by President Thomas S. Monson, first counselor in the First Presidency; 4 sessions.

Dedicatory prayer excerpt: *"Bless the youth of the land, the young men and the young women, that they may grow up in righteousness before Thee. Bless them with love for the Savior of the world, our Lord and Master, that they may pattern their lives after the pattern of His life."*

VERNAL UTAH TEMPLE

Location: The temple is the remodeled 87-year-old Tabernacle at 200 South and 500 West, Vernal, Utah.

Site: 1.6 acres.

Exterior finish: Face brick.

Temple design: Adaptation of Uintah Stake Tabernacle.

Architects: FFKR Architects of Salt Lake City, Utah.

Project manager: Lloyd Hess.

Contractor: McCullough Engineering and Construction.

Number of rooms: Two ordinance, three sealing.

Total floor area: 33,400 square feet.

District: East central Utah and parts of Wyoming and Colorado.

Groundbreaking, site dedication: May 13, 1995, by President Gordon B. Hinckley.

Dedication: Nov. 2-4, 1997, by President Gordon B. Hinckley; 11 sessions.

Dedicatory prayer excerpt: *We are grateful for this beautiful new structure which utilizes the historic tabernacle built by Thy people nearly a century ago.... Now that old and much-loved building has become the centerpiece of a new and beautiful House of the Lord. It has a quiet luster all its own. We thank Thee for the use to which it has been put."*

VILLAHERMOSA MEXICO TEMPLE

Announced: Oct. 30, 1998.

Location: 1802 27 de Febrero, Colonia Atasta, Villahermosa, Tabasco, Mexico.

Site: 1.36 acres.

Exterior finish: Blanco Guardiano white marble.

Temple Design: Classic modern.

Architects: Alvaro Iñigo and Church A&E Services.

Project manager: John Webster and Dean Fife.

Contractor: PyCSA / Okland Construction Co.

Number of rooms: Celestial room, baptistry, two ordinance rooms, two sealing rooms.

Total floor area: 12,469 square feet.

Dimensions: 84 feet by 150 feet.

District: Eight stakes and two districts.

Groundbreaking: Jan. 9, 1999, by Elder Richard E. Turley Sr. of the Seventy and first counselor in the Mexico South Area.

Dedicated: May 21, 2000, by President Thomas S. Monson, first counselor in the First Presidency; 4 sessions.

Dedicatory prayer excerpt: *"May Thy Holy*

Spirit touch the hearts of all who enter these portals. May they do so with reverence and respect. May this Thy house stand as an expression of the covenant between Thee and Thy children, and wilt Thou be constrained to look with favor upon Thy people and open the windows of heaven and shower down blessings upon them."

WASHINGTON D.C. TEMPLE

Location: Wooded site in Kensington, Md., near Exit 33 of the Capital Beltway (Interstate 495), a half-hour drive from downtown Washington, D.C.; 9900 Stoneybrook Dr., Kensington, MD.

Site: Selected in 1962; 52 acres.

Exterior finish: Reinforced concrete sheathed in 173,000 square feet of Alabama white marble.

Temple design: The total design portrays the Church as "a light to the world," with three towers to the east representing the Melchizedek Priesthood leadership, and those to the west, the Aaronic Priesthood leadership, said principal architect Keith W. Wilcox.

Architects: Fred L. Markham, Henry P. Fetzer, Harold K. Beecher, Keith W. Wilcox, under general direction of Church architect Emil B. Fetzer.

Contractor: Jacobsen, Okland, and Sidney Foulger construction companies.

Number of rooms: Six ordinance rooms, 14 sealing rooms, seven floors.

Total floor area: 160,000 square feet.

Dimensions of building: 248 feet long, 136 feet wide, not including annex or bridge to temple proper. Statue of Angel Moroni on highest spire 288 feet above ground.

District: Eastern United States, excluding New England states and New York.

Groundbreaking, site dedication: Dec. 7, 1968, by President Hugh B. Brown.

Dedication: Nov. 19-22, 1974, by President Spencer W. Kimball; 10 sessions.

Dedicatory prayer excerpt: *"We are so grateful, our Father, that Thy Son has thrown wide open the doors of the prisons for the multitudes who are waiting in the spirit world."*

WINTER QUARTERS NEBRASKA TEMPLE

Announced: June 14, 1999. **Groundbreaking:** Nov. 28, 1999.

CHRONOLOGY, NEWS IN REVIEW

HISTORICAL CHRONOLOGY OF THE CHURCH

This chronology gives a selected listing of important dates in Church history. Among items excluded are many that can be found elsewhere in this Almanac, including information on General Authorities and the establishment of stakes and missions. Italicized entries are secular events that were taking place during those periods.

1805

April 27 — *The U.S. Marines captured the port city of Derna in the Tripolitan War; the phrase "to the shores of Tripoli" in the official Marine hymn comes from this campaign.*

Dec. 23 — Joseph Smith Jr. was born in Sharon, Windsor Co., Vt., the fourth child of Joseph and Lucy Mack Smith.

1816

After living in several villages in central Vermont and New Hampshire, the Joseph Smith Sr. family moved to Palmyra, N.Y., and a few years later to a farm in nearby Manchester, N.Y.

1820

Spring — In Joseph Smith's First Vision, in answer to his prayer that was motivated by his reading of James 1:5, Joseph was visited by the Father and the Son in what is now known as the Sacred Grove near his home in upstate New York. Jesus answered his question about which church to join, opening the door to the restoration of the gospel.

March 3 — *The Missouri Compromise, allowing slavery in Missouri but not anywhere else west of the Mississippi, was passed by Congress.*

1823

Sept. 21-22 — In five visits with Joseph Smith, the resurrected Moroni revealed the existence of ancient gold plates, from which the Book of Mormon was translated, and instructed him on his role in restoring the gospel.

Dec. 2 — *The Monroe Doctrine, stating opposition to European intervention in the Americas, was announced by President James Monroe in his annual message to Congress.*

1827

Jan. 18 — Joseph Smith married Emma Hale in South Bainbridge, N.Y. The couple met while Joseph was working in Harmony, Pa., for Josiah Stowell and boarding with Emma's father, Isaac Hale.

Aug. 6 — *The United States and Great Britain signed a treaty, continuing joint occupation of the Oregon country, which extended from the California border to Alaska.*

Sept. 22 — Joseph Smith received the gold plates from the Angel Moroni at the Hill Cumorah in upstate New York. He also received the Urim and Thummim, which was used in translating the Book of Mormon.

1828

February — Martin Harris took a transcript and partial translation of the Book of Mormon to Professor Charles Anthon of Columbia College and to Dr. Samuel L. Mitchell of New York. In June, Harris borrowed and lost 116 manuscript pages.

July 4 — *The age of railroading began in the United States when the first passenger railroad in the country, the Baltimore & Ohio, started operation.*

1829

May 15 — Joseph Smith and Oliver Cowdery received the Aaronic Priesthood from John the Baptist along the banks of the Susquehanna River, near Harmony, Pa. (See D&C 13.) The two baptized one another, as instructed.

May or June — Peter, James, and John conferred the Melchizedek Priesthood upon Joseph Smith and Oliver Cowdery near the Susquehanna River between Harmony, Pa., and Colesville, N.Y.

June — The Book of Mormon translation was completed, and the three witnesses — Oliver Cowdery, David Whitmer and Martin Harris — were shown the plates by a heavenly messenger. (See D&C 17). Soon afterward, the plates were shown to eight other witnesses —Christian Whitmer, Jacob Whitmer, Peter Whitmer Jr., John Whitmer, Hiram Page, Joseph Smith Sr., Hyrum Smith, and Samuel H. Smith — by the Prophet Joseph Smith.

1830

The first covered wagons, led by Jedediah Smith and William Sublette of the Rocky Mountain Fur Company, made the trek from the Missouri River to the Rocky Mountains.

March 26 — Five thousand copies of the Book of Mormon were published by Joseph Smith and printed in Palmyra, N.Y., by E.B. Grandin at a cost of $3,000.

April — The revelation on Church government (see D&C 20) outlined procedures for organizing the Church, duties of members and officers, need for recordkeeping, and procedures for baptism and sacrament administration.

April 6 — Joseph Smith organized the "Church of Christ" at the Peter Whitmer Sr. home in Fayette, N.Y., with six incorporators as required by law — Joseph Smith, Oliver Cowdery, Hyrum Smith, Peter Whitmer Jr., David Whitmer, and Samuel H. Smith.

April 11 — Oliver Cowdery preached the first public discourse of the new Church at a meeting in the Peter Whitmer home in Fayette, N.Y.

June — The "Words of Moses," later incorporated in the Pearl of Great Price, were revealed to Joseph Smith. The prophecy of Enoch was revealed to the Prophet in December.

June — Joseph Smith was arrested on false charges of disorderly conduct but was acquitted in a trial at South Bainbridge, N.Y. This was the first of what would be many trumped-up charges against the Prophet.

June 9 — The first conference of the Church, which now numbered 27 members, convened in Fayette, N.Y.

June 30 — Samuel H. Smith left on a mission to neighboring villages, including Mendon, N.Y., where the Young and Kimball families resided.

Oct. 17 — Following a revelation received by the Prophet Joseph Smith (see D&C 32), Parley P. Pratt, Oliver Cowdery, Peter Whitmer Jr., and Ziba Peterson began a mission to the Lamanites, leaving copies of the Book of Mormon with the Cattaraugus Indians in New York, the Wyandots in Ohio, and the Shawnees and Delawares on the Missouri frontier. They stopped en route to teach and baptize Sidney Rigdon and a congregation of his followers in the Kirtland, Ohio, area.

Dec. 30 — The Saints were commanded in a revelation (see D&C 37) to gather in Ohio, the first commandment concerning a gathering in this dispensation.

1831

Feb. 4 — Edward Partridge was named "bishop unto the Church." (See D&C 41.) This was the first revelation given through the Prophet Joseph Smith at Kirtland, Ohio.

June 3-6 — At a conference in Kirtland, the first high priests were ordained, and elders were called to go to Jackson County, Mo. (See D&C 52.)

June 7 — Joseph Smith received the revelation (D&C 52) to assemble in Missouri, "the land of your inheritance."

Aug. 2 — During a ceremony in Kaw Township, 12 miles west of Independence in Jackson County, Mo., Sidney Rigdon dedicated the Land of Zion for the gathering of the Saints. The next day, on Aug. 3, Joseph Smith dedicated a temple site at Independence, Mo.

Dec. 12 — *The Republican Party held the first nominating convention of a major party in the United States.*

1832

Jan. 25 — Joseph Smith was sustained president of the high priesthood at a conference at Amherst, Ohio. Sidney Rigdon and Jesse Gause were named counselors in March 1832. Gause's service in this capacity is unconfirmed by historical records. Frederick G. Williams was called by revelation (see D&C 81) to replace him.

Feb. 16 — While working on the inspired revision of the Bible, Joseph Smith and Sidney Rigdon received a vision in Hiram, Ohio, of the three degrees of glory. (See D&C 76.)

May 21 — *The Democratic Party formally adopted its present name at a convention in Baltimore, Md.*

June — Elders began teaching the restored gospel in Canada, the first missionary effort outside the United States.

June 1 — The *Evening and Morning Star*, the first LDS publication, was issued at Independence, Mo., with William W. Phelps as editor.

Dec. 25 — Revelation and prophecy on war (see D&C 87), commencing with the Civil War some 28 years later, was given to the Prophet Joseph Smith in the Kirtland area.

Dec. 27 — The revelation known as the "Olive Leaf" (D&C 88) was presented to the Church. Included were instructions leading to the organization of the School of the Prophets on Jan. 17, 1833.

Dec. 28 — *John Calhoun became the first U.S. vice president to resign. Afterward, he won an election to fill a vacant U.S. Senate seat from South Carolina.*

1833

Feb. 27 — The revelation known as the "Word of Wisdom" (D&C 89) was received by the Prophet Joseph Smith at Kirtland, Ohio.

March 18 — The First Presidency was organized when Sidney Rigdon and Frederick G. Williams were set apart by Joseph Smith to be his counselors, to which they had previously been called.

May 6 — The Saints were commanded by revelation to build a House of the Lord at

Kirtland. (See D&C 94.) Further instructions concerning the building of the temple were given by revelation on June 1. (See D&C 95.)

July 2 — The Prophet Joseph Smith finished the translation of the New Testament.

July 20 — A mob destroyed the *Evening and Morning Star* printing office in Independence, Mo., interrupting the printing of the Book of Commandments. The *Evening and Morning Star* began publication again on Dec. 18 in Kirtland, Ohio.

Oct. 5 — The Prophet Joseph Smith left Kirtland, Ohio, for a brief mission to Canada, where he preached and baptized 16.

November — The Saints fled Jackson County, Mo., in response to mob threats and attacks and took refuge in neighboring counties, particularly Clay County.

Dec. 3 — *Oberlin College in Ohio opened, becoming the first co-educational college in the U.S.*

Dec. 18 — The Prophet Joseph Smith gave the first patriarchal blessings in this dispensation to his parents, three of his brothers, and Oliver Cowdery.

1834

Feb. 17 — The first stake in the Church was created in Kirtland, Ohio, with Joseph Smith as president, and on the same day the first high council of the Church was organized. (See D&C 102). A similar organization was created in Clay-Caldwell counties in Missouri on July 3, 1834, with David Whitmer as president.

May 3 — At a conference of elders in Kirtland, the Church was first named "The Church of Jesus Christ of Latter-day Saints."

May 8 — Zion's Camp began its march from New Portage, Ohio, to Clay County, Mo., to assist the exiled Missouri Saints. The camp dispersed June 30.

June 30 — *The Indian Territory was created by an act of Congress.*

October — The *LDS Messenger and Advocate* began publication at Kirtland and continued until the Mormon evacuation of Ohio in 1838.

1835

The Church published a collection of hymns and sacred songs selected by Emma Smith. She had been appointed to the work in July 1830 (see D&C 25), but destruction of the Independence, Mo., printing press by a mob in 1833 had delayed publication.

Feb. 14 — The Quorum of the Twelve was organized after the three witnesses to the Book of Mormon, as directed by revelation (see D&C 18), selected 12 apostles at a meeting of the members of Zion's Camp in Kirtland, Ohio.

Feb. 28 — The First Quorum of the Seventy was organized in Kirtland, and its first seven presidents, who were also selected from members of Zion's Camp, were named.

March 28 — A revelation in which various priesthood offices and powers were defined (see D&C 107) was received during a meeting of the First Presidency and Quorum of the Twelve in Kirtland.

May 4 — Members of the Quroum of the Twelve left Kirtland for the eastern states on their first mission as apostles.

July 3 — Michael H. Chandler arrived in Kirtland to exhibit four Egyptian mummies and some scrolls of papyrus. Joseph Smith's translation of the scrolls resulted in the Book of Abraham, later included in the Pearl of Great Price.

Aug. 17 — A general assembly of the Church in Kirtland accepted the revelations selected for publication as the Doctrine and Covenants. This volume contained the revelations gathered for the Book of Commandments in 1833 and others received since that time, along with articles on marriage and government and a series of Lectures on Faith written primarily by Joseph Smith for the School of the Prophets.

1836

Jan. 21 — Joseph Smith Sr. was ordained the first Patriarch to the Church.

March 27 — The Kirtland Temple, the first temple built in this dispensation, was dedicated after being under construction for nearly three years. The dedicatory prayer was given to the Prophet Joseph Smith by revelation. (See D&C 109.)

April 3 — The Savior and also Moses, Elias, and Elijah appeared in the Kirtland Temple and committed the keys of their respective dispensations to Joseph Smith and Oliver Cowdery. (See D&C 110.)

June 29 — A mass meeting of citizens at Liberty, Mo., passed a resolution to expel the Saints from Clay County. By December many had relocated on Shoal Creek (later known as Far West) in the newly established Caldwell County, located northeast of Clay County.

1837

Parley P. Pratt published his pamphlet *Voice of Warning* in New York City, the first tract published for missionary use in the Church.

June 20 — *Victoria became Queen of Great Britain.*

July 20 — The first mission in the Church — the British Mission — was organized. Apostles Heber C. Kimball and Orson Hyde, and Elders Willard Richards and Joseph Fielding had left Kirtland, Ohio, June 13 for England, opening up missionary work outside North America. They and two brethren from Canada, John Goodson and Isaac Russell, left New York on July 1 aboard the ship *Garrick*.

July 30 — Nine persons were baptized in the River Ribble at Preston, England, the first converts to the Church in Great Britain. By December, there were 1,000 LDS members in England.

1838

April 23 — *The first transatlantic steamship service began, although scheduled service was not established until 1840.*

May 19 — Joseph Smith and others visited a place on Grand River, in Missouri, about 25 miles north of Far West, called Spring Hill by the Saints, which by revelation was named Adam-ondi-Ahman because "it is the place where Adam shall come to visit his people, or the Ancient of Days shall sit, as spoken of by Daniel the prophet." (See D&C 116, Dan. 7:9-14.)

July 6 — The exodus from Kirtland, Ohio, began under the direction of the First Council of the Seventy as planned three months earlier. The Kirtland Camp arrived at Far West, Mo., Oct. 2 and at Adam-ondi-Ahman two days later.

July 8 — Revelation on the law of tithing (see D&C 119) was given at Far West, Mo.

Aug. 6 — A scuffle at the polls at Gallatin, Daviess County, Mo., intensified the mounting tension between Latter-day Saints and other area settlers.

Oct. 27 — Acting upon false reports of rebellion among the Mormons, Gov. Lilburn W. Boggs issued an order to exterminate or expel the Saints from Missouri.

Oct. 30 — Seventeen Latter-day Saints were killed and 12 severely wounded in the Haun's Mill Massacre at a small settlement on Shoal Creek, 12 miles east of Far West, Mo. The attack, by the Livingston County militia, was a reaction to the extermination order of Gov. Boggs.

Oct. 31 — Joseph Smith and others were made prisoners of the militia. The next day, a court-martial ordered the Prophet and the others shot, but Brig. Gen. A.W. Doniphan refused to carry out the order.

Nov. 9 — Joseph Smith and the other prisoners arrived in Richmond, Mo., where they were put in chains and suffered much abuse by the guards. An arraignment and a two-week trial followed, resulting in their being sent Nov. 28 to the Liberty Jail in Liberty, Mo., where they were imprisoned about Dec. 1.

1839

Jan. 26 — Brigham Young and the Quorum of the Twelve organized a committee to conduct the removal of the Saints from Missouri.

March 20 — While in Liberty Jail, Joseph Smith wrote an epistle to the Saints, which contained fervent pleadings with the Lord regarding the suffering of the Saints and words of prophecy. (See D&C 121.) A few days later, he continued the epistle, parts of which became Sections 122 and 123 of the Doctrine and Covenants.

April 16 — Joseph Smith and four other prisoners were allowed to escape while being transferred from Daviess to Boone counties in Missouri under a change of venue in their case.

April 20 — The last of the Saints left Far West, Mo. A whole community, numbering about 15,000, had been expelled from their homes on account of their religion.

April 25 — Commerce, Ill., was selected as a gathering place for the Church. On May 1, two farms were purchased by Joseph Smith and others, the first land purchased in what later became Nauvoo.

Summer — Members of the Quorum of the Twelve, as their circumstances permitted, departed from Nauvoo, Ill., for their missions to England, in accordance to a revelation concerning the Twelve. (See D&C 118).

June 11 — Joseph Smith began the task of compiling his *History of the Church.* He had the help of scribes and, later, Church historians. Segments of his history were published in Church periodicals in Nauvoo and later in Salt Lake City, and appeared in book form beginning in 1902.

Oct. 29 — Joseph Smith left Illinois for Washington, D.C., to seek redress from the president of the United States for wrongs suffered by the Saints in Missouri.

November — The first issue of the *Times and Seasons*, the fourth periodical begun by the Church, was published in Nauvoo, Ill.

Nov. 29 — In a meeting with U.S. President Martin Van Buren in Washington,

D.C., Joseph Smith was told by the president that he [Van Buren] could do nothing to relieve the oppressions in Missouri. Petitions were also presented to Congress, and a second interview was held with Van Buren, all to no avail.

1840

January — *Wilkes expedition discovered the Antarctic continent.*

April 15 — The Twelve in England named Parley P. Pratt editor of a proposed monthly periodical to be named the *Latter-day Saints Millennial Star*. The first issue was published in Manchester, England, on May 27; the publication continued until 1970.

June 6 — Forty-one members of the Church sailed for the United States from Liverpool, England, on the ship *Britannia*, being the first Saints to gather from a foreign land. By 1890, some 85,000 LDS emigrants had crossed the Atlantic Ocean in about 280 voyages.

Dec. 16 — Gov. Thomas Carlin of Illinois signed a bill creating a charter for Nauvoo, defining the city boundaries and establishing its government. Provisions included a university and a militia, the Nauvoo Legion.

1841

Jan. 19 — A revelation (see D&C 124) given at Nauvoo, Ill., outlined instructions for building a temple in Nauvoo. Baptism for the dead was introduced as a temple ordinance.

Jan. 24 — Hyrum Smith was ordained Patriarch to the Church, replacing his father, who had died Sept. 14, 1840, and also as assistant president, replacing Oliver Cowdery, who had been excommunicated.

April 4 — *John Tyler was the first vice president to become U.S. president due to death of a predecessor.*

Oct. 24 — At a site on the Mount of Olives in Jerusalem, Orson Hyde dedicated Palestine for the gathering of the Jews.

1842

Elder Lorenzo Snow presented a British edition of the Book of Mormon to Queen Victoria of England, the first head of government in the world to receive a copy of the Book of Mormon. The book, printed in Liverpool in 1841, is now in the Royal Library at Windsor.

March 1 — The Articles of Faith were published for the first time in the *Times and Seasons* in Nauvoo, Ill. Joseph Smith, in response to a request from John Wentworth, editor of the *Chicago Democrat*, wrote a summary of the Church's history, ending with 13 declarations of belief.

March 17 — Joseph Smith organized the Female Relief Society of Nauvoo, with Emma Smith, Sarah M. Cleveland, and Elizabeth Ann Whitney as its presidency, to look after the poor and sick.

May 4 — Joseph Smith introduced the temple endowment to seven men at a meeting in the room over his store in Nauvoo. A few others received endowments before completion of a temple.

Aug. 6 — Joseph Smith prophesied that the Saints would be driven to the Rocky Mountains, but that he would not go with them.

1843

Jan. 10 — *The first impeachment resolution was introduced in Congress; Virginian John Botts charged President John Tyler with corruption, misconduct in office and high crimes. It was rejected 127-83.*

May 3 — The *Nauvoo Neighbor* began publication and was voice for the Church for 2 1/2 years.

June 21 — Illinois agents, armed with a warrant from Gov. Thomas Ford, arrested Joseph Smith at Dixon, Lee County, Ill. He was released July 1, 1843, under a writ of habeas corpus.

July 12 — A revelation received in Nauvoo, Ill., on the "Eternity of the Marriage Covenant and Plural Marriage" (see D&C 132) was recorded, giving fuller meaning to the "new and everlasting covenant," which had been mentioned as early as 1831.

1844

Jan. 29 — A political convention in Nauvoo nominated Joseph Smith as a candidate for president of United States.

Feb. 20 — Joseph Smith instructed the Quorum of the Twelve to organize an exploratory expedition to look for a possible site for the Saints in California or Oregon. In meetings over the next several days, a group of volunteers was organized for the trip.

March 26 — Joseph Smith prepared a message for Congress, asking for a law protecting United States citizens immigrating to the unorganized territories, known as California and Oregon, and offered volunteers to serve in such a protective force.

April 30 — Addison Pratt landed on Tubuai, the first missionary to begin work in the South Pacific.

May 11 — Joseph Smith organized the Council of Fifty, a secret political body that directed the westward migration of the Saints and served as a "shadow government" in Utah during the 19th century.

May 24 — *Samuel Morse transmitted the first public message by telegraph from Washington, D.C., to Baltimore, opening the way for development of the first means of rapid communications.*

June 7 — The first and only edition of the anti-Mormon *Nauvoo Expositor* appeared. The city council declared the paper a nuisance three days later, and the city marshal forced entry into the print shop and destroyed the type and papers.

June 11 — Joseph Smith and the city council were charged with riot in the destruction of the *Expositor* press. A Nauvoo court absolved them of the charge, but the complainant asked for the issue to be examined by the Carthage court.

June 22 — Joseph and Hyrum Smith crossed the Mississippi River to flee to the Great Basin. But Illinois Gov. Thomas Ford promised the Prophet safety, and so at the pleadings of others, the pair returned to Nauvoo and turned themselves over to government agents.

June 27 — Joseph and Hyrum Smith were killed by a mob that rushed the Carthage Jail in Carthage, Ill. John Taylor was injured in the attack; Willard Richards escaped injury.

Aug. 4 — Sidney Rigdon advocated appointment of a guardian for the Church at a meeting in Nauvoo.

Aug. 8 — At a meeting designated for the appointment of a guardian, Rigdon again stated his views, after which Brigham Young announced an afternoon meeting. During the latter session, Young claimed the right of the Twelve Apostles to lead the Church and was sustained by a vote of the Church.

1845

January — The Illinois Legislature repealed the city charter of Nauvoo. A desperate attempt by Church leaders to reverse the action proved futile.

May — The nine accused murderers of Joseph and Hyrum Smith were acquitted upon instructions of the court.

Fall — A limestone baptismal font replaced a temporary wooden font in the basement of the Nauvoo Temple.

Sept. 9 — Church leaders stated their intent to move to the Rocky Mountains to establish a refuge for the Saints.

Sept. 22 — Citizens at a mass meeting in Quincy, Ill., endorsed a proposal requesting that the Saints leave Illinois as quickly as possible. The Twelve's reply reiterated the Latter-day Saints' intention to move to a remote area and asked for cooperation and an end of harassment in order to prepare for the move early the following summer.

Sept. 23 — *The first U.S. baseball club, the New York Knickerbocker Club, was organized.*

Dec. 10, 1845-Feb. 7, 1846 — Some 5,000 members received their endowments in the yet-to-be-finished Nauvoo Temple prior to their exodus from Nauvoo.

1846

Jan. 30 — A wind vane in the shape of an angel was put on the tower of the Nauvoo Temple.

Feb. 4 — The Mormon migration from Nauvoo began. The same day, the ship *Brooklyn* left New York for California under the direction of Samuel Brannan.

April 24 — A temporary settlement of the westward-moving Saints was established at Garden Grove, Iowa. Other camps were established at Mount Pisgah, Iowa, on May 16; at Kanesville (Council Bluffs), Iowa, on June 14; and at Winter Quarters, Neb., in September.

May 1 — The Nauvoo Temple was dedicated in public services by Apostle Orson Hyde

July 7 — *Annexation of California was proclaimed by the United States after the surrender of Mexico in the Mexican War.*

July 13 — The first of the volunteer companies of the Mormon Battalion was enlisted in response to a request delivered to Brigham Young two weeks earlier by Capt. James Allen of the United States Army. The battalion left Kanesville, Iowa, for Fort Leavenworth, Kan., on July 20.

July 31 — The ship *Brooklyn* arrived in Yerba Buena (now San Francisco), California.

August — *The Donner party blazed a trail from Henefer, Utah, to Salt Lake Valley that was used the following summer by Brigham Young's party of the original Mormon pioneers. A delay in cutting the path contributed to the Donner party losing 42 lives when they became snowbound in the Sierra Nevada, California.*

Sept. 17 — The remaining Saints in Nauvoo were driven from the city in violation of a "treaty of surrender" worked out with a citizens' committee from Quincy, Ill. The siege became known as the Battle of Nauvoo.

1847

Jan. 14 —Brigham Young presented "the word and will of the Lord," (see D&C 136) concerning the westward trek, including the pattern for organizing the wagon companies and the conduct of the participants, based on gospel principles.

Jan. 27 —The Mormon Battalion, completing its march across the Southwest, arrived at San Luis Rey, Calif., near San Diego., within view of the Pacific Ocean.

April 5 — The first pioneer company, numbering 143 men, 3 women and 2 children, left Winter Quarters, Neb., for the West, under the leadership of Brigham Young.

July 16 — Members of the Mormon Battalion were discharged at Los Angeles, Calif.

July 22-24 — Brigham Young's pioneer company arrived in the Great Salt Lake Valley. Eleven companies arrived in the valley in 1847.

July 28 — Brigham Young selected a site for the Salt Lake Temple and instructed surveyors to lay out a city on a grid pattern aligned to the compass.

Dec. 5 — The First Presidency was reorganized by the Quorum of the Twelve in Kanesville, Iowa, with Brigham Young sustained as president, and Heber C. Kimball and Willard Richards as counselors. The action was ratified in a conference in the newly constructed tabernacle in Kanesville three weeks later on Dec. 27.

December — President Brigham Young sent a highly influential general epistle calling upon members all over the world to gather in the Great Basin of the Rocky Mountains.

1848

Jan. 24 — Nine members of the discharged Mormon Battalion were at Sutter's Mill in California when gold was discovered. The millrace, or canal to the millwheel, was dug by members of the battalion. Battalion member Henry Bigler was given credit for recording in his journal the date of discovery .

Feb. 2 — *The Treaty of Guadalupe Hidalgo ended the war between Mexico and the United States that had begun in 1846. By terms of the treaty, Mexico gave up what are now the states of California, Nevada, Utah, most of Arizona, and parts of New Mexico, Colorado, and Wyoming, and relinquished all rights to Texas north of the Rio Grande.*

May — Millions of crickets descended into Salt Lake Valley and devoured the crops of the pioneers. The "miracle of the sea gulls" saved what was left of the crops by devouring the crickets.

Aug. 10— A thanksgiving feast was held in Great Salt Lake Valley to celebrate the harvest.

Aug. 13 — A conference in Manchester, England, was attended by more than 17,000 members of the British Mission.

November — The high council at Kanesville, Iowa, voted to accept a repentant Oliver Cowdery back into the Church as he requested.

1849

Jan. 1 — The first $1 denomination of "valley currency" was issued and signed by Brigham Young, Heber C. Kimball and Thomas Bullock. It was the first printing in the Salt Lake Valley.

Feb. 14 — Great Salt Lake City was divided into 19 wards of nine blocks each.

March 5 — A provisional State of Deseret was established and appeals were made to the federal government for self-government.

Aug. 28 — Capt. Howard Stansbury and Lt. John W. Gunnison arrived to survey the Great Salt Lake area.

October — A Perpetual Emigrating Fund to assist the poor to immigrate to the Salt Lake Valley was established during general conference. The system, which was incorporated a year later, continued until it was disincorporated by the Edmunds-Tucker Act in 1887.

Dec. 9 — The Sunday School was started by Richard Ballantyne in Salt Lake City. George Q. Cannon became the first general superintendent in November 1867.

1850

Missionary work took on a wider scope as missions were opened overseas in Scandinavia, France, Italy, Switzerland, and Hawaii; most, however, were discontinued after a few years.

March 26 — Col. Thomas L. Kane delivered his famous lecture to the Pennsylvania Historical Society about the Mormons and their forced exodus from Nauvoo, Ill.

June 15 — The first edition of the *Deseret News* was published in Salt Lake City.

Sept. 9 — Rather than admitting the state of Deseret into the Union, Congress created the Territory of Utah. On Sept. 20, Brigham Young was appointed governor of the territory. However, the news didn't reach Utah until Jan. 27, 1851.

Sept. 18 — *The U.S. Congress passed the Fugitive Slave Act, permitting slave owners to reclaim slaves who had escaped into other states.*

1851-1852

(See box on this page)

1853

Feb. 14 — President Brigham Young broke ground for the Salt Lake Temple and President Heber C. Kimball dedicated the site. Excavation began that day.

April 6 — The four cornerstones of the Salt Lake Temple were laid.

June 29 — *The U.S. Senate ratified the $10 million Gadsden Purchase from Mexico, which completed the modern geographical configuration of the continental United States.*

July 18 — The so-called "Walker War" began near Payson, Utah. This was one of several incidents of tension between Mormons and Indians in the Utah Territory. The war ended in May 1854.

1854

Jan. 19 — The official announcement adopting the Deseret Alphabet was made in the *Deseret News.*

May 26 — *The Kansas-Nebraska bill passed, giving territories or states freedom of choice on the question of slavery.*

Dec. 31 — It was reported that 32,627 members lived in countries comprising the European missions, of which 29,441 were in Great Britain

1855

Feb. 17 — *Congress authorized construction of a telegraph line from the Mississippi River to the Pacific.*

May 5 — The two-story adobe Endowment House in Salt Lake City was dedicated and remained in use until 1889 when it was torn down.

July 23 — The foundation of the Salt Lake Temple was finished.

Oct. 4 — The bark *Julia Ann* carrying 28 emigrating Church members from Australia ran aground on shoals near the Scilly Islands. Five were drown.

150 YEARS AGO:1851-1852

1851

Jan. 26 — The second stake in the Church and the first outside the Salt Lake Valley — since the pioneers arrived in Utah — was the Weber Stake, created by Brigham Young with headquarters in Ogden. Within the next six months, two other stakes were created, in Provo, Utah, on March 19, and in San Bernardino, Calif., on July 6.

March 24 — A company of 500 settlers called to settle in California departed from Payson, Utah. The group settled in San Bernardino, Calif., which became the first Mormon colony outside the Great Basin since the arrival of the pioneers in 1847.

May — The Book of Mormon was published in Copenhagen, Denmark, in Danish, the first language other than English in which the book was printed.

Aug. 12 — *Isaac Singer was granted a patent for his sewing machine. Singer set up business in Boston with $40 capital.*

September — Three federally appointed officials, Judge Lemuel C. Brandenbury, Judge Perry C. Brochus, and Secretary Broughton D. Harris, left Utah in protest against plural marriage, as well as what they considered unjustified influence of the Church in political affairs in the territory.

Nov. 11 — The University of the State of Deseret (now the University of Utah) in Salt Lake City was begun.

1852

During the year, areas that were opened up to missionary work included, India, China, Siam, Cape of Good Hope, Prussia, Gilbraltar, and the West Indies.

March 20 — *Harriet Beecher Stowe's influential novel about slavery,* Uncle Tom's Cabin, *was published.*

April 6 — An adobe tabernacle, built on the southwest corner of the Temple Block where the Assembly Hall now stands, was dedicated.

Aug. 28-29 — At a special conference in Salt Lake City, the doctrine of plural marriage was first publicly announced, although several of the leading brethren of the Church had been practicing the principle privately since it had been taught to them by Joseph Smith in Nauvoo.

Oct. 9 — Members, meeting in conference in the tabernacle, unanimously voted to build the Salt Lake Temple.

Oct. 29 — In a general epistle, the First Presidency proposed that Perpetual Emigrating Fund immigrants cross the plains by handcart.

1856

During the year, a general "reformation" took place throughout the Church, in which Church members were admonished strongly from the pulpit to reform their lives and rededicate themselves to the service of the Lord. As a symbol of renewed dedication, many members renewed their covenants by rebaptism. The reformation movement continued into 1857.

Feb. 10 — *An important change in U.S. citizenship laws provided that all children born abroad to U.S. citizens were assured of citizenship.*

June 9 — The first handcart company left Iowa City, Iowa. Later that year, two handcart companies, captained by James G. Willie and Edward Martin, suffered tragedy due to an early winter. More than 200 in the two companies died along the trail.

1857

March 6 — *The U.S. Supreme Court handed down its landmark ruling that a slave, Dred Scott, could not sue in federal court for his freedom.*

March 30 — Territorial Judge W.W. Drummond, who had earlier left the Territory of Utah, wrote a letter to the Attorney General of the United States, charging Mormon leaders with various crimes.

May 13 — Elder Parley P. Pratt of the Quorum of the Twelve was assassinated while on a mission in Arkansas.

May 28 — Under instructions from President James Buchanan, the United States War Department issued orders for an army to assemble at Fort Leavenworth, Kan., to march to Utah. It was assumed that the people of Utah were in rebellion against the United States. This was the beginning of the so-called "Utah War."

July 24 — While participating in the 10th anniversary celebration in Big Cottonwood Canyon of the arrival of the Pioneers, Brigham Young received word that the army, under the command of Col. Albert S. Johnston, was approaching Utah.

Sept. 7 — The Mountain Meadows Massacre took place, in which Arkansas immigrants on their way to California were killed in Southern Utah. Twenty years later, John D. Lee was executed for his part in the crime.

Sept. 15 — Brigham Young declared Utah to be under martial law and forbade the approaching troops to enter the Salt Lake Valley. An armed militia was ordered to go to various points to harass the soldiers and prevent their entry. Brigham Young also called the elders home from foreign missions and advised the Saints in many outlying settlements in the West to return to places nearer the headquarters of the Church.

1858

Feb. 24 — Col. Thomas L. Kane, a friend of the Mormons, voluntarily arrived in Salt Lake City to try to bring about a peaceful solution to the difficulties between the federal government and the Church. After meeting with President Brigham Young, he went to Ft. Scott (near Ft. Bridger) in Wyoming and met with the incoming governor of Utah, Alfred Cumming.

June 11 — The peace commissioners met with President Young and others in the Council House in Salt Lake City and peacefully worked out the difficulties between the United States and the Church.

June 26 — After having been stopped for the winter by the delaying tactics of the Mormons, Col. Johnston's army finally — and peacefully — entered the Salt Lake Valley,. The army's encampment, until 1861, was at Camp Floyd in Cedar Valley in Utah County. Most of the Saints north of Utah County had moved south, and they only returned to their homes when peace seemed assured.

Aug. 5 — *The first transatlantic telegraph cable was completed between the United States and Great Britain.*

1859

July 13 — Horace Greeley, founder and editor of the *New York Tribune*, had a two-hour interview with President Brigham Young, covering a variety of subjects from infant baptism to plurality of wives. The substance of his interview was published a year later in Greeley's *Overland Journey from New York to San Francisco.*

Aug. 27 — *The first oil well in the United States was drilled near Titusville, Pa.*

1860

Spring — Three apostles, Elders Amasa M. Lyman, Charles C. Rich, and George Q. Cannon, were appointed by President Brigham Young as the presidency of the European Mission, infusing new life into the mission.

April 3 — The Pony Express mail service began. A number of young Mormons were among the riders.

Sept. 16 — At a meeting in the bowery on the Temple Block, President Brigham Young condemned the practice of missionaries asking members in the mission field for support and, instead, said that missionary service should be financed by members at home.

Sept. 24 — The last of 10 groups of pioneers to cross the plains by handcarts arrived in Salt Lake City.

November — *Abraham Lincoln defeated Stephen A. Douglas in the presidential election.*

1861

March 2 — A bill was approved by U.S. President James Buchanan that provided for the organization of the Nevada Territory out of the western portions of Utah.

April 12 — *The Civil War began as Confederate forces fired on Ft. Sumpter in South Carolina.*

April 23 — The first of several Church wagon trains left the Salt Lake Valley with provisions for incoming Saints, whom they would meet at the Missouri River. This was the beginning of a new program to help immigrating Saints that lasted until the railroad came in 1869.

Oct. 1 — The first baptisms in the Netherlands took place near the village of Broek-Akkerwoude in the northern province of Friesland. A monument marking the site was erected in 1936.

Oct. 18 — President Brigham Young sent the first telegram over the just-completed overland telegram line.

1862

March 6 — The Salt Lake Theater, which became an important cultural center for Mormon people in the area, was dedicated. It was opened to the public two days later.

May — The Church sent 262 wagons, 292 men, 2,880 oxen, and 143,315 pounds of flour to the Missouri River to assist poor immigrants from Europe on their trek to the Great Basin.

May 20 — *The Homestead Act, granting free family farms to settlers, was passed.*

July 8 — A federal law was passed and approved by President Abraham Lincoln, defining plural marriage as bigamy and declaring it a crime. Mormons considered the law unconstitutional and refused to honor it.

1863.

March 10 — President Brigham Young was arrested on a charge of bigamy and placed under a $2,000 bond by Judge Kinney. He was never brought to trial, however.

April 14 — *A continuous roll printing press was patented, the first press to print both sides of a sheet.*

1864

April 5 — A small group of Saints bound for Utah sailed from Port Elizabeth, South Africa. Five days later another group set sail for Utah from South Africa.

1865

A war with the Indians began in central Utah, known as the Black Hawk War. It lasted until 1867.

Jan. 18 — Orson Pratt and William W. Ritter arrived in Austria. They were soon banished.

Feb. 1 — *Abraham Lincoln signed the document abolishing slavery in the United States. After ratification by 27 states, the necessary three-fourths, the measure became the 13th Amendment to the Constitution on Dec. 18, 1865.*

April 10 — In a special conference, the Church agreed to build a telegraph line connecting the settlements in Utah. The line was completed in 1867.

April 14 — *U.S. President Abraham Lincoln was assassinated by John Wilkes Booth in Ford's Theatre in Washington, D.C., while watching a performance of "Our American Cousin."*

1866

Jan. 1 — The first edition of the *Juvenile Instructor*, the official organ of the Sunday School, was published. Its name was changed to the *Instructor* in 1930, and it continued publication until 1970.

1867

July 1 — *The Dominion of Canada was created.*

Oct. 6 — The first conference to be conducted in the newly completed Tabernacle on Temple Square in Salt Lake City began. The building was dedicated eight years later on Oct. 9, 1875.

Dec. 8 — Brigham Young requested that bishops reorganize Relief Societies within their wards. The societies had been disbanded during the Utah War.

1868

Jan. 29 — The name Great Salt Lake City was changed to simply Salt Lake City.

May 26 — *President Andrew Johnson was acquitted of impeachment charges by one vote. Johnson had been accused of "high crimes and misdemeanors."*

1869

March 1 — The Church-owned ZCMI opened for business. It was the forerunner of several cooperative business ventures in Utah territory.

May 10 — The transcontinental railroad was completed with the joining of the rails at Promontory Summit, Utah. The railroad had great impact on immigration policy and on the general economy of the Church in Utah.

Nov. 17 — *The Suez Canal, linking the Mediterranean Sea and the Red Sea, was opened.*

Nov. 28 — The Young Ladies' Retrenchment Association, later renamed the Young Women's Mutual Improvement Association, was organized by Brigham Young in the Lion House in Salt Lake City. The first president, called June 19, 1880, was Elmina Shepherd Taylor. This was the forerunner of today's Young Women organization.

1870

Jan. 13 — A large mass meeting was held by the women of Salt Lake City in protest against certain anti-Mormon legislation pending in Congress. This and other such meetings demonstrated that, contrary to anti-Mormon claims, Mormon women were not antagonistic to the ecclesiastical leadership in Utah.

February — The "Liberal Party" was formed in Utah, which generally came to represent the anti-Mormon political interests, as opposed to the "People's Party," which generally represented Church interests until the end of the 19th century.

Feb. 12 — An act of the Territorial Legislature giving the elective franchise to the women of Utah was signed into law. Utah became one of the first American states or territories to grant women the right to vote.

July 24 — *The first railroad car from the Pacific Coast reached New York City, beginning transcontinental train service.*

1871

February — Judge James B. McKean, who had arrived in Utah in August 1870, made several rulings that began a bitter and antagonistic relationship between himself and Church members.

Oct. 2 — President Brigham Young was arrested on a charge of unlawful cohabitation. Various legal proceedings in the court of Judge James B. McKean lasted until April 25, 1872, during which time President Young was sometimes kept in custody in his own home. The case was dropped, however, due to a U.S. Supreme Court decision that overturned various judicial proceedings in Utah for the previous 18 months.

Oct. 8 — *Fire broke out in Patrick O'Leary's barn, which later became known as the Chicago fire, and before the blaze was put out 27 hours later, 300 persons died, 18,000 buildings were destroyed and 90,000 were left homeless.*

1872

June – The first issue of the *Woman's Exponent*, a paper owned and edited by Mormon women, was published. This periodical continued until 1914.

Nov. 5 — *Susan B. Anthony was fined $100 for voting in the presidential election, because women did not then have the right to vote.*

1873

April 8 — Due to failing health, President Brigham Young called five additional counselors in the First Presidency.

1874

May 8 — *Massachusetts enacted the first effective 10-hour work day law for women.*

May 9 — At general conference, which began on this date, the principal subject discussed was the "United Order." This resulted in the establishment of several cooperative economic ventures, the most notable of which were communities such as Orderville, Utah, where the residents owned no private property but held all property in common.

June 23 — The Poland Bill became a federal law. It had the effect of limiting the jurisdiction of probate courts in Utah. These courts had been authorized to conduct all civil and criminal cases and were generally favorable toward members of the Church, but now Mormons accused of crimes had to be tried in federal courts.

1875

March 18 — Judge James B. McKean, with whom the Mormons had been unhappy, was removed from office by U.S. President Ulysses S. Grant.

May 19 — *The first Kentucky Derby was run at Louisville, Ky.*

June 10 — The first Young Men's Mutual Improvement Association was organized in the Thirteenth Ward in Salt Lake City. On Dec. 8, 1876, a central committee was formed to coordinate all such associations. Junius F. Wells was the first superintendent. This was the forerunner of today's Young Men organization.

Oct. 16 — Brigham Young Academy, later to become Brigham Young University, was founded in Provo, Utah.

1876

March 7 — *The patent was issued for Alexander Graham Bell's telephone.*

March 23 — Advance companies of Saints from Utah who were called to settle in Arizona arrived at the Little Colorado. This was the beginning of Mormon colonization in Arizona.

1877

April 6 — The St. George Temple was dedicated by President Daniel H. Wells in connection with the 47th Annual Conference of the Church that was held in St. George. This was the first temple to be completed in Utah. The lower portion of the temple had been dedicated earlier, on Jan. 1, 1877, and ordinances for the dead had commenced.

April 24 — *Northern post-Civil War rule in the South ended as federal troops were removed from New Orleans.*

Aug. 29 — President Brigham Young died at his home in Salt Lake City at age 76.

Sept. 4 — The Quorum of the Twelve, with John Taylor as president, publicly assumed its position as the head of the Church.

1878

May 19 — The Church had previously provided for the purchase of land in Conejos County, Colo., for settlements of Saints from the Southern States. On this date the first settlers arrived, thus opening Mormon settlements in Colorado.

Aug. 25 — The Primary, founded by Aurelia Rogers, held its first meeting at Farmington, Utah. The movement spread rapidly and on June 19, 1880, a Churchwide organization was established, with Louie B. Felt as the first president.

Dec. 1 — *The first telephone was installed in the White House.*

1879

Jan. 6 — The Supreme Court of the United States, in the important Reynolds case, upheld the previous conviction of George Reynolds under the 1862 anti-bigamy law. With the ruling, the court paved the way for more intense and effective prosecution of the Mormons in the 1880s.

Oct. 4 — The first edition of the *Contributor*, which became the official publication of the Young Men's Mutual Improvement Association, was issued. It was published until 1896.

Oct. 21 — *Thomas Edison tested an electric incandescent light bulb in Menlo Park, N.J., that burned for 13 1/2 hours, marking the beginning of a new era of electric lighting.*

1880

April 6 — At general conference, a special jubilee year celebration was inaugurated. Charitable actions, reminiscent of Old Testament jubilee celebrations, included rescinding half the debt owed to the Perpetual Emigrating Fund Company, distribution of cows and sheep among the needy, and advice to the Saints to forgive the worthy poor of their debts.

Oct. 10 — The First Presidency was reorganized with President John Taylor sustained as third president of the Church, with Presidents George Q. Cannon and Joseph F. Smith as counselors.

Dec. 20 — *One mile of Broadway Street in New York City was electrically illuminated by arc lighting.*

1881

May 21 — *The American Red Cross was organized, with Clara Barton as president.*

Oct. 18 — Ngataki was the first Maori baptized in New Zealand.

1882

Jan. 8 — The Assembly Hall on Temple Square in Salt Lake City, completed in 1880 from left-over stones from the Salt Lake Temple construction, was dedicated.

March 22 — The Edmunds Anti-Polygamy bill became law when U.S. President Chester A. Arthur added his approval to that of the Senate and House of Representatives. The law defined polygamous living as "unlawful cohabitation" and made punishable the contracting of plural marriage as well as disenfranchisment of those who continued to live it. Serious prosecution under this law began in 1884.

July 17 — The Deseret Hospital, the second hospital in Utah and the first Church hospital, was opened by the Relief Society in Salt Lake City.

Aug. 18 — The Utah Commission, authorized in the Edmunds law, arrived in the territory. The five members of the commission, appointed by the U.S. president, had responsibility of supervising election procedures in Utah. Since the result of its activities was to enforce the disfranchisement of much of the Mormon population, Church members considered its work unfair.

Sept. 30 — *The first hydroelectric power station in the United States was opened at Appleton, Wis.*

1883

January — *The Pendleton Act established the U.S. Civil Service System.*

June 21 — The Council House, the first public building erected in Salt Lake City, was destroyed by fire. The structure was completed in December 1850 and was designed as a "general council house" for the Church, but was also used by the provisional State of Deseret as a statehouse. It also housed the University of Deseret for a number of years.

Aug. 26 — The first permanent branch of the Church among the Maoris in New Zealand was organized at Papawai, Wairarapa Valley, on the North Island.

Dec. 26 — Thomas L. Kane, long a friend of the Church and a champion for Mormon people, died in Philadelphia, Pa.

1884

May 1 — *Work began in Chicago on a 10-story building called a "skyscraper."*

May 17 — The Logan Temple, the second temple constructed after the Saints came west, was dedicated by President John Taylor.

June 9 — The building known as the "Cock Pit," in Preston, England, in which the first Mormon missionaries to England held meetings in 1837, tumbled down.

1885

Extensive prosecution under the Edmunds Law continued in both Utah and Idaho. Many who practiced polygamy were imprisoned, while others fled into exile, some to Mexico in 1885 and to Canada in 1887. Many of the Church leaders involved in plural marriage went into hiding, which was referred to as the "underground." Similar conditions continued for the next few years. These years are sometimes called the years of the "Crusade."

Feb. 1 — President John Taylor delivered his last public sermon in the Tabernacle in Salt Lake City. It was also his last appearance in public before he went to the "underground."

Feb. 3 — An Idaho law was approved by the governor that prohibited all Mormons from voting through the device of a "test oath." The Idaho "test oath" was upheld five years later by the U.S. Supreme Court on Feb. 3, 1890.

Feb. 21 — *The 555-foot high Washington Monument was dedicated 37 years after the cornerstone was laid.*

March 22 — The U.S. Supreme Court annulled the "test oath" formulated by the Utah Commission, thus restoring the right to vote to Saints in the territory.

May 13 — A delegation, appointed by a mass meeting held in the Tabernacle in Salt Lake City on May 2, met with U.S. President Grover Cleveland in the White House in Washington, D.C. They presented to the president a "Statement of Grievances and Protest" concerning injustices brought about because of the Edmunds law.

1886

Jan. 31 — The first Church meeting was held in the first meetinghouse built in Mexico on the Piedras Verdes River in the settlement of Colonia Juarez in northern Mexico.

March 6 — A mass meeting of 2,000 LDS women assembled in the Salt Lake Theater to protest the abuse heaped upon them by the federal courts and to protest the loss of their vote.

Oct. 28 — *The Statue of Liberty, a gift from the French people symbolizing the friendship between the United States and France, was dedicated in New York Harbor.*

1887

Feb. 17-18 — The Edmunds-Tucker Act passed Congress, and it became law without the signature of U.S. President Grover Cleveland. Among other stringent provisions, the law disincorporated the Church, dissolved the Perpetual Emigrating Fund Company and escheated its property to the government, abolished female suffrage, and provided for the confiscation of practically all the property of the Church.

June 3 — Charles O. Card, leading a contingent of eight families, pitched camp on Lee's Creek in southern Alberta, marking the beginning of the Mormon settlements in Canada. Under instructions from President John Taylor, a gathering place for Latter-day Saints in Canada was selected, and on June 17 a site was chosen for what later became Cardston.

July 25 — President John Taylor died while in "exile" at Kaysville, Utah, at age 78. The Quorum of Twelve Apostles assumed leadership of the Church until 1889.

July 30 — Under provisions of the Edmunds-Tucker Act, suits were filed against the Church and the Perpetual Emigrating Fund Company, and Church property was confiscated. A receiver for the property was appointed in November 1887, but the government allowed the Church to rent and occupy certain offices and the temple block.

Aug. 31 — *Thomas A. Edison was awarded a patent for a device he called a "kinetoscope," used to produce pictures representing objects in motion.*

1888

March 11 — *More than 400 people died as a snowstorm crippled the eastern United States during the legendary "Blizzard of '88," the most noted snowstorm in U.S. history.*

May 17 — The Manti Temple was dedicated in a private service by President Wilford Woodruff of the Quorum of the Twelve; a public service was held May 21.

June 8 — The Church General Board of Education sent a letter instructing each stake to establish an academy for secondary education. From 1888 to 1909, 35 academies were established in Utah, Idaho, Wyoming, Arizona, Mexico and Canada. The academy in Rexburg, Idaho, later became Ricks College.

1889

April 6 — The first Relief Society general conference was held in the Assembly Hall in Salt Lake City. Twenty stakes were represented.

April 7 — President Wilford Woodruff was sustained as fourth president of the Church, with Presidents George Q. Cannon and Joseph F. Smith as counselors.

May 6 — *The Eiffel Tower in Paris was officially opened at the World's Fair.*

October -- The *Young Woman's Journal,* official organ of the Young Ladies' Mutual Improvement Association, began publication. It was merged with the *Improvement Era* in 1929.

November — The Endowment House in Salt Lake City was torn down.

1890

Sept. 24 — President Wilford Woodruff issued the "Manifesto," now included in the Doctrine and Covenants as "Official Declaration — 1," that declared that no new plural marriages had been entered into with Church approval in the past year, denied that plural marriage had been taught during that time, declared the intent of the president of the Church to submit to the constitutional law of the land, and advised members of the Church to refrain from contracting any marriage forbidden by law.

Oct. 6 — The "Manifesto" was unanimously accepted by vote in general conference. This marked the beginning of reconciliation between the Church and the United States, which effectively paved the way to statehood for Utah a little more than five years later.

Oct. 25 — The First Presidency sent a letter to stake presidents and bishops directing that a week-day religious education program be established in every ward where there was not a Church school. It was recommended that classes be taught, under the direction of the Church's General Board of Education, after school hours or on Saturdays .

Dec. 31 — *Ellis Island in New York Harbor was opened as an immigration depot.*

1891

March — At the first triennial meeting of the National Council of Women of the United States, the Relief Society attended and became a charter member of that council.

1892

Jan. 4 — The new Brigham Young Academy building at Provo, Utah, was dedicated.

April 19 — *Three million acres of Cheyenne and Arapaho lands in Oklahoma were opened for settlement by presidential proclamation.*

Oct. 12 — Articles of incorporation for the Relief Society were filed, after which it became known as the National Women's Relief Society. The name was again changed in 1945 to Relief Society of The Church of Jesus Christ of Latter-day Saints.

1893

Jan. 4 — The President of the United States, Benjamin Harrison, issued a proclamation of amnesty to all polygamists who had entered into that relationship before Nov. 1, 1890. The Utah Commission soon ruled that voting restrictions in the territory should be removed.

April 6 — The Salt Lake Temple was dedicated by President Wilford Woodruff. The dedicatory services were repeated almost daily until April 24 with a total of 31 services held.

May 23 — The first ordinance work, baptisms for the dead, was performed in the Salt Lake Temple. On May 24, the first endowment work and sealings were performed.

June 27 — *The stock market crashed, resulting in four years of economic depression.*

Sept. 8 — The Salt Lake Tabernacle Choir, while competing in the choral contest at the Chicago World's Fair, won second prize ($1,000). While on this tour, the choir also held concerts at Denver, Colo.; Independence, Kansas City and St.

Louis, Mo.; and Omaha, Neb. The First Presidency, consisting of Wilford Woodruff, George Q. Cannon and Joseph F. Smith, accompanied the choir.

Oct. 25 — President Grover Cleveland signed a resolution, passed by Congress, for the return of the personal property of the Church. Three years later, on March 28, 1896, a memorial passed by Congress and approved by the president provided for the restoration of the Church's real estate.

1894

January — *The railroad age continued with railroad building by far the nation's single largest economic enterprise.*

April — President Wilford Woodruff announced in general conference that he had received a revelation that ended the law of adoption. The law of adoption was the custom of being sealed to prominent Church leaders instead of direct ancestors. He re-emphasized the need for genealogical research and sealings along natural family lines. With the termination of this type of sealings, genealogical work to trace direct ancestry increased among the members of the Church.

July 14 — President Grover Cleveland signed an act that provided for statehood for Utah. This culminated 47 years of effort on the part of Mormons in Utah to achieve this status.

Aug. 27 — President Grover Cleveland issued a proclamation granting pardons and restoring civil rights to those who had been disfranchised under anti-polygamy laws.

Nov. 13 — The genealogical society of the Church, known as the Genealogical Society of Utah, was organized.

1895

March 4 — The Utah Constitutional Convention met in Salt Lake City. John Henry Smith, a member of the Quorum of the Twelve, was elected president of that convention.

June 9 — The first stake outside the United States was created in Canada in Cardston, Alberta.

June 11 — Johan and Alma Lindelof were baptized in St. Petersburg, Russia.

Nov. 5 — By a vote of 31,305 to 7,687, the people of Utah ratified the constitution and approved statehood. The documents were later hand-delivered to President Grover Cleveland.

Dec. 9 — The first stake in Mexico, the Juarez Stake, was organized in the English-speaking Mormon colonies in northern Mexico.

Nov. 28 — *The first automobile race in the U.S. took place from the heart of Chicago to its suburbs, 54 miles at 7 1/2 miles an hour.*

1896

Jan. 4 — President Grover Cleveland signed the proclamation that admitted Utah to the Union as the 45th state. Until statehood, the affairs of the Church in the Utah Territory had been closely associated with the affairs of the civil government. With statehood and the rights of self-government secured to the people, the Church could become separate from political struggles.

Aug. 17— *Gold was discovered in Alaska on the Klondike River, sparking the second great gold rush in U.S. history.*

Nov. 5 — The First Presidency issued a formal letter of instruction directing that the first Sunday in each month be observed as fast day, rather than the first Thursday, which had been observed as fast day since the early days of the Church in the Utah territory.

1897

June 4 — Historian Andrew Jenson returned to Salt Lake City after circling the world obtaining information for Church history.

July 5 — *Soft coal miners, as ordered by the United Mine Workers, went on strike, eventually winning an 8-hour day and abolition of the company store.*

July 20-25 — The Jubilee anniversary of the arrival of the Pioneers into the Salt Lake Valley was held in Salt Lake City for six days. The celebration began with the dedication by President Wilford Woodruff of the Brigham Young statue that would later stand at the intersection of Main and South Temple streets on July 20, and ended with a celebration for the Pioneers in the Tabernacle on July 24 and memorial services honoring all deceased Pioneers on July 25.

November — The *Improvement Era* began publication as the official organ of the Young Men's Mutual Improvement Association. Other Church organizations later joined in sponsoring the monthly magazine, which continued as the official voice of the Church until 1970. It was replaced by the *Ensign* magazine.

1898

Jan. 24 — Four aged members of the Mormon Battalion took part in the 50th anniversary of the discovery of gold in California, which they had witnessed.

April 24 — *Spain declared war on the United States, and the Spanish-American War began. The war formally ended Feb. 10, 1899.*

April 28 — A First Presidency statement encouraged Latter-day Saint youth to support the American effort in the Spanish-American War. This placed the Church firmly on the side of the war de-clarations of constituted governments and ended a policy of selective pacifism.

Sept. 2 — President Wilford Woodruff died at age 91 in San Francisco, Calif., where he had gone to seek relief from his asthma problems.

Sept. 13 —President Lorenzo Snow became fifth president of the Church. He chose Presidents George Q. Cannon and Joseph F. Smith as counselors. Both had served as counselors to President Brigham Young, President John Taylor, and President Wilford Woodruff.

Oct. 15 — President Lorenzo Snow announced that the Church would issue bonds to lighten the burden of its indebtedness.

1899

May 8 — President Lorenzo Snow announced a renewed emphasis concerning the payment of tithing, which members had been neglecting for some time, at a conference in St. George, Utah.

July 2 — A solemn assembly was held in the Salt Lake Temple, attended by the Church's 26 General Authorities, presidencies of the 40 stakes, and bishops of the 478 wards of the Church. The assembly accepted the resolution that tithing is the "word and will of the Lord unto us."

Aug. 19 — Utah volunteers serving in the Philippines in the Spanish-American War returned to an enthusiastic reception from the citizens.

Oct. 14 — *The U.S. declared an "Open Door Policy" toward China, opening it as an international market.*

1900

Jan. 8 — President Lorenzo Snow issued an official statement reaffirming the Church's ban on polygamy.

Jan. 21, 28 — The mammoth Salt Lake Stake, comprised of 55 wards throughout the Salt Lake Valley, was divided and the Jordan and Granite stakes were created. It was the first stake division in the valley since the stake was created in 1847.

Jan. 25 — The U.S. House of Representatives voted to deny Utahn B.H. Roberts of the First Council of the Seventy

100 YEARS AGO: 1901-1902

1901

May 4 — Reconstruction of the Tabernacle organ was completed by the Kimball Organ Co., making the instrument one of the finest pipe organs in the world.

Aug. 12 — Elder Heber J. Grant of the Quorum of the Twelve dedicated Japan and opened a mission there as a first step in renewed emphasis on preaching the gospel in all the world.

Sept. 6 — *U.S. President William McKinley was shot by Leon Czolgosz; McKinley died eight days later.*

Oct. 10 — President Lorenzo Snow died at his home in the Beehive House in Salt Lake City at age 87.

Oct. 17 — President Joseph F. Smith was ordained and set apart as the sixth president of the Church, with Presidents John R. Winder and Anthon H. Lund as counselors. They were sustained by Church members at a special conference on Nov. 10.

1902

The Church published in book form the first volume of Joseph Smith's *History of the Church,* edited by B.H. Roberts. Publication continued over the next decade, with a seventh volume added in 1932.

January — The *Children's Friend* began publication for Primary Association teachers. The magazine later widened its audience to include children, then eliminated the teachers' departments. It was published until 1970 when it was replaced by the *Friend* magazine.

March 6 — *The Bureau of the Census was created by an act of Congress.*

Aug. 4 — The First Council of the Seventy opened a Bureau of Information and Church Literature in a small octagonal booth on Temple Square. It was replaced by a larger building in March 1904 and by the present visitors centers in 1966 and 1978.

his seat in Congress, following an investigation of the right of polygamists to hold office under the Constitution.

July 24 — Final unveiling of Brigham Young Monument at South Temple and Main in Salt Lake City was held.

1901-1902

(See box on previous page)

1903

Nov. 5 — The Carthage Jail was purchased by the Church as a historic site for $4,000.

Dec. 17 — *Orville and Wilbur Wright became the first men to fly when they managed to get their powered airplane off the ground near Kitty Hawk, N.C., for 12 seconds. They made four flights that day, the longest lasting for 59 seconds.*

1904

April 5 — President Joseph F. Smith issued an official statement upholding provisions of the 1890 Manifesto and invoking excommunication against persons violating the "law of the land" by contracting new plural marriages.

July 23 — *The first Olympic games to be held in the U.S. opened as part of the St. Louis, Mo., Exposition.*

1905

Jan. 1 — The Dr. William H. Groves Latter-day Saints Hospital opened in Salt Lake City and was dedicated three days later, the first in the Church hospital system. In 1975, the Church divested itself of its hospitals and turned them over to a private organization.

Sept. 5 — *The Treaty of Portsmouth ended the Russian-Japanese War.*

Oct. 28 — Elders John W. Taylor and Matthias F. Cowley, finding themselves out of harmony with Church policy on plural marriage, submitted resignations from the Quorum of the Twelve that were announced to the Church April 6, 1906.

Dec. 23 — President Joseph F. Smith dedicated the Joseph Smith Memorial Cottage and Monument at Sharon, Windsor County, Vt., the site of the Prophet's birth 100 years earlier. The property had been purchased by the Church earlier in the year.

1906

The Sunday School introduced a Churchwide parents' class as part of an increased emphasis on the importance of the home and of the parents' role in teaching their children the gospel.

April 18 — *San Francisco was hit by a major earthquake, measuring 8.25 on the Richter scale, which leveled 490 city blocks.*

Summer — President Joseph F. Smith traveled to Europe, the first such visit of a Church president to the area. President Smith also visited Hawaii, Canada, and Mexico during his presidency.

1907

The Church purchased the 100-acre Smith farm near Palmyra, N.Y., including the Sacred Grove.

Jan. 10 — President Joseph F. Smith announced that the Church was entirely free of debt, with the payment of the last two $500,000 bond issues sold by President Lorenzo Snow in December 1899 to fund the debt. The first had been paid in 1903. Retiring the debt was largely due to the renewed emphasis in the Church on tithing.

February — The United States Senate agreed to seat Utah Sen. Reed Smoot, a member of the Quorum of the Twelve, who was elected and sworn in March 5, 1903. The vote culminated a three-year investigation, during which Church officials testified concerning polygamy and Church involvement in politics.

April 5 — A vote of the general conference approved the First Presidency's 16-page summary statement of the Church position in the Smoot hearings.

Aug. 1 — *An aeronautical division, consisting of one officer and two enlisted men, was established by the U.S. Army, the forerunner of the U.S. Air Force.*

1908

Presiding Bishop Charles W. Nibley moved the Church to an all-cash basis and no longer issued tithing scrip.

April 8 — The First Presidency created a General Priesthood Committee on Outlines, which served until 1922. The committee created definite age groupings for priesthood offices (deacons at 12, teachers at 15, priests at 18, and elders at 21), provided systematic programs for year-round priesthood meetings, and in other ways reformed, reactivated and systematized priesthood work.

Oct. 1 — *Henry Ford introduced his famous Model-T Ford automobile.*

1909

April 6 — *The North Pole was discovered by an expedition led by Robert E. Peary.*

Sept. 26 — U.S. President William Howard Taft visited Salt Lake City en route to California and spoke in the Tabernacle.

November — As the debate on Darwinism and evolution continued in the national press, the First Presidency issued an official statement on the origin of man.

1910

The Bishop's Building, an office building for the Presiding Bishopric and auxiliary organizations of the Church at 50 N. Main St., opened. It was used for more than 50 years.

January — The first issue of the *Utah Genealogical and Historical Magazine* was published. This quarterly publication served as the voice of the Genealogical Society of Utah. It was discontinued in October 1940.

Feb. 8 — *The Boy Scouts of America was founded. It was chartered by the U.S. Congress in 1916.*

1911

The Church adopted the Boy Scout program and has since become one of the leading sponsors of this organization for young men.

April 15 — *Collier's* magazine published a letter from Theodore Roosevelt refuting many charges made against Utah Sen. Reed Smoot and the Church. This action helped defuse an anti-Mormon propaganda surge of 1910-11.

Dec. 14 — *Norwegian explorer Roald Amundsen became the first man to reach the South Pole.*

1912

The Church colonists in northern Mexico exited the country due to unsettled conditions during the revolution.

Aug. 14 — *The United States sent Marines to Nicaragua, which was in default on loans from the U.S. and Europe.*

September — The Church's first seminary began at Granite High School in Salt Lake City, marking the beginning of a released-time weekday education program for young Latter-day Saints. As the seminary program grew, the Church phased out its involvement in academies, which were Church-sponsored high schools or junior colleges. By 1924, only the Juarez Academy in Mexico remained.

Nov. 8 — The First Presidency created a Correlation Committee, headed by Elder David O. McKay of the Quorum of the Twelve, and asked it to coordinate scheduling and prevent unnecessary duplication in programs of Church auxiliaries. A Social Advisory Committee of the General Boards was merged with it in 1920. The combined committee issued a major report April 14, 1921, offering proposals for correlating priesthood and auxiliary activities; many of its recommendations were thereafter adopted.

1913

The Church established the Maori Agricultural College in New Zealand. It was destroyed by an earthquake in 1931 and was never rebuilt.

Feb. 25 — *The 16th Amendment, creating the income tax, became a part of the U.S. Constitution, the first constitutional amendment adopted in the 20th century.*

May 21 — The Boy Scout program was officially adopted by the Young Men's Mutual Improvement Association and became the activity program for boys of the Church.

1914

January — The *Relief Society Magazine* appeared as a monthly publication containing lesson material for use in the women's auxiliary of the Church. The magazine carried stories, poetry, articles, homemaking helps, news, and lesson material until it ceased publication in December 1970, when the *Ensign* magazine became the magazine for adults in the Church.

The Relief Society also introduced its first uniform courses of study, organized around four general themes. The pattern was altered in 1921 to include theology, work and business meetings, literature, and social service.

Aug. 15 — *The Panama Canal, connecting the Atlantic Ocean to the Pacific, was officially opened. Twelve days before, on Aug. 3, an ocean steamer, the* SS Acon, *passed through the canal.*

1915

April 27 — The First Presidency inaugurated the "Home Evening" program, inviting all families to participate.

May 7 — *A German submarine sank the British liner* Lusitania, *en route from New York to Liverpool, off the coast of Ireland, killing 1,198 persons.*

September — James E. Talmage's influential book *Jesus the Christ* was published.

Fall — The first college classes were taught at Ricks College, which had been Ricks Academy.

1916

Feb. 21 — *The longest and bloodiest battle of World War I, the Battle of Verdun, began in France, resulting in the death of one million soldiers.*

June 30 — The First Presidency and Quorum of the Twelve issued a doctrinal exposition clarifying the use of the title "Father" as it is applied to Jesus Christ.

1917

Oct. 2 — The Church Administration Building at 47 E. South Temple was completed.

Nov. 7 — *Nikolai Lenin and the Bolsheviks overthrew the Kerensky regime in Russia.*

1918

May — Wheat that Relief Society sisters had been gathering and storing since 1876 was sold to the U.S. government at a government price, with approval of the First Presidency and the Presiding Bishopric, to alleviate shortages during World War I.

Oct. 3 — While contemplating the meaning of Christ's atonement, President Joseph F. Smith received a manifestation on the salvation of the dead and the visit of the Savior to the spirit world after His crucifixion. A report of the experience was published in December and was added first to the Pearl of Great Price and then to the Doctrine and Covenants June 6, 1979, as Section 138.

Nov. 11 — *World War I ended, as Germany signed an armistice with the Allies.*

Nov. 19 — President Joseph F. Smith died six days after his 80th birthday. Because of an epidemic of influenza, no public funeral was held for the Church president.

Nov. 23 — President Heber J. Grant was ordained and set apart as the seventh president of the Church during a meeting of the Twelve in the Salt Lake Temple. He selected Presidents Anthon H. Lund and Charles W. Penrose as counselors.

1919

January — The 18th Amendment to the United States Constitution established prohibition. Church leaders supported the movement toward nationwide prohibition and opposed the amendment's repeal in 1933.

April — The April general conference of the Church was postponed due to the nationwide influenza epidemic. The conference was held June 1-3.

May 27 — *The first transatlantic flight (with two stopovers) was completed by a U.S. Navy seaplane.*

Oct. 10 — King Albert and Queen Elizabeth of Belgium attended a recital on Temple Square in Salt Lake City to hear the Tabernacle organ.

Nov. 27 — President Heber J. Grant dedicated the temple at Laie, Hawaii, the first temple outside the continental United States. Construction had begun soon after the site was dedicated in June 1915.

1920

In response to Church growth and need for a more cost-effective use of building funds, an "authentic form of LDS architecture" was developed. that structurally joined the previously separate chapel and classrooms with the recreational or cultural hall through a connecting foyer/office/ classroom complex.

Jan. 10 — *The League of Nations, the first permanent international body encompassing many of the nations of the world, was established as the World War I Treaty of Versailles went into effect.*

1920-1921

Elder David O. McKay of the Quorum of the Twelve and President Hugh J. Cannon of the Liberty Stake in Salt Lake City traveled 55,896 miles in a world survey of Church missions for the First Presidency. The pair visited the Saints in the Pacific Islands, New Zealand, Australia, and Asia, and then made stops in India, Egypt, and Palestine, before visiting the missions of Europe.

1921

The M-Men and Gleaner departments in the MIA were introduced Churchwide to serve the special needs of young people from ages 17 to 23.

The Doctrine and Covenants was published in Salt Lake City with double-column pages, revised footnote references, headnotes and index by Elder James. E. Talmage. For the first time, the Lectures on Faith was not included.

Oct. 5 — *The World Series was broadcast on radio for the first time.*

1922

May — Primary Children's Hospital opened in Salt Lake City.

Nov. 26 — *King Tutankhamen's tomb was opened in Egypt.*

1923

The Church purchased a part of the Hill Cumorah. Additional acquisitions in 1928 gave the Church possession of the entire hill and adjacent lands.

Aug. 26 — President Heber J. Grant

dedicated the Alberta Temple, in Cardston, Alberta, Canada, which had been under construction for nearly a decade.

Sept. 29 — *Britain began to rule Palestine under a mandate from the League of Nations.*

1924

March 21 — A First Presidency statement answered criticism of unauthorized plural marriages by once again confirming the Church's policy against the practice. Polygamists within the Church were excommunicated when discovered.

June 2 — *The U.S. Congress granted citizenship to all American Indians.*

Oct. 3 — Radio broadcast of general conference began on KSL in Salt Lake City, the Church-owned station. Coverage was expanded into Idaho in 1941.

1925

July 24 — *In the famous "Scopes Monkey Trial," John T. Scopes, a Tennessee school teacher, was found guilty of teaching evolution in a public school.*

Dec. 6 — Elder Melvin J. Ballard of the Quorum of the Twelve established a mission in South America with headquarters in Buenos Aires, Argentina, opening the Church's official work in South America, which he dedicated for the preaching of the gospel on Dec. 25.

1926

Weekday religious education was expanded to include college students with the building of the first institute of religion adjacent to the University of Idaho at Moscow.

May — Brigham Young College in Logan, Utah, founded in 1877, closed its doors and gave its library to Utah State Agriculture College and sold its buildings and land to Logan City to be used as a public high school.

May 9 — *Richard Byrd and Floyd Bennett became the first men to make an airplane flight over the North Pole.*

1927

May 21 — *Charles Lindbergh, aboard his "Spirit of St. Louis" monoplane, completed the first transatlantic solo flight from New York City to Paris, a distance of 3,610 miles, in 33 1/2 hours.*

Oct. 23 — President Heber J. Grant dedicated the Arizona Temple at Mesa, completing a project begun six years before. Dedicatory services were broadcast by radio.

1928

The YMMIA introduced a Vanguard program for 15- and 16-year-old boys. After the National Boy Scout organization created the Explorer program in 1933, patterned in part after the Vanguards, the Church adopted Explorer Scouting.

January — Priesthood quorums began meeting during the Sunday School hour for gospel instruction under a correlated experiment lasting 10 years. This priesthood Sunday School experiment included classes for all age groups, with Tuesday evening reserved as an activity night for both priesthood and young women.

May 11 — *The first regularly scheduled television programs were begun by Station WGY in Schenectady, N.Y.*

1929

July 15 — The Tabernacle Choir started a weekly network radio broadcast on NBC. Richard L. Evans joined the program with his sermonettes in June 1930. "Music and the Spoken Word" eventually switched to KSL Radio on the CBS network, and has since become the longest continuing network radio broadcast in history.

Oct. 29 — *The New York Stock Market collapsed in frantic trading, a dramatic beginning of the Great Depression.*

November — The official publication of the Sunday School began publishing under the name of *The Instructor.* From 1877 until 1929, the publication was *The Juvenile Instructor.* The name change reflected the growing use of articles on teaching methods and gospel subjects to be used by the several Church organizations.

1930

April 6 — The centennial of the Church's organization was observed at general conference in the Tabernacle in Salt Lake City. B.H. Roberts prepared his *Comprehensive History of The Church of Jesus Christ of Latter-day* Saints as a centennial memorial.

July 21 — *The U.S. Veterans Administration was established.*

1931

March 21 — A 10-reel film of the history of the Church was completed.

April 6 — The first edition of the *Church News* was printed by the Church's *Deseret News.*

May 1 — *The Empire State Building was opened in New York City.*

June — The Church Music Committee

outlined a proposal to have better choirs in every ward and stake in the Church.

1932

Jan. 10 — The first missionary training classes began, which were to be organized in every ward throughout the Church.

February — The Lion House, home of Brigham Young and a noted landmark of Salt Lake City, was turned over to the Young Ladies Mutual Improvement Association by the Church for a social center for women and young ladies. Another of Brigham Young's home, the Beehive House, was previously placed under the direction of the YLMIA as a girls' home.

April 2 — A campaign against the use of tobacco was launched by the Church.

May 12 — *Infant Charles Lindbergh Jr., kidnapped March 1, was found dead.*

May 15 — Utah Gov. George H. Dern proclaimed a special fast day in the depths of the Great Depression to gather funds for the poor.

June 12 — A marker at the site of the "Great Salt Lake Base and Meridian" was dedicated on the southeast corner of Temple Square. Apostle Orson Pratt on Aug. 3, 1847, established the base line from which all government measurements and surveys began for the West.

July 16 — The first of the Mormon Trail markers were unveiled in Henefer, Utah, and Casper, Wyo.

1933

Jan. 30 — *Adolf Hitler was named chancellor of Germany, capping a 10-year rise to power.*

Feb. 21 — The Church began a six-day commemoration of the 100th anniversary of the Word of Wisdom revelation with special observances in every ward throughout the Church.

June 1 — The Church opened a 500-foot exhibit in the Hall of Religions at the Century of Progress World's Fair in Chicago, Ill. The exhibit was prepared by famed LDS sculptor Avard Fairbanks.

July 26 — The first effort to mark the historic sites in Nauvoo, Ill., was made by the Relief Society when it placed a monument at the site of its organization in 1842 in Joseph Smith's store.

Nov. 5 — The First Presidency and four members of the Quorum of the Twelve participated in the dedication of the Washington, D.C., meetinghouse, which was adorned by a statue of the Angel Moroni atop its 165-foot spire.

1934

The general board of the Sunday School officially recognized the Junior Sunday School, which had been part of some ward programs for many years.

Jan. 17 — New headquarters of the Genealogical Society of Utah, located in the Joseph F. Smith Memorial Building on North Main Street in Salt Lake City, was formally opened. The building previously was part of the campus of the LDS College.

Feb. 3 — Stake seventies were instructed in a letter from the First Council of the Seventy that they have a duty, under the direction of the stake president, to do missionary work in the stakes.

Aug. 2 — *Adolf Hitler took control of Germany after the death of President Paul von Hindenburg.*

1935

Jan. 10 — In a change of policy, members of the Quorum of the Twelve were released from auxiliary leadership positions as presiding officers and general board members.

Jan. 11 — *American aviatrix Amelia Earhart became the first woman to fly over the Pacific, from Hawaii to California.*

March 3 — First of a series of six "Church of the Air" broadcasts was carried nationwide by the Columbia Broadcasting Co.

July 21 — President Heber J. Grant dedicated the Hill Cumorah Monument near Palmyra, N.Y.

1936

A separate Aaronic Priesthood program for adults, recommended by the General Priesthood Committee on Outlines 20 years earlier, was introduced.

Jan. 29 — *Ty Cobb, Walter Johnson, Christy Mathewson, Babe Ruth, and Honus Wagner became the first five men to be inducted into the Baseball Hall of Fame.*

April — The Church introduced a formal welfare program to assist in emergency situations needy Church members and those unemployed. Called the Church Security Program at first, it was renamed the Church Welfare Program in 1938. Later, it expanded its services with the addition of local production programs.

Also in April, supervision of stake missions was given to the First Council of the Seventy, and stake missions were soon organized in all stakes. The work had previously been under stake presidencies' direction.

1937

January — The First Presidency officially adopted the practice widely utilized over several preceding decades of ordaining worthy young men in the Aaronic Priesthood at specific ages. The recommended ages for advancement from deacon to teacher to priest to elder have changed from time to time since 1937.

Feb. 20 — A portion of the Nauvoo Temple lot in Nauvoo, Ill., returned to Church ownership when Wilford C. Wood, representing the Church, purchased the property.

April 27 — *The first Social Security payment in the U.S. was made.*

July — The Hill Cumorah pageant, "America's Witness for Christ," began on an outdoor stage on the side of the Hill Cumorah in New York. A Bureau of Information opened at the base of the hill.

Sept. 12 — President Heber J. Grant returned to Salt Lake City after a three-month tour of Europe, where he visited with Church members and missionaries in 11 countries. He dedicated nine meetinghouses and gave some 55 addresses, including the principal address at the British Mission Centennial Conference at Rochdale, England, on Aug. 1.

1938

Aug. 14 — The first Deseret Industries store opened in Salt Lake City to provide work opportunities for the elderly and handicapped. Part of the Welfare Program, a growing network of stores still offers used furniture, clothing, and other items.

Oct. 30 — *Orson Welles' fantasy radio program "War of the Worlds" was so realistic that it caused nationwide panic.*

November — The Genealogical Society of Utah had its own camera and began microfilming baptism and sealing records of the Salt Lake, Logan, Manti, and St. George temples.

1939

Feb. 18 — A miniature Salt Lake Tabernacle, with a seating capacity of about 50 persons, was built by the Church for its exhibit at the San Francisco World's Fair. The exhibit attracted 1,400 persons on opening day.

June 19 — Wilford Wood purchased the Liberty Jail in Missouri on behalf of the Church.

Aug. 24 — The First Presidency directed all missionaries in Germany to move to neutral countries. Later the missionaries were instructed to leave Europe and return to the United States. The last group arrived in New York Nov. 6, 1939.

Sept. 1 — *World War II began when Nazi Germany invaded Poland. Britain and France declared war on Germany two days later.*

Oct. 6 — The First Presidency message on world peace was delivered in general conference by President Heber J. Grant.

1940

Jan. 28 — The Mormon Battalion Monument was dedicated in San Diego, Calif.

Sept. 16 — *U.S. President Franklin D. Roosevelt signed the Selective Service Act, setting up the first peacetime military draft in the nation's history.*

1941

The Presiding Bishopric inaugurated a new membership record system. Under the new system, a master record for each member was established in the Presiding Bishopric's Office, eliminating the need for personal membership certificates.

April 6 — In general conference, the First Presidency announced the new position of Assistant to the Twelve, and the first five Assistants were called and sustained.

May — The First Presidency appointed Hugh B. Brown as the Church Army coordinator. His work with the LDS servicemen and military officials led to the development of the Church servicemen's program.

Dec. 7 — *The Japanese bombed Pearl Harbor in Hawaii, killing 2,403 Americans and wounding 1,178. The next day, President Franklin D. Roosevelt asked Congress for a declaration of war against Japan. Four days later, Germany and Italy declared war on the United States, and on the same day the U.S. declared war on the European dictatorships.*

1942

The Girls' Activity Program of the Church was introduced.

Jan. 4 — The Church observed a special fast Sunday in conjunction with a national day of prayer called by President Franklin D. Roosevelt.

Jan. 17 — The First Presidency asked all general boards and auxiliary organizations to discontinue institutes, conventions, and auxiliary stake meetings to help members meet wartime restrictions on travel and to help reduce personal expenses under increased war taxes.

Feb. 28 — It was announced that due to

World War II, the Relief Society general conference scheduled for April, which had been planned to commemorate the centennial anniversary of the founding of the Relief Society, along with centennial celebrations in the stakes, would not be held. Rather, celebrations were to be held on the ward and branch level.

March 23 — The First Presidency announced that for the duration of World War II it would call only older men who had been ordained high priests or seventies on full-time missions.

March 23 — *The forced movement of Japanese-Americans from their homes on the U.S. West Coast to inland camps during World War II began.*

April 4-6 — Because of limitations on travel, the annual April general conference was closed to the general Church membership and confined to General Authorities and presidencies of the 141 stakes. The First Presidency on April 5, 1942, closed the Tabernacle for the duration of the war. Conference sessions were held in the Assembly Hall on Temple Square and in the assembly room of the Salt Lake Temple.

April 18 — May Green Hinckley, general president of the Primary Association, announced that the presiding officers of the Primary on all levels would henceforth be known as "presidents" rather than "superintendents."

July — Church Welfare leaders urged members to plant gardens, to bottle as many fruits and vegetables as they could utilize, and to store coal.

Aug. 17 — The *USS Brigham Young,* a Liberty class ship, was christened.

1943

March 7 — The Navajo-Zuni Mission was formed, the first mission designated only for Indians.

May — The Church announced that a pocket-size Church directory had been printed for distribution in the armed forces, along with a pocket-size Book of Mormon and a compilation titled *Principles of the Gospel.*

May 22 — *USS Joseph Smith,* a Liberty class ship, was launched in Richmond, Calif. Ceremonies included a tribute to Joseph Smith and a description of the Church's part in the war effort.

July 24 — The MIA completed a war service project to purchase aircraft rescue boats by purchasing war bonds. The project began May 11 and ended with 87 stakes raising a total of $3.1 million, enough to purchase 52 boats, which cost $60,000 each.

Sept. 9 — *United States troops invaded Italy.*

1944

March — The Church announced the purchase of Spring Hill in Missouri, known in Church history as Adam-ondi-Ahman. (See D&C 116.). Final deeds for the purchase were dated June 27, 1944, the 100th anniversary of the martyrdom of the Prophet Joseph Smith. The deed to the land was passed on to the Church by Eugene Johnson, whose family had been in possession of the property for a century.

May 15 — A 12-page monthly *Church News* for the 70,000 LDS servicemen was inaugurated by the First Presidency in order to keep more closely in touch with the servicemen. This edition contained inspirational material, vital messages, answers to questions, and a summary of important news in the Church.

June 6 — *Allied forces, numbering 130,000 men, invaded Europe at Normandy, France, on "D-Day" breaking the Nazi stranglehold on the Continent and leading to the eventual surrender of Germany.*

June 25 — Memorial services were held in each ward to commemorate the 100th anniversary of the martyrdom of the Prophet Joseph Smith and Hyrum Smith. Special services were also held in Carthage Jail on June 27.

July — The Church organized the Committee on Publications comprised of General Authorities to supervise the preparation and publication of all Church literature. This committee controlled all auxiliary lessons and all publications published by and for the Church.

November — The name of the Genealogical Society of Utah was changed to the Genealogical Society of The Church of Jesus Christ of Latter-day Saints.

Nov. 28 — Young Women's Mutual Improvement Association celebrated its 75th anniversary. A plaque was dedicated by President Heber J. Grant and placed in the Lion House where the initial organization had taken place.

1945

The first microfilming of records in England was begun. Microfilming of Scandinavia records began the next year in 1946.

May 14 — President Heber J. Grant died in Salt Lake City at age 88.

May 21 — At a special meeting of the Quorum of the Twelve in the Salt Lake Temple, the First Presidency was reorganized with President George Albert

Smith ordained and set apart as the eighth president of the Church. Presidents J. Reuben Clark Jr. and David O. McKay, counselors to President Grant, were called also as counselors to President Smith.

July 16 — The First Presidency authorized monthly priesthood and auxiliary leadership meetings if they could be held without violating government restrictions concerning use of gas and rubber.

September — The First Presidency began calling mission presidents for areas vacated during the war. This process continued through 1946. The sending of missionaries soon followed the appointment of mission presidents. By the end of 1946, 3,000 missionaries were in the field.

Also, the Tabernacle was opened to the general public for the first time since March 1942.

Sept. 2 — *Formal ceremonies of surrender, ending World War II — history's deadliest and most far-reaching conflict — were held aboard the battleship* Missouri *in Tokyo Bay. Japan had surrendered on Aug. 14 (V-J Day); Germany on May 8 (V-E Day).*

Sept. 23 — The Idaho Falls Temple was dedicated by President George Albert Smith.

Oct. 5-7 — The first general, unrestricted conference of the Church in four years was held in the Tabernacle in Salt Lake City. (During World War II, general conferences were limited to general, stake, and ward priesthood leaders.)

Nov. 3 — President George Albert Smith met with U.S. President Harry S Truman in the White House and presented the Church's plans to use its welfare facilities to help relieve the suffering of Latter-day Saints in Europe.

1946

January — The Church began sending supplies to the Saints in Europe. This continued for the next several years.

Jan. 7 — *The United Nations General Assembly held its first session in London.*

Feb. 4 — Elder Ezra Taft Benson of the Quorum of the Twelve, newly called as president of the European Mission, left New York for Europe to administer to the physical and spiritual needs of members there. He traveled throughout Europe for most of the year, visiting Saints who had been isolated by the war, distributing Church welfare supplies,and setting the branches of the Church in order.

May — President George Albert Smith became the first president of the Church to visit Mexico. While in the country, he met with Manuel Avila Camacho, president of Mexico, and presented to him a copy of the Book of Mormon.

May 2 — The First Presidency instructed local Church leaders that in meetings where the sacrament is passed, it should be passed to the presiding officer first.

December — The Relief Society announced the creation of an enlarged social service and child welfare department.

1947

The Church reached the 1 million-member mark.

April 11 — *Jackie Robinson broke Major League Baseball's previous all-white color barrier when he began playing for the Brooklyn Dodgers.*

May — The vast project of revising early scripture translations and translating the scriptures into additional languages was begun by the Church offices.

July 22 — A caravan of wagon-canopied automobiles of the same number of people as the original pioneer company, arrived in Salt Lake City after following the Mormon Pioneer Trail.

July 24 — Church members celebrated the 100th anniversary of the Pioneers' arrival in Salt Lake Valley. The "This Is the Place" monument was dedicated by President George Albert Smith.

Aug. 7 — *The Kon-Tiki raft sailed by ethnologist Thor Heyerdahl arrived at the Marquesa Islands from Peru, to support his theory of the origination of the South Pacific Islanders.*

November — Some 75 tons of potatoes, raised and donated by Dutch members, were delivered to needy families in Germany. A year later, the German Saints harvested their own crop of potatoes.

December — Fast day was set aside for the relief of those in need in Europe. About $210,000 was collected and then distributed to Europeans of all faiths by an agency not connected with the Church.

Also in December, more than one million people visited Temple Square in one year for the first time.

Dec. 1 — An ambitious project to microfilm European records was started by the Genealogical Society.

Dec. 20 — President George Albert Smith announced that following the end of World War II, the Church had the responsibility to carry the gospel to the people at home and abroad, a missionary posture leading to the internationalization of the Church.

1948

Jan. 23 — Members of the Church in California took part in the centennial of the discovery of gold at the site where members of the Mormon Battalion worked under foreman John Marshall at Sutter's Mill.

April — Mission presidents from around the world reported increasing numbers of baptisms. An expanded building program was started.

May 14 — *Britain ended its rule in Palestine, and the independent state of Israel was proclaimed.*

June — It was announced that Ricks College in Rexburg, Idaho, would become a four-year college in the 1949-50 school year.

Oct. 17 — The Tabernacle Choir performed its 1,000th national broadcast over radio.

December — Significant increases were made among the Indian membership in the Southwest states.

1949

Family history efforts advanced with increased microfilming in Europe and the publication of a new manual.

April 5 — At a special welfare meeting held in conjunction with general conference, the Welfare Program was declared a permanent program of the Church.

A film made by the Church in Hollywood, *The Lord's Way*, was introduced.

May 12 — *The Berlin Blockade ended as the Soviet Union announced reopening of East German land routes.*

October — For the first time, general conference was broadcast publicly over KSL television in Salt Lake City, although since April 1948 it had been carried by closed-circuit television to other buildings on Temple Square.

The Church purchased a large property in Los Angeles, Calif., that would become another Welfare Square.

Also in October, the centennial conference of the Deseret Sunday School Union was held.

1950

Feb. 24 — The last two missionaries of the Czechoslovakian Mission were released from prison after 27 days and expelled from communist Czechoslovakia.

Feb. 25 — Missionaries returned to Hong Kong for the first time since 1853.

March — The Tahitian mission purchased an 81-foot yacht for mission travel.

June 1 — President George Albert Smith dedicated a statue of Brigham Young at the nation's Capitol.

July 1 — The responsibility of the LDS girls' program was transferred from the Presiding Bishopric to the Young Women's Mutual Improvement Association, where it remained until 1974.

September — Early morning seminaries were inaugurated in Southern California. This was the beginning of a movement that spread seminary throughout the Church on an early morning, nonreleased-time basis.

Nov. 8 — *American jets were attacked by North Korean jets in the opening days of the Korean War.*

1951-1952

(See box on next page)

1953

March 25 — The First Presidency announced that returning missionaries would no longer report directly to General Authorities but, rather, to their stake presidency and high council.

May 29 — *Sir Edmund Hillary of New Zealand became the first person to reach the top of Mount Everest.*

July 9 — Organization of the United Church School System, with Ernest L. Wilkinson as administrator, was publicly announced.

October — The semiannual conference of the Church was broadcast by television for the first time outside the Intermountain area.

1954

Utahns debated the question of ownership of Dixie, Snow, and Weber State Colleges, which had once been owned by the Church. Though the Church expressed a willingness to resume control, and the state was hard-pressed financially to operate them, voters rejected the transfer in a referendum.

Jan. 2 — President David O. McKay left Salt Lake City on a trip to London, England; South Africa; and South and Central America. He returned in mid-February, and at that point had visited every existing mission of the Church. He was the first president of the Church to visit the South African Mission.

50 YEARS AGO: 1951-52

1951

A new edition of the Servicemen's Directory was published. In addition, it was announced that the United States armed forces had authorized the use of special "LDS" identification tags (called "dog tags") for Church members in the service.

March 29 — *Julius Rosenberg and his wife, Ethel, were convicted of wartime espionage. They were executed June 19.*

April 4 — President George Albert Smith died in Salt Lake City at age 81.

April 9 — President David O. McKay was sustained as ninth president of the Church, with Presidents Stephen L Richards and J. Reuben Clark Jr. as counselors.

July 20 — Because the Korean War reduced the number of young elders being called as missionaries, the First Presidency issued a call for seventies to help fill the need. Many married men subsequently served full-time missions.

1952

A Systematic Program for Teaching the Gospel was published for use by the missionaries of the Church. This inaugurated the use of a standard plan of missionary work throughout the Church, although the specific format of the various lessons was modified from time to time after this.

March 2 — The new Primary Children's Hospital in Salt Lake City was dedicated. Half the cost of the building had been raised by children of the Church through the continuing Primary penny drive.

April 5 — The Church began carrying the priesthood session of general conference by direct telephone wire to buildings beyond Temple Square.

June — President David O. McKay made a six-week tour of European missions and branches in Holland, Denmark, Sweden, Norway, Finland, Germany, Switzerland, Wales, Scotland, and France. During this trip he announced the selection of Bern, Switzerland, as site of the first European temple.

Oct. 6 — A letter from the Presiding Bishopric introduced a new Senior Aaronic Priesthood program, with men over 21 years of age organized into separate Aaronic Priesthood quorums. Subsequently, special weekday classes were encouraged in each stake to prepare these brethren for the Melchizedek Priesthood and temple ordinances.

Nov. 1 — *The United States announced "satisfactory" experiments in developing the world's first hydrogen bomb.*

Nov. 25 — Elder Ezra Taft Benson of the Quorum of the Twelve was chosen Secretary of Agriculture by Dwight D. Eisenhower, newly elected president of the United States. Elder Benson served in that capacity for eight years.

Dec. 31 — A letter from the First Presidency announced that the Primary Association had been assigned the duty of establishing the Cub Scout program of the Boy Scouts of America for boys of the Church.

April 7 — The Church Board of Education announced that Ricks College, which had been a four-year college since 1949-50, would revert back to being a junior college, effective fall semester 1956. The final graduation of a four-year class was Aug. 10, 1956.

May 17 — *The U.S. Supreme Court ruled that racial segregation in public schools was unconstitutional.*

July — The Church announced the inauguration of the Indian Placement Program, whereby Indian students of elementary- and secondary-school age could be placed in foster homes during the school year in order for them to take advantage of better educational opportunities.

July 21 — The First Presidency announced the establishment of the Church College of Hawaii. The college commenced operation Sept. 26, 1955.

Aug. 31 — The First Presidency approved a plan to ordain young men of the Aaronic Priesthood to the office of teacher at age 14 and priest at age 16. The previous ages were 15 and 17.

1955

A special program of missionary work among the Jewish people was organized. It continued until 1959.

January-February — President David O. McKay took a trip covering more than 45,000 miles to the missions of the South Pacific, selected a site for the New Zealand

Temple and discussed plans for the building of a Church college in New Zealand.

April 5 — *British Prime Minister Winston Churchill resigned.*

July — The Church Building Committee was organized to supervise the now-vast building program of the Church throughout the world.

August-September — The Tabernacle Choir made a major concert tour of Europe.

Sept. 11 — The Swiss Temple, near Bern, was dedicated by President David O. McKay.

Sept. 26 — The Church College of Hawaii, now BYU-Hawaii, was opened.

Dec. 27 — A letter from the Presiding Bishopric announced that students at BYU would be organized into campus wards and stakes beginning Jan. 8, 1956. This move set the pattern for student wards to be organized at Church colleges and institutes of religion wherever their numbers warranted it.

1956

Jan. 1 — Frederick S. Williams, former mission president in Argentina and Uruguay, moved with his family to Peru and contacted Church headquarters for permission to organize a branch and begin missionary work. The first missionaries arrived in Peru Aug. 7, 1956.

Jan. 8 — The first campus wards and stakes in the Church were organized at BYU.

March 11 — President David O. McKay dedicated the Los Angeles Temple.

Oct. 3 — The new Relief Society Building in Salt Lake City was dedicated.

December — A new program for training priesthood leaders was inaugurated. It included quarterly stake priesthood meetings, quarterly leadership meetings, and various special leadership sessions in connection with stake conferences.

1957

Ward education committees were organized throughout the Church to encourage and enroll young people in a seminary, organize their transportation, and encourage them to attend a Church college or a college with an institute of religion. These committees functioned until 1964, when their duties were transferred to home teachers.

April — The First Presidency announced plans to move Ricks College from Rexburg to Idaho Falls, Idaho. This created much local concern and started a long debate that ended in a reversal of the decision and the announcement on April 26, 1962, of a major expansion program for the Rexburg campus.

July — The Pacific Board of Education was organized to supervise all Church schools in the Pacific area.

October — The semiannual general conference was canceled due to a flu epidemic.

Oct. 4 — *The Space Age began when the Soviet Union put the first man-made satellite into orbit around the earth.*

1958

A new program for convert integration was adopted during the year, having been previously tried on a pilot basis in several stakes.

April 20 — The New Zealand Temple was dedicated by President David O. McKay.

Aug. 3 — *The world's first atomic-powered submarine, the* USS Nautilus, *made the first voyage underneath the North Pole.*

Sept. 7 — The London Temple was dedicated by President David O. McKay.

Dec. 17 — The Church College of Hawaii in Laie, Hawaii, was dedicated by President David O. McKay.

1959

April 6 — President David O. McKay issued his famous "Every member a missionary" slogan.

June 19 — The First Presidency issued a statement entitled "The Sabbath," admonishing Latter-day Saints to keep the Sabbath day holy, and particularly to avoid shopping on Sundays.

Aug. 21 — *Hawaii was admitted as the 50th state; Alaska had gained statehood Jan. 3.*

Nov. 29 — The Tabernacle Choir received a Grammy award for its recording of the "Battle Hymn of the Republic" at the first television awards show of the National Academy of Recording Arts and Sciences in Los Angeles, Calif.

1960

Jan. 3 — The First Presidency inaugurated a three-month series of weekly Sunday evening fireside programs for youth. President David O. McKay addressed an estimated 200,000 youth at the opening fireside, carried by direct telephone wire to 290 stake centers in the United States, western Canada, and Hawaii.

Also in January, the Church began setting up the administrative framework for a large building program in Europe. By early 1961, administrative building areas outside North America had been established for all parts of the world where the Church existed, and the labor missionary program, which originated in the South Pacific in the early 1950s, was utilized in each area.

March — The First Presidency requested the General Priesthood Committee, with Elder Harold B. Lee of the Quorum of the Twelve as chairman, to make a study of Church programs and curriculum with the object of providing for better "correlation."

May 1 — *A U.S. U-2 reconnaissance airplane was shot down over the Soviet Union, typifying worsening relations between the two superpowers.*

1961

March 12 — The first non-English-speaking stake of the Church was organized at The Hague in The Netherlands.

June-July — A number of significant developments took place that revamped the missionary program of the Church. The first seminar for all mission presidents was held June 26-July 27 in Salt Lake City, at which new programs were outlined. Also, a new teaching plan of six lessons to be used in every mission of the Church was officially presented, as was the "every member a missionary" program. The missions of the world were divided into nine areas, and a General Authority was called to administer each area.

Aug. 13 — *The Soviet Union began building the Berlin Wall, dividing East and West Germany.*

November — A Language Training Institute was established at Brigham Young University for missionaries called to foreign countries. In 1963, it became the Language Training Mission.

Dec. 3 — The first Spanish-speaking stake in the Church was created in Mexico City.

1962

Feb. 20 — *John Glenn became the first American to orbit the earth, a feat he accomplished in one hour and 37 minutes aboard the Friendship 7 space capsule.*

March — The age at which young men became eligible for missions was lowered from 20 to 19.

April — At the 132nd Annual Conference, the first seminar of General Authorities and presidents of stakes outside North America was held.

Oct. 10 — The Church purchased a shortwave radio station, WRUL, with a transmitter in Boston and studios in New York City. It was subsequently used to transmit Church broadcasts to Europe and South America.

1963

July — The labor missionary program was expanded to include the United States and Canada.

Oct. 12 — The Polynesian Cultural Center, located near the Church College of Hawaii and the temple in Laie, Hawaii, was dedicated.

Nov. 22 — *John F. Kennedy became the fourth U.S. president to be assassinated; he was fatally wounded while riding in a motorcade in Dallas, Texas.*

December — Church storage vaults for records in Little Cottonwood Canyon were completed. They were dedicated on June 22, 1966.

1964

January — A new program of home teaching, replacing ward teaching, was officially inaugurated throughout the Church after having been presented in stake conferences during the last half of 1963.

Jan. 28 — Temple Square and the Lion House in Salt Lake City were recognized as National Historic Landmarks by the federal government.

March — Two LDS schools were opened in Chile, one in Santiago and the other in Vina del Mar. During the early 1970s, the Church opened an elementary school in Paraguay, one in Bolivia, and one in Peru.

April — The Mormon Pavilion opened at the New York World's Fair. The Church also built elaborate pavilions for subsequent expositions in San Antonio, Texas (1968); Japan (1970); and Spokane, Wash. (1974).

April 26 — The first meetinghouse in Asia was dedicated for the Tokyo North Branch in Japan.

July 31 — *The U.S.* Ranger 7 *spacecraft transmitted to earth the first close-up pictures of the moon.*

October — The Pacific Board of Education was discontinued. Schools under its direction became part of the Unified Church School System.

Nov. 17 — The Oakland Temple was dedicated by President David O. McKay.

1965

January — The family home evening program was inaugurated and wards had a choice of which night in the week to hold home evenings. A weekly home evening had been encouraged before by Church leaders, but now the Church published a formal family home evening manual, which was placed in every LDS home.

Jan. 18 — The Tabernacle Choir sang at the inauguration of U.S. President Lyndon B. Johnson in Washington, D.C.

February — The Italian government gave permission for LDS missionaries to proselyte in the country. No missionary work had been done there since 1862.

March — The three-generation genealogical family group-sheet program was initiated.

June 3 — *Astronaut Ed White made the first American "walk" in space during the* Gemini 4 *orbital flight.*

September — Because of the war in Vietnam, a missionary quota of two per ward was established within the United States to comply with Selective Service requests.

October — With the appointment of President Joseph Fielding Smith and Elder Thorpe B. Isaacson as counselors, President David O. McKay announced that the First Presidency would be increased to five, instead of three.

1966

May 1 — The first stake in South America was organized at Sao Paulo, Brazil.

June 29 — *North Vietnam's capital, Hanoi, and principal seaport, Haiphong, were bombed for the first time by the U.S. in the Vietnam War.*

August — A new visitors center on Temple Square was opened to tourists. While this would be the most elaborate center, it represented a trend of building visitors centers at historic sites and temples and at various other locations during the 1960s and 1970s.

1967

April — For the first time, seven Mexican television and radio stations carried a session of general conference.

June 10 — *The Six-Day War in the Middle East ended with Israel holding conquered Arab territory four times its own size.*

Sept. 1 — The beginning of the Church year was changed to Sept. 1 instead of Jan. 1 in the Southern Hemisphere, to coincide with the public school year.

Sept. 29 — The new administrative position of regional representative of the Twelve was announced, and the first 69 regional representatives were called and given their initial training.

November — Part of the Egyptian papyri owned by Joseph Smith while he was translating the Pearl of Great Price was given to the Church by the New York Metropolitan Museum of Art.

1968

Jan. 22 — *The* USS Pueblo *and its 83 crew members were seized in the Sea of Japan by North Korea.*

Feb. 2 — Six missionaries from the Taiwan and Hong Kong zones of the Southern Far East Mission were transferred to Thailand to begin missionary work.

August — A large LDS educational complex was dedicated in Mexico City. The school, Benemerito de las Americas, consisted of 11 grades for more than 1,200 students.

Oct. 17 — Relief Society Gen. Pres. Belle S. Spafford was named president of the National Council of Women for a two-year term.

Oct. 22 — The Church received official recognition in Spain. The first missionaries arrived in June, 1969.

1969

January — Two-month language training missions began. Language training for missionaries prior to their departure to their mission field first began during the early 1960s for Spanish, Portuguese, and German language missions.

Jan. 20 — The Tabernacle Choir sang at U.S. President Richard M. Nixon's inauguration in Washington, D.C.

July 20 — *U.S. astronaut Neil Armstrong became the first man to walk on the moon when he descended from the lunar module* Eagle; *he was followed 18 minutes later by Edwin Aldrin, pilot of the lunar module.*

Aug. 3-8 — A world conference on records was held in Salt Lake City, sponsored by the Church's Genealogical Society.

Nov. 1 — The Southeast Asia Mission formally opened with headquarters in Singapore. In January 1970, the first missionaries were sent to Indonesia, which was part of the mission.

1970

January — A computerized system for recording and reporting Church contributions went into operation.

Jan. 18 — President David O. McKay died in Salt Lake City at age 96.

Jan. 23 — President Joseph Fielding

Smith was ordained and set apart as the 10th president of the Church and chose Presidents Harold B. Lee and N. Eldon Tanner as his counselors.

March 15 — The first stake in Asia was organized in Tokyo, Japan.

March 22 — The first stake in Africa was organized in Transvaal, South Africa.

May — The Beehive House in Salt Lake City was placed on the register of National Historic Sites.

September — A new Aaronic Priesthood Personal Achievement Program was started, which gave young men the opportunity to set their own goals in consultation with their bishops. A similar program for young women began in January 1971.

October — Monday was designated for family home evening throughout the Church; no other Church activity was to be scheduled during that time.

1971

January — Publication of new Church magazines began: the *Ensign* for adults, the *New Era* for youth, and the *Friend* for children.

Also in January, a bishops' training program conducted by stake presidents was begun, and a new correlated teacher development program began operation.

July — The medical missionary program (later called the health missionary program) began.

Aug. 27-29 — The first Area Conference of the Church was held in Manchester, England. Before the program of holding large area conferences ended in 1980, 63 were held throughout the world.

September — All LDS women were automatically enrolled as members of the Relief Society; dues were eliminated.

Sept. 30 — *The United States and the Soviet Union signed pacts designed to avoid accidental nuclear war.*

1972

Church sports tournaments and dance festivals were directed to be held on a regional basis instead of an all-Church basis.

Jan. 14 — The Church Historical Department was formed in a reorganization of the Church Historian's Office. Church library, archives, and history divisions were created within the new department.

Jan. 18 — The Ogden Temple was dedicated by President Joseph Fielding Smith.

Feb. 9 — The Provo Temple was dedicated by President Smith.

July 2 — President Smith died in Salt Lake City at age 95.

July 7 — President Harold B. Lee was ordained and set apart as the 11th president of the Church, with Presidents N. Eldon Tanner and Marion G. Romney as his counselors.

Sept. 5 — *Eleven Israeli athletes and five of their assailants were killed in an attack on the Olympic Village at Munich, West Germany, by Arab terrorists.*

November — The MIA was realigned into the Aaronic Priesthood and Melchizedek Priesthood MIA and was placed directly under priesthood leadership.

Nov. 4 — Church departments began moving into the newly completed 28-story Church Office Building at 50 E. North Temple in Salt Lake City.

1973

A new set of missionary lessons was completed for use in all missions. It was the first change in missionary lessons since 1961.

February — The first Church agricultural missionaries to leave the United States were sent to the Guatemala-El Salvador Mission.

Feb. 4 — The Marriott Activities Center at BYU was dedicated. Seating 22,000, it was the largest such arena on any university campus in the United States.

March 8 — The first stake on mainland Asia was organized in Seoul, Korea.

April 7 — The creation of the Welfare Services Department was announced in general conference. The new organization brought the three welfare units — health services, social services, and welfare — into full correlation.

Sept. 20 — *The British-French supersonic airliner,* Concorde, *made its first landing in the United States at the Dallas-Fort Worth International Airport.*

Dec. 26 — President Harold B. Lee died in Salt Lake City at age 74.

Dec. 30 — President Spencer W. Kimball was ordained and set apart as the 12th president of the Church, with Presidents N. Eldon Tanner and Marion G. Romney as counselors.

1974

Jan. 14 — Names of stakes Churchwide were changed to reflect a consistent style identifying them with the geographical area served. Mission names were changed June 20, 1974.

March 23 — In an exchange of pioneer homes, the Church traded the Brigham Young Forest Farm home in Salt Lake City to the state of Utah for use in the state's Pioneer State Park. The Church acquired the Brigham Young winter home in St. George and the Jacob Hamblin home in nearby Santa Clara, Utah, for use as visitor and information centers.

May 9 — *Impeachment hearings began against U.S. President Richard M. Nixon.*

June 23 — MIA was dropped from the name of Church youth programs, and further modifications were implemented in the administrative structure of the Aaronic Priesthood and the Young Women organizations.

Sept. 1 — Church College of Hawaii became a branch of Brigham Young University and renamed Brigham Young University-Hawaii Campus.

Sept. 6 — The First Presidency announced that the Church was divesting itself of its 15 hospitals in three western states and turning them over to a non-Church, non-profit organization, Intermountain Health Care. The Church completed the legal steps for divesting the hospitals on March 21, 1975.

Oct. 3 — Seventies quorums were authorized in all stakes, and all quorums in the Church were renamed after the stake. Stake mission presidencies were also reorganized, with seven presidents of seventies serving in the calling, instead of three.

Nov. 19 — President Spencer W. Kimball dedicated the Washington Temple at Kensington, Md. Visitors during pre-dedication tours September through November totaled 758,327, topping the previous record of 662,401 at the Los Angeles Temple in 1956.

1975

April 20 — *South Vietnam unconditionally surrendered to North Vietnam, and the Vietnam War was officially at an end.*

May 3 — Citing accelerated growth of the Church worldwide, the First Presidency announced the creation of an area supervisory program and the assignment of six Assistants to the Twelve to oversee Church activities while residing outside the United States and Canada. The number of these foreign areas was increased to eight later in the year.

May 17 — A supervisory program for missions in the United States and Canada was announced, along with the assignment of members of the Quorum of the Twelve as advisers and other General Authorities as supervisors of the 12 areas.

June 27 — The end of auxiliary conferences was announced during the opening session of the 1975 June Conference. These conferences would be replaced with annual regional meetings for priesthood and auxiliary leaders.

July 24 — The 28-story Church Office Building in Salt Lake City was dedicated by President Spencer W. Kimball.

Aug. 8-17 — President Kimball spoke to a total of 44,500 members at five area conferences in the Far East, in Japan, the Philippines, Hong Kong, Taiwan, and Korea

Oct. 3 — President Kimball announced in general conference the organization of the First Quorum of the Seventy, and the first three members of the quorum were sustained.

Oct. 6-11 — Brigham Young University observed its 100th anniversary during homecoming week.

Nov. 7-9 — Incident to the rapid growth of the Church in Mexico, 15 stakes were created in Mexico City in one weekend.

Nov. 18 — The Church Genealogical Department was organized with five divisions, two of which were formerly known as the Genealogical Society.

1976

Feb. 15- March 2 — A total of 53,000 members in the South Pacific attended nine area conferences in American Samoa, Western Samoa, New Zealand, Fiji, Tonga, Tahiti, and Australia to hear counsel from President Spencer W. Kimball and other General Authorities.

April 3 — Members attending general conference accepted Joseph Smith's Vision of the Celestial Kingdom and Joseph F. Smith's Vision of the Redemption of the Dead for addition to the Pearl of Great Price. These scriptures became part of the Doctrine and Covenants on June 6, 1979.

June 5 — The Teton Dam in southeastern Idaho burst, sending a wall of water, between 12 and 20 feet high, onto the mostly LDS towns below. About 40,000 people, most of them members of the Church, were driven from their homes.

June 5 — The First Presidency published an official statement reaffirming the Church policy against abortion. The statement supplemented a filmstrip placed in distribution in March.

June 18-22 — President Kimball spoke at three area conferences in England and

Scotland, which were attended by more than a total of 17,000 members.

June 25 — Missouri Gov. Christopher S. Bond signed an executive order rescinding the extermination order issued in 1838 by Gov. Lilburn W. Boggs.

July 4 — President Kimball spoke at a Church-sponsored U.S. Bicentennial devotional attended by more than 23,000 people at the Capitol Centre in Landover, Md. Numerous additional activities involved Church members in the United States during the year-long Bicentennial observance.

July 31- Aug. 8 — President Kimball addressed a total of 25,000 members from 12 countries in Europe at five area conferences in France, Finland, Denmark, The Netherlands, and Germany.

Sept. 3 — Viking 2, *an American spacecraft, made a successful landing on Mars.*

Oct. 1 — Members of the First Council of the Seventy and the Assistants to the Twelve were released in general conference and called to the new First Quorum of the Seventy. Franklin D. Richards was named the first senior president.

1977

Jan. 1 — The First Presidency announced a new format for general conferences. General sessions would be held on the first Sunday of each April and October and the preceding Saturday. Regional representative seminars would be held on the preceding Friday.

Jan. 14 — The first Presiding Bishopric area supervisor, called to direct temporal affairs of the Church in Mexico, began work in Mexico City. Presiding Bishopric area supervisors for eight other areas outside the United States and Canada were announced June 4.

Feb. 5 — The First Presidency announced that the Quorum of the Twelve would oversee ecclesiastical matters and the Presiding Bishopric would have responsibility for temporal programs.

Feb. 21-March 11 — President Kimball met with heads of state in Mexico, Guatemala, Chile and Bolivia during a tour of Latin America to attend area conferences, and then visited at the White House with U.S. President Jimmy Carter March 11.

March 27 — *The worst airline disaster in history killed 581 people, as two jumbo jets collided on a runway in the Canary Islands.*

May 14 — A bishops central storehouse, the second in the Church and first outside of Salt Lake City, opened at Colton, Calif.

Also, the Young Men program was restructured. Young Men presidency and general board were given responsibility for Aaronic Priesthood curriculum, leadership training and quorum work.

May 22 — Formation of a new Church Activities Committee, with responsibility for coordinating cultural arts and physical activities, was announced. Similar groups were organized on the local levels.

May 30 — Poland granted legal status to the Church.

July 1 — In response to continued growth in membership worldwide, the geographic subdivisions of the Church, previously known as areas, were renamed zones, and the 11 zones were subdivided into areas. Members of the First Quorum of the Seventy were assigned as zone advisers and area supervisors.

July 30 — The Church Educational System was placed in the ecclesiastical line organization of the Church through an Education Executive Committee of the Quorum of the Twelve.

Oct. 1 — The Church published *A Topical Guide to the Scriptures of The Church of Jesus Christ of Latter-day Saints,* the first product of a continuing scriptural-aids project established by the First Presidency.

1978

March 31 — President Spencer W. Kimball announced that semiannual rather than quarterly stake conferences would be held starting in 1979.

April — The Church published in the *Reader's Digest* an eight-page removable insert about Church programs, the first of a series aimed at nearly 50 million *Digest* readers.

April 1 — President Kimball emphasized the four-generation program, which later became the basis for the Church's computerized Ancestral File.

June 9 — In a letter dated June 8 and made public the following day, the First Presidency announced the revelation that worthy men of all races would be eligible to receive the priesthood. On Sept. 30, members accepted the revelation by a sustaining vote at general conference. The First Presidency's announcement is now "Official Declaration – 2" in the Doctrine and Covenants.

July 1 — The Relief Society Monument to Women was dedicated in Nauvoo, Ill., by President Kimball.

July 22 — The United States Senate passed a bill, earlier approved by the House of Representatives, designating the Mormon Trail from Nauvoo, Ill., to Salt Lake City as a national historic trail.

Aug. 7 — North Dakota became the final state of the United States to have a stake headquartered within its boundaries when the Fargo North Dakota stake was created.

Sept. 9 — A new missionary training program was announced: Missionaries to English-speaking missions would receive four weeks training while those learning other languages would continue to receive eight weeks training at the new Missionary Training Center in Provo, Utah, which replaced the Language Training Mission and the Mission Home in Salt Lake City.

Sept. 16 — Women and girls 12 years of age and over gathered for a first-ever special closed-circuit audio conference, similar to general conference priesthood broadcasts.

Sept. 30 — A new special emeritus status for General Authorities was announced in general conference, and seven members of the First Quorum of the Seventy were so designated.

Oct. 22 — *Pope John Paul II formally assumed the papal throne.*

Oct. 26 — The Missionary Training Center in Provo, Utah, previously the Language Training Mission constructed in 1976, began training all missionaries.

Oct. 30 — The Sao Paulo Temple in Brazil was dedicated by President Kimball.

Nov. 9 — Elder and Sister Rendell N. Mabey and Elder and Sister Edwin Q. Cannon arrived in Nigeria as special representatives of the Church to open missionary work in West Africa.

1979

Jan. 1 — *The United States and China established diplomatic relations after decades of animosity.*

Feb. 3 — The Church Genealogical Department announced a new "family entry system" to allow submissions of names of deceased ancestors for temple work whose birthplaces and birthdates are unknown.

Feb. 18 — The Church's 1,000th stake was created at Nauvoo, Ill., by President Ezra Taft Benson of the Quorum of the Twelve.

June 6 — Joseph Smith's Vision of the Celestial Kingdom and Joseph F. Smith's Vision of the Redemption of the Dead were transferred from the Pearl of Great Price to the Doctrine and Covenants, becoming Sections 137 and 138, respectively.

Sept. 12-14 — The Tabernacle Choir, which celebrated the golden anniversary of its nationally broadcast radio program in July, toured Japan and Korea.

Sept. 29 — A new 2,400-page edition of the King James version of the Bible, with many special features, including a topical guide, a Bible dictionary, and a revolutionary footnote system, was published by the Church.

Oct. 29 — The first two converts of eastern Africa were baptized in Kenya.

Oct. 24 — President Spencer W. Kimball, on a tour of the Middle East, dedicated the Orson Hyde Memorial Gardens on the Mount of Olives in Jerusalem.

1980

Feb. 22 — The Presidency of the First Quorum of the Seventy was reorganized to strengthen the lines of administration at Church headquarters. The executive directors of the Missionary, Curriculum, Priesthood, and Genealogy departments became members of the presidency.

March 2 — U.S. and Canadian members began a new consolidated meeting schedule that put priesthood, sacrament, and auxiliary meetings into one three-hour time block on Sundays.

April 6 — Celebrating the Church's 150th anniversary, President Spencer W. Kimball conducted part of general conference from the newly restored Peter Whitmer farmhouse at Fayette, N.Y., the site where the Church was organized. The proceedings in Fayette were linked with the congregation in the Tabernacle in Salt Lake City via satellite, the first time a satellite was used in the Church for transmitting broadcasts of general conference.

May — Missionary work opened in Haiti and Belize.

May 18 — *Mt. St. Helens in Washington, one of the few active volcanoes in the United States, erupted in a violent explosion that left 10 dead and scores of others homeless.*

Oct. 18-Nov. 1 — The last of a series of large area conferences, presided over by the president of the Church, was held in six major cities in the Far East: Manila, Philippines; Hong Kong; Taipei, Taiwan; Seoul, Korea; and Tokyo and Osaka, Japan.

Oct. 27 — The Tokyo Temple was dedicated by President Kimball.

Nov. 17 — The Seattle Temple was dedicated by President Kimball.

1981

Jan. 20 — The Tabernacle Choir participated in the inaugural festivities for President Ronald Reagan.

April 1 — Plans to build nine smaller temples in the United States, Central America, Asia, Africa and Europe were announced by President Spencer W. Kimball: Chicago, Ill.; Dallas, Texas; Guatemala City, Guatemala; Lima, Peru; Frankfurt, Germany; Stockholm, Sweden; Seoul, Korea; Manila, Philippines; and Johannesburg, South Africa.

May 5 — The First Presidency publicly voiced its opposition to the proposed basing of the MX missile system in the Utah-Nevada desert.

July 23 — Elder Gordon B. Hinckley was called as a counselor in the First Presidency, the first time since the administration of President David O. McKay that a president had more than two counselors.

Sept. 12 — A smaller, less-expensive ward meetinghouse, called the Sage Plan, was announced by the First Presidency.

Sept. 26 — The first copies of a new version of the Triple Combination (Book of Mormon, Doctrine and Covenants and Pearl of Great Price), with extensive scripture helps, were made available to the public.

Oct. 3 — A network of 500 satellite dishes for stake centers outside Utah was announced. The receivers linked Church headquarters in Salt Lake City with members in the United States and Canada.

Nov. 16 — The Jordan River Temple was dedicated by President Marion G. Romney of the First Presidency.

1982

March 9 — The Spencer W. Kimball Tower, the tallest building on the BYU campus, was dedicated during ceremonies that featured President Kimball's first public appearance in six months because of illness.

March 18 — Three Church executive councils were created: the Missionary Executive Council, the Priesthood Executive Council, and the Temple and Genealogy Executive Council.

April 1 — It was announced that Church membership had reached the 5-million member mark.

April 2 — At general conference, major changes in financing Church meetinghouses were announced, shifting construction costs to general Church funds and utility costs to local units. Also, the term of service for single elders serving full-time missions was reduced from two years to 18 months.

June 30 — *The Equal Rights Amendment was defeated after a 10-year struggle for ratification.*

Sept. 5 — The Mormon Tabernacle Choir celebrated 50 years of continuous weekly broadcasts over the CBS radio network.

Sept. 10 — U.S. President Ronald Reagan visited Utah to tour a Church cannery and see the Church Welfare Program in action.

Oct. 3 — Elder Boyd K. Packer of the Quorum of the Twelve and a member of the Scriptures Publication Committee announced that a subtitle was being added to the Book of Mormon: "Another Testament of Jesus Christ."

Oct. 30 — A visitors center and historic site opened its doors in the three-story Grandin printing building in Palmyra, N.Y., where the first copies of the Book of Mormon were printed in 1830.

1983

Feb. 27 — The 150th anniversary of the Word of Wisdom was observed throughout the Church and at the Newel K. Whitney store in Kirtland, Ohio, where the original revelation was received in 1833.

June 1 — The Atlanta Georgia Temple was dedicated by President Gordon B. Hinckley of the First Presidency.

Aug. 5, 9 — For the first time in Church history, two temples were dedicated within a week's time: the Apia Samoa Temple on Aug. 5 and the Nuku'alofa Tonga Temple on Aug. 9; both by President Gordon B. Hinckley.

Sept. 15 — The Santiago Chile Temple was dedicated by President Hinckley.

Oct. 16 — The first of a series of multi-stake (later known as regional) conferences was held in London, England.

Oct. 25 — *U.S. Marines and Army Rangers invaded the Caribbean island of Grenada, deposing the island's Marxist government.*

Oct. 27 — The Papeete Tahiti Temple was dedicated by President Hinckley.

Dec. 2 — The Mexico City Temple was dedicated by President Hinckley.

1984

Jan. 7 — Premier Zhao Ziyang of the People's Republic of China visited the BYU-Hawaii campus and the adjacent Polynesian Cultural Center during the first visit of a Chinese premier to the United States since the People's Republic of China was formed in 1949.

March 25 — A new program — the Four-Phase Genealogical Facilities Program — was announced, enabling wards and branches to establish genealogical facilities in their meetinghouses.

April 7 — The first members of the First Quorum of the Seventy called for temporary three- to five-year terms were sustained. They were later sustained to the Second Quorum of the Seventy, created in 1989, and their term of service standardized at five years.

May 10 — *A federal judge in Salt Lake City ruled that the U.S. government was negligent in its above-ground testing of nuclear weapons at the Nevada test site in the 1950s and early 1960s.*

May 25 — President Gordon B. Hinckley dedicated the Boise Idaho Temple.

June 24 — Members of the First Quorum of the Seventy were appointed to serve as area presidencies in 13 major geographical areas of the Church — seven in the United States and Canada and six in other parts of the world.

Sept. 20 — The Sydney Australia Temple was dedicated by President Hinckley.

Sept. 25 — The Manila Philippines Temple was dedicated by President Hinckley.

Oct. 19 — The Dallas Texas Temple was dedicated by President Hinckley.

Oct. 28 — The Church's 1,500th stake was created 150 years after the first stake was organized in Kirtland, Ohio. The landmark stake was the Ciudad Obregon Mexico Yaqui Stake.

Nov. 17 — The Taipei Taiwan Temple was dedicated by President Hinckley.

Nov. 26 — The First Presidency announced that, beginning Jan. 1, the term of full-time missionary service for single elders would again be 24 months. It had been shortened from two years to 18 months in April 1982.

Dec. 14 — The Guatemala City Temple was dedicated by President Hinckley.

1985

Jan. 2 — BYU's football team was named national champions after being voted the No. 1 team in the nation for the 1984 season by every major poll. The Cougars had just completed a perfect 13-0 season.

Jan. 27 — Latter-day Saints in the United States and Canada participated in a special fast to benefit victims of famine in Africa and other parts of the world. The fast raised more than $6 million.

April 12 — U.S. Senator Jake Garn of Utah became the first Church member to fly in space. He was aboard the space shuttle *Challenger*. Another Church member, Don Lind, was a crew member on a space shuttle mission that blasted off April 29.

June 29 — The Freiberg Temple, located in the German Democratic Republic, then communist-controlled, was dedicated by President Gordon B. Hinckley.

July 2 — The Stockholm Sweden Temple was dedicated by President Hinckley.

July 31 — Li Xiannian, president of the People's Republic of China, and his wife, Madame Lin Jiamei, toured the Church's Polynesian Cultural Center in Hawaii as part of his tour of the United States and Canada.

Aug. 2 — A new LDS hymnbook, the first revision in 37 years, came off the presses.

Aug. 9 — The Chicago Illinois Temple was dedicated by President Hinckley.

Aug. 24 — The Johannesburg South Africa Temple was dedicated by President Hinckley. With the dedication of this building, there was now a temple on every continent except Antarctica.

Oct. 23 — The Church Genealogical Library in Salt Lake City was dedicated by President Hinckley.

Nov. 5 — President Spencer W. Kimball died in Salt Lake City at age 90.

Nov. 10 — President Ezra Taft Benson was ordained and set apart as the 13th president of the Church, with President Hinckley and President Thomas S. Monson as counselors.

Dec. 14 — The Seoul Korea Temple was dedicated by President Hinckley.

1986

Jan. 10, 17 — The Lima Peru Temple was dedicated by President Gordon B. Hinckley, and the Buenos Aires Argentina Temple was dedicated by President Thomas S. Monson.

Jan. 28 — *The space shuttle* Challenger *exploded shortly after liftoff, killing all seven people aboard, including Christa McAuliffe, the first teacher in space.*

April 30 — Church membership was estimated to have reached the 6-million member milestone.

June 22 — The 1,600th stake of the Church was created by President Monson in Kitchener, Ontario.

July 6 — New missionary discussions, which focus on "teaching from the heart," were approved for use in all English-speaking missions.

Oct. 4 — Seventies quorums in stakes throughout the Church were discontinued. Brethren serving as seventies returned to elders quorums or were ordained high priests.

Oct. 5 — The First Presidency issued a statement opposing the legalization of gambling and government sponsorship of lotteries.

Oct. 11 — In the first Churchwide Young Women activity, an estimated 300,000 gathered at sites around the world to release helium-filled balloons containing personal messages from the young women.

Oct. 24 — The Denver Colorado Temple was dedicated by President Ezra Taft Benson.

1987

Jan. 23 — Documents dealer Mark Hofmann was imprisoned after a plea bargain arrangement in which he admitted responsibility for the bombing deaths of two people in Salt Lake City in October 1985. He also confessed that he had forged the so-called Martin Harris "Salamander Letter" and other documents relating to the Church.

Jan. 27 — *Soviet Union leader Mikhail Gorbachev proposed a series of economic and social reforms that signaled the start of an era of "glasnost," or openness, in the Communist country.*

Feb. 15 — The Tabernacle Choir marked its 3,000th radio broadcast in a series that had become the longest-running network program in the free world.

March 12 — It was announced that the Church-owned Hotel Utah, a landmark in downtown Salt Lake City for 76 years, would close as a hotel Aug. 31 and be renovated as a meetinghouse and office building.

April 25 — The First Presidency announced a realignment of the Church's worldwide administrative areas, including creation of four new areas.

June 20 — The First Presidency sent a letter to priesthood leaders defining the organizational structure of ward Young Women presidencies and calling for consistent midweek activities for young women.

July 15 — The Genealogical Library celebrated the conversion of the last card from its card catalog to computer.

July 24-26 — Church members throughout Britain commemorated the 150th anniversary of the first missionary work in Great Britain. Thirteen General Authorities, including President Ezra Taft Benson and President Gordon B. Hinckley, attended various events, which included dedication of historical sites, firesides and conferences.

Aug. 15 — The Church's Genealogical Department was renamed the Family History Department.

Aug. 25 — A national Emmy award, the first-ever awarded to a public service spot, was given to the Church by the National Academy of Television Arts and Sciences.

Aug. 28 — The Frankfurt Germany Temple was dedicated by President Benson.

Sept. 4 — A letter from the First Presidency announced the discontinuance of the International Mission. Responsibility for its areas reverted to the respective area presidencies of the Church.

1988

Jan. 30-31 — Seven stakes were created in one weekend in Lima, Peru, by Elder Charles Didier of the Seventy.

March 24 — President Thomas S. Monson, second counselor in the First Presidency, and his wife, Frances, were guests of the king and queen of Sweden at a dinner commemorating the 350th year of the first Swedish settlement in the United States.

April 2 — Ricks College in Rexburg, Idaho, officially inaugurated its centennial celebration.

May 15 — Elder Neal A. Maxwell of the Quorum of the Twelve organized the Aba Nigeria Stake, the first Church stake in West Africa.

May 28 — The First Presidency issued a statement on the subject of AIDS, stressing chastity before marriage, fidelity in marriage, and abstinence from homosexual behavior, yet extending sympathy to those who have contracted the disease.

June 1 — The Church was granted legal recognition in Hungary, the first of several such steps in Eastern European nations during the next two years.

July 4 — The Tabernacle Choir completed a 21-day, 19-concert tour of Hawaii, Australia, and New Zealand.

July 16 — Monuments commemorating where the Mormon Battalion was mustered and where LDS pioneers established Nebraska's first community were dedicated near Council Bluffs, Iowa, and Florence, Neb.

August — The Church reached the milestone of having completed 100 million endowments for the dead.

Sept. 17 — The Church joined an interfaith television network (VISN) sponsored by 18 religious organizations. Also, the BYU Folk Dancers were the only North American dance company to perform at opening ceremonies of the 1988 Olympic Games in Seoul, Korea, viewed by an estimated 1 billion people worldwide.

Oct. 16 — Elder David B. Haight created the 1,700th stake of the Church. The new stake was in Manaus, Brazil, a city of 1.5 million in the heart of the Amazon jungle.

Oct. 24-28 — President Thomas S. Monson led a delegation of Church leaders that met with the German Democratic Republic's top government officials. It was announced Nov. 12 that the Church had been granted rights to send missionaries to the DDR and for LDS members from the DDR to serve as missionaries in other countries.

1989

El Salvador reached self-sufficiency in local full-time missionaries.

Jan. 19 — The Mormon Tabernacle Choir, called "The Nation's Choir," performed at events during the inauguration of President George Bush.

Jan. 28 — Elders Russell M. Nelson and Dallin H. Oaks of the Quorum of the Twelve completed an eight-day visit to China and were assured by high-level Chinese leaders that people are free to practice religious beliefs in that country.

Feb. 15 — One hundred fifty years after Quincy, Ill., residents gave aid to Church members forced to flee from Missouri, the city's mayor presented Elder Loren C. Dunn of the First Quorum of the Seventy with a key to the city and proclaimed this date "Latter-day Saints Day."

March 24 — *The* Exxon Valdez *struck a reef in Alaska's Prince William Sound and spilled 240,000 barrels of oil, the largest oil spill in U.S. history.*

April 1-2 — The Second Quorum of the Seventy was created and all General Authorities serving under a five-year call were sustained as members, along with another eight newly called General Authorities.

May 16 — The BYU Jerusalem Center for Near Eastern Studies was dedicated by President Howard W. Hunter of the Quorum of the Twelve.

June 14 — LDS missionaries and those of the Jehovah's Witnesses were expelled from Ghana, a western Africa nation where 6,000 Church members live. The Church had no advance notice of the ban. The LDS missionaries were able to return to Ghana in 1990.

June 15 — Ground was broken for the first LDS meetinghouse in Poland.

June 25 — The 100th stake in Mexico was created in Tecalco. Mexico became the first country outside the United States with 100 or more stakes.

June 27 — The renovated Carthage Jail complex in Illinois, where the Prophet Joseph Smith was martyred, was dedicated by President Gordon B. Hinckley, highlighting activities commemorating the 150th anniversary of the Mormon settlement of Nauvoo, Ill.

Aug. 19 — The Portland Oregon Temple was dedicated by President Gordon B. Hinckley.

Sept. 9 — Because of threats expressed against Americans in Colombia during increasing drug-related violence, Church leaders decided to give early releases or transfers to North American missionaries serving in that country.

Sept. 30 — The first General Authorities called under a plan to serve for five years were released in general conference.

Oct. 17 — The first LDS meetinghouse in the Republic of Hungary, located in the capital city of Budapest, was dedicated by President Thomas S. Monson.

Nov. 9 — *The Berlin Wall came down, paving the way for eventual unification of East and West Germany.*

Nov. 25 — A major change in policy for financing local Church units in the United States and Canada was announced by the First Presidency. Ward members would no longer have stake and ward budget assessments.

Dec. 16 — The Las Vegas Nevada Temple was dedicated by President Gordon B. Hinckley.

1990

Jan. 19-23 — Elder Dallin H. Oaks of the Quorum of the Twelve met with Chinese leaders and delivered a 90-minute address about the Church to the Chinese Academy of Social Sciences.

Jan. 21 — David Hsiao Hsin Chen, a professor at BYU-Hawaii who was born and raised in China, was sustained as the Church's "traveling elder" to oversee Church affairs in China.

Feb. 25 — The Church was oficially recognized in Kenya.

April 2 — A new Church software package called FamilySearch, designed to simplify the task of family history research, was released by the Church.

April 27-29 — Soviet Union's ambassador to the United States, Yuri V.

Dubinin, made a historic visit to Church sites in Utah and spoke at a conference of the Salt Lake Monument Park Stake.

May 21 — The U.S. Supreme Court handed down a unanimous decision that money given directly to missionaries was not a deductible donation under federal tax law. The Church encouraged members to follow established procedures of contributing through their wards.

July — New missions in the Eastern European countries of Czechoslovakia, Hungary, and Poland highlighted the record 29 missions created in 1990.

Aug. 7 — *International forces of "Operation Desert Shield" left for Saudi Arabia following the invasion of Kuwait by Iraq.*

Aug 25 — The Toronto Ontario Temple was dedicated by President Gordon B. Hinckley.

Sept. 13 — Registration of the Leningrad Branch of the Church was approved by the Council on Religious Affairs of the Council of Ministers in the Soviet Union.

Sept. 15 — President Hinckley spoke at a memorial service at Cedar City, Utah, that brought together descendants of the pioneers and the victims involved in the Mountain Meadows Massacre. He also dedicated a monument that had recently been erected at the site.

November — The First Presidency announced in November a new policy for United States and Canada, effective Jan. 1, 1991, that would equalize contributions required to maintain a full-time missionary.

Nov. 30 — The government of Ghana gave permission for the Church to resume activities in that West African country.

1991

Jan. 15. — Latter-day Saints were among the servicemen and women who were mobilized as part of the war in the Persian Gulf, "Operation Desert Storm." More than 100 LDS groups across the Arabian Peninsula saw to the spiritual needs of LDS servicemen and women.

Late February — Delivery of 1,800 packages of food and vitamins, designated for Church members and non-members in the Soviet Union republics of Russia and Estonia, was completed.

April 19 — Recognition of the Church in the Ivory Coast, the center of French West Africa, was announced at a special meeting of Church members in Abidjan.

April 27 — Fifty years after the Church began keeping individual membership records, it completed computerizing membership records worldwide.

May 1 — The 500,000th full-time missionary in this dispensation was called.

May 26 — The 1,800th stake in the Church, the San Francisco de Macoris Dominican Republic Stake, was created.

June 8 — The Tabernacle Choir embarked on a 21-day tour of eight European countries, including five countries in which the choir had not performed before: Hungary, Austria, Czechoslovakia, Poland and the Soviet Union.

June 22 — The Alberta Temple, after three years of renovation, was rededicated by President Gordon B. Hinckley, first counselor in the First Presidency,.

June 24 — The Russian Republic, the largest in the Soviet Union, granted formal recognition to the Church following the Tabernacle Choir's concert in Moscow's Bolshoi Theater.

Aug. 13-27 — The 100th anniversary of the founding of the Church in Tonga was observed with events in Tonga. King Taufa'ahau Tupou IV attended the major events on the main island of Tongatapu.

Sept. 1 — Membership in the Church reached 8 million, about two years after membership hit the 7 million mark in December 1989.

Nov. 5 — Twenty-two members of the Church were killed in the Philippines when a typhoon unleashed flash floods, sending a wall of mud and water through the central Philippine city of Ormoc.

December — The *Encyclopedia of Mormonism,* promoted by its New York publisher as "a landmark reference work," was published. A 13-member board of editors at BYU compiled the encyclopedia under commission from Macmillan Publishing Co.

Dec. 25 — *The Soviet Union broke up; the United States and other western countries recognized the Commonwealth of Independent States.*

1992

March 14 — The sesquicentennial of the founding of the Relief Society on March 17, 1842, was celebrated in an international satellite telecast.

May 13 — Elder Dallin H. Oaks of the Quorum of the Twelve appeared before the U.S. House Subcommittee on Civil and Constitutional Rights advocating legislation that would restore freedom of religion that was diminished in a 1990 Supreme Court decision. He testified Sept. 18 before the Senate advocating the same legislation.

May 31 — Attending specially called meetings in four Utah cities, six members of the Quorum of the Twelve and three members of the Seventy counseled stake presidents and regional representatives on moral issues.

June 9 — The new Social Hall Memorial and walkway — featuring the unearthed foundation of the historic Social Hall of Brigham Young's era — was dedicated by President Gordon B. Hinckley, first counselor in the First Presidency, in downtown Salt Lake City.

Aug. 15 — Commemorating the "second rescue" of the ill-fated Willie and Martin handcart pioneers, President Hinckley dedicated three monuments in central Wyoming . The Riverton Wyoming Stake researched family histories and performed temple ordinances for those pioneers whose work was not previously done.

Aug. 23-26 — Hurricane Andrew, the most powerful hurricane in more than 60 years, caused $30 billion in damage, including homes of Church members and some Church buildings, particularly in the Homestead Florida Stake near Miami.

Aug. 30 — The Church's 1,900th stake, the Orlando Florida South Stake, was organized by Elder Neal A. Maxwell of the Quorum of the Twelve.

Sept. 26 — The First Presidency authorized the use of humanitarian relief funds to be sent to Somalia and other African nations in the grip of the drought of the century. In an initial response, one million pounds of food was shipped.

Oct. 8 — The Church was legally recognized in Tanzania.

Oct. 18, 23 — The London and Swiss Temples were rededicated by President Hinckley following extensive remodeling and refurbishing.

Dec. 6 — The Church reached a milestone of 20,000 wards and branches with the creation of the Harvest Park Ward in the Salt Lake Granger South Stake.

Dec. 15 — A gospel literacy effort sponsored by the Relief Society to help increase literacy throughout the Church was announced in a letter from the First Presidency to priesthood and Relief Society leaders.

Dec. 26 — The Tabernacle Choir left on a tour of the Holy Land. Concerts were later held in Jerusalem, Tel Aviv, and Haifa.

1993

The Church received legal recognition in Italy, Madagascar, Cameroon, and Ethiopia.

Jan. 6 — Four Church-service missionaries entered Hanoi, Vietnam, to give humanitarian service, teaching English to doctors and staff at a children's hospital and to teachers, staff, and children at a school for young children.

April 6 — The centennial of the Salt Lake Temple was observed at a Tabernacle Choir special program, and a special mural was placed in the temple.

April 25-30 — The San Diego California Temple was dedicated by President Gordon B. Hinckley.

June 27 — After being refurbished and remodeled, the former Hotel Utah was rededicated and renamed the Joseph Smith Memorial Building, housing office and meeting facilities for the Church and a theater showing the new film "Legacy."

June 29 — The government of Mexico formally registered the LDS Church, granting it all the rights of a religious organization, including the right to own property.

Nov. 8 — TempleReady, a long-awaited software making it possible to rapidly clear names from family history research for temple work, was announced in a letter to priesthood leaders from the First Presidency.

Nov. 16 — Church leaders hailed the Religious Freedom Restoration Act passed by Congress. This act was signed into law by the U.S. president on this date as "the most historic piece of legislation dealing with religious freedom in our lifetime."

December — Members in Spanish-speaking countries received the Triple Combination of the scriptures with the scripture aids in their language. The Book of Mormon with scripture aids was published in 1992.

1994

January — A year-long commemoration of the 100th anniversary of the Church's Genealogical Society of Utah — now the Family History Department — began with an effort to invite the non-member international genealogical community to join the effort in preserving, automating, and sharing genealogical information for the benefit of all mankind.

Feb. 13 — The First Presidency announced that the 87-year-old Uintah Stake Tabernacle in Vernal, Utah, would be renovated and dedicated as Utah's 10th temple. It was the first existing building to be renovated into a temple.

May 30 — President Ezra Taft Benson, 94, president of the Church for 8 1/2 years, died in Salt Lake City.

June 5 — President Howard W. Hunter was ordained and set apart as the 14th president of the Church. Set apart as his counselors were President Gordon B. Hinckley and President Thomas S. Monson.

June 26 — President Hunter, President Hinckley, and Elder M. Russell Ballard spoke at three separate events in Nauvoo and Carthage, Ill., commemorating the 150th anniversary of the martyrdom of the Prophet Joseph Smith.

Aug. 6 — One-third of the population of the United States has been visited by Church representatives, and 36 percent have friends or relatives who are LDS, the Missionary Department announced.

Oct. 9 — The Orlando Florida Temple was dedicated by President Hunter.

December — Eighty tons of food, 20 tons of winter clothing and 2,000 winter blankets were donated to some 3,000 families of flood victims in Partiznask, Russia. Also, 20,000 food packages were sent for families in Bosnia, Croatia and Albania.

Dec. 11— The 2,000th stake in the Church, the Mexico City Mexico Contretras, was created by President Hunter near where 19 years earlier he had created 15 stakes in one weekend.

1995

Jan. 8-14 — The Bountiful Utah Temple was dedicated by President Howard W. Hunter.

Jan. 21 — The Church reached 9 million members.

March 3 — President Hunter died at his Salt Lake City home after serving as Church president for less than nine months, the shortest tenure of any president.

March 12 — President Gordon B. Hinckley was ordained and set apart as the 15th president of the Church. Set apart as his counselors were President Thomas S. Monson, first counselor, and President James E. Faust, second counselor.

April 1 — A new administrative position, Area Authority Seventy, was announced by President Hinckley during the priesthood session of general conference. The position of regional representative was discontinued after 28 years.

April 15 — President Hinckley spoke at St. Louis, Mo., at the first regional conference of dozens he would address during visits over much of the globe.

June 16 — The International Olympic Committee announced that the site for the 2002 Winter Olympics would be in Salt Lake City.

Aug. 4-5 — The Tabernacle Choir performed in the Kennedy Center in Washington, D.C. On Aug. 8-9, it performed in the Cathedral of St. John the Divine in New York City.

Aug. 23 — President Thomas S. Monson and his wife, Frances, welcomed the king and queen of Sweden to the grounds of the Stockholm Sweden Temple.

Sept. 23 — At the annual General Relief Society Meeting, the First Presidency and Quorum of the Twelve issued a Proclamation to the World on the Family, reaffirming that "the family is central to the Creator's plan for the eternal destiny of His children."

Dec. 18 — President Hinckley was interviewed by CBS television host Mike Wallace on the show *60 Minutes*. The show was broadcast in April 1996.

Dec. 20 — The Church released a new logo that emphasizes the central position of the Savior in the Church's theology.

1996

Jan. 18 — The First Presidency announced that General Authorities would no longer serve on boards of directors of businesses.

Feb. 3 — The commemoration of the sesquicentennial of the Nauvoo exodus was held on the frigid banks of the Mississippi River. This began the epic commemoration of the sesquicentennial of the pioneer migration west during 1996-97.

Feb. 28 — A milestone was reached as a majority of members, 4,720,000, now live outside the United States, compared to 4,719,000 living within.

April 6 — President Gordon B. Hinckley announced at general conference that a new assembly hall four times the size of the Tabernacle would be built.

May 26 — The Hong Kong Temple was dedicated by President Hinckley.

May 27-28 — President Hinckley, on a tour of the Orient, became the first Church president ever to visit mainland China. He also visited, from May 17 to June 1, Japan, Korea, Hong Kong, Cambodia, Vietnam, the Philippines, and Saipan.

June 11-16 — President Hinckley visited Spain, Belgium, Netherlands, Denmark, Germany, and the Holy Land.

June 17-July 12 — A commemorative wagon train crossed Iowa, retracing the path of the 1846 exodus from Nauvoo, Ill.

July 13 — President Hinckley dedicated a replica of the 1847 log tabernacle in Kanesville (Council Bluffs), Iowa, where Brigham Young was sustained as president of the Church. A re-enactment of the 1846 mustering of the Mormon Battalion was held in Council Bluffs.

Oct. 13 — President Hinckley dedicated the Mount Timpanogos Utah Temple in American Fork, Utah.

Nov. 2 The First Presidency announced the establishment of Latter-day Saint Charities, a charitable, nonprofit corporation designed to help the Church deliver humanitarian aid to the poor and needy of the world.

Nov. 8-16 — President Hinckley spoke to gatherings of Church members and missionaries in Colombia, Peru, Bolivia, Chile, Argentina, and Brazil, and broke ground for temples in Bolivia and Brazil.

Nov. 18 — Elder Joseph B. Wirthlin of the Quorum of the Twelve became the first apostle to address Latter-day Saints in Far East Russia when he spoke in Vladivostok, Russia, in the region of Siberia.

1997

January — The Church in Africa reached a milestone when the100,000th member on the continent was baptized.. The milestone marked the almost doubling of the membership in Africa in six years.

Jan. 4 — The Tabernacle Choir performed at the second inauguration of Utah Gov. Michael O. Leavitt, the second time the choir had performed at a Utah state inaugural ceremony. The first was 101 years ago when the state's first governor, Heber M. Wells, took office.

Jan. 18-27 — President Gordon B. Hinckley went on a 10-day tour that included a visit to Jacksonville, Fla., Jan. 19 for the 50th anniversary of the first stake in the South, and continued with visits to Panama, Costa Rica, Nicaragua, Honduras, El Salvador, and Guatemala.

Feb. 22 — A pioneer-style handcart, being pulled by Church members, left Krasnoyarsk in Siberia on a trek through key cities in Russia and Ukraine in commemoration of the Pioneer trek of 1847.

Feb. 28 — Some 8,500 people participated in a grand celebration commemorating the Pioneer Sesquicentennial on the grounds of the Mexico City Mexico Temple.

March 9 — Chile became the fourth nation in the world to have 100 or more stakes, with the creation of the Puerto Varas Chile Stake.

March 14-15 — Intense civil unrest in Albania, with Americans being ordered out, resulted in the evacuation for a time of the missionaries from that country.

April 4 — During general conference, the organization of the Third, Fourth, and Fifth Quorums of the Seventy was announced.

April 18 — President Hinckley dedicated two main Mormon Trail sites on the same day in two different states. First, he dedicated the Pioneer Memorial Park in Nauvoo, Ill., and later the Mormon Trail Center at Historic Winter Quarters in Omaha, Neb.,

April 19-21 — The commemorative Mormon Trail Wagon Train, which the worldwide public would view as the centerpiece of the sesquicentennial observance of the Mormon pioneer trek, left from two locations, Council Bluffs, Iowa, on April 19, and Winter Quarters (Omaha), Neb., on April 21. The two contingents would later merge.

April 23 — Tung Chee-hwa, an official of the People's Republic of China, assured President James E. Faust, second counselor in the First Presidency, and other Church leaders visiting in Hong Kong that freedom of religion in the city would remain after it reverted from British to Chinese sovereignty on July 1.

May 8-17 — President Hinckley toured the South Pacific nations of New Zealand and Australia, speaking 15 times in seven cities to a total of more than 55,000 members.

May 1 — Deseret Gymnasium in Salt Lake City, a long-standing, Church-owned enterprise, was closed and its building later demolished to make way for the Church's new assembly building. —

May 3 — Before 5,000 visitors at the Sun Ranch in central Wyoming, President Hinckley dedicated a new visitors center at Martin's Cove, Wyo., in memory of the Willie and Martin handcart pioneers of 1856.

June 1 — The St. Louis Missouri Temple was dedicated by President Hinckley.

June 1 — A letter from the First Presidency announced significant modifications to the curriculum and gospel study program for the Melchizedek Priesthood and Relief Society, providing a similar meeting and instruction schedule for both organizations.

June 15 — The 100th stake in the Church's Pacific Area, the Suva Fiji North Stake, was created.

July 22 — After 93 days on the trail, the

commemorative Mormon Trail Wagon Train from Winter Quarters, Neb., entered Salt Lake City, where they were greeted by about 50,000 cheering people at This Is the Place State Park. There, they heard an address by President Hinckley.

July 12 — It was reported that a project to restore to its 19th century appearance the Joseph Smith Farm, adjacent to the Sacred Grove, near Palmyra, N.Y., was approved by the First Presidency.

July 19 — Latter-day Saints from more than 20,000 Church units contributed some 3 million hours of service to their communities as part of Worldwide Pioneer Heritage Service Day.

July 24 — President Hinckley broke ground for the new 21,000-seat assembly building on the block north of Temple Square in Salt Lake City.

Aug. 7-14 — President Hinckley delivered 12 addresses to about 56,000 people in four nations of South America: Paraguay, Ecuador, Venezuela, and Uruguay.

Oct. 4 — It was announced in general conference by President Hinckley that the Church would construct temples in remote areas of the Church that have small LDS populations. The first were to be built in Anchorage, Alaska, in the LDS colonies of northern Mexico, and in Monticello, Utah.

Oct. 10-17 — President. Hinckley addressed a total of 52,500 members in eight islands of the Pacific: Samoa, Hawaii, American Samoa, Tonga, Fiji, and Tahiti.

November — Sometime during the first week of November, the Church reached 10 million members, according to Church estimates.

Nov. 2 — The Vernal Utah Temple, the only temple in the Church to be built from an existing structure, was dedicated by President Hinckley.

Nov. 8-13 — President Hinckley addressed 42,000 Church members in Mexico City and an additional 12,000 in Puebla, Mexico. On the trip, he met with Mexico's president, Dr. Ernesto Zedillo.

1998

Feb. 14-22 — President Gordon B. Hinckley became the first Church president ever to visit West Africa during a nine-day tour of Nigeria, Ghana, Kenya, Zimbabwe, and Suth Africa. On Feb. 16, he announced plans for the first tem;ple to be built in West Africa, in Ghana.

March 9-15 — President Hinckley addressed more than 53,000 members in 10 cities of northern Mexico: Hermosillo, Ciudad Obregon, Culiacan, Guadalajara, Torreon, Leon, Ciudad Victoria, Monterrey, Chihuahua, and Ciudad Juarez.

March 26 — The replica of the Joseph Smith Sr. family log home near Palmyra, N.Y., was dedicated by President Hinckley. The home was the location where the Prophet Joseph Smith was visited in his youth by the Angel Moroni.

March 27 — After 2 1/2 years of reconstruction, the Egbert B. Grandin Building, in Palmyra, N.Y., where the Book of Mormon was published in 1829, was dedicated as a Church historic site by President Hinckley.

April 4 — President Hinckley announced in general conference that the Church would construct an additional 30 smaller temples that would bring the total number of operating temples in the Church to 100 by the year 2000.

June 4-6 — On a tour of Europe, President Hinckley addressed Church members at meetings in Paris, France; Franfurt, Germany and Geneva, Switzerland.

June 7 — The Preston England Temple was dedicated by President Hinckley.

June 14-July 2 — The Tabernacle Choir performed in seven nations of Europe, in London, England; Brussells, Belgium; Geneva, Switzerland; Turin and Rome, Italy; Marseille, France; Barcelona and Madrid, Spain; and Lisbon, Portugal.

July 26 The Monticello Utah Temple, the prototype for a new generation of small temples in less-populous areas of the Church, was dedicated in southeast Utah by President Hinckley.

July 31-Aug. 8 — President Hinckley, on an eight-day, 12-city tour in six provinces across Canada, addressed members at meetings in Victoria, Vancouver, and Prince George, British Columbia; Lethbridge and Edmonton, Alberta; Regina, Saskatechewan; Winnipeg, Manitoba; Sudbury, Ottawa, and Hamilton, Ontario; and Montreal and Quebec City, Quebec.

Aug. 15 — Five new areas — or administrative geographical divisions — of the Church went into effect: Africa West, Brazil North, South America West, Pacific Islands, and North America East, bringing the total number of areas to 28.

Aug. 8 — The first temple to be built in the former Soviet Union was announced for Kiev, Ukraine.

Sept. 8 — President Hinckley appeared on the Cable News Network television show, "Larry King Live," answering questions on wide-ranging subjects.

NEWS IN REVIEW
October 1998-September 2000

October 1998

New family file procedures implemented in temples gave families responsibility for their own family files — as the temples no longer keep family files — and provide flexibility in performing vicarious ordinances in any temple, it was announced Oct. 3. Prior to this, when names were submitted to one temple, all ordinances generally were performed in that same temple as a cumbersome process was required to transfer names from one temple to another. The new procedures were implemented in temples in the United States, Canada, and England in 1998, and all temples worldwide in 1999.

Also in the news in October 1998:

Oct. 1: The Relief Society general presidency hosted Madame Jehan Sadat, former first lady of Egypt, in Salt Lake City.

Oct. 9: A $400,000 Encampment Mall monument, located on a seven-acre plot on the campus of Dixie College in St. George, Utah, was dedicated by President Hinckley in honor of the pioneers who first settled the area in December 1861. Five thousand people attended the dedication.

Oct. 12: One of the most visible activities of the Church in New York City took place in Manhattan when 150 members of the New York New York Stake carried flags from countries throughout the world at the 54th Annual Columbus Day Parade, attended by an estimated 1 million people.

Oct. 17: Elder Jose Manual Mackintosh of Hiko, Nev., and Elder Bradley Alan Borden of Mesa, Ariz., serving in the Russia Yetakerinburg Mission, were attacked and stabbed, resulting in the death of Elder Mackintosh and injury to Elder Borden.

Oct. 20, 1998: President James E. Faust addresses police chiefs gathered from throughout the nation.

Oct. 18: President Hinckley counseled 20,000 members, who gathered from 16 stakes in five states at a special fireside in the United Center, home of the Chicago Bulls professional basketball team, to "be not faithless, but believing," a theme taken from John 20:26-27. President Hinckley was on his way home from four days of meetings with members and missionaries from Oct. 14-17 in Burlington, Vt.; Lowell, Mass.; Worchester, Mass.; and Schenectady, N.Y.

Oct. 20: Speaking to police chiefs from throughout the world, meeting in Salt Lake City, President James E. Faust, second counselor in the First Presidency, expressed "a hope, even a prayer, that law enforcement efforts and officials all over the world could be more family friendly."

Oct. 24: Elder Parley P. Pratt was memorialized with a new heroic-size bronze sculpture and park in Salt Lake City that was dedicated by Elder M. Russell Ballard of the Quorum of the Twelve.

Oct. 28: President Thomas S. Monson,

first counselor in the First Presidency, dedicated the BYU Salt Lake Center as an "edifice of learning."

Oct. 28: The Church is playing a key role in the establishment of a new, state-of-the-art family history research facility in the Ellis Island Immigration Museum in New York City, it was announced at a news conference at the museum.

Oct. 29: A check for $100,000 was presented to Australian officials by Elder Vaughn J. Featherstone of the Seventy and president of the Australia/New Zealand Area to help alleviate damage caused by a storm.

Oct. 30: The 100,000 square-foot Deseret Industries store in Provo, Utah — by far the largest Deseret Industries facility in the Church — was dedicated by Bishop Keith McMullin, second counselor in the Presiding Bishopric.

November 1998

When Hurricane Mitch hit Central America, causing widespread devastation, the Church responded even before the winds calmed. On Nov. 2, more than 240,000 pounds of relief supplies were shipped by the Church to aid victims of the 180-mile-an-hour winds, which severely affected more than 13,000 members in Honduras, Nicaragua, and Guatemala. Within two weeks after the peak of the Oct. 27-29 hurricane, some 600,000 pounds of supplies had been sent by the Church.

On Nov. 19-21, President Hinckley, spurred by personal feelings and an intense desire to be among the people, visited hurricane-stricken areas in Nicaragua and Honduras, offering comfort and assistance to the victims, and promising them they would not be forgotten. He spoke to a total of 19,000 members in three hastily arranged meetings in Managua, Nicaragua, and in Tegucigalpa and San Pedro Sula, Honduras.

Also in the news in November 1998:

Nov. 1: Wyview Park, a new married student housing complex at BYU consisting of 30 buildings with 426 units, was dedicated by President James E. Faust.

Nov. 10: President Hinckley, speaking at BYU's weekly devotional, told 22,000 students to stand a little taller, rise a little higher, and be a little better as he encouraged them to engage in a "quest for excellence."

Nov. 14: Ricks College won an unprecedented fourth consecutive national title in the National Junior College Athletic Association's women's cross country finals in Overland Park,

Nov. 19-21, 1998: President Gordon B. Hinckley waves to child in Honduras whose father died during ravages of Hurricane Mitch. The Church leader promised members in Nicaragua and Honduras that they would not be forgotten.

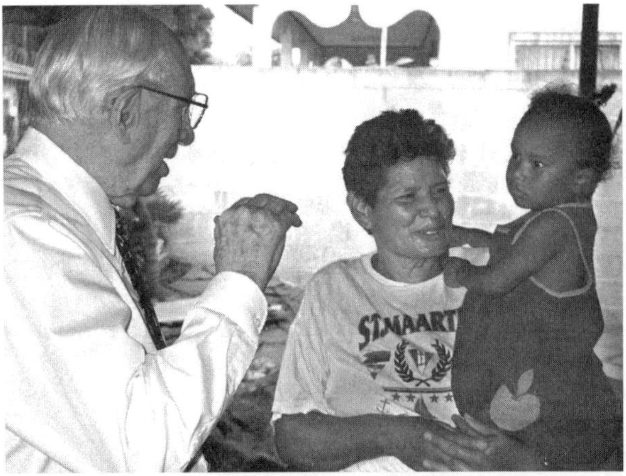

Dec. 1, 1998: Tree-lined plaza will replace asphalt between Temple Square and Church headquarters buildings, following sale of segment of street to Church.

Kan., and in the process established a new national team record.

Nov. 13-15: President Hinckley visited three mid-Atlantic states and spoke to a total of 22,600 members in meetings in Greenville, N.C.; Richmond, Va.; and Baltimore, Md.

December 1998

During 1998, President Hinckley traveled nearly 77,000 miles and met with 372,000 members on three continents, it was reported Dec. 26. During the year, he visited Central America, Mexico, Canada, Europe, many areas of the United States, and became the first president of the Church to visit West Africa.

Also in the news in December 1998:

Dec. 1: A proposal to close one block of Main Street in Salt Lake City between North Temple and South Temple and create an open-space plaza between Temple Square and the Church Administration block was announced at a press briefing in the Joseph Smith Memorial Building. The Church had agreed to pay $8,123,579 to the city for the surface rights of the one block. The proposal was approved by the Salt Lake City Council on April 13, 1999.

Dec. 2: China's ambassador to the United States, Li Zhaoxing, joined Elder John K. Carmack of the Seventy in ushering in the 21st Annual Festival of Lights at the Washington Temple Visitors Center, which was attended by diplomats from 51 countries, including 15 ambassadors.

Dec. 5: New South Wales (Australia) Gov. Gordon Samuels presented 2,000 Christmas food baskets, valued at $60,000 (Australian dollars), to the Salvation Army in behalf of the Church. The baskets were paid for with revenues from the Church's agriculture property in Australia.

Dec. 6: All three members of the First Presidency spoke about the Savior and the Christmas season at the annual First Presidency Christmas Devotional, which was attended by 6,000 Church employees and their families. Originating from the Tabernacle on Temple Square, the devotional, broadcast in 11 languages, was telecast to tens of thousands of members over the Church's satellite system throughout the United States, Canada, and the Caribbean.

Dec. 14: Elder Dallas N. Archibald of the Seventy and president of the Brazil Area drowned while fishing in the Biobio River in southern Chile, some 300 miles south of Santiago. His funeral was Dec. 28 in Salt Lake City.

Dec. 19: The Tabernacle Choir's

Jan. 9, 1999: Alaska members bundle against cold to attend dedication of northernmost temple, in Anchorage.

annual Christmas concert was telecast for the first time over the Church's satellite system.

January 1999

The 50th anniversary of the completion of the rebuilding of the organ in the Tabernacle on Temple Square was commemorated Jan. 14-17 at the Second American Classic Organ Symposium in Salt Lake City. The Tabernacle organ is one of the most famous in the world and has a long history — but many of its parts are relatively new. Jan. 16 marked the 50th anniversary of the completion of a monumental undertaking by the Aeolian-Skinner Organ Company of Boston, Mass., to rebuild the organ. When the four-year project was completed in 1949, the Tabernacle organ was practically a new instrument. Since this rebuilding, the organ was renovated again by Schoenstein & Co. of San Francisco in 1984-1988.

Also in the news in January 1999:

Jan. 9: The Anchorage Alaska Temple, the Church's northernmost temple and the second of the three smaller temples announced in general conference in October 1997, was dedicated by President Hinckley.

Jan. 15: The last surviving granddaughter of Brigham Young, Marian Morgan, celebrated her 100th birthday anniversary at a party given in her honor by members of her ward in Seal Beach, Calif.

Jan. 22: President Thomas S. Monson, during a BYU-Hawaii devotional, gave students a lesson in "home building," as he told them to build a house that would "meet the building code outlined in the Doctrine and Covenants." (Sec. 88:119).

Jan. 25: When an earthquake struck the western Colombia mountain community of Armenia, about 750 members of the Church were seriously affected. The magnitude 6 quake took the lives of more than 900 people, including three Church members, and injured 10 members. The homes of 147 LDS families were destroyed. The Church responded immediately with food, clothing, and medicine, which was shipped by welfare committees in Bogota and Cali, Colombia

Jan. 6: Sen. Harry Reid, D-Nevada, began serving as the minority whip of the U.S. Senate when the 106th Congress convened, the highest ranking position a member of the Church has held in Congress.

February 1999

At what was described as "probably the largest gathering ever convened in the cause of missionary service," President Hinckley on Feb. 21 addressed a missionary broadcast over the Church satellite system that focused on two responsibilities: the "sacred responsibility" of the local priesthood leadership and members for finding and friendshipping new investigators and "the great and serious responsibility" of holding on to each "precious convert."

Also in the news in February1999:

Feb. 9: Deseret Management Corp., the Church's holding company for commercial entities, announced that it would acquire Bookcraft Inc., a well-known Salt Lake City publisher of LDS books.

Feb. 20: The First Presidency made a landmark announcement that a temple would be built in Palmyra, N.Y., where the Prophet Joseph Smith communicated with the Father and the Son and received the early visions and revelations leading to the restoration of the Church, The announcement brought to 100 the number of temples in operation, under construction, or in planning stages.

Feb. 27: The Museum of Church History and Art in Salt Lake City commemorated its 15th anniversary with the opening of an exhibit that included favorite entries from past exhibitions since the museum opened in 1984.

March 1999

Representatives of the Screen Actors Guild were hosted at a luncheon March 5 in Salt Lake City by President James E. Faust following an agreement that was announced in January that allows professional actors who are guild members to appear in Church-produced, "in-house" motion pictures intended for instructional or visitors center use.

Also in the news in March 1999:

March 6: The last of the first three smaller temples, the Colonia Juarez Chihuahua Mexico Temple — Mexico's newest temple in its oldest stake — was dedicated by President Hinckley.

March 6: Ground was broken by Elder Wm. Rolfe Kerr of the Seventy for the first meetinghouse to be constructed for that purpose by Church in Iceland.

March 17: At a dinner and reception at the Waldorf-Astoria Hotel in New

March 6, 1999: Elder Wm. Rolfe Kerr, center, breaks ground for meetinghouse in Iceland, the first in that country. Meetinghouse was completed and dedicated in July, 2000.

March 18, 1999: President Gordon B. Hinckley, center, with President Thomas S. Monson and Elder Jeffrey R. Holland, meets with Spain's King Juan Carlos and Queen Sofia.

York City, BYU's Islamic Translation Series, which is making many important classic Islamic writings available to the Western world, was honored. Diplomats, including United Nations ambassadors and high-ranking members of the U.N. Secretariat, representing 35 Islamic countries, attended the event.

March 18: In Spain to dedicate the Madrid Spain Temple, President Hinckley, along with his first counselor, President Thomas S. Monson, and Elder Jeffrey R. Holland of the Quorum of the Twelve, visit King Juan Carlos and Queen Sofia at the royal palace.

March 18: The Church removed a senior couple and 14 full-time missionaries from Belgrade, Yugoslavia, because of escalation of tension in the Balkans, and relocated them in Croatia.

March 19: The Madrid Spain Templededicated by President Hinckley, 30 years after the first missionaries arrived in Spain to preach the restored gospel.

March 27: President Thomas S. Monson, speaking at the annual Young Women Meeting, gave four "action-packed objectives" — "gaze upward, look inward, reach outward, and press forward."

April 1999

In his closing remarks at general conference April 4, President Hinckley made a surprise announcement that the historic Nauvoo Temple, which was burned by arson fire in 1848 and later leveled by a tornado, would be rebuilt. A week later, it was announced that the temple would be built on its original site with stones quarried from the same areas in Nauvoo that produced the stone for the original temple. The Nauvoo Temple was where the pattern for sacred ordinances of salvation was set. Also at the conference, six brethren were sustained April 3 to the Second Quorum of the Seventy: Elders Adhemar Damiani, Stephen B. Oveson, David R. Stone, H. Bruce Stucki, Richard H. Winkel, and Robert S. Wood.

Also in the news in April 1999:

April 1: The pioneer cemetery at historic Winter Quarters, Neb., containing the remains of some 600 Latter-day Saints, about half of them children who died mostly during the winter of 1846-47 largely from "black canker" (a form of scurvy) and "ague" (a malarial disease) stemming from malnutrition, exhaustion, and cold, was deeded to the Church April 1 by the city of Omaha.

April 1: The sesquicentennial of the founding of the Sunday School was observed in Salt Lake City as the centennial box of the Sunday School, sealed in 1949 and containing memorabilia of 50 years ago, was opened in ceremonies attended by President Hinckley. He was called to the Sunday School general board in 1937,

After opening Sunday School centennial time storage box April 1, 1999, General Sunday School President Elder Harold G. Hillam, with counselors Elders Neil L. Andersen and John H. Groberg, later inspect globe-shaped titanium time capsule to be used for the next 50 years.

just two years after returning from his mission. The centennial box was created from 39 different woods from missions around the world,

April 10-11: Just one week after President Hinckley announced in general conference that the Church would provide assistance to refugees, a shipment of 78,500 pounds of food arrived in Kosovo. A shipment of 200,000 pounds of clothing was also sent by the Church. Later in the month, 30,000 family hygiene kits were sent by the Church for the Kosovar refugees in Macedonia and Albania.

April 11: At a fireside in BYU's Marriott Center, held in conjunction with the 150th anniversary of the founding of Provo, Utah, President Thomas S. Monson told the many thousands who attended, "We can walk in the footsteps of our forebears but we must blaze a trail for those who will follow in ours."

April 15: A gunman opened fire inside the Church Family History Library in downtown Salt Lake City. Three people were killed, including the gunman, and four others were wounded.

April 23: At a luncheon in the Joseph Smith Memorial Building in Salt Lake City, the Relief Society honored Madame Jehan Sadat, former first lady of Egypt, for her humanitarian work on issues involving women and children.

April 24: The Bogota Colombia Temple was dedicated by President Hinckley, 15 years after it was announced in 1984,

April 24: Elder Spencer J. Condie of the Seventy dedicated the site for the Copenhagen Denmark Temple, which, like the Vernal Utah Temple, will be built by remodeling an existing edifice, the Church's Priorvej Chapel in Copenhagen.

April 24: A missionary serving in the Ivory Coast Abidjan Mission in West Africa, Elder Jonathan Philip Barrett of Morgan, Utah, died after being stabbed in the chest, apparently without provocation, by a lone assailant.

April 25: President Hinckley spoke to 57,500 members, assembled in a soccer stadium, at a regional conference in Santiago, Chile.

April 15, 1999; SWAT team responds to shooting at Family History Library, where three were killed, including Church security guard Don Thomas.

April 28: Some 5,000 women who attended the annual Women's Conference gathered in two buildings on the BYU campus to make 25,000 hygiene kits and other items for needy families throughout the world during its "Worldwide Sisterhood Through Service" event — an activity called the "largest humanitarian event the Church has ever been involved with in one setting."

May 24, 1999; FamilySearch internet site for online genealogical research is started; in about one year, it had received 3 billion hits.

May 1999

The FamilySearch Internet Genealogy Service, a free Web site offered by the Church that promises to be the greatest boon to family research since the invention of microfilm, was officially launched by President Hinckley at a news conference linked by satellite between Salt Lake City and Washington, D.C., on May 24. Six months later, on Nov. 22, the site was augmented with 240 million names, enabling users to access more than 640 million entries. About a year later, the site received its 3 billionth hit on May 13, 2000.

Also in the news in May 1999:

May 3: One member was among 41 persons who were killed in the most powerful tornado ever to hit the United States that ripped through Oklahoma with winds registering 318 mph at its funnel. The winds, which also destroyed the homes of 18 LDS families, were so powerful that the National Weather Service created a new category, F6, to rank their magnitude.

May 4: The Church Family History Department announced that, after 11 years and more than 2 1/2 million hours of volunteer labor, the 1881 British Census — the largest census ever to be automated — was available on CD-ROM for home use. The automated index was the result of the collective efforts of Church-member volunteers and those from the Federation of Family History Societies of the United Kingdom.

May 8: BYU men's volleyball team won the 1999 NCAA volleyball national championship, defeating Long Beach State, in the finals in Los Angeles, Calif.

May 9: The first Church building in Madagascar, which includes the mission offices and mission home for the Madagascar Antananarivo Mission and meetinghouse facilities for the Antananarivo 2nd and 3rd branches, was dedicated by Elder Dennis E. Simmons of the Seventy and president of the Africa Southeast Area.

May 13: President Hinckley addressed 2,300 people at the Los Angeles World Affairs Council, including diplomats from 19 consulates, and told them of the worldwide operations of the Church and some challenges brought on by rapid growth.

May 17: The BYU-Hawaii women's tennis team won the NCAA Division II national championship in Pensacola, Fla, defeating Armstrong Atlantic State University.

June 1999: Mormon Youth Chorus is renamed the Temple Square Chorale and becomes a training choir for the Tabernacle Choir.

May 21-22: Before being disbanded, the Mormon Youth Chorus and Symphony performed in the Salt Lake Tabernacle its last concert of its 30-year history. The group performed its last tour May 11-13 to St. George, Utah, and southern California.

May 30: The first seminary building to be constructed in Alaska was dedicated in Chugiak, a suburb of Anchorage.

May 30: The first LDS meetinghouse in Greece was dedicated in Athens by Elder Charles Didier of the Seventy and president of the Europe East Area.

June 1999

Changes in the Church's musical organizations were implemented June 1 that affected both the Tabernacle Choir and the Mormon Youth Chorus and Symphony. The Mormon Youth Chorus, renamed The Temple Square Chorale, became a training choir for the Tabernacle Choir. The symphony orchestra was reorganized under a new name, The Orchestra at Temple Square. The three musical groups were united under one Church-service president, assisted by a full-time administrator.

Also in the news in June 1999:

June 6: More than 650 people attended two dedicatory services for the first meetinghouse in Mongolia, a well-know building in the capital city of Ulaanbaatar that has a foundation that dates back to the 1890s. Elder Richard E. Cook of the Seventy dedicated the building, which underwent an extensive renovation for two years to make it suitable for a meetinghouse.

June 14: A temple would be built adjacent to the pioneer cemetery at Winter Quarters in Omaha, Neb., the First Presidency announced

June 22-25: The annual Mission Presidents Seminar was held at the Missionary Training Center in Provo, Utah, with131 mission presidents and their wives hearing addresses from all three members of the First Presidency and other General Authorities. President Hinckley told the group that "the Church is really doing well."

June 27: President Hinckley rededicated a stake center in Salt Lake City that he, as a stake president 40 years ago, had responsibility for

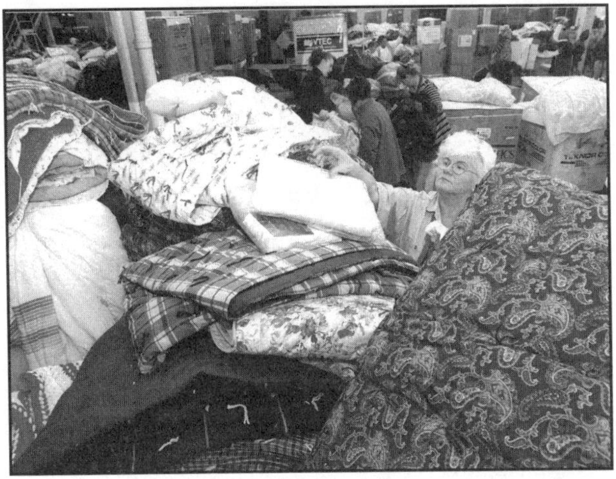

July 1999: Church members respond with enthusiasm to assist Kosovar refugees, donating more than 100,000 quilts.

constructing and which he originally dedicated on May 17, 1959, after being called as a General Authority.

July 1999

In a letter to general and local priesthood leaders in the United States and Canada, dated July 16, the Presiding Bishopric extended an invitation for individuals, families, and Relief Societies to make and donate quilts for Kosovar refugees who were returning home and facing winter months ahead. The invitation resulted in a huge response. By Oct. 12, 1999, a total of 77,391 quilts had been donated to the Latter-day Saint Humanitarian Center in Salt Lake City, and quilts were not only being sent to Kosovo, but also to Turkey, Mexico, and other areas of the world where there was a need. The quilt-making project was coordinated by the Relief Society.

Also in the news in July 1999:

July 15: The American Society of Landscape Architects honored the Church with a "once-in-a-century" medallion award for its world-renowned landscaping at Church headquarters, which includes 165,000 flowers of 460 different varieties.

July 16: After the passage of the Religious Liberty Protection Act in the U.S. House of Representatives, the Church issued a formal statement, saying the passage of the act was "an important step in restoring freedom of religion to the protected First Amendment status it enjoyed for over 200 years."

July 18: The Tabernacle Choir reached a major milestone as it performed its weekly network program, "Music and

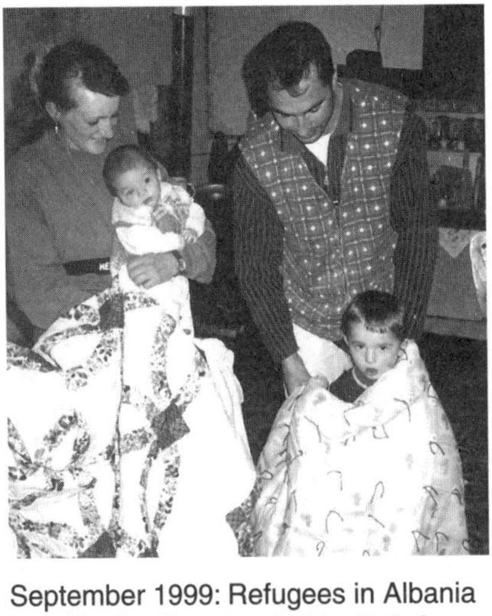

September 1999: Refugees in Albania put gift of quilts, donated by Relief Society sisters, to good use.

the Spoken Word." The program has now been on the radio for 70 years, and is the longest continuous, uninterrupted network radio broadcast in the world.

July 24: At a site near where the handcart pioneers ended their 1,300-mile journey to the Salt Lake Valley, President Hinckley dedicated a monument at This Is the Place Heritage Park in honor of the nearly 3,000 handcart pioneers who made the trek from 1856-60.

July 31: Nearly 22,000 members gathered in a large soccer stadium in Guayaquil, Ecuador, the night before the dedication of the Guayaquil temple to hear President Hinckley speak about living worthy to receive the blessings of the temple.

August 1999

In a decision made by the First Presidency and Quorum of the Twelve on Aug. 19, the Church's new 21,000-seat assembly building, under construction on the block immediately north of Temple Square, will be named the Conference Center. When completed, the building will be the site of general conferences of the Church, as well as for pageants and other events.

Also in the news in August 1999:

Aug. 1: Seventeen years after it was announced, the Guayaquil Ecuador Temple was dedicated by President Hinckley, who described the edifice as "the most beautiful building in Ecuador."

Aug. 3: President Hinckley spoke to 5,000 members at a member meeting in Maracaibo, Venezuela, urging them to be more involved in missionary work.

Aug. 11: Some damage occurred on Temple Square and at the Church's new Conference Center across the street when a rare tornado touched down in Salt Lake City, killing one person and injuring about 150.

Aug. 11, 1999: Rare tornado cuts swath of destruction across Salt Lake City, damaging trees on Temple Square but not affecting either the Tabernacle or the Assembly Hall.

Aug. 15: Elder Ben B. Banks, 67, a General Authority for 10 years, began serving in the Presidency of the Seventy. Released from the presidency was Elder Joe J. Christensen, who had served in the presidency since 1993.

Aug. 16-20: More than 30,000 Church members participated in the 1999 Campus Education Week at BYU, attending some of the more than 1,000 classes, which focused on the theme, "The quest for light and truth." (D&C 93:36).

Aug. 21: The Spokane Washington Temple, the second temple in Washington, was dedicated by President Hinckley.

Aug. 22: President Hinckley, in Spokane, Wash., to dedicate the Spokane temple, addressed some

12,000 youth and single adults at a fireside and told them that they "live in the greatest age in the history of the world."

Aug. 26: The Church contributed $50,000 to the Turkish ambassador for disaster relief in Turkey, which suffered a devastating earthquake, and $20,000 to the Chinese ambassador to help in flood relief in China.

September 1999

A declaration reaffirming the roles and values of women in the Church was introduced Sept. 25 by Relief Society Gen. Pres. Mary Ellen Smoot during the General Relief Society Meeting in the Tabernacle on Temple Square. The declaration, issued with the approval and endorsement of the First Presidency and Quorum of the Twelve, was one of two announcements concerning the 4.4 million-member Relief Society organization. The other announcement, made by Virginia U. Jensen, first counselor in the Relief Society general presidency, was that the name of the homemaking meeting would become Home, Family, and Personal Enrichment Meeting "to clearly communicate what the meeting is designed to accomplish."

Also in the news in September 1999:

Sept. 4: President Hinckley dedicated the Columbus Ohio Temple, the first temple in Ohio since the Kirtland Temple in early Church history.

Sept. 7: President Spencer W. Kimball was honored as President Hinckley dedicated a new building at Ricks College in Rexburg, Idaho, that bears the name of The Spencer W. Kimball Student and Administrative Services Building.

Sept. 11: President Hinckley spoke to 1,000 people gathered in a remote corner of southwestern Utah and dedicated a reconstructed monument, honoring the 120 people who lost their lives in the "Mountain Meadows Massacre" of 1857.

Sept. 14: Speaking to 14,000 students at BYU's weekly campus devotional, President James E. Faust talked about their search for happiness, saying it largely depends on the degree of righteousness that individuals attain.

Sept. 15: The University of Utah established "The Gordon B. Hinckley Endowment for British Studies," which will provide students an opportunity to emphasize British culture from the Middle Ages to the post-colonial period in their undergraduate studies.

Sept. 15-17: At least 20 homes of members of the Church were destroyed and hundreds of Church members were evacuated when flooding caused by Hurricane Floyd swamped several areas in Florida, Georgia, South Carolina, and North Carolina.

Sept. 19: In a land with relatively few members separated by vast distances, the Bismarck North Dakota Temple was dedicated by President Hinckley. It was his first trip ever to North Dakota.

Sept. 21: Three members were injured and the homes of 50 LDS families were seriously damaged or destroyed in an earthquake, with a magnitude of 7.6, that struck Taipei, Taiwan, killing more than 2,000 people and destroying hundreds of homes.

Sept. 25: Guests attending the 9th annual Western Family Picnic at the Marriott Family Ranch in Hume, Va., participated in one of the Church's humanitarian projects — helping to make quilts for refugees in Kosovo. The picnic was attended by diplomats from 21 countries and five members of Congress.

October 1999

The last general conference in the Tabernacle on Temple Square was held Oct. 2-3. President Hinckley, in his closing address, bid "goodbye to an old and wonderful friend." The holding of general conferences in the Tabernacle dated back 132 years to 1867.

For the first time, general conference was broadcast on a wide scale over the Internet, reaching as many as 100,000 people worldwide in 12 languages. During the conference, Elder Ben B. Banks, who had been serving as a member of the Presidency of the Seventy since Aug. 15, 1999, was sustained. Elder Joe J. Christensen was released from the presidency and, along with Elder Andrew W. Peterson, was granted emeritus status. Coleen K. Menlove was sustained as Primary general president, succeeding Patricia P. Pinegar. Sustained as first and second counselors, respectively, were Sydney S. Reynolds and Gayle M. Clegg. Anne G. Wirthlin and Susan L. Warner were released as first and second counselors, respectively.

Also in the news in October1999:

Oct. 4: In a letter addressed to members of the Church throughout the world, the First Presidency reaffirmined that Monday nights are to be reserved for family home evenings.

Oct. 5: President Hinckley dedicated BYU's renovated Ernest L. Wilkinson Student Center, which was originally completed in 1965, but, because of intense activity, was "reworked from basement to roof."

Oct. 5-7: More than 3,500 members of the Church in eight stakes were temporarily evacuated from their homes after heavy rains and flooding in southeastern Mexico.

Oct. 13: At a preview in Washington, D.C., of the PBS documentary "American Prophet: The Story of Joseph Smith," President Hinckley told an audience of 300, including diplomats from 22 countries, that Joseph Smith's "lengthened shadow extends through all the history of this Church and all across the world."

Oct. 16: The first temple in South Carolina in Columbia was dedicated by President Hinckley.

Oct. 13, 1999: Screening of PBS documentary "American Prophet: The Story of Joseph Smith" was viewed by diplomats from 22 countries.

Oct. 16: The First Presidency announced a uniform naming guideline for the temples of the world. Under the guideline, names primarily include the city and state or province, or the city and country in which they are located.

Oct. 17: After serving 24 years as director of the Tabernacle Choir, Jerold Ottley directed his final performance, before his retirement, of the choir's weekly network broadcast of "Music and the Spoken Word."

Oct. 19: The First Presidency sent a letter to general and local priesthood leaders reaffirming "the policy of strict political neutrality for the Church."

Oct. 23: President Hinckley dedicated the Detroit Michigan Temple, the first temple in Michigan.

Oct. 24: More than 5,000 people crowded onto the site of the original Nauvoo Temple to witness President

Hinckley break ground for the rebuilding of the Church's second temple in Nauvoo, Ill.

Oct. 29: The premiere concert of the Mormon Tabernacle Choir and two new musical organizations, the Temple Square Chorale and the Orchestra at Temple Square, was held in the Tabernacle in Salt Lake City.

November 1999

For the first time in the history of the Church, two temples, both of them in Canada, were dedicated on the same day. On Nov. 14, the Halifax Nova Scotia Temple was dedicated by President Hinckley, and the Regina Saskatchewan Temple was dedicated by President Boyd K. Packer, acting president of the Quorum of the Twelve.

Also in the news in November 1999:

Nov. 9: The 4-millionth visitor to the Museum of Church History and Art in Salt Lake City was recognized as part of a year-long celebration of the museum's 15th anniversary.

Nov. 14-17: Several Church members were among nearly a thousand delegates and dignitaries participating in the Second World Congress of Families in Geneva, Switzerland.

Nov. 20: The Billings Montana Temple, nestled at the base of the 300-foot-high Rimrock cliffs on the outskirts west of the city, was dedicated by President Hinckley.

Nov. 22: For the second time in three years, BYU's women's cross country team won the NCAA national championship in Bloomington, Ind., becoming the first in BYU history to win two national titles. The women's cross country team also won the national championship in 1997

Nov. 26: The documentary "American Prophet: The Story of Joseph Smith," made its national debut over the Public Broadcasting System.

Nov. 27: A name change was announced for LDS Social Services. The new name is LDS Family Services.

Nov. 30: Speaking to 18,000 BYU students at a devotional, President Hinckley urged them not to "become a weak link in the chain of your family generations."

December 1999

President Hinckley was one of three prominent religious leaders interviewed Dec. 24 by Larry King, host of CNN's national broadcast talk show "Larry King Live," which originated from the Tabernacle on Temple Square.

Nov. 14-17, 1999: Church members are among nearly a thousand delegates to Second World Conference on Families held in Geneva, Switzerland.

The other two — the Rev. Robert Schuller, television evangelist of the "Hour of Prayer," and South African Archbishop Desmond Tutu, Nobel Peace Prize laureate — were linked for the Christmas eve broadcast by satellite from Shepherds' Field near Bethlehem in the Holy Land and the National Cathedral in Washington, D.C., respectively.

Also in the news in December 1999:

Dec. 1: The First Presidency sent a letter to priesthood leaders, restating the "long-standing counsel to members of the Church to remain in their homelands rather than immigrate to the United States."

Dec. 1: Spain's ambassador to the United States, Antonio Oyarzabal, joined Elder W. Don Ladd of the Seventy in turning on the Christmas lights at the annual Festival of Lights in Washington, D.C. Ambassadors from 20 countries attended the event.

Dec. 5: President Hinckley and his counselors, President Thomas S. Monson and President James E. Faust, all spoke at the annual First Presidency Christmas Devotional in the Tabernacle on Temple Square. President Hinckley recounted the Savior's life and also paid tribute to the Prophet Joseph Smith, who was born Dec. 23, 1805.

Dec. 8: On the eve of the 150th anniversary of the founding of the Sunday School, an earth-shaped titanium sphere time capsule, containing nearly 200 pounds of mementos and artifacts gathered from all 29 areas of the Church, was sealed in ceremonies in Salt Lake City; the capsule is to be opened in 50 years, in the year 2049.

Dec. 11: The Edmonton Alberta Temple, serving members stretching hundreds of miles across the northern end of Alberta, was dedicated by President Hinckley.

Dec. 18: The Raleigh North Carolina Temple, the first temple in North Carolina, was dedicated by President Hinckley.

Dec. 25: During 1999, President Hinckley spoke to more than 197,350 members in eight countries and dedicated 14 temples on three continents, it was announced.

January 2000

The First Presidency and Quorum of the Twelve — 15 special witnesses called to testify of Christ's divinity before all the world — issued their testimony of the Savior Jan. 1 in a document titled "The Living Christ."

Dec. 24, 1999: President Gordon B. Hinckley is interviewed on CNN's national talk show "Larry King Live," along with two other prominent religious leaders.

Jan. 1, 2000: Members in Salt Lake City pack relief boxes for flood victims in northern Venezuela.

The "testimony of the apostles," which later was translated into 41 languages, was the first of two pronouncements issued by the First Presidency and Quorum of the Twelve during the year 2000. The second was a video production, "Special Witnesses of Christ," which was broadcast between general conference sessions April 1-2, 2000, and will be translated into 26 languages. It features each apostle bearing his testimony of the Savior.

Also in the news in January 2000:

Jan. 1: The first of two large shipments of food and other supplies donated by the Church arrived in northern Venezuela where floods killed thousands and left legions homeless. The first shipment was 225,000 pounds of food, hygiene kits, and medical supplies. The second shipment, which arrived in mid-January, was 200,000 pounds of food and clothing.

Jan. 9: The first temple dedicated in the year 2000, the St. Paul Minnesota Temple, was dedicated by President Hinckley.

Jan. 15: Gaston Flosse, president of the Territory of French Polynesia; Edward Fritch, vice president; and 15 Tahiti government ministers attended a dinner at the LDS mission home in Papeete, Tahiti, that was hosted by mission Pres. Ralph T. Andersen and stake and district presidents.

Jan. 22: On the first stop of a 10-day tour of the Pacific and Australia, President Hinckley spoke to more than 15,000 members in two regional meetings in Laie, Hawaii — during the sesquicentennial year of the establishment of the Church in the Hawaiian islands — and admonished them to live the gospel.

Jan. 23: The second temple in Hawaii, the Kona Hawaii Temple, was dedicated by President Hinckley.

Jan. 27: In the midst of his Pacific Rim travels, President Hinckley met with the president of Indonesia, Abdurranman Wahid, at a dinner in the presidential palace in Jakarta.

Jan. 31: Beaver Utah Stake, created in 1869 and the oldest stake in the Church after the Saints came West that had never been divided, was divided by Elder Dennis B. Neuenschwander of the Seventy and president of the Utah South Area to create the Milford Utah Stake.

February 2000

President Hinckley returned to Salt Lake City Feb. 1after an eight-stop excursion of the Pacific and Australia that took him to Hawaii, Kiribati, Indonesia, Singapore, Guam, and

Australia. During the tour, he traveled 22,670 miles and gave nine major addresses to more than 26,600 people, in addition to dedicating a temple in Hawaii and meeting with the president of Indonesia.

Also in the news in February 2000:

Feb. 13: An estimated 3,200 gathered in the Assembly Hall on Temple Square to observe the 200th anniversary of the birth of Hyrum Smith, the loyal elder brother of the Prophet Joseph Smith, who was martyred with him in Carthage, Ill., in 1844. President Hinckley and Elder M. Russell Ballard of the Quorum of the Twelve, a second-great-grandson of Hyrum, spoke.

Feb. 20: Speaking at a Missionary Satellite Broadcast that was carried throughout the United States, Canada, and the Caribbean, as well as selected sites in Latin America for the first time, President Thomas S. Monson highlighted the hallmarks of a happy home, and emphasized that happiness is found at home.

Feb. 26-27: The first two of nine temples that are expected to be dedicated in Mexico in 2000 were dedicated by President Hinckley in Ciudad Juarez, Mexico, on Feb. 26 and in Hermosillo, Sonora, Mexico, on Feb. 27. The Hermosillo temple was the 50th temple that President Hinckley has dedicated or rededicated.

March 2000

A new 60-minute movie — beyond the scale of any audiovisual product the Church has ever produced — entitled "The Testaments of One Fold and One Shepherd" opened to the public March 24 in the Legacy Theater in the Joseph Smith Memorial Building in Salt Lake City. The message of the film is the reality of the Atonement of Jesus Christ for all mankind and affirms that both the Bible and the Book of Mormon are testaments of the Savior as one fold and one shepherd. By August 2000, more than 470,000 people had seen the film.

Also in the news in March 2000:

March 5: The Albuquerque New Mexico Temple, the first in New Mexico, was dedicated by President Hinckley.

March 8: Speaking at a sold-out National Press Club Newsmakers Luncheon in Washington, D.C., President Hinckley became the first president of the Church to address the club.

March 11-12: Two more temples in Mexico were dedicated by President James E. Faust: the Oaxaca Mexico Temple on March 11 and the Tuxtla Gutierrez Mexico Temple on March 12. The temple in Tuxtla Gutierrez is the Church's 75th operating temple.

March 19: The first temple in Kentucky, the Louisville Kentucky

March 24, 2000: "The Testaments of One Fold and One Shepherd," a powerful feature movie beyond the scale of any previously produced by the Church, opens in Legacy Theater of Joseph Smith Memorial Building in Salt Lake City.

April 6, 2000: Visible from the Sacred Grove, the new Palmyra New York Temple was dedicated in services carried over the Church's satellite system to thousands of members.

Temple, was dedicated by President Thomas S. Monson.

March 20: The Church had sent 11 shipping containers of clothing, food, and medical supplies to Mozambique and 10 to Zimbabwe in Africa to help alleviate suffering caused by flooding as a result of weeks of heavy rains and cyclones, it was announced.

March 25: Addressing the annual Young Women Meeting in the Tabernacle on Temple Square, President James E. Faust told the young women of the Church that he hopes they will find joy in their womanhood during all stages of their life. In addition to being telecast over the Church satellite system, the meeting, for the first time, was available as an audio broadcast over the Internet.

April 2000

The Palmyra New York Temple, built on what was once the 100-acre Joseph Smith Sr. farm and overlooking the Sacred Grove, was dedicated April 6 by President Hinckley, exactly 170 years after the Church was organized in 1830. The first session was transmitted over the Church satellite system in 12 languages to meetinghouses in six time zones. An estimated 1.3 million members participated in the session, either the live broadcast in the morning or during a rebroadcast in the evening. The Palmyra temple was one of six temples dedicated during the month, the first time in Church history that six temples were dedicated in one month.

Also in the news in April 2000:

April 1-2: The first general conference to be held in the new Conference Center in Salt Lake City, across the street north of Temple Square, convened in the new building although it was not completed. More than 400,000 requested free tickets to attend the conference, far exceeding the 21,000-seat capacity of the hall.

During the conference, two members of the Second Quorum of the Seventy were sustained April 1 to the First Quorum of the Seventy: Elders Lynn G. Robbins and Lance B. Wickman. Also called to the First Quorum of the Seventy were Elders Donald L. Hallstrom and Ronald A. Rasband. In addition, Elders Douglas L. Callister, Darwin B. Christenson, Keith Crockett, H. Aldridge Gillespie, and Robert C. Oaks were called to the Second Quorum of the Seventy, and 39 new Area Authority Seventies were sustained to the Third, Fourth, and Fifth Quorums of the Seventy.

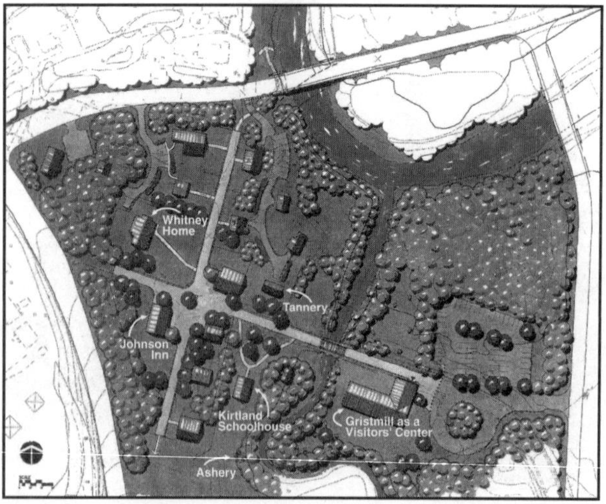

April 17, 2000: Plans are announced to reconstruct buildings in Kirtland, Ohio, prominent in Church history.

Also during conference, President Hinckley announced six new temples to be built in Africa, South America, Europe, and the United States in Aba, Nigeria; Asuncion, Paraguay; Helsinki, Finland; Lubbock, Texas; Snowflake, Ariz., and in the tri-cities area of Richland, Kennewick, and Pasco, Wash.

April 9: The Fresno California Temple, the fourth temple in California and located in an area that has been termed "the breadbasket of the nation," was dedicated by President Hinckley.

April 16: The Medford Oregon Temple, the second temple in Oregon, was dedicated by President James E. Faust.

Apil 17: At a press conference in Kirtland, Ohio, it was announced that the Church plans to restore or reconstruct six facilities in Kirtland that were prominent in Church history in the 1830s. They include the construction of a new visitors center resembling a 19th century grist mill used by Samuel Whitney, restoration of the Newel K. Whitney home, the building of a replica of the John Johnson Inn on its original foundation, and the restoration of a tannery, ashery, and school house.

April 22: The100 millionth copy of the Book of Mormon, since it was first published in 1830, has been printed, it was announced by Kay W. Briggs, director of the Church's printing and distribution services. At year-end 1999, about 99.2 million copies of the book had been distributed and with about 15,000 books sent out each day, the date for reaching 100 million was estimated to be during late February or early March. Another milestone was reached in 2000 when the Book of Mormon was printed in its 100th language, although seven of the languages are no longer in print.

April 23: For the second time in Church history, two temples were dedicated on the same day. President Thomas S. Monson dedicated the Reno Nevada Temple and President James E. Faust dedicated the Memphis Tennessee Temple.

April 23: The rebuilt Gadfield Elm Chapel, the oldest LDS chapel in England that was constructed in 1836 by members of the United Brethren and given to the Church four years later after 600 members of that faith joined the Church en masse, was rededicated by Elder Jeffrey R. Holland of the Quorum of the Twelve.

April 26: More than 10,000 women, participating in the BYU Women's Conference 2000 in Provo, Utah, on

April 27-28, gave service "across the world, across the street, and across the veil" the day before the conference began.

April 30: The Cochabamba Bolivia Temple was dedicated by President Hinckley, the sixth temple dedicated this month.

May 2000

In a meeting with Elder H. Bryan Richards of the Seventy in Jakarta, Indonesia, Alwi Shihab, the Indonesian minister of foreign affairs, expressed appreciation on May 3 to the Church for significant contributions of food, clothing, and hygiene kits donated to assist some 100,000 East Timorese refugees who fled the recent conflict in their homeland.

Also in the news in May 2000:

May 5: A major new commemorative exhibit, "From New England to the Great Salt Lake: The Mormon Legacy of Faith," opened at the prestigious Peabody Essex Museum in Salem, Mass. A joint effort of the museum and local members, the exhibit was shown through Aug. 27, 2000.

May 10-12: More than 800 Church members in two wards were among the 20,000 people, in the path of the Los Alamos, N.M., wild fire, who had to be evacuated. A total of 260 homes were destroyed in the blaze, including 10 homes of LDS families.

May 12-14: More than 200 young single adults from 11 major Russian cities, including Moscow and St. Petersburg, attended a conference in Zvenigorod, Russia.

May 20-21: Three temples were dedicated in two days, the first time in the history of the Church that has occurred. President Thomas S. Monson dedicated the Tampico Mexico Temple on May 20, and on the next day, he dedicated the Villahermosa Mexico Temple and President James E. Faust dedicated the Nashville Tennessee Temple, the second temple in Tennessee.

May 25: Near the spot where the Prophet Joseph Smith dedicated the temple lot in Independence, Mo., civic, Church and historical association leaders gathered to dedicate the first plaque in a project known as the Missouri Mormon Walking Trail.

June 2000

President Hinckley commemorated his 90th birthday June 23 by giving a party for 21,000 persons in the Conference Center in Salt Lake City and thousands of others who watched "An Evening of Celebration" over the

May 20, 2000: President Thomas S. Monson waves during dedicatory services for Tampico Mexico Temple, one of six temples he dedicated during the year.

June 23, 2000: Capacity audience enjoys "An Evening of Celebration" held in honor of President Gordon B. Hinckley's 90th birthday.

Church's satellite system. Featuring distinguished LDS musicians of international reputation, the Mormon Tabernacle Choir, and the Orchestra at Temple Square, the celebration, explained President Hinckley, was his opportunity to give something back to the community and to the "many wonderful people here and throughout the world." Performers included singers Michael Ballam, Vanessa Ballam, Stanford Olsen, Robert Peterson, Gladys Knight, Ariel Bybee, and JoAnn Ottley, and violinist Jenny Oaks Baker.

Also in the news in June 2000:

June 1: The Church's Family History and Historical Departments were consolidated into one department — the Family and Church History Department.

June 4: The Montreal Quebec Temple was dedicated by President Hinckley and the San Jose Costa Rica Temple was dedicated by President James E. Faust, the fourth time that two temple have been dedicated on the same day.

June 8-19: On an extended tour of Asia and the South Pacific, President Hinckley traveled 22,200 miles, visited six countries, dedicated four temples, met with the Thailand prime minister and Bangkok governor, and addressed more than 8,850 members in four member meetings. It was the first time in Church history that a Church president dedicated four temples during an overseas tour. He dedicated the Fukuoka Japan Temple (the 20th temple dedicated this year) June 11; the Adelaide Australia Temple June 15; the Melbourne Australia Temple (the 90th operating temple in the Church) June 16; and the Suva Fiji Temple, June 18. He held meetings with members in Bangkok, Thailand, June 13; Darwin, Australia, June 14; Noumea, New Caledonia, June 17; and Pago Pago, American Samoa, June 17 (after crossing the International Dateline). In Bangkok, a pre-birthday celebration was held in President Hinckley's honor.

June 9: Shipments of wheat, prepared by members from five stakes in England, began arriving in the drought-stricken nations of Ethiopia and Eritrea, helping those threatened with starvation in the two African countries.

June 18: The first LDS building in Bulgaria, which includes a meetinghouse, offices of the Bulgaria Sofia Mission, and a home for the mission president and his wife, was dedicated in Sofia by Elder Charles Didier of the Seventy and president of the Europe East Area.

June 21: President Hinckley announced that Church-owned Ricks College in Rexburg, Idaho, would again become a four-year college and would be renamed Brigham Young University-Idaho. Ricks, which was started in 1888 as a stake academy, has been a junior college for most of its existence, but was a four-year college for seven years, from 1949 to 1956.

June 21: At a press conference in Salt Lake City two days before his 90th birthday, President Hinckley told members of the media, "This is a great season in the history of the Church. There has never been a better season than this."

June 30: A monument, honoring 410 Icleanders who immigrated to America from 1854 to 1914 was dedicated by Elder Wm. Rolfe Kerr of the Seventy near "Mormon Pond," a tide pool on the rocky coast of the Westmann Islands where many of the early Icelander converts were baptized.

July 2000

The 150th anniversary of the Church in Scandinavia was celebrated in Denmark during the first week of July with a series of firesides, dances, reunions, and the unveiling of two statues depicting early LDS Danish emigrants. The first statue, unveiled July 4 in Denmark's only national park in the hills of Rebild, is titled "The Family" and symbolizes a Mormon family as they prepare to make the long voyage to Utah in the late 1800s. The second statue was unveiled July 6 in the harbor area of Copenhagen, where many of the Saints boarded sailing ships for the journey to America. Elder Russell M. Nelson of the Quorum of the Twelve participated in the commemorative events.

Also in the news in July 2000:

July 3-4: A museum devoted to LDS Church history was opened as part of the new Icelandic Emigration Center in Hofsos, Iceland, on July 3. The next day, on July 4, the first LDS meetinghouse in Iceland was dedicated in Garoabaer, a suburb of the capital city of Rejkjavik. Elder Wm. Rolfe Kerr of the Seventy dedicated the building, which houses two branches of the Church. Iceland's

June 9, 2000: British members ship wheat to drought-stricken nations of Ethiopia and Eritrea in Africa.

July 4, 2000: Participating in events commemorating the 150th anniversary of the Church in Denmark is Elder Russell M. Nelson, who has ancestors from Scandinavia.

president, Olafur Ragnar Grimsson, participated in both events.

July 8-9: President Thomas S. Monson dedicated two temples in Mexico, the 9th and 10th temples in that country. On July 8, he dedicated the Merida Yucatan Mexico Temple, and on July 9, the Veracruz Mexico Temple.

July 16: The Baton Rouge Louisiana Temple was dedicated by President Hinckley near a wetlands nature reserve in the state's capital city.

July 30: The Oklahoma City Oklahoma Temple, the 95th temple in operation in the Church, was dedicated by President James E. Faust.

August 2000

Legendary BYU football coach LaVell Edwards announced at a press conference Aug. 17 that he would retire at the end of the 2000 season. During his 29 years as head football coach, he has amassed the third most wins among active coaches in the United States with 251 victories. He is seventh on the all-time list in number of wins. In 1984, he coached the BYU team to a national championship.

Also in the news in August 2000:

Aug. 15: Elder Dennis B. Neuenschwander, 60, a General Authority since 1991, began serving in the Presidency of the Seventy. Released from the Presidency of the Seventy was Elder Harold G. Hillam, who had served in the presidency since Aug. 15, 1995. He was called as second counselor in the Europe West Area presidency.

Aug. 20: Announced in 1995, the Caracas Venezuela Temple was dedicated Aug. 20 by President Hinckley.

Aug. 26: The Houston Texas Temple was dedicated by President Hinckley.

September 2000

Sometime in September, two significant membership milestones were reached, according to Church statisticians. The Church reached 11 million members and, for the first time in its 170-year history, it had more non-English-speaking members than English-speaking. English, however, is still the most-spoken language in the Church with about 5.5 million English-speaking members. Spanish is second with about 3.3 million. Other languages are spoken by about 2.2 million members. Based on present membership growth rates, Spanish will become the most-spoken language in the Church by 2020.

Also in the news in September 2000:

Sept. 3: The Birmingham Alabama Temple was dedicated by President Hinckley.

Sept. 17: The Santo Domingo Dominican Republic Temple, announced in 1993, was dedicated Sept. 17, 2000, by President Hinckley.

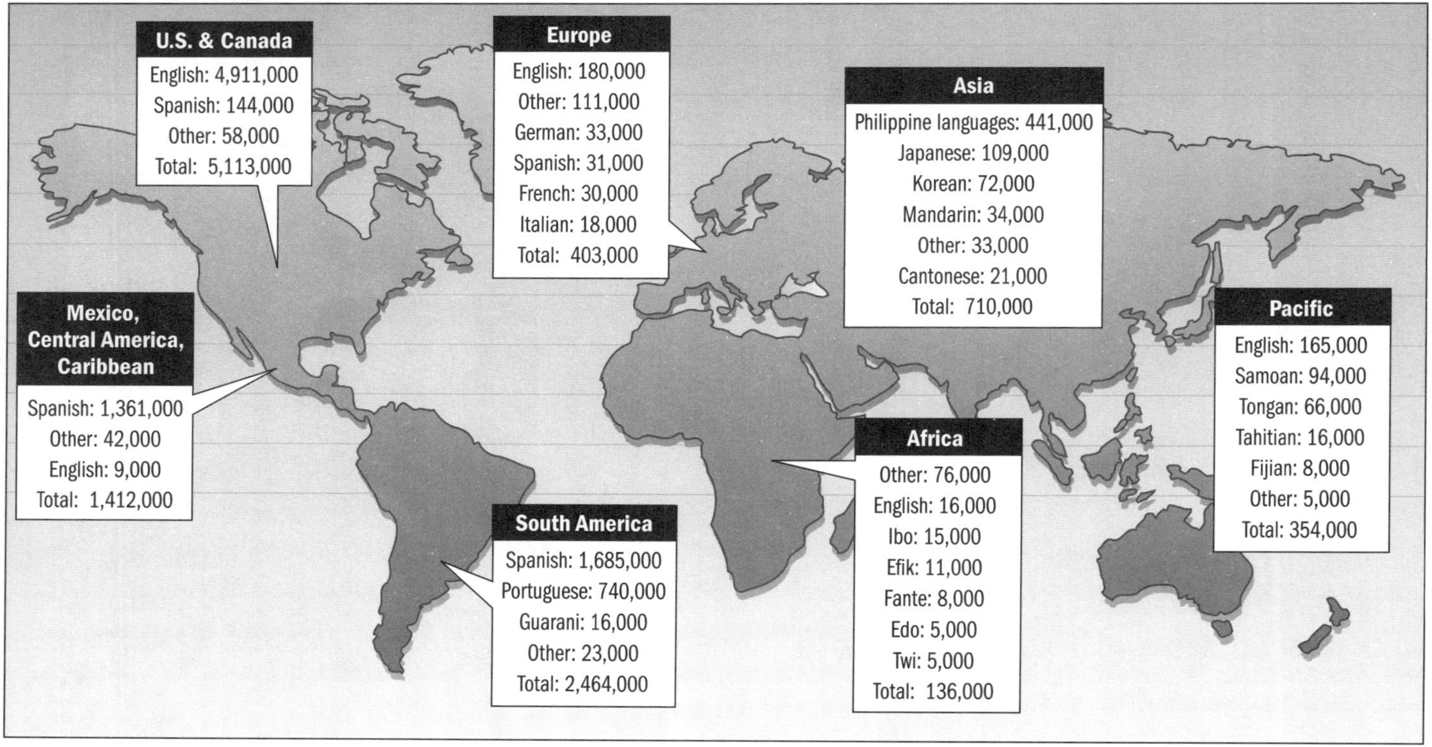

September 2000:Internationalism increases as the Church has more non-English than English-speaking members.

October 2000

The Boston Massachusetts Temple, located in the western suburbs of Boston, became the 100th operating temple in the Church when it was dedicated by President Hinckley on Oct. 1. The dedication came only 2 1/2 years after President Hinckley announced ambitious plans in general conference in April 1998 to have 100 temples in operation by the year 2000. At the time of the 1998 announcement, there were 51 temples in operation. Thirty-two of the 100 temples — in 10 countries on four continents — were dedicated during the first nine months of 2000.

Also in the news in October 2000:

Oct. 7-8: The new 21,000-seat Conference Center in Salt Lake City, across the street north of Temple Square, was dedicated during general conference by President Hinckley. The building was first announced by President Hinckley in April 1996, and ground was broken on July 24, 1997, during the sesquicentennial of the arrival of the Mormon pioneers in the Salt Lake Valley.

Also during the conference, three members of the First Quorum of the Seventy were granted emeritus status: Elders F. Enzio Busche, Loren C. Dunn, and Alexander B. Morrison; and four members of the Second Quorum of the Seventy were released: Elders Eran A. Call, W. Don Ladd, James O. Mason, and Richard E. Turley Sr. Elder Marlin K. Jensen was called as General Sunday School president, succeeding Elder Harold G. Hillam. Elders Neil L. Andersen and John H. Groberg were retained as counselors.

A new general presidency of the Sunday School was sustained at the conference. Elder marlin K. Jensenofthe Presidency of the Seventy was called as general president, succeeding Elder Harold G. Hillam. Sustained as counselors to Elder Jensen were Elder Neil L. Andersen, first counselor and Elder John H. Groberg, second counselor, both of the Seventy. They previously served as counselors to Elder Hillam.

Oct. 1, 2000: President Gordon B. Hinckley, with President Boyd K. Packer and Elder Neil L. Andersen, pauses after dedication of 100th temple in Boston, Mass.

FACTS, STATISTICS

MEMBERSHIP STATISTICS

Membership and units by Church area

As of Dec. 31, 1999; area boundaries do not necessarily follow country, state or province boundaries.; *means fewer than 100 members.

Area	Membership	Stakes	Wards	Branches in stakes	Missons	Districts	Branches in missions	Total wards, branches
Africa Southeast	50,780	10	52	43	6	9	88	183
Africa West	81,962	20	136	47	6	23	147	330
Asia	75,858	13	75	13	10	24	143	231
Asia North	182,153	47	275	93	13	26	124	492
Australia/ New Zealand	199,055	57	329	95	10	20	106	530
Brazil North	287,058	60	411	93	10	16	111	615
Brazil South	456,124	126	853	257	16	26	155	1,264
Central America	454,944	89	536	208	12	65	354	1,098
Chile	502,082	116	744	144	8	9	61	949
Europe Central	87,831	32	198	201	21	21	157	552
Europe East	20,872	0	0	0	13	29	191	191
Europe West	301,995	69	409	220	24	54	319	948
Mexico North	415,731	80	508	78	10	29	182	768
Mexico South	431,210	99	734	141	8	11	71	946
North America Central	454,075	123	852	323	16	4	33	1,208
North America East	298,541	71	476	222	14	1	6	704
North America Northeast	277,447	64	402	246	18	10	78	726
North America Northwest	733,639	196	1,473	168	9	2	11	1,652
North America Southeast (Caribbean)	110,490	16	90	61	7	18	138	289
North America Southeast (U.S. Only)	279,352	63	412	174	12	0	2	588
North America Southwest	782,340	170	1,326	272	15	3	14	1,612
North America West	787,984	173	1,247	154	18	0	2	1,403
Pacific Islands	164,311	47	315	78	5	19	111	504
Philippines	441,359	68	414	176	13	77	461	1,051
South America North	365,667	71	483	126	11	44	296	905
South America South	406,762	85	515	283	14	53	304	1,102
South America West	446,050	102	708	133	10	42	229	1,070
Utah North	1,088,885	300	2,282	98	4	1	4	2,384
Utah South	568,428	175	1,445	52	1	0	0	1,497
U.S./Canada	5,270,692	1,335	9,915	1,709	107	21	145	11,769
Outside U.S./ Canada	5,482,294	1,207	7,784	2,489	226	615	3,751	14,024
Total	**10,752,986**	**2,542**	**17,699**	**4,198**	**333**	**636**	**3,896**	**25,793**

Membership and units by countries

Countrry	Membership	Stakes	Wards	Branches in stakes	Missons	Districts	Branches in missions	Total wards, branches
AFRICA								
Angola	502	0	0	0	0	0	2	2
Botswana	700	0	2	1	0	0	0	3
Burundi	28	0	0	0	0	0	1	1
Cameroon	194	0	0	0	0	0	1	1
Cape Verde	3,893	0	0	0	0	3	19	19
Central African Republic	135	0	0	0	0	0	1	1
Democratic Republic of Congo	8,197	3	20	5	1	1	8	33
Ethiopia	257	0	0	0	0	0	1	1
Ghana	17,278	5	32	6	1	4	22	60
Ivory Coast (Cote D'ivoire)	5,402	1	11	0	1	0	3	14
Kenya	4,039	0	0	0	1	2	17	17
Lesotho	411	0	0	1	0	0	0	1
Liberia	2,694	0	0	0	0	1	12	12
Madagascar	1,349	0	0	0	1	1	6	6
Malawi	181	0	0	0	0	0	2	2
Mauritius	277	0	0	0	0	0	1	1
Mozambique	311	0	0	0	0	0	3	3
Namibia (South West Africa)	261	0	0	0	0	0	1	1
Nigeria	42,746	11	73	36	3	13	76	185
Republic of Congo	1,602	0	0	0	0	1	6	6
Reunion	695	0	0	0	0	1	4	4
Sierra Leone	3,564	0	0	0	0	3	16	16
South Africa	29,220	9	45	36	3	2	15	96
Swaziland	798	0	1	2	0	0	0	3
Tanzania	406	0	0	0	0	0	3	3
Togo	122	0	0	0	0	0	1	1
Uganda	2,375	0	0	0	0	2	12	12
Zambia	711	0	0	0	0	0	3	3
Zimbabwe	8,287	1	4	3	1	1	18	25
Africa Totals	**136,872**	**30**	**188**	**90**	**12**	**35**	**259**	**537**
ASIA								
Armenia	656	0	0	0	1	1	5	5
Cambodia (Kampuchea)1,018	0	0	0	1	1	5	5	
Cyprus	99	0	0	0	0	0	3	3
Hong Kong	20,256	5	29	2	1	2	8	39
India	2,435	0	0	0	1	4	18	18
Indonesia	5,339	0	0	0	1	3	21	21
Israel	165	0	0	0	0	1	2	2
Japan	110,987	30	170	53	8	20	94	317
Lebanon	139	0	0	0	0	0	1	1
Macau								

Countrry	Membership	Stakes	Wards	Branches in stakes	Missons	Districts	Branches in missions	Total wards, branches
(Macao) 871	0	0	0	0	0	2	2	
Malaysia	1,141	0	0	0	0	2	12	12
Mongolia	1,850	0	0	0	1	1	9	9
Papua New Guinea	8,954	1	7	0	1	2	20	27
Philippines	441,359	68	414	176	13	77	461	1,051
Singapore	2,099	1	6	2	1	0	0	8
South Korea	71,166	17	105	40	4	6	30	175
Sri Lanka	280	0	0	0	0	0	2	2
Taiwan	26,805	6	35	7	3	5	29	71
Thailand	10,808	1	5	2	1	5	22	29
Asia Totals	**710,772**	**130**	**774**	**294**	**37**	**131**	**766**	**1,834**
			CANADA					
Alberta	**63,866**	**21**	**150**	**42**	**2**	**0**	**0**	**192**
British Col.	**27,564**	**8**	**48**	**28**	**1**	**1**	**4**	**80**
Manitoba	**3,866**	**1**	**5**	**7**	**1**	**0**	**0**	**12**
New Brunswick	**2,060**	**1**	**5**	**2**	**0**	**0**	**0**	**7**
Newfoundland	**585**	**0**	**0**	**0**	**0**	**0**	**3**	**3**
Nunavat, Northwest Territories	**188**	**0**	**0**	**0**	**0**	**0**	**1**	**1**
Nova Scotia	**4,268**	**1**	**6**	**5**	**1**	**1**	**7**	**18**
Ontario	**40,289**	**9**	**57**	**25**	**2**	**2**	**10**	**92**
Prince Edward Is.	**391**	**0**	**0**	**0**	**0**	**0**	**3**	**3**
Quebec	**8,500**	**2**	**12**	**10**	**1**	**1**	**5**	**27**
Saskatchewan	**4,794**	**1**	**5**	**10**	**0**	**1**	**3**	**18**
Yukon	**204**	**0**	**0**	**1**	**0**	**0**	**0**	**1**
Totals	**156,575**	**44**	**288**	**130**	**8**	**6**	**36**	**454**
			CARIBBEAN					
Antigua and Barbuda	115	0	0	0	0	0	1	1
Aruba	230	0	0	0	0	0	2	2
Bahamas	503	0	0	0	0	0	2	2
Barbados	568	0	0	0	0	0	3	3
Bermuda	101	0	0	0	0	0	1	1
Bonaire	80	0	0	0	0	0	1	1
Cayman Islands	87	0	0	0	0	0	1	1
Curacao	348	0	0	0	0	0	1	1
Dominican Rep.	69,466	11	60	49	3	11	62	171
Grenada	109	0	0	0	0	0	1	1
Guadeloupe	195	0	0	0	0	0	2	2
Haiti	8,157	1	7	2	1	0	10	19
Jamaica	4,240	0	0	0	1	2	16	16
Martinique	143	0	0	0	0	0	1	1
Netherlands Antilles	0	.	.	.	.	.	.	.
Puerto Rico	23,223	4	23	10	1	4	22	55
Saint Kitts-Nevis	95	0	0	0	0	0	1	1
Saint Lucia	*	.	.	.	.	.	.	
Saint Maarten	138	0	0	0	0	0	1	1
Saint Martin	*	.	.	.	.	.	.	
Saint Vincent & Grenadines	342	0	0	0	0	0	1	1
Trinidad & Tobago	1,581	0	0	0	1	1	6	6

Countrry	Membership	Stakes	Wards	Branches in stakes	Missons	Districts	Branches in missions	Total wards, branches
Virgin Islands, British	11	0	0	0	0	0	1	1
Virgin Islands, USA	282	0	0	0	0	0	1	1
Caribbean Totals	**110,073**	**16**	**90**	**61**	**7**	**18**	**139**	**290**
		CENTRAL AMERICA						
Belize	2,605	0	0	0	0	3	16	16
Costa Rica	30,118	5	35	18	1	6	25	78
El Salvador	84,683	16	96	37	2	2	19	152
Guatemala	174,784	40	236	85	4	24	128	449
Honduras	95,750	20	127	41	3	11	48	216
Nicaragua	31,747	1	7	2	1	11	68	77
Panama	35,257	7	35	25	1	8	50	110
Central America Totals	**454,944**	**89**	**536**	**208**	**12**	**65**	**354**	**1,098**
EUROPE								
Albania	789	0	0	0	1	1	7	7
Andorra	64	0	0	0	0	0	1	1
Austria	3,889	2	12	10	1	0	0	22
Belarus	372	0	0	0	0	1	1	1
Belgium	5,771	2	11	12	1	1	6	29
Bulgaria	1,367	0	0	0	1	1	12	12
Corsica	49	0	0	0	0	0	1	1
Croatia	299	0	0	0	0	1	4	4
Czech Republic	1,654	0	0	0	1	4	19	19
Estonia	339	0	0	0	0	1	3	3
France	30,541	7	44	39	3	7	45	128
Germany	36,303	14	91	92	6	1	5	188
Gibraltar	24	0	0	1	0	0	0	1
Greece	479	0	0	0	1	0	5	5
Hungary	3,191	0	0	0	1	2	19	19
Italy	18,599	3	16	23	4	15	94	133
Latvia	177	0	0	0	0	1	4	4
Lithuania	500	0	0	0	1	1	3	3
Luxembourg	155	0	0	0	0	0	1	1
Malta	120	0	0	0	0	0	1	1
Netherlands	7,627	3	17	26	1	0	0	43
Poland	1,094	0	0	0	1	0	11	11
Portugal	35,248	5	28	17	3	12	60	105
Romania	1,545	0	0	0	1	2	17	17
Russia	11,092	0	0	0	8	12	103	103
Spain	30,439	7	37	24	5	16	83	144
Switzerland	7,043	3	20	19	2	0	1	40
Ukraine	6,369	0	0	0	2	8	59	59

Countrry	Membership	Stakes	Wards	Branches in stakes	Missons	Districts	Branches in missions	Total wards, branches
Europe Totals	**205,717**	**46**	**276**	**263**	**45**	**89**	**576**	**1,115**
MEXICO								
Mexico Totals	**846,931**	**179**	**1,242**	**219**	**18**	**40**	**253**	**1,714**
NORDIC COUNTRIES								
Denmark	4,527	2	14	11	1	0	0	25
Finland	4,403	2	13	5	1	3	12	30
Greenland	14	0	0	0	0	0	1	1
Iceland	248	0	0	0	0	1	2	2
Norway	4,120	1	7	3	1	3	15	25
Sweden	8,587	4	22	21	1	2	7	50
Nordic Totals	**21,899**	**9**	**56**	**40**	**4**	**9**	**37**	**133**
SOUTH AMERICA								
Argentina	288,865	64	389	205	10	37	207	801
Bolivia	112,222	21	151	25	3	9	56	232
Brazil	743,182	186	1,264	349	26	42	266	1,879
Chile	502,153	116	744	146	8	9	61	951
Colombia	129,105	23	150	29	4	20	130	309
Ecuador	146,420	32	219	67	3	11	87	373
Falkland Islands	11	0	0	0	0	0	1	1
French Guiana	209	0	0	0	0	0	2	2
Guyana	1,026	0	0	0	0	0	3	3
Paraguay	44,632	6	34	30	2	10	59	123
Peru	333,828	81	557	108	7	33	173	838
Suriname	454	0	0	0	0	0	1	1
Uruguay	73,194	15	92	46	2	6	38	176
Venezuela	89,484	16	114	30	4	13	75	219
South America Totals	**2,464,785**	**560**	**3,714**	**1,035**	**69**	**190**	**1,159**	**5,908**
SOUTH PACIFIC								
American Samoa	12,833	4	29	4	0	0	1	34
Australia	99,121	31	177	46	7	12	62	285
Cook Islands	880	0	0	0	0	1	6	6
Fiji	11,998	4	23	9	1	2	9	41
French Polynesia	16,230	6	45	7	1	3	21	73
Guam	1,476	0	0	0	1	1	4	4
Johnston Atoll	17	0	0	0	0	0	1	1
Kiribati	7,964	1	10	2	0	1	11	23
Marshall Islands	3,369	0	0	0	0	2	10	10
Micronesia Federated States	3,008	0	0	0	0	4	18	18
Nauru	96	0	0	0	0	0	1	1
New Caledonia	1,449	0	0	0	0	1	9	9
New Zealand	89,952	25	145	49	2	5	17	211
Niue	230	0	0	0	0	1	4	4
Northern Mariana Is.	870	0	0	0	0	0	1	1
Palau (Belau)	370	0	0	0	0	0	1	1
Samoa	58,477	16	108	18	1	1	4	130
Solomon Islands	148	0	0	0	0	0	1	1
Tonga	44,819	16	100	38	1	1	9	147
Tuvalu	88	0	0	0	0	0	1	1
Vanuatu	1,121	0	0	0	0	2	8	8

Country	Membership	Stakes	Wards	Branches in stakes	Missons	Districts	Branches in missions	Total wards, branches
South Pacific Totals	**354,516**	**103**	**637**	**173**	**14**	**37**	**199**	**1,009**
				U.K./IRELAND				
England	135,748	36	222	67	6	0	0	289
Ireland	2,341	1	4	4	1	1	5	13
Northern Ireland	5,516	1	8	6	0	0	0	14
Scotland	25,791	5	24	22	1	0	4	50
Wales	7,097	2	13	7	0	0	0	20
United Kingdom/ Ireland Totals	**176,493**	**45**	**271**	**106**	**8**	**1**	**9**	**386**
				UNITED STATES				
States								
Alabama	27,680	6	37	32	1	0	0	69
Alaska	25,340	6	38	20	1	1	7	65
Arizona	305,364	71	567	57	3	0	0	624
Arkansas	20,077	4	28	24	1	0	0	52
California	740,236	160	1,153	158	17	0	0	1,311
Colorado	112,232	28	204	31	2	0	3	238
Connecticut	12,163	3	22	12	1	0	0	34
Delaware	3,730	1	7	1	0	0	0	8
District of Columbia	1,660	0	0	0	0	1	5	5
Florida	108,955	24	169	32	5	0	0	201
Georgia	57,857	14	86	30	2	0	0	116
Hawaii	55,361	14	106	5	1	0	0	111
Idaho	343,489	105	791	41	2	0	0	832
Illinois	46,135	12	82	33	3	0	0	115
Indiana	33,058	10	57	31	1	0	0	88
Iowa	17,465	6	32	17	1	0	0	49
Kansas	27,232	6	45	16	0	1	8	69
Kentucky	22,952	6	32	32	2	0	0	64
Louisiana	24,143	7	37	26	1	0	0	63
Maine	8,569	2	15	11	0	0	0	26
Maryland	34,113	8	59	18	2	0	1	78
Massachusetts	21,106	4	34	15	1	0	0	49
Michigan	36,888	8	59	28	2	2	16	103
Minnesota	22,941	6	38	24	1	0	1	63
Mississippi	17,578	4	26	15	1	0	0	41
Missouri	51,187	13	96	25	2	0	0	121
Montana	39,842	11	72	42	1	0	0	114
Nebraska	18,613	4	33	20	1	0	1	54
Nevada	143,372	30	249	30	2	0	0	279
New Hampshire	7,296	3	12	8	1	0	0	20
New Jersey	25,945	5	31	24	2	1	5	60
New Mexico	57,476	12	83	32	1	1	5	120
New York	60,516	14	66	69	4	3	26	161
North Carolina	56,261	12	86	30	2	0	0	116
North Dakota	5,070	2	7	8	0	0	0	15
Ohio	47,437	10	77	38	2	0	0	115
Oklahoma	33,721	7	48	26	2	0	1	75

Countrry	Membership	Stakes	Wards	Branches in stakes	Missons	Districts	Branches in missions	Total wards, branches
Oregon	134,438	35	238	36	2	0	0	274
Pennsylvania	37,749	10	65	31	3	1	6	102
Rhode Island	3,214	0	5	2	0	0	0	7
South Carolina	27,399	4	35	20	1	0	0	55
South Dakota	8,077	2	9	13	1	1	11	33
Tennessee	31,104	9	51	22	2	0	0	73
Texas	210,892	42	324	108	7	2	9	441
Utah	1,604,686	458	3,599	144	5	1	4	3,747
Vermont	3,759	1	6	6	0	0	0	12
Virginia	66,622	17	109	32	2	0	0	141
Washington	226,411	52	425	45	3	0	0	470
West Virginia	12,290	2	17	19	1	0	0	36
Wisconsin	19,282	5	35	22	1	0	0	57
Wyoming	54,425	16	125	18	0	0	0	143
U.S.A. Totals	**5,113,409**	**1,291**	**9,627**	**1,579**	**99**	**15**	**109**	**11,315**

CHURCH STATISTICS

As of Dec. 31	Members in stakes	Members, in missions	Total	Stakes	Wards & branches	Mis-sions	Mission branches
1830							
Apr. 6	0	0	6	0	0	0	0
Dec. 31	280	0	280	0	4	0	0
1831	680	0	680	0	6	0	0
1832	1,313	1,348	2,661	0	27	0	6
1833	1,805	1,335	3,140	0	23	0	17
1834	3,050	1,322	4,372	2	22	0	18
1835	7,500	1,335	8,835	2	22	0	26
1836	12,000	1,293	13,293	2	25	0	29
1837	14,400	1,882	16,282	2	25	1	42
1838	15,300	2,581	17,881	2	26	1	65
1839	13,700	2,760	16,460	3	16	2	70
1840	11,962	4,903	16,865	10	18	2	69
1841	12,475	7,381	19,856	2	19	2	84
1842	13,549	10,015	23,564	2	26	2	199
1843	15,601	10,379	25,980	2	31	2	238
1844	16,374	9,772	26,146	2	33	3	239
1845	17,020	13,312	30,332	1	34	4	277
1846	18,960	15,033	33,993	0	30	5	311
1847	17,263	17,431	34,694	1	48	5	357
1848	16,749	23,728	40,477	1	55	5	426
1849	17,654	30,506	48,160	1	75	5	515
1850	18,756	33,083	51,839	1	61	9	637
1851	16,069	36,096	52,165	4	60	11	717
1852	15,627	37,013	52,640	5	65	13	795
1853	25,537	38,617	64,154	5	75	14	885
1854	30,817	37,612	68,429	6	79	13	859
1855	28,654	35,320	63,974	6	99	14	858
1856	31,762	32,119	63,881	7	124	12	841
1857	32,529	22,707	55,236	6	77	12	742
1858	33,880	21,875	55,755	4	81	9	661
1859	36,481	20,557	57,038	4	98	9	635
1860	39,338	21,744	61,082	4	110	8	611
1861	42,417	23,794	66,211	4	126	7	588
1862	45,565	23,215	68,780	4	135	7	563

As of Dec. 31	Members in stakes	Members, in missions	Total	Stakes	Wards & branches	Mis- sions	Mission Branches
1863	49,283	22,487	71,770	4	143	7	524
1864	53,006	21,342	74,348	4	161	8	471
1865	56,562	20,209	76,771	4	164	8	436
1866	59,803	18,081	77,884	4	167	8	420
1867	63,071	18,053	81,124	4	175	8	407
1868	66,589	18,033	84,622	5	178	8	385
1869	70,157	18,275	88,432	9	187	7	383
1870	73,747	16,383	90,130	9	195	7	363
1871	78,458	17,138	95,596	9	200	7	342
1872	81,821	16,331	98,152	9	206	7	347
1873	85,194	16,344	101,538	9	213	7	348
1874	88,567	15,349	103,916	10	216	7	309
1875	91,992	15,175	107,167	10	222	7	302
1876	95,773	15,338	111,111	10	230	8	307
1877	99,780	15,285	115,065	20	252	8	285
1878	109,894	15,152	125,046	21	254	9	272
1879	112,705	15,681	128,386	22	263	10	289
1880	117,773	15,855	133,628	23	272	10	287
1881	123,918	16,815	140,733	23	283	10	293
1882	128,779	16,825	145,604	24	292	10	291
1883	135,128	16,465	151,593	27	317	11	292
1884	142,417	15,825	158,242	29	340	13	296
1885	147,557	16,573	164,130	29	348	12	311
1886	150,602	16,051	166,653	30	342	12	315
1887	155,654	17,375	173,029	31	360	12	326
1888	162,464	17,830	180,294	32	373	13	336
1889	164,834	18,310	183,144	32	388	12	339
1890	170,653	17,610	188,263	32	395	12	330
1891	177,489	17,956	195,445	32	409	12	332
1892	182,623	18,338	200,961	33	439	14	350
1893	194,352	20,182	214,534	34	451	15	356
1894	201,047	21,322	222,369	34	457	15	356
1895	208,179	22,937	231,116	37	479	15	356
1896	215,514	25,913	241,427	37	489	17	348
1897	222,802	32,934	255,736	37	493	18	374
1898	229,428	37,823	267,251	40	516	20	401
1899	229,734	41,947	271,681	40	506	20	412
1900	236,628	47,137	283,765	43	529	20	438
1901	243,368	49,563	292,931	50	577	21	442
1902	249,927	49,178	299,105	50	595	22	481
1903	257,661	47,240	304,901	51	612	23	477
1904	275,681	48,608	324,289	55	619	21	475
1905	281,162	50,886	332,048	55	627	22	514
1906	289,377	55,637	345,014	55	636	22	541
1907	298,847	59,066	357,913	55	634	22	558
1908	307,308	64,164	371,472	59	666	22	595
1909	308,094	69,185	377,279	60	684	21	590
1910	327,017	71,461	398,478	62	699	21	611
1911	334,643	72,648	407,291	62	706	21	632
1912	341,278	76,277	417,555	65	716	22	647
1913	350,321	81,286	431,607	66	749	22	650
1914	371,729	82,989	454,718	68	772	21	601
1915	381,336	84,902	466,238	72	783	21	608
1916	390,449	86,872	477,321	73	808	22	559
1917	397,933	90,105	488,038	75	875	22	578
1918	404,030	91,932	495,962	75	893	22	559
1919	413,563	94,398	507,961	79	888	23	554
1920	426,167	99,820	525,987	83	904	24	623
1921	441,472	107,331	548,803	86	933	25	665

As of Dec. 31	Members in stakes	Members, in missions	Total	Stakes	Wards & branches	Mis-sions	Mission branches
1922	451,762	114,596	566,358	87	946	25	661
1923	463,578	112,318	575,896	90	962	26	697
1924	479,498	118,363	597.861	94	969	25	716
1925	490,688	122,884	613,572	94	985	28	720
1926	494,536	129,373	623,909	96	992	28	739
1927	510,910	133,835	644,745	99	1,005	28	758
1928	516,986	138,700	655,686	101	1,004	29	813
1929	520,339	143,313	663,652	104	1,004	30	823
1930	532,877	137,140	670,017	104	1,000	30	868
1931	544,453	143,982	688,435	104	1,004	31	861
1932	554,462	149,487	703,949	104	1,012	31	867
1933	564,042	153,577	717,619	105	1,014	31	875
1934	579,118	151,620	730,738	110	1,035	31	892
1935	595,071	151,313	746,384	115	1,064	32	900
1936	607,202	153,488	760,690	118	1,081	33	933
1937	616,088	151,664	767,752	118	1,101	35	951
1938	632,994	151,770	784,764	126	1,137	36	947
1939	645,618	157,910	803,528	129	1,154	35	1,002
1940	703,017	159,647	862,664	134	1,191	35	728
1941	736,544	155,536	892,080	139	1,224	36	757
1942	754,826	162,889	917,715	143	1,242	37	776
1943	774,161	162,889	937,050	146	1,261	38	807
1944	792,362	161,642	954,004	148	1,273	38	773
1945	811,045	168,409	979,454	153	1,295	38	909
1946	823,819	172,686	996,505	161	1,340	39	959
1947	843,021	173,149	1,016,170	169	1,425	43	1,149
1948	854,099	187,871	1,041,970	172	1,451	44	1,323
1949	876,661	202,010	1,078,671	175	1,501	46	1,327
1950	898,478	212,836	1,111,314	180	1,541	43	1,370
1951	933,792	213,365	1,147,157	191	1,666	42	1,414
1952	974,118	214,935	1,189,053	202	1,767	43	1,551
1953	1,034,381	211,981	1,246,362	211	1,884	42	1,399
1954	1,079,583	222,657	1,302,240	219	1,993	42	1,476
1955	1,126,265	213,009	1,357,274	224	2,082	44	1,471
1956	1,177,856	238,875	1,416,731	239	2,210	45	1,854
1957	1,233,397	254,917	1,488,314	251	2,362	45	1,740
1958	1,292,098	263,701	1,555,799	273	2,513	47	1,757
1959	1,336,675	279,413	1,616,088	290	2,614	50	1,895
1960	1,408,722	284,408	1,693,180	319	2,882	58	1,811
1961	1,514,551	309,110	1,823,661	345	3,143	67	1,872
1962	1,626,965	335,821	1,965,786	364	3,423	74	1,802
1963	1,736,567	380,884	2,117,451	389	3,615	77	1,782
1964	1,801,571	433,345	2,234,916	400	3,749	79	2,016
1965	1,977,418	418,514	2,395,932	412	3,897	76	2,137
1966	2,032,359	448,540	2,480,899	425	4,022	75	2,053
1967	2,144,766	469,574	2,614,340	448	4,166	77	1,987
1968	2,207,976	476,097	2,684,073	473	4,385	83	2,112
1969	2,344,635	462,821	2,807,456	496	4,592	88	2,016
1970	2,485,525	445,285	2,930,810	537	4,922	92	1,943
1971	2,645,419	445,534	3,090,953	562	5,135	98	1,942
1972	2,794,731	424,177	3,218,908	592	5,394	101	1,891
1973	2,904,244	402,414	3,306,658	630	5,707	108	1,817
1974	2,999,536	410,451	3,409,987	675	5,951	113	1,822
1975	3,188,062	384,140	3,572,202	737	6,390	134	1,761
1976	3,352,535	390,214	3,742,749	798	6,903	148	1,422
1977	3,618,331	350,889	3,969,220	885	7,466	157	1,694

As of Dec. 31	Members in stakes	Members, in missions	Total	Stakes	Wards & branches	Mis-sions	Mission branches
1978	3,829,385	337,469	4,166,854	990	8,064	166	1,790
1979	4,059,044	345,077	4,404,121	1,092	9,365	175	1,121
1980	4,328,521	311,301	4,639,822	1,218	10,324	188	2,267
1981	4,621,688	298,761	4,920,449	1,321	11,063	186	2,030
1982	4,832,158	330,461	5,162,619	1,392	11,492	180	1,979
1983	5,013,541	338,183	5,351,724	1,458	11,953	177	1,991
1984	5,278,192	362,862	5,641,054	1,507	12,422	180	2,046
1985	5,555,409	364,074	5,919,483	1,582	12,939	188	2,068
1986	5,785,324	381,650	6,166,974	1,622	13,318	193	2,064
1987	5,974,239	420,075	6,394,314	1,666	13,727	205	2,307
1988	6,271,311	449,899	6,721,210	1,707	14,069	222	2,470
1989	6,794,428	514,016	7,308,444	1,739	14,533	228	2,751
1990	7,141,477	619,702	7,761,179	1,784	15,003	256	3,079
1991	7,423,430	666,418	8,089,848	1,837	15,513	267	3,325
1992	7,673,980	730,107	8,404,087	1,919	16,292	276	3,819
1993	7,911,693	777,475	8,689,168	1,968	17,048	295	4,051
1994	8,159,995	864,373	9,024,368	2,008	17,521	303	4,311
1995	8,469,056	869,809	9,338,859	2,150	18,396	307	4,277
1996	8,855,430	837,003	9,692,441	2,296	19,522	309	3,994
1997	9,262,369	809,414	10,071,783	2,424	20,776	318	3,923
1998	9,594,010	810,439	10,404,449	2,505	21,649	331	3,904
1999	9,885,106	867,880	10,752,986	2,542	21,897	333	3,896

MISSIONARY STATISTICS

Year	No. Set apart	Year	No. Set apart	Year	No. Set apart	Year	No. Set apart
1830	16	1854	119	1878	152	1902	848
1831	58	1855	65	1879	179	1903	658
1832	72	1856	130	1880	219	1904	699
1833	41	1857	88	1881	199	1905	716
1834	111	1858	0	1882	237	1906	1,015
1835	84	1859	18	1883	248	1907	930
1836	80	1860	96	1884	205	1908	919
1837	52	1861	19	1885	235	1909	1,014
1838	16	1862	27	1886	209	1910	933
1839	67	1863	50	1887	282	1911	822
1840	80	1864	52	1888	242	1912	769
1841	100	1865	71	1889	249	1913	858
1842	45	1866	32	1890	283	1914	684
1843	374	1867	133	1891	331	1915	621
1844	586	1868	32	1892	317	1916	722
1845	84	1869	250	1893	162	1917	543
1846	32	1870	46	1894	526	1918	245
1847	40	1871	167	1895	746	1919	1,211
1848	55	1872	132	1896	922	1920	889
1849	58	1873	35	1897	943	1921	880
1850	50	1874	98	1898	1,059	1922	886
1851	44	1875	197	1899	324	1923	812
1852	158	1876	211	1900	796	1924	867
1853	33	1877	154	1901	522		

Year	No. Set apart	Year	No. Set apart	Year	No. Set apart	Year	No. Set apart
1925	1,131	1944	427	1963	5,781	1982	18,260
1926	1,236	1945	400	1964	5,886	1983	19,450
1927	1,017	1946	2,297	1965	7,139	1984	19,720
1928	1,193	1947	2,132	1966	7,021	1985	19,890
1929	1,058	1948	2,161	1967	6,475	1986	20,798
1930	896	1949	2,363	1968	7,178	1987	21,001
1931	678	1950	3,015	1969	6,967	1988	22,619
1932	399	1951	1,801	1970	7,590	1989	25,609
1933	525	1952	872	1971	8,344	1990	26,438
1934	843	1953	1,750	1972	7,874	1991	25,416
1935	960	1954	2,022	1973	9,471	1992	28,084
1936	899	1955	2,414	1974	9,811	1993	29,460
1937	1,079	1956	2,572	1975	14,446	1994	28,198
1938	1,146	1957	2,518	1976	13,928	1995	29,214
1939	1,088	1958	2,778	1977	14,561	1996	31,324
1940	1,194	1959	2,847	1978	15,860	1997	33,846
1941	1,257	1960	4,706	1979	16,590	1998	33,976
1942	629	1961	5,793	1980	16,600	1999	34,647
1943	261	1962	5,630	1981	17,800	**Total to date:**	
						814,008	

Total missionaries in the field – 1960 - 1999

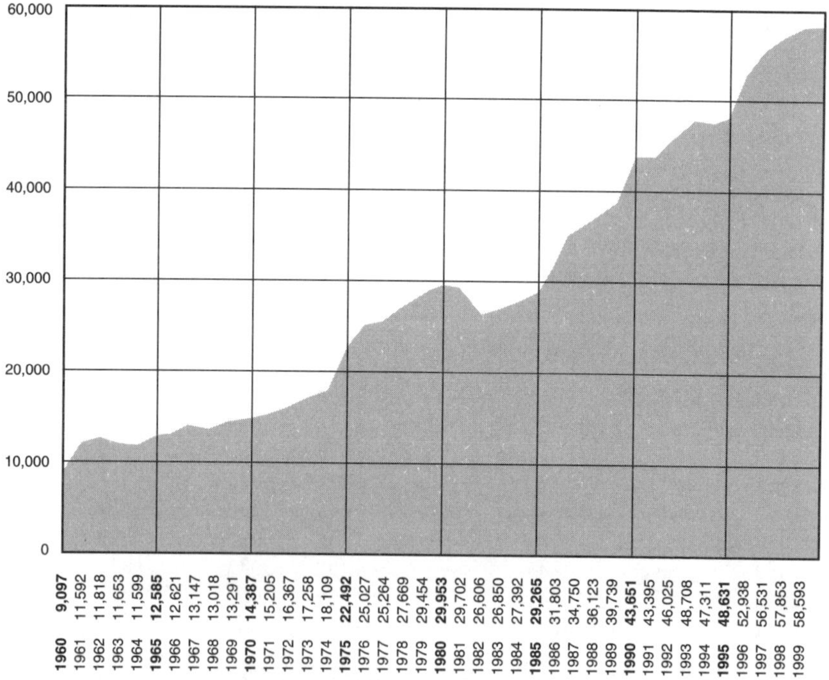

LDS Olympians

(Summer Games participants)

Year	Name	Event	Medal
1912	Alma Richards,USA	High jump	Gold
1920	Creed Haymond, USA*	Sprints	
1928	Doral W. Pilling, Canada	Javelin	
1932	Jesse Mortensen, USA**	Decathalon	
1936	M. Dale Schofield, USA	400-meter hurdles	
1948	Jay Lambert, USA	Boxing	
	Clarence Robison, USA	5,000 meter run	
1952	Paula Meyers Pope, USA***	Diving	Silver
	Robert Detweiler, USA***	Rowing Gold	
	Jane Sears, USA	Swimming	Bronze
1956	Paula Meyers Pope, USA	Diving	Silver, Bronze
1960	Paula Meyers Pope, USA	Diving	Silver
	Jack Yerman, USA***	400-meter run	
		4x100 relay	Gold
1964	L. Jay Silvester,USA	Discus	
	Dale Elizabeth McClements Kephart, USA***	Gymnastics	
	Walter E. "Ed" Red, USA***	Javelin	
1968	Wade Bell, USA	800-meter run	
	Robert Carmona, Mexico	Decathalon	
	Kresimir Cosic, Yugoslavia	Basketball	Silver
	Jackson S. Horsely, USA	Swimming	Bronze
	Canagasabi Kunulon, Singapore	Sprints	
	Kenneth Lundmark, Sweden	High jump	
	Keith Russell, USA	Diving	
	L. Jay Silvester, USA	Discus	Bronze
	Arnold Vitarbo, USA	Shooting	
1972	Anders Arrhenius, Sweden*	Shot put	
	Kresimir Cosic, Yugoslavia	Basketball	Bronze
	George Greenfield, USA	Gymnastics	
	Debbie Stark Hill, USA	Gymnastics	
	Kenneth James, Australia	Basketball	
	Canagasabi Kunulon,Singapore	Sprints	
	Eddie Palubinskas, Australia	Basketball	
	L. Jay Silvester, USA	Discus	Silver
	Usaia Sotutu, Fiji	Steeplechase	
	Saimoni Tamani, Fiji	400-meter run	
1976	Kresimir Cosic, Yugoslavia	Basketball	Silver
	Lelei Fonoimoana, Fiji	Swimming	
	Richard George, USA	Javelin	
	Henry Marsh, USA	Steeplechase	
	Laman Palma, Mexico	Marathon	
	Eddie Palubinskas, Australia	Basketball	
	L. Jay Silvester, USA	Discus	
	Phil Tollestrup, Canada	Basketball	

	Tauna Kay Vandeweghe, USA	Swimming	
	Allesandra Viero, Italy	Gymnastics	
	Wayne Young, USA	Gymnastics	
1980	Kresimir Cosic, Yugoslavia	Basketball	Gold
	Mark Albert Fuller, USA***	Greco-Roman Wrestling	
	Kenth Gardenkrans, Sweden	Discus	
	Henry Marsh, USA****	Steeplechase	
	Peter Vidmar, USA****	Gymnastics	
	Danny Vranes, USA****	Basketball	
1984	Pedro Caceres, Argentina	Steeplechase	
	Paul Cummings, USA	10,000-meter run	
	Stefan Fernholm, Sweden	Discus	
	Mark Fuller, USA	Greco-Roman wrestling	
	Bo Gustafsson, Sweden	50-kilometer walk	Silver
	Lorna Griffin, USA	Discus, shot put	
	Silo Havili, Tonga	Boxing	
	Henry Marsh, USA	Steeplechase	
	Scott Maxwell, Canada (DS)	Baseball	
	Doug Padilla, USA	5,000-meter Run	
	Villiami Pulu, Tonga	Boxing	
	Fime Sani, Tonga	Boxing	
	Timo Saarelainen, Finland***	Basketball	
	Cory Snyder, USA (DS)	Baseball	Silver
	Karl Tilleman, Canada	Basketball	
	Tauna Kay Vandeweghe, USA	Volleyball	Silver
	Peter Vidmar, USA	Gymnastics	2 Gold, 1 Silver
	Walt Zobell, USA	Trapshooting	
1988	Uati Afele, Western Samoa	Wrestling	
	Lucky Agbonsevbafe, Nigeria	Soccer	
	Troy Dalbey, USA	Swimming	2 Golds
	Mike Evans, USA	Water Polo	Silver
	James Bergeson, USA	Water Polo	Silver
	Ed Eyestone, USA	Marathon	
	Tualau Fale, Tonga	Boxing	
	Mark Fuller, USA	Greco-Roman wrestling	
	Bo Gustafsson, Sweden	50-kilometer walk	
	Viliamu Lesiva, Western Samoa	Boxing	
	Henry Marsh, USA	Steeplechase	
	Asomua Naea, Western Samoa	Boxing	
	Doug Padilla, USA	5,000-meter run	
	Fred Solovi, Western Samoa	Wrestling	
	Sione Talia'uli, Tonga	Boxing	
	Troy Tanner, USA	Volleyball	Gold
	Karl Tilleman, Canada	Basketball	
	Palako Vaka, Tonga	Boxing	
1992	Mark Albert Fuller, USA	Greco-Roman wrestling	
	Ed Eyestone, USA	Marathon	
	Julie Jenkins, USA	800-meter run	
	Mike Evans, USA	Water Polo	
1996	Kristine Quance	Swimming	Gold
	Laura Berg, USA	Softball	Gold

Year	Name	Event	Medal
2000	Kenneth Andam, Ghana	100 m run	
	Marsha Baird, Trinidad	Heptathalon	
	Maggie Chan Roper, Hong Kong	Distance runner	
	Jamie Dantzcher, USA	Gymnastics	
	Rulon Gardner, USA	Greco-Roman Wrestling	Gold
	Courtney Johnson, USA	Water polo Silver	
	Ryan Millar, USA	Volleyball	
	Leonard Myles-Mills, Ghana	100 meter run	
	Amy Palmer, USA	Hammer throw	
	Robbie Pratt, Mexico	Pole vault	
	Jason Pyrah, USA	1,500 meter run	
	Arunas Savackas, Lithuania	Swimming	
	Charlene Tagaloa, USA	Volleyball	
	Laura Berg, USA	Softball	Gold

* Injured, unable to compete
** Declared ineligible
*** Joined Church after competition
**** U.S. boycott, unable to compete
(DS) Demonstration sport

BOOK OF MORMON EDITIONS TRANSLATED AND PUBLISHED
(First editions in each language)

LANGUAGES	PLACE	YEAR	NOTES
English	Palmyra, New York	1830	
Danish	Copenhagen, Denmark	1851	Retranslated 1949
German	Hamburg, Germany	1852	Retranslated 1980
French	Paris, France	1852	Retranslated 1998
Italian	London, England	1852	Retranslated 1964, 1995
Welsh*	Merthyr Tydfil, Wales	1852	
Hawaiian	San Francisco, California	1855	Reprinted, Salt Lake City 1992
English*	New York, New York	1869	Deseret Alphabet
Spanish*(DG)	Salt Lake City, Utah	1875	Selections; full book 1886; retranslated 1952, 1986
Swedish	Copenhagen, Denmark	1878	
Maori	Auckland, New Zealand	1889	Reprinted 1989
Dutch	Amsterdam, Holland	1890	
Samoan	Salt Lake City, Utah	1903	
Tahitian	Salt Lake City, Utah	1904	
Turkish*	Boston, Massachusetts	1906	Armenian script Selections retranslated 1983, Roman letters
Japanese	Tokyo, Japan	1909	Retranslated 1957, 1995
Czech*(DG)	Prague, Czechoslovakia	1933	Selections retranslated 1980 Full book reprinted 1986
Armenian-Western*	Los Angeles, Calif.	1937	Selections retranslated 1983
English(DG)	Louisville, Kentucky	1936	Braille; revised full book 1989

Portuguese	Sao Paulo, Brazil	1939	Retranslated 1995
Tongan	Salt Lake City, Utah	1946	
Norwegian	Oslo, Norway	1950	
Finnish	Helsinki, Finland	1954	
Rarotongan	Salt Lake City, Utah	1965	
Chinese	Hong Kong	1965	
Korean	Seoul, Korea	1967	
Afrikaans	Johannesburg, So. Africa	1972	
Thai	Bangkok, Thailand	1976	
Indonesian	Jakarta, Indonesia	1977	
Aymara*(DG)	Salt Lake City, Utah	1977	Selections; full book 1986
Cakchiquel	Salt Lake City, Utah	1978	Selections; cassettes 2000
Croatian	Cakovec, Yugoslovia	1979	
Quechua-Peru	Salt Lake City, Utah	1979	Selections
Greek			
(Katharevusa)	Salt Lake City, Utah	1979	Selections
(Demotike)	Salt Lake City, Utah	1983	Selections; full book 1987
Hungarian	Salt Lake City, Utah	1979	Selections; full book 1991
Kekchi*(DG)	Salt Lake City, Utah	1979	Selections; full book 1983; cassettes 2000
Quiche	Salt Lake City, Utah	1979	Selections; cassettes 2000
Bulgarian	Salt Lake City, Utah	1980	Selections; full book, 1999
Navajo	Salt Lake City, Utah	1980	Selections; retranslated 1998 cassettes 2000
Quichua-Ecuador	Salt Lake City, Utah	1980	Selections
Arabic*(DG)	Salt Lake City, Utah	1980	Selections; full book 1986
Vietnamese*(DG)	Salt Lake City, Utah	1980	Selections (DG); full book 1982
Fijian	Salt Lake City, Utah	1980	
Russian	Salt Lake City, Utah	1981	
Catalan	Barcelona, Spain	1981	
Icelandic	Reykjavik, Iceland	1981	Retranslated 1999 (only as part of a triple)
Niuean	Salt Lake City, Utah	1981	Selections
Quechua-Bolivia	Salt Lake City, Utah	1981	Selections
Kuna	Salt Lake City, Utah	1981	Selections
Romanian	Salt Lake City, Utah	1981	Selections; full book 1998
Polish	Salt Lake City, Utah	1981	
Hindi	Hong Kong	1982	
Telugu	Salt Lake City, Utah	1982	Selections*
Tamil	Colombo, Sri Lanka	1982	Selections
Cambodian	Salt Lake City, Utah	1982	Selections
Laotian	Salt Lake City, Utah	1982	Selections
Swahili	Salt Lake City, Utah	1982	Selections; full book 2000
Guarani	Salt Lake City, Utah	1982	Selections
Maya	Salt Lake City, Utah	1983	Selections
Sinhala	Colombo, Sri Lanka	1983	Selections
Mam	Salt Lake City, Utah	1983	Selections; cassettes 2000
Efik	Salt Lake City, Utah	1983	Selections

China (Simplified characters)	Hong Kong	1983	Selections
Kisii	Salt Lake City, Utah	1983	Selections
Greek (Demotike) *(DG)	Salt Lake City, Utah	1983	Selections; full book 1987
Hmong	Salt Lake City, Utah	1983	Selections; full book 2000
Persian	Salt Lake City, Utah	1983	Selections
Haitian Creole	Salt Lake City, Utah	1983	Selections; full book 1999
Marshallese	Salt Lake City, Utah	1984	Selections
Bengali	New Delhi, India	1985	Selections
Bislama	Salt Lake City, Utah	1985	Selections
Malagasy	Salt Lake City, Utah	1986	Selections; full book 2000
Fante	Salt Lake City, Utah	1987	Selections
Greek (Demotike)	Salt Lake City, Utah	1987	
Zulu	Salt Lake City, Utah	1987	Selections
Pohnpeian	Salt Lake City, Utah	1987	Selections
Papiamento	Salt Lake City, Utah	1987	Selections
Trukese	Salt Lake City, Utah	1987	Selections
Tagalog	Salt Lake City, Utah	1987	Selections
Lingala	Salt Lake City, Utah	1988	Selections
Shona	Salt Lake City, Utah	1988	Selections
Urdu	Salt Lake City, Utah	1988	Selections
Palauan	Salt Lake City, Utah	1988	Selections
Kiribati (Gilbertese)	Salt Lake City, Utah	1988	Selections
CHamorro	Salt Lake City, Utah	1989	Selections
Ilokano	Salt Lake City, Utah	1991	Selections; full book 1995
Cebuano	Salt Lake City, Utah	1992	Selections; full book 1998
Tzotzil	Salt Lake City, Utah	1994	Selections
Hiligaynon	Salt Lake City, Utah	1994	Selections
Pampango	Salt Lake City, Utah	1994	Selections
American Sign Lang.	Salt Lake City, Utah	1995	Video tape (10 of 15 available)
Spanish-Braille	Salt Lake City, Utah	1995	(No footnotes)
Waray	Salt Lake City, Utah	1996	Selections
Ukrainian	Frankfurt, Germany	1997	Full book (reference guide edition)
Bikolano	Salt Lake City, Utah	1998	Selections
Pangasinan	Salt Lake City, Utah	1998	Full first edition
Albanian	Frankfurt, Germany	1999	
Estonian	Frankfurt, Germany	2000	
Igbo	Salt Lake City, Utah	2000	

In print 26 Sept. 2000

Full Book of Mormon	56
Selections	37
Total	93

* — Out of print (DG) — Replaced by a later edition

THE FAMILY: A PROCLAMATION TO TO THE WORLD

(Delivered by President Gordon B. Hinckley at the General Relief Society meeting, Sept. 23, 1995)

"We, the First Presidency and the Council of the Twelve Apostles of The Church of Jesus Christ of Latter-day Saints, solemnly proclaim that marriage between a man and a woman is ordained of God and that the family is central to the Creator's plan for the eternal destiny of His children.

"All human beings — male and female — are created in the image of God. Each is a beloved spirit son or daughter of heavenly parents, and, as such, each has a divine nature and destiny. Gender is an essential characteristic of individual premortal, mortal, and eternal identity and purpose.

"In the premortal realm, spirit sons and daughters knew and worshiped God as their Eternal Father and accepted His plan by which His children could obtain a physical body and gain earthly experience to progress toward perfection and ultimately realize his or her divine destiny as an heir of eternal life. The divine plan of happiness enables family relationships to be perpetuated beyond the grave. Sacred ordinances and covenants available in holy temples make it possible for individuals to return to the presence of God and for families to be united eternally.

"The first commandment that God gave to Adam and Eve pertained to their potential for parenthood as husband and wife. We declare that God's commandment for His children to multiply and replenish the earth remains in force. We further declare that God has commanded that the sacred powers of procreation are to be employed only between man and woman, lawfully wedded as husband and wife.

"We declare the means by which mortal life is created to be divinely appointed. We affirm the sanctity of life and of its importance in God's eternal plan.

"Husband and wife have a solemn responsibility to love and care for each other and for their children. 'Children are an heritage of the Lord' (Psalm 127:3). Parents have a sacred duty to rear their children in love and righteousness, to provide for their physical and spiritual needs, to teach them to love and serve one another, to observe the commandments of God and to be law-abiding citizens wherever they live. Husbands and wives — mothers and fathers — will be held accountable before God for the discharge of these obligations.

"The family is ordained of God. Marriage between man and woman is essential to His eternal plan. Children are entitled to birth within the bonds of matrimony, and to be reared by a father and a mother who honor marital vows with complete fidelity. Happiness in family life is most likely to be achieved when founded upon the teachings of the Lord Jesus Christ. Successful marriages and families are established and maintained on principles of faith, prayer, repentance, forgiveness, respect, love, compassion, work, and wholesome recreational activities. By divine design, fathers are to preside over their families in love and righteousness and are responsible to provide the necessities of life and protection for their families. Mothers are primarily responsible for the nurture of their children. In these sacred responsibilities, fathers and mothers are obligated to help one another as equal partners. Disability, death, or other circumstances may necessitate individual adaptation. Extended families should lend support when needed.

"We warn that individuals who violate covenants of chastity, who abuse spouse or offspring, or who fail to fulfill family responsibilities will one day stand accountable before God. Further, we warn that the disintegration of the family will bring upon individuals, communities, and nations the calamities foretold by ancient and modern prophets.

"We call upon responsible citizens and officers of government everywhere to promote those measures designed to maintain and strengthen the family as the fundamental unit of society."

INDEX

INDEX

A

B

F

G

I

J

K

N

O

P

Y

Z